DISCOVERING COMPUTERS 2002

Concepts for a Digital World

Web Enhanced

Complete

Gary B. Shelly
Thomas J. Cashman
Misty E. Vermaat

Contributing Authors
Susan L. Sebok
Dolores J. Wells

COURSE TECHNOLOGY
THOMSON LEARNING™

COURSE TECHNOLOGY
25 THOMSON PLACE
BOSTON MA 02210

SHELLY CASHMAN SERIES®

Australia • Canada • Denmark • Japan • Mexico • New Zealand • Philippines • Puerto Rico • Singapore
South Africa • Spain • United Kingdom • United States

COURSE TECHNOLOGY
THOMSON LEARNING

Printed in the United States of America

Asia (excluding Japan)
Thomson Learning
60 Albert Street, #15-01
Albert Complex
Singapore 189969

Japan
Thomson Learning
Palaceside Building 5F
1-1-1 Hitotsubashi, Chiyoda-ku
Tokyo 100 0003 Japan

Australia/New Zealand
Nelson/Thomson Learning
102 Dodds Street
South Melbourne, Victoria 3205
Australia

Latin America
Thomson Learning
Seneca, 53
Colonia Polanco
11560 Mexico D.F. Mexico

South Africa
Thomson Learning
Zonnebloem Building,
Constantia Square
526 Sixteenth Road
P.O. Box 2459
Halfway House, 1685
South Africa

Canada
Nelson/Thomson Learning
1120 Birchmount Road
Scarborough, Ontario
Canada M1K 5G4

UK/Europe/Middle East
Thomson Learning
Berkshire House
168-173 High Holborn
London, WC1V 7AA United Kingdom

Spain
Thomson Learning
Calle Magallanes, 25
28015-MADRID
ESPANA

For more information, contact Course Technology, 25 Thomson Place, Boston, MA 02210.

Or visit our Internet site at www.course.com

ISBN 0-7895-6185-9 (perfect bound)
ISBN 0-7895-6190-5 (case bound)

3 4 5 6 7 8 9 10 BC 05 04 03 02 01

DISCOVERING COMPUTERS 2002

Concepts for a Digital World
Web Enhanced

CONTENTS

CHAPTER 4 The Components of the System Unit

CHAPTER 5 Input

CHAPTER 6 Output

CHAPTER 7 Storage

CHAPTER 8 Operating Systems and Utility Programs

CHAPTER 9 Communications and Networks

CHAPTER 10 E-Commerce: A Revolution in the Way We Do Business

CHAPTER 11 Computers and Society: Home, Work, and Ethical Issues

CHAPTER 15
Program Development and Programming Languages

CHAPTER 16
Computer Careers and Certification

APPENDIX
Coding Schemes and Number Systems

PREFACE

The Shelly Cashman Series® offers the finest textbooks in computer education. We are proud of the fact that the previous six editions of this textbook have been runaway best-sellers. Each of the these editions included new learning innovations, such as integration of the World Wide Web, WebCT, Interactive Labs, online learning games, MyCourse.com, and Teaching Tools that set it apart from its competitors. *Discovering Computers 2002: Concepts for a Digital World, Web Enhanced* continues with the innovation, quality, timeliness, and reliability that you have come to expect from the Shelly Cashman Series. This latest edition of *Discovering Computers* includes these enhancements:

- Eight-chapter Brief edition, twelve-chapter Introductory edition, and sixteen-chapter Complete edition lets you choose the version of the textbook that fits your teaching needs
- Three new chapters round out the concepts students need to know: (1) E-Commerce; (2) Computers and Society: Home, Work, and Ethical Issues; and (3) Careers and Certification
- Students can relate to the Picture Yourself chapter openers that set the stage by providing conversational chapter-related situations
- E-Revolution two-page spreads at the end of each chapter provide a fascinating perspective of Web applications, such as e-finance, e-travel, e-arts, e-learning, e-entertainment, and e-government
- Learn It Online exercise section at the end of each chapter includes practice tests and learning games that offer a unique way for students to solidify, reinforce, and extend the concepts presented in the chapter
- Two cutting-edge companies and two technology trailblazers are spotlighted in each chapter to help students recognize the leaders and major companies in the field of computers
- Career Corner at the end of each chapter pinpoints career opportunities for all levels of students
- Apply It boxes throughout chapters help students apply the concepts presented to everyday life

OBJECTIVES OF THIS TEXTBOOK

The Complete edition of *Discovering Computers 2002: Concepts for a Digital World, Web Enhanced* is intended for use as a stand-alone textbook or in combination with an applications, Internet, or programming textbook in a one-quarter or one-semester introductory computer course. No experience with computers is assumed. The material presented provides an in-depth treatment of introductory computer subjects. Students will finish the course with a solid understanding of computers, how to use computers, and how to access information on the World Wide Web. The objectives of this book are as follows:

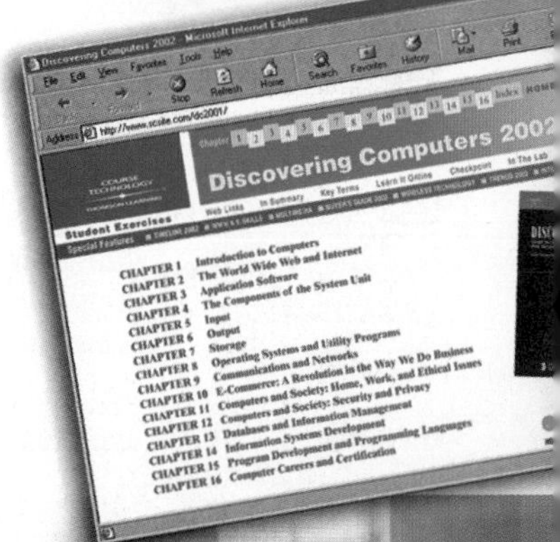

- Teach the fundamentals of computers and computer nomenclature, particularly with respect to personal computer hardware and software, and the World Wide Web
- Give students an in-depth understanding of why computers are essential components in business and society in general
- Present the material in a visually appealing and exciting manner that invites students to learn
- Provide exercises and lab assignments that allow students to interact with a computer and actually learn by using the computer and the World Wide Web
- Offer alternative learning techniques with streaming audio and video on the Web, learning games, WebCT, Blackboard, and MyCourse.com
- Present strategies for purchasing, installing, and maintaining a desktop computer, a notebook computer, and a handheld computer
- Assist students in planning a career and getting certified in the computer field

DISTINGUISHING FEATURES

The Complete edition of *Discovering Computers 2002: Concepts for a Digital World, Web Enhanced* includes the following distinguishing features.

A Proven Book

More than five million students have learned about computers using Shelly and Cashman computer fundamentals textbooks. With the additional World Wide Web integration and interactivity, streaming up-to-date audio and video, extraordinary step-by-step visual drawings and photographs, unprecedented currency, and the Shelly and Cashman touch, this book will make your computer concepts course exciting and dynamic.

World Wide Web Enhanced

This book uses the World Wide Web as a major supplement. The purpose of integrating the World Wide Web into the book is to (1) offer students additional information and currency on topics of importance; (2) make available alternative learning techniques with Web-based learning games, practice tests, and interactive labs; (3) underscore the relevance of the World Wide Web as a basic information tool that can be used in all facets of society; and (4) offer instructors the opportunity to organize and administer their traditional campus-based or distance-education-based courses on the Web using WebCT, Blackboard, or MyCourse.com.

This textbook, however, does not depend on Web access in order to be used successfully. The Web access adds to the already complete treatment of topics within the book. The World Wide Web is integrated into the book in seven ways:

- Streaming audio speaks the end-of-chapter In Summary sections to students
- End-of-chapter pages and the special features in the book are stored as Web pages on the World Wide Web; see page xv for more information
- Streaming up-to-date, computer-related CNN videos on the Web are in the end-of-chapter Web Work sections
- Throughout the text, marginal annotations titled Web Links provide suggestions on how to obtain additional information via the Web on an important topic covered on the page
- Eighteen Interactive Labs on the Web in the end-of-chapter Web Work sections
- WebCT and Blackboard Web-based course management systems for use in a traditional classroom setting or in a distance education environment
- MyCourse.com offers instructors and students an opportunity to supplement classroom learning with additional content on the Web.

A Visually Appealing Book that Maintains Student Interest

The latest technology, pictures, drawings, and text are artfully combined to produce a visually appealing and easy-to-understand book. Many of the figures show a step-by-step pedagogy, which simplifies the more complex computer concepts. Pictures and drawings reflect the latest trends in computer technology. Finally, the text is set in three columns, which research indicates is the easiest design for students to read. This combination of pictures, step-by-step drawings, and text sets a new standard for computer textbook design.

Technology Trailblazer and Company on the Cutting Edge Boxes

All students graduating from an institution of higher education should be aware of the leaders and major companies in the field of computers. Thus, interspersed throughout each chapter are boxed write-ups on two leaders in technology and two computer companies. The titles of these boxes are Technology Trailblazer and Company on the Cutting Edge. The Technology Trailblazer feature presents people who have made a difference in the computer revolution, such as Bill Gates, Lavonne Luquis, Andy Grove, Carly Fiorina, Marc Andreessen, Tim Berners-Lee, and others. The Company on the Cutting Edge feature presents the major computer companies, such as Microsoft, Intel, Yahoo!, Sun Microsystems, Gateway, IBM, and others.

Latest Computer Trends

The terms and technologies your students see in this book are those they will encounter when they start using computers. Only the latest application software packages are shown throughout the book. New topics and terms include: digital divide; wireless service provider; microbrowser; spider; wireless portal; MP3 player; m-commerce (mobile commerce); latest version of Microsoft Office; online print service; .NET; input devices for handheld computers; digital video camera; video telephone call; digital watermarks; Web bar codes; gesture recognition; Pentium 4; high-performance addressing (HPA); Internet appliance; electronic book (e-book); Digital Display Working Group (DDWG); Digital Visual Interface (DVI); Video Electronics Standards Association (VESA); interactive TV; Internet printing; Internet stamps; optically-assisted hard drive; Internet hard drive; multiread CD-ROM drive; miniature mobile storage media; Picture CD; Active Directory; Microsoft Windows 2000; Solaris; embedded operating system; Pocket PC; Pocket PC OS; utility suite; Web-based utility service; sending and receiving devices; Web cams; collaboration; online meetings; P2P; HomePLC network; phoneline network; HomeRF network; intelligent home network; DSL modem; ISDN modem; digital modem; Fast Ethernet; Gigabit Ethernet; clicks-and-mortar business; disintermediation; e-commerce business models; e-commerce revenue streams; e-procurement; electronic software distribution; Web hosting service; e-retail; shopping bot; e-commerce software; merchant account; electronic Customer Relationship Management (eCRM); e-mail publishing; creation of an online store; impact of computers in use at home and education, entertainment, finance, government, health care, science, publishing, and travel; repetitive stress injury; Internet addiction disorder; green computing; intellectual property; virus hoax; voice verification system; online backup service; S-HTTP; Secure Electronic Transaction (SET); security of e-mail messages; Pretty Good Privacy (PGP); proxy server; personal firewall; online security service; spyware; adware; spam; Web databases; Web server; CGI (common gateway interface); multidimensional databases; data mining; data marts; online analytical processing (OLAP); software engineering; Unified Modeling Language (UML); Object Management Group (OMG); CORBA (Common Object Request Broker Architecture); ActiveX controls; ActiveX technology; bytecode; Jscript; VBScript; extensible HTML (XHTML); WML (wireless markup language); WAP (wireless application protocol); computer certifications, and much more.

End-of-Chapter Exercises

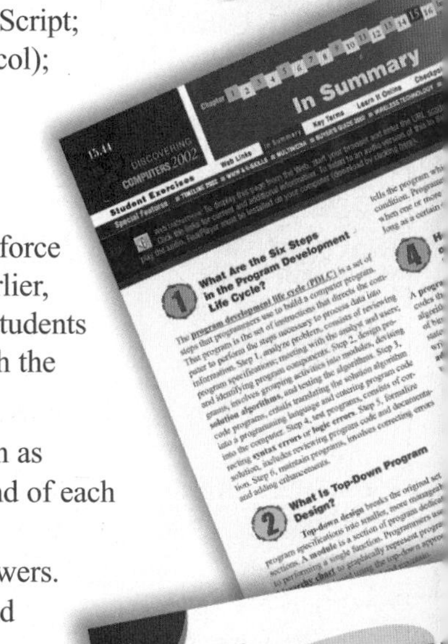

We dedicate as many resources to create the end-of-chapter material as we do to the chapter content. We believe strongly in offering exciting, rich, and thorough end-of-chapter material to reinforce the chapter objectives and assist you in making your course the finest ever offered. As indicated earlier, each of the end-of-chapter pages is stored as a Web page on the World Wide Web to provide your students in-depth information and alternative methods of preparing for examinations. Each chapter ends with the following:

- **E-Revolution** A two-page E-Revolution spread introduces students to Web applications such as e-finance, e-travel, e-arts, e-learning, e-auctions, e-entertainment, and much more. At the end of each E-Revolution are exercises that allow students to apply the topics described.
- **In Summary** This section summarizes the chapter material in the form of questions and answers. Each question addresses a chapter objective, making this section invaluable in reviewing and preparing for examinations. Links on the Web page provide additional current information. With a single-click on the Web page, the In Summary section is spoken to students using streaming audio.
- **Key Terms** This list of the key terms found in the chapter together with the page numbers on which the terms are defined will aid students in mastering the chapter material. A complete summary of all key terms in the book, together with their definitions, appears in the Index at the end of the book. On the corresponding Web page, students can click terms to view a definition and a picture and then click a link to visit a Web page that offers additional information.
- **Learn It Online** These all-new Web-based exercises include exciting activities that maintain student interest. Exercises include a scavenger hunt, search sleuth, practice tests, and learning games.

- **CheckPoint** These pencil-and-paper exercises have been expanded to two pages. Exercises include label the figure, matching, multiple choice, short answer, and working together. Students accessing the Web page can answer the questions in an interactive forum.
- **In The Lab** A series of Windows lab exercises begins with the simplest exercises within Windows. Students then are led through additional activities that, by the end of the book, enable them to be proficient using Windows.
- **Web Work** In this section, students gain an appreciation for the online technology available with the Web. The At The Movies exercise includes streaming video. The Shelly Cashman Series Interactive Labs exercises uses the latest Web technologies. Other exercises in this section, such as working with newsgroups and reviewing the latest news in technology, also use the World Wide Web.

Timeline 2002: Milestones in Computer History

A colorful, highly informative 13-page timeline following Chapter 1 steps students through the major computer technology developments during the past 60 years, including the most recent advances in 2001.

Guide to World Wide Web Sites and Searching Techniques

More than 150 popular up-to-date Web sites are listed and described in this guide to Web sites that follows Chapter 2. This guide also introduces the students to basic searching techniques.

Multimedia: A Virtual Experience

Multimedia is changing the way people work, learn, and play. This special feature following Chapter 6 introduces the students to multimedia applications, such as business presentations, computer-based training, Web-based training, electronic books, entertainment, and edutainment.

Buyer's Guide 2002

A 10-page guide following Chapter 8 introduces students to purchasing, installing, and maintaining a desktop computer, notebook computer, and handheld computer.

A World Without Wires

This special feature presents a pictorial introduction of the wireless revolution. It describes the growth of wireless technology and the latest in hardware and applications. This special feature is available in the Introductory and Complete editions.

Trends 2002: A Look to the Future

Following Chapter 16, an 11-page feature examines several trends that will influence the direction of the computer field. This special feature is available only in the Complete edition.

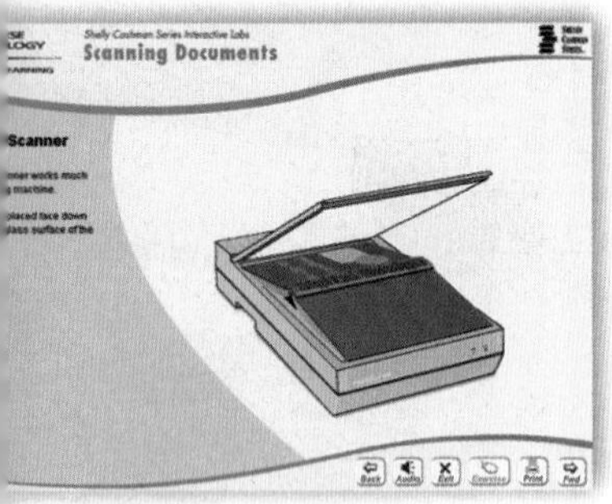

Shelly Cashman Series Interactive Labs

The Shelly Cashman Interactive Labs have been redone completely for this edition using the latest technologies. See page xvi for more information.

Data Disk

The Data Disk includes documents and executable programs used in a few of the In The Lab exercises found at the end of the chapters in this book. See the inside back cover for instructions about how to download the Data Disk.

SHELLY CASHMAN SERIES TEACHING TOOLS

Three basic ancillaries accompany this textbook: Teaching Tools (ISBN 0-7895-6261-8), Course Presenter (ISBN 0-7895-6191-3), and MyCourse.com. These ancillaries are free to adopters through your Course Technology representative or by calling one of the following telephone numbers: Colleges and Universities, 1-800-648-7450; High Schools, 1-800-824-5179; Private Career Colleges, 1-800-477-3692; Canada, 1-800-268-2222; and Corporations and Government Agencies, 1-800-340-7450.

Teaching Tools

The Teaching Tools for this textbook include both teaching and testing aids. The contents of the Teaching Tools CD-ROM are listed below.

- **Instructor's Manual** The Instructor's Manual consists of Microsoft Word files that include the following for each chapter: chapter objectives; chapter overview; detailed lesson plans with page number references; teacher notes and activities; answers to the exercises; test bank (100 true/false, 50 multiple-choice, and 70 fill-in-the-blank questions per chapter); and figure references. The figures are available in the Figures in the Book. The test bank questions are numbered the same as in the Course Test Manager. You can print a copy of the chapter test bank and use the printout to select your questions in Course Test Manager. Using your word processing software, you can generate quizzes and exams.
- **Figures in the Book** Illustrations for every picture, table, and screen in the textbook are available in electronic form. Use this ancillary to present a slide show in lecture or to print transparencies for use in lecture with an overhead projector. If you have a personal computer and LCD device, this ancillary can be an effective tool for presenting lectures.
- **Course Test Manager** Course Test Manager is a powerful testing and assessment package that enables instructors to create and print tests quickly from the 3,500 question test bank. Instructors with access to a networked computer lab (LAN) can administer, grade, and track tests online. Students also can take online practice tests, which generate customized study guides that indicate where in the textbook students can find more information for each question.
- **ExamView** ExamView is a state-of-the-art test builder. ExamView enables you to create printed tests, Internet tests, and computer (LAN-based) tests quickly. You can enter your own test questions or use the 3,500 question test bank that accompanies ExamView.
- **Course Syllabus** Any instructor who has been assigned a course at the last minute knows how difficult it is to develop a course syllabus. For this reason, a sample syllabus is included that can be customized easily to a course.
- **Student Files** A few of the exercises in the end-of-chapter In The Lab section ask students to use these files. You can distribute the files on the Teaching Tools CD-ROM to your students over a network, or you can have them follow the instructions in this preface to obtain a copy of the Discovering Computers 2002 Data Disk.
- **Interactive Labs** These are the non-audio versions of the 18 hands-on Interactive Labs exercises. Students can step through each Lab in about 15 minutes to solidify and reinforce computer concepts. Assessment requires students to answer questions about the contents of the Interactive Labs.
- **Interactive Lab Solutions** This ancillary includes the solutions to the Interactive Labs assessment quizzes.

Course Presenter with Figures, Animations, and CNN Video Clips

Course Presenter is a multimedia lecture presentation system that provides PowerPoint slides for every subject in each chapter. Use this presentation system to give well-organized lectures that are both interesting and knowledge-based. A presentation is provided for each chapter. Each file contains PowerPoint slides for every subject in each chapter together with optional choices to show any figure in the chapter as you introduce the material in class. More than 50 current, two- to three-minute up-to-date, computer-related video clips, many from CNN, and more than 35 animations that reinforce chapter material also are available for optional presentation. Course Presenter provides consistent coverage for multiple lecturers.

MyCourse.com

MyCourse.com offers instructors and students an opportunity to supplement classroom learning with additional course content. You can use MyCourse.com to expand traditional learning by accessing and completing readings, tests, and other assignments through the customized, comprehensive Web site. For additional information, visit mycourse.com and click the Help button.

SUPPLEMENTS

Five supplements can be used in combination with *Discovering Computers 2002: Concepts for a Digital World, Web Enhanced.*

Audio Chapter Review on CD-ROM

The Audio Chapter Review on CD-ROM (ISBN 0-7895-6192-1) speaks the end-of-chapter In Summary pages. Students can use this supplement with a CD player or personal computer to solidify their understanding of the concepts presented. It is a great tool for preparing for examinations. This same Audio Chapter Review also is available at no cost on the Web by clicking the Audio button on the In Summary page at the end of any chapter.

Shelly Cashman Series Interactive Labs with Audio on CD-ROM

The Shelly Cashman Series Interactive Labs with Audio on CD-ROM (ISBN 0-7895-6111-5) may be used in combination with this textbook to augment your students' learning process. See page xvi for a description of each Lab. These Interactive Labs also are available at no cost on the Web by clicking the appropriate button on the Web Work exercise pages (see page 1.47) and as a non-audio version on the Teaching Tools CD-ROM. A companion student guide for the Interactive Labs, titled *A Record of Discovery for Exploring Computers, Fourth Edition* (ISBN 0-7895-6372-X), enhances the Interactive Labs presentation, reinforces concepts, shows relationships, and provides additional facts.

Study Guide

This highly popular *Study Guide* (ISBN 0-7895-6189-1) includes a variety of activities that help students recall, review, and master introductory computer concepts. The *Study Guide* complements the end-of-chapter material with a guided chapter outline; a self-test consisting of true/false, multiple-choice, short answer, fill-in, and matching questions; an entertaining puzzle; and other challenging exercises.

WebCT Users Guide and Blackboard Users Guide

The *WebCT Users Guide* (ISBN 0-7895-6163-8) and the *Blackboard Users Guide* (ISBN 0-7895-6165-4) show students how to navigate through these course management tools.

ACKNOWLEDGMENTS

The Shelly Cashman Series would not be the leading computer education series without the contributions of outstanding publishing professionals. First, and foremost, among them is Becky Herrington, director of production and designer. She is the heart and soul of the Shelly Cashman Series, and it is only through her leadership, dedication, and tireless efforts that superior products are made possible. Becky created and produced the award-winning Windows series of books.

Under Becky's direction, the following individuals made significant contributions to these books: Doug Cowley, production manager; Ginny Harvey, series specialist; Ken Russo, senior Web and graphic designer; Mike Bodnar, associate production manager; Mark Norton, Web designer; Meena Moest, production editor; Michele French, Christy Otten, Stephanie Nance, Chris Schneider, Hector Arvizu and Kenny Tran, graphic artists; Jeanne Black and Betty Hopkins, Quark experts; Laurie Sullivan and Lyn Markowicz, copyeditors; Nancy Lamm and Rich Hansberger, proofreaders; Jeff Quasney, Teaching Tools developer; Tim Walker, Instructor's Manual and MyCourse.com author; Floyd Winters, Web content analyst; Robert Safdie, Course Presenter author; Cristina Haley, indexer; Sarah Evertson of Image Quest, photo researcher; Richard Keaveny, associate publisher; Jim Quasney, series consulting editor; Lora Wade, product manager; Erin Roberts, associate product manager; Francis Schurgot, Web product manager; Marc Ouellette, associate Web product manager; Rachel VanKirk, marketing manager; and Erin Runyon, associate product manager.

Our sincere thanks go to Dennis Tani, who together with Becky Herrington, designed this book. In addition, Dennis designed the cover, performed all the initial layout and typography and executed the magnificent drawings contained in this book.

Finally, thanks to Judy Brown, Paul Bartolomeo, Jeff Corcoran, Dr. Wil Dershimer, Susan Fry, Dr. Homa Ghajar, John G. Hoey, Joyce King, Sherry Lenhart, Dana Madison and Ed Mott, for reviewing the manuscript and to William Vermaat for researching, reviewing the manuscript, and taking photographs. Special thanks to Erin Runyon for recruiting and managing the reviewer process. We hope you find using this book an exciting and rewarding experience.

Gary B. Shelly
Thomas J. Cashman
Misty E. Vermaat

Dolores J. Wells
Susan L. Sebok

NOTES TO THE STUDENT

If you have access to the World Wide Web, you can obtain current and additional information on topics covered in this book in the five ways listed below.

1. Throughout the book, marginal annotations called Web Link (Figure 1) specify subjects about which you can obtain additional current information. Enter the designated URL and then click the appropriate term on the Web page.
2. Each chapter ends with six sections titled In Summary, Key Terms, Learn It Online, Checkpoint, In The Lab, and Web Work. These sections in your textbook are stored as pages on the Web. You can visit them by starting your browser and entering the URL listed in the Web Instructions at the top of the end-of-chapter pages. When the Web page displays, you can click links or buttons on the page to broaden your understanding of the topics and obtain current information about the topics.
3. Each chapter ends with a two-page E-Revolution spread that describes a Web application. Included in this section are URLs that let you apply what you have learned.
4. Throughout the chapters, you will find Apply It, Technology Trailblazer, Company on the Cutting Edge, and Issue boxes. Most of these boxes include URLs that point you to additional information on the topic presented.
5. More than 150 popular up-to-date Web sites are listed and described in the Guide to World Wide Web Sites that follows Chapter 2. This guide also describes basic searching techniques.

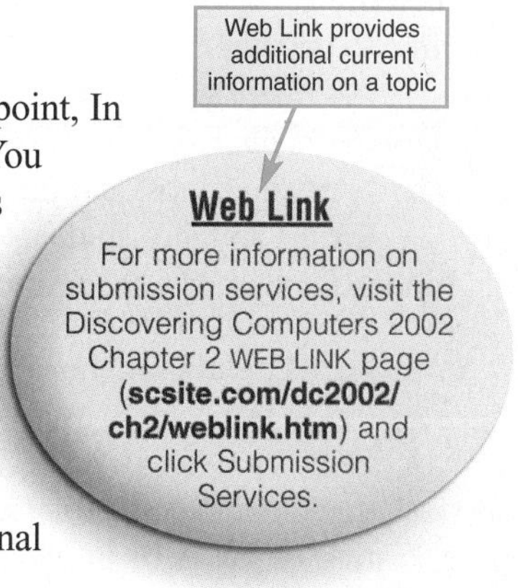

Web Link provides additional current information on a topic
Web Link
For more information on submission services, visit the Discovering Computers 2002 Chapter 2 WEB LINK page (scsite.com/dc2002/ch2/weblink.htm) and click Submission Services.

Figure 1

Each time you reference a Web page from the textbook's Web site, a navigation system displays at the top of the page (Figure 2). To display one of the Student Exercises, click the chapter number and then click the Student Exercises title at the top. To display one of the Special Features, click the desired Special Feature title at the top.

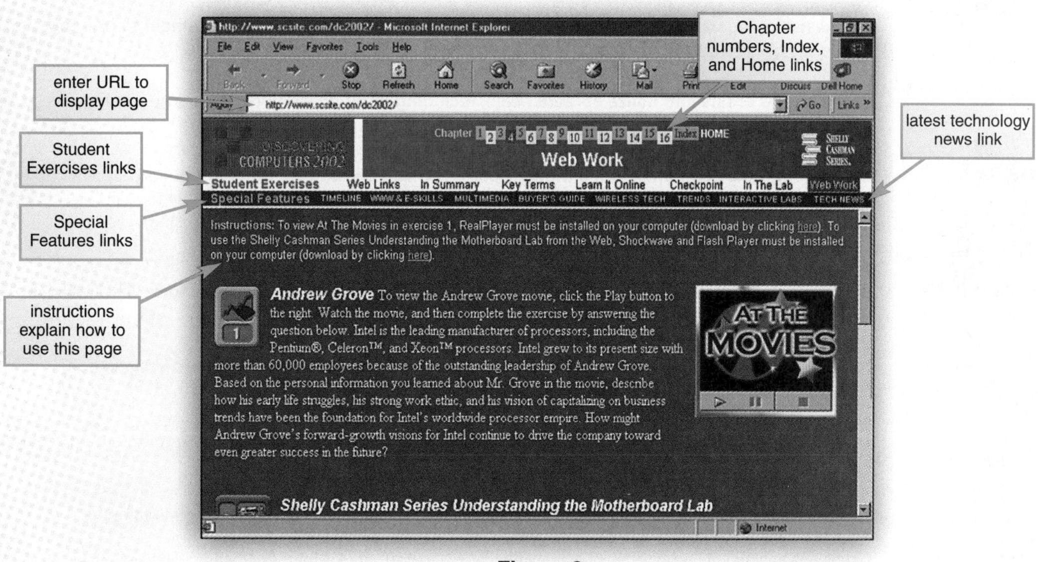

Figure 2

TO DOWNLOAD PLAYERS

For best viewing results of the Web pages referenced in this book, download Shockwave and Flash Player. To play the audio in the In Summary section and view the movie in the Web Work section at the end of each chapter, you must download RealPlayer. Follow the steps below:

Shockwave and Flash Player— (1) Start your browser; (2) enter the URL `macromedia.com`; (3) click DOWNLOADS at the top of the Macromedia home page; (4) click Macromedia Shockwave Player; (5) click the button in the Step box; (6) respond to the dialog boxes.

RealPlayer — (1) Start your browser; (2) enter the URL `real.com`; (3) scroll down and click RealPlayer 8 Basic (this is the free version of RealPlayer); (4) step through and respond to the forms, requests, and dialog boxes; (5) when the File Download dialog box displays, click the Save this program to disk option button; (6) save the file to a folder and remember the folder name; (7) if necessary, start Windows Explorer and double-click the file downloaded in Step 6.

SHELLY CASHMAN SERIES INTERACTIVE LABS WITH AUDIO

Each of the 16 chapters in this textbook includes the Web Work exercises, which utilize the World Wide Web. The 18 Shelly Cashman Series Interactive Labs described below are included as exercises in the Web Work section. These Interactive Labs are available on the Web (see page 1.47) or on CD-ROM. The audio version on CD-ROM (ISBN 0-7895-6111-5) is available at an additional cost. A non-audio version also is available on the Shelly Cashman Series Teaching Tools CD-ROM that is available free to adopters.

A student guide for the Interactive Labs is available at an additional cost. The student guide is titled *A Record of Discovery for Exploring Computers, Fourth Edition* (ISBN 0-7895-6372-X), which reviews the Interactive Labs content, shows relationships, and provides additional facts.

Each Lab takes students approximately 15 minutes to complete using a personal computer and helps them gain a better understanding of a specific subject covered in the chapter.

Shelly Cashman Series Interactive Labs with Audio		
Lab	*Function*	*Page*
Using the Mouse	Master how to use a mouse. The Lab includes exercises on pointing, clicking, double-clicking, and dragging.	1.47
Using the Keyboard	Learn how to use the keyboard. The Lab discusses different categories of keys, including the edit keys, function keys, ESC, CTRL, and ALT keys and how to press keys simultaneously.	1.47
Connecting to the Internet	Learn how a computer is connected to the Internet. The Lab presents using the Internet to access information.	2.47
The World Wide Web	Understand the significance of the World Wide Web and how to use Web browser software and search tools.	2.47
Word Processing	Gain a basic understanding of word processing concepts, from creating a document to printing and saving the final result.	3.47
Working with Spreadsheets	Learn how to create and utilize spreadsheets, including entering formulas, creating graphs, and performing what-if analysis.	3.47
Understanding the Motherboard	Step through the components of a motherboard. The Lab shows how different motherboard configurations affect the overall speed of a computer.	4.45
Scanning Documents	Understand how document scanners work.	5.43
Setting Up to Print	See how information flows from the system unit to the printer and how drivers, fonts, and physical connections play a role in generating a printout.	6.41
Configuring Your Display	Recognize the different monitor configurations available, including screen size, display cards, and number of colors.	6.41
Maintaining Your Hard Drive	Understand how files are stored on disk, what causes fragmentation, and how to maintain an efficient hard drive.	7.41
Evaluating Operating Systems	Evaluate the advantages and disadvantages of different categories of operating systems.	8.41
Working at Your Computer	Learn the basic ergonomic principles that prevent back and neck pain, eye strain, and other computer-related physical ailments.	8.41
Exploring the Computers of the Future	Learn about computers of the future and how they will work.	9.49
Understanding Multimedia	Gain an understanding of the types of media used in multimedia applications, the components of a multimedia PC, and the newest applications of multimedia.	11.47
Keeping Your Computer Virus Free	Learn what a virus is and about the different kinds of viruses. The Lab discusses how to prevent your computer from being infected with a virus.	12.45
Designing a Database	Create a database structure and optimize a database to support searching.	13.51
Choosing a Programming Language	Differentiate between traditional languages and the newer object-oriented languages.	15.51

DISCOVERING COMPUTERS 2002

Concepts for a Digital World

Web Enhanced

CHAPTER 1

Introduction to Computers

Your last final exam is complete; the semester is over! Tonight, you finally will get a good night's sleep. This semester was the most intense yet. You are a bit anxious about your grades in sociology and psychology; but ... no more waiting for mail delivery! For the first time, the school's registration department will post grades on the Internet. They should be available by the weekend.

On Friday morning, you access the Internet from your home computer to find the grades have not been posted. When you meet your sister for lunch, you discuss the anticipation of receiving your grades via the Internet. She reaches for a computer in her briefcase and accesses the Internet. Still no grades. Then while visiting a friend, you ask if he has Internet access. He pulls a handheld computer out of his coat pocket and uses it to connect to the Internet. No grades yet.

Saturday finds you relaxing with friends at the beach. With a cellular telephone in hand, one friend shouts, "Our grade reports made it to the Internet!" You cross your fingers while entering your student identification number on the telephone keypad. Yes! Three As and two Bs. Now you can enjoy the summer.

OBJECTIVES

After completing this chapter, you will be able to:

- Explain the importance of computer literacy
- Define the term computer
- Identify the components of a computer
- Explain why a computer is a powerful tool
- Differentiate among the various categories of software
- Explain the purpose of a network
- Discuss the uses of the Internet and the World Wide Web
- Describe the categories of computers and their uses
- Identify the various types of computer users
- Understand how a user can be a Web publisher

THE DIGITAL REVOLUTION

Computers are everywhere … at home, at work, and at school. Most of our daily activities either involve the use of or depend on information from a computer. Activities such as learning to read, contacting a senator, looking up a stock quote, visiting a museum, or planning a trip, could involve the use of computers (Figure 1-1).

With a home computer, you can balance your checkbook, pay bills, track personal income and expenses, transfer funds, buy or sell stocks, and evaluate financial plans. People deposit or withdraw funds through an ATM (automated teller machine). At the grocery store, a computer tracks your purchases and calculates the amount of money you owe. It also usually generates coupons customized

to your buying patterns. Many cars today include an onboard navigation system that provides directions, signals for emergency services, and tracks the vehicle if it is stolen.

In the workplace, people use computers to create correspondence such as memos and letters, calculate payroll, track inventory, and generate invoices. Both schools and homes have computers for educational purposes. Teachers use them to assist with the instruction. Students complete assignments and do research on computers in lab rooms and at home.

Many people find hours of entertainment on the computer. They play games, listen to music, watch a video or a movie, read a book or magazine, make a family tree, compose a video, re-touch a photograph, or plan a vacation.

Through computers, society has access to information from all around the globe. Instantaneously, you can find local and national news, weather reports, sports scores, stock prices, your medical records, your credit report, and countless forms of educational material. At your fingertips, you can send messages to others, meet new friends, shop, fill prescriptions, file taxes, or take a course.

Figure 1-1 Computers are present in every aspect of daily living.

Computers have become a primary tool people use to communicate with others. The brilliance of these communications is they are not limited to text. With today's technology, you also can transmit voice, sounds, video, and graphics. Use the computer to see others while you talk to them. Send family, friends, or clients videos or photographs.

The digital revolution is upon us. Technology continues to advance and computers extend into more facets of daily living. To be successful in this digital world, it is essential you are computer literate. Being **computer literate** means you have knowledge and understanding of computers and their uses.

The purpose of this book is to present the knowledge you need to understand how computers work and how computers are used. While you read, remember this chapter is an overview and many of the terms and concepts introduced will be discussed further in later chapters.

WHAT IS A COMPUTER?

A **computer** is an electronic machine, operating under the control of instructions stored in its own memory, that can accept data, manipulate the data according to specified rules, produce results, and store the results for future use.

Data and Information

Data is a collection of raw unprocessed facts, figures, and symbols. Computers process data to create information. **Information** is data that is organized, meaningful, and useful. As shown in Figure 1-2, a computer processes several data items to produce a paycheck. Another example of information is a grade report, which is generated from data items such as a student name, course names, and course grades.

A **user** is someone that communicates with a computer or uses the information it generates.

Hardware is the electric, electronic, and mechanical equipment that makes up a computer. **Software** is the series of instructions that tells the hardware how to perform tasks. Without software, most hardware is useless. The hardware needs instructions from software to process data into information.

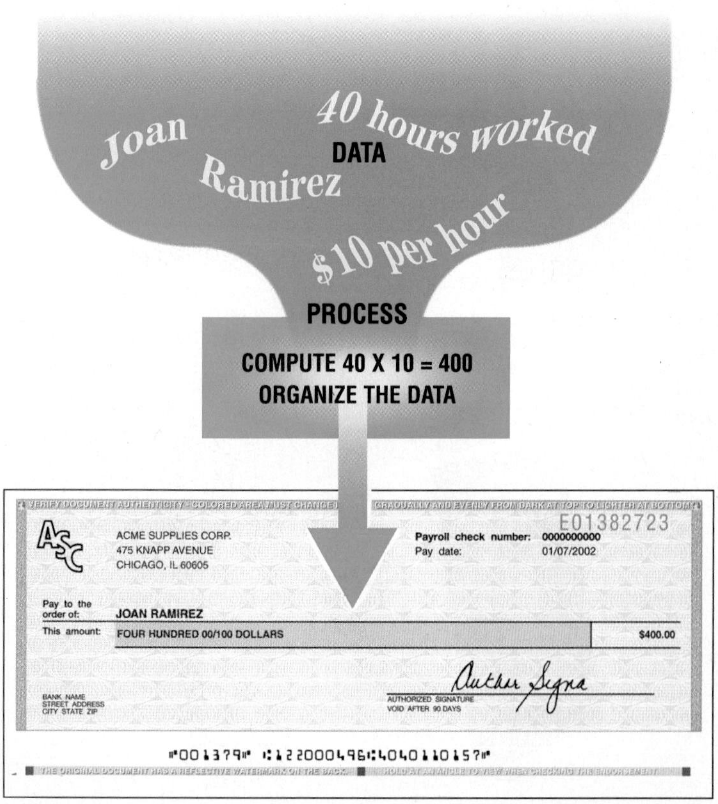

Figure 1-2 A computer processes data into information. In this example, the employee name, number of hours worked, and hourly pay rate each represent data. The computer processes these items to produce the paycheck.

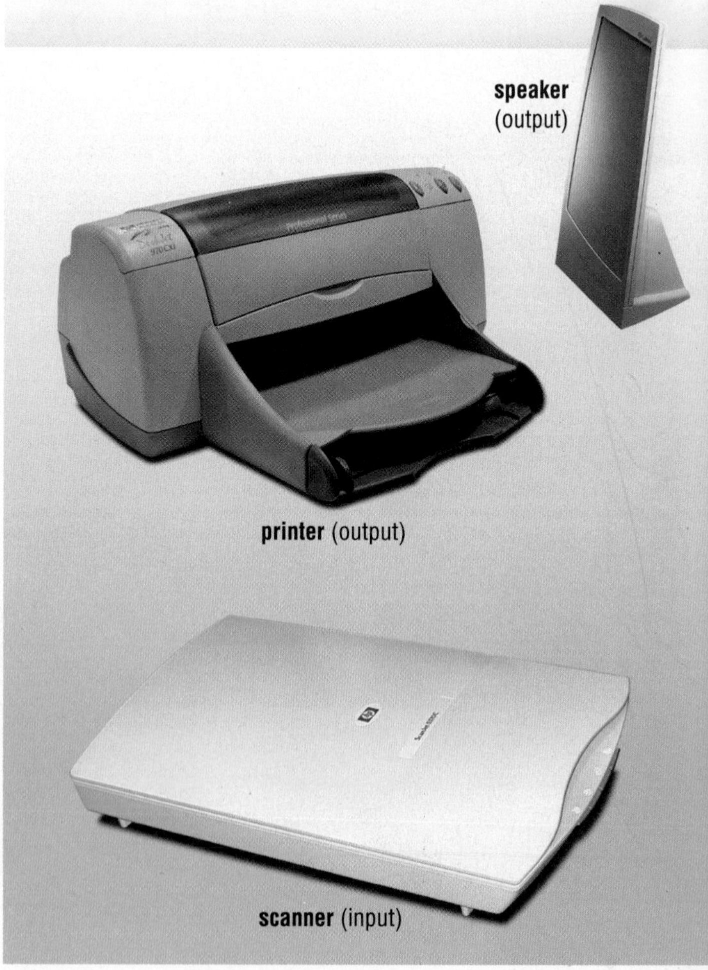

Information Processing Cycle

Input is any data or instructions you enter into a computer. **Output** is data that has been processed into information. Computers process input (data) into output (information). **Storage** is an area in a computer that can hold data and information for future use. This series of input, process, output, and storage activities sometimes is called the **information processing cycle**.

Most computers today have the capability of communicating with other computers. Thus, communications also has become an important element of the information processing cycle.

THE COMPONENTS OF A COMPUTER

A computer consists of a variety of hardware components that work together with software to perform calculations, organize data, and communicate with other computers.

These hardware components include input devices, output devices, a system unit, storage devices, and communications devices. Figure 1-3 shows some common computer hardware components.

Input Devices

An **input device** is any hardware component that allows a user to enter data and instructions into a computer. Six commonly used input devices are the keyboard, mouse, microphone, scanner, digital camera, and PC camera (see Figure 1-3).

A computer keyboard contains keys that allow you to type letters of the alphabet, numbers, spaces, punctuation marks, and other symbols. A computer keyboard also contains other keys that allow you to enter data and instructions into the computer.

A mouse is a small handheld device that contains at least one button. The mouse controls the movement of a symbol on the screen called a pointer. For example, as you move the mouse across a flat surface, the pointer on the screen also moves. With the mouse, you can make choices, initiate a process, and select objects.

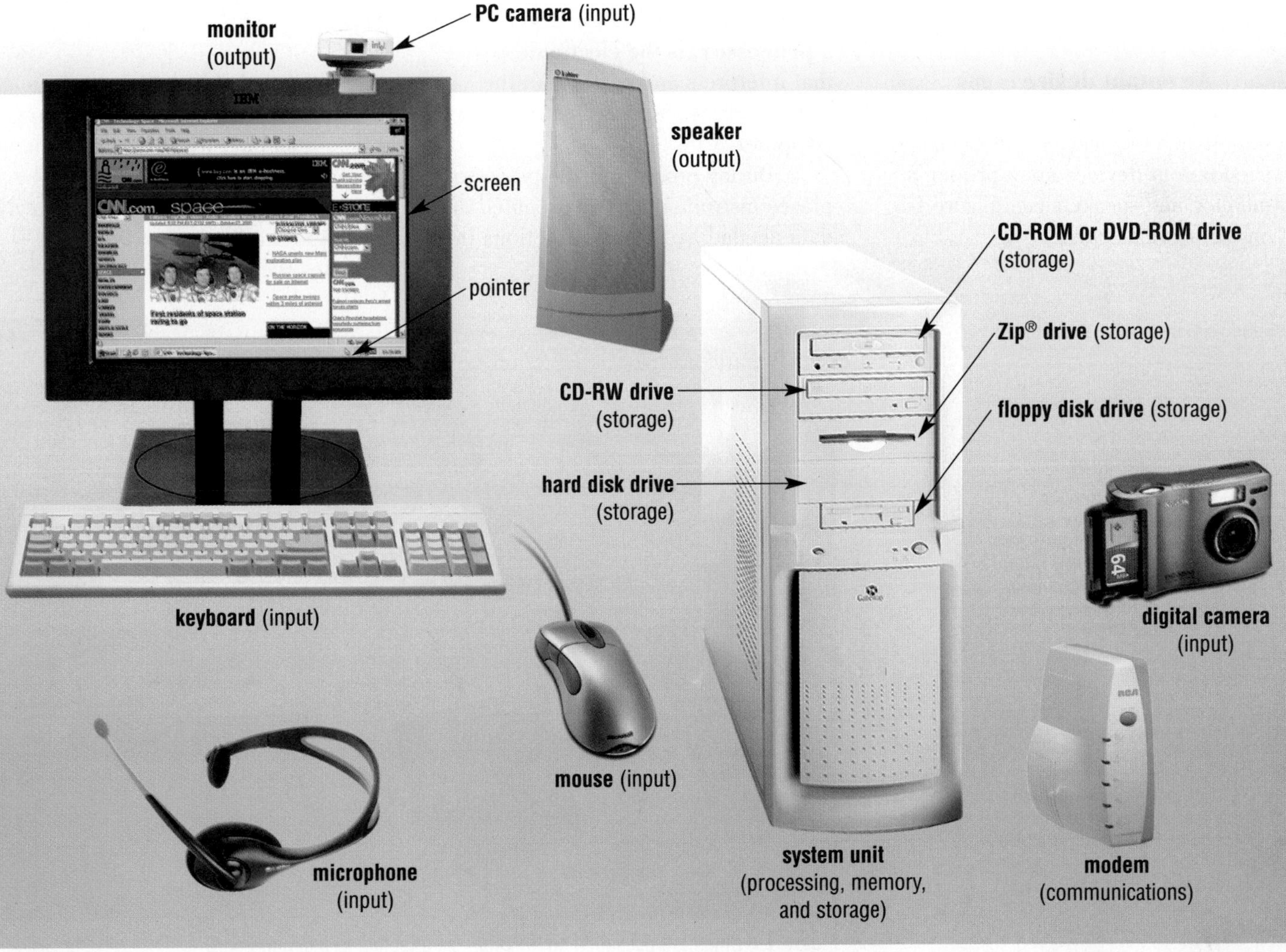

Figure 1-3 Common computer hardware components include a keyboard, mouse, microphone, PC camera, scanner, digital camera, system unit, disk drives, printer, monitor, speakers, and modem.

A microphone allows a user to speak to the computer to enter data and instructions into the computer. A scanner reads printed text and pictures and then translates the results into a form the computer can use. For example, you can scan a picture, and then include the picture when creating a brochure.

With a digital camera, you can take pictures and transfer the photographed image to the computer, instead of storing the images on traditional film. A PC camera is a digital video camera attached to a computer. This technology allows home users to edit videos, create a movie, and take digital still photographs on their computer. With a PC camera, you also can have video telephone calls — where someone can see you while communicating with you.

Output Devices

An **output device** is any hardware component that can convey information to a user. Three commonly used output devices are a printer, a monitor, and speakers (see Figure 1-3 on the previous page).

A printer produces text and graphics on a physical medium such as paper or transparency film. A monitor, which looks like a television screen, displays text, graphics, and video information. Speakers allow you to hear music, voice, and other sounds generated by the computer.

System Unit

The **system unit**, sometimes called a **chassis**, is a box-like case made from metal or plastic that protects the internal electronic components of the computer from damage (see Figure 1-3). The circuitry in the system unit usually is part of or is connected to a circuit board called the motherboard.

Two main components on the motherboard are the central processing unit and memory. The **central processing unit** (**CPU**), also called a **processor**, is the electronic device that interprets and carries out the basic instructions that operate the computer.

During processing, the processor places instructions to be executed and data needed by those instructions into memory. **Memory** is a temporary holding place for data and instructions.

Both the processor and memory consist of chips. A chip is an electronic device that contains many microscopic pathways that carry electrical current. Chips, which usually are no bigger than one-half inch square, are packaged so they can be attached to a motherboard or other circuit board (Figure 1-4).

Some computer components, such as the processor and memory, are internal and reside inside the system unit. Other components, such as the keyboard, mouse, microphone, monitor, printer, scanner, digital camera, and PC camera, often are located outside the system unit. These devices are considered external. A **peripheral** is any external device that attaches to the system unit.

Storage Devices

Storage holds data, instructions, and information for future use. Storage differs from memory, in that it can hold these items permanently. Memory, by contrast, holds items only temporarily while the processor interprets and executes them.

Web Link

For more information on input devices, visit the Discovering Computers 2002 Chapter 1 WEB LINK page (**scsite.com/dc2002/ch1/weblink.htm**) and click Input Devices.

Web Link

For more information on output devices, visit the Discovering Computers 2002 Chapter 1 WEB LINK page (**scsite.com/dc2002/ch1/weblink.htm**) and click Output Devices.

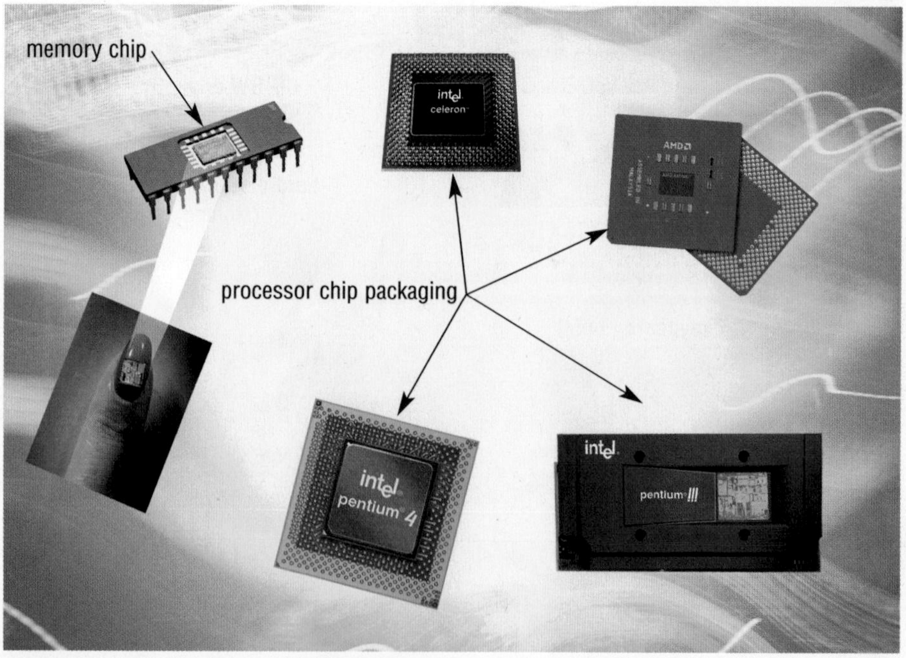

Figure 1-4 Chips are packaged so they may be attached to a circuit board.

A storage medium (media is the plural) is the physical material on which a computer keeps the data, instructions, and information. A **storage device** records and retrieves items to and from a storage medium. Storage devices often function as a source of input because they transfer items from storage into memory.

Six common storage devices are a floppy disk drive, a Zip® drive, a hard disk drive, a CD-ROM drive, a CD-RW drive, and a DVD-ROM drive (see Figure 1-3 on page 1.5). A drive is a device that reads from and may write onto a storage medium. This media includes floppy disks, Zip® disks, hard disks, and compact discs.

A floppy disk consists of a thin, circular, flexible disk enclosed in a plastic shell. A floppy disk stores data, instructions, and information using magnetic patterns. You insert and remove a floppy disk into and from a floppy disk drive (Figure 1-5). A Zip® disk is a higher capacity disk that can store the equivalent of up to 170 standard floppy disks.

A hard disk provides much greater storage capacity than a floppy disk. A hard disk usually consists of several circular platters that store items electronically. These disks are enclosed in an airtight, sealed case, which often is housed inside the system unit (Figure 1-6). Some hard disks are removable, which enables you to insert and remove the hard disk from a hard disk drive, much like a floppy disk (Figure 1-7). Removable disks are enclosed in plastic or metal cartridges so you can remove them from the drive. The advantage of removable media such as a floppy disk and removable hard disk is you can take the media out of the computer and transport or secure it.

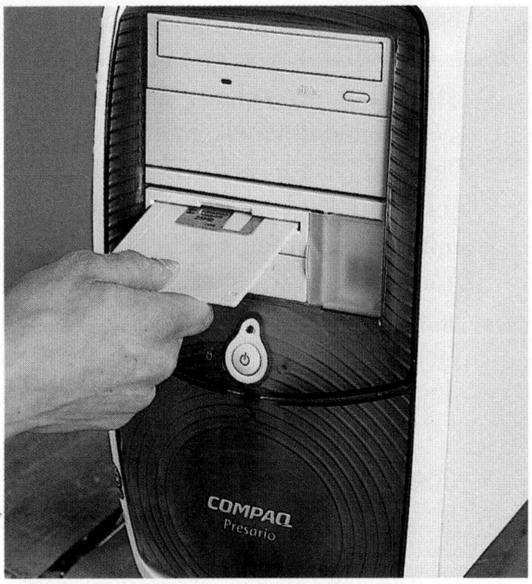

Figure 1-5 A floppy disk is inserted and removed from a floppy disk drive.

Web Link

For more information on processors, visit the Discovering Computers 2002 Chapter 1 WEB LINK page (**scsite.com/dc2002/ch1/weblink.htm**) and click Processors.

Web Link

For more information on storage devices, visit the Discovering Computers 2002 Chapter 1 WEB LINK page (**scsite.com/dc2002/ch1/weblink.htm**) and click Storage Devices.

Figure 1-6 Most hard disks are self-contained devices housed inside the system unit.

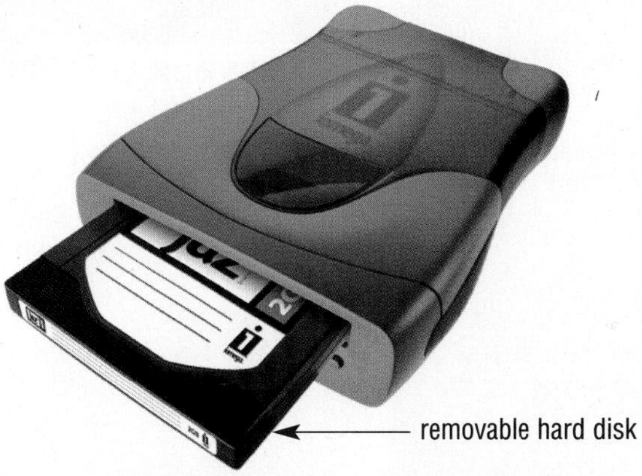

Figure 1-7 Removable hard disks are inserted and removed from a drive.

A compact disc is a flat, round, portable medium that stores data using microscopic pits, which are created by a laser light. One type of compact disc is a CD-ROM, which you access using a CD-ROM drive. A Picture CD is a special type of CD-ROM that stores digital versions of photographs for consumers.

A variation of the standard CD-ROM is the rewriteable CD, or CD-RW. In addition to accessing data, you also can erase and store data on a CD-RW. To use a CD-RW, you need a CD-RW drive. Another type of compact disc is a DVD-ROM, which has tremendous storage capacities — enough for a full-length movie. To use a DVD-ROM, you need a DVD-ROM drive (Figure 1-8).

Some devices, such as digital cameras, use miniature storage media (Figure 1-9). One popular type of miniature storage media is a card. You then can transfer the items, such as the digital photographs, from the media to your computer using a device called a card reader.

Communications Devices

Communications devices enable computer users to communicate and to exchange items such as data, instructions, and information with another computer.

A modem is a communications device that enables computers to communicate via telephone lines or cable. Modems are available as both external and internal devices.

Communications devices, such as modems, allow you to establish a connection between two computers and transmit items over transmission media, such as cables, telephone lines, or satellites.

WHY IS A COMPUTER SO POWERFUL?

A computer derives its power from its capability of performing the information processing cycle operations (input, process, output, and storage) with amazing speed, reliability, and accuracy; storing huge amounts of data and information; and communicating with other computers.

Speed

Inside the system unit, operations occur through electronic circuits. When data, instructions, and information flow along these circuits, they travel at close to the speed of light. This allows billions of operations to be carried out in a single second.

ISSUE

School's Out

Communicating Information to Your Brain

One of Billboard's top songs of 1972 was Alice Cooper's *School's Out*. Flash forward in time to the future as portrayed in the movie *Matrix*. In this world, we find "no more teacher's dirty looks" because school is out forever. Do you want to learn Chinese? Simple! Use your wireless Web-enabled watch to connect to the education portal. Download the latest Chinese language unit. Connect your brain receptor to your watch and pour the knowledge into your brain. Within minutes, you speak several Chinese dialects. At the moment, this scenario is science fiction, but could it possibly be part of our future? Will education as we now know it eventually disappear? What other methods could be used so that knowledge could be "poured" into the brain?

For more information on communications, visit the Discovering Computers 2002 Issues Web page (**scsite.com/dc2002/issues.htm**) and click Chapter 1 Issue #1.

Figure 1-8 To use a DVD-ROM, you need a DVD-ROM drive.

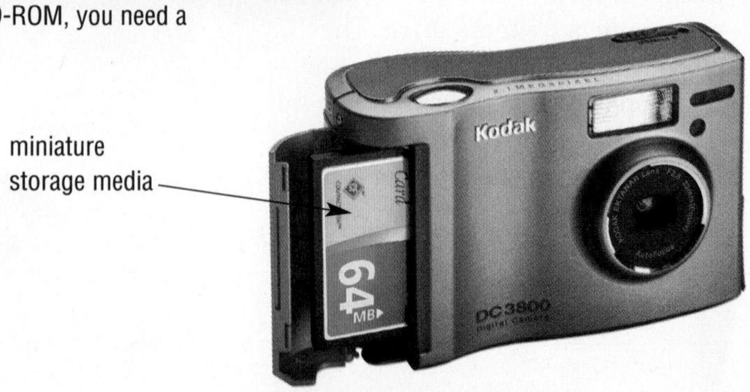

Figure 1-9 Many smaller devices, such as digital cameras, use miniature storage media.

Reliability

The electronic components in modern computers are dependable because they have a low failure rate. The high reliability of the components enables the computer to produce consistent results.

Accuracy

Computers can process large amounts of data and generate error-free results, provided the data is entered correctly and the program works properly. If data is inaccurate, the resulting output will be incorrect. A computing phrase — known as **garbage in, garbage out (GIGO)** — points out that the accuracy of a computer's output depends on the accuracy of the input.

Storage

Many computers can store enormous amounts of data and make this data available for processing any time it is needed. Using current storage devices, the computer can transfer data quickly from storage to memory, process it, and then store it again for future use.

Communications

Most computers today have the capability of communicating with other computers. Computers with this capability can share any of the four information processing cycle operations — input, process, output, and storage — with another computer. For example, two computers connected by a communications device such as a modem can share stored data, instructions, and information.

ISSUE

Computer Literacy — Important?

The Digital Revolution

In 1976, John Nevison (see URL below) coined the term computer literacy. In his article in Science magazine, he suggests an individual be called computer literate if he or she has written a computer program. Since that introduction more than 25 years ago, the definition of computer literacy has evolved, along with the numerous changes in technology. Many definitions of computer literacy exist today. These definitions range from knowing how to use the Internet, to knowing how a computer functions, to possessing the ability to use word processing software. How would you describe computer literacy? Should computer literacy be a required component of the general education requirements of a university or community college? Should computer literacy be introduced in K-12? If so, at what level? Some organizations suggest that the term information technology (IT) competency is a better description of the skills required for today's student. Do you agree? What knowledge and skills should someone have to be considered computer literate or IT competent?

For more information on computer literacy, information technology competencies, and the Web site mentioned above, visit the Discovering Computers 2002 Issues Web page (**scsite.com/dc2002/issues.htm**) and click Chapter 1 Issue #2.

Web Link

For more information on communications devices, visit the Discovering Computers 2002 Chapter 1 WEB LINK page (**scsite.com/dc2002/ch1/weblink.htm**) and click Communications Devices.

TECHNOLOGY TRAILBLAZER

BILL **GATES**

What advice does one of the richest men in the world have for students? *Get the best education you can. Take advantage of high school and college. Learn how to learn.* As Microsoft's chairman and chief software architect, Bill Gates receives hundreds of e-mail messages from students asking for insight on education. He emphasizes that college graduates know about a multitude of subjects and group dynamics. Gates dropped out of Harvard during his junior year, but he stresses that students should not quit going to school unless they are facing extraordinary prospects.

Gates began programming computers when he was 13. Early in his career he developed the BASIC programming language for the MITS Altair, one of the first microcomputers. He founded Microsoft in 1975 with Paul Allen, and five years later they developed the first operating system for the IBM PC, called MS-DOS. Under Gates' leadership, Microsoft continued to update MS-DOS and then develop Windows, Internet Explorer, and the MSNBC cable television news network and corresponding Web site. Today he is regarded as the most powerful person in the computer industry.

Gates has written two books: *Business @ the Speed of Thought* and *The Road Ahead.* All proceeds have been donated to non-profit organizations. He and his wife have endowed more than $21 billion to the Bill and Melinda Gates Foundation, which supports global health and learning.

For more information on Bill Gates, visit the Discovering Computers 2002 People Web page (**scsite.com/dc2002/people.htm**) and click Bill Gates.

When two or more computers are connected together via communications media and devices, they form a network. The most widely known network is the Internet (Figure 1-10).

COMPUTER SOFTWARE

Software, also called a **computer program** or simply a **program**, is a series of instructions that tells the hardware of a computer what to do. Some instructions allow you to input data from the keyboard and direct the computer to store the data in memory. Other instructions cause data in memory to be used in calculations such as adding a series of numbers to obtain a total. Some instructions compare two values in memory and direct the computer to perform alternative operations based on the results of the comparison. Other instructions direct the computer to print a report, display information on the monitor, draw a color picture on the monitor, or store information on a disk.

A computer carries out, or **executes**, the instructions in a program by first placing, or loading, the instructions in the memory of the computer. Usually, the computer loads the instructions from storage into memory. For example, a program might load into memory from the hard disk each time you execute the program.

When you purchase a program, such as one shown in Figure 1-11, you typically receive media such as a CD-ROM(s) or a DVD-ROM that contains the software. Some programs

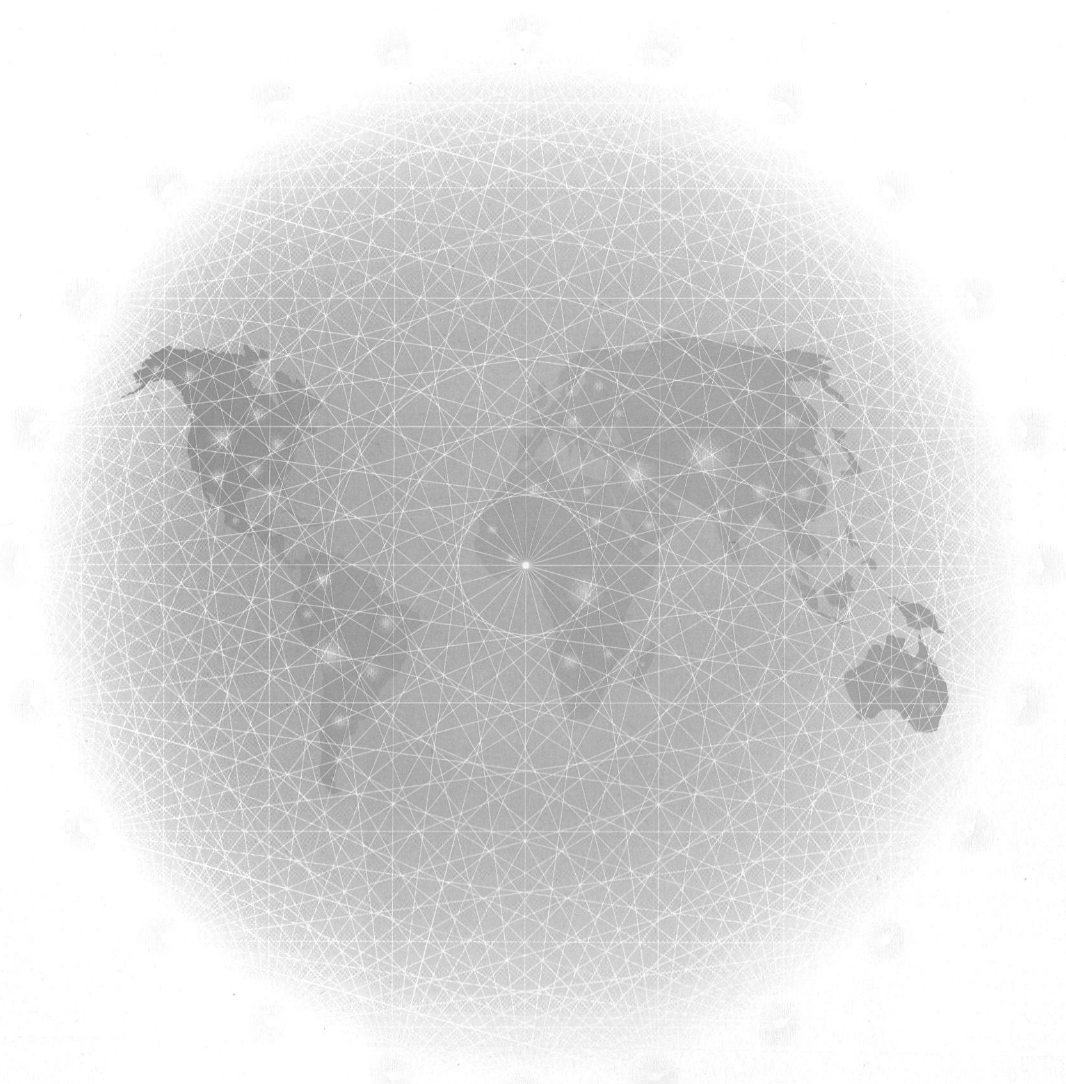

Figure 1-10 The Internet is a worldwide collection of networks that links together millions of businesses, government agencies, educational institutions, and individuals.

Figure 1-11 When you buy software, you receive media such as CD-ROMs or a DVD-ROM that contains the software program.

can load in memory directly from the media. With other programs, you must **install** a part or all of the software on the computer's hard disk before you can use the program. Some programs also require you insert the media, such as a CD-ROM, into the drive while you use, or run, the program. Others do not. Figure 1-12 shows the steps a user follows to run a computer program that allows you to create a greeting card. This program requires a CD-ROM in the CD-ROM drive.

When you buy a computer, it usually has some software pre-installed on its hard disk. This enables you to use the computer as soon as you set it up.

Software is the key to productive use of computers. With the proper software, a computer can become a valuable tool. Two types of software exist: system software and application software. The following pages describe these categories of software.

Web Link

For more information on computer programs, visit the Discovering Computers 2002 Chapter 1 WEB LINK page (**scsite.com/dc2002/ch1/weblink.htm**) and click Computer Programs.

Figure 1-12 RUNNING A COMPUTER PROGRAM FROM A CD-ROM

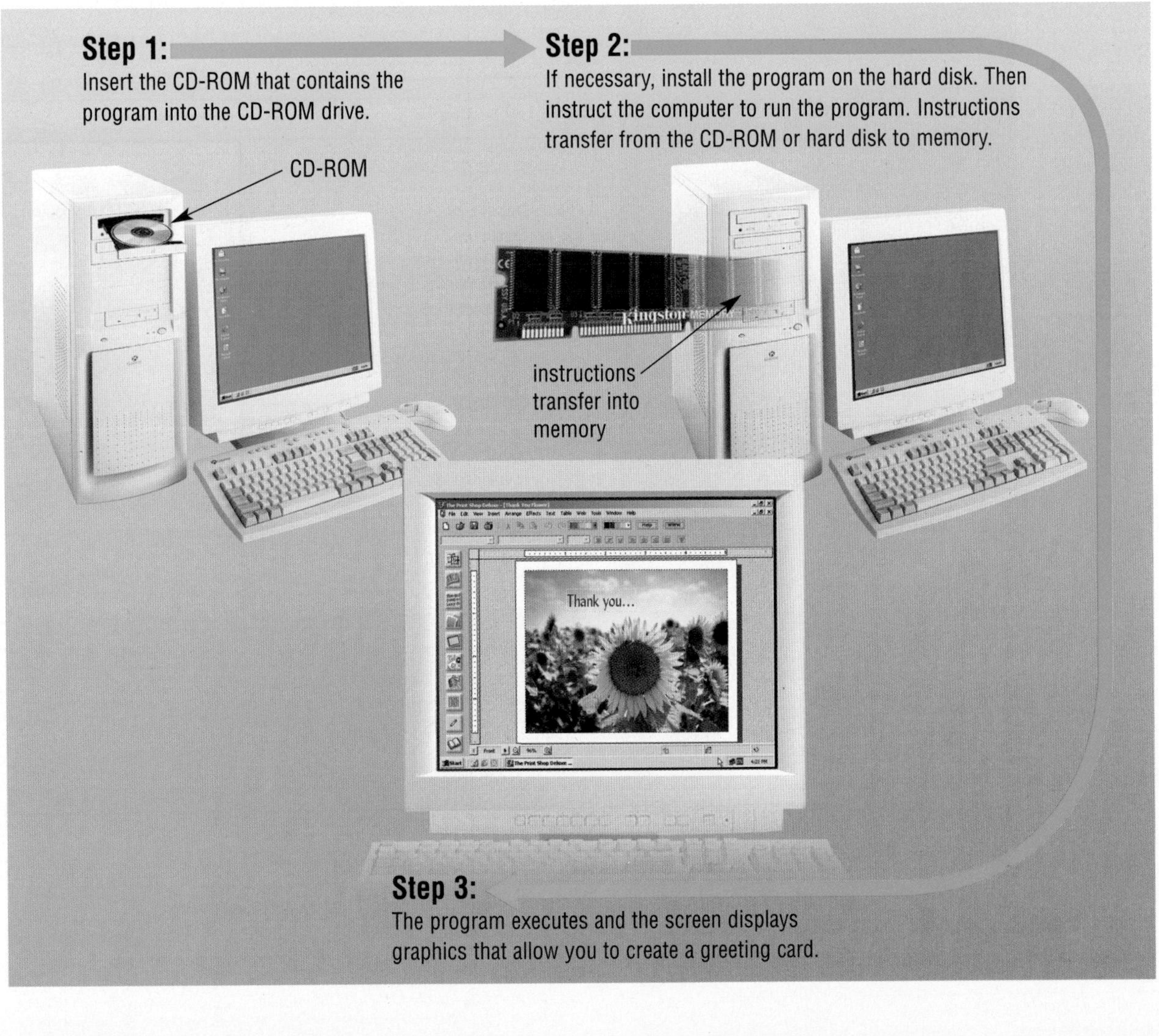

Step 1:
Insert the CD-ROM that contains the program into the CD-ROM drive.
CD-ROM
Step 2:
If necessary, install the program on the hard disk. Then instruct the computer to run the program. Instructions transfer from the CD-ROM or hard disk to memory.
instructions transfer into memory
Thank you...
Step 3:
The program executes and the screen displays graphics that allow you to create a greeting card.

System Software

System software consists of the programs that control the operations of the computer and its devices. System software serves as the interface between the user, the application software, and the computer's hardware. Two types of system software are the operating system and utility programs.

OPERATING SYSTEM An **operating system (OS)** is a set of programs containing instructions that coordinate all the activities among computer hardware devices. The operating system also contains instructions that allow you to run application software. Many of today's computers use the Microsoft Windows operating system.

When you start a computer, the operating system loads into memory from the computer's hard disk. It remains in memory while the computer is running and allows you to communicate with the computer and other software.

UTILITY PROGRAMS A **utility program** is a type of system software that performs a specific task, usually related to managing a computer, its devices, or its programs. An example of a utility program is an uninstaller, which removes a program that has been installed on a computer. Most operating systems include several utility programs for managing disk drives, printers, and other devices. You also can buy stand-alone utility programs to perform additional computer management functions.

USER INTERFACE You interact with software through its user interface. The user interface controls how you enter data and instructions and how information displays on the screen. Many of today's software programs have a graphical user interface. With a **graphical user interface (GUI** pronounced gooey), you interact with the software using visual images such as icons. An **icon** is a small image that represents a program, an instruction, or some other object. You can select icons with the mouse to perform operations such as starting a program. Figure 1-13 shows the graphical user interface of the Microsoft Windows operating system.

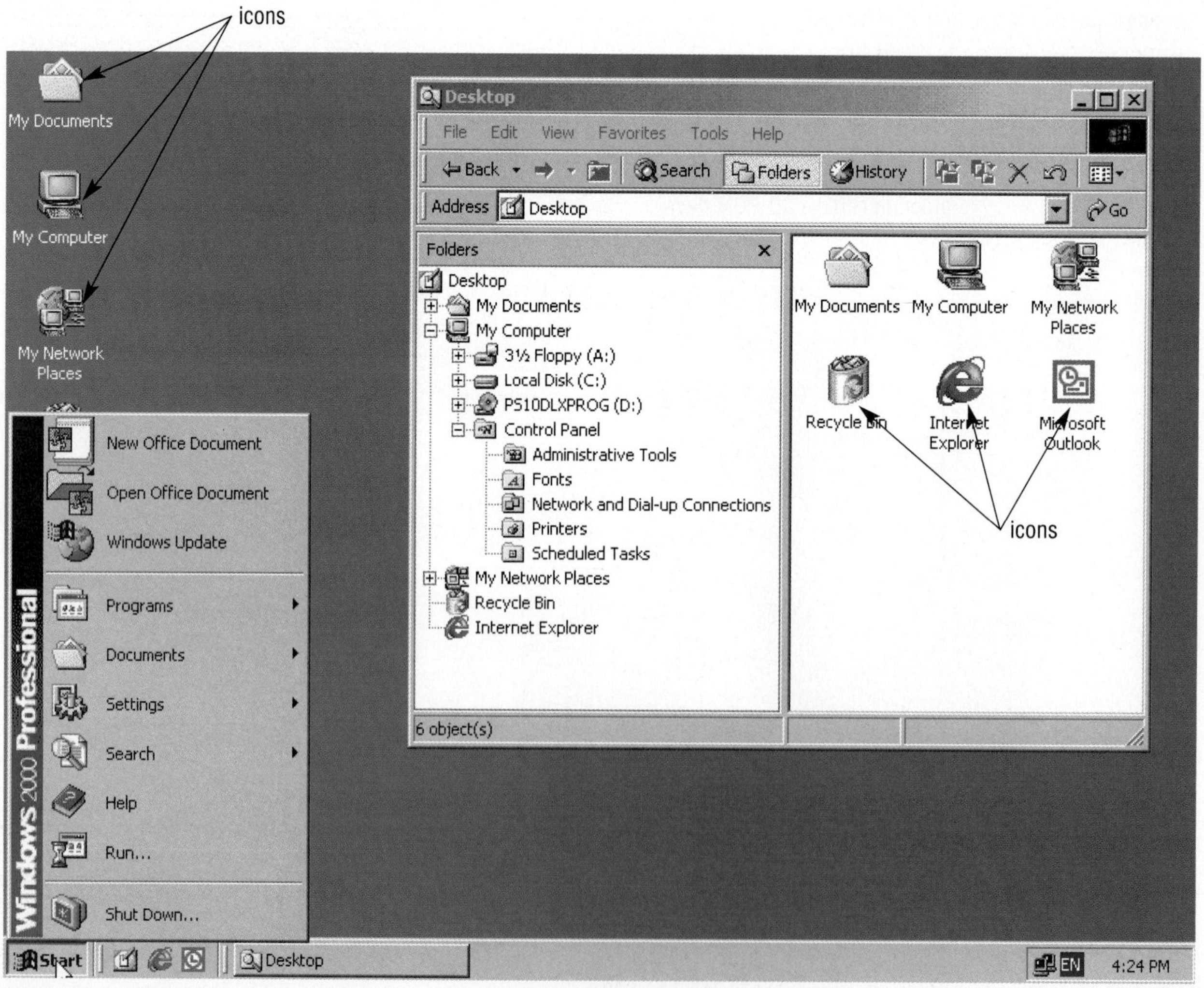

Figure 1-13 Microsoft Windows is an operating system that has a graphical user interface.

Application Software

Application software consists of programs that perform specific tasks for users. Popular application software includes word processing software, spreadsheet software, database software, and presentation graphics software. Word processing software allows you to create documents such as letters, memorandums, and brochures. Spreadsheet software allows you to calculate numbers arranged in rows and columns. Users perform financial tasks such as budgeting and forecasting with spreadsheet software. Database software allows you to store data in an organized fashion, as well as retrieve, manipulate, and display that data in a variety of formats. With presentation graphics software, you create documents called slides that add visual appeal to presentations. Software vendors often bundle and sell these four applications together as a single unit. This bundle, called a suite, costs much less than if you purchased the applications individually.

Many other types of application software exist that enable users to perform a variety of tasks. Some widely used applications include the following: reference, education, and entertainment; desktop publishing; photo and video editing; multimedia authoring; network, communications, electronic mail (e-mail), and Web browsers; accounting; project management; and personal information management. Chapter 2 discusses Web browsers and e-mail, and Chapter 3 discusses the other applications.

Application software is available in a variety of forms: packaged, custom, freeware, public domain, shareware, and from application service providers.

PACKAGED SOFTWARE **Packaged software** is copyrighted retail software that meets the needs of a wide variety of users, not just a single user or company. You can purchase packaged software from stores that sell computer products (Figure 1-14a). You also can purchase packaged software from companies on the Internet (Figure 1-14b).

Figure 1-14b (online computer store)

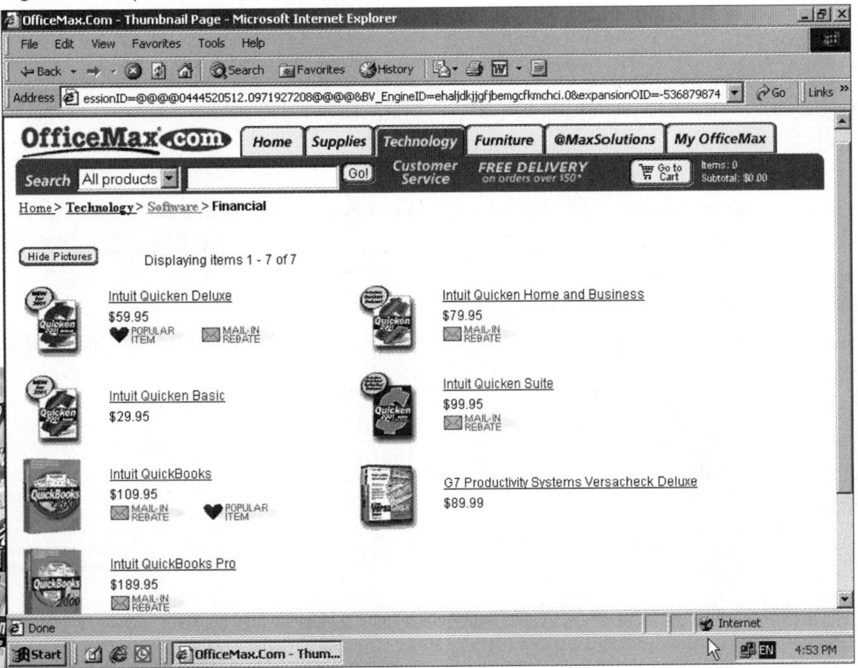

Figure 1-14a (computer store)

Figure 1-14 Packaged software programs can be purchased from computer stores, office equipment suppliers, retailers, and software vendors. Many stores, such as OfficeMax shown in this figure, allow you to purchase software programs on the Internet.

Web Link

For more information on application software, visit the Discovering Computers 2002 Chapter 1 WEB LINK page (**scsite.com/dc2002/ch1/weblink.htm**) and click Application Software.

CUSTOM SOFTWARE Sometimes a user or company with unique software requirements cannot find packaged software that meets all its needs. In this case, the person or company can opt for custom software. **Custom software**, written by a programmer, is a tailor-made program developed at a user's request to perform specific functions.

FREEWARE, PUBLIC-DOMAIN SOFTWARE, AND SHAREWARE
Freeware is software provided at no cost to a user by an individual or company. Freeware is copyrighted. You cannot resell it as your own. **Public-domain software** also is free software, but it has been donated for public use and has no copyright restrictions.

Shareware is copyrighted software that is distributed free for a trial period. If you want to use a shareware program beyond that period of time, you send a payment to the person or company that developed the program. Companies that develop shareware rely on the honor system. The company trusts you to send payment if you continue to use the software beyond the stated trial period. Upon sending this small fee, the developer registers you to receive service assistance and updates.

Examples of shareware, freeware, and public-domain software include utility programs, graphics programs, and games. Thousands of these programs are available on the Internet to download, or copy to your computer. You also can obtain copies of these programs from the developer, a coworker, or a friend.

APPLICATION SERVICE PROVIDER
Storing and maintaining programs can be a costly investment for individuals and businesses. Some opt to use an application service provider for their software needs. An **application service provider** (**ASP**) is a third-party company that manages and distributes software and services on the Internet. That is, instead of installing the software on your computer, you run the programs from the Internet. Some vendors provide access to the software at no cost. Others charge for use of the program.

Software Development

A **computer programmer**, also called a **programmer**, is someone who writes software programs. Programmers write the instructions that direct the computer to process data into information. A programmer must place instructions in the correct sequence so the computer generates the desired results. Complex programs can require hundreds of thousands of program instructions.

When writing complex programs for large businesses, programmers often follow a plan developed by a systems analyst. A **systems analyst** designs a program, working with both the user and the programmer to determine the desired output of the program.

Programmers use a programming language to write computer programs. Some programming languages, such as JavaScript, allow programmers to develop applications that run on the Internet. Figure 1-15 shows an Internet application and the instructions the programmer writes to create the application.

Figure 1-15a (JavaScript program)

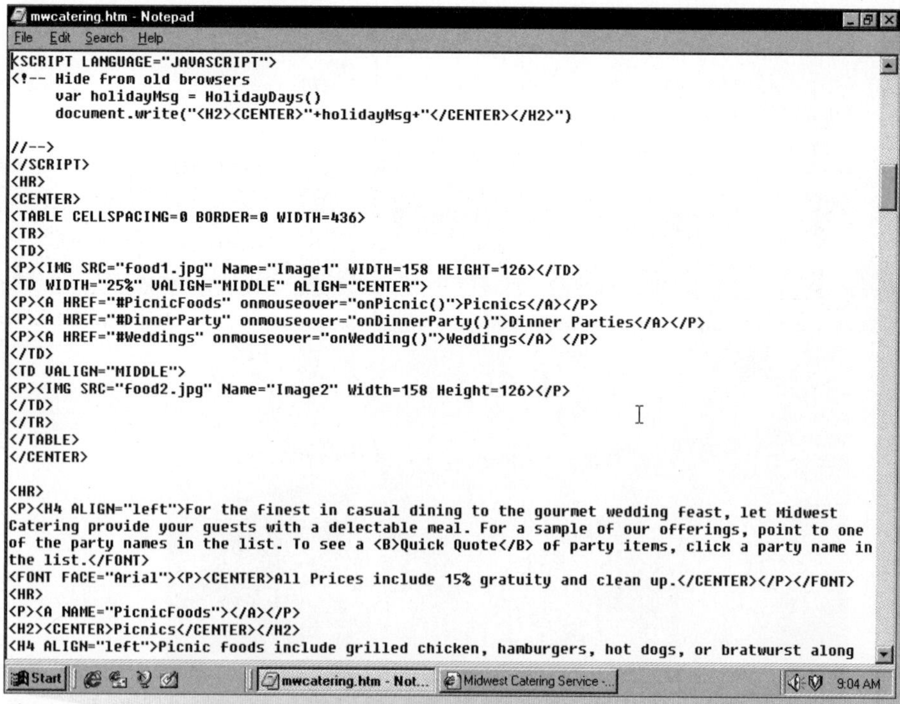

Figure 1-15 This figure illustrates an Internet application and the instructions a programmer writes in JavaScript to create the application.

ISSUE

The Computer Can Do It

Computer Software

Popular theory says that if an auditorium full of monkeys each were given a typewriter, eventually they would produce a classic novel. Monkeys may or may not be able to emulate Shakespeare, but today's computers can perform assignments once thought exclusively human. Computers have been programmed to read written work and answer questions, demonstrating comprehension. One computer has been programmed to paint, producing pictures that have sold for more than $20,000. Computer-controlled robots can play soccer. The computerized WARREN system (see URL below) helps you manage your investment portfolio. What types of activities or problems, if any, still do not embrace computer involvement? Why? Will computers someday be capable of handling these activities or problems? Why or why not?

For more information on the application of computers and the Web site mentioned above, visit the Discovering Computers 2002 Issues Web page (**scsite.com/dc2002/issues.htm**) and click Chapter 1 Issue #3.

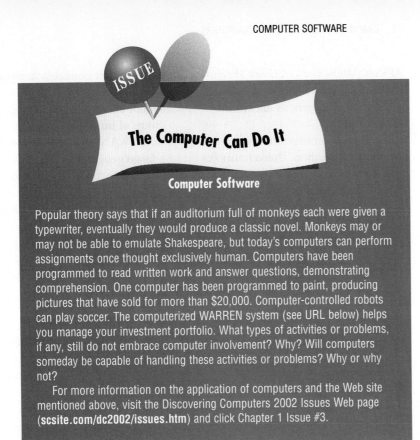

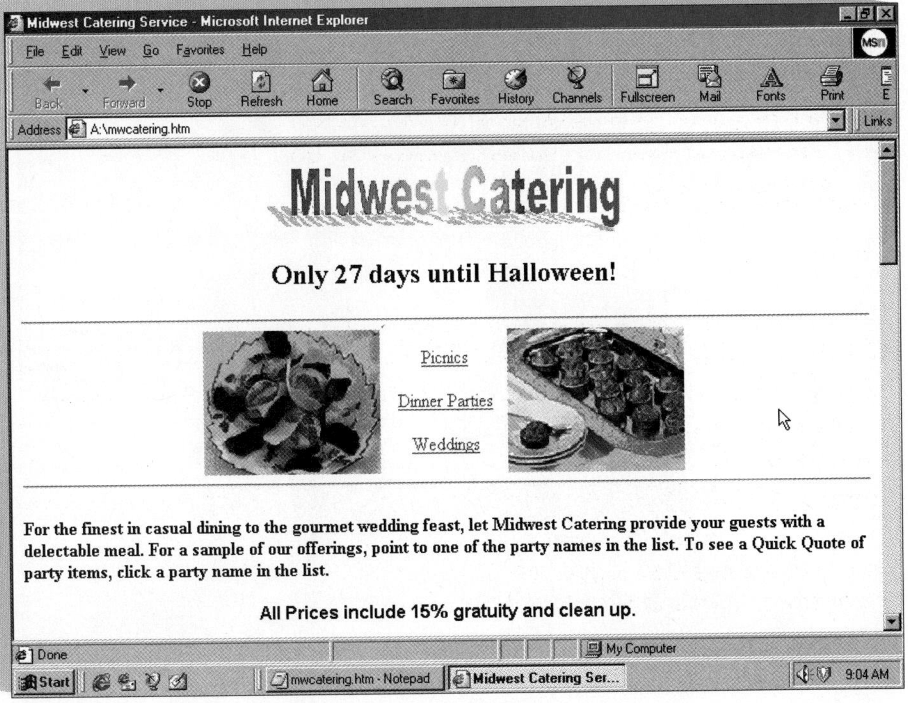

Figure 1-15b (Internet application)

APPLY IT!

Software – Purchase it Packaged, Subscribe, or Download?

Buying software used to be simple — you either purchased it from a local store or ordered it for delivery. You still have these options, but others have emerged. Providing the consumer the option to purchase and download software via the Internet, for example, is becoming standard practice for many online companies. Alternatively, Microsoft.NET is Microsoft's recent business strategy aimed at making Microsoft's existing software available on the Internet. With the Microsoft option, the user subscribes to and uses only the programs and data needed. If you are in the market to purchase or upgrade software and are unsure which option is best for you, consider the following:

- Purchasing packaged software
  - Pros: physical media in hand, easy to reinstall, does not require online access
  - Cons: limited to one computer, requires registration for upgrades, media may become damaged or lost
- Downloading from the Internet
  - Pros: easy to do, accessible 24 hours — the store is always open, easy to upgrade
  - Cons: service interruption while downloading, requires credit card information be posted online, hardware problems — reinstallation, need to download user manual
- Subscribing to and using Internet-based software
  - Pros: latest versions, accessible from any location with Internet access, access to online help, subscription not limited to one computer, use only the program and features you need
  - Cons: online access required, requires credit card information be posted online, data security, need to download user manual

For more information on software downloading or purchasing, visit the Discovering Computers 2002 Apply It Web page (**scsite.com/dc2002/apply.htm**) and click Chapter 1 Apply It #1.

NETWORKS AND THE INTERNET

A **network** is a collection of computers and devices connected together via communications devices and media. A modem is an example of a communications device. Examples of communications media are cables, telephone lines, cellular radio, and satellites. Some of these media, such as satellites and cellular radio, are wireless, which means they have no physical lines or wires. When your computer connects to a network, you are considered **online**.

Networks allow users to share **resources**, such as hardware devices, software programs, data, and information. Sharing resources saves time and money. For example, instead of purchasing one printer for every computer in a company or in a home, you can connect a single printer and all computers via a network (Figure 1-16). This type of network enables all of the computers to access the same printer.

Most businesses network their computers together. These networks can be relatively small or quite extensive. A local area network (LAN) is a network that connects computers in a limited geographic area, such as a school computer laboratory, office, or group of buildings. A wide area network (WAN) is a network that covers a large geographical area, such as one that connects the district offices across the country (Figure 1-17).

Figure 1-16 This local area network (LAN) enables two separate computers to share the same printer.

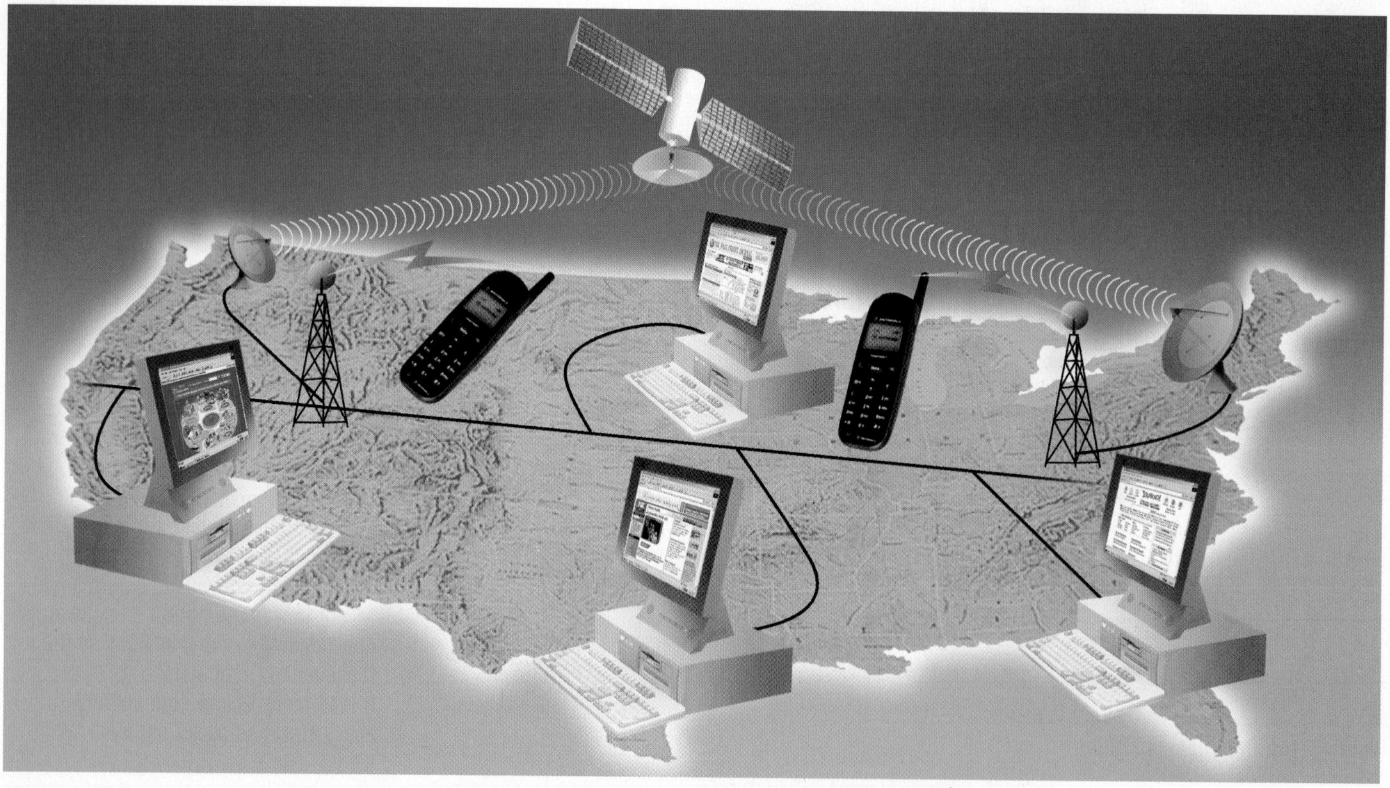

Figure 1-17 A network can be quite large and complex, connecting users in district offices around the country.

The world's largest network is the Internet. The **Internet** is a worldwide collection of networks that links together millions of businesses, government agencies, educational institutions, and individuals. With an abundance of resources and data accessible via the Internet, more than 360 million users around the world are making use of the Internet for a variety of reasons, some of which include the following (Figure 1-18):

- Sending messages to other connected users
- Accessing a wealth of information, such as news, maps, airline schedules, and stock market data
- Shopping for goods and services
- Meeting or conversing with people around the world
- Accessing sources of entertainment and leisure, such as online games, music, books, magazines, and vacation planning guides

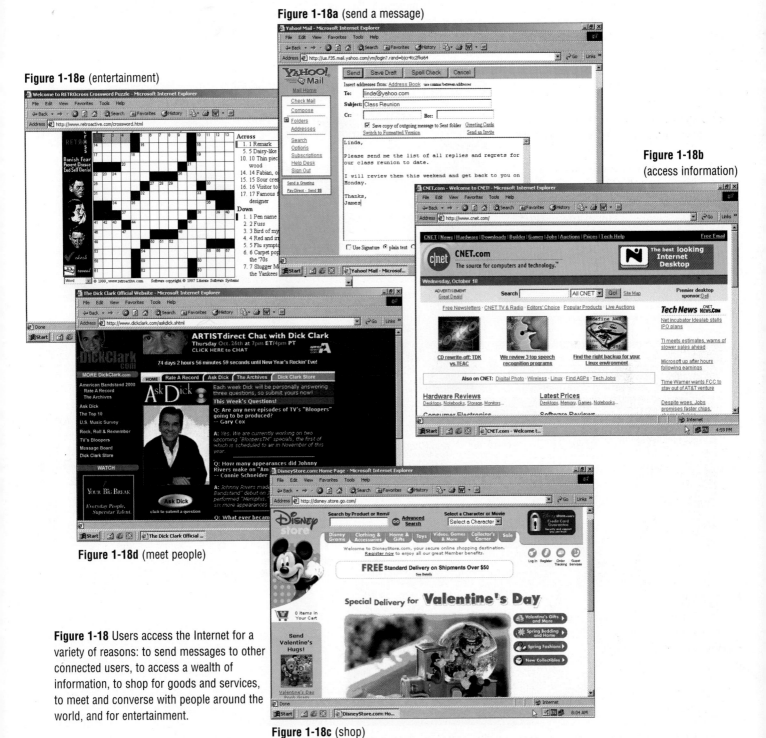

Figure 1-18a (send a message)

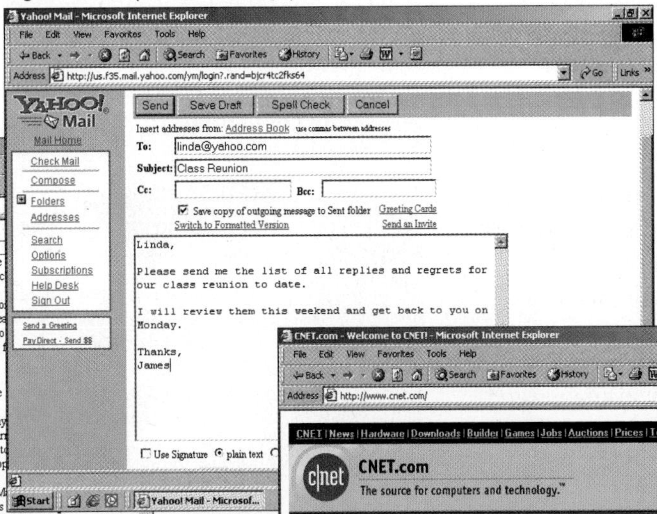

Figure 1-18e (entertainment)

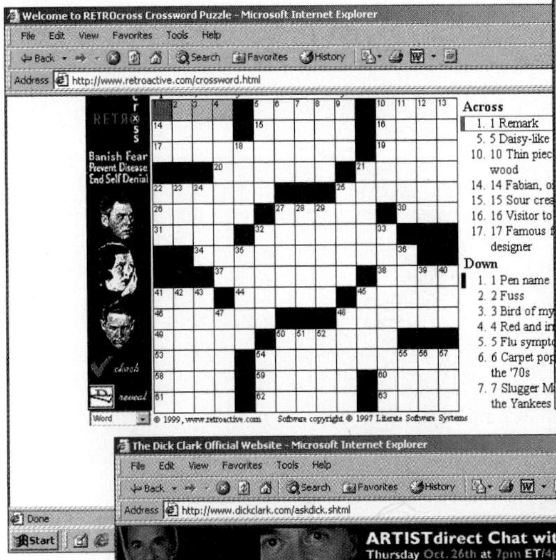

Figure 1-18b (access information)

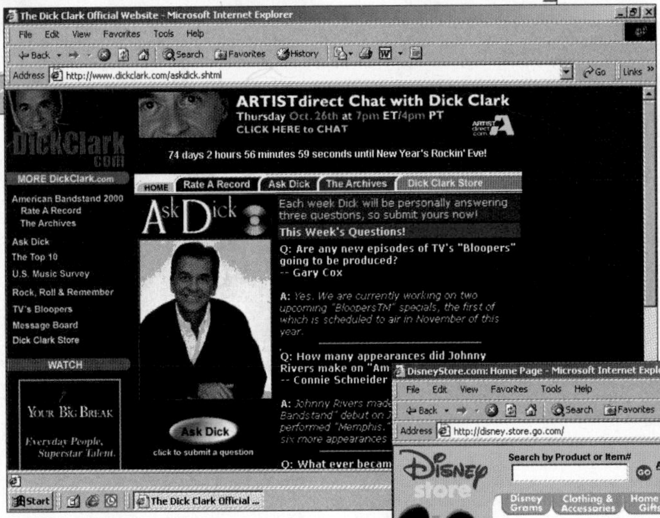

Figure 1-18d (meet people)

Figure 1-18c (shop)

Figure 1-18 Users access the Internet for a variety of reasons: to send messages to other connected users, to access a wealth of information, to shop for goods and services, to meet and converse with people around the world, and for entertainment.

Most users connect to the Internet in one of two ways: through an Internet service provider or through an online service provider. An Internet service provider (ISP) is a company that supplies connections to the Internet, usually for a monthly fee. An online service provider (OSP) also provides access to the Internet, as well as a variety of other specialized content and services such as financial data, hardware and software guides, news, weather, legal information, and other similar commodities. For this reason, the fees for using an OSP sometimes are slightly higher than fees for using an ISP. Two popular OSPs are America Online and The Microsoft Network.

One of the more popular segments of the Internet is the World Wide Web, also called the Web. The Web contains billions of documents called Web pages. A Web page contains text, graphics, sound, or video, and has built-in connections, or links, to other Web documents. Computers throughout the world store Web pages. The screens shown in Figure 1-18 on the previous page are examples of Web pages.

A Web site is a collection of related Web pages. You access and view Web pages using a software program called a Web browser. The two most popular Web browsers are Microsoft Internet Explorer and Netscape Navigator. Figure 1-19 illustrates one method of connecting to the Web and displaying a Web page.

Web Link

For more information on the Internet, visit the Discovering Computers 2002 Chapter 1 WEB LINK page (**scsite.com/dc2002/ch1/weblink.htm**) and click Internet.

Figure 1-19 CONNECTING TO THE INTERNET AND DISPLAYING A WEB PAGE

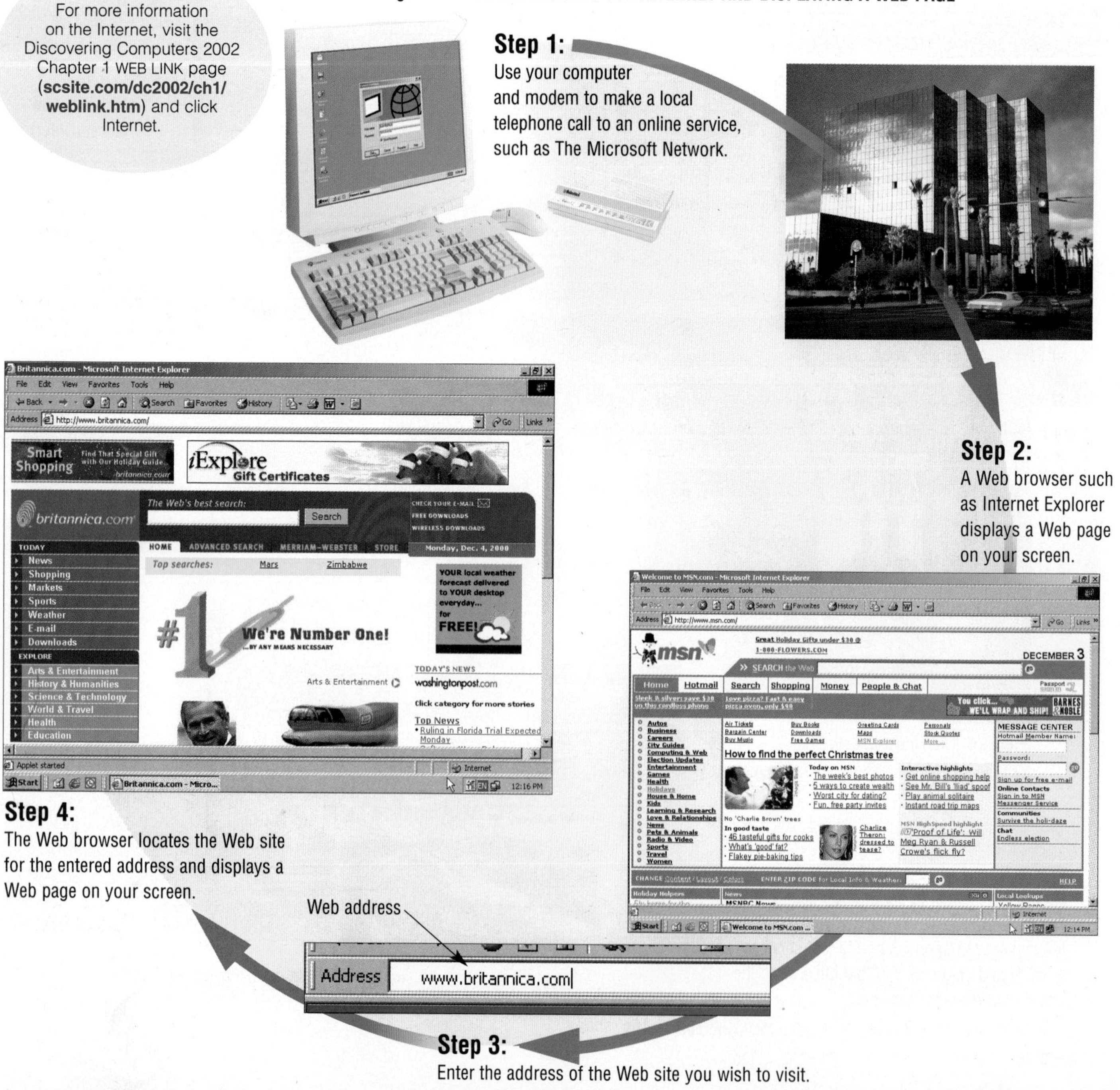

Step 1:
Use your computer and modem to make a local telephone call to an online service, such as The Microsoft Network.
Step 2:
A Web browser such as Internet Explorer displays a Web page on your screen.
Step 3:
Enter the address of the Web site you wish to visit.
Step 4:
The Web browser locates the Web site for the entered address and displays a Web page on your screen.
Web address
Address www.britannica.com

CATEGORIES OF COMPUTERS

The six major categories of computers are personal computers, handheld computers, Internet appliances, mid-range servers, mainframes, and supercomputers. These categories are based on the differences in the size, speed, processing capabilities, and price of computers. Due to rapidly changing technology, the categories cannot be defined precisely. For example, the speed that defines a mainframe today may define a mid-range server next year. Some characteristics may overlap categories. Still, many people refer to these categories when discussing computers.

Figure 1-20 summarizes the six categories of computers, and the following pages discuss them.

PERSONAL COMPUTERS

A **personal computer** is a computer that can perform all of its input, processing, output, and storage activities by itself. A personal computer contains at least one input device, one output device, one storage device, memory, and a processor. On a personal computer, all of the processor's functions typically reside on a single chip, often called a microprocessor. The processor is the basic building block of a personal computer.

Two popular series of personal computers are the PC (Figure 1-21) and the Apple Macintosh (Figure 1-22). These two types

Category	Physical size	Number of simultaneously connected users	General price range
Personal computer (desktop or notebook)	Fits on a desk or on your lap	Usually one, or many networked	Several thousand dollars or less
Handheld computer	Fits in your hand	Usually one	Several hundred dollars or less
Internet appliance	Fits on a countertop	Usually one	Several hundred dollars or less
Mid-range server	Small cabinet	Two to thousands	\$5,000 to \$150,000
Mainframe	Partial room to a full room of equipment	Hundreds to thousands	\$300,000 to several million dollars
Supercomputer	Full room of equipment	Hundreds to thousands	Several million dollars and up

Figure 1-20 This table summarizes some of the differences among the categories of computers. These should be considered general guidelines only because of rapid changes in technology.

Figure 1-21 The PC and compatibles use the Windows operating system.

Figure 1-22 The Apple Macintosh uses the Macintosh operating system.

of computers have different processors and use different operating systems. The PC and compatibles use the Windows operating system. The Apple Macintosh uses the Macintosh operating system (Mac OS). Today, the terms PC and compatible refer to any personal computer that is based on specifications of the original IBM personal computer. Companies such as Gateway, Compaq, Dell, and Toshiba all sell PC-compatible computers.

Two major categories of personal computers are desktop computers and notebook computers. The next two sections discuss these types of personal computers.

Desktop Computers

A **desktop computer** is designed so the system unit, input devices, output devices, and any other devices fit entirely on or under a desk or table (Figure 1-23). In some models, the monitor sits on top of the system unit, which is placed on top of the desk. A **tower model**, by contrast, has a tall and narrow system unit that can sit on the floor vertically — if space is limited on your desktop. Tower model desktop computers are available in a variety of heights: a full tower is at least 24 inches tall, a mid-tower is about 16 inches tall, and a mini-tower is usually 13 inches tall. The model of desktop computer you use often depends on the design of your workspace.

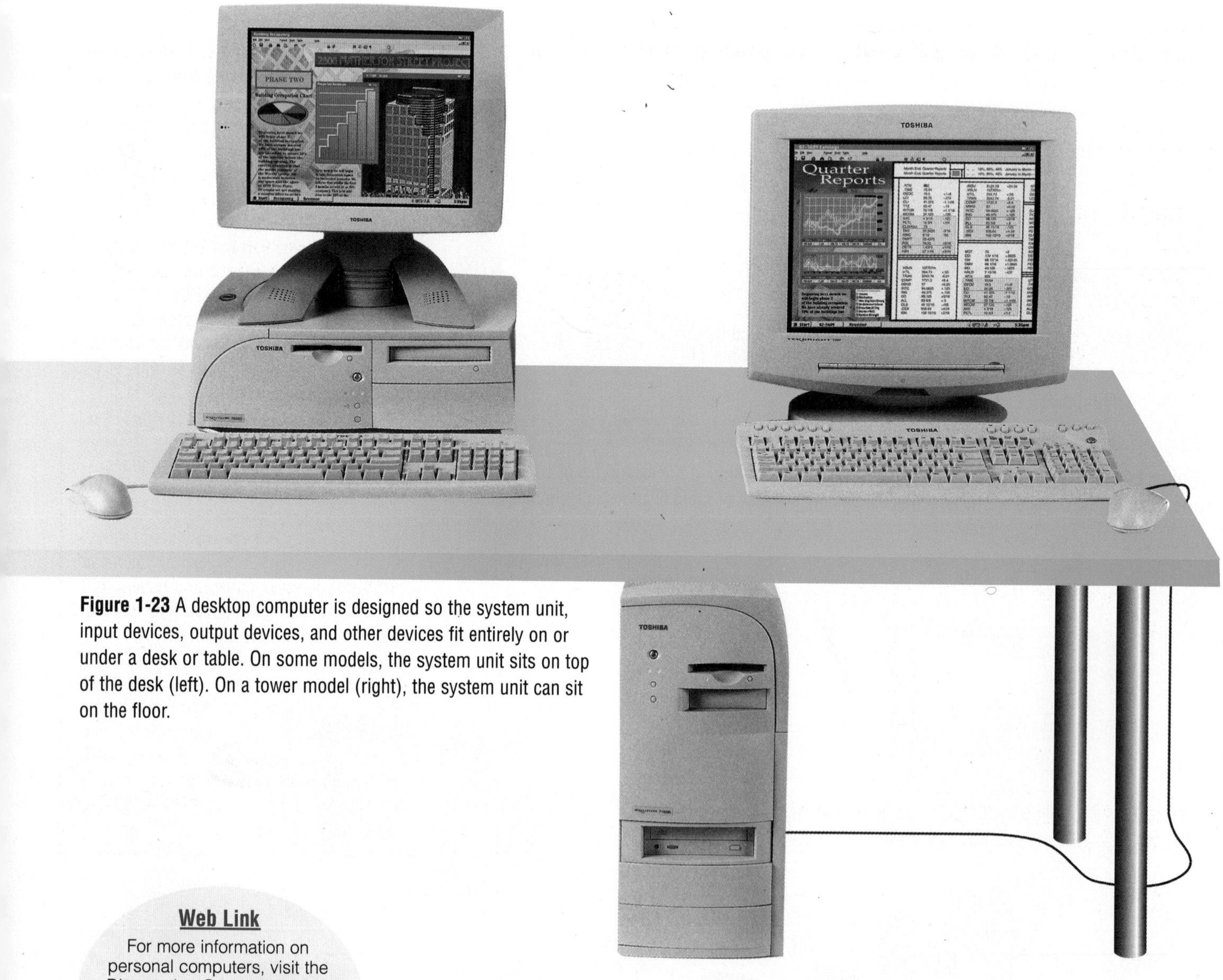

Figure 1-23 A desktop computer is designed so the system unit, input devices, output devices, and other devices fit entirely on or under a desk or table. On some models, the system unit sits on top of the desk (left). On a tower model (right), the system unit can sit on the floor.

Web Link

For more information on personal computers, visit the Discovering Computers 2002 Chapter 1 WEB LINK page (**scsite.com/dc2002/ch1/weblink.htm**) and click Personal Computers.

An **all-in-one computer** is a less expensive desktop computer that combines the monitor and system unit into a single device (Figure 1-24). These compact computers are ideal for the casual home user.

A **workstation** is a more expensive and powerful desktop computer designed for work that requires intense calculations and graphics capabilities. Users in fields such as engineering, desktop publishing, and graphic art use workstations. An architect uses a workstation to view and create maps. A graphic artist uses a workstation to create computer-animated special effects for Hollywood movies.

A **stand-alone computer** is a computer that can perform the information processing cycle operations (input, process, output, and storage) without being connected to a network. Most stand-alone desktop computers today also have networking capabilities.

Some desktop computers also are powerful enough to function as a server on a network. A **server** is a computer that manages the resources on a network. Servers control access to the software, printers, and other devices on the network. Servers also provide a centralized storage area for software programs and data. The other computers on the network, called

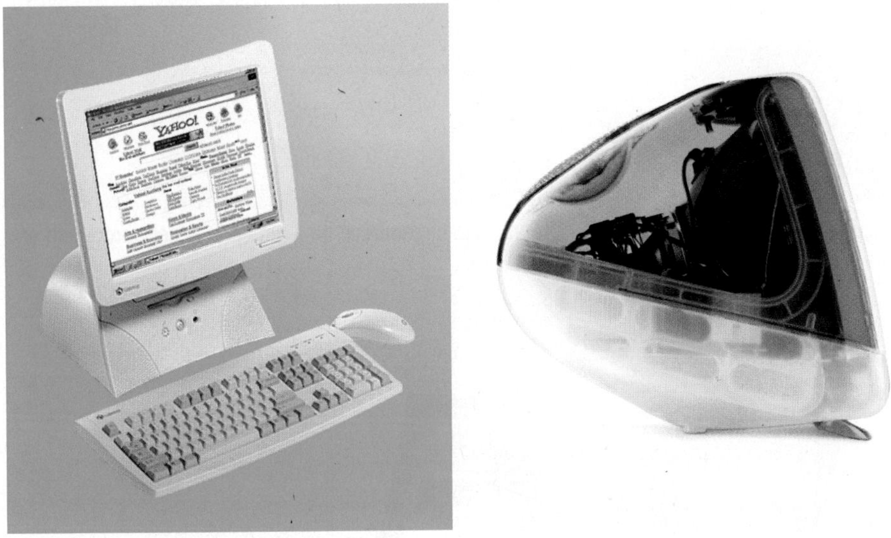

Figure 1-24 An all-in-one computer is a less expensive desktop computer that combines the monitor and system unit into a single device.

COMPANY ON THE CUTTING EDGE

Gateway

Mooo-ving Beyond the PC Box

Cow-spotted boxes are festive icons in the computer world. Gateway's trademark shipping cartons mean only one thing: a personal computer from one of the world's leading technology manufacturers.

From its humble beginnings as a two-person operation in a Sioux City, Iowa, farmhouse, Gateway has grown to a 20,000-employee Fortune 250 company. Founder Ted Waitt had the unique vision to manufacture built-to-order PCs. With a warehouse of parts to build systems, Gateway offers customers exactly what they want. Consumers from Asia, Europe, and the United States order more than 11,000 custom systems daily via the Internet, the telephone, or at Gateway Country stores. Inventory is replenished about 40 times yearly.

The company realizes that the hardware is only a tool that helps users play, work, and learn. Focusing on a lifelong relationship, its Your:)Ware program allows buyers to trade in their computers after two years and upgrade to state-of-the-art products. Gateway offers online, CD, and instructor-led training, an online software and peripheral store, and its own bundled Internet access. Indeed, Gateway is thinking beyond the box.

For more information on Gateway, visit the Discovering Computers 2002 Companies Web page (**scsite.com/dc2002/companies.htm**) and click Gateway.

clients, can access the contents of the storage area on the servers (Figure 1-25). Instead of clients, some people refer to these attached computers as workstations — giving the term workstation two entirely separate meanings.

In a network, one or more computers usually are designated as the server(s). The major difference between the server and client computers is the server ordinarily has more power and more storage space.

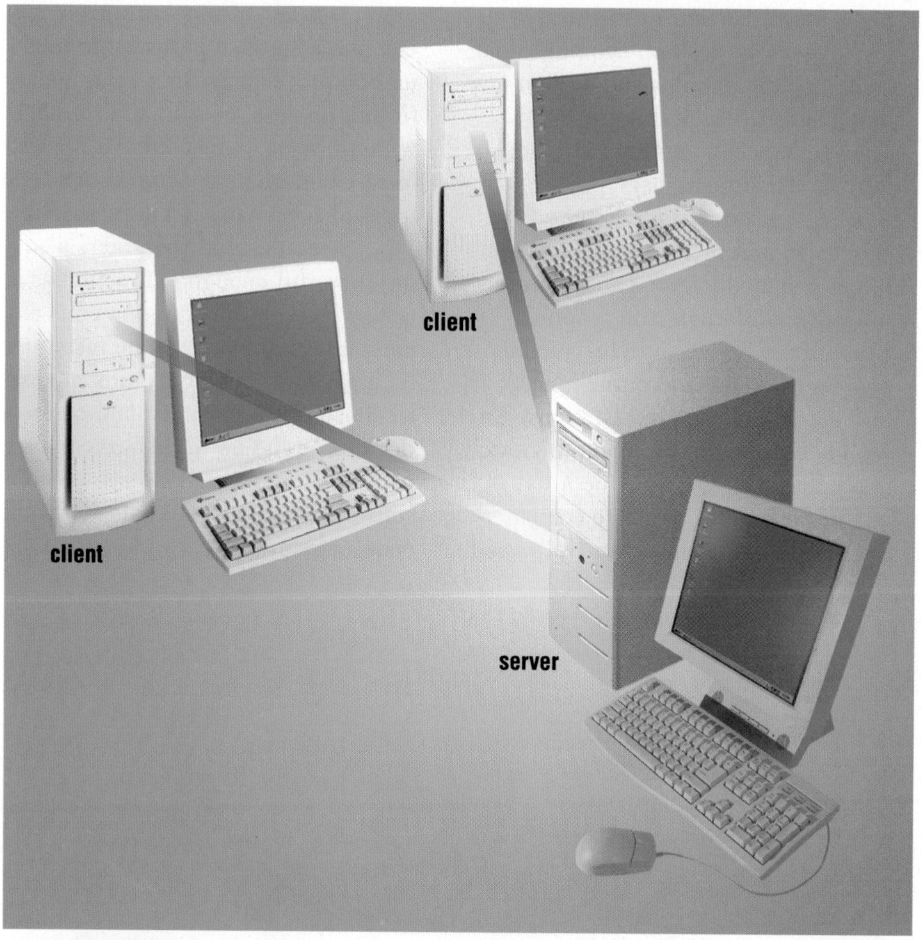

Figure 1-25 A server is a computer that manages resources on a network. Other computers on the network are called clients.

Notebook Computers

A **notebook computer**, also called a **laptop computer**, is a portable, personal computer small enough to fit on your lap. Today's notebook computers are thin, lightweight, and can be as powerful as the average desktop computer. Notebook computers generally are more expensive than desktop computers with equal capabilities.

On a typical notebook computer, the keyboard is located on top of the system unit, the monitor attaches to the system unit with a hinge, and the drives are built into the system unit (Figure 1-26). Weighing on average between 4 and 10 pounds, you easily can transport these computers from place to place. Most notebook computers can run either on batteries or a standard power supply. Users with mobile computing needs, such as business travelers, often have a notebook computer.

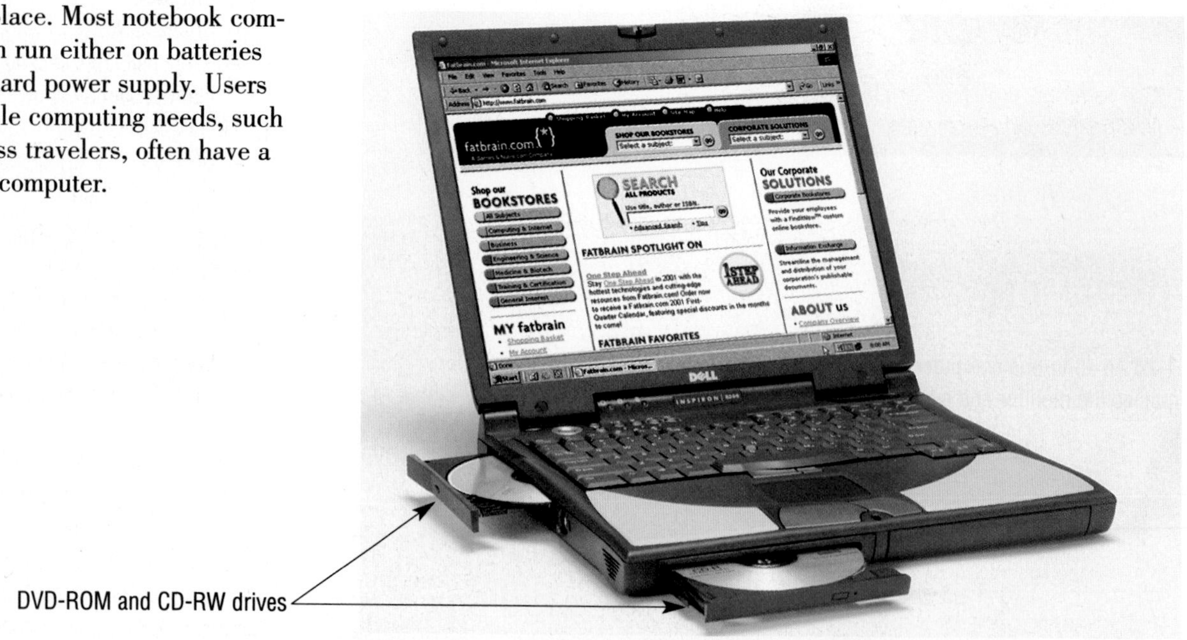

Figure 1-26 On a typical notebook computer, the keyboard is on top of the system unit, the monitor attaches to the system unit with a hinge, and the drives are built-in to the system unit.

HANDHELD COMPUTERS

A **handheld computer**, sometimes called a **palmtop computer**, is a small computer that fits in your hand (Figure 1-27). Because of their reduced size, the screens on handheld computers are quite small. Some have small keyboards. Others have no keyboard at all. Computers in the handheld category usually do not have disk drives. Instead, programs and data are stored on chips inside the system unit or on miniature storage media.

You typically can connect a handheld computer to a larger computer to exchange information between the two computers. A business traveler or other mobile user might use a handheld computer if a notebook computer is too large. Employees whose jobs require them to move from place to place such as parcel delivery people and meter readers also use specific industry-related handheld computers.

Handheld computers often include a stylus for input. A stylus looks like a ballpoint pen, but uses pressure, instead of ink, to write text and draw lines. With the stylus, also called a pen, you write on the screen instead of typing on a keyboard. These computers contain special software that permits the computer to recognize handwritten characters and other symbols. As an alternative to typing or writing, some handheld computers support voice input so you can enter text and instructions by speaking into the computer.

Figure 1-28 shows one of the most popular handheld computers in use today. Sometimes called a **PDA (personal digital assistant)**, these

Figure 1-27 A handheld computer is a small personal computer designed to fit in your hand.

Figure 1-28 With some handheld computers, you write directly on the screen with the stylus.

APPLY IT!

Lease or Purchase?

Your computer is old, and you are ready to upgrade. You discover many companies now offer a lease option — somewhat similar to what many automobile companies offer. The question is: When considering the obsolescence factor of a personal computer, does it make sense to lease rather than buy? Consider the following advantages and disadvantages when making your decision.

- Purchase Advantages
  - You own it
  - Tax deductions if used for business-related activities
  - Upgrade options
- Purchase Disadvantages
  - Obsolescence
  - Drains cash
  - Responsible for repairs
  - Interest payments
- Lease Advantages
  - Obsolescence not a factor
  - Conserves cash
  - Increases technological flexibility
- Lease Disadvantages
  - Generally more expensive
  - Will be charged for damage
  - Lease agreement might be confining or have penalty clause

Before making a decision, consider a Lease/Buy Analyzer program. Several of these are free online (see URL below).

For more information on leasing versus purchasing and the Web site mentioned above, visit the Discovering Computers 2002 Apply It Web page (**scsite.com/dc2002/apply.htm**) and click Chapter 1 Apply It #2.

lightweight handheld computers provide personal organizer functions such as a calendar, appointment book, address book, calculator, and notepad. Most of these handheld computers also offer basic software applications such as word processing and spreadsheet. Because of all these added features, many people have replaced their pocket-sized appointment book with these small handheld computers.

Some handheld computers are Web-enabled, allowing you also to access the Internet wirelessly. Other Web-enabled devices include cellular telephones and pagers (Figure 1-29). A **Web-enabled cellular telephone**, sometimes called a **smart phone**, allows you to send and receive messages on the Internet and browse Web sites specifically configured for display on the telephone. A **Web-enabled pager**, also called a **smart pager**, is a two-way radio that allows you to send and receive messages on the Internet.

INTERNET APPLIANCES

A **Internet appliance**, also called an **information appliance**, is a computer with limited fuctionality whose main purpose is to connect to the Internet from home. Internet appliances are available in a variety of styles, sizes, colors, and sleek designs.

Some Internet appliances look much like a desktop computer (Figure 1-30). Manufacturers typically pre-install all software on these Internet appliances, making it very easy for the novice user to work on the

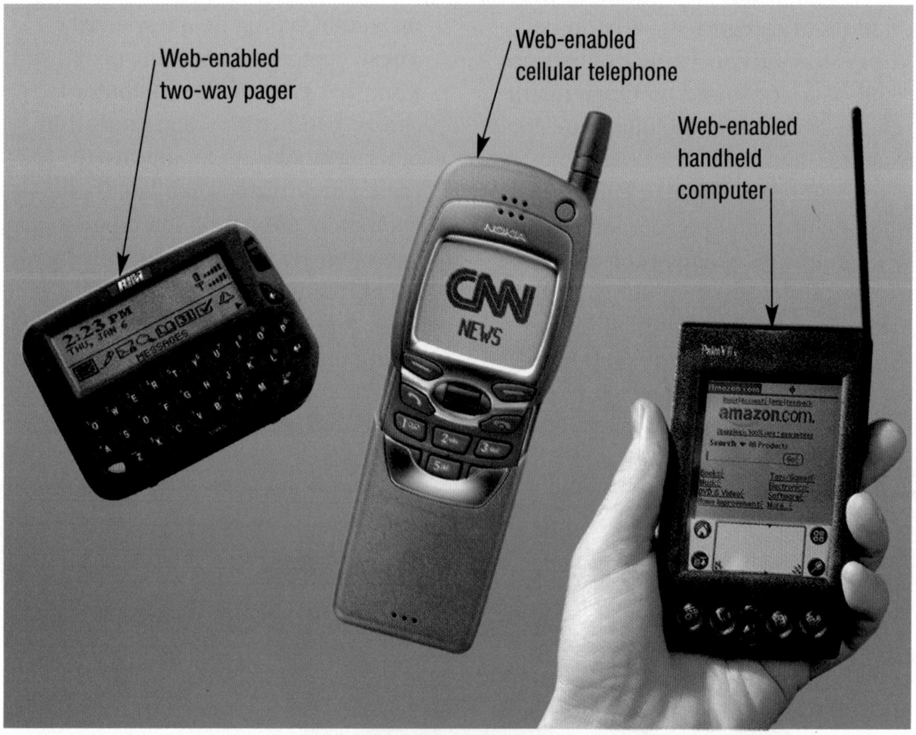

Figure 1-29 These handheld computers and devices are small enough to fit in the palm of your hand.

Figure 1-30 This Internet appliance is equipped with all the software you need to access the Internet easily from any room in the house.

Web Link

For more information on handheld computers, visit the Discovering Computers 2002 Chapter 1 WEB LINK page (**scsite.com/dc2002/ch1/weblink.htm**) and click Handheld Computers.

Internet. Another popular Internet appliance is a set-top box. A set-top box, such as WebTV™, sits on top of or next to a television set and allows you to access the Internet and navigate Web pages using a device that resembles a remote control (Figure 1-31).

MID-RANGE SERVERS

A **mid-range server** is more powerful and larger than a workstation computer (Figure 1-32). Mid-range servers often can support up to 4,000 connected users at the same time. In the past, these types of computers were known as **minicomputers**.

Users typically access a mid-range server via a personal computer or a terminal. A **terminal** is a device with a monitor and keyboard. Terminals, sometimes called **dumb terminals** because they have no processing power, cannot act as stand-alone computers and must be connected to a server to operate.

Figure 1-31 With a device such as WebTV™, you can access the Internet from the comfort of your family room or any room that has television access.

Figure 1-32 A mid-range server is more powerful than a workstation, but less powerful than a mainframe.

ISSUE

A Double-Edged Sword?

Handheld Devices

Many technological innovations are double-edged swords, with both positive and negative effects on society. Some sources say that extended use of Web-enabled cellular telephones, for instance, could lead to health problems. Storing obsolete equipment in basements and landfills is not healthy for you or the environment. Research from some health institutions indicates that people who have cardiac pacemakers could be affected by radio signals. Drivers using handheld devices are more likely to be involved in a crash. Media reports that mobile telephones have caused explosions at gasoline stations. Is the overall impact of computers and technology positive or negative for society? Do you agree adverse health effects could be related to the signals produced by the mobile devices? Should there be a law against driving and using a handheld device? What are some other negative issues related to technology?

For more information on computer effects on society, visit the Discovering Computers 2002 Issues Web page (**scsite.com/dc2002/issues.htm**) and click Chapter 1 Issue #4.

MAINFRAMES

A **mainframe** is a large, expensive, very powerful computer that can handle hundreds or thousands of connected users simultaneously (Figure 1-33). Mainframes also can act as a server in a network environment. Mainframes can store tremendous amounts of data, instructions, and information. Users often access the mainframe with terminals or personal computers.

Figure 1-33 Mainframe computers are large, expensive, powerful machines that can handle thousands of connected users simultaneously and process up to millions of instructions per second.

SUPERCOMPUTERS

A **supercomputer** is the fastest, most powerful computer — and the most expensive (Figure 1-34). Supercomputers are capable of processing more than 12 trillion instructions in a single second. Applications requiring complex, sophisticated mathematical calculations use supercomputers. For example, weather forecasting, nuclear energy research, and petroleum exploration applications use a supercomputer.

Figure 1-34 This IBM supercomputer, which covers an area the size of two basketball courts, can process up to 12 trillion calculations per second.

COMPANY ON THE CUTTING EDGE

IBM®

Big Blue PC

Checkmate. That is the word World Chess Champion Garry Kasparov heard when IBM's Deep Blue supercomputer defeated him in 1997. This six-game match marked the first time a computer had beaten a reigning world-renown chess player. But rather than emphasize the victory, IBM executives used the opportunity to focus on technology's potential.

Indeed, IBM has altered our lives since its incorporation in 1911. IBM's long record of computer successes include financial support for the Mark I in 1944, which took about 12 seconds to perform a division operation; the System/360 in 1964, which was the first family of computers with interchangeable software and peripherals; the IBM PC in 1981, with a base price of $1,565 and 16 KB of memory, a floppy disk drive, and an optional color monitor; and the ThinkPad notebook computer in 1992. For the past 40 years, IBM has been noted for its mainframe computers.

Today, IBM is the world's largest information technology company and has received numerous honors for its corporate policies, including being named by *WE Magazine* as the Top Employer of the Year for People with Disabilities and by the *Financial Times* as one of the World's Most Respected Companies.

For more information on IBM, visit the Discovering Computers 2002 Companies Web page (**scsite.com/dc2002/companies.htm**) and click IBM.

ELEMENTS OF AN INFORMATION SYSTEM

Obtaining useful and timely information from a computer requires more than just the hardware and software discussed thus far. Other elements include the input of accurate data, trained information technology (IT) personnel, knowledgeable users, and documented procedures. Together, these elements (hardware, software, data, people, and procedures) comprise an **information system** (Figure 1-35).

For an information system to provide accurate, timely, and useful information, each element in the system must be present and all of the elements must work together. The hardware must be reliable and capable of handling the expected workload. The software must be developed carefully and tested thoroughly. The data entered must be accurate. If the data is incorrect, the information it generates also will be incorrect.

Properly trained IT personnel are required to run most mid-size and large computers. Even small networks of personal computers usually have a system administrator to manage the network. Users are taking increasing responsibility for the successful operation of information systems. This includes responsibility for the accuracy of both the input and output. In addition, users are taking a more active role in the development of computer applications. They work closely with IT personnel in the development of computer applications that relate to their areas of work. Finally, all the IT applications should have documented procedures covering not only the computer operations but any other related procedures as well.

Figure 1-35 Five elements combine to make an information system: (1) hardware, (2) software, (3) data, (4) people, and (5) procedures.

Web Link

For more information on women in technology, visit the Discovering Computers 2002 Chapter 1 WEB LINK page (**scsite.com/dc2002/ch1/weblink.htm**) and click Women in Technology.

Web Link

For more information on minorities in technology, visit the Discovering Computers 2002 Chapter 1 WEB LINK page (**scsite.com/dc2002/ch1/weblink.htm**) and click Minorities in Technology.

EXAMPLES OF COMPUTER USAGE

Every day, numerous users rely on different types of computers for a variety of applications. Whether running complex application software, connecting to a network, or performing countless other functions, computers are powerful tools at home, at work, and at school.

To illustrate the variety of uses for computers, this section takes you on a visual and narrative tour of five categories of users: a home user, a small office/home office (SOHO) user, a mobile user, a large business user, and a power user (Figure 1-36). The following pages present examples of hardware and software listed in the table.

USER	HARDWARE/NETWORK	SOFTWARE
Home 	• Desktop computer • Handheld computer • Web-enabled devices • Internet	• Reference (e.g., encyclopedias, medical dictionaries, road atlas) • Entertainment (e.g., games, music composition, greeting cards) • Educational (e.g., foreign language tutorials, children's math and reading software) • Computer-based training • Productivity (word processing, spreadsheet) • Personal finance, online banking • Communications and Web browser • E-mail and instant messaging
Small Office/Home Office 	• Desktop computer • Handheld computer • Shared network printer • Local area network • Internet	• Productivity software (word processing, spreadsheet, database) • Company specific (e.g., accounting, legal reference) • Communications and Web browser • May use network versions of some software packages • E-mail
Mobile 	• Notebook computer equipped with a modem • Video projector • Web-enabled handheld computer • Internet • Local area network	• Productivity (word processing, spreadsheet, presentation graphics) • Personal information management • Communications and Web browser • E-mail
Large Business 	• Mid-range server or mainframe • Desktop or notebook computer • Handheld computer • Kiosk • Local area network or wide area network, depending on the size of the company • Internet	• Productivity (e.g., word processing, spreadsheet, database, presentation graphics) • Personal information management • Desktop publishing • Accounting • Network management software • Communications and Web browser • May use network versions of some software packages • E-mail
Power 	• Workstation or other powerful computer with multimedia capabilitities • Local area network • Internet	• Desktop publishing • Multimedia authoring • Photo, sound, and video editing • Communications and Web browser • Computer-aided design • E-mail

Figure 1-36 Today, computers are used in millions of businesses and homes to support work tasks and leisure activities. Depending on their intended usage, different computer users require different kinds of hardware and software to meet their needs effectively. The types of users are listed here together with the hardware, software, and network types mostly commonly used by each.

Home User

In a growing number of homes, the computer no longer is a convenience. Instead, it has become a basic necessity. Each family member uses the computer for different purposes. A **home user** spends time on the computer for research and education, budgeting and personal financial management, home business management, entertainment, personal and business communications, and Web access (Figure 1-37).

Once online, users can retrieve a tremendous amount of information, take college classes, pay bills, buy and sell stocks, shop, download music or movies, read a book, file taxes, book a flight, and communicate with others around the world. Some home users access the Web through the desktop computer, while others use Internet appliances and Web-enabled handheld computers and devices.

Home users also have a variety of other software. Most computers today are sold with word processing software already installed. Personal finance software helps to prepare taxes, balance a checkbook, and manage investments and family budgets. This software also allows you to connect to your bank via the Internet to pay bills online. Other software assists in organizing names and addresses, setting up home and automobile maintenance schedules, and preparing legal documents.

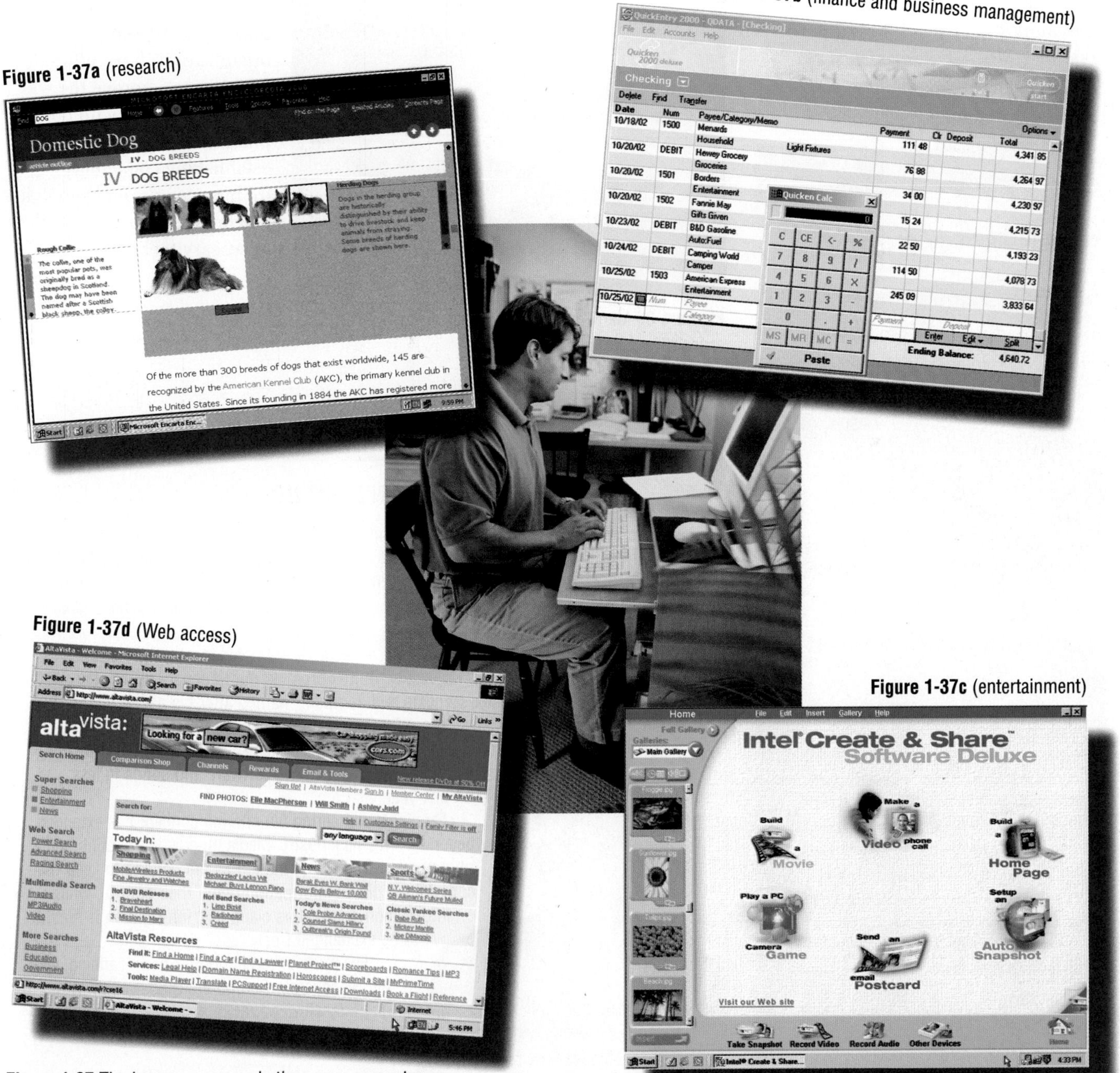

Figure 1-37a (research)

Figure 1-37b (finance and business management)

Figure 1-37c (entertainment)

Figure 1-37d (Web access)

Figure 1-37 The home user spends time on a computer for a variety of reasons.

Reference software, such as encyclopedias, medical dictionaries, or a road atlas, provides valuable and thorough information for everyone in the family. Software also provides hours of entertainment. For example, you can play games such as solitaire, chess, and Monopoly™; compose music; make a family tree; or create a greeting card. Educational software helps adults learn to speak a foreign language and youngsters to read, write, count, and spell. To make computers easier for younger people to use, many companies design special hardware just for children (Figure 1-38).

Many home users also have handheld computers to maintain daily schedules and address lists. Other special-purpose handheld computers manage and monitor the health condition of a family member.

A major concern of the United States government and many citizens around the world is the digital divide. The **digital divide** is the idea that you can separate people of the world into two distinct groups: (1) those who have access to technology with the ability to use it and (2) those who do not have access to technology or are without the ability to use it. The concern is that some of the less fortunate people in the world are not able to take advantage of the very technology that makes much of our society prosper and grow.

To narrow the gap in the digital divide, the United States government and many organizations have efforts in progress to improve the way society interacts with computers. These efforts include establishing community training centers and supplying teachers and students with necessary technology.

Figure 1-38 Many manufacturers design hardware especially for younger children.

ISSUE

Does Technology Discriminate?

Computer Usage

In California, the Technology Training Foundation of America (TTFA) (see URL below) is trying to help bridge the digital divide by providing all California public and private schools and non-profit organizations access to donated computer equipment. A study completed by the Gartner Group suggests, however, the introduction of computer technology and the Internet into the schools has served to widen the gap in educational opportunity. Michael Fleisher, Gartner chief executive, says the study indicates an experience gap exists, and an entire socioeconomic group is now one generation behind in terms of that experience. The findings of the report further imply that even if this socioeconomic group has access to computers and to the Internet at school and public libraries, they cannot catch up to their experienced counterparts. Do you agree with these findings? Does a digital divide exist? Will the gap continue to widen? What measures can be taken to eliminate the digital divide?

For more information on technology discrimination, the digital divide, and the Web site mentioned above, visit the Discovering Computers 2002 Issues Web page (**scsite.com/dc2002/issues.htm**) and click Chapter 1 Issue #5.

TECHNOLOGY TRAILBLAZER

SHAWN **FANNING**

Frustrated about not being able to download good songs, Shawn Fanning decided to take matters in his own hands. Why not allow music lovers to swap individual songs from each other? Starting in January 1999, he spent sleepless nights feverishly writing the source code on his Dell notebook computer, fearful that someone would steal his idea before he could complete the program.

One semester earlier, Fanning had been a 19-year-old freshman computer science major at Boston's Northeastern University. But he dropped out to devote his full energy toward developing the Napster software and company, named after his nappy hair. The program he wrote was an instant success, even before it was complete. More than 32 million people, including an estimated 73 percent of all U.S. students, had downloaded the software and songs in less than one year.

Fanning's pioneering file-sharing concept has extended beyond the music industry. Media moguls in the print media, photography, and movie industries are battling to keep their copyrighted digital information under their control, while information-age zealots claim that information is meant to be exchanged freely.

For more information on Shawn Fanning, visit the Discovering Computers 2002 People Web page (**scsite.com/dc2002/people.htm**) and click Shawn Fanning.

Small Office/Home Office User

Computers also play an important role in helping small business users manage their resources effectively. A **small office/home office** (**SOHO**) includes any company with fewer than 50 employees, as well as the self-employed people that work out of their home. Small offices include local law practices, accounting firms, travel agencies, and florists. SOHO users typically have a desktop personal computer to perform some or all of their duties (Figure 1-39). Many also have handheld computers to manage appointments and contact information.

SOHO users access the Web to look up information on addresses, postal codes, flights, package shipping, and rates. Nearly all SOHO users communicate with others through e-mail. Many are entering the **e-commerce** arena by conducting their financial business on the Web. These SOHO users have their own Web sites to advertise their products and services and take orders and requests from customers. Some of these Web sites use a **Web cam**, which is a video camera with output that can be displayed on a Web page. A Web cam allows the SOHO user to show the world a live view of some aspect of their business.

Small offices often have a local area network to connect the computers in the company. Networking the computers saves money on both hardware and software. For example, the small office avoids the expense of buying multiple printers by connecting a single shared printer to the network. The company also can purchase a network version of a software package. A network version usually costs less than purchasing a separate software package for each individual desktop computer. Employees then access the software on a server as needed.

For business document preparation, finances, and tracking, SOHO users often purchase basic productivity software such as word processing and spreadsheet software. They also may use other types of software, specific to their industry or company. An accounting firm, for example, will have accounting software to prepare journals, ledgers, income statements, balance sheets, and other accounting documents.

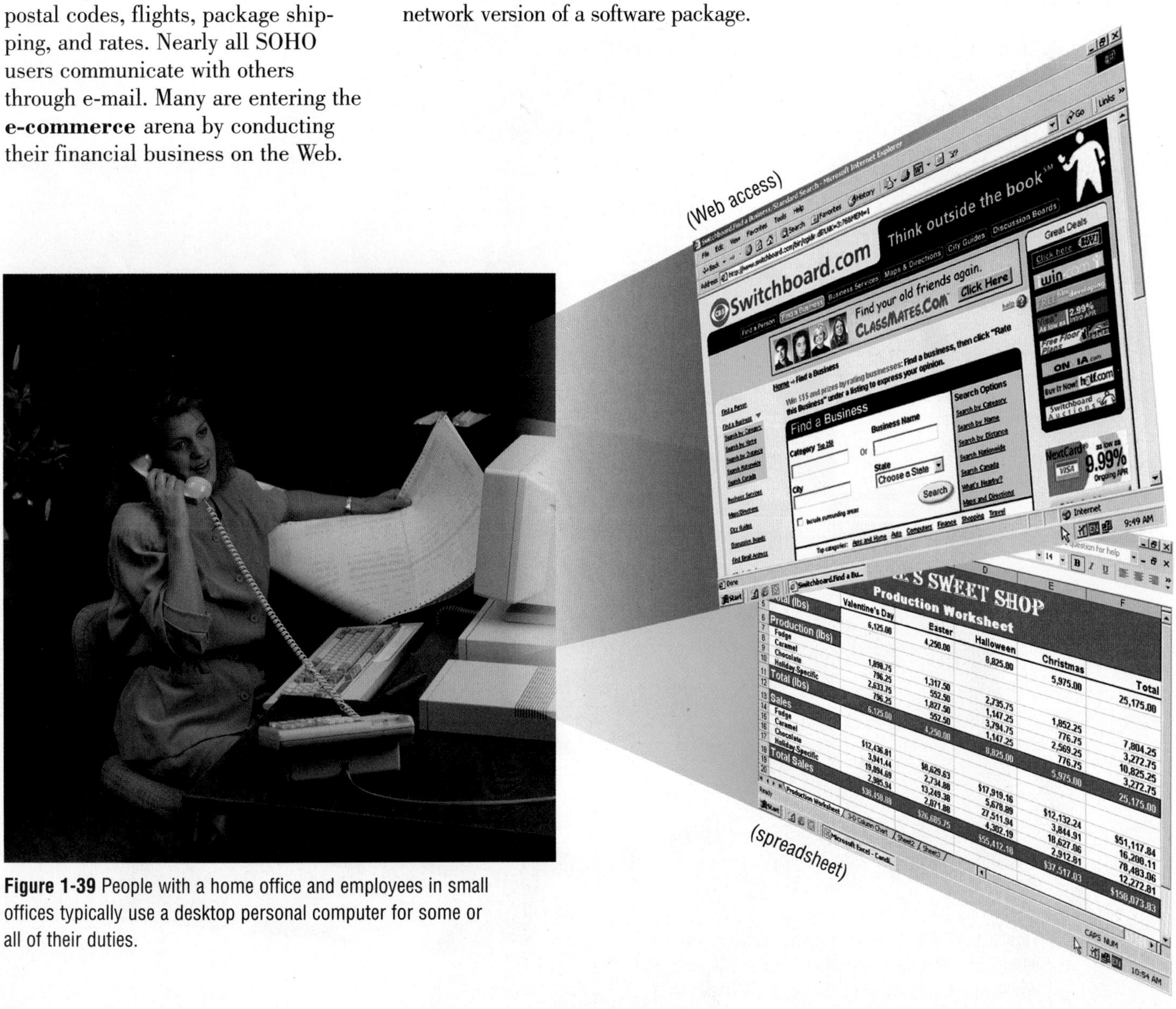

Figure 1-39 People with a home office and employees in small offices typically use a desktop personal computer for some or all of their duties.

Mobile User

As businesses expand to serve customers across the country and around the world, more and more employees have become **mobile users**, traveling to and from a main office to conduct business (Figure 1-40). Mobile users include a range of people such as sales representatives, marketing managers, real estate agents, insurance agents, meter readers, package delivery people, journalists, consultants, and students.

Mobile users often have a notebook computer equipped with a modem, which enables them to transfer information between their computer and another computer such as one at the main office. Sometimes they connect wirelessly to the Internet using a Web-enabled handheld computer or device such as a cellular telephone.

Other software utilized by mobile users includes basic productivity software such as word processing and spreadsheet software. They also use presentation graphics software to create and deliver presentations. To deliver the presentation to a large audience, the mobile user connects a notebook computer to a video projector that displays the presentation on a full screen.

Figure 1-40 Mobile users have notebook computers, handheld computers, and Web-enabled cellular telephones, so they can work while on the road.

Large Business User

A large business can have hundreds or thousands of employees in offices across a region, the country, or the world. The company usually has an equally large number of users (the **large business user**) and computers connected in a network (Figure 1-41). This network — a local area network or a wide area network depending on the size of the company — enables communications among employees at all locations.

Almost all large businesses today have their own Web sites to showcase products, services, and selected company information (Figure 1-42). Customers, vendors, and any other interested parties can access the information on the Web without having to speak to a company employee. Many large businesses also participate in e-commerce, allowing customers to conduct financial business through the Web site.

Throughout a large business, computers help employees perform a variety of job-related tasks. For example, users in a typical large company use an automated telephone system to route calls to the appropriate department or person. The inside sales representatives enter orders into desktop personal computers while on the telephone with a customer.

Figure 1-41 A large business can have hundreds or thousands of users in offices across a region, the country, or the world. Throughout the business, computers help employees perform a variety of job-related tasks.

Figure 1-42 Large businesses usually have their own Web site to showcase products, services, and company information. Many allow customers to transact business on the Web, as well.

Outside sales representatives — the mobile users in the firm — use notebook computers to conduct business while on the road. The marketing department uses desktop publishing software to prepare marketing literature such as newsletters, product brochures, and advertising material. The accounting department uses software to pay invoices, bill customers, and process payroll. The employees in the information systems department have a huge responsibility: to keep the computers and the network running and determine when and if it requires new hardware or software.

In addition to word processing, spreadsheet, database, and presentation graphics software, employees in a large firm also may use calendar programs to post their schedules on the network and handheld computers to maintain personal or company information. Electronic mail and Web browsers enable communications among employees and others around the world.

Some large businesses also use a kiosk to provide information to the public. A **kiosk** is a freestanding computer, usually with a touch screen that serves as an input device (Figure 1-43). More advanced kiosks allow customers to place orders, make payments, and access the Web.

Many employees of a large business often telecommute (Figure 1-44). **Telecommuting** is a work arrangement in which employees work away from a company's standard workplace, and often communicate with the office using some communications technology.

Figure 1-43 A kiosk is a freestanding computer, usually with multimedia capabilities and a touch screen.

Figure 1-44 Many employees of large businesses often telecommute, and communicate with the office using some form of communications technology.

Power User

Another category of user, called a **power user**, requires the capabilities of a workstation or other powerful computer. Examples of power users include engineers, architects, desktop publishers, and graphic artists (Figure 1-45). Power users typically work with **multimedia**, in which they combine text, graphics, sound, video, and other media elements into one application. All of these users need computers with extremely fast processors that have multimedia capabilities because of the nature of their work.

In addition to powerful hardware, a workstation contains software specific to the needs of the power user. For example, engineers and architects use software to draft and design items such as floor plans, mechanical assemblies, and computer chips. The desktop publisher uses specialized software to prepare marketing literature such as newsletters, brochures, and annual reports. This software usually is quite expensive because of its specialized design.

Power users are found in all types of businesses, both large and small. Some also work at home. Depending on where they work, power users might fit into one of the previously discussed categories, as well. Thus, in addition to their specific needs, these users often have additional hardware and software requirements such as network capabilities and Internet access.

Figure 1-45 Examples of power users are engineers, architects, desktop publishers, graphic artists, and multimedia authors.

COMPUTER USER AS A WEB PUBLISHER

Individuals in each of the five categories of users (home, SOHO, mobile, large business, and power) access the Internet for a wealth of information and to shop for goods and services. In addition to being a recipient of information, however, users have the ability to *provide* information to other connected users around the world. Embracing this growing service of the Internet, users now can be active participants that provide personal and business information, photographs, items for sale, and even live conversation.

To accomplish this, many users create Web pages with word processing software or with Web page authoring software. Once you have created a Web page, you publish it. **Publishing** a Web page is the process of making it available on the Internet. Many Internet service providers (ISPs) and online service providers (OSPs) will store personal Web pages for their subscribers and members at no cost. Through your application software, you can copy Web pages from your computer to the ISPs or OSPs to make your Web pages available to the world.

Users publish Web pages for a variety of reasons:

- Home users publish Web pages that provide information about their family
- Small business users publish Web pages that provide information about their business
- Job seekers often publish Web pages that resemble a resume (Figure 1-46)
- Educators publish online courses, called distance-learning courses

Home and small business users also display photographs, videos, artwork, and other images on personal Web pages or as advertisements on other's Web pages. To display photographs, you use a scanner, a digital camera, or a PC camera. To create and modify graphical images, many easy-to-use paint/image editing programs exist. Some of these programs even include photo-editing capabilities so you can touch-up digital photographs such as removing red-eye. Some Web sites are called **photo communities** because they allow you to create an online photo album, and they store your digital photographs free of charge.

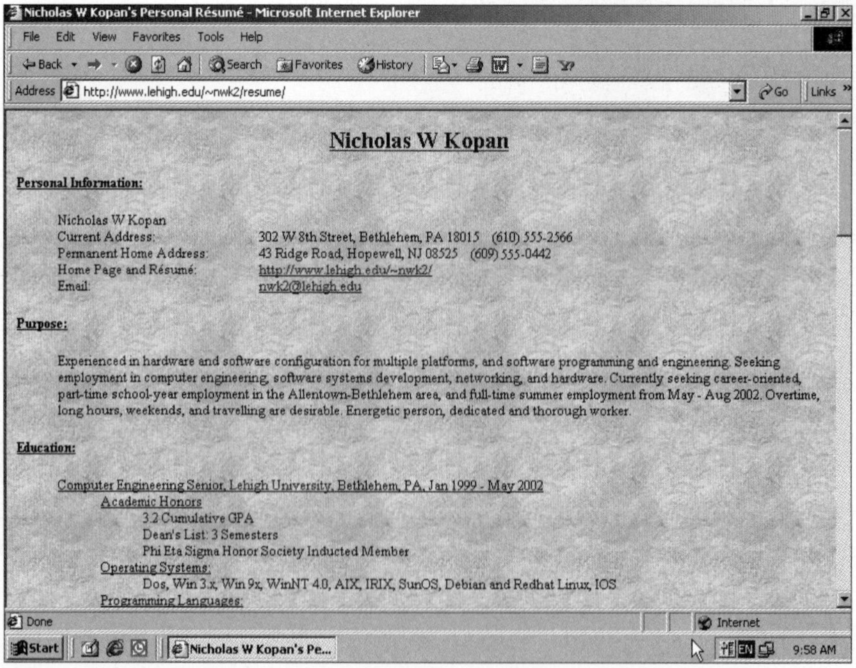

Figure 1-46 Job seekers often publish Web pages, so potential employers easily can locate their resume on the Web.

APPLY IT!

Share Your Photos Online

Digital cameras have opened a new world of photo sharing online. Photo communities are all the rage. At these photo sharing Web sites, you store and share pictures. You can elect to share your Web site with the world, protect it with a password, or keep the site private. Many of the Web sites offer a variety of other services, including advice on how to take better pictures, tools, products, and more. Some let you share other items too, including calendars and stories.

WebShots (see URL below) is one of the many popular photo communities. To join WebShot and other free photo communities, you first must complete a registration process. Most of these sites require you provide your name and e-mail address, and that you select a user name and password. Some communities, such as WebShot, require you to download a software program, which includes an automatic Web connection that downloads new photos each day from a category of your choice. PhotoPoint (see URL below) is another popular community. This site provides helpful links and how-to guides and does not require a software download. Some sites limit the amount of space, while others offer unlimited space. Before joining one of these communities (see URLs below), evaluate several of them and determine the one or ones that best meets your needs.

For more information on photo communities, photo albums online, and the Web sites mentioned above, visit the Discovering Computers 2002 Apply It Web page (**scsite.com/dc2002/apply.htm**) and click Chapter 1 Apply It #3.

If you are a small business and you would like to advertise and take orders on the Web, you can sell your products at an electronic storefront. Some Web sites provide a means for you to create a storefront directly at their site, from which users around the world can view and make purchases (Figure 1-47). If you have only a single item for sale, you instead might consider putting it for sale on an online auction.

If you simply want to communicate with others on the Web, you can use e-mail, chat rooms, or instant messaging. Many Web sites offer online calendars and address books so that you can share your appointments and contacts with others. The next chapter presents a more detailed discussion of these Internet services.

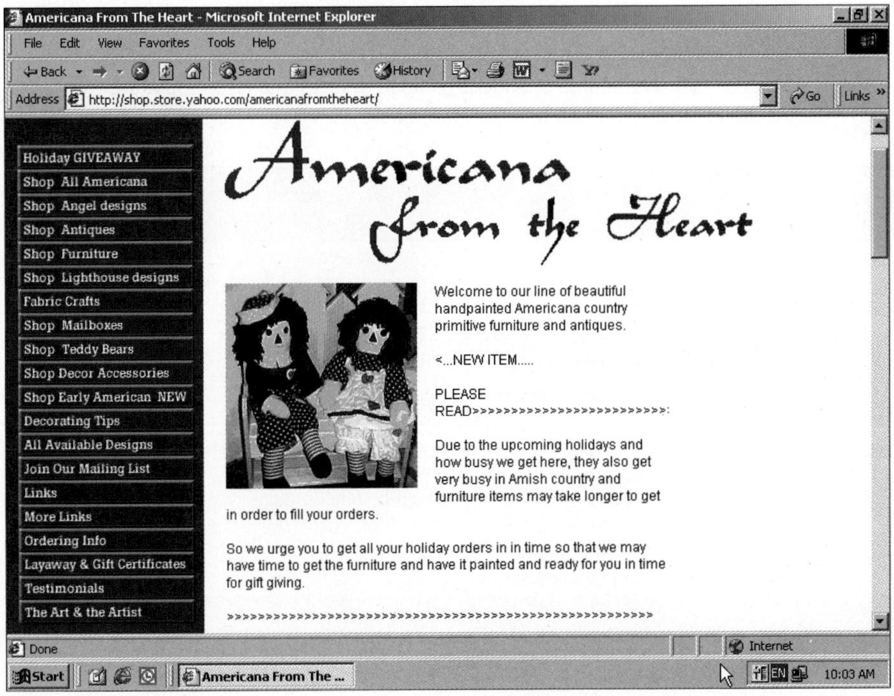

Figure 1-47 Users can create an electronic storefront for their home or small business.

CHAPTER SUMMARY

Chapter 1 introduced you to basic computer concepts such as what a computer is, how it works, and what makes it a powerful tool. You learned about the components of a computer. Next, the chapter discussed computer software, networks, and the Internet. The many different categories of computers and computer users also were presented. This chapter was an overview. Many of the terms and concepts introduced will be discussed further in later chapters.

Help Desk Specialist

A Help Desk Specialist is an entryway into the information technology (IT) field. Almost all organizations provide their employees with some type of help desk assistance. Within most companies, this job is one of the least technical. Some of the job requirements may include the following:

- Solve procedural and software questions both in person and over the telephone
- Develop and maintain Help Desk Operations Manuals
- Assist in training new Help Desk personnel

The type of questions one may encounter as a Help Desk Specialist depends on the setting. Someone who works in the computing center of a school would be required to have a broad knowledge of each computing platform used. In most instances, regardless of the setting, this job requires the specialist to be knowledgeable about major software packages in use.

Educational requirements are not as stringent as they are for other jobs in the computer field. In some cases, a high school diploma is sufficient. Advancement within the field requires a minimum of a two-year degree, while management generally requires a bachelor's degree in Information Systems or a related field. Entry-level salaries average $20,000 per year. Managers average between $42,000 and $50,000.

To learn more about the field of Help Desk Specialist as a career, visit the Discovering Computers 2002 Careers Web page (**scsite.com/dc2002/careers.htm**) and click Help Desk Specialist.

E-FUN E-ENTERTAINMENT

THAT'S ENTERTAINMENT

Surf's Up for Fun Web Sites

Girls just want to have fun, according to singer Cindy Lauper. The Internet abounds with fun sites for both gals and guys, with everything from the Rock and Roll Hall of Fame and Museum to the Rock of Gibraltar.

Do you want to see the attractions at Walt Disney World? Or, how about wild animals at a game preserve in Africa, pandas at the San Diego Zoo, and surfers in Hawaii (Figure 1-48)? Travel to the South Pole and hear the frigid wind blow, to Yellowstone Park to see the Old Faithful geyser, and to Loch Ness for a possible glimpse of the famous monster. Web cams take armchair travelers across the world for views of natural attractions, historical monuments, colleges, and cities. Some of the world's Web cams are listed in Figure 1-49.

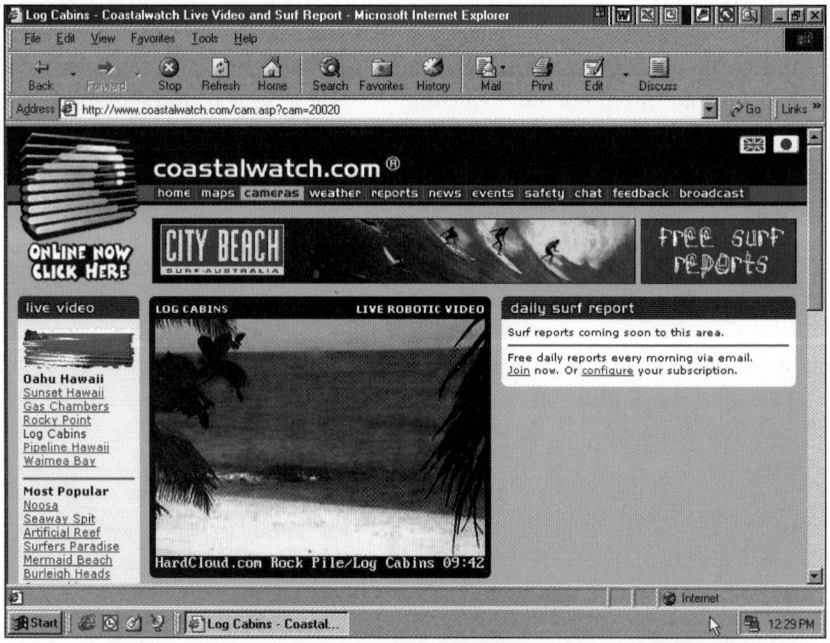

Figure 1-48 Web cams provide a glimpse of locations throughout the world, including famous surfing beaches in Hawaii.

FUN AND ENTERTAINMENT WEB SITES	URL
Web Cams	
AfriCam - The World's First Virtual Game Reserve	africam.com/
Discovery.com Cams	discovery.com/cams/cams.html
Iowa State Insect Zoo Live Camera	zoocam.ent.iastate.edu
Nesse on the Net! (Loch Ness Monster)	www.lochness.co.uk/livecam
OnlineWeather.com Webcams Index	onlineweather.com/webcams
Panda Cam San Diego Zoo	sandiegozoo.org/special/pandas/pandacam/index.html
The Automated Astrophysical Site-Testing Observatory (AASTO) (South Pole)	bat.phys.unsw.edu.au/~aasto
The Old Faithful Geyser WebCam	www.nps.gov/yell/oldfaithfulcam.htm
Walt Disney World - Theme Park Live Camera	home.disney.com/DisneyWorld/cgi-bin/oneShot.cgi?type=st&park=ds
Wild Birds Unlimited Bird FeederCam	wbu.com/feedercam_home.htm
World Map of Live Webcams	dove.mtx.net.au/~punky/World.html
World Wide Surf Cameras	goan.com/surfcam.shtml
Entertainment	
AMG All Music Guide	allmusic.com
Entertainment Tonight Online	etonline.com
Entertainment Weekly Online	ew.com/ew
Mr. Showbiz: Celebrities	mrshowbiz.go.com/celebrities/index.html
RadioDigest.com	radiodigest.com
Rock and Roll Hall of Fame and Museum	rockhall.com
Spinner.com	spinner.com
The Internet Movie Database (IMDb)	imdb.com
Welcome to E! Online	eonline.com
World Radio Network WRN	wrn.org

For an updated list of fun and entertainment Web sites, visit scsite.com/dc2002/e-rev.htm.

Figure 1-49 When you visit Web sites offering fun and entertainment resources, you can be both amused and informed.

If you need an update on what happened to Victor and Nikki on *The Young and the Restless* or a preview of the upcoming Julia Roberts movie, the Web can satisfy your entertainment thirst. E! Online, Entertainment Tonight Online (Figure 1-50), and Mr. Showbiz provide the latest features on television and movie stars. The Internet Movie Database contains credits and reviews of more than 120,000 movies.

If your passion is music and radio, the AMG All Music Guide provides backgrounds on new releases and top artists. See and hear the musicians inducted into the Rock and Roll Hall of Fame and Museum (Figure 1-51). The World Radio Network features international public radio programs, such as *The Voice of Russia* and *UN Radio*.

For more information on fun and entertainment Web sites, visit the Discovering Computers 2002 E-Revolution Web page (scsite.com/dc2002/e-rev.htm) and click Fun/Entertainment.

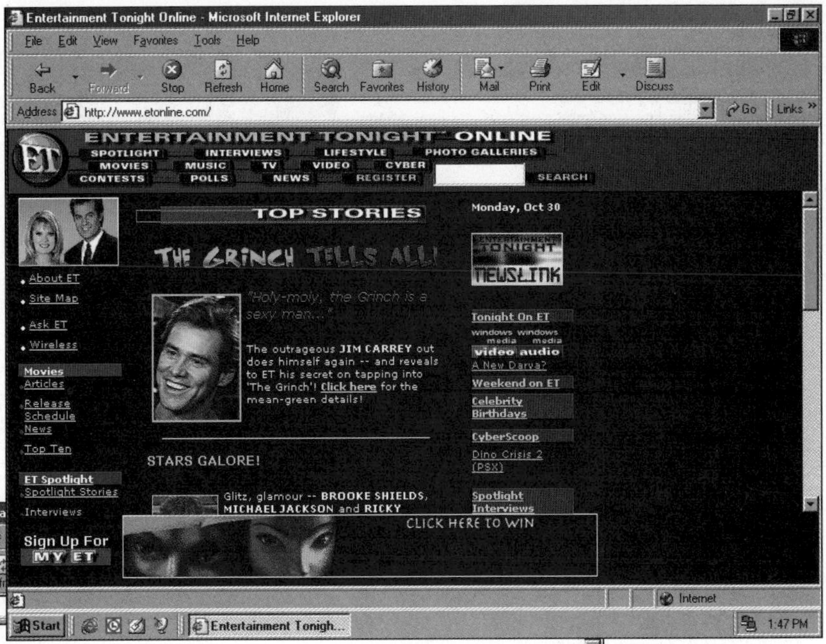

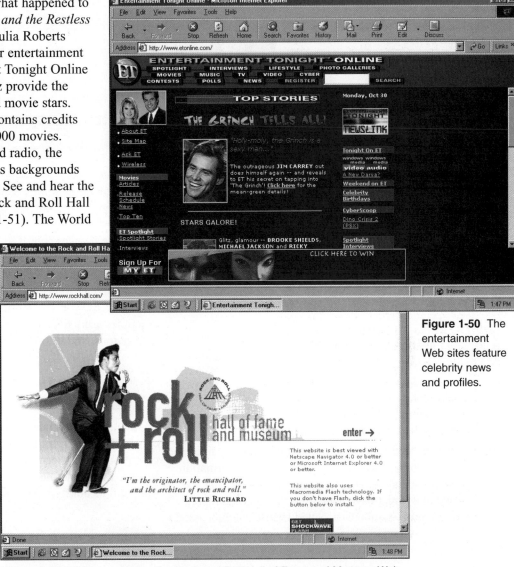

Figure 1-50 The entertainment Web sites feature celebrity news and profiles.

Figure 1-51 Visitors exploring the Rock and Roll Hall of Fame and Museum Web site will find history, exhibitions, programs, and the names and particulars of the latest inductees.

eREVOLUTION E-FUN E-ENTERTAINMENT *applied:*

1. Visit the World Map of Live Webcams and the Culture Connect Web sites listed in Figure 1-49. View two of the Web cams closest to your hometown, and describe the scenes. Then, visit the Discovery.com Cams Web site and view two of the animal cams in the Cam Universe. What do you observe? Visit another Web site listed in Figure 1-49 and describe the view. What are the benefits of having Web cams at these locations throughout the world?

2. What are your favorite movies? Use The Internet Movie Database Web site listed in Figure 1-49 to search for information about two of these films, and write a brief description of the biographies of the major stars and director for each movie. Then, visit one of the entertainment Web sites and describe three of the featured stories. At the Rock and Roll Hall of Fame and Museum Web site, view the information on Elvis and one of your favorite musicians. Write a paragraph describing the information available on these rock stars.

In Summary

Web Instructions: To display this page from the Web, start your browser and enter the URL scsite.com/dc2002/ch1/summary.htm. Click the links for current and additional information. To listen to an audio version of this In Summary, click the Audio button. To play the audio, RealPlayer must be installed on your computer (download by clicking here).

1 Why Is Computer Literacy Important?

To be successful in today's world, it is crucial to have knowledge and understanding of computers and their uses. Being computer literate is essential as technology advances and computers extend into every facet of daily living.

2 What Is a Computer?

A computer is an electronic machine that operates under the control of instructions stored in its own memory, that can accept data (input), manipulate the data according to specified rules (process), produce results (output), and store the results for future use (**storage**). **Data** is a collection of unorganized facts, figures, and symbols. Computers process data to create information. **Information** is data that is organized, meaningful, and useful. Examples are a paycheck or a student grade report. Data entered into a computer is called **input**. The processed results are called **output**. The cycle of input, process, output, and storage is called the **information processing cycle**.

3 What Are the Components of a Computer?

Hardware is the electric, electronic, and mechanical equipment that makes up a computer. An **input device** allows a user to enter data and commands into the memory of a computer. Six commonly used input devices are a keyboard, mouse, microphone, scanner, PC camera, and digital camera. An **output device** conveys information generated by a computer to the user. Three commonly used output devices are a printer, a monitor, and speakers. The **system unit**, sometimes called a **chassis**, is a box-like case made from metal or plastic that houses the computer circuitry. The two main components of the motherboard are the central processing unit (CPU), which interprets and carries out the instructions that operate a computer, including computations; and **memory**, which is a series of electronic elements that temporarily holds the data and instructions while the processor is processing them. A **storage device** records and retrieves data, information, and instructions to and from a storage medium. Six common storage devices are a floppy disk drive, hard disk drive, CD-ROM drive, Zip® drive, CD-RW drive, and DVD-ROM drive. **Communications devices** allow computer users to exchange items such as data, instructions, and information with another computer.

4 Why Is a Computer a Powerful Tool?

A computer's power is derived from its capability of performing the information processing cycle operations with speed, reliability, and accuracy; its capacity to store huge amounts of data, instructions, and information; and its ability to communicate with other computers.

5 What Are the Categories of Computer Software?

Software, also called a computer program, is the series of instructions that tells the hardware of a computer what to do. Software can be categorized into two types: system software and application software. **System software** controls the operation of the computer and its devices and serves as the interface between a user and the computer's hardware. Two types of system software are the **operating system (OS)**, which contains instructions that coordinate the activities of hardware devices; and **utility programs**, which perform specific tasks usually related to managing a computer. **Application software** performs specific tasks for users, such as creating word processing documents, spreadsheets, databases, or presentation graphics. A **computer programmer** writes software programs, often following a plan developed by a **systems analyst**.

6 What Is the Purpose of a Network?

A network is a collection of computers and devices connected together via communications media. Computers are networked so users can share **resources** such as hardware devices, software programs, data, and information. When your computer connects to a network, you are **online**.

7 How Are the Internet and the World Wide Web Used?

The world's largest network is the **Internet**, which is a worldwide collection of networks that links together millions of computers. The Internet is used to send messages to other users, obtain information, shop for goods and services, meet or converse with people around the world, and access sources of entertainment and leisure. The World Wide Web, which contains billions of Web pages with text, graphics, sound, video, and links to other Web pages, is one of the more popular segments of the Internet.

8 What Are the Categories of Computers and Their Uses?

The six major categories of computers are personal computers, handheld computers, Internet appliances, mid-range servers, mainframes, and supercomputers. These categories are based on differences in size, speed, processing capabilities, and price. A **personal computer** can perform all of its input, processing, output, and storage activities by itself. Two categories of personal computers are **desktop computers**, which are designed to fit entirely on or under a desk or table, and **notebook computers**, which are small enough to fit on your lap. A **handheld computer**, also called a **palmtop computer**, is a small computer that fits in your hand. One of the most popular handheld computers is the **PDA (personal digital assistant)**. An **Internet appliance** is a device designed specifically to connect to the Internet. A **mid-range server**, formerly called a **minicomputer**, is larger and more powerful than a workstation computer and often can support up to 4,000 connected users. A **mainframe** is a large, expensive, very powerful computer that can handle hundreds or thousands of connected users simultaneously. A **supercomputer** — the fastest, most powerful, and most expensive computer — is capable of processing more than 12 trillion instructions in a single second.

9 Who Are Computer Users?

Every day, people depend on different types of computers for a variety of applications. A **home user** relies on the computer for entertainment; communications, Web access, and e-mail; reference, research, and education; personal finance; and productivity software. A **small office/home office (SOHO)** includes small companies (under 50 employees) and self-employed individuals working from home. These users access the Web; utilize productivity and specialized software; and use e-mail and communications software. **Mobile users** have notebook computers often equipped with a modem so they can work on the road. They often use presentation software and other productivity software. **Large business users** utilize computers to run their businesses by using productivity software, communications software, automated systems for most departments in the company, and large networks. **Power users** require the capabilities of workstations or other powerful computers to design plans, produce publications, create graphic art, and work with **multimedia** that includes text, graphics, sound, video, and other media elements.

10 How Can a User Be a Web Publisher?

Through the Internet, each category of user can access a wealth of information and has the ability to provide information to other connected users around the world. Many users create Web pages. **Publishing** a Web page is the process of making it available on the Internet.

Key Terms

Web Instructions: To display this page from the Web, start your browser and enter the URL scsite.com/dc2002/ch1/terms.htm. Scroll through the list of terms. Click a term to display its definition and a picture. Click the To WEB button for current and additional information about the term from the Web. To see animations, Shockwave and Flash Player must be installed on your computer (download by clicking here).

all-in-one computer (1.21)
application service provider (ASP) (1.14)
application software (1.13)
central processing unit (CPU) (1.6)
chassis (1.6)
communications devices (1.8)
computer (1.4)
computer literate (1.4)
computer program (1.10)
computer programmer (1.14)
custom software (1.14)
data (1.4)
desktop computer (1.20)
digital divide (1.30)
dumb terminals (1.25)
e-commerce (1.31)
executes (1.10)
freeware (1.14)
garbage in, garbage out (GIGO) (1.9)

WORKSTATION
Desktop computer designed for work that requires intense calculations and graphics capabilities; sometimes used to refer to any computer connected to a network. (1.21)

graphical user interface (GUI) (1.12)
handheld computer (1.23)
hardware (1.4)
home user (1.29)
icon (1.12)
information (1.4)
information appliance (1.24)
information processing cycle (1.5)
information system (1.27)
input (1.5)
input device (1.5)
install (1.11)
Internet (1.17)
Internet appliance (1.24)
kiosk (1.34)
laptop computer (1.22)
large business user (1.32)
mainframe (1.26)
memory (1.6)
mid-range server (1.25)
minicomputers (1.25)
mobile users (1.32)
multimedia (1.35)
network (1.16)
notebook computer (1.22)
online (1.16)
operating system (OS) (1.12)
output (1.5)
output device (1.6)
packaged software (1.13)
palmtop computer (1.23)
PDA (Personal Digital Assistant) (1.23)
peripheral (1.6)
personal computer (1.19)
photo communities (1.37)
power user (1.35)
processor (1.6)
program (1.10)
programmer (1.14)
public-domain software (1.14)
publishing (1.36)
resources (1.16)

INFORMATION
Information is data that is organized, meaningful, and useful. A computer processes data into information. (1.4)

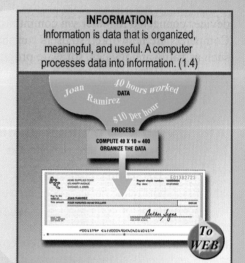

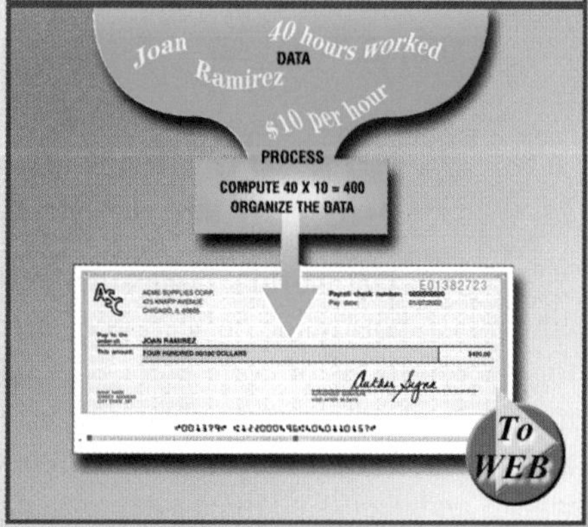

server (1.21)
shareware (1.14)
small office/home office (SOHO) (1.29)
smart pager (1.24)
smart phone (1.24)
software (1.4)
stand-alone computer (1.21)
storage (1.5)
storage device (1.7)
supercomputer (1.26)
system software (1.12)
system unit (1.6)
systems analyst (1.14)
telecommuting (1.34)
terminal (1.25)
tower model (1.20)
user (1.4)
utility program (1.12)
Web cam (1.29)
Web-enabled cellular telephone (1.24)
Web-enabled pager (1.24)
workstation (1.21)

Learn It Online

Web Instructions: To display this page from the Web, start your browser and then enter the URL scsite.com/dc2002/ch1/learn.htm.

1. Web Guide

Click Web Guide to display the Guide to World Wide Web Sites and Searching Techniques Web page. Click Reference and then click AskEric Virtual Library. Click AskEric InfoGuides and search for Computer Literacy. Click a search results link of your choice. Use your word processing program to prepare a brief report on what you learned and submit your assignment to your instructor.

2. Scavenger Hunt

Click Scavenger Hunt. Print a copy of the Scavenger Hunt page; use this page to write down your answers as you search the Web. Submit your completed page to your instructor.

3. Who Wants to Be a Computer Genius?

Click Computer Genius to find out if you are a computer genius. Directions on how to play the game will display. When you are ready to play, click the PLAY button. Submit your score to your instructor.

4. Wheel of Terms

Click Wheel of Terms to reinforce important terms you learned in this chapter by playing the Shelly Cashman Series version of this popular game. Directions on how to play the game will display. When you are ready to play, click the PLAY button. Submit your score to your instructor.

5. Career Corner

Click Career Corner to display the Hire-Ed page. Search for jobs in your state. Write a brief report on the jobs you found. Submit the report to your instructor.

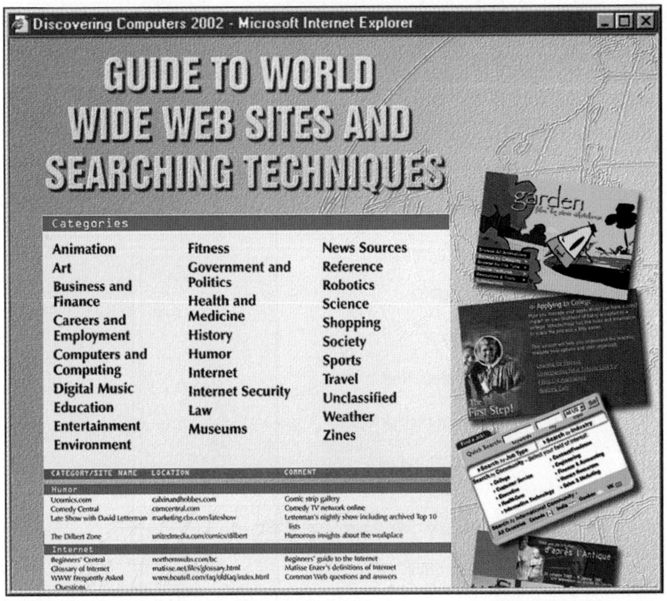

6. Search Sleuth

Click Search Sleuth to learn search techniques that will help make you a research expert. Submit the completed assignment to your instructor.

7. Crossword Puzzle Challenge

Click Crossword Puzzle Challenge. Complete the puzzle to reinforce skills you learned in this chapter. Directions on how to play the game will display. When you are ready to play, click the PLAY button. Submit the completed puzzle to your instructor.

8. Practice Test

Click Practice Test. Answer each question. When completed, enter your name and click the Grade Test button to submit the quiz for grading. Make a note of any missed questions. If required, print a copy to submit to your instructor.

Checkpoint

Web Instructions: To display this page from the Web, start your browser and enter the URL scsite.com/dc2002/ch1/check.htm. Click the links for current and additional information. To experience the animation and interactivity, Shockwave and Flash Player must be installed on your computer (download by clicking here.)

LABEL THE FIGURE

Instructions: Categorize these common computer hardware components.

Write the letter next to each component on the right in an appropriate blue box. Then write the words from the list on the left in the appropriate yellow boxes to identify the hardware components.

monitor
speakers
keyboard
mouse
printer
system unit
hard disk drive
CD-ROM or DVD-ROM drive
floppy disk drive
Zip drive
modem
digital camera
microphone
PC video camera
scanner
CD-RW drive

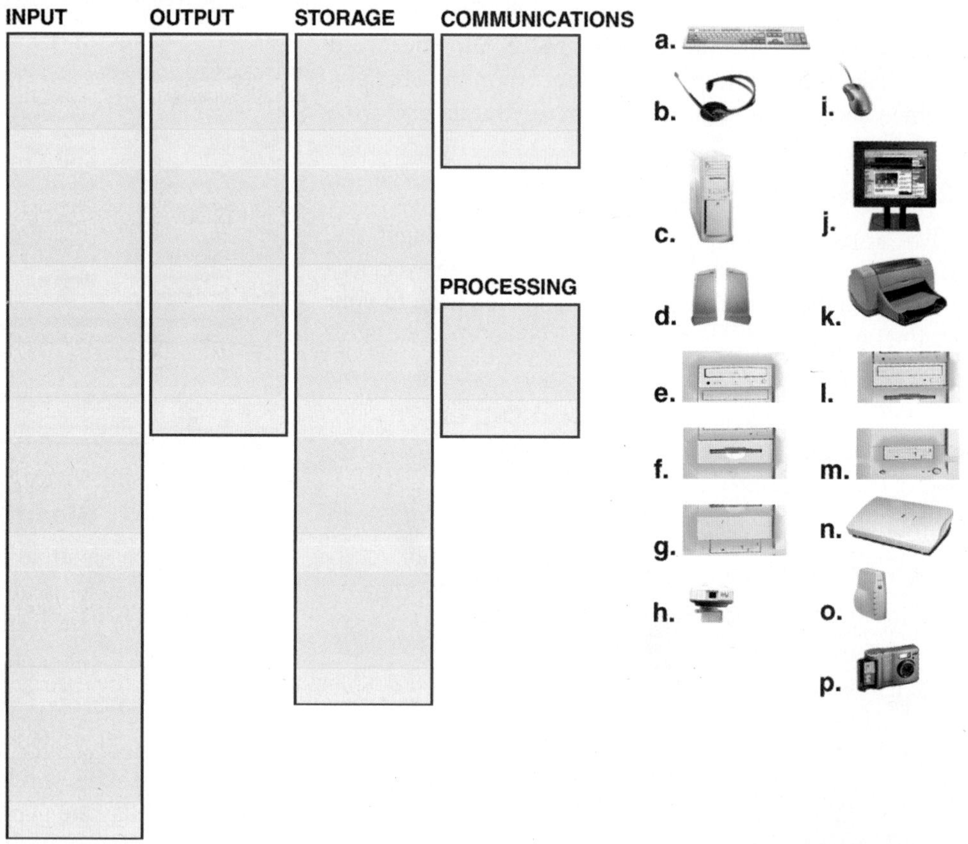

MATCHING

Instructions: Match each term from the column on the left with the best description from the column on the right.

_______ 1. data
_______ 2. information
_______ 3. output
_______ 4. storage
_______ 5. input

a. An area in a computer that can hold data and information for future use.
b. Someone who communicates with a computer or uses the information it generates.
c. A collection of raw unprocessed facts, figures, and symbols.
d. Data or instructions a user enters into a computer.
e. Data that is organized, meaningful, and useful.
f. Data that has been processed into information.
g. The series of instructions that tells the hardware how to perform tasks.

Checkpoint

MULTIPLE CHOICE

Instructions: Select the letter of the correct answer for each of the following questions.

1. ___________ is the electric, electronic, and mechanical equipment that makes up a computer.
   a. Hardware
   b. Software
   c. The operating system
   d. The GUI
2. A(n) ___________ is software that consists of programs that perform specific tasks for users.
   a. operating system
   b. virus
   c. application
   d. GUI
3. Software donated for public use that has no software restrictions is ___________ .
   a. shareware
   b. public domain software
   c. freeware
   d. copyrighted
4. Someone who writes software programs is called a ___________ .
   a. systems analyst
   b. hardware specialist
   c. network manager
   d. programmer
5. A Web ___________ is a collection of related **Web pages**.
   a. site
   b. browser
   c. interface
   d. set

SHORT ANSWER

Instructions: Write a brief answer to each of the following questions.

1. What are some ways people use computers in the home, at work, and at school? ___________ What does it mean to be computer literate? ___________
2. How is hardware different from software? ___________ Why is hardware useless without software? ___________
3. What is a peripheral device? ___________ What hardware components are considered peripheral devices? ___________
4. What are six common storage devices? ___________ How are they different? ___________
5. Why do people use the Internet? ___________ How do most users connect to the Internet? ___________

WORKING TOGETHER

Instructions: Working with a group of your classmates, complete the following team exercise.

Six commonly used input devices are listed in this chapter. These devices include a keyboard, mouse, microphone, scanner, PC camera, and digital camera. Using the Internet or other resources, prepare a report on each of the devices. Discuss how and when you would use one device instead of another. What are some of the different features available in each device? How would you determine which keyboard, mouse, and so on is the best for your particular needs? Share your reports with the class.

In The Lab

Web Instructions: To display this page from the Web, start your browser and enter the URL scsite.com/dc2002/ch1/lab.htm. Click the links for current and additional information.

1. Using Windows Help

This exercise uses Windows 98 or Windows 2000 procedures. In the past, when you purchased computer software, you also received large printed manuals that attempted to answer any questions you might have. Today, Help usually is offered directly on the computer. To make it easy to find exactly the Help you need, Windows Help is arranged on three sheets: Contents, Index, and Search. Windows 2000 includes a fourth sheet, Favorites. Click the Start button on the taskbar and then click Help on the Start menu. Click the Contents tab in the Help window. What do you see? When would you use the Contents sheet to find Help? Click the Index tab. What do you see? When would you use the Index sheet to find Help? Click the Search tab. What do you see? When would you use the Search sheet to find Help? If you are using Windows 2000, click the Favorites tab. What do you see? When would you use the Favorites sheet to find Help? Close the Help window.

2. What's New in Microsoft Windows?

This exercise uses Windows 98 or Windows 2000 procedures. Click the Start button on the taskbar and then click Help on the Start menu. Click the Contents tab in the Windows Help window. Click the Introducing Windows 98 or Windows 2000 book, and then click the What's New in Windows 98 or Windows 2000 book. Click a topic in which you are interested. Click each topic in the right pane. How is this version of Windows better than previous versions of Windows? Will the improvement make your work more efficient? Why or why not? What improvement, if any, would you still like to see? Close the Windows Help window.

3. Improving Mouse Skills

This exercise uses Windows 98 or Windows 2000 procedures. Click the Start button on the taskbar. Point to Programs on the Start menu, point to Accessories on the Programs submenu, point to Games on the Accessories submenu, and then click Solitaire on the Games submenu. When the Solitaire window displays, click the Maximize button. Click Help on the Solitaire menu bar, and then click Help Topics. Click the Contents tab. Click the The object of Solitaire topic and read the information. Click the Playing Solitaire topic. Read and print the information by clicking the Solitaire Help window's Options button, clicking Print, and then clicking the OK button. Click the Close button in the Solitaire Help window. Play the game of Solitaire. Close the Solitaire window.

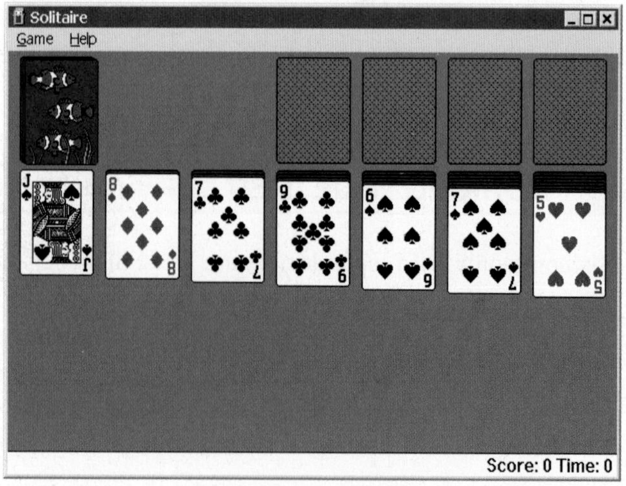

4. Learning About Your System

You can learn some important information about your computer system by studying the system properties. Click the Start button. Point to Settings on the Start menu, and then click Control Panel on the Settings submenu. Double-click the System icon in the Control Panel window. Click the General tab in the System Properties dialog box. Use the General sheet to find out the answers to these questions:

- What operating system does your computer use?
- To whom is your system registered?
- What type of processor does your computer have?
- How much memory (RAM) does your computer have?

Close the System Properties dialog box. Close the Control Panel window.

Web Work

Web Instructions: To display this page from the Web, start your browser and enter the URL scsite.com/dc2002/ch1/web.htm. To view At The Movies in exercise 1, RealPlayer must be installed on your computer (download by clicking here). To use the Shelly Cashman Series Using the Mouse Lab and Using the Keyboard Lab from the Web, Shockwave and Flash Player must be installed on your computer (download by clicking here).

1 Technosaurs

To view the Technosaurs movie, click the button to the left or click the Play button to the right. Watch the movie, and then complete the exercise by answering the questions below. Just as rapid, massive climate changes are said to have rendered dinosaurs extinct, dizzying changes in computer technology challenge today's companies to evolve, adapt, or… die off. Traditional brokerages are losing billions of dollars to online trading. Travel Web sites on the Internet are siphoning billions of dollars from bricks-and-mortar travel agencies. Changes in communications hardware and software for sales and service functions threaten companies as well. What are some of the new technologies that radically can improve the competitiveness of a company's sales force? What are some of the new software programs to manage customer relationships better?

2 Shelly Cashman Series Using the Mouse Lab

1. To start the Shelly Cashman Series Using the Mouse Lab, complete the step that applies to you.
   a. Running from the World Wide Web: Enter the URL, www.scsite.com/sclabs/menu.htm; or display the Web Work page (see instructions at the top of this page) and then click the button to the left.
   b. Running from a CD-ROM: Insert the Shelly Cashman Series Labs with Audio CD-ROM in your CD-ROM drive.
   c. Running the No-Audio Version from a Hard Disk or Network: Click the Start button on the taskbar, point to Shelly Cashman Series Labs on the Programs submenu, and then click Interactive Labs.
2. When the Shelly Cashman Series IN THE LAB screen shown in the figure to the right displays, follow the instructions on the screen to start the Using the Mouse Lab.
3. When the Using the Mouse screen displays, read the objectives.
4. If assigned, follow the instructions on the screen to print the questions associated with the Lab.
5. Follow the instructions on the screen to continue in the Lab.
6. When completed, follow the instructions on the screen to quit the lab.
7. If assigned, submit your answers for the printed questions to your instructor.

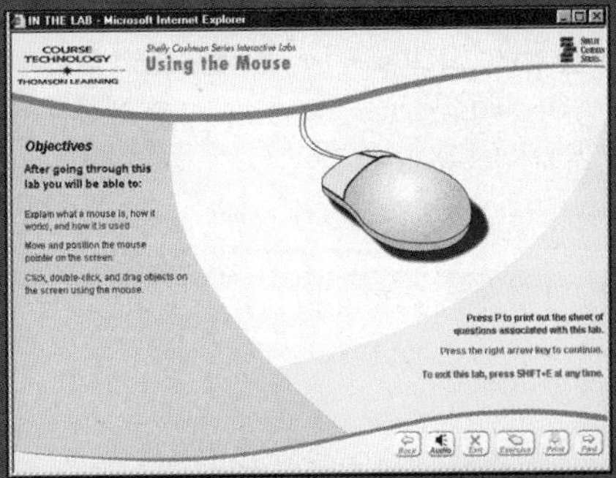

3 Shelly Cashman Series Using the Keyboard Lab

Follow the appropriate instructions in Web Work Exercise 2 above to start and use the Shelly Cashman Series Using the Keyboard Lab. If you are running from the Web, enter the URL, www.scsite.com/sclabs/menu.htm; or display the Web Work page (see instructions at the top of this page) and then click the button to the left.

4 Learn the Net

No matter how much computer experience you have, navigating the Net for the first time can be intimidating. How do you get started? Click the button to the left and complete this exercise to discover how you can find out everything you want to know about the Internet.

scsite.com/dc2002/ch1/timeline1.htm

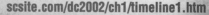

TIME Line 2002

Milestones in Computer History

1937 Dr. John V. Atanasoff and Clifford Berry design and build the first electronic digital computer. Their machine, the Atanasoff-Berry-Computer, or ABC, provides the foundation for advances in electronic digital computers.

1946 Dr. John W. Mauchly and J. Presper Eckert, Jr. complete work on the first large-scale electronic, general-purpose digital computer. The ENIAC (Electronic Numerical Integrator And Computer) weighs thirty tons, contains 18,000 vacuum tubes, occupies a thirty-by-fifty-foot space, and consumes 160 kilowatts of power. The first time it is turned on, lights dim in an entire section of Philadelphia.

1945 Dr. John von Neumann writes a brilliant paper describing the stored program concept. His breakthrough idea, where memory holds both data and stored programs, lays the foundation for all digital computers that have since been built.

1943 During World War II, British scientist Alan Turing designs the Colossus, an electronic computer created for the military to break German codes. The computer's existence is kept secret until the 1970s.

Web Instructions: *To gain World Wide Web access to additional and up-to-date information regarding this special feature, start your browser and enter the URLs at the top of each page.*

William Shockley, John Bardeen, and Walter Brattain invent the transfer resistance device, eventually called the transistor. The transistor would revolutionize computers, proving much more reliable than vacuum tubes.

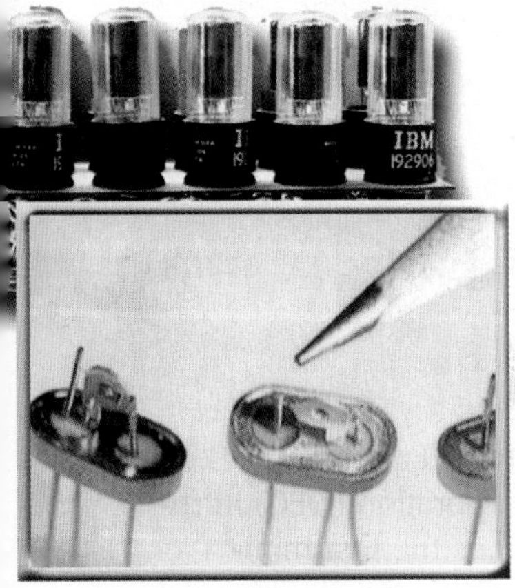

1947

1952

Dr. Grace Hopper considers the concept of reusable software in her paper, "The Education of a Computer." The paper describes how to program a computer with symbolic notation instead of the detailed machine language that had been used.

FORTRAN (FORmula TRANslation), an efficient, easy-to-use programming language, is introduced by John Backus.

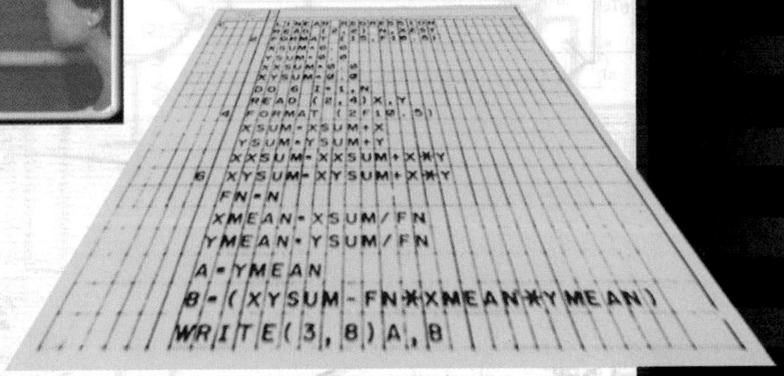

1957

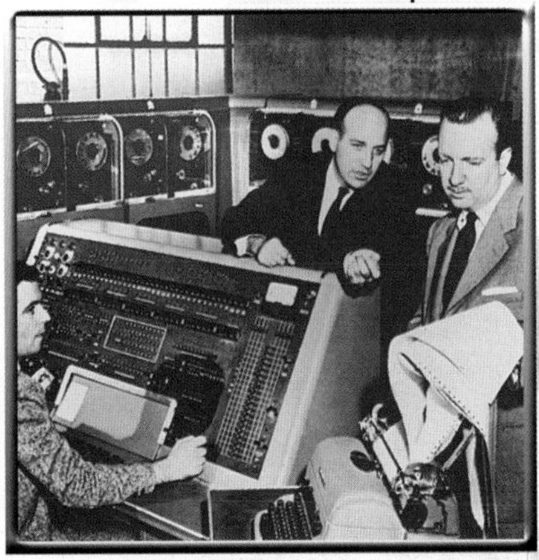

1951

The first commercially available electronic digital computer, the UNIVAC I (UNIVersal Automatic Computer), is introduced by Remington Rand. Public awareness of computers increases when the UNIVAC I, after analyzing only 5 percent of the popular vote, correctly predicts that Dwight D. Eisenhower will win the presidential election.

1953

The IBM model 650 is one of the first widely used computer systems. Originally planning to produce only 50 machines, the system is so successful that eventually IBM manufactures more than 1,000. With the IBM 700 series of machines, the company will dominate the mainframe market for the next decade.

Core memory, developed in the early 1950s, provides much larger storage capacity than vacuum tube memory.

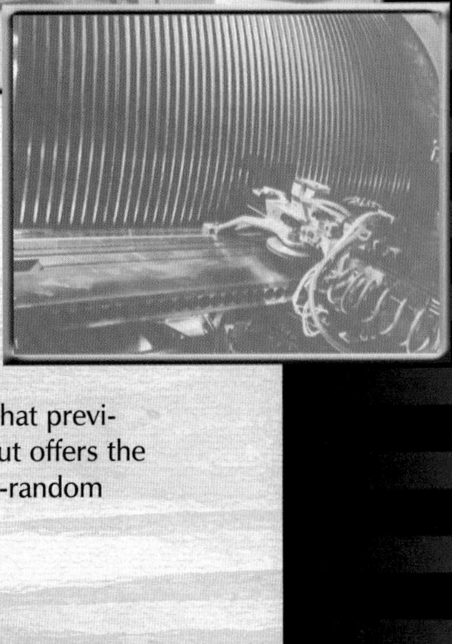

The IBM 305 RAMAC system is the first to use magnetic disk for external storage. The system provides storage capacity similar to magnetic tape that previously was used, but offers the advantage of semi-random access capability.

scsite.com/dc2002/ch1/timeline3.htm

IBM introduces two smaller, desk-sized computers: the IBM 1401 for business and the IBM 1602 for scientists. The IBM 1602 initially is called the CADET, but IBM drops the name when campus wags claim it is an acronym for, Can't Add, Doesn't Even Try.

More than 200 programming languages have been created.

1959

1960

COBOL, a high-level business application language, is developed by a committee headed by Dr. Grace Hopper. COBOL uses English-like phrases and runs on most business computers, making it one of the more widely used programming languages.

Dr. John Kemeny of Dartmouth leads the development of the BASIC programming language. BASIC will be widely used on personal computers.

BASIC

1965

Digital Equipment Corporation (DEC) introduces the first minicomputer, the PDP-8. The machine is used extensively as an interface for time-sharing systems.

1958

Computers built with transistors mark the beginning of the second generation of computer hardware.

1964

The number of computers has grown to 18,000.

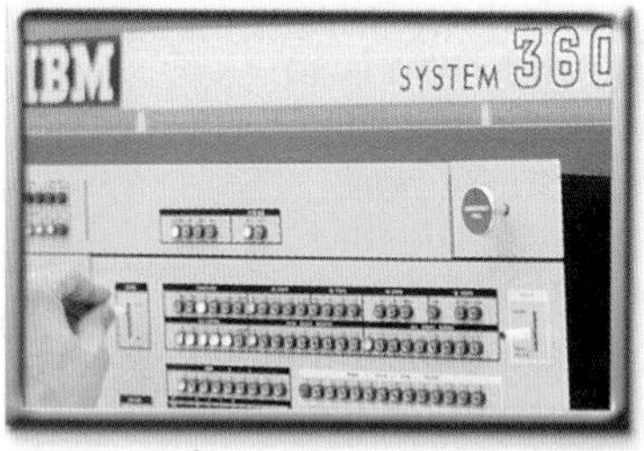

Third-generation computers, with their controlling circuitry stored on chips, are introduced. The IBM System/360 computer is the first family of compatible machines, merging science and business lines.

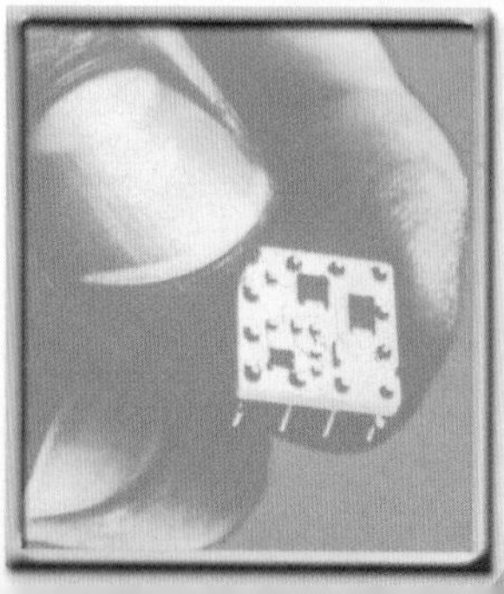

1968

Computer Science Corporation becomes the first software company listed on the New York Stock Exchange.

In a letter to the editor titled, "GO TO Statements Considered Harmful," Dr. Edsger Dijsktra introduces the concept of structured programming, developing standards for constructing computer programs.

Alan Shugart at IBM demonstrates the first regular use of an 8-inch floppy (magnetic storage) disk.

Fourth-generation computers, built with chips that use LSI (large-scale integration) arrive. While the chips used in 1965 contained as many as 1,000 circuits, the LSI chip contains as many as 15,000.

1970

Ethernet, the first local area network (LAN), is developed at Xerox PARC (Palo Alto Research Center) by Robert Metcalf. The LAN allows computers to communicate and share software, data, and peripherals. Initially designed to link minicomputers, Ethernet will be extended to personal computers.

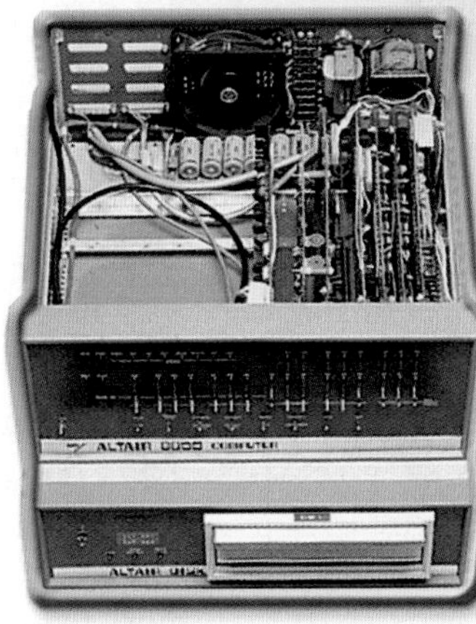

MITS, Inc. advertises one of the first microcomputers, the Altair. Named for the destination in an episode of Star Trek, the Altair is sold in kits for less than $400. Although initially it has no keyboard, no monitor, no permanent memory, and no software, 4,000 orders are taken within the first three months.

1975

1969

The ARPANET network, a predecessor of the Internet, is established.

ArpaNet

Under pressure from the industry, IBM announces that some of its software will be priced separately from the computer hardware. This unbundling allows software firms to emerge in the industry.

IBM

1971

Dr. Ted Hoff of Intel Corporation develops a microprocessor, or microprogrammable computer chip, the Intel 4004.

1976

Steve Wozniak and Steve Jobs build the first Apple computer. A subsequent version, the Apple II, is an immediate success. Adopted by elementary schools, high schools, and colleges, for many students the Apple II is their first contact with the world of computers.

scsite.com/dc2002/ch1/timeline5.htm

1979

The first public online information services, CompuServe and the Source, are founded.

VisiCalc, a spreadsheet program written by Bob Frankston and Dan Bricklin, is introduced. Originally written to run on Apple II computers, VisiCalc will be seen as the most important reason for the acceptance of personal computers in the business world.

1980

Alan Shugart presents the Winchester hard drive, revolutionizing storage for personal computers.

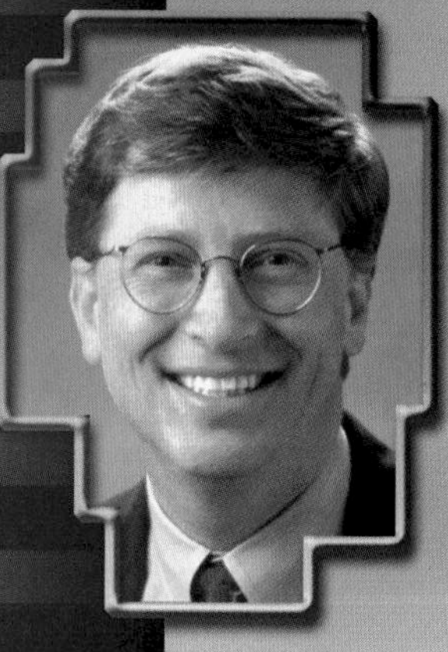

IBM offers Microsoft Corporation co-founder, Bill Gates, the opportunity to develop the operating system for the soon-to-be announced IBM personal computer. With the development of MS-DOS, Microsoft achieves tremendous growth and success.

1981

The IBM PC is introduced, signaling IBM's entrance into the personal computer marketplace. The IBM PC quickly garners the largest share of the personal computer market and becomes the personal computer of choice in business.

1982

Hayes introduces the 300 bps smart modem. The modem is an immediate success.

COMPAQ

Compaq, Inc. is founded to develop and market IBM-compatible PCs.

3,275,000 personal computers are sold, almost 3,000,000 more than in 1981.

1983

Instead of choosing a person for its annual award, TIME magazine names the computer Machine of the Year for 1982, acknowledging the impact of computers on society.

Lotus Development Corporation is founded. Its spreadsheet software, Lotus 1-2-3, which combines spreadsheet, graphics, and database programs in one package, becomes the best-selling program for IBM personal computers.

1984

IBM introduces a personal computer, called the PC AT, that uses the Intel 80286 microprocessor.

Apple introduces the Macintosh computer, which incorporates a unique, easy-to-learn, graphical user interface.

Hewlett-Packard announces the first LaserJet printer for personal computers.

1987

Several personal computers utilizing the powerful Intel 80386 microprocessor are introduced. These machines perform processing that once only large systems could handle.

1988

Microsoft surpasses Lotus Development Corporation to become the world's top software vendor.

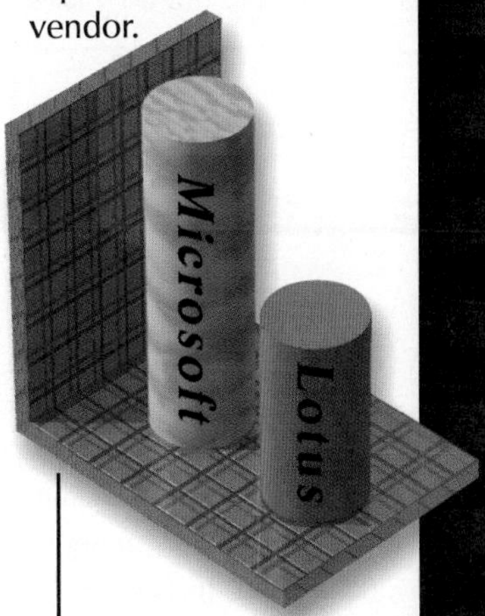

1989

The Intel 486 becomes the world's first 1,000,000 transistor microprocessor. It crams 1.2 million transistors on a .4" x .6" sliver of silicon and executes 15,000,000 instructions per second — four times as fast as its predecessor, the 80386 chip.

While working at CERN, Switzerland, Tim Berners-Lee invents an Internet-based hypermedia enterprise for information sharing. Berners-Lee will call this innovation the World Wide Web.

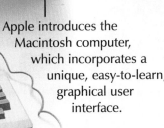

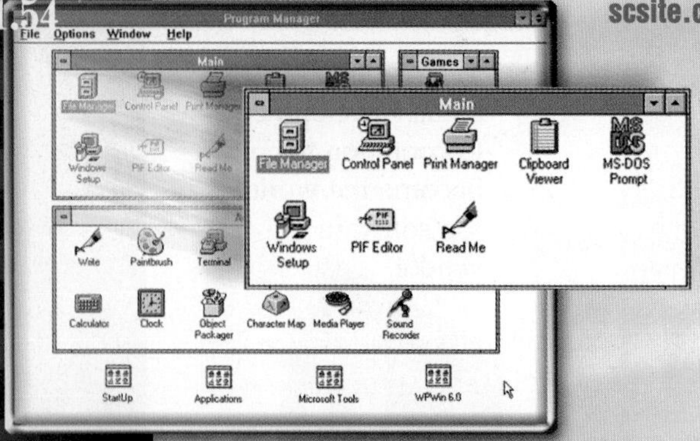

1992

Microsoft releases Windows 3.1, the latest version of its Windows operating system. Windows 3.1 offers improvements such as TrueType fonts, multimedia capability, and object linking and embedding (OLE). In two months, 3,000,000 copies of Windows 3.1 are sold.

1993

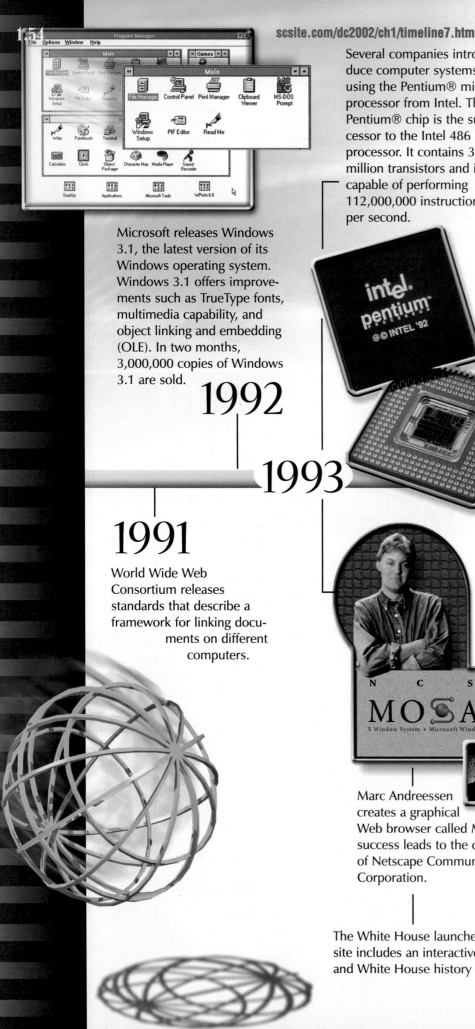

Several companies introduce computer systems using the Pentium® microprocessor from Intel. The Pentium® chip is the successor to the Intel 486 processor. It contains 3.1 million transistors and is capable of performing 112,000,000 instructions per second.

1994

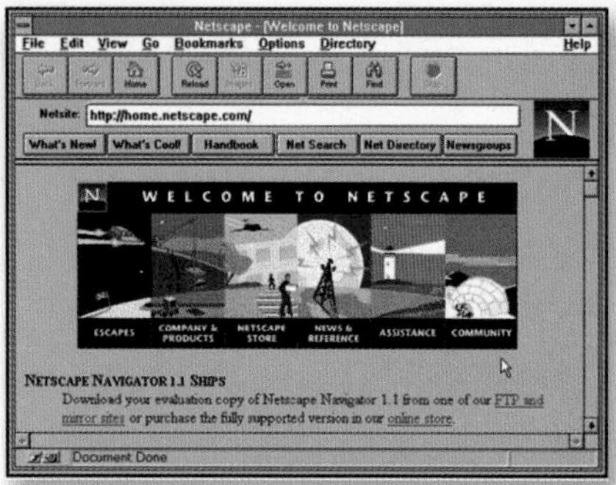

Jim Clark and Marc Andreessen found Netscape and launch Netscape Navigator 1.0, a browser for the World Wide Web.

1991

World Wide Web Consortium releases standards that describe a framework for linking documents on different computers.

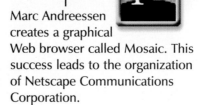

Marc Andreessen creates a graphical Web browser called Mosaic. This success leads to the organization of Netscape Communications Corporation.

The White House launches its Web page. The site includes an interactive citizens' handbook and White House history and tours.

Linus Torvalds creates the Linux kernel, a UNIX-like operating system that he releases free across the Internet for further enhancement by other programmers.

Sun Microsystems launches Java, an object-oriented programming language that allows users to write one application for a variety of computer platforms. Java becomes one of the hottest Internet technologies.

U.S. Robotics introduces PalmPilot, a handheld personal organizer. The PalmPilot's user friendliness and low price make it a standout next to more expensive personal digital assistants (PDAs).

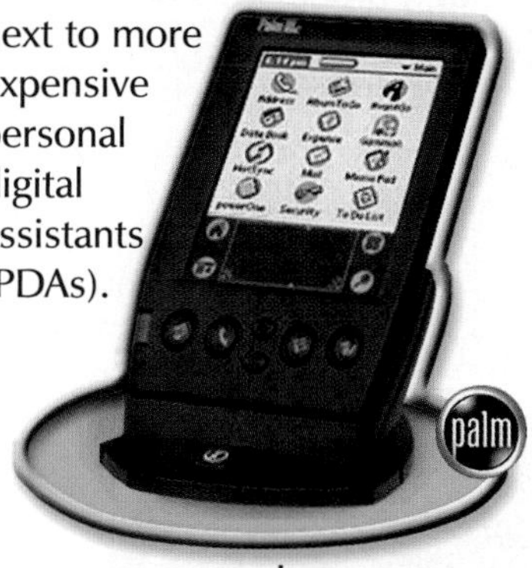

Microsoft releases Windows NT 4.0, an operating system for client-server networks. Windows NT's management tools and Wizards make it easier for developers to build and deploy business applications.

The Summer Olympics in Atlanta makes extensive use of computer technology, using an IBM network of 7,000 personal computers, 2,000 pagers and wireless devices, and 90 industrial-strength computers to share information with more than 150,000 athletes, coaches, journalists, and Olympics staff members, and millions of Web users.

1995

1996

Microsoft releases Windows 95, a major upgrade to its Windows operating system. Windows 95 consists of more than 10,000,000 lines of computer instructions developed by 300 person-years of effort. More than 50,000 individuals and companies test the software before it is released.

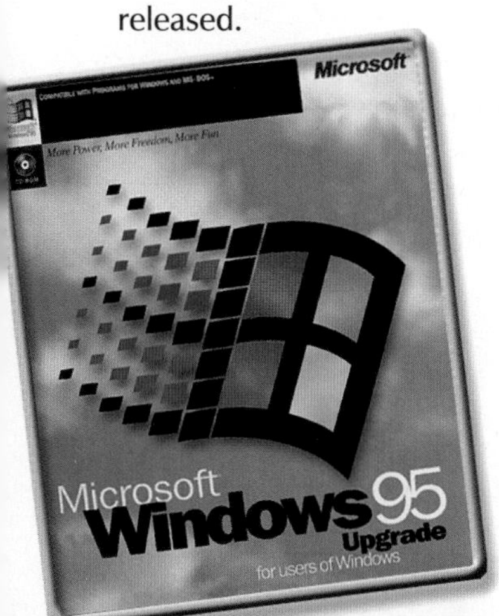

Two out of three employees in the United States have access to a personal computer, and one out of every three homes has a personal computer. Fifty million personal computers are sold worldwide and more than 250,000,000 are in use.

An innovative technology called webtv combines television and the Internet by providing viewers with tools to navigate the Web.

scsite.com/dc2002/ch1/timeline9.htm

Deep Blue, an IBM supercomputer, defeats world chess champion Gary Kasparov in a six-game chess competition. Millions of people follow the 9-day long rematch on IBM's Web site.

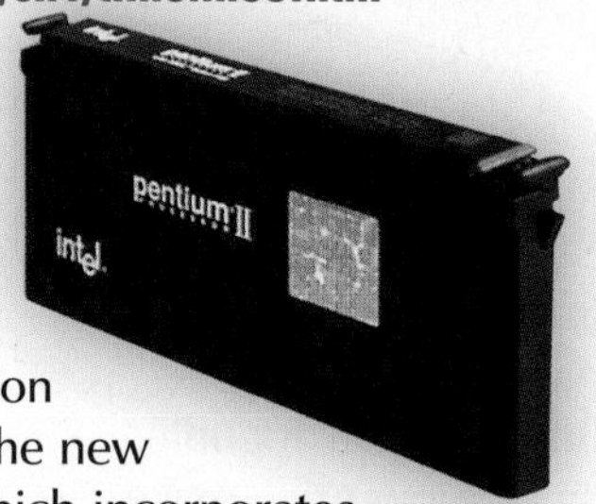

Intel introduces the Pentium® II processor with 7.5 million transistors. The new processor, which incorporates MMX™ technology, processes video, audio, and graphics data more efficiently and supports applications such as movie-editing, gaming, and more.

Fifty million users are connected to the Internet and World Wide Web.

More than 10,000,000 people take up telecommuting the capability of working at home and communicating with an office via computer. More and more firms embrace telecommuting to help increase productivity, reduce absenteeism, and provide greater job satisfaction.

1997

Apple and Microsoft sign a joint technology development agreement. Microsoft buys $150,000,000 of Apple stock.

Microsoft releases Internet Explorer 4.0 and seizes a key place in the Internet arena. This new Web browser is greeted with tremendous customer demand.

DVD (Digital Video Disc), the next generation of optical disc storage technology, is introduced. DVD can store computer, audio, and video data in a single format, with the capability of producing near-studio quality. By year's end, 500,000 DVD players are shipped worldwide.

1998

E-commerce, or electronic commerce – the marketing of goods and services over the Internet – booms. Companies such as Dell, E*TRADE, and Amazon.com spur online shopping, allowing buyers to obtain everything from hardware and software to financial and travel services, insurance, automobiles, books, and more.

Microsoft ships Windows 98, an upgrade to Windows 95. Windows 98 offers improved Internet access, better system performance, and support for a new generation of hardware and software. In six months, more than 10,000,000 copies of Windows 98 are sold worldwide.

The Department of Justice's broad antitrust lawsuit asks that Microsoft offer Windows 98 without the Internet Explorer browser or that it bundle the competing Netscape Navigator browser with the operating system.

Intel releases its Pentium® III processor, which provides enhanced multimedia capabilities.

Governments and businesses frantically work to make their computer systems Y2K (Year 2000) compliant, spending more than $500 billion worldwide. Y2K non-compliant computers cannot distinguish if 01/01/00 refers to 1900 or 2000, and thus may operate using a wrong date. This Y2K bug can affect any application that relies on computer chips, such as ATMs, airplanes, energy companies, and the telephone system.

U.S. District Judge Thomas Penfield Jackson rules in the antitrust lawsuit brought by the Department of Justice and 19 states that Microsoft used its monopoly power to stifle competition.

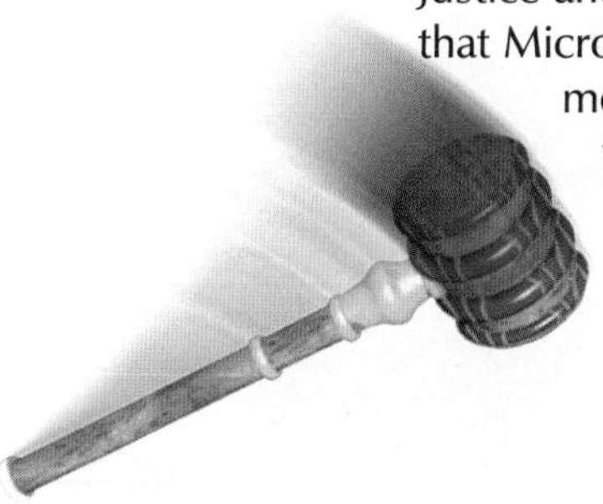

1998

Compaq Computer, the United States' leading personal computer manufacturer, buys Digital Equipment Corporation in the biggest take-over in the history of the computer industry. Compaq becomes the world's second largest computer firm, behind IBM.

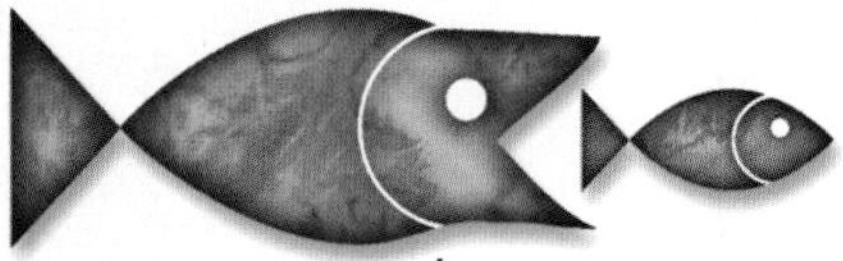

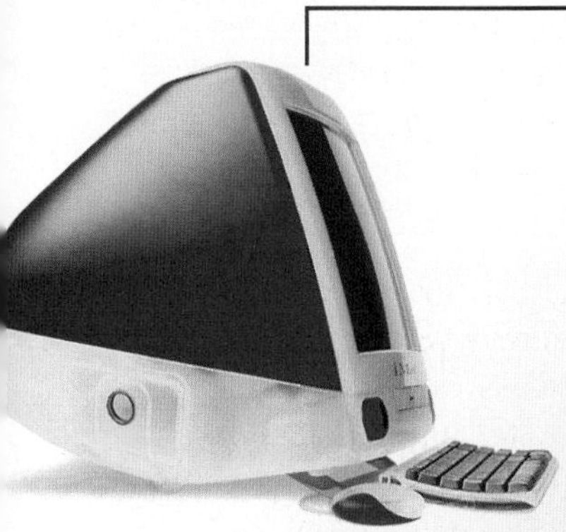

Apple Computer introduces the iMac, the latest version of its popular Macintosh computer. The iMac abandons such conventional features as a floppy disk drive but wins customers with its futuristic design, see-through case, and easy setup. Consumer demand outstrips Apple's production capabilities, and some vendors are forced to begin waiting lists.

1999

Microsoft introduces Office 2000, its premier productivity suite, offering new tools for users to create content and save it directly to a Web site without any file conversion or special steps.

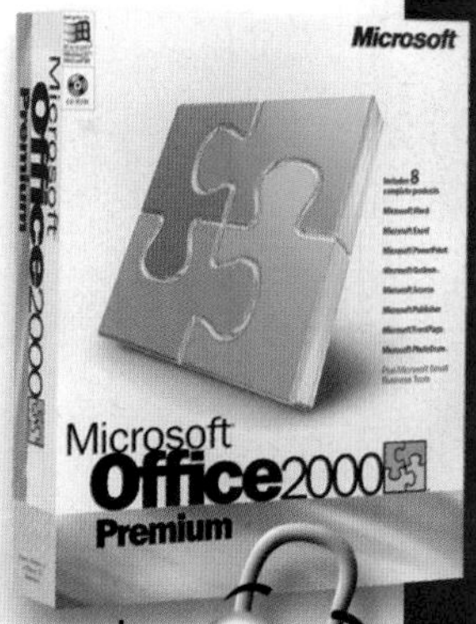

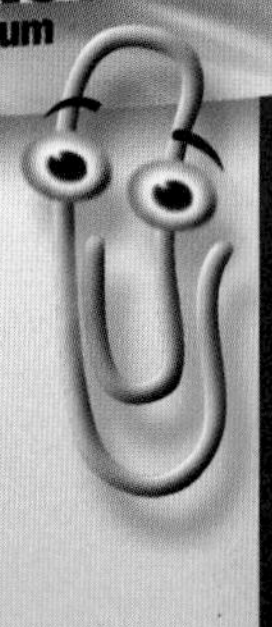

Open Source Code software, such as the Linux operating system and the Apache Web server created by unpaid volunteers, begin to gain wide acceptance among computer users.

Shawn Fanning, 19, and his company, Napster, turn the music industry upside down by developing software that allows computer users to swap music files with one another without going through a centralized file server. The Recording Industry of America, on behalf of five media companies, sues Napster for copyright infringement.

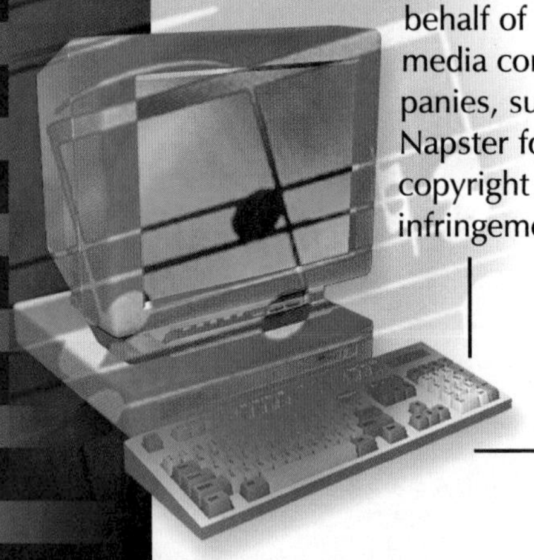

Microsoft ships Windows 2000 and Windows Me. Windows 2000 offers improved behind-the-scene security and reliability. Windows Me is designed for home users and lets them edit home movies, share digital photos, index music, and create a home network.

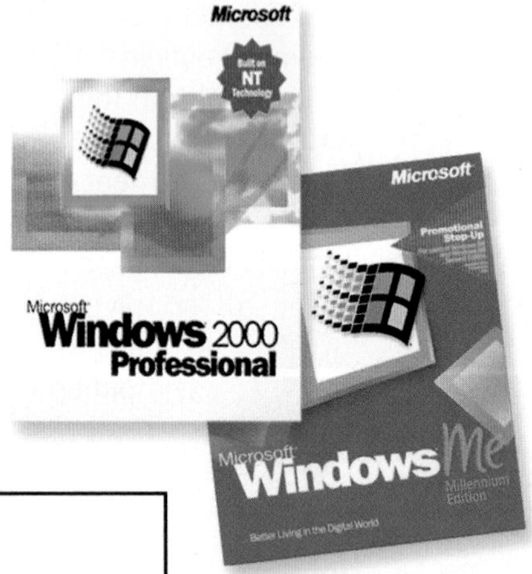

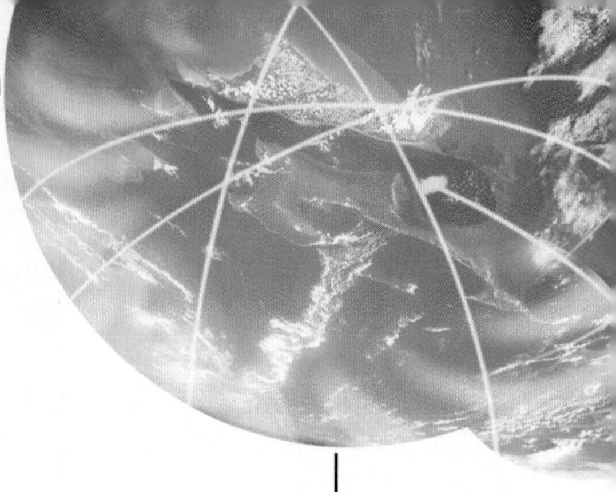

According to the U.S. Commerce Department, Internet traffic is doubling every 100 days, resulting in an annual growth rate of more than 700 percent. It has taken radio and television 30 years and 15 years to reach 60 million people, respectively. The Internet has achieved the same audience base in three years.

2000

Intel unveils its Pentium 4 chip with clock speeds starting at 1.4 GHz. The Pentium 4 includes 42 million transistors, nearly twice as many contained on its predecessor, the Pentium III.

E-commerce achieves mainstream acceptance. Annual e-commerce sales exceed $100 billion, and Internet advertising expenditures reach more than $5 billion.

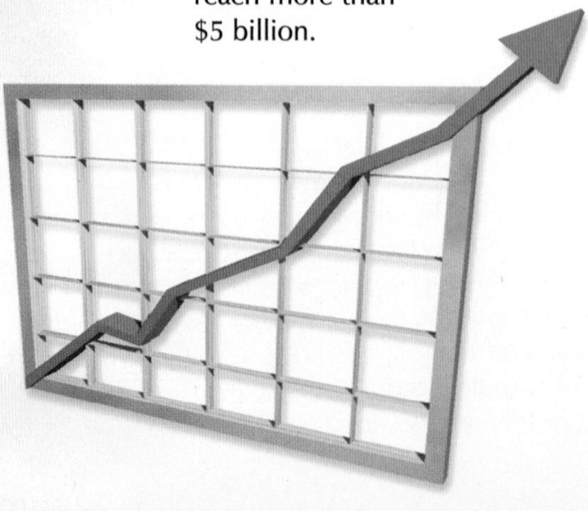

Dot com companies (Internet based) go out of business at a record pace — nearly one per day — as financial investors withhold funding due to the companies' unprofitability.

Telemedicine uses satellite technology and videoconferencing to broadcast consultations and to perform distant surgeries. Robots are used for complex and precise tasks. Computer-aided surgery uses virtual reality to assist with training and planning procedures.

Microsoft introduces a new version of Office, which includes voice recognition and speech capabilities. Its Subscription mode lets users register the software over the Internet and renew or extend the amount of time it will run.

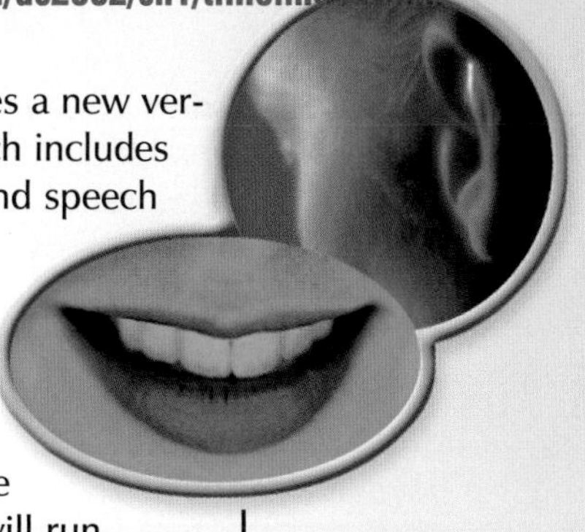

Microsoft .net

Microsoft launches its .NET strategy, which is a new environment for developing and running software applications featuring ease of development of Web-based services. As a user of applications, you will see the benefit of .NET as instant access to data and services in the context of your current task.

More than 25 million computer users subscribe to America Online and take advantage of its AOL Anywhere features, including Instant Messenger, e-mail, and customized news and information pages. AOL's merger with Time Warner combines the strengths of the Internet, entertainment, and communications industries.

AOL Anywhere

TIME WARNER

2001

Application service providers offer a return to a centralized computing environment, in which large megaservers warehouse your data, information, and software, so it is accessible using a variety of devices from any location.

Wireless technology, especially handheld computers, achieves significant market penetration. Prices drop, usage increases, and wireless carriers scramble for new services, particularly for a mobile workforce that can access the Internet anywhere at any time.

Avid readers enjoy e-books, which are digital texts read on compact computer screens. E-books can hold the equivalent of 10 traditional books containing text and graphics. Readers can search, highlight text, and add notes.

CHAPTER 2

The Internet and World Wide Web

Ecstatic. Relieved. Exhausted. With graduation day approaching, these are only a few of your emotions. The day after commencement exercises, you and six friends from school are driving to Hidden Lake National Park to enjoy fresh air in the great outdoors on a two-week camping trip.

Before the semester ends, though, you plan to line up a job. This way, you can embark on your new career just as soon as you return from the outing. Today, you meet with an adviser in the Office of Career Development. Among other resources, the office maintains a Resume Forwarding system. The adviser shows you how to enter your resume into the system, and then automatically, it sends yours and all current resumes on file to potential employers. He also recommends that you attend the Campus Career Fair next week, and suggests you publish your resume on the Web.

Computer Technology was not your major. You tell the adviser that publishing on the Web sounds a little too high-tech for you. He says publishing a personal Web page is fairly simple … as long as you have the right tools. His office is conducting a three-hour seminar next Wednesday called How to Publish a Resume. You immediately sign up.

OBJECTIVES

After completing this chapter, you will be able to:

- Discuss how the Internet works
- Understand ways to access the Internet
- Identify a URL
- Know how to search for information on the Web
- Describe the types of Web pages
- Recognize how Web pages use graphics, animation, audio, video, and virtual reality
- Define Webcasting
- Describe the uses of electronic commerce (e-commerce)
- Identify the tools required for Web publishing
- Explain how e-mail, FTP, newsgroups and message boards, mailing lists, chat rooms, and instant messaging work
- Identify the rules of netiquette

THE INTERNET

One of the major reasons business, home, and other users purchase computers is for Internet access. Through the Internet, society has access to information from all around the globe. Instantaneously, you can find local and national news, weather reports, sports scores, stock prices, your medical records, your credit report, and countless forms of educational material. The Internet also offers many conveniences. At your fingertips, you can send messages to others, meet new friends, bank, invest, shop, fill prescriptions, file taxes, take a course, play a game, listen to music, or watch a movie. The magnificence of the Internet is you can access it from a computer anywhere: at home, at work, at school, at the beach, in a restaurant, and even on an airplane.

Success today in the business world requires an understanding of the Internet. Without it, you are missing a tremendous resource for goods, services, information, and communications.

As discussed in Chapter 1, the Internet is the world's largest network. A **network** is a collection of computers and devices connected together via communications devices and media such as modems, cables, telephone lines, and satellites. The **Internet**, also called the **Net**, is a worldwide collection of networks that links millions of businesses, government agencies, educational institutions, and individuals. Each of the networks on the Internet provides resources that add to the abundance of goods, services, and information accessible via the Internet.

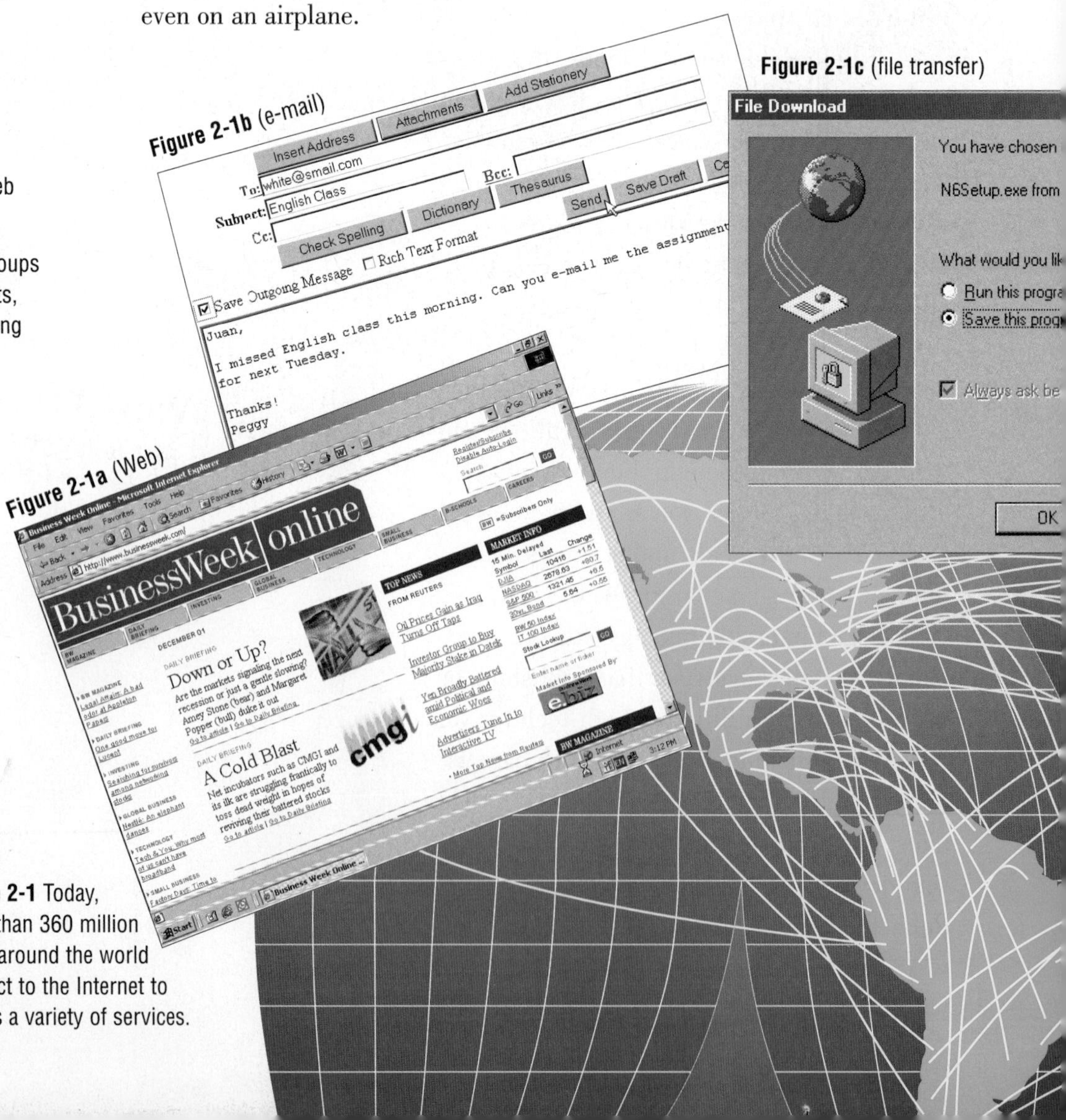

Figure 2-1b (e-mail)

Figure 2-1c (file transfer)

Figure 2-1a (Web)

Figure 2-1 Today, more than 360 million users around the world connect to the Internet to access a variety of services.

The Internet consists of many local, regional, national, and international networks. Although each of these networks on the Internet is owned by a public or private organization, no single organization owns or controls the Internet. Each organization on the Internet is responsible only for maintaining its own network.

Today, more than 360 million users around the world connect to the Internet for a variety of reasons. Some of the uses of the Internet are as follows:

- Access a wealth of information, news, and research material
- Communicate with others around the world
- Bank and invest
- Shop for goods and services
- Download and listen to music or download and watch movies
- Take a course or access other educational material
- Access sources of entertainment and leisure such as online games, magazines, and vacation planning guides
- Access other computers and exchange files
- Share and edit documents with others in real time
- Provide information, photographs, audio clips, or video clips

To support these and other activities, the Internet provides a variety of services (Figure 2-1). One of the most widely accessed of the Internet services is the World Wide Web. Other services include electronic mail (e-mail), file transfer, newsgroups and message boards, mailing lists, chat rooms, and instant messaging. The following pages explain these services, along with a discussion of the history of the Internet and how the Internet works.

HISTORY OF THE INTERNET

The Internet has it roots in a networking project started by the Pentagon's **Advanced Research Projects Agency** (**ARPA**), an agency of the U.S. Department of Defense. ARPA's goal was to build a network that (1) would allow scientists at different

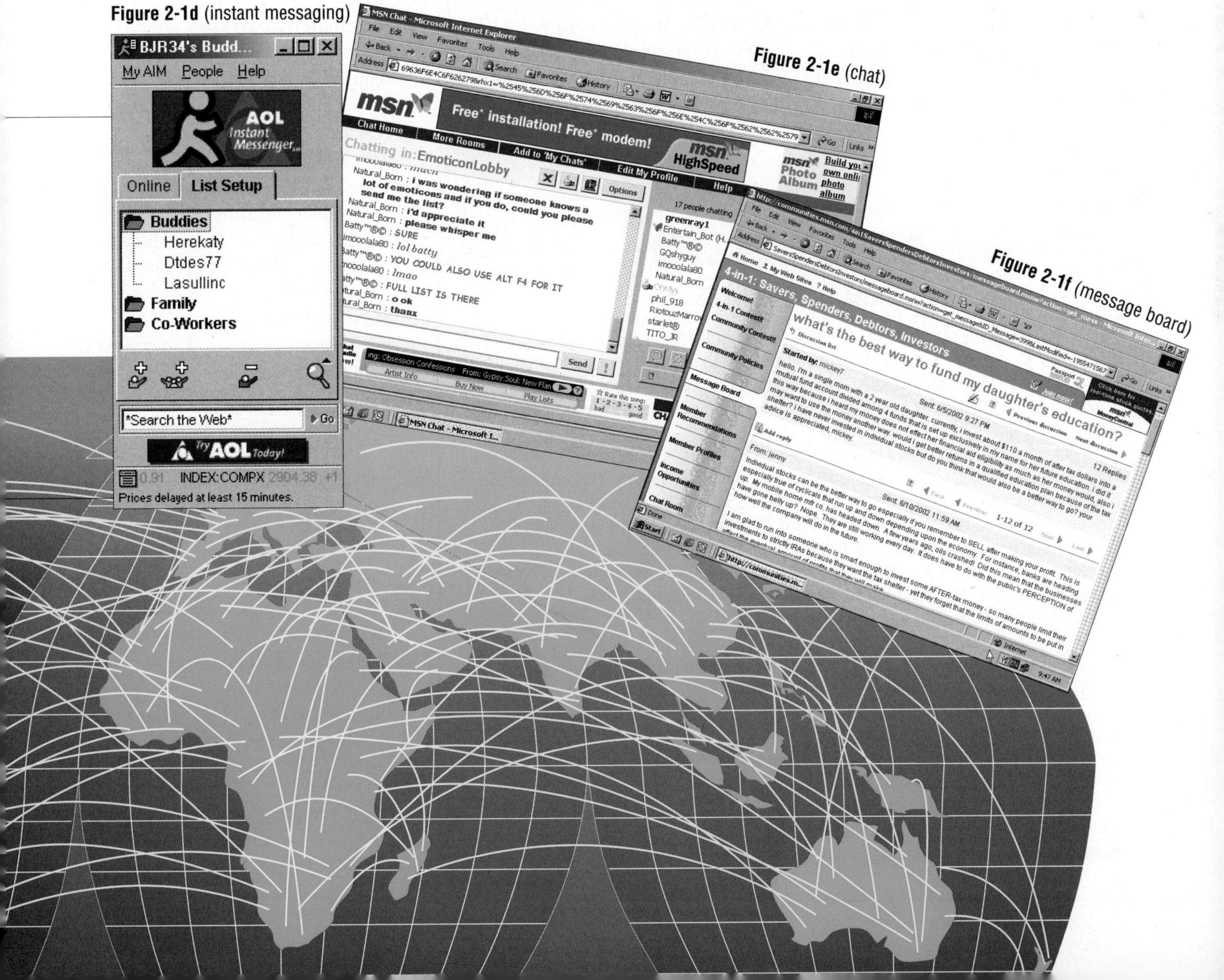

Figure 2-1d (instant messaging)
Figure 2-1e (chat)
Figure 2-1f (message board)

locations to share information and work together on military and scientific projects and (2) could function even if part of the network were disabled or destroyed by a disaster such as a nuclear attack. That network, called **ARPANET**, became functional in September 1969, linking scientific and academic researchers in the United States.

The original ARPANET was a wide area network (WAN) consisting of four main computers, one each located at the University of California at Los Angeles, the Stanford Research Institute, the University of California at Santa Barbara, and the University of Utah. Each of these four computers served as the network's host nodes. In a network, a host **node**, or **host**, is any computer that directly connects to the network. A host often stores and transfers data and messages on high-speed communications lines and provides network connections for other computers.

As researchers and others realized the great benefit of using ARPANET's electronic mail to share information, ARPANET underwent phenomenal growth. By 1984, ARPANET had more than 1,000 individual computers linked as hosts. (Today, more than 100 million hosts connect to the Internet.)

Some organizations connected entire networks to ARPANET to take advantage of the high-speed communications it offered. In 1986, for example, the National Science Foundation (NSF) connected its huge network of five supercomputer centers, called **NSFnet**, to ARPANET. This configuration of complex networks and hosts became known as the Internet.

Until 1995, NSFnet handled the bulk of the communications activity, or **traffic**, on the Internet. In 1995, NSFnet terminated its network on the Internet and returned its status to a research network.

Today, a variety of corporations, commercial firms, and other companies provide networks to handle the traffic on the Internet. These networks, along with telephone companies, cable and satellite companies, and the government all contribute toward the internal structure of the Internet. Many donate resources, such as servers, communications lines, and technical specialists — making the Internet truly collaborative.

Even as the Internet grows, it remains a public, cooperative, and independent network. Although no single person, company, institution, or government agency controls or owns the Internet, several organizations contribute toward its success by advising, defining standards, and addressing other issues. The **World Wide Web Consortium (W3C)** is the group that oversees research and sets standards and guidelines for many areas of the Internet.

Internet2 is an Internet-related research and development project. Through an extremely high-speed network, **Internet2 (I2)** develops and tests advanced Internet technologies for research, teaching, and learning. Members of I2 include more than 180 universities in the United States, along with several industry and government partners. The goal of I2 is to enhance tomorrow's Internet with its advanced technologies.

TECHNOLOGY TRAILBLAZER

TIM BERNERS-LEE

WWW. You see those letters everywhere, thanks to Tim Berners-Lee. This unsung hero created the World Wide Web, although he refuses to step into the limelight to profit from his invention. In his words, commercializing his brainchild would suggest that people would be respecting him "as a function of [his] net worth. That's not an assumption I was brought up with."

Instead, Berners-Lee prefers to work quietly in academia as director of the World Wide Web Consortium (W3C) at the Massachusetts Institute of Technology. This organization consists of hundreds of representatives from the world's leading Internet companies, including Microsoft, IBM, and Hewlett-Packard. W3C considers issues in the Web's evolution and hopes to realize its full potential and ensure its reliability.

Berners-Lee learned these values as a child in London. His parents, who met while working with one of the first commercially sold computers, sparked his interest in both electronics and mathematics. He graduated with a degree in physics from Queen's College at Oxford University, where he created his first working computer with an old television, an M6800 processor, and a soldering iron.

For more information on Tim Berners-Lee, visit the Discovering Computers 2002 People Web page (**scsite.com/dc2002/people.htm**) and click Tim Berners-Lee.

HOW THE INTERNET WORKS

Data sent over the Internet travels via networks and communications channels owned and operated by many companies. The following sections preset various ways to connect to these networks.

Service Providers

An **Internet service provider** (**ISP**) is a business that has a permanent Internet connection and provides temporary connections to individuals and companies for free or for a fee. The most common ISP fee arrangement is a fixed amount, usually about \$10 to \$20 per month for an individual account. For this amount, many ISPs offer unlimited Internet access. Others specify a set number of access hours per month. With these arrangements, you pay an additional amount for each hour you connect in excess of an allotted number of access hours.

If you use a telephone line to access the Internet, the telephone number you dial connects you to an access point on the Internet, called a **point of presence** (**POP**). When selecting a service provider, ensure it provides at least one local POP telephone number. Otherwise, you will pay long-distance telephone bills for the time you connect to the Internet.

Two types of ISPs are regional and national (Figure 2-2). A **regional ISP** usually provides access to the Internet through one or more telephone numbers local to a specific geographic area. A **national ISP** is a larger business that provides local telephone numbers in most major cities and towns nationwide. Some national ISPs also provide a toll-free telephone number. Due to their larger size, national ISPs usually offer more services and generally have a larger technical support staff than regional ISPs. Examples of national ISPs are AT&T, Earthlink, and WorldCom.

Like an ISP, an **online service provider** (**OSP**) supplies Internet access, but an OSP also has many members-only features that offer a variety of special content and services such as news; weather; legal information; financial data; hardware and software guides; games; and travel guides. For this reason, the fees for using an OSP sometimes are slightly

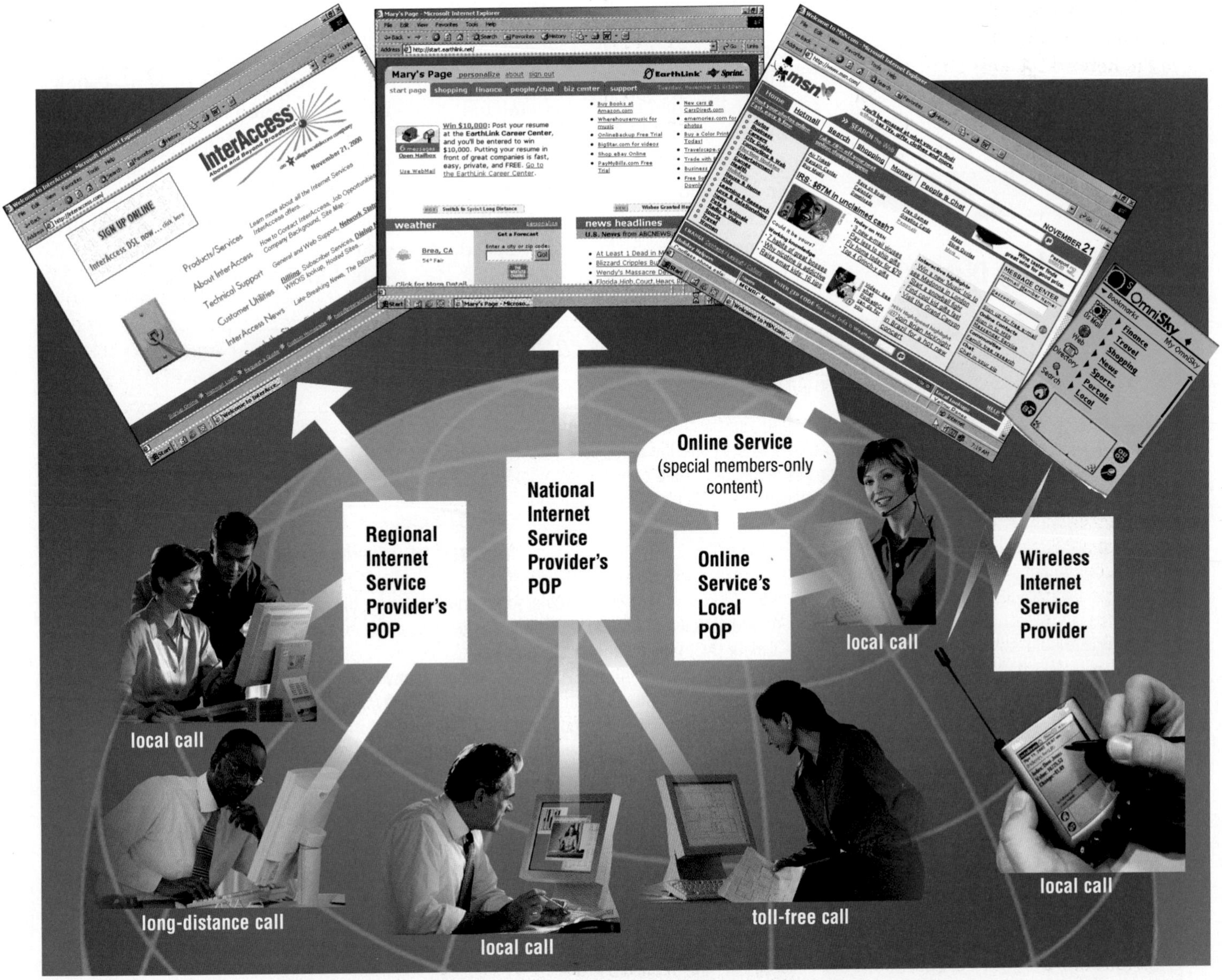

Figure 2-2 Common ways to access the Internet are through a regional or national Internet service provider, an online service provider, or a wireless service provider.

higher than fees for an ISP. The two most popular OSPs are America Online (AOL) and the Microsoft Network (MSN).

A **wireless service provider (WSP)** is a company that provides wireless Internet access to users with wireless modems or Web-enabled handheld computers or devices. Notebook computers can use wireless modems. Web-enabled devices include cellular telephones, two-way pagers, and hands-free (voice activated) Internet devices in automobiles. An antenna on the wireless modem or Web-enabled device typically sends signals through the airwaves to communicate with a WSP. Examples of WSPs include GoAmerica Communications, OmniSky, and SprintPCS.

Connecting to the Internet

Employees and students often connect to the Internet through a business or school network. In this case, the computers usually are part of a local area network (LAN) that connects to a service provider through a high-speed connection line leased from the local telephone company.

Home or small business users often connect to the Internet through dial-up access. With **dial-up access**, you use a computer, a modem, and a regular telephone line to dial into an ISP or OSP. Dial-up access provides an easy and inexpensive way for users to connect to the Internet. A dial-up connection, however, is slow-speed technology.

Some home and small business users opt for newer high-speed technologies such as digital subscriber lines or cable television Internet services. **DSL (digital subscriber line)** provides high-speed connections over a regular copper telephone line. A **cable modem** provides high-speed Internet connections through the cable television network. These services cost about twice as much as dial-up access.

How Data Travels the Internet

Computers connected to the Internet work together to transfer data and information around the world using servers and clients. As discussed in Chapter 1, a **server** is a computer that manages the resources on a network and provides a centralized storage area for resources such as programs and data. A **client** is a computer that can access the contents of the storage area on the server. On the Internet, for example, your computer is a client that can access files and services on a variety of servers, called **host computers**.

Web Link

For more information on service providers, visit the Discovering Computers 2002 Chapter 2 WEB LINK page (**scsite.com/dc2002/ch2/weblink.htm**) and click Service Providers.

ISSUE

Local or Long Distance?

Fees and Taxes for Internet Access

In early 1999, the Federal Communications Commission (FCC) (see URL below) ruled that dial-up Internet calls are interstate in nature and not local. The FCC concluded that calls to Internet service providers (ISPs) should be regarded as interstate transactions, because Internet traffic is not, strictly speaking, local. Many people feel this 4-0 vote by the FCC could open the way for new fees for ISPs, which eventually would be passed on to users. If this ruling is implemented, Internet users will pay a fee and tax similar to the charges for long-distance telephone calls. Should Internet users be required to pay a long-distance fee? Should they be taxed while online? Will Internet usage diminish if users are required to pay additional per minute charges?

For more information on Internet charges, online access, and the Web site mentioned above, visit the Discovering Computers 2002 Issues Web page (**scsite.com/dc2002/issues.htm**) and click Chapter 2 Issue #1.

COMPANY ON THE CUTTING EDGE

AMERICA Online

Interacting Anywhere

Meg Ryan and Tom Hanks fostered an online relationship in their hit movie, *You've Got Mail.* Worldwide, more than 25 million users likewise cultivate associations by using America Online (AOL) for their interactive needs.

With a strategy of *AOL Anywhere*, the company is the world's leading online service provider, with features such as electronic mail, software, computer support services, and Internet access. Each day members send 110 million e-mail messages, seek 200 million stock quotes, and browse 5.2 billion Web pages. At any given time, nearly 1.2 million users can be online simultaneously.

Stephen M. Case founded the company in 1985 as Quantum Computer Services Corporation with a vision of simplifying the Internet for people other than computer scholars and specialists. He partnered with a series of companies, including Commodore International, Ltd., Tandy Corporation, and Apple Computer. Case changed the company name to America Online in 1991.

AOL experienced tremendous growth throughout the 1990s partly due to its aggressive marketing campaign using direct mail, membership kits, and magazine inserts. It acquired Netscape Communications in 1998 and proposed the largest corporate merger with Time Warner, one of the world's leading media conglomerates, in 2000.

For more information on America Online, visit the Discovering Computers 2002 Companies Web page (**scsite.com/dc2002/companies.htm**) and click AOL.

The inner structure of the Internet works much like a transportation system. Just as highways connect major cities and carry the bulk of the automotive traffic across the country, several main communications lines carry the heaviest amount of traffic on the Internet. These communications lines are referred to collectively as the Internet **backbone**.

In the United States, the communications lines that make up the Internet backbone exchange data at several different major cities across the country. The high-speed equipment in these major cities functions similar to a highway interchange, transferring data from one network to another until it reaches its final destination (Figure 2-3).

Web Link

For more information on the Internet backbone, visit the Discovering Computers 2002 Chapter 2 WEB LINK page (**scsite.com/dc2002/ch2/weblink.htm**) and click Internet Backbone.

Figure 2-3 HOW DATA MIGHT TRAVEL THE INTERNET USING A TELEPHONE LINE CONNECTION

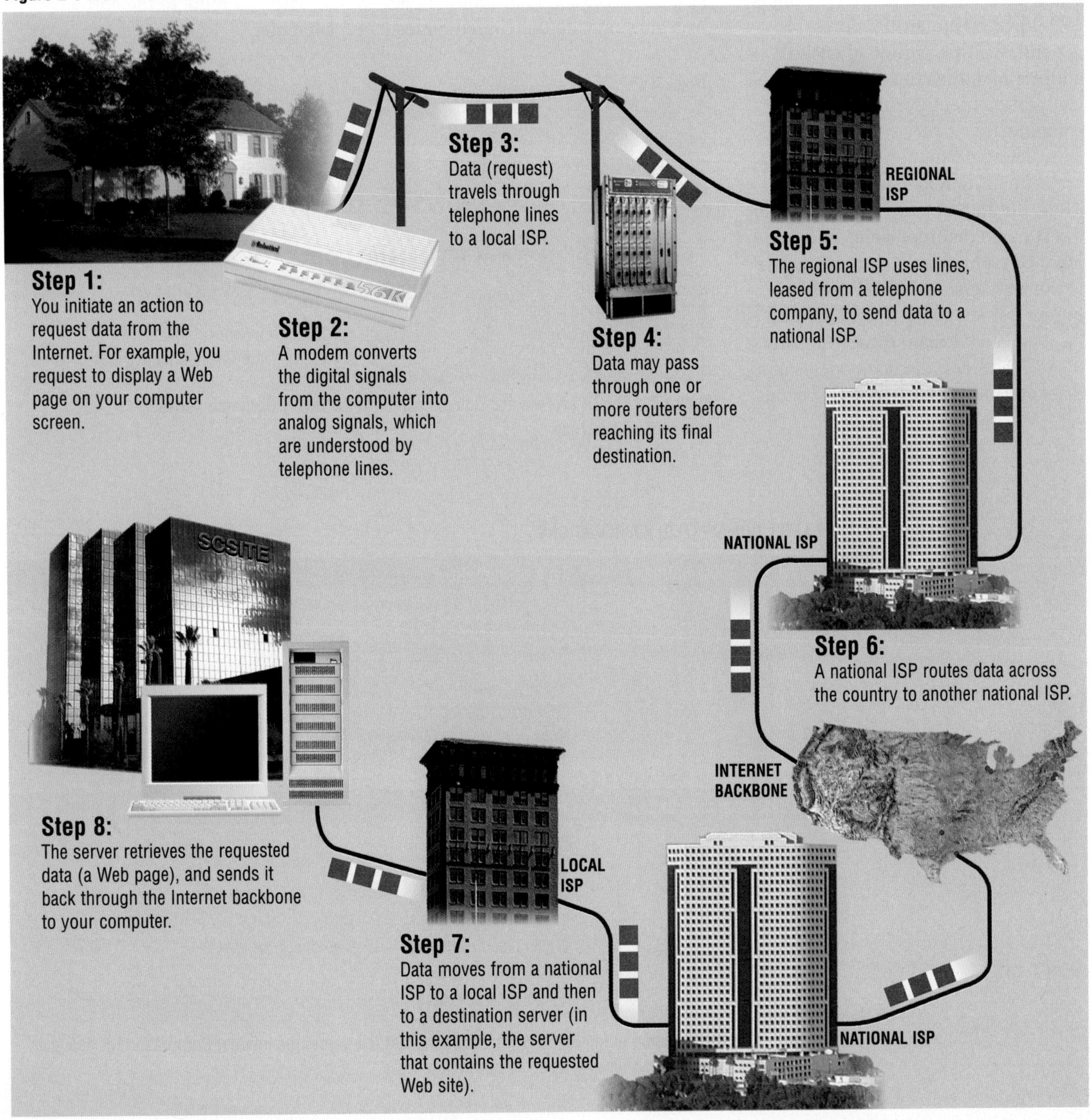
Step 1:
You initiate an action to request data from the Internet. For example, you request to display a Web page on your computer screen.
Step 2:
A modem converts the digital signals from the computer into analog signals, which are understood by telephone lines.
Step 3:
Data (request) travels through telephone lines to a local ISP.
Step 4:
Data may pass through one or more routers before reaching its final destination.
REGIONAL ISP
Step 5:
The regional ISP uses lines, leased from a telephone company, to send data to a national ISP.
NATIONAL ISP
Step 6:
A national ISP routes data across the country to another national ISP.
INTERNET BACKBONE
NATIONAL ISP
LOCAL ISP
Step 7:
Data moves from a national ISP to a local ISP and then to a destination server (in this example, the server that contains the requested Web site).
Step 8:
The server retrieves the requested data (a Web page), and sends it back through the Internet backbone to your computer.
SCSITE
56K

Internet Addresses

The Internet relies on an addressing system much like the postal service to send data to a computer at a specific destination. An **IP address**, short for Internet protocol address, is a number that uniquely identifies each computer or device connected to the Internet. The IP address consists of four groups of numbers, each separated by a period. The number in each group is between 0 and 255. For example, the numbers 199.95.72.10 are an IP address. In general, the first portion of each IP address identifies the network and the last portion identifies the specific computer.

These all-numeric IP addresses are difficult to remember and use. Thus, the Internet supports the use of a text name that represents one or more IP addresses. A **domain name** is the text version of an IP address. Figure 2-4 shows an IP address and its associated domain name. Similarly to an IP address, the components of a domain name are separated by periods.

Every domain name contains a **top-level domain** (**TLD**) abbreviation that identifies the type of organization that is associated with the domain. In Figure 2-4, the abbreviation, com, is a top-level domain. **Dot com** is the name sometimes used to describe an organization that has a TLD of com.

The group that assigns and controls TLDs is the **Internet Corporation for Assigned Names and Numbers** (**ICANN** pronounced EYE-can). Figure 2-5 lists current TLD abbreviations. For international Web sites outside the United States, the domain name also includes a country code. In these cases, the domain name ends with the country code, such as au for Australia or fr for France.

The **domain name system** (**DNS**) is the system on the Internet that stores the domain names and their corresponding IP addresses. Every time you specify a domain name, an Internet server called the **DNS server** translates the domain name into its associated IP address, so data can route to the correct computer.

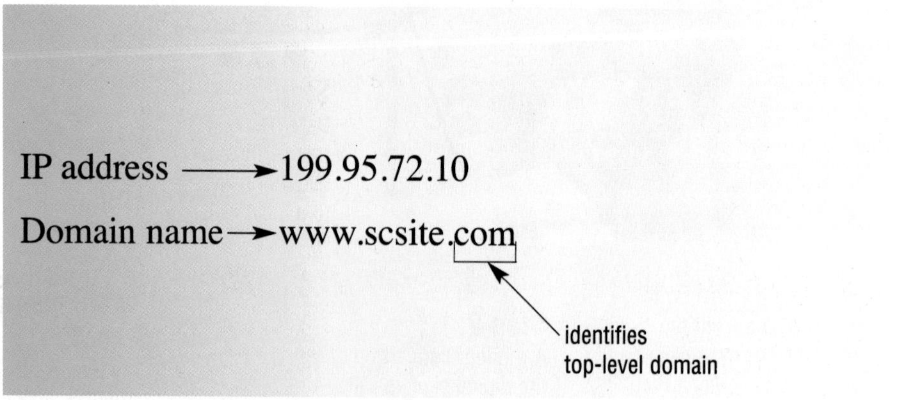

Figure 2-4 The IP address and domain name for the Shelly Cashman Series® Instructional Web site.

TOP-LEVEL DOMAIN (TLD) ABBREVIATIONS

Original TLD Abbreviations	Type of Domain
com	Commercial organizations, businesses, and companies
edu	Educational institutions
gov	Government agencies
mil	Military organizations
net	Network provider
org	Non-profit organizations

Newer TLD Abbreviations	Type of Domain
museum	Accredited museum
biz	Business
info	Information service
name	Individuals or families
pro	Credentialed professional such as doctor or lawyer
aero	Air transport company
coop	Business cooperative such as credit unions and rural electric coops

Figure 2-5 With the explosion of Internet growth during the last few years, the Internet Corporation for Assigned Names and Numbers (ICANN) recently adopted seven new TLDs.

THE WORLD WIDE WEB

Many people use the terms World Wide Web and Internet interchangeably. The World Wide Web, however, is just one of the many services available on the Internet. The World Wide Web actually is a relatively new aspect of the Internet. While the Internet was developed in the late 1960s, the World Wide Web emerged less than a decade ago — in the early 1990s. Since then, however, it has grown phenomenally to become the most widely used service on the Internet.

The **World Wide Web** (**WWW**), or **Web**, consists of a worldwide collection of electronic documents. Each of these electronic documents on the Web is called a **Web page**. A Web page can contain text, graphics, sound, and video, as well as built-in connections to other documents. A **Web site** is a collection of related Web pages.

Do not assume that information presented on a Web page is correct or accurate. You always should evaluate the value of a Web page before relying on its content.

Browsing the Web

A **Web browser**, or **browser**, is a software program that allows you to access and view Web pages. The more widely used Web browsers for personal computers are Microsoft Internet Explorer and Netscape. Figure 2-6 shows Netscape and

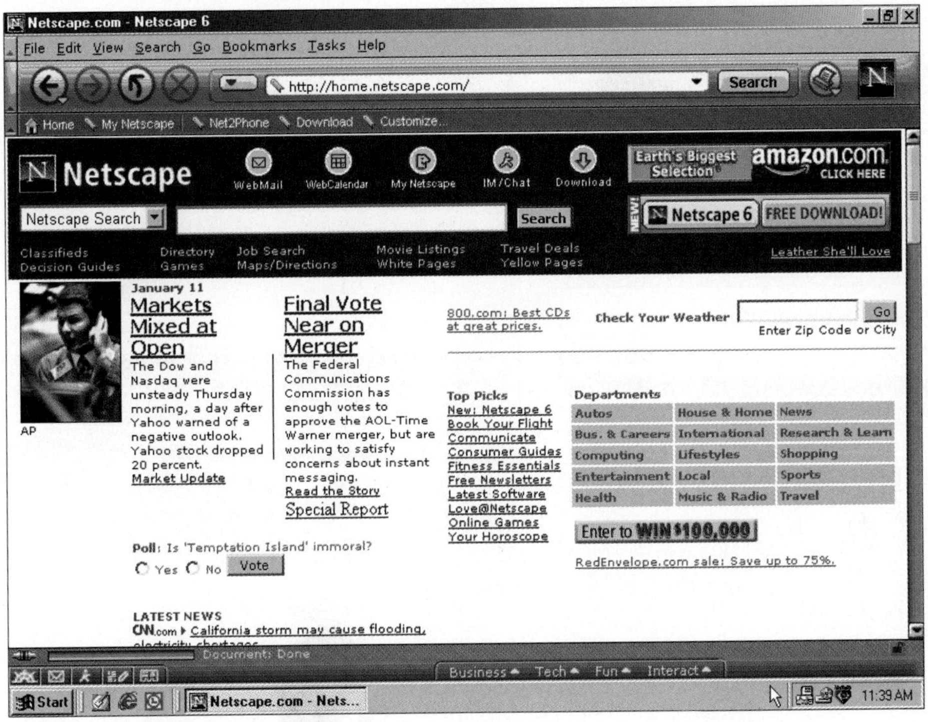

Figure 2-6 Netscape is a widely used Web browser. Shown here is the Netscape Web site, which displays when you start the Netscape browser.

APPLY IT!

Browser Tips and Tricks

When browsing the Web, most people use either Internet Explorer or Netscape. Similar to many other software applications, both browsers contain several seldom-used features. Learning how to use some of these features can enhance and enrich your computing experience. The list below pertains to Internet Explorer (IE). If you use Netscape, search Help to find similar features.

- Keyboard Shortcuts – following are a few of the many IE keyboard shortcuts for the PC: F1 – display Help; F5 – refresh the screen; F11 – toggle between full-screen and regular views of the browser window; CTRL+C – copy selected items to the Clipboard; CTRL+V – paste the contents of the Clipboard at the current location; CTRL+A – select all items on the current Web page. For a more detailed list, search for the words, keyboard shortcuts, in the online Help system.
- Links Toolbar – convenient place to add links to Web pages that you use frequently. Click the link on the Links toolbar to display the page. Add a link to the Links toolbar by using any of the following techniques: drag the icon from the Address bar to the Links bar; drag a link from a Web page to the Links bar; or drag a link to the Links bar from your Favorites list.
- Export your Favorites list to a Web page – Use this option to display your Favorites list on a Web page, share the list with someone, or use the list with Netscape. After exporting, open the list in your browser.
  1. In IE, click File on the menu bar and then click Import/Export to display the Import/Export Wizard.
  2. Click the Next button and then click Export Favorites in the list.
  3. Select your Favorites folder, click the Next button, and then click the Browse button.
  4. Determine where you want to save the file, type a file name, and then click the Save button.

For more information on subscribing to an online tips service and other Netscape and Internet Explorer tips and tricks, visit the Discovering Computers 2002 Apply It Web page (**scsite.com/dc2002/apply.htm**) and click Chapter 2 Apply It #1.

the final screen in Figure 2-7 shows Internet Explorer, which in this case displays the AOL Web site.

To browse the Web, you need a Web browser and a computer that is connected to the Internet. To establish the connection and start the Web browser, you typically use the mouse to select an icon on your desktop (Figure 2-7). If you use a standard telephone line for an Internet connection, a modem dials the telephone number to the ISP or OSP. Once the telephone connection is established, the browser retrieves and displays a home page.

A **home page**, which is the starting page for a browser, is similar to a book cover or a table of contents for a Web site. It provides information about the site's purpose and content. The initial home page that displays is one selected by your Web browser.

Figure 2-7 ONE METHOD OF CONNECTING TO THE INTERNET

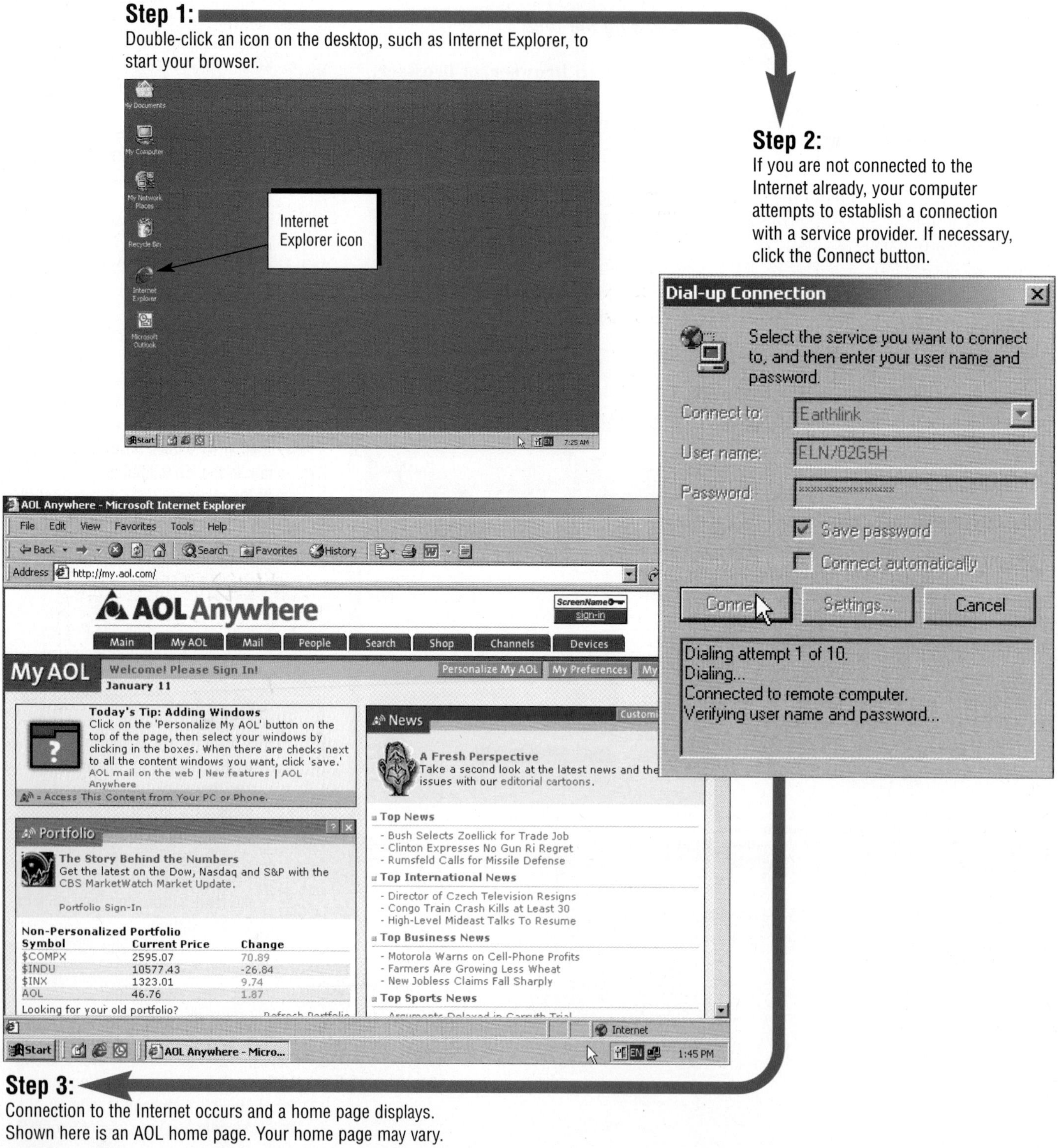

You can change the home page at any time. Many sites also allow you to personalize the home page so it displays areas of interest to you. Some Web sites also refer to their starting page as a home page.

Downloading is the process of receiving information, such as a Web page, onto your computer from a server on the Internet. While your browser downloads a page, such as the home page, it typically displays an animated logo or icon in the top-right corner of the browser window. When the download finishes, the animation stops.

Downloading a Web page can take from a few seconds to several minutes, depending on the speed of your Internet connection and the amount of graphics on the Web page. To speed up the display of pages, you can turn off the graphics and display only text in most Web browsers.

Web-enabled handheld computers and devices such as cellular telephones use a special type of browser designed for their small screens. A **microbrowser**, also called a **minibrowser**, is a software program that accesses and displays Web pages that contain mostly text (Figure 2-8). Many Web sites design Web pages specifically for display on a Web-enabled handheld computer or device.

Navigating Web Pages

Most Web pages contain hyperlinks. A **hyperlink**, also called a **link**, is a built-in connection to another related Web page or part of a Web page. Links allow you to obtain information in a nonlinear way. That is, you make associations between topics instead of moving sequentially through the topics. Reading a book from cover to cover is a linear way of learning. Branching off and investigating related topics as you encounter them is a nonlinear way of learning. Looking up definitions in a dictionary is a nonlinear way of learning.

While reading an article online about nutrition, you might want to learn more about counting calories. Having linked to and read information on counting calories, you might want to find several low-fat, low-calorie recipes. Reading these might inspire you to learn about a chef that specializes in healthy but tasty food preparation. The capability of branching from one related topic to another in a nonlinear fashion is what makes links so powerful, and the Web such an interesting place to explore.

Figure 2-8a (microbrowser for a Web-enabled handheld computer)

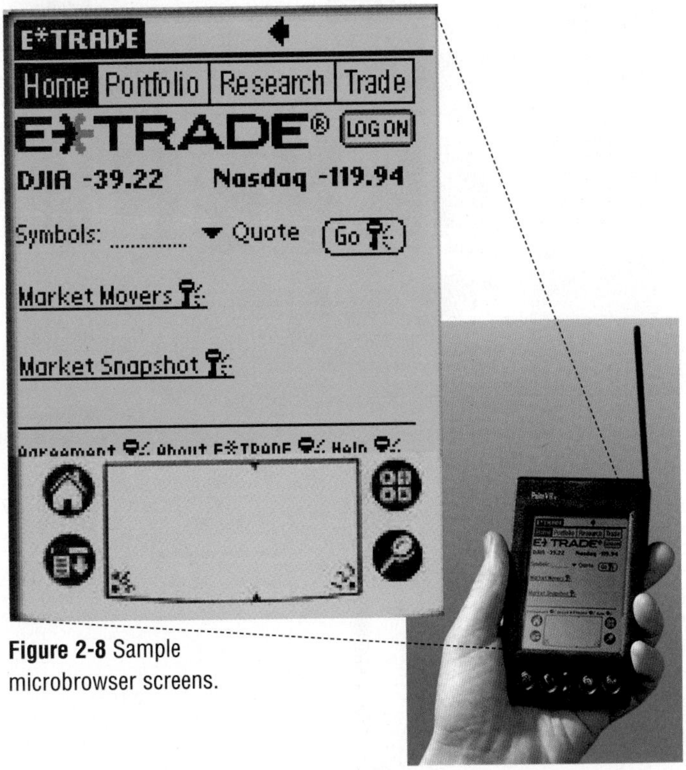

Figure 2-8b (microbrowser for a Web-enabled cellular telephone)

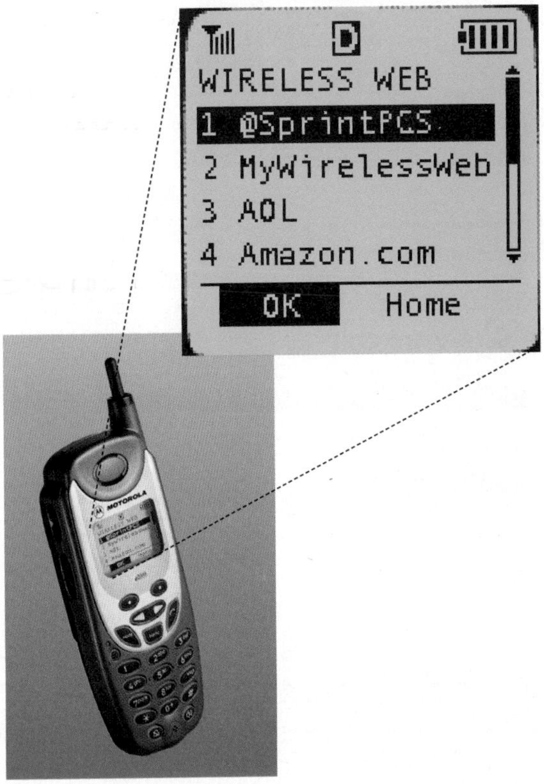

Figure 2-8 Sample microbrowser screens.

On the Web, a link can be a word, phrase, or image. You often can identify a link by its appearance. Text links usually are underlined or in a color different from the rest of the document. When you point to a graphical link, it may change its look in some way. As shown in Figure 2-9, the shape of the pointer on the screen changes to a small hand with a pointing index finger when you position it on a link, or point to the link.

To activate a link, you point to it and then press the mouse button, or click the link. This causes the item associated with the link to display on the screen. The link can point to an item on the same Web page, a different Web page at the same Web site, or a separate Web page at a different Web site in another city or country. In most cases, when you navigate using links, you are jumping from Web page to Web page. Some people refer to this activity of jumping from one Web page to another as **surfing the Web**. To remind you visually that you have visited a location or document, some browsers change the color of a text link after you click it.

Using a URL

A Web page has a unique address, called a **Uniform Resource Locator (URL)**. A browser retrieves

Figure 2-9 NAVIGATING USING A VARIETY OF LINKS

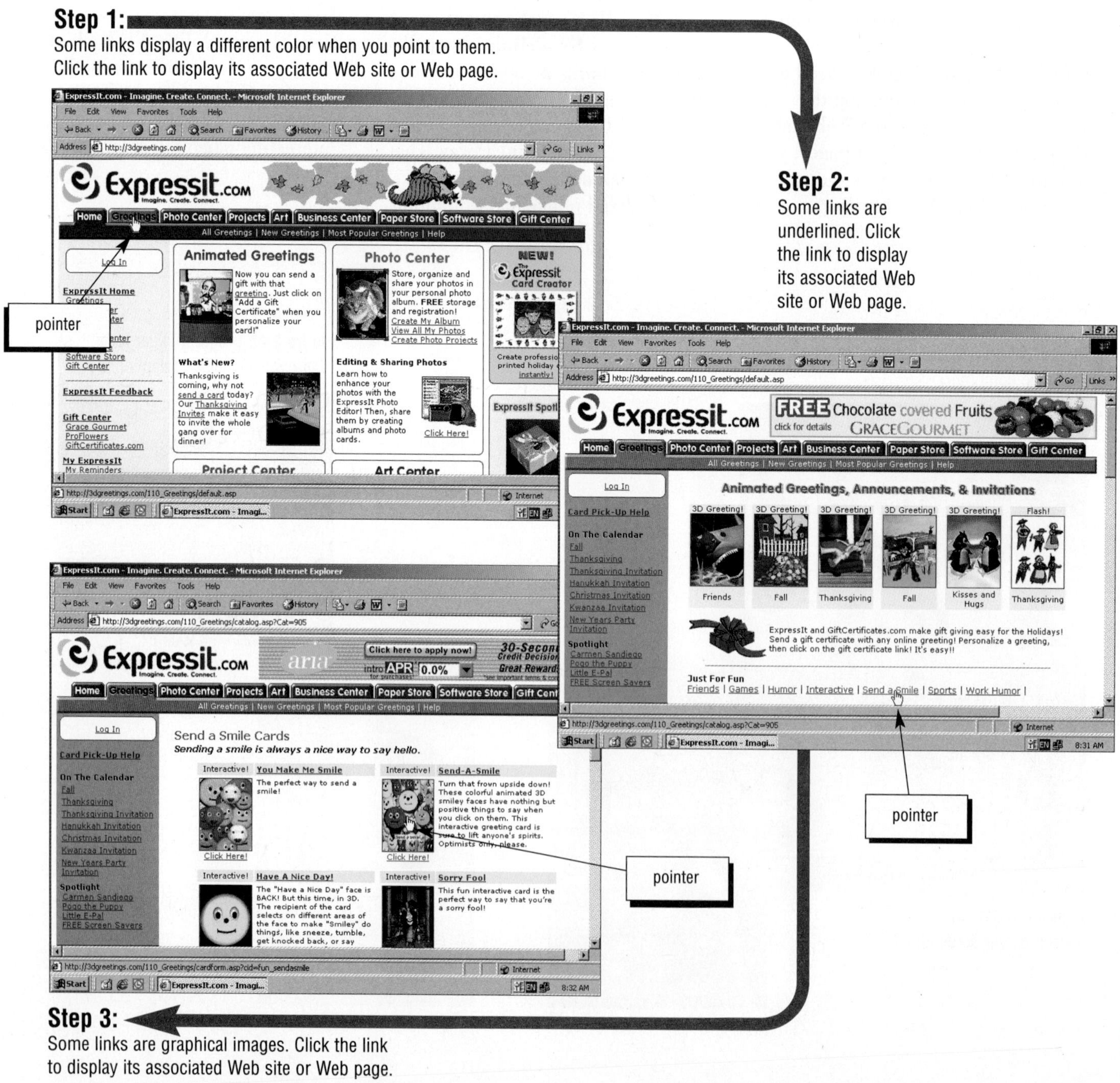
Step 1:
Some links display a different color when you point to them. Click the link to display its associated Web site or Web page.
pointer
Step 2:
Some links are underlined. Click the link to display its associated Web site or Web page.
pointer
pointer
Step 3:
Some links are graphical images. Click the link to display its associated Web site or Web page.

a Web page by using its URL, also called a **Web address**. The URL tells the browser where to locate the document. URLs make it possible for you to navigate using links because a link is associated with a URL. When you click a link, you are issuing a request to display the Web site or the document associated with the URL.

Many companies and organizations assume the public is familiar with URLs. Web addresses appear on television, in radio broadcasts, in printed newspapers, magazines, and other forms of advertising.

If you know the URL of a Web page, you can type it into a text box at the top of the browser window. For example, if you type the URL of http://www.nationalgeographic.com/travel/index.html in the Address text box and then press the ENTER key, the browser downloads and displays the Travel page of the National Geographic Web site (Figure 2-10).

As shown in Figure 2-10, a URL consists of a protocol, domain name, and sometimes the path to a specific Web page or location on a Web page. Most Web page URLs begin with http://. The **http** stands for **hypertext transfer protocol**, which is the communications standard that enables pages to transfer on the Web.

If you do not enter a URL exactly, your browser will not locate the site or Web page you want to visit (view). To help minimize errors, most current browsers and Web sites allow you to omit the http:// and www portions of the URL. For example, you can type nationalgeographic.com/travel/index.html instead of http://www.nationalgeographic.com/travel/index.html. If you enter an incorrect URL, some browsers search for similar addresses and provide a list from which you can select.

A **Web server** is a computer that delivers (serves) Web pages you request. For example, when you enter the URL, nationalgeographic.com/travel/index.html in the browser, it sends a request to the server that stores the Web site of www.nationalgeographic.com. The server then retrieves the Web page named index.html in the travel path and sends it to your browser.

The same Web server can store multiple Web sites. For example, many Internet service providers grant their subscribers free storage space on a Web server for personal or company Web sites.

Figure 2-10 The URL for the Travel page of the National Geographic Web site is www.nationalgeographic.com/travel/index.html. When you enter this URL in the Address text box, the Web page shown displays.

Web Link

For more information on URLs, visit the Discovering Computers 2002 Chapter 2 WEB LINK page (**scsite.com/dc2002/ch2/weblink.htm**) and click URLs.

ISSUE

Beware of Stealth URLs

Navigating the Web

A father sat down at a computer with his young child, typed what he thought was the URL for a site of national interest, and was surprised to encounter pornographic material. "I should have paid closer attention to the (URL) suffix," he admitted. Stealth URLs — addresses similar to those of other Web pages — attract visitors and potential subscribers. Some Web pages adopt the URLs of popular Web sites, with minor changes in spelling or domain name. Critics claim this misleads consumers and weakens the value of the original name. Defendants counter that restrictions on URLs would violate rights to free speech. Similar to stealth URLs, some *adult* Web sites include words such as Nintendo 64, Sega, Barbie, and others within the Web site descriptions, often called meta tags. Many search engines examine the meta tags content and return these Web sites as a suggested link. Do you think URLs should be regulated? Why or why not? How else can people deal with the problem of stealth URLs? Should Web site developers be permitted to include phrases within the meta tags that do not relate to the Web site? How could this be regulated?

For more information on stealth URLs and meta tags, visit the Discovering Computers 2002 Issues Web page (**scsite.com/dc2002/issues.htm**) and click Chapter 2 Issue #2.

Searching for Information on the Web

No single organization controls additions, deletions, and changes to Web sites. This means no central menu or catalog of Web site content and addresses exists. Several companies, however, maintain organized directories of Web sites to help you find information on specific topics.

A **search engine** is a software program you can use to find Web sites, Web pages, and Internet files. Search engines are particularly helpful in locating Web pages on certain topics or in locating specific pages for which you do not know the exact URL. To find a page or pages, you enter a word or phrase, called **search text** or **keywords**, in the search engine's text box. Many search engines use a program called a spider to display a list of all Web pages that contain the word or phrase you entered. A **spider**, also called a **crawler** or **bot**, is a program that reads pages on Web sites in order to create a catalog, or index, of hits.

A **hit** is any Web page name that lists as the result of a search. For example, if you want a listing of ski resorts in Colorado, you could enter Colorado ski resort as your search text. The search engine would return a list of hits, or Web page names, that contain the phrase Colorado ski resort (Figure 2-11). You then click an appropriate link in the list to display the associated Web site or Web page.

When you enter search text that contains multiple keywords, the search engine usually locates sites that

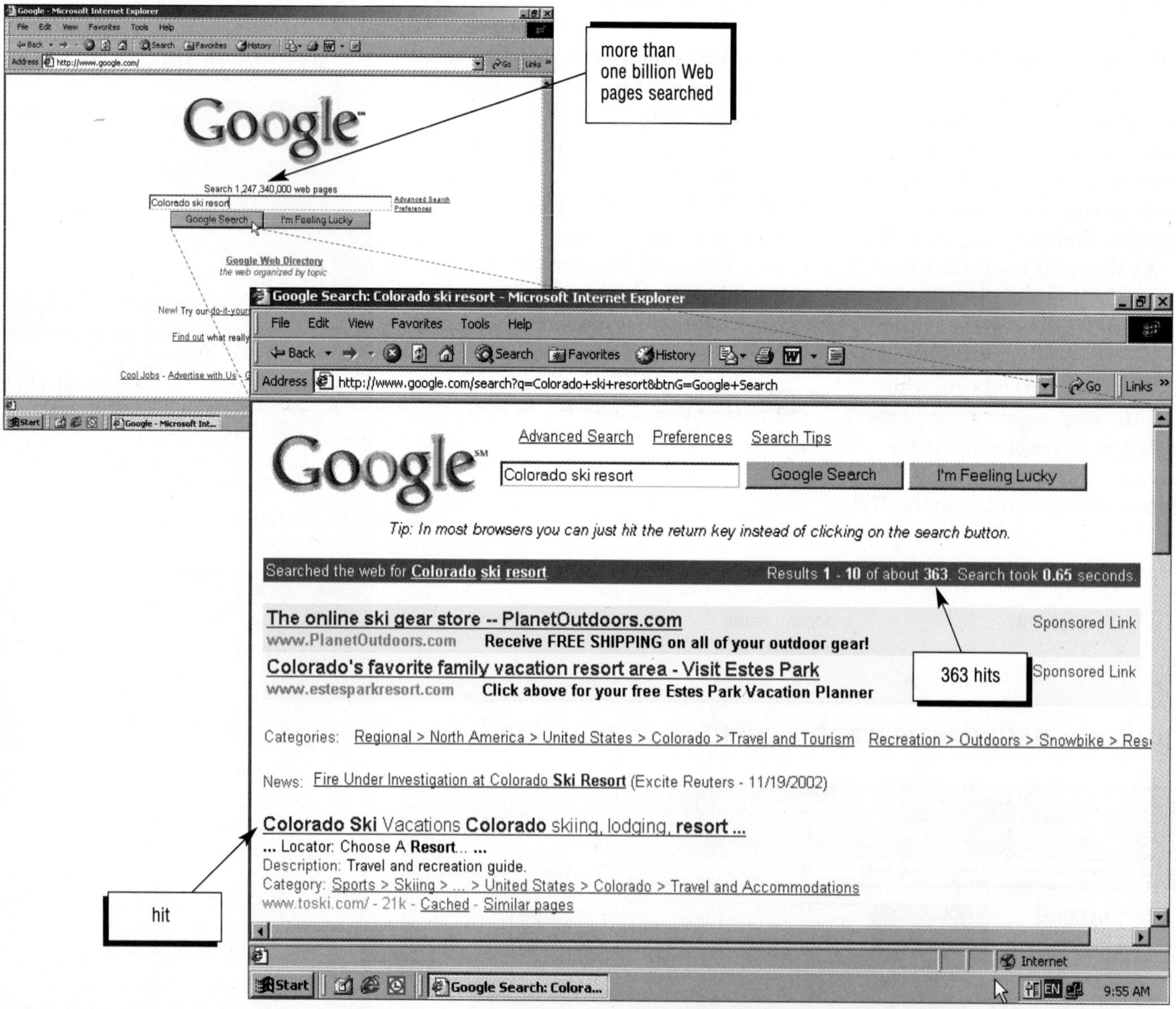

Figure 2-11 When you enter search text into a search engine, such as Google, a list of hits will display.

contain all of the words. For example, a search with the keywords, ski resort, results in 368,000 hits, or Web pages, that contain the word ski and the word resort. To reduce the number of hits, you should be more specific in the search. For example, the search text, Colorado ski resort, reduces the number of hits to 363.

The table in Figure 2-12 lists the Web site addresses of several Internet search engines. Most of these sites also provide directories of Web sites. On the Web, a **directory** is an organized set of topics, such as arts, reference, sports, and subtopics. Figure 2-13 shows Yahoo!'s directory Web page. If you wanted information on major league baseball parks, you could use a directory to display the topic sports, then the subtopic baseball, and then the subtopic major league.

Widely Used Search Engines	
AltaVista	altavista.com
Excite	excite.com
Google	google.com
GoTo.com	goto.com
HotBot	hotbot.com
Lycos	lycos.com
WebCrawler	webcrawler.com
Yahoo!	yahoo.com

Figure 2-12 Widely used search engines.

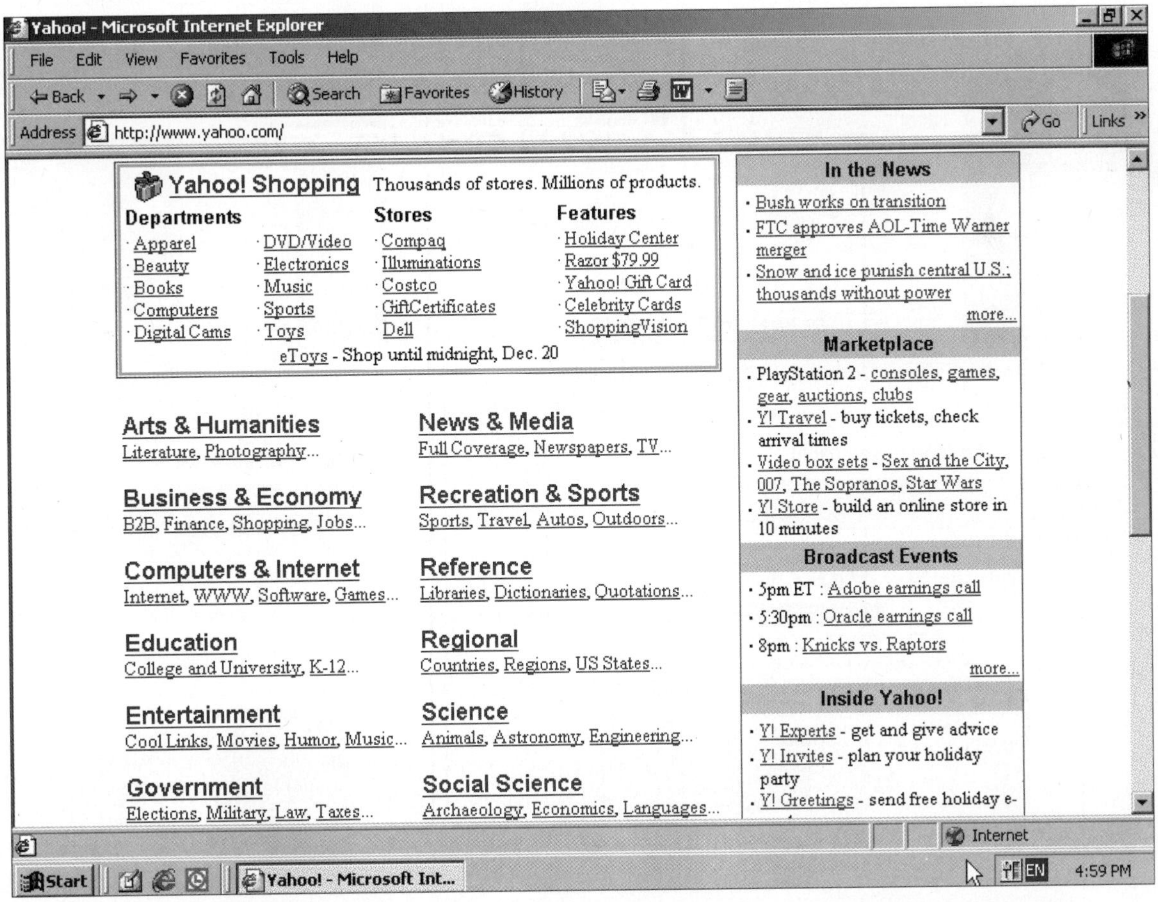

Figure 2-13 An example of a directory Web page.

Types of Web Pages

Six basic types of Web pages exist: advocacy, business/marketing, informational, news, portal, and personal (Figure 2-14). Many Web pages fall into more than one of these categories. The following paragraphs discuss each of these types of Web pages.

ADVOCACY WEB PAGE An **advocacy Web page** contains content that describes a cause, opinion, or idea. The purpose of an advocacy Web page is to convince the reader of the validity

Figure 2-14a (advocacy Web page)

Figure 2-14b (business/marketing Web page)

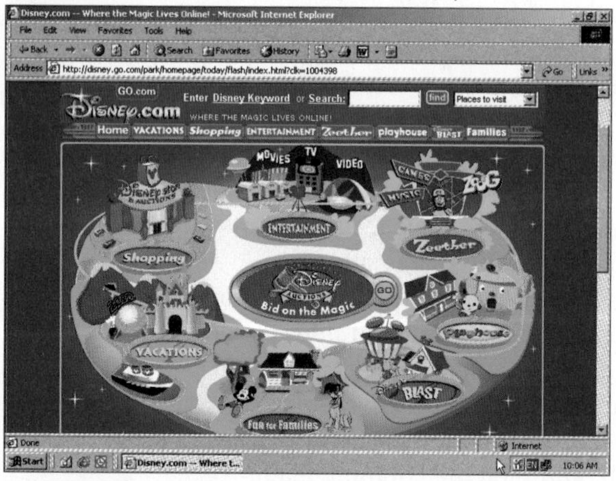

Figure 2-14c (informational Web page)

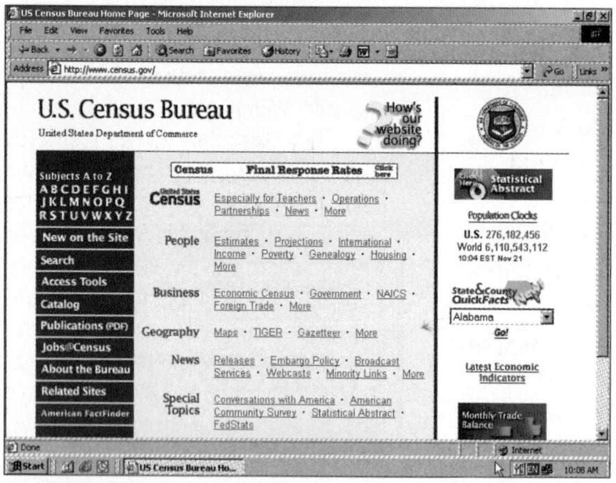

Figure 2-14d (news Web page)

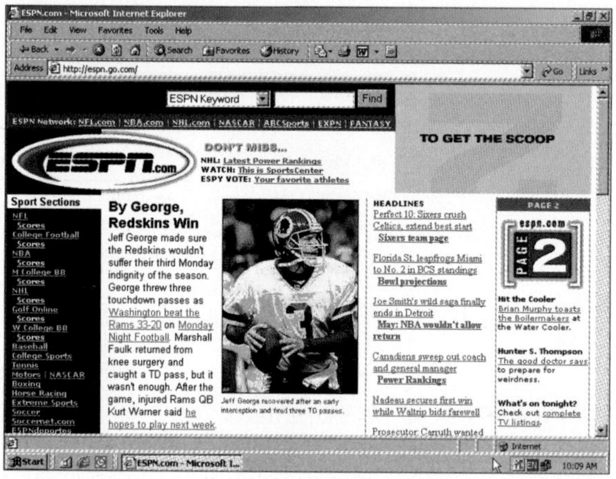

Figure 2-14e (portal Web page)

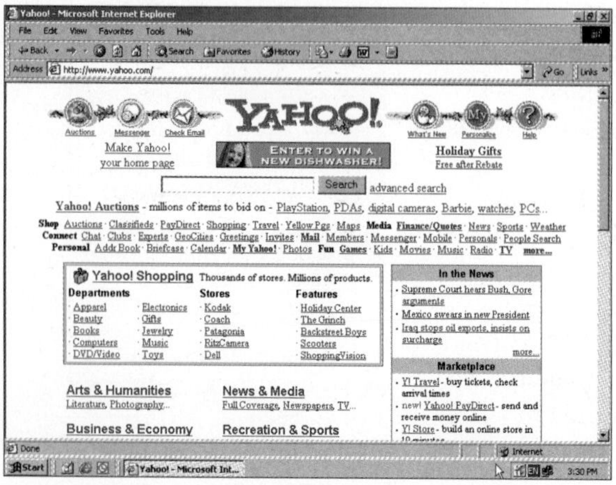

Figure 2-14f (personal Web page)

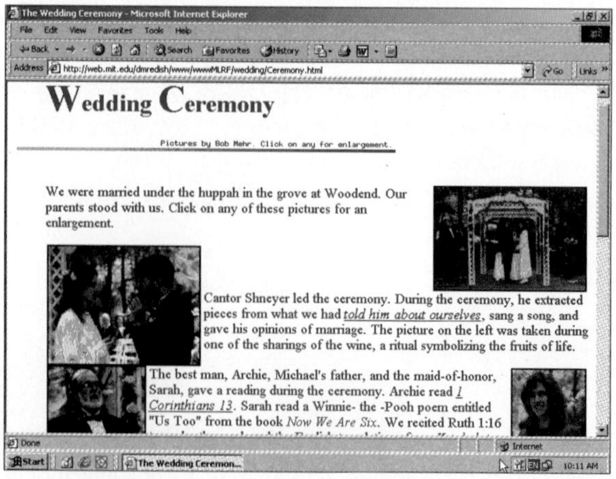

Figure 2-14 Types of Web pages.

of the cause, opinion, or idea. These Web pages usually present views of a particular group or association. Sponsors of advocacy Web pages include the Democratic Party, the Republican Party, the Society for the Prevention of Cruelty to Animals, and the Society to Protect Human Rights.

BUSINESS/MARKETING WEB PAGE A **business/marketing Web page** contains content that promotes or sells products or services. Nearly every business today has a business/marketing Web page. AT&T, Dell Computer Corporation, General Motors Corporation, Kraft Foods Inc., and Walt Disney Company all have business/marketing Web pages. Many of these companies also allow you to purchase their products or services online.

INFORMATIONAL WEB PAGE An **informational Web page** contains factual information. Many United States government agencies have informational Web pages providing information such as census data, tax codes, and the congressional budget. Other organizations provide information such as public transportation schedules and published research findings.

NEWS WEB PAGE A **news Web page** contains newsworthy material including stories and articles relating to current events, life, money, sports, and the weather. Many magazines and newspapers sponsor Web sites that provide summaries of printed articles, as well as articles not included in the printed versions. Newspapers and television and radio stations are some of the media that maintain news Web pages.

PORTAL WEB PAGE A **portal Web page**, often called a **portal**, offers a variety of Internet services from a single, convenient location. Most portals offer the following free services: search engine; local, national, and worldwide news; sports and weather; free personal Web pages; reference tools such as yellow pages, stock quotes, and maps; shopping malls and auctions; e-mail; instant messaging, newsgroups or message boards, calendars, and chat rooms.

Some portals also have Web communities. A **Web community** is a Web site that joins a specific group of people with similar interests or relationships. These communities usually offer a newsgroup or message board, chat room, e-mail, and online photo albums to facilitate communications among members.

Popular portals include AltaVista, America Online, Dogpile, Euroseek, Excite, GO.com, Google, HotBot, looksmart, Lycos, Microsoft Network, Netscape Netcenter, and Yahoo!. You may notice that many portals also are Internet service providers or online service providers, and offer search engines and directories. The goal of these portals is to be designated as your browser's home page, the first page that displays when you connect to the Internet.

A **wireless portal** is a portal specifically designed for Web-enabled handheld computers and devices. Wireless portals attempt to provide all information a wireless user might require. These portals offer services such as search engines, news, stock quotes, weather, maps, e-mail, calendar, instant messaging, and shopping.

PERSONAL WEB PAGE A private individual who normally is not associated with any organization often maintains a **personal Web page**. People publish personal Web pages for a variety of reasons. Some are job hunting. Others simply want to share life experiences with the world.

COMPANY ON THE CUTTING EDGE

YAHOO!®

Indexing the World Wide Web

The Yahoos were a primitive society in Jonathan Swift's *Gulliver's Travels*. Like those Yahoos, the contemporary Yahoo!'s co-founders, Jerry Yang and David Filo, were involved in the early phases of a society — the Internet society. These Stanford University students started creating lists in 1994 as an attempt to organize their favorite Web sites. One list branched into another, and before they knew it, they had created a tree-style database and a method of searching for specific Web pages.

They claim they named their creation Yahoo! because they considered themselves two tough guys, or yahoos. Yang maintained the lists on his Stanford student workstation, and Filo kept the search engine on his computer. They shared their creation with thousands of other information seekers and continued to add new categories and sites. In 1995, they moved their operation to large computers at Netscape Communications Corporation.

Today, the lists still are maintained by Yahoo!'s employees. More than 166 million visitors access 180 million pages daily, including the network's e-mail, chat rooms, shopping site, and personal Web pages. These services, which are supported by 3,000 advertisers, are free to users.

For more information on Yahoo!, visit the Discovering Computers 2002 Companies Web page (**scsite.com/dc2002/companies.htm**) and click Yahoo!.

Multimedia on the Web

Most Web pages include more than formatted text and links. In fact, some of the more exciting Web pages use multimedia. **Multimedia** refers to any application that integrates text with one or more of the following elements: graphics, sound, video, virtual reality, or other media elements. A Web page that uses multimedia has much more appeal than one with text on a gray background. It brings a Web page to life, increases the types of information available on the Web, expands the Web's potential uses, and makes the Internet a more entertaining place to explore. Multimedia Web pages often require more time to download because they contain large graphics and video or audio clips. These multimedia pages, however, usually are worth the wait.

The following sections discuss how the Web uses graphics, animation, audio, video, and virtual reality.

GRAPHICS A **graphic**, or **graphical image**, is a digital representation of information such as a drawing, chart, or photograph. Graphics were the first media used to enhance the text-based Internet. The introduction of graphical Web browsers allowed Web page developers to incorporate illustrations, logos, and other images into Web pages. Today, many Web pages use colorful graphical designs and images to convey messages (Figure 2-15).

The Web contains thousands of image files on countless subjects. You can download many of these images at no cost and use them for noncommercial purposes. Recall that downloading is the process of transferring an object from the Web to your computer. For example, you can incorporate them into your own Web pages.

To use graphics files on the Web, they must be saved in a certain format (Figure 2-16). A saved image, known as a file, is stored on a medium such as a floppy disk or hard disk. The next chapter discusses files and saving in more depth.

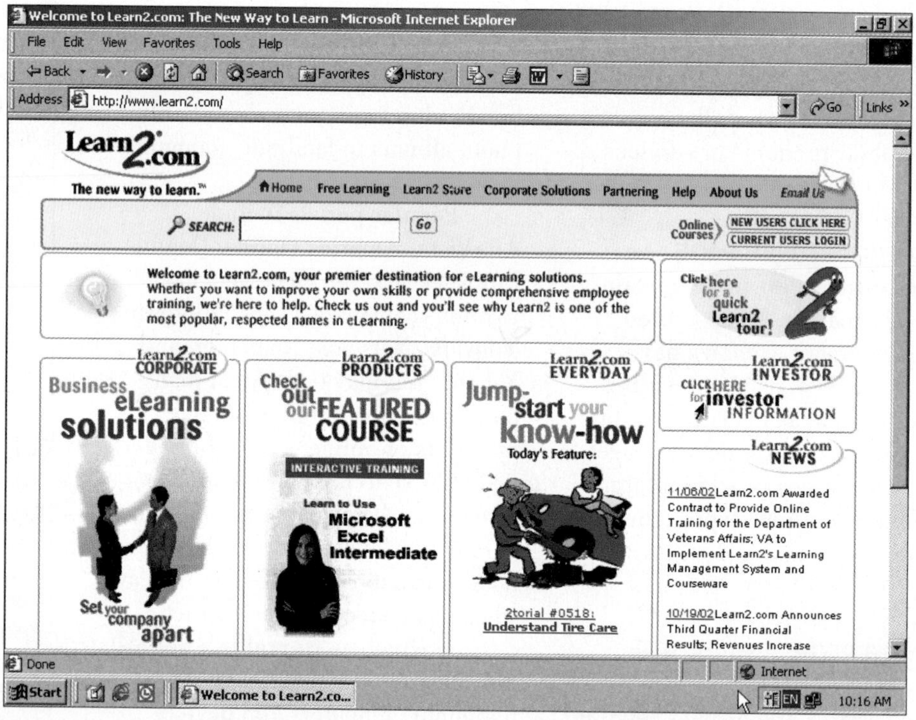

Figure 2-15 Many Web pages use colorful graphical designs and images to convey their messages.

GRAPHICS FORMATS USED ON THE INTERNET

Acronym	Name	File Extension
BMP	Bit Map	.bmp
GIF (pronounced JIFF)	Graphics Interchange Format	.gif
JPEG (pronounced JAY-peg)	Joint Photographic Experts Group	.jpg
PCX	PC Paintbrush	.pcx
PNG (pronounced ping)	Portable Network Graphics	.png
TIFF	Tagged Image File Format	.tif

Figure 2-16 Graphics formats used on the Internet. Some users look on their computer at a file's extension to determine the type of file.

Two of the more common file formats in Figure 2-16 for graphical images on the Web are JPEG and GIF. A **JPEG** (pronounced JAY-peg) file, which stands for **Joint Photographic Experts Group**, is a graphical image that uses compression techniques to reduce the file size. These smaller sizes result in faster downloading of Web pages. The more compressed the file, the smaller the file, but the lower the quality. The goal with JPEG files is to reach a balance between image quality and file size.

A graphical image saved as a **GIF** (pronounced jiff or giff) file, which stands for **Graphics Interchange Format**, also uses compression techniques to reduce file sizes. The GIF format works best for images with only a few distinct colors, such as line drawings, single-color borders, and simple cartoons.

The BMP, PCX, and TIFF formats listed in Figure 2-16 have larger file sizes and thus are not used on the Web as frequently as JPEG and GIF.

Some Web sites use thumbnails on their pages because graphics files can be time consuming to display. A **thumbnail** is a small version of a larger graphical image you usually can click to display the full-sized image (Figure 2-17).

ANIMATION Many Web pages use animated graphics, or animation. **Animation** is the appearance of motion created by displaying a series of still images in rapid sequence. Animated graphics can make Web pages more visually interesting or draw attention to important information or links. For example, text that animates by scrolling across the screen, called a **marquee** (pronounced mar-KEE), can serve as a ticker to display stock updates, news, sports scores, weather, or other information. Web-based games often use animation. Some animations even contain links to a different page.

One popular type of animation, called an **animated GIF**, uses computer animation and graphics software to combine several images into a single GIF file.

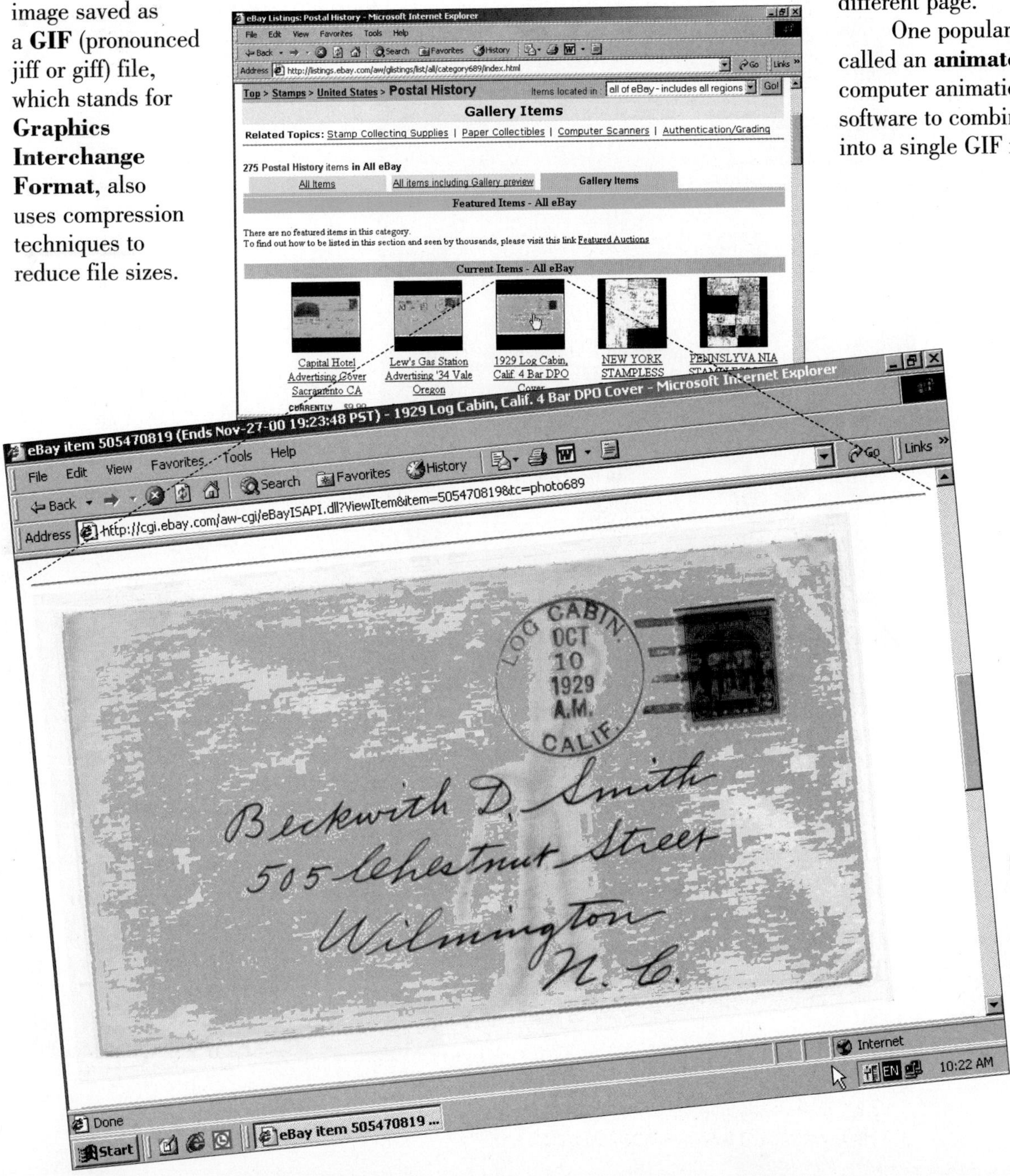

Figure 2-17 If you click the thumbnail of the envelope with the stamp in the screen above, a full-sized image of the envelope displays in a separate window.

AUDIO On the Web, you can listen to audio clips and live audio. **Audio** is music, speech, or any other sound.

Simple audio applications on the Web consist of individual sound files that you download to your computer. Once downloaded, you can play (listen) to the contents of these files. As with graphics files, audio files must be saved in a certain format. A common format for audio files on the Web is MP3.

MP3 is a popular technology that compresses audio. MP3 reduces an audio file to about one-tenth of its original size — while preserving the original quality of the sound. You easily can copy these smaller files from the Web to your computer — even with a slow Internet connection. This capability of transferring music across the Internet has stirred much controversy with respect to copyright infringement of music because it provides users with an easy method of copying MP3 music files from one computer to another.

Most current operating systems contain a program, called a **player**, that can play the audio in MP3 files on your computer. You also can buy portable audio devices, called **MP3 players**, that can play MP3 files stored on CD or miniature storage media (Figure 2-18).

More advanced audio applications on the Web use streaming audio. **Streaming** is the process of transferring data in a continuous and even flow. Streaming allows users to access and use a file while it is transmitting. Streaming is important because most users do not have fast enough Internet connections to download a large multimedia file quickly.

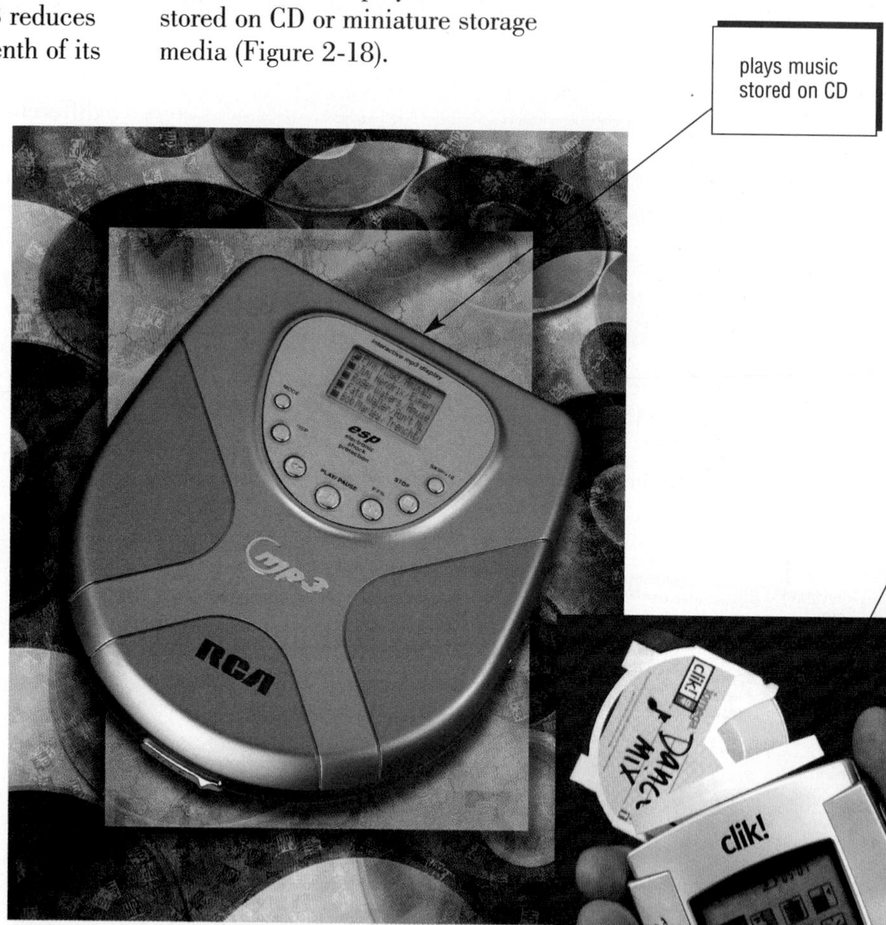

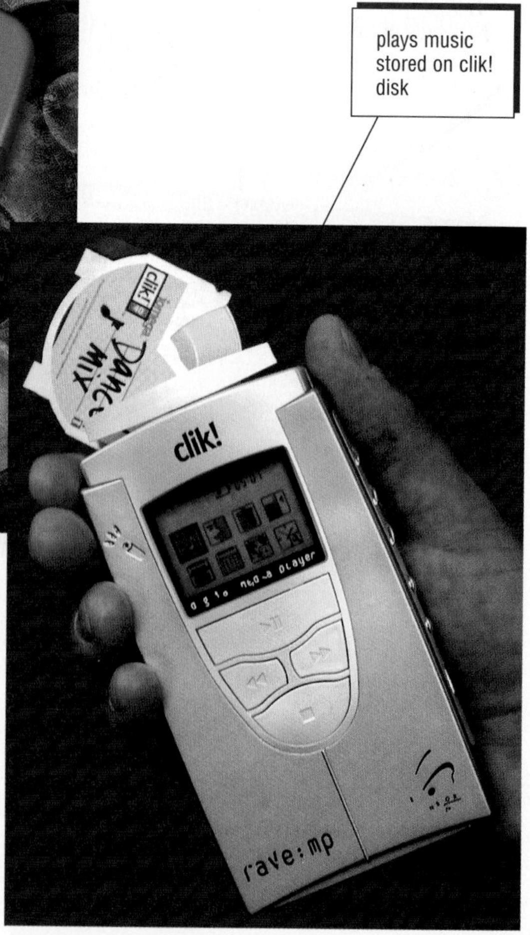

Figure 2-18 You can buy an MP3 player, which is a portable audio device that can play MP3 files stored on a CD or miniature storage media.

Web Link

For more information on MP3, visit the Discovering Computers 2002 Chapter 2 WEB LINK page (**scsite.com/dc2002/ch2/weblink.htm**) and click MP3.

Streaming audio, also called **streaming sound**, enables you to listen to the sound (the data) as it downloads to your computer. Many radio and television stations use streaming audio to broadcast music, interviews, talk shows, sporting events, music videos, news, live concerts, and other segments (Figure 2-19). Two accepted standards supported by most Web browsers for transmitting streaming audio data on the Internet are Windows Media Player and RealAudio. RealAudio is a component of RealPlayer, which is a streaming media program. You also can use MP3 for streaming audio.

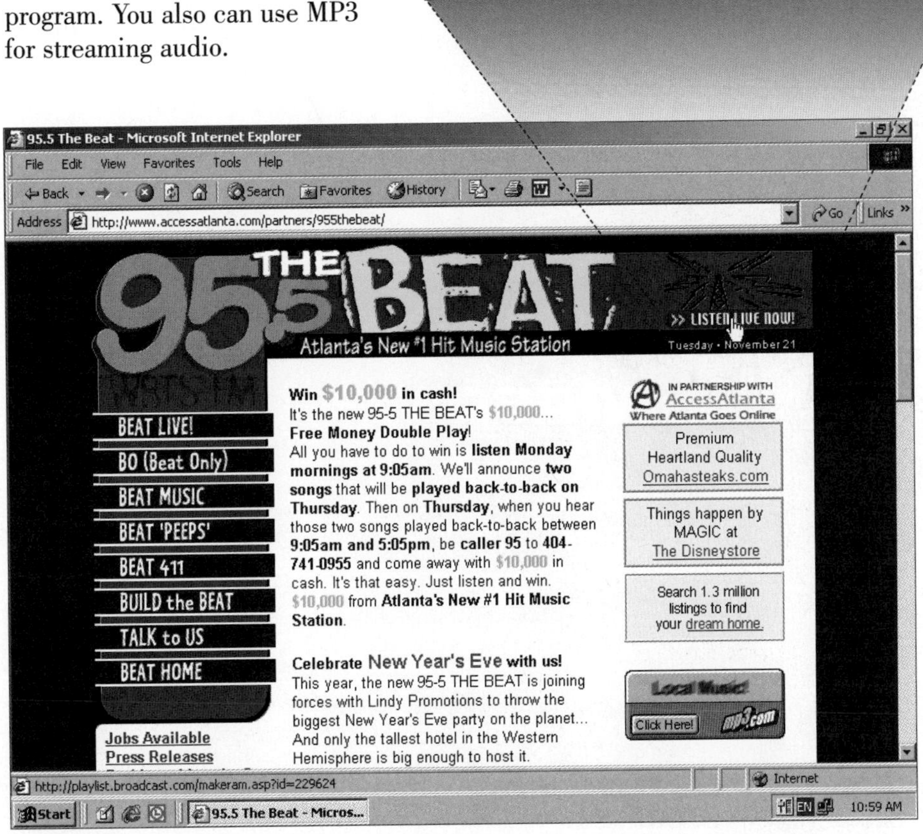

Figure 2-19 Many radio and television stations use streaming audio. Radio station 95.5 The Beat broadcasts using RealAudio, which is a component of RealPlayer.

APPLY IT!

Now Playing – Online Radio

Regardless of your taste in music — jazz, country, rock, classical, hip hop — you can find it on the Internet. Thousands of radio stations now are broadcasting in real-time on the World Wide Web. You can listen to almost any station in the world for free as long as you have the right software and an Internet connection. The three most popular software programs are RealNetwork's RealPlayer software (see URL below), Apple Computer's QuickTime (see URL below), and Microsoft's Windows Media Player (see URL below).

You can download each of these programs at no cost from the Internet. After downloading and installing the software, you are ready to tune in and listen to a radio station of choice. You can find online radio stations on the Web in a variety of places. Some sites, such as Yahoo! Broadcast.com (see URL below) and Starting Page (see URL below) function as clearinghouses, archiving many radio programs in one area for you to sample. Or, in a search engine, type `radio stations` and then click the Find or Search button to display hundreds of links. Select your favorite station, click the link to activate your software, and then listen to the music.

For more information on online radio and the Web sites mentioned above, visit the Discovering Computers 2002 Apply It Web page (**scsite.com/dc2002/apply.htm**) and click Chapter 2 Apply It #2.

VIDEO **Video** consists of full-motion images that are played back at various speeds. Most video also has accompanying audio. As with audio, many Web sites include video to enhance your understanding or for entertainment purposes. Watch a news report as it is being reported (Figure 2-20) or enjoy a live performance of your favorite vocalist.

Like audio, simple video applications on the Web consist of individual video files, such as movie or television clips, that you must download completely before you can play them on the computer. Video files often are compressed because they are quite large in size. These clips also are quite short in length because they can take a long time to download. The **Moving Pictures Experts Group (MPEG)** defines a popular video compression standard.

As with streaming audio, **streaming video** allows you to view longer or live video images as they download to your computer. Two widely used standards supported by most Web browsers for transmitting streaming video data on the Internet are RealVideo and Windows Media Player. Like RealAudio, RealVideo is a component of RealPlayer.

Another use of video on the Web is for a Web cam. A **Web cam**, also called a **cam**, is a video camera whose output displays on a Web page. A Web cam attracts Web site visitors by showing images that change regularly. Chapter 6 discusses Web cams in more depth.

Web Link

For more information on streaming media, visit the Discovering Computers 2002 Chapter 2 WEB LINK page (**scsite.com/dc2002/ch2/weblink.htm**) and click Streaming Media.

VIRTUAL REALITY **Virtual reality (VR)** is the use of computers to simulate a real or imagined environment that appears as a three-dimensional (3-D) space. On the Web, VR involves the display of 3-D images that you can explore and manipulate interactively.

Using special VR software, a Web developer creates an entire 3-D site that contains infinite space and depth, called a **VR world**. A VR world, for example, might show a room with furniture. You can walk through such a VR room by moving an input device forward, backward, or to the side.

VR often is used for games, but it has many practical applications as well. Science educators can create VR models of molecules, organisms, and other structures for students to examine (Figure 2-21). Companies can use VR to showcase products or create advertisements. Architects can create VR models of buildings and rooms so clients can see how a completed construction project will look before it is built.

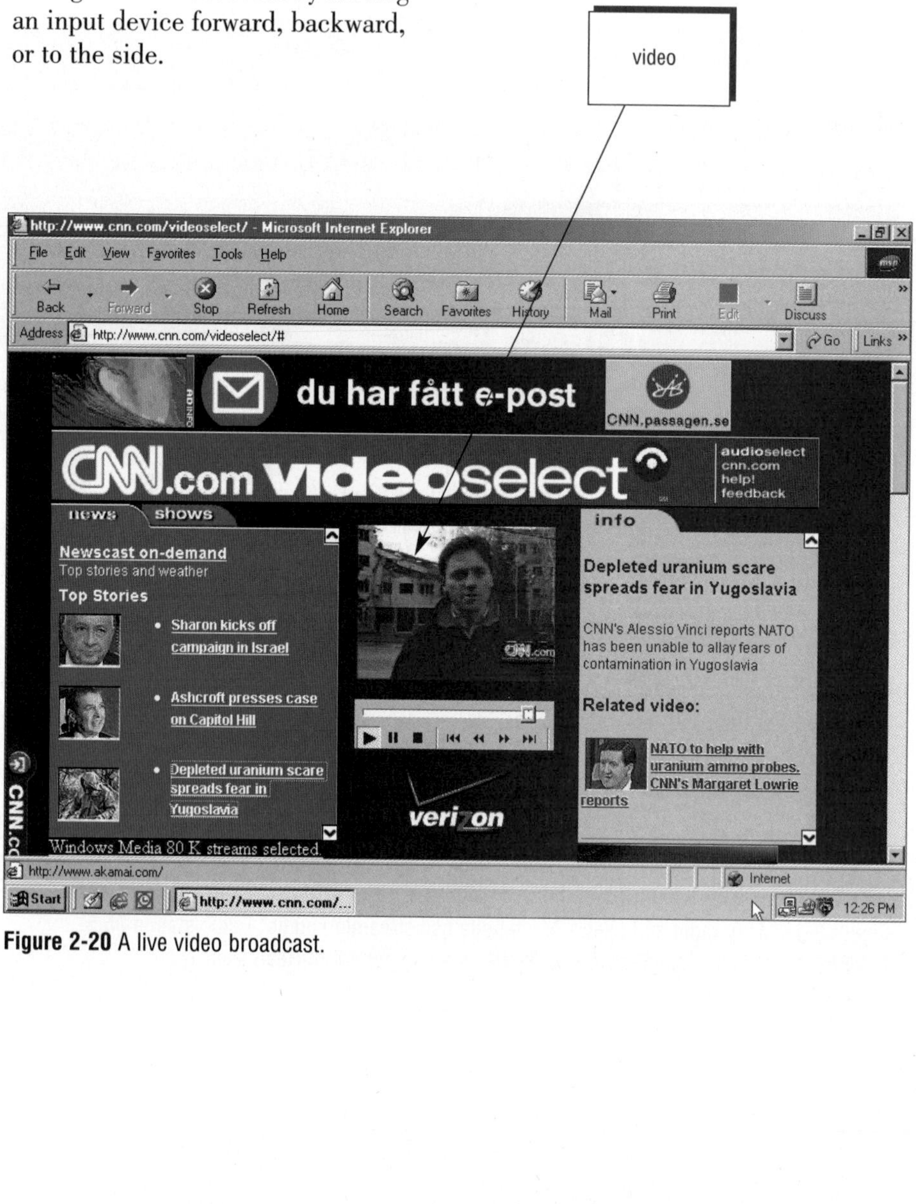

Figure 2-20 A live video broadcast.

Webcasting

When you want information from a Web site, you often request it from the site. This method of obtaining information, known as **pull technology**, relies on a client such as your computer to request a Web page from a server. For example, you enter a URL in your browser or click a link to display a particular Web page.

Today's browsers also support push technology. Using **push technology**, also called **Webcasting**, a server automatically downloads content to your computer at regular intervals or whenever updates are made to the site. A Web server can push an entire Web site or just a portion of one, such as the latest news, to your computer. For example, a Webcast can display stock prices and financial headlines on your desktop in the form of a continuously running ticker tape (Figure 2-22). Webcasting saves time by delivering information at regular intervals, without you having to request it.

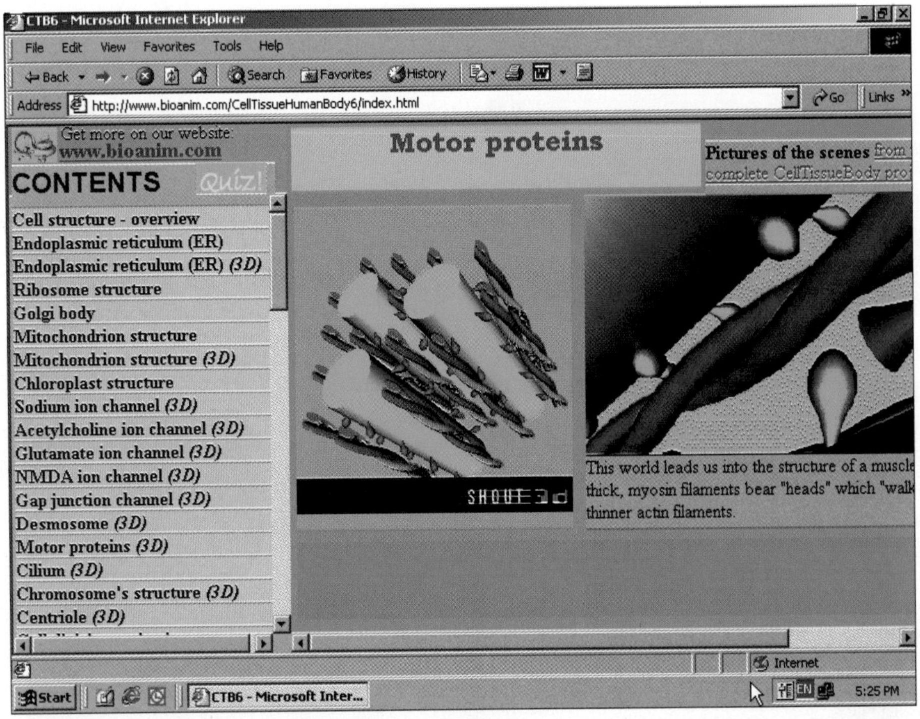

Figure 2-21 This instructional site uses VR to teach biology students about cells and body tissue.

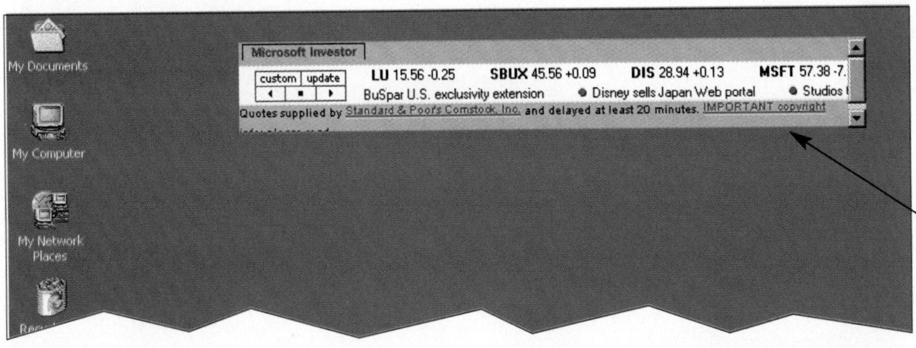

Figure 2-22 On this screen, stock prices and financial headlines are pushed onto the desktop.

ISSUE

Downloading Copyrighted Material

Text, Graphics, Audio, and Video on the Web

You may be familiar with the term intellectual property (IP), the ownership of ideas and knowledge. This term has become more commonplace during the past few years, especially in the context of computer ethics and copyright. The Library of Congress (see URL below) defines copyright as follows: "Copyright is a form of protection provided by the laws of the United States (title 17, U.S. Code) to the authors of 'original works of authorship,' including literary, dramatic, musical, artistic, and certain other intellectual works." The Internet contains an abundance of IP or copyrighted material: text, pictures, music, video, and so on. With a mouse click or two, anyone can download these copyrighted media. If it were available on a Web site, would you download copyrighted music? a copyrighted book? a copyrighted video? Would you put copyrighted material on the Web? What steps would you take to prevent someone from copying your intellectual property?

For more information on the Internet, copyrighted issues, and the Web site mentioned above, visit the Discovering Computers 2002 Issues Web page (**scsite.com/dc2002/issues.htm**) and click Chapter 2 Issue #3.

Another advantage of Webcasting is that once the Web server pushes Web content to your computer, you can view it whether you are online or offline. (**Offline** means you are not connected to the Internet.) With Webcasting, the Web server downloads the contents of one or more Web sites to your hard disk while you are online. This downloaded information also is available for browsing while you are offline. Offline browsing is ideal for mobile users because they do not always have access to the Internet.

ELECTRONIC COMMERCE

Electronic commerce, also known as **e-commerce**, is a financial business transaction that occurs over an electronic network such as the Internet. Anyone with access to a computer, an Internet connection, and a means to pay for purchased goods or services can participate in e-commerce (Figure 2-23).

In the past, e-commerce transactions were conducted primarily through desktop computers. Today, many laptop computers, handheld computers, pagers, and cellular telephones also can access the Web wirelessly. Some people use the term **m-commerce** (**mobile commerce**) to identify e-commerce that takes place using mobile devices.

E-commerce has changed the way people conduct business. It virtually eliminates the barriers of time and distance that slow traditional transactions. Now, with e-commerce, transactions can occur instantaneously and globally. This saves time for participants on both ends.

Two of the most popular uses of e-commerce by consumers are investing and shopping. Through online investing, you buy and sell stocks or

Figure 2-23 E-commerce activities include shopping for goods from a retailer.

Web Link

For more information on e-commerce, visit the Discovering Computers 2002 Chapter 2 WEB LINK page (**scsite.com/dc2002/ch2/weblink.htm**) and click E-Commerce.

bonds without using a broker. Thus, the transaction fees for online trading usually are reduced greatly.

You can purchase just about any good or service on the Web. Examples include flowers, books, groceries, computers, prescription drugs, music, movies, cars, airline tickets, and concert tickets.

Today, three types of e-commerce exist: business to consumer, consumer to consumer, and business to business. **Business-to-consumer** (**B-to-C** or **B2C**) e-commerce consists of the sale of goods to the general public. For example, instead of visiting a computer retailer to purchase a computer, you can order one that meets your specifications directly from the manufacturer's Web site.

A customer (consumer) visits an online business through an electronic storefront. An **electronic storefront** contains descriptions, graphics, and a shopping cart. The **shopping cart** allows the customer to collect purchases. When ready to complete the sale, the customer enters personal and financial data through a secure Web connection.

Instead of purchasing from a business, consumers can purchase from each other. For example, with an **online auction**, you bid on an item being sold by someone else. The highest bidder at the end of the bidding period purchases the item. **Consumer-to-consumer** (**C-to-C** or **C2C**) e-commerce occurs when one consumer sells directly to another, such as in an online auction.

Most e-commerce, though, actually takes place between businesses, which is called **business-to-business** (**B-to-B** or **B2B**) **e-commerce**. Businesses often provide goods and services to other businesses, such as online advertising, recruiting, credit, sales, market research, technical support, and training.

ISSUE

To Tax or Not to Tax?

Electronic Commerce

The Supreme Court has ruled buyers must pay state and local sales taxes only when merchants have a physical presence, such as a store or office building, in the buyer's state. Internet purchases usually are sales tax free because most Internet merchants do not have a physical presence in a buyer's state. Some believe this tax-free status has a negative impact on local businesses (that must charge sales tax), state and local tax coffers (one estimate claims $60 billion in revenues is lost annually), and lower-income families (who are less likely to buy online). Yet, others feel any tax on e-commerce would be unmanageable (forcing vendors to adjust to varying sales tax rates) and unjustified. Should a sales tax be applied to Internet purchases? Why or why not? How can the problems of taxing, or not taxing, Internet purchases be addressed?

For more information on e-commerce and taxing issues, visit the Discovering Computers 2002 Issues Web page (**scsite.com/dc2002/issues.htm**) and click Chapter 2 Issue #4.

TECHNOLOGY TRAILBLAZER

MASAYOSHI **SON**

Often called "the Bill Gates of Japan," Masayoshi Son has helped bring that country to the forefront of the digital age.

When he was 16 years old, the second-generation Korean-Japanese moved from Japan to California to learn English. He then majored in economics at the University of California, Berkeley. While in school, he earned his first $1 million by importing arcade games from Japan for the campus, developing computer games, and selling a patent for a multilingual pocket translator to Sharp Corporation.

At age 23, he founded Softbank Corporation, a software distribution operation, in 1981. By 1995, the company controlled one-half of the personal computer software in Japan. Profits from this company have served as the primary basis for other profitable investments, including Yahoo!, Kingston Technologies, Ziff-Davis, and E*Trade. Besides these software investments, Son now has holdings in more than 50 international technology companies, including publishing, electronic banking, and broadcasting.

Son is a leading member of Japan's Prime Minister's IT Strategy Council. Though criticized for heavy investment in U.S. Internet companies, Son sees such alliances as helpful to both countries' economies.

For more information on Masayoshi Son, visit the Discovering Computers 2002 People Web page (**scsite.com/dc2002/people.htm**) and click Masayoshi Son.

Web Link

For more information on Web publishing, visit the Discovering Computers 2002 Chapter 2 WEB LINK page (**scsite.com/dc2002/ch2/weblink.htm**) and click Web Publishing.

ISSUE

Ink or Link?

Web Publishing

With the exception of the printed book, the Twentieth Century was predominantly visual — photography, film, television, video. As we begin the Twenty-First Century, are we entering a brave new world of all digital media? Digital communications technologies no doubt are spurring fundamental changes within all publishing businesses. Many magazines provide both a printed subscription service and an online presence. A printed version provides the flexibility of any time, anywhere reading. Many people who read for enjoyment assert they prefer reading that includes the ability to carry, hold, and manipulate the material. On the other hand, the online version offers benefits not found in the printed version. For instance, one can search and display an index of past articles or link to other relevant and updated topics. Do most people prefer reading online or reading printed materials? What impact will the Internet have on printed media within the next five years? with books? with magazines? with newspapers? Which will be better for the environment — online reading or printed media? Why?

For more information on electronic media and Web publishing, visit the Discovering Computers 2002 Issues Web page (**scsite.com/dc2002/issues.htm**) and click Chapter 2 Issue #5.

WEB PUBLISHING

Before the advent of the Web, the means to share opinions and ideas with others easily and inexpensively was limited to the media, classroom, work, or social environments. Generating an advertisement or publication that could reach a massive audience required much expense. Today, businesses and individuals can convey information to millions of people by creating their own Web pages.

Web publishing is the development and maintenance of Web pages. To develop a Web page, you do not have to be a computer programmer. For the small business or home user, Web publishing is fairly easy as long as you have the proper tools.

The five major steps to Web publishing are as follows:

(1) planning the Web site
(2) analyzing and designing the Web site
(3) creating the Web site
(4) deploying the Web site
(5) maintaining the Web site

Figure 2-24 illustrates these steps with respect to a personal Web site. The following paragraphs describe these steps in more depth.

Planning the Web Site

Planning a personal Web site involves thinking about issues that could affect the design of the Web site. You should identify the purpose of the Web site and the characteristics of the people that you want to visit the Web site. Determine ways to differentiate your Web site from similar ones. Decide how to keep the content of the Web site current and exciting. With these types of issues resolved, you can move to the next step of Analyzing and Designing the Web Site.

Analyzing and Designing the Web Site

A Web site can be simple or complex. In this step, you determine specific ways to meet the goals identified in the previous step. You design the layout of elements of the Web page such as text, graphics, audio, video, and virtual reality. Decide if you have the means to include all the elements of the design into the Web site.

Hardware you may need includes a digital camera, scanner, sound card, microphone, and PC camera. To incorporate pictures in your Web pages, you can take digital photographs with a digital camera or scan existing photographs and other graphics into a digital format with a scanner. You also can download images from the Web or purchase a CD-ROM or DVD-ROM that contains a collection of images. With a sound card, you can add sounds to your Web pages. A microphone allows you to include your voice in a Web page. To incorporate videos, you could use a PC camera or purchase special hardware that captures still photographs from videos.

Figure 2-24 HOW TO PUBLISH YOUR RESUME ON THE WEB

Step 1:
Think about issues that could affect the design of the Web site.

Step 2:
Sketch a design of the Web page on paper.

Step 3:
Create the Web site in a software package such as word processing.

Step 4:
Copy (upload) the Web site from your hard disk to a Web server.

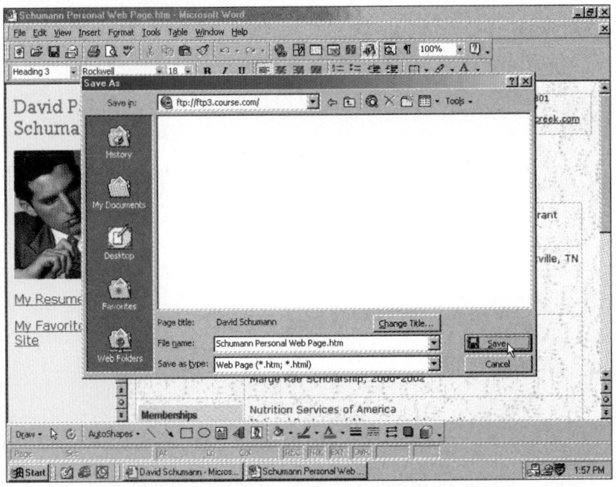

Step 5:
Visit and revise your Web site regularly to be sure it is working and current.

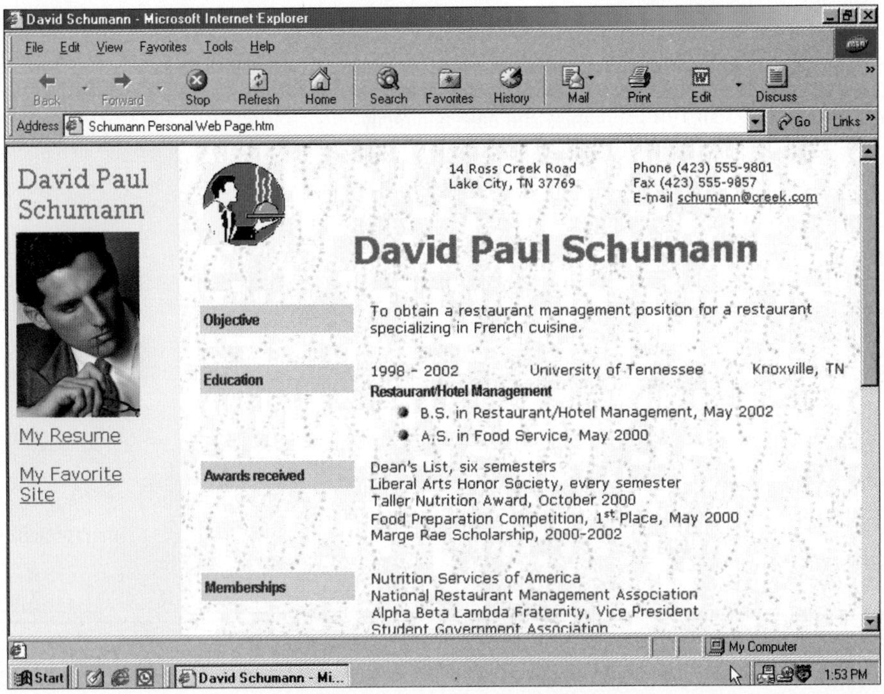

Most browsers have the capability of displaying basic multimedia elements on a Web page. Sometimes, a browser might need an additional program, called a plug-in. A **plug-in** is a program that extends the capability of a browser. You can download many plug-ins at no cost from various sites on the Web (Figure 2-25). If your Web page uses multimedia elements that require a plug-in, you may want to include a link to the Web site that contains the plug-in so that visitors can download it.

Web Link

For more information on plug-ins, visit the Discovering Computers 2002 Chapter 2 WEB LINK page (**scsite.com/dc2002/ch2/weblink.htm**) and click Plug-ins.

Creating a Web Site

Creating a Web site, sometimes called **Web page authoring**, involves working on the computer to compose the Web site. Many current word processing packages include Web page authoring features that help you to create basic Web pages that contain text and graphics. Millions of people use word processing software every day to develop documents, including Web pages.

To create more sophisticated Web pages that include video, sound, animation, and other special effects, you can use Web page authoring software. **Web page authoring software** is software specifically designed to help you create Web pages. Both new and experienced users can create fascinating Web sites with this software. Popular Web page authoring software packages include Microsoft FrontPage, Adobe GoLive, Lotus FastSite, Macromedia Dreamweaver, and Macromedia Flash.

When you save a Web page using word processing or Web page authoring software, the software saves the Web page in an HTML format.

POPULAR PLUG-IN APPLICATION

Plug-In Application		Description	Web Site
Get Acrobat Reader (Adobe)	**Acrobat Reader**	View, navigate, and print Portable Document Format (PDF) files — documents formatted to look just as they look in print	adobe.com
macromedia FLASH PLAYER	**Flash Player**	View dazzling graphics and animation, hear outstanding sound and music, display Web pages across entire screen	macromedia.com
supports mp3s liquid player five	**Liquid Player**	Listen and purchase CD-quality music tracks and audio CDs over the Internet; access MP3 files	liquidaudio.com
	QuickTime	View animation, music, audio, video, and VR panoramas and objects directly in a Web page	apple.com
real jukebox FREE	**RealJukebox**	Play MP3 files; create music CDs	real.com
real player plus	**RealPlayer**	Listen to live and on-demand near-CD-quality audio and newscast-quality video; stream audio and video content for faster viewing	real.com
macromedia SHOCKWAVE	**Shockwave**	Experience dynamic interactive multimedia, graphics, and streaming audio	macromedia.com

Figure 2-25 Most plug-ins can be downloaded free from the Web.

HTML (hypertext markup language) is a set of special codes that format a file for use as a Web page. These codes, called **tags**, specify how the text and other elements display in a browser and where the links lead. For an example of HTML, see Figure 1-15a on page 1.14. Your Web browser translates the document with HTML tags into a functional Web page. Some experienced programmers modify the HTML generated by Web page authoring software or even write the entire HTML codes from scratch.

Deploying a Web Site

After your Web pages are created, you store them on a Web server. Many ISPs and OSPs provide their customers with a Web address and storage space on a Web server for the Web site at no additional cost. If your service provider does not include this service, companies called **Web hosting services** provide storage for your Web pages for a reasonable monthly fee. The fee charged by a Web hosting service varies based on factors such as the amount of storage your Web pages require, whether your pages use streaming or other multimedia, and whether the pages are personal or for business use.

If your service provider does not supply you with a Web address or if you want to obtain a different domain name, you apply to an official registrar for a specific domain name such as countryflorist.com. You then pay a small annual fee to continue using the domain name.

Once you have created a Web site and located a Web server to store it, you need to **upload** the Web site, or copy it from your computer to the Web server. One procedure used to upload files is FTP, discussed later in this chapter. Another procedure is to save the Web site to a Web folder, which is a location on a Web server. You must contact the network administrator or technical support staff at your ISP or OSP to determine if the Web server supports FTP or Web folders and then obtain necessary permissions to access the Web server.

To help others locate your Web site, you should register it with various search engines. Doing so ensures your site will appear in the hit lists for searches on related keywords. Many search engines allow you to register your URL and keywords at no cost.

Registering your site with the various search engines, however, can be an extremely time-consuming task. Instead, you can use a submission service. A **submission service** is a Web-based business that offers a registration package in which you pay to register with hundreds of search engines.

In addition to supplying a title for your site, the URL, and a site description, the submission service might require you to identify several features of your site, such as whether it is commercial or personal; a category and subcategory; and search keywords. For example, if your Web site business sells greeting cards, you could register under the Products and Services subcategory in the Business and Economy category, and specify keywords such as greeting cards, birthday cards, and anniversary cards.

Maintaining the Web Site

A **Webmaster** is the individual responsible for maintaining a Web site and developing Web pages. Webmasters and other Web page developers maintain Web sites using software products. Most Web page authoring software packages provide basic Web site management tools, allowing you to add and modify Web pages within the Web site. For more advanced features such as managing users, passwords, chat rooms, and e-mail, you need to purchase specialized Web site management software.

OTHER INTERNET SERVICES

Although the World Wide Web is the most talked about service on the Internet, many other Internet services are used widely. These include e-mail, FTP, newsgroups and message boards, mailing lists, chat rooms, and instant messaging. The following pages discuss each of these services.

Web Link

For more information on submission services, visit the Discovering Computers 2002 Chapter 2 WEB LINK page (**scsite.com/dc2002/ch2/weblink.htm**) and click Submission Services.

E-Mail

E-mail (**electronic mail**) is the transmission of messages and files via a computer network. E-mail was one of the original services on the Internet, enabling scientists and researchers working on government-sponsored projects to communicate with colleagues at other locations. Today, e-mail quickly is becoming a primary communications method for both personal and business use.

You can create, send, receive, forward, store, print, and delete messages using an **e-mail program**. The steps in Figure 2-26 illustrate how to

Figure 2-26 HOW TO SEND AN E-MAIL MESSAGE

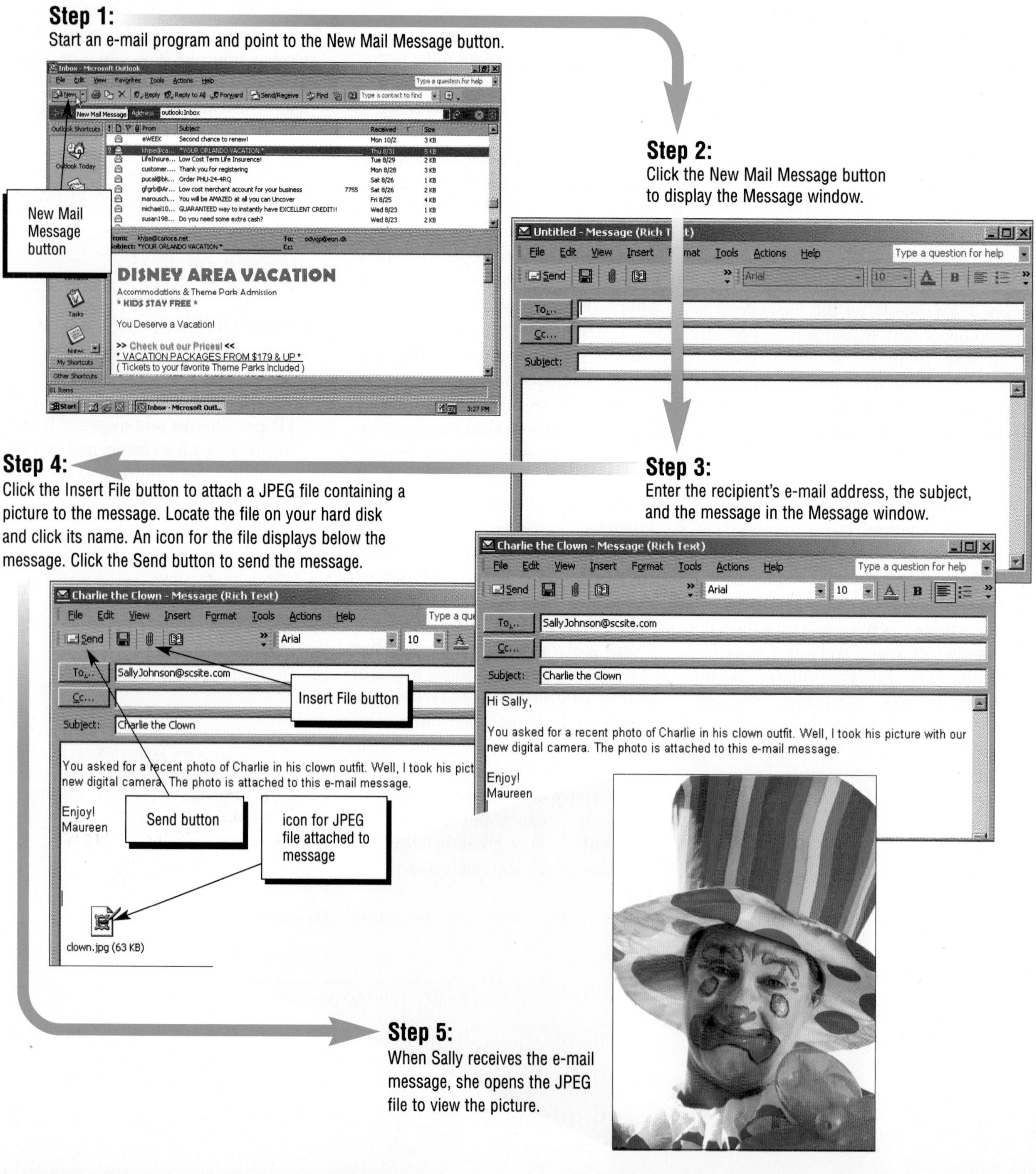
Step 1:
Start an e-mail program and point to the New Mail Message button.
New Mail Message button
Step 2:
Click the New Mail Message button to display the Message window.
Step 3:
Enter the recipient's e-mail address, the subject, and the message in the Message window.
Step 4:
Click the Insert File button to attach a JPEG file containing a picture to the message. Locate the file on your hard disk and click its name. An icon for the file displays below the message. Click the Send button to send the message.
Insert File button
Send button
icon for JPEG file attached to message
Step 5:
When Sally receives the e-mail message, she opens the JPEG file to view the picture.
Charlie the Clown - Message (Rich Text)
SallyJohnson@scsite.com
Charlie the Clown
Hi Sally,
You asked for a recent photo of Charlie in his clown outfit. Well, I took his picture with our new digital camera. The photo is attached to this e-mail message.
Enjoy!
Maureen
clown.jpg (63 KB)

send an e-mail message. The message can be simple text or can include an attachment such as a word processing document, a graphical image, or an audio or video clip.

Just as you address a letter when using the postal system, you must address an e-mail message with the e-mail address of your intended recipient. To receive messages, you need an e-mail address. Likewise, when someone sends you a message, they must have your e-mail address. An **e-mail address** is a combination of a user name and a domain name that identifies a user, so he or she can receive Internet e-mail (Figure 2-27).

A **user name**, or **user-ID**, is a unique combination of characters, such as letters of the alphabet or numbers, that identifies you. Your user name must be different from the other user names in the same domain. For example, a user named Sally Johnson whose server has a domain name of scsite.com might select S_Johnson as her user name. If scsite.com already has a user S_Johnson (for Sam Johnson), Sally would have to select a different user name, such as SallyJohnson or Sally_Johnson. You select your user name. Although you can select a nickname or any other combination of characters for your user name, many users select a combination of their first and last names so others can remember it easily.

In an Internet e-mail address, an @ symbol (pronounced at) separates the user name from the domain name. Your service provider supplies you with the domain name. Using the example in Figure 2-27, a possible e-mail address would be SallyJohnson@scsite.com, which would be read as follows: Sally Johnson at s c site dot com. Most e-mail programs allow you to create an **address book**, which contains a list of names and e-mail addresses.

Although no complete listing of Internet e-mail addresses exists, several Internet sites list addresses collected from public sources. These sites also allow you to list your e-mail address voluntarily so others can find it. The site also might ask for other information, such as your high school or college, so others can determine if you are the person they want to reach.

Most e-mail programs have a mail notification alert that informs you via a message or sound when you receive new mail, even if you are working in another application. As you receive e-mail messages, they are placed in your mailbox. A **mailbox** is a storage location usually residing on the computer that connects you to the Internet, such as the server operated by your ISP or OSP. The server that contains the mailboxes often is called a **mail server**. Most ISPs and OSPs provide an Internet e-mail program and a mailbox on a mail server as a standard part of their Internet access services.

Figure 2-27 An e-mail address is a combination of a user name and a domain name.

APPLY IT!

Hello from Your Personal Computer

The convenience of voice communications now is available online. In traditional voice mail, the caller leaves a message in your voice mailbox; similarly, with voice e-mail, you speak instead of typing an e-mail message. Most computers can handle voice messages once you install the proper software or services. In addition to a computer, you will need software that can record sound, a sound card, and a microphone. Most likely, you will want a set of external speakers, though you can use the computer's internal speakers. Cool Edit Pro (see URL below) is a good software choice for the Windows user, and Sound Edit (see URL below) works well for the Macintosh user. You also can find many other software packages by searching on the term, voice messaging, at CNET's download site (see URL below). Most voice messaging software packages require you to pay a fee. Some software manufacturers, however, provide free versions, but they do not have as many capabilities as the full versions.

Once you are set up and ready to go, prepare your room for recording by making sure it is quiet. Speak directly into the microphone as though you are talking to someone else in the room. When you finish with a recording, reduce the file size by saving your message as a mono sound file. Generally, it is best to keep the message length no longer than 30 seconds.

To send a sound file, open your e-mail program and attach the sound file, using the same process you use to attach any other file. Click the Send button and the voice message is on its way.

For more information on computer voice messages and the Web sites mentioned above, visit the Discovering Computers 2002 Apply It Web page (**scsite.com/dc2002/apply.htm**) and click Chapter 2 Apply It #3.

Web Link

For more information on e-mail, visit the Discovering Computers 2002 Chapter 2 WEB LINK page (**scsite.com/dc2002/ch2/weblink.htm**) and click E-Mail.

Some Web sites provide e-mail services free of charge. To use these Web-based e-mail programs, you connect to the Web site and set up an e-mail account, which typically includes an e-mail address and a password. Instead of sending e-mail messages, several Web sites provide services that allow you to send other items such as online invitations and greetings. These Web sites have a server that stores your messages, invitations, and greetings.

When you send an e-mail message, a program on the mail server determines how to route the message through the Internet and then sends the message. When the message arrives at the recipient's mail server, the message transfers to a POP or POP3 server. **POP (Post Office Protocol)** is a communications technology for retrieving e-mail from a mail server. The POP server holds the message until the recipient retrieves it with his or her e-mail software (Figure 2-28). The newest version of POP is **POP3**, or **Post Office Protocol 3**.

FTP

FTP (File Transfer Protocol) is an Internet standard that allows you to upload and download files with other computers on the Internet. For example, if you click a link on a Web page that begins to download a file to

Figure 2-28 HOW AN E-MAIL MESSAGE TRAVELS FROM THE SENDER TO THE RECEIVER

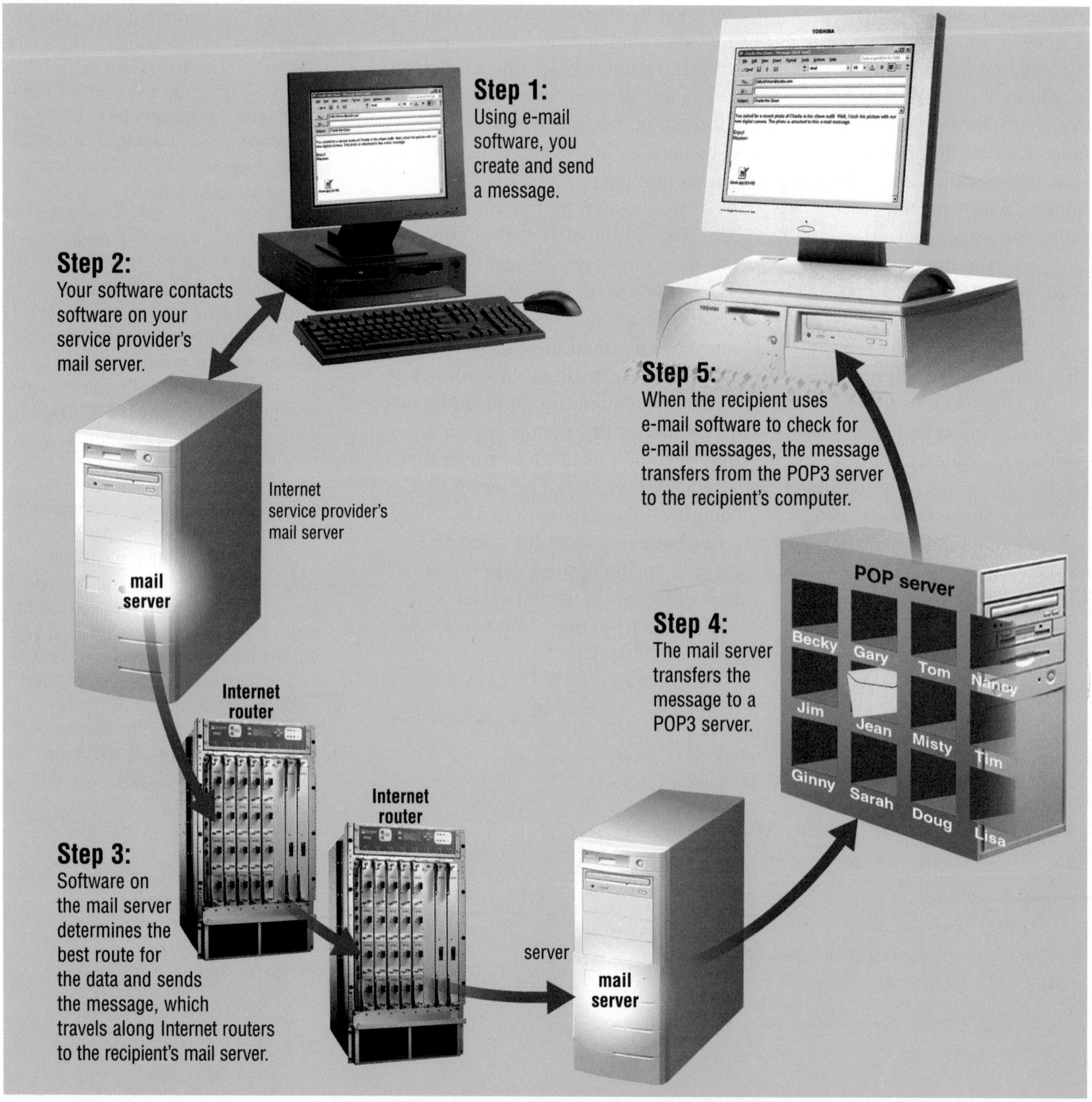

your hard disk, you probably are using FTP (Figure 2-29).

An **FTP server** is a computer that allows users to upload and download files using FTP. An **FTP site** is a collection of files including text, graphics, audio, video, and program files that reside on an FTP server. Some FTP sites limit file transfers to individuals who have authorized accounts (user names and passwords) on the FTP server. Many FTP sites allow **anonymous FTP**, whereby anyone can transfer some, if not all, available files. Many program files on anonymous FTP sites are freeware or public domain software. Others are shareware.

Large files on FTP sites often are compressed to reduce storage space and download time. Before you use a compressed file, you must expand it with a decompression program, such as WinZip. Such programs usually also are available for download from an FTP site (see Figure 2-29). Chapter 8 discusses compression and decompression programs.

In some cases, you may want to upload a file to an FTP site. For example, if you create a personal Web site, you will want to publish it on a Web server. Many Web servers require you to upload the files using FTP. To upload files from your computer to an FTP site, you use an FTP program. Some ISPs and OSPs include an FTP program as part of their Internet access service. You also can download FTP programs from the Web.

Newsgroups and Message Boards

A **newsgroup** is an online area in which users conduct written discussions about a particular subject. To participate in a discussion, a user sends a message to the newsgroup, and other users in the newsgroup read and reply to the message. The entire collection of Internet newsgroups is called **Usenet**, which contains thousands of newsgroups on a multitude of topics. Some major topic areas include news, recreation, business, science, and computers.

A computer that stores and distributes newsgroup messages is called a **news server**. Many universities, corporations, ISPs, OSPs, and other large organizations have a news server. Some newsgroups require you to enter your user name and password to participate in the discussion. Only authorized members can use this type of newsgroup. For example, a newsgroup for students taking a college course may require a user name and password to access the newsgroup. This ensures that only students in the course participate in the discussion.

To participate in a newsgroup, you use a program called a **newsreader**, which is included with most browsers. The newsreader enables you to access a newsgroup to read a previously entered message, called an **article**. You also can **post**, or add, an article of your own. The newsreader also keeps track of which articles you have and have not read.

Newsgroup members frequently post articles as a reply to another article — either to answer a question or to comment on material in the original article. These replies may cause the author of the original article, or others, to post additional articles related to the original article. A **thread** or **threaded discussion** consists of the original article and all subsequent related replies. A thread can be short-lived or continue for some time, depending on the nature of the topic and the interest of the participants.

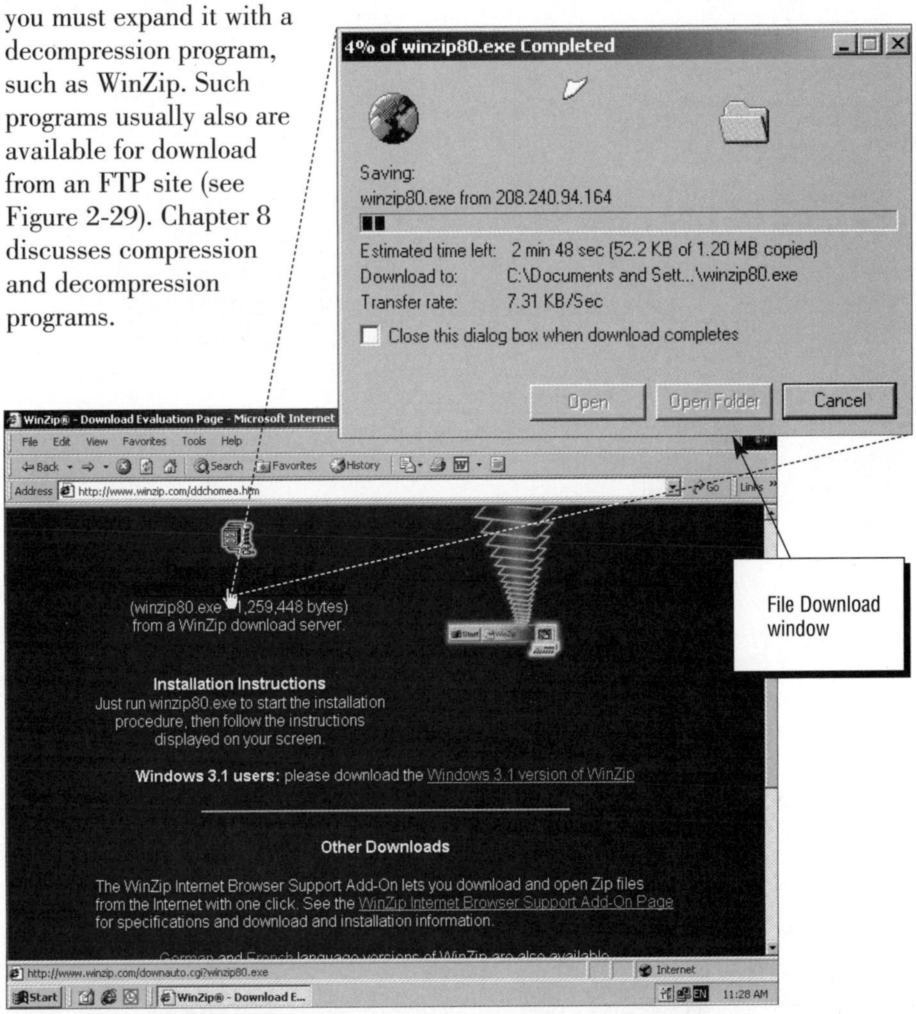

Figure 2-29 The File Download window indicates the estimated time for the download, as well as where the file is being saved on your hard disk.

Using a newsreader, you can search for newsgroups discussing a particular subject such as a type of musical instrument, brand of sports equipment, or employment opportunities. If you like the discussion in a particular newsgroup, you can **subscribe** to it, which means its location is saved in your newsreader for easy future access.

In some newsgroups, when you post an article, it is sent to a moderator instead of immediately displaying on the newsgroup. The **moderator** reviews the contents of the article and then posts it, if appropriate. Called a **moderated newsgroup**, the moderator decides if the article is relevant to the discussion. The moderator may choose to edit or discard inappropriate articles. For this reason, the content of a moderated newsgroup is considered more valuable.

A popular Web-based type of discussion group that does not require a newsreader is a message board (Figure 2-30). Many Web sites provide a **message board**, also called a **discussion board**. Message boards typically are easier to use than newsgroups.

Mailing Lists

A **mailing list** is a group of e-mail names and addresses given a single name. When a message is sent to a mailing list, every person on the list receives a copy of the message in his or her mailbox. To add your e-mail name and address to a mailing list, you **subscribe** to it (Figure 2-31). To remove your name, you **unsubscribe** from the mailing list. Some mailing lists are called **LISTSERVs**, named

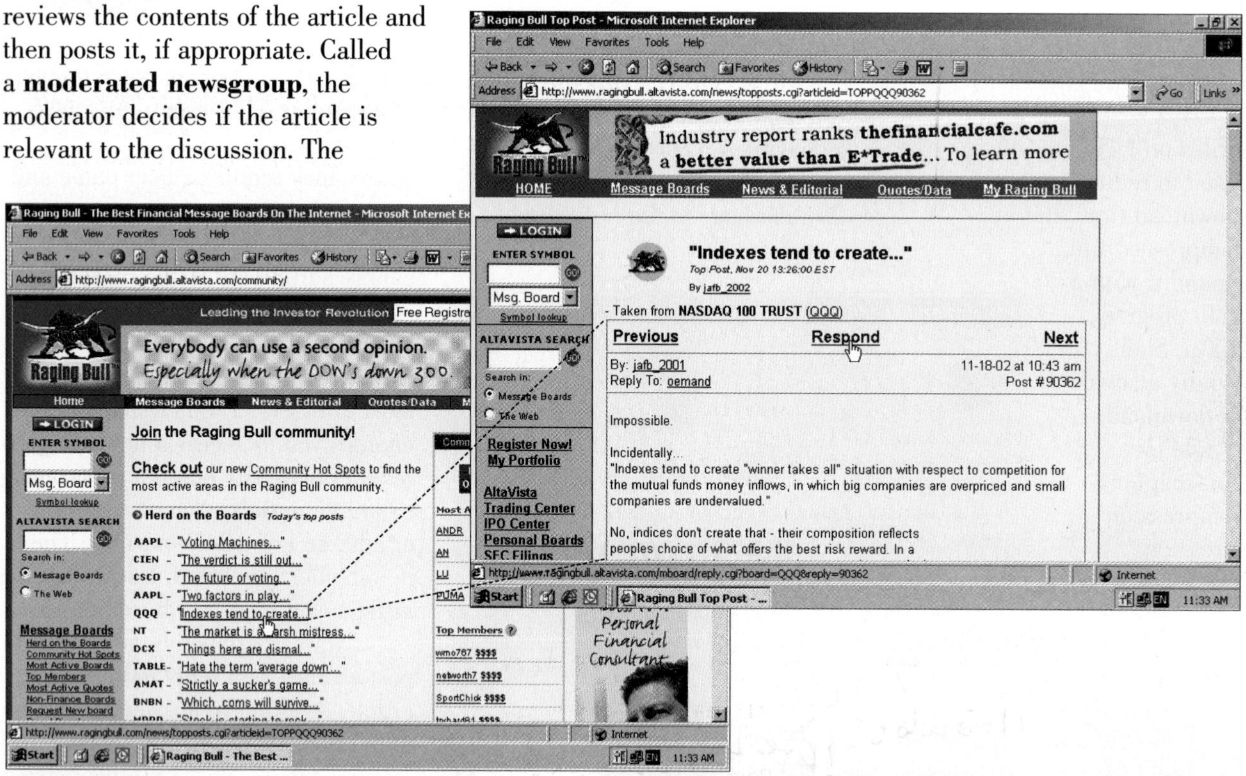

Figure 2-30 This message board allows users to discuss financial issues.

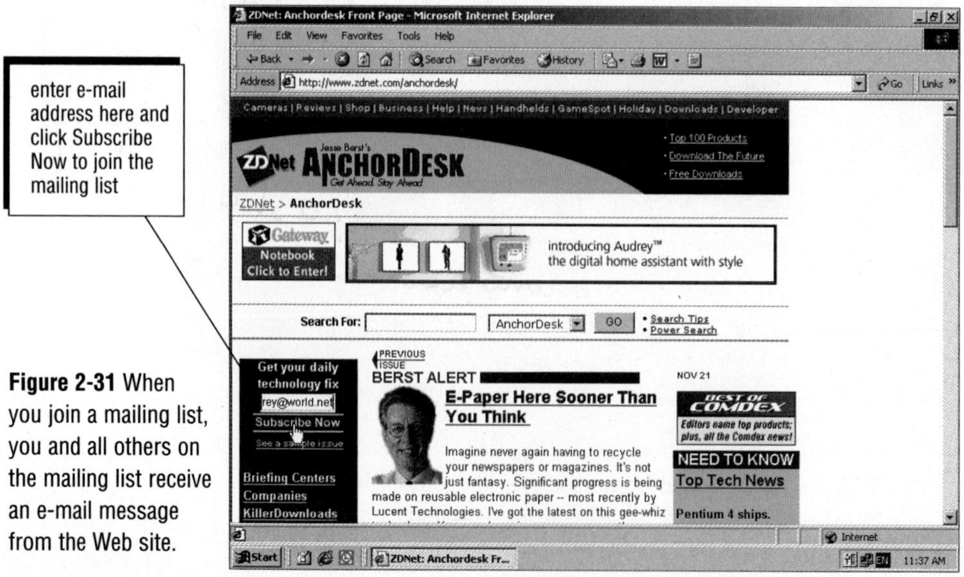

Figure 2-31 When you join a mailing list, you and all others on the mailing list receive an e-mail message from the Web site.

Web Link

For more information on newsgroups and message boards, visit the Discovering Computers 2002 Chapter 2 WEB LINK page (**scsite.com/dc2002/ch2/weblink.htm**) and click Newsgroups and Message Boards.

after a popular mailing list software product.

Thousands of mailing lists exist on a variety of topics in areas of entertainment, business, computers, society, culture, health, recreation, and education. To locate a mailing list dealing with a particular topic, you can search for the keywords, mailing lists or LISTSERVs, using your Web browser.

Chat Rooms

A **chat** is a real-time typed conversation that takes place on a computer. **Real-time** means that you and the people with whom you are conversing are online at the same time. As you type on your keyboard, a line of characters and symbols display on the computer screen. Others connected to the same chat room server also can see what you have typed (Figure 2-32). In some chat rooms, you can click a button to see a profile of someone in the chat room.

A **chat room** is a location on an Internet server that permits users to chat with each other. Anyone in the chat room can participate in the conversation, which usually is specific to a particular topic. Some chat rooms support **voice chats** and **video chats**, where you hear or see others and they can hear or see you as you chat.

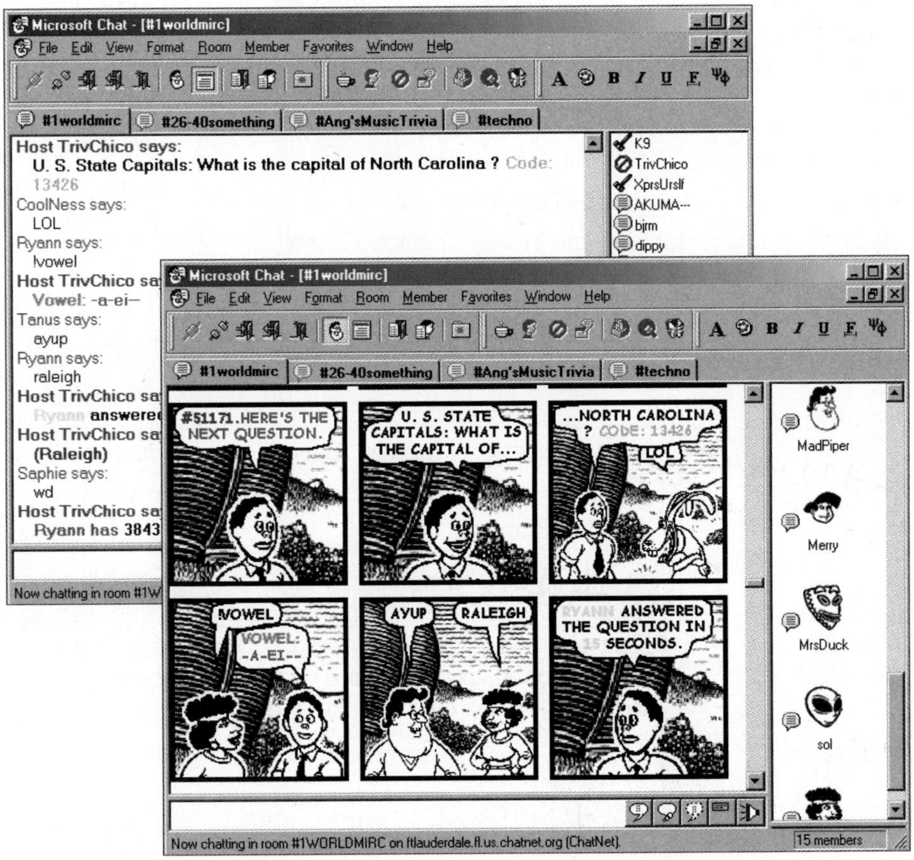

Figure 2-32 Most browsers include chat software. Some allow you to use a fictitious character.

TECHNOLOGY TRAILBLAZER

LAVONNE **LUQUIS**

Journalists are trained to conduct research and report their findings clearly to an audience. With a bachelor's degree with honors from the University of Colorado and seven years of solid print journalism experience, Lavonne Luquis researched the Internet in 1994 to find sites about her native Puerto Rico. When she found only one page, she decided to start *LatinoLink*, the first general interest Web magazine with "a space for Latinos on the Web."

With high-quality content and feature articles, the site fit the classic print magazine model. It did not, however, attract a large audience. Luquis' viewers inundated her with e-mail messages requesting a chat feature. She listened to her audience and added news, commentary, reviews, and bulletin boards, along with the ability to chat. Today, the site, renamed Latino.com, boasts more than 280,000 visitors each month.

Luquis believes the site's value is its material, and she has established content partnerships with Netscape, Yahoo!, and Snap Online. She has been recognized for her efforts by winning the U.S. Hispanic Chamber of Commerce's National Hispanic Businesswoman of the Year award and *Hispanic* magazine's Hispanic Achievements Award.

For more information on Lavonne Luquis, visit the Discovering Computers 2002 People Web page (**scsite.com/dc2002/people.htm**) and click Lavonne Luquis.

Web Link

For more information on chat rooms, visit the Discovering Computers 2002 Chapter 2 WEB LINK page (**scsite.com/dc2002/ch2/weblink.htm**) and click Chat Rooms.

To start a chat session, you connect to a chat server through a chat client. A **chat client** is a program on your computer. Today's browsers usually include a chat client. If yours does not, you can download a chat client from the Web. Some chat clients are text-based. Others support graphical chats also, where you can assume the appearance of a fictitious character.

Once you have installed a chat client, you can create or join a conversation on the chat server to which you are connected. The chat room should indicate the topic of discussion. The person who creates a chat room acts as the operator and has responsibility for monitoring the conversation and disconnecting anyone whom becomes disruptive. Operator status can be shared or transferred to someone else.

Instant Messaging

Instant messaging (**IM**) is a real-time Internet communications service that notifies you when one or more people are online and then allows you to exchange messages or files or join a private chat room with them (Figure 2-33). Many IM services also can alert you to information such as calendar appointments, stock quotes, weather, or sports scores. People use IM on all types of computers, including desktop computers, notebook computers, handheld computers, and Web-enabled devices.

To use IM, you install software from an instant messaging service, sometimes called an **instant messenger**, onto the computer or device with which you wish to use IM. No standards currently exist for IM. Thus, you and all those individuals on your notification list need to use the same or a compatible instant messenger to guarantee successful communications.

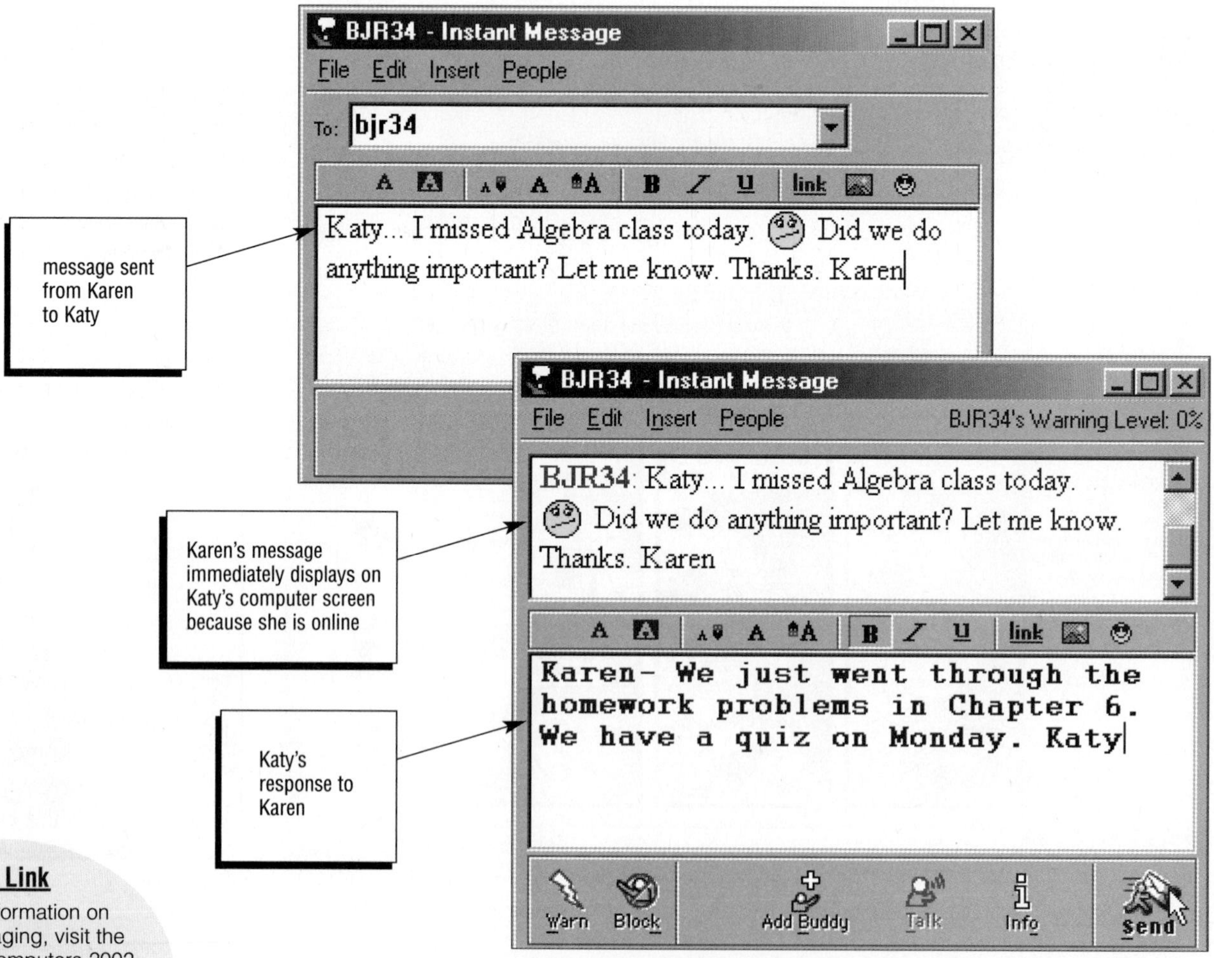

Figure 2-33 Instant messaging is a real-time Internet communications service that notifies you when one or more people are online and then allows you to exchange messages or files or join a private chat room with them.

Web Link

For more information on instant messaging, visit the Discovering Computers 2002 Chapter 2 WEB LINK page (**scsite.com/dc2002/ch2/weblink.htm**) and click Instant Messaging.

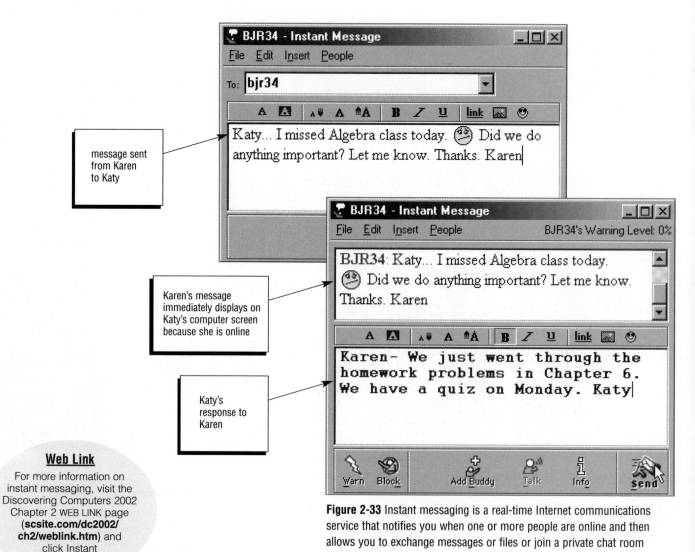

NETIQUETTE

Netiquette, which is short for Internet etiquette, is the code of acceptable behaviors users should follow while on the Internet; that is, the conduct expected of individuals while online. Netiquette includes rules for all aspects of the Internet, including the World Wide Web, e-mail, FTP, newsgroups and message boards, chat rooms, and instant messaging. Figure 2-34 outlines the rules of netiquette.

CHAPTER SUMMARY

This chapter discussed the history and structure of the Internet. It discussed at length the World Wide Web, including topics such as browsing, navigating, e-commerce, and Web publishing. It also presented other various services available on the Internet, such as e-mail, FTP, newsgroups and message boards, chat rooms, and instant messaging. Finally, the chapter listed rules of netiquette.

Netiquette

Golden Rule: *Treat others as you would like them to treat you.*

1. In e-mail, newsgroups, and chat rooms:
   - Keep messages brief using proper grammar and spelling.
   - Be careful when using sarcasm and humor, as it might be misinterpreted.
   - Be polite. Avoid offensive language.
   - Avoid sending or posting **flames**, which are abusive or insulting messages. Do not participate in **flame wars**, which are exchanges of flames.
   - Avoid sending spam, which is the Internet's version of junk mail. **Spam** is an unsolicited e-mail message or newsgroup posting sent to many recipients or newsgroups at once.
   - Do not use all capital letters, which is the equivalent of SHOUTING!
   - Use **emoticons** to express emotion. Popular emoticons include

:)	Smile
:(	Frown
:|	Indifference
:\	Undecided
:o	Surprised

   - Use abbreviations and acronyms for phrases such as

BTW	by the way
FYI	for your information
FWIW	for what it's worth
IMHO	in my humble opinion
TTFN	ta ta for now
TYVM	thank you very much

   - Clearly identify a **spoiler**, which is a message that reveals a solution to a game or ending to a movie or program.
2. Read the **FAQ** (frequently asked questions) document, if one exists. Many newsgroups and Web pages have a FAQ.
3. Use your user name for your personal use only.
4. Do not assume material is accurate or up to date. Be forgiving of other's mistakes.
5. Never read someone's private e-mail.

Figure 2-34 Some of the rules of netiquette.

Webmaster

What is a Webmaster? Although, typically, a Webmaster's responsibility is related to maintaining a company's Web site, no single definitive answer exists to this question. If your goal is to become a Webmaster, you will want to master most of these skills:

- Identify goals, objectives, and budget requirements
- Develop Web sites using HTML, Java, JavaScript, and other programming tools
- Determine the best software and hardware for presentation of information
- Work with others to coordinate the workflow of the Web site
- Develop a uniform standard for the company Web site
- Maintain the home page and certain other primary site documents as well as a Frequently Asked Questions (FAQ) document where necessary
- Actively participate in departmental advisory committees to provide input to help establish objectives and to establish standards and guidelines for content
- Promote the site

Many educational institutions offer Internet-related courses, certifications, and degrees. Salaries vary, depending on education and location. ZDNet (see URL below) reports that Webmasters earn an average annual salary of $40,000 to $53,000. Real Salary Survey (see URL below) shows a range of $40,000 to $93,000, with a median of $54,000.

To learn more about the field of Webmaster as a career and the Web sites mentioned above, visit the Discovering Computers 2002 Careers Web page (**scsite.com/dc2002/careers.htm**) and click Webmaster.

E-TRAVEL

GET PACKING!

Explore the World without Leaving Home

Balmy beaches. Majestic mountains. Exotic destinations. Just dreaming of experiencing these locales can lift your spirits. Researchers conclude that vacations are healthy for your mind and body because they help eliminate stress, offer opportunities to spend quality time with family and friends, and provide exercise. Whether you are ready to arrange your next travel adventure or just want to explore destination possibilities, the Internet provides ample resources to set your plans in motion.

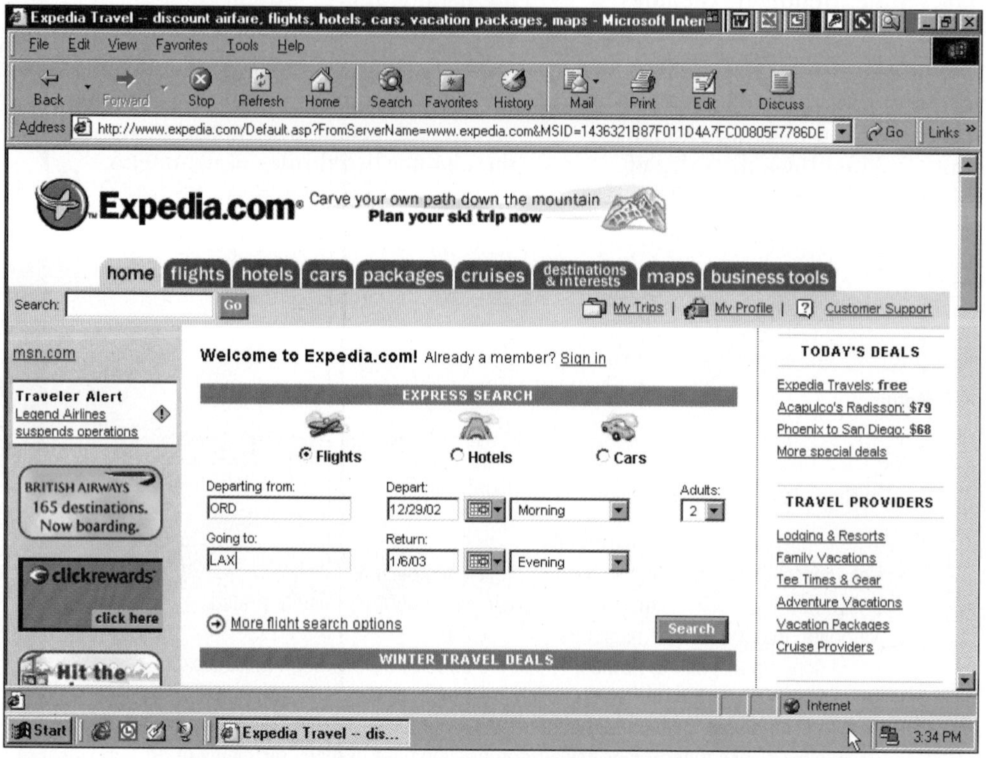

Figure 2-35 Book flights, cruises, and ski trips with all-encompassing travel resources.

Some good starting places are all-encompassing Web sites such as Travelocity, which is owned by Sabre, the electronic booking service travel agents use, Expedia (Figure 2-35), and TRIP.com (Figure 2-36). These general travel Web sites have tools to help you find the lowest prices and details on flights, cruises, car rentals, and hotels, and they include such features as airplane seating maps, local weather, popular restaurants, and photos. Each of the major airlines and cruise lines also has a Web site where you can check prices, purchase tickets and tour packages, and sign up for weekly e-mail alerts on specials and new services.

To discover exactly where your destination is on this planet, cartography Web sites, including MapQuest (Figure 2-37), maps.com, mapsindex.com, and

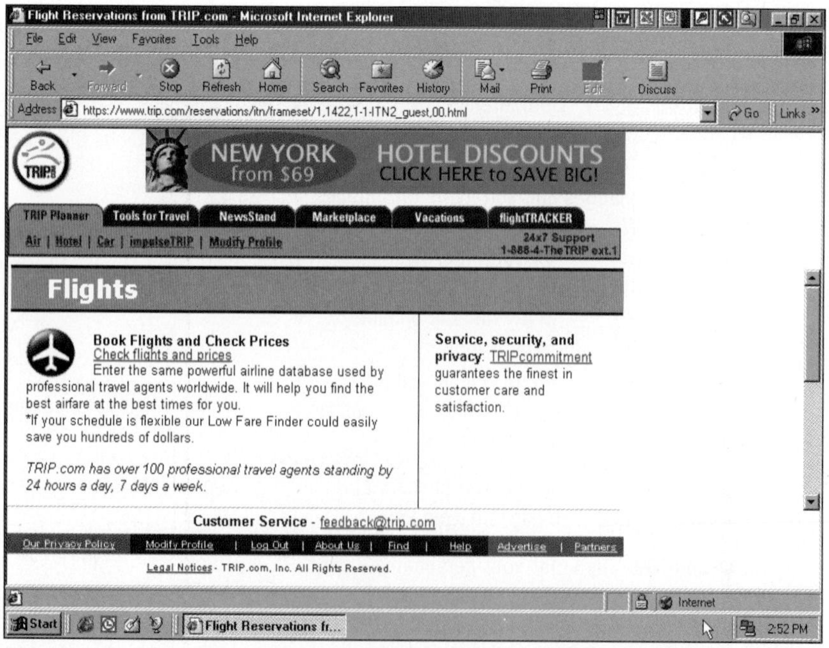

Figure 2-36 General travel Web sites allow users to check fares to your favorite destinations.

Rand McNally, let you pinpoint your destination. These Web pages generally are divided into geographical areas, such as North America and Europe. When you choose an area, you see a subject-based index that lists helpful tools such as route planners, subway maps, entertainment, and ski trails.

For more information on travel sites, visit the Discovering Computers 2002 E-Revolution Web page (scsite.com/dc2002/e-rev.htm) and click Travel.

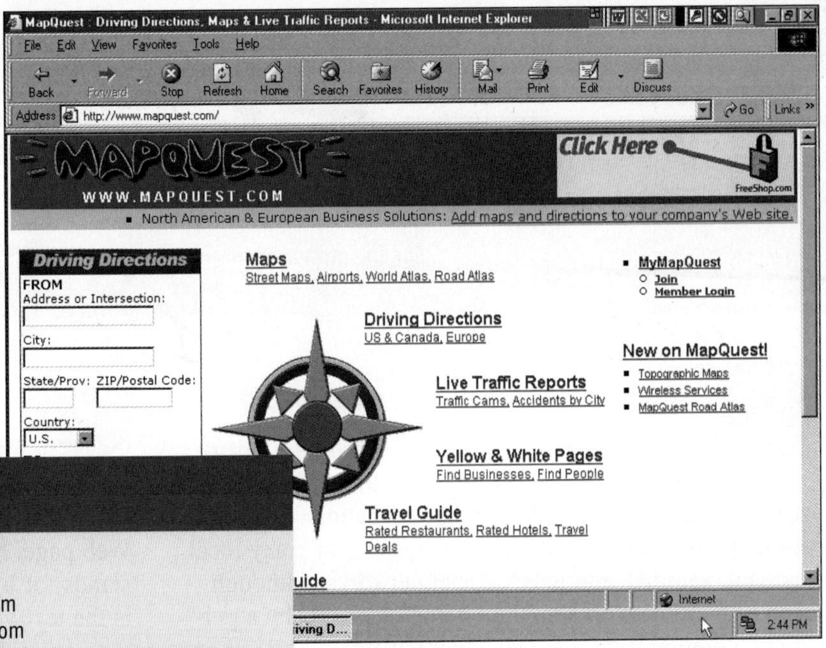

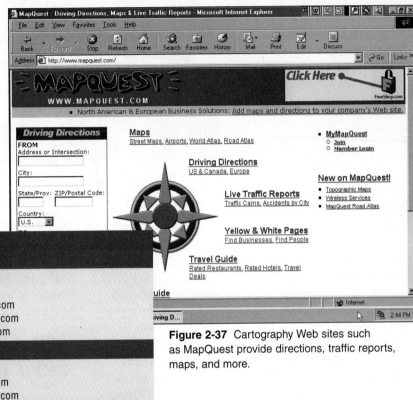

Figure 2-37 Cartography Web sites such as MapQuest provide directions, traffic reports, maps, and more.

TRAVEL WEB SITES	URL
General Travel	
TRIP.com	trip.com
Expedia Travel	expedia.com
Travelscape.com	travelscape.com
Yahoo! Travel	travel.yahoo.com
Travelocity.com	travelocity.com
Cartography	
Maps.com	maps.com
MapQuest	mapquest.com
Rand McNally	randmcnally.com
Travel and City Guides	
All the Greatest Cities of the World	greatestcities.com
U.S. National Parks Info	us-parks.com
10Best: City Guides	10best.com

For an updated list of travel Web sites, visit scsite.com/dc2002/e-rev.htm.

Figure 2-38 These travel resources Web sites offer travel information to exciting destinations throughout the world.

E-REVOLUTION E-TRAVEL *applied:*

1. Visit one of the cartography Web sites listed in Figure 2-38 and print directions from your campus to one of these destinations: the White House in Washington, DC; Elvis's home in Memphis, Tennessee; Disney World in Orlando, Florida; or the Grand Old Opry in Nashville, Tennessee. How many miles is it to your destination? What is the estimated driving time? Then, visit one of the general travel Web sites listed in the table and plan a flight from the nearest major airport to one of the four destinations for the week after finals and a return trip one week later. What is the lowest coach fare for this round-trip flight? What airline, flight numbers, and departure and arrival times did you select? Finally, explore car rental rates for a subcompact car for this one-week vacation. What rental agency and rate did you choose?

2. Visit one of the travel and city guide Web sites listed in Figure 2-38, and choose a destination for a getaway this coming weekend. Write a one-page paper giving details about this location, such as popular hotels and lodging, expected weather, population, local colleges and universities, parks and recreation, ancient and modern history, and tours. Print a map of this place. Why did you select this destination? How would you travel there and back? What is the breakdown of expected costs for this weekend, including travel expenditures, meals, lodging, and tickets to events and activities? What URLs did you use to complete this exercise?

In Summary

Web Instructions: To display this page from the Web, start your browser and enter the URL scsite.com/dc2002/ch2/summary.htm. Click the links for current and additional information. To listen to an audio version of this In Summary, click the Audio button. To play the audio, RealPlayer must be installed on your computer (download by clicking here).

1 How Does the Internet Work?

The Internet, also called the **Net**, is a worldwide collection of networks that links millions of businesses, government agencies, educational institutions, and individuals. The Internet consists of many local, regional, national, and international networks. Although each of these networks on the Internet is owned by a public or private organization, no single organization owns or controls the Internet. Each organization on the Internet is responsible only for maintaining its own network. The Internet provides a variety of services, including access to the World Wide Web, electronic mail (e-mail), FTP, newsgroups and message boards, mailing lists, chat rooms, and instant messaging.

2 What Are the Ways to Access the Internet?

An **Internet service provider** (**ISP**) provides temporary Internet connections to individuals and companies. An **online service provider** (**OSP**) also supplies Internet access, in addition to a variety of special services. Those users with wireless modems or Web-enabled devices communicate through an antenna with a **wireless service provider** (**WSP**). At a business or school, users connect to the Internet through a local area network (LAN) that is connected to an ISP. At home, individuals often use their computers and a modem to dial into an ISP or OSP over a regular telephone line. Some home and small businesses also use high-speed technologies such as a **DSL** (**digital subscriber line**) and cable modem.

Data is transferred over the Internet using a **server**, which is a computer that manages network resources and provides centralized storage areas, and a client, which is a computer that can access the contents of the storage areas. Each computer destination has a unique numeric address called an **IP address**, the text version of which is called a **domain name**.

3 How Do You Identify a URL?

The **Uniform Resource Locator** (**URL**) is the Web page address. A URL consists of a protocol, a domain name, and sometimes the path to a specific Web page. Most Web pages begin with http://. The **http** stands for **hypertext transfer protocol**. The **domain name** is the text version of an IP address.

4 How Do You Search for Information on the Web?

To find Web sites, you use a **search engine** software program. To locate a Web page, you enter a keyword or **search text** in the search engine's text box. Another search option is a **directory**, which on the Web, is an organized set of topics and subtopics.

5 What Are the Types of Web Pages?

Six basic types of Web pages exist. An **advocacy Web page** contains content that describes a cause, opinion, or idea and attempts to convince the reader of the validity of the idea or opinion. A **business/marketing Web page** contains content that promotes or sells products or services. An **informational Web page** contains factual information. A **news Web page** contains stories and articles relating to current events, life, money, sports, and the weather. A portal Web page provides a variety of Internet services, many of which are free. These services may include search engines; local, national, and worldwide news; sports and weather; free personal Web pages; reference tools; shopping malls and auctions; e-mail; instant messaging, newsgroups, calendars, and chat rooms. A **wireless portal** is specifically designed for Web-enabled devices. Private individuals may maintain a **personal Web page** for a variety of general uses such as job hunting.

In Summary

6 How Are Graphics, Animation, Audio, Video, and Virtual Reality Used on the World Wide Web?

Most Web pages have built-in **links** to related Web pages. A Web page can contain **multimedia** features that include graphics, animation, audio, video, and virtual reality. A **graphic**, which is a digital representation of information, was the first medium used to enhance the text-based Internet. **Animation** is the appearance of motion that is created by displaying a series of still images in rapid sequence. Simple Web **audio** and Web **video** applications consist of individual sound and video files that must be downloaded completely before they can be played on your computer. Streaming audio and **streaming video** allow you to listen and/or view the sound and/or images as they download to your computer. **Virtual reality** (**VR**) is the simulation of a real or imagined environment that appears as a three-dimensional (3-D) space.

7 What is Webcasting?

Webcasting also is known as push technology. A server automatically downloads content to your computer at regular intervals or whenever updates are made to the Web site. Once the content is pushed to your computer, you can view it online or **offline**.

8 How Is Electronic Commerce Used?

Electronic commerce (**e-commerce**) is the performance of business activities online. Three types of e-commerce exist. **Business to consumer** (**B-to-C** or **B2C**) e-commerce consists of the sale of goods to the general public. Consumer to consumer (C-to-C or C2C) e-commerce occurs when one consumer sells directly to another, such as in an online auction. **Business to business** (**B-to-B** or **B2B**) e-commerce, which is the most prevalent type of e-commerce, takes place between businesses, with businesses typically providing services to other businesses.

9 What Tools Are Required for Web Publishing?

Web publishing is the development and maintenance of Web pages. Web pages are created and formatted using a set of codes called **HTML** (**hypertext markup language**). These codes, called tags, stipulate how elements display and where links lead. Developers use tags to create HTML documents with a text editor or word processing software. Many word processing packages generate HTML tags and include authoring features that help users create basic Web pages. **Web page authoring software** can be used to create more sophisticated Web pages. Other Web publishing tools include digital cameras, scanners, and/or CD-ROM or DVD-ROM image collections to incorporate pictures; sound cards and microphones to incorporate sound; and PC cameras and video cameras to incorporate videos.

10 How Do E-Mail, FTP, Newsgroups and Message Boards, Mailing Lists, Chat Rooms, and Instant Messaging Work?

A variety of services are used widely on the Internet. **E-mail** (**electronic mail**), which is the transmission of messages and files via a computer network, is a primary method of communication. FTP (file transfer protocol) is an Internet standard that allows you to upload and download files with other computers. A **newsgroup** is an online area in which users conduct written discussions about a particular subject. A **message board**, also called a **discussion board**, is a Web-based discussion group that is easier to use than newsgroups. A **mailing list** is a group of e-mail names and addresses given a single name. A **chat** is **real-time** typed conversation that takes place on a computer through a **chat room**, or communications medium. **Instant messaging** (**IM**) is a service that notifies you when one or more people are online and then allows you to exchange messages or join a private chat room.

11 What Are the Rules of Netiquette?

Netiquette, which is short for Internet etiquette, is the code of acceptable behaviors when using the Internet. Rules for e-mail, newsgroups, and chat rooms include keeping messages short and polite; avoiding sarcasm, **flames** (abusive messages), and spam (unsolicited junk mail); and reading the **FAQs** (frequently asked questions). When using the Internet, do not assume all material is accurate or up to date, and never read private e-mail.

Key Terms

Web Instructions: To display this page from the Web, start your browser and enter the URL scsite.com/dc2002/ch2/terms.htm. Scroll through the list of terms. Click a term to display its definition and a picture. Click the To WEB button for current and additional information about the term from the Web. To see animations, Shockwave and Flash Player must be installed on your computer (download by clicking here).

VR WORLD
3-D site that contains infinite space and depth. (2.22)

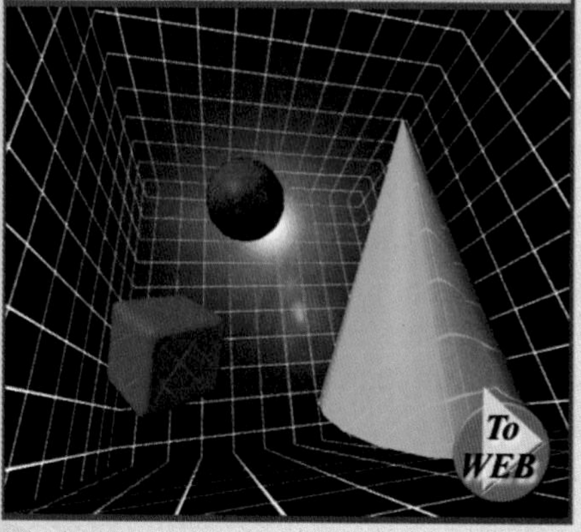

Learn It Online

Web Instructions: To display this page from the Web, start your browser, and then enter the URL scsite.com/dc2002/ch2/learn.htm.

1. Web Guide

Click Web Guide to display the Guide to World Wide Web Sites and Searching Techniques Web page. Click Reference and then click AskJeeves. Ask Jeeves about the history of the Internet. Click an answer of your choice. Use your word processing program to prepare a brief report on what you discovered and submit your assignment to your instructor.

2. Scavenger Hunt

Click Scavenger Hunt. Print a copy of the Scavenger Hunt page; use this page to write down your answers as you search the Web. Submit your completed page to your instructor.

3. Who Wants to Be a Computer Genius?

Click Computer Genius to find out if you are a computer genius. Directions on how to play the game will display. When you are ready to play, click the PLAY button. Submit your score to your instructor.

4. Wheel of Terms

Click Wheel of Terms to reinforce important terms you learned in this chapter by playing the Shelly Cashman Series version of this popular game. Directions on how to play the game will display. When you are ready to play, click the PLAY button. Submit your score to your instructor.

5. Career Corner

Click Career Corner to display the USA TODAY page. Scroll down, click Career Center, and click a link of interest. Write a brief report on what you discovered. Submit the report to your instructor.

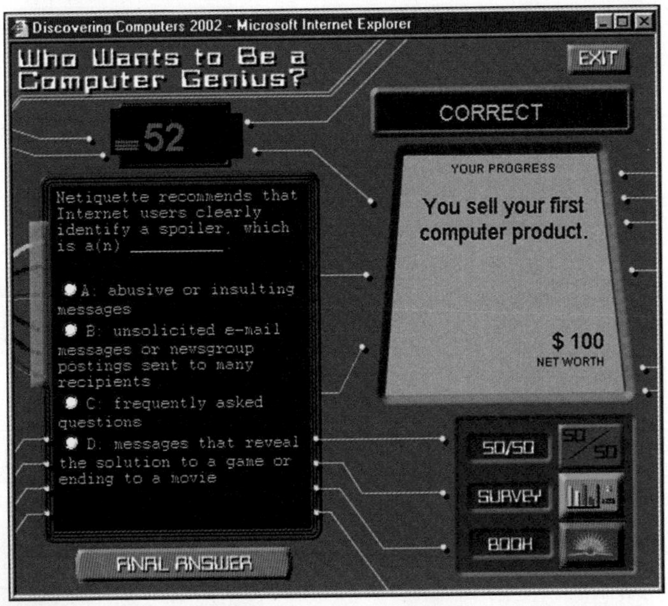

6. Search Sleuth

Click Search Sleuth to learn search techniques that will help make you a research expert. Submit the completed assignment to your instructor.

7. Crossword Puzzle Challenge

Click Crossword Puzzle Challenge. Complete the puzzle to reinforce skills you learned in this chapter. Directions on how to play the game will display. When you are ready to play, click the PLAY button. Submit the completed puzzle to your instructor.

8. Practice Test

Click Practice Test. Answer each question. When completed, enter your name and click the Grade Test button to submit the quiz for grading. Make a note of any missed questions. If required, print a copy to submit to your instructor.

Checkpoint

Web Instructions: To display this page from the Web, start your browser and enter the URL scsite.com/dc2002/ch2/check.htm. Click the links for current and additional information. To experience the animation and interactivity, Shockwave and Flash Player must be installed on your computer (download by clicking here.).

LABEL THE FIGURE

Instructions: Identify each part of the URL and e-mail address.

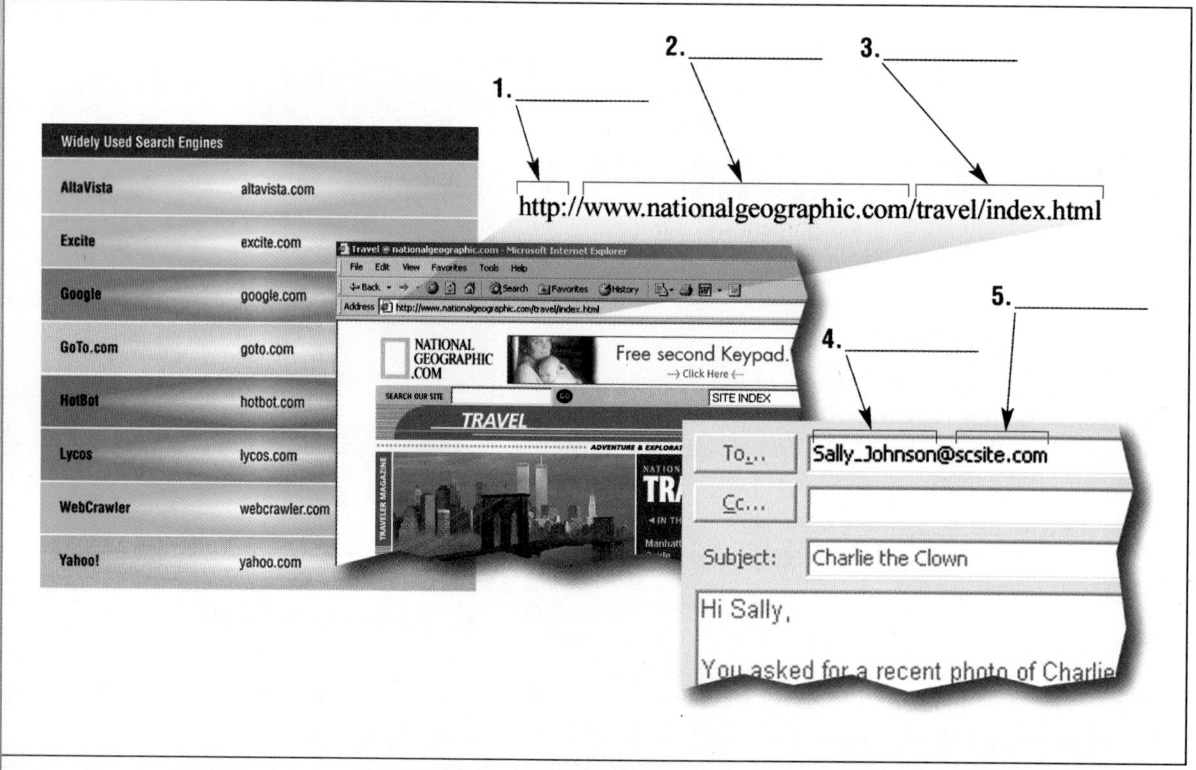

MATCHING

Instructions: Match each term from the column on the left with the best description from the column on the right.

_______ 1. FTP
_______ 2. chat
_______ 3. mailing list
_______ 4. newsgroup
_______ 5. e-mail

a. A real-time typed conversation that takes place on a computer.
b. A list of names and addresses.
c. An Internet standard that allows you to upload and download files with other computers.
d. The transmission of messages and files via a computer network.
e. A group of e-mail names and addresses given a single name.
f. A real-time Internet communications service that notifies you when one or more people are online.
g. An online area in which users conduct written discussions about a particular subject.

Checkpoint

MULTIPLE CHOICE

Instructions: Select the letter of the correct answer for each of the following questions.

1. On a Web page, a(n) __________ is a built-in connection to another related Web page or part of a Web page.
   a. graphic
   b. animation
   c. link
   d. keyword
2. A(n) __________ is a computer that delivers Web pages you request.
   a. Web server
   b. client
   c. FTP server
   d. mail server
3. To participate in a newsgroup, you use a program called a __________ .
   a. discussion
   b. thread
   c. newsreader
   d. message board
4. A Web page that offers a variety of Internet services from a single, convenient location is called a(n) __________ .
   a. Web community
   b. informational Web page
   c. news Web page
   d. portal
5. __________ occurs when a server automatically downloads content to your computer at regular intervals.
   a. Pull technology
   b. Push technology
   c. Online technology
   d. M-commerce

SHORT ANSWER

Instructions: Write a brief answer to each of the following questions.

1. What is a network? __________ What is a node? __________ What is an ISP? __________
2. How are a Web page, Web site, and home page different? __________ What is a URL? __________
3. What is a search engine? __________ What is a plug-in? __________ Why would you need a plug-in? __________
4. What does it mean to subscribe to a newsgroup? __________ What is the difference between a newsgroup and Usenet? __________ What is a threaded discussion? __________
5. What is FTP? __________ What is an FTP site? __________ Why would someone use an FTP server? __________

WORKING TOGETHER

Instructions: Working with a group of your classmates, complete the following team exercise.

Your textbook lists six different types of Web pages. Use the Internet to find at least two examples of each type of Web page. Create a report listing the type of Web page, the URL or Web site address, and an explanation of why the Web page fits the particular category. Then, describe what multimedia elements your team found on each Web page. Share your report and/or a PowerPoint presentation with the class.

Web Instructions: To display this page from the Web, start your browser and enter the URL scsite.com/dc2002/ch2/lab.htm. Click the links or current and additional information.

1 Online Services

This exercise uses Windows 98 procedures. What online services are available on your computer? Right-click the Online Services icon on the desktop and then click Open on the shortcut menu. What online services have shortcut icons in the Online Services window? Right-click each icon and then click Properties on each shortcut menu. Click the General tab. When was each icon created? Close the dialog box and then click the Close button to close the Online Services window.

Understanding Internet Properties

2 Right-click an icon for a Web browser that displays on your desktop. Click Properties on the shortcut menu. When the Internet Properties dialog box or Netscape Properties dialog box displays, click the General tab. Click the Question Mark button on the title bar and then click one of the buttons. Read the information in the pop-up window and then click the pop-up window to close it. Repeat the process for other areas of the dialog box. Click the Cancel button in the Internet Properties dialog box.

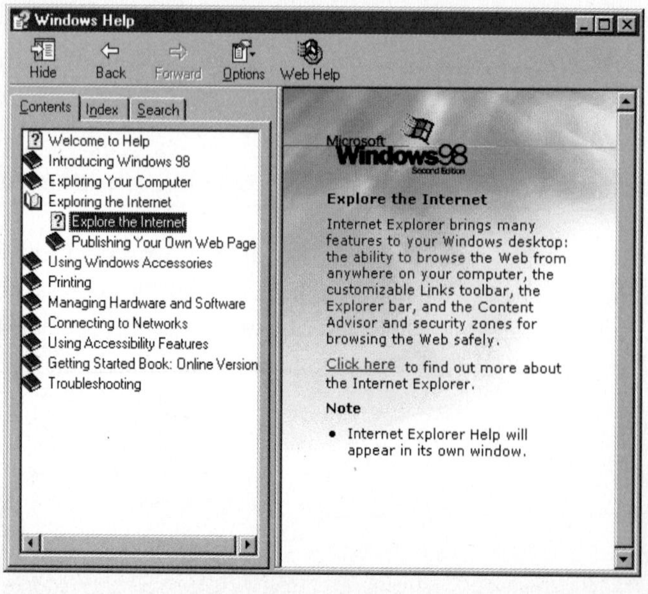

3 Determining Dial-Up Networking Connections

This exercise uses Windows 98 procedures. Click the Start button on the taskbar. Point to Programs on the Start menu, point to Accessories on the Program submenu, point to Communications on the Accessories submenu, and then click Dial-Up Networking on the Accessories submenu. When the Dial-Up Networking window opens, right-click an icon displayed in the window and then click Connect on the shortcut menu. Write down the User name and the Phone number. Close the Connect To dialog box and the Dial-Up Networking window.

Using Help to Understand the Internet

4 This exercise uses Windows 98 procedures. Click the Start button on the taskbar and then click Help on the Start menu. Click the Contents tab. Click the Exploring the Internet book and then click the Explore the Internet topic. Click the Click here link to find out more about Internet Explorer. Answer the following questions:

- How can you update your favorite Web sites and view them at your leisure?
- How can you move around the Web faster and easier with the Explorer bar?
- How can you browse the Web safely?
- How can you view Web pages in other languages?

Close the Microsoft Internet Explorer Help window and the Windows Help window.

5 Streaming Audio and Streaming Video

Review the chapter section on streaming audio and streaming video. Use PowerPoint to create a presentation describing the basics of streaming media. Search the Web for additional information and include what you discover as part of your presentation. Share your presentation with your class.

Web Work

Web Instructions: To display this page from the Web, start your browser and enter the URL scsite.com/dc2002/ch2/web.htm. To view At The Movies in exercise 1, RealPlayer must be installed on your computer (download by clicking here). To use the Shelly Cashman Series Connecting to the Internet Lab and The World Wide Web Lab from the Web, Shockwave and Flash Player must be installed on your computer (download by clicking here).

Chat Room Lawsuit

To view the Chat room Lawsuit movie, click the button to the left or click the Play button to the right. Watch the movie, and then complete the exercise by answering the questions below. Many companies are fed up with being trashed online and are fighting back with lawsuits. Most chat room posters offer legitimate criticisms and warnings, but instances of outright lies and intentional sabotage are a reality. In some cases, unsubstantiated comments have caused a company's stock to nose-dive and even caused bankruptcy. Tracking down the anonymous posters (by filing subpoenas against Internet providers, such as Yahoo! or America Online) raises free speech issues and threatens the free flow of information on the Web. Who deserves greater protection: the companies and their products, or individuals and the free flow of information on the Web? What agency should be the judge?

Shelly Cashman Series Connecting to the Internet Lab

Follow the instructions in Web Work 2 on page 1.47 to start and use the Shelly Cashman Series Connecting to the Internet Lab. If you are running from the Web, enter the URL www.scsite.com/sclabs/menu.htm or display the Web Work page (see instructions at the top of this page) and then click the button to the left.

Shelly Cashman Series The World Wide Web Lab

Follow the instructions in Web Work 2 on page 1.47 to start and use the Shelly Cashman Series the World Wide Web lab. If you are running from the Web, enter the URL, www.scsite.com/sclabs/menu.htm or display the Web Work page (see instructions at the top of this page) and then click the button to the left.

Internet Newsgroups

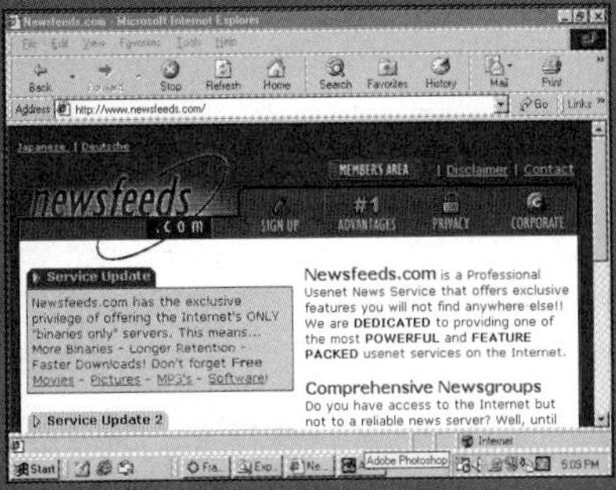

One of the more popular topics for Internet newsgroups is the Internet. Click the button to the left for a list of newsgroups. Find one or more newsgroups that discuss something about the Internet. Read the newsgroup postings and briefly summarize the topic under discussion. If you like, post a reply to a message.

In the News

In her book, *Caught in the Net*, Kimberly S. Young argues that the Internet can be addictive. Young's methodology and conclusions have been questioned by several critics, but Young remains resolute. She points out that at one time, no one admitted the existence of alcoholism. Click the button to the left and read a news article about the impact of Internet use on human behavior. What affect did the Internet have? Why? In your opinion, is the Internet's influence positive or negative? Why?

"When I was a child in Philadelphia, my father told me that I didn't need to memorize the contents of the Encyclopedia Britannica; I just needed to know how to find what is in it."

– Richard Saul Wurman, "Information Anxiety," 1989

GUIDE TO WORLD WIDE WEB SITES AND SEARCHING TECHNIQUES

The World Wide Web is an exciting and highly dynamic medium that has revolutionized the way people access information. You can display information on virtually any topic you can imagine, if you know the URL. If you do not know the URL, you must use a search tool because the Web has no bibliographic control. Statistics from the NEC Research Institute indicate that every second, 25 new Web pages are added to the more than 5.5 billion Web pages already on the Internet. Given this, finding the information you want can be a massive chore if you don't know the URL or how to use Web search tools.

To help you locate information, this special feature provides three resources: a topical list of some of the more popular Web sites, an introduction to searching techniques, and a list of portals with search capabilities.

WEB INSTRUCTIONS: *To gain World Wide Web access to additional and up-to-date information regarding this special feature, start your browser and enter the URL shown at the top of this page.*

Categories

Animation
Art
Business and Finance
Careers and Employment
Computers and Computing
Digital Music
Education
Entertainment
Environment
Fitness
Government and Politics
Health and Medicine
History
Humor
Internet
Internet Security
Law
Museums
News Sources
Reference
Robotics
Science
Shopping
Society
Sports
Travel
Unclassified
Weather
Zines

CATEGORY/SITE NAME	LOCATION	COMMENT
Animation		
Animation Express	animationexpress.com	Cool animations
RGB gallery	hotwired.lycos.com/rgb	Art animations
Shockwave	shockwave.com	Cool Shockwave animations
Art		
Fine Art Forum	msstate.edu/fineart_online/home.html	Art and technology net news
Leonardo da Vinci	metalab.unc.edu/wm/paint/auth/vinci	Works of the famous Italian artist and thinker
The Andy Warhol Museum	warhol.org	Famous American pop artist
WebMuseum	www.louvre.fr/louvrea.htm	Web version of Louvre Museum, Paris
World Wide Arts Resources	wwar.com	Links to many art sites
Business and Finance		
All Business Network	all-biz.com	Links to Web business information
FinanCenter.com	financenter.com	Personal finance information
MSN MoneyCentral	moneycentral.msn.com	Microsoft's Financial portal
Morningstar, Inc.	morningstar.com	Mutual fund site
PC Quote	www.pcquote.com	Free delayed stock quotes
Quicken	quicken.com	Personal financial advice
Raging Bull	ragingbull.com	Real-time stock quotes
SiliconInvestor	siliconinvestor.com	Stock chat for technology investors
SmartMoney	smartmoney.com	Live snapshot of the stock market
Stockgroup Research	smallcapcenter.com	Investment information
The Wall Street Journal	interactive.wsj.com	Financial news page
Yahoo! Finance	quote.yahoo.com	Free delayed stock quotes
Careers and Employment		
CareerMagazine	careermag.com	Career articles and information
CareerBuilder	careerpath.com	Job listings from U.S. newspapers
Headhunter	headhunter.net	Jobs from around the world
Job Options	joboptions.com	Searchable job database
Monster.com	monster.com	Job finder

For an updated list: scsite.com/dc2002/ch2/websites.htm

CATEGORY/SITE NAME	LOCATION	COMMENT
Computers and Computing		
Computer companies	Insert name or initials of most computer companies before .com to find their Web sites. Examples: ibm.com, microsoft.com, dell.com	
Expertcity	expertcity.com	Live experts offer technical support
Internet.com	internet.com	E-Business and Technology Network
MIT Media Lab	www.media.mit.edu	Information on computer trends
The Computer Museum	computerhistory.org	Exhibits and history of computing
The PC Guide	pcguide.com	PC Reference Information
Virtual Computer Library	www.utexas.edu/computer/vcl	Information on computers and computing
Virtual Museum of Computing	www.museums.reading.ac.uk/vmoc	History of computing and online computer-base exhibits
ZDNet	zdnet.com	Downloads and product reviews
Digital Music		
Live Concerts	liveconcerts.com	RealMedia streamed concerts
MP3.com	mp3.com	Music files
Sonique	sonique.com	MP3 player made by aliens!!
This American Life	thislife.org	Public Radio program
Education		
CollegeNET	collegenet.com	Searchable database of more than 2,000 colleges and universities
EdLinks	webpages.marshall.edu/~jmullens/edlinks.html	Links to many educational sites
The Open University	www.open.ac.uk	Independent study courses from the U.K.
UMUC Distance Education	umuc.edu/distance	University of Maryland distance education
WiredScholar	www.wiredscholar.com	Information on financing an education
Entertainment		
Classics World	bmgclassics.com	Classical music information
Internet Movie Database	imdb.com	Movies
Internet Underground Music Archive	www.iuma.com	Underground music database
Mr. Showbiz	mrshowbiz.com	Information on latest films
Music Boulevard	musicblvd.com	Search for and buy all types of music
Playbill Online	playbill.com	Theater news
Rock & Roll Hall of Fame	rockhall.com	Cleveland museum site

For an updated list: scsite.com/dc2002/ch2/websites.htm

CATEGORY/SITE NAME	LOCATION	COMMENT
Environment		
EnviroLink Network	envirolink.org	Environmental information
Greenpeace	greenpeace.org	Environmental activism
U.S. Environmental Protection Agency (EPA)	epa.gov	U.S. government environmental news
Fitness		
24 Hour Fitness	24hourfitness.com	A health and fitness community
GlobalFitness.com	globalfitness.com	Health and fitness
Government and Politics		
CIA	www.odci.gov	Political and economic information on countries
Democratic National Committee	democrats.org	Democratic party news
FedWorld	fedworld.gov	Links to U.S. government sites
PoliSci.com	polisci.com	Politics on the Web
Republican National Committee	rnc.org	GOP party news
The Library of Congress	www.loc.gov	Variety of U.S. government information
The White House	www.whitehouse.gov	Take a tour and learn about the occupants
U.S. Census Bureau	www.census.gov	Population and other statistics
United Nations	www.un.org	Latest UN projects and information
Health and Medicine		
Centers for Disease Control and Prevention (CDC)	www.cdc.gov	How to prevent and control disease
Cornucopia of Disability Information (CODI)	codi.buffalo.edu	Resource for disability products and services
The Interactive Patient	medicus.marshall.edu/medicus.htm	Simulates visit to doctor
Women's Medical Health Page	cbull.com/health.htm	Articles and links to other sites
History		
American Memory	rs6.loc.gov/amhome.html	American history
Don Mabry's Historical Text Archive	geocities.com/Athens/Forum/9061/USA/usa.html	U.S. documents, photos, and databases
Virtual Library History	www.ukans.edu/history/VL	Organized links to history sites
World History Archives	www.hartford-hwp.com/archives	Links to history sites

For an updated list: scsite.com/dc2002/ch2/websites.htm

CATEGORY/SITE NAME	LOCATION	COMMENT
Humor		
Ucomics.com	calvinandhobbes.com	Comic strip gallery
Comedy Central	comcentral.com	Comedy TV network online
Late Show with David Letterman	marketing.cbs.com/lateshow	Letterman's nightly show including archived Top 10 lists
The Dilbert Zone	unitedmedia.com/comics/dilbert	Humorous insights about the workplace
Internet		
Beginners' Central	northernwebs.com/bc	Beginners' guide to the Internet
Glossary of Internet	matisse.net/files/glossary.html	Matisse Enzer's definitions of Internet
WWW Frequently Asked Questions	www.boutell.com/faq/oldfaq/index.html	Common Web questions and answers
Internet Security		
F-secure Hoax warnings	datafellows.com/news/hoax.htm	Industry standard information source for new virus hoaxes and false alerts
Secure Solutions Experts (SSE)	www.sse.ie/securitynews.html	Over 100 of the best information security news sites, many of which are updated daily
Law		
APB News.com	apbnews.com	Crime, justice, and safety news
Copyright Website	benedict.com	Provides copyright information
FindLaw	findlaw.com	Law resource portal
KuesterLaw	kuesterlaw.com	Technology law resource
Privacy Rights Clearinghouse	privacyrights.org	Information on privacy issues
Museums		
Smithsonian Institution	www.si.edu	Information and links to Smithsonian museums
The National Gallery of Art, Washington	aga.gov	Plan a visit or take an online tour
U.S. Holocaust Memorial Museum	ushmm.org	Dedicated to World War II victims
University of California Museum of Paleontology	www.ucmp.berkeley.edu	Information on dinosaurs and other exhibits

For an updated list: scsite.com/dc2002/ch2/websites.htm

CATEGORY/SITE NAME	LOCATION	COMMENT
News Sources		
CNET	cnet.com	Technology news
Cable News Network	cnn.com	CNN all-news network
Enews.com, Inc.	enews.com	An electronic newstand
Time	time.com	Excerpts from Time-Warner magazines
USA TODAY	usatoday.com	Latest U.S. and international news
Wired News	wired.com	Wired magazine online and HotWired network
Reference		
About.com, Inc.	about.com	Search engine and portal
AskEric Virtual Library	askeric.org/Virtual	Educational resources
AskJeeves	askjeeves.com	Search engine
Bartlett's Quotations	www.columbia.edu/acis/bartleby/bartlett	Organized, searchable database of famous quotes
Internet Public Library	ipl.org	Literature and reference works
The New York Public Library	www.nypl.org	Extensive reference and research material
Webopedia	webopedia.com	Online dictionary and search engine
Robotics		
Remotebot.net	remotebot.net	Control a robot with your Netscape Web browser; interactive Robotic Museum
Robotics and Intelligent Machines Laboratory	robotics.eecs.berkeley.edu	Robotics and mechanical and electrical engineering
University of Massachusetts Robotics Information	www-robotics.cs.umass.edu/robotics.html	Robotics resource index page
Science		
American Institute of Physics	www.aip.org	Physics research information
Exploratorium	exploratorium.edu	Interactive science exhibits
Internet Chemistry Index	chemie.de	List of chemistry information sites
National Institute for Discovery Science (NIDS)	www.accessnv.com/nids	Research of anomalous phenomena
Solar System Simulator	space.jpl.nasa.gov	JPL's spyglass on the cosmos
The NASA Homepage	www.nasa.gov	Information on U.S. space program
The Nine Planets	www.nineplanets.org	Tour the solar system's nine planets

For an updated list: scsite.com/dc2002/ch2/websites.htm

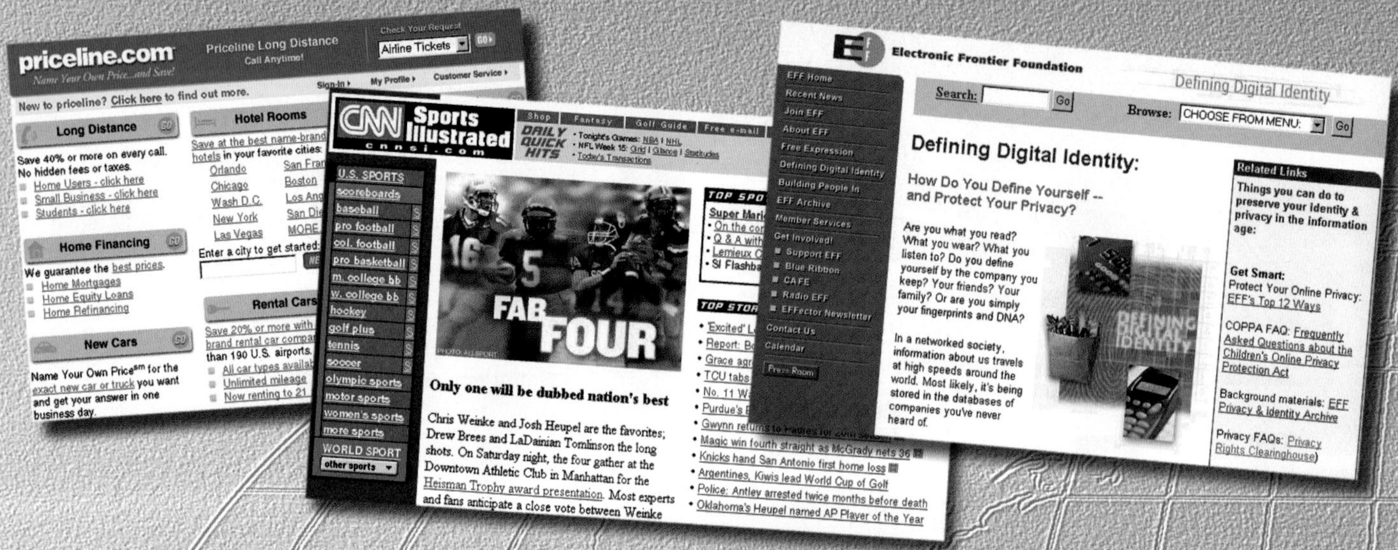

CATEGORY/SITE NAME	LOCATION	COMMENT
Shopping		
Amazon.com	amazon.com	Books and gifts
Bartleby	bartleby.com	Great Books online
BizRate	bizrate.com	Rates e-commerce sites
BizWeb	bizweb.com	Search for products from more than 45,753 companies
CNET Shopper	shopper.com	Computer and electronic products
CommerceNet	www.commerce.net	Non-profit with focus on B2B e-commerce
Consumer World	consumerworld.org	Consumer information
Ebay	ebay.com	Online auctions
Greenlight	greenlight.com	Automobile buying site
Internet Bookshop	www.bookshop.co.uk	780,000 titles on more than 2,000 subjects
PriceLine.com	priceline.com	Merchandise from groceries to airfare; name your price
ShopNow	Shopnow.com	Specialty stores, hot deals, computer products
Society		
Association for Computing Machinery (ACM)	acm.org	World's first educational and scientific computing society
Center for Applied Ethics	www.ethics.ubc.ca/resources/computer	Computer and information ethic resources
Center for Computing and Society Responsibility	www.ccsr.cse.dmu.ac.uk/index.html	Social and ethical impacts of information and communication technologies
Civil Society Democracy Project	cpsr.org	A public-interest alliance of computer scientists and others concerned about the impact of computer technology on society
Computers and Society	acm.org/sigcas	Special interest group within Association for Computing Machinery (ACM)
Electronic Frontier Foundation	eff.org	Protecting rights and promoting freedom
Electronic Privacy Information Center	epic.org	Links to latest new regarding privacy issues
International Center for Information Ethics (ICIE)	infoethics.net	An academic Web site on information ethics
International Federation for Information Processing (IFIP)	www.info.fundp.ac.be/~jbl/IFIP/cadresIFIP.html	Computers and social accountability
ISWorld Net Professional Ethics	www.cityu.edu.hk/is/ethics/ethics.htm	Practice of ethics in the information systems profession
The Privacy Page	privacy.org	Current privacy issues

For an updated list: scsite.com/dc2002/ch2/websites.htm

CATEGORY/SITE NAME	LOCATION	COMMENT
Sports		
ESPN SportsZone	espn.com	Latest sports news
NBA Basketball	nba.com	Information and links to team sites
NFL Football	nfl.com	Information and links to team sites
Sports Illustrated	cnnsi.com	Leading sports magazine
Travel		
CitySearch	citysearch.com	United States and international city guides
Excite City.Net	excite.com/travel	Guide to world cities
InfoHub Specialty Travel Guide	infohub.com	Worldwide travel information
Lonely Planet Online	www.lonelyplanet.com	Budget travel guides and stories
Expedia.com	expedia.msn.com	Complete travel resource
Travelocity.com	travelocity.com	Online travel agency
TravelWebSM	travelweb.com	Places to stay
Unclassified		
Cool site of the Day	cool.infi.net	Different site each day
Cupid's Network™	cupidnet.com	Links to dating resources
Taxi Cam	ny-taxi.com	NYC from a taxi Web cam
Where's George?	wheresgeorge.com	Dollar bill locator
Zing	zing.com	Online photo community
Weather		
Intellicast	intellicast.com	International weather and skiing information
The Weather Channel	weather.com	National and local forecasts
Weather Underground	wunderground.com	Weather maps
Zines		
AFU & Urban Legends Archive	urbanlegends.com	Urban legends
Breakup Girl	breakupgirl.com	Saving love lives all over the world
Rock School	rockschool.com	Everything you need to know about being in a rock band
The Smoking Gun	thesmokinggun.com	Confidential documents

For an updated list: scsite.com/dc2002/ch2/websites.htm

WORLD WIDE WEB SEARCH TOOLS

Successful searching of the Web involves two key steps:

1. Briefly describe the information you are seeking. Start by identifying the main idea or concept in your topic and determine any synonyms, alternate spellings, or variant word forms for the concept.
2. Use the brief description with a search tool to display links to pages containing the desired information.

The two most common search tools are subject directories and search engines. You use a **subject directory** by clicking through its collection of categories and sub-categories until you reach the information you want. You use a **search engine** to search for a keyword. The following sections describe how to use a subject directory and a search engine.

Using a Subject Directory

A subject directory provides categorized lists of links. These categorized lists are arranged by subject and then displayed in a series of menus. Using this type of search tool, you can locate a particular topic by starting from the top and clicking links through the different levels, going from the general to the specific. Each time you click a category link, the search tool displays a page of sub-category links from which you again choose. You continue in this fashion until the search tool displays a list of Web pages on the desired topic. Browsing a subject directory requires that you make assumptions about the topic's hierarchical placement within the categorized list.

For the following example, assume you have been assigned the task of writing a research paper on Mark Twain's childhood. The assignment requires that you include at least one Web page citation. This example uses the Yahoo! (yahoo.com) search directory to locate information on Mark Twain's childhood.

1 Launch your browser and enter the URL yahoo.com in the Address box. When the Yahoo! home page displays, point to the Literature link below Arts & Humanities as shown in Figure 1. You point to Literature because that is the category in which Mark Twain made his contributions.

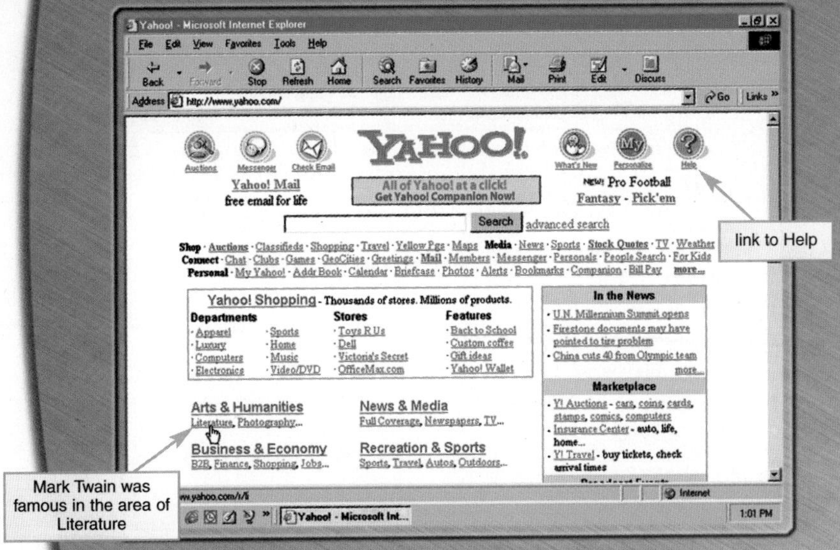

Figure 1 Yahoo! home page.

2 Click Literature. When the Literature page displays, scroll down and point to the Authors link as shown in Figure 2. You point to Authors because Mark Twain was an author. Each time you click a category link, you move closer to the topic.

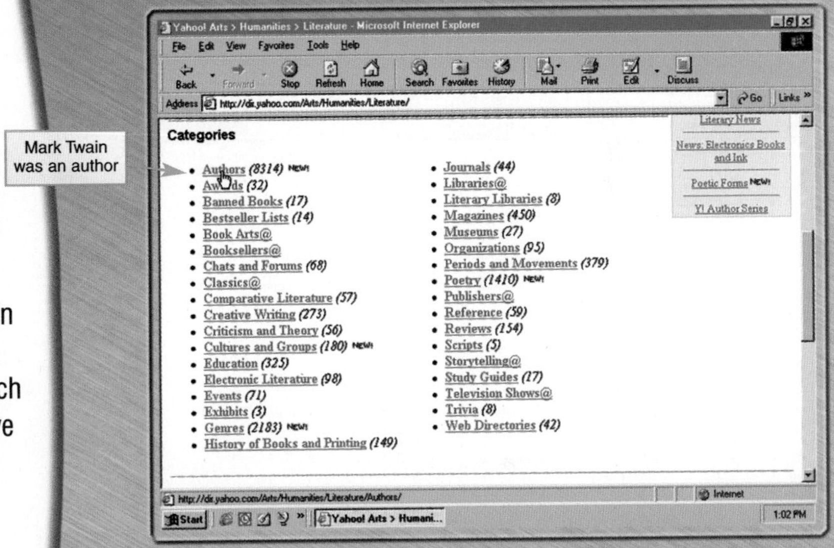

Figure 2 Literature categories.

3 Click Authors. When the Authors page displays, point to the Literary Fiction link as shown in Figure 3. You point to Literary Fiction because that is the area of literature in which Mark Twain specialized.

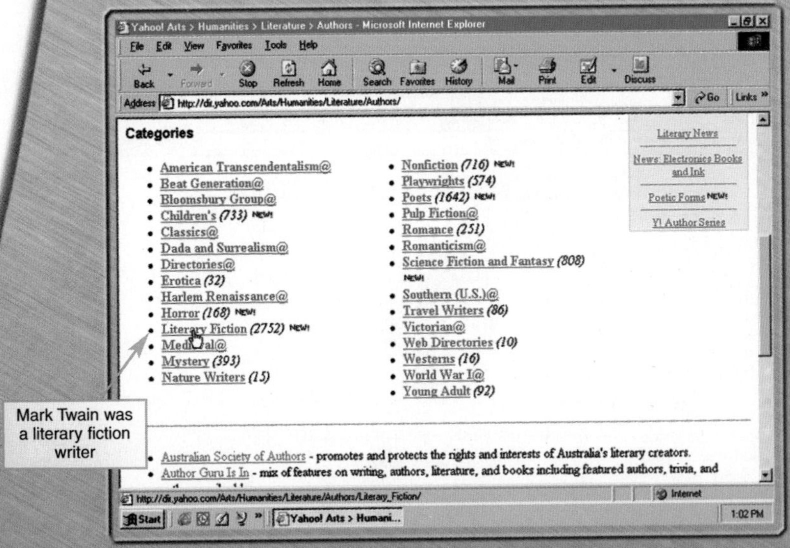

Figure 3 Authors categories.

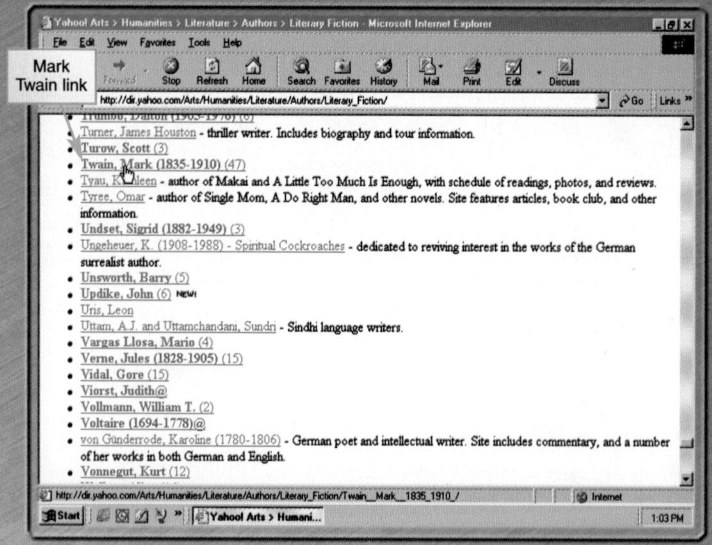

Figure 4 Literary Fiction categories.

4

Click Literary Fiction. When the Literary Fiction page displays, scroll down and point to the Twain, Mark (1835 - 1910) link as shown in Figure 4.

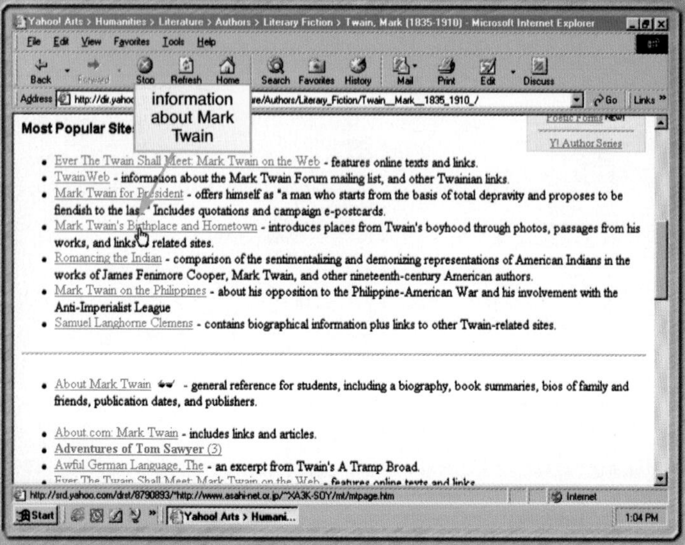

Figure 5 Twain, Mark (1835-1910) categories.

5

Click Twain, Mark (1835 - 1910). When the Twain, Mark (1835 - 1910) page displays, scroll down and point to the Mark Twain's Birthplace and Hometown link as shown in Figure 5.

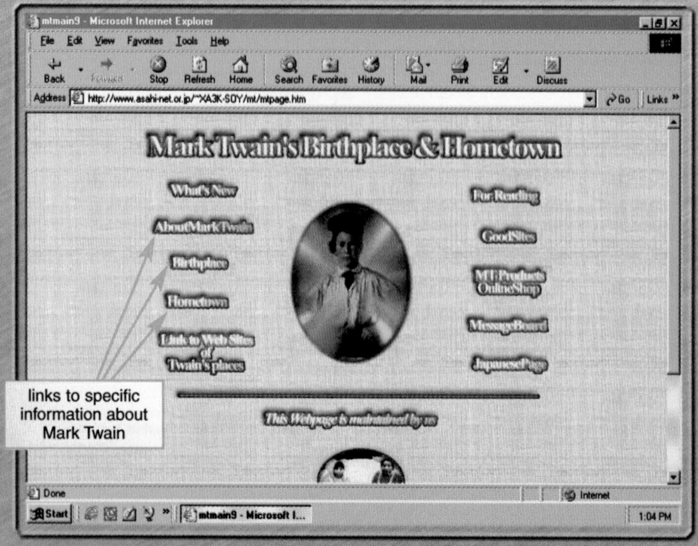

Figure 6 Mark Twain's Birthplace and Hometown Web page.

6

Click Mark Twain's Birthplace and Hometown. When the Mark Twain's Birthplace and Hometown page displays (Figure 6), one at a time, click the links. Use the browser's Back button to return to Mark Twain's Birthplace and Hometown page after viewing the page associated with each link.

With just a few clicks, the Yahoo! search directory displays information about Mark Twain's childhood. The Mark Twain sub-category page in Figure 6 shows several links to his writings, as well as to pages describing his life and times.

The major problem with a search directory is deciding which categories to choose as you work through the menus of links presented. For additional information on how to use the Yahoo! search directory, click the Help link in the upper-right corner of its home page (Figure 1).

Using a Search Engine

Search engines require that you enter search text or keywords (single word, words, or phrase) that defines what you are looking for, rather than clicking through menus of links. Search engines often respond with results that include thousands of links to Web pages, many of which have little or no bearing on the information you are seeking. You can eliminate the superfluous pages by carefully crafting a keyword that limits the search. The following example uses the Google search engine to search for the phrase, mark twain childhood.

1 Launch your browser and enter the URL `google.com` in the Address box. When the Google home page displays, type `mark twain childhood` in the Search box and then point to the Google Search button as shown in Figure 7.

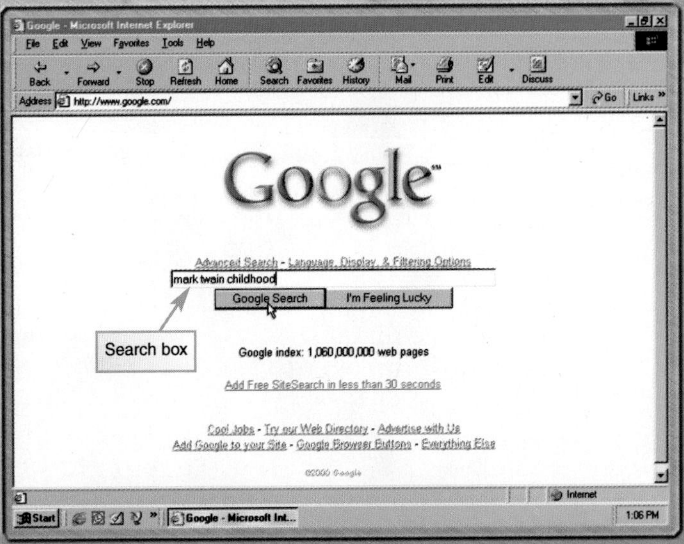

Figure 7 Google home page

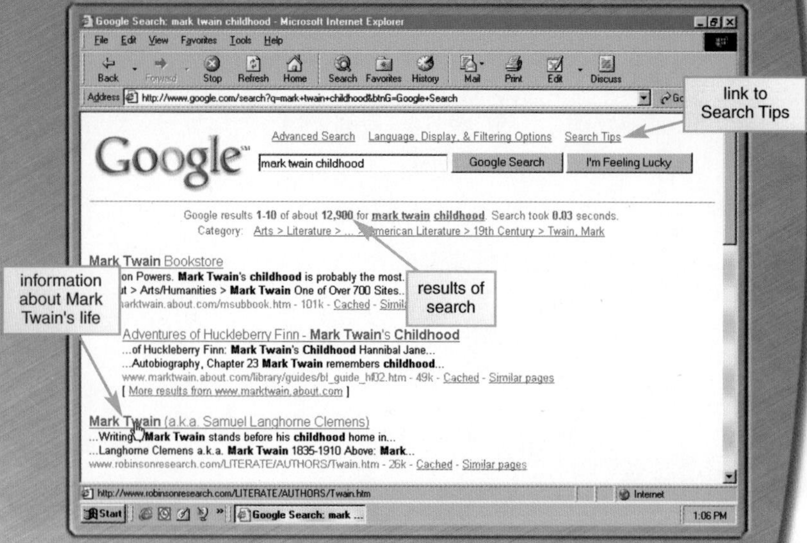

Figure 8 Google search results.

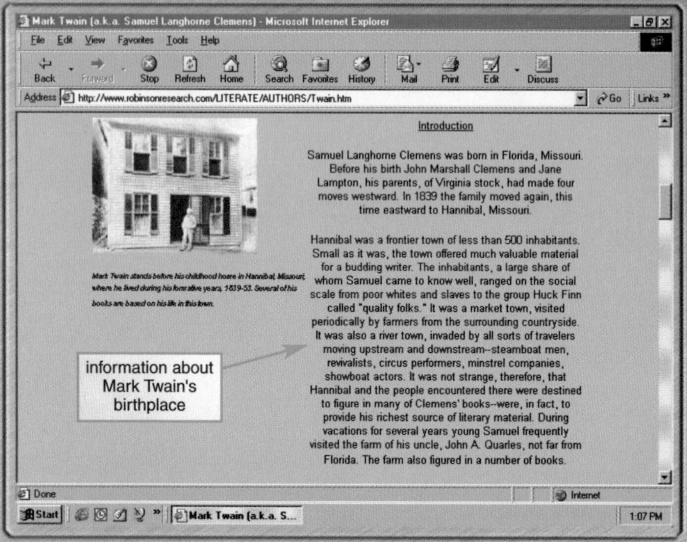

Figure 9 Web page describing Mark Twain's early years.

Click the Google Search button. When the results of the search display, scroll through the links and read the descriptions. Point to the Mark Twain (a.k.a. Samuel Langhorne Clemens) link as shown in Figure 8.

Click the Mark Twain (a.k.a. Samuel Langhorne Clemens) link. A Web page displays describing Mark Twain's birthplace (Hannibal, Missouri) and early life (Figure 9).

The results in Figure 8 include nearly 13,000 links to Web pages concerning Mark Twain's childhood. Most search engines sequence the results based on how close the words in the keyword are to one another in the Web page titles and their descriptions. Thus, the first few links probably contain more relevant information. For additional information on how to use the Goggle search engine, click the Search Tips link in the upper-right corner of its home page (Figure 8).

Limiting the Search

If you enter a phrase with spaces between the keywords, most search engines return links to pages that include all of the words. Figure 10 lists some common operators, commands, and special characters you can use to refine your search.

Guidelines to Successful Searching

You can improve your Web searches by following these guidelines.

1. Use nouns as keywords, and put the most important terms first in your keyword.
2. Use the asterisk (*) to find plurals of words. For example: retriev* returns retrieves, retrieval, retriever, and any other variation.
3. Type keywords in lowercase to find both lowercase and uppercase variations.
4. Use quotation marks to create phrases so the search engine finds the exact sequence of words.
5. Use a hyphen alternative. For example, use email e-mail.
6. Limit the search by language.
7. Use uppercase characters for Boolean operators in your search statements to differentiate between the words and operators.
8. Before you use a search engine, read its Help.
9. The Internet contains many search engines. If your search is unsuccessful with one search engine, try another.

CATEGORY OF OPERATOR	OPERATOR	KEYWORD EXAMPLES	DESCRIPTION
Boolean	AND (+)	art AND music smoking health hazards fish +pollutants +runoff	Requires both words to be in the page. No operator between words or the plus sign (+) are shortcuts for the Boolean operator AND.
	OR	mental illness OR insane canine OR dog OR puppy flight attendant OR stewardess OR steward	Requires only one of the words to be in the page.
	AND NOT (-)	auto AND NOT SUV AND NOT convertible computers -programming shakespeare -hamlet -(romeo+juliet)	Excludes page with the word following AND NOT. The minus sign (-) is a shortcut for the Boolean operator AND NOT.
Parentheses	( )	physics AND (relativity OR einstein)	Parentheses group portions of Boolean operators together.
Phrase Searching	" "	"harry potter" "19th century literature"	Requires the exact phrase within quotation marks to be in the page.
Wildcard	*	writ* clou*	The asterisk (*) at the end of words substitutes for any combination of characters.

Figure 10 Search engine keyword operators, commands, and special characters.

Popular Portals

Most portals include both a search engine and subject directory. Figure 11 contains a list of portals and their URLs where you can access search engines and subject directories to search the Web.

PORTALS	URL
AltaVista	altavista.com
Direct Hit	directhit.com
Excite	excite.com
GO	go.com
Google	google.com
HotBot	hotbot.com
LookSmart	looksmart.com
Netscape Search	search.netscape.com
MSN	search.msn.com
Yahoo!	yahoo.com

Figure 11 List of portals with search engines and directories.

CHAPTER 3

Application Software

The doorbell rings on Saturday afternoon. Surprised to see the mail carrier after opening the door, she hands you a huge stack of mail. She jokes about the quantity and that you are so popular the mail no longer fits in the mailbox. Sifting through the pile, you notice your bank statement and think back when it took hours to balance a statement.

Today, so much has changed. Checkbook registers are a thing of the past. Every other day you connect to the bank and copy your personal account transactions from the bank's computer to your computer. Your computerized checkbook balance always is up to date. It shows cleared checks, ATM withdrawals, debit card transactions, and automatic payments. Statement reconciliations literally take minutes.

The online payment feature also saves you time. Your bank automatically transfers the specified funds on certain dates from your checking account to the payees' accounts, assuring accurate and timely bill paying.

In the mail, you see an advertisement from your checkbook software vendor. Their new software version includes tax preparation capabilities. Now you can get help organizing and filing taxes electronically. This could mean no more endless days completing tax forms. You wonder what innovation might be next to help save you time.

OBJECTIVES

After completing this chapter, you will be able to:

- Define application software
- Understand how system software interacts with application software
- Identify the role of the user interface
- Explain how to start a software application
- Identify the widely used products and explain key features of productivity/business software applications, graphic design/multimedia software applications, home/personal/educational software applications, and communications software applications
- Identify various products available as Web applications
- Describe the learning aids available with many software applications

APPLICATION SOFTWARE

Application software, also called a **software application** or an **application**, consists of programs that perform specific tasks for users. Application software is used for a variety of reasons:

1. As a productivity/business tool
2. To assist with graphics and multimedia projects
3. To support household activities, for personal business, or for education
4. To facilitate communications

The table in Figure 3-1 categorizes popular types of application software by their general use. You likely will find yourself using software from more than one of these categories.

These four categories are not mutually exclusive. For example, an e-mail program is a communications tool and a productivity tool. A software suite is a productivity tool that also can include Web page authoring software. Both home users and business users have legal software.

A variety of application software is available as packaged software that you can purchase from software vendors in retail stores or on the Web. A **software package** is a specific software product, such as Microsoft Word. As discussed in Chapter 1, many software packages also are available as shareware, freeware, and public-domain software. These packages, however, usually have fewer capabilities than retail software packages.

CATEGORIES OF APPLICATION SOFTWARE

Productivity/ Business	Graphic Design/ Multimedia	Home/Personal/ Educational	Communications
• Word Processing	• Computer-Aided Design	• Integrated Software	• E-Mail
• Spreadsheet	• Desktop Publishing (Professional)	• Personal Finance	• Web Browser
• Presentation Graphics	• Paint/Image Editing (Professional)	• Legal	• Chat Rooms
• Database	• Video and Audio Editing	• Tax Preparation	• Newsgroups
• Personal Information Management	• Multimedia Authoring	• Desktop Publishing (Personal)	• Instant Messaging
• Software Suite	• Web Page Authoring	• Paint/Image Editing (Personal)	• Groupware
• Project Management		• Home Design/ Landscaping	• Videoconferencing
• Accounting		• Educational	
		• Reference	
		• Entertainment	

Figure 3-1 This table outlines the four major categories of popular application software. You probably will use software from more than one of these categories.

The Role of the System Software

Like most computer users, you probably are somewhat familiar with application software. To run any application software, however, your computer must be running another type of software — system software.

As described in Chapter 1, **system software** consists of programs that control the operations of the computer and its devices. As shown in Figure 3-2, system software serves as the interface between the user, the application software, and the computer's hardware. One type of system software, the **operating system**, contains instructions that coordinate all the activities among computer hardware devices. The operating system also contains instructions that allow you to run application software.

Before a computer can run any application software, the operating system must load from the hard disk (storage) into the computer's memory. Each time you start the computer, the operating system loads, or copies, into memory from the computer's hard disk. Once the operating system loads, it tells the computer how to perform functions. These functions include controlling computer resources and transferring data among input and output devices and memory.

While the computer is running, the operating system remains in memory. The operating system continues to run until power is removed from the computer.

Another type of system software is a utility program. A **utility program**, also called a **utility**, is a type of system software that performs a specific task, usually related to managing a computer, its devices, or its programs. One utility that every computer should have is an antivirus program. An **antivirus program** is a utility that prevents, detects, and removes viruses from a computer's memory or storage devices. A **virus** is a program that copies itself into other programs and spreads through multiple computers. Some malicious programmers intentionally write virus programs that destroy or corrupt data

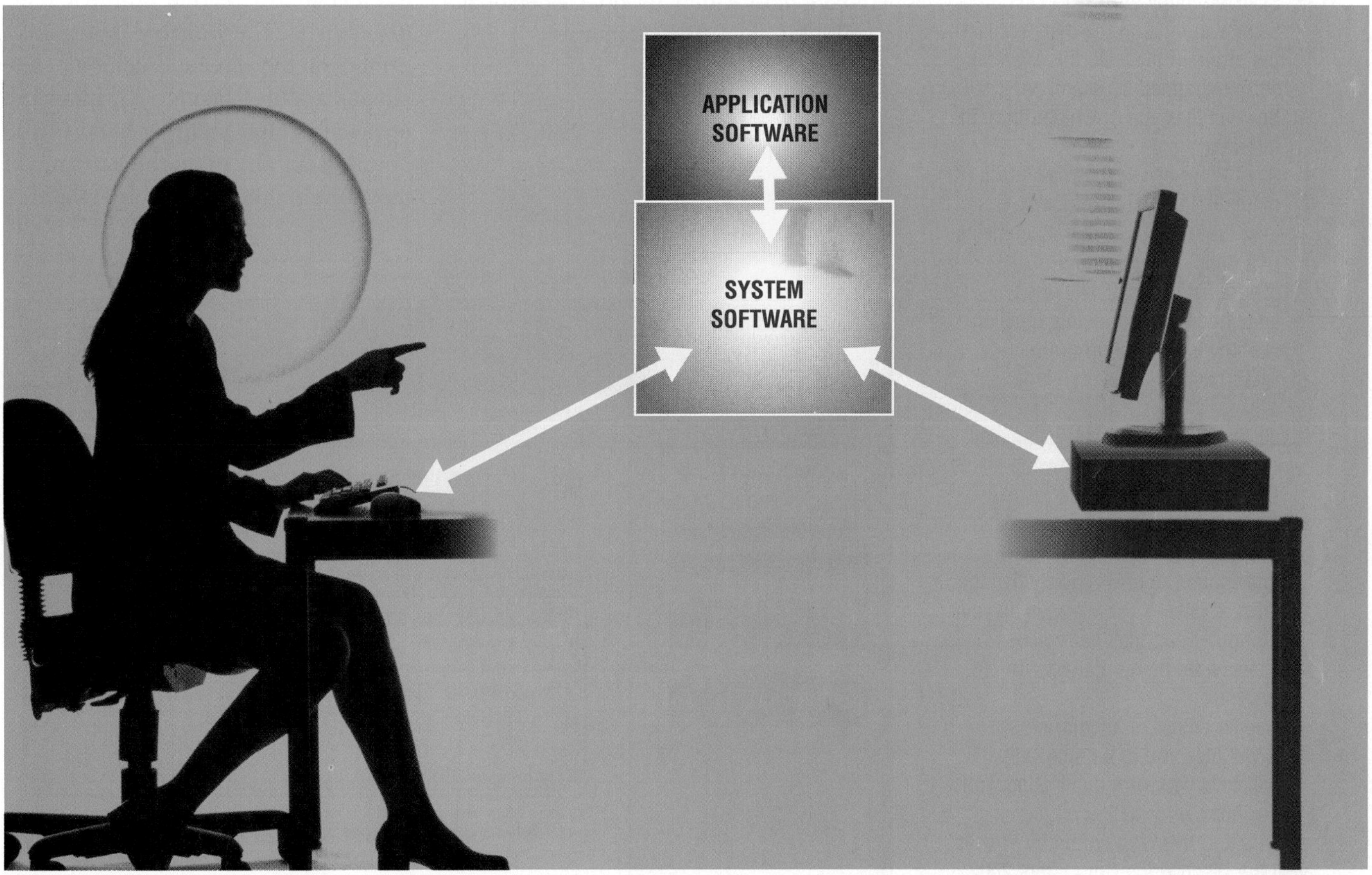

Figure 3-2 The user interacts with the system software or with the application software to control the hardware.

APPLY IT!

Virus Alert!

The number of computer viruses developed each day is astounding. Viruses can range from simply annoying ones to downright disastrous ones. If you read e-mail attachments, access shared files, insert disks into your computer, or download software from the Internet, you eventually will encounter a virus. Consider the following tips for preventing virus infections:

- Use a high-quality anti-virus program, and be sure to update it regularly. Use it to scan any files, programs, software, or floppy disks before you use them on your computer.
- Do not start your computer with a floppy disk in drive A, unless it is an uninfected rescue disk (see Chapter 8).
- Scan all floppy disks and Zip® disks. Scan every file on the disk, not just the program files. Do this even for shrink-wrapped software.
- Scan all files you download from the Internet.
- Scan Word or Excel e-mail attachments before you read them. It is best first to copy these attachments to a floppy disk. Some e-mail programs automatically open attachments. Disable this function within your e-mail program.
- Make backups of everything.

If you think your computer is infected, take special note of the following points:

- Do not panic.
- Do not erase or format everything in sight. You may lose valuable information. It is very likely that the virus is only in a few places on your computer and may be removed easily with the right anti-virus program.
- Keep a record of all your steps. It will help you to be thorough and will save you from duplicating work.

For more information on learning about and preventing computer viruses, visit the Discovering Computers 2002 Apply It Web page (**scsite.com/dc2002/apply.htm**) and click Chapter 3 Apply It #1.

on a computer. When you purchase a new computer, it often includes an antivirus software program (Figure 3-3). Chapter 8 discusses other commonly used utility programs.

The Role of the User Interface

You interact with software through its user interface. The **user interface** controls how you enter data or instructions and how information displays on the screen. Many of today's software programs have a graphical user interface. A **graphical user interface** (**GUI**) combines text, graphics, and other visual images to make software easier to use.

In 1984, Apple Computer introduced the Macintosh operating system, which used a GUI. Many software companies recognized the value of this easy-to-use interface and developed their own GUI software. Today's most widely used GUI personal computer operating system is Microsoft Windows.

Starting a Software Application

Both the Apple Macintosh and Microsoft Windows operating systems use the concept of a desktop to make the computer easier to use. The **desktop** is an on-screen work area that can display graphical elements such as icons, buttons, windows, menus, links, and dialog boxes. The Windows desktop shown in Figure 3-4 contains many icons and buttons.

An **icon** is a small image that displays on the screen to represent a program, a document, or some other object. A **button** is a graphical element that you activate to cause a specific action to take place. For example, one button may start the Web browser and another may start an e-mail program. Buttons usually are rectangular or circular in shape.

One way to activate a button is to click it with a mouse. As you move the mouse, the pointer on the screen also moves. The **pointer** is a small symbol on the screen. Common pointer shapes are an I-beam (I), block arrow ( ), and pointing hand ( ). To **click** an object on the screen, you move the pointer to the object and

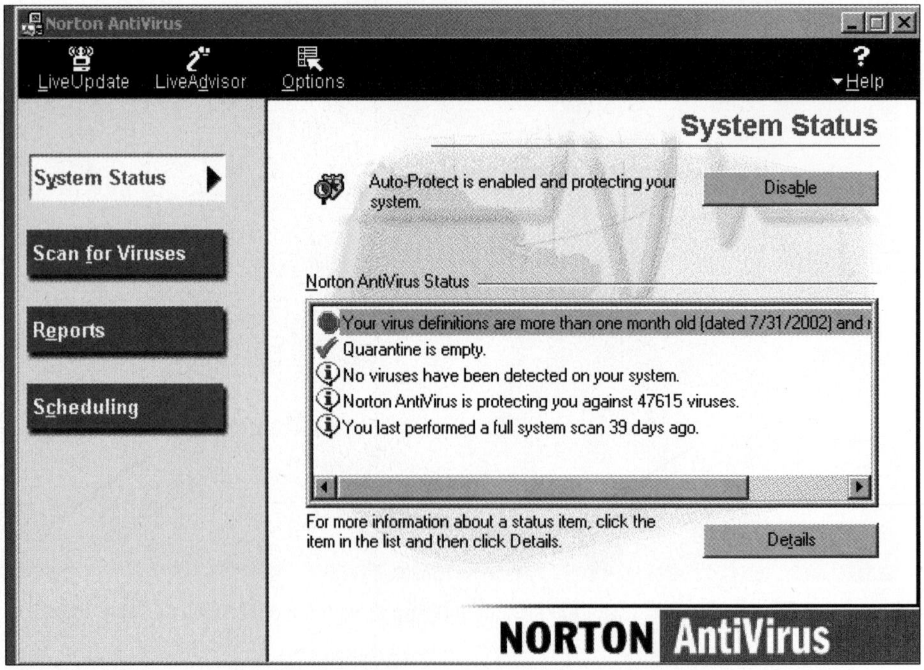

Figure 3-3 An antivirus program prevents, detects, and removes viruses from a computer's memory or storage devices.

then press and release a button on the mouse.

The Windows desktop contains a Start button in its lower-left corner. You can use the Start button to start an application. When you click the Start button, the Start menu displays on the desktop. A **menu** contains commands you can select. A **command** is an instruction that causes a computer program to perform a specific action.

Some menus have a submenu. A **submenu** is a menu that displays when you point to a command on a previous menu. As shown in Figure 3-5, when you click the Start button and point to the Programs command on the Start menu, the Programs submenu displays. Pointing to the Accessories command on the Programs submenu displays the Accessories submenu. Notice that the Accessories submenu contains several applications such as Calculator, Paint, and WordPad.

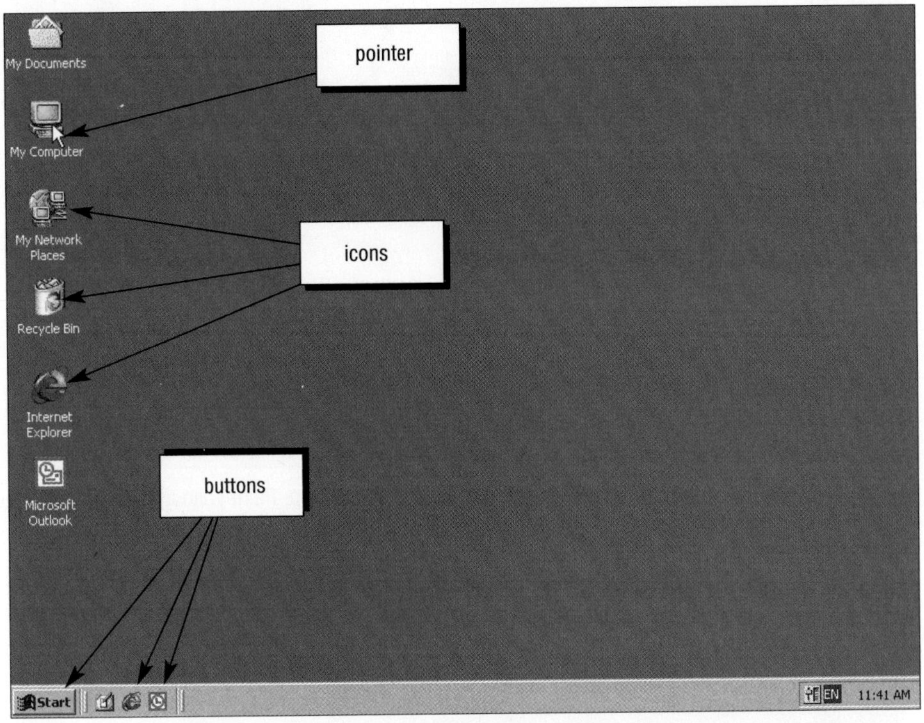

Figure 3-4 This Windows desktop shows a variety of icons and buttons.

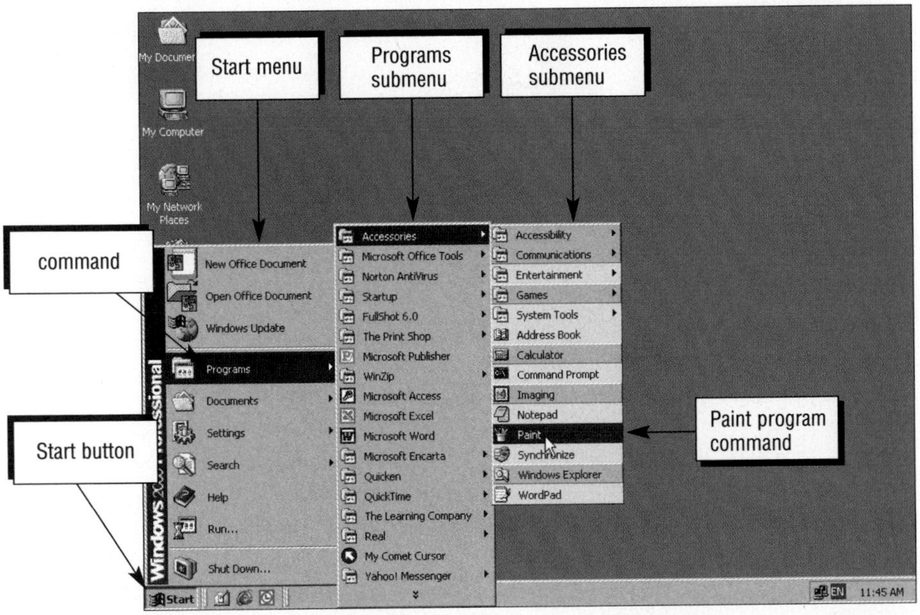

Figure 3-5 This figure shows the Start menu and the Programs and Accessories submenus. Some commands in menus are followed by a right arrowhead (▶), which indicates a submenu of additional commands exists.

TECHNOLOGY TRAILBLAZER

PAUL **ALLEN**

Owning the Portland Trail Blazers and the Seattle Seahawks may seem unlikely investments for an individual who helped create one of the world's largest computer companies. But for Microsoft co-founder Paul Allen, these NBA and NFL franchises are opportunities to showcase his savvy business skills. So are Allen's 140 other diverse technology, entertainment, and new media enterprises. He is chairman of Vulcan Northwest, owns a 24 percent equity stake in Dreamworks SKG, and is responsible for Experience Music Project, a shrine for electric guitarist Jimi Hendrix. He also shares his expertise with the community through his six charitable foundations.

Allen met Bill Gates when they attended high school together in Seattle in the late 1960s. Allen was working in Boston in 1975 as a programmer at Honeywell when he saw an advertisement for the first microcomputer. He went to Gates' dorm room at Harvard and convinced Gates to help him develop software for this machine. Their creation laid Microsoft's foundation.

Allen became the company's head of research and new product development and helped bring many of the company's highest-profile products to market. Today he serves as a senior strategy adviser to top Microsoft executives.

For more information on Paul Allen, visit the Discovering Computers 2002 People Web page (**scsite.com/dc2002/people.htm**) and click Paul Allen.

You can start an application by clicking its program name on a menu or submenu. Doing so instructs the operating system to start the application by transferring the program's instructions from a storage medium into memory. For example, if you click Paint on the Accessories submenu, Windows transfers the Paint program instructions from the computer's hard disk into memory.

Once started, an application displays in a window on the desktop. A **window** is a rectangular area of the screen that displays a program, data, and/or information. The top of a window has a **title bar**, which is a horizontal space that contains the window's name. Figure 3-6 shows the Paint window. This window contains an image that has been photographed with a digital camera.

In some cases, when you instruct a program to perform an activity such as printing, a dialog box displays. A **dialog box** is a special window a program displays to provide information, present available options, or request a response (Figure 3-7). For example, a Print dialog box gives you many printing options such as specifying a different printer, printing all or part of a document, or printing multiple copies.

Many applications use shortcut menus. A **shortcut menu**, also called a **context-sensitive menu**, is a menu that displays a list of commonly used commands for completing a task related to the current activity or selected item.

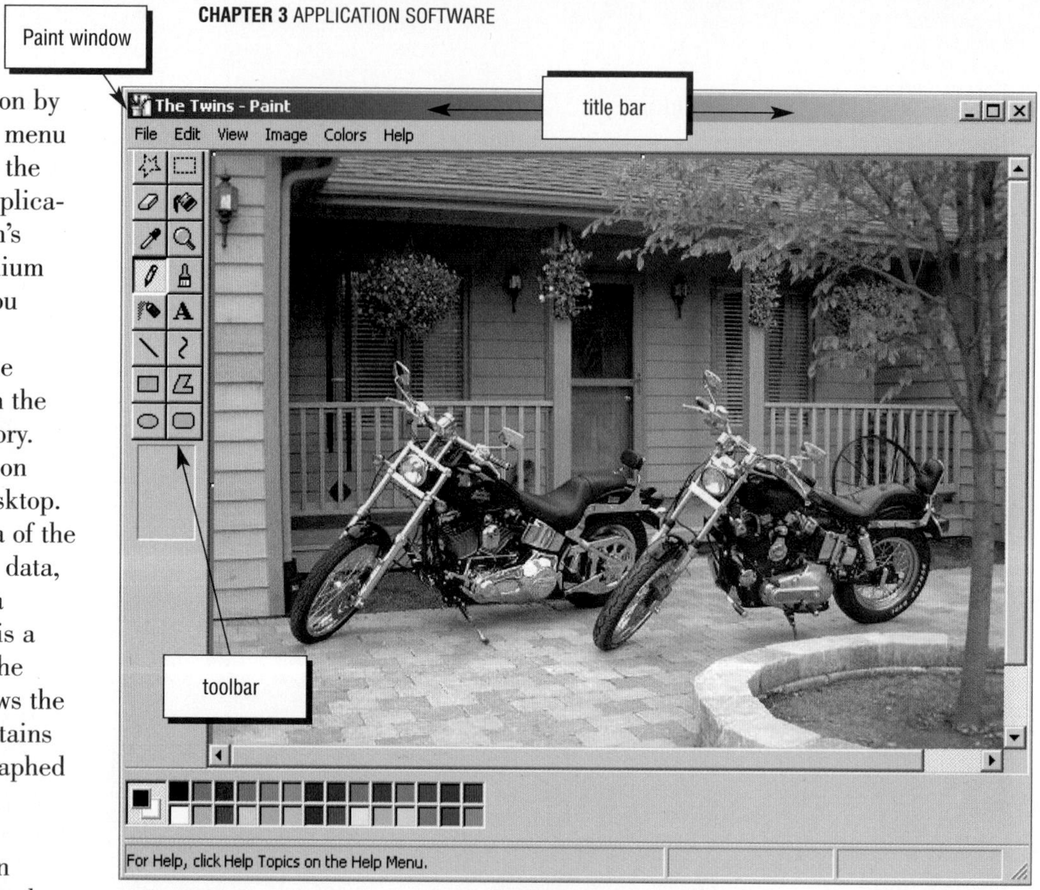

Figure 3-6 The Paint program displays in a window on the desktop. Paint is an application included with Windows that allows you to work with, manipulate, and print graphical images. Many applications contain a toolbar, which is a row or column of buttons for commonly used tasks.

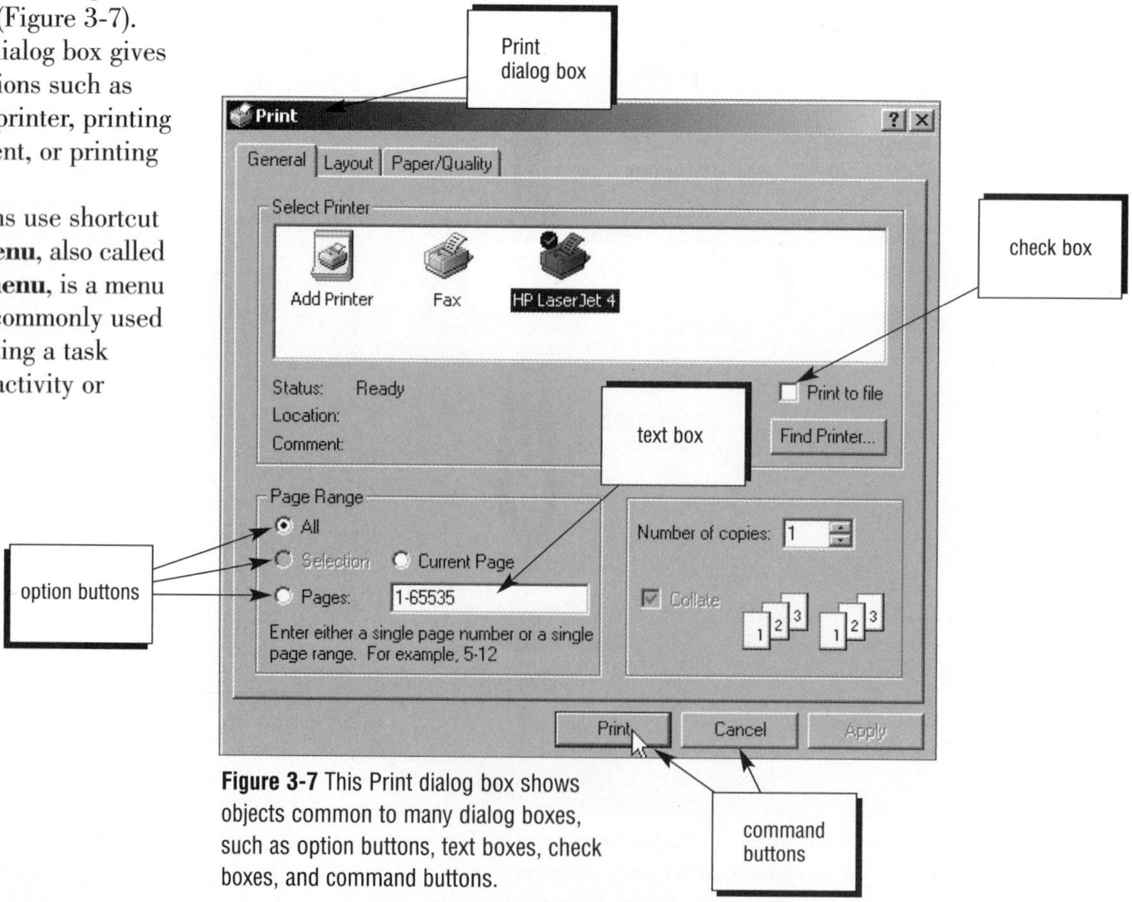

Figure 3-7 This Print dialog box shows objects common to many dialog boxes, such as option buttons, text boxes, check boxes, and command buttons.

Many elements shown on the previous pages, such as icons, buttons, and menus are part of the graphical user interface (GUI). One of the major advantages of a GUI is that these elements usually are similar across most applications. Once you learn the purpose and functionality of these elements, you can apply that knowledge to other software applications.

PRODUCTIVITY SOFTWARE

Productivity software is software that assists people in becoming more effective and efficient while performing daily activities. Productivity software includes applications such as word processing, spreadsheet, database, presentation graphics, personal information manager, software suite, accounting, and project management. Figure 3-8 lists popular software packages for each of these applications and the following sections discuss the features and functions of these applications.

POPULAR PRODUCTIVITY SOFTWARE PACKAGES

Software Application	Popular Packages
Word Processing	• Microsoft Word • Corel WordPerfect • Lotus Word Pro • Microsoft Pocket Word
Spreadsheet	• Microsoft Excel • Corel Quattro Pro • Lotus 1-2-3 • Microsoft Pocket Excel
Database	• Microsoft Access • Corel Paradox • Lotus Approach • Microsoft Visual FoxPro • Oracle
Presentation Graphics	• Microsoft PowerPoint • Corel Presentations • Lotus Freelance Graphics
Personal Information Manager	• Microsoft Outlook • CorelCENTRAL • Lotus Organizer • Palm Desktop
Software Suite	• Microsoft Office • Corel WordPerfect Suite • Lotus SmartSuite
Project Management	• Corel CATALYST • Microsoft Project • Primavera SureTrak Project Manager
Accounting	• Intuit QuickBooks • Peachtree Complete Accounting

Figure 3-8 Popular productivity software products.

COMPANY ON THE CUTTING EDGE

Microsoft

Productivity Software Gives Directions

If someone asks "Where do you want to go today?" you might answer, "Microsoft." Indeed, Microsoft attributes its worldwide success to helping customers achieve their goals. Whether these people need help creating a letter, organizing their data, or playing a game, Microsoft supplies top-rated software to help them "any time, any place, and on any device."

Bill Gates, Microsoft's current chairman and chief software architect, founded the company in 1975 with Paul Allen, his former schoolmate. Today, the Redmond, Washington-based corporation employs nearly 40,000 people and has subsidiary offices in more than 55 countries.

Ninety-five percent of personal computers run at least one Microsoft application, making the company the world's leading productivity software developer. Equally popular is its family of operating system software, including Windows 2000 Professional for business customers and Windows Millennium Edition for consumers. Several million users across the globe use MSN, which includes Internet access, Hotmail e-mail, and instant messaging. Microsoft's games, especially Flight Simulator and Age of Empires, are best-sellers. The corporation also is making technological advances in the television, wireless, and small business fields.

For more information on Microsoft, visit the Discovering Computers 2002 Companies Web page (**scsite.com/dc2002/companies.htm**) and click Microsoft.

Word Processing Software

Word processing software is one of the most widely used types of application software. **Word processing software**, sometimes called a **word processor**, allows users to create and manipulate documents that contain text and graphics (Figure 3-9). Millions of people use word processing software every day to develop documents such as letters, memos, reports, fax cover sheets, mailing labels, newsletters, and Web pages.

Word processing software has many features to make documents look professional and visually appealing. You can change the shape and size of characters in headlines and headings, change the color of characters, and organize text into newspaper-style columns. When you use colors for characters, they will print as black or gray unless you have a color printer.

Most word processing software allows you to incorporate audio clips, video clips, and many types of graphical images into documents. One popular type of graphical image is clip art. **Clip art** is a collection of drawings, diagrams, and photographs that you can insert into documents. Figure 3-9 includes eight clip art images related to camping. Some clip art is stored on your hard disk, a CD-ROM, or a DVD-ROM. In other cases, you access the clip art on the Web.

All word processing software provides at least some basic capabilities to help you create and modify documents. For example, you can define the size of the paper on which to print. You also can specify the **margins** – that is, the portion of the page outside the main body of text, including the top, the bottom, and both sides of the paper. The word processing software automatically re-adjusts text so it fits within the adjusted paper size and margins.

Word wrap allows you to type words in a paragraph continually without pressing the ENTER key at

ISSUE

Words, Words, and More Words

Word Processing

Two schools of thought exist when it comes to writing and computers. Many people believe word processing software greatly improves the quality of written material by making it easier to create, modify, and print documents. Some word processing software even provides templates — patterns or blueprints for a document — that produce reports, memos, cover letters, resumes, legal pleadings, and even letters to mom! Yet, other people argue word processing software has become a crutch, making it unnecessary for students to learn the rudiments and nuances of languages. These people feel that much of the work produced with word processing software is *processed*, lacking the beauty, artistry, and individuality of great literature. What effect do you think word processing software has on written communications? Does it result in better work or simply more correct mediocre work? What word processing features, if any, do you feel are particularly valuable to an author?

For more information on word processing and the writing process, visit the Discovering Computers 2002 Issues Web page (**scsite.com/dc2002/issues.htm**) and click Chapter 3 Issue #1.

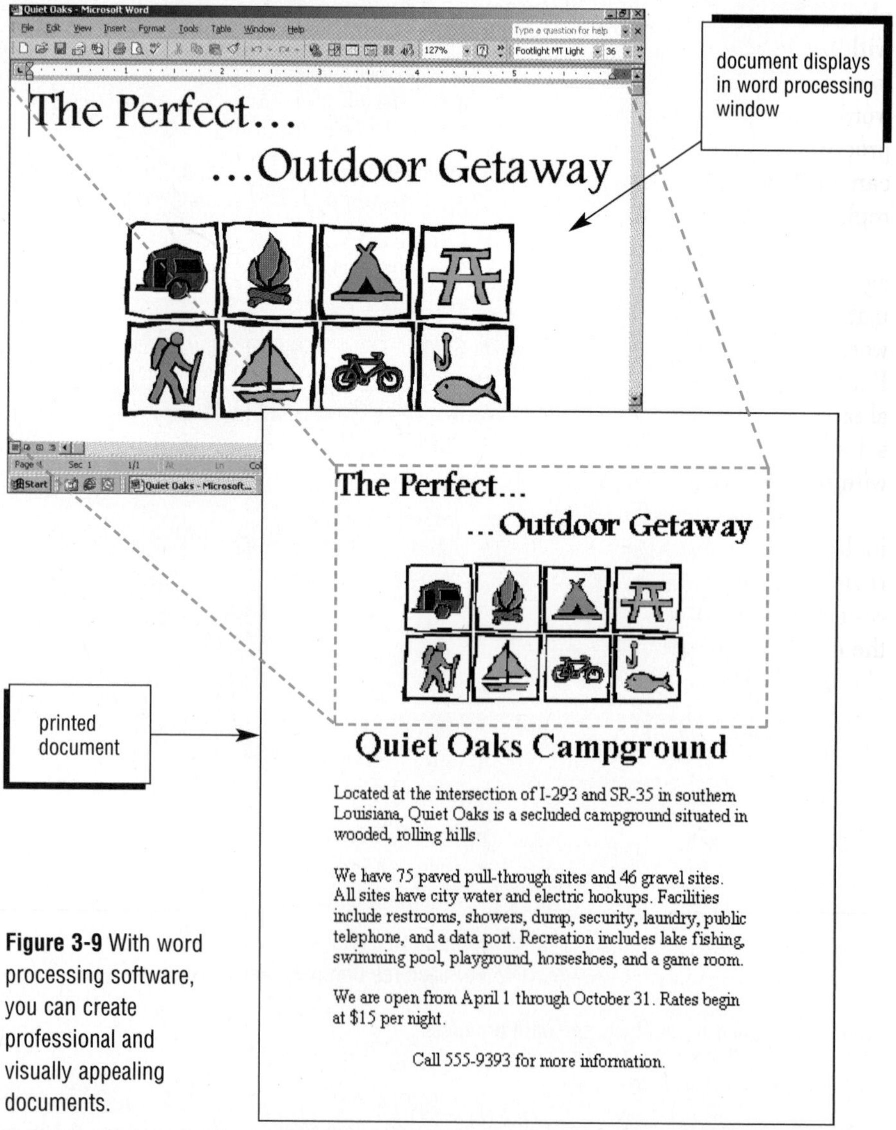

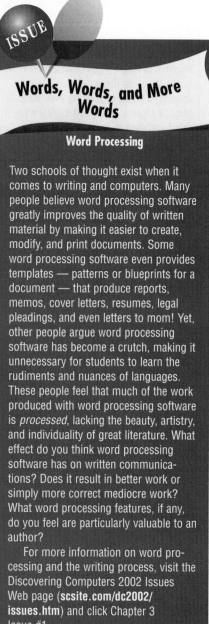

Figure 3-9 With word processing software, you can create professional and visually appealing documents.

the end of each line. With **word wrap**, if you type text that extends beyond the right page margin, the word processing software automatically positions text at the beginning of the next line.

As you type more lines of text than can display on the screen, the top portion of the document moves upward, or scrolls, off the screen. **Scrolling** is the process of moving different portions of the document on the screen into view.

A major advantage of using word processing software is you easily can change what you have written. You can insert, delete, or rearrange words, sentences, paragraphs, or entire sections. The **find** or **search** feature allows you to locate all occurrences of a certain character, word, or phrase. This feature in combination with the **replace** feature allows you to substitute existing characters or words with new ones. The word processing software, for example, can locate the word, secluded, and replace it with the word, remote.

Current word processing packages even have a feature that automatically corrects errors and makes word substitutions as you type text. For instance, when you type the abbreviation asap, the word processing software replaces the abbreviation with the phrase, as soon as possible.

Word processing packages include a **spelling checker**, which reviews the spelling of individual words, sections of a document, or the entire document. The spelling checker compares the words in the document to an electronic dictionary that is part of the word processing software. You can customize the electronic dictionary by adding words such as companies, streets, cities, and personal names, so the software can check the spelling of those words too. Many word processing software packages allow you to check the spelling of a whole document at one time, or to check the spelling of individual words as you type them.

You also can insert headers and footers into a word processing document. A **header** is text that appears at the top of each page. A **footer** is text that appears at the bottom of each page. Page numbers, company names, report titles, and dates are examples of items often included in headers and footers.

In addition to these basic features, most current word processing packages provide numerous additional features. The table in Figure 3-10 lists these additional features.

POPULAR WORD PROCESSING FEATURES

AutoCorrect	As you type words, the AutoCorrect feature corrects common spelling errors. AutoCorrect also corrects capitalization mistakes.
AutoFormat	As you type, the AutoFormat feature automatically applies formatting to your text. For example, it automatically can number a list or convert a Web address to a hyperlink.
Collaboration	Collaboration includes discussions and online meetings. Discussions allow multiple users to enter comments in a document and read and reply to each other's comments. Through an online meeting, you share documents with others in real time and view changes as they are being made.
Columns	Most word processing software can arrange text in two or more columns to look similar to a newspaper or magazine. The text from the bottom of one column automatically flows to the top of the next column.
Grammar Checker	You can use the grammar checker to proofread documents for grammar, writing style, and sentence structure errors in a document.
Macros	A macro is a sequence of keystrokes and instructions that you record and save. When you wish to execute the same series of instructions, execute the macro instead.
Mail Merge	Create form letters, mailing labels, and envelopes.
Tables	Tables are a way of organizing information into rows and columns. Instead of evenly spaced rows and columns, some word processing packages allow you to draw the tables, any size or shape, directly into the document.
Templates	A template is a document that contains the formatting necessary for a specific document type. Templates usually exist for memos, fax cover sheets, and letters.
Thesaurus	With a thesaurus, you can look up a synonym (word with the same meaning) for a word in a document.
Tracking Changes	If multiple users work with a document, the word processing software can highlight or color-code changes made by various users. You also can add comments to a document, without changing the text itself. Comments allow you to communicate with the other users working on the document.
Voice Recognition	With some word processing packages, you can speak into the computer's microphone and watch the spoken words display on your screen as you talk. With these packages, you also can speak commands such as editing and formatting the document.
Web Page Development	Most word processing software supports Internet connectivity, allowing you to create, edit, and format documents for the World Wide Web. You automatically can convert an existing word processing document into the standard document format for the World Wide Web.

Figure 3-10 Some of the additional features included with word processing software.

DEVELOPING A DOCUMENT

Many software applications, such as word processing, allow you to create, edit, format, print, and save documents. During the process of developing a document, you likely will switch back and forth among all of these activities.

Creating involves developing the document by entering text or numbers, inserting graphical images, and performing other tasks using an input device such as a keyboard, mouse, or microphone. If you are designing an announcement in Microsoft Word, for example, you are creating a document.

Editing is the process of making changes to a document's existing content. Common editing features include inserting, deleting, cutting, copying, and pasting items into a document. In Microsoft Word, you can insert (add) text to a document, such as listing additional facilities at a campground. Deleting is the process of removing text or other content. To cut involves removing a portion of the document and storing it in a temporary storage location called the **Clipboard**. Copying occurs when you duplicate a portion of the document and store it on the Clipboard. To paste items involves placing items stored on the Clipboard into the document.

When you **format** a document, you change its appearance. Formatting is important because the overall look of a document significantly can affect its ability to communicate effectively.

Examples of formatting tasks are changing the font, font size, or font style of text (Figure 3-11). A **font** is a name assigned to a specific design of characters. Times New Roman and Arial are examples of fonts. **Font size** specifies the size of the characters in a particular font. Font size is gauged by a measurement system called points. A single **point** is about 1/72 of an inch in height. The text you are reading in this book is 11 point. Thus, each character is about 11/72 of an inch in height. A **font style** adds emphasis to a font. Examples of font styles are **bold**, *italic*, and underline.

While you create, edit, and format a document, the computer temporarily holds it in memory. Once you complete these steps, you may want to save your document for future use. **Saving** is the process of copying a document from memory to a storage medium such as a floppy disk or hard disk. While working on a document, you should save it frequently. Doing so ensures you will not lose much work in case of a power failure or other system failure. Many applications have an optional AutoSave feature that automatically saves open documents at specified time intervals.

Once you save a document, it exists as a file on a storage medium such as a floppy disk or hard disk. A **file** is a named collection of data, instructions, or information. To distinguish among various files, each file has a file name. A **file name** is a unique combination of letters of the alphabet, numbers, and other characters that identifies the file.

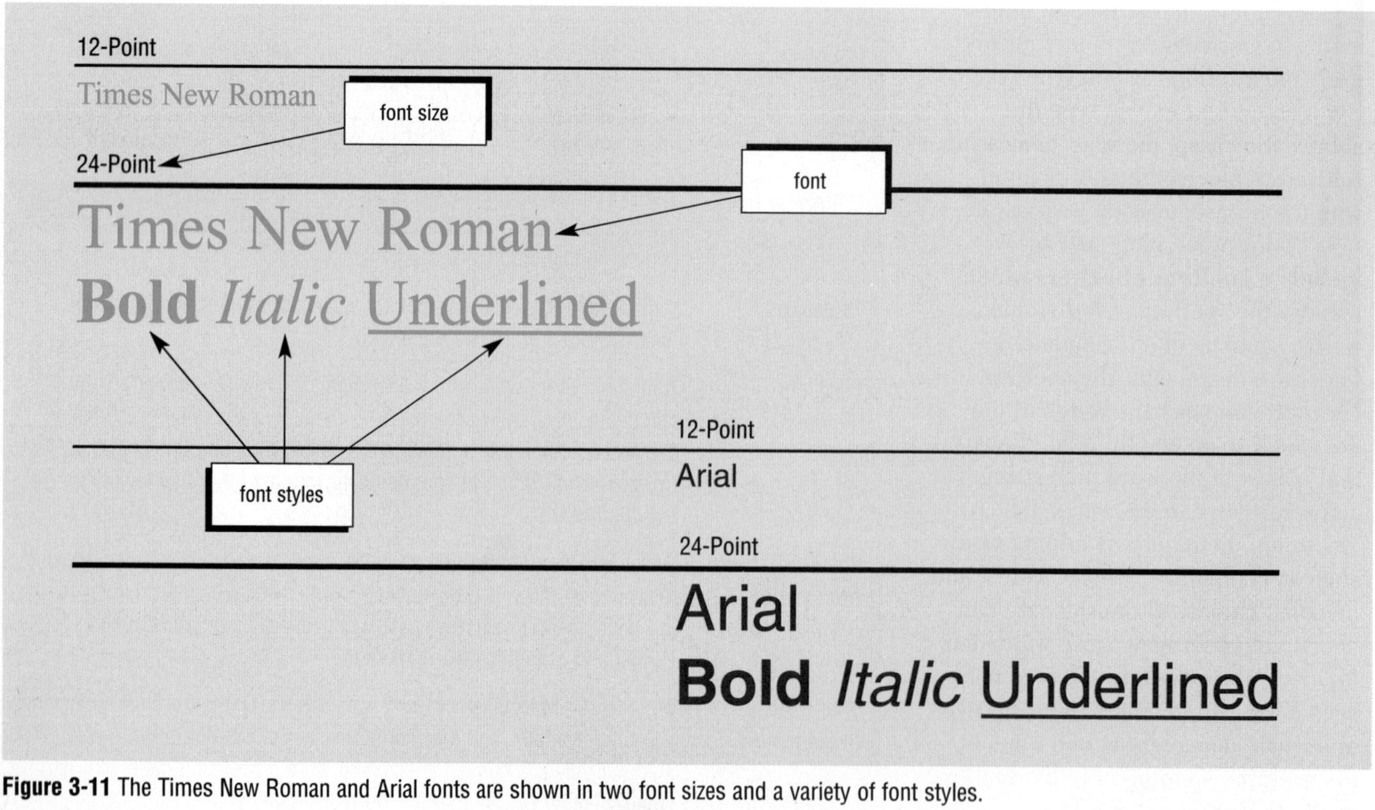

Figure 3-11 The Times New Roman and Arial fonts are shown in two font sizes and a variety of font styles.

The file name for the announcement in Figure 3-9 on page 3.8 is Quiet Oaks. The title bar of the document window usually displays a document's file name.

Once you have created a document, you can print it many times, with each copy looking just like the first. **Printing** is the process of sending a file to a printer to generate output on a medium such as paper. Instead of printing a document and mailing it, some users e-mail the document to others. That is, they send the document electronically to others on a network such as the Internet.

Many software applications support voice recognition. **Voice recognition**, also called **speech recognition**, is the computer's capability of distinguishing spoken words. You speak into the computer's microphone and watch the spoken words display on your screen as you talk. You also can edit and format a document by speaking or spelling instructions. Figure 3-12 shows how to dictate words and issue voice commands in Microsoft Word.

Figure 3-12 HOW TO DICTATE WORDS AND COMMANDS

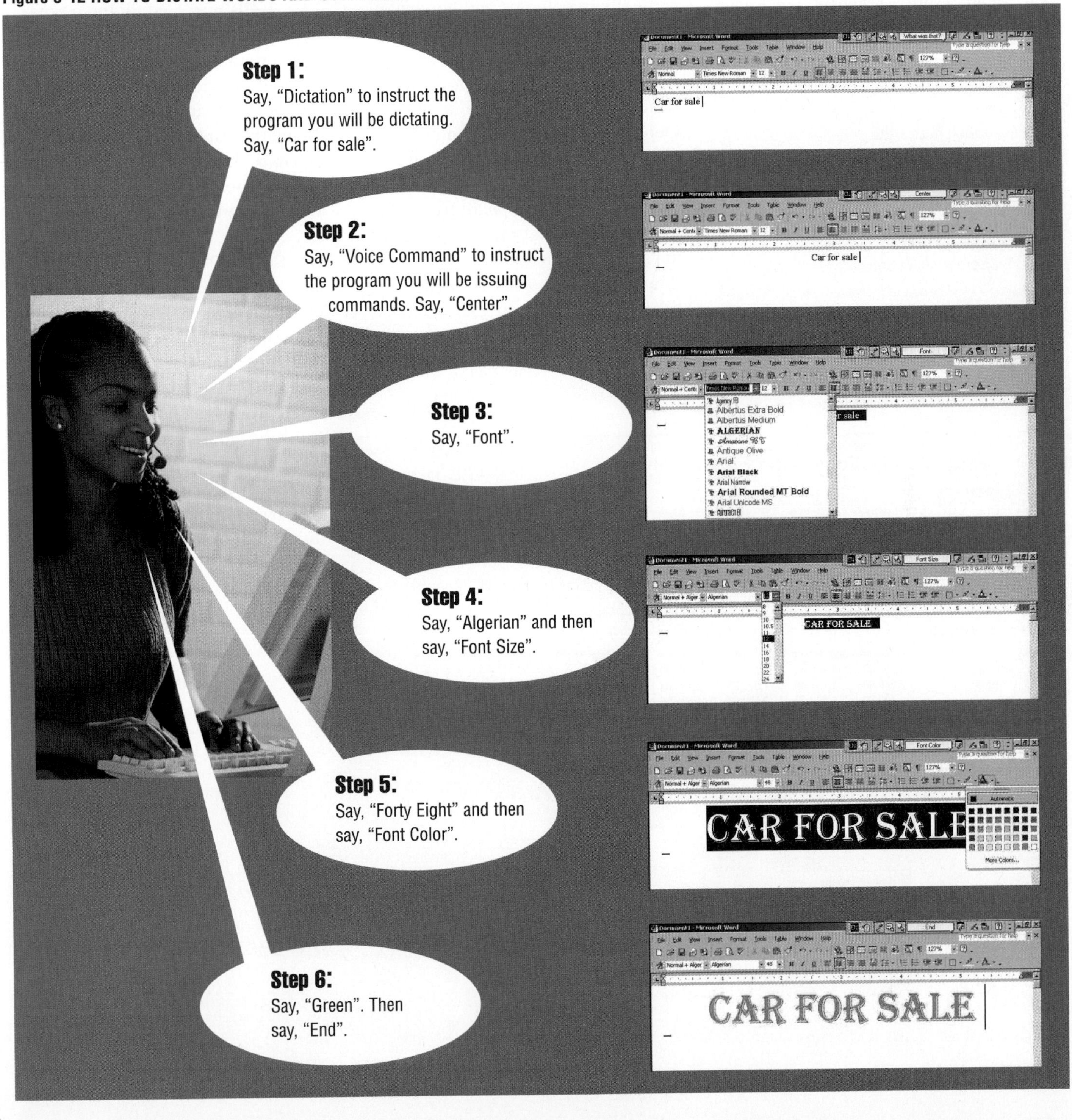
Step 1:
Say, "Dictation" to instruct the program you will be dictating. Say, "Car for sale".
Car for sale
Step 2:
Say, "Voice Command" to instruct the program you will be issuing commands. Say, "Center".
Car for sale
Step 3:
Say, "Font".
Step 4:
Say, "Algerian" and then say, "Font Size".
CAR FOR SALE
Step 5:
Say, "Forty Eight" and then say, "Font Color".
CAR FOR SALE
Step 6:
Say, "Green". Then say, "End".
CAR FOR SALE

Spreadsheet Software

Spreadsheet software is another widely used application. With **spreadsheet software**, you can organize data in rows and columns and perform calculations on this data. These rows and columns collectively are called a **worksheet**. For years, people used manual methods, such as those performed with pencil and paper, to organize data in rows and columns. In an electronic worksheet, you organize data in the same manner as in a manual worksheet (Figure 3-13).

Web Link

For more information on spreadsheet software, visit the Discovering Computers 2002 Chapter 3 WEB LINK page (**scsite.com/dc2002/ch3/weblink.htm**) and click Spreadsheet Software.

As with word processing software, most spreadsheet software has basic features to help you create, edit, and format worksheets. The following sections describe the features that are included in several popular spreadsheet software packages.

SPREADSHEET ORGANIZATION A spreadsheet file is similar to a notebook with up to 255 related individual worksheets. Data is organized vertically in columns and horizontally in rows on each worksheet. Each worksheet typically has 256 columns and 65,536 rows. One or more letters identify each column, and a number identifies each row. The column letters begin with A and end with IV. The row numbers begin with 1 and end with 65,536. Only a small fraction of these columns and rows displays on the screen at one time. You scroll through the worksheet to display different parts of it on your screen.

A **cell** is the intersection of a column and row. Each worksheet has more than 16 million (256 x 65,536) cells in which you can enter data. The spreadsheet software identifies cells by the column and row in which they are located. For example, the intersection of column C and row 5 is referred to as cell C5. In Figure 3-13, cell C5 contains the number, 5,092.50, which represents the Sophomore Tuition & Books expenses.

Cells may contain three types of data: labels (text), values (numbers), and formulas. The text, or **label**, entered in a cell identifies the data and helps organize the worksheet. Using descriptive labels, such as Room & Board, Tuition & Books, and Clothes, helps make a worksheet more meaningful.

CALCULATIONS Many of the worksheet cells shown in Figure 3-13 contain a number, also called a **value**. Other cells, however, contain formulas that generate values. A **formula** performs calculations on the data in the worksheet and displays the resulting value in a cell, usually the cell containing the formula. When creating a worksheet, you can enter your own formulas. In Figure 3-13, for example, cell C9 could contain the formula =C4+C5+C6+C7+C8 to

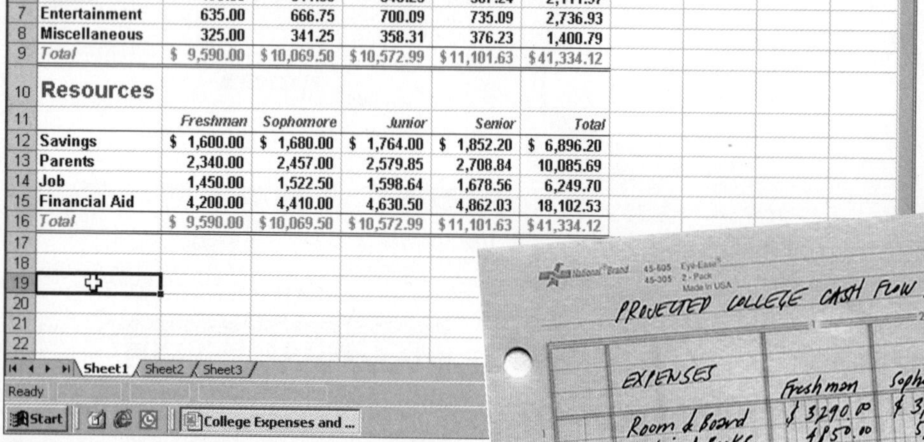

	A	B	C	D	E	F
1	Projected College Cash Flow Analysis					
2	Expenses					
3		Freshman	Sophomore	Junior	Senior	Total
4	Room & Board	$ 3,290.00	$ 3,454.50	$ 3,627.23	$ 3,808.59	$14,180.32
5	Tuition & Books	4,850.00	5,092.50	5,347.13	5,614.48	20,904.11
6	Clothes	490.00	514.50	540.23	567.24	2,111.97
7	Entertainment	635.00	666.75	700.09	735.09	2,736.93
8	Miscellaneous	325.00	341.25	358.31	376.23	1,400.79
9	Total	$ 9,590.00	$10,069.50	$10,572.99	$11,101.63	$41,334.12
10	Resources					
11		Freshman	Sophomore	Junior	Senior	Total
12	Savings	$ 1,600.00	$ 1,680.00	$ 1,764.00	$ 1,852.20	$ 6,896.20
13	Parents	2,340.00	2,457.00	2,579.85	2,708.84	10,085.69
14	Job	1,450.00	1,522.50	1,598.64	1,678.56	6,249.70
15	Financial Aid	4,200.00	4,410.00	4,630.50	4,862.03	18,102.53
16	Total	$ 9,590.00	$10,069.50	$10,572.99	$11,101.63	$41,334.12

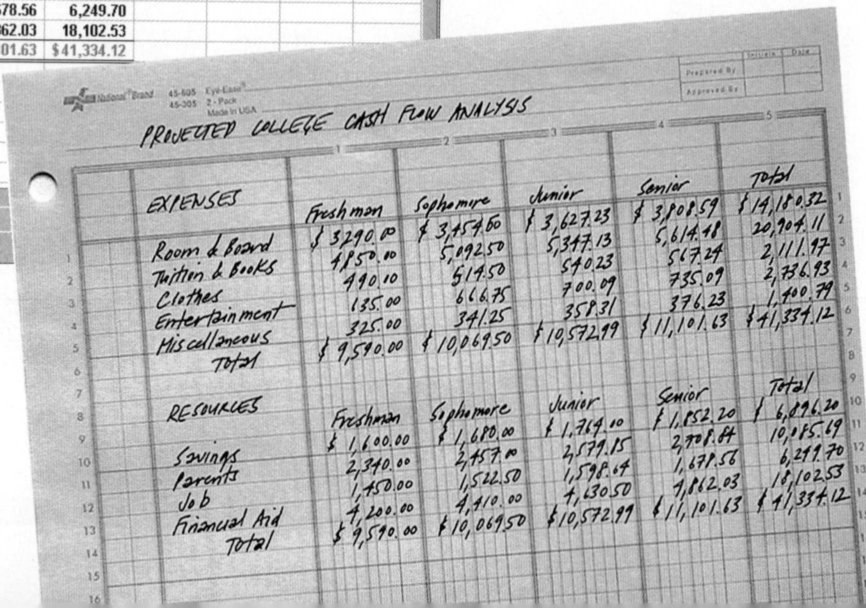

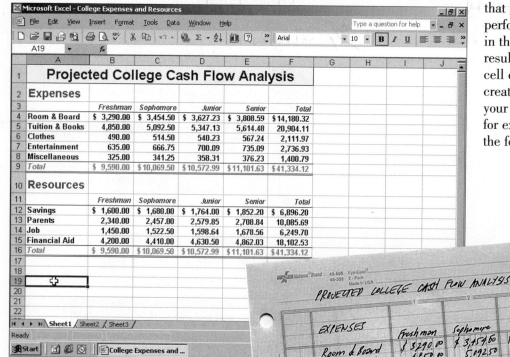

Figure 3-13 With spreadsheet software, you create worksheets that contain data arranged in rows and columns.

calculate the projected total expense for the student's sophomore year. A much more efficient way to sum the contents of cells is to use a function included with the spreadsheet software.

A **function** is a predefined formula that performs common calculations such as adding the values in a group of cells or generating a value such as the time or date. For example, instead of using the formula =C4+C5+C6+C7+C8 to calculate the projected total expense for the student's sophomore year, you should use the function =SUM(C4:C8), which adds, or sums, the contents of cells C4, C5, C6, C7, and C8. Figure 3-14 is a list of functions commonly included in spreadsheet software packages.

MACROS Spreadsheet software and other programs often include a timesaving feature called a macro. A **macro** is a sequence of keystrokes and instructions you record and save. When you run the macro, it performs the sequence of saved keystrokes and instructions. Creating a macro can help save you time by allowing you to enter a single character or word to perform frequently used tasks. For example, you can create a macro to format cells or print a portion of a worksheet.

RECALCULATION One of the more powerful features of spreadsheet software is its capability of recalculating the rest of the worksheet when data in a worksheet changes. To appreciate this capability, consider what happens each time you change a value in a manual worksheet. You must erase the old value, write in a new value, erase any totals that contain calculations referring to the changed value, and then recalculate these totals and enter the new results. When working with a manual worksheet, accurately making changes and updating the affected values can be time consuming and may result in new errors.

Making changes in an electronic worksheet is much easier and faster. When you enter a new value to change data in a cell, any value that is affected by the change is updated

SPREADSHEET FUNCTIONS

FINANCIAL	
FV (rate, number of periods, payment)	Calculates the future value of an investment
NPV (rate, range)	Calculates the net present value of an investment
PMT (rate, number of periods, present value)	Calculates the periodic payment for an annuity
PV (rate, number of periods, payment)	Calculates the present value of an investment
RATE (number of periods, payment, present value)	Calculates the periodic interest rate of an annuity
DAY & TIME	
DATE	Returns the current date
NOW	Returns the current date and time
TIME	Returns the current time
MATHEMATICAL	
ABS (number)	Returns the absolute value of a number
INT (number)	Rounds a number down to the nearest integer
LN (number)	Calculates the natural logarithm of a number
LOG (number, base)	Calculates the logarithm of a number to a specified base
ROUND (number, number of digits)	Rounds a number to a specified number of digits
SQRT (number)	Calculates the square root of a number
SUM (range)	Calculates the total of a range of numbers
STATISTICAL	
AVERAGE (range)	Calculates the average value of a range of numbers
COUNT (range)	Counts how many cells in the range have entries
MAX (range)	Returns the maximum value in a range
MIN (range)	Returns the minimum value in a range
STDEV (range)	Calculates the standard deviation of a range of numbers
LOGICAL	
IF (logical test, value if true, value if false)	Performs a test and returns one value if the result of the test is true and another value if the result is false

Figure 3-14 Functions typically found in spreadsheet software.

automatically and instantaneously. In Figure 3-13 on page 3.12 for example, if you change the Room & Board Expenses for Sophomore from 3,454.50 to 3,554.50, the total in cell C9 automatically changes to $10,169.50.

Spreadsheet software's capability of recalculating data also makes it a valuable tool for decision-making by using what-if analysis. **What-if analysis** is a process in which you change certain values in a spreadsheet in order to reveal the effects of those changes.

CHARTING **Charting**, another standard feature of spreadsheet software, allows you to display data in a chart that shows the relationship of data in graphical form. A visual representation of data through charts often makes it easier for users to analyze and interpret information.

Three popular chart types are line charts, column charts, and pie charts. Figure 3-15 shows examples of these charts that were plotted from the data in Figure 3-13. **Line charts** show a trend during a period of time, as indicated by a rising or falling line. A line chart indicating college resources could show the total for each year the student attends college. **Column charts**, also called **bar charts**, display bars of various lengths to show the relationship of data. The bars can be horizontal, vertical, or stacked on top of one another. A column chart might show the college expense breakdown by category, with each bar representing a different category. **Pie charts**, which have the shape of round pies cut into pieces or slices, show the relationship of parts to a whole. You might use a pie chart to show what percentage (part) each

TECHNOLOGY TRAILBLAZER

DAN BRICKLIN

The next time you use your calculator to balance your checkbook, think about Dan Bricklin. He used his Texas Instruments calculator constantly in the late 1970s while developing VisiCalc (Visible Calculator), the first electronic spreadsheet, in graduate school. He still owns that calculator, along with the original VisiCalc code.

Bricklin and his friend, Bob Frankston, formed a company called Software Arts and programmed the VisiCalc prototype using Apple Basic on an Apple II computer. The final version sold for $100 in 1979, and this small program included many of the features found in today's spreadsheet software. VisiCalc still runs on personal computers, and Bricklin includes the program on his personal Web site (see URL below).

Lotus Software purchased Software Arts in 1985. After serving as a consultant to Lotus, Bricklin turned his attention to starting a new company, Software Garden, Inc., and developing new software that focuses on pen-based computing and interactive videoconferencing. His current venture, Trellix, helps consumers and small businesses create and edit documents for the Internet.

For more information on Dan Bricklin and the Web site mentioned above, visit the Discovering Computers 2002 People Web page (**scsite.com/dc2002/people.htm**) and click Dan Bricklin.

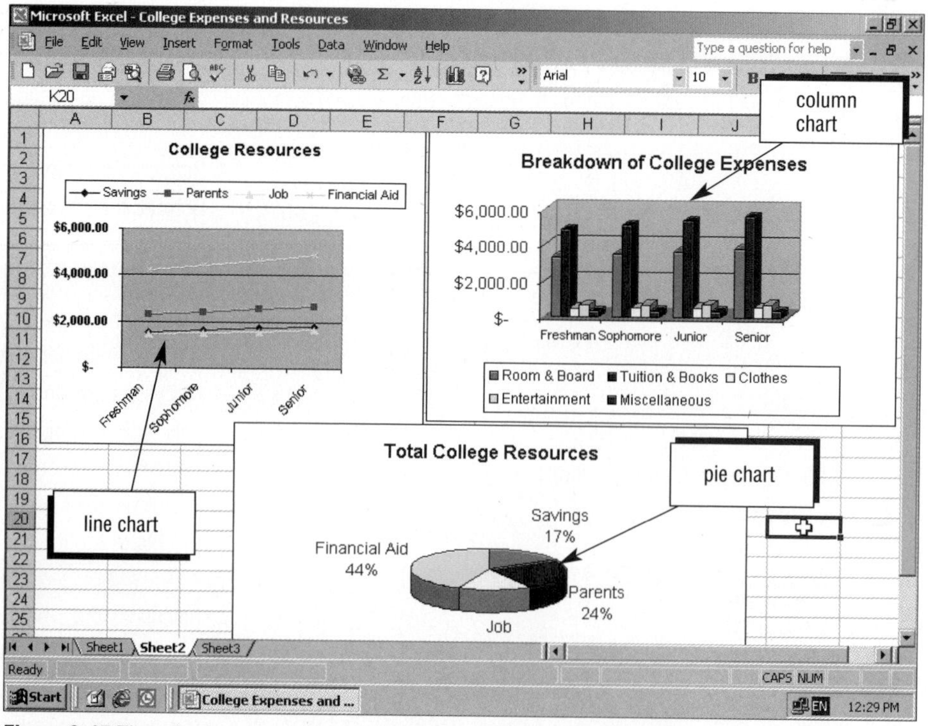

Figure 3-15 Three basic types of charts provided with spreadsheet software are line charts, column charts, and pie charts. The line chart, column chart, and pie chart were created from the data in the worksheet in Figure 3-13 on page 3.12.

resource category contributed to the total resources (whole) for a time period.

Spreadsheet software also incorporates many of the features found in word processing software such as checking spelling, changing fonts and font sizes, adding colors, tracking changes, recognizing voice input, including audio and video clips, and converting an existing spreadsheet document into a format for the World Wide Web.

Database Software

A **database** is a collection of data organized in a manner that allows access, retrieval, and use of that data. In a manual database, you might record data on paper and store it in a filing cabinet. With a computerized database, such as the one shown in Figure 3-16, the computer stores the data in an electronic format on a storage medium such as a floppy disk or a hard disk.

APPLY IT!

A Tip a Day

Today's software applications include many, many features that can improve your productivity. So how do you learn about all of these features? One option is to join a mailing list and receive daily or weekly tips for an application or applications of your choice. It is easy to subscribe to these newsletters. Just select the topics you want, fill in your e-mail address, and click the Subscribe button. Some of the more popular Web sites providing this free service are as follows:

- TipWorld (see URL below) offers daily tips. Tips on this site are not limited to software. Other categories include music, literature, cooking, business, science, personal finance, and entertainment.
- DummiesDaily (see URL below) offers daily eTips. Similarly to TipWorld, a variety of categories, in addition to computers, are available. Some other categories include Sports and Recreation, Pets, and Investing.
- CyberTips (see URL below) provides an option for how often you receive tips — daily, three times a week, or once a week. In addition to the Computers category, you also will find Health and Fitness, Home and Family, Golf, and other categories.
- PCShowAndTell (see URL below) is somewhat different from the other above listed services. This site offers multimedia tutorials for more than 100 different software applications, with a library of more than 35,000 tutorials. Signing up for their free newsletter brings random weekly tips to your mailbox. Ten tutorials per product are available free of charge. The company charges a $15 yearly fee, which provides access to their full library.

With the exception of PCShowAndTell, expect to see sponsor advertising within the newsletters you receive.

For more information on subscribing to an online tips service and the Web sites mentioned above, visit the Discovering Computers 2002 Apply It Web page (**scsite.com/dc2002/apply.htm**) and click Chapter 3 Apply It #2.

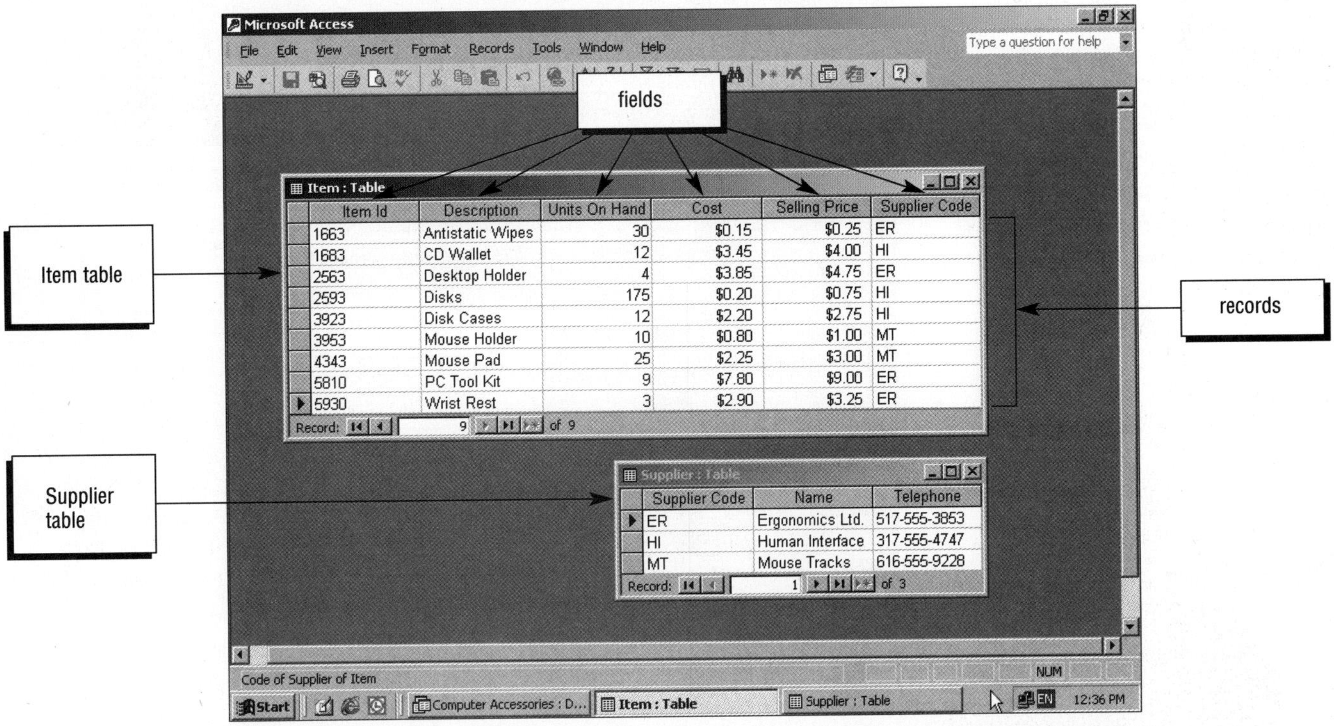

Figure 3-16 This database contains two tables: one for items and one for suppliers. The Item table has 9 records and 6 fields; the Supplier table has 3 records and 3 fields.

Database software, also called a **database management system (DBMS),** is software that allows you to create, access, and manage a database. Using database software, you can add, change, and delete data in the database; sort and retrieve data from the database; and create forms and reports using the data in the database.

With most popular personal computer database software packages, a database consists of a collection of **tables,** organized in rows and columns. A **record** is a row in a table that contains information about a given person, product, or event. A **field** is a column in a table that contains a specific piece of information within a record.

The Computer Warehouse database shown in Figure 3-16 on the previous page consists of two tables: an Item table and a Supplier table. The Item table contains nine records (rows), each storing data about one item. The item data exists in six fields (columns): item identification number, description, units on hand, cost, selling price, and supplier code. The description field, for instance, contains a name of a particular item.

DATABASE ORGANIZATION Before creating a database, you should perform some preliminary tasks. Make a list of the data items you want to organize. Each of these data items will become a field in the database. To identify the different fields, assign each field a unique name that is short, yet descriptive. For example, the field name for an item identification number could be Item Id.

Once you determine the fields and field names, you also must decide the field size and data type for each field. The **field size** is the maximum number of characters that a particular field can contain. The Description field, for instance, may be defined as 25 characters in length. The **data type** specifies the kind of data a field can contain and how the field is used. Common data types include the following:

- **Text**: letters, numbers, or special characters
- **Numeric**: numbers only
- **Currency**: dollar and cent amounts
- **Date**: month, day, and year information
- **Memo**: lengthy text entries
- **Hyperlink**: Web address that links to a document or a Web page
- **Object**: picture, audio, video, or a document created in other applications such as word processing or spreadsheet

Completing these steps provides a general description of the records and fields in a table, including the number of fields, field names, field sizes, and data types. These items collectively are known as the table **structure** (Figure 3-17).

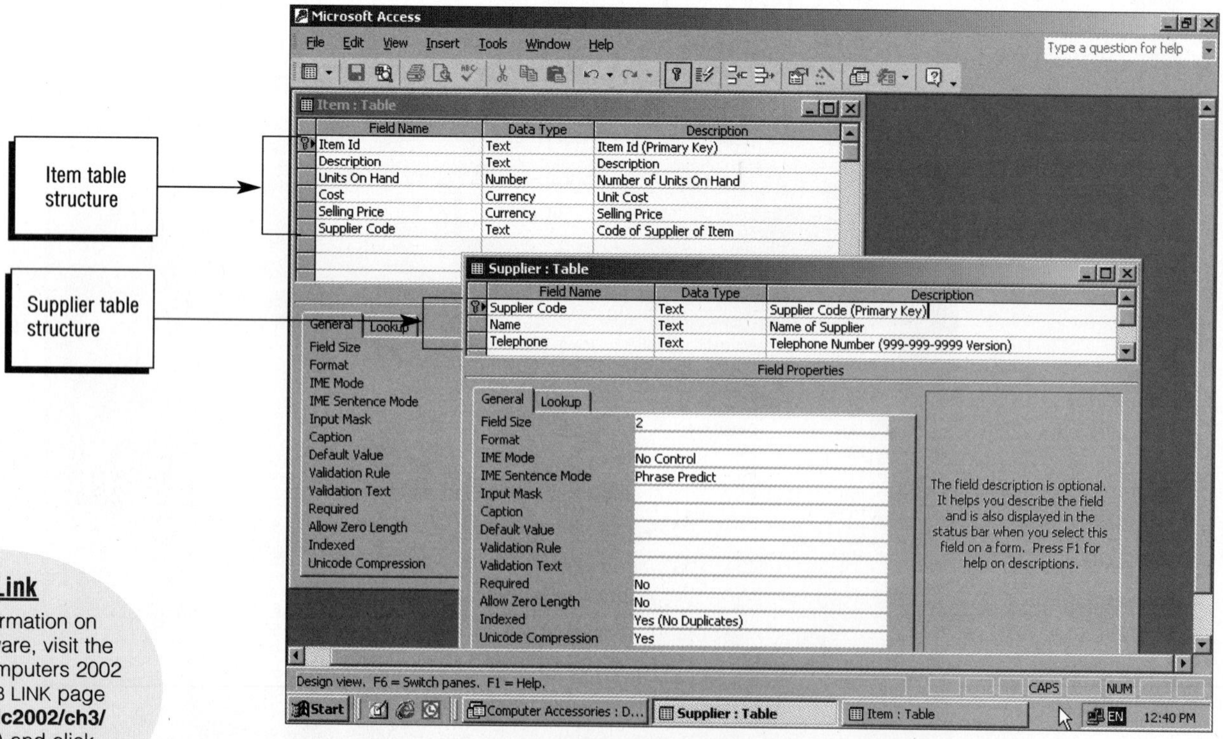

Figure 3-17 The structure of a table includes the field names, field sizes, and data types. This Microsoft Access screen illustrates the structures for the Item and the Supplier tables.

Web Link

For more information on database software, visit the Discovering Computers 2002 Chapter 3 WEB LINK page (**scsite.com/dc2002/ch3/weblink.htm**) and click Database Software.

ENTERING DATA After you create a table structure, the next step is to enter individual records into a table, called **populating** the table. The database software usually allows you to create a data entry form, through which you can enter or modify records using the keyboard (Figure 3-18). As you are entering the data, the database software checks, or validates, the data. **Validation** is the process of comparing the data to a set of rules or values to determine if the data is correct. For example, a field with a numeric data type restricts a user to entering only numbers into the field. Validation is important because it helps to ensure that data entered into the database is error free.

Another way to enter data into a database is to import data from an existing file. For example, you can import data from a spreadsheet file into a database.

MANIPULATING DATA Once the records are in the database, you can use the database software to manipulate the data to generate information. You can **sort**, or organize a set of records in a particular order, such as alphabetical or by date.

You also can retrieve information from the database by running a query. A **query** is a request for specific data from the database. You can specify which data the query retrieves by identifying **criteria**, which are restrictions the data must meet. For example, suppose you wanted to generate a list of all items that have a selling price less than $15.00. You could set up a query to list the Supplier Code, Name, Item Id, Description, Units On Hand, Cost, and Selling Price for all records that meet the criteria. Then, you can sort the list by supplier name (Figure 3-19), and instruct the database software to print or store the results of the query.

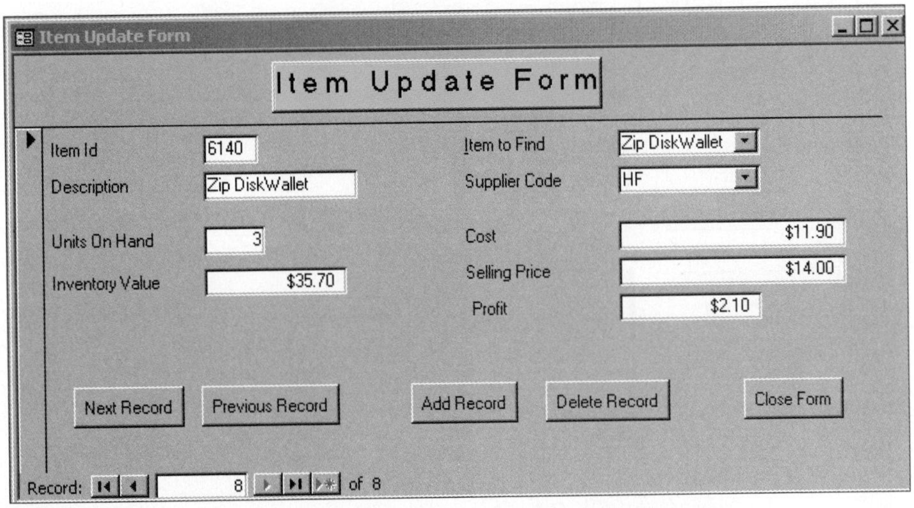

Figure 3-18 Once the table structure is defined, you can enter or modify data in a database using a data entry form. Most database software allows you to create a data entry form, based on the way you define fields. This data entry form allows you to enter or modify data in the Item table.

Suppliers and Items : Select Query

Supplier Code	Name	Item Id	Description	Units On Hand	Cost	Selling Price
ER	Ergonomics Inc.	2563	Desktop Holder	4	$3.85	$4.75
HF	Human Interface	1683	CD Wallet	8	$3.45	$4.00
HF	Human Interface	2593	Disks	145	$0.20	$0.75
HF	Human Interface	3923	Disk Cases	12	$2.20	$2.75
HF	Human Interface	6140	Zip DiskWallet	3	$11.90	$14.00
MT	Mouse Trails	3953	Mouse Holder	10	$0.80	$1.00
MT	Mouse Trails	4343	Mouse Pad-Plain	16	$2.25	$3.00
MT	Mouse Trails	5810	Mouse Pad-Logo	25	$3.45	$5.00

Record: 8 of 8

Figure 3-19 Database software can produce reports based on criteria a user specifies. This screen shows the result of a query to list the Supplier Code, Name, Item Id, Description, Units On Hand, Cost, and Selling Price fields for all records that have a Selling Price less than $15.00. The results of the query can be displayed or printed.

Presentation Graphics Software

Presentation graphics software allows you to create documents called presentations, which are used to communicate ideas, messages, and other information to a group. The presentations can be viewed as slides, sometimes called a **slide show**, that display on a large monitor or on a projection screen (Figure 3-20).

Presentation graphics software typically provides a variety of predefined presentation formats that define complementary colors for backgrounds, text, and other items on the slides. This software also provides a variety of layouts for each individual slide such as a title slide, a two-column slide, and a slide with clip art, a chart, or a table. You can enhance any text, charts, and graphical images on a slide with 3-D and other special effects such as shading, shadows, and textures.

Presentation graphics software typically includes a clip gallery, allowing you to create multimedia presentations. A **clip gallery** includes clip art images, pictures, video clips, and audio clips. A clip gallery can be stored on your hard disk, a CD-ROM, or a DVD-ROM. In some cases, you access the clip gallery on the Web. As with clip art collections, a clip gallery typically is organized by categories that can include academic, business, entertainment, transportation, and so on. For example, the Healthcare & Medicine category may contain a clip art image of a treadmill, a photograph of a person jogging, a video clip of a person exercising, and an audio clip of a heartbeat.

If you have an artistic ability, you can create clip art and other graphics using Paint or a similar application. Then, you **import** (bring in) the clip art into the slide. Once you insert or import a clip art image or other graphical image into a document, you can move it, resize it, rotate it, crop it, and adjust its color.

When building a presentation, you also can set the slide timing so the presentation automatically displays the next slide after a preset delay. Presentation graphics software allows you to apply special effects to the transition between each slide. One slide, for example, might fade away slowly as the next slide displays.

To help organize the presentation, you can view small versions of all the slides in slide sorter view (Figure 3-21). Slide sorter view presents a screen view similar to how 35mm slides would look on a photographer's light table. The slide sorter allows you to arrange the slides in any order.

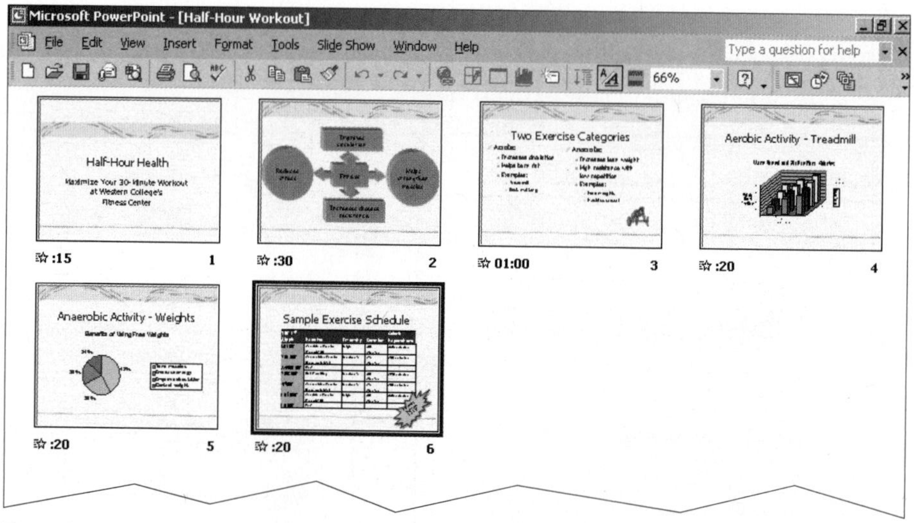

Figure 3-21 Slide sorter view shows a small version of each slide. Using a device, such as the mouse or the keyboard, you can rearrange the slides to change the sequence of the presentation.

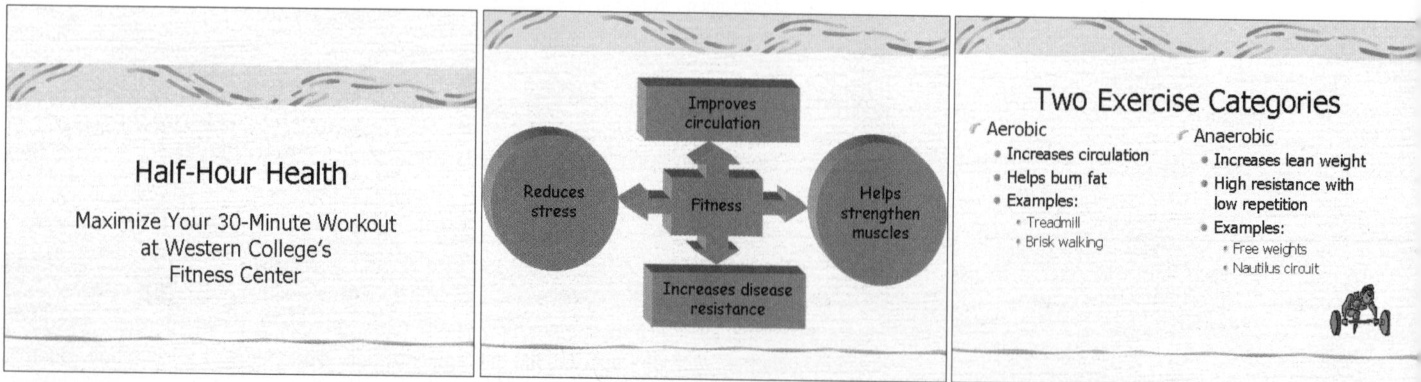

Figure 3-20 Using presentation graphics software, you can develop a presentation that can be projected onto a screen or displayed on a large monitor. This presentation consists of six slides.

Once a presentation is created, you can view or print the presentation as slides or in several other formats. An outline includes only the text from each slide such as the slide title and the key points (Figure 3-22a). Audience handouts include images of two or more slides on a page that you can distribute to audience members (Figure 3-22b). Speakers sometimes print a notes page to help them deliver the presentation. A notes page shows a picture of the slide along with any additional notes a presenter wants to see while discussing a topic or slide (Figure 3-22c).

Presentation graphics software incorporates some of the features found in word processing software such as checking spelling, formatting, recognizing voice input, and converting an existing slide show into a format for the World Wide Web.

Figure 3-22a (outline of presentation)

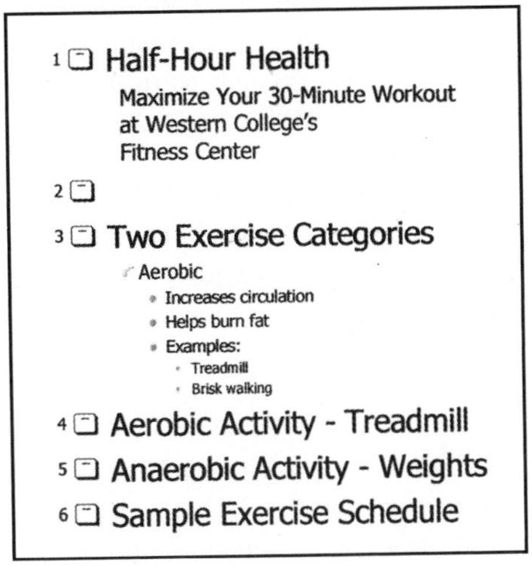

Figure 3-22b (audience handouts)

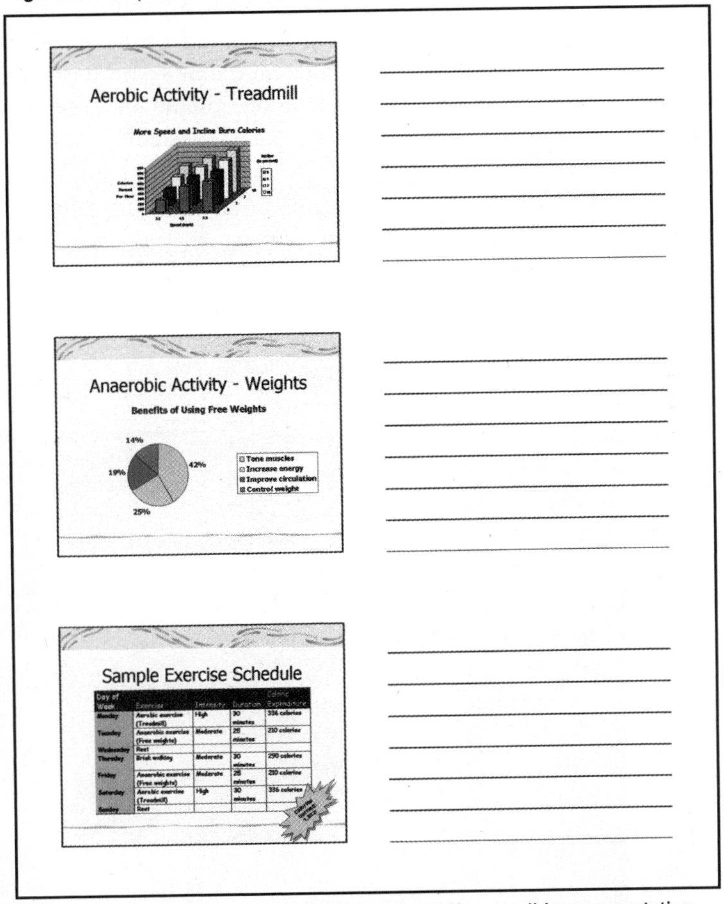

Figure 3-22c (notes page for speaker)

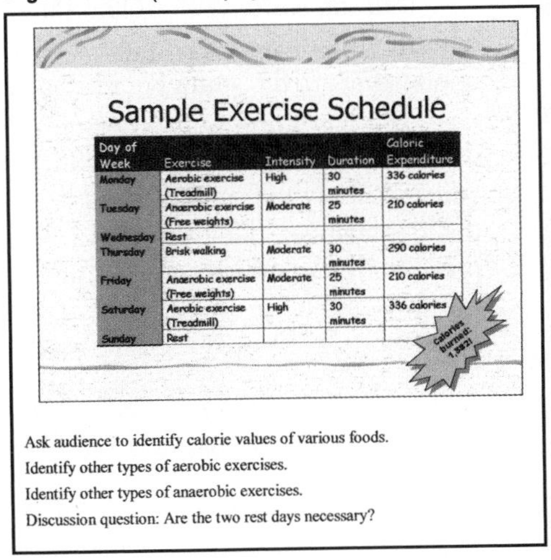

Figure 3-22 In addition to viewing the presentation as slides, presentation graphics packages allow you to view or print the presentation as an outline, as audience handouts, or as notes pages for the speaker.

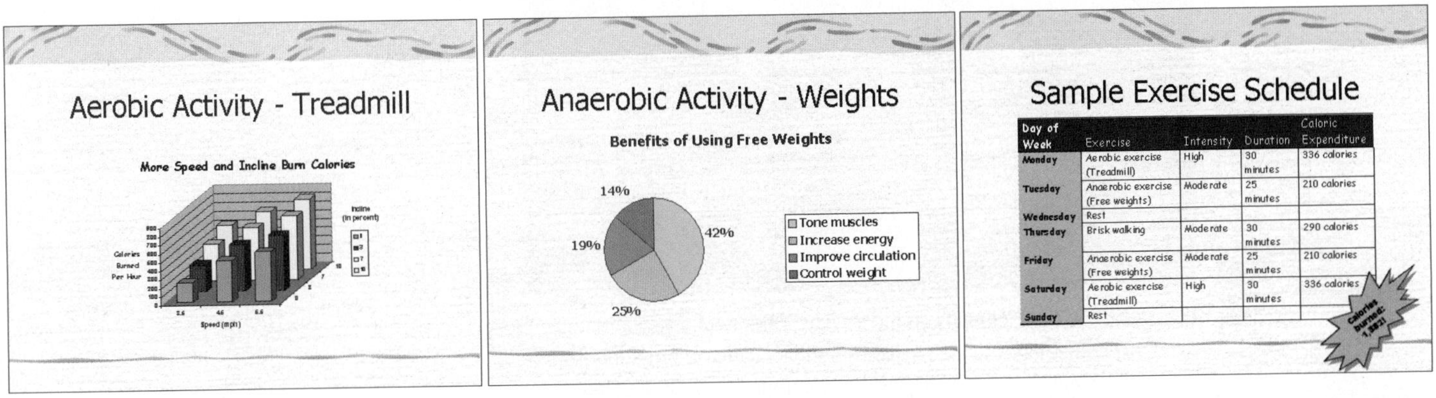

Personal Information Managers

A **personal information manager (PIM)** is a software application that includes an appointment calendar, address book, notepad, and other features to help you organize personal information. A PIM allows you to take information previously tracked in a weekly or daily calendar, and organize and store it on your computer. PIMs can manage many different types of information such as telephone messages, project notes, reminders, task and address lists, important dates, and appointments.

PIMs offer a range of capabilities. Most include at least an appointment calendar, address book, and notepad. An **appointment calendar** allows you to schedule activities for a particular day and time. With an **address book**, you can enter and maintain names, addresses, and telephone numbers of customers, co-workers, family members, and friends. Instead of writing notes on a piece of paper, you can use a **notepad** to record ideas, reminders, and other important information.

Most handheld computers have PIM functions, as well as many other features. These features often include a calculator, simple word processing application, simple spreadsheet application, games, e-mail capabilities, and Web browsing capabilities. Using a handheld computer, you can **synchronize**, or transfer information between the handheld computer and a desktop computer so the same information is available on both computers (Figure 3-23).

Software Suite

A software **suite** is a collection of individual applications sold as a single package. When you install the suite, you install the entire collection of applications at once instead of installing each application individually. At a minimum, productivity suites typically include the following software applications: word processing, spreadsheet, database, and presentation graphics. Two popular software suites are Microsoft Office and Lotus SmartSuite.

Software suites offer two major advantages: lower cost and ease of use. Buying a collection of software packages in a suite usually costs significantly less than purchasing each of the application packages separately. Software suites provide ease of use because the applications within a suite normally use a similar interface and have some common features. Once you learn how to use one application in the suite, you are familiar with the interface in the other applications in the suite. For example, once you learn how to print using the suite's word processing package, you can apply the same skill to the spreadsheet, database, and presentation graphics software in the suite.

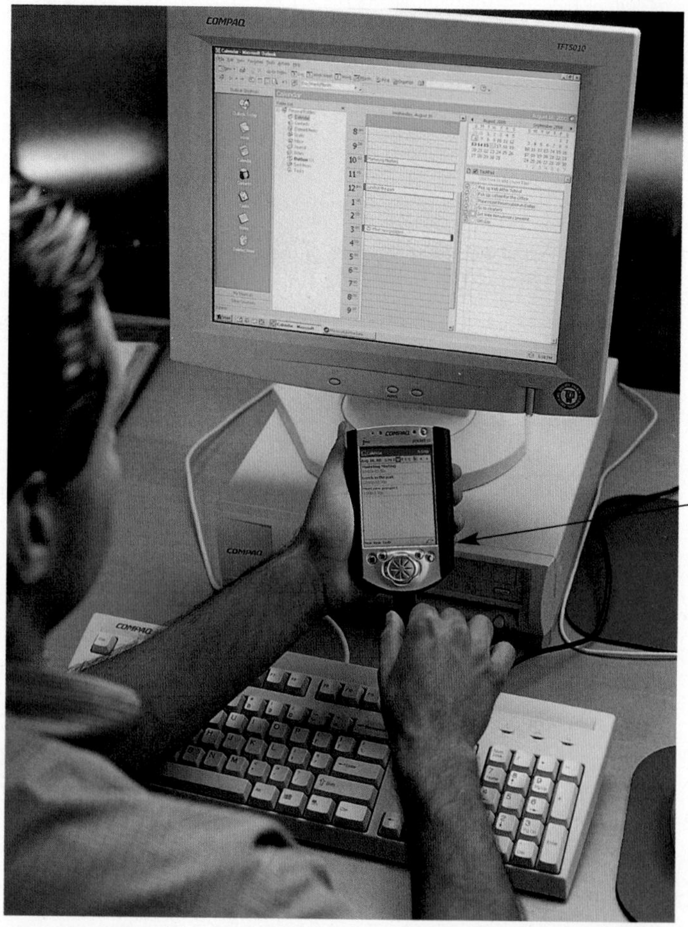

Figure 3-23 Most handheld computers have PIM functions. With most handheld computers, you can synchronize or transfer information from the handheld computer to your desktop computer, so your appointments, address lists, and other important information always are available.

Project Management Software

Project management software allows you to plan, schedule, track, and analyze the events, resources, and costs of a project (Figure 3-24). A general contractor, for example, might use project management software to manage a home-remodeling schedule. A publisher might use it to coordinate the process of producing a textbook.

Project management software helps users track, control, and manage project variables, allowing them to complete a project on time and within budget.

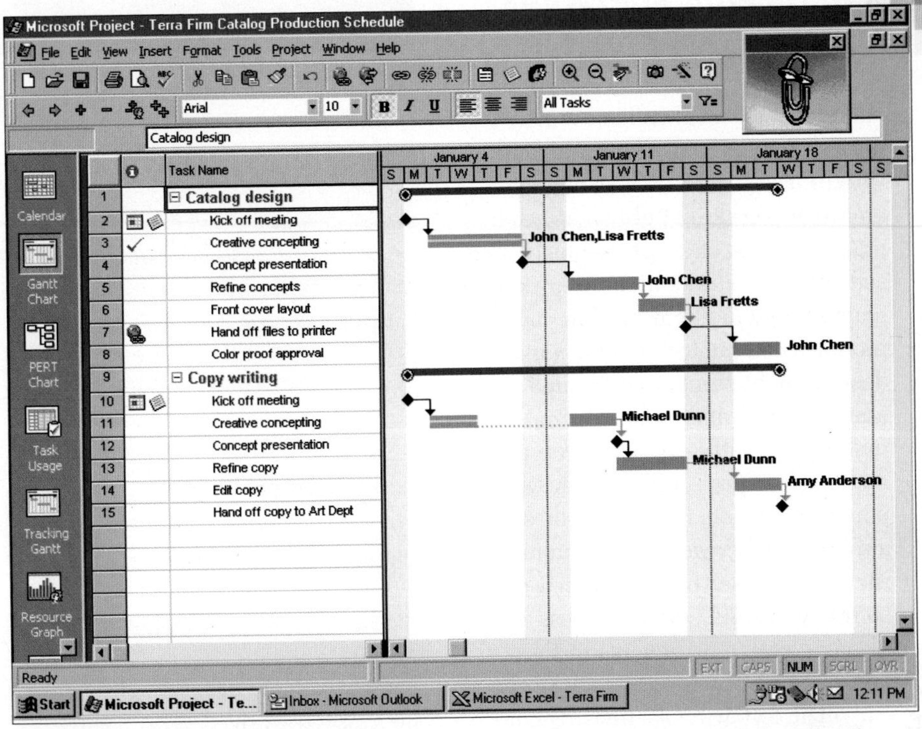

Figure 3-24 Project management software allows you to plan, schedule, track, and analyze the events, resources, and costs of a project.

Accounting Software

Accounting software helps companies record and report their financial transactions (Figure 3-25). With accounting software, small and large business users perform accounting activities related to the general ledger, accounts receivable, accounts payable, purchasing, invoicing, job costing, and payroll functions. Accounting software also enables users to write and print checks, track checking account activity, and update and reconcile balances on demand.

Newer accounting software packages support online direct deposit and payroll services. These services make it possible for a company to deposit paychecks directly into employees' checking accounts and pay employee taxes electronically.

Some accounting software offers more complex features such as multiple company reporting, foreign currency reporting, and forecasting the amount of raw materials needed for products. The cost of accounting software for small businesses ranges from less than one hundred to several thousand dollars. Accounting software for large businesses can cost several hundred thousand dollars.

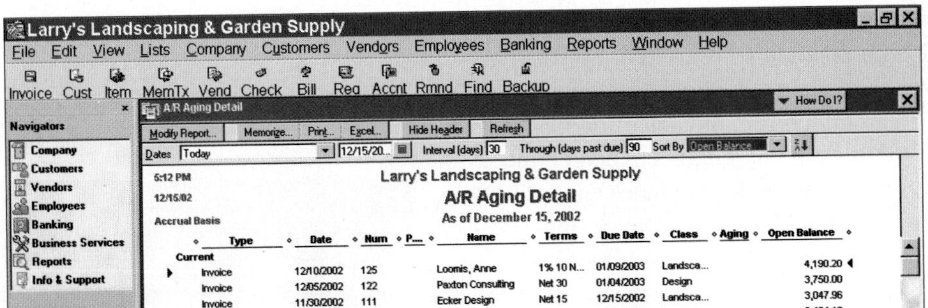

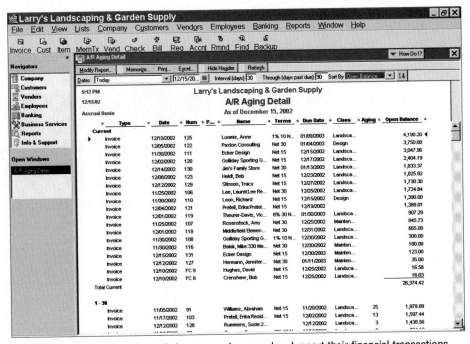

Figure 3-25 Accounting software helps companies record and report their financial transactions.

GRAPHICS AND MULTIMEDIA SOFTWARE

In addition to productivity software, many people work with software designed specifically for their field of work. Power users such as engineers, architects, desktop publishers, and graphic artists often use sophisticated software that allows them to work with graphics and multimedia. This software includes computer-aided design, desktop publishing, paint/image editing, video and audio editing, multimedia authoring, and Web page authoring. Figure 3-26 lists the more popular products for each of these applications. Some of these products incorporate user-friendly interfaces, so the home and small business user also can create documents in these applications.

The following sections discuss the features and functions of these applications.

POPULAR GRAPHICS AND MULTIMEDIA SOFTWARE PACKAGES

Software Application	Popular Packages
Computer-Aided Design (CAD)	• Autodesk AutoCAD • Microsoft Visio Technical
Desktop Publishing (Professional)	• Adobe InDesign • Adobe PageMaker • Corel VENTURA • QuarkXPress
Paint/Image Editing (Professional)	• Adobe Illustrator • Adobe Photoshop • CorelDRAW • Macromedia FreeHand
Video and Audio Editing	• Adobe Premiere • Ulead Systems MediaStudio Pro
Multimedia Authoring	• click2learn.com ToolBook • Macromedia Authorware • Macromedia Director
Web Page Authoring	• Adobe GoLive • Lotus FastSite • Macromedia Dreamweaver • Macromedia Flash • Microsoft FrontPage

Figure 3-26 Popular graphics and multimedia software products.

Computer-Aided Design

Computer-aided design (CAD) software is a sophisticated type of application software that assists a professional user in creating engineering, architectural, and scientific designs. For example, engineers can create design plans for airplanes and security systems. Architects can design building structures and floor plans. Scientists can design drawings of molecular structures.

CAD software eliminates the laborious manual drafting that design processes can require. With CAD, designers can make changes to a drawing or design and immediately view the results. Three-dimensional CAD programs allow designers to rotate designs of 3-D objects to view them from any angle (Figure 3-27). Some CAD software even can generate material lists for building designs.

Some manufacturers of CAD software sell a scaled-down product that is designed for the home user or small business user.

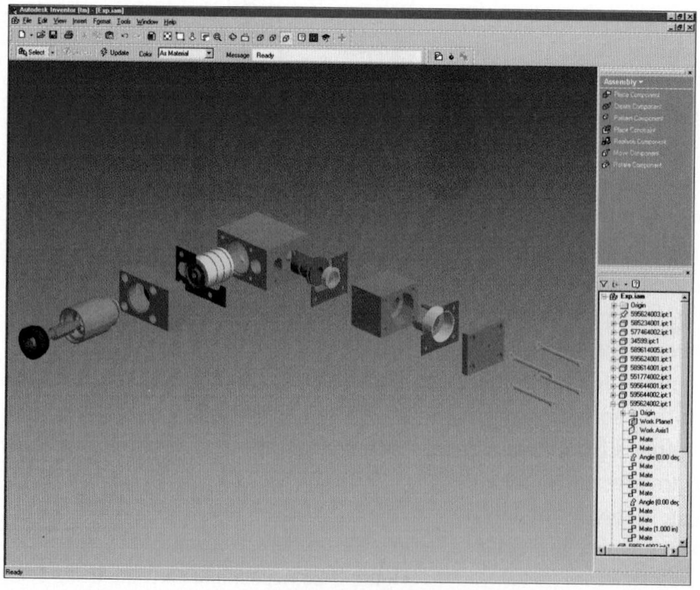

Figure 3-27 CAD software is sophisticated software that assists engineers, architects, and scientists in creating designs.

Desktop Publishing Software (Professional)

Desktop publishing (DTP) software enables professional designers to design and produce sophisticated documents that contain text, graphics, and brilliant colors (Figure 3-28). Professional DTP software is ideal for the production of high-quality color documents such as textbooks, corporate newsletters, marketing literature, product catalogs, and annual reports. In the past, documents of this type were created by slower, more expensive traditional publishing methods such as typesetting. Today's DTP software allows you to convert a color document into a format for use on the World Wide Web.

Although many word processing packages have some of the capabilities of DTP software, professional designers and graphic artists use DTP software because it supports page layout. **Page layout** is the process of arranging text and graphics in a document on a page-by-page basis.

With DTP software, users can add text and graphical images directly into the document or import existing text and graphics from other files. For example, text from a word processing file can be imported into a DTP document. Graphics files such as illustrations and photographs also can be imported into a DTP document. Another alternative is to use a scanner to convert printed graphics such as photographs and drawings into files that DTP software can use.

Once an artist or designer has created or inserted a graphical image into a document, the DTP software can crop, sharpen, and change the colors in the image by adding tints or percentages of colors. DTP software packages include color libraries to assist in color selections for graphical images and text. A **color library** is a standard set of colors used by designers and printers to ensure that colors will print exactly as specified.

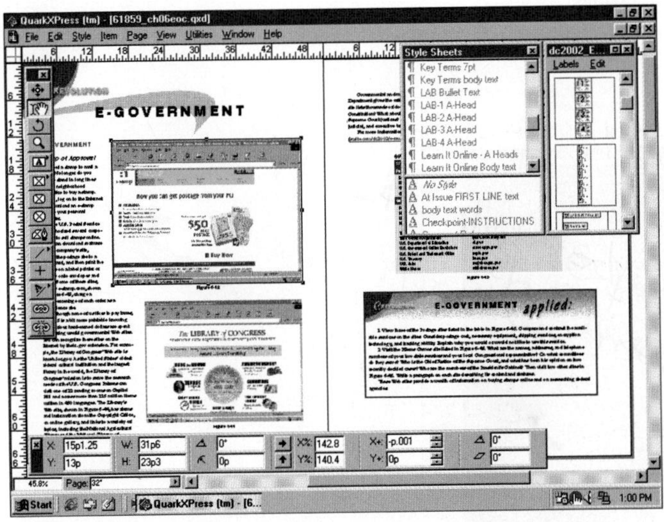

Figure 3-28 Professional designers and graphic artists use DTP software to produce sophisticated publications such as textbooks, marketing literature, product catalogs, and annual reports.

COMPANY ON THE CUTTING EDGE

Adobe

Breakthrough Desktop Publishing Software

Chances are when you view Web pages, you see images that were developed or enhanced with one of the products developed by Adobe Systems. The company's award-winning software, including Photoshop, Illustrator, GoLive, LiveMotion, PageMill, and Streamline, is used to create and deliver the majority of Web images today.

In the early 1980s, each software package had its own set of commands, called drivers, needed to communicate with printers. John Warnock and Charles Geschke saw the opportunity to create software using a common page-description language that would work with a variety of programs and printers. Warnock and Geschke founded Adobe Systems in 1982, and today Adobe is the third largest personal computer software company in the United States.

One of the reasons for the company's success is PageMaker, its desktop publishing (DTP) product. This software was the first DTP program, released in 1985 by the Aldus Corporation for the Macintosh and in 1986 for the PC. In 1994, Adobe acquired Aldus. PageMaker continues to be a popular DTP product today.

For more information on Adobe, visit the Discovering Computers 2002 Companies Web page (**scsite.com/dc2002/companies.htm**) and click Adobe.

Paint/Image Editing Software (Professional)

Graphic artists, multimedia professionals, technical illustrators, and desktop publishers use paint software and image editing software to create and modify graphical images such as those used in DTP documents and Web pages. **Paint software**, sometimes called **illustration software**, allows these users to draw pictures, shapes, and other graphical images with various on-screen tools such as a pen, brush, eyedropper, and paint bucket. **Image editing software** provides the capabilities of paint software as well as the capability to modify existing images (Figure 3-29). For example, you can retouch photographs, adjust or enhance image colors, and add special effects such as shadows and glows.

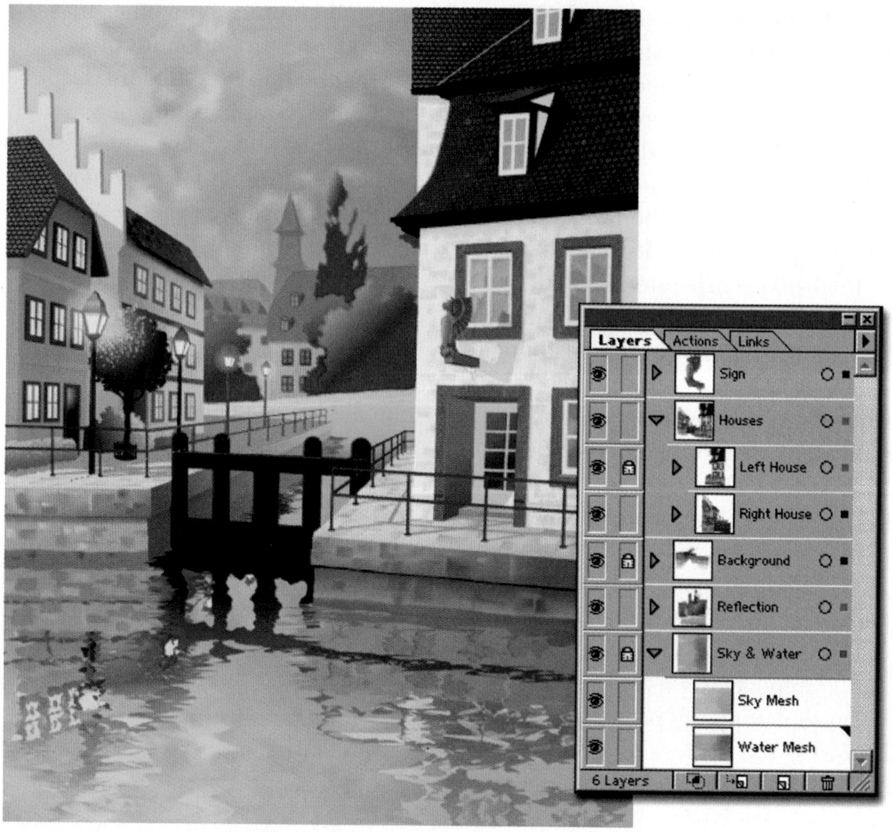

Figure 3-29 With image editing software, artists can create and modify a variety of graphic images.

Web Link

For more information on paint/image editing software, visit the Discovering Computers 2002 Chapter 3 WEB LINK page (**scsite.com/dc2002/ch3/weblink.htm**) and click Paint/Image Editing Software.

ISSUE

Image Altering

Paint and Image Editing Software

Today, many photojournalists, commercial artists, creators of cartoons, book covers, and billboards designers use paint and image editing software. With this software, an artist can convert photographs to a digital form that can be colorized, stretched, squeezed, texturized, or otherwise altered. They can import graphics files and manipulate the images in ways that previously were unachievable. For example, you can add clouds to a blue sky, or manipulate a picture of a person so it appears the person is standing in front of the Great Pyramids of Egypt. The National Press Photographers Association endorses the following: "As [photo] journalists we believe the guiding principle of our profession is accuracy; therefore, we believe it is wrong to alter the content of a photograph in any way, electronically or in the darkroom, that deceives the public." Do you agree with this guideline? Should professional graphic artists be able to alter photographs or other existing illustrations with paint and image editing software? Is it ethical? Is altering someone else's photograph a copyright issue?

For more information on paint and image editing software and photograph altering, visit the Discovering Computers 2002 Issues Web page (**scsite.com/dc2002/issues.htm**) and click Chapter 3 Issue #2.

Video and Audio Editing Software

Video consists of full-motion images played back at various speeds. With **video editing software** (Figure 3-30), you can modify a segment of a video, called a clip. For example, you can reduce the length of a video clip, reorder a series of clips, or add special effects such as words that move horizontally across the screen. Video editing software typically includes audio editing capabilities.

Audio is any music, speech, or other sound stored and produced by the computer. With **audio editing software**, you can modify audio clips and produce studio quality soundtracks. Audio editing software usually includes filters, which are designed to enhance audio quality. A filter might remove a distracting background noise from the audio clip.

Some operating systems include audio editing and video editing capabilities. These operating systems give the home user the ability to edit home movies and share clips on the Web.

Multimedia Authoring Software

Multimedia authoring software, sometimes called **authorware**, allows you to combine text, graphics, audio, video, and animation into an interactive presentation (Figure 3-31). With this software, you can control the placement of text and images and the duration of sounds, video, and animation. Once created, multimedia presentations often take the form of interactive computer-based presentations or Web-based presentations designed to facilitate learning and elicit direct student participation. Multimedia presentations usually are stored and delivered via a CD-ROM or DVD-ROM, over a local area network, or via the Internet. The Multimedia special feature following Chapter 6 discusses multimedia authoring software in more depth.

Web Page Authoring Software

As discussed in Chapter 2, Web page authoring software helps users of all skill levels create fascinating Web pages that include graphical images, video, audio, animation, and other special effects. In addition, many Web page authoring packages allow users to organize, manage, and maintain Web sites.

Many application software packages include Web page authoring features. This allows home users to create basic Web pages using packages such as Microsoft Word or Microsoft Excel. For more sophisticated Web pages, users work with Web page authoring software. Many Web page developers also use multimedia authoring software along with, or instead of, Web page authoring software for Web page development.

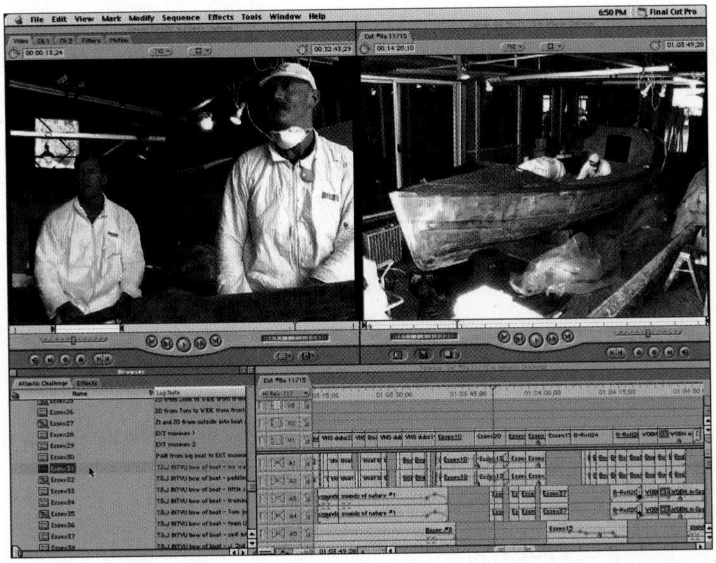

Figure 3-30 With video editing software, users can modify video images.

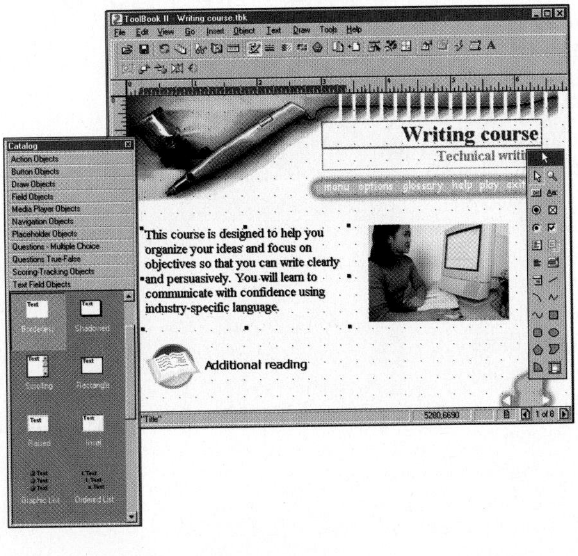

Figure 3-31 Multimedia authoring software allows you to create dynamic presentations that include text, graphics, audio, video, and animation.

SOFTWARE FOR HOME, PERSONAL, AND EDUCATIONAL USE

Many software applications are designed specifically for use at home or for personal or educational use. Integrated software is an example of a package for the home user that includes word processing, spreadsheet, database, and other software in a single package. Other packages for home, personal, and educational use include applications for finance, legal, tax preparation, desktop publishing, paint image/editing, clip art/image gallery, home design/landscaping, educational, reference, and entertainment.

Most of the products in this category are relatively inexpensive, often priced less than $100. Figure 3-32 lists popular software packages for many of these applications. The following sections discuss the features and functions of these applications.

POPULAR SOFTWARE PACKAGES FOR HOME/PERSONAL/EDUCATIONAL USE

Software Application	Popular Packages
Integrated Software	• Microsoft Works
Personal Finance	• Intuit Quicken • Microsoft Money
Legal	• E-Z Legal Advisor • Kiplinger's WILL Power • Nolo WillMaker
Tax Preparation	• Intuit TurboTax • Kiplinger TaxCut
Desktop Publishing (Personal)	• Broderbund Print Shop Pro Publisher • Microsoft Publisher
Paint/Image Editing (Personal)	• Adobe PhotoDeluxe • Broderbund Print Shop • Corel PHOTO-PAINT • Jasc Paint Shop Pro • Microsoft PhotoDraw • Microsoft Picture It! Photo
Clip Art/Image Gallery	• Corel GALLERY • Nova Development Art Explosion
Home Design/Landscaping	• Bob Vila's Home Design • Broderbund 3D Home Design Suite • Quality Plans Complete LandDesign
Reference	• Compton's American Heritage Talking Dictionary • Microsoft Encarta • Microsoft Pocket Streets • Microsoft Streets & Trips • Rand McNally StreetFinder • Rand McNally TripMaker

Figure 3-32 Popular software products for home, personal, and educational use.

APPLY IT!
Office and the Web

If you want to create a Web page, but do not have the time to learn HTML, then consider using one of the Office applications. Word, for instance, provides two techniques for creating Web pages. You can save an existing document as a Web page or you can use the Web Page Wizard.

To save an existing document as a Web page:

- Start Word and open the document.
- Click File on the menu bar and then click Save as Web Page.
- When the Save As dialog box displays, type the file name in the File name text box.
- Click the Change Title button, type a title name, and then click the OK button. This name displays in the browser's title bar. Many search engines use the title for cataloging Web pages, so the title should be as descriptive as possible.

By asking you a series of questions, the Web Page Wizard designs a Web page that can contain frames. A frame is a rectangular section of a Web page that can display another separate Web page. A Web page that contains frames can display multiple Web pages simultaneously on the same screen. If you wish to create a Web page that contains frames, use the Word Help system for assistance on using the Web Page Wizard.

Once you have created Web pages, you can publish them. Publishing is the process of making Web pages available to others, for example on the World Wide Web. Using the Office applications, you can publish Web pages by saving them to a Web folder or to an FTP location.

All Office applications provide options for saving files as Web pages. Word, however, is the only application that provides the Web Page Wizard.

For more information on using Office to create Web pages, visit the Discovering Computers 2002 Apply It Web page (**scsite.com/dc2002/apply.htm**) and click Chapter 3 Apply It #3.

Integrated Software

Integrated software is software that combines applications such as word processing, spreadsheet, and database into a single, easy-to-use package. Like a software suite, the applications within the integrated software package use a similar interface and share some common features. Once you learn how to use one application in the integrated software package, you are familiar with the interface in the other applications.

Unlike a software suite, however, you cannot purchase the applications in the integrated software package individually. Each application in an integrated software package is available only through the integrated software package.

The applications within the integrated software package typically do not have all the capabilities of stand-alone productivity software applications such as Microsoft Word and Microsoft Excel. Integrated software thus is less expensive than a more powerful software suite. For many home and personal users, however, the capabilities of an integrated software package more than meet their needs.

Personal Finance Software

Personal finance software is a simplified accounting program that helps home users and small office/home office users balance their checkbook, pay bills, track personal income and expenses, track investments, and evaluate financial plans (Figure 3-33). Using personal finance software can help you determine where, and for what purpose, you are spending money so you can manage your finances. Reports can

Web Link

For more information on personal finance software, visit the Discovering Computers 2002 Chapter 3 WEB LINK page (**scsite.com/dc2002/ch3/weblink.htm**) and click Personal Finance Software.

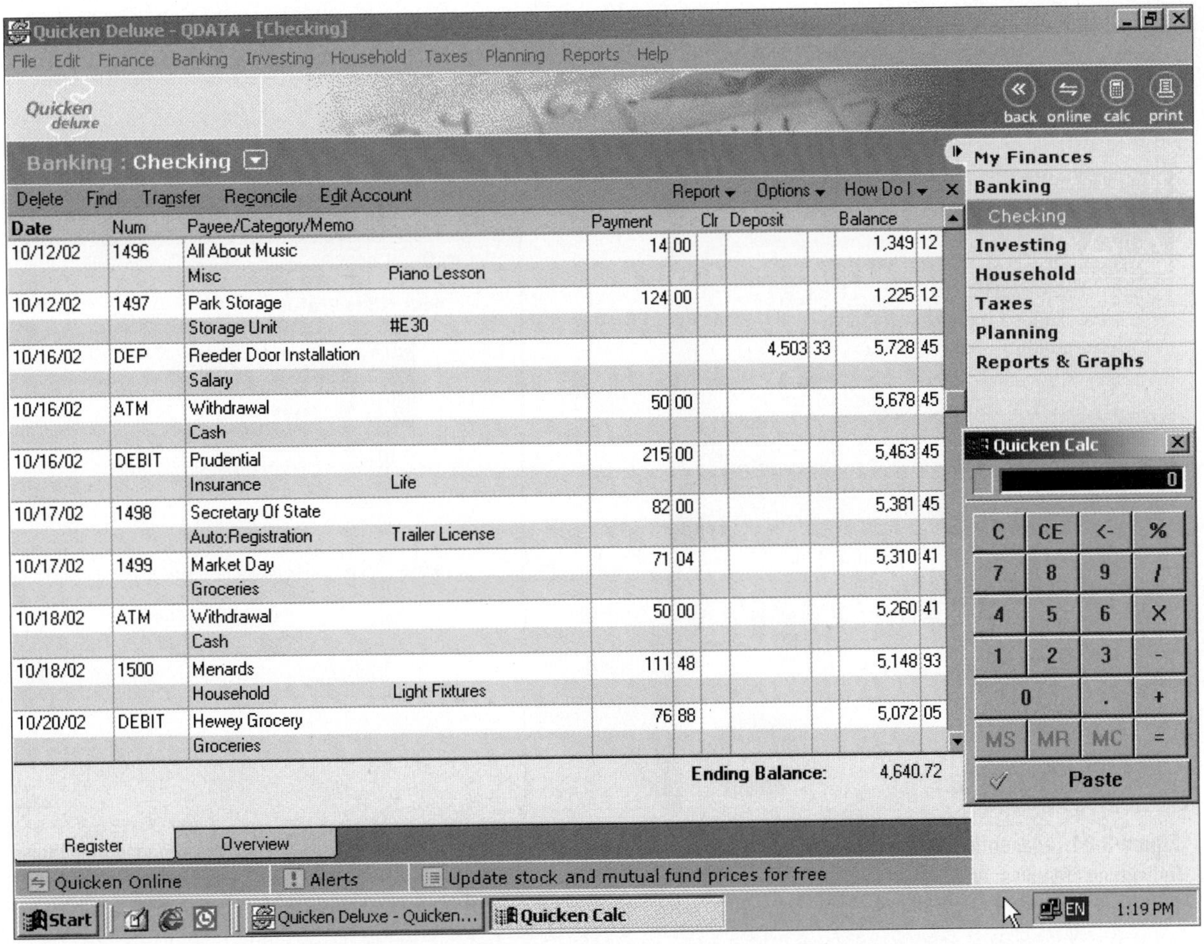

Figure 3-33 Many home users work with personal finance software to assist them with balancing their checkbook and paying bills.

summarize transactions by category (such as dining), by payee (such as the electric company), or by time period (such as the last two months).

Most of these packages offer a variety of online services, which require access to the Web. For example, you can track your investments online, compare insurance rates from leading insurance companies, and even do online banking. With **online banking**, you transfer money electronically from your checking or credit card accounts to payees' accounts. You also can download monthly transactions and statements from the Web right into your computer.

Financial planning features include analyzing home and personal loans, preparing income taxes, and managing retirement savings. Other features found in many personal finance packages include home inventory, budgeting, and tax preparation.

Legal Software

Legal software assists in the preparation of legal documents and provides legal advice to individuals, families, and small businesses (Figure 3-34). Legal software provides standard contracts and documents associated with buying, selling, and renting property; estate planning; marriage and divorce; and preparing a will or living trust. By answering a series of questions or completing a form, the legal software tailors the legal document to your needs.

Once the legal document is created, you can file the paperwork with the appropriate agency, court, or office; or you can take the document to your attorney for his or her review and signature. Before using one of these software packages to create a document, you may want to check with your local bar association for its legality.

Tax Preparation Software

Tax preparation software guides individuals, families, or small businesses through the process of filing federal taxes (Figure 3-35). These software packages offer money saving tax tips, designed to lower your tax bill. After you answer a series of questions and complete basic forms, the software creates and analyzes your tax forms to search for missed potential errors and deduction opportunities.

Once the forms are complete, you can print any necessary paperwork, completed and ready for you to file. Some tax preparation packages even allow you to file your tax forms electronically.

Desktop Publishing (Personal)

Instead of using professional DTP software (as discussed earlier in this chapter), many home and small

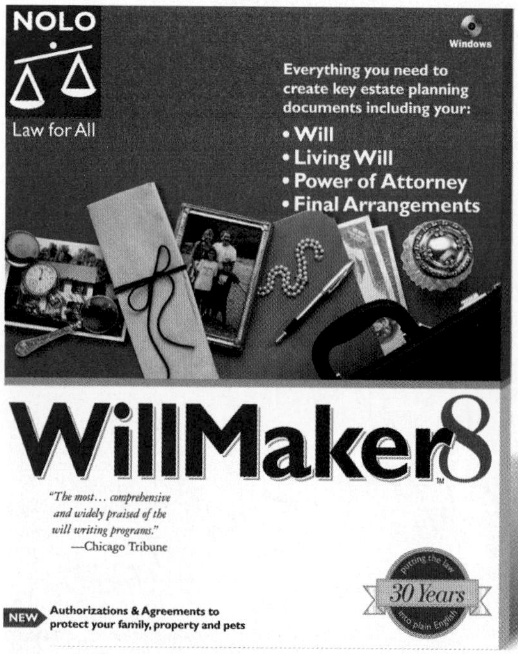

Figure 3-34 Legal software provides legal advice to individuals, families, and small businesses and assists in the preparation of legal documents.

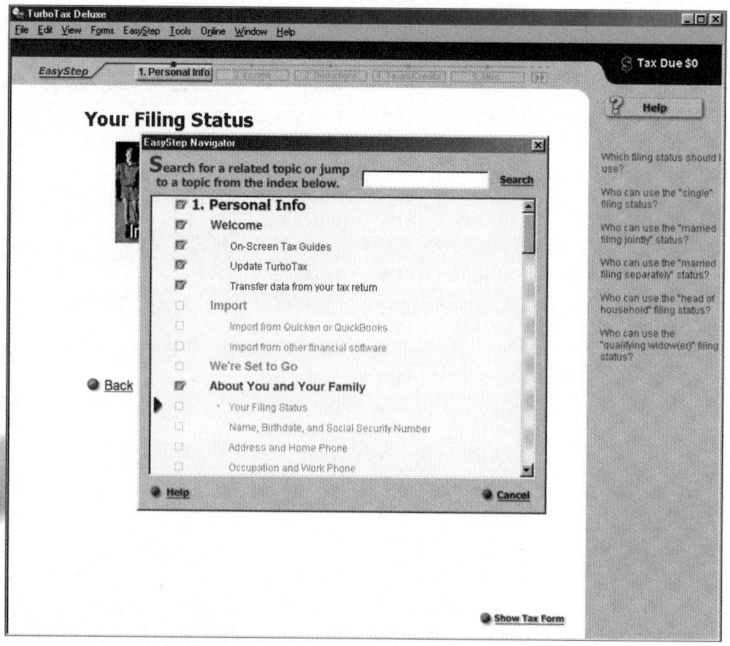

Figure 3-35 Tax preparation software guides individuals, families, or small businesses through the process of filing federal taxes.

business users utilize much simpler, easy-to-understand DTP software designed for smaller-scale desktop publishing projects (Figure 3-36). Using **personal DTP software**, you can create newsletters, brochures, and advertisements; postcards and greeting cards; letterhead and business cards; banners, calendars, and logos; and Web pages.

Personal DTP software packages provide hundreds of thousands of graphical images. You also can import your own digital photographs into the documents. These packages typically guide you through the development of a document by asking a series of questions, offering numerous predefined layouts, and providing standard text you can add to documents. In some packages, as you enter text, the personal DTP software checks your spelling. Then, you can print your finished publications on a color printer or place them on the Web.

Many personal DTP packages also include paint/image editing software and photo-editing software.

Paint/Image Editing Software (Personal)

Personal paint/image editing software provides an easy-to-use interface, usually with more simplified capabilities than its professional counterpart, including functions tailored to meet the needs of the home and small business user.

Like the professional versions, personal paint software includes various simplified tools that allow you to draw pictures, shapes, and other images. Personal image editing software provides the capabilities of paint software and the capability of modifying existing graphics. These products also include many templates to assist you in adding an image to documents such as greeting cards, banners, calendars, signs, labels, business cards, and letterhead.

One popular type of image editing software, called **photo-editing software**, allows you to edit digital photographs by removing red-eye (Figure 3-37), adding special effects, or creating electronic photo albums. When the photograph is complete, you can print it on labels, calendars, business cards, and banners; or place it on a Web page. Some of these software packages allow you to send digital photographs to an **online print service**, which will send high-resolution printed images through the postal service. Many have a photo community where you can post photographs on the Web for others to view.

Figure 3-36 With Microsoft Publisher, home and small business users can create professional looking publications such as this announcement.

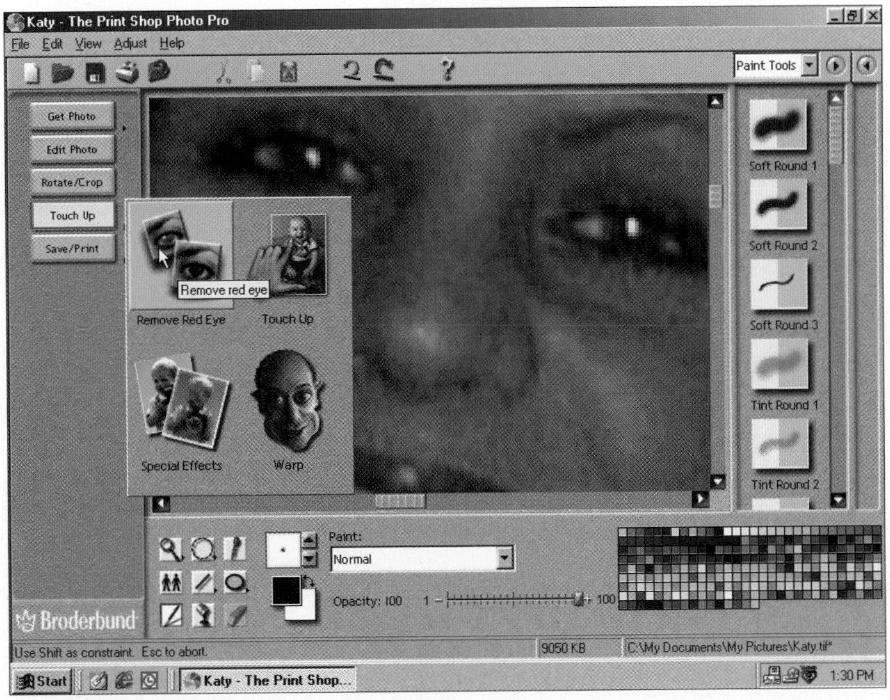

Figure 3-37 Photo-editing software allows the home user to remove red-eye from digital images.

Web Link

For more information on clip art/image galleries, visit the Discovering Computers 2002 Chapter 3 WEB LINK page (**scsite.com/dc2002/ch3/weblink.htm**) and click Clip Art/Image Galleries.

Clip Art/Image Gallery

Many applications include a **clip art/image gallery**, which is a collection of clip art and photographs (Figure 3-38). Some applications have links to additional clips available on the Web. You also can purchase clip art/image galleries if you need a wider selection of images.

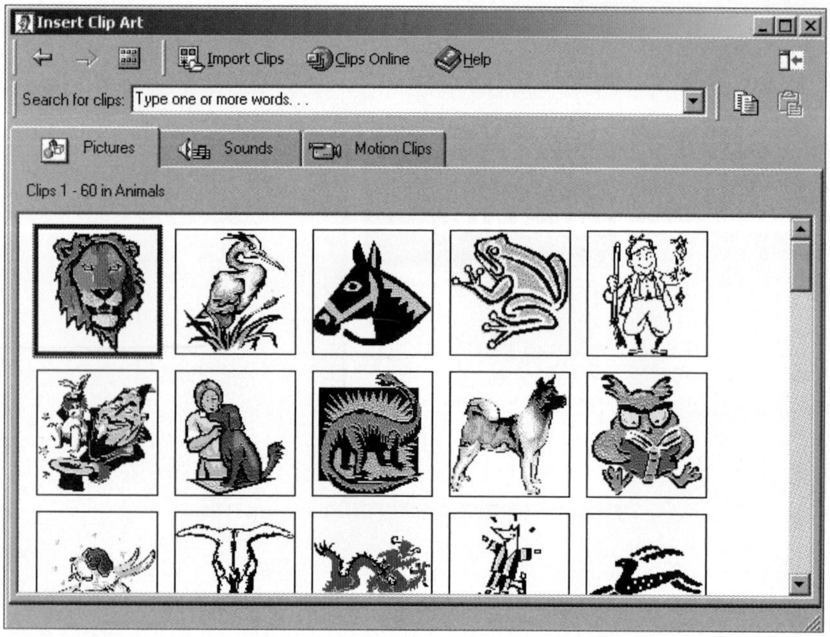

Figure 3-38 Many applications have a clip art/image gallery, such as the one shown in this figure, built in to the package.

ISSUE

Personal Publishing

Application Software

Johann Guttenberg's invention of the printing press had a profound impact on Western thought. Guttenberg's influence on moveable type evolving to the printing press greatly impacted society. Books once available only to a privileged elite became accessible to a much wider audience, thereby broadening the distribution of ideas. Some believe Web page authoring software, desktop publishing software, presentation graphics software, multimedia authoring software, and other applications that help people communicate more effectively will have a similar impact. Unpublished authors can use these applications to produce works that, because of their professional looking appearance, are considered thoughtfully and circulated extensively. Will these applications really help give previously unheard speakers a louder voice? Why or why not? What effect, if any, will these applications have on the delivery, and possible acceptance, of material that reflects unconventional, or not generally accepted, ideas?

For more information on desktop and Web publishing, visit the Discovering Computers 2002 Issues Web page (**scsite.com/dc2002/issues.htm**) and click Chapter 3 Issue #3.

In addition to clip art, many clip art/image galleries provide fonts, animations, sounds, video clips, and audio clips. You can use the images, fonts, and other items from the clip art/image gallery in all types of documents, including word processing, desktop publishing, spreadsheet, and presentation graphics.

Home Design/Landscaping Software

Homeowners or potential homeowners can use **home design/landscaping software** to assist with the design or remodeling of a home, deck, or landscape (Figure 3-39). Home design/landscaping software includes hundreds of predrawn plans which you can customize to meet your needs. Once designed, many home design/landscaping packages will print a material list outlining costs and quantities for the entire project.

Educational/Reference/Entertainment Software

Educational software is software that teaches a particular skill. Educational software exists for just about any subject, from learning a foreign language to learning how to cook. Preschool to high school learners also use educational software to assist them with subjects such as reading and math, or to prepare them for class or college entry exams.

Many educational software products use a computer-based training approach. **Computer-based training (CBT)**, also called **computer-aided instruction**, is a type of education in which students learn by using and completing exercises with instructional software. CBT typically consists of self-directed, self-paced instruction on a topic. CBT is popular in business, industry, and schools for teaching new skills or enhancing existing skills of employees, teachers, or students.

Reference software provides valuable and thorough information for all individuals (Figure 3-40). Popular reference software includes encyclopedias, dictionaries, health/medical guides, and travel directories.

Entertainment software for personal computers includes interactive games, videos, and other programs designed to support a hobby or provide amusement and enjoyment. For example, you can use entertainment software to play games, make a family tree, compose music, or fly an aircraft.

Web Link

For more information on reference software, visit the Discovering Computers 2002 Chapter 3 WEB LINK page (**scsite.com/dc2002/ch3/weblink.htm**) and click Reference Software.

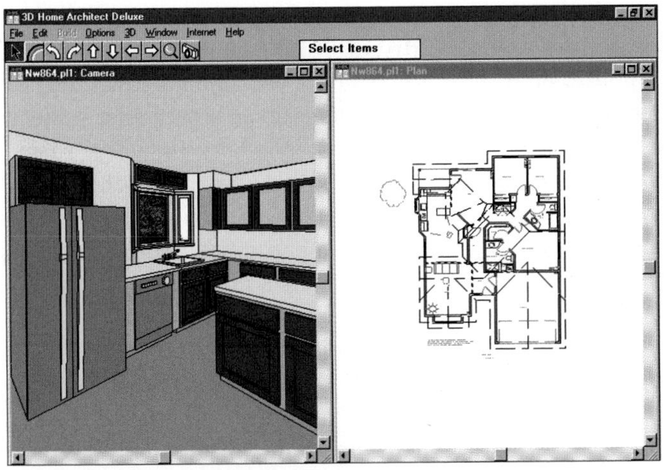

Figure 3-39 Home design/landscaping software can help you design or remodel a home, deck, or landscape.

Figure 3-40 Reference software provides valuable and thorough information for all types of users. This figure shows text you can read about evolution. It includes a variety of pictures, videos, and links to the Web.

ISSUE

How Young Is Too Young?

Educational Software

Software developed for elementary school children, kindergartners, and even preschoolers has won the praise of educators and child psychologists. Yet, controversy has erupted about how young is too young over Knowledge Adventure's® JumpStart Baby™ program, which targets children six- to twenty-four-months old. According to developers, JumpStart Baby™ makes even young children comfortable with computers. The software is tailored to tots and, supporters insist, certainly is more beneficial than an equal amount of time spent watching television. Knowledge Adventure® advocates the software is designed as lapware, meaning it is intended to be used by baby and parent together. It can serve as a springboard to stimulate activities rich in communications and social interaction during the critical developmental years. Critics feel, however, that digital blocks are not a substitute for the real thing. Children need to experience the real world, not a cyber representation. When should children be introduced to computers? Why? How can parents ensure that a child's computer experience is worthwhile?

For more information on children and software, visit the Discovering Computers 2002 Issues Web page (**scsite.com/dc2002/issues.htm**) and click Chapter 3 Issue #4.

SOFTWARE FOR COMMUNICATIONS

One of the main reasons people use computers is to communicate and share information with others. Home and business users have a variety of software options relative to communications. These include e-mail, Web browsers, chat rooms, newsgroups, instant messaging, groupware, and videoconferencing. Chapter 2 presented many of these products. The following sections briefly review these services.

ISSUE

Privacy at Work?

E-Mail

A recent survey indicates that more than 75 percent of Fortune 500 companies routinely monitor employees' e-mail and Web browsing habits. About one company in four has fired an employee based on their discoveries. Some companies even use automated software that searches e-mail messages for derogatory language. One unidentified woman, for example, was fired for using her office e-mail system to complain about her boss. Although she felt her e-mail conversations were private and would not be monitored, she learned, to her chagrin, that she was wrong. Do you think that employers have the right to monitor e-mail? Why or why not? If you knew that a fellow employee criticized the company through the e-mail system, would you tell your boss? What if you heard the same employee planning a theft of company products? Where do you draw the line?

For more information on employee monitoring, visit the Discovering Computers 2002 Issues Web page (**scsite.com/dc2002/issues.htm**) and click Chapter 3 Issue #5.

E-Mail

Today, e-mail quickly is becoming a primary communications method for both personal and business use. **E-mail (electronic mail)** is the transmission of messages via a computer network such as a local area network or the Internet. The message can be simple text or can include an attachment such as a word processing document, a graphical image, or an audio or video clip. You use **e-mail software** to create, send, receive, forward, store, print, and delete e-mail messages (see Figure 2-26 on page 2.30). Most e-mail software has a mail notification alert that informs via a message or sound that you have received new mail, even while you are working in another application.

Web Browsers

A software application called a **Web browser**, or **browser**, allows you to access and view Web pages on the Internet (see Figure 2-6 on page 2.9). Today's browsers have graphical user interfaces and are quite easy to learn and use. Browsers have many special features including buttons and navigation to help guide you through Web sites. In addition to displaying Web pages, most browsers allow you to use other Internet services such as e-mail and chat rooms.

Chat Rooms

A **chat room** permits users to chat with each other via the computer (see Figure 2-32 on 2.35). As you type a line of text on your computer, your entered words display on the computer screens of other people in the same chat room. Chats typically are specific to a certain topic, such as computers or cooking. Some chat rooms support **voice chats** and **video chats**, where you hear and see others and they can hear or see you as you chat.

To start a chat session, you connect to a chat server through a chat client. A **chat client** is software on your computer. Most Web browsers include a chat client. If yours does not, you can download one from the Web.

Newsgroups

A **newsgroup**, also called a **discussion**, is an online area on the Web where users conduct written discussions about a particular subject. The difference between a chat room and a newsgroup is that a chat room is a live conversation. The newsgroup is not. To participate in a newsgroup, a user sends a message to the newsgroup. Other users in the newsgroup read and reply to the message.

Some newsgroups require you enter a user name and password to participate in a discussion. These types of newsgroups are used when messages are to be viewed only by authorized members, such as students taking a college course.

To participate in a newsgroup, you use a software program called a **newsreader**. Most browsers include a newsreader.

Instant Messaging

Instant messaging (IM) is a real-time communications service that notifies you when one or more people are online and then allows you to exchange messages or files with them or join a private chat room (see Figure 2-33 on page 2.36). Many IM services also can alert you to information such as calendar appointments, stock quotes, weather, or sports scores. People use IM on all types of computers, including desktop computers, notebook computers, handheld computers, and Web-enabled devices.

To use IM, you install software from an instant messaging service, sometimes called an **instant messenger**, onto the computer or device with which you wish to use IM. No standards currently exist for IM. Thus, you and all those individuals on your notification list need to use the same or a compatible instant messenger to guarantee successful communications.

Groupware

Groupware is a software application that helps groups of people work together and share information over a network. To assist with these activities, most groupware provides PIM (personal information manager) functions, such as an address book and appointment calendar. A major feature of groupware is group scheduling, in which a group calendar tracks the schedules of multiple users and helps coordinate appointments and meeting times.

Videoconferencing

A **videoconference** is a meeting between two or more geographically separated people who use a network or the Internet to transmit audio and video data (see Figure 1-44 on page 1.34). A videoconference allows participants to collaborate as if they were in the same room.

To participate in a videoconference, you need videoconferencing software along with a microphone, speakers, and a video camera attached to your computer. As you speak, members of the meeting hear your voice on their speakers. Any image in front of the video camera, such as a person's face, displays in a window on each participant's screen.

Using a similar technology, home users today can make a **video telephone call**, where both parties see each other as they talk.

APPLICATIONS ON THE WEB

As discussed in Chapter 1, you often purchase packaged software from a software vendor, retail store, or Web-based business. In this case, you usually install the software onto your computer before you can run it. Using packaged software has the disadvantages of requiring disk space on your computer and being costly to upgrade as vendors release new versions. Realizing these disadvantages, some companies today offer products and services on the Web. A **Web application** is a software application that exists on a Web site. Some Web application sites also store your data and information at their site.

To access a Web application, you simply visit the Web site that offers the program. Some Web sites provide access to the program for free. For example, one site creates a map and driving directions when you enter a starting and destination point (Figure 3-41).

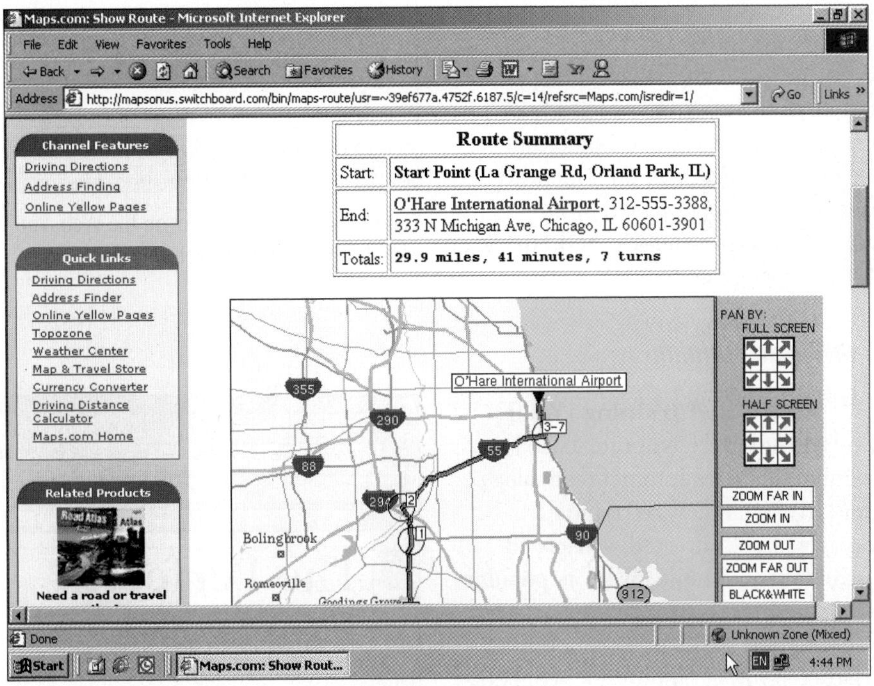

Figure 3-41 This Web site creates a map and provides directions when you enter a starting and destination point.

Web Link

For more information on Web applications, visit the Discovering Computers 2002 Chapter 3 WEB LINK page (**scsite.com/dc2002/ch3/weblink.htm**) and click Web Applications.

Web Link

For more information on groupware, visit the Discovering Computers 2002 Chapter 3 WEB LINK page (**scsite.com/dc2002/ch3/weblink.htm**) and click Groupware.

Other Web sites allow you to use the program for free and pay a fee when a certain action occurs. For example, you can prepare your tax return for free using TurboTax on the Web (Figure 3-42), but if you elect to file it electronically, you pay a small fee (under $10).

Some companies, instead, charge only for service and support — allowing you to use or download the software for free (Figure 3-43). Microsoft's Web applications, called **.NET**, enable users to access Microsoft software on the Web from any type of device or computer that can connect to the Internet.

For those sites that charge for use of the program, a variety of payment schemes exist. Some rent use of the application on a monthly basis, some charge based on the number of user accesses, and others charge a one-time fee.

Figure 3-42 With TurboTax on the Web, you prepare your taxes for free but pay a small fee if you elect to file them electronically.

Web-Based Training

Web-based training (WBT) is a type of CBT (computer-based training) that uses Internet technology. Similarly to CBT, WBT typically consists of self-directed, self-paced instruction on a topic. WBT is popular in business, industry, and schools for teaching new skills or enhancing existing skills of employees, teachers, or students. When using a WBT product, students actively become involved in the learning process instead of passive recipients of information.

Many Web sites offer WBT to the general public. Such training covers a wide range of topics, from how to change a flat tire to creating documents in Word. Many of these Web sites are free. Others ask you to register and pay a fee to take the complete Web-based course.

Figure 3-43 Sun Microsystems only charges for service and support of its StarOffice™ product, which is an integrated word processing, spreadsheet, presentation graphics, database, photo-editing, personal information manager, and communications suite.

WBT often is combined with other materials for distance learning courses. **Distance learning** (**DL**), also called **distance education** (**DE**) or **online learning**, is the delivery of education at one location while the learning takes place at other locations. DL courses provide many time, distance, and place advantages for students who live far from a college campus or work full time. These courses enable students to attend class from anywhere in the world and at times that fit their schedule. Many national and international companies offer DL training. These training courses eliminate the costs of airfare, hotels, and meals for centralized training sessions.

Some Web-based companies specialize in providing instructors with the tools for preparation, distribution, and management of DL courses (Figure 3-44). These tools enable instructors to create rich, educational Web-based training sites and allow the students to interact with a powerful Web learning environment. Through the training site, students can check their progress, take practice tests, search for topics, send e-mail, and participate in discussions and chats. The appeal of these products is they generally are quite easy to learn and use for both the instructors and the students.

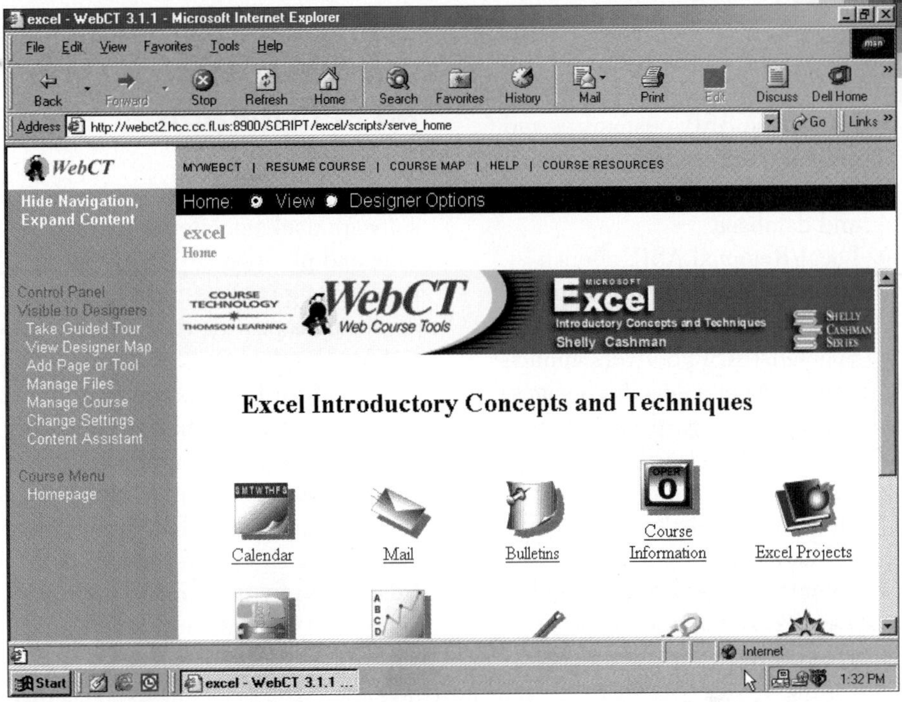

Figure 3-44 WebCT is a tool that enables instructors to create Web-based training courses.

Application Service Providers

Storing and maintaining programs can be a costly investment for businesses. Thus, some have elected to outsource one or more facets of their information technology (IT) needs to an application service provider. An **application service provider** (**ASP**) is a third-party organization that manages and distributes software and services on the Web. For example, Metier is an ASP that provides project management software on the Web (Figure 3-45).

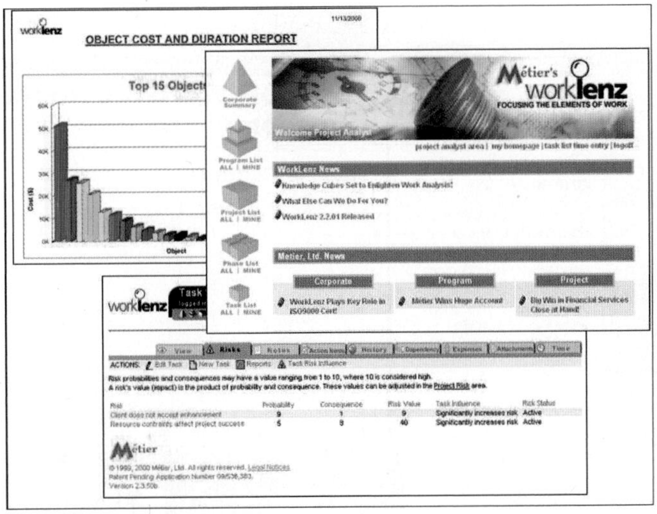

Figure 3-45 WorkLenz is project management software offered by Metier, an application service provider. Using WorkLenz, customers can pinpoint inefficiencies in processes.

Web Link

For more information on distance learning, visit the Discovering Computers 2002 Chapter 3 WEB LINK page (**scsite.com/dc2002/ch3/weblink.htm**) and click Distance Learning.

Five categories of ASPs have emerged:

- Enterprise ASP: customizes and delivers high-end business applications, such as finance and database
- Local/Regional ASP: offers a variety of software applications to a specific geographic region
- Specialist ASP: delivers applications to meet a specific business need, such as preparing taxes
- Vertical Market ASP: provides applications for a particular industry, such as construction or healthcare
- Volume Business ASP: supplies prepackaged applications, such as accounting, to businesses

Despite the advantages, some companies will wait to outsource to an ASP until they have faster Internet connections.

LEARNING AIDS AND SUPPORT TOOLS WITHIN AN APPLICATION

Learning how to use an application software package effectively involves time and practice. To assist you in the learning process, many software applications provide online Help, links to FAQs, and wizards (Figure 3-46).

Online Help is the electronic equivalent of a user manual. It usually is integrated into an application software package. Online Help provides assistance that can increase your productivity and reduce your frustrations by minimizing the time you spend learning how to use an application software package.

In most packages, a function key or a button on the screen starts the Help feature. When you are using an application and have a question, you can use the Help feature to ask a question or access the Help topics in subject or alphabetical order. Often the Help is **context-sensitive**, meaning that the Help information relates to the current task being attempted. Most online Help also points you to Web sites that provide updates and more comprehensive resources to answer your software questions. These Web sites usually have a **FAQs** (Frequently Asked Questions) page to help you find answers to common questions.

In many cases, online Help has replaced the user manual altogether. Most software developers no longer

Figure 3-46b (FAQ)

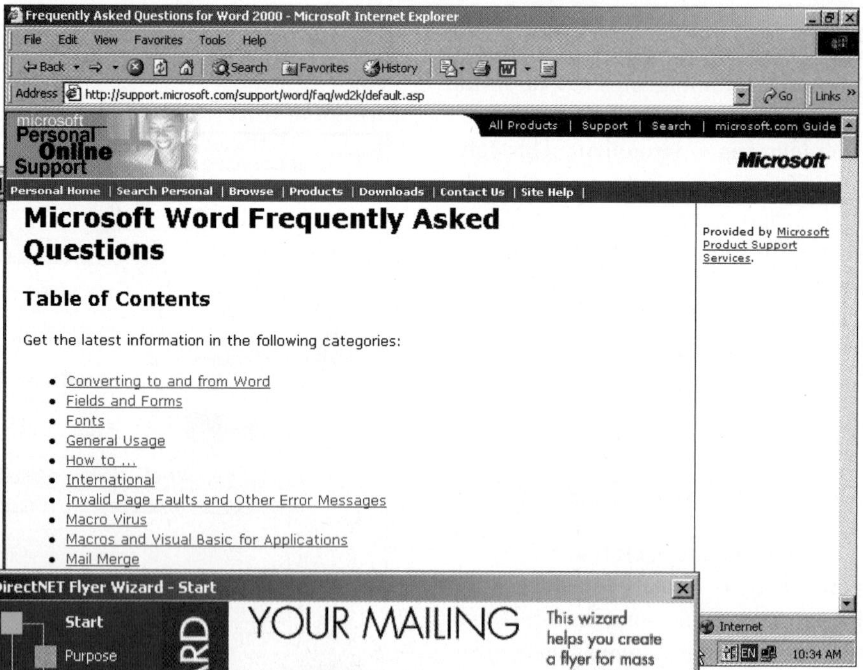

Figure 3-46a (online Help)

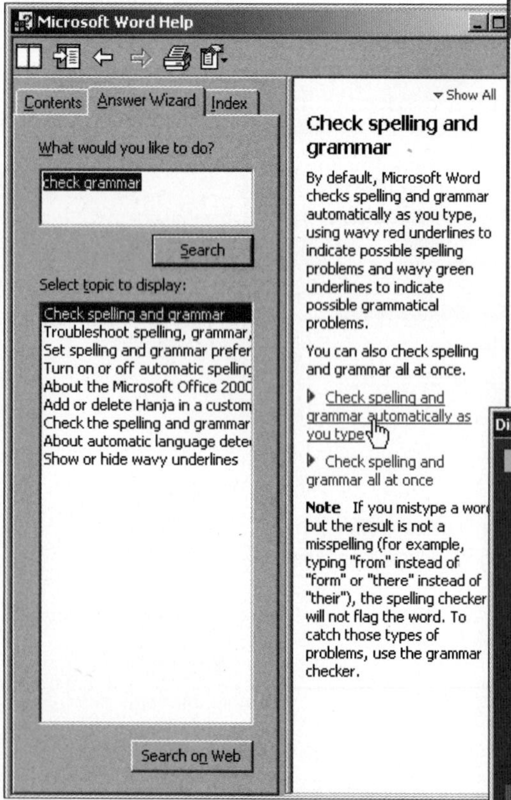

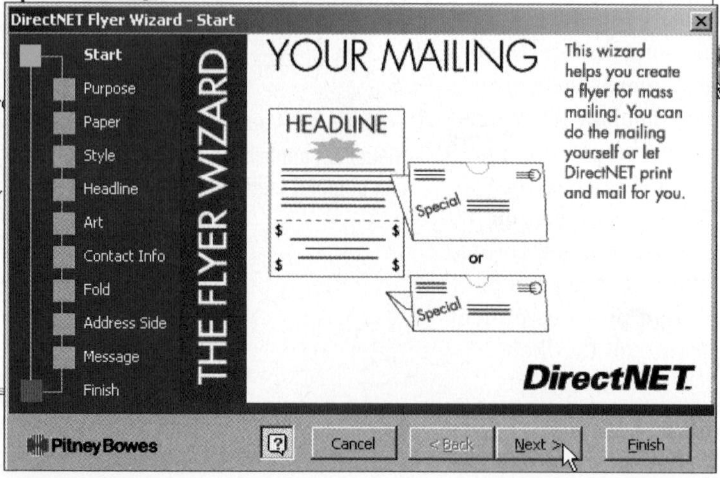

Figure 3-46c (wizard)

Figure 3-46 Many software applications include online Help, links to FAQs, and wizards.

include user's manuals with the software. If you want to learn more about the software package from a printed manual, however, many books are available to help you learn to use the features of personal computer application packages (Figure 3-47). These books typically are available in bookstores and software stores.

A **wizard** is an automated assistant that helps you complete a task by asking you questions and then automatically performing actions based on your answers. Many software applications include wizards. For example, word processing software uses wizards to help you create memorandums, meeting agendas, fax cover sheets, flyers, letters, and resumes. Spreadsheet software includes chart and function wizards. Database software has form and report wizards.

Many colleges and schools provide training on several of the applications discussed in this chapter. If you would like more direction than is provided in online Help, FAQs, wizards, and trade books, contact your local school for a list of class offerings.

Figure 3-47 Many bookstores sell trade books to help you learn to use the features of personal computer application packages.

CHAPTER SUMMARY

This chapter discussed the role of the system software with respect to application software. It then presented an overview of several productivity software applications, graphic design/multimedia software applications, home/personal/educational software applications, and communications software applications. The chapter identified various Web applications. Finally, learning aids and support tools within application software products were presented.

Word Processing Technician

Someone with word processing skills can look for career opportunities as a word processing technician or specialist. Other job titles that involve word processing may include word processing operator, clerk typist, general office clerk, data entry clerk, billing clerk, or file clerk. Job responsibilities may include the following:

- Prepares word processing materials that include correspondence, reports, brochures, and other documents.
- Formats and proofreads materials and makes corrections or changes as directed.
- Maintains filing system based on departmental needs as applicable to word processing procedures.

As a word processing technician, you generally work with a team of people. Word processing operators may find employment opportunities in a wide variety of office settings that include business, industry, government agencies, and non-profit agencies. Generally, a high school diploma is the minimum requirement. Entry-level salaries range from $15,000 to $30,000. Microsoft offers the Microsoft Office Users Specialist (MOUS) certification designed to measure and validate users' skills. Those individuals with more experience and advanced skills may find opportunities as word processing supervisors and office supervisors.

To learn more about the field of word processing as a career, visit the Discovering Computers 2002 Careers Web page (**scsite.com/dc2002/careers.htm**) and click Word Processing Technician.

E-FINANCE

KA-CHING, KA-CHING

Cashing In on Financial Advice

"Money makes the world go 'round," according to Liza Minnelli and her friends in the 1972 hit musical, *Cabaret*. If that musical were written today, the lyrics would be updated to "Money makes the World Wide Web go 'round," based on the volume of financial Web sites available to Internet users.

When Doug Lebda became thoroughly disgusted with all the red tape he encountered trying to apply for a home mortgage, he took matters into his own hands. He started LendingTree, a Web site that helps consumers conveniently obtain mortgages, loans, and credit cards, as shown in Figure 3-54. This Web site and a growing number of other Internet companies work with hundreds of national lenders to match consumers' needs with the marketplaces' lenders. One of the fastest-growing online banks is Wells Fargo (Figure 3-55), with a Web site that features online banking, tax help, and wanted posters of people who have defrauded the bank.

If you do not have a personal banker or a financial planner, consider a Web adviser to guide your investment decisions. Three highly recognized financial Web

Figure 3-54 Online lending Web sites can help consumers seeking assistance with financial matters, including obtaining loans or comparing mortgage rates.

FINANCE WEB SITES	URL
Advice and Education	
MSN MoneyCentral	moneycentral.msn.com
The Motley Fool	fool.com
Yahoo Finance	finance.yahoo.com
Bankrate.com	bankrate.com
E-Loan	loan.com
LendingTree	lendingtree.com
Wells Fargo	wellsfargo.com
Stock Market	
DLJdirect	dljdirect.com
E*TRADE	etrade.com
Financial Engines	financialengines.com
FreeEdgar	www.freeedgar.com
Merrill Lynch Direct	mldirect.ml.com
MeVC	mevc.com
Morningstar	morningstar.com
Vanguard Group	vanguard.com
Taxes	
IRS - The Digital Daily	www.irs.gov
H&R Block	hrblock.com

For an updated list of finance Web sites, visit scsite.com/dc2002/e-rev.htm.

Figure 3-55 Financial resources Web sites offer general information, stock market analyses, and tax advice, as well as guidance and tips.

sites are MSN MoneyCentral, Yahoo Finance, and The Motley Fool (Figure 3-56) for commentary and education on investing strategies, financial news, and taxes.

You likely have heard stories of people who have made — and lost — their fortunes in the stock market. If you are ready to ride the ups and downs of the NASDAQ and the Dow, an abundance of Web sites can help you pick companies that fit your interests and financial needs. For example, FreeEdgar allows you to read company filings with the SEC. DLJdirect gives you the latest market news from Wall Street's Donaldson, Lufkin & Jenrette.

Figure 3-56 The Fool.com Web site contains strategies and news stories related to personal financing and investing.

Figure 3-57 Income tax forms, employment opportunities, and filing procedures and regulations are posted on the Internal Revenue Service THE DIGITAL DAILY Web page.

When April 15 rolls around, many taxpayers mutter the words, Internal Revenue Service. But the IRS can be a friend, too, when you visit, THE DIGITAL DAILY (Figure 3-57). Claiming to be the fastest, easiest tax publication on the planet, this Web page contains procedures for filing tax appeals, and contains IRS forms, publications, and legal regulations. H&R Block also offers tax information in its Tax Center.

For more information on financial Web sites, visit the Discovering Computers 2002 E-Revolution Web page (scsite.com/dc2002/e-rev.htm) and click Finance.

eREVOLUTION E-FINANCE *applied:*

1. Visit the three advice and education Web sites listed in Figure 3-55 and read their top business world reports. Write a paragraph on each, summarizing these stories. Which stocks or mutual funds do these Web sites predict as being sound investments today? What are the current market indexes for the DJIA (Dow Jones Industrial Average), S&P 500, and NASDAQ, and how do these figures compare with the previous day's numbers?

2. Using two of the stock market Web sites listed in Figure 3-55, search for information about Microsoft, Adobe Systems, and one other software vendor discussed in this chapter. Write a paragraph on each of these stocks describing the revenues, net incomes, total assets for the previous year, current stock price per share, highest and lowest prices of each stock during the past year, and other relevant investment information.

In Summary

Web Instructions: To display this page from the Web, start your browser and enter the URL scsite.com/dc2002/ch3/summary.htm. Click the links for current and additional information. To listen to an audio version of this In Summary, click the Audio button. To play the audio, RealPlayer must be installed on your computer (download by clicking here).

1 What Is Application Software?

Application software, also called a **software application** or an **application**, consists of programs designed to perform specific tasks for users. Application software can be grouped into four major categories: productivity software; graphics design and multimedia software; home, personal, and educational software; and communications software.

2 How Does System Software Interact with Application Software?

System software controls the operations of the computer and its devices. It serves as the interface between the user, the application software, and the computer's hardware. The operating system, one type of system software, contains instructions that allow the user to run application software. The operating system must load from storage into the computer's memory before you can run any application software. A **utility** is a type of system program that performs a specific task.

3 What Is the Role of the User Interface?

Users interact with software through a user interface. Both the Microsoft Windows and the Apple Macintosh operating systems use the concept of a **graphical user interface (GUI)**. This type of interface combines text, graphics, and other visual images to make software easier to use.

4 How Do You Start a Software Application?

The desktop is an onscreen work area with common graphical elements such as **icons**, **buttons**, menus, links, windows, and dialog boxes. A software application can be started by clicking its program name on a **menu** or list of **commands**. Clicking the program name instructs the operating system to transfer the program's instructions from a storage medium into memory. Once started, the application displays in a window on the desktop. A **window** is a rectangular area of the screen used to show the program, data, and/or information.

5 What Are the Widely Used Products and Key Features of Productivity/Business Software Applications and Graphic Design/Multimedia Software Applications?

Productivity software helps people become more effective and efficient while performing daily activities. **Word processing software** is used for **creating** and **editing** documents that consist primarily of text. In addition, you can **format** a document to improve its appearance and then print and save it to use again. **Spreadsheet software** organizes numeric data in a **worksheet** made up of rows and columns. **Database software** is used to create a **database**, which is an organized collection of data that can be accessed, retrieved, and used. Presentation graphics software creates documents called presentations that communicate ideas, messages, and other information to a group. A **personal information manager (PIM)** is software that includes an **appointment calendar**, **address book**, and **notepad** to help organize personal information. **Project management software** is used to plan, schedule, track, and analyze the progress of a project. **Accounting software** helps companies record and report their financial transactions.

Power users often use software that allows them to work with graphics and multimedia. **Computer-aided design (CAD) software** assists in creating engineering, architectural, and scientific designs. **Desktop publishing (DTP)** software is used in designing and producing sophisticated documents. **Paint software** is used to draw graphical images with various tools, while **image editing software** provides the capability of modifying existing images. Video editing software and **audio editing software** modify **video** and **audio** segments called clips.

Multimedia authoring software creates electronic interactive presentations that can include text, images, video, audio, and animation. Web page authoring software is designed to help users create Web pages and to organize, manage, and maintain Web sites.

6 What Are the Widely Used Products and Key Features of Home/Personal/Educational Software Applications and Communications Software Applications?

Many applications are designed for use at home, or for personal or educational use. **Integrated software** combines several productivity software applications into a single package. Personal finance software is an accounting program that helps users pay bills, balance a checkbook, track income and expenses, follow investments, and evaluate financial plans. **Legal software** assists in the creation of legal documents and provides legal advice. **Tax preparation software** guides users through the process of filing federal taxes. **Personal DTP software** helps develop conventional documents by asking questions, offering predefined layouts, and providing standard text. **Photo-editing software** is used to edit digital photographs. A **clip art/image gallery** is a collection of clip art and photographs. **Home design/landscaping software** assists with design or remodeling a home, deck, or landscape. **Educational software** teaches a particular skill, **reference software** provides information, and **entertainment software** is designed to support a hobby or provide amusement.

One of the primary reasons people use computers is to communicate and share information. A variety of software options are available. **E-mail software** is used to create, send, receive, forward, store, print, and delete **e-mail** (**electronic mail**) messages. A **Web browser**, or **browser**, is a software application used to access and view Web pages. **Newsgroups**, or online **discussions**, are areas on the Web where users can participate in discussions about a particular topic. **Instant messaging** provides real-time communications by permitting you to exchange messages or files with other online users. Groupware identifies any type of software that helps groups of people on a network collaborate on projects and share information. A **videoconference** is a meeting between two or more people separated geographically who use a network or the Internet to transmit audio and video data.

7 What Products Are Available as Web Applications?

A **Web application** is a software application that exists on a Web site. To access the program, you visit the Web site that offers the program. Some examples of Web applications include the capability of creating a map and viewing driving directions; viewing your credit card transactions; and preparing your tax return. **Web-based training** (**WBT**) is a type of computer-based training that uses Internet technology and often is combined with **distance learning** (**DL**).

8 What Learning Aids Are Available with Software Applications?

Many software applications and Web sites provide learning aids such as online Help, FAQs, and wizards. Online Help is the electronic equivalent of a user manual. **FAQs** (Frequently Asked Questions) provide answers to common queries. A **wizard** is an automated assistant that helps users complete a task by asking questions and then performing actions based on the answers.

Key Terms

Web Instructions: To display this page from the Web, start your browser and enter the URL scsite.com/dc2002/ch3/terms.htm. Scroll through the list of terms. Click a term to display its definition and a picture. Click the To WEB button for current and additional information about the term from the Web. To see animations, Shockwave and Flash Player must be installed on your computer (download by clicking here).

accounting software (3.21)
address book (3.20)
antivirus program (3.3)
application (3.2)
application service provider (ASP) (3.35)
application software (3.2)
appointment calendar (3.20)
audio (3.25)
audio editing software (3.25)
authorware (3.25)
bar charts (3.14)
browser (3.32)
button (3.4)
cell (3.12)
charting (3.14)
chat client (3.32)
chat room (3.32)
click (3.4)
clip art (3.8)
clip art/image gallery (3.30)
clip gallery (3.18)
Clipboard (3.10)
color library (3.23)
column charts (3.14)
command (3.5)
computer-aided design (CAD) software (3.22)
computer-aided instruction (3.30)
computer-based training (CBT) (3.30)
context-sensitive (3.36)
context-sensitive menu (3.6)
creating (3.10)
criteria (3.17)
currency (3.16)
data type (3.16)
database (3.15)
database management system (DBMS) (3.16)
database software (3.16)
date (3.16)
desktop (3.4)
desktop publishing (DTP) software (3.23)
dialog box (3.6)
discussion (3.32)
distance education (DE) (3.35)
distance learning (DL) (3.35)
editing (3.10)
educational software (3.30)
e-mail (electronic mail) (3.32)
e-mail software (3.32)
entertainment software (3.31)
FAQs (3.36)
field (3.16)
field size (3.16)
file (3.10)
file name (3.10)
find (3.9)
font (3.10)
font size (3.10)
font style (3.10)
footer (3.9)
format (3.10)
formula (3.12)
function (3.13)
graphical user interface (GUI) (3.4)
groupware (3.33)
header (3.9)
home design/landscaping software (3.30)
hyperlink (3.16)
icon (3.4)
illustration software (3.24)
image editing software (3.24)
import (3.18)
instant messaging (IM) (3.33)
instant messenger (3.33)
integrated software (3.27)
label (3.12)

PRINTING
The process of sending a file to a printer to generate output on a medium such as paper. (3.11)

legal software (3.28)
line charts (3.14)
macro (3.13)
margins (3.8)
memo (3.16)
menu (3.5)
multimedia authoring software (3.25)
.NET (3.34)
newsgroup (3.32)
newsreader (3.32)
notepad (3.20)
numeric (3.16)
object (3.16)
online banking (3.28)
online Help (3.36)
online learning (3.35)
online print service (3.29)
operating system (3.3)
page layout (3.23)
paint software (3.24)
personal DTP software (3.29)
personal finance software (3.27)
personal information manager (PIM) (3.20)
photo-editing software (3.29)
pie charts (3.14)
point (3.10)
pointer (3.4)
populating (3.17)
presentation graphics software (3.18)
printing (3.11)
productivity software (3.7)
project management software (3.21)
query (3.17)
record (3.16)
reference software (3.31)
replace (3.9)
saving (3.10)
scrolling (3.9)
search (3.9)
shortcut menu (3.6)
slide show (3.18)
software application (3.2)
software package (3.2)
sort (3.17)
speech recognition (3.11)
spelling checker (3.9)
spreadsheet software (3.12)
structure (3.16)
submenu (3.5)
suite (3.20)
synchronize (3.20)
system software (3.3)
tables (3.16)
tax preparation software (3.28)
text (3.16)
title bar (3.6)
user interface (3.4)
utility (3.3)
utility program (3.3)
validation (3.17)
value (3.12)
video (3.25)
video chats (3.32)
video editing software (3.25)
video telephone call (3.33)
videoconference (3.33)
virus (3.3)
voice chats (3.32)
voice recognition (3.11)
Web application (3.33)
Web browser (3.32)
Web-based training (WBT) (3.34)
what-if analysis (3.14)
window (3.6)
wizard (3.37)
word processing software (3.8)
word processor (3.8)
word wrap (3.9)
worksheet (3.12)

Learn It Online

Web Instructions: To display this page from the Web, start your browser and enter the URL scsite.com/dc2002/ch3/learn.htm.

1. Web Guide

Click Web Guide to display the Guide to World Wide Web Sites and Searching Techniques Web page. Click Shopping and then click eBay. Search for Software. Use your word processing program to prepare a brief report on the software programs you found. Submit your assignment to your instructor.

2. Scavenger Hunt

Click Scavenger Hunt. Print a copy of the Scavenger Hunt page; use this page to write down your answers as you search the Web. Submit your completed page to your instructor.

3. Who Wants to Be a Computer Genius?

Click Computer Genius to find out if you are a computer genius. Directions on how to play the game will display. When you are ready to play, click the PLAY button. Submit your score to your instructor.

4. Wheel of Terms

Click Wheel of Terms to reinforce important terms you learned in this chapter by playing the Shelly Cashman Series version of this popular game. Directions on how to play the game will display. When you are ready to play, click the PLAY button. Submit your score to your instructor.

5. Career Corner

Click Career Corner to display the Penn State's Career Services Web page. Click a link of your choice. Write a brief report on the information you found. Submit the report to your instructor.

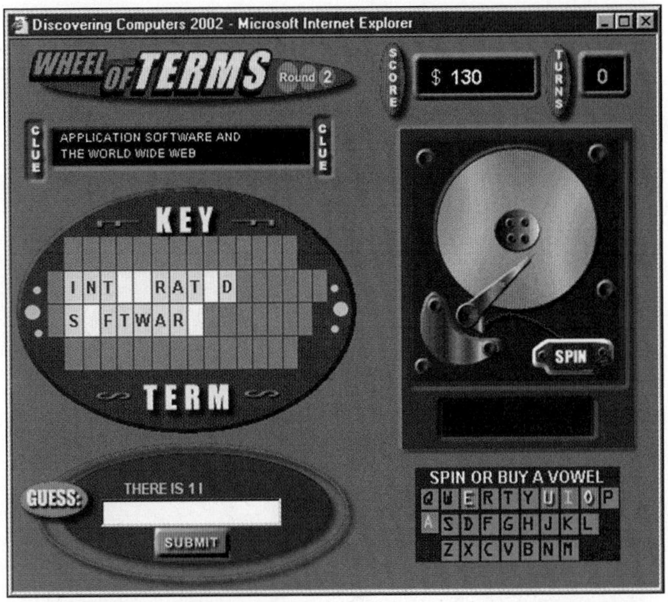

6. Search Sleuth

Click the Search Sleuth to learn search techniques that will help make you a research expert. Submit the completed assignment to your instructor.

7. Crossword Puzzle Challenge

Click Crossword Puzzle Challenge. Complete the puzzle to reinforce skills you learned in this chapter. Directions on how to play the game will display. When you are ready to play, click the PLAY button. Submit the completed puzzle to your instructor.

8. Practice Test

Click Practice Test. Answer each question. When completed, enter your name and click the Grade Test button to submit the quiz for grading. Make a note of any missed questions. If required, print a copy to submit to your instructor.

Web Instructions: To display this page from the Web, start your browser and enter the URL scsite.com/dc2002/ch3/check.htm. Click the links for current and additional information. To experience the animation and interactivity, Shockwave and Flash Player must be installed on your computer (download by clicking here.)

LABEL THE FIGURE

Instructions: Identify the indicated elements in the Windows graphical user interface.

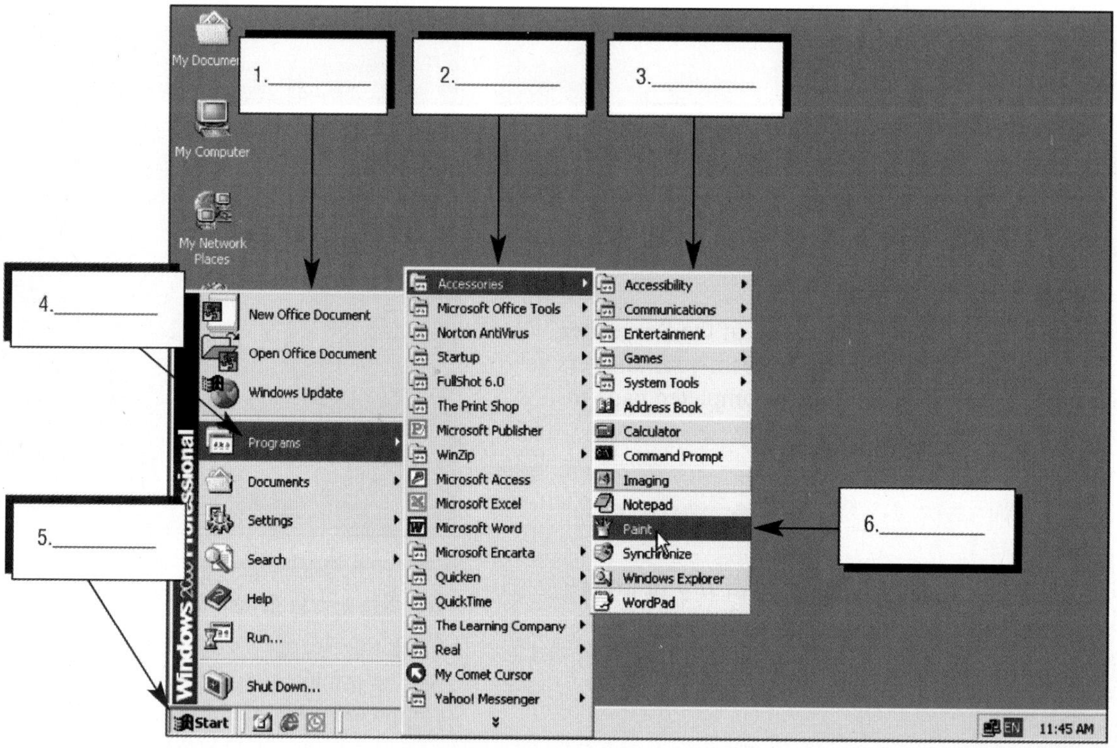

MATCHING

Instructions: Match each term from the column on the left with the best description from the column on the right.

_______ 1. word wrap
_______ 2. what-if analysis
_______ 3. validation
_______ 4. clip gallery
_______ 5. query

a. Spreadsheet feature that displays data relationships in a graphical, rather than numerical, form.
b. Word processing feature used to locate all occurrences of a particular character, word, or phrase.
c. Word processing feature that allows typing continually without pressing the ENTER key at the end of each line.
d. Database feature that is a specific set of instructions for retrieving data.
e. Database feature that compares data to a set of defined rules or values to determine if it is acceptable.
f. Spreadsheet feature in which certain values are altered to reveal the effects of those changes.
g. Presentation graphics feature consisting of images, pictures, and clips that can be incorporated into slides.

Checkpoint

MULTIPLE CHOICE

Instructions: Select the letter of the correct answer for each of the following questions.

1. A(n) __________ is a utility that prevents, detects, and removes viruses from a computer's memory or storage devices.
   a. macro
   b. operating system
   c. antivirus program
   d. virus program
2. A small symbol on the screen is called a(n) __________.
   a. pointer
   b. mouse
   c. menu
   d. icon
3. A __________ is a special window a program displays to provide information, present available options, or request a response.
   a. dialog box
   b. shortcut menu
   c. context-sensitive menu
   d. function
4. A __________ is a unique combination of letters of the alphabet, numbers, and other characters that identifies the file.
   a. title bar
   b. file
   c. file name
   d. program name
5. __________ software enables professional designers to design and produce sophisticated documents that contain text, graphics, and brilliant colors.
   a. Spreadsheet
   b. Desktop publishing
   c. Word processing
   d. Paint

SHORT ANSWER

Instructions: Write a brief answer to each of the following questions.

1. How are creating, editing, and formatting a word processing document different? __________ What is the Clipboard? __________ How does the Clipboard work? __________
2. What is a personal information manager? __________ Describe some of the features that are available in a PIM. __________
3. Why do professional designers and graphic artists use DTP software instead of word processing packages? __________ What is a color library? __________ What is page layout? __________
4. What is an Internet e-mail address? __________ What two parts of an e-mail address are separated by the at (@) sign? __________
5. What is online Help? __________ How do FAQs and wizards help software users? __________

WORKING TOGETHER

Instructions: Working with a group of your classmates, complete the following team exercise.

A Web application is a software application that exists on a Web site. With your group, develop a report describing at least three of these Web applications and how an individual could use these various applications effectively. Include in your report a description of each application, a short overview of any online Help or FAQs, and the URL for all applications within your report. Share your findings with your class.

Web Instructions: To display this page from the Web, start your browser and enter the URL scsite.com/dc2002/ch3/lab.htm. Click the links for current and additional information.

1. Working with Application Programs

This exercise uses Windows 98 procedures. Windows is a multitasking operating system, meaning you can work on two or more applications that reside in memory at the same time. To find out how to work with multiple application programs, click the Start button on the taskbar, and then click Help on the Start menu. Click the Contents tab. Click the Exploring Your Computer book. Click the Work with Programs book. Click an appropriate topic to answer each of the following questions:

- How do you start a program?
- How do you switch between programs?
- How do you quit a program that is not responding?
- How do you quit a program?

Close the Windows Help window.

2. Creating a Word Processing Document

WordPad is a simple word processing program included with the Windows operating system. To create a document with WordPad, click the Start button on the taskbar, point to Programs on the Start menu, point to Accessories on the Programs submenu, and then click WordPad on the Accessories submenu. If necessary, when the WordPad window opens, click its Maximize button. Click View on the menu bar. If a check mark does not display to the left of the Toolbar command, click the toolbar command. Type a complete answer to one of the E-Revolution applied questions posed in this chapter. Your answer should be at least two paragraphs long. Press the TAB key to indent the first line of each paragraph and the ENTER key to begin a new paragraph. To correct errors, press the BACKSPACE key to erase to the left of the insertion point and press the DELETE key to erase to the right. To insert text, position the I-beam mouse pointer at the location where the text should be inserted, and then begin typing. At the end of your document, press the ENTER key twice and then type your name. When your document is complete, save it on a floppy disk inserted into drive A. Click the Save button on the toolbar, type `a:\h3-2` in the File name text box in the Save As dialog box, and then click the Save button. Click the Print button on the toolbar to print your document. Quit WordPad.

3. Using WordPad Help

This exercise uses Windows 98 procedures. Start WordPad as described in In The Lab 2 above. Click Help on the WordPad menu bar and then click Help Topics. When the WordPad Help window opens, click the Index tab. Type `saving documents` in the text box and then press the ENTER key. Click To save changes to a document in the Topics Found dialog box and then click the Display button.

- How can you save changes to a document?
- How can you save an existing document with a new name?

Close the WordPad Help window and quit WordPad.

4. Productivity Software Products

What productivity software packages are on your computer? Click the Start button on the taskbar and point to Programs on the Start menu. Scan the Programs submenu (if necessary, point to the arrow at the top or bottom of the submenu to move the submenu up or down) for the names of popular productivity packages. Write the package name and the type of software application (see the chart on page 3.7 for help). When you are finished, click an empty area of the desktop.

Web Work

Web Instructions: To display this page from the Web, start your browser and enter the URL scsite.com/dc2002/ch3/web.htm. To view At The Movies in exercise 1, RealPlayer must be installed on your computer (download by clicking here). To use the Shelly Cashman Series Word Processing Lab and the Working with Spreadsheets Lab from the Web, Shockwave and Flash Player must be installed on your computer (download by clicking here).

What Is Microsoft?

To view the What Is Microsoft? movie, click the button to the left or click the Play button to the right. Watch the movie, and then complete the exercise by answering the questions below. Founded in 1975, Microsoft is a $25 billion company. It is divided into three main business groups: operating systems, software products, and consumer products, which include games, Web browsers, and other home, personal, and educational products. With this exposure, Microsoft dominates in many markets. Nine out of ten personal computers run some version of the Microsoft Windows operating system. In addition, Microsoft has 90 percent of the office/spreadsheet/graphics software market. Its MSN Internet Explorer comprises more than 60 percent of the Web-browser market. And, because Microsoft bundles and interlocks its systems and programs, organizations with a network of computers are compelled to buy Microsoft products continually. What do you think should be done, if anything, and why?

Shelly Cashman Series Word Processing Lab

Follow the instructions in Web Work 2 on page 1.47 to start and use the Shelly Cashman Series Word Processing Lab. If you are running from the Web, enter the URL www.scsite.com/sclabs/menu.htm or display this Web Work page (see instructions at the top of this page) and then click the button to the left.

Shelly Cashman Series Working with Spreadsheets Lab

Follow the instructions in Web Work 2 on page 1.47 to start and use the Shelly Cashman Series Working with Spreadsheets Lab. If you are running from the Web, enter the URL www.scsite.com/sclabs/menu.htm or display the Web Work page (see instructions at the top of this page) and then click the button to the left.

Setting Up an E-Mail Account

The fastest growing software application may be electronic mail (e-mail). One free e-mail service reports 30 million current subscribers with an additional 80,000 joining every day. To set up a free e-mail account, click the button to the left. Follow the procedures to establish an e-mail account. When you are finished, send yourself an e-mail.

In the News

It is a computer user's nightmare — a button is clicked accidentally or a key is pressed unintentionally and an important message, document, or presentation is deleted. Happily, some software can restore a sound night's sleep by continuously copying open files to the hard drive. Not only are files kept safe, but you always can return to earlier versions of a project. Click the button to the left and read a news article about a new software program. Who is introducing the program? What is the program called? What does it do? Who will benefit from using this software? Why? Where can the software be obtained? Would you be interested in this software? Why or why not?

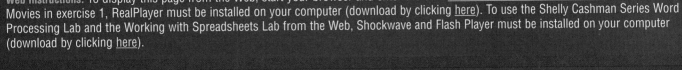

CHAPTER 4

The Components of the System Unit

The doorbell rings. As you open the door, your niece and nephew politely greet you and then head straight for the computer. Weekend visits have become part of their regular routine. You would like to think it is because of your great personality! The real draw is your computer and all the cool game software.

Lately, though, you have heard complaining. Videos and actions on the screen are choppy. The computer is slow, and it freezes in the middle of some programs.

What can you do? You cannot afford a new computer. A visit to the electronics store where you purchased the computer seems like the solution. After explaining the situation to a technician, she suggests you upgrade the memory inside the computer for a cost of a hundred dollars. It sounds great, but you have one very big problem. You do not have the slightest idea how to install memory inside a computer. The technician assures you the memory upgrade kit includes thorough instructions with detailed pictures. The store also has a 24-hour toll-free help line.

Leaving the store with the upgrade memory kit in hand, you will tackle this project on the weekend — when you can recruit help from your niece and nephew!

OBJECTIVES

After completing this chapter, you will be able to:

- Describe the components in the system unit
- Explain how the CPU uses the four steps of a machine cycle to process data
- Compare and contrast various personal computer processors on the market today
- Define a bit and describe how a series of bits represents data
- Differentiate between the various types of memory
- Describe the types of expansion slots and cards in the system unit
- Explain the difference between a serial, a parallel, and a USB port
- Describe how buses contribute to a computer's processing speed
- Identify components in a notebook computer
- Identify components in a handheld computer

THE SYSTEM UNIT

Whether you are a home or a business user, you most likely will make the decision to purchase a new computer or upgrade an existing computer within your lifetime. Thus, understanding the purpose of each component in a computer is important. As discussed in Chapter 1, a computer includes devices used for input, processing, output, storage, and communications. Many of these components reside in the system unit.

The **system unit** is a box-like case that houses the electronic components of the computer used to process data. Sometimes called a **chassis**, the system unit is made of metal or plastic and protects the internal electronic components from damage. All computers have a system unit (Figure 4-1).

On a personal computer, the electronic components and most storage devices reside inside the

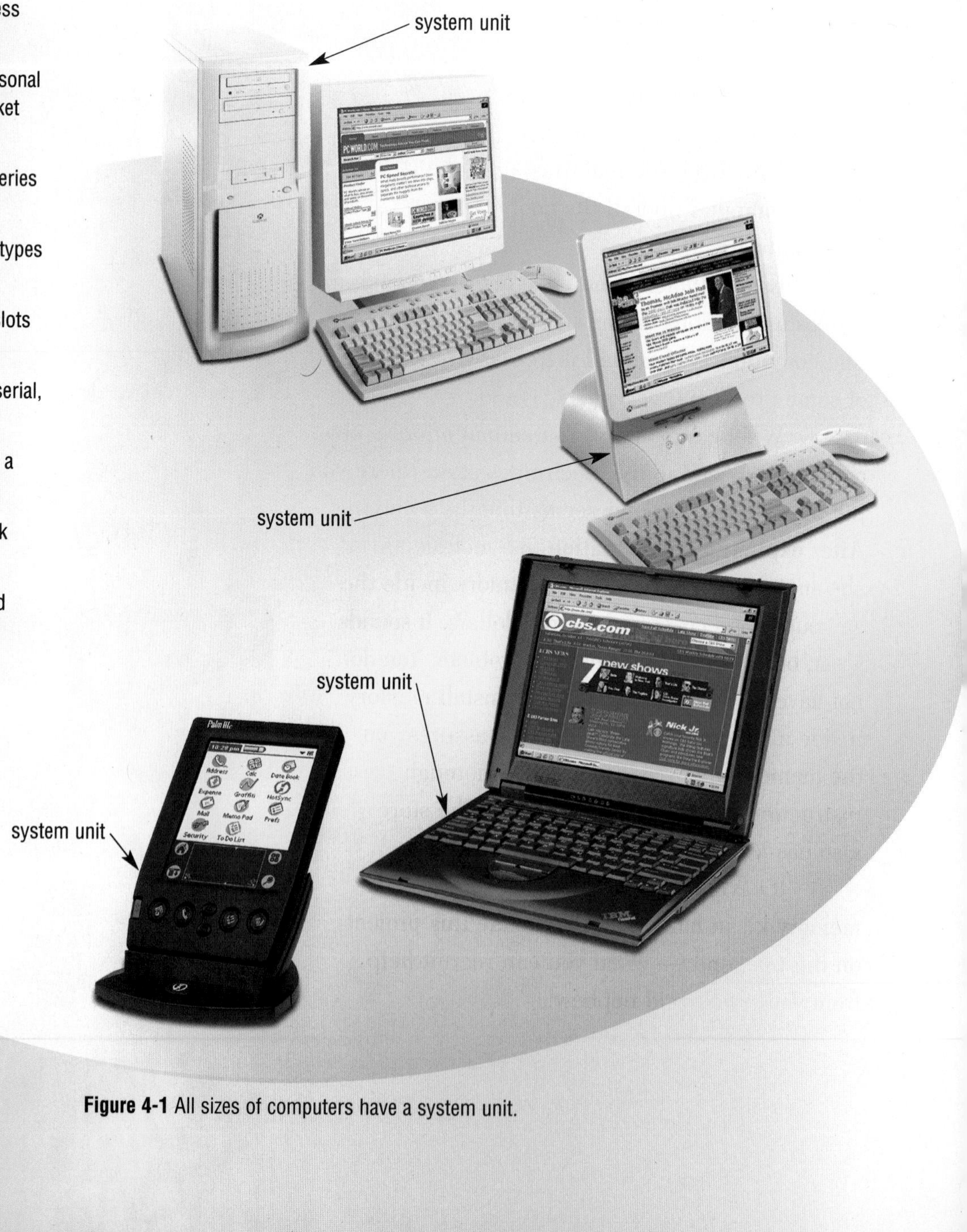

Figure 4-1 All sizes of computers have a system unit.

system unit. Other devices, such as a keyboard, mouse, microphone, monitor, printer, speakers, scanner, and PC camera normally occupy space outside the system unit. On a desktop personal computer, the system unit usually is a device separate from the monitor and keyboard. Some system units sit on top of a desk. Other models, called **tower models**, can stand vertically on the floor.

To conserve on space, an **all-in-one computer** houses the system unit in the same physical case as the monitor. On notebook computers, the keyboard and pointing device often occupy the area on the top of the system unit. The display attaches to the system unit by a hinge. The system unit on a handheld computer usually consumes the entire device. On these devices, the display is part of the system unit too.

At some point, you might have to open the system unit on a desktop personal computer to replace or install a new component. For this reason, you should be somewhat familiar with the inside of the system unit.

Figure 4-2 identifies some of the components inside a system unit on a desktop personal computer. Components inside the system unit include the processor, memory module, cards, ports, and connectors. The

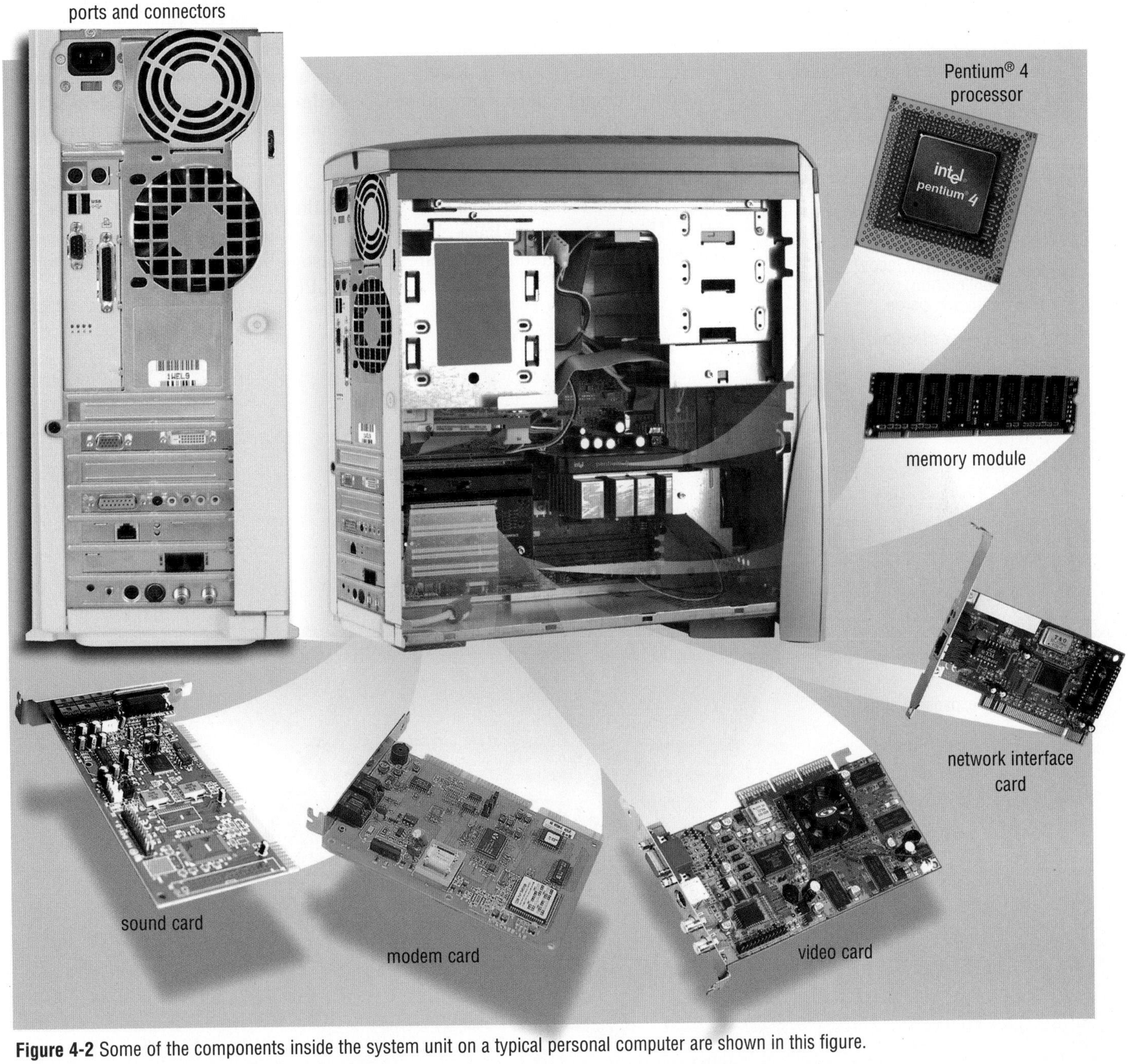

Figure 4-2 Some of the components inside the system unit on a typical personal computer are shown in this figure.

processor interprets and carries out the basic instructions that operate a computer. A memory module is a package that houses memory. Memory temporarily holds data and instructions. A card, also called an expansion card, is a circuit board that adds devices or capabilities to the computer. Four types of cards found in most desktop personal computers today are a sound card, a modem card, a video card, and a network interface card.

Devices outside the system unit attach to a port on the system unit by a cable. These devices may include a keyboard, mouse, microphone, monitor, printer, scanner, speakers, and PC camera.

Web Link

For more information on motherboards, visit the Discovering Computers 2002 Chapter 4 WEB LINK page (**scsite.com/dc2002/ch4/weblink.htm**) and click Motherboards.

The Motherboard

The **motherboard**, sometimes called **system board**, is the main circuit board in the system unit. Figure 4-3 shows a photograph of a desktop personal computer motherboard and identifies some of its components, including different types of chips.

A **chip** is a small piece of semi-conducting material, usually no bigger than one-half-inch square, on which integrated circuits are etched. An **integrated circuit** (**IC**) is a microscopic pathway capable of carrying electrical current. Each integrated circuit can contain millions of elements such as transistors. A **transistor** acts as an electronic switch, or gate, that opens or closes the circuit for electronic signals.

Manufacturers package chips so the chips can be attached to a circuit board such as a motherboard, memory module, or card. A variety of chip packages exist (Figure 4-4). One type, called a **dual inline package** (**DIP**), consists of two parallel rows of downward-pointing thin metal feet (pins). The pins attach the chip package to the circuit board. A **pin grid array** (**PGA**) **package** holds a larger number of pins because the pins are mounted on the surface of the package. A **flip chip-PGA** (**FC-PGA**) **package** is a higher-performance PGA packaging that places the chip on the opposite side (flip side) of the pins. Another high performance packaging technique does not use pins. A **single edge contact** (**SEC**) **cartridge** connects to the motherboard on one of its edges.

The motherboard contains many different types of chips. Of these, one of the most important is the processor, also called the central processing unit (CPU).

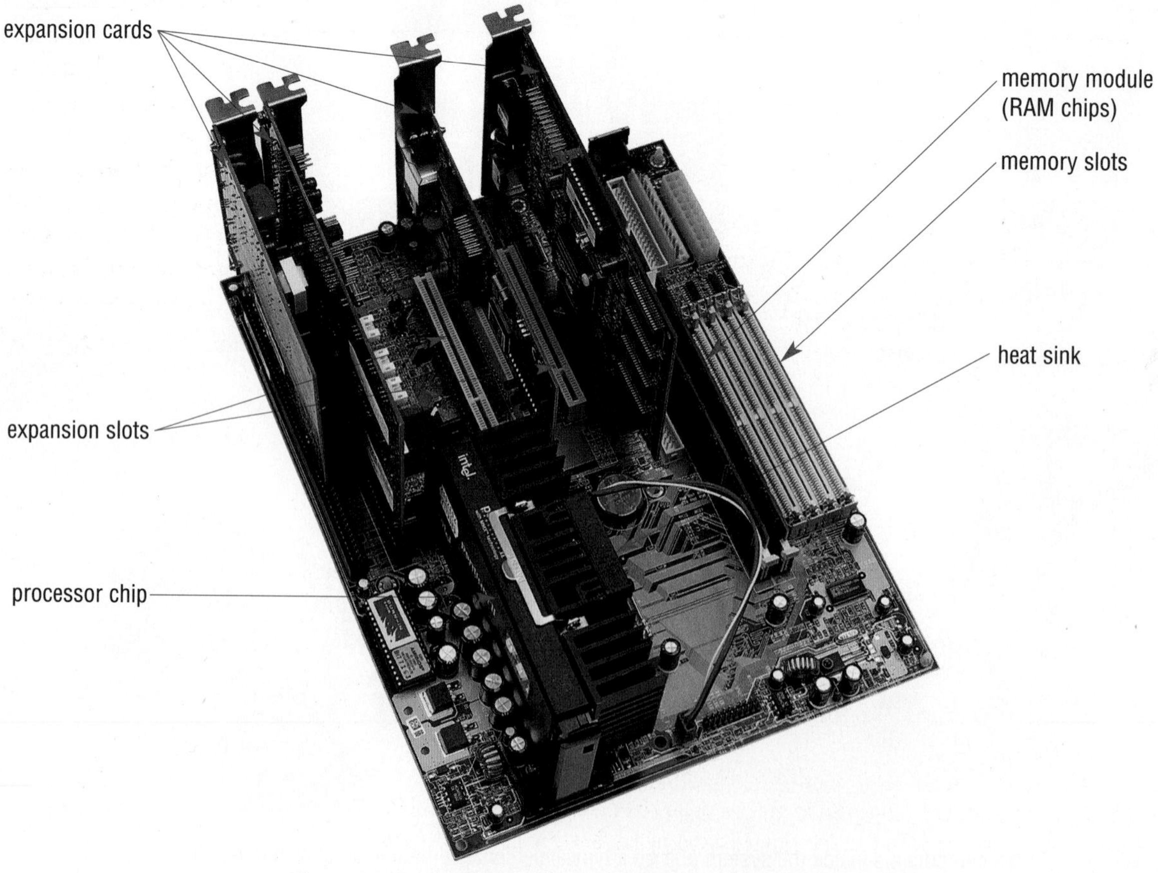

Figure 4-3 The motherboard in a desktop personal computer contains chips and many other electronic components.

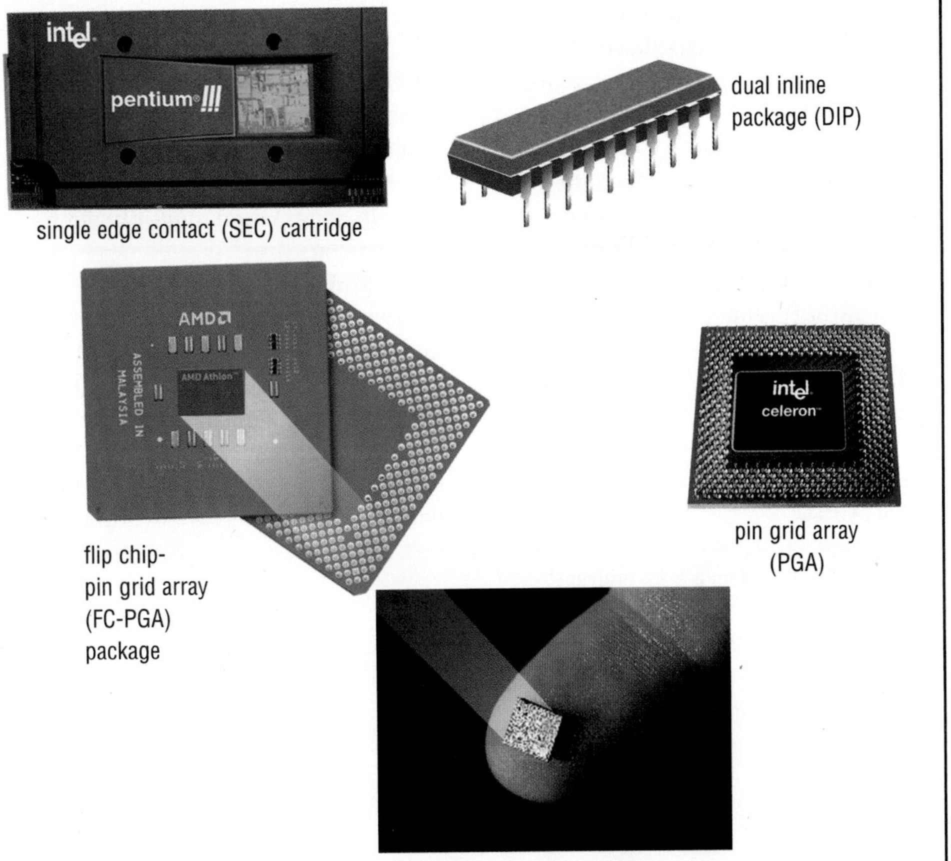

Figure 4-4 Various chip packages.

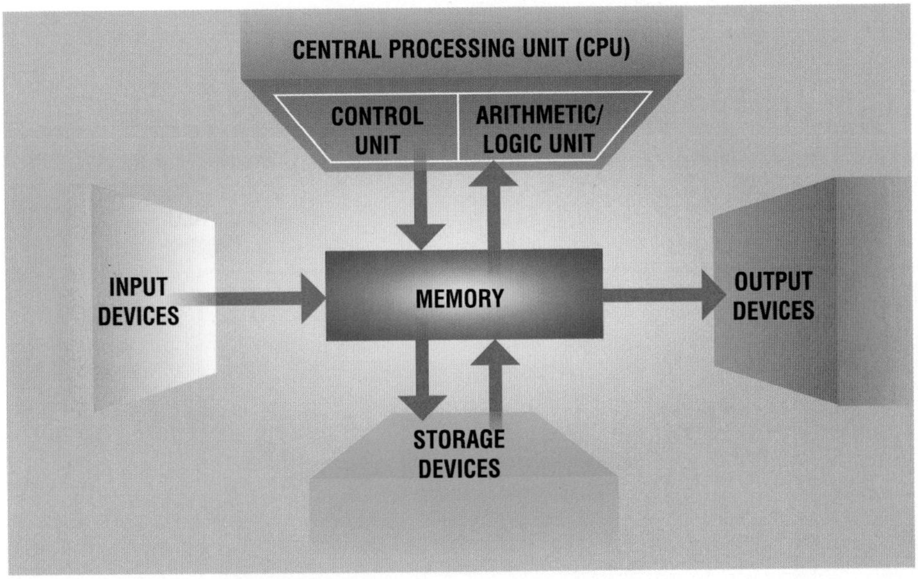

Figure 4-5 Most of the devices connected to the computer communicate with the CPU in order to carry out a task. The arrows in this figure represent the flow of data, instructions, and information.

CENTRAL PROCESSING UNIT

The **central processing unit (CPU)**, often called a **processor**, interprets and carries out the basic instructions that operate a computer. The CPU significantly impacts overall computing power and manages most of a computer's operations. Most of the devices connected to the computer communicate with the CPU in order to carry out a task (Figure 4-5).

The CPU contains the control unit and the arithmetic/logic unit. These two components work together to perform processing operations.

The Control Unit

The **control unit**, one component of the CPU, directs and coordinates most of the operations in the computer. The control unit has a role much like a traffic cop: it interprets each instruction issued by a program and then initiates the appropriate action to carry out the instruction.

For every instruction, the control unit repeats a set of four basic operations: (1) fetching, (2) decoding, (3) executing, and, if necessary, (4) storing. **Fetching** is the process of obtaining a program instruction or data item from memory. **Decoding** is the process of translating the instruction into commands the computer can execute. **Executing** is the process of carrying out the commands. **Storing** is the process of writing the result to memory.

Together, these four operations (fetching, decoding, executing, and storing) comprise a **machine cycle** or **instruction cycle** (Figure 4-6). **Instruction time (i-time)** is the time it takes the control unit to fetch and decode. **Execution time (e-time)** is the time it takes the control unit to execute and store. You can compute the total time required for a machine cycle by adding together the i-time and e-time.

Some computer professionals measure a CPU's speed according to how many **m**illions of **i**nstructions **p**er **s**econd (**MIPS**) it can process. Current desktop personal computers, for example, can process more than 300 MIPS. No real standard for measuring MIPS exists, however, because different instructions require varying amounts of processing time.

CPUs use either a CISC or RISC design. **CISC (complex instruction set computing)** supports a large number of instructions. **RISC (reduced instruction set computing)** reduces the instructions to only those used more frequently. A RISC CPU executes simple instructions more quickly than a CISC CPU. A CISC CPU executes complex instructions more quickly than a RISC CPU.

The Arithmetic/Logic Unit

The **arithmetic/logic unit (ALU)**, another component of the CPU, performs arithmetic, comparison, and logical operations.

Arithmetic operations include addition, subtraction, multiplication, and division.

Comparison operations involve comparing one data item to another to determine if the first item is greater than, equal to, or less than the other item. Depending on the result of the comparison, different actions may occur. To determine if an employee should receive overtime

Figure 4-6 THE STEPS IN A MACHINE CYCLE

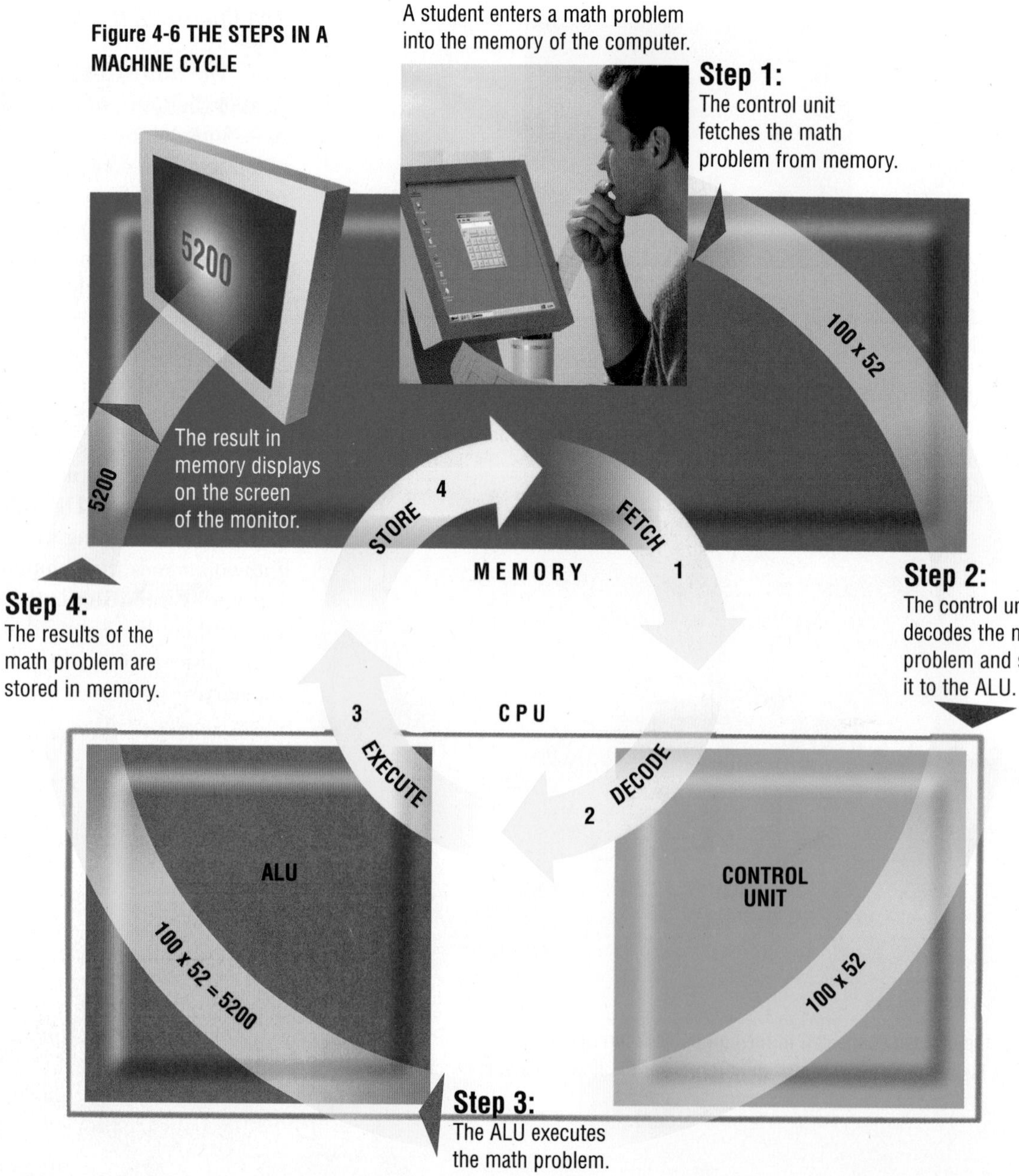
A student enters a math problem into the memory of the computer.
Step 1:
The control unit fetches the math problem from memory.
5200
100 x 52
The result in memory displays on the screen of the monitor.
5200
4
STORE
FETCH
MEMORY
1
Step 2:
The control unit decodes the math problem and sends it to the ALU.
Step 4:
The results of the math problem are stored in memory.
3
CPU
EXECUTE
DECODE
2
ALU
CONTROL UNIT
100 x 52 = 5200
100 x 52
Step 3:
The ALU executes the math problem.

pay, the ALU compares the number of hours an employee worked during the week to the regular time hours allowed (40 hours, for instance). If the hours worked is greater than 40, the ALU calculates an overtime wage. If hours worked is not greater than 40, the ALU does not calculate an overtime wage.

Logical operations use conditions along with logical operators such as AND, OR, and NOT. For example, if only non-salaried employees can receive overtime pay, the ALU must verify that the employee is non-salaried AND worked more than 40 hours before computing an overtime wage.

Pipelining

In some computers, the CPU processes only one instruction at a time. In these computers, the CPU waits until an instruction completes all four stages of the machine cycle (fetch, decode, execute, and store) before beginning work on the next instruction.

With **pipelining**, the CPU begins executing a second instruction before it completes the first instruction. Pipelining results in faster processing because the CPU does not have to wait for one instruction to complete the machine cycle before fetching the next. Think of a pipeline as an assembly line. By the time the first instruction is in the last stage of the machine cycle, three other instructions could have been fetched and started through the machine cycle (Figure 4-7).

Although formerly used only in high-performance computers, today's personal computers commonly use pipelining. Most current personal computer CPU chips can pipeline up to four instructions.

Registers

The CPU contains high-speed storage locations, called **registers**, that temporarily hold data and instructions. A CPU has many different types of registers, each with a specific function. These functions include storing the location from where an instruction was fetched, storing an instruction while the control unit decodes it, storing data while the ALU processes it, and storing the results of a calculation.

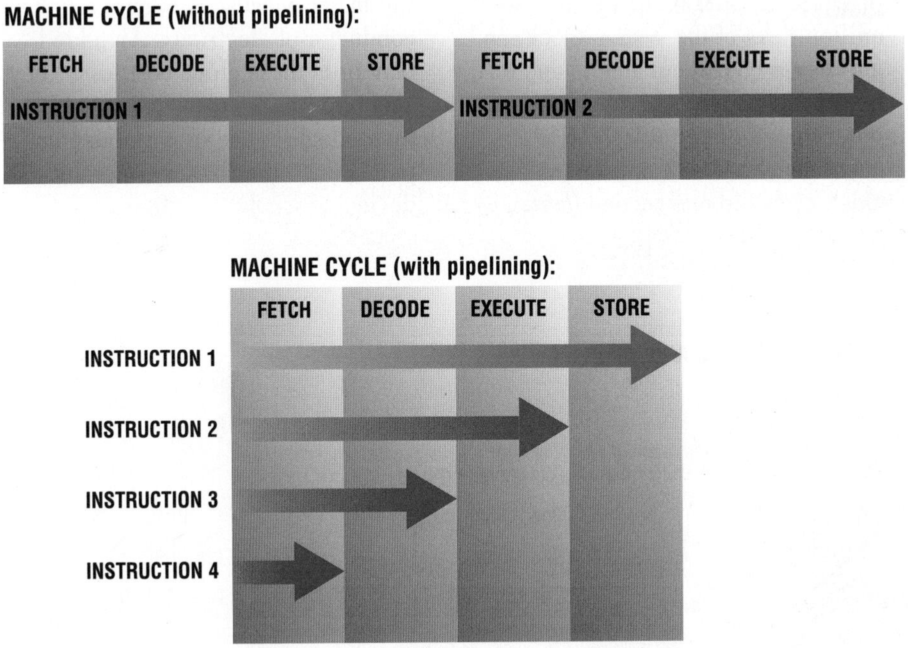

Figure 4-7 Most modern personal computers support pipelining. With pipelining, the CPU begins executing a second instruction before the first instruction is completed. The result is faster processing.

Functions of the Control Unit

The control unit's function is to direct and coordinate most of the operations in the computer. For each instruction, the control unit repeats a set of four operations: fetching, decoding, executing, and storing. These four operations may seem new to you, but in a sense you carry out these same operations each time you complete certain ordinary tasks. You input data through one of your five senses; you decode this data, changing it into information; you execute the task in some way; and you store this information for later retrieval. Do people solve problems the same way in which a computer solves a problem? Do you agree that the human brain is similar to a computer? Why or why not? Describe a simple task in which you perform operations like those in the machine cycle. What is different and why? If the human brain can perform all of these functions, do we really need computers? Explain your answer.

For more information on the control unit vs. the human brain, visit the Discovering Computers 2002 Issues Web page (**scsite.com/dc2002/issues.htm**) and click Chapter 4 Issue #1.

APPLY IT!

Clock Speed – How Much Is Enough?

If you have considered purchasing a computer recently, you are aware of the many available models and that each of these models provides several options from which to choose. The market for personal computer hardware is incredible, making your options on what type of machine you want to buy just as impressive. One primary option to consider is processing power. What clock speed should you purchase? Do you need the latest and greatest dream machine? Is 1 GHz necessary for your processing needs or can you accomplish as much with less power? How fast do you want to go? The answers to these questions are directly related to how you intend to use the computer and what software applications you need. You can select a machine just for the basics or select one used by professional graphic artists or game players.

- Level I – Below 600 MHz
  This computer should provide more than adequate processing power for at least the next couple of years for the typical home user — someone who primarily uses a standard Office suite, edits home photographs, and plays a game now and then.
- Level II – 600 MHz to 1 GHz
  If your interest is in graphics and design, you play some of the multimedia games that include simulated 3-D and virtual reality, or you use voice recognition, your needs would be met best by a Level II computer.
- Level III – 1 GHz and above
  This computer is for the power user. If your goal is to create 3-D applications, run sophisticated graphics software or CAD programs, then you definitely want to purchase the fastest computer you can afford.

For more information on computer processing power, visit the Discovering Computers 2002 Apply It Web page (**scsite.com/dc2002/apply.htm**) and click Chapter 4 Apply It #1.

Web Link

For more information on clock speed, visit the Discovering Computers 2002 Chapter 4 WEB LINK page (**scsite.com/dc2002/ch4/weblink.htm**) and click Clock Speed.

The System Clock

The CPU relies on a small chip called the **system clock** to synchronize, or control the timing of, all computer operations. Just as your heart beats at a regular rate to keep your body functioning, the system clock generates regular electronic pulses, or ticks, that set the operating pace of components in the system unit.

Each tick is a **clock cycle**. In the past, CPUs used one or more clock cycles to execute each instruction. Many of today's CPUs are **superscalar** and can execute more than one instruction per clock cycle.

Clock speed, also called **clock rate**, is the speed at which a processor executes instructions. The faster the clock, the more instructions the CPU can execute per second. Manufacturers state clock speed in megahertz and gigahertz. A **hertz** is one cycle per second. Mega is a prefix that stands for million. Giga is a prefix that stands for billion. Thus, **megahertz (MHz)** equates to one million ticks of the system clock, and **gigahertz (GHz)** equates to one billion ticks of the system clock. A computer that operates at 933 MHz (*megahertz*) has 933 million (*mega*) clock cycles in one second (*hertz*). The table in Figure 4-8 identifies these and other prefixes commonly used in the computer industry.

The power of a CPU frequently is determined by how fast it processes data. The system clock is one of the major factors that influence a computer's speed. A CPU with higher clock speed can process more instructions per second than a CPU with a lower clock speed. For example, a 1 GHz CPU is faster than a CPU operating at 800 MHz. Keep in mind that the speed of the system clock affects only the CPU. It has no effect on peripherals such as a printer or disk drive.

The speed of the system clock varies among CPUs. A technological breakthrough by IBM enables CPUs today to operate at speeds well beyond 400 MHz. For nearly 30 years, aluminum was used to create the electronic circuitry on a single chip of silicon crystal. Now, a process exists that uses copper instead of aluminum. CPU chips that use copper run faster because copper is a better conductor of electricity. An added benefit is these chips cost less. They also require less electricity, making them ideal for use in portable computers and other battery-operated devices.

COMMON PREFIXES AND THEIR MEANINGS

Prefixes for Small Amounts	Meaning	Decimal Notation
MILLI	One thousandth of	.001
MICRO	One millionth of	.000001
NANO	One billionth of	.000000001
PICO	One trillionth of	.000000000001

Prefixes for Large Amounts	Meaning	Decimal Notation
KILO	One thousand	1,000
MEGA	One million	1,000,000
GIGA	One billion	1,000,000,000
TERA	One trillion	1,000,000,000,000

Figure 4-8 The table above outlines prefixes commonly used in the computer industry.

Comparison of Personal Computer Processors

On larger computers, such as mainframes and supercomputers, the various functions performed by the CPU, also called a processor, span many separate chips and sometimes multiple circuit boards. On a personal computer, because all functions of the processor usually are on a single chip, some call the chip a **microprocessor**. Most advertisements, however, refer to the chip as a processor. Figure 4-9 shows several popular personal computer processors.

Manufacturers often identify their personal computer processors by a model name or model number. Figure 4-10 summarizes the historical development of the personal computer processor and documents the increases in clock speed and number of transistors in chips since 1982. The greater the number of transistors, the more complex and powerful the chip.

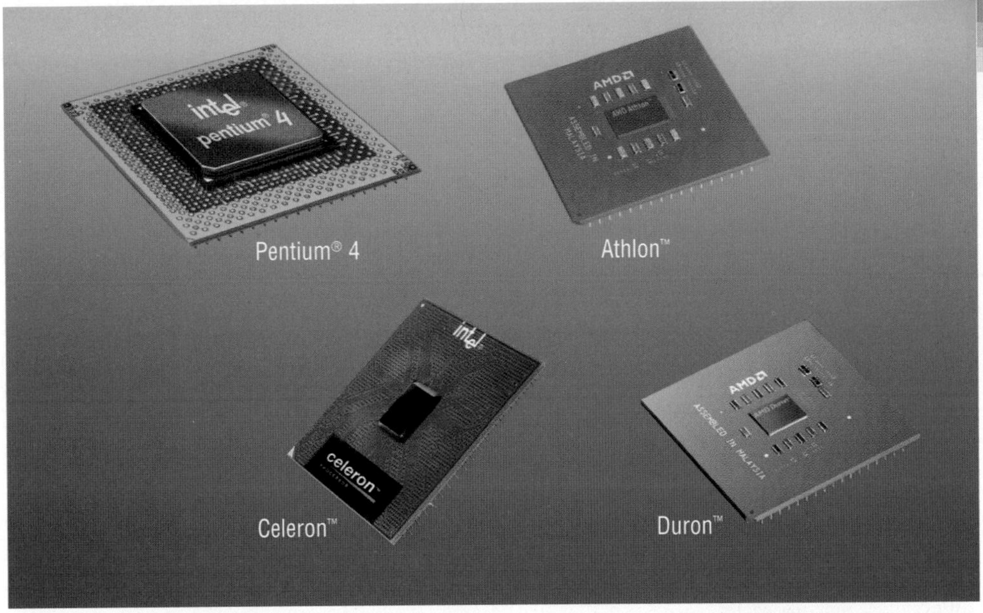

Figure 4-9 Most high-performance PCs use Pentium® and Athlon™ processors. Basic PCs have a Celeron™ or Duron™ processor.

COMPARISON OF WIDELY USED PERSONAL COMPUTER PROCESSORS

NAME	DATE INTRODUCED	MANUFACTURER	CLOCK SPEED	NUMBER OF TRANSISTORS
Pentium® 4	2000	Intel	1.4 GHz and up	42 million
Itanium™	2000	Intel	800 MHz and up	25.4-60 million
Pentium® III Xeon™	1999	Intel	500 MHz - 1 GHz	9.5-28 million
Pentium® III	1999	Intel	400 MHz - 1.2 GHz	9.5-28 million
Athlon™	1999	AMD	500 MHz - 1.2 GHz	22-37 million
Duron™	1999	AMD	600 - 800 MHz	18 million
AMD-K6® III	1999	AMD	400 - 450 MHz	21.3 million
Celeron™	1998	Intel	266 - 800 MHz	7.5-19 million
Pentium® II Xeon	1998	Intel	400 - 450 MHz	7.5-27 million
AMD-K6® II	1998	AMD	366 - 550 MHz	9.3 million
AMD-K6®	1998	AMD	300 MHz	8.8 million
Pentium® II	1997	Intel	234 - 450 MHz	7.5 million
Pentium® with MMX™ technology	1997	Intel	166 - 233 MHz	4.5 million
Pentium® Pro	1995	Intel	150 - 200 MHz	5.5 million
Pentium®	1993	Intel	75 - 200 MHz	3.3 million
80486DX	1989	Intel	25 - 100 MHz	1.2 million
80386DX	1985	Intel	16 - 33 MHz	275,000
80286	1982	Intel	6 - 12 MHz	134,000
PowerPC	1994	Motorola	50 - 500 MHz	Up to 50 million
68040	1989	Motorola	25 - 40 MHz	1.2 million
68030	1987	Motorola	16 - 50 MHz	270,000
68020	1984	Motorola	16 - 33 MHz	190,000
Alpha	1993	Digital; Compaq	150 - 700 MHz	Up to 100 million

Figure 4-10 A comparison of some of the more widely used personal computer processors.

COMPANY ON THE CUTTING EDGE

intel®

Chips Dominate Computer Market

Answer: This company's chips power 85 percent of all desktop computers.
Question: What is Intel?

Jeopardy television series contestants faced this question in 1994, and today Intel still is the world's largest chip maker. The company also is a major producer of boards, systems, and software for the personal computer, network, and communications industries.

When Gordon Moore and Robert Noyce started Intel in 1968, their goal was to build semiconductor memory to replace magnetic core memory. Intel refined the process of placing thousands of tiny electronic devices on a silicon chip; in 1970, Intel successfully introduced the 1103. One year later, this product became the world's best-selling semiconductor device. In 1971 Intel developed the 4004, the world's first processor.

This innovative spirit and attention to detail remain part of Intel's corporate culture. The company has grown to more than 70,000 employees in more than 40 countries. Intel supports the values of responding to customer needs, working with discipline and quality, taking risks, working in an open and satisfying environment, and striving for optimum results.

For more information on Intel, visit the Discovering Computers 2002 Companies Web page (**scsite.com/dc2002/companies.htm**) and click Intel.

COMPANY ON THE CUTTING EDGE

AMD

Intel-Compatible Processor Leader

In the 18th century, philosophers spoke of The Age of Enlightenment. In 1969, The Fifth Dimension sang of The Age of Aquarius. But could today be The Age of Asparagus? In the early 1980s, Advanced Micro Devices (AMD) adopted the phrase to characterize its commitment to develop increasing numbers of proprietary products for the computer industry. Executives identified this goal with asparagus farming because the crop grows slowly, but it is very lucrative once it takes hold.

The company's seeds sprouted and grew into the world's second-largest manufacturer of processors for Microsoft Windows-compatible personal computers. Along with the AMD-K6® and Athlon™ processors with 3DNow!™ technology, AMD also develops flash memory, programmable logic, communications, and networking devices. One-half of the company's nearly $3 billion in revenues is generated from sales outside the United States.

Co-founders Jerry Sanders and John Carey laid the foundation for AMD in Carey's living room in 1968. From the beginning, AMD guaranteed its microchips for every customer would meet or exceed stringent standards. More than three decades later, the company continues this commitment to "parametric superiority."

For more information on AMD, visit the Discovering Computers 2002 Companies Web page (**scsite.com/dc2002/companies.htm**) and click AMD.

Intel is a leading manufacturer of personal computer processors. With their earlier processors, Intel used a model number to identify the various chips. After learning that processor model numbers could not be trademarked and protected from use by competitors, Intel began identifying their processors with names — thus emerged their series of processors known as the Pentium®. Most high-performance PCs use a **Pentium®** processor. Less expensive, basic PCs use a brand of Intel processor called the **Celeron™**. Two more brands, called the **Xeon™** and **Itanium™** processors, are ideal for workstations and low-end servers.

Other companies such as AMD also make **Intel-compatible processors**. These processors have the same internal design or architecture as Intel processors and perform the same functions, but often are less expensive. Intel and Intel-compatible processors are used in PCs.

Apple Macintosh and Power Macintosh systems use a **Motorola processor**, which has a design different from the Intel-style processor. For Apple's PowerPC, Motorola introduced a new processor architecture that increased the speed of the computer.

The **Alpha processor**, which originally was developed by Digital Equipment Corporation, is used primarily in workstations and high-end servers. Current models of the Alpha chip run at clock speeds up to 700 MHz.

A new type of personal computer processor, called an **integrated CPU**, combines functions of a processor, memory, and a video card on a single chip. Lower-costing personal computers and Internet appliances such as a set-top box sometimes use an integrated CPU.

Determining which processor is right for you will depend on how you plan to use the computer. If you purchase a PC (IBM-compatible), you will choose an Intel processor or an Intel-compatible processor. Apple Macintosh and Power Macintosh users will choose a PowerPC processor.

Your intended use also will determine the clock speed of the processor you choose. Processor speed is an important consideration. A home user surfing the Web, for example, will not need as fast a processor as an artist working with graphics or applications requiring multimedia capabilities such as full-motion video. Figure 4-11 describes guidelines for selecting an Intel processor. Remember, the higher the clock speed, the faster the processor — but also the more expensive the computer.

Today's processors use **MMX™ (multimedia extensions)** technology, which is a set of instructions built into the processor that allows it to manipulate and process multimedia data more efficiently. In addition to MMX, Intel's latest processors include **SSE instructions (streaming single-instruction, multiple-data instructions)**, and AMD's latest processors have **3DNow!™** technology. These two technologies further improve the processor's performance of multimedia, the Web, and 3-D graphics.

Processor Installation and Upgrades

Instead of buying an entirely new computer, you might be able to upgrade your processor to increase the computer's performance. Processor upgrades are one of three forms: chip for chip, piggyback, or daughterboard. With a **chip for chip upgrade**, you replace the existing processor chip with a new one. With a **piggyback upgrade**, you stack the new processor chip on top of the old one. With a **daughterboard upgrade**, the new processor chip is on a daughterboard. A **daughterboard** is a small circuit board that plugs into the motherboard, often to add additional capabilities to the motherboard.

INTEL PROCESSOR	DESIRED CLOCK SPEED	USE
Itanium™ or Xeon™	1 GHz and up	Power users with workstations; low-end servers on a network
Pentium® family	1 GHz and up	Power users or users that design professional drawings, produce and edit videos, record and edit music, participate in videoconference calls, create professional Web sites, play graphic-intensive multiplayer Internet games
	800 MHz - 1 GHz	Users that design professional documents containing graphics such as newsletters or number intensive spreadsheets; produce multimedia presentations; use the Web as an intensive research tool; edit photographs; send documents and graphics via the Web; watch videos; play graphic-intensive games on CD or DVD; create personal Web sites
	600 - 800 MHz	Home users that manage personal finances; create basic documents with word processing and spreadsheet software; communicate with others on the Web via e-mail, chat rooms, and discussions; shop on the Web; create basic Web pages
Celeron™	600 MHz and up	Home users that manage personal finances; create basic documents with word processing and spreadsheet software; edit photographs; make greeting cards and calendars; use educational or entertainment CD-ROMs; communicate with others on the Web via e-mail, chat rooms, and discussions

Figure 4-11 Determining which processor to obtain when you purchase a computer depends on your computer usage.

APPLY IT!

The Upgrade Dilemma

If you purchased your computer more than two years ago, then you probably have started to wonder if it is time to buy a new one. You might want one with a few additional options, such as a DVD drive, and a lot more power, especially because today's applications demand speed. The question is should you purchase a new computer or upgrade your current computer. The following list should help with your decision.

- If the processor is a 486 or older, donate it and purchase a new computer.
- If you have a computer with a slow processor, then consider the following upgrade options:
  - If the motherboard will accept a faster processor, replace it.
  - If the motherboard will not accept a faster processor, then consider an upgrade kit. The advantage of buying an upgrade kit is that memory and the processor are pre-installed on the motherboard.
  - Purchase a motherboard and processor of your choice. This option is for the more technical people who know the strengths and weaknesses of the various motherboards and which one will go well with the processor they are purchasing. Also, keep in mind that replacing the motherboard, even using an upgrade kit, is time-consuming.
- Additional items to consider are other devices that may need to be upgraded on your system. Some possibilities include more memory, a new monitor, more video RAM, USB ports, more hard disk storage, new or faster CD-ROM drive, and other storage devices such as a Zip® drive.

For more information on upgrading versus purchasing a new computer, visit the Discovering Computers 2002 Apply It Web page (**scsite.com/dc2002/apply.htm**) and click Chapter 4 Apply It #2.

A processor chip is inserted into an opening, or **socket**, on the motherboard. Many PGA (pin grid array) chips use a zero-insertion force socket. A **zero-insertion force (ZIF) socket** has a small lever or screw that facilitates the installation and removal of processor chips (Figure 4-12). Users easily can upgrade the processor on computers with a ZIF socket because this type of socket requires no force to remove and install a chip. Some motherboards have a second ZIF socket that holds an upgrade chip. In this case, the existing processor chip remains on the motherboard, and you install the upgrade chip into the second ZIF socket.

Heat Sinks and Heat Pipes

Newer processor chips generate a lot of heat, which could cause the chip to burn up. Often, the computer's main fan generates enough airflow to cool the processor. Sometimes, however, the processor requires a heat sink — especially when upgrading to a more powerful processor. A **heat sink** is a small ceramic or metal component with fins on its surface that absorbs and ventilates heat produced by electrical components. Some heat sinks are packaged as part of the processor chip. Others are installed on top or the side of the chip. Because a heat sink consumes a lot of room, a smaller device called a **heat pipe** cools processors in notebook computers.

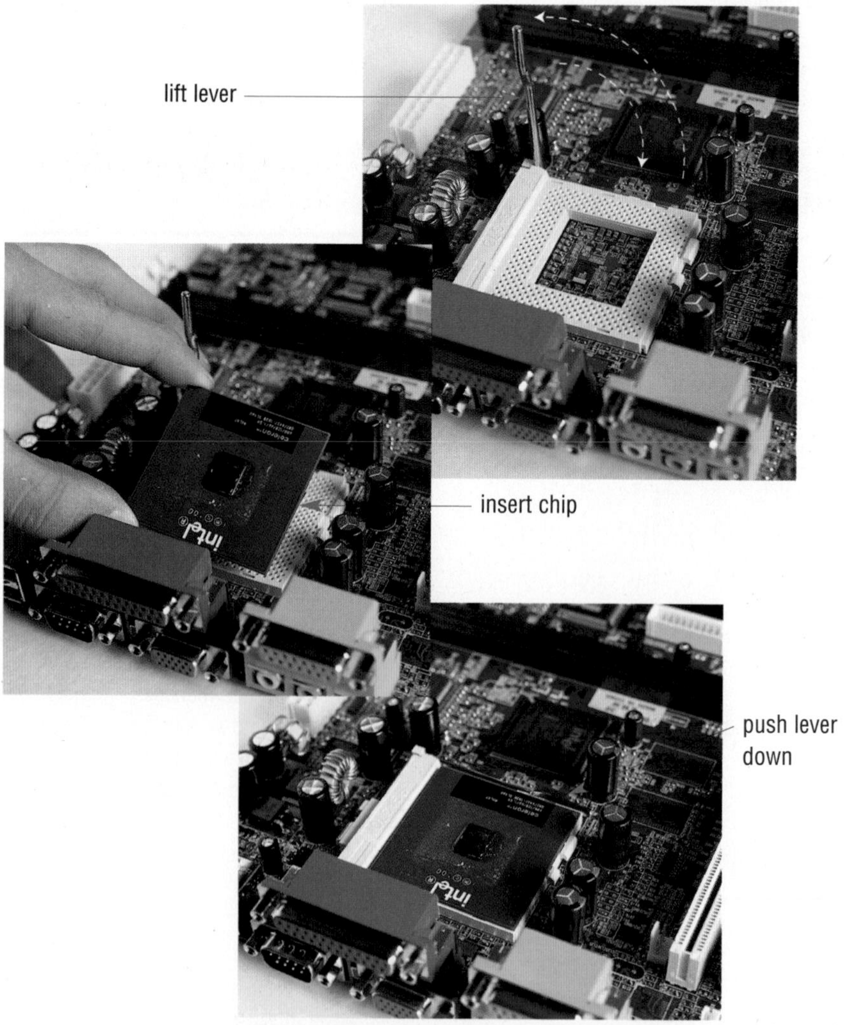

Figure 4-12 A zero-insertion force socket makes it easy to remove and re-install processor chips.

Coprocessors

Another way to increase the performance of a computer is through the use of a coprocessor. A **coprocessor** is a special processor chip or circuit board that assists the processor in performing specific tasks. Users running engineering, scientific, or graphics applications, for instance, will notice a dramatic increase in speed in applications that take advantage of a **floating-point coprocessor**. Floating-point coprocessors sometimes are called math or numeric coprocessors. Most of today's computers include a floating-point coprocessor.

Parallel Processing

Some computers use more than one processor to speed processing times. Known as **parallel processing**, this method uses multiple processors simultaneously to execute a program (Figure 4-13). Parallel processing divides up a problem so that multiple processors work on their assigned portion of the problem at the same time. As you might expect, parallel processing requires special software that recognizes how to divide up the problem and then bring the results back together again. Supercomputers use parallel processing for applications such as weather forecasting.

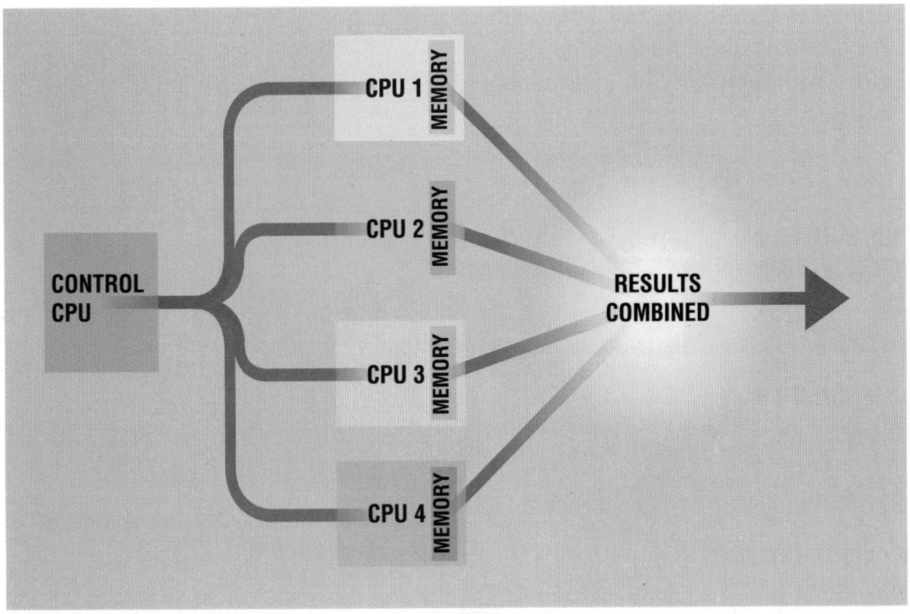

Figure 4-13 Parallel processing divides up a problem so that multiple processors work on their assigned portion of a problem at the same time.

DATA REPRESENTATION

To understand fully the way a computer processes data, it is important to know how a computer represents data. People communicate through speech by combining words into sentences. Human speech is **analog** because it uses continuous signals that vary in strength and quality. Most computers are **digital**. They recognize only two discrete states: on and off. This is because computers are electronic devices powered by electricity, which also has only two states: on or off.

Web Link

For more information on processors, visit the Discovering Computers 2002 Chapter 4 WEB LINK page (**scsite.com/dc2002/ch4/weblink.htm**) and click Processors.

TECHNOLOGY TRAILBLAZER

ANDY **GROVE**

Psychologists classify paranoia as a serious mental disorder; Intel Chairman Andy Grove classifies it as an essential component of business success. In Grove's book, *Only the Paranoid Survive*, he states that successful corporate managers constantly need to be on the lookout for competitors' threats. He personally worries about flawed products, unproductive factories, and low employee morale.

He advises college students to make career choices based on a variety of factors, including their strengths and weaknesses, their responsibilities at a particular company, to whom they would report, and their ability to adapt to new environments. He explains that after graduating from the University of California at Berkeley in 1963, he chose to work at Fairchild Semiconductor because he desired the California location and he wanted to work with Gordon Moore.

Five years later, he helped found Intel Corporation and was named president in 1979. From 1987 to 1998 he served as chief executive officer. He was named *Time* magazine's Man of the Year in 1997 for his innovative work on microchips, entrepreneurial spirit, and sharp, brilliant mind.

For more information on Andy Grove, visit the Discovering Computers 2002 People Web page (**scsite.com/dc2002/people.htm**) and click Andy Grove.

The two digits, zero and one, easily can represent these two states (Figure 4-14). The digit zero (0) represents the electronic state of off (absence of an electronic charge). The digit one (1) represents the electronic state of on (presence of an electronic charge).

When people count, they use the digits in the decimal system (0 through 9). The computer uses a binary system because it only understands two states. The **binary system** is a number system that has just two unique digits, 0 and 1, called bits. A **bit** (short for **bi**nary digi**t**) is the smallest unit of data the computer can represent. By itself, a bit is not very informative.

When eight bits are grouped together as a unit, they form a **byte**. A byte is informative because it provides enough different combinations of 0s and 1s to represent 256 individual characters. These characters include numbers, uppercase and lowercase letters of the alphabet, punctuation marks, and others such as the letters of the Greek alphabet.

The combinations of 0s and 1s that represent characters are defined by patterns called a coding scheme. In one coding scheme, the number 3 is represented as 00110011, the number 5 as 00110101, and the capital letter T as 01010100 (Figure 4-15). Two popular coding schemes are ASCII and EBCDIC (Figure 4-16). The **American Standard Code for Information Interchange**, or **ASCII** (pronounced ASK-ee), is the most widely used coding system to represent data. Most personal computers and mid-range servers use the ASCII coding scheme. The **Extended Binary Coded Decimal Interchange Code**, or **EBCDIC** (pronounced EB-see-dic) is used primarily on mainframe computers.

The ASCII and EBCDIC coding schemes are sufficient for English and Western European languages but are not large enough for Asian and other languages that use different alphabets. **Unicode** is a coding scheme capable of representing all the world's current languages. The appendix of this book discusses the ASCII, EBCDIC, and Unicode schemes in more depth, along with the parity bit and number systems.

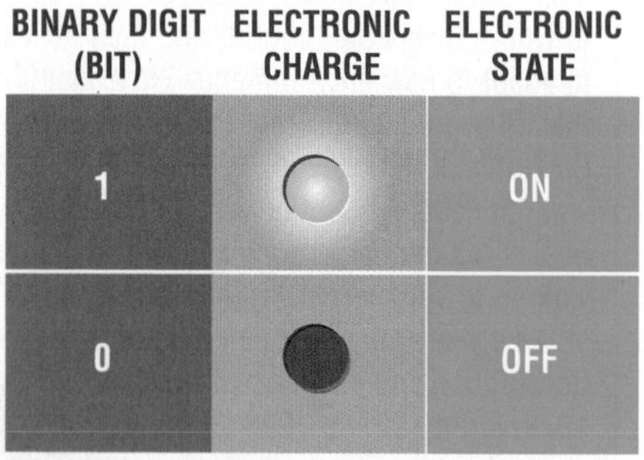

Figure 4-14 A computer circuit represents the 0 or the 1 electronically by the presence or absence of an electronic charge.

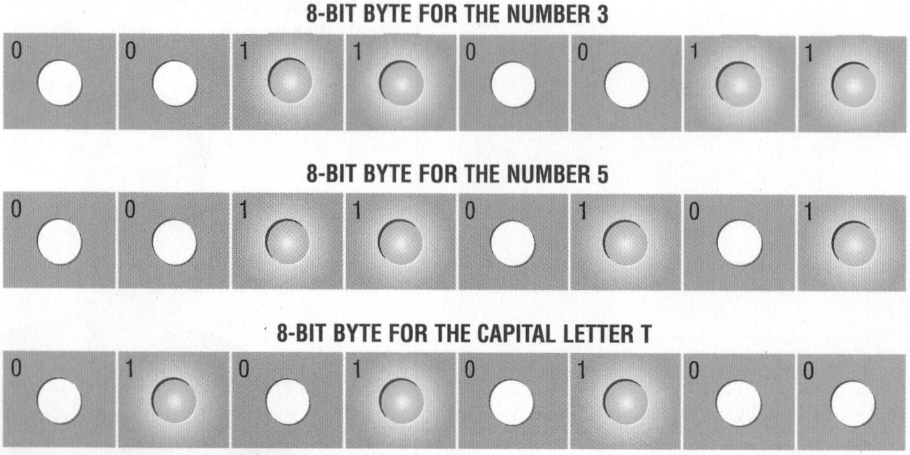

Figure 4-15 Eight bits grouped together as a unit are called a byte. A byte represents a single character in the computer.

ASCII	SYMBOL	EBCDIC
00110000	0	11110000
00110001	1	11110001
00110010	2	11110010
00110011	3	11110011
00110100	4	11110100
00110101	5	11110101
00110110	6	11110110
00110111	7	11110111
00111000	8	11111000
00111001	9	11111001
01000001	A	11000001
01000010	B	11000010
01000011	C	11000011
01000100	D	11000100
01000101	E	11000101
01000110	F	11000110
01000111	G	11000111
01001000	H	11001000
01001001	I	11001001
01001010	J	11010001
01001011	K	11010010
01001100	L	11010011
01001101	M	11010100
01001110	N	11010101
01001111	O	11010110
01010000	P	11010111
01010001	Q	11011000
01010010	R	11011001
01010011	S	11100010
01010100	T	11100011
01010101	U	11100100
01010110	V	11100101
01010111	W	11100110
01011000	X	11100111
01011001	Y	11101000
01011010	Z	11101001
00100001	!	01011010
00100010	"	01111111
00100011	#	01111011
00100100	$	01011011
00100101	%	01101100
00100110	&	01010000
00101000	(	01001101
00101001	)	01011101
00101010	*	01011100
00101011	+	01001110

Figure 4-16 Two popular coding schemes are ASCII and EBCDIC.

Coding schemes such as ASCII make it possible for humans to interact with a digital computer that recognizes only bits. When you press a key on a keyboard, the electronic signal is converted into a binary form the computer recognizes and is stored in memory. Every character is converted to its corresponding byte. The computer then processes the data as bytes, which actually is a series of on/off electrical states. When processing is finished, software converts the bytes back into numbers, letters of the alphabet, or special characters so they can display on a screen or be printed (Figure 4-17). All of these conversions take place so quickly that you do not realize they are occurring.

Standards, such as those defined by ASCII and EBCDIC, make it possible for components within computers to communicate with each other successfully. These and other standards allow various manufacturers to produce a component and be assured that it will operate correctly in a computer – as long as it meets the defined standard. Standards also enable consumers to purchase components that are compatible with their computer configuration.

Figure 4-17 HOW A LETTER IS CONVERTED TO BINARY FORM AND BACK

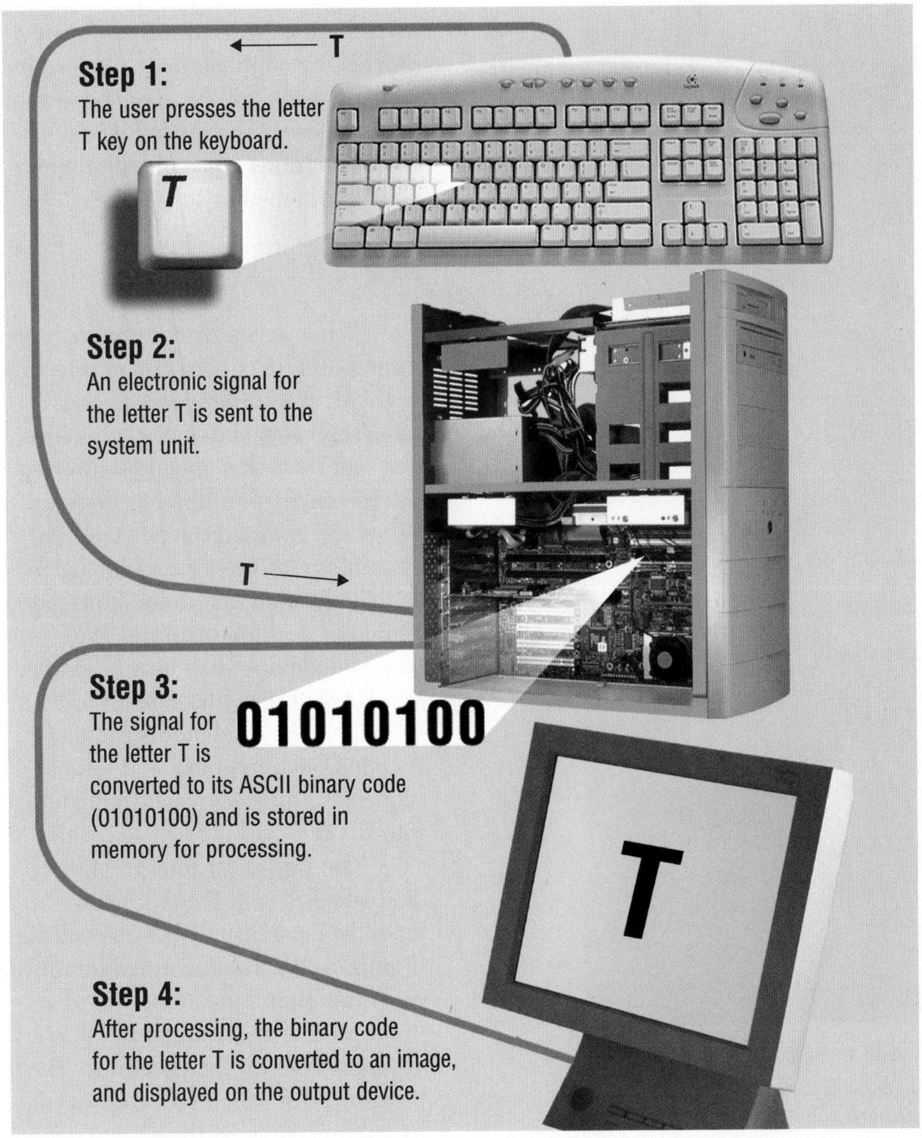

T
Step 1:
The user presses the letter T key on the keyboard.
T
Step 2:
An electronic signal for the letter T is sent to the system unit.
T
Step 3:
The signal for the letter T is converted to its ASCII binary code (01010100) and is stored in memory for processing.
01010100
T
Step 4:
After processing, the binary code for the letter T is converted to an image, and displayed on the output device.

MEMORY

During processing, the processor places instructions to be executed and data needed by those instructions into memory. This **memory** is a temporary storage place for data, instructions, and information. Sometimes called primary storage, this and other types of memory consist of one or more chips on the motherboard or some other circuit board in the computer.

TECHNOLOGY TRAILBLAZER

GORDON **MOORE**

A $15 million watch would be extravagant for most people, but not for Gordon Moore, Intel's chairman emeritus. Although he no longer wears his timepiece, it serves as a reminder of Intel's venture into manufacturing and selling digital watches with liquid crystal displays for approximately $150 — until competitors started selling theirs for less than one-tenth the cost. Intel stopped making the watches in 1978.

As a co-founder of Intel in 1968, he witnessed a geometric growth in technology so consistent he could set his watch by it. When writing an article for *Electronics* magazine in 1965 to predict the growth of component technology for the next 10 years, he graphed data about memory chip performance. He predicted the number of transistors and resistors placed on computer chips would double every year, with a proportional increase in computing power and decrease in cost. This principle, Moore's Law, held true until 1975, when he changed the prediction to doubling every two years.

For more information on Gordon Moore, visit the Discovering Computers 2002 People Web page (**scsite.com/dc2002/people.htm**) and click Gordon Moore.

Memory stores three basic items: (1) the operating system and other system software that control the usage of the computer equipment; (2) application programs that carry out a specific task such as word processing; and (3) the data being processed by the application programs. This role of memory to store both data and programs is known as the **stored program concept**.

A byte (character) is the basic storage unit in memory. When application program instructions and data transfer into memory from storage devices, the instructions and data exist as bytes. Each byte resides temporarily in a location in memory, called an **address**. An address is simply a unique number that identifies the location of the byte in memory. The illustration in Figure 4-18 shows how seats in an airplane are similar to addresses in memory: (1) a seat holds one person at a time and an address in memory holds a single byte, (2) both a seat and an address can be empty, and (3) a seat has a unique identifying number and so does a memory address. To access data or instructions in memory, the computer references the addresses that contain bytes of data.

Figure 4-18 This figure shows how seats in an airplane are similar to addresses in memory: (1) a seat holds one person at a time and an address in memory holds a single byte, (2) both a seat and an address can be empty, and (3) a seat has a unique identifying number and so does a memory address.

Manufacturers state memory and storage sizes in terms of the number of bytes the device has available for storage (Figure 4-19). A **kilobyte** of memory, abbreviated **KB** or **K**, is equal to exactly 1,024 bytes. To make memory and storage definitions easier to identify, computer users often round a kilobyte down to 1,000 bytes. For example, if a memory chip can store 100 KB, it can hold approximately 100,000 bytes (characters). A **megabyte** (**MB**) is equal to approximately one million bytes. A **gigabyte** (**GB**) equals approximately one billion bytes.

The system unit contains two types of memory: volatile and nonvolatile. When the computer's power is turned off, **volatile memory** loses its contents. **Nonvolatile memory** (**NVM**), by contrast, does not lose its contents when power is removed from the computer. The following sections discuss various types of volatile and nonvolatile memory.

RAM

When users discuss memory in a computer, they usually are referring to RAM. **RAM (random access memory)** consists of memory chips that can be read from and written to by the processor and other devices. When the computer is powered on, certain operating system files (such as the files that determine how your Windows desktop displays) load from a storage device such as a hard disk into RAM. These files remain in RAM as long as the computer is running. As additional programs and data are requested, they also load from storage into RAM.

The processor interprets the data while it is in RAM. During this time, the contents of RAM may change (Figure 4-20). RAM can hold multiple programs simultaneously, provided the computer has enough RAM to accommodate all the programs. The program with which you are working usually displays on the screen.

MEMORY AND STORAGE SIZES

Term	Abbreviation	Approximate Memory Size	Exact Memory Amount	Approximate Number of Pages of Text
Kilobyte	KB or K	1 thousand bytes	1,024 bytes	1/2
Megabyte	MB	1 million bytes	1,048,576 bytes	500
Gigabyte	GB	1 billion bytes	1,073,741,824 bytes	500,000
Terabyte	TB	1 trillion bytes	1,099,511,627,776 bytes	500,000,000

Figure 4-19 This table outlines terms used to define memory and storage sizes.

Figure 4-20 HOW APPLICATION PROGRAMS TRANSFER IN AND OUT OF RAM

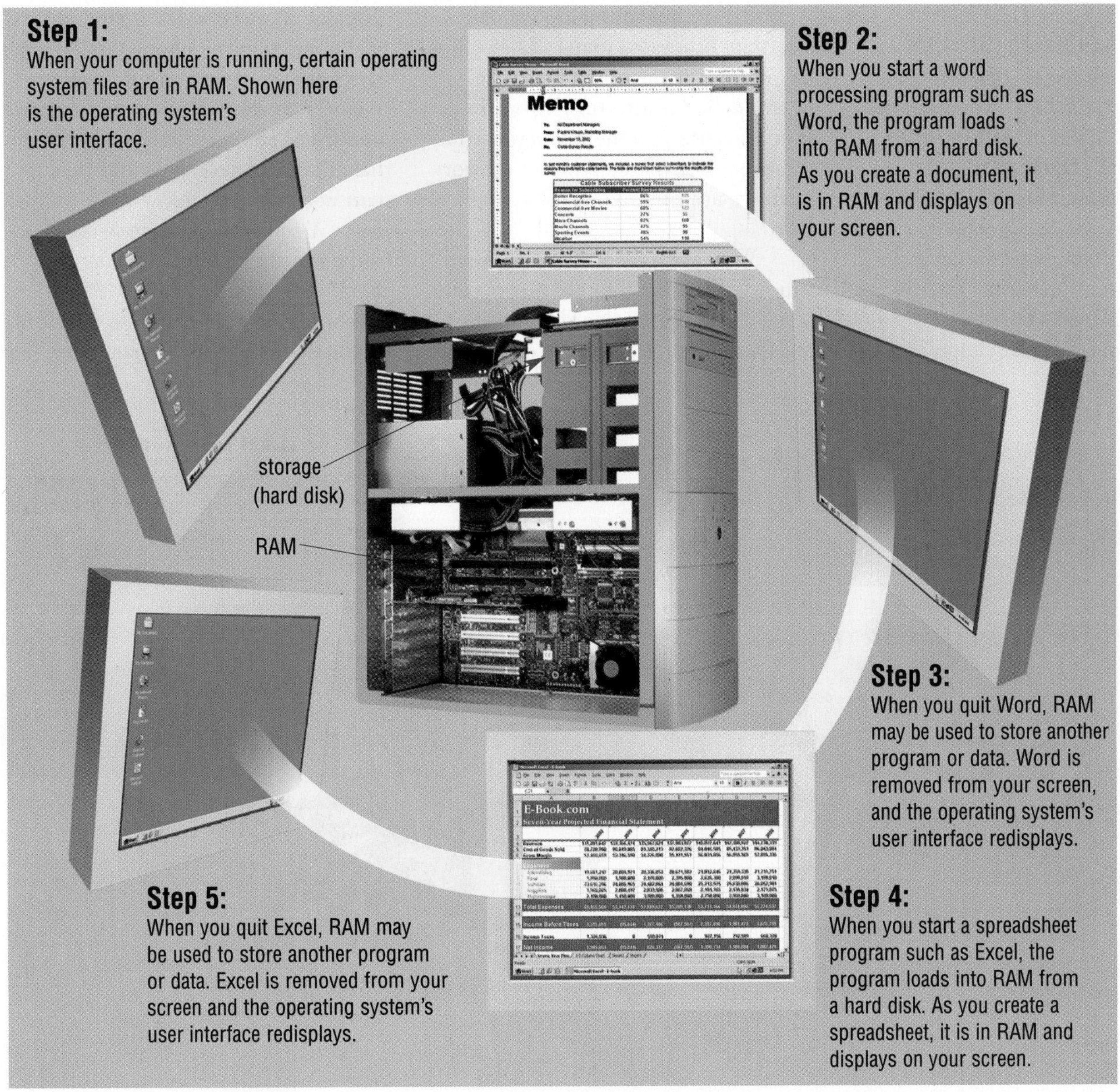
Step 1:
When your computer is running, certain operating system files are in RAM. Shown here is the operating system's user interface.
Step 2:
When you start a word processing program such as Word, the program loads into RAM from a hard disk. As you create a document, it is in RAM and displays on your screen.
Memo
storage (hard disk)
RAM
Step 3:
When you quit Word, RAM may be used to store another program or data. Word is removed from your screen, and the operating system's user interface redisplays.
E-Book.com
Seven-Year Projected Financial Statement
Step 4:
When you start a spreadsheet program such as Excel, the program loads into RAM from a hard disk. As you create a spreadsheet, it is in RAM and displays on your screen.
Step 5:
When you quit Excel, RAM may be used to store another program or data. Excel is removed from your screen and the operating system's user interface redisplays.

Most RAM is volatile. It loses its contents when the power is removed from the computer. For this reason, you must save any items you may need in the future. **Saving** is the process of copying items from RAM to a storage device such as a hard disk.

Two basic types of RAM chips exist: dynamic RAM chips and static RAM chips. Sometimes called **main memory**, dynamic RAM chips are the most common type of RAM. **Dynamic RAM**, or **DRAM** (pronounced DEE-ram), chips must be re-energized constantly or they lose their contents. Many variations of DRAM chips exist, most of which are faster than the basic DRAM. **Synchronous DRAM (SDRAM)** chips are much faster than DRAM chips because they are synchronized to the system clock. **Double data rate SDRAM (DDR SDRAM)** chips, also called **SDRAM II** chips, are faster than SDRAM chips because they transfer data twice for each clock cycle, instead of just once. **Direct Rambus® DRAM (Direct RDRAM®)** chips are yet another type of DRAM chips that are much faster than SDRAM chips because they use pipelining techniques. Most computers today use some form of SDRAM chips or RDRAM chips.

Static RAM chips, also called **SRAM** (pronounced ESS-ram) chips, are faster and more reliable than any variation of DRAM chips. These chips do not have to be re-energized as often as DRAM chips; thus, the term static is used. SRAM chips, however, are much more expensive than DRAM chips. Special applications such as cache use SRAM chips. A later section in this chapter discusses cache.

RAM chips often are smaller in size than processor chips. RAM chips usually reside on a small circuit board, called a **memory module**, which inserts into the motherboard (Figure 4-21). Three types of memory modules are SIMMs, DIMMs, and RIMMs.

With a **single inline memory module (SIMM)**, the pins on opposite sides of the circuit board connect together to form a single set of contacts. With a **dual inline memory module (DIMM)**, the pins on opposite sides of the circuit board do not connect and thus form two sets of contacts. SIMMs and DIMMs typically use SDRAM chips. A **Rambus® inline memory module (RIMM)** houses RDRAM chips.

RAM REQUIREMENTS The amount of RAM a computer requires often depends on the types of applications you plan to use on the computer. A computer only can manipulate data that is in memory. RAM is similar to the workspace on the top of your desk. Just as a desktop needs a certain amount of space to hold papers, pens, a stapler, your telephone, and so on, a computer needs a certain amount of memory to store application programs and files. The more RAM a computer has, the more programs and files it can work on at once.

A software package usually indicates the minimum amount of RAM it requires (Figure 4-22). If you want the application to perform optimally, you usually need more than

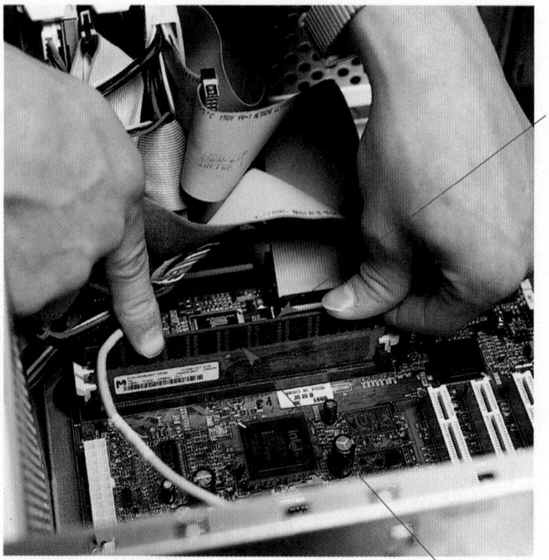

Figure 4-21 This photo shows a dual inline memory module (DIMM).

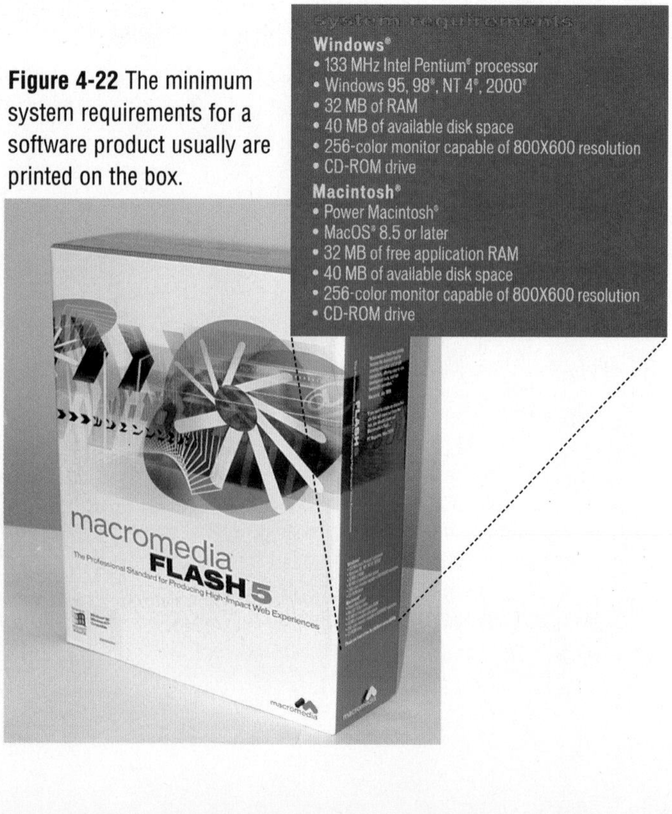

Figure 4-22 The minimum system requirements for a software product usually are printed on the box.

the minimum specifications on the software package.

Generally, home users running Windows and using standard application software such as word processing should have at least 32 MB of RAM. Most business users that work with accounting, financial, or spreadsheet programs, voice recognition, and programs requiring multimedia capabilities should have a minimum of 64 MB of RAM. Users composing multimedia presentations or using graphics-intensive applications will want at least 256 MB of RAM.

Figure 4-23a provides guidelines for the amount of RAM for various types of users. Figure 4-23b shows advertisements that match to each user requirement. Advertisements normally list the type of processor, the clock speed of the processor in MHz or GHz, and the amount of RAM in the computer. The amount of RAM in computers purchased today ranges from 64 MB to 512 MB.

The amount of RAM on the computer determines the amount of programs and data a computer can handle at one time, which affects overall performance. The more RAM, the faster the computer will respond.

Cache

Most of today's computers improve processing times with cache (pronounced cash). Two types of **cache** are memory cache and disk cache. This chapter discusses memory cache. Chapter 7 discusses disk cache.

Memory cache, also called a **cache store** or **RAM cache**, helps speed the processes of the computer because it stores frequently used instructions and data. The processor is likely to request these items repeatedly, so the items are stored for quick access. When the processor needs an instruction or data, it first searches cache. If it cannot locate the item in cache, then it searches RAM.

Most modern computers have two or three types, or layers, of memory cache: Level 1, Level 2, and Level 3. **Level 1 (L1) cache**, also called **primary cache** or **internal cache**, is built directly into the processor chip. L1 cache usually has a very small capacity, ranging from 8 KB to 64 KB. The most common size is 16 KB.

When discussing cache, most users are referring to L2 cache. **Level 2 (L2) cache**, or **external cache**, is slightly slower than L1 cache but has a much larger capacity, ranging from 64 KB to 4 MB. On older computers, L2 cache was not part of the processor chip. Instead, it

Web Link

For more information on cache, visit the Discovering Computers 2002 Chapter 4 WEB LINK page (**scsite.com/dc2002/ch4/weblink.htm**) and click Cache.

Figure 4-23a (RAM guidelines)

RAM (in MB)	**64 to 128 MB** (minimum)	**128 to 256 MB** (minimum)	**256 MB and up**
Use	Home and business users managing personal finances, using standard application software such as word processing; using educational or entertainment CD-ROMs; communicating with others on the Web	Users requiring more advanced multimedia capabilites; running number-intensive accounting, financial, or spreadsheet programs; using voice recognition; working with videos, music, and digital imaging; creating Web sites; participating in video-conferences; playing Internet games	Power users creating professional Web sites; running sophisticated CAD, 3-D design, or other graphics-intensive software

Figure 4-23b (computers for sale)

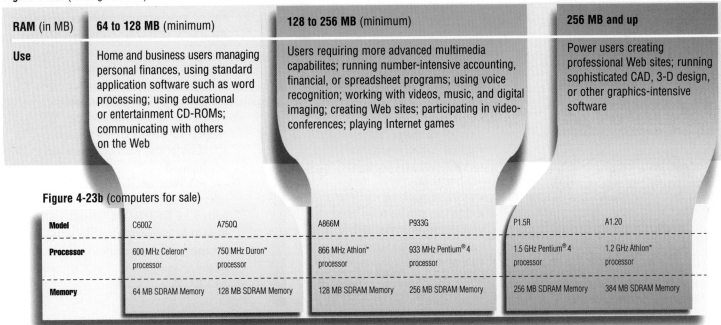

Model	C600Z	A750Q	A866M	P933G	P1.5R	A1.20
Processor	600 MHz Celeron™ processor	750 MHz Duron™ processor	866 MHz Athlon™ processor	933 MHz Pentium® 4 processor	1.5 GHz Pentium® 4 processor	1.2 GHz Athlon™ processor
Memory	64 MB SDRAM Memory	128 MB SDRAM Memory	128 MB SDRAM Memory	256 MB SDRAM Memory	256 MB SDRAM Memory	384 MB SDRAM Memory

Figure 4-23 Determining how much RAM you need depends on the applications you intend to run on your computer. Advertisements for computers normally list the type of processor, the speed of the computer measured in MHz or GHz, as well as the amount of RAM installed.

consisted of high-speed SRAM chips on the motherboard or a separate card of chips inserted into a slot in the computer. Current processors include **advanced transfer cache**, a type of L2 cache built directly on the processor chip. Processors that use advanced transfer cache perform at much faster rates than those that do not use it. The common size of advanced transfer cache is 256 KB.

If a processor has L2 advanced transfer cache, it also can use L3 cache. **L3 cache** is a cache separate from the processor chips on the motherboard. L3 cache only exists on computers that use L2 advanced transfer cache.

Cache speeds up processing time because it stores frequently used instructions and data. When the processor needs an instruction or data, it searches memory in this order: L1 cache, then L2 cache, then L3 cache (if it exists), then RAM — with a greater delay in processing for each level of memory it must search. If the instruction or data is not found in memory, then it must search a slower speed storage device such as a hard disk or CD-ROM.

A computer with L2 cache usually performs at speeds 10- to 40-percent faster than those without cache. To realize the largest increase in performance, a desktop computer should have at least 256 KB of L2 advanced transfer cache (Figure 4-24). Servers and workstations have at least 2 MB of L2 advanced transfer cache.

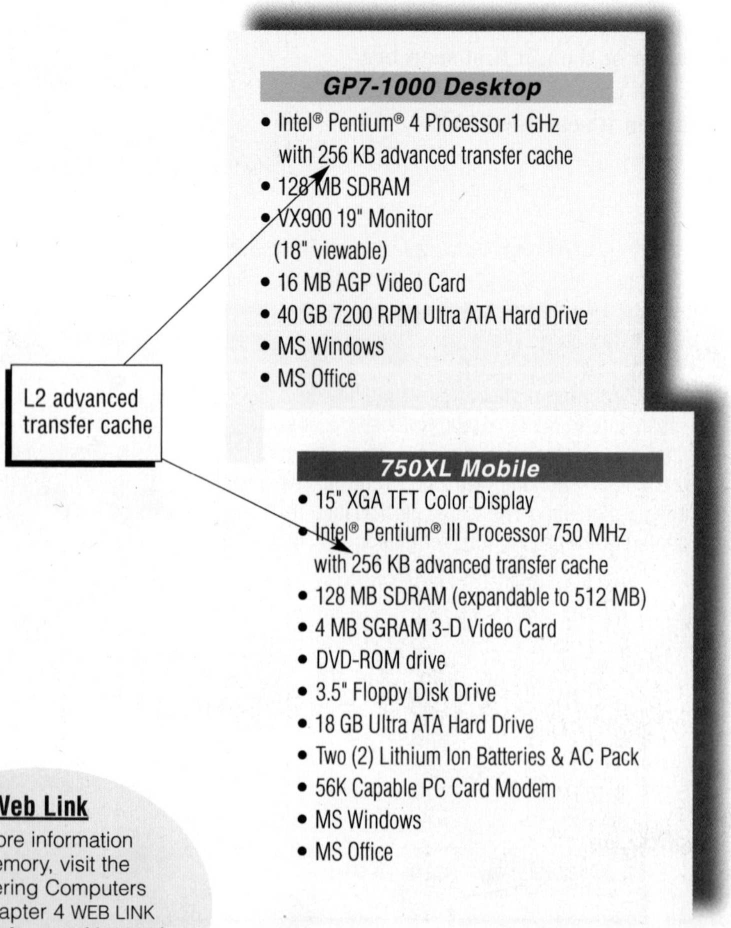

Figure 4-24 As shown in these advertisements, most current systems are equipped with at least 256 KB of L2 advanced transfer cache.

Web Link

For more information on memory, visit the Discovering Computers 2002 Chapter 4 WEB LINK page (**scsite.com/dc2002/ch4/weblink.htm**) and click Memory.

ROM

Read-only memory (**ROM** pronounced rahm) refers to memory chips storing data that only can be read. The data on ROM chips cannot be modified — hence, the name read only. ROM is nonvolatile. Its contents are not lost when power is removed from the computer.

ROM chips contain data, instructions, or information that is recorded permanently. For example, ROM contains the **basic input/output system** (**BIOS** pronounced BYE-ohss), which is a sequence of instructions the computer follows to load the operating system and other files when you first turn on the computer. Many other devices also contain ROM chips. For example, ROM chips in many printers contain data for fonts.

Manufacturers of ROM chips often record the data, instructions, or information on the chips when they manufacture the chip. These ROM chips, called **firmware,** contain permanently written data, instructions, or information. The BIOS is firmware that contains the computer's startup instructions.

A variation of the ROM chip, called a **programmable read-only memory** (**PROM**) chip, is a blank ROM chip on which you can place items permanently. Programmers use **microcode** instructions to program a PROM chip. Once a programmer writes the microcode onto the PROM chip, it functions like a regular ROM chip and cannot be erased or changed.

A programmer can erase microcode on a type of PROM chip, called an **EEPROM** (**electrically erasable programmable read-only memory**). Flash memory, discussed in the next section, uses a variation of EEPROM.

Flash Memory

Flash memory, also known as **flash ROM** or **flash RAM**, is a type of nonvolatile memory that can be erased electronically and reprogrammed. Many current computers use flash BIOS. With **flash BIOS**, the computer easily can update the contents of the BIOS chip, if necessary.

Flash memory chips store data and programs on many handheld computers and devices, such as digital cellular telephones, printers, set-top boxes, digital cameras, automotive devices, digital voice recorders, and pagers (Figure 4-25). **Flash memory cards** store flash memory on a removable device instead of a chip. Removable flash memory allows users to transfer data and information conveniently from these small devices to their desktop computers. A later section in this chapter discusses these cards in more depth. Flash memory is available in sizes up to 128 MB.

CMOS

Another type of memory chip in the system unit is complementary metal-oxide semiconductor memory. **Complementary metal-oxide semiconductor memory**, abbreviated **CMOS** (pronounced SEE-moss), stores configuration information about the computer. This information includes the type of disk drives, keyboard, and monitor; the current date and time; and other startup information needed when you turn on the computer.

CMOS chips use battery power to retain information even when the power to the computer is off. Battery-backed CMOS memory thus keeps the calendar, date, and time current even when the computer is off. Unlike standard ROM, the computer can change information in CMOS, such as when you change from standard time to daylight savings time or when you add new hardware devices to the computer.

Figure 4-25 Flash memory chips are used in personal and handheld computers, digital cellular telephones, printers, set-top boxes, digital cameras, automotive devices, digital voice recorders, and pagers.

APPLY IT!

Your Computer's Battery

Is your computer clock losing time? If so, that is a warning that your CMOS battery is about to go. Moreover, when it does, you will have a difficult time accessing your computer until you change the battery. The CMOS battery powers both the computer's internal clock and a CMOS memory chip that holds all the computer's crucial setup information, such as hard disk parameters, types of floppy drives, and memory size. The battery is easy to replace. Just follow these steps:

1. Obtain a replacement battery from a local vendor or online computer parts dealer.
2. Record your computer's setup information. You can do this by booting your computer and entering its setup mode. Write down all of the settings from the various menus. Alternatively, you can use a software program, such as Norton Utilities, that stores a backup copy of your computer's CMOS settings on a floppy disk.
3. Turn off the computer.
4. Open the case and locate the battery on the motherboard. See your user manual for specifications about the battery and its location.
5. Remove the old battery and replace it with the new one. You may have to move some cables around.
6. Document the date you replaced the battery.
7. Replace the case and turn on the computer. An error message will display.
8. Enter your computer's setup mode.
9. Reenter the settings you recorded from the various setup menus. If you used a program such as Norton Utilities, restore the settings from the floppy disk.

Caution: Do not forget to observe proper anti-static precautions when working inside the case of your computer.

For more information on CMOS and replacing the battery, visit the Discovering Computers 2002 Apply It Web page (**scsite.com/dc2002/apply.htm**) and click Chapter 4 Apply It #3.

Memory Access Times

Access time is the amount of time it takes the processor to read data, instructions, and information from memory. A computer's access time directly affects how fast the computer processes data. Manufacturers use a variety of terminology to state access times (Figure 4-26). Some use fractions of a second, which for memory, occurs in nanoseconds. A **nanosecond** (abbreviated **ns**) is one billionth of a second. A nanosecond is extremely fast (Figure 4-27). In fact, electricity travels about one foot in a nanosecond.

Other manufacturers state access times in MHz, e.g., an 83 MHz SDRAM. If a manufacturer states access time in megahertz, you can convert it to nanoseconds by dividing the megahertz number into 1 billion ns. For example, 133 MHz equals approximately 7.5 ns.

The access time (speed) of memory contributes to the overall performance of the computer. SDRAM chips can have access times up to 133 MHz (7.5 ns). The faster RDRAM chips can have access times up to 800 MHz (1.25 ns). ROM's access times range from 25 to 250 ns. Accessing data in memory can be more than 200,000 times faster than accessing data on a hard disk.

While access times of memory greatly affect overall computer performance, manufacturers and retailers usually list a computer's memory in terms of its size, not its access time. Thus, an advertisement might describe a computer as having 32 MB of SDRAM expandable to 512 MB.

You can expand memory capacity in a number of ways, such as installing additional memory in an expansion slot or inserting a memory card into a card slot.

ISSUE

Chip Recall

Processor Chip Flaws

A glitch within a single computer chip can cause untold problems. In 1994, a design flaw in Intel's Pentium® chip caused a rounding error once in every nine billion division operations. For most users, this would result in a mistake only once in every 27,000 years, so Intel initially ignored the problem. After an unexpected public outcry, Intel supplied replacements to anyone who asked, which cost the company nearly $500 million. Did people overreact? Did the demand for perfection divert funds that could have been spent better elsewhere? (Intel's costs were equivalent to half a year's research and development budget.) How much perfection do consumers have a right to expect? How serious should a problem be before a chip is recalled?

For more information on processor chips and flaw issues, visit the Discovering Computers 2002 Issues Web page (**scsite.com/dc2002/issues.htm**) and click Chapter 4 Issue #2.

ACCESS TIME TERMINOLOGY

TERM	ABBREVIATION	SPEED
Millisecond	ms	One-thousandth of a second
Microsecond	μs	One-millionth of a second
Nanosecond	ns	One-billionth of a second
Picosecond	ps	One-trillionth of a second

Figure 4-26 Access times are measured in fractions of a second. This table outlines terms used to define access times.

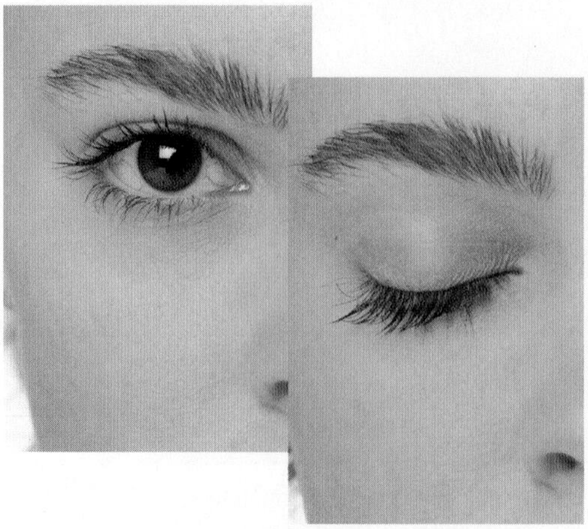

10 million operations = 1 blink

Figure 4-27 It takes about one-tenth of a second to blink your eye, which is the equivalent of 100 million nanoseconds. A computer can perform some operations in as little as 10 nanoseconds. In the time it takes to blink your eye, a computer can perform some operations 10 million times.

Web Link

For more information on flash memory, visit the Discovering Computers 2002 Chapter 4 WEB LINK page (**scsite.com/dc2002/ch4/weblink.htm**) and click Flash Memory.

EXPANSION SLOTS AND EXPANSION CARDS

An **expansion slot** is an opening, or socket, where you can insert a circuit board into the motherboard. These circuit boards add new devices or capabilities to the computer such as more memory, higher-quality sound devices, a modem, or graphics capabilities (Figure 4-28). A variety of terms identify a circuit board that fits in an expansion slot: **card**, **expansion card**, **expansion board**, **board**, **adapter card**, **adapter**, **interface card**, **add-in**, and **add-on**.

Sometimes a device or feature is built into a card. With other cards, a cable connects the expansion card to a device, such as a scanner, outside the system unit. Figure 4-29 shows someone inserting an expansion card into an expansion slot on a personal computer motherboard.

Four types of expansion cards found in most of today's computers are a video card, a sound card, a network interface card, and a modem card. A **video card**, also called a **video adapter** or **graphics card**, converts computer output into a video signal that is sent through a cable to the monitor, which displays an image on the screen. A **sound card** enhances the sound-generating capabilities of a personal computer by allowing sound to be input through a microphone and output through speakers. A **network interface card** (**NIC** pronounced nick), also called a **network card**, is a communications device that allows the computer to communicate via a network. A **modem card**, also called an **internal modem**, is a communications device that enables computers to communicate via telephone lines or other means.

TYPES OF EXPANSION CARDS

EXPANSION CARD	PURPOSE
Accelerator	To increase the speed of the processor
Controller	To connect disk drives; being phased out because newer motherboards support these connections
Game	To connect a joystick
I/O	To connect input and output devices such as a printer or mouse; being phased out because newer motherboards support these connections
Interface	To connect other peripherals such as a mouse, CD-ROM, or scanner
Memory	To add more memory to the computer
Modem	To connect to other computers through telephone lines
Network Interface	To connect to other computers and peripherals
PC-to-TV converter	To connect to a television
Sound	To connect speakers or microphone
TV Tuner	To view television channels on your monitor
Video	To connect a monitor
Video Capture	To connect a camcorder

Figure 4-28 This table lists some of the types of expansion cards and their functions.

Figure 4-29 This figure shows an expansion card being inserted into an expansion slot on the motherboard of a personal computer.

Web Link

For more information on expansion cards, visit the Discovering Computers 2002 Chapter 4 WEB LINK page (**scsite.com/dc2002/ch4/weblink.htm**) and click Expansion Cards.

In the past installing a card was not easy and required you set switches and other elements on the motherboard. Many of today's computers support Plug and Play. With **Plug and Play**, the computer automatically can configure cards and other devices as you install them. Having Plug and Play support means you can plug in a device, turn on the computer, and then use, or *play*, the device without having to configure the computer manually.

PC Cards and Flash Memory Cards

Notebook and other mobile computers have a special type of expansion slot for installing PC Cards. A **PC Card** is a thin credit card-sized device that adds memory, disk drives, sound, fax/modem, communications, and other capabilities to a mobile computer such as a notebook computer (Figure 4-30). Because of their small size and versatility, many consumer electronics products such as digital cameras, cable TV, and automobiles use PC Cards.

All PC Cards conform to standards developed by the **P**ersonal **C**omputer **M**emory **C**ard **I**nternational **A**ssociation (these cards originally were called **PCMCIA cards**). This helps to ensure that you can interchange PC Cards among handheld computers. PC Cards are all the same length and width, and fit in a standard PC Card slot. A notebook computer usually has a PC card slot on one of its edges.

The three types of PC Cards are Type I, Type II, and Type III. The only difference in size among the three types is their thickness. The thinnest **Type I cards** add memory capabilities to the computer. **Type II cards** contain communications devices such as modems. The thickest **Type III cards** house devices such as hard disks.

Web Link

For more information on PC Cards, visit the Discovering Computers 2002 Chapter 4 WEB LINK page (**scsite.com/dc2002/ch4/weblink.htm**) and click PC Cards.

Figure 4-30 This picture shows a PC Card sticking out of a PC Card slot on a notebook computer.

ISSUE

Is Cheaper Just as Good?

Personal Computer Prices

Today, you can buy a personal computer for less than $1,000 that has as much functionality as one nearly twice its cost two years ago. These low prices allow consumers today to shop for computer bargains. Many consumers want inexpensive computers that are adequate for basic tasks, such as word processing and Internet access. They feel that spending higher prices on computers with faster processors and more hard disk space is an unnecessary, frivolous expense. As one industry analyst asks, "Why buy a Porsche when you are going to drive only 55 miles per hour?" How might a greater availability of lower costing personal computers change the way schools and businesses use them? Does a higher price mean better quality, with respect to computers? Is it necessary to have the latest and greatest technology in a personal computer?

For more information on prices of personal computers, visit the Discovering Computers 2002 Issues Web page (**scsite.com/dc2002/issues.htm**) and click Chapter 4 Issue #3.

Flash memory cards are available in a variety of sizes (Figure 4-31). Many handheld computers and devices, such as digital computers, digital music players, and cellular telephones, use these memory cards. Some printers and computers have built-in card readers or slots. You also can purchase an external card reader that attaches to any computer. The type of card you have will determine the type of card reader you need.

Unlike other cards that require you to open the system unit and install the card onto the motherboard, you can change a PC Card or flash memory card without having to open the system unit or restart the computer. For example, if you need to connect to the Internet, you can just insert the modem card in the PC Card slot of your notebook computer while the computer is running. The operating system automatically recognizes the new card and allows you to connect to the Internet.

This feature of PC Cards and flash memory cards, called **hot plugging** or **hot swapping**, allows you to add and remove devices while a computer is running.

PORTS

External devices such as a keyboard, monitor, printer, mouse, and microphone, often attach by a cable to the system unit. A **port** is the interface, or point of attachment, to the system unit. The back of the system unit contains many ports (Figure 4-32).

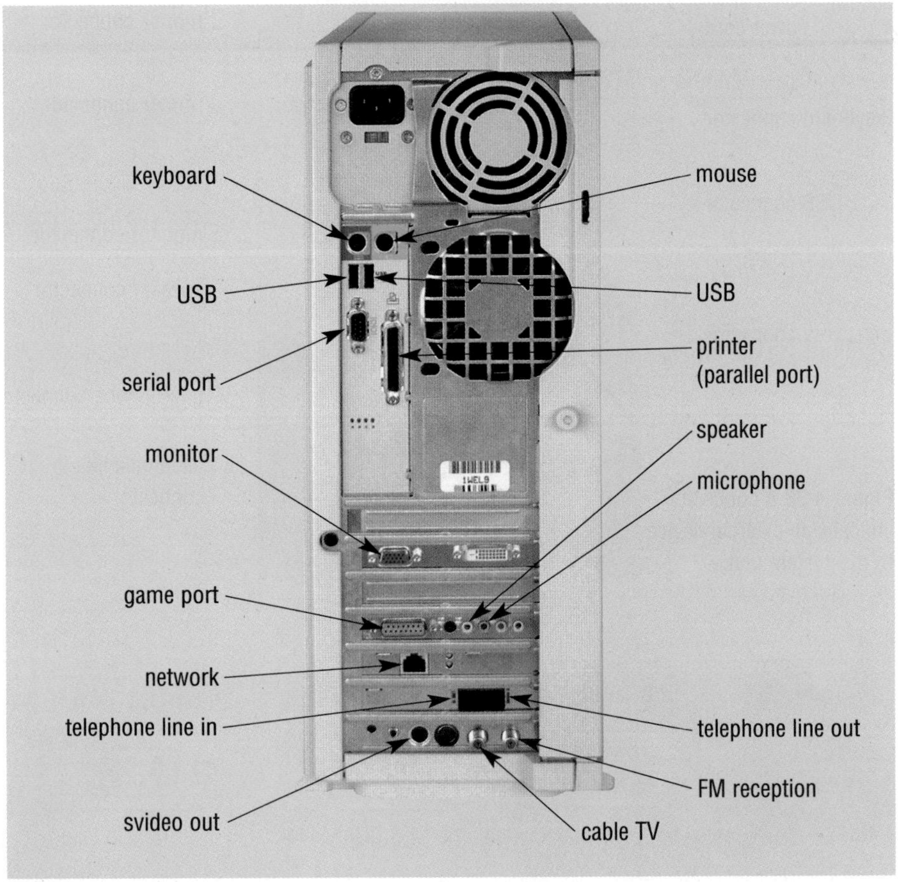

Figure 4-32 A port is an interface that allows you to connect a peripheral device such as a printer, mouse, or keyboard to the computer. The back of the system unit has many ports.

Figure 4-31 Flash memory cards are available in a wide range of sizes.

Web Link

For more information on ports and connectors, visit the Discovering Computers 2002 Chapter 4 WEB LINK page (**scsite.com/dc2002/ch4/weblink.htm**) and click Ports and Connectors.

Ports have different types of connectors. A **connector** joins a cable to a device (Figure 4-33). One end of a cable attaches to the connector on the system unit and the other end of the cable attaches to a connector on the peripheral device. Most connectors are available in one of two genders: male or female. **Male connectors** have one or more exposed pins, like the end of an electrical cord you plug into the wall. **Female connectors** have matching holes to accept the pins on a male connector, like an electrical wall outlet.

Figure 4-34 shows the different types of connectors on a system unit. Some system units include these connectors when you buy the computer. You add other connectors by inserting cards into the computer. The card has a port that allows you to attach a device to the card.

When you purchase a cable to connect your computer to a peripheral, the manufacturers often identify the cables by their connector types. For example, a printer port might use any

power cord
keyboard connector
USB connector
network connector
mouse connector
printer connector
monitor connector
speaker connector
microphone connector
telephone line in connector

Figure 4-33 A connector attaches an external device to the system unit.

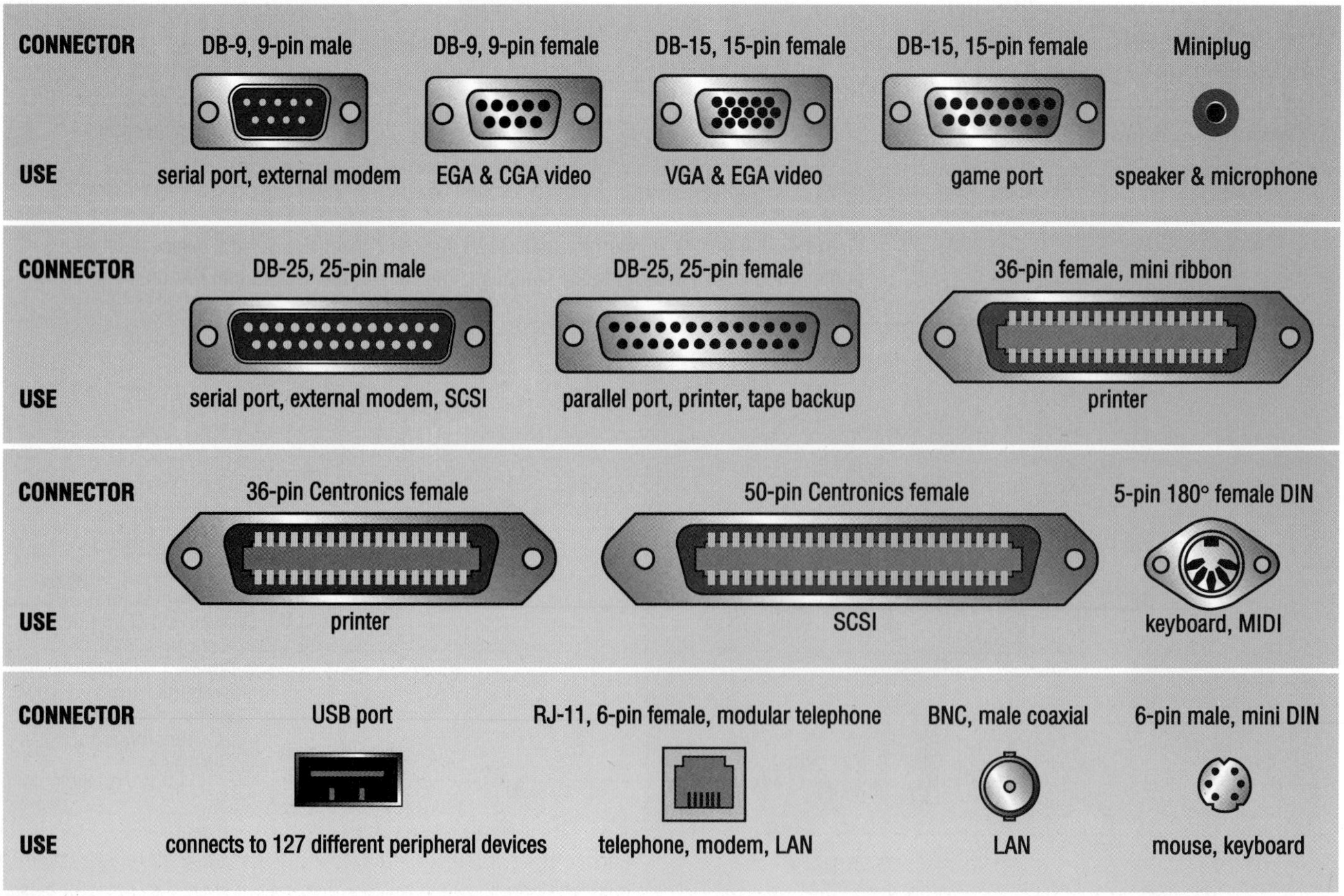
CONNECTOR
DB-9, 9-pin male
DB-9, 9-pin female
DB-15, 15-pin female
DB-15, 15-pin female
Miniplug
USE
serial port, external modem
EGA & CGA video
VGA & EGA video
game port
speaker & microphone
CONNECTOR
DB-25, 25-pin male
DB-25, 25-pin female
36-pin female, mini ribbon
USE
serial port, external modem, SCSI
parallel port, printer, tape backup
printer
CONNECTOR
36-pin Centronics female
50-pin Centronics female
5-pin 180° female DIN
USE
printer
SCSI
keyboard, MIDI
CONNECTOR
USB port
RJ-11, 6-pin female, modular telephone
BNC, male coaxial
6-pin male, mini DIN
USE
connects to 127 different peripheral devices
telephone, modem, LAN
LAN
mouse, keyboard

Figure 4-34 Examples of different types of connectors on a system unit.

one of these connectors: 25-pin female, 36-pin female, 36-pin Centronics female, or USB. Thus, you should understand the differences among connector types.

Sometimes you cannot attach a new peripheral device to the computer because the connector on the system unit is the same gender as the connector on the cable. You can use a gender changer to solve this problem. A **gender changer** is a device that enables you to join two connectors that are either both female or both male.

Most computers have three types of ports: serial, parallel, and USB. The next section discusses each of these ports.

Serial Ports

A **serial port** is one type of interface that connects a device to the system unit by transmitting data one bit at a time (Figure 4-35). Serial ports usually connect devices that do not require fast data transmission rates, such as a mouse, keyboard, or modem. The COM port on the system unit is one type of serial port.

Some modems that connect the system unit to a telephone line use a serial port because the telephone line expects the data in a specific frequency. Serial ports conform to either the RS-232 or RS-422 standard, which specifies the number of pins used on the port's connector. Two common connectors for serial ports are a male 25-pin connector and a male 9-pin connector.

Parallel Ports

Unlike a serial port, a **parallel port** is an interface that connects devices by transferring more than one bit at a time (Figure 4-36). Parallel ports originally were developed as an alternative to the slower speed serial ports.

Many printers connect to the system unit using a parallel port with a 25-pin female connector. This parallel port can transfer eight bits of data (one byte) simultaneously through eight separate lines in a single cable. A parallel port sometimes is

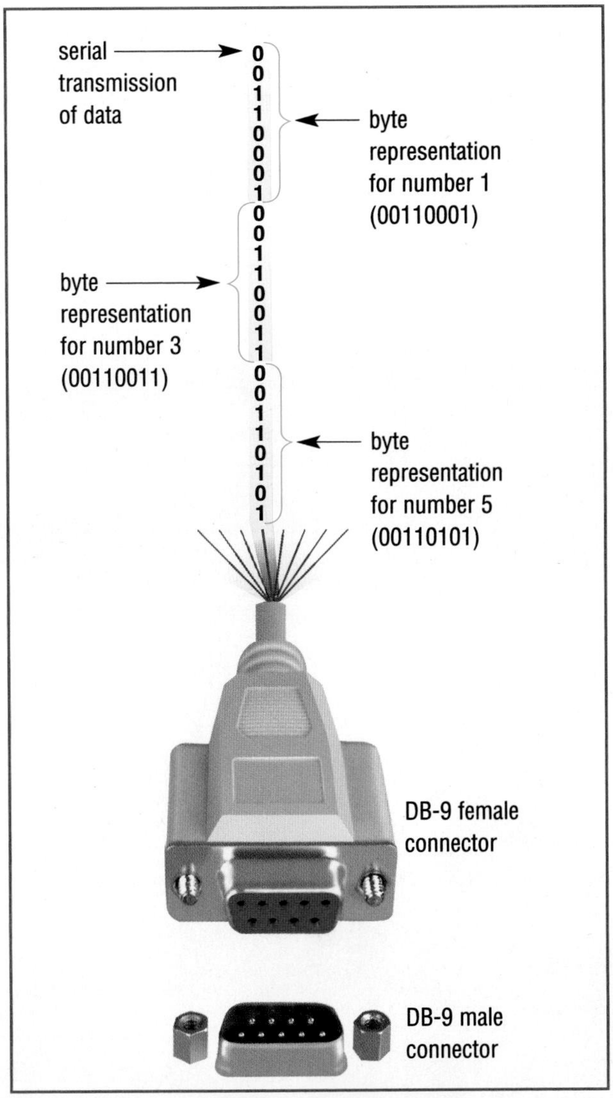

Figure 4-35 A serial port transmits data one bit at a time. One wire sends data; another receives data; and the remaining wires are used for other communications operations.

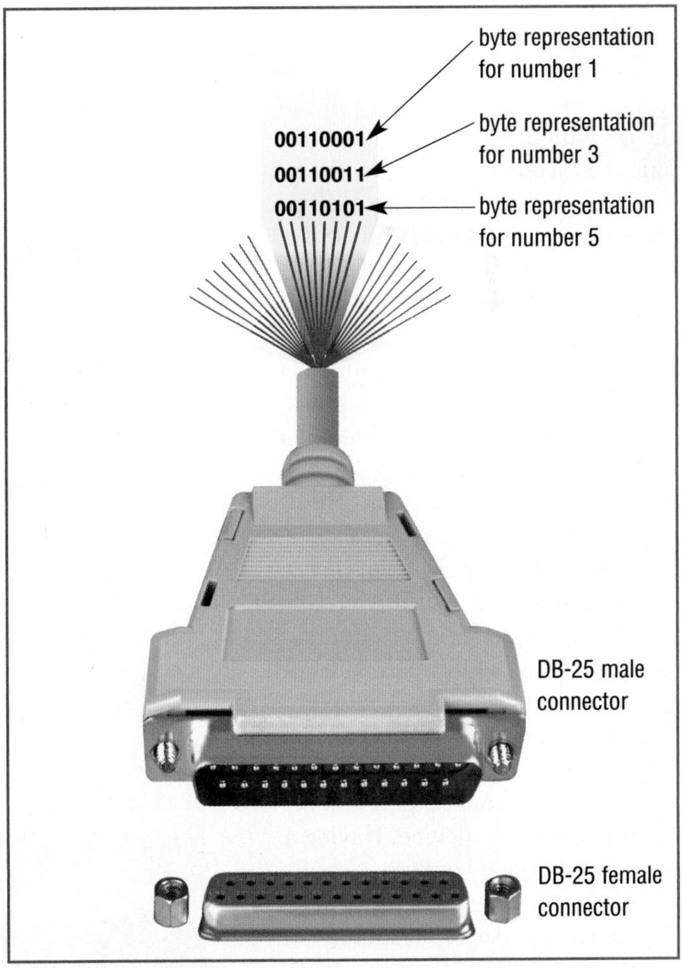

Figure 4-36 A parallel port is capable of transmitting more than one bit at a time. The port shown in this figure has eight wires that transmit data; the remaining wires are used for other communications operations.

called a Centronics interface, after the company that first defined the standard for communications between the system unit and a printer.

Two newer types of parallel ports, the EPP (Enhanced Parallel Port) and the ECP (Extended Capabilities Port), use the same connectors as the Centronics port, but are more than 10 times faster. Both EPP and ECP are part of the IEEE (Institute of Electrical and Electronics Engineers) 1284 standard. The **IEEE 1284** standard specifies how older and newer peripheral devices that use a parallel port should transfer data to and from a computer.

Universal Serial Bus Port

A **universal serial bus (USB) port** can connect up to 127 different peripheral devices with a single connector type. Many system units have one or two USB ports (see Figure 4-32 on page 4.25). To attach multiple devices using a single port, you can daisy chain the devices together outside the system unit. That is, the first USB device connects to the USB port on the computer, the second USB device connects to the first USB device, the third USB device connects to the second USB device, and so on. An alternative to daisy chaining is to use a USB hub. A **USB hub** plugs into the USB port on the system unit and contains multiple USB ports into which you plug cables from USB devices.

Some newer peripheral devices may attach only to a USB port. Others attach to either a serial or parallel port, as well as a USB port. When connecting a device to a USB port, you do not need to install a card in the computer. Simply plug one end of the cable into the USB port and the other end into the device. Having a standard port and connector greatly simplifies the process of attaching devices to a personal computer.

The USB also supports hot plugging and Plug and Play, which means you can attach peripherals while the computer is running. With serial and parallel port connections, by contrast, you often must restart the computer after you attach the device.

Special-Purpose Ports

Four special-purpose ports used on many of today's computers are 1394, MIDI, SCSI, and IrDA. The following section discusses each of these ports.

1394 PORT Similarly to the USB port, the IEEE **1394 port**, also called **FireWire**, can connect multiple types of devices that require faster data transmission speeds such as digital video cameras, digital VCRs, color printers, scanners, digital cameras, and DVD drives to a single connector. You can connect up to 63 devices together using a 1394 port. The 1394 port also supports Plug and Play. The Macintosh G4 computer has a 1394 port.

Many computer professionals believe that ports such as USB and 1394 someday will replace serial and parallel ports completely (Figure 4-37).

MIDI PORT A special type of serial port, called a **musical instrument digital interface**, or **MIDI** (pronounced MID-dee) port, connects the system unit to a musical instrument, such as an electronic keyboard. The electronic music industry has adopted MIDI as a standard to define how devices, such as sound cards and synthesizers, represent sounds electronically. A **synthesizer**, which can be a peripheral or a chip, creates sound from digital instructions.

A system unit with a MIDI port has the capability of recording sounds that have been created by a synthesizer and then processing the sounds (the data) to create new sounds. Just about every sound card supports the MIDI standard, so you can play and manipulate sounds on a computer that were created originally on another computer.

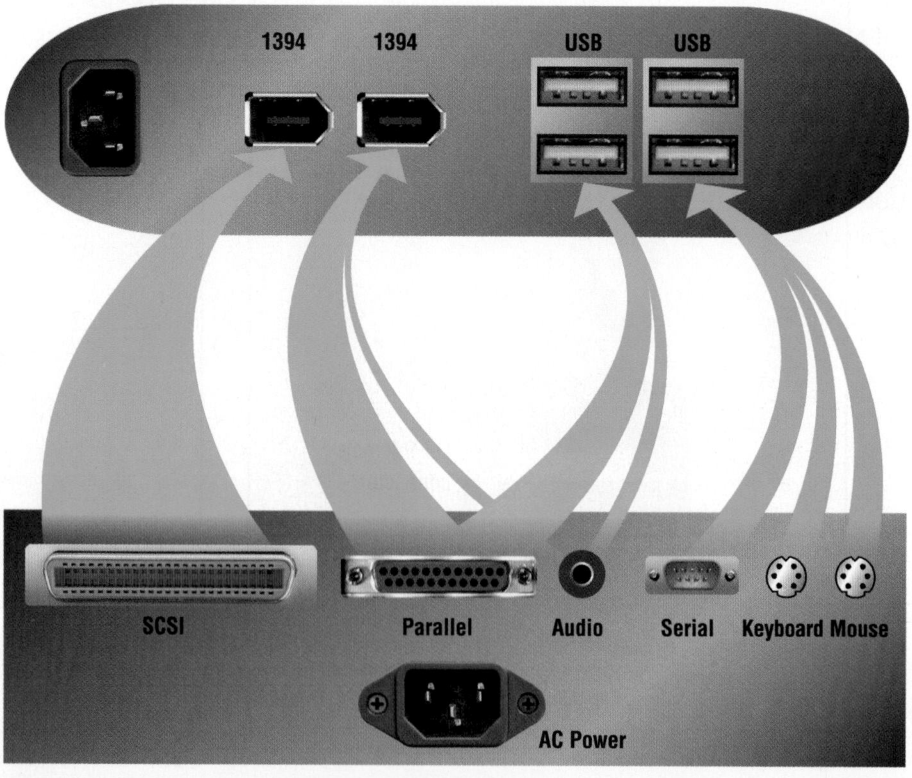

Figure 4-37 Many computer professionals believe that ports such as USB and 1394 someday will replace serial and parallel ports completely.

SCSI PORT A **small computer system interface** (**SCSI** pronounced skuzzy) port is a special high-speed parallel port that allows you to attach SCSI peripheral devices such as disk drives and printers. Depending on the type of SCSI interface, you can daisy chain either up to 7 or 15 devices together. That is, the first SCSI device connects to the computer, the second SCSI device connects to the first SCSI device, and so on. Some new computers include a SCSI port. Others have a slot that supports a SCSI card.

IrDA PORT Peripheral devices may not use any cables. Instead, some transmit data via infrared light waves. For these wireless devices to transmit signals to a computer, both the computer and the device must have an **IrDA port** (Figure 4-38). These ports conform to standards developed by the **IrDA** (**Infrared Data Association**).

Operating similar to a television remote control, you must align the IrDA port on the peripheral device with the IrDA port on the computer so that nothing obstructs the path of the infrared light wave. Devices that use IrDA ports include the keyboard, mouse, printer, digital cameras, digital telephones, and pagers. Several of these devices use a high-speed IrDA port, sometimes called a **FIR** (**fast infrared**) port.

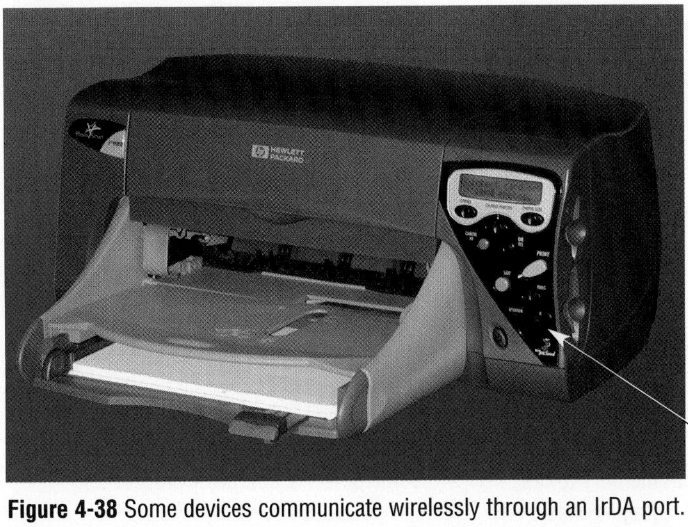

Figure 4-38 Some devices communicate wirelessly through an IrDA port.

BUSES

As previously explained, a computer processes and stores data as a series of electronic bits. These bits transfer internally within the circuitry of the computer along electrical channels. Each channel, called a **bus**, allows the various devices inside and attached to the system unit to communicate with each other. Just as vehicles travel on a highway to move from one destination to another, bits travel on a bus (Figure 4-39 on the next page).

Buses transfer bits from input devices to memory, from memory to the processor, from the processor to memory, and from memory to output or storage devices. Buses consist of two parts: a data bus and an address bus. The data bus transfers actual data and the address bus transfers information about where the data should go in memory.

The size of a bus, called the **bus width**, determines the number of bits that the computer can transmit at one time. For example, a 32-bit bus can transmit 32 bits (four bytes) at a time. On a 64-bit bus, bits transmit from one location to another 64 bits (eight bytes) at a time. The larger the number of bits handled by the bus, the faster the computer transfers data.

Web Link

For more information on buses, visit the Discovering Computers 2002 Chapter 4 WEB LINK page (**scsite.com/dc2002/ch4/weblink.htm**) and click Buses.

ISSUE

High-Speed Ports

USB and 1394

In 1996, a few computer manufacturers started to include universal serial bus (USB) support in newer machines. With the release of the iMac in 1998 the USB became widespread. Many consider the USB to be the most important advance to date in connectivity standards for the personal computer. The primary selling point of USB is Plug and Play. Another selling point is that you can daisy chain up to 127 different peripheral devices. It is important to note that 127 is a theoretical limit. In reality, the number of devices is limited by their need for bandwidth and power needs. Another Plug and Play port that supports high speed data transfer rates is the IEEE 1394, also known as FireWire. A 1394 port can handle up to 63 daisy-chained devices. The primary difference between USB and 1394 is that 1394 is more expensive and supports faster data transfer rates. For those with the newest computers and the latest version of Windows 98, USB and 1394 devices should prove much easier to install and use than devices dependent on expansion cards. Will USB and 1394 eventually replace serial and parallel ports? Will consumers be willing to pay more for a 1394 port for faster transfer rates? Why or why not?

For more information on the USB and 1394 devices, visit the Discovering Computers 2002 Issues Web page (**scsite.com/dc2002/issues.htm**) and click Chapter 4 Issue #4.

Using the highway analogy again, assume that one lane on a highway can carry one bit. A 32-bit bus is like a 32-lane highway. A 64-bit bus is like a 64-lane highway.

If a number in memory occupies 8 bytes, or 64 bits, the computer must transmit it in two separate steps when using a 32-bit bus: once for the first 32 bits and once for the second 32 bits. Using a 64-bit bus, the computer can transmit the number in a single step, transferring all 64 bits at once. The wider the bus, the fewer number of transfer steps required and the faster the transfer of data. Figure 4-40 lists some personal computer processors and their bus widths.

In conjunction with the bus width, many computer professionals discuss a computer's word size. **Word size** is the number of bits the processor can interpret and execute at a given time. That is, a 64-bit processor can manipulate 64 bits at a time. Computers with a larger word size can process more data in the same amount of time than computers with a smaller word size. In most computers, the word size is the same as the bus width.

Every bus also has a clock speed. Just like the processor, manufacturers state the clock speed for a bus in megahertz. Recall that one megahertz (MHz) is equal to one million ticks per second. Most of today's processors have a bus speed of either 100 MHz or 133 MHz. The higher the bus clock speed, the faster the transmission of data, which results in applications running faster.

A computer has two basic types of buses: a system bus and an expansion bus. A **system bus** is part of the motherboard and connects the processor to main memory. An **expansion bus** allows the processor to communicate with peripheral devices. When computer professionals use the term bus by itself, they usually are referring to the system bus.

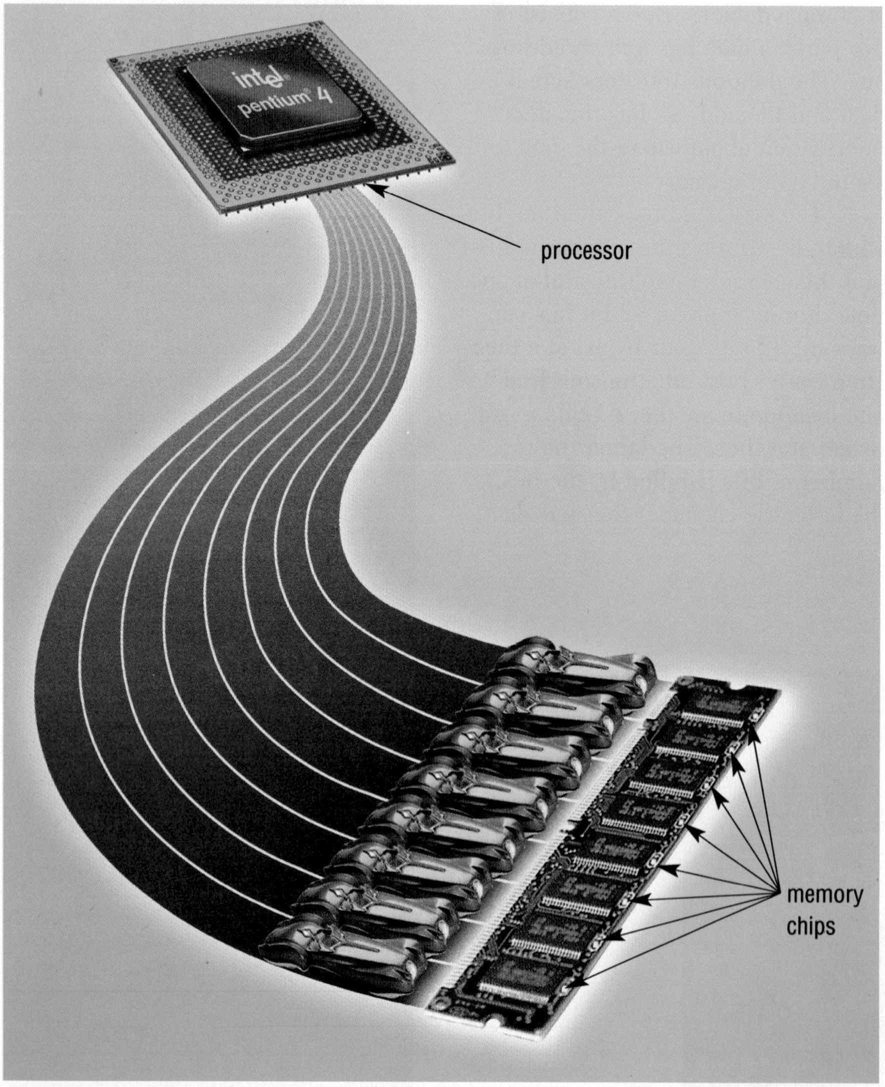

Figure 4-39 Just as vehicles travel on a highway to move from one destination to another, bits travel on a bus. Buses transfer bits from input devices to memory, from memory to the processor, from the processor to memory, and from memory to output or storage devices.

COMPARISON OF BUS WIDTHS

NAME	BUS WIDTH*
Pentium® 4	64
Itanium™	64
Pentium® III Xeon™	64
Pentium® III	64
Celeron™	64
Pentium® II Xeon™	64
Pentium® II	64
Pentium® with MMX™ technology	64
Pentium® Pro	64
Pentium®	64
80486DX	32
80386DX	32
80286	16
PowerPC	64
68040	32
68030	32
68020	32

Figure 4-40 A comparison of bus widths on some personal computer processors.

Expansion Bus

Some devices outside the system unit connect to a port on a card, which is inserted into an expansion slot. This expansion slot connects to the expansion bus, which allows the processor to communicate with the peripheral device attached to the card. Data transmitted to memory or the processor travels from the expansion bus via the expansion bus and the system bus (Figure 4-41).

The types of expansion buses on a motherboard determine the types of cards you can add to your computer. Thus, you should understand the following types of expansion buses: ISA bus, PCI bus, AGP bus, USB, 1394 bus, and PC Card bus.

- The most common and slowest expansion bus is the **ISA (Industry Standard Architecture) bus**. A mouse, modem card, sound card, and low-speed network interface card are examples of devices that connect to the ISA bus directly or through an ISA bus expansion slot.
- A **local bus** is a high-speed expansion bus that connects higher speed devices such as hard disks. The first standard local bus was the **VESA local bus**, which was used primarily for video cards. The current local bus standard is the **PCI (Peripheral Component Interconnect) bus** because it is more versatile than the VESA local bus. Types of cards you can insert into a PCI bus expansion slot include video cards, sound cards, SCSI cards, and high-speed network interface cards. The PCI bus transfers data about four times faster than the ISA bus. Most current personal computers have a PCI bus as well as an ISA bus.
- The **Accelerated Graphics Port (AGP)** is a bus designed by Intel to improve the speed with which 3-D graphics and video transmit. With an AGP video card in an AGP bus slot, the AGP bus provides a faster, dedicated interface between the video card and memory. Newer processors support AGP technology.

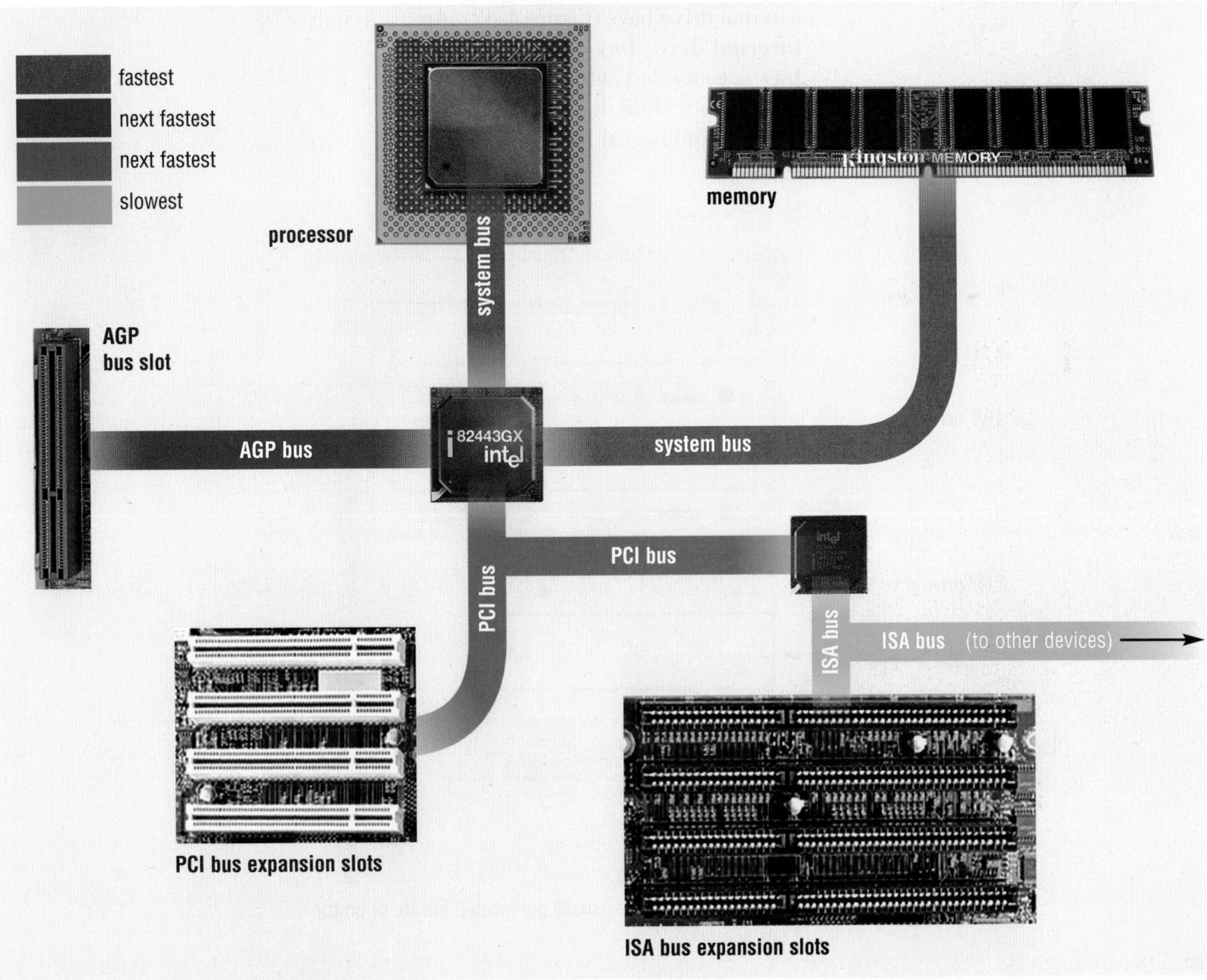

Figure 4-41 Buses allow the various devices inside and attached to the system unit to communicate with each other. Shown here, the buses in order of speed, from fastest to slowest, are the system bus, the AGP bus, the PCI bus, and the ISA bus.

- The **universal serial bus (USB)** and **1394 bus** are buses that eliminate the need to install cards into expansion slots. In a computer with a USB, for example, USB devices connect to each other outside the system unit and then a single cable attaches to the USB port. The USB port then connects to the USB, which connects to the PCI bus on the motherboard. The 1394 bus works in a similar fashion. With these buses, expansion slots are available for devices not compatible with USB or 1394.
- The expansion bus for a PC Card is the **PC Card bus**. With a PC Card inserted into a PC Card slot, data travels on the PC Card bus to the PCI bus.

BAYS

After you purchase a computer, you may want to install an additional device such as a disk drive to add storage capabilities to the system unit. A **bay** is an open area inside the system unit in which you can install additional equipment. A bay is different from a slot, which is used for the installation of cards. These spaces, commonly called **drive bays**, most often hold disk drives.

Two types of drive bays exist: internal and external. An **external drive bay** or **exposed drive bay** allows access to the drive from outside the system unit. Floppy disk drives, CD-ROM drives, DVD-ROM drives, Zip® drives, and tape drives are examples of devices installed in external drive bays (Figure 4-42). An **internal drive bay** or **hidden drive bay** is concealed entirely within the system unit. Hard disk drives are installed in internal bays.

POWER SUPPLY

Many personal computers plug into standard wall outlets, which supply an alternating current (AC) of 115 to 120 volts. This type of power is unsuitable for use with a computer, which requires a direct current (DC) ranging from 5 to 12 volts. The **power supply** is the component in the system unit that converts the wall outlet AC power into DC power.

Some external peripheral devices such as an external modem or tape drive have an **AC adapter**, which is an external power supply. One end of the AC adapter plugs into the wall outlet and the other end attaches to the peripheral device. The AC adapter converts the AC power into DC power that the device requires.

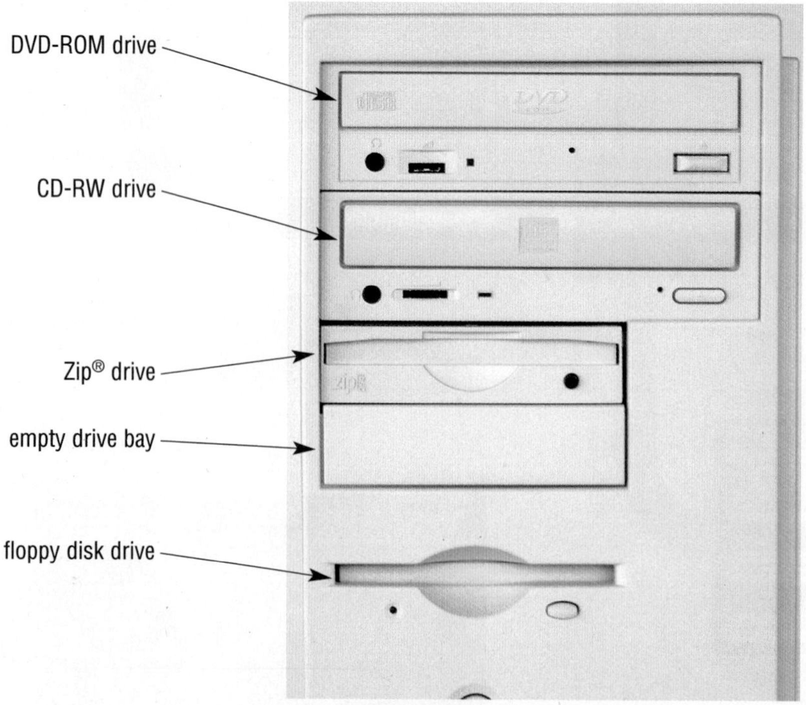

Figure 4-42 Drive bays usually are located beside or on top of one another.

MOBILE COMPUTERS

As businesses expand to serve customers across the country and around the world, more and more people need to use a computer while traveling to and from a main office to conduct business. As noted in Chapter 1, users with such mobile computing needs — known as mobile users — often have a mobile computer such as a notebook and/or handheld computer (Figure 4-43).

Weighing on average between 4 and 10 pounds, notebook computers can run either using batteries or using a standard power supply. Smaller handheld computers, run strictly on battery.

Like their desktop counterparts, notebook computers and handheld computers have a system unit that contains electronic components that processes data (Figure 4-44). The difference is many other devices also are part of the system unit. In addition to the motherboard, processor, memory, sound card, PC Card slot, and drive bay, the system unit also houses devices such as the keyboard, pointing device, speakers, and display.

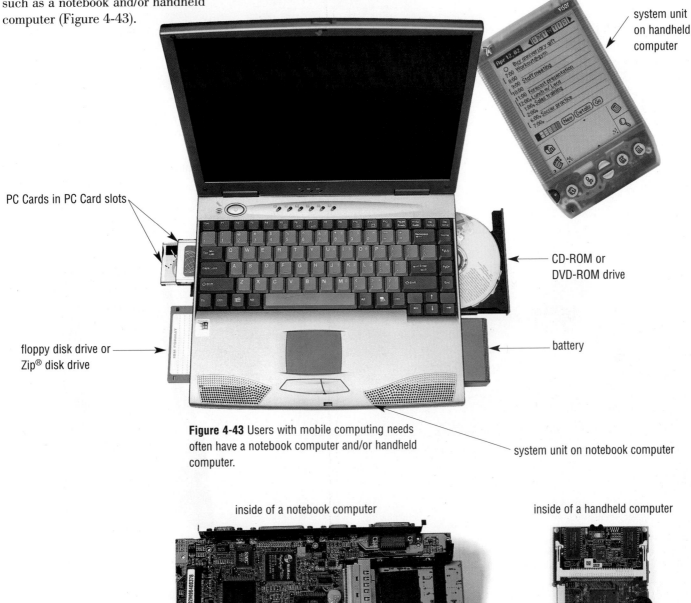

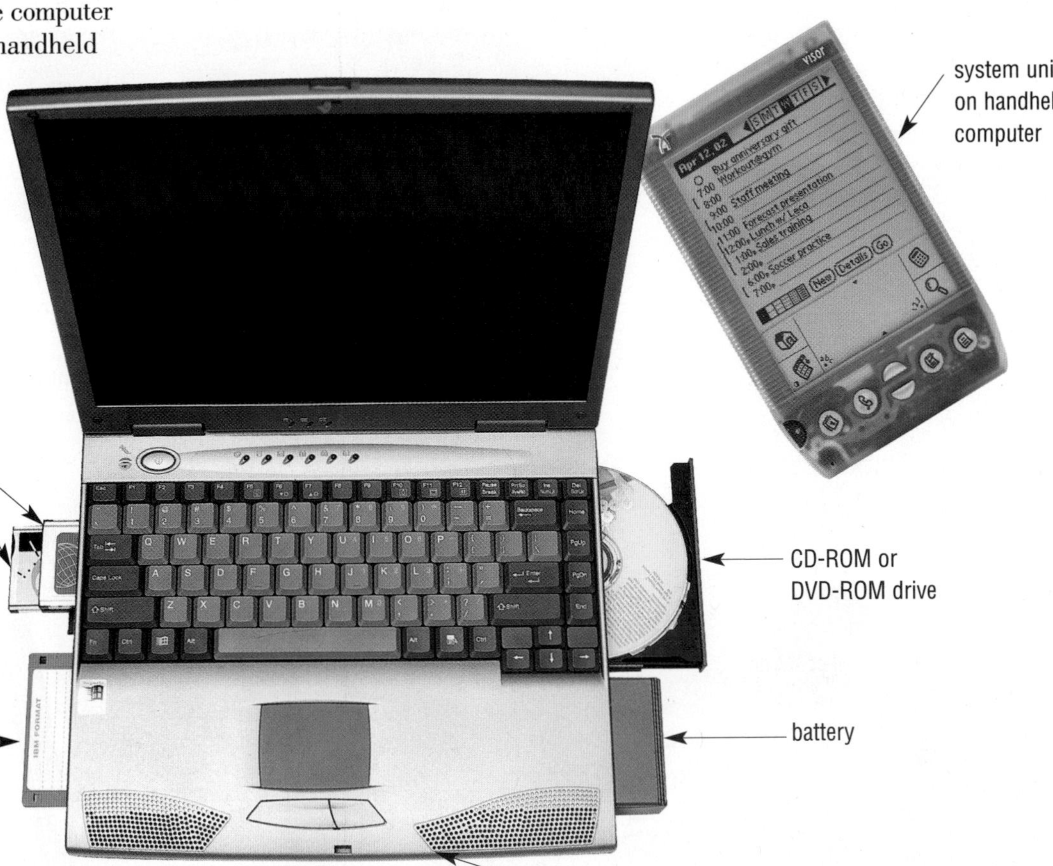

Figure 4-43 Users with mobile computing needs often have a notebook computer and/or handheld computer.

Figure 4-44 Notebook and handheld computers contain electronic components that process data.

A notebook computer usually is more expensive than a desktop computer with the same capabilities. Handheld computers are more affordable, usually costing a few hundred dollars.

The typical notebook computer often has a keyboard/mouse, IrDA, serial, parallel, video, and USB ports (Figure 4-45).

Handheld computers often have an IrDA port so you can communicate wirelessly with other computers or devices such as a printer. Many include a serial port. Handheld computers also can rest in a cradle, so you can transfer data to your desktop computer (Figure 4-46).

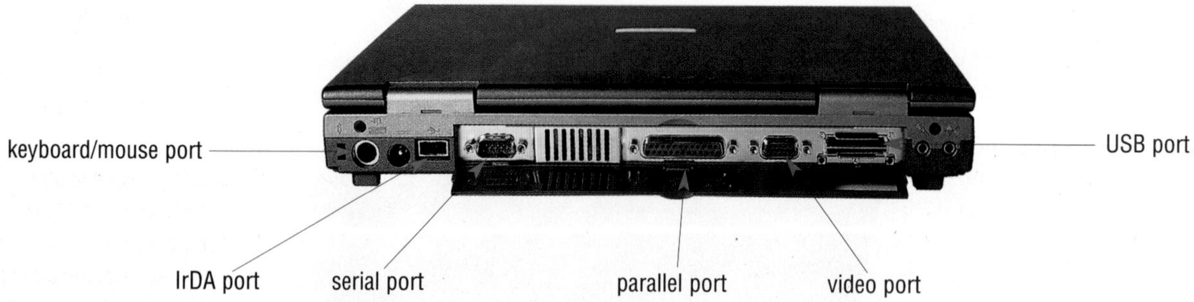

Figure 4-45 A notebook computer often has a keyboard/mouse, IrDA, serial, parallel, video, and USB ports.

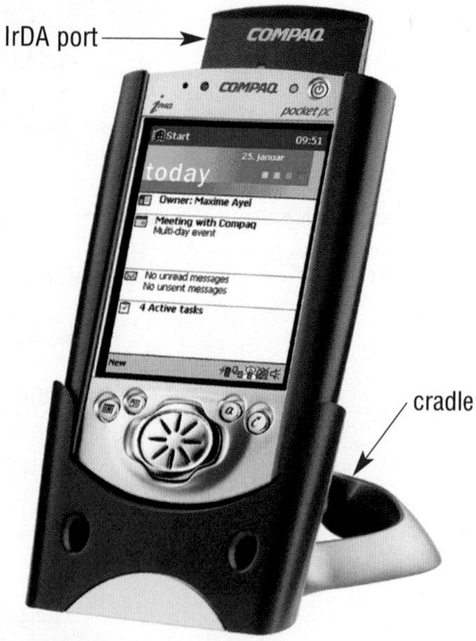

Figure 4-46 You transfer data from a smaller handheld computer, through a cradle or an IrDA port.

ISSUE

On the Go

Mobile Computers

Mobile computers are everywhere. Handheld computers and Web-enabled cellular telephones are ideal for the person on the go. A typical handheld computer can function as a fax sender and personal organizer. Handheld computers often use a stylus instead of a keyboard for input, which allows you to write directly on the device's screen. Thus, many handheld computers incorporate handwriting recognition features. Some handheld computers are capable of voice input using voice recognition technology. Software for many of these devices can turn your handheld organizer into a miniature version of the Web. And, handheld computers are inexpensive. If a mobile device can perform all the same functions, including Web access, of a desktop or notebook computer, is it necessary to spend more money on these higher priced devices? What advantages does a desktop or notebook computer provide? What advantages does a handheld computer provide? Is it necessary to have both a desktop or notebook computer and a handheld computer? Why or why not?

For more information on mobile computers, visit the Discovering Computers 2002 Issues Web page (**scsite.com/dc2002/issues.htm**) and click Chapter 4 Issue #5.

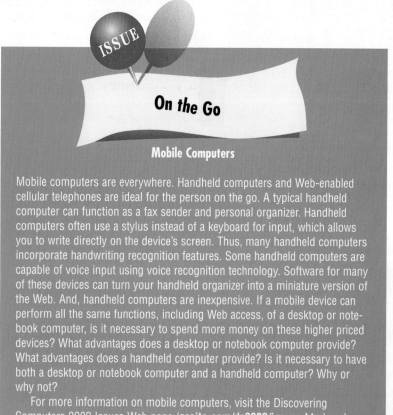

PUTTING IT ALL TOGETHER

When purchasing a computer, it is important to understand how the components in the system unit work. Many factors inside the system unit influence the speed and power of a computer. The type of computer configuration you require depends on your intended use. The table in Figure 4-47 lists the suggested processor, clock speed, and RAM requirements based on the needs of various types of computer users.

CHAPTER SUMMARY

Chapter 4 presented the components in the system unit, described how memory stores data, instructions, and information, and discussed the sequence of operations that occur when a computer executes an instruction. The chapter included a comparison of various personal computer processors on the market today.

SUGGESTED CONFIGURATIONS BY USER

USER	PROCESSOR AND CLOCK SPEED	MINIMUM RAM
Home 	Pentium® 4 or Athlon™ 600 MHz or higher; or Celeron™ or Duron™ – 600 MHz or higher	64 MB
Small Office/Home Office 	Pentium® 4 or Athlon™ – 800 MHz or higher	128 MB
Mobile 	Pentium® III or AMD-K6®-2-P 500 MHz or higher	64 MB
Large Business 	Pentium® 4 or Athlon™ – 700 MHz or higher	128 MB
Power 	Pentium® 4 or Itanium™ or Athlon™ – 1 GHz or higher	256 MB

Figure 4-47 This table recommends suggested processor, clock speed, and RAM configurations.

Software Engineer

Software engineering is a dynamic and exciting field. You have your choice of a number of professions from robotics to operating systems and application software development to personal communications systems to intelligent agents to computer animation to computational biology. In many universities, software engineering is a sub-component of computer science. The field of software engineering is concerned with the processes, methods, and tools for the development of high-quality software systems. Students study the application of software specification, design, implementation, testing, and documentation of software.

A minimum of a bachelor's degree is required to work as a software engineer, but many people continue on for their masters and even a Ph.D. A strong mathematics background is required, and the road to the top of this field is a rigorous one. Expect to work hard and put in many years before you obtain your degree. When you finally achieve your goal, do not relax too quickly; computer science is ever changing. To stay in this field, you can expect to upgrade continually your skills and knowledge. The benefits are worth the effort. Software engineers can expect salaries of $75,000 and up.

To learn more about the field of software engineering as a career, visit the Discovering Computers 2002 Careers Web page (**scsite.com/dc2002/careers.htm**) and click Software Engineering.

E-RESOURCES

LOOK IT UP

Web Resources Ease System Concerns

Have you heard of a Diffie-Hellman or a mouse potato? If you do not know a JDK from an OSS, then an online computer technology dictionary may be the tool you need. From dictionaries and encyclopedias to online technical support, the Web is filled with a plethora of resources, including those listed in Figure 4-48, to answer your computer questions and resolve specialized problems.

Chapter 4 describes the components of the system unit including the different processors, various types of memory, and other devices associated with it, as well as the components of notebook and handheld computers. With the continual developments in technology and communications, new products reach the marketplace daily.

A way to keep up with the latest developments is to look to online dictionaries that add to their collections of computer and product terms on a regular basis and include thousands of descriptions and designations. An example is the whatis?com Web site listed in the table in Figure 4-48 and shown in Figure 4-49. The whatis?com Web site contains more than 2,500 cyberterms, with daily updates to the words and definitions. This Web site and many other reference Web pages feature a word of the day that identifies a new product or industry standard as well as highlight recently added or revised terms.

Shopping for a new computer can be a daunting experience, but many online guides can help you select the components that best fit your needs and budget. Most of these Web sites, including NetGuide (Figure 4-50),

RESOURCES WEB SITES	URL
Dictionaries and Encyclopedias	
CDT's Guide to Online Privacy	www.cdt.org/privacy/guide/terms
ComputerUser High-Tech Dictionary	computeruser.com/resources/dictionary
Webopedia: Online Computer Dictionary for Internet Terms and Technical Support	webopedia.com
whatis?com	whatis.com
ZD Webopædia	www.zdwebopedia.com
Computer Shopping Guides	
BizRate.com®	bizrate.com/marketplace
Computer Shopper	zdnet.com/computershopper
NetGuide	netguide.com
The CPU Scorecard	cpuscorecard.com
The Online Computer Buying Guide™	grohol.com/computers
Upgrading Guides	
CNET Shopper	shopper.cnet.com
eHow™	ehow.com
PC World.com	pcworld.com/heres_how
Upgrade Source	upgradesource.com
Focus on MacSupport	macsupport.miningco.com/compute/macsupport
Online Technical Support	
Dux Computer Digest	duxcw.com
MSN Computing Central	computingcentral.msn.com
PC911	pcnineoneone.com
PC-Help Online	pchelponline.com
Learnlots.com	www.learnlots.com
Technical and Consumer Information	
CNET	cnet.com
newsday.com	newsday.com/plugin/c101main.htm
The Standard.com	thestandard.com
Wired News	wirednews.com
ZDNet	zdnet.com

For an updated list of resources Web sites, visit scsite.com/dc2002/e-rev.htm.

Figure 4-48 A variety of Web resources can provide information on buying, repairing, and upgrading computers.

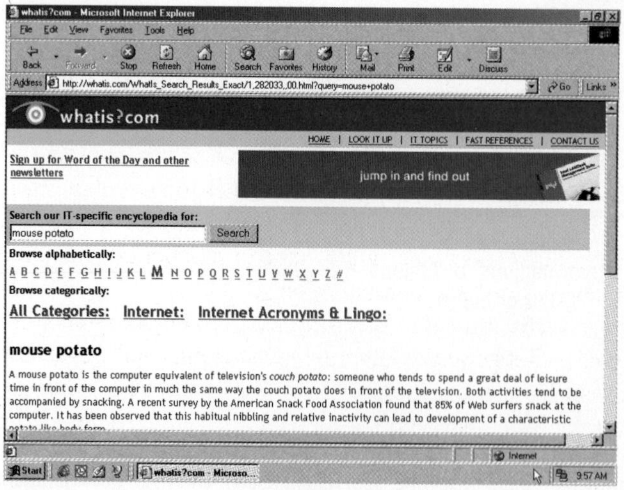

Figure 4-49 Thousands of technology terms are defined at the whatis?com Website.

feature the latest desktop and notebook computer prices, hardware reviews, bargains, and links to popular manufacturers' sale Web pages. If you want to upgrade your present computer, several online guides, such as CNET Shopper and Upgrade Source, give current prices for these components and list the more popular products.

If you are not confident in your ability to work a problem alone, turn to online technical support. Such Web sites, including Learnlots.com (Figure 4-51), often provide streaming how-to video lessons, tutorials, and real-time chats with experienced technicians.

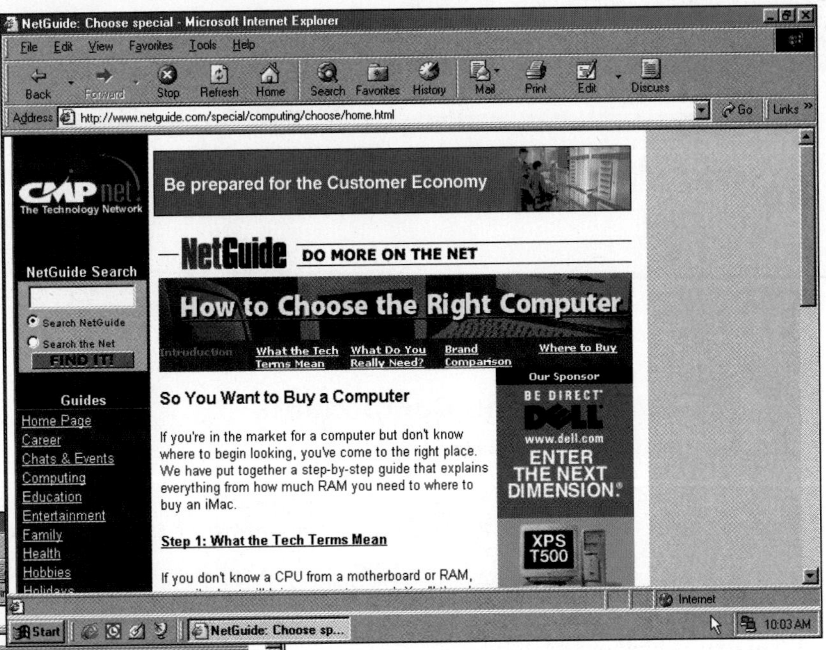

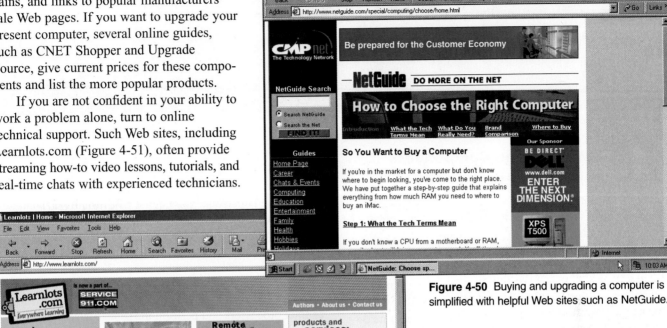

Figure 4-50 Buying and upgrading a computer is simplified with helpful Web sites such as NetGuide.

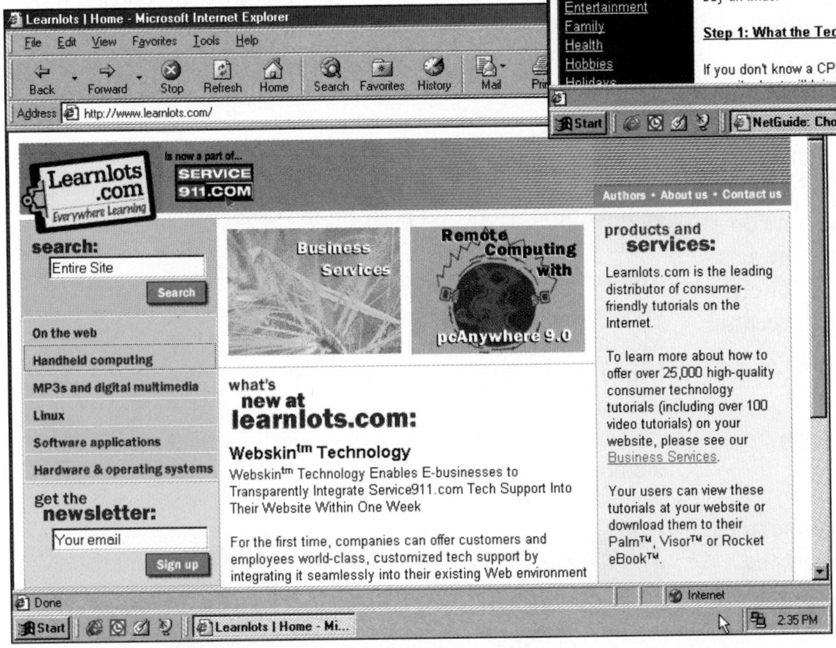

Figure 4-51 Practical tutorials at the Learnlots.com Web site provide useful technological information.

The Web offers a variety of technical and consumer information. Hardware and software reviews, price comparisons, shareware, technical questions and answers, and breaking technology news are found on comprehensive portals such as CNET and ZDNET.

For more information on Web resources sites, visit the Discovering Computers 2002 E-Revolution Web page (scsite.com/dc2002/e-rev.htm) and click Resources.

eREVOLUTION E-RESOURCES applied:

1. Visit the dictionary and encyclopedia Web sites listed in Figure 4-48. Search these resources for five terms. Create a table with two columns: one for the cyberterm and one for the Web definition. Then, create a second table listing five recently added or updated words and their definitions on these sites. Next, visit two of the listed computer shopping guide Web sites to choose the components you would buy if you were building a customized desktop computer and notebook computer. Create a table for both systems listing the computer manufacturer, processor model name or number and manufacturer, clock speed, RAM, cache, number of expansion slots, and number of bays.

2. Visit three upgrading guide Web sites listed in Figure 4-48. Write a paragraph describing available advice for buying a motherboard. Describe the strengths and weaknesses of these Web sites, focusing on such criteria as clarity of instructions, thoroughness, and ease of navigation. Would you use these Web sites as a resource to troubleshoot computer problems? Then, view two technical and consumer information Web sites listed in the table and write a paragraph on each describing the top two news stories of the day.

In Summary

Web Instructions: To display this page from the Web, start your browser and enter the URL scsite.com/dc2002/ch4/summary.htm. Click the links for current and additional information. To listen to an audio version of this In Summary, click the Audio button. To play the audio, RealPlayer must be installed on your computer (download by clicking here).

1 What Are the Components in the System Unit?

The **system unit**, sometimes called a **chassis**, is a box-like case that houses the electronic components of a computer that are used to process data. System unit components include the processor, memory module, expansion cards, ports, and connectors. Many components reside on a circuit board called the **motherboard**, or **system board**. The motherboard contains different types of **chips**, or small pieces of semi-conducting material on which one or more **integrated circuits** (**IC**) are etched. A **transistor** acts as an electronic gate that opens or closes the circuit for electronic signals. One of the more important chips is the central processing unit (CPU).

2 How Does the CPU Process Data?

The **central processing unit** (**CPU**), sometimes referred to as the **processor**, interprets and carries out the basic instructions that operate a computer. The **control unit**, which is one component of the CPU, directs and coordinates most of the operations in the computer. For every instruction, the control unit repeats a set of four basic operations called the **machine cycle**: (1) **fetching** the instruction or data item from memory; (2) **decoding** the instruction into commands the computer understands; (3) **executing**, or carrying out, the commands; and, if necessary, (4) **storing**, or writing, the result to memory. The **arithmetic/logic unit** (**ALU**), another component of the CPU, performs the arithmetic, comparison, and logical operations.

3 What Are Some Processors Available Today?

A personal computer's CPU usually is contained on a single chip called a **processor**. Intel, a leading manufacturer of processors, produces **Pentium®** processors for high-end personal computers, the **Celeron™** processor for less expensive personal computers, and the **Xeon™** and **Itanium™** processors for workstations and servers. **Intel-compatible processors** have the same internal design as Intel processors and perform the same functions, but are made by other companies and often are less expensive. The **Motorola processor** is an alternative to the Intel-style processor and is found in Apple Macintosh and Power Macintosh systems. The **Alpha processor**, originally from Digital Equipment Corporation, is used primarily in workstations and high-end servers. A new type of processor, called an **integrated CPU**, combines functions of a CPU, memory, and a video card on a single chip.

4 How Do Series of Bits Represent Data?

Most computers are **digital**, meaning they understand only two discrete states: on and off. These states are represented using two digits, 0 (off) and 1 (on). Each on or off value is called a **bit** (short for **bin**ary dig**it**), which is the smallest unit of data a computer can handle. Eight bits grouped together as a unit are called a **byte**. A byte can represent 256 individual characters including numbers, letters of the alphabet, punctuation marks, and other characters. Combinations of 0s and 1s used to represent data are defined by patterns called coding schemes. Popular coding schemes are **ASCII**, **EBCDIC**, and **Unicode**.

In Summary

5 What Are Different Types of Memory?

In the processor, a computer's **memory** stores data, instructions, and information. Memory and storage size are measured by the number of bytes — a **kilobyte** (**K** or **KB**) is approximately one thousand bytes, a **megabyte** (**MB**) is approximately one million bytes, and a **gigabyte** (**GB**) is approximately one billion bytes. **RAM (random access memory)** consists of memory chips that can be read from and written to by the processor and other devices. Two types of RAM chips exist: **dynamic RAM (DRAM)**, which must be reenergized constantly; and **static RAM (SRAM)**, which must be reenergized less often but is more expensive. Most computers improve processing times by using **memory cache** to store frequently used instructions and data. **ROM (read-only memory)** is a memory chip that only can be read; it cannot be modified. **Flash memory**, also called **flash ROM** or **flash RAM**, is nonvolatile memory that can be erased electronically and reprogrammed. **CMOS** memory is used to store configuration information about the computer.

6 What Are Expansion Slots and Expansion Cards?

An **expansion slot** is an opening, or socket, where a circuit board can be inserted into the motherboard. These circuit boards, sometimes referred to as **expansion boards** or **expansion cards** and several other terms, are used to add new devices or capabilities to the computer, such as a modem or more memory. **Plug and Play** refers to a computer's capability of automatically configuring expansion cards and other devices as they are installed.

7 How Are Serial Ports, Parallel Ports, and USB Ports Different?

A cable often attaches external devices to the system unit. The interface, or point of attachment, to the system unit is called a **port**. Ports have different types of **connectors** used to join a cable to a device. A **serial port** is an interface that transmits only one bit of data at a time. Serial ports usually connect devices that do not require fast data transmission rates, such as a mouse, keyboard, or modem. A **parallel port** is an interface used to connect devices that are capable of transferring more than one bit at a time. Many printers connect to the system unit using a parallel port. A **universal serial bus (USB) port** can connect up to 127 different peripheral devices with a single connector type. To attach multiple devices to a single port, you daisy chain the devices.

8 How Do Buses Contribute to a Computer's Processing Speed?

Bits are transferred internally within the circuitry of the computer along electrical channels. Each channel, called a **bus**, allows various devices inside and attached to the system unit to communicate with each other. The **bus width**, or size of the bus, determines the number of bits that can be transferred at one time. The larger the bus width, the faster the computer transfers data. **Word size** is the number of bits the CPU can process at one time.

9 What Are the Components in a Notebook Computer?

Notebook computers have a system unit that contains electronic components — the same as those found in a desktop computer. Additionally, the system unit houses the keyboard, pointing device, speakers, and display. A notebook computer often has serial, parallel, keyboard, mouse, USB, video, and IrDA ports.

10 What Are the Components in a Handheld Computer?

Handheld computers have a system unit that contains electronic components — the same as those found in a desktop computer. Most handheld computers contain an IrDA port to communicate with other handheld computers, desktop and notebook computers, or devices such as a printer.

Key Terms

Web Instructions: To display this page from the Web, start your browser and enter the URL scsite.com/dc2002/ch4/terms.htm. Scroll through the list of terms. Click a term to display its definition and a picture. Click the To WEB button for current and additional information about the term from the Web. To see animations, Shockwave and Flash Player must be installed on your computer (download by clicking here).

SYSTEMBOARD
Circuit board that contains most of the electronic components in the system unit. Also called motherboard. (4.4)

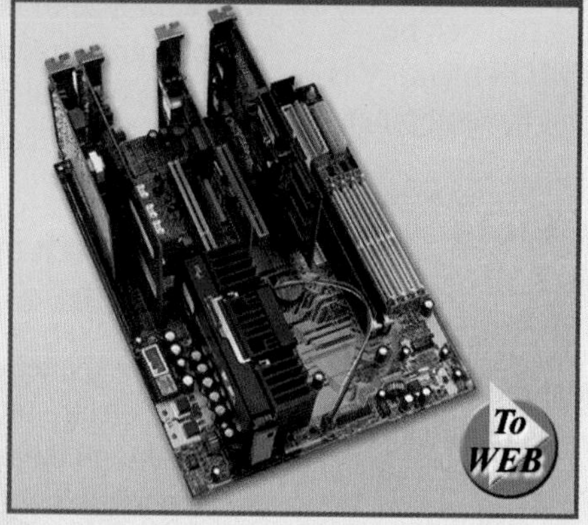

Learn It Online

Web Instructions: To display this page from the Web, start your browser and enter the URL scsite.com/dc2002/ch1/learn.htm.

1. Web Guide

Click Web Guide to display the Guide to World Wide Web Sites and Searching Techniques Web page. Click Computers and Computing and then click Virtual Museum of Computing. Scroll down the page and locate General Historical Information. Click a link of your choice. Use your word processing program to prepare a brief report on your tour and submit your assignment to your instructor.

2. Scavenger Hunt

Click Scavenger Hunt. Print a copy of the Scavenger Hunt page; use this page to write down your answers as you search the Web. Submit your completed page to your instructor.

3. Who Wants to Be a Computer Genius?

Click Computer Genius to find out if you are a computer genius. Directions on how to play the game will display. When you are ready to play, click the PLAY button. Submit your score to your instructor.

4. Wheel of Terms

Click Wheel of Terms to reinforce important terms you learned in this chapter by playing the Shelly Cashman Series version of this popular game. Directions on how to play the game will display. When you are ready to play, click the PLAY button. Submit your score to your instructor.

5. Career Corner

Click Career Corner to display the Making College Count page. Click a link of your choice and review the page. Write a brief report describing what you learned. Submit the report to your instructor.

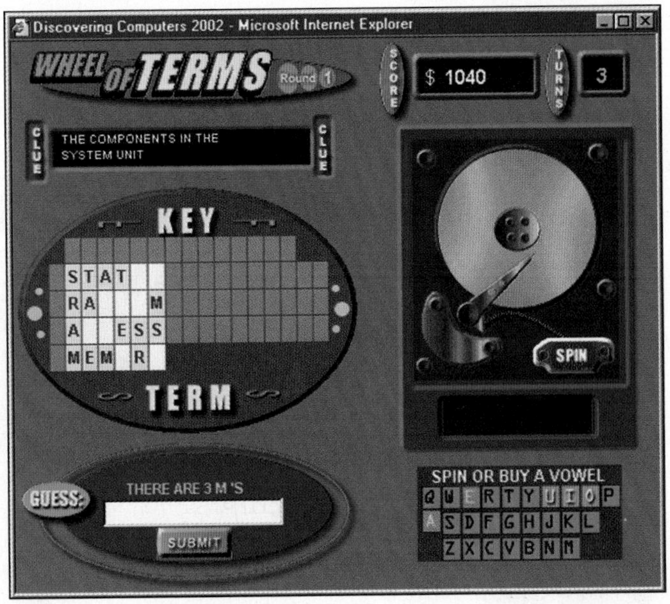

6. Search Sleuth

Click Search Sleuth to learn search techniques that will help make you a research expert. Submit the completed assignment to your instructor.

7. Crossword Puzzle Challenge

Click Crossword Puzzle Challenge. Complete the puzzle to reinforce skills you learned in this chapter. Directions on how to play the game will display. When you are ready to play, click the PLAY button. Submit the completed puzzle to your instructor.

8. Practice Test

Click Practice Test. Answer each question. When completed enter your name and click the Grade Test button to submit the quiz for grading. Make a note of any missed questions. If required, print a copy to submit to your instructor.

Checkpoint

Web Instructions: To display this page from the Web, start your browser and enter the URL scsite.com/dc2002/ch4/check.htm. Click the links for current and additional information. To experience the animation and interactivity, Shockwave and Flash Player must be installed on your computer (download by clicking here.)

LABEL THE FIGURE

Instructions: Identify these components of the motherboard.

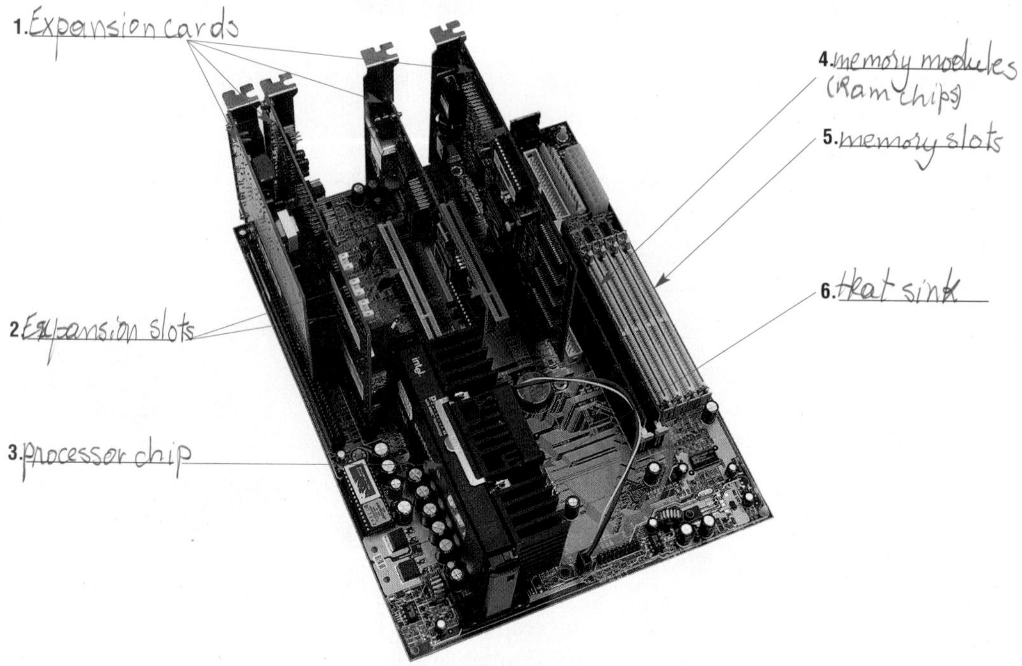

MATCHING

Instructions: Match each term from the column on the left with the best description from the column on the right.

_______1. PC card
_______2. sound card
_______3. expansion slot
_______4. video card
_______5. network interface card

a. Converts computer output into a video signal.
b. A communications device that allows the computer to communicate via a network.
c. Enhances the sound-generating capabilities of a personal computer.
d. A device that can connect up to 127 different peripheral devices with a single connector type.
e. A device that enables you to join two connectors that are either both female or both male.
f. A thin, credit card-sized device.
g. An opening, or socket, where you can insert a circuit board into the motherboard.

Checkpoint

MULTIPLE CHOICE

Instructions: Select the letter of the correct answer for each of the following questions.

1. A(n) ___________ is a small piece of semi-conducting material on which one or more integrated circuits are etched.
   a. chip
   b. system board
   c. control unit
   d. arithmetic/logic unit
2. The process of translating instructions into commands is called ___________.
   a. fetching
   b. decoding
   c. executing
   d. storing
3. Most RAM is ___________.
   a. volatile
   b. nonvolatile
   c. read-only
   d. both a and c
4. A ___________ cache helps speed the processes of the computer by storing frequently used instructions and data.
   a. disk
   b. memory
   c. ROM
   d. PROM
5. A ___________ port can support up to 127 different devices.
   a. serial
   b. parallel
   c. SCSI
   d. USB

SHORT ANSWER

Instructions: Write a brief answer to each of the following questions.

1. What is the purpose of the CPU? ___________ What is the control unit's job? ___________ What are the four basic operations? ___________
2. How is instruction time, or i-time, different from execution time, or e-time? ___________ In what unit is a computer's speed measured? ___________
3. How are arithmetic operations, comparison operations, and logical operations different? ___________ In what part of the CPU do these operations occur? ___________
4. What are some of the different processors used in today's personal computers? ___________ What is a new type of processor? ___________
5. How are the components different among a desktop computer, a notebook computer, and a handheld computer? ___________

WORKING TOGETHER

Instructions: Working with a group of your classmates, complete the following team exercise.

Prepare a report on the different types of ports and the way you connect peripheral devices to a computer. As part of your report, include the following subheadings and an overview of each subheading topic: (1) What is a port? (2) What is a connector? (3) What is a serial port and how does it work? (4) What is a parallel port and how does it work? (5) What is a USB port and how does it work? Expand your report so that it includes information beyond that in your textbook. Create a PowerPoint presentation from your report.

Web Instructions: To display this page from the Web, start your browser and enter the URL scsite.com/dc2002/ch4/lab.htm. Click the links for current and additional information.

1 Installing New Hardware

This exercise uses Windows 98 procedures. Plug and Play technology, a key feature of the Windows operating system, allows users to install new devices without having to reconfigure the system manually. To find out how to install a new device with Plug and Play technology, click the Start button on the taskbar, and then click Help on the Start menu. When the Windows Help window displays, if necessary, click the Contents tab. Click the Managing Hardware and Software book and then click the Installing New Hardware and Software book. Click Install a Plug and Play device.

- What are the three steps in installing a Plug and Play device?
- When would Windows not detect a Plug and Play device?
- How is a device that is not Plug and Play installed?

Close Windows Help.

2 Setting the System Clock

Double-click the time on the taskbar. In the Date/Time Properties dialog box, click the Question Mark button on its title bar, and then click the picture of the calendar. Read the information in the pop-up window and then click the pop-up window to close it. Repeat this process for other areas of the dialog box and then answer these questions:

- What is the purpose of the calendar?
- How do you change the time zone?
- What is the difference between the Close and Apply buttons?

Close the Date/Time Properties dialog box.

3 Using Calculator to Perform Number System Conversion

Instead of the decimal (base 10) number system that people use, computers use the binary (base 2) or hexadecimal (base 16) number systems. It is not necessary to understand these number systems to use a computer, but it is interesting to see how decimal numbers look when in binary or hexadecimal form. Click the Start button on the taskbar, point to Programs on the Start menu, point to Accessories on the Programs submenu, and then click Calculator on the Accessories submenu. Click View on the menu bar and then click Scientific to display the scientific calculator. Perform the following tasks:

- Click Dec to select decimal. Enter 35 by clicking the numeric buttons or using the numeric keypad. Click Bin to select binary. What number displays? Click Hex to select hexadecimal. What number displays? Click the C (Clear) button.
- Convert the following decimal numbers to binary and hexadecimal: 7,256, and 3,421.
- What decimal number is equal to 10010 in the binary system? What decimal number is equal to 2DA9 in the hexadecimal system?

Close the Calculator window.

4 Power Management

This exercise uses Windows 98 or Windows 2000 procedures. Environmental and financial considerations make it important to manage the amount of power a computer uses. Click the Start button on the taskbar, point to Settings on the Start menu, and then click Control Panel on the Settings submenu. Double-click the Power Management icon in the Control Panel window. In the Power Management Properties dialog box, if necessary, click the Power Schemes tab.

- What is a power scheme?
- What power scheme currently is being used on your computer?
- After how many minutes of inactivity is the monitor turned off?
- After how many minutes of inactivity are the hard disks turned off?

Close the Power Management Properties dialog box and the Control Panel window. How can the Power Management Properties dialog box be used to make a computer more energy efficient?

Web Work

Web Instructions: To display this page from the Web, start your browser and enter the URL scsite.com/dc2002/ch4/web.htm. To view At The Movies in exercise 1, RealPlayer must be installed on your computer (download by clicking here). To use the Shelly Cashman Series Understanding the Motherboard Lab from the Web, Shockwave and Flash Player must be installed on your computer (download by clicking here).

1

Andrew Grove

To view the Andrew Grove movie, click the button to the left or click the Play button to the right. Watch the movie, and then complete the exercise by answering the question below. Intel is the leading manufacturer of processors, including the Pentium®, Celeron™, and Xeon™ processors. Intel grew to its present size with more than 60,000 employees because of the outstanding leadership of Andrew Grove. Based on the personal information you learned about Mr. Grove in the movie, describe how his early life struggles, his strong work ethic, and his vision of capitalizing on business trends have been the foundation for Intel's worldwide processor empire. How might Andrew Grove's forward-growth visions for Intel continue to drive the company toward even greater success in the future?

2

Shelly Cashman Series Understanding the Motherboard Lab

Follow the appropriate instructions in Web Work 2 on page 1.47 to start and use the Shelly Cashman Series Understanding the Motherboard Lab. If you are running from the Web, enter the URL scsite.com/sclabs/menu.htm, or display the Web Work page (see instructions at the top of this page) and then click the button to the left.

3

How a Processor Works

After reading about what a processor does and the way it interacts with other system unit components, it still can be difficult to understand how a processor performs even a simple task such as adding two plus three. Click the button to the left, and complete this exercise to learn what a processor does to find the answer.

4

Newsgroups

Would you like more information about a special interest? Perhaps you would like to share opinions and advice with people who have the same interests. If so, you might be interested in newsgroups, also called discussion groups or forums. A newsgroup offers the opportunity to read articles on a specific subject, respond to the articles, and even post your own articles. Click the button to the left to find out more about newsgroups. What is lurking? What is Usenet? Click the how do I find a newsgroup? link at the bottom of the page. Read and print the how do I find a newsgroup? Web page. How can you locate a newsgroup on a particular topic?

5

In the News

The ENIAC (Electronic Numerical Integrator and Computer) often is considered the first modern computer. Invented in 1946, the ENIAC weighed 30 tons and filled a 30-by-50-foot room, yet its capabilities are dwarfed by current notebook computers. The ENIAC performed fewer than 1,000 calculations per minute; today, personal computers can process more than 300 million instructions per second. The rapid development of computing power and capabilities is astonishing, and that development is accelerating. Click the button to the left and read a news article about the introduction of a new or improved computer component. What is the component? Who is introducing it? Will the component change the way people use computers? If so, how?

CHAPTER 5

Input

As the semester ends, schoolwork is becoming more intense. Your term paper on the American Revolution is due next week. The research is complete, but you still need to type and format your document. Written summaries of biology labs also are due. Your partner just e-mailed you the spreadsheet analysis for your marketing case study. You have to write a report that summarizes these findings.

Before sitting down at the computer, you decide to get some fresh air and take your dog, Bandit, for a walk. First thing out the door, Bandit wraps his leash around your legs as he takes off after a cat. Trying to free yourself, you fall down and break your right arm and two fingers. After a lengthy delay in the emergency room, you now have a cast from your shoulder to your fingertips.

You are beside yourself wondering how you are going to finish all your papers. You barely can type and cannot use the mouse at all. Your friend suggests voice recognition software. Just talk to the computer and it writes what you say. This sounds perfect! You spend some of your savings on the software thinking — this is going to be cool!

WHAT IS INPUT?

Input is any data or instructions you enter into the memory of a computer. Users can input data and instructions using a variety of techniques (Figure 5-1). A keyboard allows you to type characters. Using a mouse, you can click a button or roll a wheel to input instructions to the computer. A microphone allows you to speak into the computer. You can write on some computer screens with a special writing device. With others, you touch the screen to make selections. You can send images into the computer using a digital camera, video camera, or a scanner.

Once input is in memory, the processor can access it and process it into output. As mentioned, two types of input are data and instructions (Figure 5-2).

OBJECTIVES

After completing this chapter, you will be able to:

- Describe the two types of input
- List the characteristics of a keyboard
- Identify various types of keyboards
- Identify various types of pointing devices
- Explain how a mouse works
- Describe different mouse types
- Explain how voice recognition works
- Understand how to input data into a handheld computer
- Identify the uses of a digital camera
- Describe the various techniques used for video input
- Describe the uses of PC video cameras and Web cams
- Explain how scanners and other reading devices work
- Identify alternative input devices for physically challenged users

Figure 5-1 Data can be input into a computer in a variety of ways.

Data is a collection of raw unprocessed facts, figures, and symbols. In addition to words and numbers, data also includes sounds, images, and video. Technically speaking, a datum is a single item of data. The term data, however, commonly is used and accepted as both the singular and plural form of the word.

A computer processes data into information. **Information** is data that is organized, meaningful, and useful to a particular user or group of users. The timecards for a given week are an example of data. A company might process this data into a report (information) that summarizes the total hours worked and the payroll expense for the week.

Instructions can be in the form of programs, commands, and user responses. Following is a description of each type of instruction.

A **program** is a series of instructions that tells a computer how to perform the tasks necessary to process data into information. Programs are kept on storage media such as a floppy disk, hard disk, CD-ROM, or DVD-ROM. Programs are input into the memory of the computer, as they are needed. Programs respond to commands that a user issues.

A **command** is an instruction given to a computer program. Users can issue commands by typing or pressing keys on the keyboard, clicking a mouse button, speaking into a microphone, or touching an area of a screen.

Most programs today are menu driven and have a graphical user interface. A **menu-driven** program provides menus as a means of entering commands. Menus contain a list of options from which you select. A **graphical user interface** (**GUI**) has icons, buttons, and other graphical objects that allow you to select and issue commands. A GUI is the most user-friendly way to interact with a computer.

A **user response** is an instruction you issue by replying to a question that a computer program displays. Your response to the question instructs the program to perform certain actions. Assume the program asks the question, Are the timecard entries correct? If you answer Yes, the program saves the timecard entries on a storage device. If you answer No, the program gives you the opportunity to modify the entries.

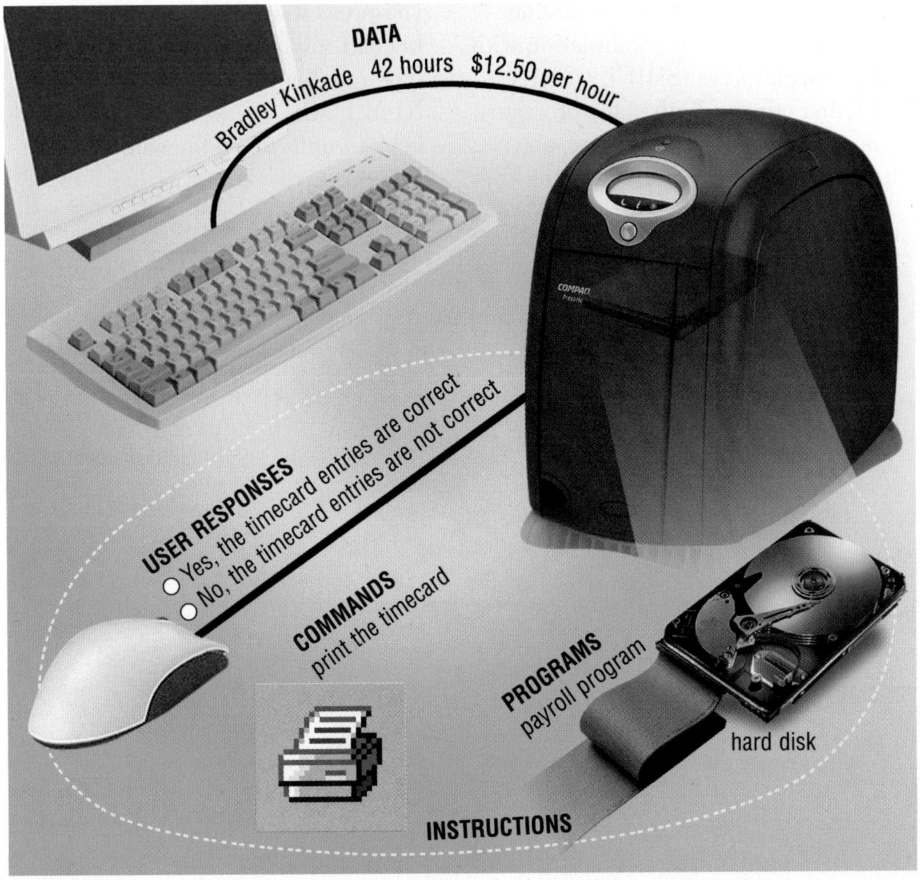

Figure 5-2 Two types of input are data and instructions. Instructions can be in the form of user responses, commands, and programs.

ISSUE

Watching Your Emotions

Emotional Input and Your Privacy

In addition to data, programs, commands, and user responses, researchers are experimenting with a fifth type of input – human emotions. A development called affective computing uses input devices such as video cameras and skin sensors with software similar to voice recognition programs, allowing a computer to read a user's emotions. For example, a furrowed brow and sweaty palms might indicate frustration. Emotional input could be invaluable in conjunction with computer-aided instruction, letting a computer know whether to speed up or slow down tutorials. Some people, however, see affective computing as an invasion of privacy. Do you agree? In what areas might affective computing be useful? Why? Would you be comfortable with a computer knowing how you feel? Why or why not?

For more information on affective computing, visit the Discovering Computers 2002 Issues Web page (**scsite.com/dc2002/issues.htm**) and click Chapter 5 Issue #1.

WHAT ARE INPUT DEVICES?

An **input device** is any hardware component that allows you to enter data, programs, commands, and user responses into a computer. Depending on your particular application and requirement, the input device you use may vary. Popular input devices include the keyboard, mouse, stylus, microphone, digital camera, and scanner. The following pages discuss these and other input devices.

Storage devices, such as disk drives, serve as both input and output devices. Chapter 7 discusses storage devices.

THE KEYBOARD

Many people use a keyboard as one of their input devices. A **keyboard** is an input device that contains keys you press to enter data into the computer (Figure 5-3).

Desktop computer keyboards typically have from 101 to 105 keys. Keyboards for smaller computers such as notebook computers contain fewer keys. A computer keyboard includes keys that allow you to type letters of the alphabet, numbers, spaces, punctuation marks, and other symbols such as the dollar sign ($) and asterisk (*). A keyboard also contains other keys that allow you to enter data and instructions into the computer.

All computer keyboards have a typing area that includes the letters of the alphabet, numbers, punctuation marks, and other basic keys. Many desktop computer keyboards also have a numeric keypad on the right side of the keyboard. A **numeric keypad** is a calculator-style arrangement of keys that includes numbers, a decimal point, and some basic mathematical operators (see Figure 5-3). Many users prefer to use the numbers on the numeric keypad instead of the numbers at the top of the typing area.

Across the top of most keyboards are function keys, which are labeled with the letter F followed by a number (see Figure 5-3). **Function keys** are special keys programmed to issue commands to a computer. The command associated with a function key depends on the program you are using. For example, in many programs, pressing the function key F1 displays a Help window. When instructed to press a function key such as F1, do not press the letter F followed by the number 1. Instead, press the key labeled F1.

To issue commands, you often use function keys in combination with other special keys (SHIFT, CTRL, ALT, and others). With many programs, you can use a button, a menu, a function key, or a combination of keys to obtain the same result (Figure 5-4).

Keyboards also contain keys that allow you to position the insertion point. The **insertion point** is a symbol that indicates where on the screen the next character you type will display (Figure 5-5). Depending on the program, the symbol may be a vertical bar, a rectangle, or an underline. You can move the insertion point left, right, up, or down by pressing the arrow keys on the keyboard.

Keyboards typically contain at least four **arrow keys**: one pointing up, one pointing down, one pointing left, and one pointing right. Most keyboards also contain keys such as HOME, END, PAGE UP, and PAGE DOWN, that you can press to move the insertion point to the beginning or end of a line, page, or document.

Nearly all keyboards have toggle keys. A **toggle key** is a key that switches between two different states. The NUM LOCK key, for example, is a toggle key (see Figure 5-3). When you press it once, it locks the numeric keypad so you can use this keypad to type numbers. When you press the NUM LOCK key again, the numeric keypad unlocks so the same keys serve as arrow keys that move the

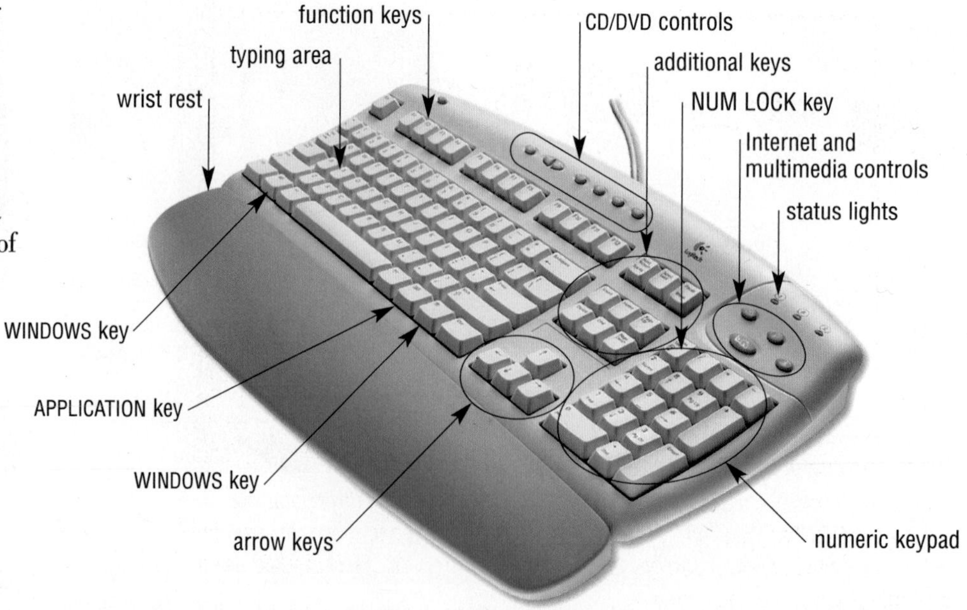

Figure 5-3 A desktop computer keyboard. You type using keys in the typing area and on the numeric keypad.

Web Link

For more information on keyboards, visit the Discovering Computers 2002 Chapter 5 WEB LINK page (**scsite.com/dc2002/ch5/weblink.htm**) and click Keyboards.

insertion point. Many keyboards have status lights that light up when you activate a toggle key.

Most keyboards have a WINDOWS key and an APPLICATION key. The WINDOWS key displays the Start menu. The APPLICATION key displays an item's shortcut menu.

Newer keyboards also include buttons that allow you to access your CD/DVD drive, adjust speaker volume, open your e-mail program, start your Web browser, and search the Internet. Some keyboards even have USB ports so you can plug USB devices directly into the keyboard instead of the back of the system unit.

Keyboard Types

A standard computer keyboard sometimes is called a **QWERTY keyboard** because of the layout of its typing area. That is, the first six leftmost letters on the top alphabetic line of the keyboard spell QWERTY (pronounced KWER-tee).

Most of today's desktop computer keyboards are enhanced keyboards. An **enhanced keyboard** has 12 function keys along the top, 2 CTRL keys, 2 ALT keys, and a set of arrow and additional keys between the typing area and the numeric keypad (see Figure 5-3).

Most keyboards attach to a serial port, or a keyboard port, or a USB port on the system unit via a cable. Some keyboards, however, do not use wires at all. A **cordless keyboard** is a battery-powered device that transmits data using wireless technology, such as radio waves or infrared light waves. These cordless devices communicate with a receiver that attaches to a port on the system unit. The port type varies depending on the type of wireless technology.

On notebook and many handheld computers, the keyboard is built into the top of the system unit (Figure 5-6). To fit in these smaller computers, the keyboards usually are smaller and have fewer keys. Most desktop computer keyboards have at least 101 keys. A typical notebook computer keyboard, by contrast, usually has about 85 keys. To provide all of the functionality of a desktop computer keyboard, manufacturers design many of the keys to serve two or three different purposes.

Command	Button	Menu	Function Key(s)
Copy		Edit|Copy	SHIFT+F2
Open		File|Open	CTRL+F12
Print		File|Print	CTRL+SHIFT+F12

Figure 5-4 Many programs allow you to use a button, a menu, or a function key to obtain the same result, as shown by these examples from Microsoft Word.

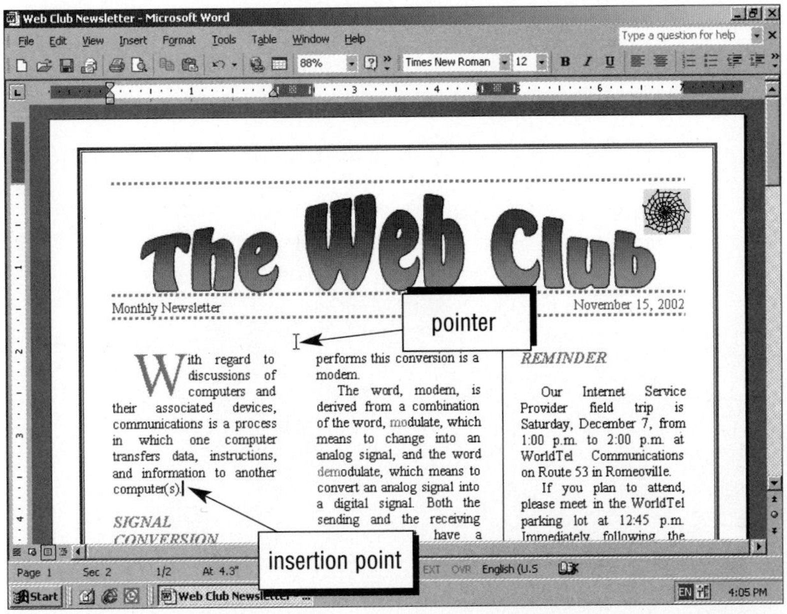

Figure 5-5 In most Windows programs, such as Word, the insertion point is a blinking vertical bar. You can use the keyboard or the mouse to move the insertion point. The pointer, another symbol that displays on the screen, is controlled using a pointing device such as a mouse.

Figure 5-6 On notebook and many handheld computers, the keyboard is built into the top of the system unit.

Users of handheld computers that do not have keyboards sometimes prefer to work with a portable keyboard to enter data. A **portable keyboard** is a full-sized keyboard you conveniently can attach and remove from a handheld computer. Figure 5-7 shows a pocket-sized portable keyboard that unfolds into a full-sized keyboard.

Regardless of size, many keyboards have a rectangular shape with the keys aligned in rows. Users who spend a large amount of time typing on these keyboards sometimes experience repetitive strain injuries (RSI) of their wrists. For this reason, some manufacturers offer ergonomic keyboards. An **ergonomic keyboard** has a design that reduces the chance of these wrist injuries (Figure 5-8). Even keyboards that are not ergonomically designed attempt to offer a user more comfort. For example, many keyboards today include a wrist rest or palm rest to reduce strain on your wrist while typing (see Figure 5-3 on page 5.4).

The goal of **ergonomics** is to incorporate comfort, efficiency, and safety into the design of items in the workplace. Employees can be injured or develop disorders of the muscles, nerves, tendons, ligaments, and joints from working in an area that is not ergonomically designed. Thus, OSHA (Occupational Safety & Health Administration) has proposed standards whereby employers must establish programs that prevent these types of injuries or disorders.

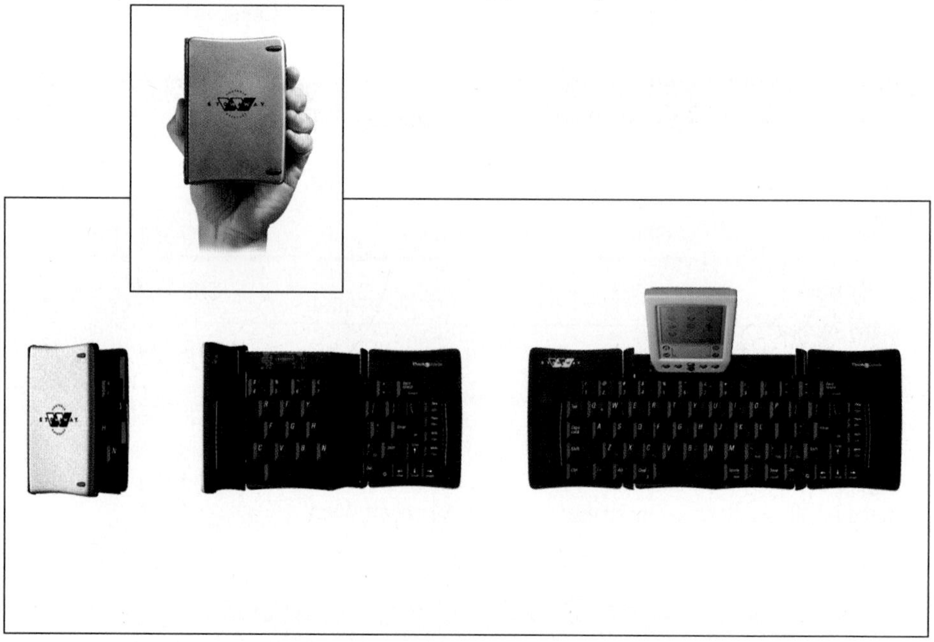

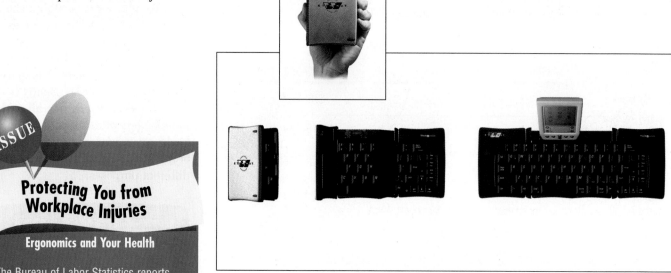

Figure 5-7 This convenient, portable keyboard unfolds into a full-sized keyboard that you can attach to a handheld computer.

Figure 5-8 The Microsoft Natural Keyboard Pro is an ergonomic keyboard designed to minimize strain on your hands and wrists.

ISSUE

Protecting You from Workplace Injuries

Ergonomics and Your Health

The Bureau of Labor Statistics reports that work-related musculoskeletal disorders (MSDs) account for one-third of all occupational injuries and illnesses. These disorders are the largest job-related injury and illness problem in the United States today. OSHA (see URL below) has proposed standards whereby employers must establish programs that prevent workplace injuries with respect to computer usage. If these standards are approved and initiated, the cost to employers and society will be millions of dollars. What is your opinion of this proposal? Should this proposal be implemented? Whose responsibility is this — employees or employer? Will this have a detrimental affect on small businesses?

For more information on OSHA, ergonomics, and the Web site mentioned above, visit the Discovering Computers 2002 Issues Web page (**scsite.com/dc2002/issues.htm**) and click Chapter 5 Issue #2.

POINTING DEVICES

A **pointing device** is an input device that allows you to control a pointer on the screen. In a graphical user interface, a **pointer** is a small symbol on the screen (see Figure 5-5 on page 5.5). A pointer often takes the shape of an I-beam (I), a block arrow (↖), or a pointing hand (☝). Using a pointing device, you can position the pointer to move or select items on the screen. For example, you can use a pointing device to move the insertion point; select text, graphics, and other objects; and click buttons, icons, links, and menu commands.

The following sections discuss common pointing devices.

MOUSE

A **mouse** is a pointing device that fits comfortably under the palm of your hand. The mouse is the most widely used pointing device on desktop computers.

With a mouse, you control the movement of the pointer, often called a **mouse pointer**, on the screen and make selections from the screen. The top of a mouse has one to four buttons; some also have a small wheel. The bottom of a mouse is flat and contains a mechanism that detects movement of the mouse.

Mouse Types

A **mechanical mouse** has a rubber or metal ball on its underside (Figure 5-9). When the ball rolls in a certain direction, electronic circuits in the mouse translate the movement of the mouse into signals the computer understands. You should place a mechanical mouse on a mouse pad. A **mouse pad** is a rectangular rubber or foam pad that provides better traction than the top of a desk. The mouse pad also protects the ball in the mouse from a build up of dust and dirt, which could cause it to malfunction.

An optical mouse, by contrast, has no moving mechanical parts inside. Instead, an **optical mouse** uses devices that emit and sense light to detect the mouse's movement (Figure 5-10). Some use optical sensors; others use laser. You can place an optical mouse that uses optical sensors on nearly all types of surfaces, eliminating the need for a mouse pad. An optical mouse that uses laser usually requires a special mouse pad. An optical mouse is more precise than a mechanical mouse and does not require cleaning like a mechanical mouse, but it also is slightly more expensive.

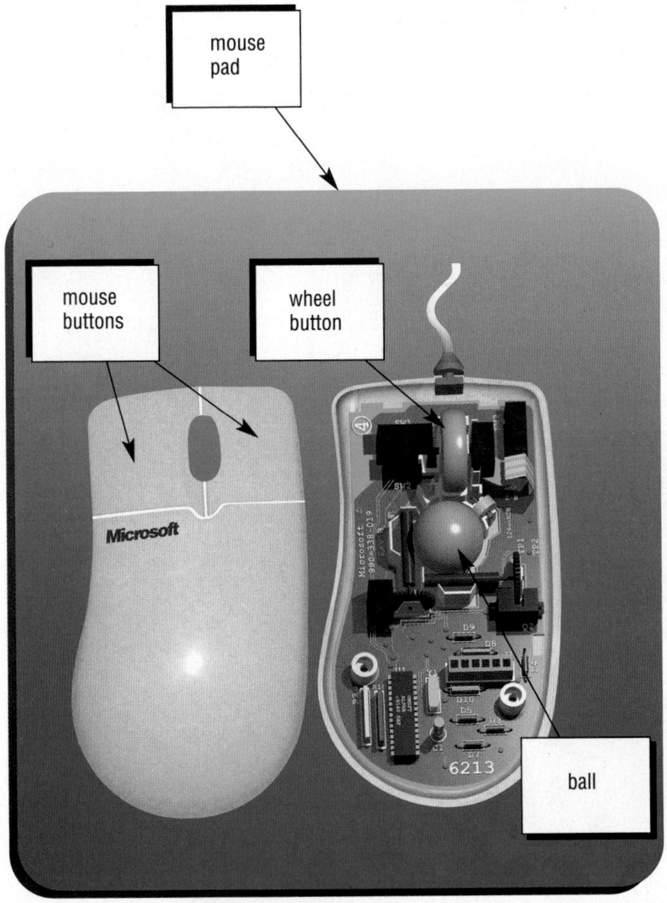

Figure 5-9 A mechanical mouse contains a small ball.

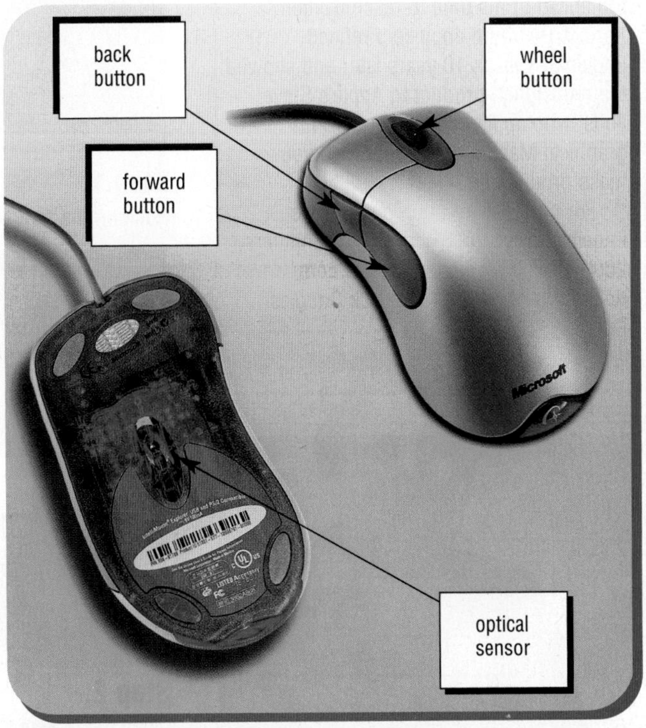

Figure 5-10 This optical mouse uses an optical sensor. It also includes buttons you push with your thumb that enable you to navigate forward and backward through Web pages.

Web Link

For more information on a mouse, visit the Discovering Computers 2002 Chapter 5 WEB LINK page (**scsite.com/dc2002/ch5/weblink.htm**) and click Mouse.

TECHNOLOGY TRAILBLAZER

DOUGLAS **ENGELBART**

Without Douglas Engelbart, it is unlikely the phrase *point and click* would be part of our vocabulary. As a scientist at the Stanford Research Institute in the 1960s, Engelbart was part of a team that designed the first mouse with funding from NASA and the U.S. Department of Defense. The mouse prototype had a cord in the front, but Engelbart switched it to the rear to move it out of the way. He would tilt or rock that mouse to draw straight lines, and then he would push it and lift it off the desk to let the two perpendicular wheels on the bottom spin, which moved the cursor across the screen.

Even though he filed a patent for his design in 1965, Engelbart's thinking was too ahead of his time to reach fruition. Xerox's Palo Alto engineers refined Engelbart's ideas 10 years later and showed the redesigned product to Apple's Steve Jobs, who applied the concept to his graphical Macintosh and had the mouse mass produced in the mid-1980s.

For more information on Douglas Engelbart, visit the Discovering Computers 2002 People Web page (**scsite.com/dc2002/people.htm**) and click Douglas Engelbart.

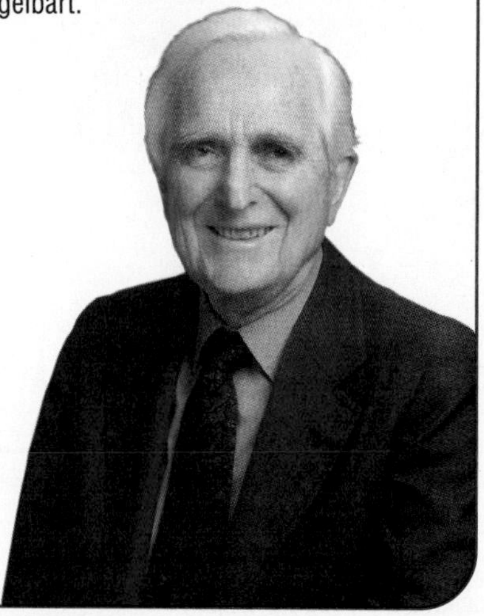

A mouse can connect to your computer in several ways. Most have a cable that attaches to a serial port, a mouse port, or USB port on the computer. A **cordless mouse** or **wireless mouse** is a battery-powered device that transmits data using wireless technology, such as radio waves or infrared light waves. The wireless technology used for a cordless mouse is very similar to that of a cordless keyboard discussed earlier. Some users prefer a cordless mouse because it frees up desk space and eliminates the clutter of a cord.

Using a Mouse

As you move the mouse, the pointer on the screen also moves. For example, when you move the mouse to the left, the pointer moves left on the screen (Figure 5-11). When you move the mouse to the right, the pointer moves right on the screen, and so on. If you have never worked with a mouse, you might find it a little awkward at first. With a little practice, however, you will discover that a mouse is quite easy to use.

Generally, you use the mouse to move the pointer on the screen to an object such as a button, a menu, an icon, a link, or text. Then, you press a mouse button to perform a certain

Figure 5-11 HOW TO MOVE THE POINTER WITH A MOUSE

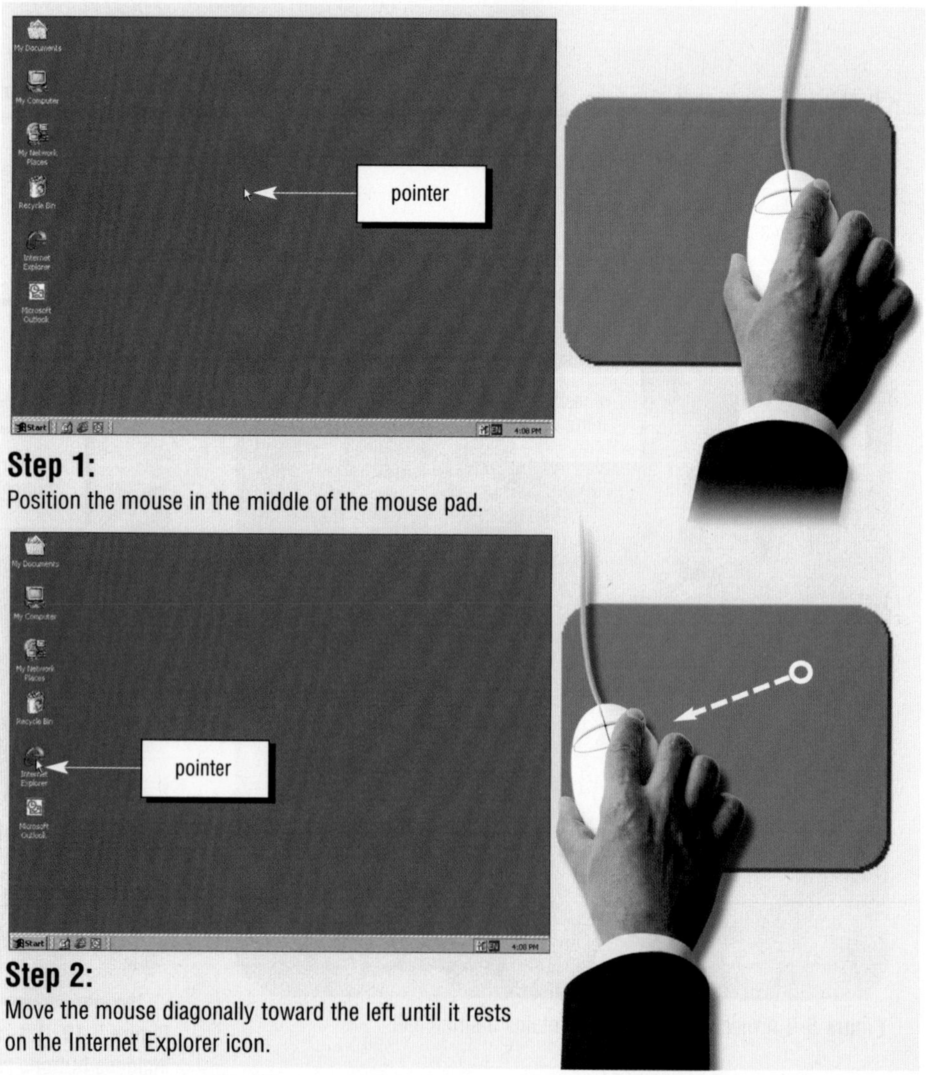

Step 1:
Position the mouse in the middle of the mouse pad.

Step 2:
Move the mouse diagonally toward the left until it rests on the Internet Explorer icon.

action on that object. Windows users work with a mouse that has at least two buttons. For example, if you point to the Internet Explorer button on the taskbar and then press, or *click*, the primary mouse button, the browser displays a Web page on the screen. For a right-handed user, the left button usually is the primary mouse button and the right mouse button is the secondary mouse button. Left-handed people, however, can reverse the function of these buttons.

In addition to clicking, you can perform other operations using the mouse. These operations include point, right-click, double-click, drag, and right-drag. The table in Figure 5-12 explains how to perform these and other mouse operations. Some programs also use keys in combination with the mouse to perform certain actions.

As mentioned earlier, sometimes a mouse has a wheel that you can use with certain programs (see Figure 5-9 on page 5.7 and Figure 5-10 on page 5.7). You rotate or press the wheel to move text and objects on the screen. The function of the mouse buttons and the wheel varies depending on the program.

COMPANY ON THE CUTTING EDGE

Logitech

Mice Are Welcome Here

Thinking about a room full of mice can send chills down your spine. But Logitech employees are not bothered by all the mice in their offices; in fact, they smile when they think of these creatures.

Logitech is the world's largest manufacturer of the mouse, having created more than 200-million corded and cordless devices since 1981. The company also designs, produces, and markets a variety of other input devices, including keyboards, optical trackballs, joysticks, gamepads, and Internet video cameras. Cordless products account for more than one-third of the devices sold.

More than one-half of Logitech's engineers are software engineers, and they have used their innovative design and technological expertise to help the company win more than 50 worldwide awards. Among their 25 industry firsts are the cordless and opto-mechanical mouse devices, the color handheld scanner, and the digital still camera.

For more information on Logitech, visit the Discovering Computers 2002 Companies Web page (**scsite.com/dc2002/companies.htm**) and click Logitech.

Operation	Mouse Action	Example
Point	Move the mouse across a flat surface until the pointer on the desktop rests on the item of choice.	Position the pointer on the screen.
Click	Press and release the primary mouse button, which usually is the left mouse button.	Select or deselect items on the screen or start a program or program feature.
Right-click	Press and release the secondary mouse button, which usually is the right mouse button.	Display a shortcut menu.
Double-click	Quickly press and release the left mouse button twice without moving the mouse.	Start a program or program feature.
Drag	Point to an item, hold down the left mouse button, move the item to the desired location on the screen, and then release the left mouse button.	Move an object from one location to another or draw pictures.
Right-drag	Point to an item, hold down the right mouse button, move the item to the desired location on the screen, and then release the right mouse button.	Display a shortcut menu after moving an object from one location to another.
Rotate wheel	Roll the wheel forward or backward.	Scroll up or down a few lines.
Press wheel button	Press the wheel button while moving the mouse on the desktop.	Scroll continuously.

Figure 5-12 The more common mouse operations.

OTHER POINTING DEVICES

The mouse is the most widely used pointing device today. Some users, however, work with other pointing devices. These include the trackball, touchpad, pointing stick, joystick, wheel, light pen, touch screen, and stylus. The following sections discuss each of these pointing devices.

Trackball

Whereas a mechanical mouse has a ball on the bottom, a **trackball** is a stationary pointing device with a ball on its top (Figure 5-13). The ball in most trackballs is about the size of a Ping-Pong ball.

To move the pointer using a trackball, you rotate the ball with your thumb, fingers, or the palm of your hand. In addition to the ball, a trackball usually has one or more buttons that work just like mouse buttons.

A trackball requires frequent cleaning because it picks up oils from your fingers and dust from the environment. If you have limited desk space, however, a trackball is a good alternative to a mouse because you do not have to move the entire device.

Touchpad

A **touchpad** or **trackpad** is a small, flat, rectangular pointing device that is sensitive to pressure and motion (Figure 5-14). To move the pointer using a touchpad, you slide your fingertip across the surface of the pad. Some touchpads have one or more buttons around the edge of the pad that work like mouse buttons. On many touchpads, you also can tap the pad's surface to imitate mouse operations such as clicking.

You can attach a stand-alone touchpad to any personal computer. You find them more often on notebook computers.

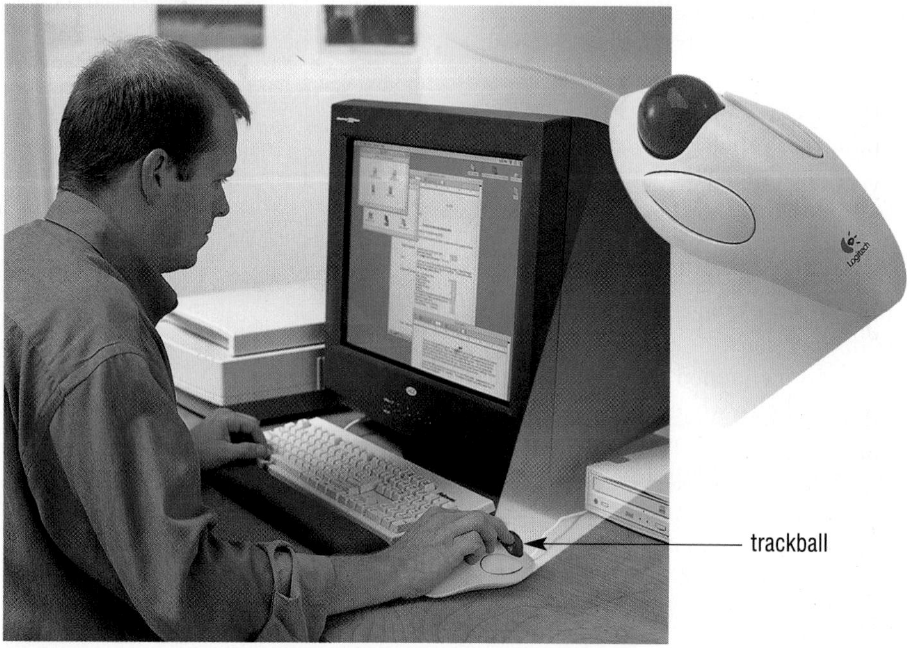

Figure 5-13 A trackball is like an upside-down mouse. You rotate the ball with your thumb, fingers, or palm of your hand to move the pointer.

Web Link

For more information on trackballs, visit the Discovering Computers 2002 Chapter 5 WEB LINK page (**scsite.com/dc2002/ch5/weblink.htm**) and click Trackballs.

Web Link

For more information on touchpads, visit the Discovering Computers 2002 Chapter 5 WEB LINK page (**scsite.com/dc2002/ch5/weblink.htm**) and click Touchpads.

Figure 5-14 Many notebook computers have a touchpad that you can use to control the movement of the pointer.

Pointing Stick

A **pointing stick** is a pressure-sensitive pointing device shaped like a pencil eraser that is positioned between keys on the keyboard (Figure 5-15). To move the pointer using a pointing stick, you push the pointing stick with your finger. The pointer on the screen moves in the direction you push the pointing stick.

A pointing stick does not require any additional desk space. In addition, it does not require cleaning like a mechanical mouse or trackball. IBM first developed the pointing stick for its notebook computers. Whether you select a notebook computer that has a touchpad or pointing stick is a matter of personal preference.

Figure 5-15 Some notebook computers use a pointing stick to control the movement of the pointer.

Web Link

For more information on pointing sticks, visit the Discovering Computers 2002 Chapter 5 WEB LINK page (**scsite.com/dc2002/ch5/weblink.htm**) and click Pointing Sticks.

Joysticks and Wheels

Users running game software or flight and driving simulation software often use a joystick or wheel as a pointing device (Figure 5-16). A **joystick** is a vertical lever mounted on a base. You move the lever in different directions to control the actions of a vehicle or player. The lever usually includes buttons called triggers you can press to activate certain events. Some joysticks also have additional buttons you can set to perform other actions.

A **wheel** is a steering-wheel type input device. You turn the wheel to drive a car, truck, or other vehicle. Most wheels also include foot pedals for acceleration and braking actions. A joystick and wheel typically attach via a cable to the game port on a sound card or game card or to a USB port.

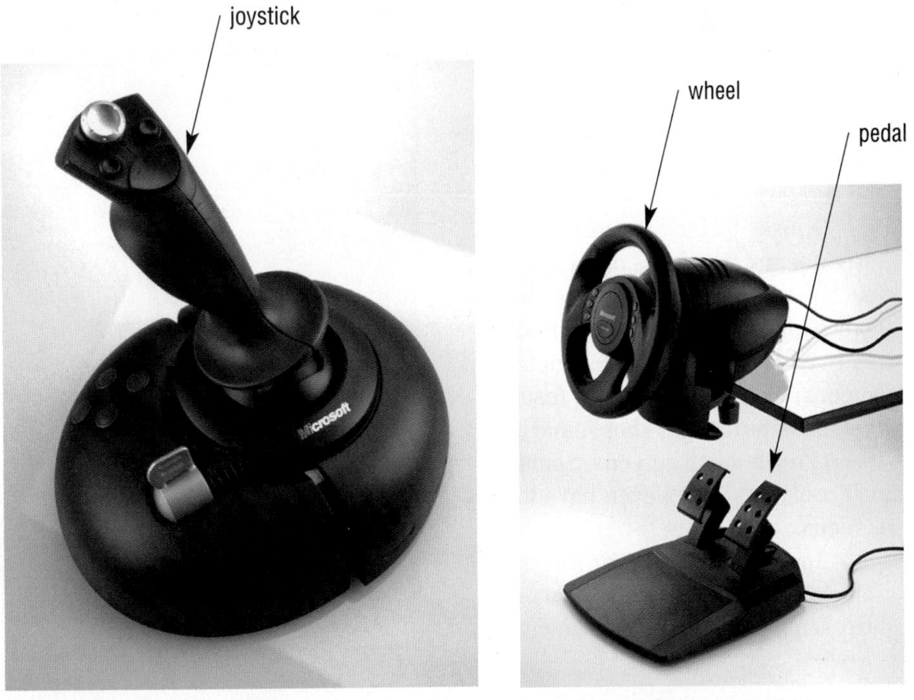

Figure 5-16 Joysticks and wheels help the user control the actions of players and vehicles in game and simulation software.

Light Pen

A **light pen** is a handheld input device that contains a light source or can detect light. Some light pens require a specially designed monitor, while others work with a standard monitor. To select objects on the screen, you press the light pen against the surface of the screen or point the light pen at the screen and then press a button on the pen.

Health care professionals, such as doctors and dentists, use light pens because they can slide a protective sleeve over the pen — keeping their fingers free of contaminants (Figure 5-17). Light pens also are ideal for areas where employees hands might contain food, dirt, grease, or other chemicals that could damage the computer. Applications with limited desktop space such as industrial or manufacturing environments find light pens convenient, as well.

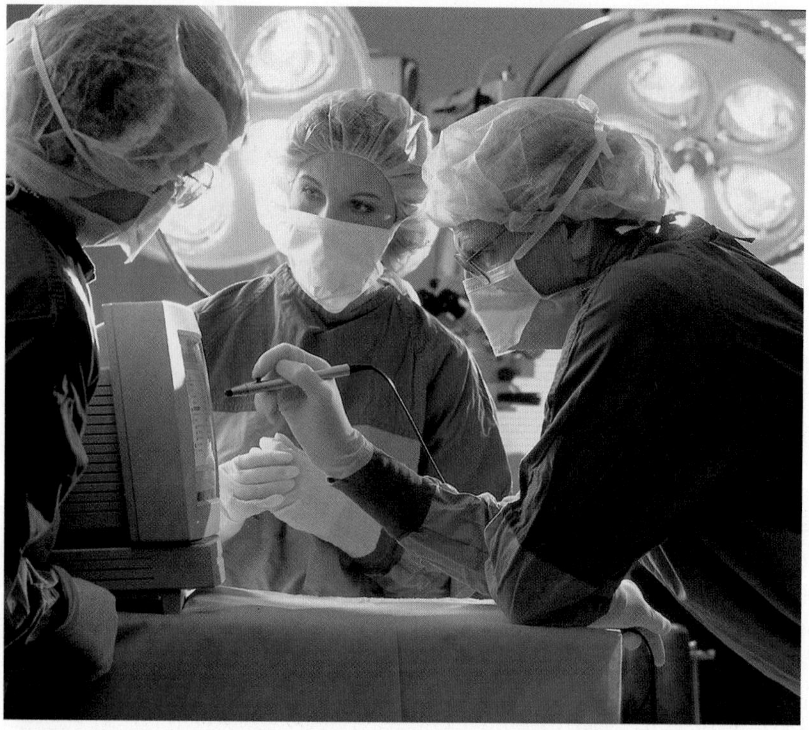

Figure 5-17 To make selections with a light pen, you touch the pen against the surface of the screen or point the pen at the screen and then press a button on the pen.

Touch Screen

A **touch screen** is a touch-sensitive display. You interact with the device by touching areas of the screen with your finger (Figure 5-18). Because they require a lot of arm movements, you do not enter large amounts of data into touch screens. Instead, you touch words, pictures, numbers, or locations identified on the screen.

Kiosks located in stores, hotels, airports, and museums often have touch screens. So you easily can access your bank account from your car, many ATM machines have touch screens. Many computers in restaurants, cafeterias, gift shops, and resorts have touch screens. Some notebook computers even have touch screens.

Instead of using your finger, some touch screens use a stylus. The next section discusses this device.

Figure 5-18 You interact with a touch screen by touching areas of the screen with your finger.

Stylus

A **stylus** looks like a ballpoint pen, but uses pressure, instead of ink, to write text and draw lines. This device, originally called a **pen** or electronic pen, was used in professional graphical applications such as computer-aided design and drafting. The following paragraphs describe how these and many other applications today use a pen, also known as a stylus.

Architects, mapmakers, artists, and designers create drawings and sketches by using an electronic pen on a graphics tablet. A **graphics tablet**, also called a **digitizer** or **digitizing tablet**, is a flat, rectangular, electronic plastic board. Each location on the graphics tablet corresponds to a specific location on the screen. When you draw on the tablet with the pen, the tablet detects and converts the movements into digital signals that are sent into the computer. These pens are quite sophisticated, featuring erasers and programmable buttons. In addition to a pen, some graphics tablets also use a cursor. A **cursor** is a device that looks similar to a mouse, except it has a window with cross hairs, so the user can see through to the tablet (Figure 5-19).

Pens used for handwriting recognition have grown in popularity. Using special software along with a pen and graphics tablet, you can send handwritten notes via e-mail or sign your name electronically (Figure 5-20). Upon receipt, the receiver sees your handwritten note or signature in its original form. Businesses save time using **electronic signatures**, also called **e-signatures**, which are just as legal as an ink signature.

Web Link

For more information on a stylus, visit the Discovering Computers 2002 Chapter 5 WEB LINK page (**scsite.com/dc2002/ch5/weblink.htm**) and click Stylus.

Web Link

For more information on e-signatures, visit the Discovering Computers 2002 Chapter 5 WEB LINK page (**scsite.com/dc2002/ch5/weblink.htm**) and click E-signatures.

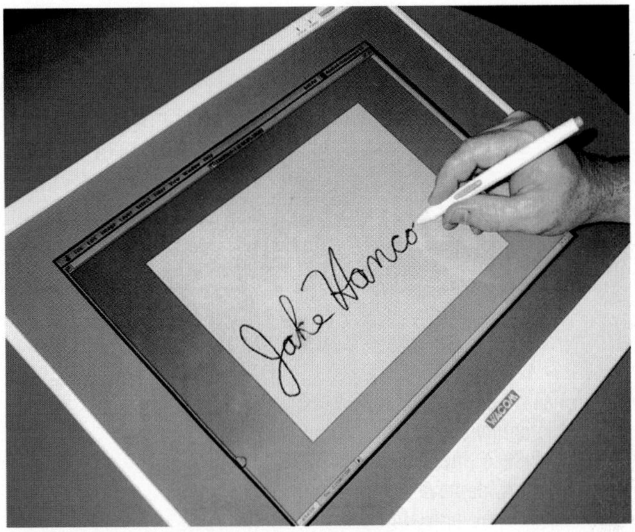

Figure 5-20 With digital signatures just as legal as ink signatures, the demand for graphics tablets and pens is growing.

Figure 5-19 Architects, mapmakers, artists, and designers create drawings and sketches with an electronic pen on a graphics tablet. Other tablets use a cursor as the input device.

Some notebook and many handheld computers have touch screens that allow you to input data using a stylus (Figure 5-21). Instead of using a keyboard, you write or make selections on the computer screen with the stylus. These computers use **handwriting recognition software** that translates handwritten letters and symbols into characters that the computer understands. A later section in this chapter discusses handheld computer input and handwriting recognition software in more depth.

VOICE INPUT

Voice input is the process of entering data by speaking into a microphone that is attached to the sound card on the computer. As an alternative to using a keyboard to input data, many users are talking to their computers.

Voice recognition, also called **speech recognition**, is the computer's capability of distinguishing spoken words (Figure 5-22). Voice recognition programs do not understand speech. They only recognize a vocabulary of pre-programmed words. The vocabulary of voice recognition programs can range from two words to millions of words. The automated telephone system at your bank may ask you to answer questions by speaking the words Yes or No into the telephone. A voice recognition program on your computer, by contrast, may recognize up to two million words!

In the past, voice recognition systems were found only in specialized applications in which a user's hands were occupied or disabled. Today, voice recognition applications are affordable and easy to use, providing all types of users with a convenient form of input. Some productivity software, such as word processing and spreadsheet, include voice recognition as part of the product. For example, you can dictate memos and letters into your word processing program instead of typing them. You can issue commands to your software applications, search the Web, participate in chat rooms, and send and receive e-mail and instant messages — all by speaking into a microphone.

The first voice recognition programs were speaker dependent. Today, most are speaker independent. With **speaker-dependent software**, the computer makes a profile of your voice, which means you have to train the computer to recognize your voice.

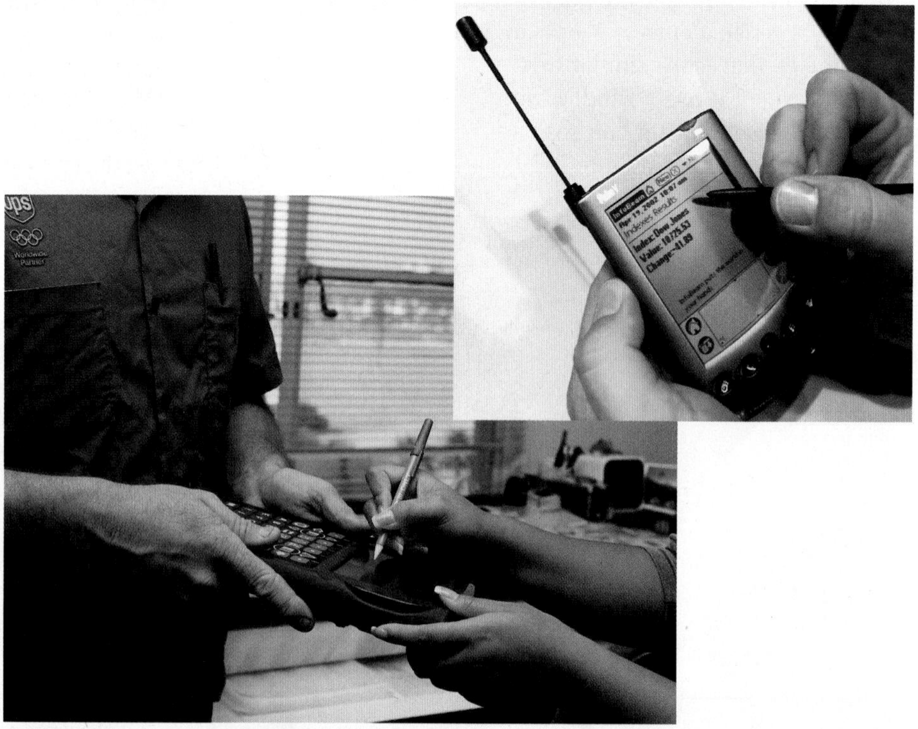

Figure 5-21 Many handheld computers support handwriting input through a stylus.

COMPANY ON THE CUTTING EDGE

Ubiquitous Palm Is a Phenomenon

Oprah has one. So do Murphy Brown and the media spinners in the hit movie, *Wag the Dog*. Indeed, more than two million people worldwide have a Palm handheld computer in their pocket or purse or briefcase to help them manage and organize their professional and personal lives.

The Palm handheld computer, manufactured by Palm, Inc., commands more than three-fourths of the handheld computer market. More than 43,000 developers are working on new software applications and hardware add-ons for this versatile and stylish product. Currently, software for Palm handhelds enables users to perform a multitude of tasks, including read e-books, record golf scores, and play games.

Palm was founded in 1992 and acquired by U.S. Robotics in 1995. One year later, the company introduced the Pilot 1000 and 5000 products, which blazed a trail for the handheld market. In 1997, 3Com acquired U.S. Robotics and made Palm a subsidiary of the corporation. Two years later, 3Com made Palm an independent, publicly traded company.

For more information on Palm, visit the Discovering Computers 2002 Companies Web page (**scsite.com/dc2002/companies.htm**) and click Palm.

To train the computer, you must speak each of the words in the vocabulary into the computer repeatedly. After hearing the spoken word repeatedly, the program develops and stores a digital pattern for the word. When you later speak a word, the program compares the spoken word to those stored. **Speaker-independent software** has a built-in set of word patterns. That is, you do not have to train a computer to recognize your voice. Many products today include a built-in set of words that grows as the software learns your words.

Some voice recognition software requires **discrete speech**, which means you have to speak slowly and separate each word with a short pause. Most of today's products, however, allow you to speak in a flowing conversational tone, called **continuous speech**.

ISSUE

Talk to Your Computer

The Accuracy of Voice Recognition Software

Voice recognition is a process accomplished through software that allows users to interact with their computer by voice. Even though improvements have been made within voice recognition software, it still is not perfect. Experts agree voice recognition capability represents the future of software. Experts do not agree, however, that the future is now. The best voice recognition programs are 90 to 95 percent accurate. Yet, advocates admit this assessment is based on expected speech and vocabulary. When confronted with unusual dialogue, accuracy drops. Even a 90 percent accuracy rate means 1 out of 10 words will be wrong. Before we can use voice recognition software effectively, how accurate must it be? When would voice recognition be an advantage? Might it ever be a disadvantage? Why? Would you use voice recognition software?

For more information on voice recognition, visit the Discovering Computers 2002 Issues Web page (**scsite.com/dc2002/issues.htm**) and and click Chapter 5 Issue #3.

Figure 5-22 HOW VOICE RECOGNITION WORKS

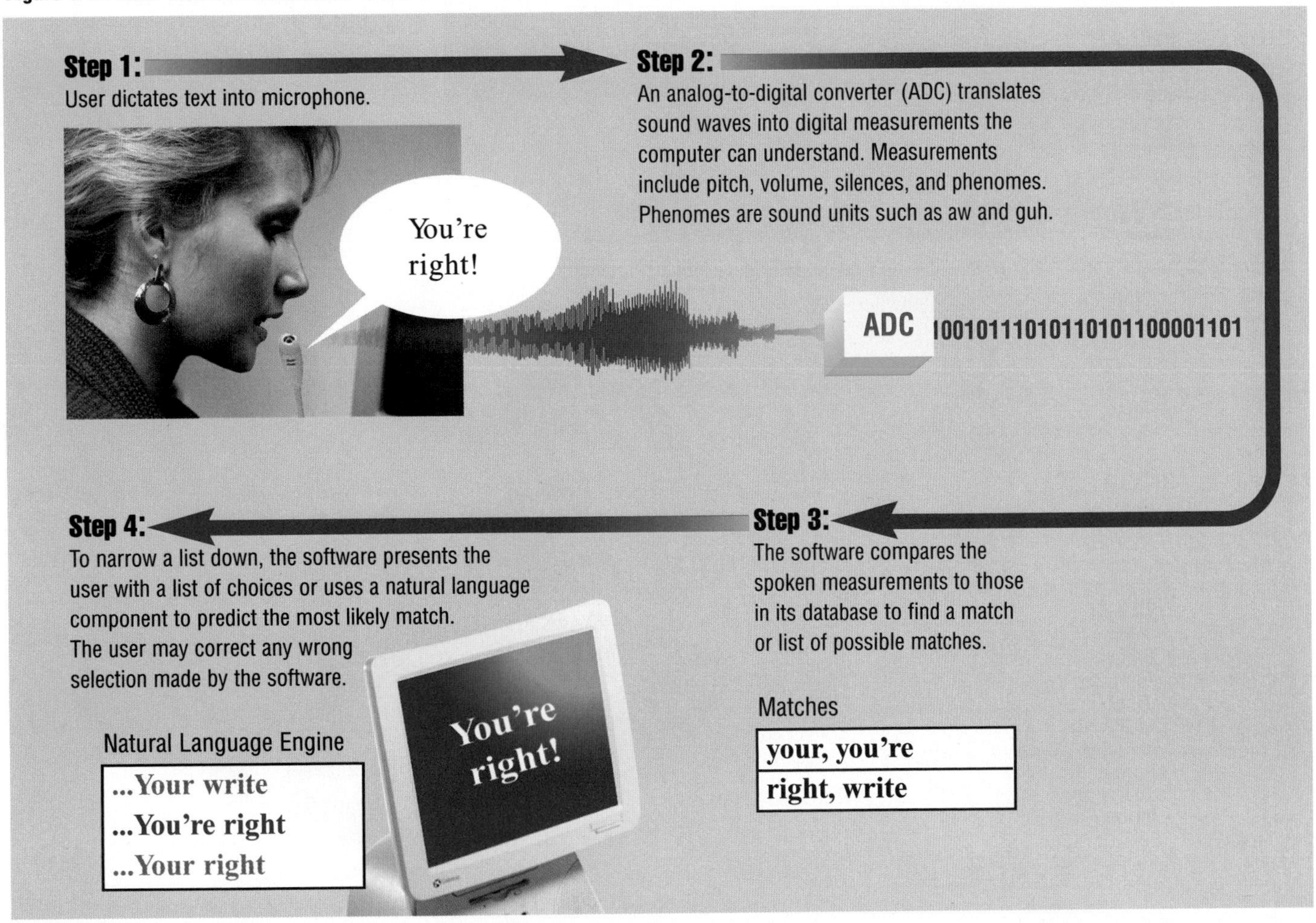

Step 1:
User dictates text into microphone.
You're right!
Step 2:
An analog-to-digital converter (ADC) translates sound waves into digital measurements the computer can understand. Measurements include pitch, volume, silences, and phenomes. Phenomes are sound units such as aw and guh.
ADC
1001011101011010110000110
Step 3:
The software compares the spoken measurements to those in its database to find a match or list of possible matches.
Matches
your, you're
right, write
Step 4:
To narrow a list down, the software presents the user with a list of choices or uses a natural language component to predict the most likely match. The user may correct any wrong selection made by the software.
Natural Language Engine
...Your write
...You're right
...Your right
You're right!

Audio Input

Voice input is part of a larger category of input called audio input. **Audio input** is the process of entering any sound into the computer such as speech, music, and sound effects. To input high-quality sound, your personal computer must have a sound card. You can input sound via a device such as a microphone, tape player, CD player, or radio, each of which plugs into a port on the sound card.

With a microphone plugged into the microphone port on the sound card, you can record any sound, including speech. Windows stores audio files as **waveforms**, which are called **WAV** files and have a .wav extension. Once you save the sound in a file, you can play it using the Sound Recorder. You can attach the audio file to an e-mail message or include it in a document such as a word processing report or presentation graphics slide show.

WAV files often are large – requiring more than 1 MB of storage space for a single minute of audio. For this reason, WAV files often are compressed so they take up less storage space.

You can input music and other sound effects using external MIDI devices such as an electronic piano keyboard (Figure 5-23). Discussed in the previous chapter, in addition to being a port, MIDI (musical instrument digital interface) is the electronic music industry's standard that defines how digital musical devices represent sounds electronically. These devices connect to the sound card on your computer. Software programs that conform to the MIDI standard allow you to compose and edit music and other sounds. For example, you can change the speed, add notes, or rearrange the score to produce an entirely new sound.

Figure 5-23 An electronic piano keyboard is an external MIDI device that can record music. You can store the music in the computer.

INPUT DEVICES FOR HANDHELD COMPUTERS

Handheld computers today are very popular for both home and business users (Figure 5-24). Available in a variety of sleek colors, they include many features such as a calendar, appointment book, calculator, memo pad, and wireless Web and e-mail access.

Web Link

For more information on handheld computer input, visit the Discovering Computers 2002 Chapter 5 WEB LINK page (**scsite.com/dc2002/ch5/weblink.htm**) and click Handheld Computer Input.

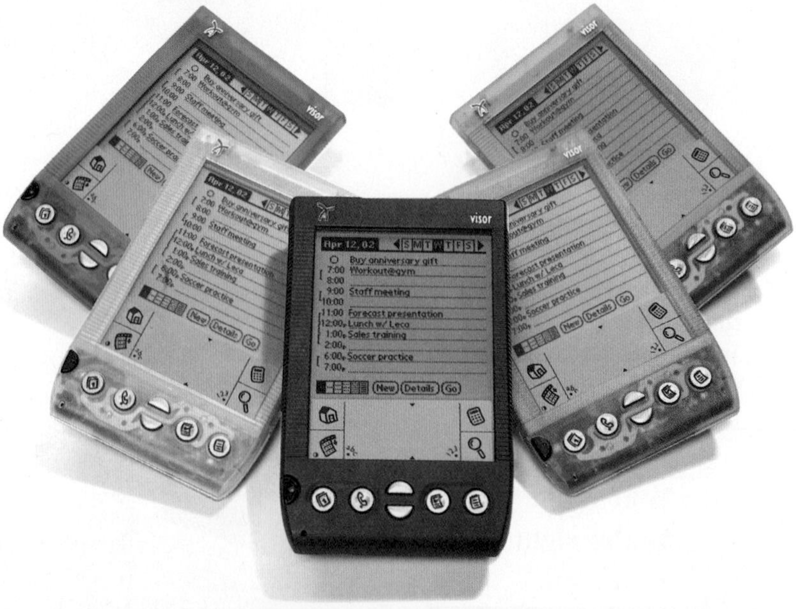

Figure 5-24 Handheld computers today are available in a wide range of colors.

To satisfy the input needs of many different types of users, handheld computers provide many different ways to input data (Figure 5-25). The primary input method on most is the stylus. A handheld computer typically includes a basic stylus. You can purchase more elaborate models that have a ballpoint pen at one end and a stylus at the other. With the stylus, you can enter data in two ways: use an on-screen keyboard or use handwriting recognition software. Each handheld computer uses its own handwriting recognition software. For example, the Palm products use Graffiti®.

Instead of using a stylus, you can attach a full-sized keyboard to your handheld computer. You also can type onto your desktop computer and transfer the data into your handheld computer and vice-versa. As an alternative to typing, many handheld computers support voice input so you can enter data and instructions by speaking into the device. If you want to take photographs and view them on your handheld computer, you can attach a digital camera directly to many handheld computer models.

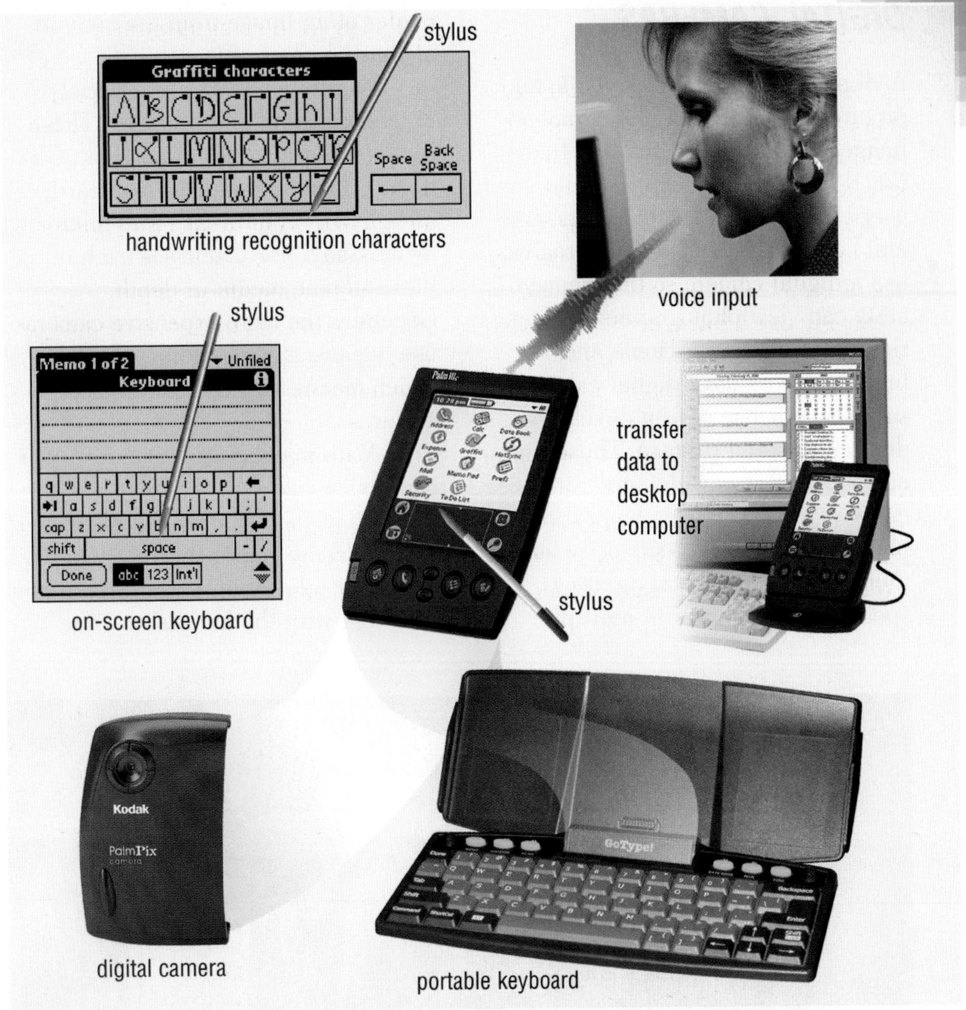

Figure 5-25 Data can be input into a handheld computer using a variety of techniques.

TECHNOLOGY TRAILBLAZER

DONNA **DUBINSKY**

As if being the president and CEO of 3Com's Palm Computing Division were not enough of a challenge, Donna Dubinsky founded Handspring with Jeff Hawkins in 1998 with the goal of becoming the leading handheld computing device maker for the consumer market.

Before coming to Palm Computing, Dubinsky had served as director of distribution at Apple Computer and as an international vice president at Claris. At Palm, she and Hawkins introduced the PalmPilot personal organizer in 1996; sales of more than two million units make it the most-rapidly adopted new computing product ever manufactured. In an effort to learn how consumers actually use the Palm, she watched consumers open the PalmPilot boxes and read the manuals. She even took some technical support calls herself to see what questions they were asking.

Craving her independence and autonomy at Handspring, Dubinsky is using the Palm operating system on its Visor handheld computer. She stresses that size, connectivity to a personal computer, usability, and an economical price are the factors that make handheld computers successful.

For more information on Donna Dubinsky, visit the Discovering Computers 2002 People Web page (**scsite.com/dc2002/people.htm**) and click Donna Dubinsky.

DIGITAL CAMERAS

A **digital camera** allows you to take pictures and store the photographed images digitally, instead of on traditional film (Figure 5-26). Mobile users such as real estate agents, general contractors, and photojournalists use a digital camera so they immediately can view photographed images right on the camera. Home and business users have digital cameras to save the expense of film developing, duplication, and postage. These users can share images with family, friends, co-workers, and clients by posting the photographs on a Web site or e-mailing them. You also can add dazzling special effects and print multiple copies of an image from the comfort of your home or office.

Digital cameras use a variety of techniques to store images. These include floppy disk, SuperDisk, Clik! disk, PC Card, compact flash card, memory stick, mini-CD, and microdrive. Chapter 7 discusses each of these storage media in depth. Generally, the more expensive cameras use higher-capacity storage devices, which means they can hold more pictures.

With many digital cameras, you can review and edit the images while they are in the camera. You also can connect some cameras directly to a printer or television. If you prefer, you can work with the images on your desktop personal computer. To do this, you **download**, or transfer a copy of, the pictures from the digital camera to the computer. With some cameras, you connect a cable between the digital camera and a serial port or USB port on the computer and then use special software included with the camera. As a faster alternative, some users purchase a reading device that attaches to a parallel port or USB port on the computer. With the media in a reading device, you can transfer the images from the media to the computer. For cameras that use a floppy disk, you simply insert the disk into the computer's disk drive and then copy the pictures to the computer.

Figure 5-26 Digital cameras are used for a variety of reasons. The images are viewable immediately on the camera. They also can be edited, printed, or posted on a Web page or photo community.

Once the pictures are on your computer, you can edit them with photo-editing software, print them, fax them, send them via e-mail, include them in another document, or post them to a Web site or photo community for everyone to see. You can add pictures to greeting cards, a computerized photo album, a family newsletter, certificates, and awards. Figure 5-27 illustrates how a digital camera transforms the captured image into a screen display on your computer.

The three basic types of digital cameras are studio cameras, field cameras, and point-and-shoot cameras. The most expensive and highest quality of the three, a **studio camera** is a stationary camera used for professional studio work. Often used by photojournalists, a **field camera** is a portable camera that has many lenses and other attachments. Similarly to the studio camera, a field camera can be quite expensive. A **point-and-shoot camera** is more affordable and lightweight and provides acceptable quality photographic images for the home or small business user.

A point-and-shoot camera often features flash, zoom, automatic focus, and special effects. With some, you can record short narrations for your pictures. Several of these cameras have a built-in TV out port that allows

Figure 5-27 HOW A DIGITAL CAMERA WORKS

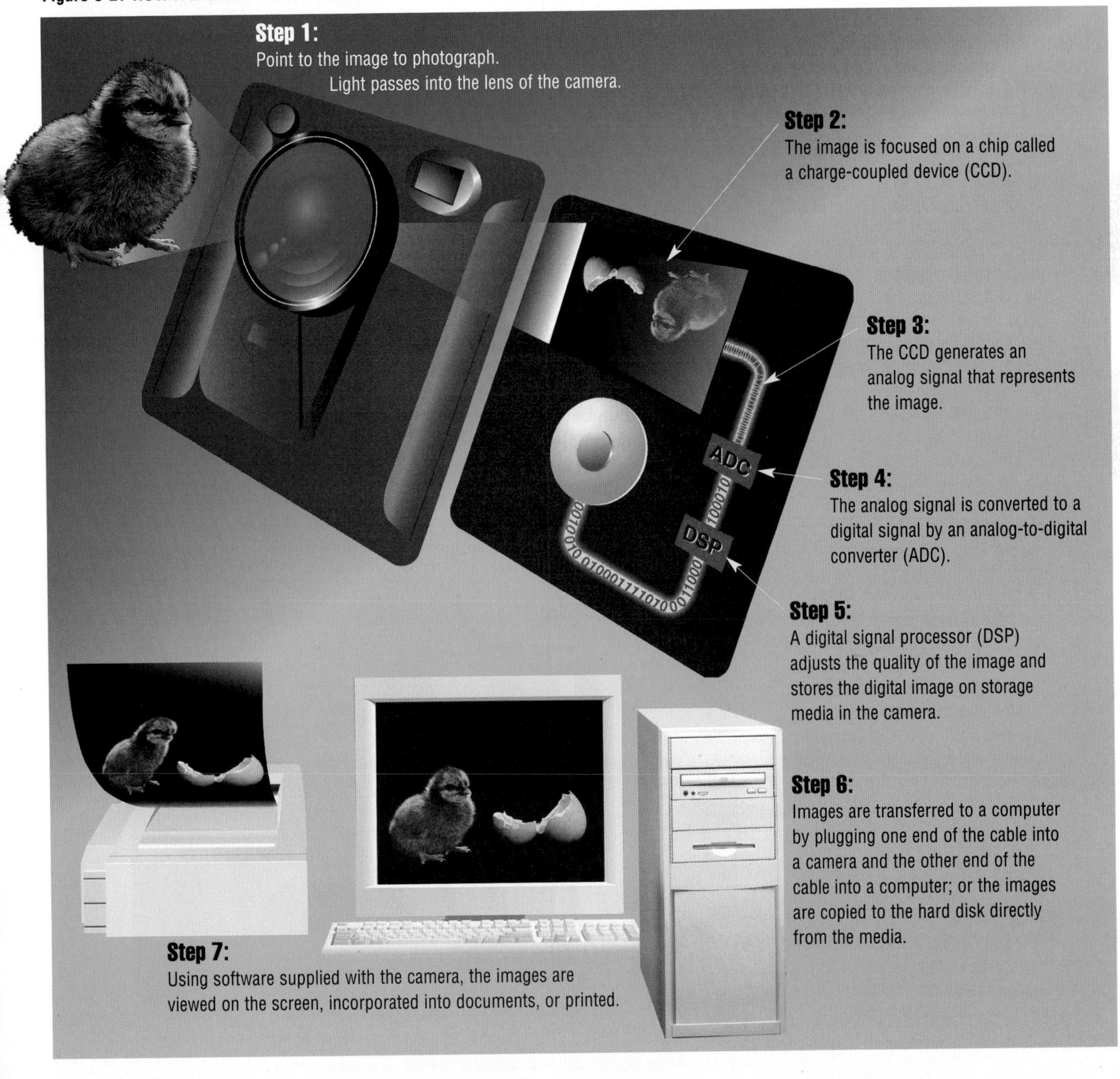

Step 1:
Point to the image to photograph.
Light passes into the lens of the camera.
Step 2:
The image is focused on a chip called a charge-coupled device (CCD).
Step 3:
The CCD generates an analog signal that represents the image.
ADC
DSP
Step 4:
The analog signal is converted to a digital signal by an analog-to-digital converter (ADC).
Step 5:
A digital signal processor (DSP) adjusts the quality of the image and stores the digital image on storage media in the camera.
Step 6:
Images are transferred to a computer by plugging one end of the cable into a camera and the other end of the cable into a computer; or the images are copied to the hard disk directly from the media.
Step 7:
Using software supplied with the camera, the images are viewed on the screen, incorporated into documents, or printed.

you to display their pictures directly on your television screen. This camera is ideal for the home user and mobile users such as real estate agents, insurance agents, and general contractors.

One factor that affects the quality of a digital camera is its resolution. **Resolution** describes the sharpness and clearness of an image. The higher the resolution, the better the image quality, but the more expensive the camera. Some digital camera resolutions today exceed three million pixels. A **pixel** (short for *pic*ture *el*ement) is a single point in an electronic image (Figure 5-28). The greater the number of pixels the camera uses to capture an image, the better the quality of the image.

As a rule, a 1-megapixel (million pixel) camera is fine for screen displays such as photo communities, Web pages, and e-mail attachments. These low-end cameras cost a few hundred dollars. If you plan to print photographs larger than 5 x 7 inches, you should have at least a 2-megapixel (million pixel) camera. For images as good as film-based cameras, use a 3-megapixel camera. These high-end point-and-shoot cameras cost less than $1,000.

Some manufacturers use dots per inch to represent a digital camera's resolution. **Dots per inch (dpi)** is the number of pixels in an inch of screen display. For example, a 1,600 x 1,200 (pronounced 1600 by 1200) dpi camera has 1,600 pixels per vertical inch and 1,200 pixels per horizontal inch. If just one number is stated, such as 1,200 dpi, then both the vertical and horizontal numbers are the same. Digital cameras for the consumer range from 640 x 480 dpi to 1,792 x 1,200 dpi. On some cameras, you can adjust the dpi to the resolution you need. With a lower dpi, you can capture more images. For example, a camera set at 800 x 600 dpi might capture and store 61 images. The number of images reduces to 24 on the same camera set at 1,600 x 1,200 dpi.

The actual photographed resolution is known as the **optical resolution**. Some manufacturers state **enhanced resolution**, or **interpolated resolution**, instead of or in addition to optical resolution. Optical resolution is different from enhanced resolution. The enhanced resolution usually is higher because it uses a special formula to add pixels between those generated by the optical resolution.

Another measure of a digital camera's quality is the number of bits it stores in a dot. Each dot consists of one or more bits of data. The more bits used to represent a dot, the more colors and shades of gray that can be represented. One bit per dot is enough for simple one-color images. For multiple colors and shades of gray, each dot requires more than one bit of data. Your point-and-shoot camera should be at least 24 bit.

Figure 5-28 A pixel is a single point in an electronic image. In digital images, the pixel is a tiny square. When images are printed, pixels are circles of color.

APPLY IT!

Going Digital with Pictures

If you are considering purchasing a new camera in the near future, then consider going digital. Taking pictures with a digital camera is fast and easy. Similar to a traditional camera, you will find a wide price range for digital cameras. For a better idea of what you should purchase to fit your budget and lifestyle, consider the following:

1. If you want to print or publish your images on the Web, then resolution is important. Similar to your monitor, the higher the resolution, the better and sharper the picture.
2. Image storage is another feature to consider. Most digital cameras include some type of miniature removable storage media. The most popular of these media is flash memory, but some cameras use small hard disks or even the venerable floppy disk. The number of images you can store on one of these devices depends on the capacity, the resolution, and the amount of compression.
3. The type of lens you select affects how your pictures look. If you are going to be backpacking in the Rockies and want to take a close-up picture of a newly bloomed wildflower, then a macro lens is what you need. Or, if you want to take a picture of the moose on the next hill over, consider a zoom lens.
4. Perhaps the most important factor to consider is how much money you plan to spend. Determine your price and do some comparison shopping, using the above listed features as guidelines.

For links to digital camera sites, visit the Discovering Computers 2002 Apply It Web page (**scsite.com/dc2002/apply.htm**) and click Chapter 5 Apply It #1.

VIDEO INPUT

Video input or **video capture** is the process of entering a full-motion recording into a computer and storing it on a storage medium. Many video devices use analog video signals. Computers, by contrast, use digital signals. To input video from these analog devices, the analog signal must be converted to a digital signal. To do this, you plug a video camera, VCR, or other analog video device into a video-in plug that is attached to the computer. One card that has a video-in plug is a video capture card. A **video capture card** is an expansion card that converts the analog video signal into a digital signal that a computer can understand. (Most new computers are not equipped with a video capture card because not all users need this type of card.)

A new generation of video cameras produces digital signals. A **digital video (DV) camera** is a video camera that records video as digital signals, instead of analog signals. In addition to video, you also can capture still frames with these cameras. A DV camera connects directly to a parallel port or USB port on the computer. Many DV cameras have a video-in plug. Thus, with a DV camera, you do not need a video capture card (Figure 5-29).

Once you connect the video device to the computer, you can begin recording. After you save the video on a storage medium, you can play it or edit it using video-editing software.

Just as with audio files, video files can require huge amounts of storage space. A three-minute segment, or clip, of high-quality video can require an entire gigabyte of storage (equal to approximately 50 million pages of text). To decrease the size of the files, video often is compressed.

Video compression works by recognizing that only a small portion of a video image changes from frame to frame. A video compression program might store the first frame and then store only the changes from one frame to the next. The program assumes the next frames will be almost identical to the first. Before you view the video, the program decompresses the video segment. Instead of using software to decompress video, some computers have a video decoder. A **video decoder** is a card that decompresses video data. A video decoder is more effective and efficient than software.

If you do not want to save an entire video clip on your computer, you can use a **video digitizer** to capture an individual frame from an analog video and then save the still

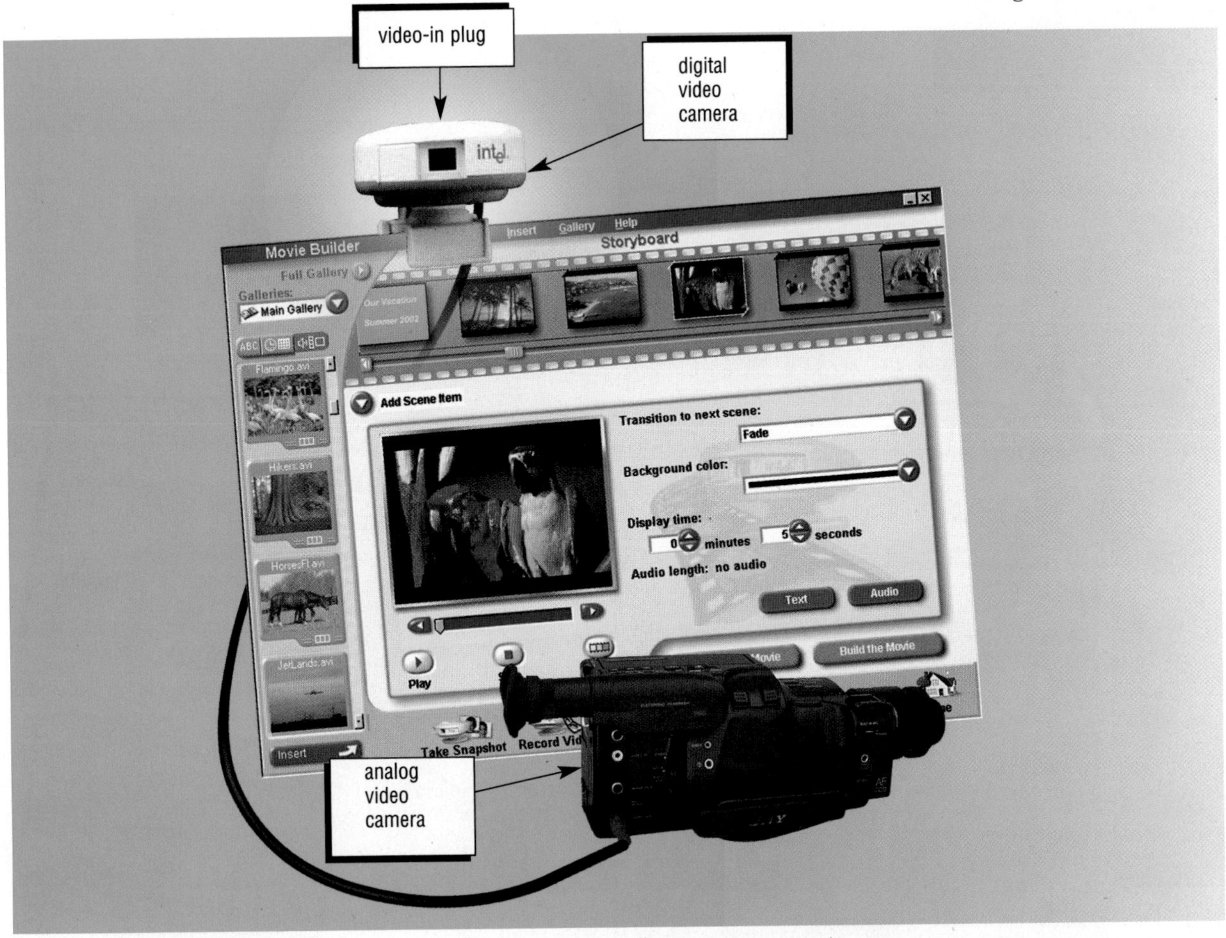

Figure 5-29 You can capture home videos on VHS tapes by attaching an analog video camera to the video-in plug on a digital video camera.

ISSUE

Watching the Babysitter

PC Cameras and Your Privacy

Many of the computers you purchase today include a PC camera, which allows you to make video telephone calls or take snapshots. But how valuable is this? Is it really worth the extra money or the hidden cost built into the price of the computer? Some people may argue once you use this technology it will become a part of your repertoire and you will discover many uses. Do you think this is true? For instance, you could use the camera to monitor the babysitter or housekeeper. Do you agree with this? Why would the home user need or even want a PC camera? Can you list some other ways that you would use this technology?

For more information on PC cameras, visit the Discovering Computers 2002 Issues Web page (**scsite.com/dc2002/issues.htm**) and click Chapter 5 Issue #4.

picture in a file. To do this, plug the analog recording device such as a video camera, VCR, or television into the video digitizer. The video digitizer then usually connects to a parallel port or USB port. While watching the video using special software, you can stop it and capture any single frame. The resulting files are similar to those that a digital camera generates.

PC Video Cameras

A **PC video camera**, or **PC camera**, is a DV camera that allows the home user to record, edit, and capture video and still images and to make video telephone calls on the Internet (Figure 5-30). During a **video telephone call**, both parties see each other as they talk. To provide security in your home, the PC camera can be set to take digital photographs at preset time intervals or whenever it detects motion.

Attached to your computer's USB port, a PC camera usually sits on top of your monitor. For more flexibility, some PC cameras are portable. That is, you can detach them from the computer and use them anywhere.

Some PC cameras have a video-in plug, allowing you to attach a video camera or VCR directly to it. This enables you to create movies from existing videos. The cost of these cameras usually is less than a hundred dollars.

Many magazines and textbooks are beginning to use digital watermarks and PC cameras to connect printed media to the Web. A **digital watermark** is a small digital image that when held in front of a PC camera, displays an associated Web page on the computer screen.

Figure 5-30 A PC video camera can be used to capture, edit, and record video and to make video telephone calls on the Internet.

Web Cams

A **Web cam**, also called a **cam**, is a video camera whose output displays on a Web page. A Web cam attracts Web site visitors by showing images that change regularly (Figure 5-31). You could use a Web cam to show a work in progress, weather and traffic information, employees at work, photographs of a vacation, or any other images you wish to display.

Some Web sites have live Web cams that display still pictures and update the displayed image at a specified time or time intervals, such as 30 seconds. Another type of Web cam, called **streaming cam**, shows moving images by sending a continual stream of pictures.

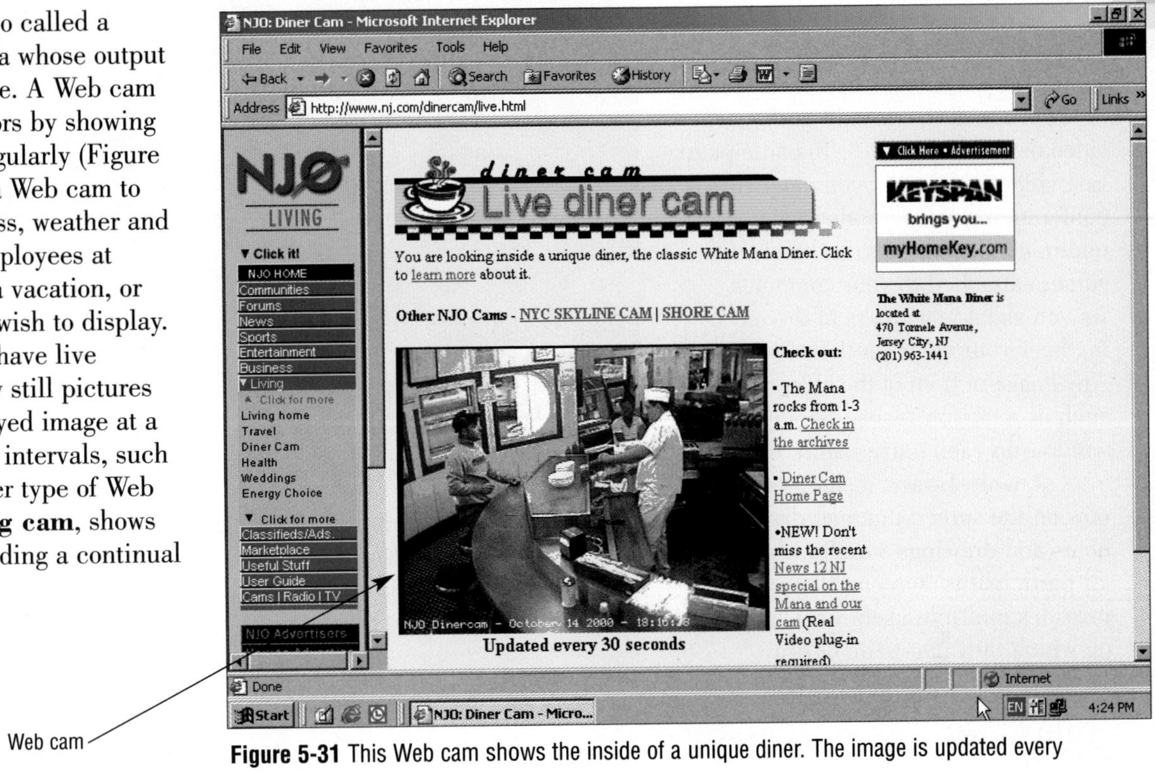

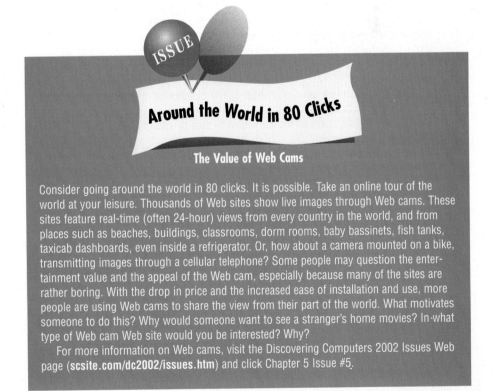

Figure 5-31 This Web cam shows the inside of a unique diner. The image is updated every 30 seconds.

The Value of Web Cams

Consider going around the world in 80 clicks. It is possible. Take an online tour of the world at your leisure. Thousands of Web sites show live images through Web cams. These sites feature real-time (often 24-hour) views from every country in the world, and from places such as beaches, buildings, classrooms, dorm rooms, baby bassinets, fish tanks, taxicab dashboards, even inside a refrigerator. Or, how about a camera mounted on a bike, transmitting images through a cellular telephone? Some people may question the entertainment value and the appeal of the Web cam, especially because many of the sites are rather boring. With the drop in price and the increased ease of installation and use, more people are using Web cams to share the view from their part of the world. What motivates someone to do this? Why would someone want to see a stranger's home movies? In what type of Web cam Web site would you be interested? Why?

For more information on Web cams, visit the Discovering Computers 2002 Issues Web page (**scsite.com/dc2002/issues.htm**) and click Chapter 5 Issue #5.

Videoconferencing

A **videoconference** is a meeting between two or more geographically separated people who use a network or the Internet to transmit audio and video data (Figure 5-32). To participate in a videoconference, you need videoconferencing software along with a microphone, speakers, and a video camera attached to your computer. As you speak, members of the meeting hear your voice on their speakers. Any image in front of the video camera, such as a person's face, displays in a window on each participant's screen.

A **whiteboard** is another window on the screen that can display notes and drawings simultaneously on all participants' screens. This window provides multiple users with an area on which they can write or draw.

Figure 5-32 As you speak, members of a videoconference hear your voice on their speakers. With the video camera facing you, an image of your face displays in a window on each participant's screen.

The costs of videoconferencing hardware and software continue to decrease. Thus, videoconferencing is becoming a cost-effective way to conduct business meetings, corporate training, and educational classes.

APPLY IT!

Setting Up a Web Cam

Web cams are the Internet craze of today. Live Web cam images provide Web site visitors an inside view of your world. Setting up a Web cam is much easier than you might think.

1. The first step is to select a camera. If you use an analog camcorder, you need a card such as a video capture card that converts the analog video signal into a digital signal. Another alternative is a digital video camera that connects directly to your computer's USB port or parallel port. If the camera connects to the parallel port, you also will need a device such as a switchbox that enables you to use the camera and printer at the same time.

   Be sure your camera can capture high-quality pictures for areas with poor lighting. A camera with an inadequate sensitivity to light often generates murky Web cam images. Many cameras are on the market, so be sure to read reviews prior to purchasing.
2. To display Web cam images on a Web page, you send the images from your camera to a Web server. With many Web cam software programs, you FTP images (frames) at specified times or time intervals. Some programs also allow you to set up streaming video from the camera. Popular Web cam software products include Webcam32 and Ispy WebCam (see URL below). Price range for this software is from $25 to $75.
3. Next, you create a Web page that will display your Web cam images. On the Web page, you need to add HTML code that instructs the Web server to display your images. Most Web cam software products provide sample code.
4. For the Web cam images to display on the Web, you need access to a Web server. Many ISPs or OSPs provide this service at no cost. With your Web page on the Web server, the world can see your Web cam images.

Several all-in-one kits also are available that supply the camera, the software, and sometimes access to a Web server. These kits are convenient and easy to use but may not provide the extras that are available when you purchase individual components.

For more information on Web cams and the Web addresses mentioned above, visit the Discovering Computers 2002 Apply It Web page (**scsite.com/dc2002/apply.htm**) and click Chapter 5 Apply It #2.

SCANNERS AND READING DEVICES

Some input devices save you time by eliminating the manual entry of data. With these devices, you do not type or speak into the computer. Instead, these devices capture data from a **source document**, which is the original form of the data. Examples of source documents are timecards, order forms, invoices, paychecks, advertisements, brochures, photographs, inventory tags, or any other document that contains data to be processed.

Devices that capture data directly from source documents include optical scanners, optical character recognition devices, optical mark recognition devices, bar code scanners, and magnetic-ink character recognition readers. The following pages discuss each of these devices.

Optical Scanner

An **optical scanner**, usually called a **scanner**, is a light-sensing input device that reads printed text and graphics and then translates the results into a form the computer can use.

One of the more popular types of scanners is a flatbed scanner. A **flatbed scanner** works similarly to a copy machine except it creates a file of the document in memory instead of a paper copy (Figure 5-33). Once an object is scanned, you can display it on the screen, store it on a storage medium, print it, fax it, attach it to an e-mail message, include it in another document, or post it to a Web site or photo community for everyone to see. For example, you can scan a picture and then include the picture when creating a brochure.

Web Link

For more information on scanners, visit the Discovering Computers 2002 Chapter 5 WEB LINK page (**scsite.com/dc2002/ch5/weblink.htm**) and click Scanners.

Figure 5-33 HOW A FLATBED SCANNER WORKS

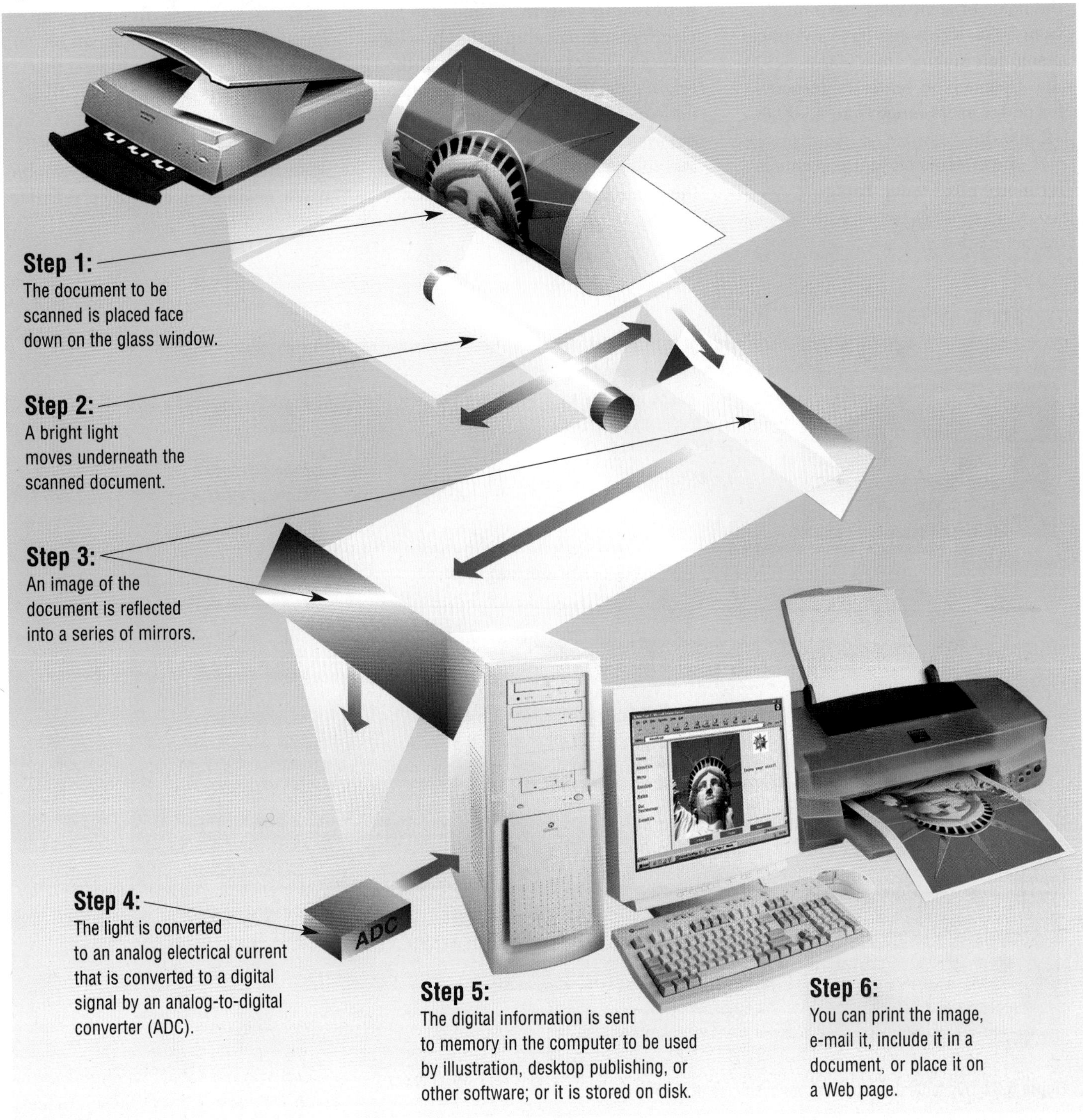

Step 1:
The document to be scanned is placed face down on the glass window.
Step 2:
A bright light moves underneath the scanned document.
Step 3:
An image of the document is reflected into a series of mirrors.
Step 4:
The light is converted to an analog electrical current that is converted to a digital signal by an analog-to-digital converter (ADC).
ADC
Step 5:
The digital information is sent to memory in the computer to be used by illustration, desktop publishing, or other software; or it is stored on disk.
Step 6:
You can print the image, e-mail it, include it in a document, or place it on a Web page.

Three other types of scanners are pen, sheet-fed, and drum. The table in Figure 5-34 summarizes the four types of scanners.

As with a digital camera, the quality of a scanner is measured by the number of bits it stores in a dot and the number of dots per inch, or resolution. The higher each number, the better quality, but the more expensive the scanner. Most of today's affordable color desktop scanners for the home or small business range from 30 to 48 bit and have an optical resolution ranging from 600 to 3,000 dpi. Commercial scanners designed for power users range from 4,000 to 12,500 dpi.

Businesses often use scanners for image processing. **Image processing**, or **imaging**, consists of capturing, storing, analyzing, displaying, printing, and manipulating images. Image processing allows you to convert paper documents such as reports, memos, and procedure manuals into an electronic form. Once saved electronically, you can distribute these documents electronically.

Many business users store and index these documents with an image processing system. An **image processing system** is similar to an electronic filing cabinet that provides access to exact reproductions of the original documents. The government, for example, uses an image processing system to store property deeds and titles to provide quick access to the public, lawyers, and loan officers.

Many scanners also include OCR (optical character recognition) software. **OCR software** can read and convert many types of text documents. Suppose you need to modify a business report, but do not have the original word processing file. You could scan the document with a flatbed scanner, but you still would not be able to edit the report. The scanner, which does not differentiate between text and graphics, saves the report as an image. To convert the image into a text file that can be edited, you use OCR software that works with the scanner. You will be able to edit the resulting text file in a word processing program. The OCR software typically places any graphics in the scanned image into a separate graphics file.

TYPES OF SCANNERS

Scanner	Method of Scanning/ Use	Scannable Items
Flatbed 	• Similar to a copy machine • Scanning mechanism passes under the item to be scanned, which is placed on a glass surface	• Single sheet documents • Bound material • Photographs • Some models include trays for slides, transparencies, and negatives
Pen or handheld 	• Move pen over text to be scanned, then transfer data to computer • Ideal for mobile users, students, researchers • Some connect to a handheld computer • Some read Web bar codes	• Any printed text • Web bar codes
Sheet-fed 	• Item to be scanned is pulled into a stationary scanning mechanism • Smaller and less expensive than a flatbed scanner	• Single sheet documents • Photographs • Slides (with an adapter)
Drum 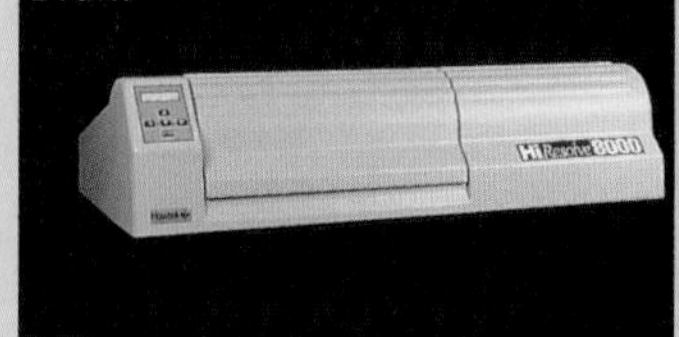	• Item to be scanned rotates around a stationary scanning mechanism • Very large and expensive • Used in publishing industry	• Single sheet documents • Photographs • Slides • Negatives

Figure 5-34 This table describes the various types of scanners.

Current OCR software has a very high success rate and usually can identify more than 99 percent of scanned material. OCR software also marks text it cannot read, allowing you to make corrections easily.

Optical Readers

An **optical reader** is a device that uses a light source to read characters, marks, and codes and then converts them into digital data that a computer can process. The following sections discuss three types of optical readers: optical character recognition, optical mark recognition, and bar code scanner.

OPTICAL CHARACTER RECOGNITION

Optical character recognition (**OCR**) is a technology that involves reading typewritten, computer-printed, or handwritten characters from ordinary documents and translating the images into a form that the computer can understand. Most **OCR devices** include a small optical scanner for reading characters and sophisticated software for analyzing what is read.

OCR devices range from large machines that can read thousands of documents per minute to handheld wands that read one document at a time. OCR devices read characters printed using an OCR font. A widely used OCR font is called OCR-A (Figure 5-35). During the scan of a document, an OCR device determines the shapes of characters by detecting patterns of light and dark. OCR software then compares these shapes with predefined shapes stored in memory and converts the shapes into characters the computer can understand.

Many companies use OCR characters on turnaround documents. A **turnaround document** is a document that you return (turn around) to the company that creates and sends it. For example, when you receive a bill, you tear off a portion of the bill and send it back to the company with your payment (Figure 5-36). The portion of the bill you return usually has your account number, payment amount, and other information printed in optical characters.

ABCDEFGHIJKLMNOPQRSTUVWXYZ
1234567890-=▮;',./

Figure 5-35 A portion of the characters in the OCR-A font. Notice how characters such as the number 0 and the letter O are shaped differently so the reading device easily can distinguish between them.

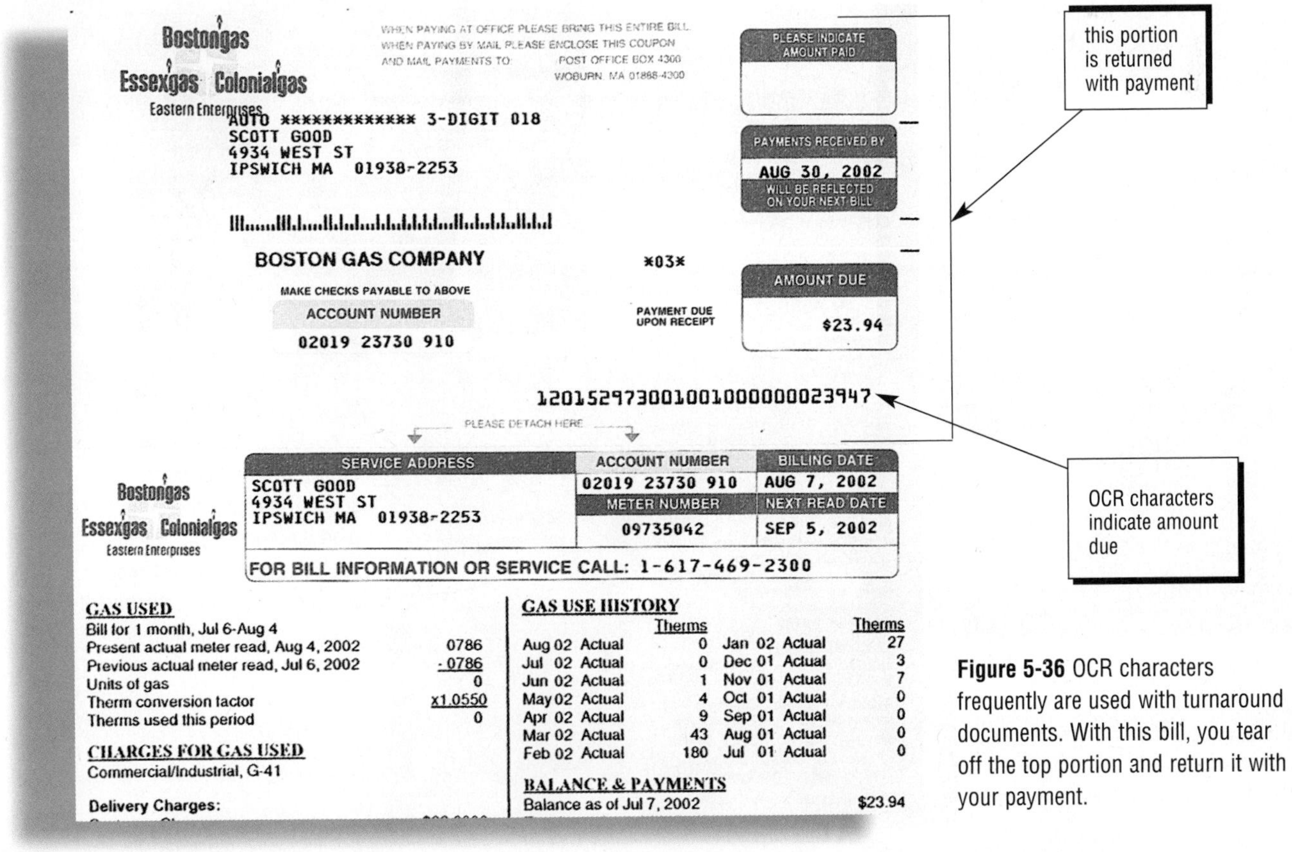
Bostongas Essexgas Colonialgas Eastern Enterprises
WHEN PAYING AT OFFICE PLEASE BRING THIS ENTIRE BILL
WHEN PAYING BY MAIL PLEASE ENCLOSE THIS COUPON AND MAIL PAYMENTS TO: POST OFFICE BOX 4300 WOBURN MA 01888-4300

PLEASE INDICATE AMOUNT PAID

AUTO ************* 3-DIGIT 018
SCOTT GOOD
4934 WEST ST
IPSWICH MA 01938-2253

PAYMENTS RECEIVED BY AUG 30, 2002 WILL BE REFLECTED ON YOUR NEXT BILL

BOSTON GAS COMPANY *03*
MAKE CHECKS PAYABLE TO ABOVE
ACCOUNT NUMBER 02019 23730 910
PAYMENT DUE UPON RECEIPT
AMOUNT DUE $23.94

120152973001001000000023947

PLEASE DETACH HERE

Bostongas Essexgas Colonialgas Eastern Enterprises

SERVICE ADDRESS	ACCOUNT NUMBER	BILLING DATE
SCOTT GOOD 4934 WEST ST IPSWICH MA 01938-2253	02019 23730 910	AUG 7, 2002
	METER NUMBER	NEXT READ DATE
	09735042	SEP 5, 2002

FOR BILL INFORMATION OR SERVICE CALL: 1-617-469-2300

GAS USED

Bill for 1 month, Jul 6-Aug 4	
Present actual meter read, Aug 4, 2002	0786
Previous actual meter read, Jul 6, 2002	- 0786
Units of gas	0
Therm conversion factor	x1.0550
Therms used this period	0

CHARGES FOR GAS USED
Commercial/Industrial, G-41

Delivery Charges:

GAS USE HISTORY

	Therms		Therms
Aug 02 Actual	0	Jan 02 Actual	27
Jul 02 Actual	0	Dec 01 Actual	3
Jun 02 Actual	1	Nov 01 Actual	7
May 02 Actual	4	Oct 01 Actual	0
Apr 02 Actual	9	Sep 01 Actual	0
Mar 02 Actual	43	Aug 01 Actual	0
Feb 02 Actual	180	Jul 01 Actual	0

BALANCE & PAYMENTS
Balance as of Jul 7, 2002 $23.94

Figure 5-36 OCR characters frequently are used with turnaround documents. With this bill, you tear off the top portion and return it with your payment.

OPTICAL MARK RECOGNITION

Optical mark recognition (OMR) devices read hand-drawn marks such as small circles or rectangles. A person places these marks on a form, such as a test, survey, or questionnaire answer sheet (Figure 5-37). With a test, the OMR device first reads the answer key sheet to record correct answers based on patterns of light. The OMR device then reads the remaining documents and matches their patterns of light against the answer key sheet.

BAR CODE SCANNER A **bar code scanner** uses laser beams to read bar codes (Figure 5-38). A **bar code** is an identification code that consists of a set of vertical lines and spaces of different widths. The bar code represents data that identifies the manufacturer and the item. Manufacturers either print a bar code on a product's package or on

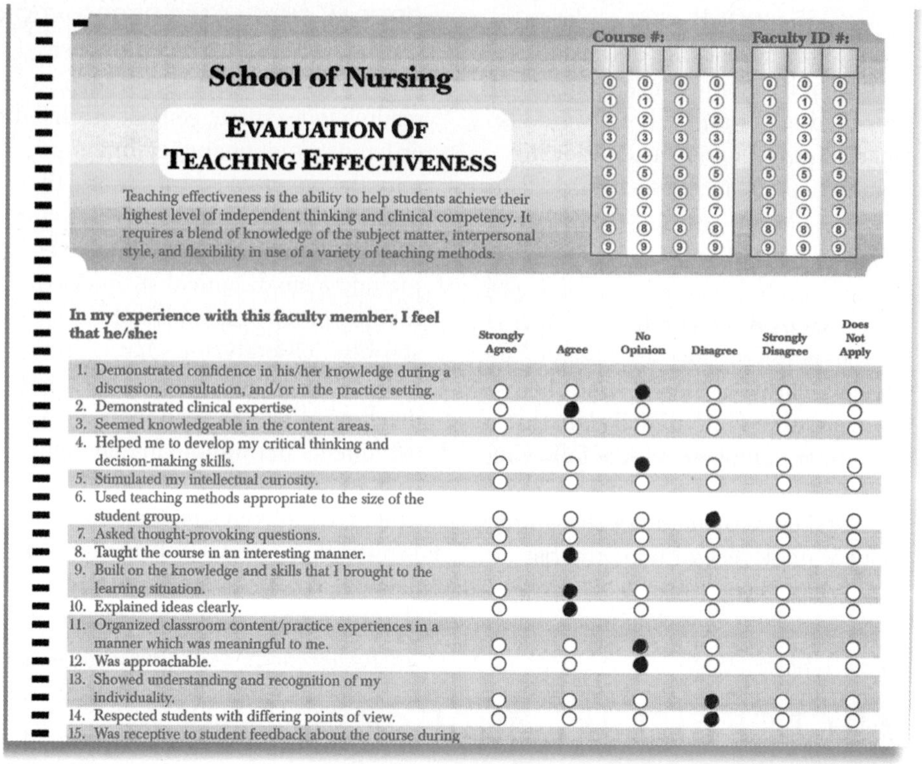

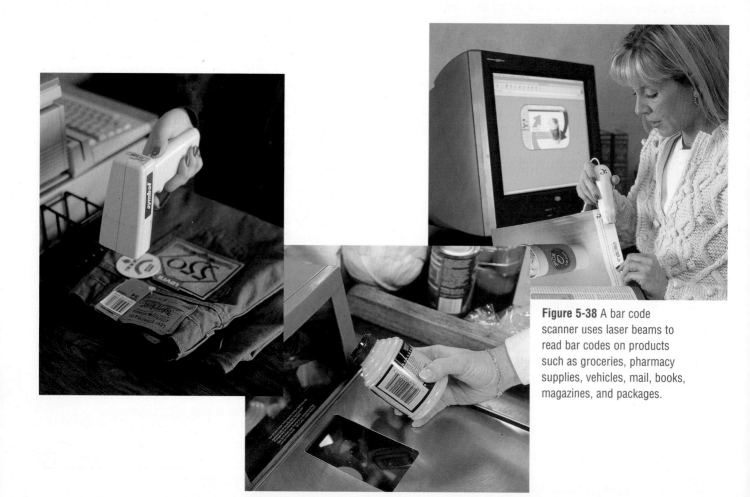

School of Nursing

EVALUATION OF TEACHING EFFECTIVENESS

Teaching effectiveness is the ability to help students achieve their highest level of independent thinking and clinical competency. It requires a blend of knowledge of the subject matter, interpersonal style, and flexibility in use of a variety of teaching methods.

Course #: 0 1 2 3 4 5 6 7 8 9

Faculty ID #: 0 1 2 3 4 5 6 7 8 9

In my experience with this faculty member, I feel that he/she:	Strongly Agree	Agree	No Opinion	Disagree	Strongly Disagree	Does Not Apply
1. Demonstrated confidence in his/her knowledge during a discussion, consultation, and/or in the practice setting.	○	○	●	○	○	○
2. Demonstrated clinical expertise.	○	●	○	○	○	○
3. Seemed knowledgeable in the content areas.	○	○	○	○	○	○
4. Helped me to develop my critical thinking and decision-making skills.	○	○	●	○	○	○
5. Stimulated my intellectual curiosity.	○	○	○	○	○	○
6. Used teaching methods appropriate to the size of the student group.	○	○	○	●	○	○
7. Asked thought-provoking questions.	○	○	○	○	○	○
8. Taught the course in an interesting manner.	○	●	○	○	○	○
9. Built on the knowledge and skills that I brought to the learning situation.	○	●	○	○	○	○
10. Explained ideas clearly.	○	●	○	○	○	○
11. Organized classroom content/practice experiences in a manner which was meaningful to me.	○	○	●	○	○	○
12. Was approachable.	○	○	●	○	○	○
13. Showed understanding and recognition of my individuality.	○	○	○	●	○	○
14. Respected students with differing points of view.	○	○	○	●	○	○
15. Was receptive to student feedback about the course during						

Figure 5-37 On many surveys and questionnaires, you draw small circles to indicate your answers. These forms are read by optical mark recognition (OMR) devices.

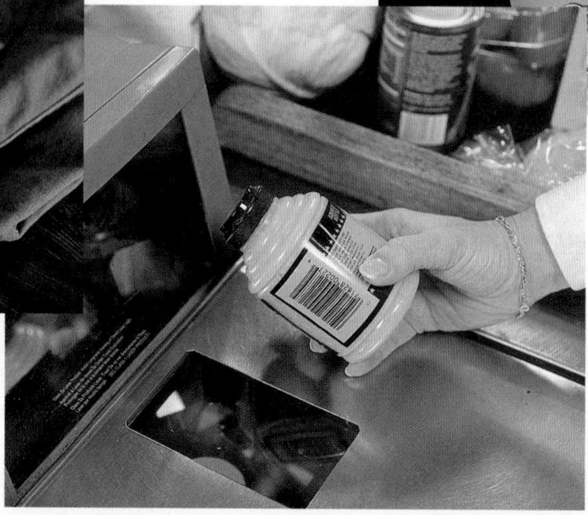

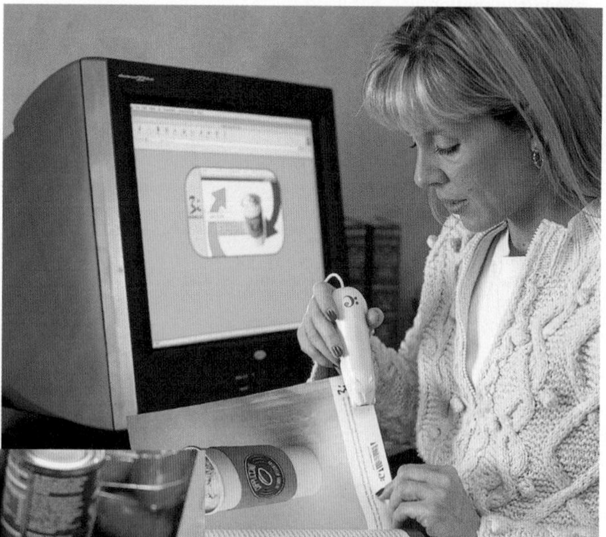

Figure 5-38 A bar code scanner uses laser beams to read bar codes on products such as groceries, pharmacy supplies, vehicles, mail, books, magazines, and packages.

a label that is affixed to a product. A bar code scanner reads a bar code by using light patterns that pass through the bar code lines.

A variety of products such as groceries, pharmacy supplies, vehicles, mail, magazines, and books have bar codes. Each industry uses its own type of bar code. The U.S. Postal Service uses a POSTNET bar code. Retail and grocery stores use the Universal Product Code, or UPC (Figure 5-39). The table in Figure 5-40 summarizes some of the more widely used bar codes.

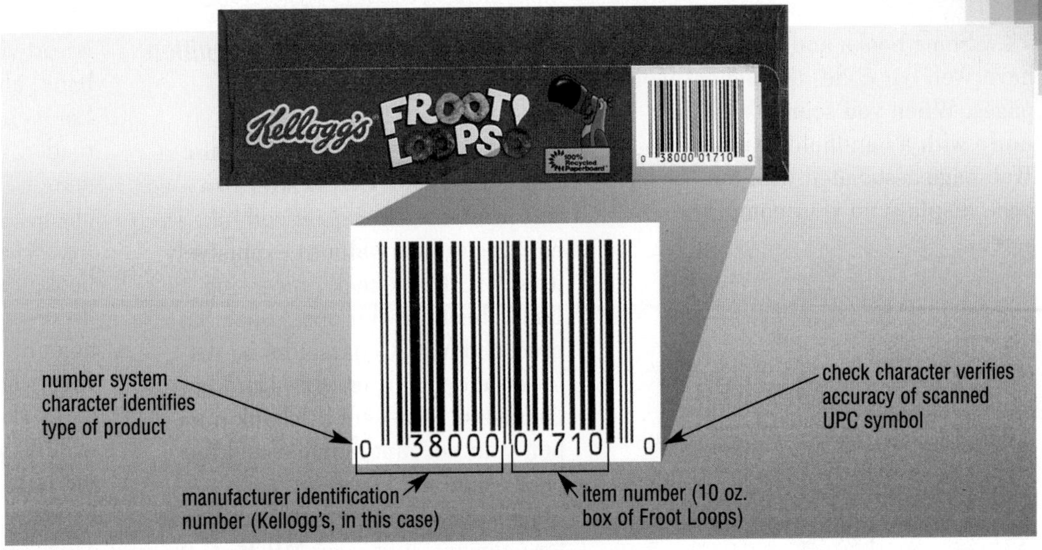

Figure 5-39 This UPC identifies a box of Kellogg's Froot Loops™.

TYPES OF BAR CODES

Bar Code Name	Sample Bar Code	Primary Market
Codabar	Codabar A 1 2 3 4 5 6 7 8 9 0 1 2 A	Libraries, blood banks, and air parcel carriers.
Code 39	C O D E 3 9	Nonretail applications such as manufacturing, inventory, military, and health applications requiring numbers and letters in the bar code.
EAN – European Article Numbering	EAN-13 1 234567 890128	Similar to UPC, except used in Europe. A variation of EAN is used for ISBN numbers on books.
Interleaved 2 of 5	Interleaved 2 of 5 1 2 3 4 5 6 7 8 9 0 1 2	Nonretail applications, such as game tickets, requiring only numbers in the bar code.
POSTNET – Postal Numeric Encoding Technique		U.S. Postal Service to represent a postal code or delivery point code.
UPC – Universal Product Code	UPC-A with Supplemental 0 12345 67890 5	Supermarkets, convenience, and specialty stores used to identify manufacturers and products.
Web bar code	:C	Magazines and books to display a Web page.

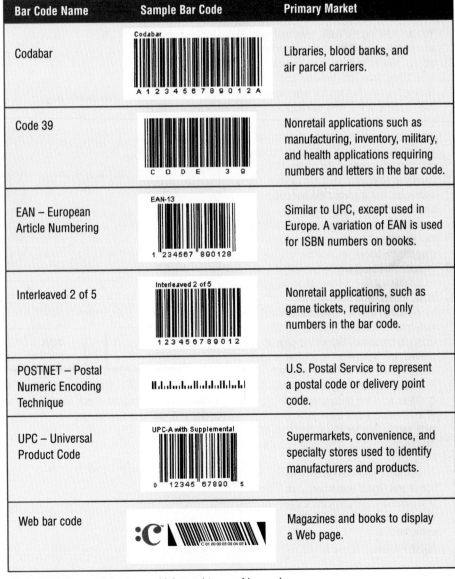

Figure 5-40 Some of the more widely used types of bar codes.

Some books and magazines have Web bar codes throughout their pages. When you scan a **Web bar code** with a handheld scanner, the Web page associated with the bar code displays on your computer screen.

APPLY IT!

Web Bar Codes Can Save You Time

You are reading the daily news and run across a Web address that looks interesting. You write it down so you can type it later into your browser and review the site. But what if you did not have to type in the Web site address? If you live in Charleston, South Carolina and subscribe to one of the daily newspapers, you may have noticed bar codes displayed throughout the pages. Use a handheld scanner connected to your computer, run it across the bar code, and a related Web page pops up on the screen. This technology is not limited to newspapers. It has been extended to magazines, books, postcards, or any imaginable object where one might want to establish a direct connection between static objects and the Internet.

A related technology is the digital watermark. Consider the way a photograph is produced. Before the page is printed, the watermark is applied to the electronic version of the photograph. Run your scanner across the photograph or hold the photograph in front of a PC camera and up pops a related Web page. Look for this technology in magazines such as Wired and Popular Mechanics.

For more information on Web bar codes and digital watermarks, visit the Discovering Computers 2002 Apply It Web page (**scsite.com/dc2002/apply.htm**) and click Chapter 5 Apply It #3.

Magnetic Ink Character Recognition Reader

A **magnetic-ink character recognition (MICR) reader** can read text printed with magnetized ink. The banking industry almost exclusively uses MICR for check processing. Each check in your checkbook has precoded MICR characters on the lower-left edge (Figure 5-41). These characters represent the bank number, your account number, and the check number.

When a bank receives a check for payment, it uses an MICR inscriber to print the amount of the check in MICR characters in the lower-right corner. The check then is sorted or routed to the customer's bank, along with thousands of others. Each check is inserted into an MICR reader, which sends the check information — including the amount of the check — to a computer for processing. When you balance your checkbook, verify the amount printed in the lower-right corner is the same as the amount written on the check; otherwise, your statement will not balance.

The banking industry has established an international standard not only for bank numbers, but also for the font of the MICR characters. This standardization makes it possible for you to write checks in another country.

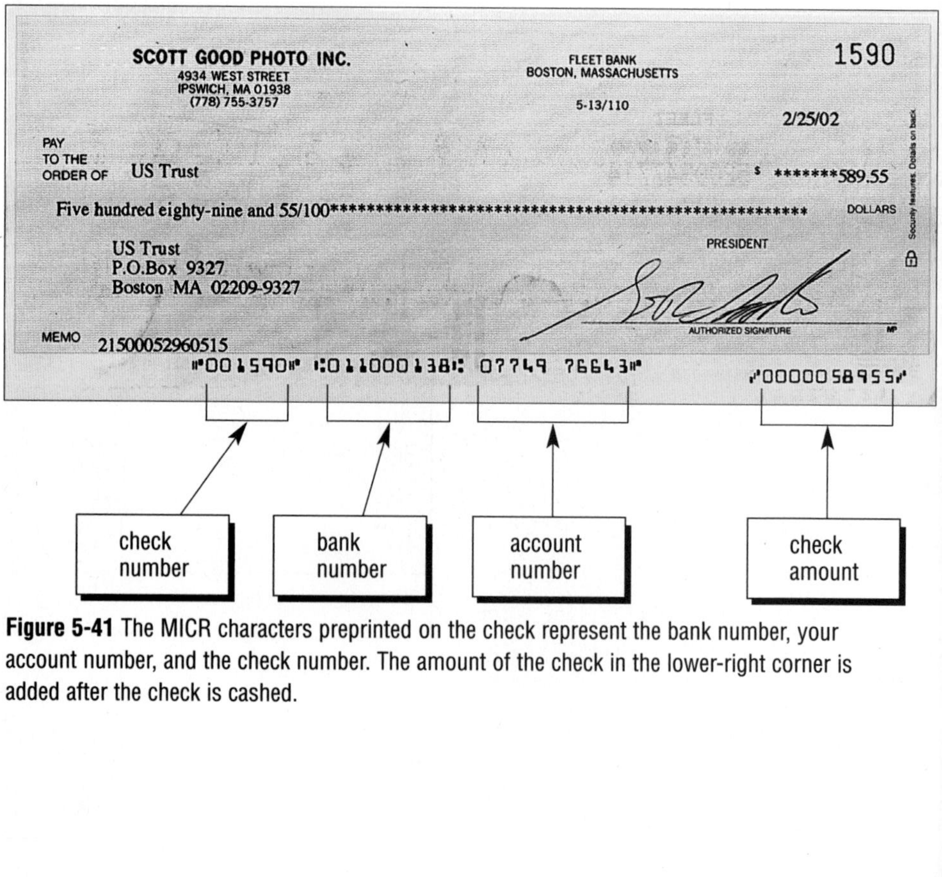

Figure 5-41 The MICR characters preprinted on the check represent the bank number, your account number, and the check number. The amount of the check in the lower-right corner is added after the check is cashed.

Wireless Input

Instead of reading or scanning data from a source document, you can use a wireless input technology to obtain data directly at the location where the transaction or event takes place. Factories, warehouses, the outdoors, or other locations where heat, humidity, and cleanliness are difficult to control use wireless input. The employee uses a handheld computer or device to collect data wirelessly.

As shown in Figure 5-42, an employee can enter product inventory data into a handheld device and then later transfer the data to a desktop computer through a docking station.

Many users have Web-enabled computers and devices such as cellular telephones and pagers, which allow wireless connections to the Web. More and more users today send data wirelessly to central office computers using these devices.

Figure 5-42 This employee enters product data into a handheld device and then later transfers the data to a desktop computer through a docking station.

INPUT DEVICES FOR PHYSICALLY CHALLENGED USERS

The growing presence of computers in everyone's lives has generated an awareness of the need to address computing requirements for those with physical limitations. The **Americans with Disabilities Act (ADA)** requires any company with 15 or more employees make reasonable attempts to accommodate the needs of physically challenged workers. Whether at work or at home, you may find it necessary to obtain input devices that address physical limitations. Besides voice recognition, which is ideal for blind or visually impaired users, several other input devices are available.

Users with limited hand mobility that wish to use a keyboard have several options. A **keyguard** is a metal or plastic plate placed over the keyboard that allows users to rest their hands on the keyboard without accidentally pressing any keys. A keyguard also guides a finger or pointing device so a user presses only one key at a time (Figure 5-43).

Figure 5-43 A keyguard allows users to rest their hands on the keyboard without accidentally pressing any keys. It also guides a finger or pointing device onto a key so a user presses only a single key at a time.

Keyboards with larger keys also are available. Still another option is the **on-screen keyboard**, in which a graphic of a standard keyboard displays on the user's screen. Figure 5-44 shows an on-screen keyboard in Microsoft Word. In Figure 5-45, a woman uses a pointing device in her lap to press the keys on the on-screen keyboard.

Various pointing devices are available for users with motor disabilities. Small trackballs that you control with a thumb or one finger can be attached to a table, mounted to a wheelchair, or held in a user's hand. People with limited hand movement can use a **head-mounted pointer** to control the pointer or insertion point. To simulate the functions of a mouse button, a user can work with switches that control the pointer. The switch might be a pad you press with your hand, a foot pedal, a receptor that detects facial motions, or a pneumatic instrument controlled by puffs of air.

Two exciting developments in this area are gesture recognition and computerized implant devices. Both in the prototype stage, they attempt to provide users with a natural computer interface. With **gesture recognition**, the computer will be able to detect human motions. Computers with this capability have the potential to recognize sign language, read lips, track facial movements, or follow eye gazes. For paralyzed or speech impaired individuals, a doctor will implant a computerized device into the brain. This device will contain a transmitter. As the user thinks thoughts, the transmitter will send signals to the computer.

PUTTING IT ALL TOGETHER

When you purchase a computer, you should have an understanding of the input devices included with the computer, as well as those you may need that are not included. Many factors influence the type of input devices you may use: the type of input desired, the hardware and software in use, and the desired cost. The type of input devices you require depends on your intended use. Figure 5-46 outlines several suggested input devices for specific computer users.

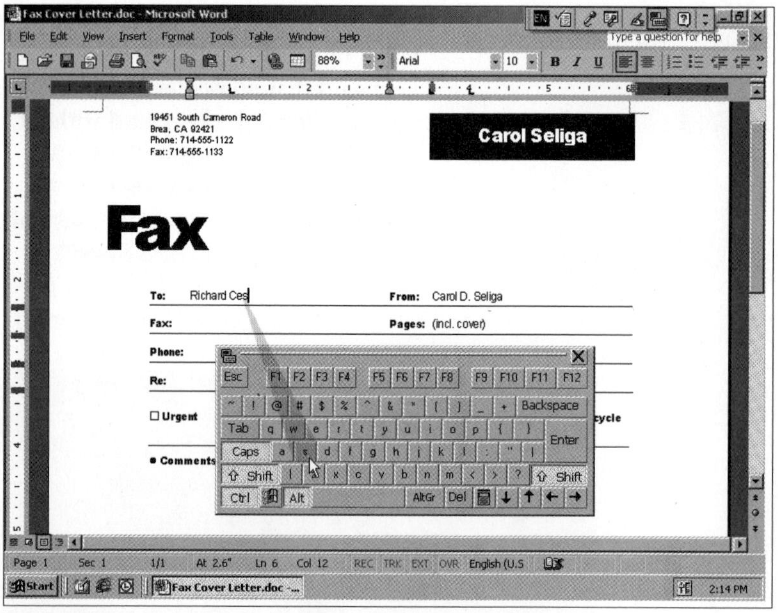

Figure 5-44 As you click letters on the on-screen keyboard, they display in the document at the location of the insertion point.

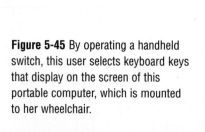

Figure 5-45 By operating a handheld switch, this user selects keyboard keys that display on the screen of this portable computer, which is mounted to her wheelchair.

SUGGESTED INPUT DEVICES BY USER

USER	INPUT DEVICE
Home 	• Enhanced keyboard or ergonomic keyboard • Mouse • Joystick or wheel • 30-bit 600 x 1,200 dpi color scanner • 1- or 2-megapixel digital camera • Microphone • Voice recognition software • PC video camera
Small Office/Home Office 	• Enhanced keyboard or ergonomic keyboard • Mouse • Stylus and portable keyboard for handheld computer • 36-bit 600 x 1,200 dpi color scanner • 1- or 2-megapixel digital camera • Microphone • Voice recognition software • PC video camera
Mobile 	• Wireless mouse for notebook computer • Trackball, touchpad, or pointing stick on notebook computer • Stylus and portable keyboard for handheld computer • 2- or 3-megapixel digital camera • Voice recognition software
Large Business 	• Enhanced keyboard or ergonomic keyboard • Mouse • Touch screen • Light pen for point-of-sale terminals • 42-bit 1,200 x 1,200 dpi color scanner • OCR or OMR or bar code reader or MICR reader • Microphone • Voice recognition software • Video camera for videoconferences
Power 	• Enhanced keyboard or ergonomic keyboard • Mouse • Stylus and cursor for graphics tablet • 48-bit 1,200 x 1,200 dpi color scanner • 3-megapixel digital camera • Microphone • PC video camera

Figure 5-46 This table recommends suggested input devices.

Webcasting

Webcasting is a form of communications that features streaming rich media, including audio, video, and Web-based multimedia. It quickly is becoming a mainstream Internet application. Similar to a television broadcast, a Webcast airs exclusively on the Internet. The advantage is Webcasting can be done at anytime, anywhere in the world.

With broadband communications becoming more widely used, digital video and digital audio quickly are becoming in-demand technologies. As a result, Webcasting is a growing niche industry. Because creating and delivering a Webcast requires diverse skills, employment opportunities are available for people with knowledge in a range of fields, including production and camera use, content development and technical writing, audio/visual expertise, engineering, networking, or other technical areas. Dual skill sets are an asset. Salaries within this industry vary widely, anywhere from $25,000 to $100,000 or more, depending on the job and the skills.

Currently no certifications are available in this field, but you can look for these in the near future. The International Webmasters Association (IWA) will most likely sponsor the certifications (see URL below).

To learn more about Webcasting as a career and the Web site mentioned above, visit the Discovering Computers 2002 Careers Web page (**scsite.com/dc2002/careers.htm**) and click Webcasting.

E-COMMUNITIES

PICTURE THIS!

Share Your Community Pride

The family welcomes a new baby, a cousin graduates from college, good friends tie the knot, and grandma and grandpa celebrate their 50th wedding anniversary. Share these kinds of announcements, memories, and activities, and photographs of each event, by joining a Web community or creating your own. Virtual communities allow family, friends, and others with similar interests to connect and disseminate information with the Internet world.

Web communities connect computer users around the globe and make exchanging ideas and viewpoints easy and convenient. Thousands of virtual communities permit groups to play games, offer support, entertain each other, and work on collective projects.

Several Web sites bridge the gap between conventional and digital photography. These photo-sharing services allow shutterbugs to create virtual photo albums and share these images online.

Most Web sites, such as Zing shown in Figure 5-47, provide free, unlimited storage space with the hope that users will view the advertisements and order paper reprints and personalized gifts. Other photo Web sites are listed in Figure 5-48.

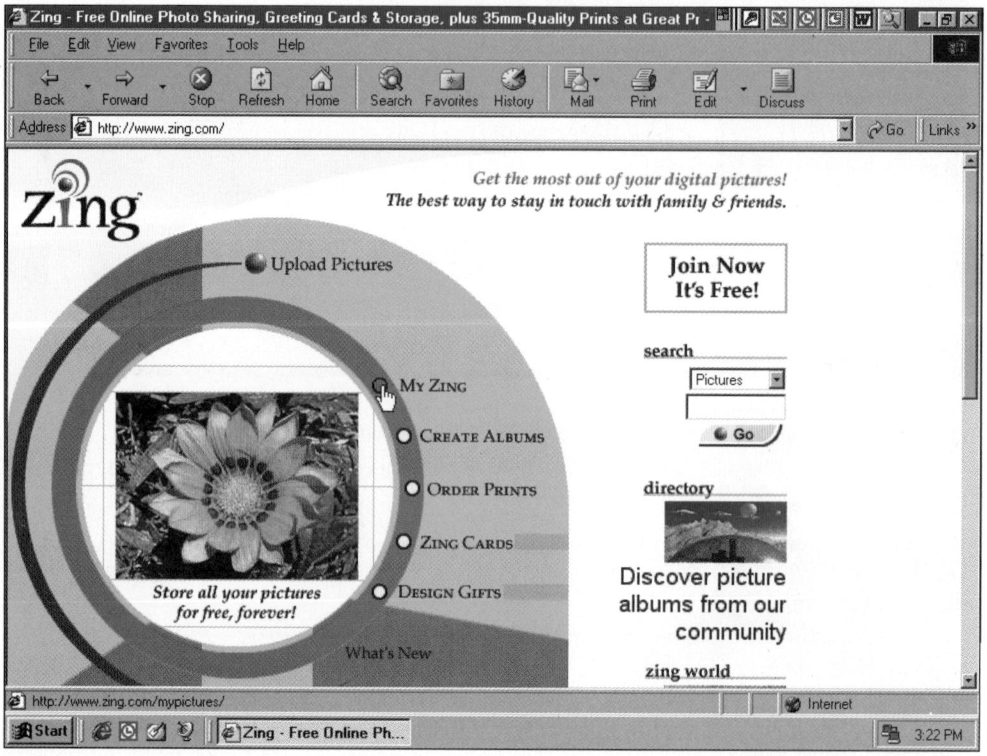

Figure 5-47 Zing and other photo Web sites provide a setting where family and friends can view digital pictures online.

PHOTO AND COMMUNITY WEB SITES	URL
Photos	
GatherRound.com℠	gatherround.com
Kodak PhotoNet Online	www.photonet.com
MSN PictureIt Photo Center	communities.msn.com/photoalbums
PhotoWorks	photoworks.com
Shutterfly	shutterfly.com
Zing	zing.com
Web Communities	
Canterbury Net	www.canterbury.net.nz
CyberErie	cybererie.com
MSN Web Communities	communities.msn.com/webcommunities
Redstone Colorado Online	redstonecolorado.com
Run the Planet	runtheplanet.com
Yahoo! GeoCities Neighborhoods	geocities.yahoo.com/cgi-bin/hood/geo

For an updated list of photo and community Web sites, visit scsite.com/dc2002/e-rev.htm.

Figure 5-48 These photo and community Web sites allow you to share your pictures and meet people with similar interests.

Another type of virtual community allows people with related interests to share information. The categories of these Web communities are wide-ranging and include health support groups and vintage Corvettes to cruise ships and the Chicago Cubs. The Yahoo! GeoCities CollegePark community displayed in Figure 5-49 allows users to converse on such topics as distance learning, sports, and music. Runners can jump to Run the Planet, billed as the largest world-wide running community on the Internet.

Residents in entire towns have developed Web communities that promote businesses, permit parents to communicate with teachers, and inform citizens about the town council's meetings. One of the first communities was developed in Montana in the late 1980s to connect teachers, many of whom taught in one-room schools. Today, residents throughout the world have virtual communities. Citizens in Canterbury, New Zealand, for example, share information on genealogy, psychology, and community activities on their Canterbury Net; Redstone, Colorado, residents share community news and activities by logging on to Redstone Colorado Online (Figure 5-50); and CyberErie citizens in Erie, Pennsylvania, take coffee breaks in their cyber café, share their pets in the virtual zoo, and relax in the CyberLibrary.

For more information on Web communities, visit the Discovering Computers 2002 E-Revolution Web page (scsite.com/dc2002/e-rev.htm) and click Communities.

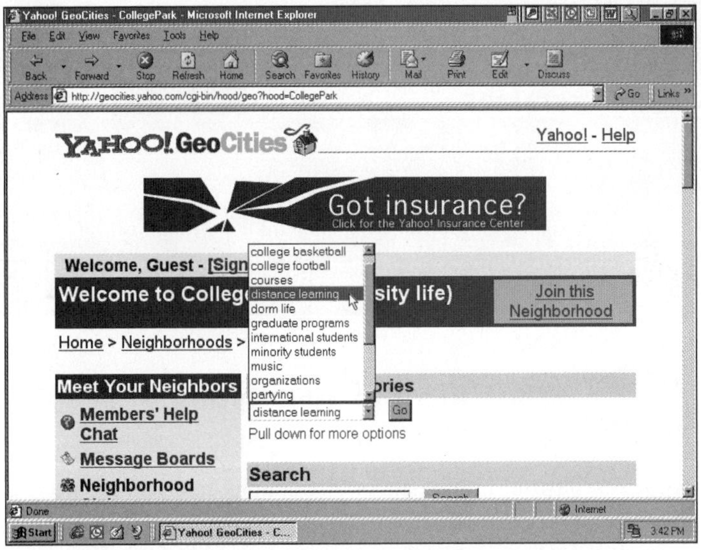

Figure 5-49 Cyber residents of Yahoo!'s GeoCities CollegePark discuss hundreds of collegiate topics, including distance learning, assignments, sports, and activities.

Figure 5-50 Redstone, Colorado, residents share information on local events, shopping, and the environment through their community Web site.

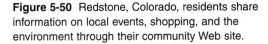

eREVOLUTION E-COMMUNITIES *applied:*

1. View three of the photos Web sites listed in Figure 5-48. Make a table that lists the Web site names, categories of photo albums, amount of storage space, cost, resolution constraints, and length of time photos are permitted to stay online. Explain why you would or would not like to view photos online.

2. Visit two of the community Web sites listed in Figure 5-48. Write a paragraph on each Web site describing its content, ease of use, and features. Then, describe what content you would include in a Web community of your hometown. Would you, for example, include a Web cam? A list of businesses and services? Hours when public offices are open? What advertisers, if any, would you contact to obtain revenue?

In Summary

Web Instructions: To display this page from the Web, start your browser and enter the URL scsite.com/dc2002/ch5/summary.htm. Click the links for current and additional information. To listen to an audio version of this In Summary, click the Audio button. To play the audio RealPlayer must be installed on your computer (download by clicking here).

1 What Are the Two Types of Input?

Input is any data or instructions entered into the memory of a computer. The two types of input are data and programs. **Data** is a collection of unorganized facts that can include words, numbers, pictures, sounds, and video. A computer processes data into information. A **program** is a series of instructions that tell a computer how to process data into information.

2 What Are the Characteristics of a Keyboard?

The **keyboard**, a primary input device on a computer, is an input device that contains keys you press to enter data into the computer. All keyboards have a typing area used to type letters of the alphabet, numbers, punctuation marks, and other basic characters. A keyboard also may include a **numeric keypad** designed to make it easier to enter numbers, **function keys** programmed to issue commands and accomplish certain tasks, **arrow keys** used to move the **insertion point**, and **toggle keys** that can be switched between two different states.

3 Describe the Various Types of Keyboards

A standard computer keyboard sometimes is called a **QWERTY keyboard** because of the layout of its typing area. An **enhanced keyboard** has function keys, CTRL keys, ALT keys, and a set of arrow and additional keys. A **cordless keyboard** transmits data using wireless technology such as infrared light or radio waves. A **portable keyboard** is a full-sized keyboard you can attach and remove from a handheld computer. An **ergonomic keyboard** is designed to reduce the risk of wrist injuries.

4 What Are the Various Types of Pointing Devices?

A **pointing device** controls the movement of a pointer on the screen. A **mouse** is a pointing device that is moved across a flat surface, controls the movement of the pointer on the screen, and is used to make selections from the screen. A **trackball** is a stationary pointing device with a ball mechanism on its top. A **touchpad** or **trackpad** is a flat, rectangular pointing device that is sensitive to pressure and motion. A **pointing stick** is a pressure-sensitive pointing device shaped like a pencil eraser. Other pointing devices include a **joystick** (a vertical lever mounted on a base), a **wheel** (a steering-wheel type of device), a **light pen** (a handheld device that contains a light source or can detect light), a **touch screen** (a monitor with a touch-sensitive panel on the screen), a **stylus** or **pen** (a pen to write text and draw lines), a **graphics tablet** or **digitizer** or **digitizing tablet** (an electronic plastic board used to input graphical data) and a **cursor** (a mouse-like device that has a window with cross hairs).

5 How Does a Mouse Work?

The bottom of a mouse is flat and contains a multidirectional mechanism, either a small ball or an optical sensor, which detects movement of the mouse. As the mouse is moved across a flat surface, electronic circuits in the mouse translate the movement into signals that are sent to the computer. You use the mouse to move the pointer on the screen. To operate the mouse, you point, click, right-click, double-click, drag, and right-drag.

6 What Are the Different Mouse Types?

A **mechanical mouse** has a rubber or metal ball on its underside. An **optical mouse** uses devices that emit light to detect the mouse's movement. A **cordless mouse**, or **wireless mouse**, relies on battery power and uses infrared light or radio waves to communicate with a receiver.

7 How Does Voice Recognition Work?

Voice input is the process of entering data by speaking into a computer-attached microphone and is part of a larger category of input called audio input. **Audio input** is the process of entering any sound into the computer such as speech, music, and sound effects. To input voice requires **voice recognition** or **speech recognition** software. The program may be **speaker-dependent** (the computer makes a profile of your voice) or **speaker-independent** (contains a built-in set of word patterns). Some programs require **discrete speech**, which means you have to speak slowly, whereas others support **continuous speech**, allowing you to talk in a normal conversational tone.

8 How Is Data Input into a Handheld Computer?

Handheld computers are popular for both home and business users. Using the stylus, the primary input method, you can enter data through an onscreen keyboard or use handwriting recognition software. Other input methods include attaching a full-sized keyboard, using voice input, or attaching a digital camera to the handheld computer.

9 What Are the Uses of a Digital Camera?

You use a **digital camera** to take pictures and digitally store the photographed images. The three basic types are **studio camera**, **field camera**, and **point-and-shoot camera**. You can **download**, or transfer, the photographed images to a computer by a connecting cable; or they can be stored and copied on a computer. Once on a computer, pictures can be edited with photo-editing software, printed, faxed, sent via electronic mail, included in another document, or posted on a Web site.

10 What Are Various Techniques Used for Video Input?

Video input or **video capture** is the process of entering a full-motion recording into a computer and storing the video on a hard disk or some other medium. To capture video, a video camera is plugged into a **video capture card**, which is an expansion card that converts the analog video signal into a digital signal. A **digital video (DV) camera** is a video camera that records video as digital signals, instead of analog signals. A **video digitizer** can be used to capture an individual frame from a video and save the still picture in a file.

11 What Are Uses of PC Video Cameras and Web Cams?

A **PC video camera**, or **PC camera**, is a DV camera that allows the home user to record, edit, and capture video and still images and to make video telephone calls on the Internet. You can use the PC camera for security by setting it to take digital photographs at preset times. To attract visitors to your Web site, use your video camera to display a **Web cam** image on your Web page.

12 How Do Scanners and Other Reading Devices Work?

A **scanner** is a light-sensing input device that reads printed text and graphics and then translates the results into a form the computer can use. An **optical reader** uses a light source to read characters, marks, and codes and converts them into digital data that can be processed by a computer. Three types of optical readers are **optical character recognition (OCR)**, **optical mark recognition (OMR)**, **bar code scanners**, and **magnetic-ink character recognition (MICR) reader**.

13 What Are Some Alternative Input Devices for Physically Challenged Users?

Speech recognition, or the computer's capability of distinguishing spoken words, is ideal for blind or visually impaired computer users. A **keyguard**, which is placed over the keyboard, allows people with limited hand mobility to rest their hands on the keyboard and guides a finger or pointing device so a user presses only one key at a time. Keyboards with larger keys and screen-displayed keyboards on which keys are pressed using a pointing device also can help. Pointing devices such as small trackballs that can be controlled with a thumb or one finger and **head-mounted pointers** also are available for users with motor disabilities.

Key Terms

Web Instructions: To display this page from the Web, start your browser and enter the URL scsite.com/dc2002/ch5/terms.htm. Scroll through the list of terms. Click a term to display its definition and a picture. Click the To WEB button for current and additional information about the term from the Web. To see animations, Shockwave and Flash Player must be installed on your computer (download by clicking here).

Americans with Disabilities Act (ADA) (5.31)
arrow keys (5.4)
audio input (5.16)
bar code (5.28)
bar code scanner (5.28)
cam (5.23)
command (5.3)
continuous speech (5.15)
cordless keyboard (5.5)
cordless mouse (5.8)
cursor (5.13)
data (5.3)
digital camera (5.18)
digital video (DV) camera (5.21)
digital watermark (5.22)
digitizer (5.13)
digitizing tablet (5.13)
discrete speech (5.15)
dots per inch (dpi) (5.20)
download (5.18)
electronic signatures (5.13)
enhanced keyboard (5.5)
enhanced resolution (5.20)
ergonomic keyboard (5.6)
ergonomics (5.6)
e-signatures (5.13)
field camera (5.19)
flatbed scanner (5.25)
function keys (5.4)
gesture recognition (5.32)
graphical user interface (GUI) (5.3)
graphics tablet (5.13)
handwriting recognition software (5.14)
head-mounted pointer (5.32)
image processing (5.26)
image processing system (5.26)
imaging (5.26)
information (5.3)
input (5.2)
input device (5.4)
insertion point (5.4)
instructions (5.3)
interpolated resolution (5.20)
joystick (5.11)
keyboard (5.4)
keyguard (5.31)
light pen (5.12)
magnetic-ink character recognition (MICR) reader (5.30)
mechanical mouse (5.7)
menu-driven (5.3)
mouse (5.7)
mouse pad (5.7)
mouse pointer (5.7)
numeric keypad (5.4)
OCR devices (5.27)
OCR software (5.26)
on-screen keyboard (5.32)
optical character recognition (OCR) (5.27)
optical mark recognition (OMR) (5.28)
optical mouse (5.7)

SCANNER
Light-sensing input device that reads printed text and graphics, then translates the results into a form the computer can use; similar to a copy machine except it creates a file of the document instead of a paper copy. Also called an optical scanner. (5.25)

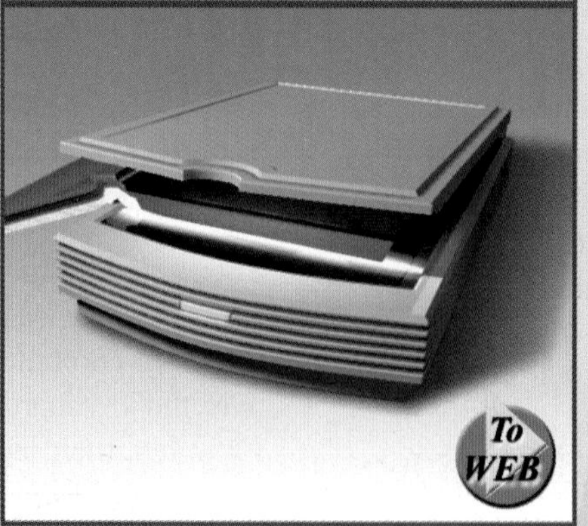

optical reader (5.27)
optical resolution (5.20)
optical scanner (5.25)
PC camera (5.22)
PC video camera (5.22)
pen (5.13)
pixel (5.20)
point-and-shoot camera (5.19)
pointer (5.7)
pointing device (5.7)
pointing stick (5.11)
portable keyboard (5.6)
program (5.3)
QWERTY keyboard (5.5)
resolution (5.20)
scanner (5.25)
source document (5.24)
speaker-dependent software (5.14)
speaker-independent software (5.15)
speech recognition (5.14)
streaming cam (5.23)
studio camera (5.19)
stylus (5.13)
toggle key (5.4)
touch screen (5.12)
touchpad (5.10)
trackball (5.10)
trackpad (5.10)
turnaround document (5.27)
user response (5.3)
video capture (5.21)
video capture card (5.21)
video compression (5.21)
video decoder (5.21)
video digitizer (5.21)
video input (5.21)
video telephone call (5.22)
videoconference (5.24)
voice input (5.14)
voice recognition (5.14)
WAV (5.16)
waveforms (5.16)
Web bar code (5.30)
Web cam (5.23)
wheel (5.11)
whiteboard (5.24)
wireless mouse (5.8)

Learn It Online

Web Instructions: To display this page from the Web, start your browser and enter the URL scsite.com/dc2002/ch5/learn.htm.

1. Web Guide

Click Web Guide to display the Guide to World Wide Web Sites and Searching Techniques Web page. Click Reference and then click About.com. Search for data dictionary. In the Find It Now text box, type digital camera. Scroll through the results and then click a link of your choice. Use your word processing program to prepare a brief report on your findings and submit your assignment to your instructor.

2. Scavenger Hunt

Click Scavenger Hunt. Print a copy of the Scavenger Hunt page; use this page to write down your answers as you search the Web. Submit your completed page to your instructor.

3. Who Wants to Be a Computer Genius?

Click Computer Genius to find out if you are a computer genius. Directions on how to play the game will display. When you are ready to play, click the PLAY button. Submit your score to your instructor.

4. Wheel of Terms

Click Wheel of Terms to reinforce important terms you learned in this chapter by playing the Shelly Cashman Series version of this popular game. Directions on how to play the game will display. When you are ready to play, click the PLAY button. Submit your score to your instructor.

5. Career Corner

Click Career Corner to display the Career Magazine page. Review this page. Click the links that you find interesting. Write a brief report on the topics you found to be the most interesting. Submit the report to your instructor.

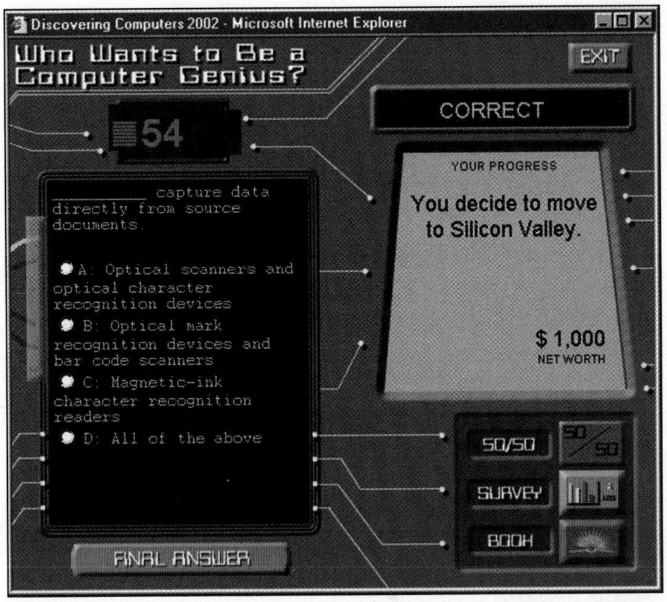

6. Search Sleuth

Click Search Sleuth to learn search techniques that will help make you a research expert. Submit the completed assignment to your instructor.

7. Crossword Puzzle Challenge

Click Crossword Puzzle Challenge. Complete the puzzle to reinforce skills you learned in this chapter. Directions on how to play the game will display. When you are ready to play, click the PLAY button. Submit the completed puzzle to your instructor.

8. Practice Test

Click Practice Test. Answer each question. When completed, click the Grade Test button to submit the quiz for grading. Make a note of any missed questions. If required, print a copy to submit to your instructor.

Web Instructions: To display this page from the Web, start your browser and enter the URL scsite.com/dc2002/ch5/check.htm. Click the links for current and additional information. To experience the animation and interactivity, Shockwave and Flash Player must be installed on your computer (download by clicking here.)

LABEL THE FIGURE

Instructions: Identify these areas and keys on a typical desktop computer keyboard.

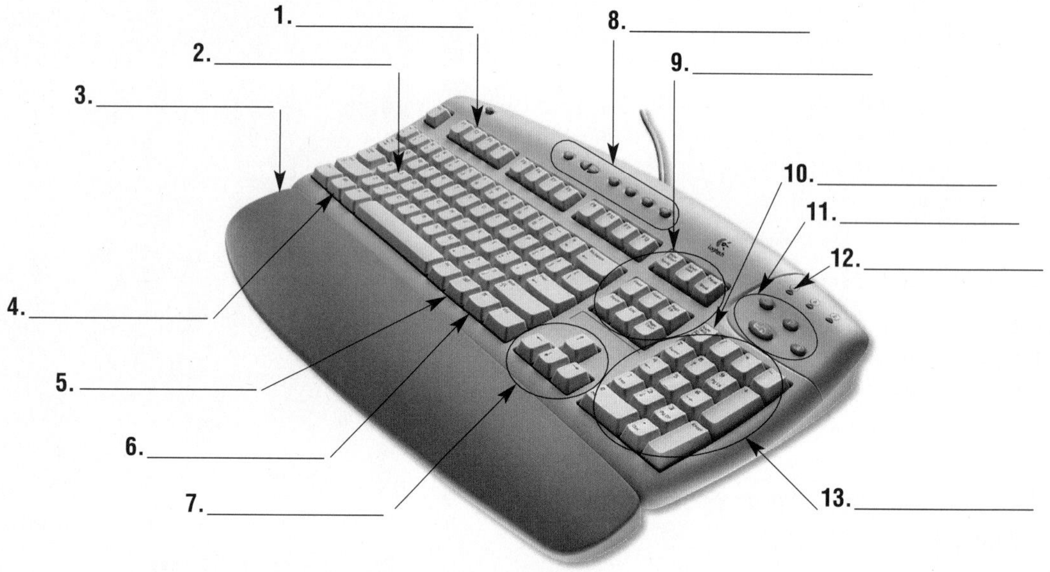

MATCHING

Instructions: Match each term from the column on the left with the best description from the column on the right.

_______1. Trackball
_______2. Pointing stick
_______3. Joystick
_______4. Mouse
_______5. Touchpad

a. The most widely used pointing device on desktop computers.
b. A stationary pointing device with a ball on its top.
c. A vertical lever mounted on a base.
d. A steering-wheel type input device.
e. A handheld input device that contains a light source.
f. A small, flat, rectangular pointing device that is sensitive to pressure and motion.
g. A pressure-sensitive pointing device shaped like a pencil eraser that is positioned between keys on the keyboard.

Checkpoint

MULTIPLE CHOICE

Instructions: Select the letter of the correct answer for each of the following questions.

1. A(n) __________ is a device that looks similar to a mouse, except it has a window with cross hairs, so the user can see through to the tablet.
   a. optical scanner
   b. cursor
   c. stylus
   d. trackball
2. __________ is speaking slowly and pausing between each word when using voice recognition software.
   a. Discrete speech
   b. Continuous speech
   c. Speaker-independent
   d. Speaker-dependent
3. An architect may use an electronic pen and a ______________ to create drawings.
   a. graphics tablet
   c. touchpad
   b. touch screen
   d. trackball
4. The most expensive type of digital camera is a __________ .
   a. field
   b. point-and-shoot
   c. studio
   d. Web cam
5. A light-sensing input device that reads printed text and graphics and then translates the results into a form the computer can use is called a __________ .
   a. camera
   b. microphone
   c. handheld computer
   d. scanner

SHORT ANSWER

Instructions: Write a brief answer to each of the following questions.

1. Why is resolution important when using a scanner? __________ How is resolution typically measured and stated? __________
2. How is optical character recognition different from optical mark recognition? __________ What is MICR? __________
3. What is a bar code? __________ How are bar codes read? __________ On what products are they used? __________ What is the difference between a bar code and a Web bar code? __________
4. How is speaker-dependent software different from speaker-independent software? __________ How is discrete speech recognition different from continuous speech recognition? __________
5. What is videoconferencing? __________ How does a whiteboard enhance videoconferencing? __________ What hardware is required for a videoconference? __________

WORKING TOGETHER

Instructions: Working with a group of your classmates, complete the following team exercise.

The Occupational and Safety Health Association (OSHA) defines ergonomics as the science of fitting the job to the worker. Investigate the difference between carpal tunnel syndrome and repetitive strain injury. Prepare a report and a PowerPoint presentation to share with the class. Include suggestions on proper workstation ergonomics.

Web Instructions: To display this page from the Web, start your browser and enter the URL scsite.com/dc2002/ch5/lab.htm. Click the links or current and additional information.

About Your Computer

1 This exercise uses Window 95 or Windows 98 procedures. Your computer probably has more than one input device. To learn about the input devices on your computer, right-click the My Computer icon on the desktop. Click Properties on the shortcut menu. When the System Properties dialog box displays, click the Device Manager tab. Click View devices by type. Below Computer, a list of hardware device categories displays. What input devices appear in the list? Click the plus sign next to each category. What specific input devices in each category are connected to your computer? Click the Cancel button in the System Properties dialog box.

Customizing the Keyboard

2 The Windows operating system provides several ways to customize the keyboard for people with physical limitations. Some of these options are StickyKeys, FilterKeys, and ToggleKeys. To discover more about each option, click the Start button on the taskbar, point to Settings on the Start menu, and then click Control Panel on the Settings submenu. Double-click the Accessibility Options icon in the Control Panel window. Click the Keyboard tab in the Accessibility Properties dialog box. Click the Question Mark button in the title bar, click StickyKeys, read the information on the pop-up window, and then click the pop-up window to close it. Repeat this process for FilterKeys and ToggleKeys. What is the purpose of each option? How might each option benefit someone with a physical disability? Click the Cancel button in the Accessibility Properties dialog box and then click the Close button in the Control Panel window.

Using the Mouse and Keyboard to Interact with an Online Program

3 See your instructor for the location of the Loan Payment Calculator program. Click the Start button on the taskbar, and then click Run on the Start menu to display the Run dialog box. In the Run text box, type the path and file name of the program. For example, type `a:loancalc.exe` and then press the ENTER key to display the Loan Payment Calculator window. Type `12500` in the LOAN AMOUNT text box. Click the YEARS right scroll arrow or drag the scroll box until YEARS equals 15. Click the APR right scroll arrow or drag the scroll box until APR equals 8.5. Click the Calculate button. Write down the monthly payment and sum of payments. Click the Clear button. What are the monthly payment and sum of payments for each of these loan amounts, years, and APRs: (1) 28000, 5, 7.25; (2) 98750, 30, 9; (3) 6000, 3, 8.75; (4) 62500, 15, 9.25. Close the Loan Payment Calculator.

MouseKeys

4 A graphical user interface allows you to perform many tasks with just the point and click of a mouse. Yet, what if you do not have, or cannot use, a mouse? The Windows operating system is prepared to accommodate this possibility with an option called MouseKeys. When the MouseKeys option is turned on, you can use numeric keypad keys to move the mouse pointer, click, right-click, double-click, and drag. To find out how, click the Start button on the taskbar and then click Help on the Start menu. Click the Index tab in the Help window. Type `MouseKeys` in the text box and then click the Display button. To answer each of the following questions, click an appropriate topic in the Topics Found dialog box, click the Display button, and read the Help information. To display a different topic, click the topic and then click the Display button.

- How do you turn on MouseKeys?
- How do you use MouseKeys to move the mouse pointer?
- How do you perform each of these operations using MouseKeys: click, right-click, double-click, drag?

Click the Close button to close the Help window.

Web Work

Web Instructions: To display this page from the Web, start your browser and enter the URL scsite.com/dc2002/ch5/web.htm. To view At The Movies in exercise 1, RealPlayer must be installed on your computer (download by clicking here). To use the Shelly Cashman Series Scanning Documents Lab from the Web, Shockwave and Flash Player must be installed on your computer (download by clicking here).

Web Cam Virtual World

To view the Web Cam Virtual World movie, click the button to the left or click the Play button to the right. Watch the movie, and then complete the exercise by answering the questions below. The Internet is where the curious meet the pretentious. With the availability of mobile cameras, Web cams, and PC video cameras, images reach millions of people. From around the globe, you can watch gorillas from Namibia, the miracle of birth at a hospital, or a toddler's birthday party next door. Some of this Web cam virtual world is informative, some serves a useful purpose, some of it is just entertainment, and some of it is intrusive. A more open society sounds like a good thing, but what about the privacy issues? Are there limits to what should be on the Web, or only limits to who should have access? Is access to this virtual world too easy or distracting? Will it help or hinder efforts to solve the problems of the real world?

Shelly Cashman Series Scanning Documents Lab

Follow the appropriate instructions in Web Work 2 on page 1.47 to start and use the Shelly Cashman Series Scanning Documents Lab. If you are running from the Web, enter the URL, www.scsite.com/sclabs/menu.htm; or display the Web Work page (see instructions at the top of this page) and then click the button to the left.

Sending E-Mail

E-mail allows you to send messages anywhere in the world. Use the e-mail account you set up in Web Work 4 in Chapter 3 to send a message. Click the button to the left to display your e-mail service. Log in to your e-mail service and then follow the instructions for composing a message. The subject of the message should be input devices. Type the e-mail address of one of your classmates. In the message itself, type something your classmate should know about input devices, and then send the message. Next, follow the instructions to read and reply to any messages you have received. When you are finished, quit your e-mail service.

In the News

Input devices can enhance user productivity and increase the number of potential users. The U.S. Army recently discovered this by replacing the many buttons used to operate a tank's onboard computer with a joystick and just three buttons. To the Army's delight, tank-driver performance has improved, and even individuals who scored poorly on Army intelligence tests handled the tanks effectively. Click the button to the left and read a news article about a new or improved input device, an input device being used in a new way, or an input device being made more available. What is the device? Who is promoting it? How will it be used? Will the input device change the

CHAPTER 6

Output

One day a week during a break between classes, you go home to make a nutritious lunch. You enjoy preparing meals now because your refrigerator's screen displays a digital cookbook with recipes suitable for the food currently stored in it.

The telephone rings as you sit down to eat. After taking the call, you turn to the refrigerator's door and press a button on its screen to record a video message: "John, the dealership called. Your car is ready. The number is 555-1029." When John returns home, he will retrieve the message you recorded.

With a few minutes to relax, you press a button on the refrigerator's screen to view your own video messages. John's face appears on the screen. He says, "Samantha called. She needs help with algebra." When the message ends, you press another button to watch the daily news directly on the refrigerator's screen.

Before heading back, you check your e-mail messages with the touch of a button; compose a message to Samantha pressing on-screen keyboard keys; and then reach for a soda.

This not-so-ordinary refrigerator has become communications central at your house. Now, if only your car could drive itself to school, you could study on the way!

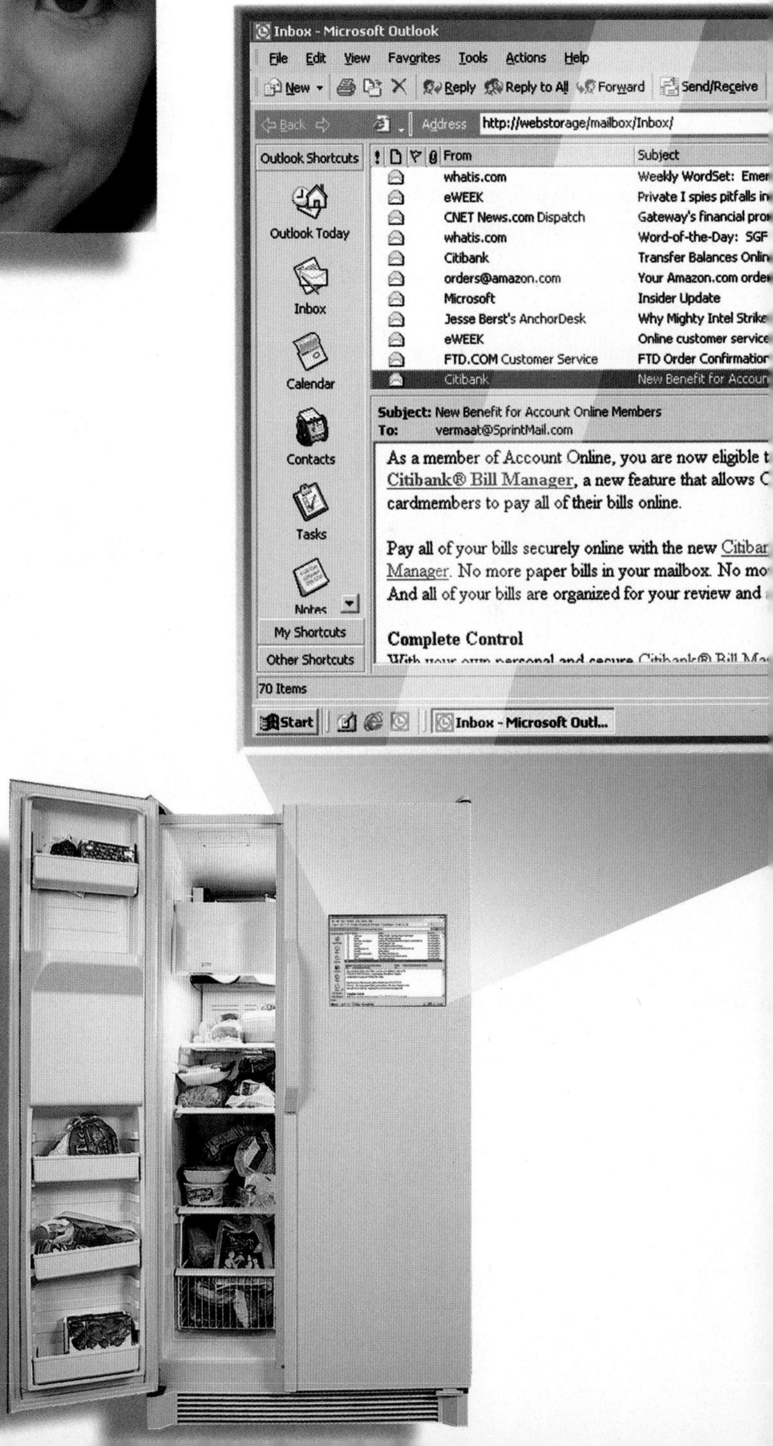

OBJECTIVES

After completing this chapter, you will be able to:

- Define the four categories of output
- Identify the different types of display devices
- Describe factors that affect the quality of a monitor
- Identify monitor ergonomic issues
- Explain the differences among various types of printers
- Describe the uses of speakers and headsets
- Identify the purpose of data projectors, fax machines, and multifunction devices
- Explain how a terminal is both an input and output device
- Identify output options for physically challenged users

WHAT IS OUTPUT?

Output is data that has been processed into a useful form, called information. That is, computers process input into output. A computer generates several types of output, depending on the hardware and software being used and the requirements of the user.

You view, print, or hear output. Looking at a monitor on your desktop, you see information on the screen. Notebook computers, handheld computers, cellular telephones, and many other similar devices also have screens that allow mobile users to view information such as documents, Web sites, and e-mail messages while away from a desk. Some printers produce black-and-white documents. Others produce brilliant colors, so you can print color documents, photographs, and transparencies. Through the computer's speakers or a headset, you can hear sounds, music, and voice.

While using a computer, you will encounter four basic categories of output: text, graphics, audio, and video (Figure 6-1). Very often, documents and Web sites include more than one of these types of output.

- **Text** consists of characters that create words, sentences, and paragraphs. Examples of text-based documents are memorandums, letters, announcements, press releases, advertisements, newsletters, envelopes, and mailing labels.

  By accessing the Web, you can view and print many other types of text-based documents. These include newspapers, magazines, books, play or television show transcripts, stock quotes, famous speeches, and historical lectures.

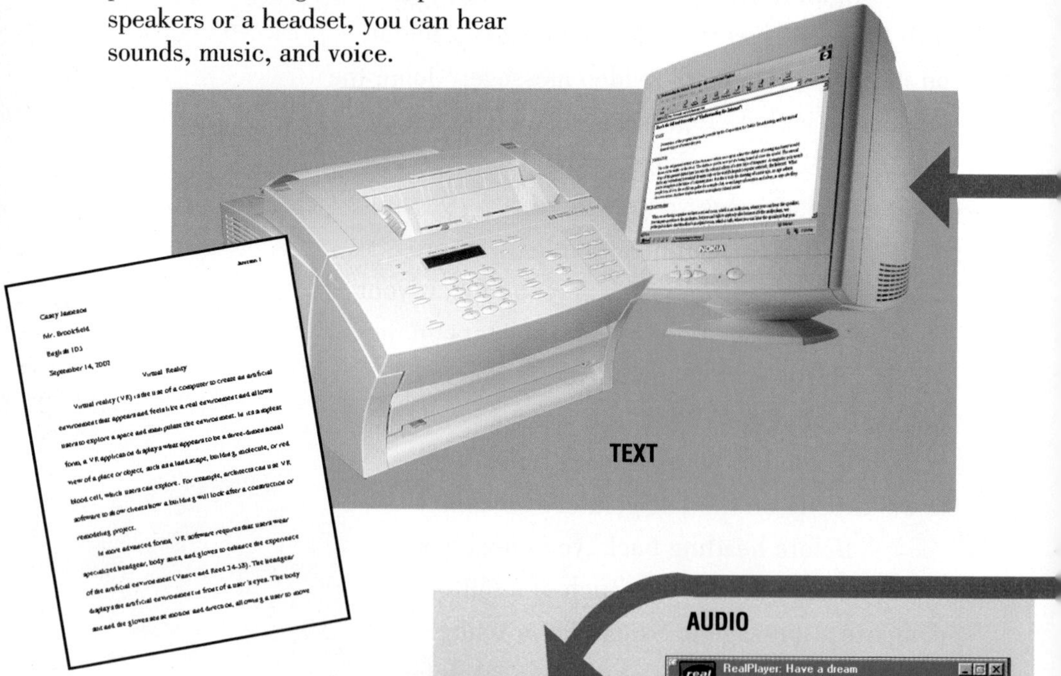

- A **graphic**, or **graphical image**, is a digital representation of non-text information such as a drawing, chart, and photograph. Many text-based documents include graphical images to enhance their visual appeal and convey information. Business letters have logos. Reports include charts. Newsletters use drawings, clip art, and photographs. You even can print high-quality photographs right from your digital camera, eliminating the need for film or film developers.

  Many Web sites use animated graphics, giving images the appearance of motion. Some sites have simple animations such as blinking icons and scrolling messages. Others use sophisticated animations such as a simulation that shows how an avalanche starts.

- **Audio** is music, speech, or any other sound. You can put your favorite music CD in the CD-ROM or DVD-ROM drive and listen to the music while working on the computer. Many software programs such as games, encyclopedias, and simulations have musical accompaniments for entertainment and audio clips, such as narrations and speeches, to enhance understanding. For example, you can listen to Martin Luther King recite his "I Have a Dream" speech.

  On the Web, you can tune into radio and television stations and listen to audio clips or live broadcasts of interviews, talk shows, sporting events, news, music, and concerts. You also can have a conversation with a friend, co-worker, or family member over the Web, just as if you were on the telephone.

- **Video** consists of full-motion images that are played back at various speeds. Most video also has accompanying audio. By attaching your video camera to the computer, you can watch home movies on the computer. You also can attach your television's antenna or cable to your computer and watch your favorite television programs right on the computer.

  As with audio, many software programs and Web sites include video clips to enhance your understanding. See doctors perform a life-saving surgery, watch a prerecorded news report, observe a hurricane in action, or enjoy a live performance of your favorite jazz band — right on your computer!

Figure 6-1 Four common types of output are text, graphics, audio, and video.

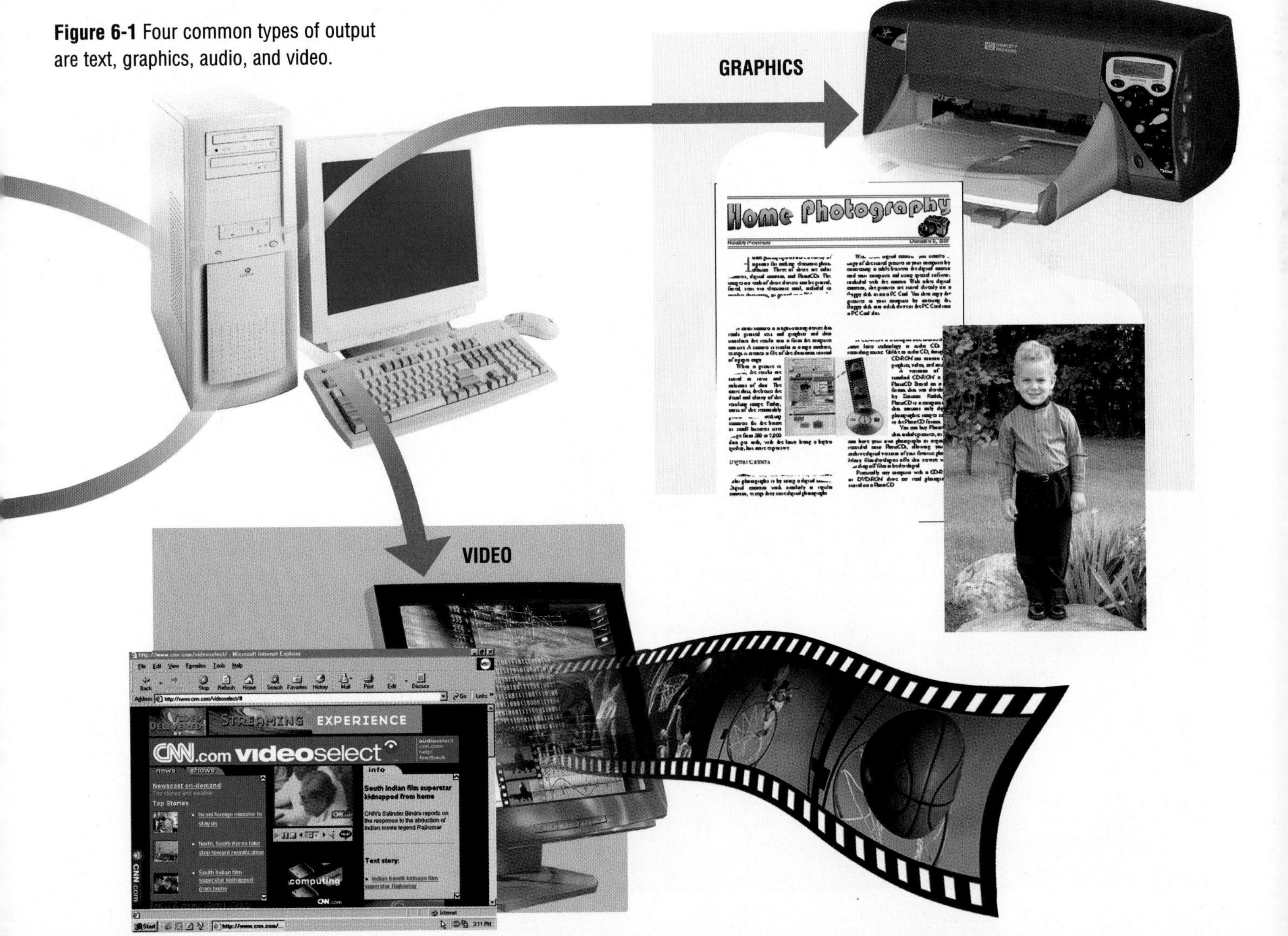

WHAT ARE OUTPUT DEVICES?

An **output device** is any hardware component that can convey information to a user. Commonly used output devices include display devices, printers, speakers, headsets, data projectors, facsimile machines, and multifunction devices. The following pages discuss each of these output devices.

DISPLAY DEVICES

A **display device**, or simply **display**, is an output device that visually conveys text, graphics, and video information. Information on a display device, sometimes called **soft copy**, exists electronically and displays for a temporary period of time.

The display device consists of the **screen**, or projection surface, and the components that produce the information on the screen. Many computers use a monitor as their display device. A **monitor** is a separate plastic or metal case that houses the screen. Most mobile computers, however, integrate the display and other components into the same physical case. For example, the display on a notebook computer attaches with a hinge, and the display on a handheld computer is part of the computer case.

Most display devices project text, graphics, and video information in color (Figure 6-2). Some, however, are monochrome. **Monochrome** means the information displays in one color (such as white, amber, green, black, blue, or gray) on a different color background, possibly black or grayish-white. Some handheld computers and devices use monochrome displays to save on battery power. To enhance the quality of their graphics, monochrome displays often use gray scaling. **Gray scaling** involves using many shades of gray from white to black, which provides better contrast on the images.

Figure 6-2 Most desktop monitors display information in color.

Web Link

For more information on monitors, visit the Discovering Computers 2002 Chapter 6 WEB LINK page (**scsite.com/dc2002/ch6/weblink.htm**) and click Monitors.

ISSUE

The Paper Chase

Use a Display Device instead of a Printer

In 1975, George Pake, the head of Xerox Corporation's Research Center in Palo Alto, California, predicted the use of printed paper would decline dramatically as offices turned to electronic files accessed at the touch of a button. Futurist Alvin Toffler wrote in 1970 that making paper copies of anything is a primitive use of machines and violates their very spirit. Instead of these predictions coming true, the opposite happened. Paper use has risen more than 40 percent during the past 30 years. Statistics indicate a major portion of this increase is tied directly to e-mail. Additionally, every office has computer printers, copy machines, and facsimile machines that reproduce documents at an ever-increasing rate. Can and should people and organizations try to reduce paper use? Why or why not? If society cannot create a paperless office, what can be done to promote a less-paper office?

For more information on the paperless office, visit the Discovering Computers 2002 Issues Web page (**scsite.com/dc2002/issues.htm**) and click Chapter 6 Issue #1.

Display devices include CRT monitors, LCD monitors and displays, gas plasma monitors, and televisions. The following sections describe each of these display devices.

CRT Monitors

A **CRT monitor** is a monitor that is similar to a standard television set because it contains a cathode ray tube (Figure 6-3). A **cathode ray tube (CRT)** is a large, sealed, glass tube. The front of the tube is the screen. Tiny dots of phosphor material coat the screen on a CRT. Each dot consists of a red, a green, and a blue phosphor. The three dots combine to make up each pixel. Recall from Chapter 5 that a **pixel** (short for *pic*ture *el*ement) is a single point in an electronic image. Inside the CRT, an electron beam moves back and forth across the back of the screen. This causes the dots on the front of the screen to glow, which produces an image on the screen.

CRT monitors for desktop computers are available in various sizes, with the more common being 15, 17, 19, 21, and 22 inches. You measure a monitor diagonally, from one corner of the casing to the other. In addition to monitor size, advertisements also list a monitor's viewable size. The **viewable size** is the diagonal measurement of the actual viewing area provided by the monitor. A 21-inch monitor, for example, may have a viewable size of only 19.8 inches.

Determining what size monitor to use depends on your intended use. A large monitor allows you to view more information on the screen at once, but usually is more expensive. If you work on the Web or use multiple applications at one time, you may want to invest in a 19-inch monitor. If you use your computer for intense graphing applications, such as desktop publishing and engineering, you may want an even larger monitor.

In the past, CRT monitor screens were curved slightly. Current models have flat screens. A flat screen reduces glare, reflection, and distortion of images. With a flat screen, you will not have as much eyestrain and fatigue. Thus, a flat screen is an ergonomic screen. Recall from Chapter 5 that the goal of ergonomics is to incorporate comfort, efficiency, and safety into the design of items in the workplace.

LCD Monitors and Displays

LCD monitors and **LCD displays** use liquid crystal, instead of a cathode ray tube, to present information on the screen. A **liquid crystal display (LCD)** has liquid crystals between two sheets of material. When an electric current passes through the crystals, they twist. This causes some light waves to be blocked and allows others to pass through, which creates the images on the screen.

LCD monitors and LCD displays are a type of flat-panel display. A **flat-panel display** has a lightweight, compact screen that consumes less than one-third of the power than does a CRT monitor. This feature makes the LCD monitors and displays ideal for mobile users or users with space limitations.

Like CRT monitors, LCD monitors are available in a variety of sizes, with the more common being 15, 17, 18, and 20 inches. LCD monitors have a much smaller footprint than do traditional CRT monitors; that is, they take up much less desk space (Figure 6-4). You even can mount some LCD monitors on the wall for increased space savings. LCD monitors typically are more expensive than CRT monitors.

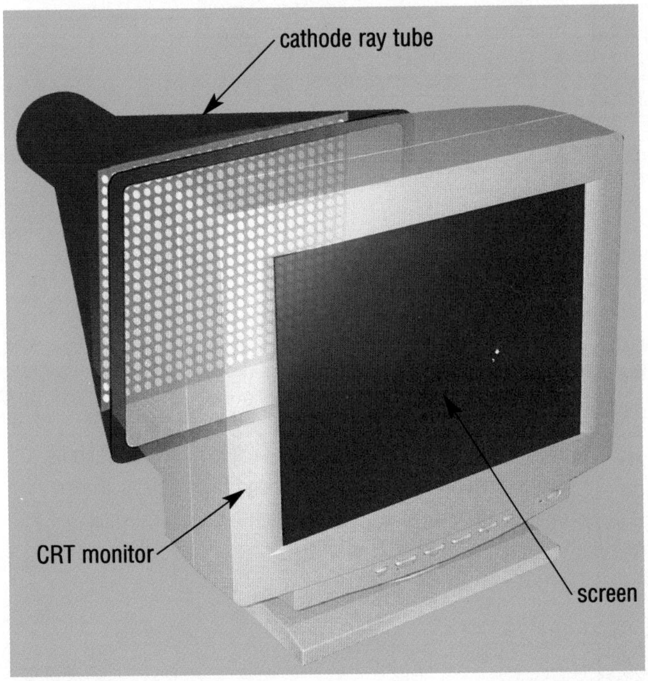

Figure 6-3 The core of many desktop monitors is a cathode ray tube.

Figure 6-4 An LCD monitor is much thinner and lighter than a CRT monitor.

Many current LCD monitors have built-in television tuners. These monitors allow you to watch television programs without having to install a TV tuner card in the system unit. Simply plug your television antenna or cable into the port on the monitor.

Notebook and handheld computers often use LCD displays. The display device is built into these mobile computers (Figure 6-5). The LCD displays for notebook computers are available in a variety of sizes, with the more common being 14.1, 15.0, and 15.4 inches.

Many Web-enabled devices such as cellular telephones and pagers also use LCD displays (Figure 6-6).

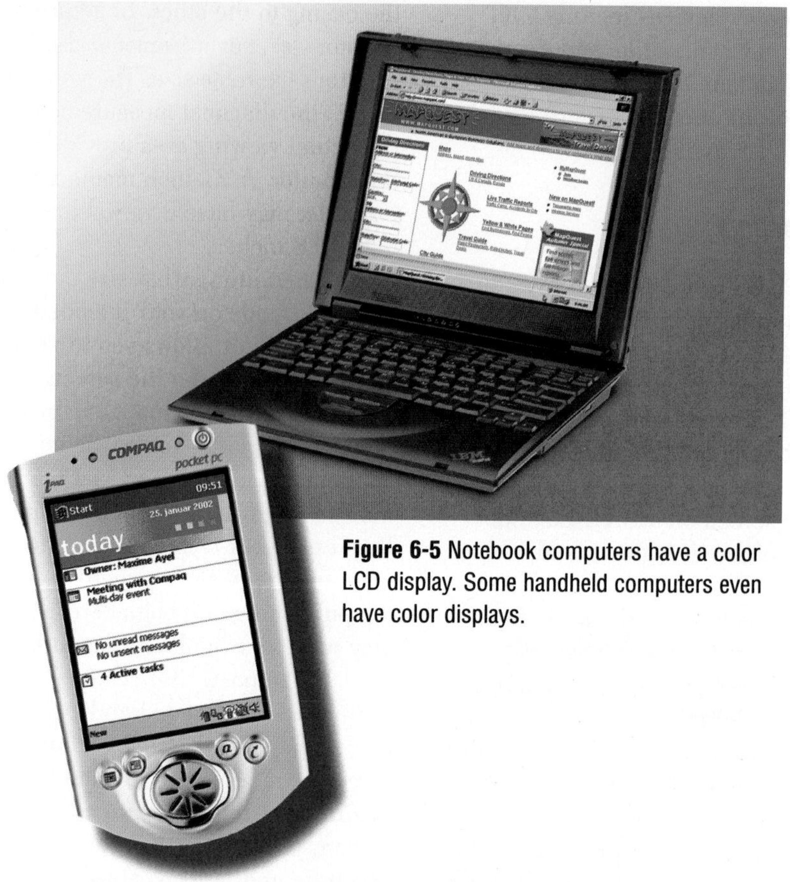

Figure 6-5 Notebook computers have a color LCD display. Some handheld computers even have color displays.

Web Link

For more information on Web-enabled devices, visit the Discovering Computers 2002 Chapter 6 WEB LINK page (**scsite.com/dc2002/ch6/weblink.htm**) and click Web-enabled Devices.

Figure 6-6 Most handheld Web-enabled devices such as cellular telephones and pagers use LCD displays. These devices provide access to the Internet and/or e-mail.

COMPANY ON THE CUTTING EDGE

MOTOROLA

Wireless Products for Web Access

The next time you listen to your favorite radio station in your car, give thanks to Paul and Joseph Galvin for making it possible. These two brothers developed the first practical and affordable car radio and created the Galvin Manufacturing Corporation in Chicago in 1928.

Paul Galvin named the company's products Motorola, combining the ideas of motion and radio. This trademark became so familiar that the company officially changed its name in 1947. Although the corporation branched out into other products, such as two-way radios for the military and for police departments, televisions, and microprocessor chips, its development of early communications devices made them the formidable leader they are today in wireless communications.

Today, Motorola's wireless telephones and word pagers allow you to receive Internet content, send e-mail, and connect to personal and company databases. Mya, the cyber-generated personal assistant, even will read you your e-mail, appointments, and weather and traffic reports.

For more information on Motorola, visit the Discovering Computers 2002 Companies Web page (**scsite.com/dc2002/companies.htm**) and click Motorola.

A Web-enabled device is a device that provides access to the Web and/or e-mail. Many Web-enabled handheld computers and devices use monochrome displays to save battery power. Some handheld computers, however, do have a color display.

Another popular handheld Web-enabled device that uses an LCD screen is an electronic book. An **electronic book (e-book)** is a small, book-sized computer that allows users to read, save, highlight, bookmark, and add notes to online text (Figure 6-7). You download new book content to your e-book from the Web.

To improve the quality of reading material on LCD screens, such as an e-book, Microsoft has developed a new technology called ClearType. The goal of **ClearType** is to make onscreen reading as natural as reading from printed material.

ISSUE

Read any Good E-Books Lately?

Electronic Books

Imagine a library on your lap. Read your favorite Stephen King novel, delete it, and download the complete works of Hemingway. The electronic book (e-book) has arrived. Analysts predict electronic books will revolutionize the publishing industry. An electronic book is primarily a digital storage and display unit. This small, handheld device plugs into a cradle that attaches to your computer, letting you download textbooks or novels from Web-based publishers. Some of these include a built-in modem that allows you to connect directly to the Internet. They range in size and weight from a paperback to a two-pound textbook and can hold thousands of pages or the equivalent to 10 or more books. Keeping with some traits of traditional books, you can move forward or backward one page at a time, or use a stylus to write notes in the margin. What is your opinion of the electronic book? Will it replace the printed book? Why not just buy the book? Is there a place in society for the electronic book? Who will use electronic books and how will they use them?

For more information on electronic books, visit the Discovering Computers 2002 Issues Web page (**scsite.com/dc2002/issues.htm**) and click Chapter 6 Issue #2.

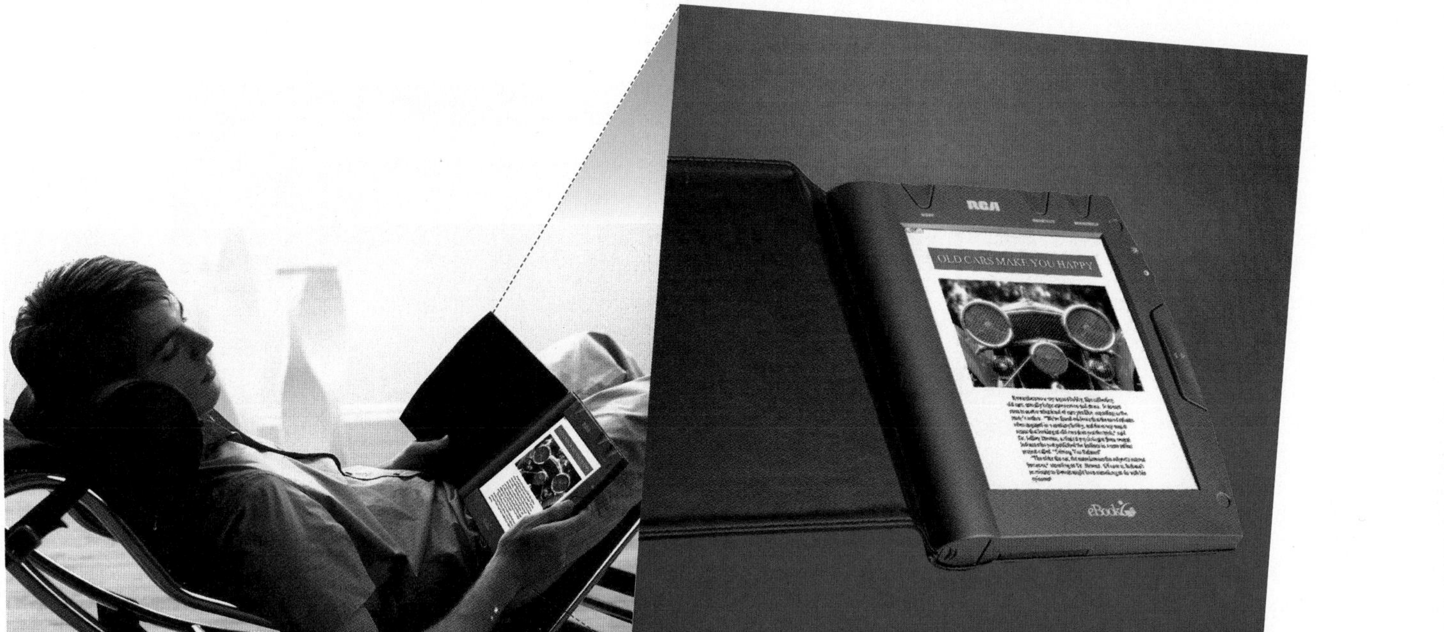

Figure 6-7 E-books typically use an LCD display. You can read books, magazines, newspapers, Web pages, or any other printed material on an e-book, which is about the size of a paperback book.

LCD monitors and displays produce color using either passive matrix or active matrix technology. An **active-matrix display**, also known as a **thin-film transistor (TFT) display**, uses a separate transistor for each color pixel and thus can display high-quality color that is viewable from all angles. Active-matrix displays require more power than passive-matrix displays because they use many transistors.

A **passive-matrix display**, now often called a **dual-scan display**, uses fewer transistors and requires less power than an active-matrix display. The color on a passive-matrix display often is not as bright as an active-matrix display. You can view images on a passive-matrix display best when working directly in front of the display. The latest passive-matrix displays use **high-performance addressing (HPA)**, which provide image quality near that of TFT displays. Passive-matrix displays are less expensive than active-matrix displays.

Gas Plasma Monitors

For even larger displays, some large business or power users prefer gas plasma monitors, which can measure more than 42 inches wide (Figure 6-8). Many of these monitors also can hang directly on a wall.

A **gas plasma monitor** is a flat-panel display that uses gas plasma technology, which substitutes a layer of gas for the liquid crystal material in an LCD monitor. When voltage is applied, the gas releases ultraviolet (UV) light. This UV light causes the pixels on the screen to glow and form an image. Gas plasma monitors offer larger screen sizes and higher display quality than LCD monitors but are much more expensive.

Quality of Display Devices

The quality of a monitor or display depends largely on its resolution, dot pitch, and refresh rate. As described in Chapter 5, **resolution** describes the sharpness and clearness of an image. Manufacturers state the resolution of a display device as dots, or pixels. The greater the number of pixels the display uses, the better the quality of the image. For example, an 800 x 600 monitor can display up to 800 horizontal pixels and 600 vertical pixels, for a total of 480,000 pixels to create a screen image. Most monitors today can display up to 1280 x 1024 pixels, with 800 x 600 typically the standard. High-end monitors can display up to 2048 x 1536 pixels.

Figure 6-8 Large gas plasma monitors can measure more than 42 inches wide.

Displays with higher resolutions use a greater number of pixels, providing a smoother image. As the resolution increases, however, the images on the screen appear smaller (Figure 6-9). For this reason, you would not use a high resolution on a small display, such as a 15-inch monitor, because the small characters would be difficult to read. The display resolution you choose is a matter of preference. Larger monitors typically use a higher resolution, and smaller monitors use a lower resolution. For example, a 21-inch monitor may use a 1600 x 1200 resolution, and a 17-inch monitor may use a resolution of 800 x 600. A higher resolution also is desirable for graphics applications. A lower resolution usually is satisfactory for business applications such as word processing.

Dot pitch is another factor which you can use to measure image clarity. **Dot pitch**, sometimes called **pixel pitch**, is the distance between each pixel on a display. The smaller the distance between the pixels, the sharper the image. Text created with a smaller dot pitch is easier to read. To minimize eye fatigue, you should use a monitor with a dot pitch of .29 millimeters or lower.

Refresh rate is yet another factor in a monitor's quality. **Refresh rate**, also called **vertical frequency** or **vertical scan rate**, is the speed that a monitor redraws images on the screen. Ideally, a monitor's refresh rate should be fast enough to maintain a constant, flicker-free image. A slower refresh rate causes the image to fade and then flicker as it is redrawn. This flicker can lead to eye fatigue and cause headaches for users. Refresh rate is measured according to **hertz**, which is the number of times per second the screen is redrawn. Although most people can tolerate a refresh rate of 60 hertz, a high-quality monitor will provide a refresh rate of at least 75 hertz. This means the image on the screen redraws itself 75 times in a second.

Figure 6-9a (screen resolution at 800 x 600)

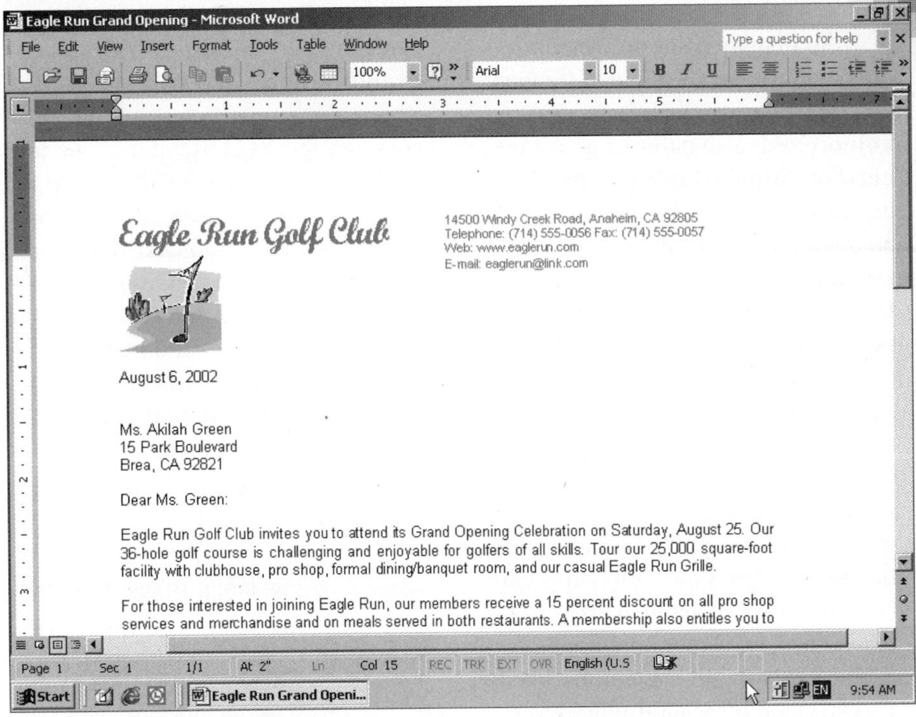

Figure 6-9b (screen resolution at 1024 x 768)

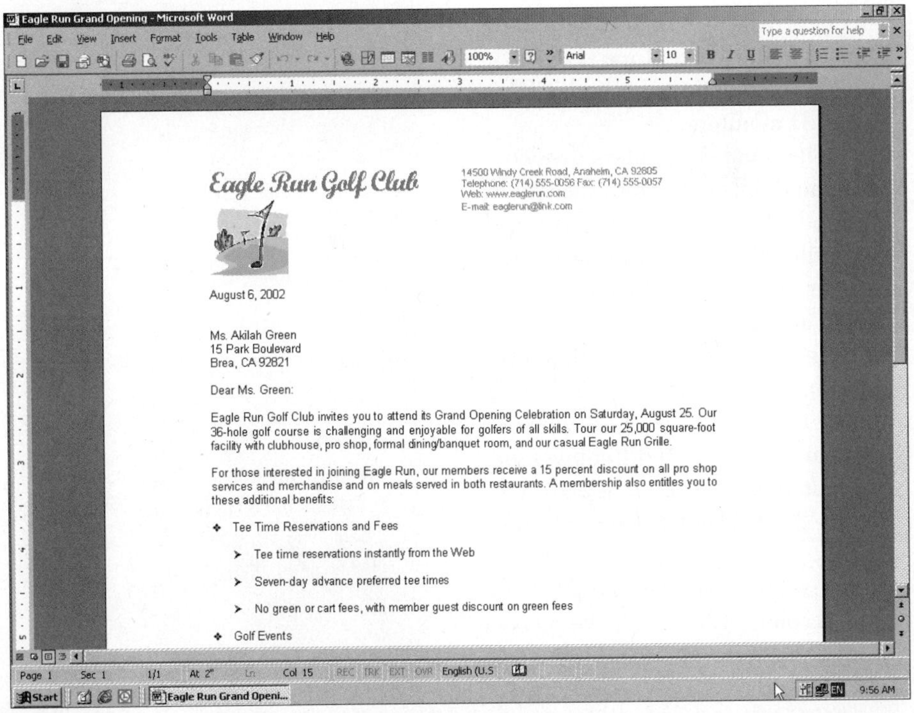

Figure 6-9 The higher a screen's resolution, the smaller the images display on the screen. This figure illustrates that all elements on the screen become smaller when the resolution is increased from 800 x 600 to 1024 x 768. Notice also that more text displays on the screen with the higher resolution.

Video Cards and Monitors

To display color on a monitor, the computer sends a signal through the video card in the system unit. A **video card**, also called a **graphics card** or **video adapter**, converts digital output from the computer into an analog video signal and sends the signal through a cable to the monitor. How the display device produces the picture varies depending on the type of display.

CRT monitors use the analog signal to produce a picture (Figure 6-10). LCD monitors use a digital signal to produce a picture. The LCD monitor contains circuitry that converts the analog signal from the video card back to a digital signal. This is one reason why LCD monitors are more expensive than CRT monitors. Ideally, an LCD monitor should plug into a digital interface on the computer. The **Digital Display Working Group (DDWG)**, which is led by several industry companies, is developing a standard interface for all displays. This new digital interface, called the **Digital Video Interface (DVI)**, provides connections for both CRT and LCD monitors.

The number of colors a video card can display is determined by its bit depth. The video card's **bit depth**, also called the **color depth**, is the number of bits it uses to store information about each pixel. For example, an 8-bit video card (also called 8-bit color) uses 8 bits to store information about each pixel. Thus, this video card can display 256 different colors (computed as 2^8 or 2 x 2 x 2 x 2 x 2 x 2 x 2 x 2). A 24-bit video card uses 24 bits to store information about each pixel and can display 2^{24} or 16.7 million colors. The greater the number of bits, the better the resulting image.

Over the years, several video standards have been developed to define the resolution, number of colors, and other display properties. Today, the **Video Electronics Standards Association (VESA)**, which consists of video card and monitor manufacturers, develops video standards. Most current video cards support the **super video graphics array (SVGA)** standard, which also supports resolutions and colors in the VGA standard. The table in Figure 6-11 outlines the suggested resolution and number of displayed colors in the MDA, VGA, XGA, SVGA, and beyond SVGA standards.

For a monitor to display images using the resolution and number of colors defined by a video standard, the monitor must support the same video standard *and* the video card must be capable of communicating appropriate signals to the monitor. Both the video card and the monitor must support the video standard to generate the desired resolution and number of colors.

Your video card also must have enough memory to generate the resolution and number of colors you want to display. The memory in video cards stores information about each pixel. Video cards use a variety of video memory: VRAM, WRAM, SGRAM, or SDRAM. Manufacturers state video memory in megabytes. The table in Figure 6-12 outlines the amount of video memory required for various screen resolutions and color depth configurations. For example, if you

Figure 6-10 HOW VIDEO TRAVELS FROM THE PROCESSOR TO A CRT MONITOR

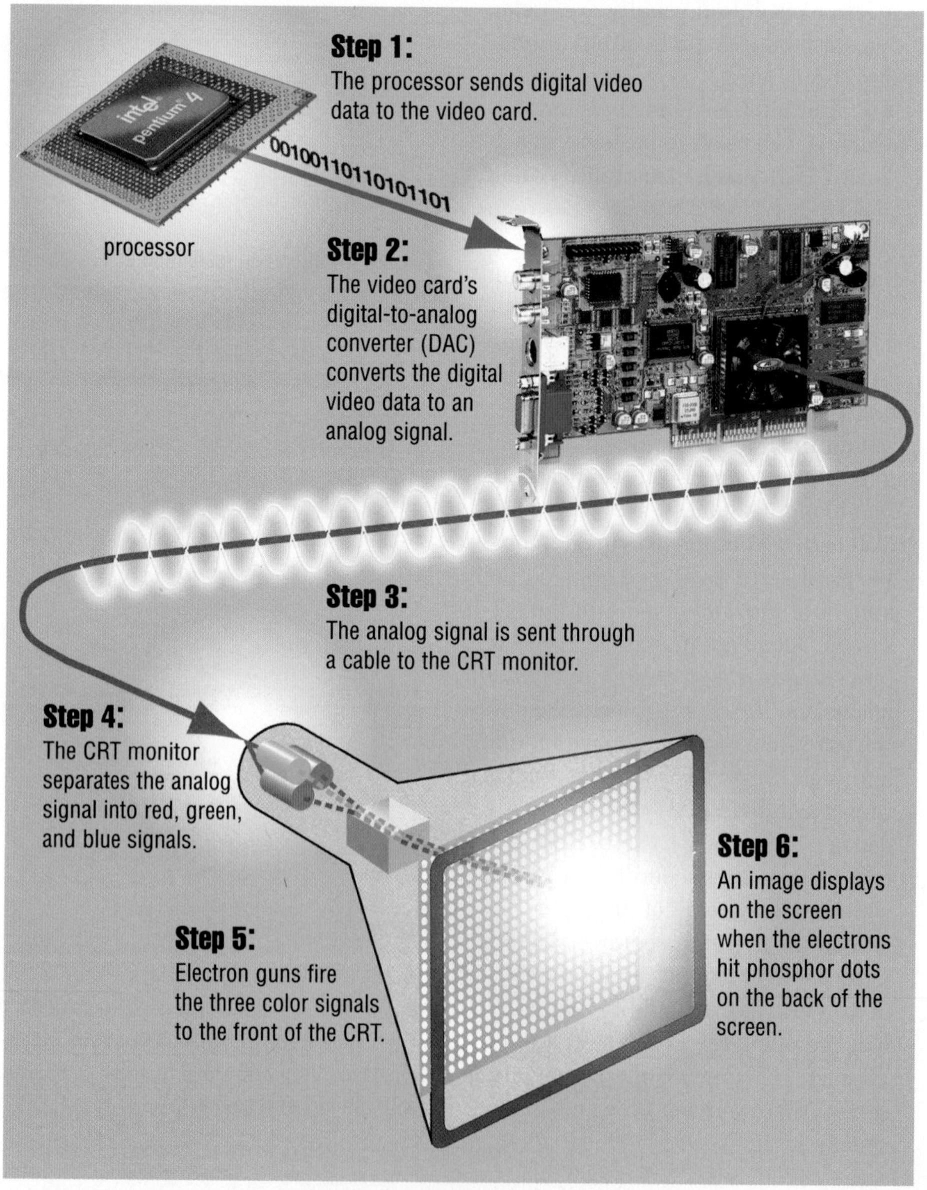
Step 1:
The processor sends digital video data to the video card.
intel pentium 4
0010011011010101101
processor
Step 2:
The video card's digital-to-analog converter (DAC) converts the digital video data to an analog signal.
Step 3:
The analog signal is sent through a cable to the CRT monitor.
Step 4:
The CRT monitor separates the analog signal into red, green, and blue signals.
Step 5:
Electron guns fire the three color signals to the front of the CRT.
Step 6:
An image displays on the screen when the electrons hit phosphor dots on the back of the screen.

wanted an 800 x 600 resolution with 24-bit color (16.7 million colors), then your video card should have at least 2 MB of video memory.

Monitor Ergonomics

The goal of ergonomics is to incorporate comfort, efficiency, and safety into the design of items in the workplace. Many monitors have features that help address ergonomic issues. Most monitors have a tilt-and-swivel base, so you can adjust the angle of the screen to minimize neck strain and reduce glare from overhead lighting.

Monitors also have controls that allow you to adjust the brightness, contrast, positioning, height, and width of images. These controls usually are on the front of the monitor for easy access. Newer monitors have digital controls that allow you to fine-tune the display in small increments. An advantage of digital controls is you quickly can return to the default settings by pressing the reset button.

CRT monitors produce a small amount of electromagnetic radiation. **Electromagnetic radiation** (**EMR**) is a magnetic field that travels at the speed of light. No solid evidence exists to prove that EMR poses a health risk. To be safe, however, all high-quality CRT monitors comply with MPR II standards. **MPR II** is a set of standards that defines acceptable levels of EMR for a monitor. To protect yourself even further, sit at arm's length from the CRT monitor because EMR only travels a short distance. In addition, EMR is greatest on the sides and back of the CRT monitor. LCD monitors do not pose this risk.

VIDEO STANDARDS

Standard	Suggested Resolution	Possible Simultaneous Colors
Monochrome Display Adapter (MDA)	720 x 350	1 for text
Video Graphics Array (VGA)	640 x 480	16
	320 x 200	256
Extended Graphics Array (XGA)	1024 x 768	256
	640 x 480	65,536
Super Video Graphics Array (SVGA)	800 x 600	16.7 million
	1024 x 768	16.7 million
	1280 x 1024	16.7 million
	1600 x 1200	16.7 million
Beyond SVGA	1920 x 1440	16.7 million
	2048 x 1536	16.7 million

Figure 6-11 The various video standards.

VARIOUS VIDEO CARD CONFIGURATIONS

Video Memory	Color Depth	Number of Colors	Resolution
1 MB	8-bit	256	1024 x 768
	16-bit	65,536	800 x 600
2 MB	8-bit	256	1024 x 768
	16-bit	65,536	1280 x 1024
	24-bit	16.7 million	800 x 600
4 MB	24-bit	16.7 million	1024 x 768
6 MB	24-bit	16.7 million	1280 x 1024
8 MB	32-bit	16.7 million	1600 x 1200
16 MB	32-bit	16.7 million	1920 x 1440
32 MB	32-bit	16.7 million	2048 x 1536

Figure 6-12 The amount of video memory required for various screen resolutions.

APPLY IT!

Monitor Ergonomics – All Strain, No Gain

Your desktop computer can cause you more problems than you know. Many computer users are unaware of computer vision syndrome (CVS). The Mayo Clinic (see URL below) advises that if you have some or all of these symptoms, you may have CVS: sore, tired, burning, itching or dry eyes; blurred or double vision; distance vision blurred after prolonged staring at monitor; headache or sore neck; difficulty shifting focus between monitor and source documents; difficulty focusing on the screen image; color fringes or afterimages when you look away from the monitor; and increased sensitivity to light. Although eyestrain associated with CVS is not thought to have serious or long-term consequences, it is disruptive and unpleasant.

Following are some hints that may help ease the strain:

- Take an eye break – every 10 minutes or so, look away from the monitor
- Close your eyes and rest them for at least a minute
- Blink your eyes – the Mayo Clinic suggests blinking every five seconds
- Place your monitor about an arm's length away from your eyes with the top of the screen at eye level or below
- Use a glare screen
- Use large fonts
- If you wear glasses, ask your doctor for computer glasses
- Adjust the lighting

For links to computer health issues and the Web site mentioned above, visit the Discovering Computers 2002 Apply It Web page (**scsite.com/dc2002/apply.htm**) and click Chapter 6 Apply It #1.

To help reduce the amount of electricity used by monitors and other computer components, the United States Department of Energy (DOE) and the United States Environmental Protection Agency (EPA) developed the **ENERGY STAR program**. This program encourages manufacturers to create energy-efficient devices that require little power when they are not in use. Monitors and devices that meet ENERGY STAR guidelines display an ENERGY STAR® label (Figure 6-13).

Televisions

Many home and business users have a television set as a monitor for their computer. Connecting a computer to a standard television set requires an **NTSC converter**, which converts the digital signal from the computer into an analog signal that the television set can display. NTSC stands for **National Television Standards Committee** and consists of industry members that have technical expertise about television-related issues.

High-definition television (HDTV) is a type of television set that works with digital broadcasting signals and supports a wider screen and higher resolution display than a standard television set. With HDTV, the broadcast signals are digitized when they are sent. Digital television signals provide two major advantages over analog signals. First, digital signals produce a higher-quality picture. Second, many programs can be broadcast on a single digital channel, whereas only one program can be broadcast on an analog channel. Currently, only a few U.S. television stations broadcast digital signals. By 2006, all stations must be broadcasting digital signals, as mandated by the FCC.

As the cost of HDTV becomes more reasonable, home users will begin to use it as their computer's display device. HDTV also is ideal for presenting material to a large group.

HDTV technology also makes interactive TV more feasible. **Interactive TV** is a two-way communications technology in which users interact with television programming. Instead of adding special equipment to your standard television, HDTV works directly with interactive TV. Uses of interactive TV include selecting a movie from a central library of movies, voting or responding to network questionnaires, banking and shopping, and playing games.

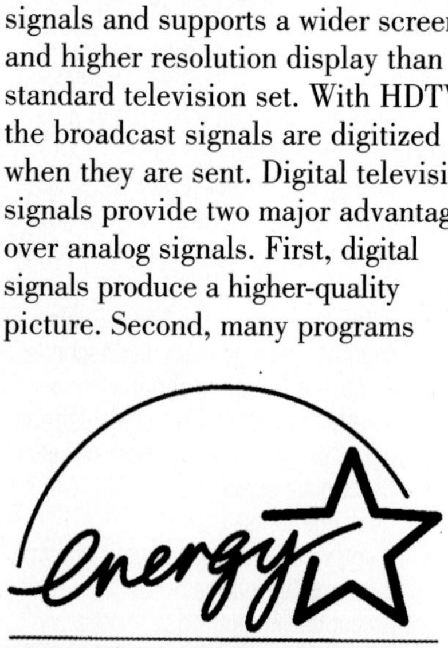

Figure 6-13 Products with an Energy Star label are energy efficient as defined by the Environmental Protection Agency (EPA).

PRINTERS

A **printer** is an output device that produces text and graphics on a physical medium such as paper or transparency film. Printed information, called **hard copy**, exists physically and is a more permanent form of output than that presented on a display device (soft copy).

A hard copy, also called a **printout**, can be portrait or landscape orientation (Figure 6-14). A page in **portrait orientation** is taller than it is wide, with information printed across the shorter width of the paper. A page in **landscape orientation** is wider than it is tall, with information printed across the widest part of the paper. Letters, reports, and books typically use portrait orientation. Spreadsheets, slide shows, and graphics often use landscape orientation.

Figure 6-14a (portrait orientation)

Figure 6-14 Portrait orientation is taller than it is wide. Landscape orientation is wider than it is tall.

Figure 6-14b (landscape orientation)

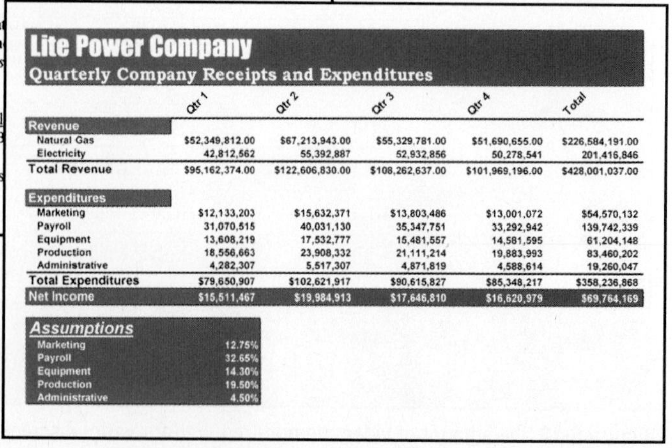

Lite Power Company
Quarterly Company Receipts and Expenditures

	Qtr 1	Qtr 2	Qtr 3	Qtr 4	Total
Revenue					
Natural Gas	$52,349,812.00	$67,213,943.00	$55,329,781.00	$51,690,655.00	$226,584,191.00
Electricity	42,812,562	55,392,887	52,932,856	50,278,541	201,416,846
Total Revenue	$95,162,374.00	$122,606,830.00	$108,262,637.00	$101,969,196.00	$428,001,037.00
Expenditures					
Marketing	$12,133,203	$15,632,371	$13,803,486	$13,001,072	$54,570,132
Payroll	31,070,515	40,031,130	35,347,751	33,292,942	139,742,339
Equipment	13,608,219	17,532,777	15,481,557	14,581,595	61,204,148
Production	18,556,663	23,908,332	21,111,214	19,883,993	83,460,202
Administrative	4,282,307	5,517,307	4,871,819	4,588,614	19,260,047
Total Expenditures	$79,650,907	$102,621,917	$90,615,827	$85,348,217	$358,236,868
Net Income	$15,511,467	$19,984,913	$17,646,810	$16,620,979	$69,764,169

Assumptions	
Marketing	12.75%
Payroll	32.65%
Equipment	14.30%
Production	19.50%
Administrative	4.50%

Home computer users might print a hundred pages or fewer a week. Small business computer users might print several hundred pages a day. Users of mainframe computers, such as large utility companies that send printed statements to hundreds of thousands of customers each month, require printers that are capable of printing thousands of pages per hour.

To meet this range of printing needs, many different printers exist with varying speeds, capabilities, and printing methods. Figure 6-15 presents a list of questions to help you decide on the printer best suited to your needs.

Many printers today handle Internet printing. With **Internet printing**, an Internet service on the Web sends a print instruction to your printer, which may be at a location different from your computer or device that accessed the Web site (Figure 6-16). A printer with Internet printing capability can receive print instructions from an Internet printing service so it can print documents from desktop and wireless computers and devices, such as cellular telephones. For example, you can print items such as postage, package shipping labels, newspaper articles, and event tickets from a Web-enabled cellular telephone. The goal of Internet printing is to make every computer and Web-enabled device capable of printing.

Generally, printers are either impact or nonimpact. The following pages discuss printers in both of these categories.

1. How fast must my printer print?
2. Do I need a color printer?
3. What is the cost per page for printing?
4. Do I need multiple copies of documents?
5. Will I print graphics?
6. Do I want to print photographs?
7. What types of paper does the printer use?
8. What sizes of paper does the printer accept?
9. How much paper can the printer tray hold?
10. Will the printer work with my computer and software?
11. How much do supplies such as ink and paper cost?
12. Can the printer print on envelopes and transparencies?
13. What is my budget?
14. How much do I print now, and what will I be printing in a year or two?

Figure 6-15 Questions to ask when purchasing a printer.

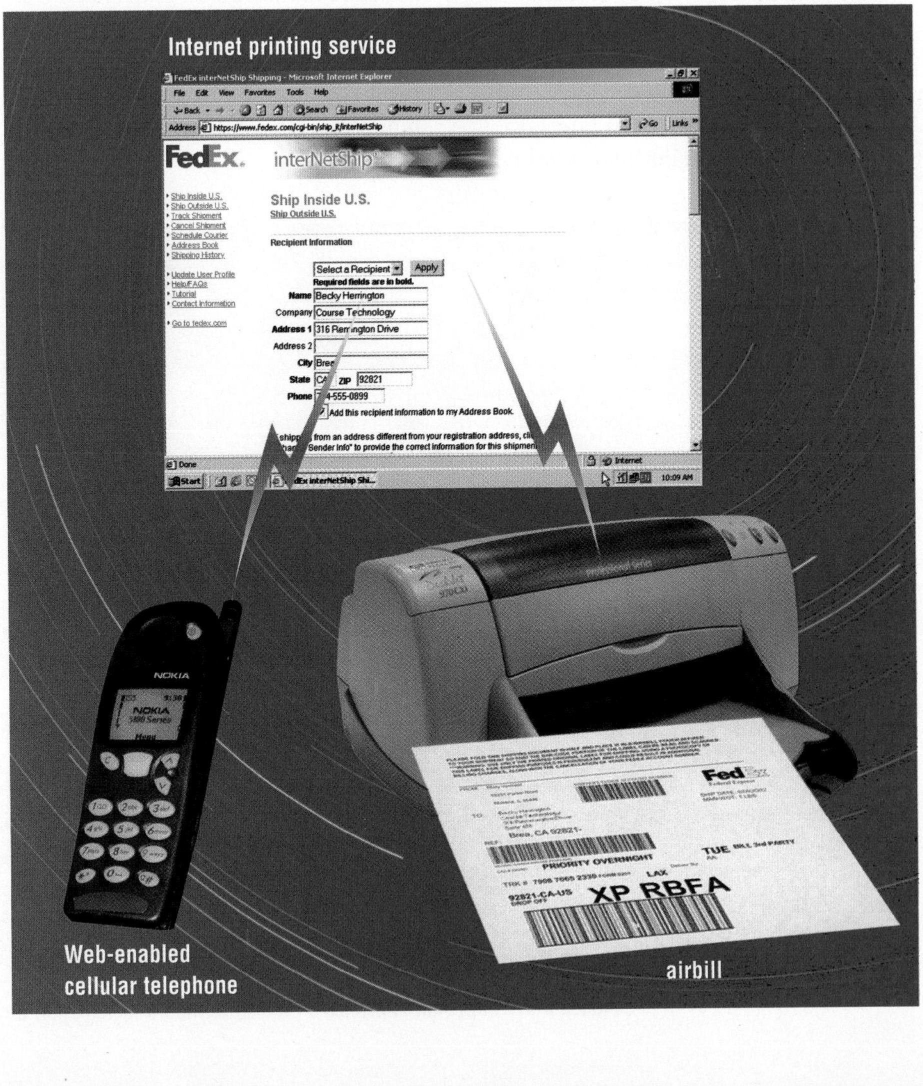

Figure 6-16 Internet printing allows printers to print documents from desktop and wireless computers and devices. The device sends the print instruction to an Internet service, which sends the print instruction to the printer.

Impact Printers

An **impact printer** forms characters and graphics on a piece of paper by striking a mechanism against an ink ribbon that physically contacts the paper. Impact printers generally are noisy because of this striking activity.

Impact printers typically do not provide letter quality print. **Letter quality (LQ)** output is a quality of print acceptable for business letters. Many impact printers produce **near letter quality (NLQ)** print, which is slightly less clear than letter quality. Some companies use NLQ impact printers for routine jobs such as printing mailing labels, envelopes, and invoices.

Impact printers are ideal for printing multipart forms because they easily can print through many layers of paper. Factories and retail counters use impact printers because these printers can withstand dusty environments, vibrations, and extreme temperatures.

Two commonly used types of impact printers are dot-matrix printers and line printers. The following paragraphs discuss each of these printers.

DOT-MATRIX PRINTERS A **dot-matrix printer** is an impact printer that produces printed images when tiny wire pins on a print head mechanism strike an inked ribbon (Figure 6-17). When the ribbon presses against the paper, it creates dots that form characters and graphics.

Most dot-matrix printers use **continuous-form paper**, in which each sheet of paper is connected together. The pages have holes along the sides to help feed the paper through the printer. Perforations along the inside of the holes and at each fold allow you to separate the sheets into standard-sized sheets of paper, such as $8^{1}/_{2}$-by-11-inches. With continuous-form paper, you do not have to change the paper often because thousands of sheets are connected together. You also can adjust many dot-matrix printers to print pages in either portrait or landscape orientation.

The print head mechanism on a dot-matrix printer can contain 9 to 24 pins, depending on the manufacturer and the printer model. A higher number of pins means the printer prints more dots per character, which results in higher print quality.

The speed of a dot-matrix printer is measured by the number of characters per second (cps) it can print. The speed of dot-matrix printers ranges from 50 to 700 characters per second (cps), depending on the desired print quality.

LINE PRINTERS A **line printer** is a high-speed impact printer that prints an entire line at a time (Figure 6-18). The speed of a line printer is measured by the number of lines per minute (lpm) it can print. These printers are capable of printing up to 3,000 lines per minute (lpm).

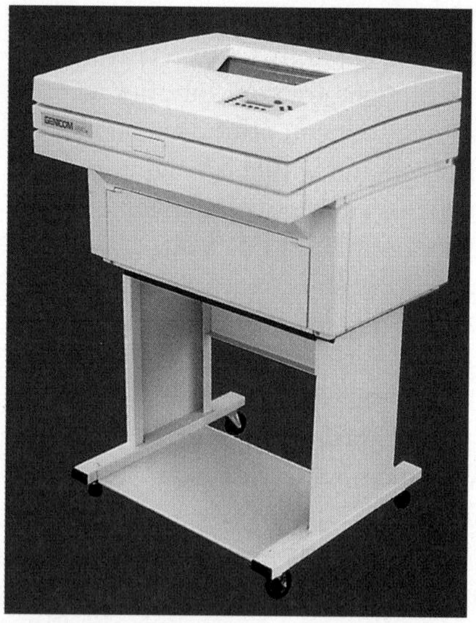

Figure 6-18 A line printer is a high-speed printer often connected to a mainframe, mid-range server, or network.

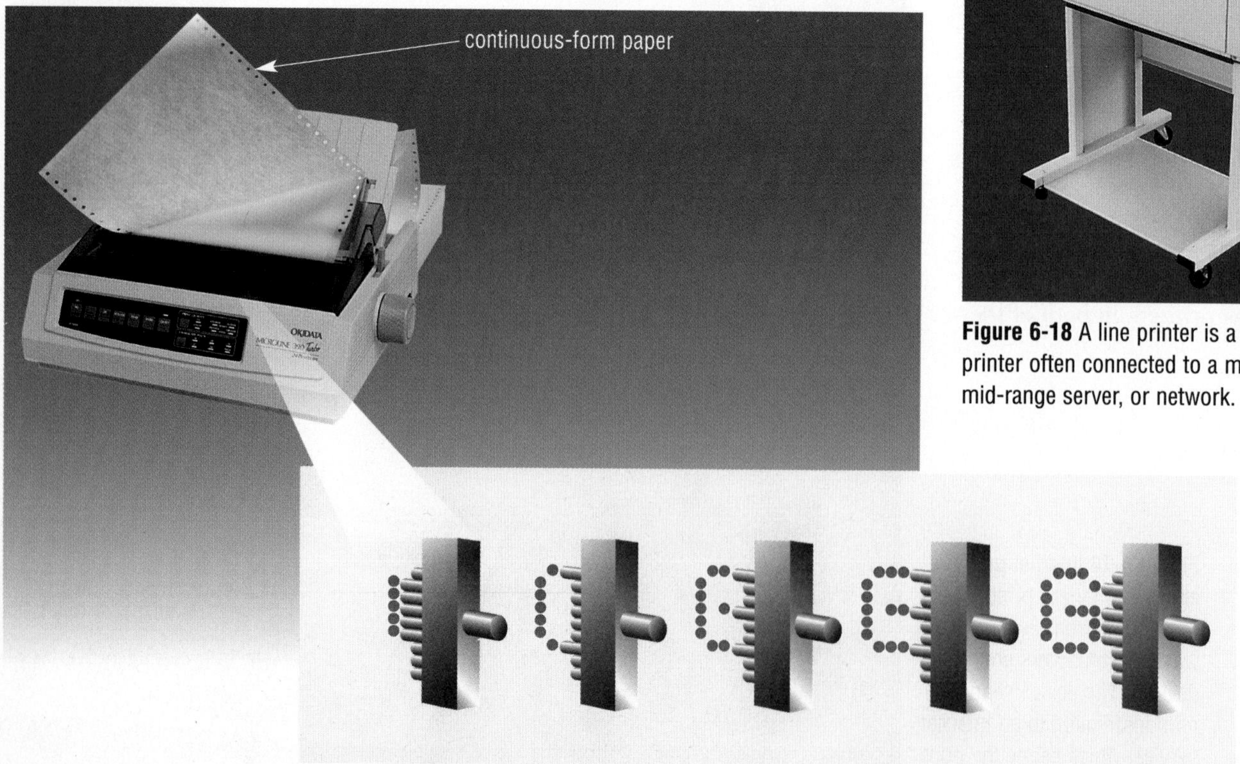

Figure 6-17 A dot-matrix printer produces printed images when tiny pins strike an inked ribbon.

Mainframes, mid-range servers, or networked applications, such as manufacturing, distribution, or shipping, often use line printers. These printers typically use 11-by-17-inch continuous-form paper. For example, mainframe computers often use greenbar paper to print reports.

Two popular types of line printers used for high-volume output are band and shuttle-matrix. A **band printer** prints fully-formed characters when hammers strike a horizontal, rotating band that contains shapes of numbers, letters of the alphabet, and other characters. A shuttle-matrix printer works more like a dot-matrix printer. The difference is the **shuttle-matrix printer** moves a series of print hammers back and forth horizontally at incredibly high speeds, as compared to standard line printers. Unlike a band printer, a shuttle-matrix printer can print characters in various fonts and font sizes.

Nonimpact Printers

A **nonimpact printer** forms characters and graphics on a piece of paper without actually striking the paper. Some spray ink, while others use heat and pressure to create images. Because these printers do not strike the paper, they are much quieter than the previously discussed impact printers.

Three commonly used types of nonimpact printers are ink-jet printers, laser printers, and thermal printers. The following sections discuss each of these printers.

Ink-Jet Printers

An **ink-jet printer** is a type of nonimpact printer that forms characters and graphics by spraying tiny drops of liquid ink onto a piece of paper. Ink-jet printers usually use individual sheets of paper stored in a removable or stationary tray.

Ink-jet printers can produce letter-quality text and graphics in both black-and-white and color print on a variety of paper types (Figure 6-19). Available paper types include plain paper, ink-jet, photo paper, glossy paper, and banner paper. Some ink-jet printers can print photographic-quality images on any of these types of paper. Others require the heavier weight ink-jet paper for better-looking color documents.

These printers also print on other materials such as envelopes, labels, index cards, greeting card paper, transparencies, and iron-on t-shirt transfers. Many ink-jet printers include software for creating greeting cards, banners, business cards, letterheads, and transparencies.

Ink-jet printers have become the most popular type of color printer for use in the home because of their lower cost and letter-quality print. You can purchase an ink-jet printer of reasonable quality for a few hundred dollars.

As with many other input and output devices, one factor that determines the quality of an ink-jet printer is its resolution, or sharpness and clarity. Printer resolution is measured by the number of dots per inch (dpi) a printer can output. As shown in Figure 6-20, the higher the dpi, the better the print quality. With an ink-jet printer, a dot is a drop of ink. A higher dpi means the drops of ink are smaller, which provides a higher quality image. Most ink-jet printers have a dpi that ranges from 300 to 2,400 dpi. Printers with a higher dpi usually are more expensive.

The speed of an ink-jet printer is measured by the number of pages per minute (ppm) it can print. Most ink-jet printers print from 1 to 12 pages per minute (ppm). Graphics and colors print at the slower rate.

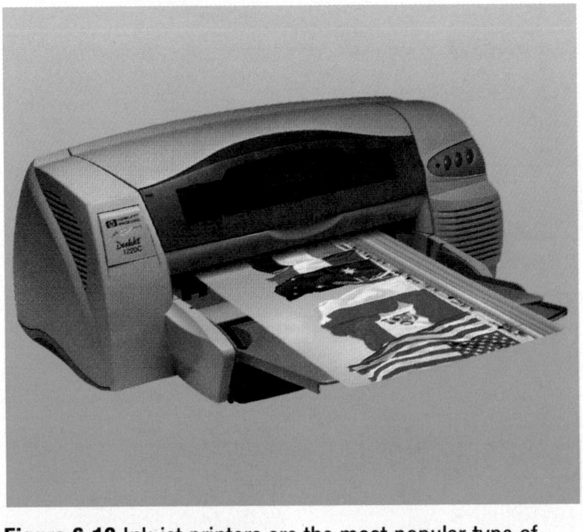

Figure 6-19 Ink-jet printers are the most popular type of color printer used in the home.

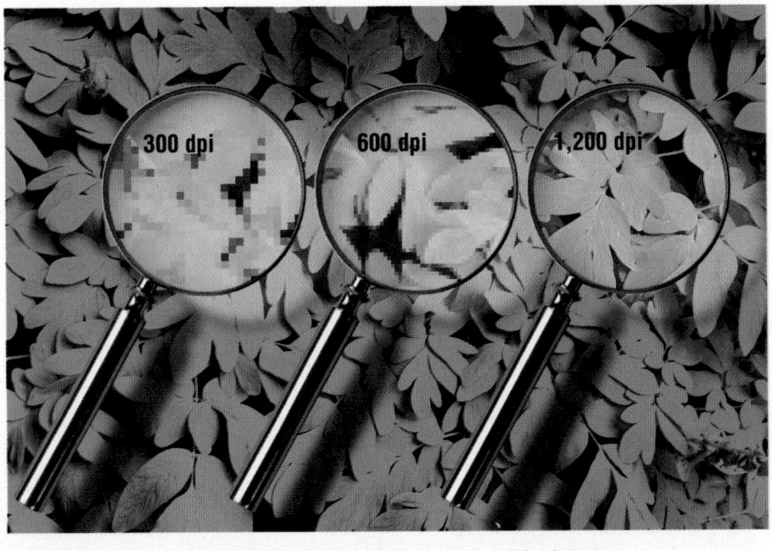

Figure 6-20 The higher the dpi, the better the quality of the image.

The print head mechanism in an ink-jet printer contains ink-filled print cartridges. Each cartridge has fifty to several hundred small ink holes, or nozzles. The steps in Figure 6-21 illustrate how a drop of ink appears on a page. Each nozzle in the print cartridge is similar to an individual pin on a dot-matrix printer. Just as any combination of dot-matrix pins can be activated, heat or pressure propels ink through any combination of the nozzles to form a character or image on the paper.

Web Link

For more information on ink-jet printers, visit the Discovering Computers 2002 Chapter 6 WEB LINK page (**scsite.com/dc2002/ch6/weblink.htm**) and click Ink-Jet Printers.

When the print cartridge runs out of ink, you simply replace the cartridge. Most ink-jet printers have at least two print cartridges: one containing black ink and the other(s) containing colors. These cartridges usually cost from $20 to $40 per cartridge. The number of pages you can print from a single cartridge varies by manufacturer. Some print as few as 20 pages, while others print as many as 300 pages.

On average, it costs from $.03 to $.05 per page for black ink and $.10 to $.15 per page for color ink. When coupled with premium photo paper, the cost for a high-quality photograph can increase to about $1.00 per page.

Laser Printers

A **laser printer** is a high-speed, high-quality nonimpact printer (Figure 6-22). Laser printers for personal computers usually use individual sheets of paper stored in a removable tray that slides into the printer case. Some laser printers have trays that can accommodate different sizes of paper, while others require separate trays for letter- and legal-sized paper. Most laser printers have a manual feed slot where you can insert individual sheets and envelopes. You also can print transparencies on a laser printer.

Figure 6-21 HOW AN INK-JET PRINTER WORKS

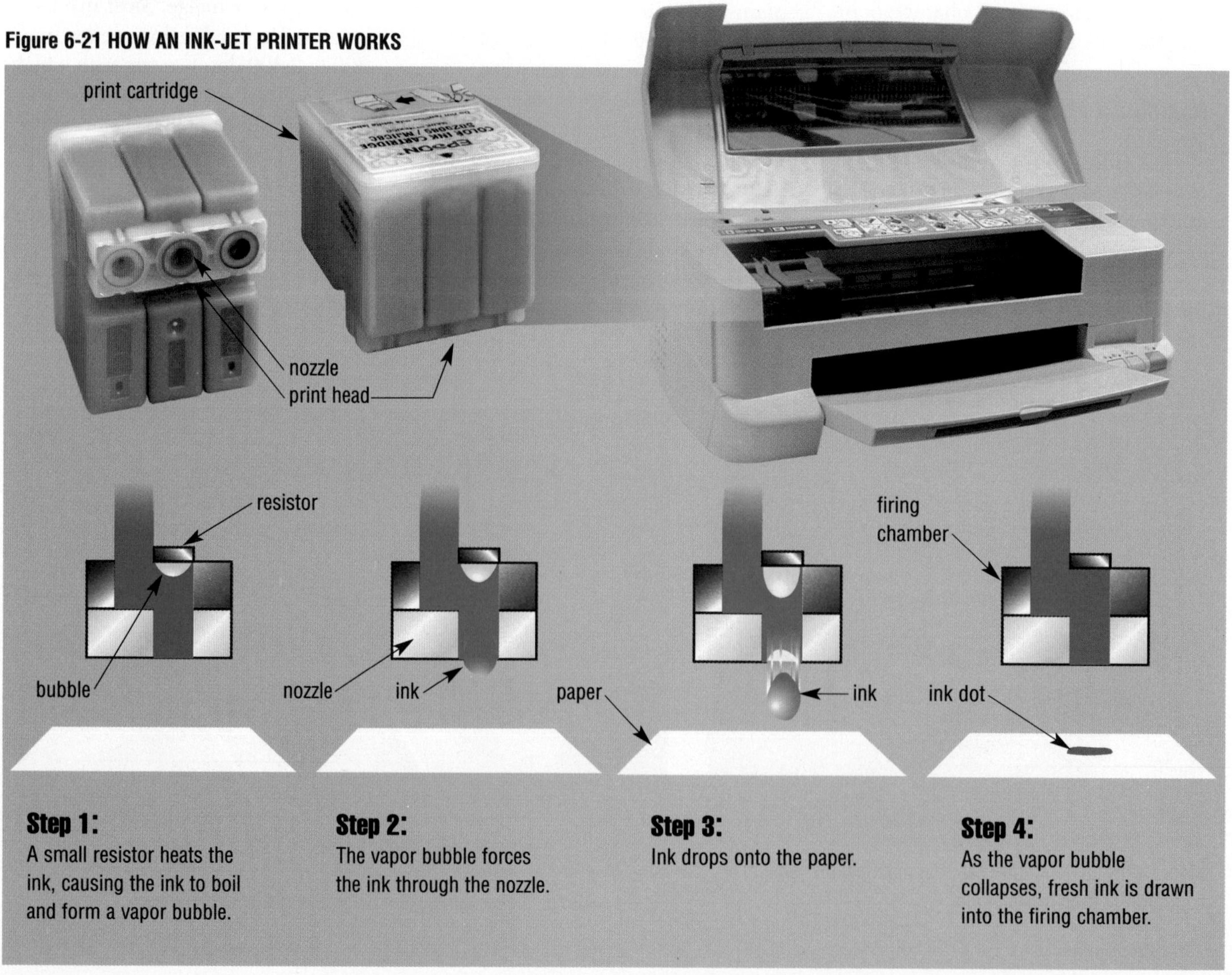

Step 1: A small resistor heats the ink, causing the ink to boil and form a vapor bubble.

Step 2: The vapor bubble forces the ink through the nozzle.

Step 3: Ink drops onto the paper.

Step 4: As the vapor bubble collapses, fresh ink is drawn into the firing chamber.

Figure 6-22 Laser printers are used with personal computers, as well as larger computers.

Laser printers can print text and graphics in very high quality resolutions, ranging from 600 to 1,200 dpi. While laser printers typically cost more than ink-jet printers, they also are much faster. A high-end laser printer can print text at speeds of up to 40 pages per minute.

Depending on the quality and speed of the printer, the cost of a black-and-white laser printer ranges from a few hundred to several thousand dollars. The higher the resolution and speed, the more expensive the printer. Mainframe computers use high-end fast laser printers. Although color laser printers are available, they are relatively expensive, with prices often exceeding a thousand dollars.

Operating in a manner similar to a copy machine, a laser printer creates images using a laser beam and powdered ink, called **toner**. The laser beam produces an image on a special drum inside the printer. The light of the laser alters the electrical charge on the drum wherever it hits. When this occurs, the toner sticks to the drum and then transfers to the paper through a combination of pressure and heat (Figure 6-23).

Web Link

For more information on laser printers, visit the Discovering Computers 2002 Chapter 6 WEB LINK page (**scsite.com/dc2002/ch6/weblink.htm**) and click Laser Printers.

Figure 6-23 HOW A LASER PRINTER WORKS

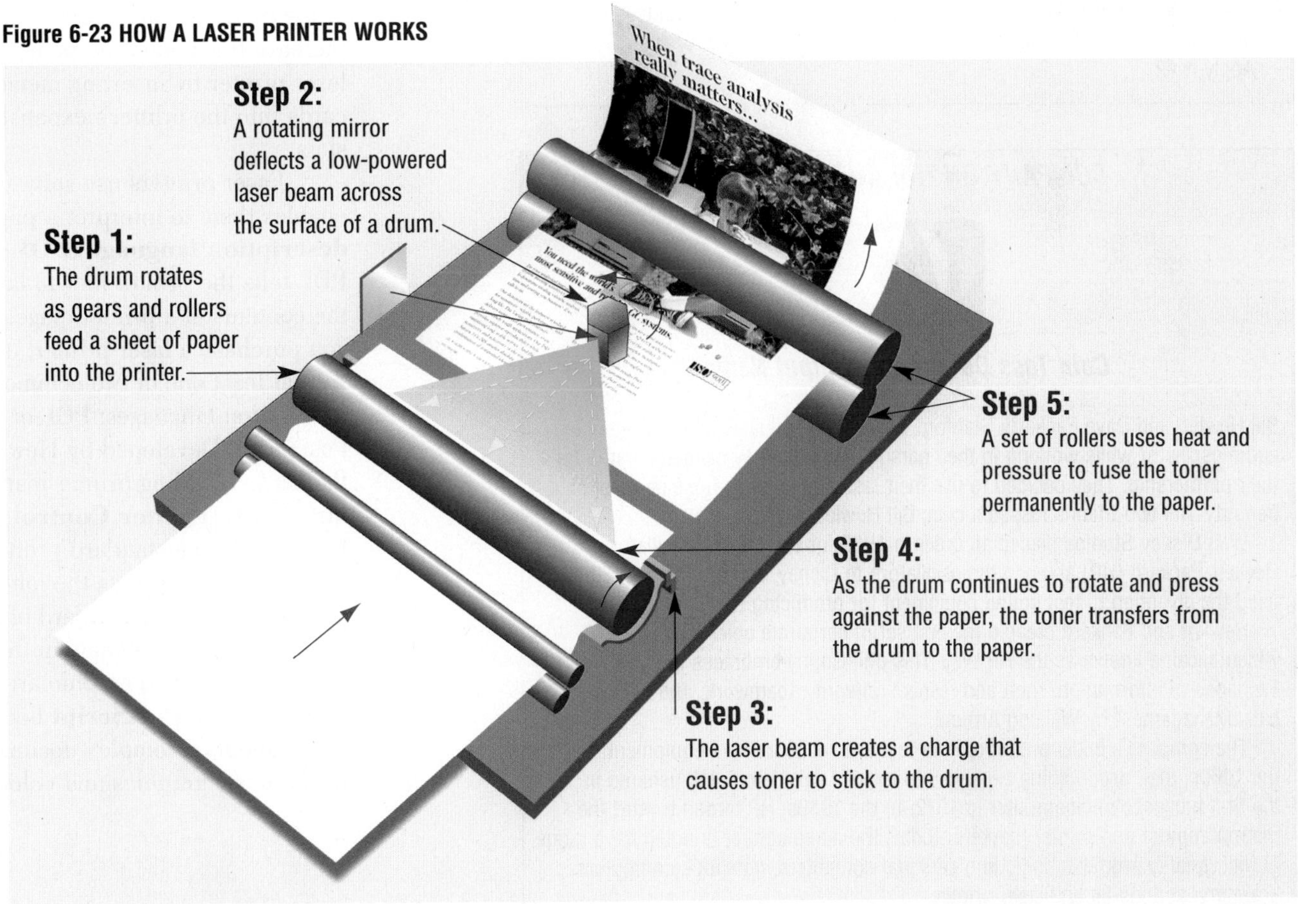
When trace analysis really matters...
Step 1:
The drum rotates as gears and rollers feed a sheet of paper into the printer.
Step 2:
A rotating mirror deflects a low-powered laser beam across the surface of a drum.
Step 3:
The laser beam creates a charge that causes toner to stick to the drum.
Step 4:
As the drum continues to rotate and press against the paper, the toner transfers from the drum to the paper.
Step 5:
A set of rollers uses heat and pressure to fuse the toner permanently to the paper.

APPLY IT!

Printed Matters

Printers are available in various shapes and sizes and a range of prices. The type of printer you purchase depends on the type of printing you want to do. If the printer is for your business, it either can enhance the professional image you want the world to see — or detract from it. If the printer is for personal use, high-quality output may not be a major factor.

For most people, the choice is between two categories: laser printers and ink-jet printers. A laser printer generally prints at a relatively fast speed and produces high-quality black and white or color output. Resolution continues to improve from the original 300 dots per inch (dpi) to as much as 1,200 dpi. The price per page of a text-oriented document is $.02 to $.03. The printer trays for most laser printers can hold as many as 250 sheets of paper, and the printer can handle thousands of pages of output per month. Color laser printers are available and prices have decreased, but they still are expensive.

Although slower, ink-jet printers are less expensive than laser printers. The big advantage is the availability of color printing and entry-level units with low price tags. The price for a page of black-and-white text is around $.04 per page.

Some factors to consider when purchasing a printer are as follows:

- Primary use
- Space and noise
- Speed or pages per minute (PPM)
- Color capabilities
- Price of consumables
- Print quality and resolution
- Interface – parallel or USB
- Paper handling features

For more information on printers, visit the Discovering Computers 2002 Apply It Web page (**scsite.com/dc2002/apply.htm**) and click Chapter 6 Apply It #2.

COMPANY ON THE CUTTING EDGE

Coin Toss Determines Output Name

Bill Hewlett and Dave Packard, Stanford University graduates, had invented an audio oscillator while working in their garage, and now they needed a name for their partnership. They decided to use their last names, but whose name should be first? The two friends tossed a coin; Bill Hewlett won.

Walt Disney Studios placed an order in 1939 for eight audio oscillators. Hewlett-Packard (HP) shipped the oscillators to Disney, and the movie studios used the invention to test sound equipment for producing the film *Fantasia*.

Hewlett and Packard created the first set of corporate objectives in 1957, which became known as the HP Way. This philosophy embraces the free exchange of information, trust and respect, integrity, teamwork, and what HP calls Management by Walking Around.

The company's initial products were test and measurement equipment. In the 1960s, their product line expanded to include calculators. HP ushered in the first business minicomputer in 1972. In the 1980s, HP turned toward the microcomputer and printer markets. Today, the manufacturer is noted for a range of high-quality products, including personal computers, notebook computers, scanners, and ink-jet and laser printers.

For more information on Hewlett-Packard, visit the Discovering Computers 2002 Companies Web page (**scsite.com/dc2002/companies.htm**) and click HP.

When the toner runs out, you can replace the toner cartridge. Toner cartridge prices range from $50 to $100 for about 5,000 printed pages. On average, the cost per printed page on a black-and-white laser printer is $.02 to $.03.

When printing a document, laser printers process and store the entire page before they actually print it. For this reason, laser printers sometimes are called page printers. Storing a page before printing requires the laser printer has a certain amount of memory in the device.

Depending on the amount of graphics you intend to print, a laser printer can have up to 200 MB of memory. To print a full-page 600-dpi picture, for instance, you might need 16 MB of memory on the printer. If your printer does not have enough memory to print the picture, it either will print as much of the picture as its memory will allow, or it will display an error message and not print any of the picture. You usually can increase the amount of memory in a laser printer by inserting memory cards into the printer's expansion slots.

Laser printers use software that enables them to interpret a **page description language** (**PDL**). A PDL tells the printer how to layout the contents of a printed page. When you purchase a laser printer, it comes with at least one of two common page description languages: PCL or PostScript. Developed by Hewlett-Packard, a leading printer manufacturer, **PCL** (**Printer Control Language**) is a standard printer language that supports the fonts and layout used in standard office documents. Professionals in the desktop publishing and graphic art fields commonly use **PostScript** because it is designed for complex documents with intense graphics and colors.

Thermal Printers

A **thermal printer** generates images by pushing electrically heated pins against heat-sensitive paper. Basic thermal printers are inexpensive, but the print quality is low and the images tend to fade over time. Thermal printers, however, are ideal for use in small devices such as adding machines.

Two special types of thermal printers have a much higher print quality. A **thermal wax-transfer printer**, also called a **thermal transfer printer**, generates rich, nonsmearing images by using heat to melt colored wax onto heat-sensitive paper. Thermal wax-transfer printers are more expensive than ink-jet printers, but less expensive than many color laser printers. A **dye-sublimation printer**, also called a **thermal dye transfer printer**, uses heat to transfer colored dye to specially coated paper. Costing several thousand dollars, dye-sublimation printers can create images that are of photographic quality (Figure 6-24). Applications requiring very high image quality, such as medical or security applications, use these printers.

Some manufacturers offer a near dye-sublimation quality printer for the home user that costs several hundred dollars. Most home users, however, purchase a photo printer instead of these inexpensive dye-sublimation quality printers. The next page discusses photo printers.

Figure 6-24 This printer uses dye sublimation technology, which creates photographic quality output.

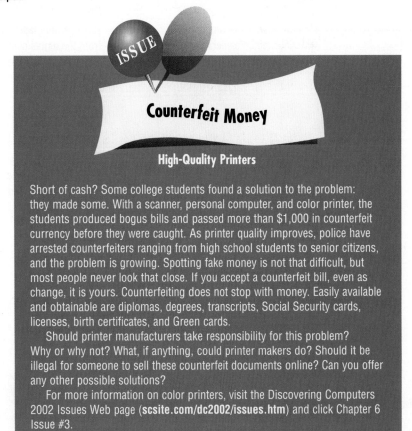

Counterfeit Money

High-Quality Printers

Short of cash? Some college students found a solution to the problem: they made some. With a scanner, personal computer, and color printer, the students produced bogus bills and passed more than $1,000 in counterfeit currency before they were caught. As printer quality improves, police have arrested counterfeiters ranging from high school students to senior citizens, and the problem is growing. Spotting fake money is not that difficult, but most people never look that close. If you accept a counterfeit bill, even as change, it is yours. Counterfeiting does not stop with money. Easily available and obtainable are diplomas, degrees, transcripts, Social Security cards, licenses, birth certificates, and Green cards.

Should printer manufacturers take responsibility for this problem? Why or why not? What, if anything, could printer makers do? Should it be illegal for someone to sell these counterfeit documents online? Can you offer any other possible solutions?

For more information on color printers, visit the Discovering Computers 2002 Issues Web page (**scsite.com/dc2002/issues.htm**) and click Chapter 6 Issue #3.

Web Link

For more information on photo printers, visit the Discovering Computers 2002 Chapter 6 WEB LINK page (**scsite.com/dc2002/ch6/weblink.htm**) and click Photo Printers.

Photo Printers

A **photo printer** is a color printer that can produce photo lab quality pictures as well as printing everyday documents. In addition, many photo printers can read media directly from a digital camera (Figure 6-25). That is, you do not need to attach the printer to your computer. Simply remove the storage device, such as a media card, from the digital camera and insert it into the printer. Then, push buttons on the printer to select the desired photo, specify the number of copies, and indicate the size of the printed image. Size options for printed photographs can range from 3 x 3 inches to 13 x 19 inches. Some even print panoramic photographs.

Many photo printers use ink-jet technology. Thus, you can connect a photo printer to your computer and use it for all your printing needs. For a few hundred dollars, this printer is ideal for the home or small business user.

Figure 6-25 HOW SOME PHOTO PRINTERS WORK WITH A DIGITAL CAMERA

CASIO
Step 1:
Insert media card into digital camera. Take the photograph with your digital camera.
Step 2:
Remove the media card from the digital camera and insert it into the card slot on the photo printer.
Step 3:
Select desired image to print, number of copies, and size of print by pushing buttons on the photo printer.
Step 4:
Remove the photo from the photo printer.

Label and Postage Printers

A **label printer** is a small printer that prints on an adhesive-type material that can be placed on a variety of items such as envelopes, packages, floppy disks, CDs, DVDs, audiocassettes, photographs, file folders, and toys. Most label printers also print bar codes.

Some newer model label printers have built-in digital scales and can print e-stamps (Figure 6-26). An **e-stamp**, also called **Internet postage**, is digital postage you buy and print right from your personal computer. That is, you purchase an amount of postage from an authorized postal service Web site and download it directly to the label printer. As you need stamps, you print them on the label printer.

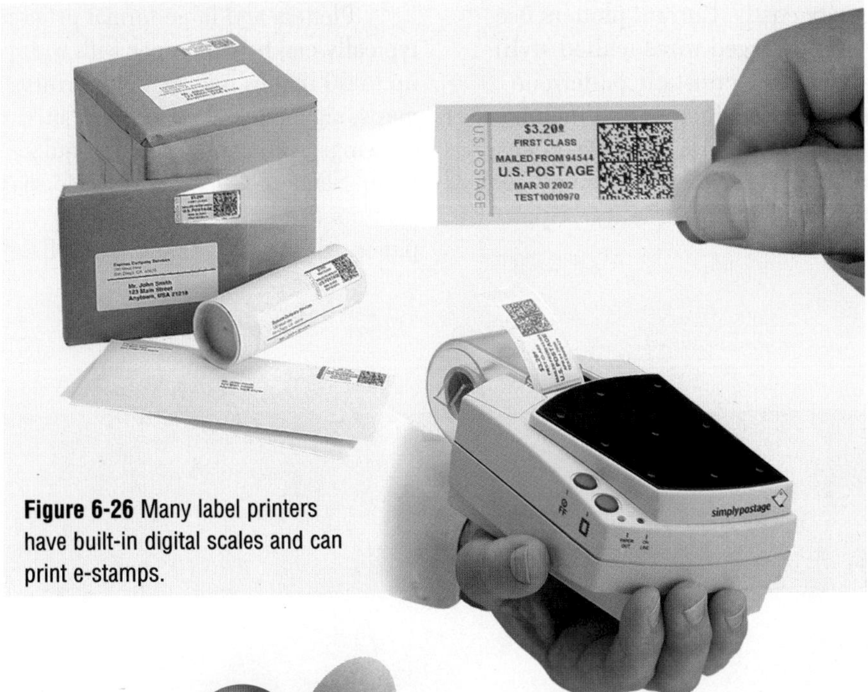

Figure 6-26 Many label printers have built-in digital scales and can print e-stamps.

ISSUE

Print Your Own Photographs

Digital Cameras and Photo Printers

As with any technology, the price of digital cameras and photo printers continues to decrease. Lower prices are an enticement for more and more people to turn away from traditional cameras and film developing to digital photography. Digital cameras radically have simplified the process of getting your pictures into your personal computer. Even so, all cameras live or die on image quality. Some experts suggest that the 35mm still is king and the traditional camera rules, especially when making photographs for glossy reports or other high-quality publications. How much quality is lost by using a digital camera? Maybe none. Other experts argue that a digital camera produces better quality than a film camera in many important respects and praise the digital camera as the answer to all photographic needs.

So whom can you believe? Does this mean one should throw away the 35mm camera? Is this the end of the traditional camera? What is your opinion of the digital camera? How much longer before the demise of purchasing rolls of films and print development? Alternatively, will traditional cameras continue for many more years?

For more information on digital cameras and photo printers, visit the Discovering Computers 2002 Issues Web page (**scsite.com/dc2002/issues.htm**) and click Chapter 6 Issue #4.

TECHNOLOGY TRAILBLAZER

CARLY **FIORINA**

It seems somewhat improbable that a shipping department secretary would someday return to become the company's chairman of the board, but it is a true story for Carly Fiorina. As Hewlett-Packard's leader, she is focusing on improving profitability, innovation, customer service, and Internet applications.

Fiorina credits her liberal arts undergraduate studies at Stanford University, with majors in philosophy and medieval history, with helping her learn how to think and make choices. She urges college graduates to love what they do, not to make choices to please someone else.

After a brief stint in law school, she became a sales representative for AT&T. That short-term job eventually grew into leading and guiding Lucent Technologies, Inc., the AT&T spin-off, to one of the most successful IPO stock offerings. Fiorina says leadership involves influencing others and mastering change. It also empowers people to reach their full potential and make decisions.

For more information on Carly Fiorina, visit the Discovering Computers 2002 People Web page (**scsite.com/dc2002/people.htm**) and click Carly Fiorina.

Portable Printers

A **portable printer** is a small, lightweight printer that allows a mobile user to print from a notebook or handheld computer while traveling (Figure 6-27). Barely wider than the paper on which they print, portable printers easily can fit in a briefcase alongside a notebook computer.

Some portable printers use ink-jet technology. Others are thermal or thermal wax-transfer. Many of these printers connect to a parallel port or USB port. Others have a built-in wireless infrared port through which they communicate with the computer.

Plotters and Large-Format Printers

Plotters are sophisticated printers used to produce high-quality drawings such as blueprints, maps, and circuit diagrams. These printers are used in specialized fields such as engineering and drafting, and usually are very costly. Current plotters use a row of charged wires (called styli) to draw an electrostatic pattern on specially coated paper and then fuse toner to the pattern. The printed image consists of a series of very small dots, which provide high-quality output.

Operating like an ink-jet printer, but on a much larger scale, a **large-format printer** creates photo-realistic quality color prints. Used by graphic artists, these high costing, high performance printers are used for signs, posters, and other displays (Figure 6-28).

Plotters and large-format printers typically can handle paper with widths up to 60 inches because blueprints, maps, signs, posters and other such drawings and displays can be quite large. Some plotters and large-format printers use individual sheets of paper, while others take large rolls.

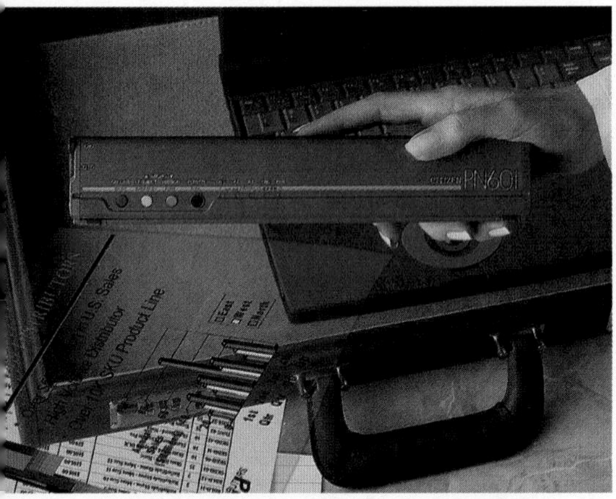

Figure 6-27 A portable printer is a small, compact printer that allows the mobile user to print from a notebook or handheld computer while traveling.

Figure 6-28 Graphic artists use large-format printers to print signs, posters, and other displays.

SPEAKERS AND HEADSETS

An **audio output device** is a component of a computer that produces music, speech, or other sounds, such as beeps. Two commonly used audio output devices are speakers and headsets.

Most personal computers have a small internal speaker that usually outputs only low-quality sound. For this reason, many personal computer users add sophisticated stereo **speakers** to their computers to generate a higher-quality sound (Figure 6-29). Some monitors even have larger speakers built into the sides of the monitor.

To boost the low bass sounds, some users add a **woofer** (also called a subwoofer). You connect the stereo speakers and woofer to ports on the sound card. Most speakers have tone and volume controls so you can adjust settings.

When using speakers, anyone within listening distance can hear the output. If you are in a computer laboratory or some other crowded environment, speakers might not be practical. Instead, you can plug a headset into a port on the sound card. With the **headset**, only you can hear the sound from the computer (Figure 6-30).

Figure 6-29 Many personal computer users have high-quality stereo speakers and a woofer for their computers.

Figure 6-30 In a crowded environment where speakers are not practical, you can use a headset for audio output.

APPLY IT!

Plug into Sound

Before purchasing a new computer or upgrading an existing one, you should consider the ways in which you will use it. Unless sound plays a minor role in your life, you will want to consider a stand-alone sound card. Most inexpensive computers integrate a sound chip with the motherboard. Look at the back of the computer. If the microphone and speaker ports are grouped together with the keyboard/mouse connector and the serial port, you have an integrated onboard sound chip.

Until recently, Creative Lab's Sound Blaster (see URL below) card has dominated the computer sound market. If a sound card were not Sound Blaster compatible, it would not sell. This is because most games require a Sound Blaster compatible sound card. Even though new technology opened the door for other options, Sound Blaster is still the de facto standard. Today's cards make games and multimedia applications sound great and provide users with the capability to compose, edit, and print their own music; learn to play the piano; record and edit digital audio; and play audio CDs.

The biggest change in sound card architecture was the introduction of 3D-positional audio. Primarily used with games, the 3D-positional audio algorithm fools your brain into thinking sounds are emanating from somewhere other than the speakers sitting in front of you.

Purchasing a sound card is an individual decision. To get a better idea of what you should purchase to fit your budget and lifestyle, consider the following:

1. How much money do you plan to spend?
2. Will you use the sound card for playing games or music, recording digital audio?
3. Select two or three cards and then read online reviews (see URL below).

For more information on computer sound systems and the Web sites mentioned above, visit the Discovering Computers 2002 Apply It Web page (**scsite.com/dc2002/apply.htm**) and click Chapter 6 Apply It #3.

Electronically produced voice output is growing in popularity. **Voice output** occurs when you hear a person's voice or when the computer talks to you through the speakers on the computer. As discussed in Chapter 2, you can listen to interviews, talk shows, sporting events, news, recorded music, and live concerts from many radio and television stations on the Web. Some Web sites dedicate themselves to providing voice output, where you can hear songs, quotes, and historical speeches and lectures (Figure 6-31).

Very often, voice output works with voice input. **Internet telephony**, for example, allows you to have a conversation over the Web, just as if you were on the telephone.

Sophisticated programs enable the computer to converse with you. Talk into the microphone and say, "I'd like today's weather report." The computer replies, "For which city?" You reply, "Chicago." The computer says, "Sunny and 80 degrees."

OTHER OUTPUT DEVICES

Although monitors, printers, and speakers are the more widely used output devices, many other output devices are available for particular uses and applications. These include data projectors, facsimiles, and multifunction devices. The following pages discuss each of these devices.

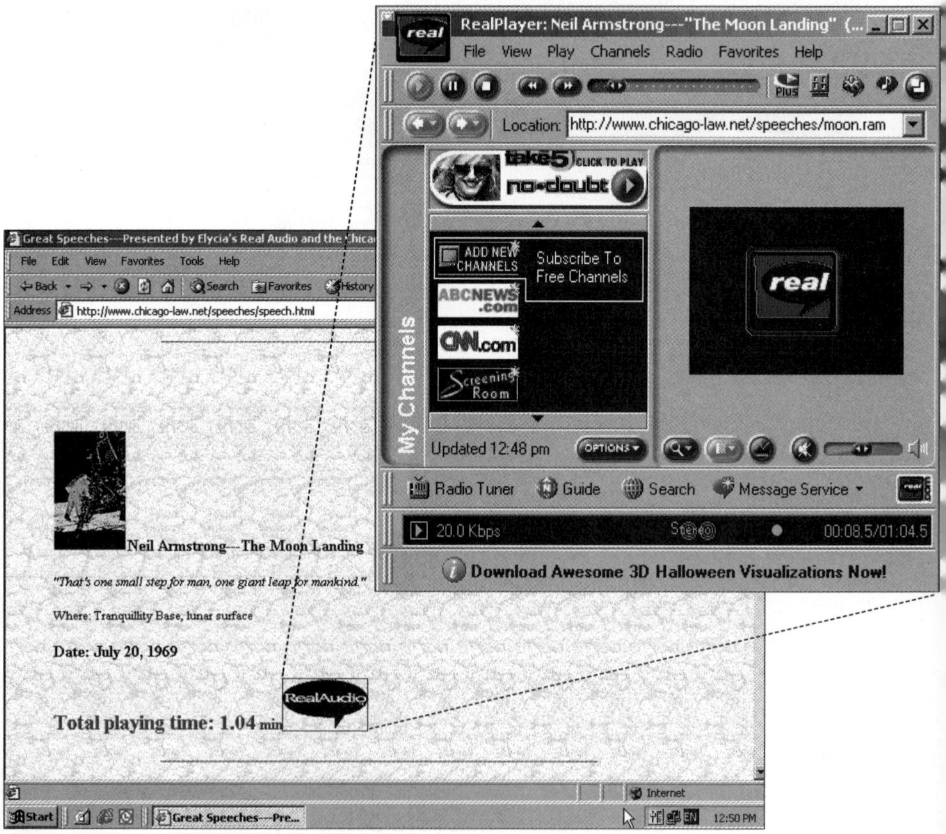

Figure 6-31 You can listen to historical speeches and lectures from the Web. Playing here is an audio broadcast made by Neil Armstrong as he walked on the moon for the first time.

Data Projectors

A **data projector** is a device that takes the image from a computer screen and projects it onto a larger screen so an audience of people can see the image clearly. For example, many classrooms use data projectors so all students easily can see an instructor's presentation on the screen (Figure 6-32).

Some data projectors are large devices that attach to a ceiling or wall in an auditorium. Others are small portable devices. Two types of smaller, lower-cost units are LCD projectors and DLP projectors.

An **LCD projector**, which uses liquid crystal display technology, attaches directly to a computer and uses its own light source to display the information shown on the computer screen. Because LCD projectors tend to produce lower-quality images, some users prefer to use a DLP projector for sharper, brighter images.

A **digital light processing (DLP) projector** uses tiny mirrors to reflect light, which produces crisp, bright, colorful images that remain in focus and can be seen clearly even in a well-lit room.

Facsimile (Fax) Machine

A **facsimile (fax) machine** is a device that transmits and receives documents over telephone lines. The documents can contain text, drawings, or photographs, or can be handwritten. The term fax also refers to a document that you send or receive via a fax machine.

A stand-alone fax machine scans an original document, converts the image into digitized data, and transmits the digitized image (Figure 6-33). A fax machine at the receiving end reads the incoming data, converts the digitized data into an image, and prints or stores a copy of the original image.

Figure 6-33 A stand-alone fax machine.

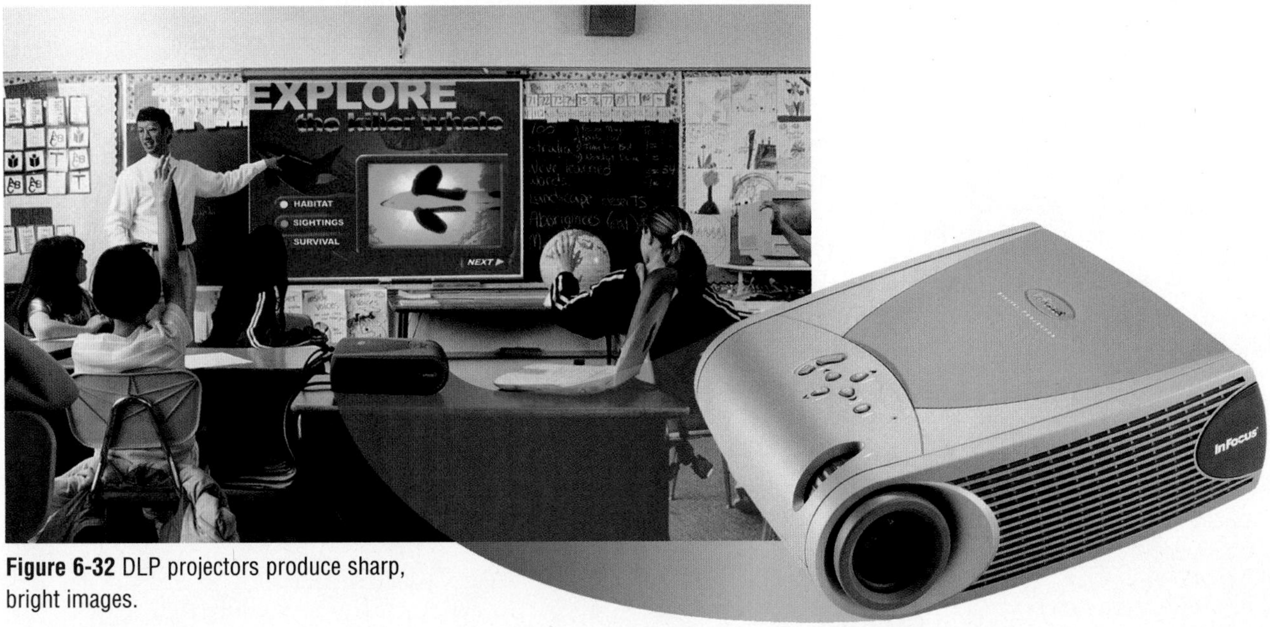

Figure 6-32 DLP projectors produce sharp, bright images.

Many computers include fax capability by using a fax modem. A **fax modem** is a modem that also allows you to send (and sometimes receive) electronic documents as faxes (Figure 6-34). A fax modem transmits computer-prepared documents, such as a word processing letter, or documents that have been digitized with a scanner or digital camera. A fax modem transmits these faxes to a fax machine or to another fax modem.

When a computer (instead of a fax machine) receives a fax, you can view the fax on the screen, saving the time and expense of printing it. If you wish, you also can print the fax using special fax software. The quality of the viewed or printed fax is less than that of a word processing document because the fax actually is a large image. Optical character recognition (OCR) software enables you to convert the image to text and then edit it.

A fax modem can be an external device that plugs into a port on the back of the system unit or an internal card you insert into an expansion slot on the motherboard.

Multifunction Devices

A **multifunction device** (**MFD**) is a single piece of equipment that looks like a copy machine, but provides the functionality of a printer, scanner, copy machine, and perhaps a fax machine (Figure 6-35). The features of these devices, which are sometimes called multifunction peripherals (MFPs) or all-in-one devices, vary widely. For example, some use color ink-jet printer technology, while others include a black-and-white laser printer.

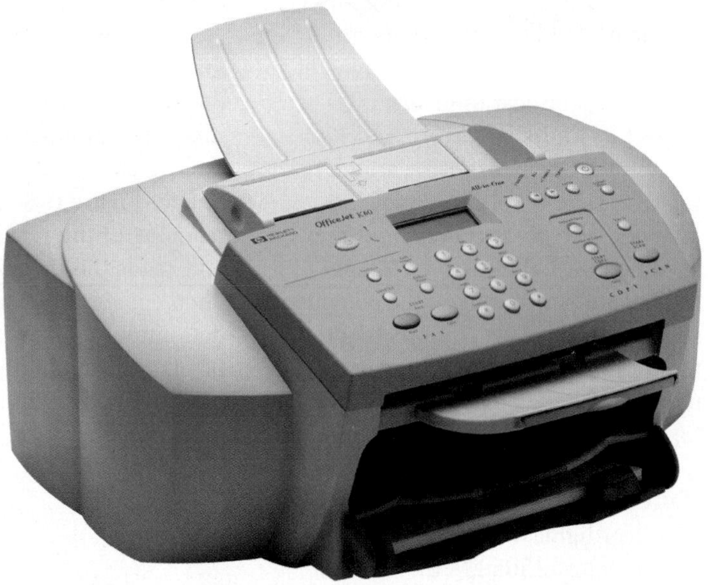

Figure 6-35 This multifunction device is a color printer, scanner, copy machine, and fax machine all in one.

Web Link
For more information on fax modems, visit the Discovering Computers 2002 Chapter 6 WEB LINK page (**scsite.com/dc2002/ch6/weblink.htm**) and click Fax Modems.

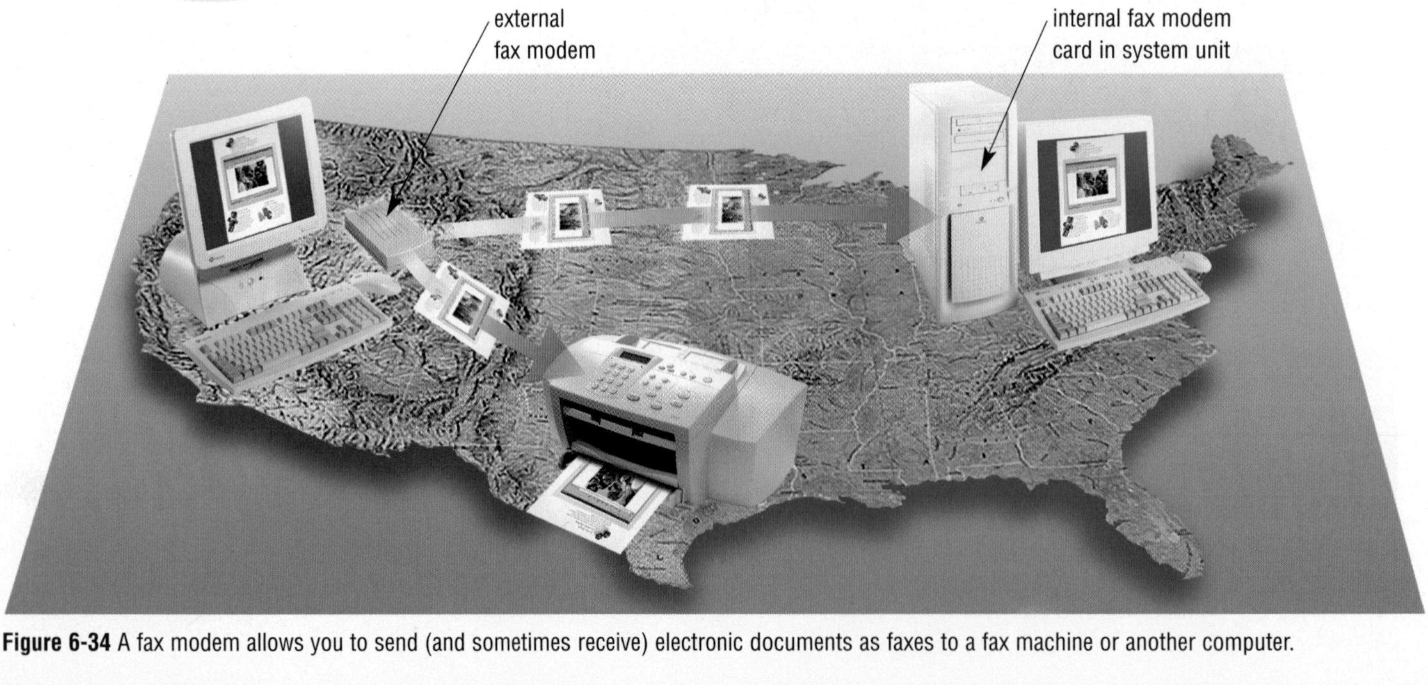

Figure 6-34 A fax modem allows you to send (and sometimes receive) electronic documents as faxes to a fax machine or another computer.

Small offices and home offices (SOHOs) use MFDs because they require less space than having a separate printer, scanner, copy machine, and fax machine. Another advantage of an MFD is that it is significantly less expensive than if you purchase each device separately. If the device breaks down, however, you lose all four functions, which is the primary disadvantage. Given all the advantages, more users are bringing MFDs into their offices and homes.

TERMINALS

A **terminal** is a device that performs both input and output because it consists of a monitor (output), a keyboard (input), and a video card. Terminals fall into three basic categories: dumb terminals, intelligent terminals, and special-purpose terminals.

A **dumb terminal** has no processing power; thus, cannot function as an independent device (Figure 6-36). A dumb terminal can enter and transmit data to, or receive and display information from, a computer to which it is connected. Dumb terminals connect to a **host computer** that performs the processing and then sends the output back to the dumb terminal. The host computer usually is a mid-range server, mainframe, or supercomputer.

Figure 6-36 Dumb terminals have no processing power and usually are connected to larger computer systems.

Web Link

For more information on multifunction devices, visit the Discovering Computers 2002 Chapter 6 WEB LINK page (**scsite.com/dc2002/ch6/weblink.htm**) and click Multifunction Devices.

ISSUE

Jack of *all* Trades

Multifunction Devices

Designing and setting up a home office is a challenge. In addition to a computer, other required hardware most likely includes a printer, fax machine, copy machine, and scanner. When selecting these components, you have several options to consider. One option is to purchase each of these as a separate device. A second option is to purchase a combination printer and scanner or combination printer and fax machine. A third option is to purchase a multi-function device that contains all four of these hardware devices. Generally, a multifunction device represents a convenient and efficient way to expand the type of document input and output facilities. On the other hand, performance offered by multifunction devices rarely matches individual devices that are designed specifically for the job. Which option would be best? How would budget and workspace affect your choice? Why? What advantages or disadvantages are there in relation to connecting these devices to a personal computer?

For more information on multifunction devices, visit the Discovering Computers 2002 Issues Web page (**scsite.com/dc2002/issues.htm**) and and click Chapter 6 Issue #5.

In addition to a monitor and keyboard, an **intelligent terminal** also has memory and a processor that has the capability of performing some functions independent of the host computer. Intelligent terminals sometimes are called **programmable terminals** because they can be programmed by the software developer to perform basic tasks. In recent years, personal computers have replaced most intelligent terminals.

Other special-purpose terminals perform specific tasks and contain features uniquely designed for use in a particular industry. Two of these special-purpose terminals are point-of-sale terminals and automated teller machines (Figure 6-37).

A **point-of-sale (POS)** terminal records purchases at the point where the consumer purchases a product or service. The POS terminal used in a grocery store, for example, is a combination of an electronic cash register and bar code reader. As described in Chapter 5, grocery store UPC bar codes contain data that identify the manufacturer and item of a product. When the check out clerk scans the bar code on the food product (input), the computer uses the manufacturer and item numbers to look up the price of the item and the complete product name in the database. Then, the price of the item from the database displays on the monitor (output), the name of the item and its price print on a receipt (output), and the item being sold is recorded so the inventory can be updated. Thus, the output from POS terminals serves as input to other computers to maintain sales records, update inventory, verify credit, and perform other activities associated with the sales transactions that are critical to running the business.

Many POS terminals handle credit card or debit card payments. Simply swipe your card through the reader (input) and the system processes your credit or debit card. Once approved, the terminal usually prints a receipt for a customer (output).

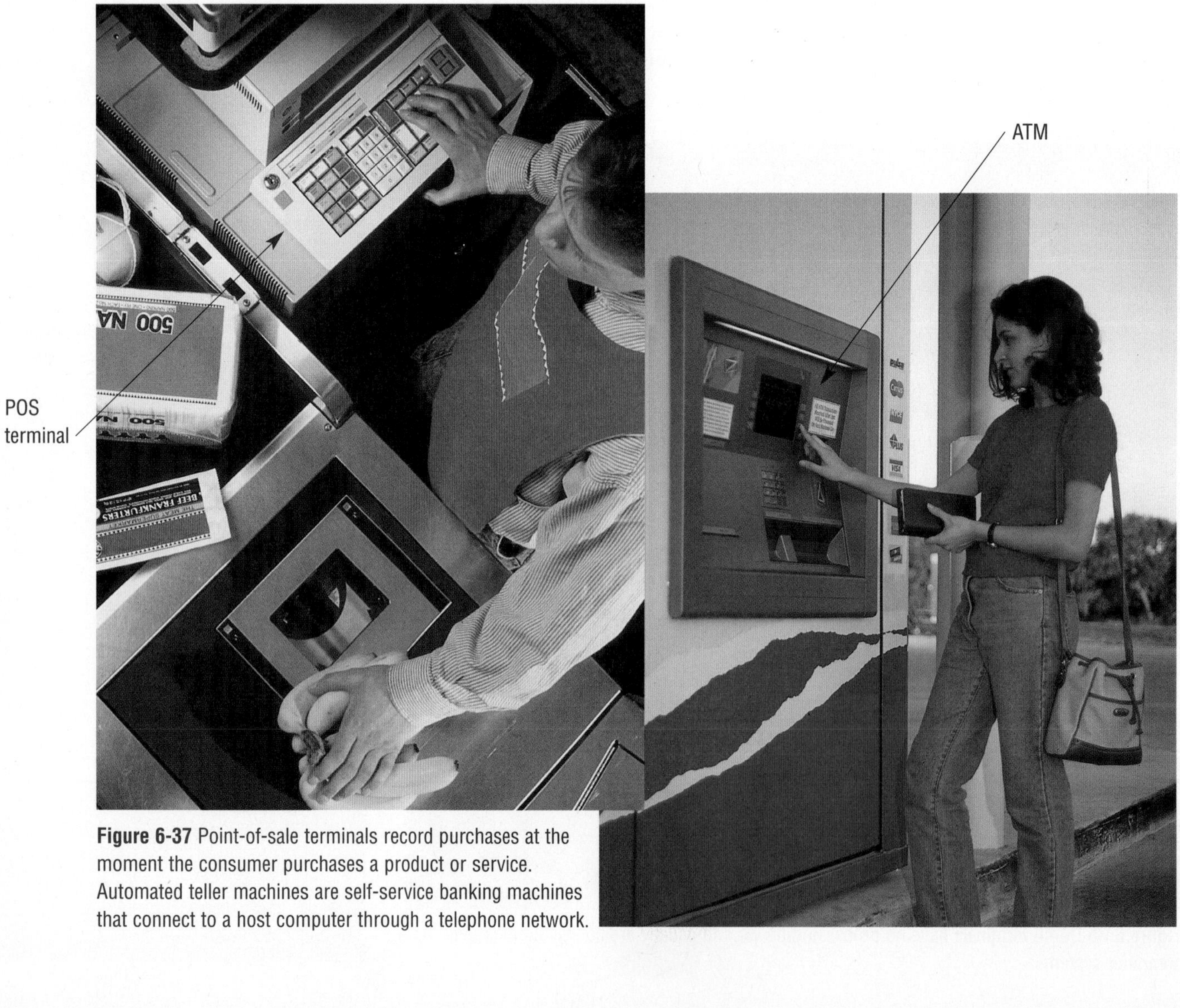

Figure 6-37 Point-of-sale terminals record purchases at the moment the consumer purchases a product or service. Automated teller machines are self-service banking machines that connect to a host computer through a telephone network.

An **automated teller machine (ATM)** is a self-service banking machine that connects to a host computer through a telephone network. You insert a plastic bankcard with a magnetic strip into the ATM and enter your password, called a personal identification number (PIN), to access your bank account. Some ATMs have touch screens, while others have special keyboards for input. Using an ATM, you can withdraw cash, deposit money, transfer funds, or inquire about an account balance. When your transaction is complete, the ATM prints a receipt for your records.

OUTPUT DEVICES FOR PHYSICALLY CHALLENGED USERS

As discussed in Chapter 5, the growing presence of computers in people's lives has generated an awareness of the need to address computing requirements for those with physical limitations. For users with mobility, hearing, or vision disabilities, many different types of output devices are available. Hearing-impaired users, for example, can instruct programs to display words instead of sounds. With the Windows operating system, these users also can set options to make programs easier to use. For example, the Magnifier command enlarges text and other items in a window on the screen (Figure 6-38).

Web Link

For more information on POS terminals visit the Discovering Computers 2002 Chapter 6 WEB LINK page (**scsite.com/dc2002/ch6/weblink.htm**) and click POS Terminals.

Web Link

For more information on automated teller machines, visit the Discovering Computers 2002 Chapter 6 WEB LINK page (**scsite.com/dc2002/ch6/weblink.htm**) and click Automated Teller Machines.

Figure 6-38a (Magnifier command)

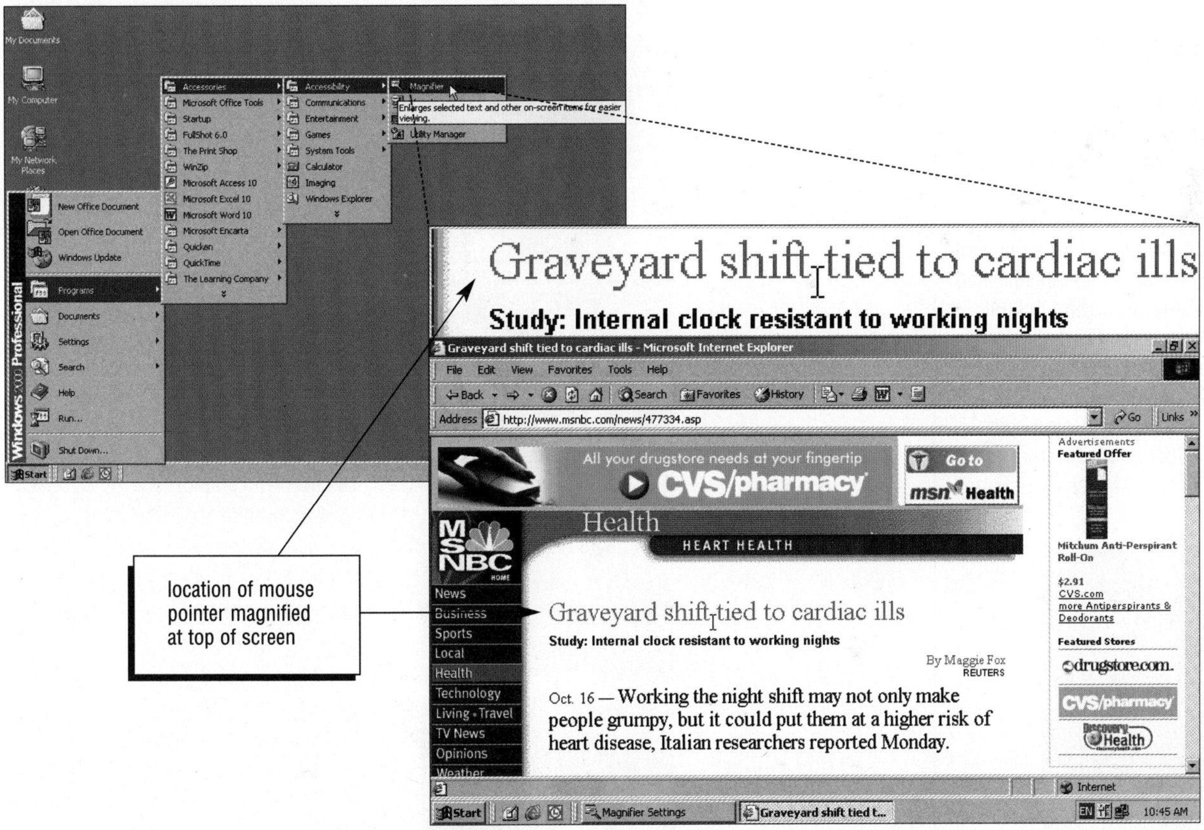

Figure 6-38b (screen with magnification window at top)

Figure 6-38 The Magnifier command in Windows enlarges text and other on-screen items for individuals with vision disabilities.

Visually impaired users can change Windows settings such as increasing the size or changing the color of the text to make the words easier to read. Instead of using a monitor, blind users can work with voice output. That is, the computer reads the information that displays on the screen. Another alternative is a **Braille printer**, which outputs information in Braille onto paper (Figure 6-39).

Figure 6-39
A Braille printer.

TECHNOLOGY TRAILBLAZER

HEIDI **VAN ARNEM**

The needs of the disability community often go unmet, but Heidi Van Arnem is helping to enhance the lives of people with disabilities and the individuals and organizations that support them. As chairman and CEO of iCan.com, she helps to bring together businesses, the medical industry, government-led efforts, and nonprofits.

As a successful businesswoman, entrepreneur, and inventor, Van Arnem is recognized as one of the Top 25 Women on the Web. She was the first recipient of the Evan Kemp Entrepreneur of the Year award by the President's Committee on Employment of People with Disabilities and has received numerous awards for her business achievements and community outreach by organizations such as the U.S. Chamber of Commerce. In addition, Van Arnem's Spend a Day in a Wheelchair program has received national acclaim for helping sensitize students to the difficulties wheelchair users face.

A quadriplegic since 16 from a gunshot wound to the neck, Van Arnem established the Heidi Van Arnem foundation in 1992. This nonprofit organization is dedicated to helping find a cure for paralysis.

For more information on Heidi Van Arnem, visit the Discovering Computers 2002 People Web page (**scsite.com/dc2002/people.htm**) and click Heidi Van Arnem.

SUGGESTED OUTPUT DEVICES BY USER

USER	MONITOR
Home 	• 17- or 19-inch color CRT monitor • High-definition television
Small Office/Home Office 	• 19- or 21-inch color CRT monitor • Color LCD display for handheld computer
Mobile 	• 15.4-inch color LCD display with a notebook computer • 19-inch color CRT monitor for a notebook computer docking station • Color LCD display for handheld computer
Large Business 	• 19- or 21-inch color CRT or LCD monitor • 15.4-inch color LCD display for a notebook computer • Color LCD display for handheld computer
Power 	• 21-inch color LCD monitor

Figure 6-40 This table recommends suggested output devices for various types of users.

PUTTING IT ALL TOGETHER

Many factors influence the type of output devices you should use: the type of output desired, the hardware and software in use, and the desired cost. Figure 6-40 outlines several suggested monitors, printers, and other output devices for various types of computer users.

CHAPTER SUMMARY

Data is a collection of raw, unprocessed facts, figures, and symbols. Computers process and organize data into information, which has meaning and is useful. This chapter described the various methods of output and several commonly used output devices. Output devices presented included display devices, printers, speakers, data projectors, fax machines, multifunction devices, and terminals.

PRINTER	OTHER
• Ink-jet color printer; *or* • Photo printer • Label printer	• Speakers • Headset
• Multifunction device; *or* • Ink-jet color printer; *or* • Laser printer, black and white • Label printer	• Fax machine • Speakers
• Portable printer • Ink-jet color printer; *or* • Laser printer, black and white, for in-office use; *or* • Photo printer	• Fax modem • Headset • DLP data projector
• Laser printer, black and white • Line printer (for large reports from a mainframe) • Label printer	• Fax machine *or* fax modem • Speakers • DLP data projector • Dumb terminal
• Laser printer, black and white • Plotter • Photo printer; *or* • Dye sublimation printer	• Fax machine *or* fax modem • Speakers • Headset

Graphics Designer/Illustrator

A designer or illustrator is an artist, but generally does not create original works. Instead, their job is to portray visually the ideas of their clients. Illustrators work in fields such as fashion, technical, medical, animation, or even that of a cartoonist. Designers create visual impressions of products and advertisements. Some of these are as follows:

- Graphic designers – design book covers, stationery, CD covers, and CD embossments
- Costume and theater designers – design costumes and settings for theater and television
- Interior designers – design the layout, decor, and furnishings of homes and buildings
- Jewelry designers – design jewelry, including some one of a kind
- Fashion designers – design clothing, shoes, and other fashion accessories

Education-wise, you can find certificate, two-year, four-year, and master level programs within the design area. Many individuals choose to freelance, while others work with ad agencies, publishing companies, design studios, or specialized departments within large companies. Salaries may range anywhere from $25,000 to $75,000 plus, based on experience and educational background.

Adobe (see URL below) offers a Certified Expert Program. To become an Adobe® Certified Expert, you must pass an Adobe Product Proficiency Exam for the product for which you want to be certified.

To learn more about graphics design and illustration as a career and the Web site mentioned above, visit the Discovering Computers 2002 Careers Web page (**scsite.com/dc2002/careers.htm**) and click Graphics Designer/Illustrator.

E-GOVERNMENT

STAMP OF APPROVAL

Making a Federal Case for Useful Information

When it is time to buy stamps to mail your correspondence, you no longer need to wait in long lines at your local post office. Instead, log on to the Internet and download a stamp right to your personal computer.

The U.S. Postal Service has authorized several corporations to sell stamps online. Users can download software from a company's Web site, charge the postage fee to a credit card, and then print the postage on a label printer or directly onto envelopes and labels. Some of these Web sites, such as Stamps.com, shown in Figure 6-41, charge a small percentage of each order as a convenience fee.

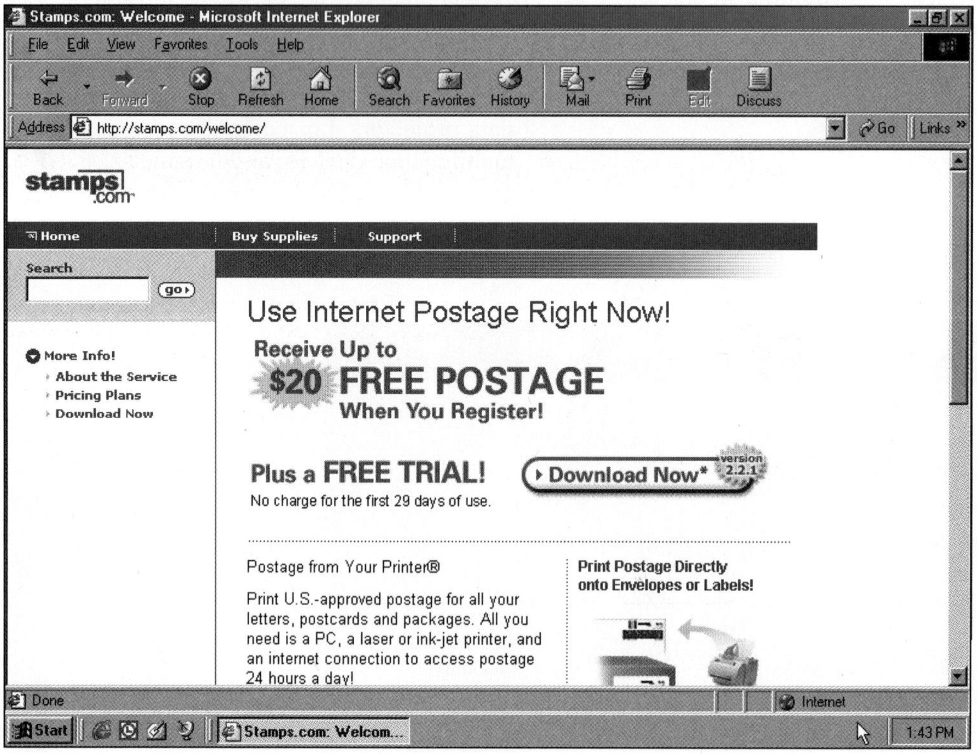

Figure 6-41 Purchasing stamps on the Internet eliminates making a trip to the post office and waiting in long lines.

Although citizens may not be enthusiastic about paying income taxes, April 15 can be more tolerable knowing that some of their hard-earned dollars are spent subsidizing useful government Web sites.

You can recognize these Web sites on the Internet by their .gov top-level domain abbreviation. For example, the Library of Congress Web site is lcweb.loc.gov. As the oldest federal cultural institution in the United States and the largest library in the world, the mission of the Library of Congress is to serve the research needs of the U.S. Congress. Patrons can visit one of 22 reading rooms on Capitol Hill and access more than 115 million items written in 450 languages. The Library of Congress Web site, shown in Figure 6-42, has forms and information from the Copyright Office, an

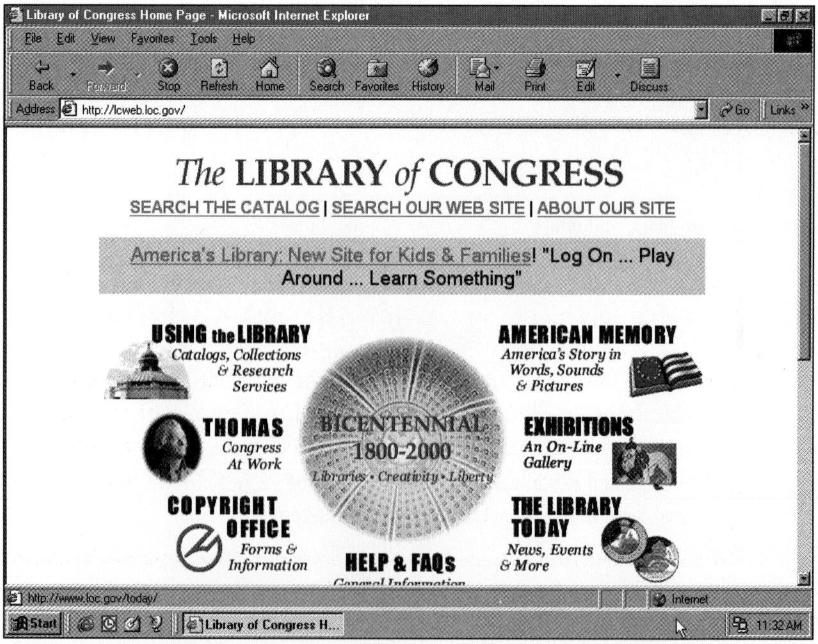

Figure 6-42 The Library of Congress Web site contains more than 115 million items written in 450 languages.

online gallery, and links to a variety of topics, including the National Agricultural Library and the National Library of Medicine. These and other government resources Web sites are listed in Figure 6-43.

Government and military Web sites offer a wide range of information. The Time Service Department Web site will provide you with the correct time. If you are looking for a federal document, the FedWorld Information Network lists thousands of documents distributed by the government on its Web site. For access to the names of your congressional representatives, the president's cabinet members, and the Supreme Court justices; or to read portions of a federal statute or the U.S. Constitution, visit the extensive Hieros Gamos Web site, which is a governmental and legal portal with links to the legislative, judicial, and executive branches of government.

For more information on government resources Web sites, visit the Discovering Computers 2002 E-Revolution Web page (scsite.com/dc2002/e-rev.htm) and click Government.

GOVERNMENT RESOURCES WEB SITES	URL
Postage	
Pitney Bowes	pitneybowes.com
Simply Postage	simplypostage.com
Stamps.com	stamps.com
Government	
FedWorld Information Network	fedworld.gov
Hieros Gamos	hg.org
Library of Congress	lcweb.loc.gov
National Archives and Records Administration	www.nara.gov
National Agricultural Library	www.nal.usda.gov
National Library of Medicine	www.nlm.nih.gov
The White House	www.whitehouse.gov
Thomas Legislative Information	thomas.loc.gov
Time Service Department	tycho.usno.navy.mil
U.S. Department of Education	ed.gov
U.S. Government Printing Office	www.access.gpo.gov
U.S. Patent and Trademark Office	www.uspto.gov
U.S. Treasury	treas.gov
USA Jobs	www.usajobs.opm.gov

For an updated list of government resources Web sites, visit scsite.com/dc2002/e-rev.htm.

Figure 6-43 These Web sites offer information on buying U.S.-approved postage online and researching federal agencies.

eREVOLUTION E-GOVERNMENT applied:

1. View the three postage Web sites listed in Figure 6-43. Compare and contrast the available services on each one. Consider postage cost, necessary equipment, shipping services, security techniques, and tracking capability. Explain why you would or would not like to use this service.

2. Visit the Hieros Gamos Web site listed in Figure 6-43. What are the names, addresses, and telephone numbers of your two state senators and your local congressional representative? On what committees do they serve? Who is the chief justice of the Supreme Court, and what has been this justice's opinion on two recently decided cases? Who are the members of the president's cabinet? Then, visit two other Web sites listed in Figure 6-43. Write a paragraph on each Web site describing its content and features.

In Summary

Web Instructions: To display this page from the Web, start your browser and enter the URL scsite.com/dc2002/ch6/summary.htm. Click the links for current and additional information. To listen to an audio version of this In Summary, click the Audio button. To play the audio, RealPlayer must be installed on your computer (download by clicking here).

1 What Are the Four Types of Output?

Output is data that has been processed into a useful form, called information. Four types of output are text, graphics, audio, and video. **Text** consists of characters used to create words, sentences, and paragraphs. A **graphic** or **graphical image** is a digital representation of nontext information such as a drawing, chart, or photograph. **Audio** is music, speech, or any other sound. **Video** consists of full-motion images that are played back at various speeds.

2 What Are the Different Types of Output Devices?

An **output device** is any hardware component capable of conveying information to a user. A **display device** is an output device that visually conveys text, graphics, and video information. A **printer** is an output device that produces text and graphics on a physical medium such as paper or transparency film. An **audio output device** produces music, speech, or other sounds. Other output devices include data projectors, facsimile (fax) machines, and multifunction devices.

3 What Factors Affect the Quality of a Monitor?

A **monitor** is a display device that consists of a screen housed in a plastic or metal case. The quality of the display depends on a monitor's resolution, dot pitch, and refresh rate. **Resolution**, or sharpness, is related to the number of pixels a monitor can display. **Dot pitch**, a measure of image clarity, is the distance between each pixel. **Refresh rate** is the speed with which a monitor redraws images on the screen. Refresh rate should be fast enough to maintain a constant, flicker-free image. A **video card** converts digital output into an analog video signal that is sent through a cable to the monitor. How the picture is produced is determined by the display device. Several standards define resolution, the number of colors, and other monitor properties. Today, most monitors and video cards support the **super video graphics array (SVGA)** standard.

4 What Are Monitor Ergonomic Issues?

Features that address monitor ergonomic issues include controls to adjust the brightness, contrast, positioning, height, and width of images. Many monitors have a tilt-and-swivel base so the angle of the screen can be altered to minimize neck strain and glare. CRT monitors produce a small amount of **electromagnetic radiation (EMR)**, which is a magnetic field that travels at the speed of light. High-quality CRT monitors should comply with **MPR II standards**, which define acceptable levels of EMR for a monitor.

5 How Are Various Types of Printers Different?

Printers produce printed information, called **hard copy**. Generally printers are grouped into two categories: impact and nonimpact. An **impact printer** forms characters and graphics by striking a mechanism against an ink ribbon that physically contacts the paper. A **dot-matrix printer** is an impact printer that prints images when tiny wire pins on a print head mechanism strike an inked ribbon. A **line printer** is a high-speed impact printer that prints an entire line at one time. A **nonimpact printer** creates characters and graphics without actually striking the paper. An **ink-jet printer** is a high-speed, high-quality nonimpact printer that sprays drops of ink onto a piece of paper. A **laser printer** is a nonimpact printer that operates in a manner similar to a copy machine. A **thermal printer** generates images by pushing electrically heated pins against heat-sensitive paper. A printer capable of **Internet printing** receives print instructions from an Internet service, allowing it to print documents from desktop and wireless devices. Other types of printers include **photo printers**, **label printers**, **portable printers**, and **plotters**.

In Summary

6 What Are Various Types of Audio Output Devices?

Two commonly used audio output devices are **speakers** and **headsets**. Most personal computers have an internal speaker that outputs low-quality sound. Many users add high-quality stereo speakers or purchase personal computers with larger speakers built into the sides of the monitor. A woofer can be added to boost low bass sounds. A headset plugged into a port on the sound card allows only the user to hear sound from the computer.

7 Why Are Data Projectors, Fax Machines, and Multifunction Devices Used?

A data projector takes the image on a computer screen and projects it onto a large screen so an audience of people can see the image. A **facsimile (fax) machine** transmits and receives documents over telephone lines. A **fax modem** is a communications device that sends (and sometimes receives) electronic documents as faxes. A **multifunction device (MFD)** is a single piece of equipment that looks like a copy machine, but provides the functionality of a printer, scanner, copy machine, and sometimes a fax machine.

8 How Is a Terminal Both an Input and Output Device?

A **terminal** is a device that consists of a keyboard (input), a monitor (output), and a video card. A terminal is used to input and transmit data to, or receive and output information from, a host computer that performs the processing. Three basic categories of terminals are **dumb terminals**, **intelligent terminals**, and **point-of-sale (POS)** terminals.

9 What Are Output Options for Physically Challenged Users?

For users with mobility, hearing, or vision disabilities, many different types of output devices are available. Hearing-impaired users can instruct programs to display words instead of produce sounds. Visually impaired users can change the size or color of text to make words easier to read. Blind users can utilize voice output, where the computer reads information that displays on the screen. A Braille printer outputs information in Braille onto paper.

Key Terms

Web Instructions: To display this page from the Web, start your browser and enter the URL scsite.com/dc2002/ch6/terms.htm. Scroll through the list of terms. Click a term to display its definition and a picture. Click the To WEB button for current and additional information about the term from the Web. To see animations, Shockwave and Flash Player must be installed on your computer (download by clicking here).

active-matrix display (6.8)
audio (6.3)
audio output device (6.23)
automatic teller machine (ATM) (6.29)
band printer (6.15)
bit depth (6.10)
Braille printer (6.30)
cathode ray tube (CRT) (6.5)
ClearType (6.7)
color depth (6.10)
continuous-form paper (6.14)
CRT monitor (6.5)
data projector (6.25)
Digital Display Working Group (DDWG) (6.10)
digital light processing (DLP) projector (6.25)
Digital Video Interface (DVI) (6.10)
display (6.4)
display device (6.4)
dot pitch (6.9)
dot-matrix printer (6.14)
dual-scan display (6.8)
dumb terminal (6.27)
dye-sublimation printer (6.19)
electromagnetic radiation (EMR) (6.11)
electronic book (e-book) (6.7)
ENERGY STAR program (6.12)
e-stamp (6.21)
facsimile (fax) machine (6.25)
fax modem (6.26)
flat-panel display (6.5)
gas plasma monitor (6.8)
graphic (6.3)
graphical image (6.3)
graphics card (6.10)
gray scaling (6.4)
hard copy (6.12)
headset (6.23)
hertz (6.9)
high-definition television (HDTV) (6.12)
high-performance addressing (HPA) (6.8)
host computer (6.27)
impact printer (6.14)
ink-jet printer (6.15)
intelligent terminal (6.28)
interactive TV (6.12)
Internet postage (6.21)
Internet printing (6.13)

BRAILLE PRINTER
Printer for blind users that outputs information in Braille onto paper. (6.30)

Internet telephony (6.24)
label printer (6.21)
landscape orientation (6.12)
large-format printer (6.22)
laser printer (6.16)
LCD displays (6.5)
LCD monitors (6.5)
LCD projector (6.25)
letter quality (LQ) (6.14)
line printer (6.14)
liquid crystal display (LCD) (6.5)
monitor (6.4)
monochrome (6.4)
MPR II (6.11)
multifunction device (MFD) (6.26)
National Television Standards Committee (6.12)
near letter quality (NLQ) (6.14)
nonimpact printer (6.15)
NTSC converter (6.12)
output (6.2)
output device (6.4)
page description language (PDL) (6.18)
passive-matrix display (6.8)
PCL (Printer Control Language) (6.18)
photo printer (6.20)
pixel (6.5)
pixel pitch (6.9)
plotters (6.22)
point-of-sale (POS) terminal (6.28)
portable printer (6.22)
portrait orientation (6.12)
PostScript (6.18)
printer (6.12)
printout (6.12)
programmable terminals (6.28)
refresh rate (6.9)
resolution (6.8)
screen (6.4)
shuttle-matrix printer (6.15)
soft copy (6.4)
speakers (6.23)
super video graphics array (SVGA) (6.10)
terminal (6.27)
text (6.2)
thermal dye transfer printer (6.19)
thermal printer (6.19)
thermal transfer printer (6.19)
thermal wax-transfer printer (6.19)
thin-film transistor (TFT) display (6.8)
toner (6.17)
vertical frequency (6.9)
vertical scan rate (6.9)
video (6.3)
video adapter (6.10)
video card (6.10)
Video Electronics Standards Association (VESA) (6.10)

LARGE FORMAT PRINTER
Nonimpact printer that creates photo-realistic quality color prints; operates like an ink-jet printer, but on a much larger scale. (6.22)

viewable size (6.5)
voice output (6.24)
woofer (6.23)

Learn It Online

Web Instructions: To display this page from the Web, start your browser and enter the URL scsite.com/dc2002/ch6/learn.htm.

1. Web Guide

Click Web Guide to display the Guide to World Wide Web Sites and Searching Techniques Web page. Click Computers and Computing. Click PC Guide and then search for monitors. Click monitors and then review the information. Use your word processing program to prepare a brief report on your findings and submit your assignment to your instructor.

2. Scavenger Hunt

Click Scavenger Hunt. Print a copy of the Scavenger Hunt page; use this page to write down your answers as you search the Web. Submit your completed page to your instructor.

3. Who Wants to Be a Computer Genius?

Click Computer Genius to find out if you are a computer genius. Directions on how to play the game will display. When you are ready to play, click the PLAY button. Submit your score to your instructor.

4. Wheel of Terms

Click Wheel of Terms to reinforce important terms you learned in this chapter by playing the Shelly Cashman Series version of this popular game. Directions on how to play the game will display. When you are ready to play, click the PLAY button. Submit your score to your instructor.

5. Career Corner

Click Career Corner to display the MSN Career page. Review this page. Click the links that you find interesting. Write a brief report on the topics you found to be the most helpful. Submit the report to your instructor.

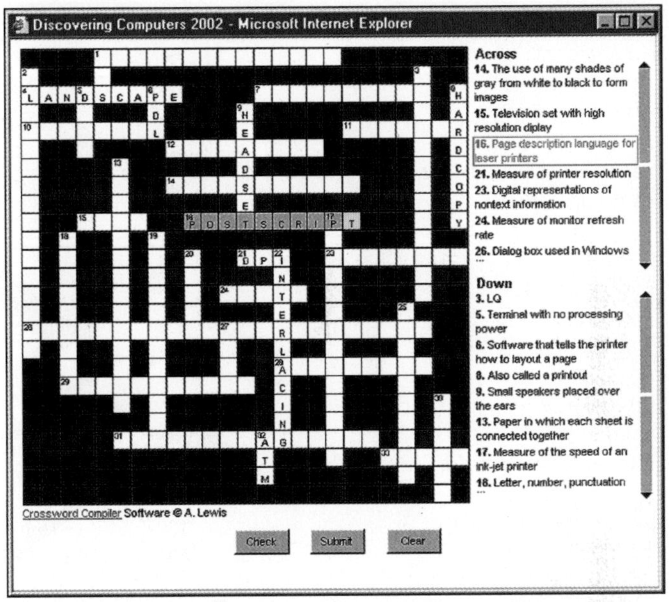

6. Search Sleuth

Click Search Sleuth to learn search techniques that will help make you a research expert. Submit the completed assignment to your instructor.

7. Crossword Puzzle Challenge

Click Crossword Puzzle Challenge. Complete the puzzle to reinforce skills you learned in this chapter. Directions on how to play the game will display. When you are ready to play, click the PLAY button. Submit the completed puzzle to your instructor.

8. Practice Test

Click Practice Test. Answer each question. When completed, enter your name and click the Grade Test button to submit the quiz for grading. Make a note of any missed questions. If required, print a copy to submit to your instructor.

Checkpoint

Web Instructions: To display this page from the Web, start your browser and enter the URL scsite.com/dc2002/ch6/check.htm. Click the links for current and additional information. To experience the animation and interactivity, Shockwave and Flash Player must be installed on your computer (download by clicking here.)

LABEL THE FIGURE

Instructions: Identify each step in how a laser printer works.

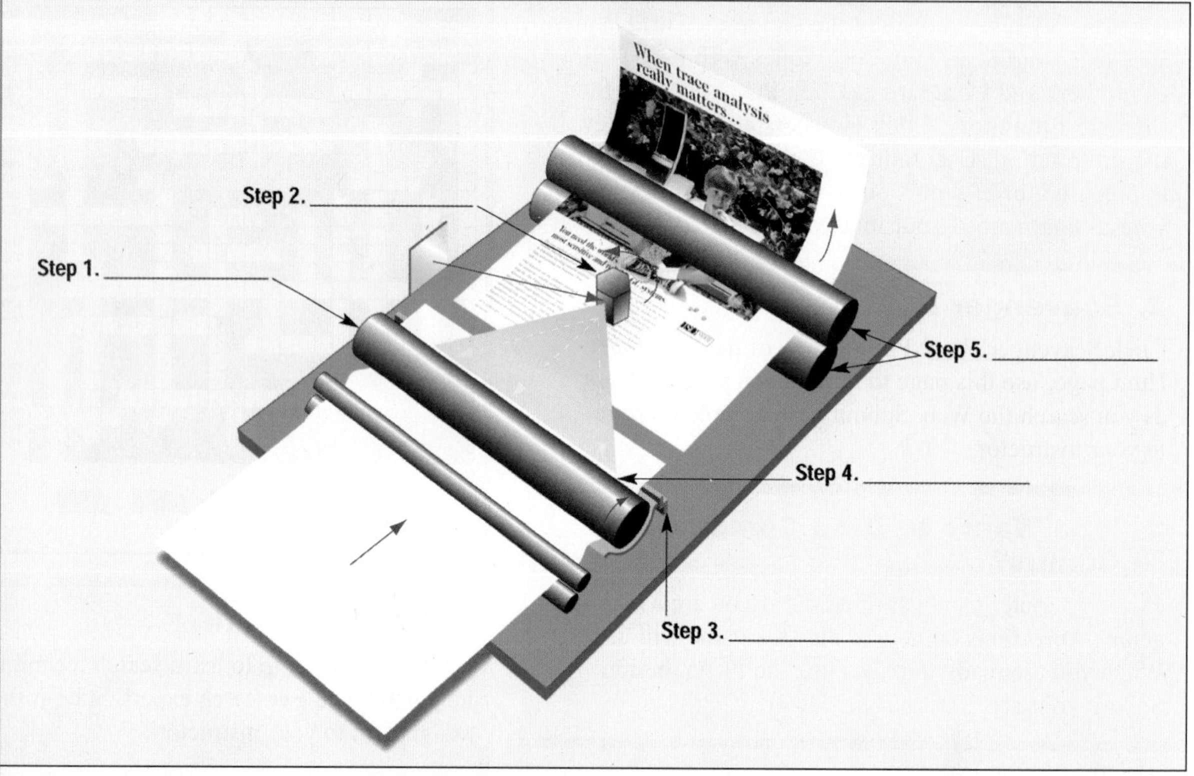

MATCHING

Instructions: Match each term from the column on the left with the best description from the column on the right.

_______ 1. thermal
_______ 2. dot-matrix
_______ 3. laser
_______ 4. portable
_______ 5. ink-jet

a. Generates images by pushing electrically heated pins against heat-sensitive paper.
b. Uses heat to transfer colored dye to specially coated paper.
c. An impact printer.
d. Sprays droplets of ink to form characters and graphics.
e. Prints an entire line at one time.
f. Processes and stores the entire page before printing it.
g. Lightweight printer for a mobile user.

Checkpoint

MULTIPLE CHOICE

Instructions: Select the letter of the correct answers for each of the following questions.

1. Output is data that has been processed into a useful form, called __________.
   a. ClearType
   b. MPR II
   c. information
   d. gray scaling
2. A display device __________.
   a. displays in two colors on a black background
   b. is an output device that visually conveys text, graphics, and video information
   c. meets ENERGY STAR guidelines
   d. none of the above
3. A display screen that uses a separate transistor for each color pixel is a(n) __________.
   a. dual-scan display
   b. passive-matrix display
   c. terminal
   d. active-matrix display
4. A printer produces __________.
   a. soft copy
   b. hard copy
   c. both hard copy and soft copy
   d. color depth
5. Using __________, you can have a conversation over the Web.
   a. DLP
   b. EMR
   c. the ENERGY STAR program
   d. Internet telephony

SHORT ANSWER

Instructions: Write a brief answer to each of the following questions.

1. How is an active-matrix display different from a passive-matrix display? __________ What is a gas plasma monitor? __________
2. How do LCD monitors and LCD displays present information on the screen? __________ What is a flat-panel display? __________ What is an electronic book (e-book) and how does it use ClearType? __________
3. What is high-definition television (HDTV)? __________ What advantages does HDTV provide over analog signals? __________
4. What is monitor ergonomics? __________ Why is monitor ergonomics important? __________ What is the ENERGY STAR program? __________
5. How is a dumb terminal different from an intelligent terminal? __________ For what purpose is a point-of-sale terminal used? __________ What is a programmable terminal? __________

WORKING TOGETHER

Instructions: Working with a group of your classmates, complete the following team exercise.

A group of business employees would like to set up a small accounting office, with 10 to 12 employees. They have hired you and your group as consultants to help with the setup. Your primary responsibility is to determine the type of output devices you think they will need within the office. Items to consider are type and number of printers, type and number of display devices, audio and video devices, and whether fax machines, fax modems, and/or multifunction devices are needed. Use the Internet to research information for this project. Prepare a report to share with the class. Include a table listing the pros and cons of the various devices and a short explanation why you selected each device.

Web Instructions: To display this page from the Web, start your browser and enter the URL scsite.com/dc2002/ch1/lab.htm. Click the links or current and additional information.

About Your Computer

1 This exercise uses Windows 98 procedures. Your computer probably has more than one output device. To learn about the output devices on your computer, right-click the My Computer icon on the desktop. Click Properties on the shortcut menu. When the System Properties dialog box displays, click the Device Manager tab. If necessary, click View devices by type. Below Computer, a list of hardware device categories displays. What output devices display in the list? Click the plus sign next to each category. What specific output devices in each category are connected to your computer? Close the System Properties dialog box.

Accessibility Options

2 This exercise uses Windows 98 procedures. The Windows operating system offers several output options for people with hearing or visual impairments. Three of these options are SoundSentry, ShowSounds, and High Contrast. To find out more about each option, click the Start button, point to Settings on the Start menu, and then click Control Panel on the Settings submenu. Double-click the Accessibility Options icon in the Control Panel window. Click the Sound tab in the Accessibility Properties dialog box. Click the Question Mark button on the title bar, click SoundSentry, read the information in the pop-up window, and then click the pop-up window to close it. Repeat this process for ShowSounds. Click the Display tab. Click the Question Mark button on the title bar and then click High Contrast. Read the information in the pop-up window, and then click the pop-up window to close it. What is the purpose of each option? Click the Cancel button. Click the Close button to close the Control Panel window.

Self-Portrait

3 Windows includes a drawing program called Paint. The quality of graphics produced with this program depends on a variety of factors, including the quality of your printer, your understanding of the software, and (to some extent) your artistic talent. In this exercise, you use Paint to create a self-portrait. To access Paint, click the Start button, point to Programs on the Start menu, point to Accessories on the Programs submenu, and then click Paint on the Accessories submenu. When the Paint window opens, the Paint toolbox displays on the left side of the window. Point to a toolbox button to see a tool's name; click a button to use that tool. Use the tools and colors available in Paint to draw a picture of yourself. If you make a mistake, you can click Undo on the Edit menu to undo your most recent action, you can erase part of your picture using the Eraser/Color Eraser tool, or you can clear the entire picture by clicking Clear Image on the Image menu. When your self-portrait is finished, print it by clicking Print on the File menu. Close Paint.

Magnifier

4 This exercise uses Windows 2000 procedures. Magnifier is a Windows utility for the visually impaired. To find out about the Magnifier capabilities, click the Start button on the taskbar and then click Help on the Start menu. Click the Index tab in the Windows 2000 window and then type `magnifier` in the Type in the keyword to find text box. Click the overview subentry below the Magnifier entry in the list of topics and then click the Display button. Click Magnifier overview in the Topics Found dialog box and then click the Display button. Read the Help information in the right pane of the Windows 2000 window and answer the following questions:

- How does Magnifier make the screen more readable for the visually impaired?
- What viewing options does Magnifier have?
- What tracking options does Magnifier have?

Click the Close button to close the Windows 2000 window.

Web Work

Web Instructions: To display this page from the Web, start your browser and enter the URL scsite.com/dc2002/ch6/web.htm. To view At The Movies in exercise 1, RealPlayer must be installed on your computer (download by clicking here). To use the Shelly Cashman Series Setting Up to Print Lab and the Configuring Your Display Lab from the Web, Shockwave and Flash Player must be installed on your computer (download by clicking here).

1 *E-Books*

To view the E-Books movie, click the button to the left or click the Play button to the right. Watch the movie, and then complete the exercise by answering the questions below. Electronic books are here. Holding a half-dozen novels, a semester's worth of textbooks, or a library of sales and service manuals, they promise a new world of portability, access, and convenience. Book files can be downloaded easily from the Internet. Prices range from $300 to $500 for the e-book itself, with thousands of titles currently available for $5 to$25 each. The technology and the market for e-books continue to improve in parallel. Better screens and voice recognition already are in the works. What other features might you suggest? What, if anything, do you think inhibits consumer acceptance of this technology?

2 *Shelly Cashman Series Setting Up to Print Lab*

Follow the appropriate instructions in Web Work 2 on page 1.47 to start and use the Shelly Cashman Series Setting Up to Print Lab. If you are running from the Web, enter the URL, www.scsite.com/sclabs/menu.htm; or display the Web Work page (see instructions at the top of this page) and then click the button to the left.

3 *Shelly Cashman Series Configuring Your Display Lab*

Follow the appropriate instructions in Web Work 2 on page 1.47 to start and use the Shelly Cashman Series Configuring Your Display Lab. If you are running from the Web, enter the URL, www.scsite.com/sclabs/menu.htm; or display the Web Work page (see instructions at the top of this page) and then click the button to the left.

4 *Choosing a Monitor*

The monitor is a key component of any new personal computer that you purchase. Everything you see is influenced by the monitor you select. Determining which monitor is best for your individual needs requires some research. Monitors are available in a range of sizes and a variety of resolutions. Click the button to the left for a tutorial on how to select the monitor that is best for your particular requirements.

5 *In the News*

Monitors continue to grow clearer and thinner. A newly introduced 50-inch gas plasma display presents near-photographic images and is less than four inches thick. At a cost of $25,000, the monitors probably will be seen first at stadiums, in airports, and as touch screens in stores. Yet, as prices fall, consumers surely will purchase the monitors for HDTV and crystal-clear Internet access. Click the button to the left and then read a news article about a new or improved output device. What is the device? Who manufactures it? How is the output device better than, or different from, earlier devices? Who do you think is most likely to use the device? Why?

MULTIMEDIA a VIRTUAL experience

Web Instructions: To gain World Wide Web access to additional and up-to-date information regarding this special feature, launch your browser and enter the URL shown at the top of this page.

INTERACTIVE MULTIMEDIA
Changing the Way People Work, Learn, and Play

Watch the Air Force Thunderbirds perform their daring aerobatic feats. Travel to Egypt and view King Tut's tomb. Watch the space shuttle blast into orbit. With multimedia, you can have all these adventures without setting foot outside your house (Figure 1). **Multimedia** refers to using computers to integrate text, graphics, animation, audio, and video into one application.

Unlike television, which combines and presents these media in a predefined order, most multimedia applications are interactive. Users participate directly with the application. **Interactive multimedia** presents information in various ways with a variety of media elements. Users choose the material to view, define the order in which it is presented, and obtain feedback on their actions. The computer accepts input through a keyboard, voice, or pointing device — such as a mouse — and performs an action in response.

Interactivity makes multimedia well suited for applications such as video games, flight simulators, virtual reality, electronic magazines, and educational and training tutorials. The multimedia application shown in Figure 2, for example, allows you to select from numerous geographical locations to learn about diving expeditions into the U.S. National Marine Sanctuaries and other regions.

Figure 1
Today, interactive multimedia plays an increasingly important role in business, industry, education, and entertainment.

MULTIMEDIA APPLICATIONS

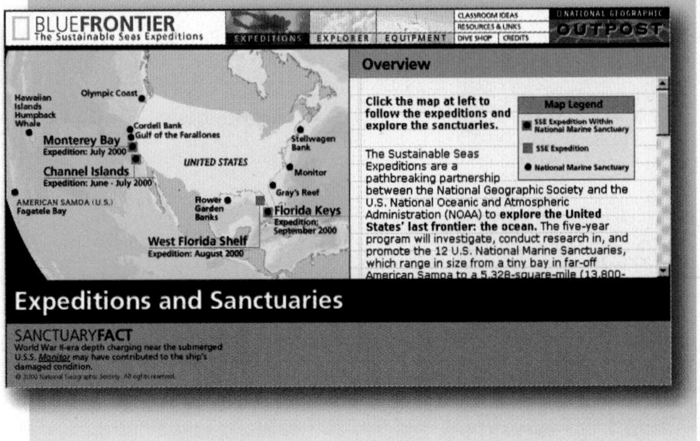

Figure 2
This National Geographic Web site consists of text, graphics, and links to diving expeditions.

A **multimedia application** uses technology for business, education, and entertainment. Businesses use multimedia, for example, in interactive advertisements and for job- and skill-training applications. Teachers use multimedia applications to deliver classroom presentations that enhance student learning.

Students, in turn, use multimedia applications to learn by reading, seeing, hearing, and interacting with the subject content. A wide variety of computer games and other types of entertainment also use multimedia applications.

Another important application of multimedia is to create **simulations**, which are computer-based models of real-life situations. Multimedia simulations often replace costly and sometimes hazardous demonstrations and training in areas such as chemistry, biology, medicine, and aviation.

The following sections provide a more detailed look at the various types of multimedia applications, such as business presentations, computer- and Web-based training, distant learning, classroom and special education, electronic books and references, how-to guides, and newspapers and magazines. These sections also address the use of multimedia for entertainment and edutainment, virtual reality, and kiosks, as well as its importance on the World Wide Web.

Business Presentations

Many businesses and industries use multimedia to create marketing presentations that advertise and sell products. Advertisers, for instance, save time and money by using this software to produce television commercials with unique media effects. Sales representatives also use multimedia in marketing presentations created using presentation graphics software. To deliver these presentations to a large audience, users can connect their computer to a video projector that displays the presentation on a full screen (Figure 3).

Figure 3
Video projectors connected to a computer can display images brightly and clearly. Some projectors are as small and lightweight as a notebook computer.

WORK • LEARN • PLAY

Computer-Based Training

Students use **computer-based training** (**CBT**) to learn and complete exercises with instructional software, such as the Learn By Series shown in Figure 4. Also called **computer-aided instruction** (**CAI**), computer-based training is popular in business, industry, and schools to teach new skills or to enhance the existing skills of employees, teachers, or students. Athletes, for example, use multimedia computer-based training programs to learn the intricacies of baseball, football, soccer, tennis, and golf, while airlines use multimedia CBT simulations to train employees for emergency situations. Schools use CBT to train teachers in various disciplines and to teach students math, language, and software skills. Interactive CBT software called **courseware** usually is available on CD-ROM or DVD-ROM or shared over a network.

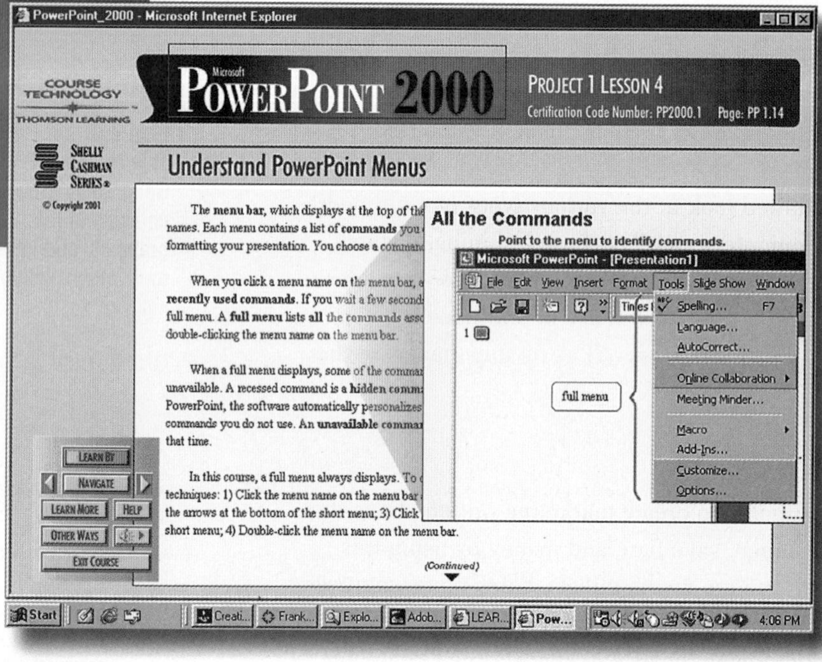

Figure 4
Computer-based training, such as the Learn By Series, is designed so students can choose learning activities that complement their learning styles.

Computer-based training allows for flexible, on-the-spot training. Businesses, for example, can set up corporate training labs, so employees can update their skills without leaving the workplace. Installing CBT software on an employee's computer or on the company network provides even more flexibility by allowing employees to update their job skills at their desks, at home, or while traveling.

Computer-based training provides a unique learning experience because learners receive instant feedback in the form of positive responses for correct answers or actions, additional information on incorrect answers, and immediate scoring and results. Testing and self-diagnostic features allow instructors to verify that a learner has mastered curriculum objectives and identify those who need additional instruction or practice. CBT is especially effective for teaching software skills if the CBT is integrated with the software application because it allows students to practice using the software as they learn.

Some of the many other advantages of CBT over traditional training include self-paced study, reduced training time and costs, and unique multimedia content. Many CBT trainers find they can increase their time helping trainees because computers handle test delivery and grading.

Web-Based Training (WBT) and Distance Learning

Web-based training (**WBT**) is an approach to computer-based training (CBT) that employs the technologies of the Internet and the World Wide Web. As with CBT, Web-based training typically consists of self-directed, self-paced instruction on a topic. Because it is delivered via the Web, however, WBT has the advantage of being able to offer up-to-date content on any type of computer platform.

During the past few years, the number of organizations using Web-based training has exploded. Today, many major corporations in the United States provide employees with some type of Web-based training to teach new skills or to upgrade their current skills.

Web-based training, computer-based training, and other materials often are used as materials for distance learning courses. **Distance learning**, also called **distance education**, is the delivery of education from one location while the learning takes place at other locations. Some national and international corporations also save millions of dollars by using distance learning to train employees, thus eliminating the costs of airfare, hotels, and meals for centralized training sessions.

Many colleges and universities offer numerous distance learning courses, usually in the form of Web-based or Web-enhanced courses (Figure 5). Web-based courses offer many advantages for students who live far from a college campus or work full time, allowing them to complete coursework from home or at any time that fits their schedules. A number of colleges and universities now offer master's and doctorate degree programs in which every required course is taught over the Web.

Web-based training also is available for individuals at home or at work. Today, anyone with access to the Web can take advantage of hundreds of multimedia tutorials offered online. Such tutorials cover a wide range of topics, from how to change a flat tire to creating presentations in Microsoft PowerPoint. Many of these Web sites are free (Figure 6); others ask users to register and pay a fee to take the complete Web-based course.

Classroom and Special Education

Multimedia applications are used to teach students of all ages. From interactive CD-ROMs and DVD-ROMs to presentations, multimedia can be an effective tool for delivering educational material to potential learners, making learning more exciting and interesting. Often, isolated rural schools are leaders in connecting classrooms to the Internet and using multimedia applications to enhance learning.

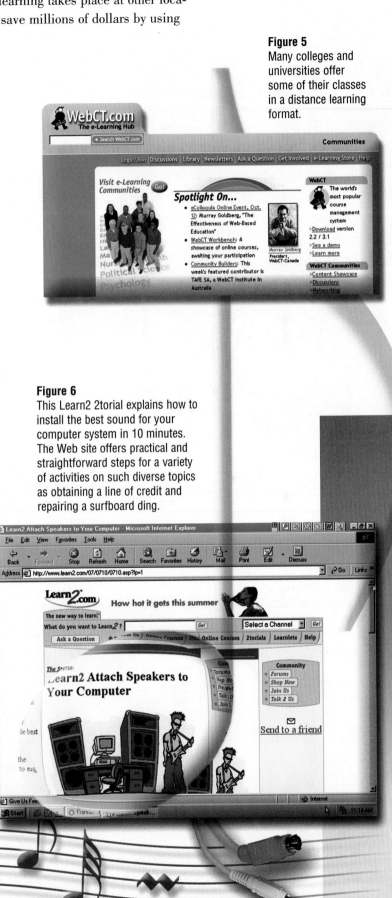

Figure 5
Many colleges and universities offer some of their classes in a distance learning format.

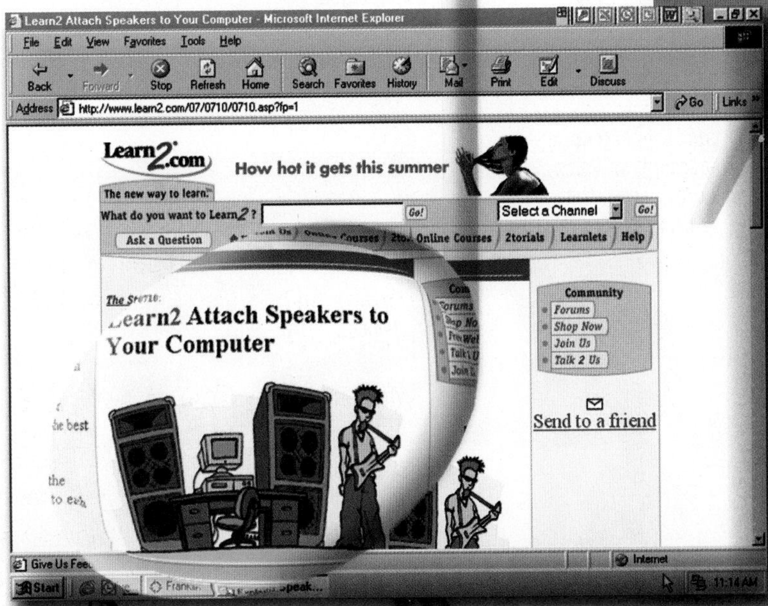

Figure 6
This Learn2 2torial explains how to install the best sound for your computer system in 10 minutes. The Web site offers practical and straightforward steps for a variety of activities on such diverse topics as obtaining a line of credit and repairing a surfboard ding.

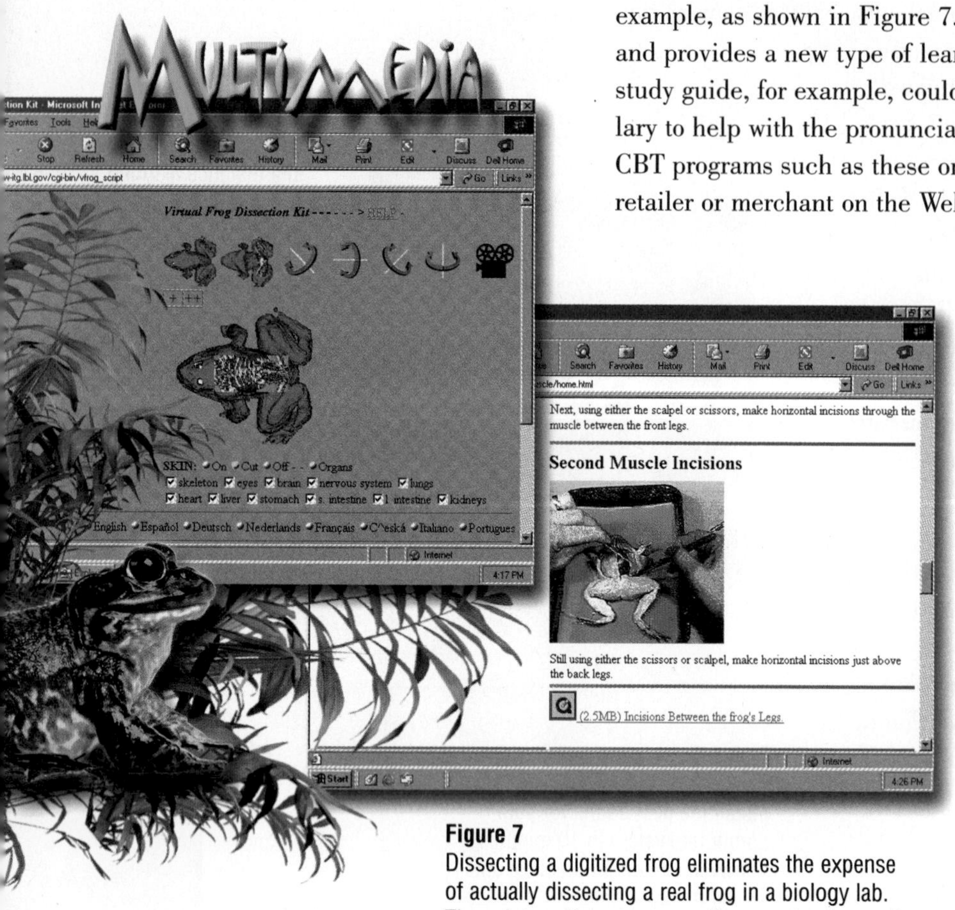

Figure 7
Dissecting a digitized frog eliminates the expense of actually dissecting a real frog in a biology lab. These interactive programs allow you to view and remove organs and to make a movie of your progress. The Web pages are available in various languages.

This software makes the learning process more interesting, allows students to perform experiments in a risk-free environment, and provides instant feedback and testing. Virtual dissection of a frog is possible, for example, as shown in Figure 7. CBT also appeals to various learning styles and provides a new type of learning experience. A student using a CBT study guide, for example, could listen to a speaker reciting French vocabulary to help with the pronunciation of difficult words. You can buy many CBT programs such as these on CD-ROM or DVD-ROM from a local retailer or merchant on the Web.

Research has shown that, when properly evaluated and integrated into teaching at the point of instruction, multimedia applications are a highly effective teaching tool. When using a multimedia application, students become actively involved in the learning process instead of passive recipients of information. Interactive multimedia applications engage students by asking them to define their own paths through an application, which often lead them to explore many related topics.

Multimedia applications also are well suited for both physically impaired and learning disabled students. Students who are visually impaired, for example, benefit from the audio capabilities of multimedia applications, as well as the use of graphics and larger font sizes (Figure 8). Visual materials, such as graphics, animation, and video, also make learning easier for students who are hearing impaired. Many educational software companies offer multimedia products with closed captioning or sign language to enhance the learning experience for hearing-impaired students. The ability of individuals to work, practice, and review at their own pace is a major benefit for the learning disabled.

FIGURE 8
Physically impaired and learning disabled students benefit from multimedia software rich in graphics, animation, and video. These students are using software developed by ClickIt!, which allows them to choose objects on the screen without using a mouse.

Electronic Books

One type of **electronic book** is a digital text that gives the user access to information through links, which often are bold or underlined words. These electronic books have many of the elements of a regular book, including pages of text and graphics. Users generally click icons to turn pages of this type of electronic book. A table of contents, glossary, and index also are available at the click of a button. To display a definition or a graphic, play a sound or a video sequence, or connect to a Web site, users simply can click a link.

A newer type of electronic book, called an **e-book**, uses a small book-sized computer that can hold up to 4,000 pages, or about 10 book's worth of text and small graphics. By clicking a button, users move forward or backward, add notes, and highlight text stored in the e-book. Figure 6-7 on page 6.7 shows a photograph of an e-book. Readers also can view e-books on a small personal computer, such as a Palm™ handheld computer, with the text supplied from various sources. One of these sources is **Project Gutenberg**, which makes thousands of literary and reference books and materials available free to the general public (Figure 9).

Publishers are developing innovative methods of getting authors' words to the public. Some publishers, for example, create purely digital books sold online or in single copies when customers place orders through online booksellers' and organizations' Web sites. These e-books are not sold in bookstores. For example, readers desiring chapters of Stephen King's novel, *The Plant*, ordered them for $1 each through Amazon.com. Other publishers are creating **electronic paper**, which feels like real paper but is coated with electronic ink so that the characters can change. When you finish reading one of these books, you can plug it into a telephone line or a wireless receiver and then download another book.

FIGURE 9
Geoffrey Chaucer's *Canterbury Tales* is among the thousands of public domain reference and literary works available from Project Gutenberg. One new book is added to the Web site almost daily.

FIGURE 10
Microsoft Encarta is a popular multimedia encyclopedia that includes graphics, audio, video, and Web links.

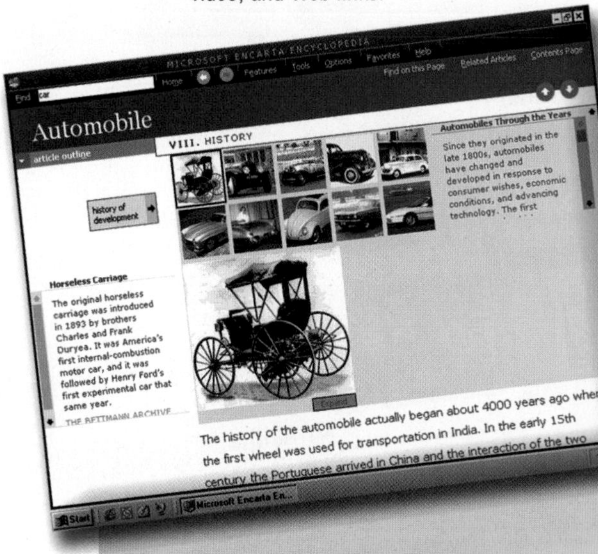

Electronic Reference Texts

An **electronic reference text**, sometimes called an **e-text**, is a digital version of a reference book, which uses text, graphics, sound, animation, and video to explain a topic or to provide additional information. The multimedia encyclopedia, Microsoft Encarta, for example, includes the complete text of a multivolume encyclopedia. In addition to text-based information, Microsoft Encarta includes thousands of photographs, animations, audio and video clips, and detailed illustrations (Figure 10). This array of multimedia information is accessible via menus and links.

Many other reference texts are used in a variety of fields and professions (Figure 11). Health and medicine are two areas in which multimedia reference texts play an important role. Instead of using volumes of books, health professionals and students rely on reference CD-ROMs and DVD-ROMs for information, illustrations, animations, and photographs on hundreds of health and first-aid topics.

ELECTRONIC REFERENCE TEXTS

Name	Publisher	URL	Description
American Heritage Talking Dictionary	Compton's NewMedia, Inc.	www.comptons.com	Uses a human-sounding voice to pronounce more than 90,000 words; contains more than 200,000 definitions, an integrated thesaurus, and 3,000 images, photographs, maps, and flags.
Compton's® Encyclopedia	Compton's NewMedia, Inc.	www.comptons.com	Features more than 40,000 articles, interactive science activities, monthly updates via the Internet, 360-degree views and virtual tours, more than 8,000 photos, and 100 videos, animations, and slide shows.
Encarta Encyclopedia Deluxe	Microsoft	microsoft.com	Contains more than 42,000 articles, 170 videos and animations, a natural language search function, a dynamic timeline, virtual tours, 360-degree views, and text-to-speech capabilities.
Library of the Future	AbleSoft	kidsoft.com	Contains descriptions of more than 5,000 literary works, authors' biographies, and film clips.
American Sign Language for Kids	Multimedia 2000	m-2k.com	Uses text, QuickTime video, animations, and illustrations to teach 2,600 signs, and includes learning games and lessons on fingerspelling.

For an updated list of electronic reference text Web sites, enter the URL at the top of this page.

FIGURE 11 These e-texts use multimedia to clarify topics and supply additional information on thousands of subjects.

How-To Guides

Numerous interactive multimedia applications are available to help individuals in their daily lives. These multimedia applications fall into the broad category of how-to guides. **How-to guides** are multimedia applications that include step-by-step instructions and interactive demonstrations to teach practical new skills (Figure 12). Much like the computer-based training applications used by businesses, how-to guides allow users to acquire and test new skills in a risk-free environment. The skills learned with a how-to guide, however, usually are oriented toward personal enrichment, rather than workplace skills.

How-to guides can help with activities such as buying a home or a car, designing a garden, planning a vacation, improving a home, and repairing a car or computer. The CD-ROM how-to-guides listed in Figure 13 show the wide variety of instructional guides. Multimedia how-to guides also are available on DVD-ROM and the Web.

FIGURE 12
Web users can learn American Sign Language via the HandSpeak online dictionary. This Web site features video clips of individuals signing words, including words with several definitions.

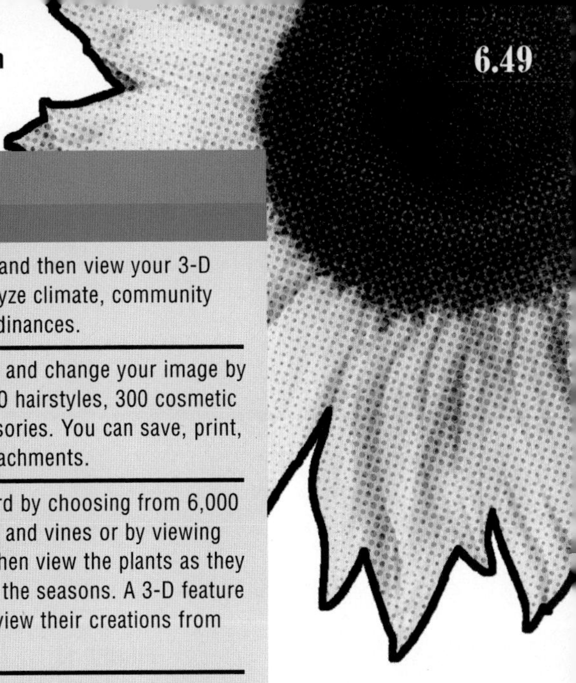

CD-ROM HOW-TO GUIDES

Name	Publisher	URL	Description
3D Home Architect®	Mattel Interactive™	www.mattelinteractive.com	Customize floor plans and then view your 3-D design. The plans analyze climate, community growth, and zoning ordinances.
Cosmopolitan™ Virtual Makeover™	Mattel Interactive™	www.mattelinteractive.com	Input your photograph and change your image by experimenting with 500 hairstyles, 300 cosmetic colors, and 200 accessories. You can save, print, and send as e-mail attachments.
Complete LandDesigner 3D	SierraHome Network	sierra.com/sierrahome	Design a garden or yard by choosing from 6,000 trees, shrubs, flowers, and vines or by viewing sample gardens, and then view the plants as they grow and change with the seasons. A 3-D feature lets virtual gardeners view their creations from any angle.
MasterCook Deluxe	SierraHome Network	sierra.com/sierrahome	Prepare one of 5,000 dishes based on nutritional value and ingredients on hand. Watch instructional videos, and adjust the portions to the number of servings needed.
Teach Yourself PC Maintenance	Learn2.com, Inc.	learn2.com	Learn such computer concepts as motherboard ports, the OS and processor, hardware, installing SIMMs, modem standards, baud vs. bit rates, maintenance tools, keyboard cleaning, and the ScanDisk utility from four interactive multimedia CD-ROM tutorials.

For an updated list of CD-ROM how-to guide Web sites, enter the URL at the top of this page.

FIGURE 13
These how-to guides teach useful skills by using videos, interactive demonstrations, and animations.

Newspapers and Magazines

A **multimedia newspaper** and a **multimedia magazine** are digital versions of a newspaper or magazine distributed on CD-ROM, DVD-ROM, or via the World Wide Web. Today, many print-based magazines and newspapers have companion Web sites that provide multimedia versions of some or all of their printed content (Figure 14). An **electronic magazine**, or **e-zine**, is a digital publication available via the Web (Figure 15 on the next page).

Multimedia newspapers and magazines usually include the sections and articles found in their print-based versions, including departments, editorials, and more. Unlike printed publications, however, multimedia magazines and newspapers use many types of media to convey information. Audio and video clips, for example, can showcase recent album or movie releases, and animations can depict weather patterns or election results.

MULTIMEDIA MAGAZINES AND NEWSPAPERS

Name	URL
Independent Newspapers (South Africa)	iol.co.za
Kyodo News (Tokyo)	home.kyodo.co.jp
National Geographic	nationalgeographic.com
Newsweek	newsweek.msnbc.com
The Daily Telegraph (London)	www.telegraph.co.uk
The Globe and Mail (Canada)	globeandmail.ca
The New York Times	nytimes.com
The Wall Street Journal	wsj.com
Time	time.com
USA TODAY	usatoday.com
Washington Post	washingtonpost.com

For an updated list of multimedia magazine and newspaper Web sites, enter the URL at the top of this page.

FIGURE 14
Multimedia magazines and newspapers from various countries use video and audio clips, animations, and other interactive multimedia tools to bring the world to personal computers.

FIGURE 15 E-zines are produced for the Web and often contain multimedia applications.

E-ZINES		
Name	**URL**	**Description**
AMC's American Pop!	ampop.com	Programming devoted to vintage music, movies, toys, fashions, and pop culture. Shockwave and Flash are used extensively.
OS/2 eZine	www.os2ezine.com	Articles and forums focusing on IBM's OS/2 multitasking operating system.
The Western Flyfisher	westernflyfisher.com	Numerous audio and video clips for flyfishing enthusiasts.
WebReference.com	webreference.com	Reference material on a wide variety of Web topics, including effective authoring, browsing, coding HTML, and designing Web sites.
ZENtertainment	zentertainment.com	Latest entertainment news, including sections for music, TV, movies, toys, comics, and food.

For an updated list of e-zines Web sites, enter the URL at the top of this page.

Entertainment and Edutainment

Multimedia combines the media elements of television and interactivity, thus making it ideal for entertainment. Multimedia computer games, for example, use a combination of graphics, audio, and video to create a realistic and entertaining game situation. Often the game simulates a real or fictitious world, in which users play the role of a character and have direct control of what happens in the game. The music industry also sells interactive multimedia applications on CD-ROM and DVD-ROM. Some interactive music CD-ROMs, for example, allow budding musicians to play musical instruments along with their favorite musician, read about the musician's life and interests, and even create their own versions of popular songs. Like interactive games, these applications give users a character role and put them in control of the application (Figure 16).

ENTERTAINMENT APPLICATIONS			
Name	**Publisher**	**URL**	**Description**
Backyard Baseball	Humongous Entertainment	humongous.com	Select players from 30 Major League Baseball teams or create your own team colors, ballpark, and strategy. Play online with other Windows users.
Dogz®	Mattel Interactive™	www.mattelinteractive.com	Use voice recognition to train your Dogz to sit, fetch, or roll over; create custom scenes with the Play Scene Editor.
Motocross Madness	Microsoft	microsoft.com	Perform stunts on your motorbike while you race up to eight opponents online via the MSN Gaming Zone.
RollerCoaster Tycoon™	Hasbro Interactive	hasbro-interactive.com	Use 14 styles to construct roller coasters with accurate motion dynamics and physics principles. Analyze their excitement and nausea ratings.
The Sims	Electronic Arts	thesims.com	Develop characters in a neighborhood, build their homes, and display your creations on the World Wide Web with these open-ended games.

For an updated list of entertainment application Web sites, enter the URL at the top of this page.

FIGURE 16 Entertainment applications, rich in multimedia content, provide fun and relaxation for children and adults.

Other multimedia applications are used for **edutainment**, which is an experience meant to be both educational and entertaining. Many edutainment CD-ROMs and DVD-ROMs provide content for individuals of all ages, while others are created specifically to teach children in a fun and appealing way. Some of these edutainment applications are listed in Figure 17.

EDUTAINMENT APPLICATIONS

Name	Publisher	URL	Description
Carmen Sandiego	Mattel Interactive	www.mattelinteractive.com	Discover geography by searching for criminals in various locales using foreign languages and Internet links to maps and satellite pictures. The police chief gives updates using real-time video.
James Cameron's Titanic Explorer	20th Century Fox	foxinteractive.com/games/titanicexplorer	Witness James Cameron's diving expedition of the Titanic and use interactive 3-D models to examine the ship and the wreck. View a computer simulation of how the ship sank, and then browse through more than 1,200 pages of survivors' testimony.
Kaplan GMAT, LSAT, and GRE™	Encore Software	encoresoftware.com	View personalized interactive lessons and links to graduate schools.
Reader Rabbit	Mattel Interactive	www.mattelinteractive.com	Teaches young children problem solving, decision making, and logic skills; learning technology monitors performance, offers help, and prints reports.
The New Way Things Work	DK Multimedia	www.dk.com	Discover how more than 150 machines work by viewing animations, illustrations, and videos.

For an updated list of edutainment application Web sites, enter the URL at the top of this page.

FIGURE 17
Edutainment applications offer adults and children both education and entertainment.

Virtual Reality

Virtual reality (VR) is the use of a computer to create an artificial environment that appears and feels like a real environment and allows users to explore a space and manipulate the surroundings (Figure 18). In its simplest form, a virtual reality application displays a three-dimensional view of a place or object, such as a landscape, building, molecule, or red blood cell, which users can explore. Architects use this type of software to show clients how a building will look after a construction or remodeling project.

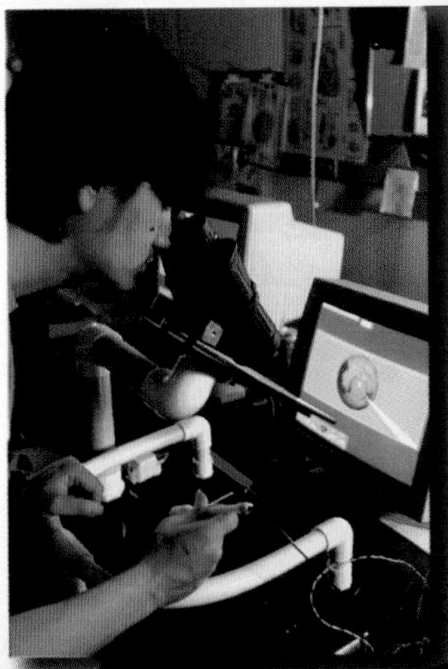

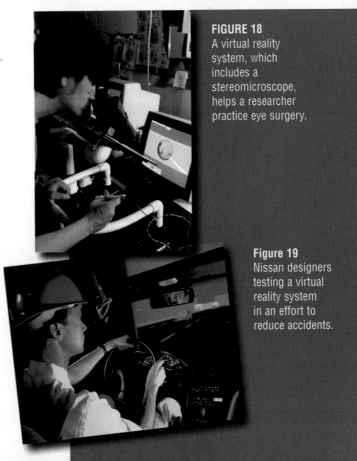

FIGURE 18
A virtual reality system, which includes a stereomicroscope, helps a researcher practice eye surgery.

In more advanced forms, VR software users wear specialized headgear, body suits, and gloves to enhance the experience of the artificial environment (Figure 19). The headgear displays the artificial environment in front of both eyes. The body suit and the gloves sense motion and direction, allowing users to move, pick up, and hold virtually displayed items. Experts predict that eventually the body suits will provide tactile feedback, so users can experience the touch and feel of the virtual world.

Figure 19
Nissan designers testing a virtual reality system in an effort to reduce accidents.

Your first encounter with VR likely will be a virtual reality game such as a flight simulator. In these games, special visors allow you to see the computer-generated environment. As you walk around the game's electronic landscape, sensors in the surrounding game machine record your movements and change your view of the landscape accordingly. You also might use a Web-based VR application developed using **virtual reality modeling language (VRML)**. Web sites, such as the U.S. Capitol Web site shown in Figure 20, use virtual reality to allow you to take tours of a city, view real estate for sale, or interact with local attractions.

Some companies use VR for more practical, commercial applications, as well. Automobile companies, for example, have created virtual showrooms in which customers can view the exterior and interior of vehicles (Figure 21). In addition, airplane manufacturers are using virtual prototypes to test new models and shorten product design time. Telecommunications firms use personal computer-based VR applications for employee training. As computing power and the use of the Web increase, practical applications of VR will continue to emerge in education, business, and entertainment.

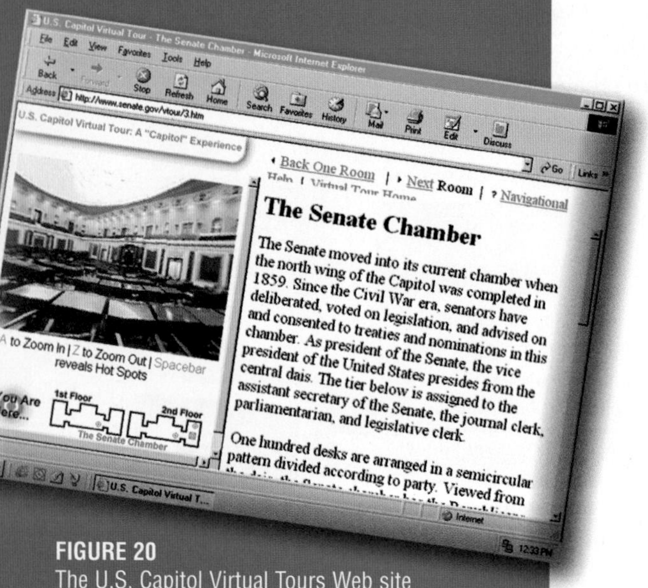

FIGURE 20
The U.S. Capitol Virtual Tours Web site give visitors 360-degree views of the Senate and House of Representative chambers, also included are details about objects found in those rooms and historical information.

Kiosks

A **kiosk** is a computerized information or reference center that allows users to select various options to browse through or find specific information. A typical kiosk is a self-service structure equipped with computer hardware and software. Kiosks often use touch screen monitors or keyboards for input devices and contain all of the data and information needed for the application stored directly on the computer.

Kiosks often provide information in public places where visitors or customers have common questions. Locations such as shopping centers, airports, museums, and libraries, for example, use kiosks to provide information on available services, product and exhibit locations, maps, and other information (Figure 22). Kiosks also are used for marketing. A kiosk might contain an interactive multimedia application that allows you to try options and explore scenarios related to a product or service. For example, you might be able to try different color combinations or take short quizzes to determine which product best meets your needs. The interactive multimedia involves customers with the product, thus increasing the likelihood of purchase.

FIGURE 21
Lexus is one of the auto manufacturers that allows Internet users to build a specific car, including selecting colors and accessories, and then price their designed vehicle. Nearly one-half of U.S. households that buy vehicles turn to the Internet to research their purchases.

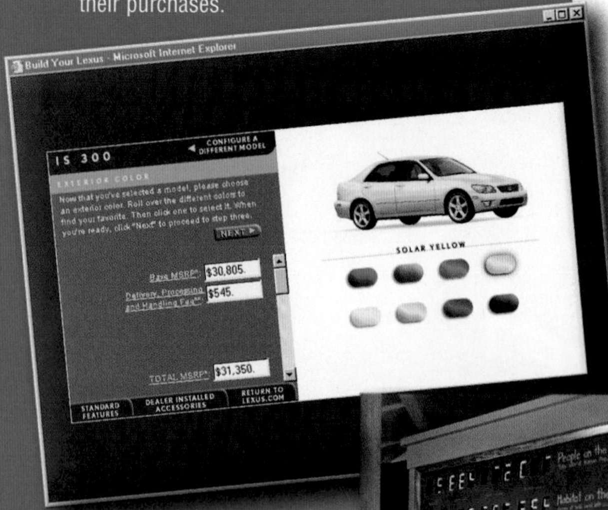

FIGURE 22
Seattle's Woodland Park Zoo features an interactive kiosk for its *Touch the Earth . . . Gently* exhibit. The 11-by-9-foot exhibit contains a laser disc player, touch screen monitor, and counters that calculate the net gain in world population and the net loss of wild animals' habitats.

The World Wide Web

Multimedia applications also play an important role on the **World Wide Web**, which is the part of the Internet that supports multimedia. In fact, much of the information on the Web today relies on multimedia. Using multimedia brings a Web page to life, increases the types of information available on the Web, expands the Web's potential uses, and makes the Internet a more entertaining place to explore. As described in Chapter 2, the Web uses many types of media to deliver information and enhance a user's Web experience (Figure 23). Graphics and animations reinforce text-based content and provide updated information. Online radio stations, movie rental Web sites, and games use audio and video clips to provide movie and music clips or to deliver the latest news.

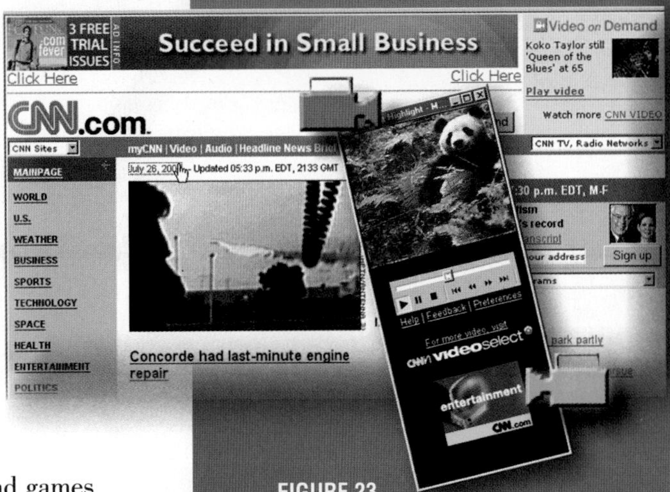

FIGURE 23
CNN is one of the many Web sites that incorporates multimedia features to report daily news events, weather, health tips, and entertainment.

Many of the multimedia applications previously described, including computer- and Web-based training, newspapers, e-zines, games, and virtual reality, are deliverable via the Web. New multimedia authoring software packages include tools for creating and delivering multimedia applications via the World Wide Web. Some of these authoring software packages allow users to create applications in the Windows environment and then convert them to HTML and Java for Web use.

DEVELOPING MULTIMEDIA APPLICATIONS

You can create a multimedia application using a variety of software applications. With PowerPoint, for example, you can create a presentation that combines text, graphics, animation, and audio and video clips (Figure 24). Developing these applications follows a standard process with several phases. While some

FIGURE 24
This PowerPoint slide features an animated sun and a sound file with the crash of waves.

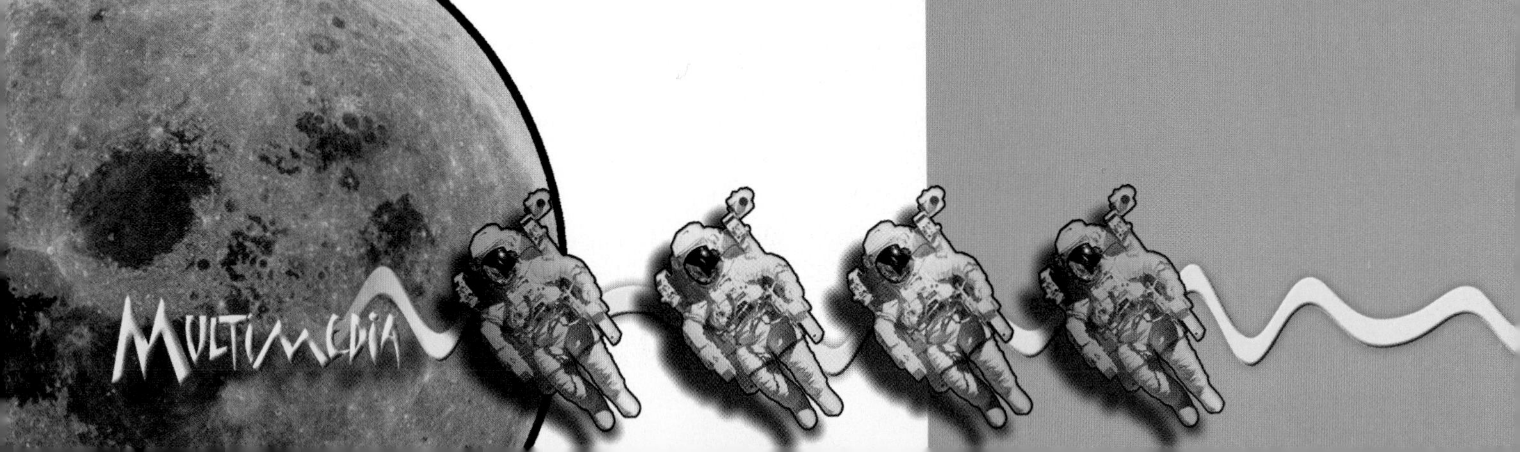

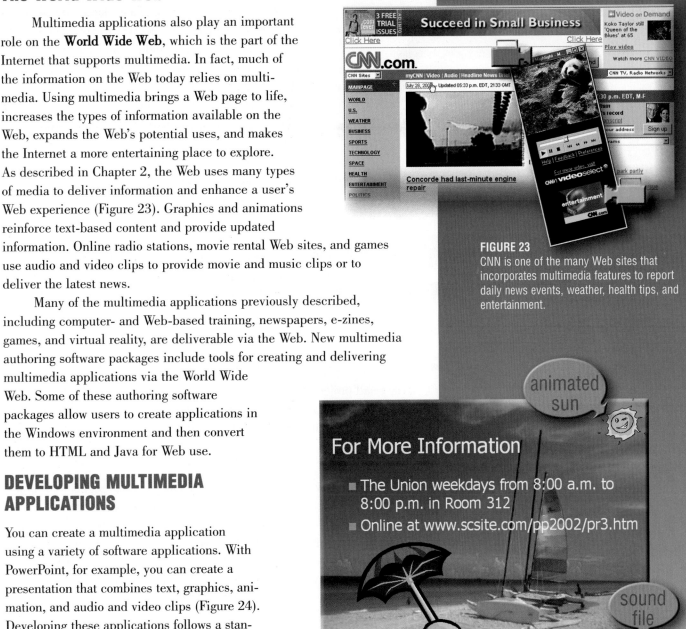

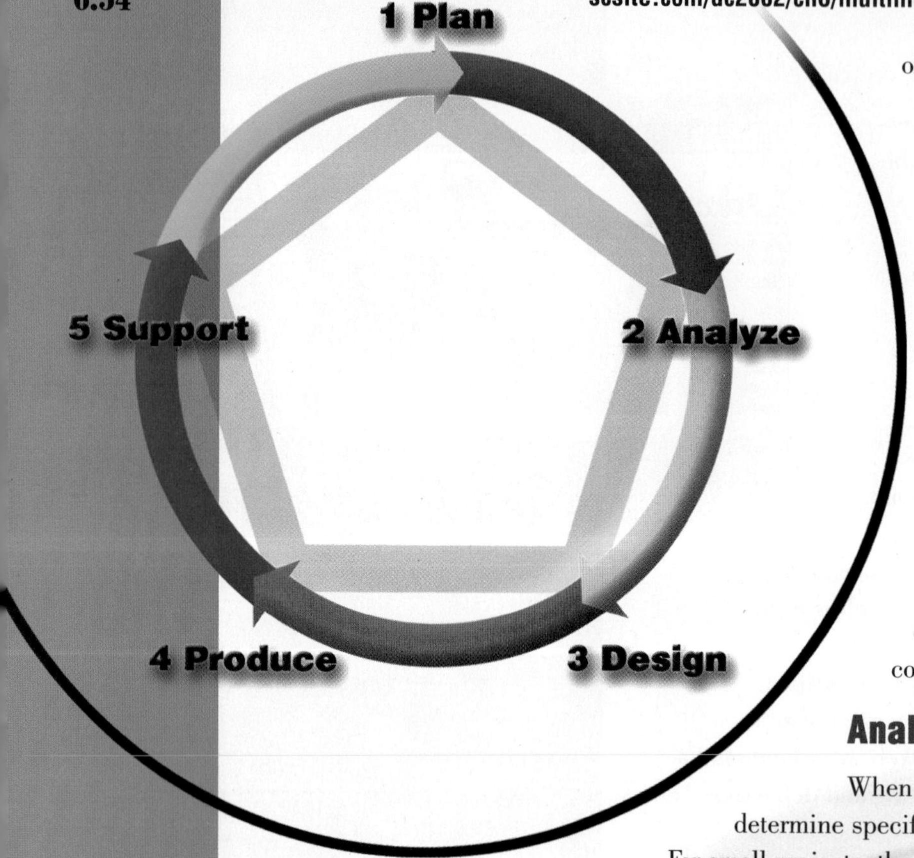

of the terminology is different, the basic activities completed within each phase closely follow those of the program development life cycle: plan, analyze, design, produce, and support (Figure 25).

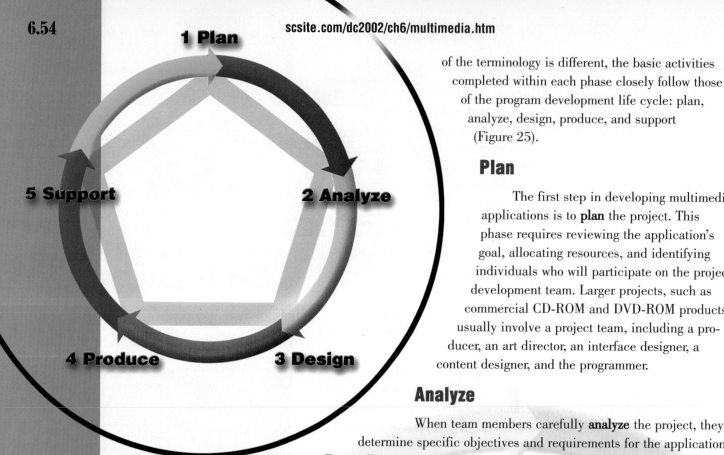

FIGURE 25 Developing effective multimedia presentations involves a five-step process.

Plan

The first step in developing multimedia applications is to **plan** the project. This phase requires reviewing the application's goal, allocating resources, and identifying individuals who will participate on the project development team. Larger projects, such as commercial CD-ROM and DVD-ROM products, usually involve a project team, including a producer, an art director, an interface designer, a content designer, and the programmer.

Analyze

When team members carefully **analyze** the project, they determine specific objectives and requirements for the application. For small projects, the developer may play a variety of roles, which may include content developer, interface designer, and programmer. For larger projects with specific learning objectives, analysis is extremely important.

Design

Once basic requirements have been determined, the **design** phase begins. A vital tool for the project team is a flowchart, or map, which includes all of the various media elements in the application and serves as a blueprint to which the project team or individual developer can refer. Another important tool is the **project script**, which provides detailed information to supplement the flowchart and records how the various media elements will be used in the production. Screen design is another crucial part of designing an effective multimedia application. The colors and layout used for individual screens greatly influence the overall effect of the finished product.

Produce

Project team members **produce** the multimedia application by creating the various media elements used in the application and combining them using multimedia authoring software. Artists develop original graphics and animations using drawing and illustration software, add photographs by using a digital camera, a PhotoCD, or a scanner, and record digital video and audio clips using recording devices and a video capture or sound card. Authoring begins when they have obtained all of the media elements. Finally, the developer tests the program to verify it performs according to design specifications.

Support

During the **support** phase, the developer reviews the project to ensure all objectives have been met. In addition, errors are identified and corrected. At this point, plans may be made to modify or enhance the application with additional features. If so, the cycle begins again at the planning phase.

Multimedia Authoring Software

Developing an interactive multimedia application involves using **multimedia authoring software** to combine text, graphics, animation, audio, and video into an application. Authoring programs also allow you to design interactive areas on the screen that respond to user input. Once various media elements are added to the program, the multimedia authoring software assigns relationships and actions to elements. The programs also help create a structure that lets the user navigate through the material presented.

One of the more important activities of the production phase of multimedia development is selecting the multimedia authoring software package. Factors to consider when selecting a multimedia authoring software package are quality of application developed, ease of use, clear documentation, responsiveness of vendor's service and technical support, compatibility with other applications, ease of programming, functionality, and system requirements for both user and developer.

Most popular authoring packages share similar features and are capable of creating similar applications. The major differences exist in the ease of use for development. Four popular multimedia authoring packages — Authorware, Director, Flash, and ToolBook — are described in Figure 26. Developers can use these products to create spectacular Web sites.

FIGURE 26
These popular multimedia authoring software packages allow users to create interactive elements that respond to user input.

MULTIMEDIA AUTHORING SOFTWARE

Product	Publisher	URL	Use
Authorware	Macromedia	macromedia.com	Uses flowchart metaphor to build a multimedia application.
Director	Macromedia	macromedia.com	Uses a theater or movie production metaphor to build a multimedia application. Three integrated windows — Cast, Score, and Stage — are used to create and sequence text and other media elements.
Flash	Macromedia	macromedia.com	Creates dazzling Web sites that display across a user's entire screen — regardless of monitor size — and include input, interactivity, sounds, music, graphics, and animations.
ToolBook	click2learn.com	click2learn.com	Uses a graphical user interface and an object-oriented approach to design applications using basic objects such as buttons, fields, graphics, backgrounds, and pages.

For an updated list of multimedia authoring software Web sites, enter the URL at the top of this page.

FEATURE SUMMARY

Interactive multimedia distributed on CD-ROM, DVD-ROM, and via the World Wide Web influences people's everyday experiences in the workplace, at school, and in recreational activities. In today's office, employees and clients prepare and view multimedia business presentations. Using drill-and-practice or exploration activities, learners of all ages are able to define their own learning paths, investigate topics in depth, and get immediate feedback. Students gain knowledge of the world in and out of the classroom using computer-based training, Web-based training, distance learning, electronic books and reference texts, how-to guides, virtual reality, and multimedia magazines and newspapers. Entertainment and edutainment interactive multimedia programs enrich the way people relax and have fun. Interacting with well-designed multimedia applications is a positive experience and engages and challenges users, thus encouraging them to think independently and creatively.

CHAPTER 7

Storage

Wedding bells are ringing. It is just two weeks until your big day! With all your wedding arrangements confirmed, the reception planned, and the honeymoon booked, you are happily humming the tune... "Going to the chapel and we're gonna get married."

Of the 247 invited family members and friends, 192 guests have responded, yes. Most of the regrets are guests who live too far away and cannot afford airfare and hotel expenses.

Even though you knew this would happen, it is disappointing that anyone must miss this special occasion. That is why you ordered digital photographs as part of your wedding package. At the end of your big day, the photographer will present you with a memory card containing at least 30 digital photographs of the wedding. You plan to post these photographs to your Internet hard drive before you leave for your Caribbean cruise.

For this very reason, your wedding invitations requested a reply with your guests' e-mail addresses. With the response cards in hand, you sit down at the computer and e-mail the Web address of your Internet hard drive to all those on your guest list. As you finish the first e-mail message, you hum, "Today's the day we'll say I do."

MEMORY VERSUS STORAGE

Storage refers to the media on which data, instructions, and information are kept, as well as the devices that record and retrieve these items (Figure 7-1). It is important you understand the difference between storage and memory, which was discussed in Chapter 4. The next section reviews the definition of memory and then discusses basic storage concepts.

OBJECTIVES

After completing this chapter, you will be able to:

- Differentiate between storage and memory
- Identify various types of storage media and storage devices
- Explain how a floppy disk stores data
- Identify the advantages of using high-capacity disks
- Describe how a hard disk organizes data
- Identify the advantages of using an Internet hard drive
- Explain how a compact disc stores data
- Understand how to care for a compact disc
- Differentiate between CD-ROMs, CD-RWs, and DVD-ROMs
- Identify the uses of tape
- Understand how an enterprise storage system works
- Explain how to use PC Cards and other miniature storage media
- Identify uses of microfilm and microfiche

Figure 7-1 Data, instructions, and information are stored on a variety of storage media.

floppy disk

miniature mobile storage media

PC Card

tape library

Memory

During processing, the processor places instructions to be executed and data needed by those instructions into memory. Memory is a temporary holding place for data and instructions. Sometimes called primary storage, memory consists of one or more chips on the motherboard or some other circuit board in the computer.

The two basic types of memory are volatile and nonvolatile. When the computer's power is turned off, **volatile memory** loses its contents. Almost all RAM is volatile.

Nonvolatile memory, by contrast, does not lose its contents when power is removed from the computer. For example, when a manufacturer permanently records data and instructions onto a non-volatile ROM chip, the contents of the chip remain intact when you turn off the computer.

hard disk

RAID

CD-ROM, DVD-ROM, or CD-RW

Storage

eo • Pictures • Text • Graphics • Audio • Video
ures • Text • Graphics • Audio • Video • Pictures
xt • Graphics • Audio • Video • Pictures • Text
ics • Audio • Video • Pictures • Text • Graphics
dio • Video • Pictures • Text • Graphics • Audio
eo • Pictures • Text • Graphics • Audio • Video
ures • Text • Graphics • Audio • Video • Pictures
xt • Graphics • Audio • Video • Pictures • Text
ics • Audio • Video • Pictures • Text • Graphics
dio • Video • Pictures • Text • Graphics • Audio

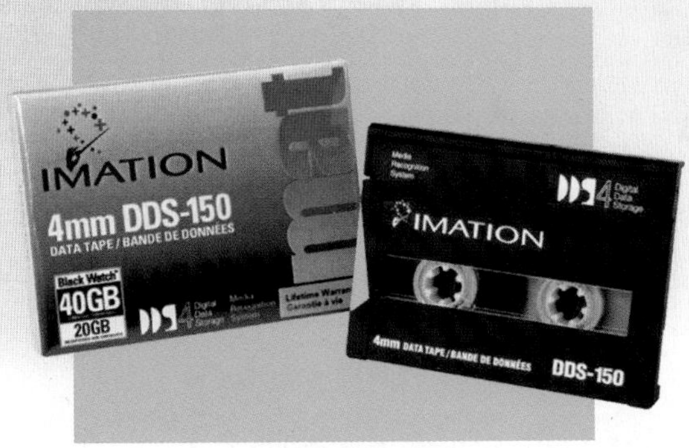

tape backup

CD-ROM jukeboxes

Storage

Storage, also called **secondary storage, auxiliary storage, permanent storage**, or **mass storage**, holds items such as data, instructions, and information for future use.

Think of storage as a filing cabinet that holds file folders, and memory as the top of your desk. When you want to work with a file, you remove it from the filing cabinet (storage) and place it on your desk (memory). When you are finished with the file, you remove it from your desk (memory) and return it to the filing cabinet (storage).

Storage is nonvolatile. Items in storage remain intact even when power is removed from the computer (Figure 7-2). A **storage medium** (media is the plural) is the physical material on which a computer keeps data, instructions, and information. Examples of storage media are floppy disks, hard disks, compact discs, and tape. A **storage device** is the computer hardware that records and retrieves items to and from a storage medium.

Storage devices serve as a source of input when they read and a source of output when they write. **Reading** is the process of transferring data, instructions, and information from a storage medium into memory. **Writing** is the process of transferring these items from memory to a storage medium.

The speed of a disk storage device is defined by its access time. **Access time** is the amount of time it takes the device to locate an item on a disk. The access time of storage devices is slow, compared with memory. Memory devices access items in billionths of a second (nanoseconds). Storage devices, by contrast, access items in thousandths of a second (milliseconds).

Capacity is the number of bytes (characters) a storage medium can hold. Figure 7-3 lists the terms

AN ILLUSTRATION OF VOLATILITY

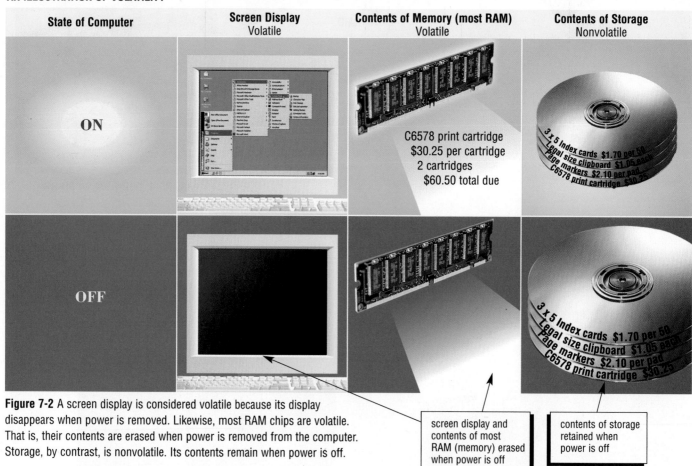

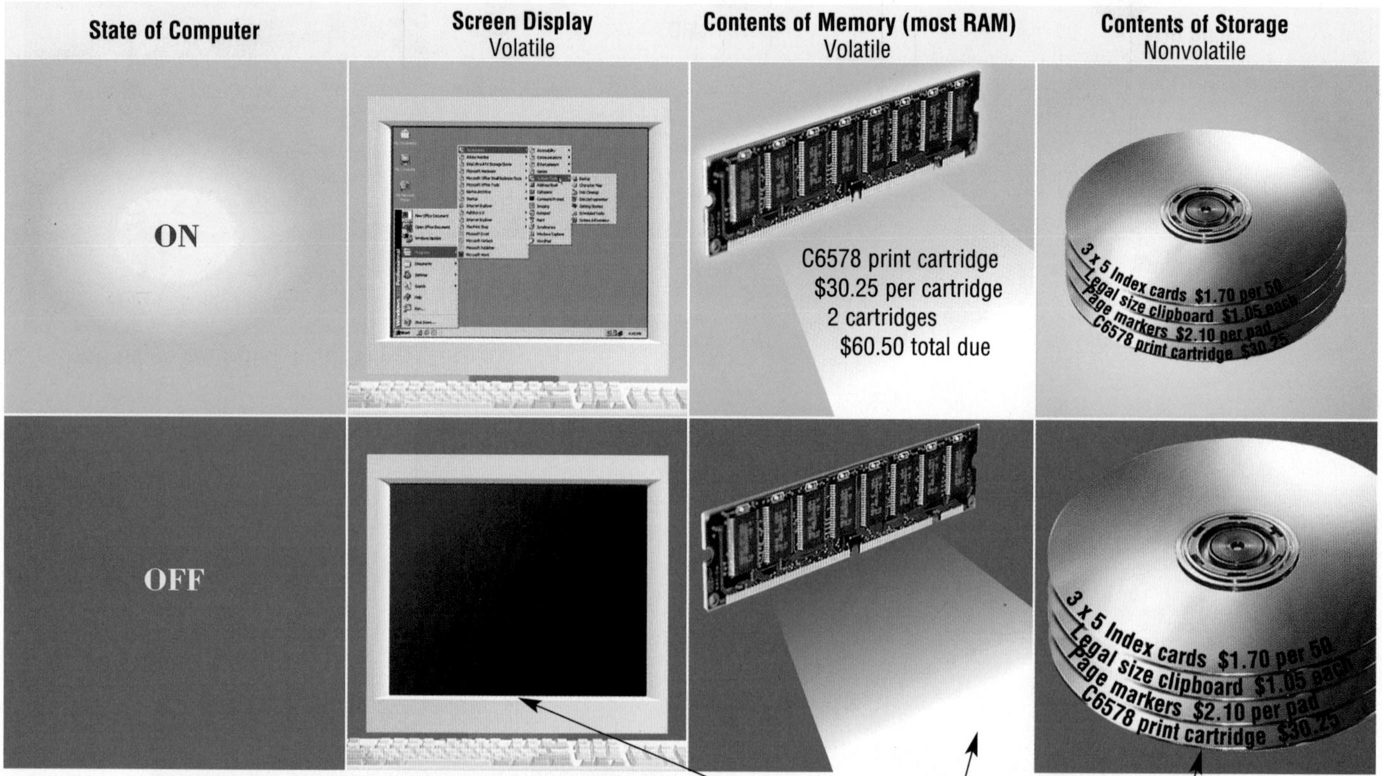

Figure 7-2 A screen display is considered volatile because its display disappears when power is removed. Likewise, most RAM chips are volatile. That is, their contents are erased when power is removed from the computer. Storage, by contrast, is nonvolatile. Its contents remain when power is off.

STORAGE TERMS

Storage Term	Abbreviation	Number of Bytes
Kilobyte	KB	1 thousand
Megabyte	MB	1 million
Gigabyte	GB	1 billion
Terabyte	TB	1 trillion
Petabyte	PB	1 quadrillion

Figure 7-3 The capacity of a storage device is measured by the amount of bytes it can hold.

manufacturers use to define the capacity of storage media. A typical floppy disk can store up to 1.44 MB of data (approximately 1.4 million bytes) and a typical hard disk stores 30 GB of data (approximately 30 billion bytes).

Storage requirements among users vary greatly. Small office home office (SOHO) users might need to store a relatively small amount of data. A field sales representative might have a list of names, addresses, and telephone numbers of 50 customers, which he or she uses on a daily basis. Such a list might require no more than a few thousand bytes of storage. Large business users, such as banks, libraries, or insurance companies, often process data for millions of customers and thus might need to store trillions of bytes worth of historical or financial records in their archives.

Numerous types of storage media and storage devices exist to meet a variety of users' needs. Figure 7-4 shows how different types of storage media and memory compare in terms of relative cost and speed. This chapter discusses the storage media in the pyramid, as well as other media.

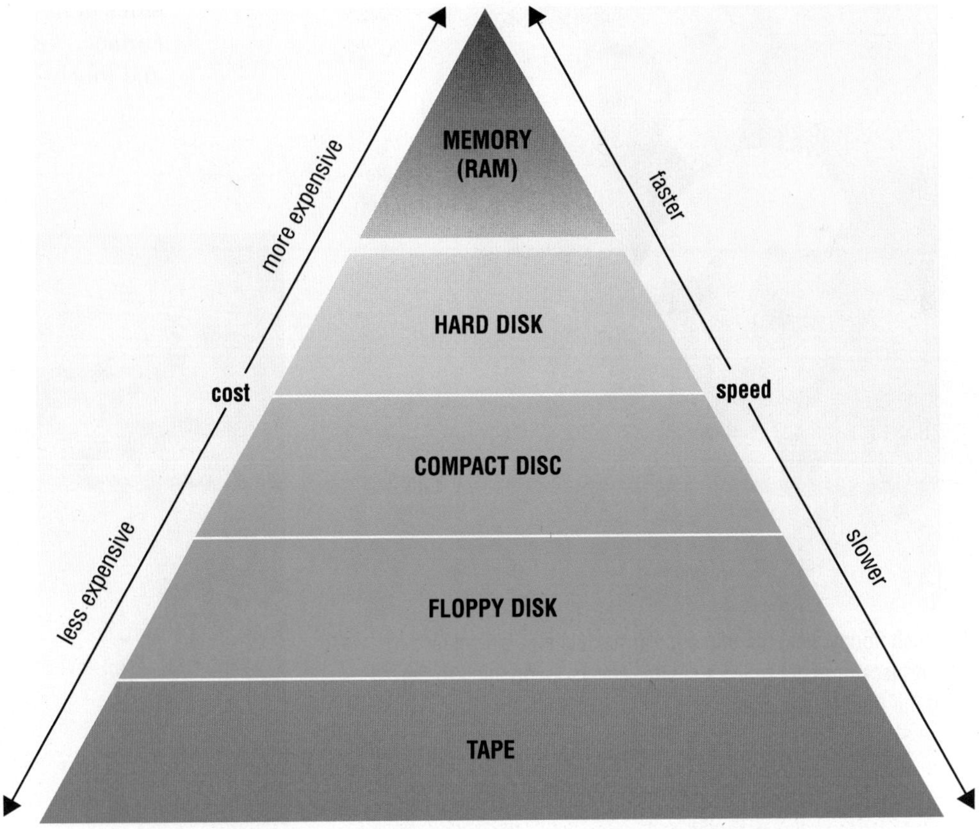

Figure 7-4 This pyramid shows how different types of storage media and memory compare in terms of relative cost and speed. Memory is faster than storage, but is expensive and not practical for all storage requirements. Storage is less expensive but is slower than memory.

FLOPPY DISKS

A **floppy disk**, or **diskette**, is a portable, inexpensive storage medium that consists of a thin, circular, flexible plastic disk with a magnetic coating enclosed in a square-shaped plastic shell (Figure 7-5). In the early 1970s, IBM introduced the floppy disk as a new type of storage. These 8-inch wide disks were known as floppies because they had flexible plastic covers. The next generation of floppies looked much the same, but they were only 5.25-inches wide.

Today, the standard floppy disk is 3.5-inches wide and has a rigid plastic outer cover. Although the exterior of the 3.5-inch disk is not floppy, users still refer to them as floppy disks.

A floppy disk is a portable storage medium. When discussing a storage medium, the term portable means you can remove the medium from one computer and carry it to another computer. For example, most personal computers have a floppy disk drive, in which you insert and remove a floppy disk (Figure 7-6).

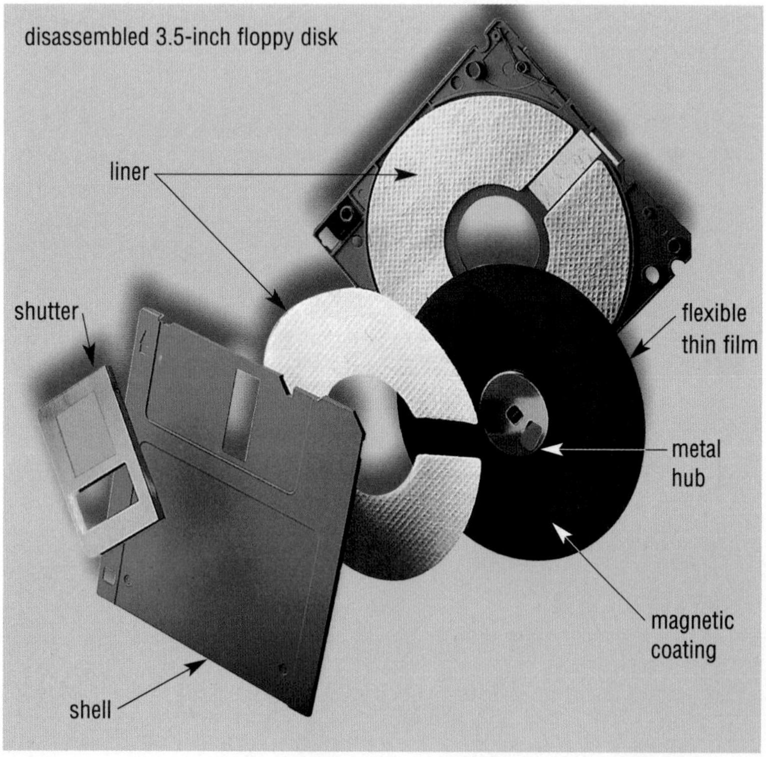

Figure 7-5 In a 3.5-inch floppy disk, the thin circular flexible film is enclosed between two liners. A piece of metal called a shutter covers an opening to the recording surface in the rigid plastic shell.

Floppy Disk Drives

A **floppy disk drive** (**FDD**) is a device that can read from and write on a floppy disk. Desktop personal computers and many notebook computers have a floppy disk drive installed inside the system unit. Some notebook computers have a removable floppy disk drive, where you can remove the entire drive and replace it with another type of drive or device.

Computers with one floppy disk drive refer to it as *drive A*. Computers that have two floppy disk drives designate the second one as *drive B*.

On a 3.5-inch floppy disk, a piece of metal called the **shutter** covers an opening in the rigid plastic shell (see Figure 7-5). When you insert a floppy disk into a floppy disk drive, the drive slides the shutter to the side to expose a portion of both sides of the floppy disk's recording surface. Never open the disk's shutter and touch its recording surface.

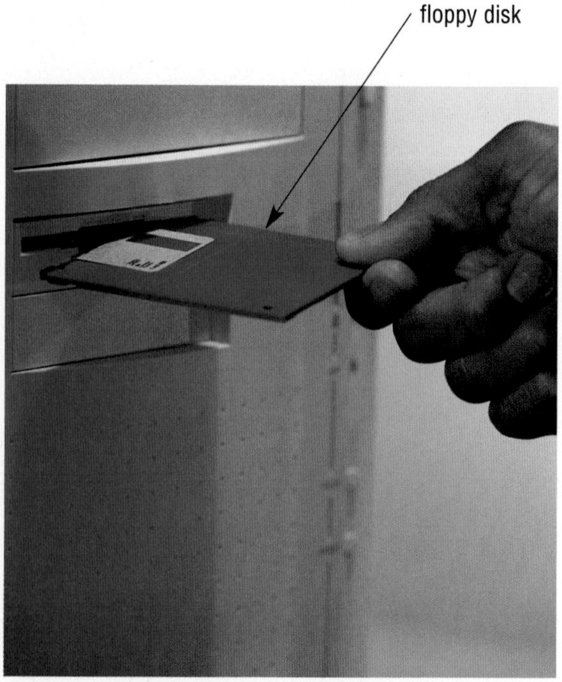

Figure 7-6 On a personal computer, you insert and remove a floppy disk from a floppy disk drive.

On the front of most floppy disk drives is a light emitting diode (LED) that lights up when the drive is accessing the floppy disk. You should not remove a floppy disk when the LED is lit.

The read/write head in the floppy disk drive is the mechanism that actually reads items from or writes items on the floppy disk. Figure 7-7 illustrates the steps for reading from and writing on a floppy disk. The average time it takes a current floppy disk drive to locate an item on a disk is 84 milliseconds, or approximately 1/12 of a second.

Sometimes, a floppy disk drive will malfunction when it is attempting to access a floppy disk and will display an error message on the screen. If the same error occurs with multiple floppy disks, the read/write heads in the floppy disk drive may have a buildup of dust or dirt. In this case, you can try cleaning the read/write heads using a floppy disk cleaning kit.

To read from or write on a floppy disk, a floppy disk drive must support that floppy disk's density. **Density** is the number of bits in an area on a storage medium. A disk with a higher density has more bits in an area and thus has a larger storage capacity. Most disks today are high density (HD). To access an HD floppy disk, you must have an HD floppy disk drive. An HD floppy disk has a capacity of 1.44 MB. That is, an HD floppy disk can hold up to approximately 1.44 million bytes.

Floppy disk drives are **downward compatible**, which means they recognize and can use earlier media. Floppy disk drives are not **upward compatible**, and thus cannot recognize newer media. For example, a lower-density floppy disk drive cannot read from or write on a high-density floppy disk.

Figure 7-7 HOW A FLOPPY DISK DRIVE WORKS

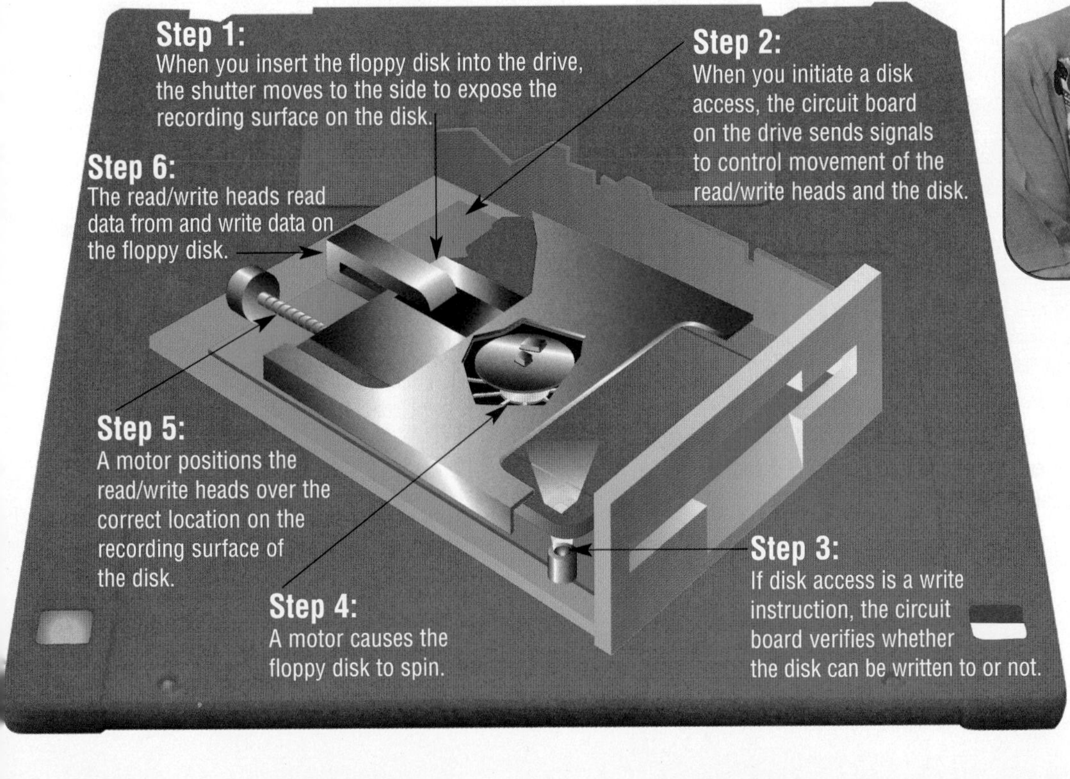
Step 1:
When you insert the floppy disk into the drive, the shutter moves to the side to expose the recording surface on the disk.
Step 2:
When you initiate a disk access, the circuit board on the drive sends signals to control movement of the read/write heads and the disk.
Step 6:
The read/write heads read data from and write data on the floppy disk.
Step 5:
A motor positions the read/write heads over the correct location on the recording surface of the disk.
Step 4:
A motor causes the floppy disk to spin.
Step 3:
If disk access is a write instruction, the circuit board verifies whether the disk can be written to or not.

TECHNOLOGY TRAILBLAZER

AL SHUGART

Al Shugart has more than 45 years experience in the technology industry.

In 1951, Shugart joined IBM as a customer engineer. In 1955, he became part of a product development program that would have a profound impact on the computer industry. As the company's product manager for random-access memory projects worldwide, Shugart supervised a team in 1967 responsible for developing a removable, portable data storage device. This effort led to the construction of an 8-inch, read-only disk and later to the first read-write disk drive. Shugart left IBM in 1969 and spent the next four years as vice president of product development for Memorex. He founded Shugart Associates in 1973 with the mission to popularize the 8-inch disk drive and mass produce it for the commercial market. The following year, Shugart left the company bearing his name and worked as a private consultant to the technology industry until 1979, when he founded Seagate Technology.

For more information on Al Shugart, visit the Discovering Computers 2002 People Web page (**scsite.com/dc2002/people.htm**) and click Al Shugart.

Web Link

For more information on floppy disks, visit the Discovering Computers 2002 Chapter 7 WEB LINK page (**scsite.com/dc2002/ch7/weblink.htm**) and click Floppy Disks.

How a Floppy Disk Stores Data

A floppy disk is a type of magnetic media. **Magnetic media** uses magnetic patterns to store items such as data, instructions, and information on a disk's surface. Most magnetic disks are read/write storage media. This enables you to access (read) data from and place (write) data on a magnetic disk any number of times, just as you can with an audiocassette tape.

A floppy disk stores data in tracks and sectors (Figure 7-8). A **track** is a narrow recording band that forms a full circle on the surface of the disk. The disk's storage locations consist of pie-shaped sections, which break the tracks into small arcs called **sectors**. A sector can store up to 512 bytes of data. A typical floppy disk stores data on both sides of the disk, has 80 tracks on each side of the recording surface, and 18 sectors per track.

You can compute a disk's storage capacity by multiplying together the number of sides on the disk, the number of tracks on the disk, the number of sectors per track, and the number of bytes in a sector. For example, the formula for a high-density 3.5-inch floppy disk is as follows: 2 (sides) x 80 (tracks) x 18 (sectors per track) x 512 (bytes per sector) = 1,474,560 bytes (Figure 7-9). Some disks store system files in some tracks, which means the available capacity on a disk may be less than the total possible capacity.

Given the actual number of available bytes on a floppy disk (1,474,560), you may question why manufacturers call them 1.44 MB disks. The 1.44 MB is not a rounding of the 1,474,560. Instead, it is a result of doubling 720 MB, which is the capacity of a low-density 3.5-inch floppy disk.

For reading and writing purposes, sectors are grouped into clusters. A **cluster** is the smallest unit of disk space that stores data. Each cluster, also called an **allocation unit**, consists of two to eight sectors (the number varies depending on the operating system). Even if a file consists of only a few bytes, it uses an entire cluster. Each cluster holds data from only one file. One file, however, can span many clusters.

Sometimes, a sector has a flaw and cannot store data. When you format a disk, the operating system marks these bad sectors as unusable. **Formatting** is the process of preparing a disk for reading and writing. Chapter 8 discusses the formatting process in more depth.

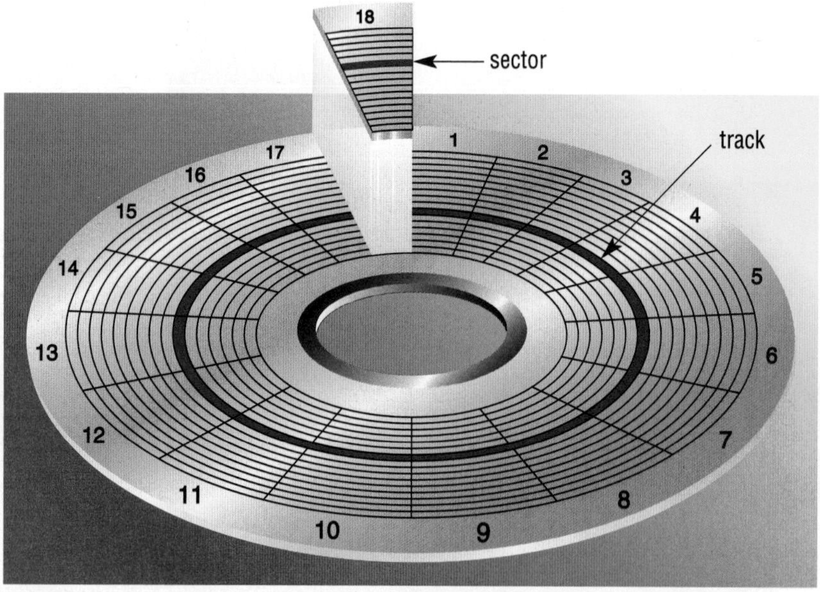

Figure 7-8 A track is a narrow recording band that forms a full circle on the surface of a disk. The disk's storage locations then are divided into pie-shaped sections, which break the tracks into small arcs called sectors.

CHARACTERISTICS OF A 3.5-INCH HIGH-DENSITY FLOPPY DISK

Capacity	1.44 MB
Sides	2
Tracks	80
Sectors per track	18
Bytes per sector	512
Sector per disk	2880

Figure 7-9 Most of today's personal computers use high-density disks.

Care of Floppy Disks

Floppy disks provide an inexpensive and reliable form of storage. Disk manufacturers state that a floppy disk can last at least seven years, with reasonable care. In many cases, the disks do not have that long of a life span.

To maximize a disk's life, you should take proper care of it. When handling a floppy disk, avoid exposing it to heat, cold, magnetic fields, and contaminants such as dust, smoke, or salt air. Exposure to any of these elements could damage or destroy the data, instructions, and information stored on the floppy disk. To protect disks further, keep the disks in a storage tray when not using them.

To protect floppy disks from accidentally being erased, the disk's plastic outer cover has a write-protect notch in its corner. A **write-protect notch** is a small opening that has a tab you slide to cover or expose the notch (Figure 7-10). The write-protect notch works much like the recording tab on a VHS tape: if you remove the recording tab, a VCR cannot record onto the VHS tape.

On a floppy disk, if the write-protect notch is open, the drive cannot write on the floppy disk. If the write-protect notch is covered, or closed, the drive can write on the floppy disk. The write-protect notch only affects the floppy disk drive's capability of *writing* on the disk. A floppy disk drive can read from a floppy disk whether the write-protect notch is open or closed. Some floppy disks have a second opening on the opposite side of the disk that does not have the small tab. This opening identifies the disk as an HD (high-density) floppy disk.

HIGH-CAPACITY DISKS

A **high-capacity disk drive** is a disk drive that uses disks with capacities of 100 MB and greater. High-capacity disks allow you easily to transport a large number of files from one computer to another. These disks also can store large graphics, audio, or video files. Another popular use of these disks is to back up important data and information. A **backup** is a duplicate of a file, program, or disk that you can use if the original is lost, damaged, or destroyed.

Three types of high-capacity disk drives are the SuperDisk™ drive, the HiFD™ drive, and the Zip® drive. The first two are downward compatible with floppy disks. That is, SuperDisk™ and HiFD™ drives can read from and write on standard 3.5-inch floppy disks, as well as their own high-capacity disks.

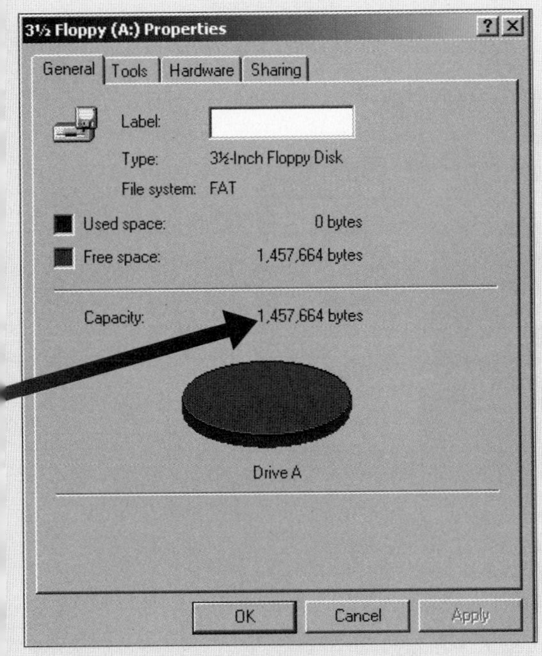

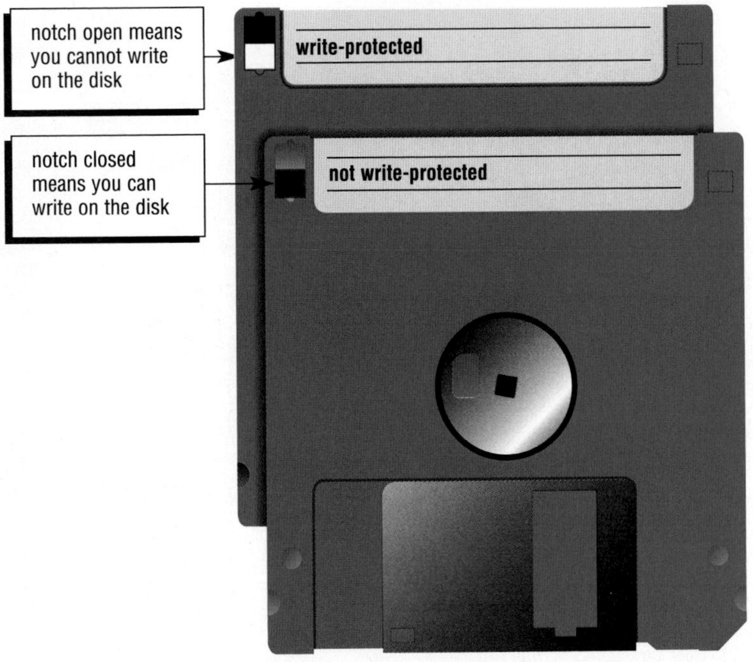

Figure 7-10 To protect data from being erased accidentally, floppy disks have a write-protect notch. By sliding a small tab, you either can cover or expose the notch.

Many notebook computers offer a SuperDisk™ drive or a HiFD™ drive as an option. Developed by Imation, a **SuperDisk™ drive** reads from and writes on a 120 MB or a 250 MB SuperDisk™. Some digital cameras have built-in SuperDisk drives to allow storage of hundreds of photographs on a single disk. The **HiFD™ (High-Capacity Floppy Disk) drive**, developed by Sony Electronics Inc., reads from and writes on a 200 MB HiFD™ disk.

A **Zip® drive** is a high-capacity disk drive developed by Iomega Corporation that uses a Zip® disk. A **Zip® disk** is slightly larger than and about twice as thick as a 3.5-inch floppy disk, and can store 100 MB or 250 MB of data. Many desktop computers have a built-in Zip® drive as a standard feature (Figure 7-11). Others offer it as an option. You also can connect an external Zip® drive to a notebook or desktop computer to provide even more portability.

HARD DISKS

When personal computers were introduced, software programs and their related files fit easily on a single floppy disk. With these programs, you simply inserted the disk to use the program. Throughout time, software became more complex and included graphical user interfaces and multimedia. Users no longer could run programs from a floppy disk. Instead, they installed the program, which consumed many floppy disks, onto the hard disk. Hard disks provide far greater storage capacities and much faster access times than floppy disks.

A **hard disk**, also called a **hard disk drive**, consists of several inflexible, circular platters that store items electronically. Made of aluminum, glass, or ceramic, a **platter** is coated with a material that allows items to be recorded magnetically on its surface. The platters, along with the read/write heads, and the mechanism for moving the heads across the surface of the hard disk, are enclosed in an airtight, sealed case to protect them from contamination.

Most desktop personal computers contain at least one hard disk. The hard disk inside the system unit, sometimes called a **fixed disk**, is not portable (Figure 7-12). A section later in this chapter discusses another type of hard disk: a removable hard disk.

Current personal computer hard disks can store from 10 to 75 GB of data, instructions, and information. Like floppy disks, these hard disks store data magnetically. Hard disks also are read/write storage media. That is, you can both read from and write on a hard disk any number of times. A recently developed hard disk, called an **optically-assisted hard drive**, combines laser and optic technologies with the magnetic media. These optically-assisted hard drives have potential storage capacities of up to 280 GB.

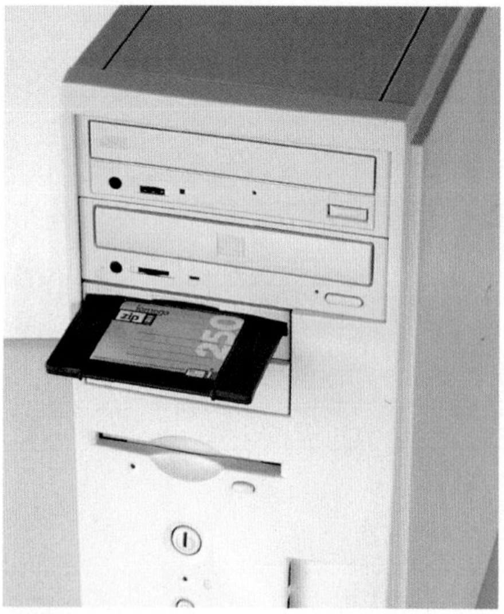

Figure 7-11 Many new computers have a built-in Zip® drive.

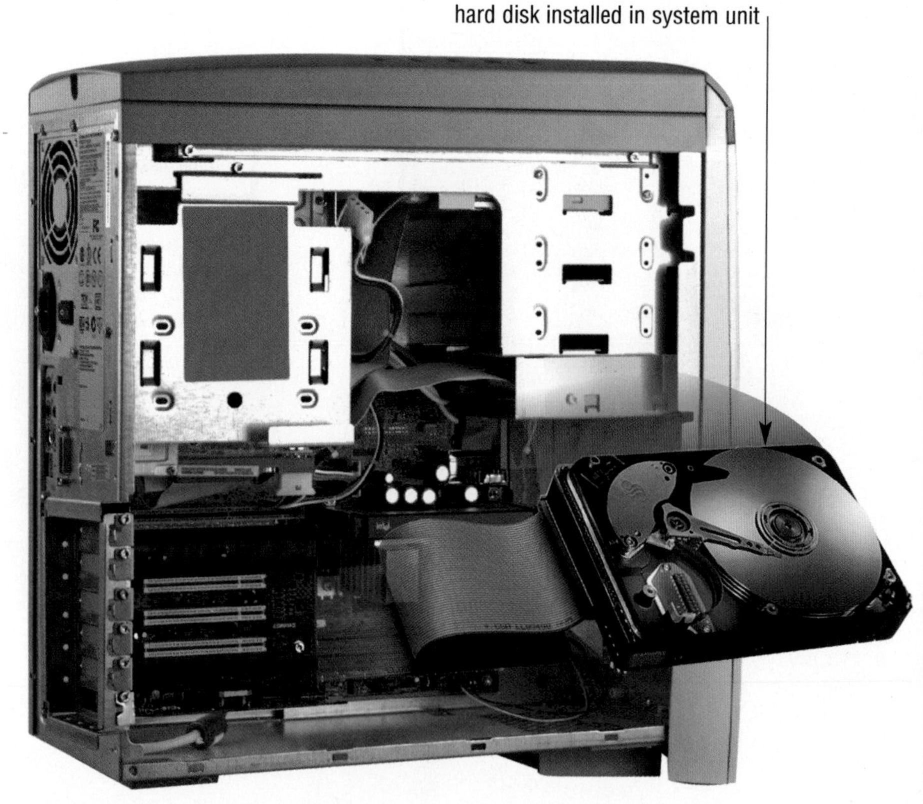

Figure 7-12 The hard disk in a desktop personal computer normally resides permanently inside the system unit. That is, it is not portable.

Web Link

For more information on Zip® drives, visit the Discovering Computers 2002 Chapter 7 WEB LINK page (**scsite.com/dc2002/ch7/weblink.htm**) and click Zip® Drives.

How a Hard Disk Works

Most hard disks have multiple platters stacked on top of one another. Each platter has two read/write heads, one for each side. The hard disk has arms that move the read/write heads to the proper location on the platter (Figure 7-13).

The location of the read/write heads often is referred to by its cylinder. A **cylinder** is the location of a single track through all platters (Figure 7-14). For example, if a hard disk has 4 platters (8 sides), each with 1,000 tracks, then it will have 1,000 cylinders with each cylinder consisting of 8 tracks (2 for each platter). A single movement of the read/write head arms can read all the platters of data.

While your computer is running, the platters in the hard disk rotate at a high rate of speed, usually 5,400 to 7,200 revolutions per minute. The platters typically continue spinning until power is removed from the computer. (On some computers, the hard disk turns off after a specified time period to save power.) The spinning motion creates a cushion of air between the platter and its read/write head. This cushion ensures that the read/write head floats above the platter instead of making direct contact with the platter surface. The distance between the read/write head and the platter is approximately two millionths of an inch.

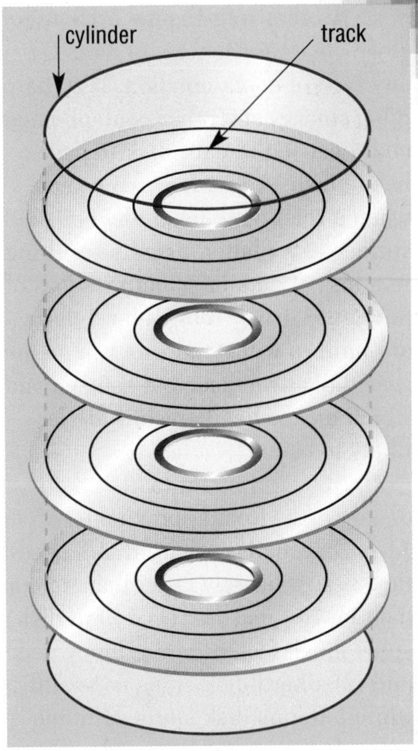

Figure 7-14 A cylinder is the location of a single track through all platters on a hard disk.

Figure 7-13 HOW A HARD DISK WORKS

Step 1:
The circuit board controls the movement of the head actuator and a small motor.
Step 2:
A small motor spins the platters while the computer is running.
Step 3:
When software requests a disk access, the read/write heads determine the current or new location of the data.
Step 4:
The head actuator positions the read/write head arms over the correct location on the platters to read or write data.

Web Link

For more information on hard disks, visit the Discovering Computers 2002 Chapter 7 WEB LINK page (**scsite.com/dc2002/ch7/weblink.htm**) and click Hard Disks.

As shown in Figure 7-15, this close clearance leaves no room for any type of contamination. Dirt, hair, dust, smoke, and other contaminants could cause the hard disk to have a head crash. A **head crash** occurs when a read/write head touches the surface of a platter, usually resulting in a loss of data or sometimes loss of the entire drive. Today's hard disks are built to withstand shocks and are sealed tightly to keep out contaminants, which means head crashes are less likely to occur.

Access time for today's hard disks ranges from approximately 5 to 11 milliseconds. A hard disk's access time is significantly faster than a floppy disk for two reasons: (1) a hard disk spins much faster than a floppy disk and (2) a hard disk spins constantly, while a floppy disk starts spinning only when it receives a read or write command.

Some computers improve hard disk access time by using disk caching. **Disk cache** (pronounced cash) is a portion of memory that the processor uses to store frequently accessed items (Figure 7-16). Disk cache works similarly to memory cache. When a program needs data, instructions, or information, the processor checks the disk cache. If the item is in disk cache, the processor uses that item and completes the process. If the processor does not find the requested item in the disk cache, then the processor must wait for the hard disk drive to locate and transfer the item from the disk to the processor.

A **cache controller** manages cache and thus determines which items cache should store. On newer processors, the cache controller is part of the processor.

Some disk caching systems also attempt to predict what data, instructions, or information might be needed and place them into cache before the processor requests them. Almost all new disk drives work with some amount of disk cache because it significantly improves disk access times.

You can divide a formatted hard disk into separate areas called **partitions** by issuing a special operating system command. Each partition functions as if it were a separate hard disk drive. Users often partition a hard disk so they can install multiple operating systems on the same hard disk.

If a hard disk has only one partition, the operating system designates it as *drive C*. If the hard disk has two partitions, the first partition is *drive C* and the second is *drive D*. Unless specifically requested by the consumer, most manufacturers define a single partition (drive C) on the hard disk.

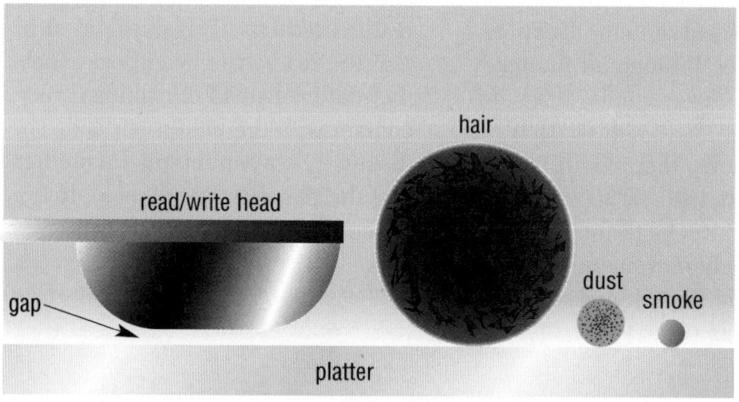

Figure 7-15 The clearance between a disk read/write head and the platter is about two millionths of an inch. Contaminants, such as a smoke particle, dust particle, or human hair, could render the drive unusable.

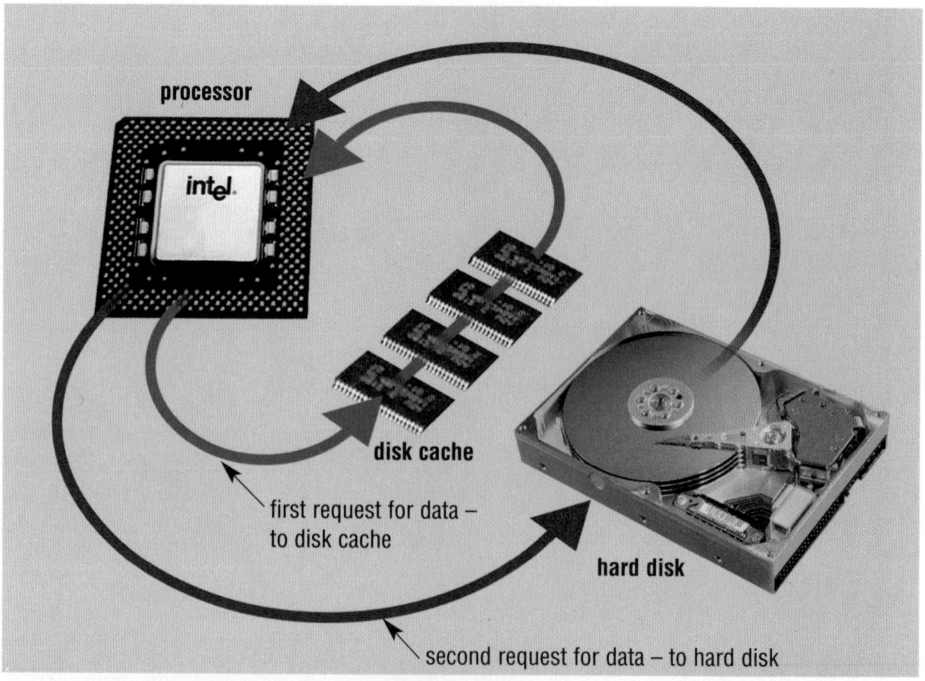

Figure 7-16 When a program needs an item such as data, instructions, or information, the processor checks the disk cache. If the item is located, the processor uses it. If the processor does not find the item in the disk cache, then the processor must wait for the disk drive to locate and transfer the item from the disk.

Hard Disk Controllers

A **disk controller** is a special-purpose chip and associated electronic circuits that control the transfer of data, instructions, and information from a disk to the rest of the computer. Some users refer to the disk controller as an interface.

On a personal computer, a **hard disk controller** (**HDC**) is the interface for a hard disk. The HDC may be part of a disk drive or may be a separate card inside in the system unit. Many external hard drives use a USB port as their interface.

Vendors usually state the HDC interface in their computer advertisements. Thus, you should understand the types of available interfaces. In addition to USB, two types of HDCs for personal computers are EIDE and SCSI.

EIDE One of the most widely used controllers for hard disks is the **Enhanced Integrated Drive Electronics** (**EIDE**) controller. EIDE controllers can support up to four hard disks at 137 GB per disk. They can transfer data, instructions, and information to and from the disk at rates of up to 66 MB per second.

An earlier type of EIDE controller was **ATA**, which is short for AT Attachment. Some manufacturers market their EIDE controllers as Fast ATA. EIDE controllers are backward compatible with earlier IDE and ATA controllers. Various versions include ATA, ATA-4, Ultra ATA, Ultra DMA, and ATA/66.

SCSI **Small computer system interface**, or **SCSI**, (pronounced scuzzy) controllers can support multiple disk drives, as well as other peripherals such as scanners high-capacity disk drives, CD-ROM drives, CD-RW drives, DVD-ROM drives, tape drives, printers, scanners, network interface cards, and much more. When using SCSI devices, you can daisy chain devices together by connecting the first SCSI device to the computer, the second SCSI device to the first SCSI device, and so on. Some computers have a built in SCSI controller, while others use an expansion card to add a SCSI controller.

SCSI controllers are faster than EIDE controllers, providing up to 160 MB per second transfer rates. SCSI controllers typically cost a few hundred dollars more than do EIDE controllers. Many versions of SCSI controllers exist, including SCSI-3, Wide SCSI, Fast SCSI, Fast Wide SCSI, Ultra SCSI, Ultra2 SCSI, and Ultra 160 SCSI. These SCSI controllers typically are backward compatible with earlier SCSI devices.

Removable Hard Disks

Some hard disks are removable, which enables you to insert and remove the hard disk from a hard disk drive, much like a floppy disk. A **removable hard disk**, also called a **disk cartridge**, is a disk drive in which a plastic or metal case surrounds the hard disk so you can remove it from the drive (Figure 7-17). A popular, reasonably priced, removable hard disk is the **Jaz® disk** by Iomega. A Jaz® disk can store up to 2 GB of data, instructions, and information.

Figure 7-17 The Jaz® disk by Iomega is a removable hard disk with a storage capacity of up to 2 GB.

COMPANY ON THE CUTTING EDGE

Kingston TECHNOLOGY
COMPUTING WITHOUT LIMITS®

Memory in the Making

Ever sit down to take a test, have your mind go blank, and wonder if you were losing your memory?

The computer industry also thought it was losing its memory in 1987. At that time, memory for personal computers was scarce. John Tu and David Sun knew they could help solve the problem. They founded Kingston Technology and designed a standard single inline memory module (SIMM) using a readily available alternative chip.

As the memory shortage eased a few years later, Kingston branched into manufacturing processor upgrades, storage subsystems, and networking solutions. Today, Kingston is the world's leading independent manufacturer of memory products for computers, servers, digital cameras, and other electronic devices. With annual sales of more than $1.5 million in 1999, Kingston markets more than 2,000 products.

Fortune magazine has honored Kingston as one of the 100 Best Companies to Work for in the United States. Part of this honor is due to Kingston's company philosophy of treating all employees as family members and of displaying such traits as courtesy, honesty, and compassion.

For more information on Kingston Technology, visit the Discovering Computers 2002 Companies Web page (**scsite.com/dc2002/companies.htm**) and click Kingston.

Portable media, such as floppy disks and other removable disks, have several advantages over fixed disks. First, you can use a removable disk to transport a large number of files or to make backup copies of important files. You also can use removable disks when data security is an issue. For example, at the end of a work session, you can remove the hard disk and lock it up, leaving no data in the computer.

RAID

For applications that depend on reliable data access, it is crucial the data is available when a user attempts to access it. Some manufacturers develop a type of hard disk system that connects several smaller disks into a single unit that acts like a single large hard disk. A group of two or more integrated hard disks is called a **RAID (redundant array of independent disks)**. Although quite expensive, a RAID system is more reliable than a traditional disk system (Figure 7-18). Thus, networks and Internet servers often use RAID.

RAID duplicates data, instructions, and information to improve data reliability. RAID systems implement this duplication in different ways, depending on the storage design, or level, used. (These levels are not hierarchical. That is, higher levels are not necessarily better than lower levels.) The simplest RAID storage design is **level 1**, called **mirroring**, which has one backup disk for each disk (Figure 7-19a). A level 1 configuration enhances system reliability because, if a drive should fail, a duplicate of the requested item is available elsewhere within the array of disks.

Levels beyond level 1 use a technique called **striping**, which splits data, instructions, and information across multiple disks in the array (Figure 7-19b). Striping improves disk access times, but does not offer data duplication. For this reason, some RAID levels combine both mirroring and striping.

Figure 7-18 A group of two or more integrated hard disks, called a RAID (redundant array of independent disks), often is used with network servers. Shown here is a desktop RAID. Figure 7-1 on page 7.3 shows a rack-mount RAID.

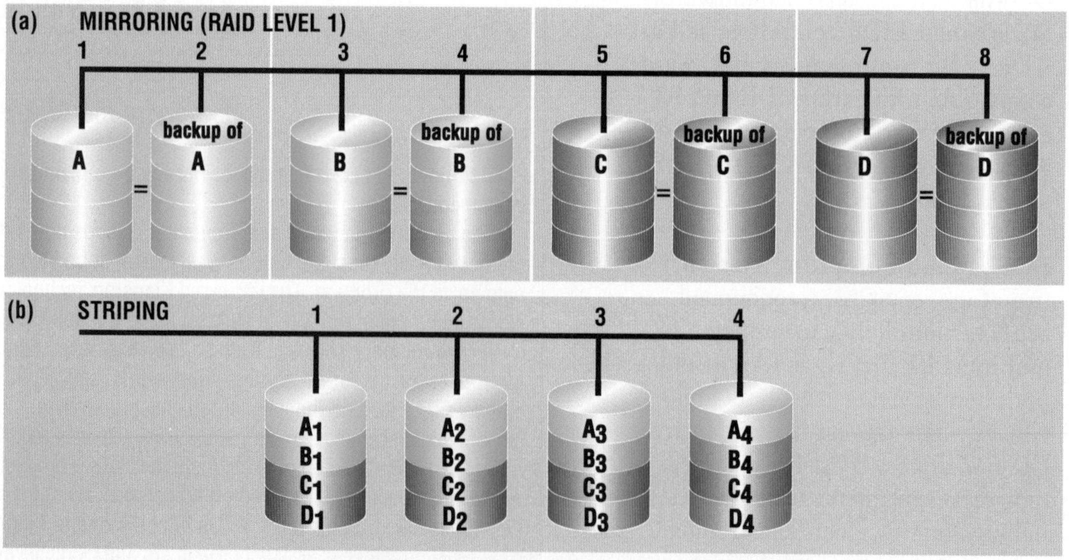

Figure 7-19 In RAID level 1, called mirroring, a backup disk exists for each disk. Higher RAID levels use striping; that is, portions of each disk are placed on multiple disks.

Maintaining Data Stored on a Hard Disk

Most manufacturers guarantee their hard disks to last somewhere between three and five years. Many last much longer with proper care. To prevent the loss of items stored on a hard disk, you should perform preventative maintenance such as defragmenting or scanning the disk for errors. As shown in the table in Figure 7-20, operating systems such as Windows provide many maintenance and monitoring utilities. Chapter 8 discusses these and other utilities in more depth.

Web Link

For more information on disk utilities, visit the Discovering Computers 2002 Chapter 7 WEB LINK page (**scsite.com/dc2002/ch7/weblink.htm**) and click Disk Utilities.

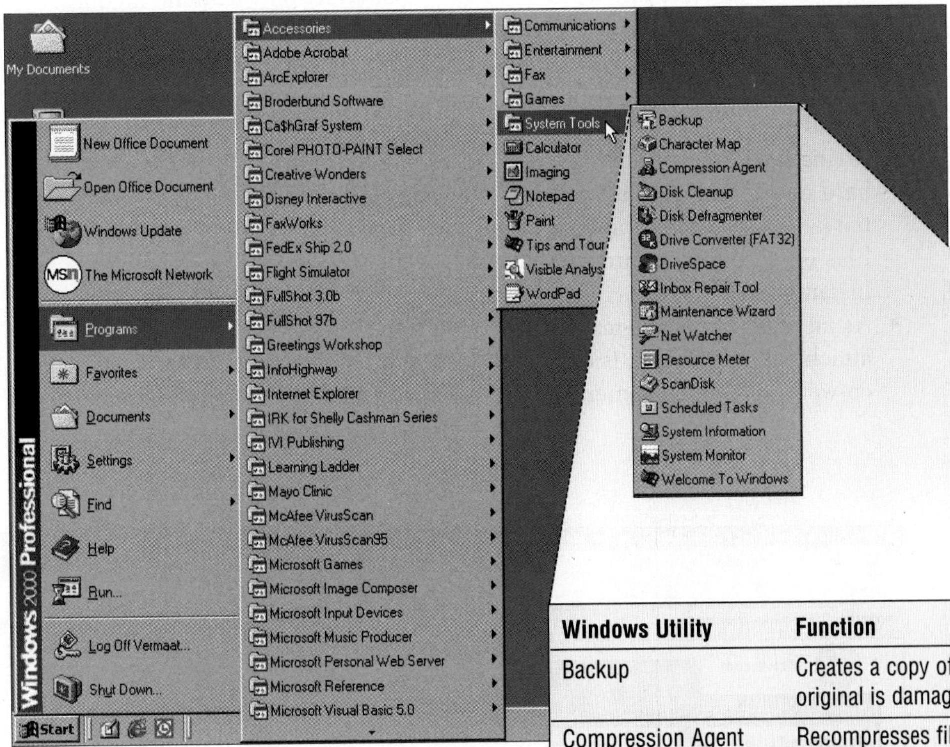

Windows Utility	Function
Backup	Creates a copy of files on a hard disk in case the original is damaged or destroyed.
Compression Agent	Recompresses files according to settings in DriveSpace (see below).
Disk Cleanup	Frees up space on a hard disk by listing files that can be deleted safely.
Disk Defragmenter	Reorganizes files and unused space on a hard disk so programs run faster.
Drive Converter (FAT 32)	Improves the FAT method of storing data, which frees up hard disk space and makes programs load faster.
DriveSpace	Compresses a hard disk or floppy disk to create free space on the disk.
Maintenance Wizard	Runs utilities that optimize your computer's performance.
Net Watcher	Monitors users and disk/file usage when computers are networked.
Resource Meter	Monitors system, user, and graphics resources being used by programs.
ScanDisk	Detects errors on a disk and then repairs the damaged areas.
Scheduled Tasks	Automatically runs a utility at a specified time.
System Monitor	Monitors disk access, the processor, memory, and network usage.

Figure 7-20 Windows provides many maintenance and monitoring utilities on the System Tools submenu. The table in this figure briefly describes some of these utilities.

Internet Hard Drives

Instead of storing data locally on your fixed or removable hard disk, you can opt to store it on an Internet hard drive. An **Internet hard drive**, sometimes called **online storage**, is a service on the Web that provides storage to computer users (Figure 7-21). Many offer storage free of charge to the consumer. Revenues come from advertisers on the site.

Users store data and information on an Internet hard drive for a variety of reasons:

- You no longer need to transport files while away from your desktop computer. Simply copy files to an Internet hard drive and access them from any computer or device that has Web access.
- As you surf the Web, you may spend a lot of time downloading or saving files on your computer's hard disk. Instead, you can save the large audio, video, and graphics files on an Internet hard drive instantaneously.
- As an alternative to e-mailing attachments to family, friends, co-workers, and customers, you can save the attachment on an Internet hard drive. Recipients of your e-mail message can visit your Internet hard drive to play an audio file, watch the video clip, or view a picture.
- View time-critical data and images immediately while away from the main office or location. For example, doctors can view x-ray images from another hospital, home, office, or while on vacation.
- You easily can store offsite backups of data. Chapter 8 presents this and other backup strategies.

In addition to storage space, these Web sites offer other services. These services often include e-mail, calendar, address book, and task list applications. As with other files on the Internet hard drive, you can share your calendars, address books, and tasks lists with others that have Web access.

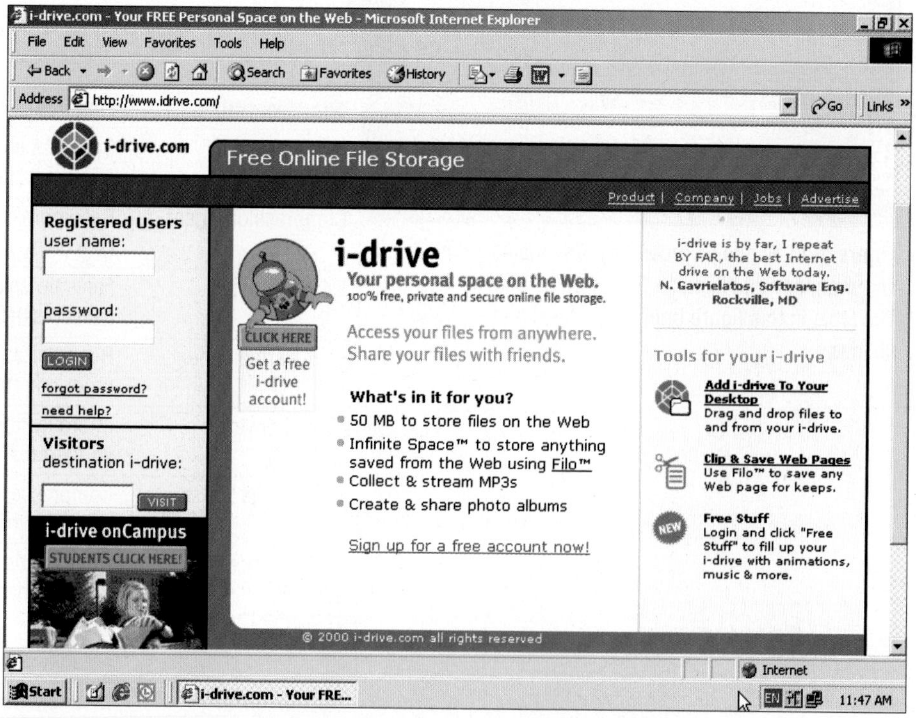

Figure 7-21 Shown here is an example of a free Internet hard drive service.

APPLY IT!

Use an Internet Hard Drive to Extend Your Disk Drive Space

If you are looking for extra disk drive space, a file backup service, or a way to share files with others, you may want to consider one of the free Internet hard drive services. One of the most popular of these is i-drive (see URL below). Using i-drive, you can do the following:

- Save music files, create a play list, and play the songs from i-drive
- Create an online photo album to share with your family and friends
- Save games and other software programs
- Save entire Web pages

To use i-drive, first set up your free account by filling out a short online form. Record your ID and password, log on, and you are ready to go. Click a button to access, setup, and use the following features:

1. Add an i-drive icon to your desktop so that you can drag-and-drop files to your i-drive the same way you drag-and-drop within Windows.
2. Create a Play List folder or a New Photo Album and make these available for public, private, or shared access.
3. Download and install Filo, free downloadable software that lets you clip Web pages, images, files, and links straight to your i-drive or bookmark directly to your i-drive.
4. Use i-drive and access your files from any computer with Web access.

For links to Internet hard drive services and the Web site mentioned above, visit the Discovering Computers 2002 Apply It Web page (**scsite.com/dc2002/apply.htm**) and click Chapter 7 Apply It #1.

COMPACT DISCS

In the past, when you purchased software, you received one or more floppy disks that contained the files needed to install or run the software program. As software programs became more and more complex, the number of floppy disks required to store the programs increased, sometimes exceeding 30 disks. These more complex programs required a storage medium with greater capacity. This is why most manufacturers today distribute software programs on compact discs.

A **compact disc (CD)**, also called an **optical disc**, is a flat, round, portable, metal storage medium that usually is 4.75 inches in diameter and less than one-twentieth of an inch thick. Just about every personal computer today includes some type of compact disc drive installed in a drive bay. These drives read compact discs, including audio CDs.

On these drives, you push a button to slide out a tray, insert your compact disc with the label side up, and then push the same button to close the tray (Figure 7-22). Other convenient features on most of these drives include a volume control button and a headphone jack so you can use stereo headphones to listen to audio without disturbing others nearby.

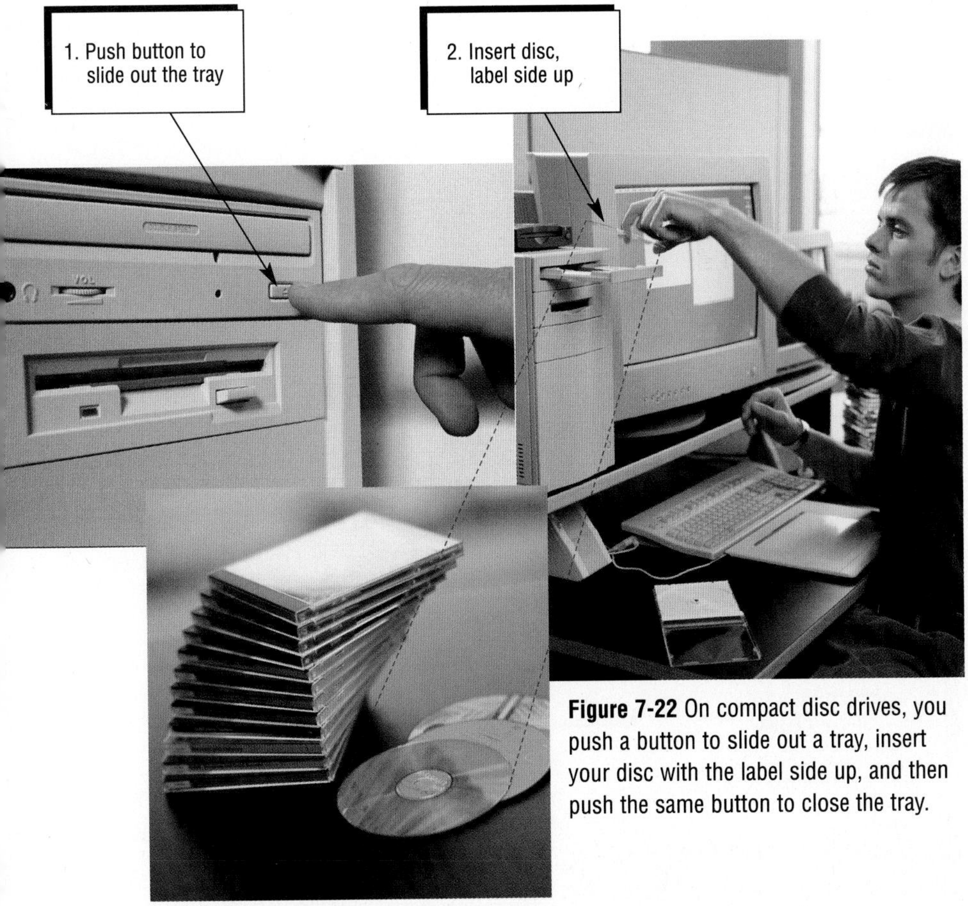
1. Push button to slide out the tray
2. Insert disc, label side up

Figure 7-22 On compact disc drives, you push a button to slide out a tray, insert your disc with the label side up, and then push the same button to close the tray.

ISSUE

Web Warehouses

Online Storage

Consider the following scenarios:
a) You are at work and realize you forgot the electronic files at home for your meeting today; b) You just returned from a fabulous vacation and want to share vacation pictures; or, c) Your computer's hard disk is almost full and you cannot afford to purchase additional storage. One solution is to use one of the free Internet hard drive storage services. Ease of use, number of features, and amount of storage space varies, based on the specific Web site, but you can store information and access it from any Web-enabled computer in the world. Would you store your information on the Internet, instead of on your hard disk? If so, what types of information would you store online? Do you trust the security of these online storage services? What negatives and/or positives could someone encounter with this type of service?

For more information on online storage, visit the Discovering Computers 2002 Issues Web page (**scsite.com/dc2002/issues.htm**) and click Chapter 7 Issue #1.

Recall that a floppy disk drive is designated as drive A. The drive designation of a compact disc drive usually follows alphabetically after that of the hard disk. For example, if the hard disk is drive C, then the compact disc is drive D.

Compact discs store items such as data, instructions, and information by using microscopic pits (indentations) and land (flat areas) that are in the middle layer of the disc (Figure 7-23). (Most manufacturers place a silk-screened label on the top layer of the disc so you can identify it.) A high-powered laser light creates the pits. A lower-powered laser light reads items from the compact disc by reflecting light through the bottom of the disc, which usually is either solid gold or silver in color. The reflected light is converted into a series of bits the computer can process. Land causes light to reflect, which is read as binary digit 1. Pits absorb the light; this absence of light is read as binary digit 0.

A compact disc typically stores items in a single track that spirals from the center of the disc to the edge of the disc. As with a hard disk, this single track is divided into evenly sized sectors in which items are stored (Figure 7-24).

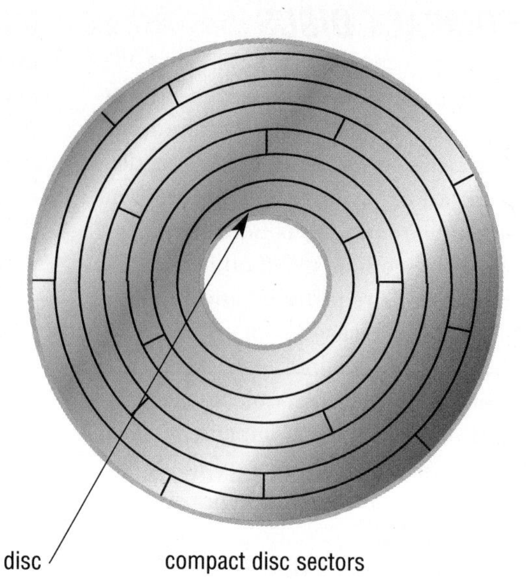

Figure 7-24 The data on a compact disc often is stored in a single track that spirals from the center of the disc to the edge of a disc.

Figure 7-23 HOW A LASER READS DATA ON A COMPACT DISC

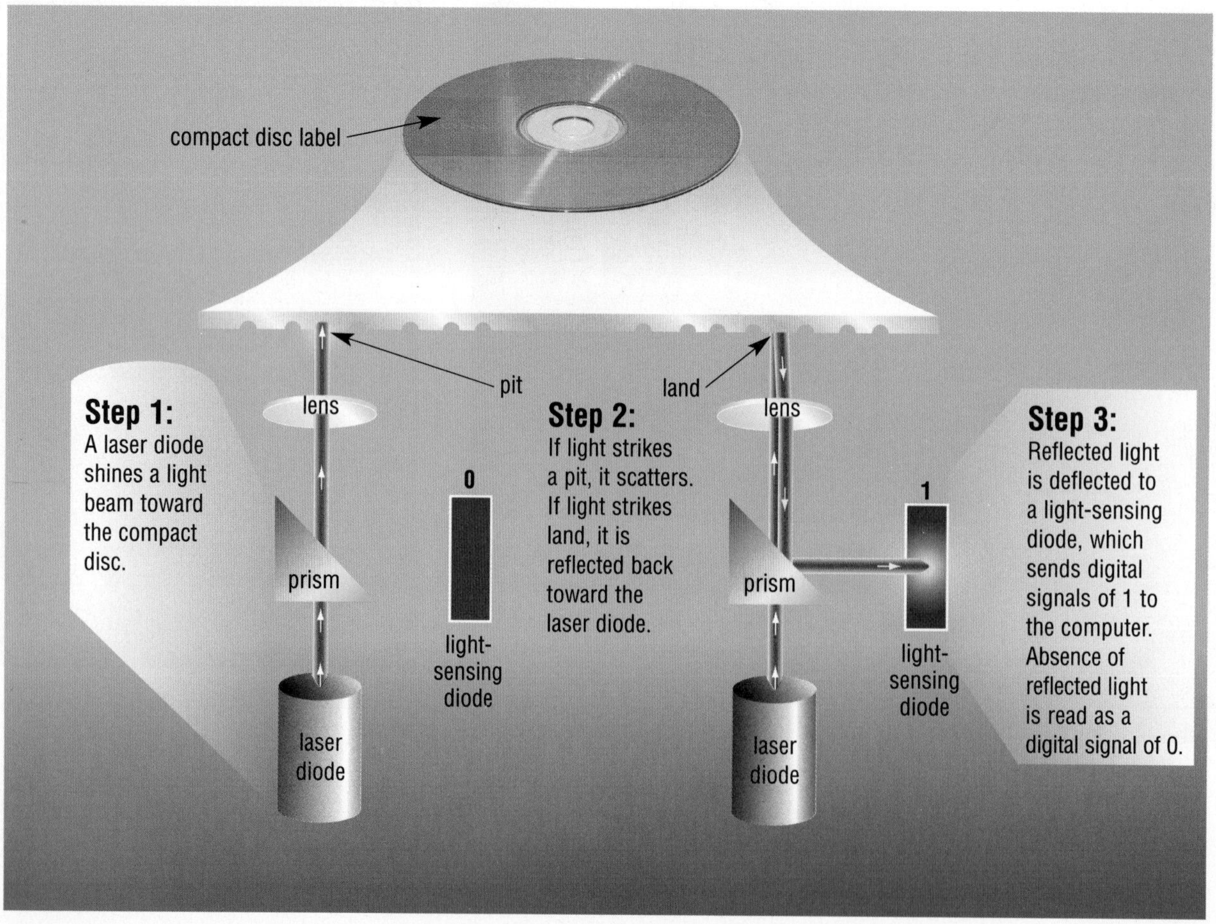

compact disc label
pit
land
lens
lens
Step 1:
A laser diode shines a light beam toward the compact disc.
prism
0
light-
sensing
diode
laser
diode
Step 2:
If light strikes a pit, it scatters. If light strikes land, it is reflected back toward the laser diode.
prism
1
light-
sensing
diode
laser
diode
Step 3:
Reflected light is deflected to a light-sensing diode, which sends digital signals of 1 to the computer. Absence of reflected light is read as a digital signal of 0.

Manufacturers guarantee that a properly cared for compact disc will last five years, but could last up to 50 years. To protect data on any type of compact disc, you should place it in its protective case, called a **jewel box**, when you are finished using it (Figure 7-25). When handling compact discs, you should avoid stacking them and exposing them to heat, cold, and contaminants. Figure 7-26 outlines some guidelines for the proper care of compact discs.

Figure 7-25 To protect data on a CD, you should place it in a jewel box when you are finished using it.

You can clean the bottom surface of a compact disc with a soft cloth and warm water or a specialized compact disc cleaning kit. You also can repair scratches on the bottom surface with a specialized compact disc repair kit.

Compact discs are available in a variety of formats, including CD-ROM, CD-R, CD-RW, and DVD-ROM. The following pages discuss these basic formats.

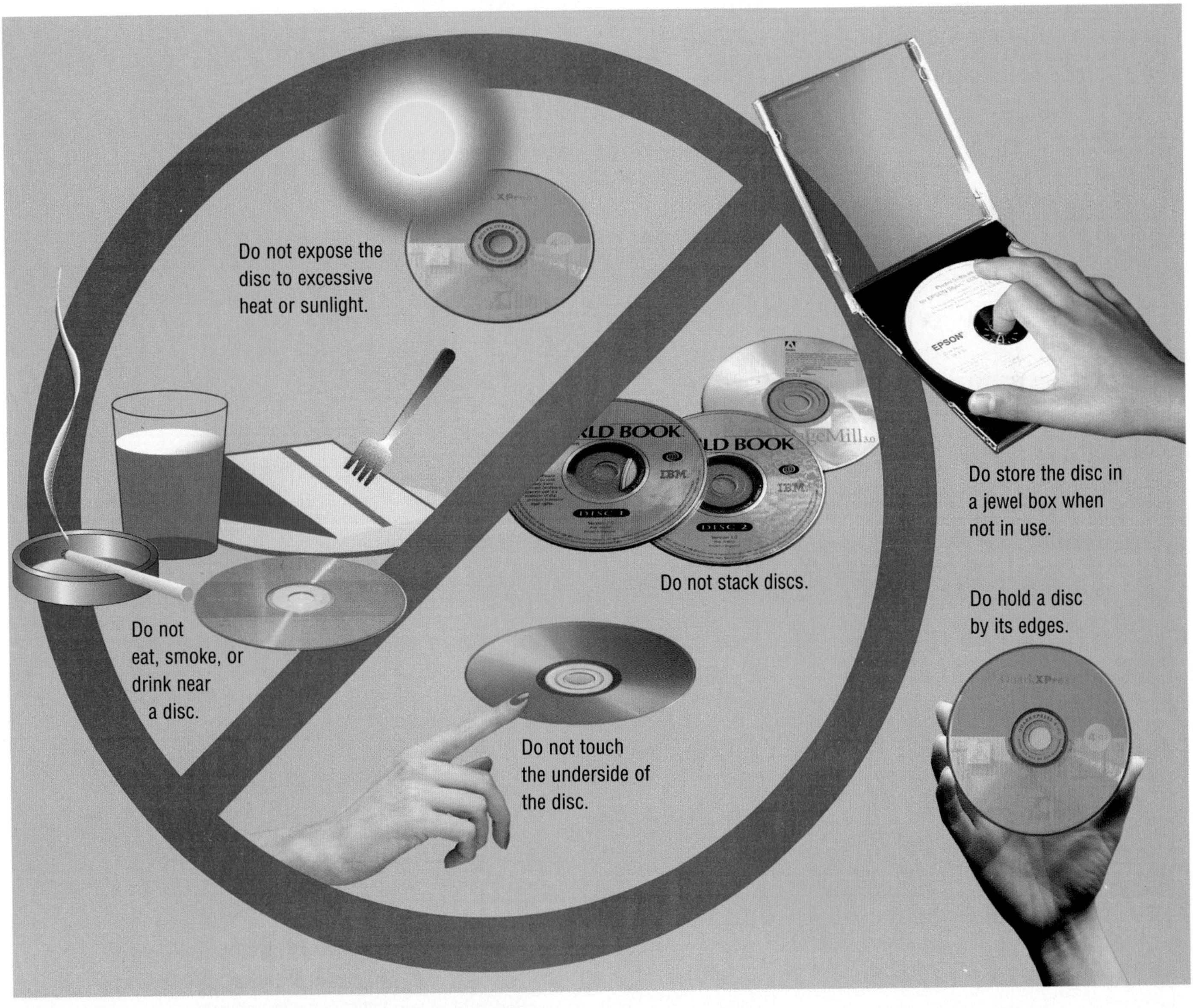

Do not expose the disc to excessive heat or sunlight.
Do not stack discs.
Do store the disc in a jewel box when not in use.
Do hold a disc by its edges.
Do not eat, smoke, or drink near a disc.
Do not touch the underside of the disc.
EPSON
IBM

Figure 7-26 Some guidelines for the proper care of compact discs.

CD-ROMs

A **CD-ROM** (pronounced SEE-DEE-rom), or **compact disc read-only memory,** is a silver-colored compact disc that uses the same laser technology as audio CDs for recording music. In addition to audio, a CD-ROM can contain text, graphics, and video. The manufacturer writes, or **records**, the contents of standard CD-ROMs. You only can read the contents of these discs. That is, you cannot erase or modify their contents — hence, the name read-only.

For a computer to read items on a CD-ROM, you must place it into a **CD-ROM drive** or **CD-ROM player**. Because audio CDs and CD-ROMs use the same laser technology, you also can use your CD-ROM drive to listen to an audio CD while working on your computer.

A typical CD-ROM holds about 650 MB of data, instructions, and information. This is about 450 times more than you can store on a high-density 3.5-inch floppy disk. Manufacturers use CD-ROMs to store and distribute today's multimedia and other complex software because these discs have such high storage capacities (Figure 7-27). Some programs even require that the disc be in the drive each time you use the program.

CD-ROM Drive Speed

The speed of a CD-ROM drive is extremely important when viewing animation or video such as those found in multimedia encyclopedias and games. A slower CD-ROM drive results in choppy images or sound. The data transfer rate is the time it takes a drive to transmit data, instructions, and information from the

Web Link

For more information on CD-ROMs, visit the Discovering Computers 2002 Chapter 7 WEB LINK page (**scsite.com/dc2002/ch7/weblink.htm**) and click CD-ROMs.

Figure 7-27 CD-ROMs are used to store and distribute multimedia and other complex software.

drive to another device. The original CD-ROM drives were single-speed drives with a data transfer rate of 150 KB per second. Manufacturers measure all CD-ROM drives relative to the first CD-ROM drive. An X denotes the original transfer rate of 150 KB per second. For example, a 40X CD-ROM drive has a data transfer rate of 6,000 (40 x 150) KB per second or 6 MB per second.

Current CD-ROM drives have data transfer rates, or speeds, ranging from 40X to 75X. The higher the number, the faster the CD-ROM drive, which results in smoother playback of images and sounds. Faster CD-ROM drives, however, are more expensive than slower drives.

Figure 7-28 Many film developers offer a Picture CD service when you drop off film to be developed.

PhotoCDs and Picture CDs

Based on a file format developed by Eastman Kodak, a **PhotoCD** is a compact disc that contains digital photographic images saved in the PhotoCD format. Commercial and professional users work with PhotoCDs. Most professional desktop publishing software packages can read the PhotoCD format.

A PhotoCD is a **multisession** disc, which means you can write additional data, instructions, and information to the disc at a later time. Thus, as users capture more photographs, they can add them to the PhotoCD. (Most standard CD-ROMs are **single-session** because manufacturers write all items to the disc at one time.)

For the home user, Kodak has a Picture CD. A **Picture CD** is a single-session disc that stores digital versions of photographs for consumers. Many film developers offer this service when you drop off film to be developed. That is, in addition to printed photographs and negatives, you also receive a disc containing your pictures (Figure 7-28). The additional cost for a Picture CD is about $10 per roll of film.

ISSUE

And Your Choice Is?

CD-ROM or Printed Brochure

Instead of printed brochures, companies increasingly now mail or give marketing CD-ROMs to their potential customers. CD-ROMs are more expensive than conventional advertisements, but the companies feel the storage medium's interactivity is worth the cost in most instances. Some automobile manufacturers, for example, offer a CD-ROM that introduces new vehicles to prospective buyers. The CD-ROM shows photographs, statistics, option packages, and pricing information. Using a mouse, automobile shoppers can *walk around and kick the tires*, view the car from different angles, obtain close-ups of special features, and even go on a figurative test drive. Should companies advertise on CD-ROMs and mail the CD-ROMs to the public? Do people install and read the information on these CD-ROMs? Is a printed brochure more effective? What products are best suited to promotion on CD-ROM? Why? What products are least suited? Why? Will marketing CD-ROMs ever replace printed advertising materials? Why or why not?

For more information on CD-ROMs, visit the Discovering Computers 2002 Issues Web page (**scsite.com/dc2002/issues.htm**) and click Chapter 7 Issue #2.

Using photo-editing software and the photographs on the Picture CD, you can remove red eye, crop the photograph, trim away edges, enhance colors, adjust the lighting, and edit just about any aspect of a photograph. You also can print copies of the photographs on glossy paper with your ink-jet printer. If you want to share the photographs, you can e-mail them, copy them to an Internet hard drive, or post them on a photo community.

Web Link

For more information on Picture CDs, visit the Discovering Computers 2002 Chapter 7 WEB LINK page (**scsite.com/dc2002/ch7/weblink.htm**) and click Picture CDs.

CD-R AND CD-RW

Most computers today include either a CD-R or CD-RW drive as a standard feature. Others offer one of these drives as an option. Unlike standard CD-ROM drives, you can record, or write, your own data onto a disc with a CD-R or CD-RW drive.

A **CD-R (compact disc-recordable)** is a multisession compact disc onto which you can record your own items such as text, graphics, and audio. With a CD-R, you can write on part of the disc at one time and another part at a later time. Once you have recorded the CD-R, you can read from it as many times as you wish. You can write on each part only one time, and you cannot erase the disc's contents. Most CD-ROM drives can read a CD-R.

You write on the CD-R using a **CD recorder** or a **CD-R drive** and special software. A CD-R drive can read and write both audio CDs and standard CD-ROMs. These drives read at speeds of up to 24X and write at speeds of up to 8X. Manufacturers often list the write speed first, for example, as 8/24. CD-R drives are slightly more expensive than standard CD-ROM drives.

Instead of CD-R drives, many users opt for CD-RW drives. A **CD-RW (compact disc-rewritable)** is an erasable disc you can write on multiple times. Originally called an **erasable CD (CD-E)**, a CD-RW overcomes the major disadvantage of CD-R disks, which is you can write on them only once. With CD-RW, the disc acts like a floppy or hard disk, allowing you to write and rewrite data, instructions, and information onto it multiple times. To write on a CD-RW disc, you must have CD-RW software and a **CD-RW drive**. These drives have a write speed up to 12X, rewrite speed up to 4X, and a read speed up to 32X. Manufacturers typically state the speeds in this order, for example, as 12/4/32.

CD-RW discs can be read only by multiread CD-ROM drives. A **multiread CD-ROM drive** is a drive that can read audio CDs, data CDs, CD-Rs, and CD-RWs. Most recent CD-ROM drives are multiread.

APPLY IT!

Digital Photographs

Internet evangelists have long predicted the move to digital and online photograph storage. These predictions now are coming true. One does not even need a scanner or digital camera to participate in the fun.

Picture CD is a new film digitation service from Kodak (see URL below). This technology bridges the film-digital gap by providing a solution that gives people the benefit of both film and digital pictures. Use a Picture CD to view pictures on your computer. You can print or modify, improve, and enhance your photographs, and send e-mail postcards. To purchase a Picture CD, just check the box for KODAK Picture CD on your processing envelope when you take in your film or one-time-use cameras for processing.

Many sites on the Web allow you to create a photo album similar to an album you may have at home. Most of these sites offer free unlimited storage. If you choose, you can share your albums with friends, family, or the entire Internet community. Some sites provide the option of sending electronic greeting cards or postcards.

For more information on Picture CDs, online photograph storage, and the Web site mentioned above, visit the Discovering Computers 2002 Apply It Web page (**scsite.com/dc2002/apply.htm**) and click Chapter 7 Apply It #2.

Using a CD-RW disc, you easily can backup large files from your hard disk. You also can share data and information with other users that have a CD-ROM drive.

A very popular use of CD-RW and CD-R discs is to create audio CDs. That is, you can make your own music disc. Users have two basic options to create an audio CD: copy the song(s) from an existing audio CD or download the song(s) from the Web. The steps in Figure 7-29 illustrate these techniques.

Web Link

For more information on CD-RWs, visit the Discovering Computers 2002 Chapter 7 WEB LINK page (**scsite.com/dc2002/ch7/weblink.htm**) and click CD-RWs.

Figure 7-29 HOW TO CREATE AN AUDIO CD

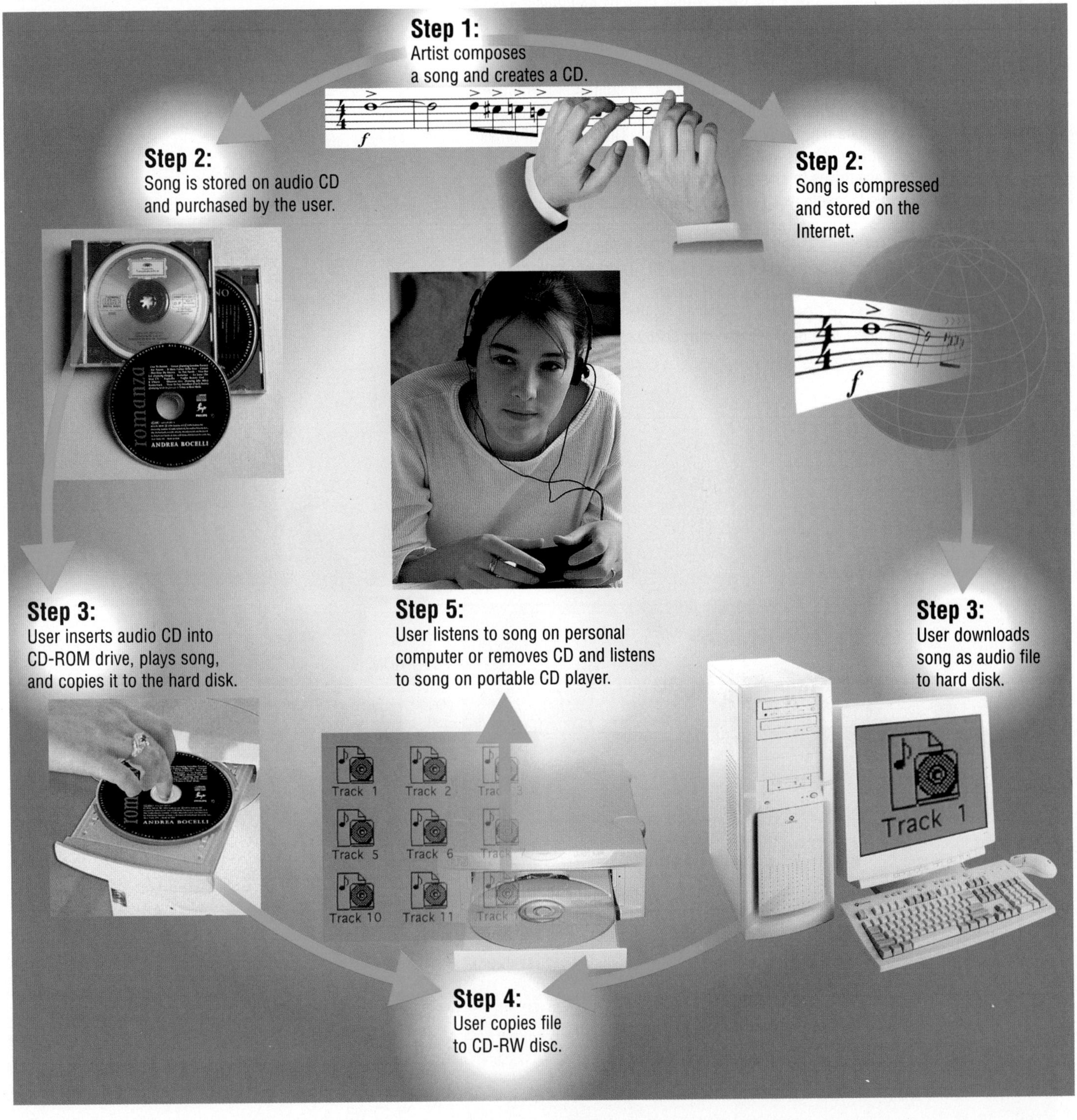
Step 1:
Artist composes a song and creates a CD.
Step 2:
Song is stored on audio CD and purchased by the user.
Step 2:
Song is compressed and stored on the Internet.
romanza
ANDREA BOCELLI
Step 3:
User inserts audio CD into CD-ROM drive, plays song, and copies it to the hard disk.
Step 5:
User listens to song on personal computer or removes CD and listens to song on portable CD player.
Step 3:
User downloads song as audio file to hard disk.
Track 1
Track 2
Track 5
Track 6
Track 10
Track 11
Step 4:
User copies file to CD-RW disc.

APPLY IT!

The Future of CD-RW Discs

You probably have seen ads and read about CD-R and CD-RW discs. You may have considered purchasing one of these drives, but wondered how you could use this technology. Consider that 10 years ago the common method of sharing files was via a 5.25-inch floppy disk. Depending on the disk's density, you could store either 360 or 1.2 million characters. With today's increasing need for removable storage, CD-R and CD-RW may become as popular as the floppy disk in its heyday. These drives have more than 400 times the capacity of a floppy disk. They combine the compatibility, flexibility, and storage capacity of a CD with the drag-and-drop ease of a floppy.

CD-R and CD-RW add a new dimension to CD use in computers. You use CD technology to store your data and record your own CDs. With CD-RW, you can erase and rewrite data repeatedly on the same disc. The number of times the disc can be rewritten depends upon the quality of the disc.

Adding one of these drives to any new or existing computer is easy to do. You may find that this technology is perfect for backing up a large set of files, creating music CDs, or creating multimedia presentations. CD-RW drives are able to write both CD-R and CD-RW disc formats. CD-RW discs, however, have two disadvantages: a) they cannot be read by all CD drives; and b) CD-RW discs cannot be written to by CD-R drives.

For more information on CD-R and CD-RW discs, visit the Discovering Computers 2002 Apply It Web page (**scsite.com/dc2002/apply.htm**) and click Chapter 7 Apply It #3.

ISSUE

Make Your Own Music

CD-RW Storage

The CD-RW disc opened new possibilities. For multimedia designers and home recording artists, the recordable CD format offers a range of powerful storage applications. Price decreases and ease of use make these devices even more attractive. Along with almost any new technology, negatives exist. At many schools, for example, some students use college servers to create their own music sites and download copyrighted music. Using CD-RW storage, they record the songs and distribute unauthorized copies. Many people think the Internet is a new frontier and copyright rules do not apply. Do you agree with this? Is it ethical to copy a CD and share it with a friend? Is it the responsibility of schools to educate students about such ethical issues? Why or why not?

For more information on CD-RWs, visit the Discovering Computers 2002 Issues Web page (**scsite.com/dc2002/issues.htm**) and click Chapter 7 Issue #3.

DVD-ROMS

Although CD-ROMs have huge storage capacities, even a CD-ROM is not large enough for many of today's complex programs. Some multimedia software, for example, requires five or more CD-ROMs. To meet these tremendous storage requirements, some manufacturers store and distribute software using a DVD-ROM (Figure 7-30). The goal of DVD technology is to meet the needs of home entertainment, computer usage,

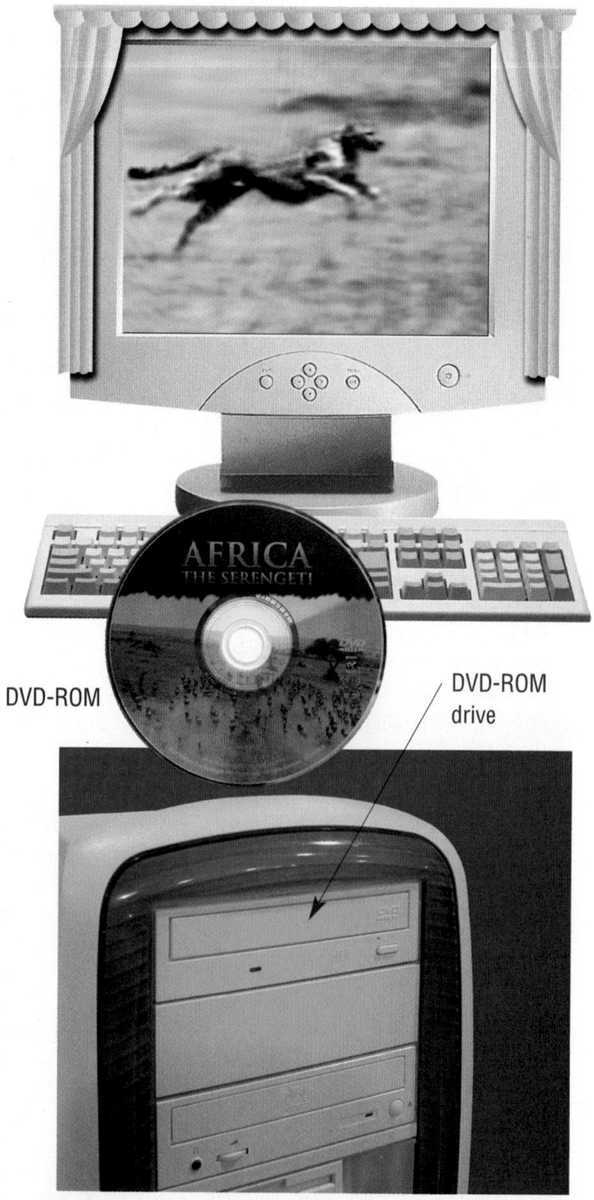

Figure 7-30 A DVD-ROM is an extremely high-capacity compact disc capable of storing 4.7 GB to 17 GB.

and business data and information storage with a single medium. When you rent or buy a DVD movie, it uses a DVD-Video format to store the motion picture digitally.

A **DVD-ROM (digital video disc-ROM)** is an extremely high capacity compact disc capable of storing from 4.7 GB to 17 GB. The storage capacity of a DVD-ROM is more than enough to hold a telephone book containing every resident in the United States. Not only is the storage capacity of a DVD-ROM greater than a CD-ROM, a DVD-ROM's quality also far surpasses that of a CD-ROM.

In order to read a DVD-ROM, you must have a **DVD-ROM drive** or **DVD player**. These drives can read at speeds up to 40X. Newer DVD-ROM drives also can read audio CDs, CD-ROMs, CD-Rs, and CD-RWs.

At a glance, a DVD-ROM looks just like a CD-ROM. Although the size and shape are similar, a DVD-ROM stores data, instructions, and information in a slightly different manner and thus achieves a higher storage capacity.

A DVD-ROM uses one of three storage techniques. The first technique involves making the disc more dense by packing the pits closer together. A second technique involves using two layers of pits. For this technique to work, the lower layer of pits is semitransparent so the laser can read through it to the upper layer. This technique doubles the capacity of the disc. Finally, some DVD-ROMs are double-sided, which means you remove the DVD-ROM and turn it over to read the other side. The storage capacities of various types of DVD-ROMs are shown in the table in Figure 7-31.

DVD Variations

DVDs are available in a variety of formats, one of which stores digital motion pictures. To view a movie on a DVD, insert the DVD movie disc into a DVD player connected to your television set or into a DVD-ROM drive to view the movie on your computer screen. Movies on DVD have near-studio-quality video, which far surpasses VHS tapes. When music is stored on a DVD, it includes surround sound and has a much better quality than that on an audio CD.

You also can obtain recordable and rewritable versions of DVD. With a **DVD-R (DVD-recordable)**, you can write once on it and read (play) it many times. A DVD-R is similar to a CD-R. DVD-R drives have a read speed of up to 32X and a write speed of up to 8X. With a rewritable DVD, called a **DVD-RAM**, you can erase and record on the disc multiple times. A DVD-RAM is similar to a CD-RW, except it has storage capacities up to 5.2 GB. DVD-RAM drives typically can read DVD-ROM, DVD-R, and all CD media. A competing technology to DVD-RAM is **DVD+RW**. As the cost of DVD technologies becomes more reasonable, many industry professionals expect that DVD eventually will replace all CD media.

DVD-ROM STORAGE CAPACITIES

Sides	Layers	Storage Capacity
1	1	4.7 GB
1	2	8.5 GB
2	1	9.4 GB
2	2	17 GB

Figure 7-31 Storage capacities of DVD-ROMS.

TECHNOLOGY TRAILBLAZER

MARK **DEAN**

Not many first graders can handle algebra problems. But Mark Dean was no ordinary first grader. Along with solving fourth-grade math equations in his first year of school, he also tutored older students. In high school, he was a straight-A student and a star athlete.

He also spent hours inventing new products. As a youth, he and his dad built a tractor from scratch. After graduating at the top of his class from the University of Tennessee, he joined IBM and helped design the improvements in architecture that allow components, such as modems and printers, to communicate with personal computers. This technology is used in more than 40 million personal computers manufactured each year. After earning his Ph.D. degree at Stanford, he headed a team at IBM that invented the first CMOS microprocessor chip to operate at one gigahertz (1,000 MHz). As an IBM idea man, he currently is developing an electronic tablet that functions as an e-book, DVD player, radio, wireless telephone, and Web-enabled device.

Dean is the first African-American to receive an IBM Fellowship, the company's highest technical ranking. He has been inducted into the National Inventor's Hall of Fame, an honor he shares with fewer than 150 other people.

For more information on Mark Dean, visit the Discovering Computers 2002 People Web page (**scsite.com/dc2002/people.htm**) and click Mark Dean.

TAPES

One of the first storage media used with mainframe computers was tape. **Tape** is a magnetically coated ribbon of plastic capable of storing large amounts of data and information at a low cost.

Similar to a tape recorder, a **tape drive** reads from and writes data and information on a tape.

Although older computers used reel-to-reel tape drives, today's tape drives use tape cartridges. A **tape cartridge** is a small, rectangular, plastic housing for tape (Figure 7-32). Tape cartridges containing one-quarter-inch wide tape are slightly larger than audiocassette tapes. Business and home users sometimes backup personal computer hard disks onto tape.

Some personal computers have external tape units. Others have the tape drive built into the system unit. On larger computers, tape cartridges are mounted in a separate cabinet called a tape library.

Three common types of tape drives are quarter-inch cartridge (QIC), digital audio tape (DAT), and digital linear tape (DLT). The fastest and most expensive of the three is DLT. The table in Figure 7-33 summarizes each of these types of tapes.

Tape storage requires **sequential access**, which refers to reading or writing data consecutively. Like a music tape, you must forward or rewind the tape to a specific point to access a specific piece of data. For example, to access item W, you must pass sequentially through points A through V.

Floppy disks, hard disks, and compact discs all use direct access. **Direct access**, also called **random access**, means you can locate a particular data item or file immediately, without having to move consecutively through items stored in front of the desired data item or file. Sequential access is much slower than direct access. Tapes no longer are used as a primary method of storage. Instead, business and home users utilize tapes most often for long-term storage and backup.

COMPANY ON THE CUTTING EDGE

EMC²

where information lives

Big-Time Storage Solutions

When your closet gets too small for your wardrobe, you have two choices: discard some clothes you no longer wear, or find a larger closet. When the world's largest corporations run out of space to store their data, they, too, have two choices: discard some of the files they no longer need, or find additional storage locations. When they choose the latter, chances are they might consider EMC Corporation, a provider of storage systems.

Richard Egan and Roger Marino (the "E" and "M" in EMC) founded EMC in 1979 to fill a demand for add-on memory boards in the minicomputer market. Soon, the company expanded to provide small disk drives using RAID technology for mainframe computers, the industry standard for storage systems today. Other ventures include Symmetrix Remote Data Facility, which provides business continuity and disaster recovery, and more than a dozen storage-based software solutions.

For more information on the EMC Corporation, visit the Discovering Computers 2002 Companies Web page (**scsite.com/dc2002/companies.htm**) and click EMC.

Web Link

For more information on tapes, visit the Discovering Computers 2002 Chapter 7 WEB LINK page (**scsite.com/dc2002/ch7/weblink.htm**) and click Tapes.

Figure 7-32 A tape cartridge and a tape drive.

POPULAR TYPES OF TAPES

Name	Abbreviation	Storage Capacity
Quarter-inch cartridge	QIC	40 MB to 20 GB
Digital audio tape	DAT	2 to 40 GB
Digital linear tape	DLT	20 to 80 GB

Figure 7-33 Common types of tapes.

ENTERPRISE STORAGE SYSTEMS

Many companies use networks. Data, information, and instructions stored on the network must be accessible easily to all authorized users. The data, information, and instructions also must be secure, so unauthorized users do not have access. An **enterprise storage system** is a strategy that focuses on the availability, protection, organization, and backup of storage in a company. The goal of an enterprise storage system is to consolidate storage so operations run as efficiently as possible. Large business users often utilize an enterprise storage system strategy.

To implement an enterprise storage system, a company uses a combination of techniques. As shown in Figure 7-34, an enterprise storage system may use servers, a RAID system, a tape library, CD-ROM jukeboxes, Internet backup, NAS devices, and/or a storage area network. The following paragraphs briefly discuss each of these storage techniques.

- A server stores data, information, and instructions needed by users on the network.
- A RAID system ensures that data is not lost if one drive fails.
- A **tape library** is a high-capacity tape system that works with multiple tape cartridges for storing backups of data, information, and instructions.
- A CD-ROM server, also called a **CD-ROM jukebox**, holds hundreds of CD-ROMs that can contain application programs and data.
- Companies using **Internet backup** store data, information, and instructions on the Web.
- A **network-attached storage (NAS)** device is an easy way to add additional hard disk space to the network.
- A **storage area network (SAN)** is a high-speed network that connects storage devices.

Some companies manage an enterprise storage system in house. Other larger applications elect to offload all (or at least the backup) storage management to an outside

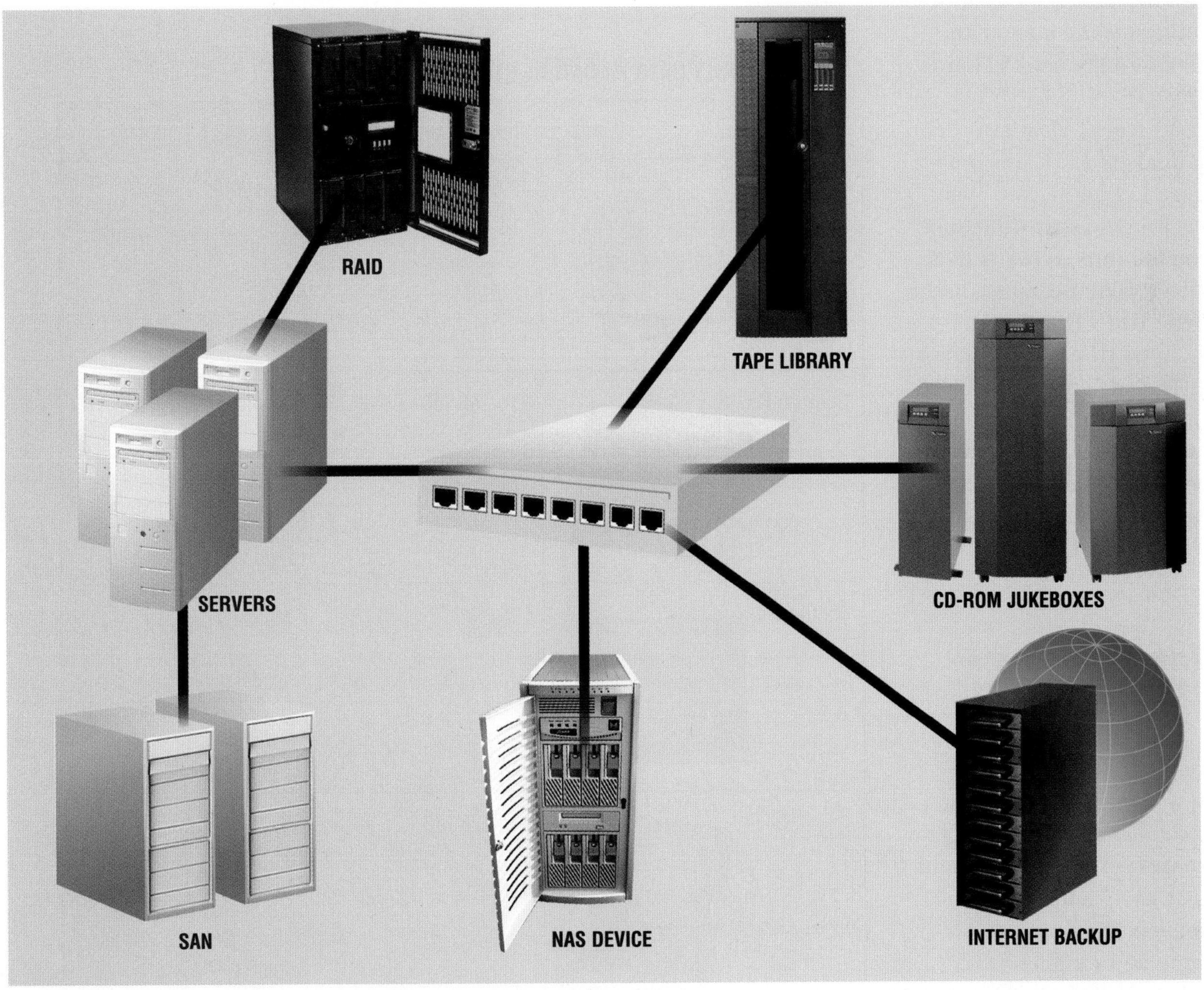

Figure 7-34 An enterprise storage system uses a variety of storage techniques.

organization or online Web service. Some vendors focus on providing enterprise storage systems to clients. A data warehouse might seek this type of outside service. A **data warehouse** is a huge database system that stores and manages historical and current transaction data. For example, a credit card company that stores and manages millions of customer transactions probably uses a data warehouse.

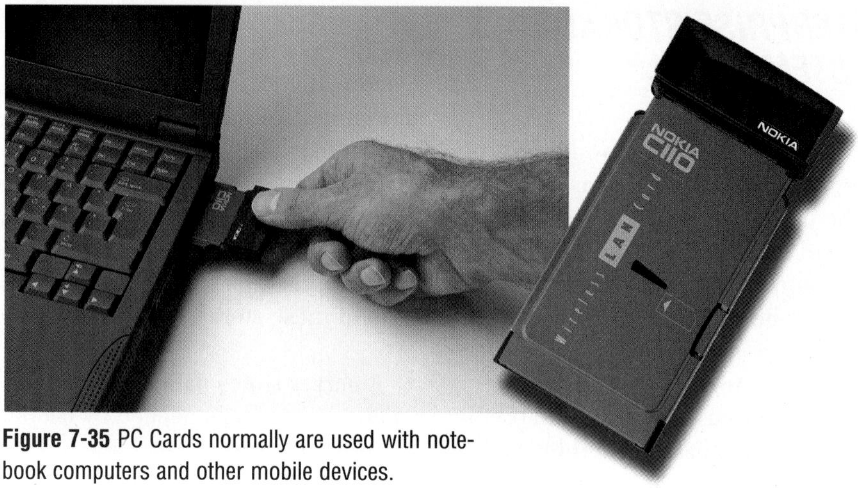

Figure 7-35 PC Cards normally are used with notebook computers and other mobile devices.

PC CARDS

As discussed in Chapter 4, a **PC Card** is a thin, credit card-sized device that fits into a PC Card slot on a notebook or other personal computer. Different types and sizes of PC Cards add storage, additional memory, communications, and sound capabilities to a computer. Notebook computers and other mobile computers and devices most often use PC Cards (Figure 7-35).

Originally called PCMCIA cards, three kinds of PC Cards are available: Type I, Type II, and Type III (Figure 7-36). The only difference in size among the three types is their thickness. Some digital cameras use a Type II or Type III PC Card to store photographs. Type III cards can house a hard disk. The advantage of a PC Card for storage is portability. You easily can transport large amounts of data, instructions, and information from one machine to another using a Type II or Type III PC Card.

PC CARDS

Category	Thickness	Use
Type I	3.3 mm	RAM, SRAM, flash memory
Type II	5.0 mm	Modem, LAN, SCSI, sound, TV tuner, storage
Type III	10.5 mm	Rotating storage such as a hard disk

Figure 7-36 The above table outlines the various uses of PC Cards.

MINIATURE MOBILE STORAGE MEDIA

Handheld computers and digital cameras are wonderful devices that provide the mobile user with immediate access to technology. These handheld devices do not have much internal storage. Some use PC Cards. As shown in the table in Figure 7-37, other types of miniature storage media also are available.

SOME COMMONLY USED MINIATURE STORAGE MEDIA

Device Name	Storage Capacity	Type, Use
Clik! Disk 	40 MB	Cartridge Digital cameras, notebook computers
CompactFlash 	2 to 256 MB	Memory Card Digital cameras, handheld computers, notebook computers, printers, cellular telephones
Microdrive 	1 GB	Memory Card Digital cameras, handheld computers, music players, video cameras
SmartMedia 	2 to 128 MB	Memory Card Digital cameras, handheld computers, photo printers, cellular telephones

Figure 7-37 Miniature storage used with digital cameras and other handheld devices.

To view images and other information captured on a miniature mobile medium, you can transfer its contents to your desktop computer or other device. Some printers read PC cards and other miniature storage media. Handheld devices, such as players and wallets, read or display the contents of miniature storage media such as memory cards (Figure 7-38).

Figure 7-38 This wallet displays the contents of a memory card.

Smart Cards

A **smart card**, which is similar in size to a credit card or ATM card, stores data on a thin microprocessor embedded in the card (Figure 7-39). When you insert the smart card into a specialized card reader, the information on the smart card is read and, if necessary, updated.

Two types of smart cards exist: intelligent and memory. An **intelligent smart card** contains a processor and has input, process, output, and storage capabilities. A **memory card**, by contrast, has only storage capabilities. A memory card can store a variety of data and information including photographs, music, books, and video clips. As shown earlier, many digital cameras and other handheld devices use memory cards.

One popular use of smart cards is to store a prepaid dollar amount, as in a prepaid telephone calling card. You receive the card with a specific dollar amount stored in the microprocessor. Each time you use the card, it reduces the available amount of money. Using these cards provides convenience to the caller, eliminates the telephone company's need to collect coins from telephones, and reduces vandalism of pay telephones. Other uses of smart cards include storing patient records, vaccination data, and other health-care information; tracking information such as customer purchases or employee attendance; and storing a prepaid amount such as electronic money.

Electronic money (e-money), also called **digital cash**, is a means of paying for goods and services over the Internet. As discussed in Chapter 2, a bank issues unique digital cash numbers that represent an amount of money. When you purchase digital cash, the amount of money is withdrawn from your bank account. One implementation of e-money places the digital cash on a smart card. To use the card, you swipe it through a card reader on your computer or one that is attached to your computer.

Figure 7-39 This doctor of pediatrics looks up the confidential patient records on her computer by sliding the smart card through a smart card reader. The smart card reader attaches to the serial port on the computer.

ISSUE

Will Money Become Obsolete?

E-Money Society

The first e-commerce transaction from one personal computer to another computer occurred in May 1994. When you conduct a business activity online, you are participating in e-commerce. One method of paying for the goods or services purchased online is e-money. Digital signatures and encryption techniques make e-money possible. This technology is recognized widely by banks as the most secure measure for protecting financial information. Financial institutions tout the many benefits of e-money for the consumer. Some of these include convenient and easy one-button payment, easy refunds, shop online without a credit card, privacy protection, and wireless access. With all of these benefits of e-money, will paper money disappear? Is e-money just a step on the way to tomorrow's payment system technology or is it already here? Would you feel comfortable using e-money? Will society in general accept this technology?

For more information on e-money, visit the Discovering Computers 2002 Issues Web page (**scsite.com/dc2002/issues.htm**) and click Chapter 7 Issue #4.

Web Link

For more information on PC Cards, visit the Discovering Computers 2002 Chapter 7 WEB LINK page (**scsite.com/dc2002/ch7/weblink.htm**) and click PC Cards.

MICROFILM AND MICROFICHE

Microfilm and microfiche store microscopic images of documents on roll or sheet film (Figure 7-40). **Microfilm** uses a 100- to 215-foot roll of film. **Microfiche** uses a small sheet of film, usually about four inches by six inches. A **computer output microfilm (COM) recorder** is the device that records the images on the film. The stored images are so small that you only can read them with a microfilm or microfiche reader.

Applications of microfilm and microfiche are widespread. Libraries use these media to store back issues of newspapers, magazines, and genealogy records. Large organizations use microfilm and microfiche to archive inactive files. Banks use it to store transactions and cancelled checks. The U.S. Army uses it to store personnel records.

Using microfilm and microfiche provides a number of advantages. It greatly reduces the amount of paper firms must handle. It is inexpensive, and it has the longest life of any storage medium (Figure 7-41).

Figure 7-40 Microfilm and microfiche store microscopic images of documents on roll or sheet film.

MEDIA LIFE EXPECTANCIES

Media Type	Guaranteed Life Expectancy	Potential Life Expectancy
Tape	2 to 5 years	20 years
Compact Disc	5 years	50 to 100 years
Microfilm	100 years	200 years

Figure 7-41 Microfilm is the medium with the longest life.

ISSUE

Nothing Lasts Forever

Digital Information Deterioration

This aphorism is true even with respect to computer storage. The industry has just begun to realize the magnitude of digital information deterioration. NASA discovered almost 20 percent of the data collected during the Viking mission was lost on decaying magnetic tape. Veterans' files, census statistics, and toxic-waste records also have been lost on deteriorating storage media. One computer scientist admits that digital information lasts forever or five years — whichever comes first. A major problem with digital data is that, unlike the visible deterioration in a faded document, the extent of decay on a storage medium such as a CD-ROM may be invisible until it is too late. If you were the leader of an information-intensive organization, what medium would you choose to store your records? Why? What steps would you take to ensure the records were intact 10 years from now? Twenty years from now?

For more information on digital storage, visit the Discovering Computers 2002 Issues Web page (**scsite.com/dc2002/issues.htm**) and click Chapter 7 Issue #5.

PUTTING IT ALL TOGETHER

Many factors influence the type of storage devices you should use: the amount of data, instructions, and information to be stored; the hardware and software in use; and the desired cost. The table in Figure 7-42 outlines several suggested storage devices for various types of computer users.

CHAPTER SUMMARY

Storage refers to the media on which data, instructions, and information are kept, as well as the devices that record and retrieve these items. This chapter explained various storage media and storage devices. Storage media covered included floppy disks, high-capacity disks, hard disks, CD-ROMs, CD-RWs, DVD-ROMs, tape, and PC Cards and other miniature forms of storage. Enterprise storage systems also were covered.

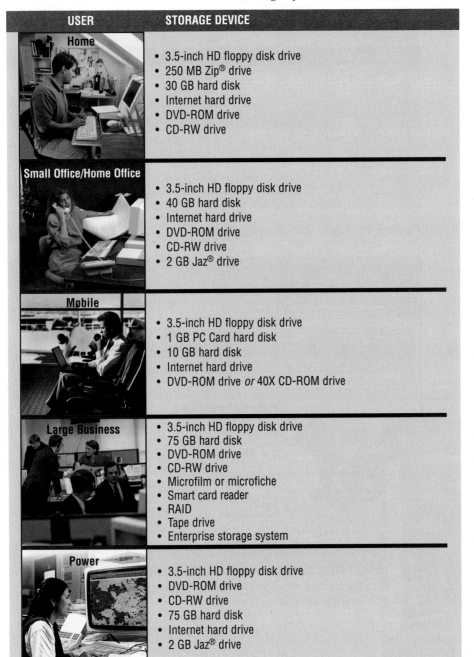

USER	STORAGE DEVICE
Home 	• 3.5-inch HD floppy disk drive • 250 MB Zip® drive • 30 GB hard disk • Internet hard drive • DVD-ROM drive • CD-RW drive
Small Office/Home Office 	• 3.5-inch HD floppy disk drive • 40 GB hard disk • Internet hard drive • DVD-ROM drive • CD-RW drive • 2 GB Jaz® drive
Mobile 	• 3.5-inch HD floppy disk drive • 1 GB PC Card hard disk • 10 GB hard disk • Internet hard drive • DVD-ROM drive *or* 40X CD-ROM drive
Large Business 	• 3.5-inch HD floppy disk drive • 75 GB hard disk • DVD-ROM drive • CD-RW drive • Microfilm or microfiche • Smart card reader • RAID • Tape drive • Enterprise storage system
Power 	• 3.5-inch HD floppy disk drive • DVD-ROM drive • CD-RW drive • 75 GB hard disk • Internet hard drive • 2 GB Jaz® drive

Figure 7-42 This table recommends suggested storage devices.

Computer Technician

Computer technicians are in great demand in every organization and industry. For many, this is the entry point for a career in the computer/information technology field. The responsibilities of a computer technician or a computer service technician can include a variety of duties. Most companies who employ someone with this title expect the technician to have basic across-the-board knowledge of concepts in the computer electronics field. Some of these tasks are hardware repair and installation; software installation, upgrade, and configuration; and troubleshooting client and/or server problems.

Technicians generally work with a variety of users, so people skills are an important asset, especially the ability to work with groups of non-technical users. Because this is an entry-level position, salaries are not quite as high as other more demanding and skilled positions. Individuals with these skills can expect an average annual starting salary of around $25,000 to $35,000.

The Electronics Technicians Association (see URL below) provides a Computer Service Technician (CST) certification program.

To learn more about the field of computer technician as a career and the Web site mentioned above, visit the Discovering Computers 2002 Careers Web page (**scsite.com/dc2002/careers.htm**) and click Computer Technician.

E-SHOPPING

CYBERMALL MANIA

Let Your Mouse Do Your Shopping

From groceries to clothing to computers, you can buy just about everything you need with just a few clicks of your mouse. Electronic retailers (e-tailers), especially those listed in Figure 7-43, are cashing in from cybershoppers' purchases with books, computer software and hardware, and music being the hottest commodities. Online sales in the United States exceed $60 billion yearly. E-shoppers can browse for a variety of goods at these popular Web sites.

Holiday sales account for a large portion of Internet purchases with nearly nine million households doing some of their holiday shopping online. During the holiday season, some Web sites such as KBkids.com (Figure 7-44) have more than 235,000 hits per day. Macy's, Bloomingdale's, and other e-tailers ship more than 300,000 boxes daily out of warehouses that are the size of 20 football fields and are stocked with five million items.

The two categories of Internet shopping Web sites are those with physical counterparts, such as Eddie Bauer (Figure 7-45),

SHOPPING WEB SITES	URL
Apparel	
Eddie Bauer	eddiebauer.com
J. Crew	jcrew.com
Lands' End	landsend.com
Books and Music	
Amazon.com	amazon.com
Barnes & Noble	barnesandnoble.com
Borders	borders.com
Computers and Electronics	
Crutchfield	crutchfield.com
Best Buy	bestbuy.com
Buy.com	buy.com
Miscellaneous	
1-800-Flowers.com	1800flowers.com
drugstore.com	drugstore.com
Toys "R" Us	toysrus.com
Wal-Mart	walmart.com

For an updated list of shopping Web sites, visit scsite.com/dc2002/e-rev.htm.

Figure 7-43 Popular Web shopping sites.

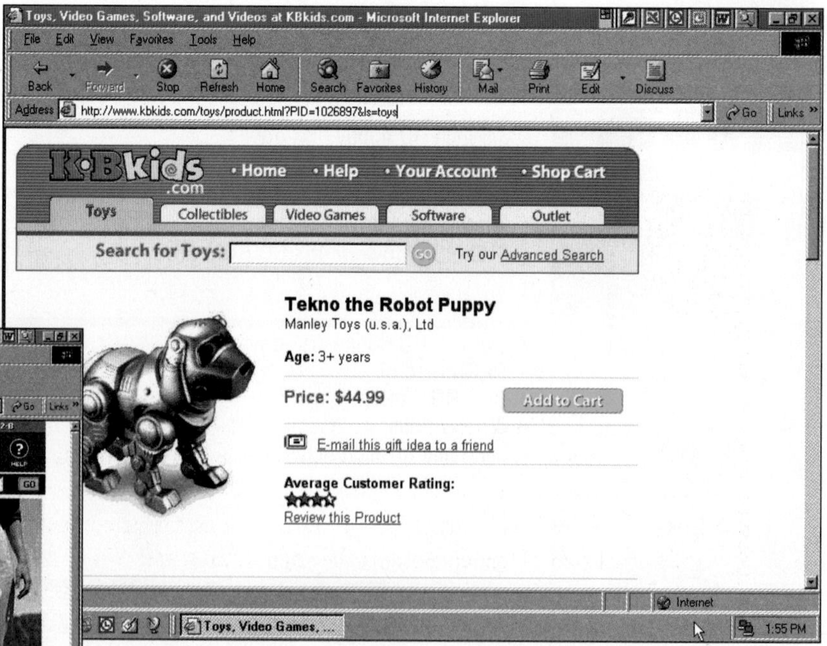

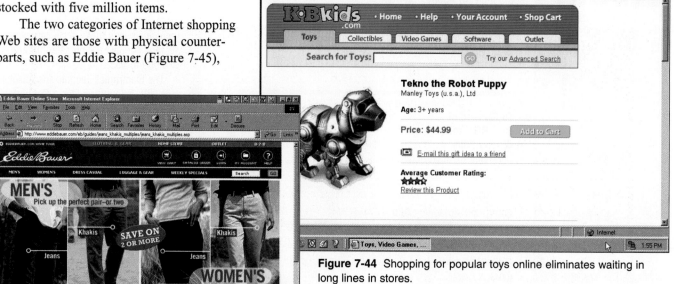

Figure 7-44 Shopping for popular toys online eliminates waiting in long lines in stores.

Figure 7-45 Stores such as Eddie Bauer have both a physical and an Internet presence.

Wal-Mart, and Nordstrom, and those with only a Web presence, such as Egghead.com (Figure 7-46), and amazon.com.

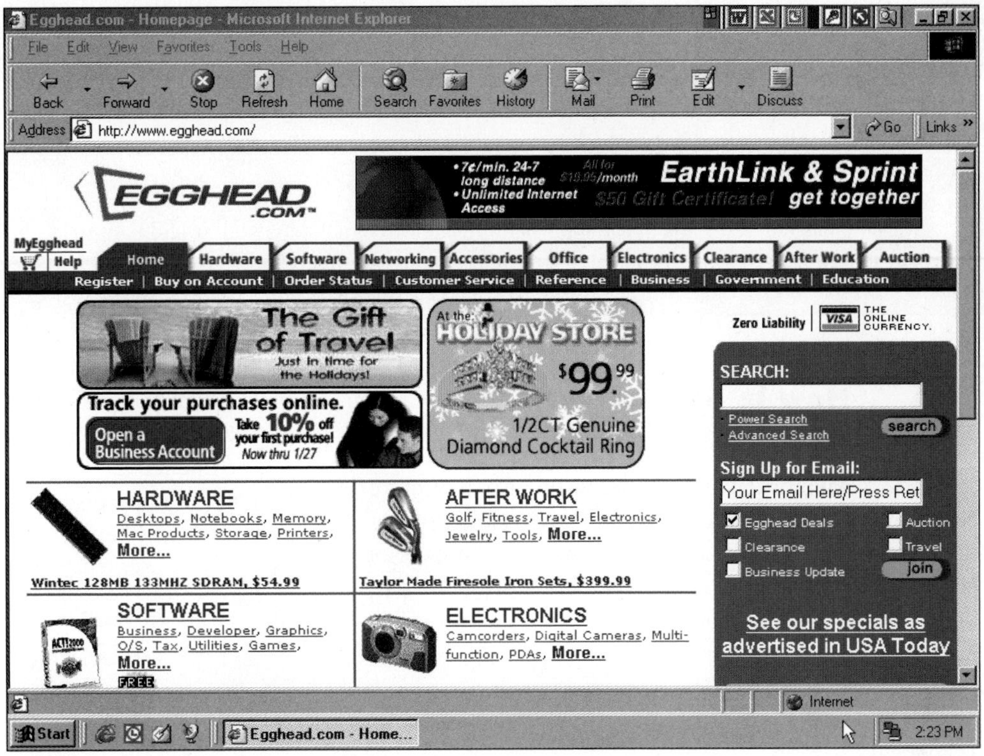

Figure 7-46 Egghead.com is a business with only an Internet presence.

Some e-shoppers, however, are finding online shopping even more frustrating than finding a convenient parking space at the neighborhood mall on Saturday afternoon. Delayed shipments, out-of-stock merchandise, poor customer service, and difficult return policies have left some savvy shoppers with a poor impression of their Internet experience. As e-tailers rush to set up an Internet site, they sometimes overlook important considerations, such as customer service telephone numbers and e-mail addresses, adequate staff to answer queries quickly and courteously, and sufficient in-stock merchandise.

Paying for the merchandise online causes concern for many e-shoppers. Although online merchants promise secure transactions, some users are wary of cyberthieves. One way of calming their fears may be through the use of e-money, which is a payment system that allows consumers to purchase goods and services anonymously. Several computer companies, Web merchants, and credit card companies are collaborating to develop a standard method of transferring money securely and quickly from electronic wallets, which verify a user's identity.

For more information on shopping Web sites, visit the Discovering Computers 2002 E-Revolution Web page (scsite.com/dc2002/e-rev.htm) and click Shopping.

eREVOLUTION E-SHOPPING *applied:*

1. Visit two of the three apparel Web sites listed in the table in Figure 7-43 and select a specific pair of jeans and a shirt from each one. Create a table with these headings: e-tailer, style, fabric, features, price, tax, and shipping fee. Enter details about your selections in the table. Then, visit two of the books and music Web sites and search for a CD you would consider purchasing. Create another table with the names of the Web site, artist, and CD, as well as the price, tax, and shipping fee.

2. Visit two of the computers and electronics and two of the miscellaneous Web sites listed in Figure 7-43. Write a paragraph describing the features these Web sites offer compared with the same offerings from stores. In another paragraph, describe any disadvantages of shopping at these Web sites instead of actually seeing the merchandise. Then, describe their policies for returning unwanted merchandise and for handling complaints.

In Summary

Web Instructions: To display this page from the Web, start your browser and enter the URL scsite.com/dc2002/ch7/summary.htm. Click the links for current and additional information. To listen to an audio version of this In Summary, click the Audio button. To play the audio, RealPlayer must be installed on your computer (download by clicking here).

1 How Is Storage Different from Memory?

Memory, which is composed of one or more chips on the motherboard, holds data and instructions while they are being interpreted and executed by the processor. Memory can be **volatile** or **nonvolatile**. Storage holds items such as data, instructions, and information for future use.

2 What Are Storage Media and Storage Devices?

A **storage medium** (media is the plural) is the physical material on which items such as data, instructions, and information are kept. A **storage device** is the mechanism used to record and retrieve items to and from a storage medium. When a storage device transfers items from a storage medium into memory — a process called reading — it functions as an input device. When a storage device transfers items from memory to a storage medium — a process called **writing** — it functions as an output device.

3 How Is Data Stored on a Floppy Disk?

A **floppy disk** is a portable, inexpensive storage medium that consists of a thin, circular, flexible disk with a plastic magnetic coating enclosed in a square-shaped plastic shell. Formatting prepares a disk for reading and writing by organizing the disk into storage locations called **tracks** and **sectors**. A **floppy disk drive (FDD)** is a device that reads from and writes on a floppy disk. The drive slides the **shutter** to the side to expose a portion of both sides of the floppy disk's recording surface. A circuit board on the drive sends signals to control the movement of the read/write head, which is the mechanism that reads items from or writes items on the floppy disk. A motor causes the floppy disk to spin and positions the read/write head over the correct location on the recording surface. The read/write head then writes data on the floppy disk. Floppy disks should not be exposed to heat, cold, magnetic fields, or contaminants such as dust, smoke, or salt air. The disk's shutter should not be opened and the recording surface should not be touched. Floppy disks should be inserted carefully into the disk drive and kept in a storage tray when not in use.

4 What Are the Advantages of Using High-Capacity Disks?

A disk with capacities of 100 MB or greater is called a high-capacity disk. To store large graphics, audio, video, or other large files and for data **backup**, high-capacity disks are the best choice for storage. Three types of high-capacity disk drives are the **SuperDisk™ drive**, the **HiFD™** (High-Capacity Floppy Disk) **drive**, and the **Zip® drive**.

5 How Does a Hard Disk Organize Data?

A **hard disk** consists of several inflexible, circular disks called platters on which items are stored electronically. A hard disk can be divided into separate areas called **partitions** with each partition functioning as if it were a separate hard disk drive. An **optically-assisted hard drive** combines laser and optic technologies with the magnetic media.

6 What Are the Advantages of Using an Internet Hard Drive?

An **Internet hard drive** is a service on the Web that provides storage to computer users. Many offer this service without charge. Users may store information on an **Internet hard drive** so they can access files from any computer or device that has Web access, download and save large files, share files with others, view time-critical data and images, and store offsite backup of data.

In Summary

7 How Is Data Stored on Compact Discs?

A **compact disc** (**CD**) is a flat, round, portable metal storage medium that usually is 4.75 inches in diameter and less than one-twentieth of an inch thick. Compact discs store items in microscopic pits (indentations) and land (flat areas) that are located in the middle layer, usually under the printed label on the disc. A high-powered laser light creates the pits in a single track, divided into evenly sized sectors, that spirals from the center of the disc to the edge of the disc. A lower-powered laser reads items from the compact disc by reflecting light through the bottom of the disc surface. The reflected light is converted into a series of bits that the computer can process.

8 How Do You Care for a Compact Disc?

Compact discs should not be stacked or exposed to heat, cold, and contaminants. The underside should not be touched. A compact disc should be held by its edges and placed in its protective case, called a **jewel box**, when it is not being used. The bottom surface of the compact disc can be cleaned with a soft cloth and warm water or a specialized CD cleaning kit.

9 How Are CD-ROMs, CD-RWs, and DVD-ROMs Different?

A **CD-ROM** is a compact disc that uses the same laser technology as audio CDs for recording music. A typical CD-ROM can hold about 650 MB of data, instructions, and information. A **CD-RW** is an erasable disc on which you can write multiple times. These discs can be read only by multiread CD-ROM drives. A **DVD-ROM** is an extremely high capacity compact disc capable of storing from 4.7 GB to 17 GB. Both the storage capacity and quality of a DVD-ROM surpass that of a CD-ROM. A DVD-ROM stores data in a different manner than a CD-ROM, making the disc more dense by packing pits closer together, by using two layers of pits, or by using both sides of the disc. You must have a **DVD-ROM drive** or **DVD player** to read a DVD-ROM disc.

10 What Are Some Uses for Tape?

Tape is a magnetically coated ribbon of plastic capable of storing large amounts of data and information at a low cost. Tape storage requires sequential access, which refers to reading or writing data consecutively. Tape mainly is used for long-term storage and backup.

11 How Does an Enterprise Storage System Work?

An **enterprise storage system** is a strategy that focuses on the availability, protection, organization, and backup of storage in a company. It is implemented using the following techniques: a server for the users, a RAID system, a **storage area network** (**SAN**), a **network-attached storage** (NAS) device, a CD-ROM jukebox, **Internet backup**, and a **tape library**.

12 How Do You Use PC Cards and Other Miniature Storage Media?

A **PC Card** is a thin, credit card-sized device that fits into a PC Card slot on a notebook computer or personal computer. PC Cards are used to add storage, memory, communications, and sound capabilities. A smart card, similar in size to an ATM card, stores data on a thin processor embedded in the card. Smart cards are used to store prepaid dollar amounts, such as electronic money; patient records in the health-care industry; and tracking information, such as customer purchases.

13 What Are Some Uses for Microfilm and Microfiche?

Microfilm and microfiche store microscopic images of documents on roll (microfilm) or sheet (microfiche) film. Libraries and large organizations use microfilm and microfiche to archive relatively inactive documents and files.

Key Terms

Web Instructions: To display this page from the Web, start your browser and enter the URL scsite.com/dc2002/ch7/terms.htm. Scroll through the list of terms. Click a term to display its definition and a picture. Click the To WEB button for current and additional information about the term from the Web. To see animations, Shockwave and Flash Player must be installed on your computer (download by clicking here).

access time (7.4)
allocation unit (7.8)
ATA (7.13)
auxiliary storage (7.4)
backup (7.9)
cache controller (7.12)
capacity (7.4)
CD recorder (7.22)
CD-R (compact disc-recordable) (7.22)
CD-R drive (7.22)
CD-ROM (7.20)
CD-ROM drive (7.20)
CD-ROM jukebox (7.27)
CD-ROM player (7.20)
CD-RW (compact disc-rewritable) (7.22)
CD-RW drive (7.22)
cluster (7.8)
compact disc (CD) (7.17)

PhotoCD

Compact disc that contains only digital photographic images saved in PhotoCD format. PhotoCDs containing pictures can be purchased, or a user can have his or her own pictures or negatives recorded on a PhotoCD in order to have digital versions of photographs. (7.21)

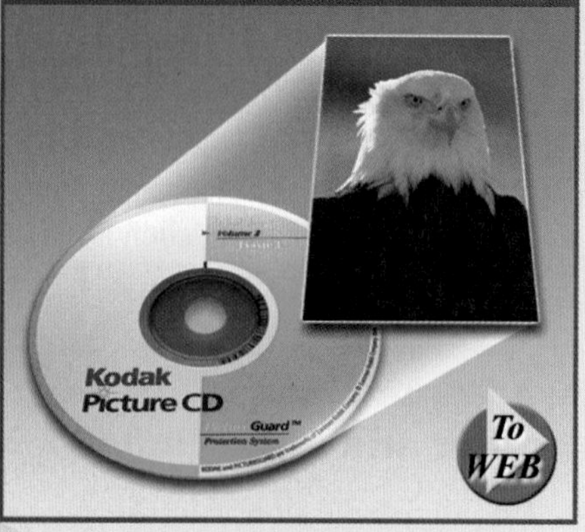

compact disc read-only memory (7.20)
computer output microfilm (COM) recorder (7.30)
cylinder (7.11)
data warehouse (7.28)
density (7.7)
digital cash (7.29)
direct access (7.26)
disk cache (7.12)
disk cartridge (7.13)
disk controller (7.13)
diskette (7.6)
downward compatible (7.7)
DVD player (7.25)
DVD+RW (7.25)
DVD-R (DVD-recordable) (7.25)
DVD-RAM (7.25)
DVD-ROM (digital video disc-ROM) (7.25)
DVD-ROM drive (7.25)
electronic money (e-money) (7.29)
Enhanced Integrated Drive Electronics (EIDE) (7.13)
enterprise storage system (7.27)
erasable CD (CD-E) (7.22)
fixed disk (7.10)
floppy disk (7.6)
floppy disk drive (FDD) (7.6)
formatting (7.8)
hard disk (7.10)
hard disk controller (HDC) (7.13)
hard disk drive (7.10)
head crash (7.12)
HiFD™ (High-Capacity Floppy Disk) drive (7.10)
high-capacity disk drive (7.9)
intelligent smart card (7.29)
Internet backup (7.27)
Internet hard drive (7.16)
Jaz® disk (7.13)
jewel box (7.19)
level 1 (7.14)
magnetic media (7.8)
mass storage (7.4)
memory card (7.29)
microfiche (7.30)
microfilm (7.30)
mirroring (7.14)
multiread CD-ROM drive (7.22)
multisession (7.21)
network-attached storage (NAS) (7.27)
nonvolatile memory (7.3)
online storage (7.16)
optical disc (7.17)
optically-assisted hard drive (7.10)
partitions (7.12)
PC Card (7.28)
permanent storage (7.4)
PhotoCD (7.21)
Picture CD (7.21)
platter (7.10)
RAID (redundant array of independent disks) (7.14)

Floppy Disk

Portable, inexpensive storage medium that consists of a thin, circular, flexible plastic disk with a magnetic coating. (7.5)

random access (7.26)
reading (7.4)
records (7.20)
removable hard disk (7.13)
secondary storage (7.4)
sectors (7.8)
sequential access (7.26)
shutter (7.6)
single-session (7.21)
small computer system interface (SCSI) (7.13)
smart card (7.29)
storage (7.4)
storage area network (SAN) (7.27)
storage device (7.4)
storage medium (7.4)
striping (7.14)
SuperDisk™ drive (7.10)
tape (7.26)
tape cartridge (7.26)
tape drive (7.26)
tape library (7.27)
track (7.8)
upward compatible (7.7)
volatile memory (7.3)
write-protect notch (7.9)
writing (7.4)
Zip® disk (7.10)
Zip® drive (7.10)

Learn It Online

Web Instructions: To display this page from the Web, start your browser and enter the URL scsite.com/dc2002/ch7/learn.htm.

1. Web Guide

Click Web Guide to display the Guide to World Wide Web Sites and Searching Techniques Web page. Click Reference and then click Webopedia. Search for optical disc. Click one of the optical disc links. Use your word processing program to prepare a brief report on your findings and submit your assignment to your instructor.

2. Scavenger Hunt

Click Scavenger Hunt. Print a copy of the Scavenger Hunt page; use this page to write down your answers as you search the Web. Submit your completed page to your instructor.

3. Who Wants to Be a Computer Genius?

Click Computer Genius to find out if you are a computer genius. Directions on how to play the game will display. When you are ready to play, click the PLAY button. Submit your score to your instructor.

4. Wheel of Terms

Click Wheel of Terms to reinforce important terms you learned in this chapter by playing the Shelly Cashman Series version of this popular game. Directions on how to play the game will display. When you are ready to play, click the PLAY button. Submit your score to your instructor.

5. Career Corner

Click Career Corner to display the Campus Career page. Click a link of an area of interest and review the information. Write a brief report describing what you discovered. Submit the report to your instructor.

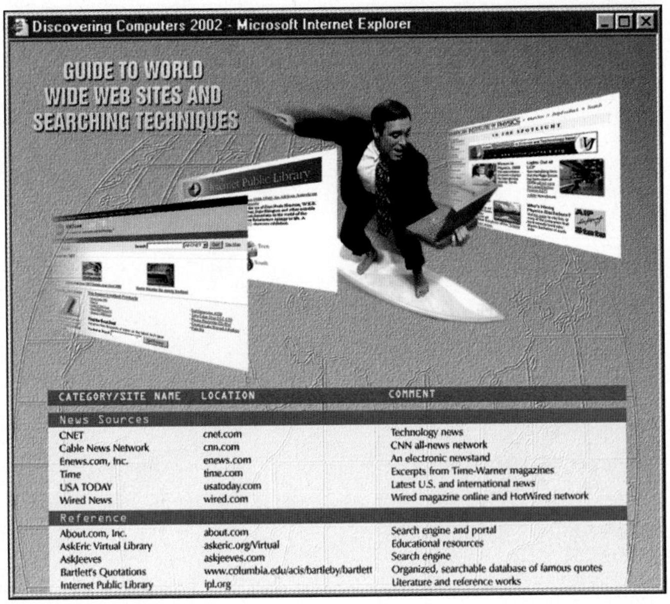

6. Search Sleuth

Click Search Sleuth to learn search techniques that will help make you a research expert. Submit the completed assignment to your instructor.

7. Crossword Puzzle Challenge

Click Crossword Puzzle Challenge. Complete the puzzle to reinforce skills you learned in this chapter. Directions on how to play the game will display. When you are ready to play, click the PLAY button. Submit the completed puzzle to your instructor.

8. Practice Test

Click Practice Test. Answer each question. When completed, enter your name and click the Grade Test button to submit the quiz for grading. Make a note of any missed questions. If required, print a copy to submit to your instructor.

Checkpoint

Web Instructions: To display this page from the Web, launch your browser and enter the URL scsite.com/dc2002/ch7/check.htm. Click the links for current and additional information. To experience the animation and interactivity, Shockwave and Flash Player must be installed on your computer (download by clicking here.)

LABEL THE FIGURE

Instructions: Identify each step of how a hard disk works.

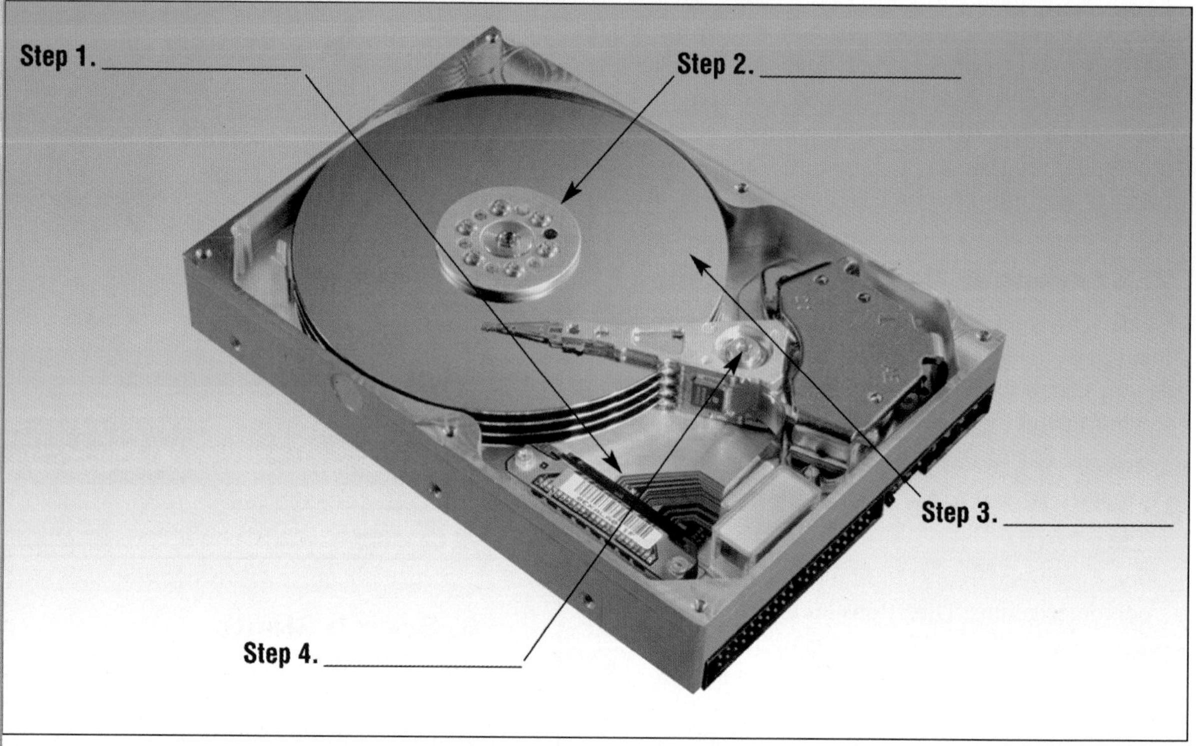

MATCHING

Instructions: Match each term from the column on the left with the best description from the column on the right.

_______ 1. CD-ROM
_______ 2. hard disk
_______ 3. floppy disk
_______ 4. Zip® disk
_______ 5. CD-RW

a. Typically stores data on both sides of the disk, has 80 tracks on each side of the recording surface, and 18 sectors per track.
b. An erasable optical disc you can write on multiple times.
c. A silver-colored compact disc that uses the same laser technology as audio CDs.
d. Consists of several inflexible, circular platters that store items electronically.
e. A drive that can read audio CDs, data CD-ROMs, CD-Rs, and CD-RWs.
f. Slightly larger than and about twice as thick as a 3.5-inch floppy disk, and can store 100 MB or 250 MB of data.
g. A multisession compact disc onto which you can record your own items such as text, graphics, and audio.

MULTIPLE CHOICE

Instructions: Select the letter of the correct answer for each of the following questions.

1. Secondary storage is ___________ .
   a. volatile
   b. nonvolatile
   c. permanent
   d. both b and c
2. The amount of time it takes the device to locate an item on a disk is called ___________ .
   a. reading time
   b. writing time
   c. access time
   d. locating time
3. Most ___________ have multiple platters stacked on top of one another.
   a. hard disks
   b. floppy disks
   c. CD-ROMs
   d. Zip® disks
4. An Internet hard drive is a service on the Web that provides ___________ to computer users.
   a. a multiread CD-ROM drive
   b. a CD-ROM jukebox
   c. online storage
   d. sectors
5. A ___________ is an extremely high-capacity compact disc capable of storing from 4.7 GB to 17 GB.
   a. CD-RW
   b. DVD-ROM
   c. CD-R
   d. PhotoCD

SHORT ANSWER

Instructions: Write a brief answer to each of the following questions.

1. What is access time? ___________ Why is hard disk access time faster than floppy disk access time? ___________
2. What is disk density? ___________ What does it mean to say that floppy disk drives are downward compatible but not upward compatible? ___________
3. What is a head crash? ___________ How does a disk cache improve hard disk access time? ___________
4. How does an Internet hard drive work? ___________ Why would someone want to use one of these? ___________ What disadvantages could there be? ___________
5. How are multisession CD-ROMs different from single-session CD-ROMs? ___________ What are the four basic formats of compact discs? ___________ How are CD-Rs and CD-RWs different? ___________

WORKING TOGETHER

Instructions: Working with a group of your classmates, complete the following team exercise.

Data and information backup is as important for people with personal computers as it is for companies. Develop a report detailing what your group would consider to be the ideal backup system and devices for the following scenarios: (1) a home computer for personal use; (2) a computer used in a home-based business; (3) a small business with six to eight computers; (4) a business or organization with up to 100 computers; and (5) a business or organization with more than 100 computers. Include information that supports why you selected the particular options. Develop a PowerPoint presentation and present your information to the class.

Web Instructions: To display this page from the Web, start your browser and enter the URL scsite.com/dc2002/ch7/lab.htm. Click the links for current and additional information.

1 Examining My Computer

How many disk drives does your computer have? What letter is used for each? To find out more about the disk drives on your computer, right-click the My Computer icon on the desktop. Click Open on the shortcut menu. What is the drive letter for the floppy disk drive on your computer? What letter(s) are used for the hard disk drives on your computer? If you have a CD-ROM drive, what letter is used for it? Double-click the Hard disk (C:) drive icon in the My Computer window. The Hard disk (C:) window shows the file folders (yellow folder icons) stored on your hard disk. How many folders are on the hard disk? Click the Close button to close the Hard disk (C:) window. Close the My Computer window.

2 Working with Files

Insert the Discover Data Disk into drive A. See the inside back cover of this book for instructions for downloading the Data Disk or see your instructor for information on accessing the files required in this book. Double-click the My Computer icon on the desktop. When the My Computer window opens, right-click the 3½ Floppy (A:) icon. Click Open on the shortcut menu. Click View on the menu bar and then click Large Icons. Right-click the h3-2 icon. If h3-2 is not on the floppy disk, ask your instructor for a copy. Click Copy on the shortcut menu. Click Edit on the menu bar and then click Paste. How has the 3½ Floppy (A:) window changed? Right-click the new icon (Copy of h3-2) and then click Rename on the shortcut menu. Type `h7-2` and then press the ENTER key. Right-click the h7-2 icon and then click Print on the shortcut menu. Close the 3½ Floppy (A:) window. Close the My Computer window.

3 Learning About Your Hard Disk

What are the characteristics of your hard disk? To find out, right-click the My Computer icon on the desktop. Click Open on the shortcut menu. Right-click the Hard disk (C:) icon in the My Computer window. Click Properties on the shortcut menu. If necessary, click the General tab and then answer the following questions:

- What Label is on the disk?
- What Type of disk is it?
- How much of the hard disk is Used space?
- How much of the hard disk is Free space?
- What is the total Capacity of the hard disk?

Close the Hard disk (C:) Properties dialog box and the My Computer window.

4 Disk Cleanup

This exercise uses Windows 2000 procedures. Just as people maintain they never can have too much money, computer users insist that you never can have too much hard disk space. Fortunately, Windows includes a utility program called Disk Cleanup that can increase available hard disk space. To find out more about Disk Cleanup, click the Start button on the taskbar and then click Help on the Start menu. Click the Index tab in the Windows 2000 window and then type `disk cleanup` in the Type in the keyword to find text box. Click the overview subentry below the Disk Cleanup entry in the list of topics and then click the Display button. Read the Help information in the right pane of the Windows 2000 window and answer the following questions:

- How does Disk Cleanup help to free up space on the hard disk?
- How do you start Disk Cleanup using the Start button?

Click the Close button to close the Windows 2000 window.

Web Work

Web Instructions: To display this page from the Web, start your browser and enter the URL scsite.com/dc2002/ch7/web.htm. To view At The Movies in exercise 1, RealPlayer must be installed on your computer (download by clicking here). To use the Shelly Cashman Series Maintaining Your Hard Drive Lab from the Web, Shockwave and Flash Player must be installed on your computer (download by clicking here).

Pocket Card

To view the Pocket Card movie, click the button to the left or click the Play button to the right. Watch the movie, and then complete the exercise by answering the questions below. The dangers of too-easy credit are all too obvious, and often personally painful. Addressing these dangers, the pocket card (actually a debit card) was developed to provide access to a fixed-dollar limit, corresponding to a pre-deposited amount. In emergencies (or perhaps with a heartrending story to one's parent) it is possible to increase the amount with a deposit or transfer, either online or using a Touch-Tone telephone. Pocket cards also offer monitoring and accountability, because purchases trigger e-mail notification to the card's owner. The budgeting and monitoring features have attracted two prime markets: parents of out-of-town students, and employers of salespeople. Why these two markets? What other target opportunities can you see?

Shelly Cashman Series Maintaining Your Hard Drive Lab

Follow the appropriate instructions in Web Work 2 on page 1.47 to start and use the Shelly Cashman Series Maintaining Your Hard Drive Lab. If you are running from the Web, enter the URL, www.scsite.com/sclabs/menu.htm; or display the Web Work page (see instructions at the top of this page) and then click the button to the left.

Digital Video Disc (DVD)

A DVD can hold almost 25 times more data than a CD. This translates into richer sound and images than ever seen or heard before. The quality of DVD storage is beginning to have a major impact on the market. Some expect that the sales of DVD optical drives soon will pass the $4 billion mark. Click the button to the left and complete this exercise to learn more about DVDs.

Personal Information Management

Are you tired of forgetting birthdays, missing meetings, overlooking appointments, or neglecting to complete important tasks? If so, then personal information management software may be perfect for you. Click the button to the left to find out about a free, Internet-based calendar. How could this calendar help you organize your life? How might the calendar help you have more fun? After reading the information, you may sign up to create your own Internet-based calendar.

In the News

IBM recently unveiled a small disk drive, about the size of a quarter, that is capable of storing 1 GB of information, as much as 690 floppy disks. The drive will be used in devices such as digital cameras. What other storage devices are on the horizon? Click the button to the left and read a news article about a new or improved storage device. What is the device? Who manufactures it? How is the storage device better than, or different from, earlier devices? How will the device be used? Why?

CHAPTER 8

Operating Systems and Utility Programs

At last, your chemistry lab is finished. Now you have time to relax and respond to e-mail messages, some of which relate to your distance learning course. As you click the Send button, replying to the first of 22 unread messages, the computer freezes. You click the button on the mouse. Nothing happens. You press a key on the keyboard. The computer beeps. You click the mouse again. Still no response. With reluctance, you restart the computer.

While you are waiting, you ponder the work ahead and hope nothing is wrong. After all, you no longer can get by in school without your computer. By now, you expect to see the Windows desktop. Something *is* wrong. It is time to call for help. You dial the toll-free number for technical support, but the automated system places you on hold. Your thoughts turn to that distance learning homework.

Finally, a live person answers your call! You explain the problem to the technician. She tells you the first step in solving this problem is to start the computer again — this time with the boot disk in the floppy disk drive. Now you know you are in trouble… what's a boot disk?

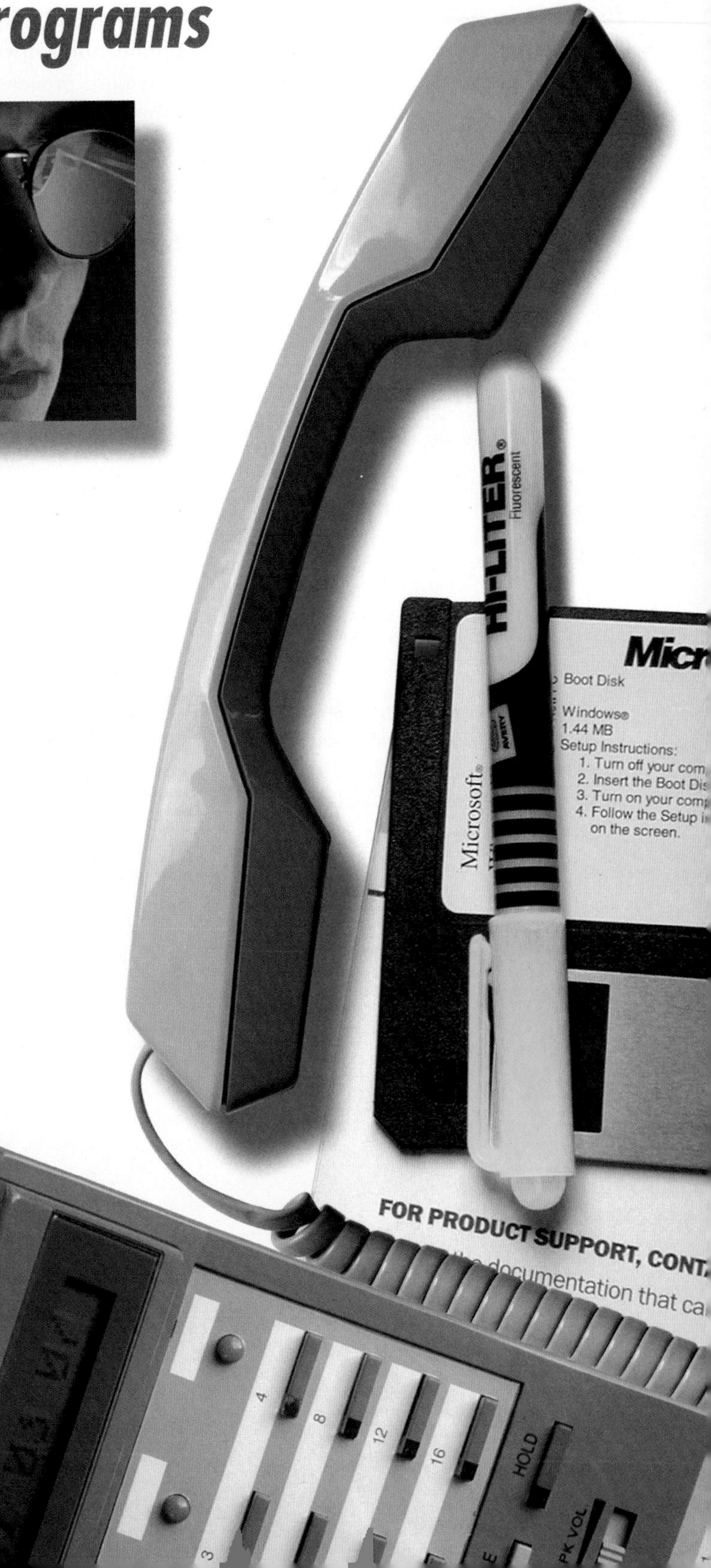

OBJECTIVES

After completing this chapter, you will be able to:

- Describe the two types of software
- Understand the startup process for a personal computer
- Describe the term user interface
- Explain features common to most operating systems
- Know the difference between stand-alone operating systems and network operating systems
- Identify various stand-alone operating systems
- Identify various network operating systems
- Recognize devices that use embedded operating systems
- Discuss the purpose of the following utilities: file viewer, file compression, diagnostic, uninstaller, disk scanner, disk defragmenter, backup, and screen saver

SYSTEM SOFTWARE

Software is the series of computer-language coded instructions that tells the computer how to perform tasks. Two types of software are application software and system software. Like most computer users, you probably interact with a variety of application software products such as a word processing program, an e-mail program, and a Web browser. You also interact with system software.

System software consists of the programs that control the operations of the computer and its devices. System software serves as the interface between the user, the application software, and the computer's hardware.

Two types of system software include operating systems and utility programs. This chapter discusses the operating system and its functions, as well as several utility programs for personal computers.

Figure 8-1 Most operating systems perform the functions illustrated in this figure.

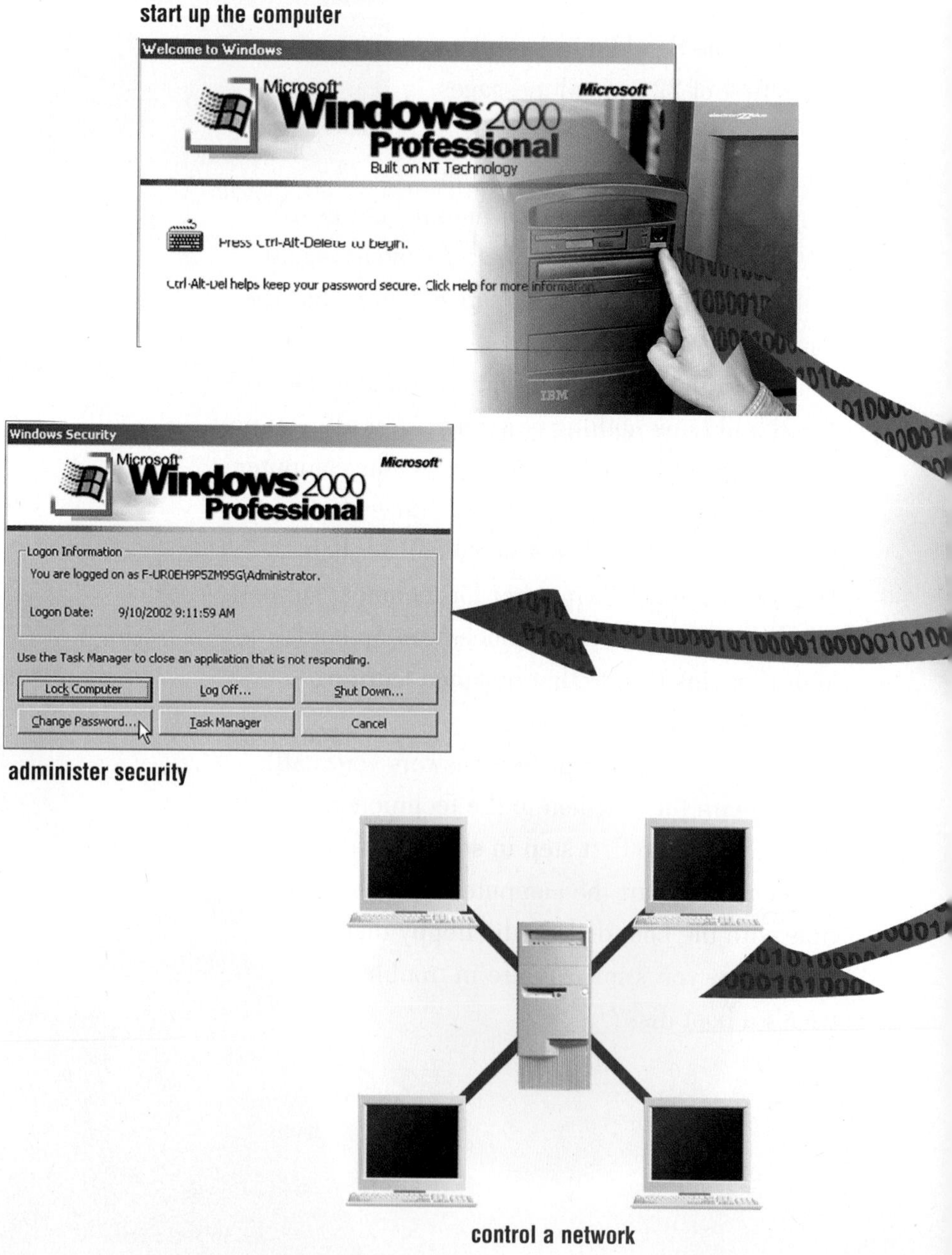

OPERATING SYSTEMS

An **operating system** (**OS**) is a set of programs containing instructions that coordinate all the activities among computer hardware resources. For example, the operating system recognizes input from an input device such as the keyboard, mouse, microphone, or PC camera; coordinates the display of output on the monitor; instructs a printer how and when to print information; and manages data and instructions in memory and information stored on disk. A computer needs an operating system to work.

Many different operating systems exist. Most perform similar functions that include starting the computer, providing a user interface, managing programs, managing memory, scheduling jobs, configuring devices, accessing the Web, monitoring performance, and providing housekeeping services (Figure 8-1). Some operating systems also allow you to control a network and administer security.

In most cases, the operating system resides on the computer's hard disk. On smaller handheld computers, the operating system may reside on a ROM chip.

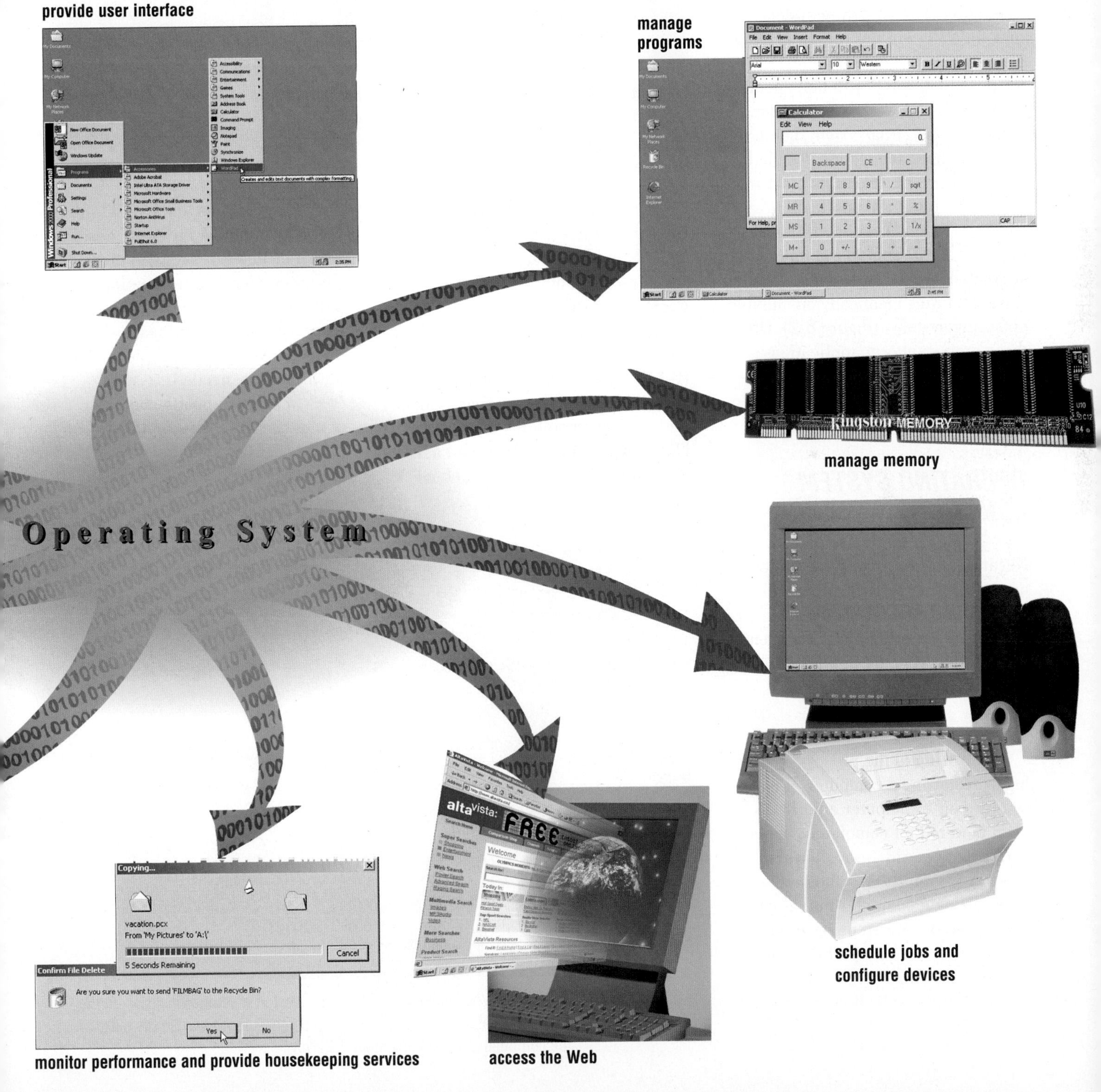

Different sizes of computers typically use different operating systems. For example, a mainframe computer does not use the same operating system as a desktop computer. Even the same types of computers, such as desktop computers, may not use the same operating system. One personal computer may use Windows and another may use Mac OS. Furthermore, these various operating systems often are not compatible with each other. The operating system that runs on a PC will not run on an Apple computer. In addition, application software that works with one operating system may not work with another.

The operating system that a computer uses sometimes is called the **software platform** or **platform**. When you purchase application software, the package identifies the required software platform (operating system). A **cross-platform** application is one that runs identically on multiple operating systems (Figure 8-2). Often, these cross-platform applications have multiple versions, each corresponding to a different operating system.

Figure 8-2 Some applications run on multiple software platforms (operating systems). This box shows that FileMaker runs on Windows 98 and Windows NT.

OPERATING SYSTEM FUNCTIONS

Regardless of the size of computer, most operating systems provide similar functions. The following sections discuss functions common to operating systems.

Starting a Computer

Booting is the process of starting or restarting a computer. When you turn on a computer after it has been powered off completely, you are performing a **cold boot**. A **warm boot** or **warm start** is the process of restarting a computer that already is powered on. When using Windows, for example, you can perform a warm boot by pressing a combination of keyboard keys, selecting options from a menu, or pressing a Reset button on the computer.

Each time you boot a computer, the kernel and other frequently used operating system instructions are *loaded*, or copied from the hard disk (storage) to the computer's memory (RAM). The **kernel** is the core of an operating system that manages memory and devices; maintains the computer's clock; starts applications; and assigns the computer's resources, such as devices, programs, data, and information. The kernel is **memory resident**, which means it remains in memory while the computer is running. Other parts of the operating system are **nonresident**, which means their instructions remain on the hard disk until they are needed.

When you boot a computer, a set of messages displays on the screen (Figure 8-3). The actual information

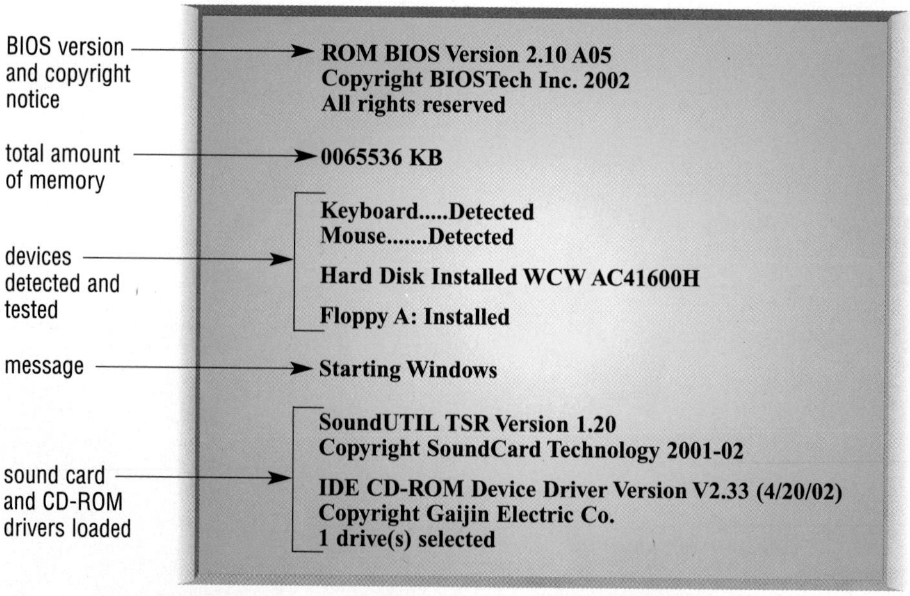

Figure 8-3 When you boot a computer, a set of messages displays on the screen. The actual information displayed varies depending on the make of the computer and the equipment installed.

displayed varies depending on the make of the computer and the equipment installed. The boot process, however, is similar for large and small computers.

The following steps explain what occurs during a cold boot on a personal computer using the Windows operating system (Figure 8-4).

1. When you turn on the computer, the power supply sends an electrical signal to the motherboard and the other devices located in the system unit.
2. The surge of electricity causes the processor chip to reset itself and look for the ROM chip(s) that contains the BIOS. The **BIOS** (pronounced BYE-ohss), which stands for **basic input/output system**, is firmware that contains the computer's startup instructions.

Figure 8-4 HOW A PERSONAL COMPUTER BOOTS UP

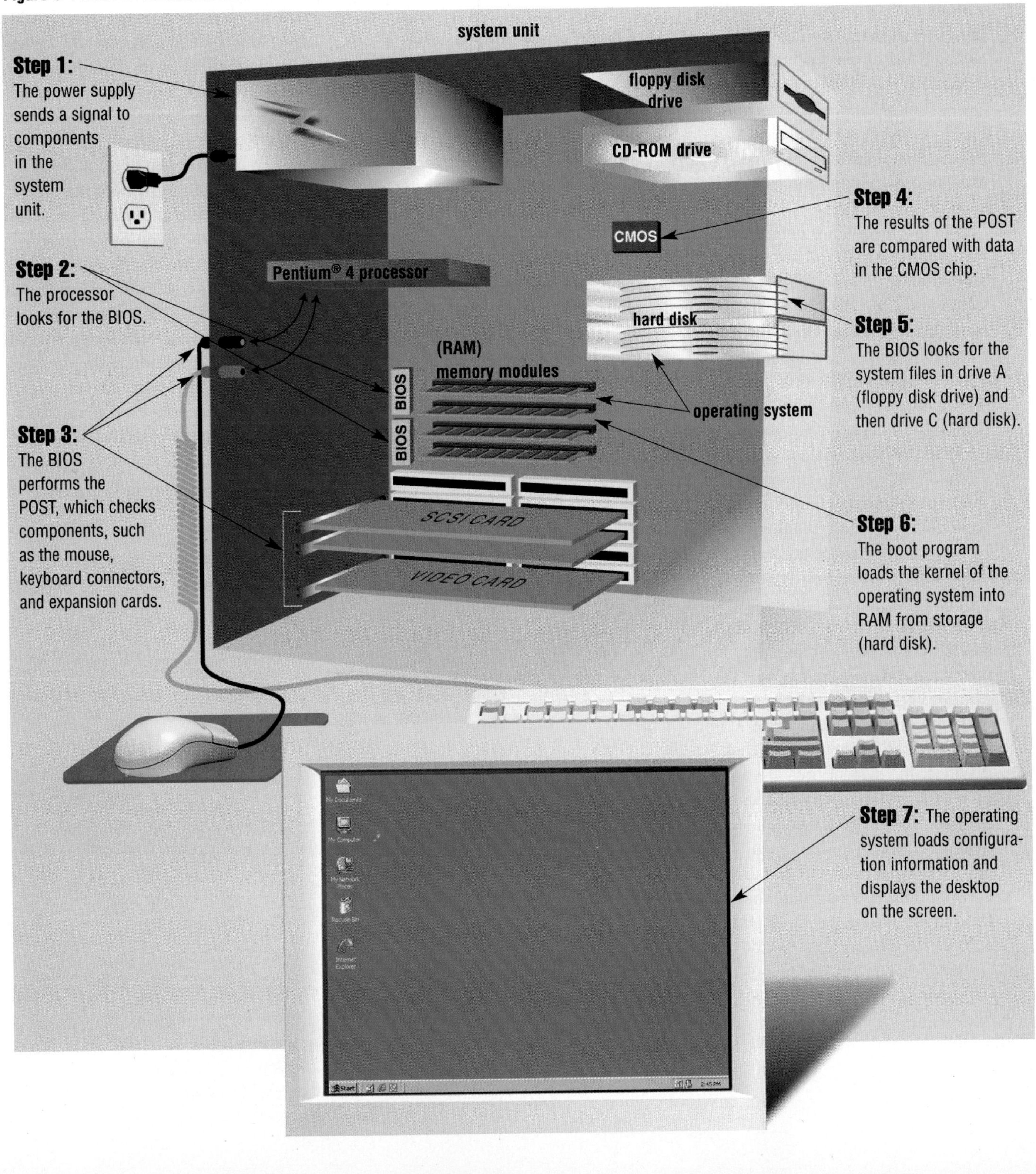
system unit
Step 1: The power supply sends a signal to components in the system unit.
floppy disk drive
CD-ROM drive
Step 4: The results of the POST are compared with data in the CMOS chip.
CMOS
Step 2: The processor looks for the BIOS.
Pentium® 4 processor
hard disk
Step 5: The BIOS looks for the system files in drive A (floppy disk drive) and then drive C (hard disk).
(RAM) memory modules
BIOS
BIOS
operating system
Step 3: The BIOS performs the POST, which checks components, such as the mouse, keyboard connectors, and expansion cards.
SCSI CARD
VIDEO CARD
Step 6: The boot program loads the kernel of the operating system into RAM from storage (hard disk).
Step 7: The operating system loads configuration information and displays the desktop on the screen.

As discussed in Chapter 4, firmware consists of ROM chips that contain permanently written instructions.

3. The BIOS executes a series of tests to make sure the computer hardware is connected properly and operating correctly. The tests, collectively called the **power-on self test** (**POST**), check the various system components such as the buses, system clock, expansion cards, RAM chips, keyboard, and drives. As the POST executes, LEDs flicker on devices, including the disk drives and keyboard. Several beeps also sound, and messages display on the monitor's screen.
4. The POST results are compared with data in a CMOS chip on the motherboard. As discussed in Chapter 4, the CMOS chip stores configuration information about the computer, such as the amount of memory; type of disk drives, keyboard, and monitor; the current date and time; and other startup information. It also detects any new devices connected to the computer. If any problems are found, the computer may beep, display error messages, or cease operating — depending on the severity of the problem.
5. If the POST completes successfully, the BIOS searches for specific operating system files called **system files**. Usually, the operating system will look first in drive A (the designation for a floppy disk drive). If the system files are not on a disk in drive A, the BIOS looks in drive C (the designation usually given to the first hard disk). If neither drive A nor drive C contain the system files, some computers look to the CD-ROM or DVD-ROM drive.
6. Once located, the system files load into memory and execute. Next, the kernel of the operating system loads into memory. Then, the operating system in memory takes control of the computer.
7. The operating system loads system configuration information. In Windows, the **registry** consists of several files that contain the system configuration information. Windows constantly accesses the registry during the computer's operation for information such as installed hardware and software devices and individual user preferences for mouse speed, passwords, and other user-specific information.

Necessary operating system files load into memory. When complete, the Windows desktop and icons display on the screen. The operating system executes programs in the StartUp folder. The **StartUp folder** contains a list of programs that open automatically when you boot the computer.

EMERGENCY REPAIR DISK A **boot drive** is the drive from which your personal computer boots (starts). In most cases, drive C (the hard disk) is the boot drive. Sometimes a hard disk becomes damaged and the computer cannot boot from the hard disk. In this case, you can boot from a special disk. An **emergency repair disk**, sometimes called a **boot disk** or a **rescue disk**, is a floppy disk, Zip® disk, or CD-ROM that contains system files that will start the computer. For this reason, it is crucial you have an emergency repair disk available and ready for use.

When you install an operating system, one of the installation steps involves making an emergency repair disk. Often when you purchase a computer, the manufacturer pre-installs the operating system. If you did not install the operating system, you may not have an emergency repair disk. In this case, you should create one and keep it in a safe place. The steps in Figure 8-5 show how to create an emergency repair disk in Windows.

Figure 8-5 HOW TO CREATE AN EMERGENCY REPAIR DISK IN WINDOWS

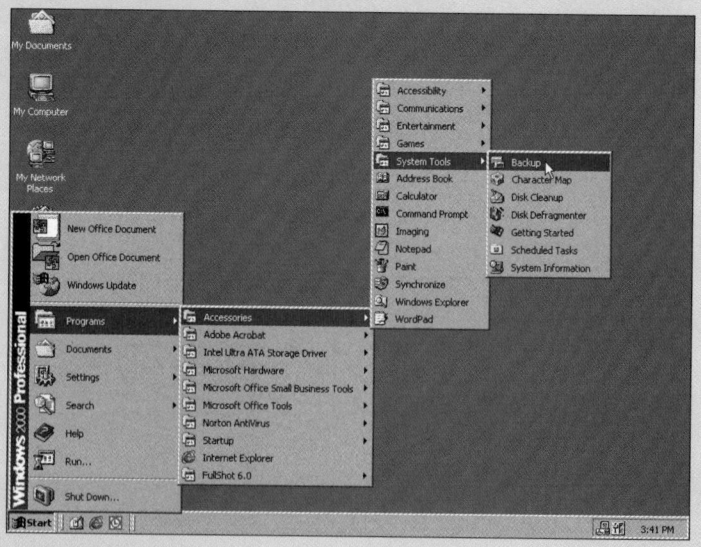

Step 1:

Click the Start button on the taskbar, point to Programs on the Start menu, point to Accessories on the Programs submenu, point to System Tools on the Accessories submenu, and then point to Backup.

The User Interface

You interact with software through its user interface. A **user interface** controls how you enter data and instructions and how information displays on the screen. Two types of user interfaces are command-line and graphical (Figure 8-6). Many operating systems use a combination of these two interfaces to define how you interact with your computer.

Figure 8-6b (graphical user interface)

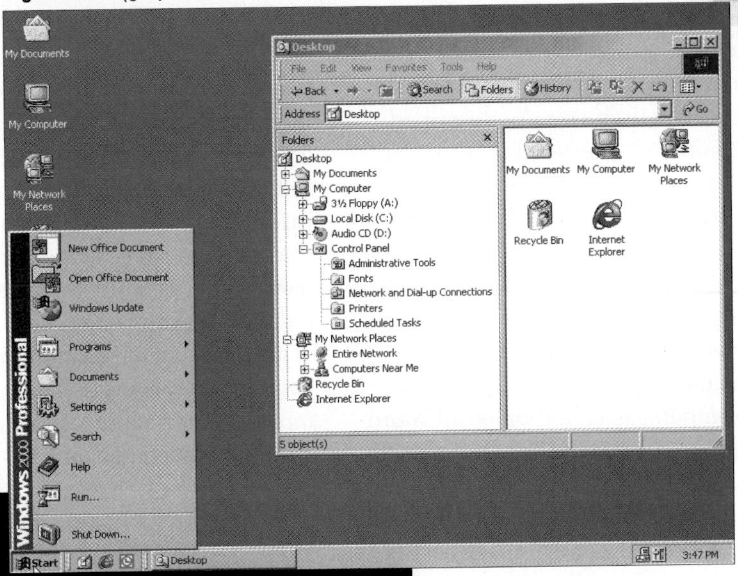

Figure 8-6a (command-line interface)

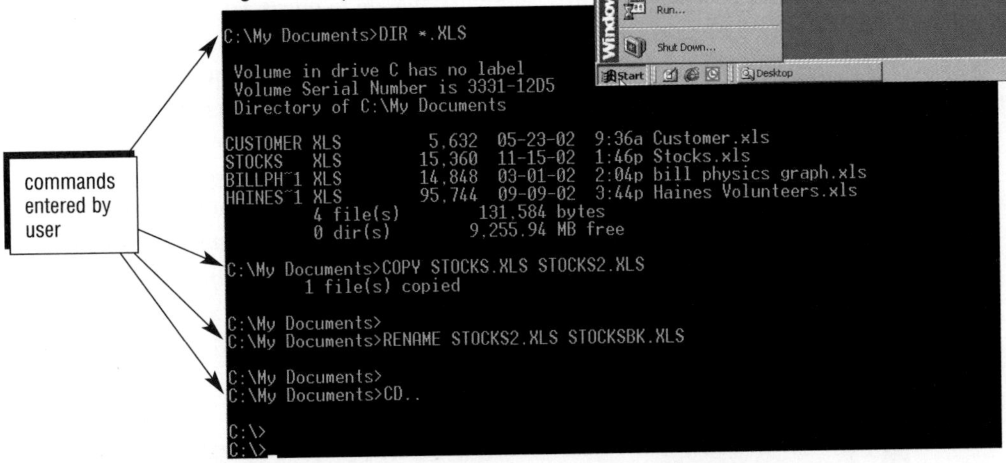

Figure 8-6 Examples of command-line and graphical user interfaces.

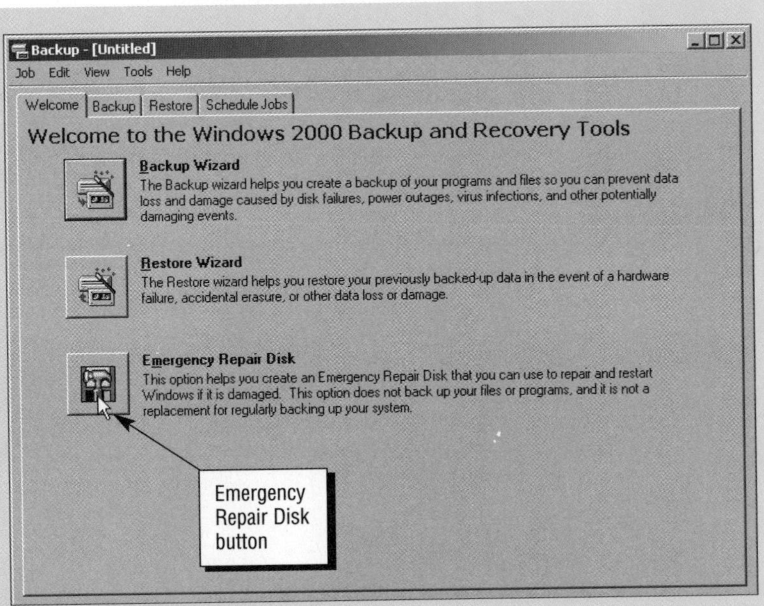

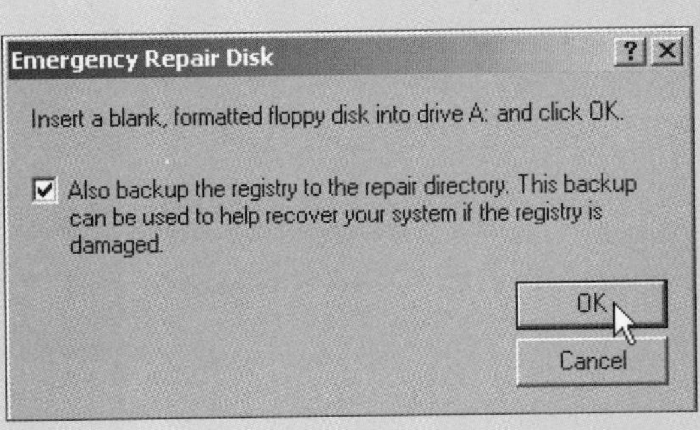

Step 2:
Click Backup on the System Tools submenu to open the Backup window. Point to the Emergency Repair Disk button.

Step 3:
Click the Emergency Repair Disk button to create the emergency repair disk. Follow the on-screen instructions.

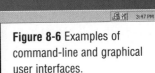

With a **command-line interface**, you type keywords or press special keys on the keyboard to enter data and instructions. As described in Chapter 3, a keyword is a special word, phrase, or code that a program understands as an instruction. Some keyboards also include keys that send a command to a program when you press them. When working with a command-line interface, the set of commands you use to interact with the computer is called the **command language**. Command-line interfaces often are difficult to use because they require exact spelling, grammar, and punctuation. Minor errors, such as a missing period, will generate an error message.

A graphical user interface typically is easier to learn and use than a command-line interface because it does not require you memorize a command language. As discussed in Chapter 1, a **graphical user interface (GUI)** allows you to use menus and visual images such as icons, buttons, and other graphical objects to issue commands. A **menu** is a set of commands from which you choose. An **icon** is a small image that represents a program, an instruction, a file, or some other object. You can use a keyboard, mouse, or any other pointing device to interact with menus, icons, buttons, and other onscreen objects.

Today, many GUIs incorporate features similar to that of a Web browser. For example, icons function as Web links, and Web pages can be delivered or *pushed* automatically to your screen (Figure 8-7).

Managing Programs

Some operating systems have single-user functionality and can support only one running program. Others support thousands of users running multiple programs. How an operating system handles programs directly affects your productivity.

A **single user/single tasking** operating system allows only one user to run one program at a time. Suppose, for example, you are creating a poster in a graphics program and then decide to check your e-mail messages. With a single tasking operating system, you must quit the graphics program before you can run the e-mail program. You then must close the e-mail program and restart the graphics program to finish the poster. Early systems were single user. Most operating systems today are multitasking.

ISSUE

OS Innovations

Types of Operating Systems

Today's operating systems include a variety of features. They support a graphical user interface, monitor performance, and administer security. Most operating systems also include a variety of utility programs. These utilities offer functions such as compressing files, diagnosing problems, scanning disks, defragmenting disks, checking for viruses, backing up files and disks, and displaying screen savers. Do you think an operating system should include these features? Are these features useful? What other features should be included in an operating system? If you were to write an overview of the perfect operating system, which innovative features would you include?

For more information on operating systems and operating systems features, visit the Discovering Computers 2002 Issues Web page (**scsite.com/dc2002/issues.htm**) and click Chapter 8 Issue #1.

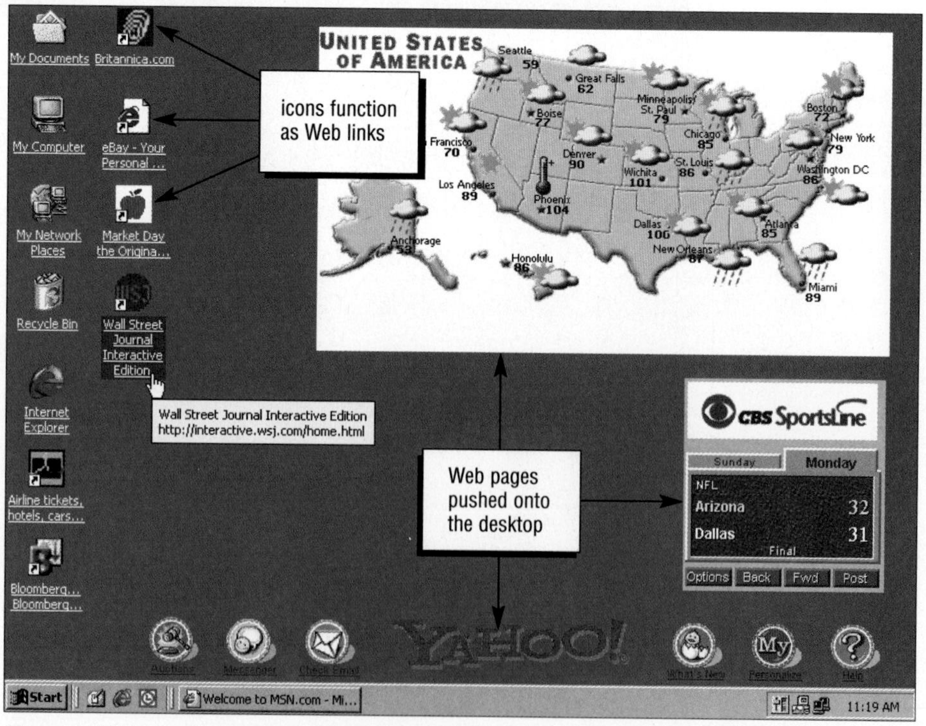

Figure 8-7 This graphical user interface incorporates icons that function like Web links, and Web pages that are *pushed* onto the desktop.

A **multitasking** operating system allows a single user to work on two or more applications that reside in memory at the same time. Using the example just cited, if you are working with a multitasking operating system, you do not have to quit the graphics program to run your e-mail program. Both programs can run concurrently.

Most users today run multiple programs simultaneously. It is common to have an e-mail program and Web browser open at all times, while working in applications such as word processing or graphics.

When you run multiple applications at the same time, one is in the foreground and others are in the background (Figure 8-8). The **foreground** contains the active application; that is, the one you currently are using. The others that are running, but not in use, are in the **background**. You easily can switch between foreground and background applications. To make an application active (in the foreground), you click its name on the taskbar. This causes the operating system to place all other applications in the background.

A **multiuser** operating system enables two or more users to run a program simultaneously. Networks, mid-range servers, mainframes, and supercomputers allow hundreds to thousands of users to connect at the same time, and thus are multiuser.

A **multiprocessing** operating system can support two or more processors running programs at the same time. Multiprocessing works much like parallel processing, which was discussed in Chapter 3. Multiprocessing involves the coordinated processing of programs by more than one processor. As with parallel processing, multi-processing increases a computer's processing speed.

A computer with separate processors also can serve as a fault-tolerant computer. A **fault-tolerant computer** continues to operate even if one of its components fails. Fault-tolerant computers have duplicate components such as processors, memory, and disk drives. If any one of these components fails, the computer switches to the duplicate component and continues to operate. Airline reservation systems, communications networks, and automated teller machines and other systems that must be operational at all times use fault-tolerant computers.

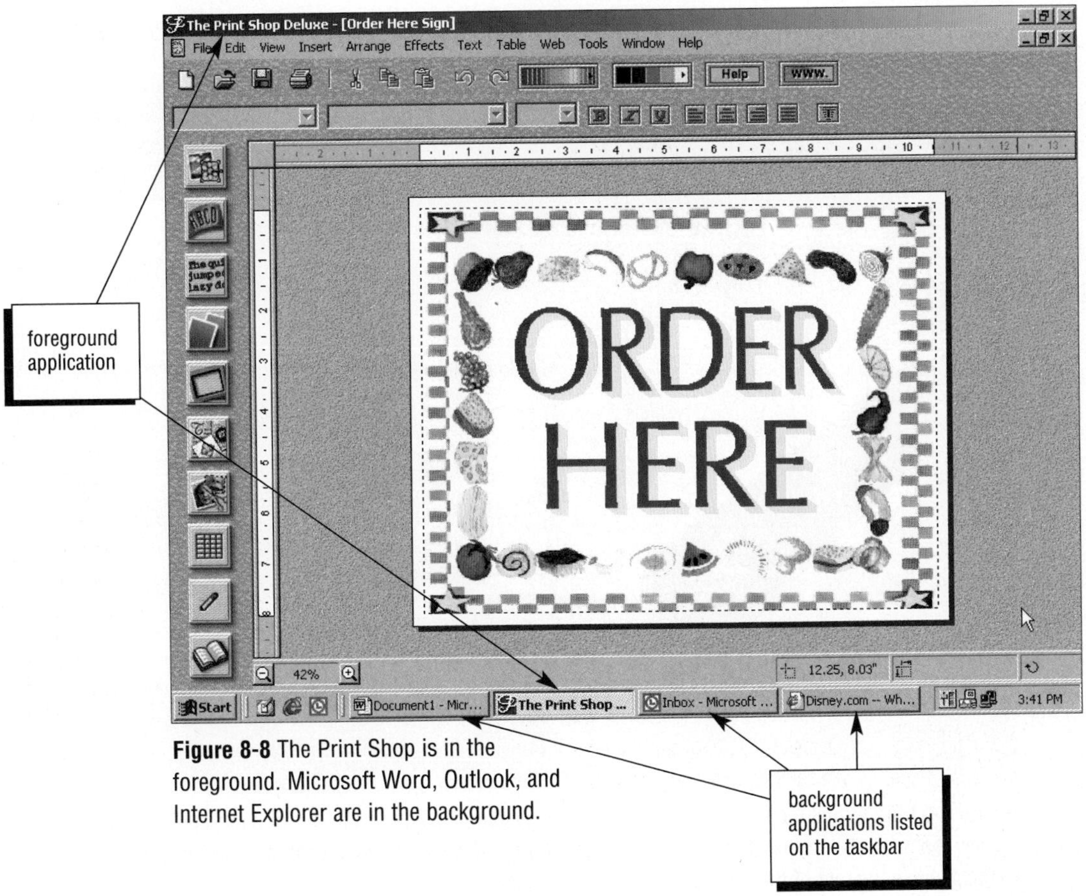

Figure 8-8 The Print Shop is in the foreground. Microsoft Word, Outlook, and Internet Explorer are in the background.

Managing Memory

The purpose of **memory management** is to optimize use of random access memory (RAM). As discussed in Chapter 4, RAM consists of one or more chips on the motherboard that temporarily hold items such as data and instructions while the processor interprets and executes them. The operating system allocates, or assigns, these items to an area of memory while they are being processed. Then, it carefully monitors the contents of memory. Finally, the operating system clears these items from memory when the processor no longer requires them.

Some operating systems use virtual memory to optimize RAM. With **virtual memory** (**VM**), the operating system allocates a portion of a storage medium, usually the hard disk, to function as additional RAM (Figure 8-9). As you interact with a program, part of it may be in RAM, while the rest of the program is on the hard disk as virtual memory.

The area of the hard disk used for virtual memory is called a **swap file** because it swaps (exchanges) data, information, and instructions between memory and storage. A **page** is the amount of data and program instructions that can swap at a given time. Thus, the technique of swapping items between memory and storage often is called **paging**.

When an operating system spends much of its time paging, instead of executing application software, it is said to be **thrashing**. If application software, such as a Web browser, has stopped responding and your hard disk's LED blinks repeatedly, the operating system probably is thrashing. To stop it from thrashing, quit the application that stopped responding. If thrashing occurs frequently, one possibility is you may need to install more RAM in your computer.

Scheduling Jobs

The operating system determines the order in which jobs are processed. A **job** is an operation the processor manages. Jobs include receiving data from an input device, processing

VIRTUAL MEMORY MANAGEMENT

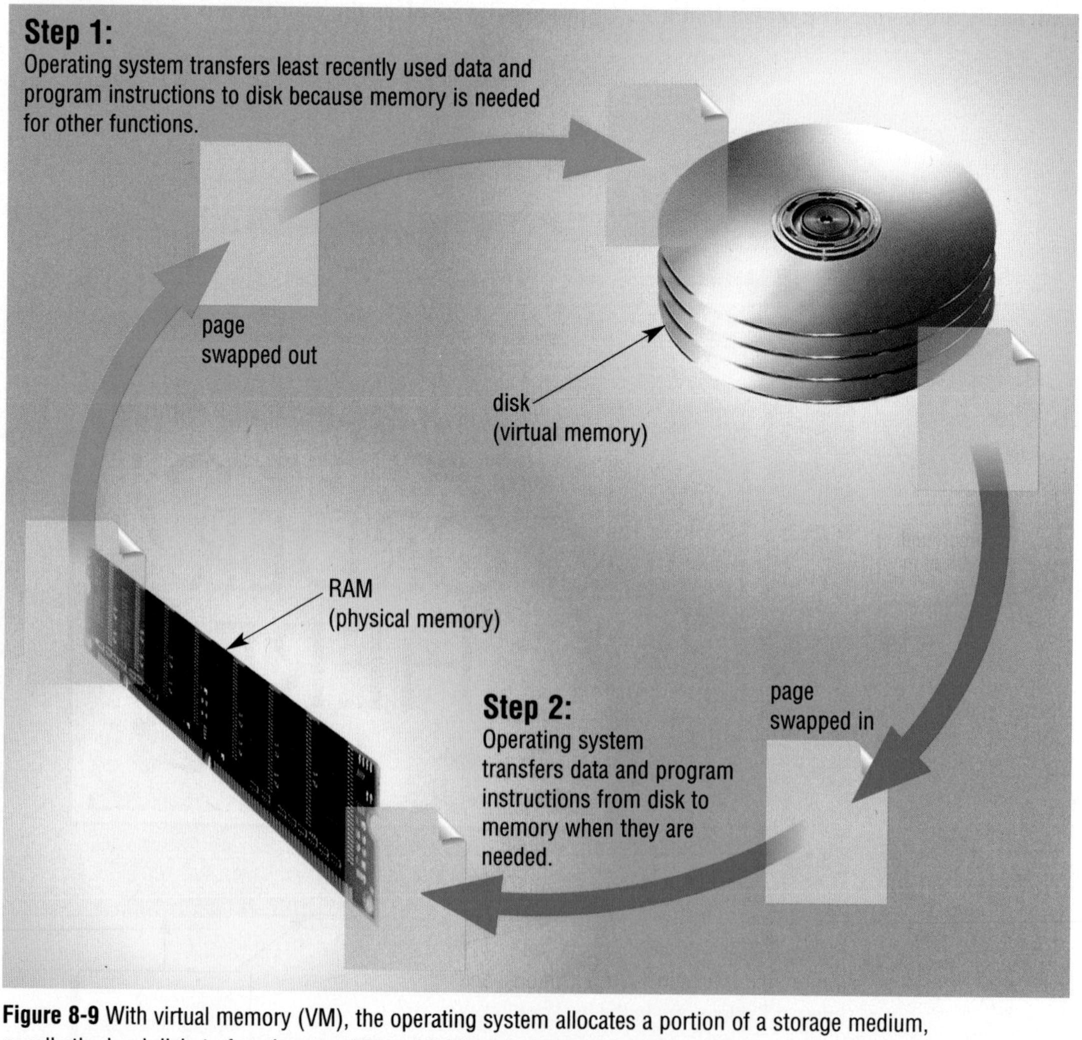
Step 1:
Operating system transfers least recently used data and program instructions to disk because memory is needed for other functions.
page swapped out
disk (virtual memory)
RAM (physical memory)
Step 2:
Operating system transfers data and program instructions from disk to memory when they are needed.
page swapped in

Figure 8-9 With virtual memory (VM), the operating system allocates a portion of a storage medium, usually the hard disk, to function as additional RAM. As you interact with a program, part of it may be in RAM, while the rest of the program is on the hard disk as virtual memory.

instructions, sending information to an output device, and transferring items from storage to memory and from memory to storage.

The operating system does not always process jobs on a first-come, first-served basis. Sometimes, one user may have higher priority than other users. In this case, the operating system has to adjust the schedule of jobs. Other times, a device may already be busy processing one job when it receives another job. This occurs because the processor operates at a much faster rate of speed than peripheral devices. For example, if the processor sends five print jobs to a printer, the printer only can print one document at a time.

While waiting for devices to become idle, the operating system places items in buffers. A **buffer** is an area of memory or storage in which items are placed while waiting to be transferred to or from an input or output device.

The operating system commonly uses buffers with print jobs. This process, called **spooling,** sends print jobs to a buffer instead of sending them immediately to the printer. The buffer holds the information waiting to print while the printer prints from the buffer at its own speed. By spooling print jobs to a buffer, the processor can interpret and execute instructions while the printer is printing documents. Once a print job is in the buffer, you can use the computer for other tasks.

Another advantage of spooling is it allows you to send a second job to the printer without waiting for the first job to finish printing. Multiple print jobs line up in a **queue** within the buffer. A program, called a **print spooler**, intercepts print jobs from the operating system and places them in the queue (Figure 8-10).

Configuring Devices

To communicate with each device in the computer, the operating system relies on device drivers. A **device driver**, also called a **driver**, is a small program that tells the operating system how to communicate with a device. Each device on a computer, such as the mouse, keyboard, monitor, and printer, has its own specialized set of commands and thus requires its own specific driver. When you boot a computer, the operating system loads each device's driver. These devices will not function without their correct drivers. In Windows environments, most device drivers have a .drv extension.

Web Link

For more information on device drivers, visit the Discovering Computers 2002 Chapter 8 WEB LINK page (**scsite.com/dc2002/ch8/weblink.htm**) and click Device Drivers.

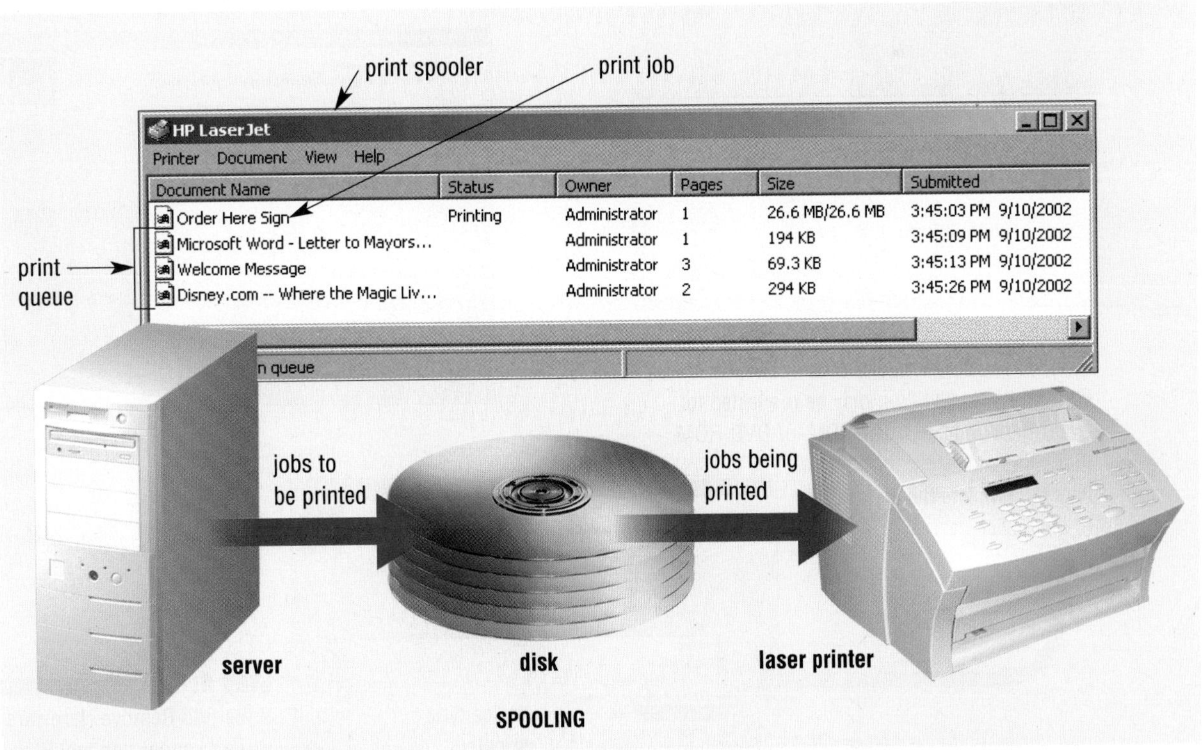

Figure 8-10 Spooling increases both processor and printer efficiency by writing print jobs to a disk before they are printed. In this figure, three jobs are in the queue and one is printing.

If you attach a new device to your computer, such as a printer or scanner, its driver must be installed before you can use the device. Windows provides a wizard to guide you through the installation steps. Figure 8-11 shows how to install a device driver for a Kodak digital camera. You follow the same general steps to install device drivers for any type of hardware. For many devices, your computer's operating system already may include the necessary drivers. If it does not, you can install the drivers from the disk included with the device upon purchase.

If you need a driver for your device and do not have the original disk, you can obtain the driver by contacting the vendor that sold you the device or contacting the manufacturer directly. Many manufacturers post device drivers on their Web site for anyone to download.

Figure 8-11 HOW TO INSTALL DRIVERS FOR NEW HARDWARE IN WINDOWS

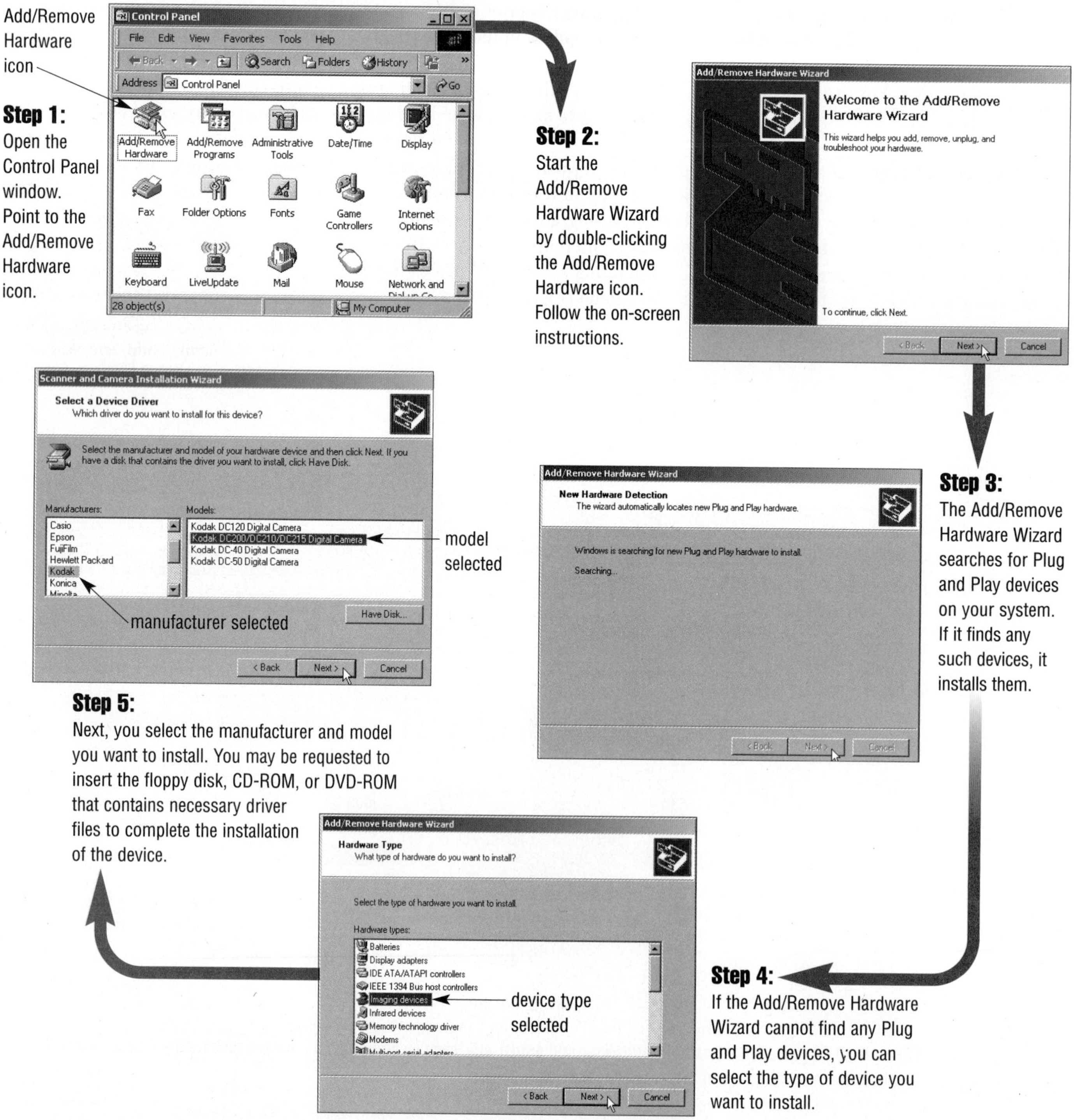
Add/Remove Hardware icon
Step 1:
Open the Control Panel window. Point to the Add/Remove Hardware icon.
Control Panel
Step 2:
Start the Add/Remove Hardware Wizard by double-clicking the Add/Remove Hardware icon. Follow the on-screen instructions.
Add/Remove Hardware Wizard
Welcome to the Add/Remove Hardware Wizard
This wizard helps you add, remove, unplug, and troubleshoot your hardware.
To continue, click Next.
Step 3:
The Add/Remove Hardware Wizard searches for Plug and Play devices on your system. If it finds any such devices, it installs them.
New Hardware Detection
The wizard automatically locates new Plug and Play hardware.
Windows is searching for new Plug and Play hardware to install.
Searching...
Step 4:
If the Add/Remove Hardware Wizard cannot find any Plug and Play devices, you can select the type of device you want to install.
Hardware Type
What type of hardware do you want to install?
Select the type of hardware you want to install.
device type selected
Scanner and Camera Installation Wizard
Select a Device Driver
Which driver do you want to install for this device?
Select the manufacturer and model of your hardware device and then click Next. If you have a disk that contains the driver you want to install, click Have Disk.
model selected
manufacturer selected
Step 5:
Next, you select the manufacturer and model you want to install. You may be requested to insert the floppy disk, CD-ROM, or DVD-ROM that contains necessary driver files to complete the installation of the device.

In the past, installing a new hardware device often required setting switches and other elements on the motherboard. Today, installation is easier because most devices and operating systems support Plug and Play. As discussed in Chapter 4, **Plug and Play** means the computer can recognize a new device and assist you in its installation by loading the necessary drivers automatically and checking for conflicts with other devices. With Plug and Play, a user can plug in a device, turn on the computer, and then use, or play, the device without having to configure the system manually.

When installing some components, occasionally you have to know which interrupt request the device should use for communications. An **interrupt request** (**IRQ**) is a communications line between a device and the processor. Most computers have 16 IRQs, numbered 0 through 15 (Figure 8-12). With Plug and Play, the operating system determines the best IRQ to use for these communications. If your operating system uses an IRQ that already is assigned to another device, an IRQ conflict will occur and the computer will not work properly. If an IRQ conflict occurs, you will have to obtain the correct IRQ for the device. You usually can find this information in the installation directions that accompany the device.

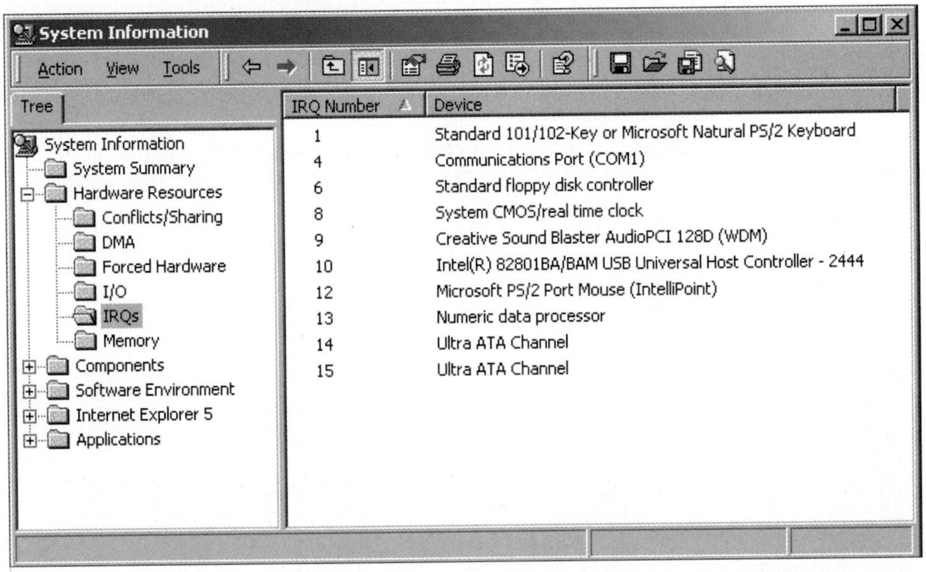

Figure 8-12 An interrupt request (IRQ) is a communication line between a device and the processor. In this example, only 10 of the 16 IRQs are being used (1, 4, 6, 8, 9, 10, 12, 13, 14, and 15).

Accessing the Web

Operating systems typically provide a means to establish Web connections. For example, Windows includes an Internet Connection Wizard that guides you through the process of setting up a connection between your computer and your Internet service provider (Figure 8-13).

Some operating systems include a Web browser and an e-mail program, enabling you to begin using the Web and communicate with others as soon as you set up the connections. This feature saves time because you do not have to install any additional software.

Web Link

For more information on Plug and Play, visit the Discovering Computers 2002 Chapter 8 WEB LINK page (**scsite.com/dc2002/ch8/weblink.htm**) and click Plug and Play.

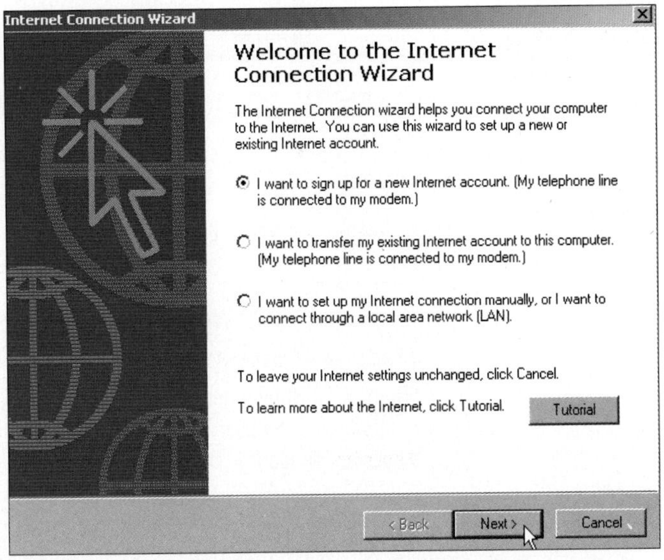

Figure 8-13 The Internet Connection Wizard allows you to set up a connection between your computer and your Internet service provider.

Monitoring Performance

Operating systems typically contain a performance monitor. A **performance monitor** is a program that assesses and reports information about various system resources and devices (Figure 8-14). For example, you can monitor the processor, disks, memory, and network usage. A performance monitor also can check the number of reads and writes to a file.

The information in performance reports can help you identify problems with resources so you can attempt to resolve the problem. If your computer is running extremely slow, the performance monitor may determine that you are using the computer's memory to its maximum. Thus, you might consider installing additional memory.

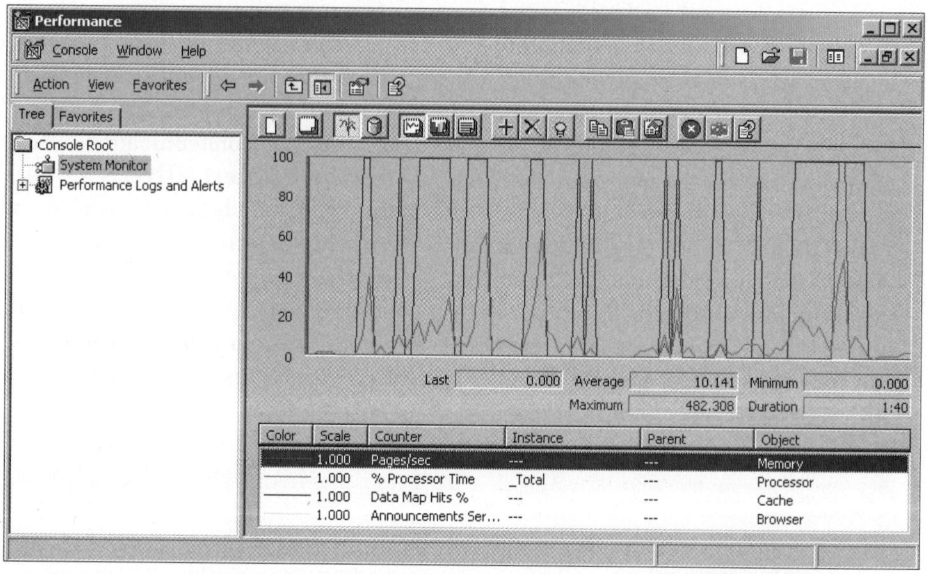

Figure 8-14 A performance monitor is a program that assesses and reports information about various system resources and devices. The System Monitor is a performance monitor in Windows. Shown above it is tracking memory, processor, cache, and browser usage.

Providing Housekeeping Services

Operating systems contain a program called a file manager. A **file manager** performs functions related to storage and file management (Figure 8-15). Some of the storage and file management functions that a file manager performs are formatting and copying disks; displaying a list of files on a storage medium; checking the amount of used or free space on a storage medium; organizing, copying, renaming, deleting, moving, and sorting files; and creating shortcuts. A **shortcut** is an icon on the desktop that runs a program when you click it.

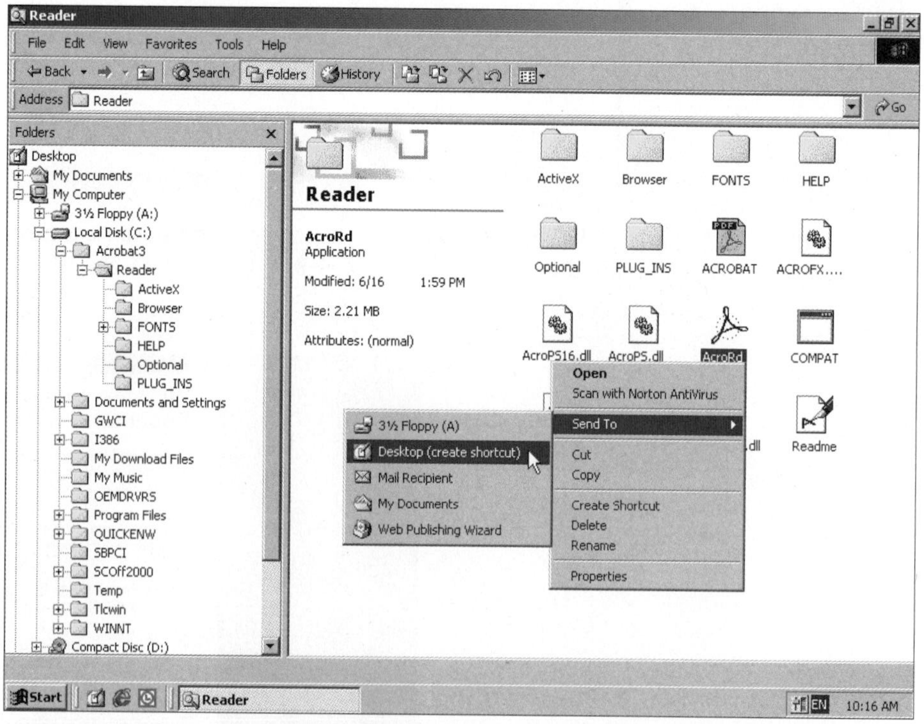

Figure 8-15 Shown here is Windows Explorer, which is a file manager included with Windows. In this figure, the user is creating a shortcut for the Acrobat Reader program. The shortcut will display as an icon on the desktop.

Formatting is the process of preparing a disk for reading and writing. Most floppy and hard disk manufacturers preformat their disks. If you must format a floppy disk, do so by issuing a formatting command to the operating system. Various operating systems format disks differently. Thus, you typically cannot use a disk formatted in one operating system in a computer that has a different operating system. For example, you cannot use a Mac OS floppy disk in a computer that uses the Windows operating system — without special hardware and software.

With the Windows operating system, the formatting process also defines the file allocation table. The **file allocation table** (**FAT**) is a table of information that the operating system uses to locate files on a disk. The FAT is like a library card catalog for your disk, which contains a listing of all files, file types, and locations. If you format a disk that already contains data, instructions, or information, the formatting process erases the file location information and redefines the file allocation table for these items. Thus, formatting does not erase the actual files on the disk. For this reason, if you accidentally format a disk, you often can unformat it with a utility program.

Controlling a Network

Some operating systems are network operating systems. A **network operating system**, also called a **network OS** or **NOS** (pronounced nauce), is an operating system that supports a network. As discussed in Chapter 1, a **network** is a collection of computers and devices connected together via communications media and devices such as cables, telephone lines, and modems. Some networks are wireless, that is, use no physical lines or wires.

In some networks, the **server** is the computer that controls access to the hardware and software on the network and provides a centralized storage area for programs, data, and information. The other computers on the network, called **clients**, rely on the server(s) for resources such as files, devices, processing power, and storage (Figure 8-16).

A network OS organizes and coordinates how multiple users access and share resources on the network. Resources include programs, files, and devices such as printers and drives. The network administrator uses the network OS to add and remove users, computers, and other devices to and from the network.

Some operating systems have network features built into them. In other cases, the network OS is a set of programs separate from the operating system on the client computers. When they are not connected to the network, the client computers use their own operating system. When connected to the network, the network OS assumes most of the functions of the operating system.

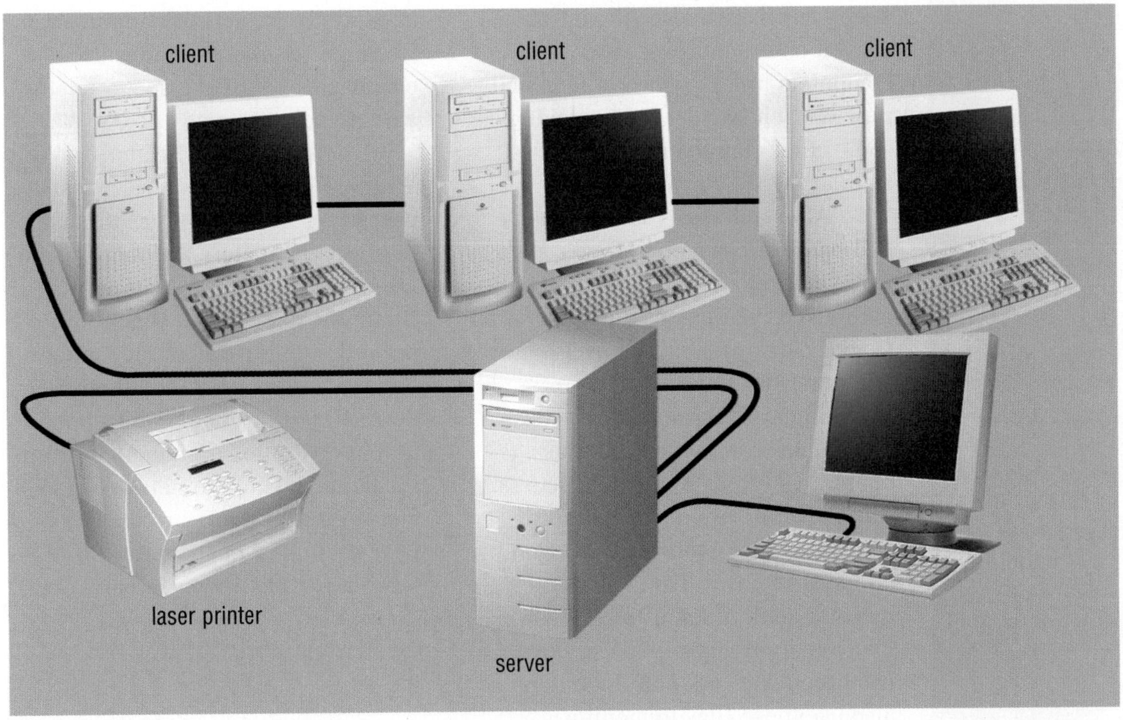

Figure 8-16 On a client/server network, one or more computers are designated as a server, and the other computers on the network are called clients.

Administering Security

When network administrators establish user accounts, each account typically requires a user name and password to access, or **log on**, to the network (Figure 8-17). A **user name**, or **user ID**, is a unique combination of characters, such as letters of the alphabet or numbers, that identifies one specific user. Many users select a combination of their first and last names as their user name. A user named Katy Bollini might choose kbollini as her user name.

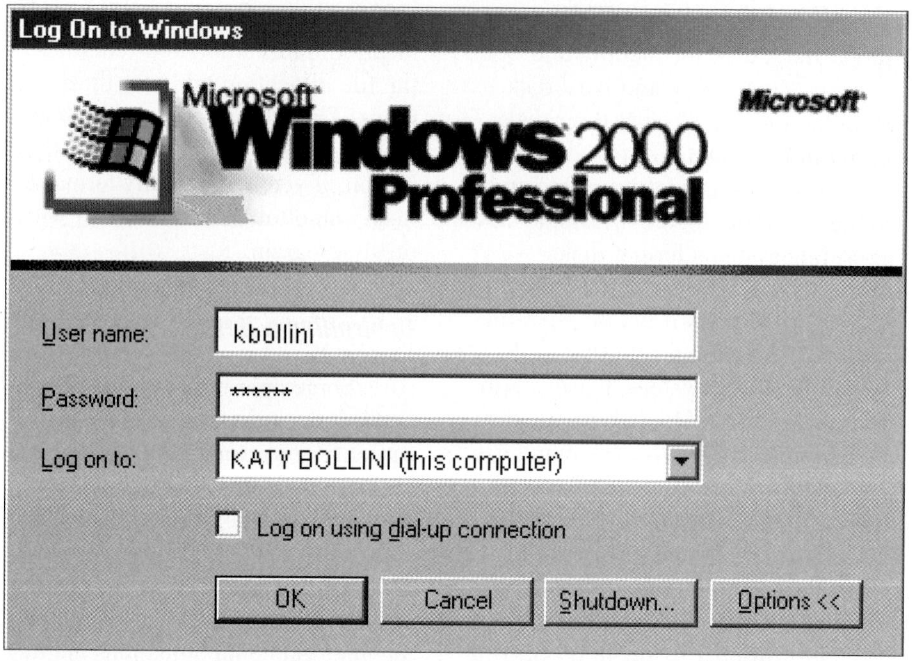

Figure 8-17 Most multiuser operating systems allow each user to log on, which is the process of entering a user name and a password into the computer.

A **password** is a combination of characters associated with the user name that allows access to certain computer resources. To prevent unauthorized users from accessing those computer resources, you should keep your password confidential. As you enter your password, most computers hide, or mask, the actual password characters by displaying some other characters, such as asterisks (*).

After entering your user name and password, the operating system compares your entries with a list of authorized user names and passwords. If your entries match the user name and password kept on file, the operating system grants you access. If the entries do not match, the operating system denies you access. The operating system also records successful and unsuccessful logon attempts in a file. This allows the network administrator to review who is using or attempting to use the computer. Network administrators also use these files to monitor computer usage.

The network administrator uses the network OS to establish permissions to resources. These permissions define who can access certain resources and when they can access those resources. Some operating systems allow the network administrator to assign passwords to files and commands, restricting access to only authorized users.

Network administrators using Windows 2000 Server easily manage user access and resources through its Active Directory service. **Active Directory** (**AD**) is a feature of Windows 2000 Server that allows network administrators to manage all network information including users, devices, settings, and connections from a central environment — even if components of the network are not located in the same physical areas. A later section in this chapter discusses Windows 2000 Server in more depth.

ISSUE

Three Tries and You're Out

Password Authentication

If your educational institution uses a network to access the system, you most likely must enter a user name and password. The password helps ensure that unauthorized users do not gain access. User names and passwords, however, do not necessarily guarantee proper network security. A recent survey by the Computer Security Institute reported that some 70 percent of the organizations polled said that their network defenses had been breached. Some organizations address this issue by requiring the user's password to be several characters long. They also enforce a limit on the number of password entry attempts. What is your opinion of this security measure? Do you think the number of attempts should be limited to three? Why or why not? Does a long password add to security measures? Many Web sites also require passwords. Can a Web site be secure? Why or why not? Should a Web site limit the number of password entry attempts to three?

For more information on network security and password authentication, visit the Discovering Computers 2002 Issues Web page (**scsite.com/dc2002/issues.htm**) and click Chapter 8 Issue #2.

TYPES OF OPERATING SYSTEMS

Many of the first operating systems were device dependent and proprietary. A **device-dependent** software product is one that runs only on a specific type of computer. **Proprietary software** is privately owned and limited to a specific vendor or computer model. When manufacturers introduced a new computer or model, they often produced an improved and different proprietary operating system. Problems arose, however, when a user wanted to switch computer models or manufacturers. The user's application software often would not work on the new computer because the applications were designed to work with a specific operating system.

Some operating systems still are device dependent. The trend today, however, is toward **device-independent** operating systems that run on many manufacturers' computers. The advantage of device independent operating systems is you can retain existing application software and data files even if you change computer models or vendors. This feature generally represents a sizable savings in time and money.

New versions of an operating system usually are downward compatible. A **downward-compatible** operating system is one that recognizes and works with application software written for an earlier version of the operating system. The application software, by contrast, is said to be upward compatible. An **upward-compatible** product is written for an earlier version of the operating system, but also runs with the new version.

Three basic categories of operating systems exist today: stand-alone, network, and embedded. The table in Figure 8-18 lists examples of operating systems in each category. The following pages discuss the operating systems listed in the table.

STAND-ALONE OPERATING SYSTEMS

A **stand-alone operating system** is a complete operating system that works on a desktop or notebook computer. Some stand-alone operating systems, called **client operating systems**, also work in conjunction with a network operating system. That is, client operating systems can operate with or without a network.

Examples of stand-alone operating systems are DOS, Windows 3.x, Windows 95, Windows NT Workstation, Windows 98, Windows 2000 Professional, Windows Millennium Edition, Mac OS, OS/2 Warp, UNIX, and Linux. The following paragraphs briefly discuss most of these operating systems. The section that covers network operating systems discusses UNIX and Linux.

DOS

The term **DOS (Disk Operating System)** refers to several single user operating systems developed in the early 1980s for personal computers. The two more widely used versions of DOS were PC-DOS and MS-DOS. Microsoft Corporation developed both PC-DOS and MS-DOS. The functionality of these two operating systems was essentially the same. The basic difference was the type of computer on which they were installed. Microsoft developed PC-DOS (Personal Computer DOS) for IBM, which in turn installed and sold PC-DOS on its computers. At the same time, Microsoft marketed and sold MS-DOS (Microsoft DOS) to makers of IBM-compatible PCs.

CATEGORIES OF OPERATING SYSTEMS

Stand-alone	• DOS • Windows 3.x • Windows 95 • Windows NT Workstation • Windows 98 • Windows 2000 Professional • Windows Millennium Edition • Mac OS • OS/2 Warp • UNIX • Linux
Network	• NetWare • Windows NT Server • Windows 2000 Server • OS/2 Warp Server for E-business • UNIX • Linux • Solaris
Embedded	• Windows CE • Pocket PC OS • Palm OS

Figure 8-18 Examples of stand-alone, network, and embedded operating systems.

DOS used a command-line interface when Microsoft first developed it. Later versions included both command-line and menu-driven user interfaces, as well as improved memory and disk management.

At its peak, DOS was a widely used operating system, with an estimated 70 million computers running it. Today, DOS no longer is widely used because it does not offer a graphical user interface (GUI) and it cannot take full advantage of modern 32-bit personal computer processors.

Windows 3.x

To meet the need for an operating system that had a GUI, Microsoft developed **Windows**. **Windows 3.x** refers to three early versions of Microsoft Windows: Windows 3.0, Windows 3.1, and Windows 3.11. These Windows 3.x versions were not operating systems. They were operating environments. An **operating environment** is a GUI that works in combination with an operating system to simplify its use. Windows 3.x was designed to work as an operating environment with DOS.

Windows 95

With **Windows 95**, Microsoft developed a true multitasking operating system — not an operating environment like early versions of Windows. Windows 95 thus did not require DOS to run. It did include, however, some DOS and Windows 3.x features to allow for downward compatibility.

One advantage of Windows 95 was its improved GUI, which made working with files and programs easier than the earlier versions. In addition, most programs ran faster under Windows 95 because it was written to take advantage of the processing speed in 32-bit processors (versus 16-bit processors). Windows 95 also included support for networking, Plug and Play technology, longer file names, and e-mail.

Windows NT Workstation

Microsoft developed **Windows NT Workstation** as a client operating system that could connect to a Windows NT Server. **Windows NT**, also referred to as **NT**, was an operating system designed for client/server networks. Windows NT Workstation had a Windows 95 interface. Thus, users familiar with Windows 95 easily could migrate to Windows NT Workstation. Businesses most often used Windows NT Workstation.

Windows 98

Microsoft developed an upgrade to the Windows 95 operating system, called Windows 98. The **Windows 98** operating system was more integrated with the Internet than Windows 95. For example, Windows 98 included Microsoft **Internet Explorer**, a popular Web browser. The Windows 98 file manager, called **Windows Explorer**, also had a Web browser look and feel. With Windows 98, you could have an **Active Desktop**™ interface, which allowed you to set up Windows so icons on the desktop and file names in Windows Explorer worked similar to Web links.

Windows 98 also provided faster system startup and shutdown, better file management, and support for multimedia technologies such as DVD and WebTV™. Windows 98 supported the Universal Serial Bus (USB) so you easily could add and remove devices on your computer.

Windows 2000 Professional

Microsoft Windows 2000 Professional is an upgrade to the Windows NT Workstation operating system. **Windows 2000 Professional** is a complete multitasking client operating system that has a GUI (Figure 8-19). Windows 2000 Professional is a reliable operating system for desktop and laptop business computers.

Windows 2000 Professional includes features of previous Windows versions (Figure 8-20). Additionally, Windows 2000 Professional includes these features:

- Windows Installer Service guides you through installation or upgrade of applications
- Windows File Protection safeguards operating system files from being overwritten during installation of applications
- Certifies device drivers to safeguard them from tampering
- Faster performance than Windows 98
- Adapts Start menu to display applications you use most frequently
- Preview multimedia files in Windows Explorer before opening them
- Enhanced technology to increase efficiency and productivity of mobile users

Windows 2000 does require more disk space, memory, and a faster processor than previous versions of Windows because its features are more complex.

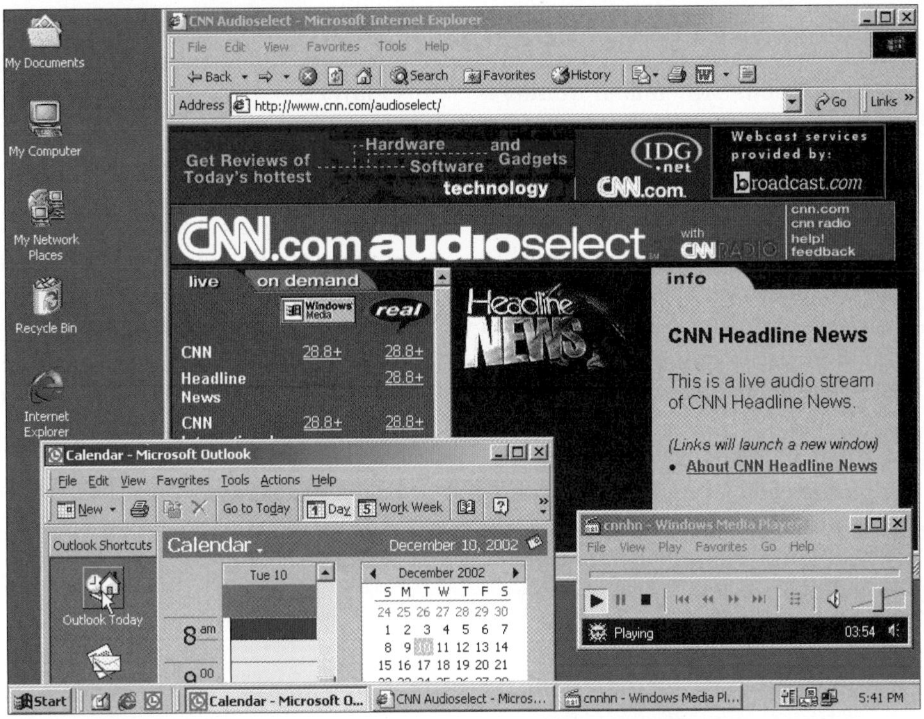

Figure 8-19 Microsoft Windows 2000 is easy to use, fast, and integrated with the Internet.

Web Link

For more information on Windows, visit the Discovering Computers 2002 Chapter 8 WEB LINK page (**scsite.com/dc2002/ch8/weblink.htm**) and click Windows.

WINDOWS FEATURES

Feature	Description
1. Active Desktop™	Active Desktop™ allows you to set up Windows so icons on the desktop and file names in Windows Explorer work like links (single-click), and create real-time windows that display television-style news or an animated ticker that provides stock updates, news, or other information.
2. Taskbar/toolbars	Several new toolbars can be added to the taskbar by right-clicking the taskbar.
3. Windows Explorer has a Web browser look and feel	Several Web browser tools have been added to Windows Explorer so your hard disk is viewed as an extension of the World Wide Web. For example, Back and Forward buttons allow you easily to revisit folders you have selected previously. A Favorites menu enables you to view quickly your favorite folders.
4. Increased speed	Faster startup and shutdown of Windows. Also, loads 32-bit applications faster.
5. Tune-Up Wizard	Makes your program run faster, checks for hard disk problems, and frees up hard disk space.
6. Multiple display support	Makes it possible for you to use several monitors at the same time to increase the size of your desktop, run different programs on separate monitors, and run programs or play games with multiple views.
7. Universal Serial Bus	Add devices to your computer easily without having to restart.
8. Accessibility Settings Wizard	Accessibility options, such as StickyKeys, ShowSounds, and MouseKeys, are Wizard designed to help users with specific disabilities make full use of the computer.
9. Update Wizard	Reviews device drivers and system software on your computer, compares findings with a master database on the Web, and then recommends and installs updates specific to your computer.
10. Registry Checker	Maintenance program that finds and fixes Registry problems.
11. FAT32	FAT32 is an improved version of the File Allocation Table (file system) that allows hard drives larger than 2 GB to be formatted as a single drive.
12. Hardware support	Supports a variety of new hardware devices, such as DVD, force-feedback joysticks, digital audio speakers, and recording devices. Improved Plug and Play capabilities make installing new hardware easy.

Figure 8-20 Most of the Windows operating systems include these features.

ISSUE

To Change or Not?

Operating Systems

At a recent technical conference, a speaker from a noted software company told an audience of IT professionals that upgrading to a new operating system would be seamless. His listeners responded with uncontrollable laughter. Adopting a new operating system seldom is easy. As a result, no matter what the benefits, people often are reluctant to give up their old operating systems. Although reviewers agree each new Windows version offers several advantages over previous versions, one of the earlier versions of the operating system, Windows 95, is still in use. Why might people be unwilling to embrace new operating system versions? How could developers hasten acceptance of a new operating system? If you generally are satisfied with your current operating system, would you upgrade? Why or why not?

For more information on operating systems and Windows, visit the Discovering Computers 2002 Issues Web page (**scsite.com/dc2002/issues.htm**) and click Chapter 8 Issue #3.

Windows Millennium Edition

Windows Millennium Edition is an upgrade to the Windows 98 operating system. **Windows Millennium Edition**, also called **Windows Me** (pronounced EM-ee), is an operating system that has features specifically for the home user (Figure 8-21). In addition to providing the capabilities in Windows 98, Windows Me offers these additional features:

- Digitize, edit, and store home movies and still photographs using Windows Movie Maker
- Easily transfer photographs from a digital camera with Windows Image Acquisition
- Listen to audio CDs or Web radio stations with Windows Media Player
- Use Windows Restore to recover previous computer settings when a problem occurs
- Deliver the latest system updates automatically to your desktop when you are connected to the Internet
- Easily set up a home network
- Use Internet Connection Sharing so that multiple members of the house can all connect to the Internet at the same time
- Send instant messages
- Use NetMeeting to have a video telephone call

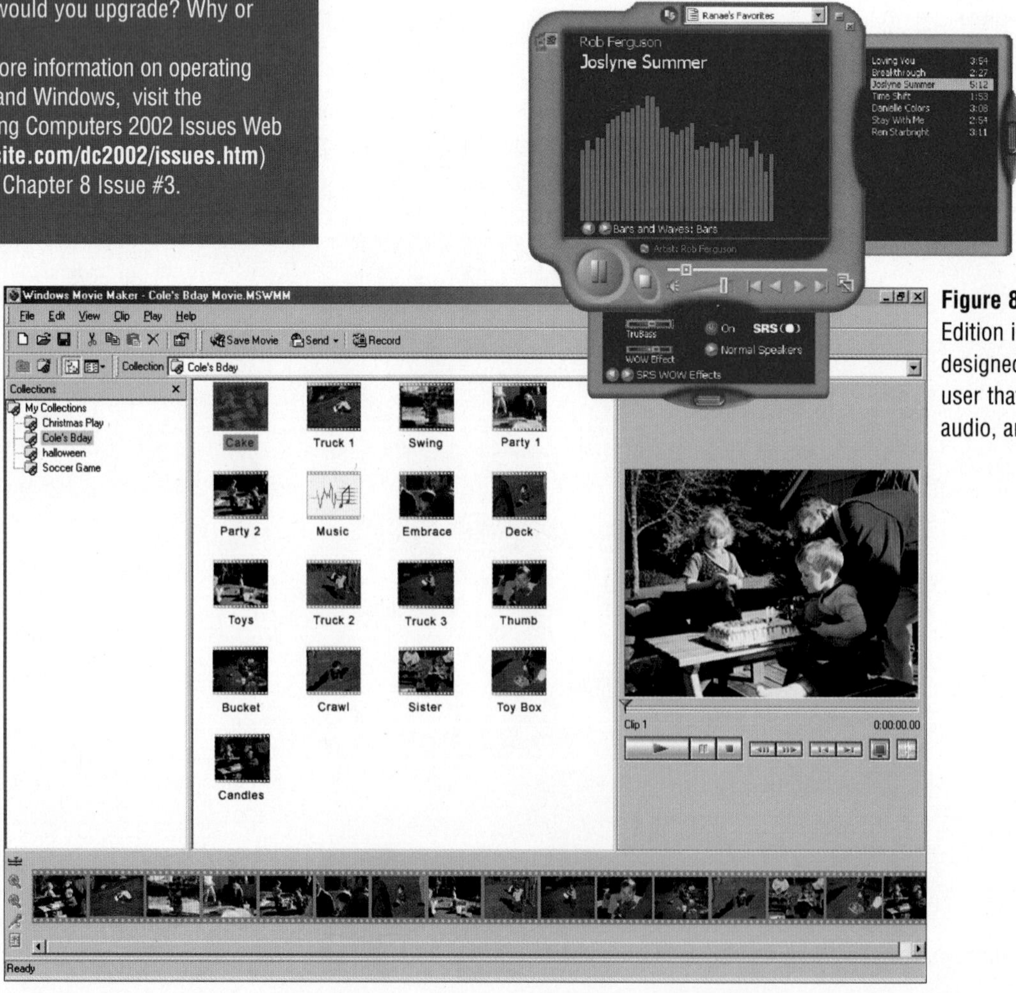

Figure 8-21 Windows Millennium Edition is an operating system designed specifically for the home user that includes many graphic, audio, and video applications.

Mac OS

Apple's **Macintosh operating system** was the first commercially successful GUI. It was released with Macintosh computers in 1984. Since then, it has set the standard for operating system ease of use and has been the model for most of the new GUIs developed for non-Macintosh systems.

Recently, Apple changed the name of the operating system from Macintosh operating system to Mac OS. **Mac OS** is a multitasking operating system available only for computers manufactured by Apple. Figure 8-22 shows a screen of the latest version of Mac OS. This version includes two popular Web browsers: Netscape Navigator and Microsoft Internet Explorer. It also has the capability of opening, editing, and saving files created using the Windows and DOS platforms. Other features of the latest version of Mac OS include large photo-quality icons, built-in networking support, electronic mail, online shopping, enhanced speech recognition, and enhanced multimedia capabilities.

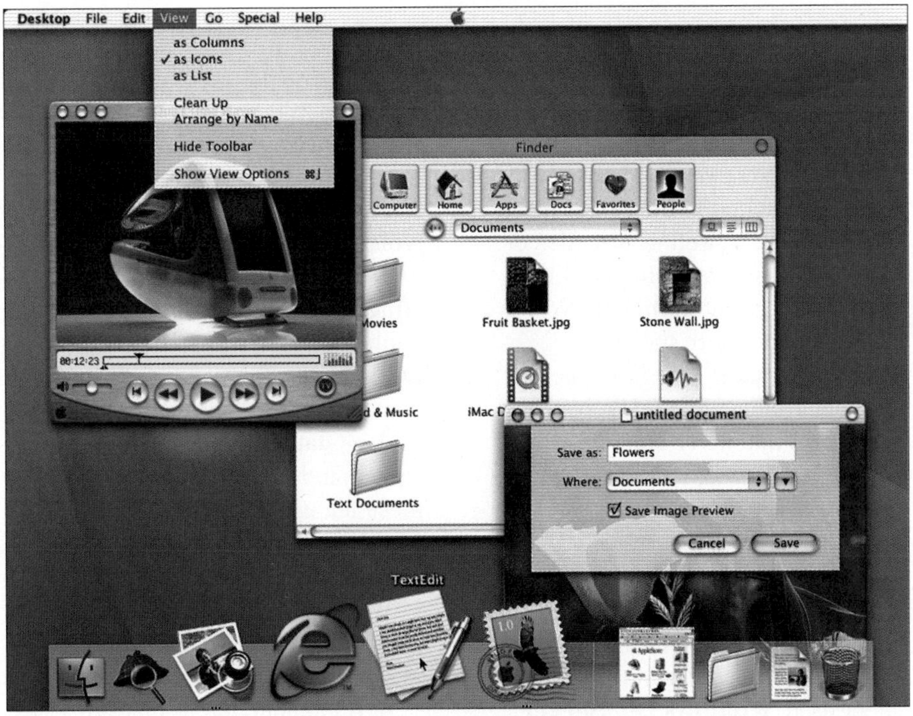

Figure 8-22 Mac OS is the operating system used with Apple Macintosh computers.

Web Link

For more information on Mac OS, visit the Discovering Computers 2002 Chapter 8 WEB LINK page (**scsite.com/dc2002/ch8/weblink.htm**) and click Mac OS.

COMPANY ON THE CUTTING EDGE

Apple Computer, Inc.

Mac OS X Introduces Technologies

Actor Richard Dreyfuss says his Apple Macintosh makes him a thousand times more productive. Humanitarian and boxing champion Muhammed Ali uses his Mac for philanthropic efforts. Comedian Sinbad would select Apple's QuickTime software if he could have only one application. These AppleMasters praise Apple's hardware and software virtues, as do millions of users in more than 120 countries.

Steven Jobs and Stephen Wozniak formed Apple in 1976 when they decided to market the Apple I, a circuit board they had developed in Jobs' garage. They incorporated one year later and introduced the Apple II, the personal computer that helped generate more than $1 billion in annual sales.

The Apple II product line was discontinued in 1993, and the following year Apple introduced the high-performance Power Macintosh line. Apple then licensed its operating system to other computer manufacturers. This decision was reversed later, however, as other manufacturers reduced Apple's market share and revenues dropped. After a series of personnel changes, Jobs became Apple's CEO. Under his direction, Apple introduced the iBook, the PowerMac G4, and the Mac OS X, which includes iTools, an Internet search feature called Sherlock, and QuickTime TV.

For more information on Apple Computers, visit the Discovering Computers 2002 Companies Web page (**scsite.com/dc2002/companies.htm**) and click Apple.

OS/2 Warp

OS/2 Warp is IBM's GUI multitasking client operating system that supports networking, the Internet, Java, and speech recognition (Figure 8-23). In addition to running programs written specifically for OS/2 (pronounced OH-ESS-too), the operating system also can run DOS and most Windows programs.

OS/2 has been used by businesses because of IBM's long association with business computing and OS/2's strong networking support.

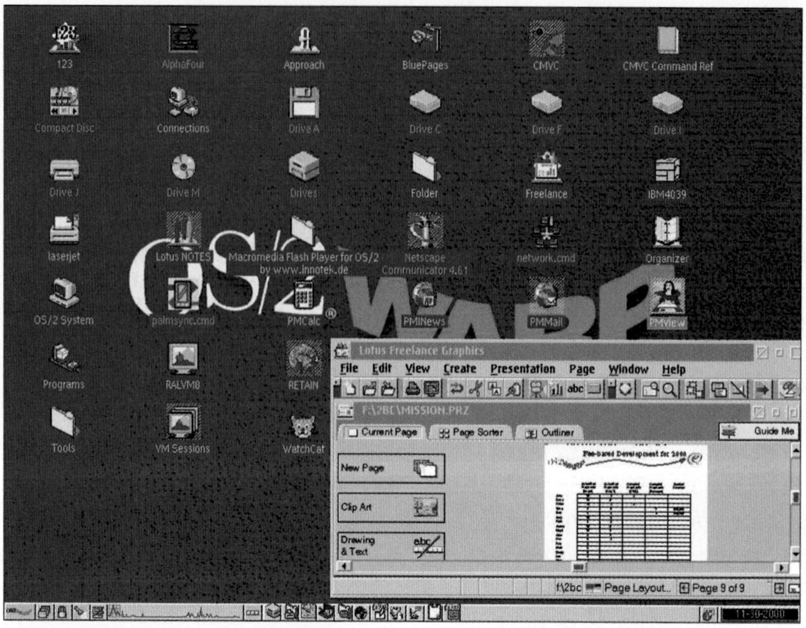

Figure 8-23 OS/2 is IBM's multitasking GUI operating system designed to work with 32-bit personal computer processors.

NETWORK OPERATING SYSTEMS

As discussed earlier in this chapter, a network operating system is an operating system that supports a network. A network operating system typically resides on a server. Recall the server is the computer that controls access to the hardware and software on the network and provides a centralized storage area for programs, data, and information. The client computers on the network rely on the server(s) for resources. Many of the client operating systems discussed in the previous section work in conjunction with a network operating system.

Examples of network operating systems include NetWare, Windows NT Server, Windows 2000 Server, OS/2 Warp Server for E-business, UNIX, Linux, and Solaris™. The following pages briefly discuss these operating systems.

NetWare

Novell's **NetWare** is a widely used network operating system designed for client/server networks. NetWare has a server portion that resides on the network server and a client portion that resides on each client computer connected to the network. The server portion of NetWare allows you to share hardware devices attached to the server (such as a printer), as well as any files or application software stored on the server. The client portion of NetWare communicates with the server. Client computers also have their own stand-alone operating system such as Windows or Mac OS.

Windows NT Server

As previously mentioned, Microsoft developed Windows NT as an operating system for client/server networks. The server in this environment used **Windows NT Server**. The client computers used Windows NT Workstation or some other stand-alone version of Windows.

Windows 2000 Server

Windows 2000 Server is an upgrade to Windows NT Server. To meet various levels of server requirements, the **Windows 2000 Server family** consists of three products: Windows 2000 Server, Windows 2000 Advanced Server, and Windows 2000 Datacenter Server. **Windows 2000 Server** is the operating system for the typical business network. **Windows 2000 Advanced Server** is an operating system designed for e-commerce applications. **Windows 2000 Datacenter Server** is best for demanding, large-scale applications such as data warehousing.

Windows 2000 Server offers these features:

- Host and manage Web sites
- Windows Distributed interNet Applications (DNA) Architecture provides a tool for easy application development across platforms
- Deliver and manage multimedia across intranets and the Internet
- Enable users to store documents in Web folders
- Manage information about network users and resources with Active Directory™
- Support clients using Windows 2000 Professional, Windows NT, Windows 98, Windows 95, Windows 3.x, Mac OS, and UNIX

OS/2 Warp Server for E-business

OS/2 Warp Server for E-business is IBM's network operating system designed for all sizes of business. Many e-commerce applications use OS/2 Warp Server for E-business. For its Web browser and e-mail program, OS/2 Warp Server for E-business includes Netscape. Clients use OS/2 Warp or some version of Windows.

UNIX

UNIX (pronounced YOU-nix) is a multitasking operating system developed in the early 1970s by scientists at Bell Laboratories. Bell Labs (a subsidiary of AT&T) was prohibited from actively promoting UNIX in the commercial marketplace because of federal regulations. Bell Labs instead licensed UNIX for a low fee to numerous colleges and universities, where UNIX obtained a wide following. UNIX was implemented on many different types of computers. After deregulation of the telephone companies in the 1980s, UNIX was licensed to many hardware and software companies.

UNIX lacks interoperability across multiple platforms. Several versions of this operating system exist, each slightly different. When you move application software from one UNIX version to another, you must rewrite some of the programs. Another weakness of UNIX is that it has a command-line interface (Figure 8-24).

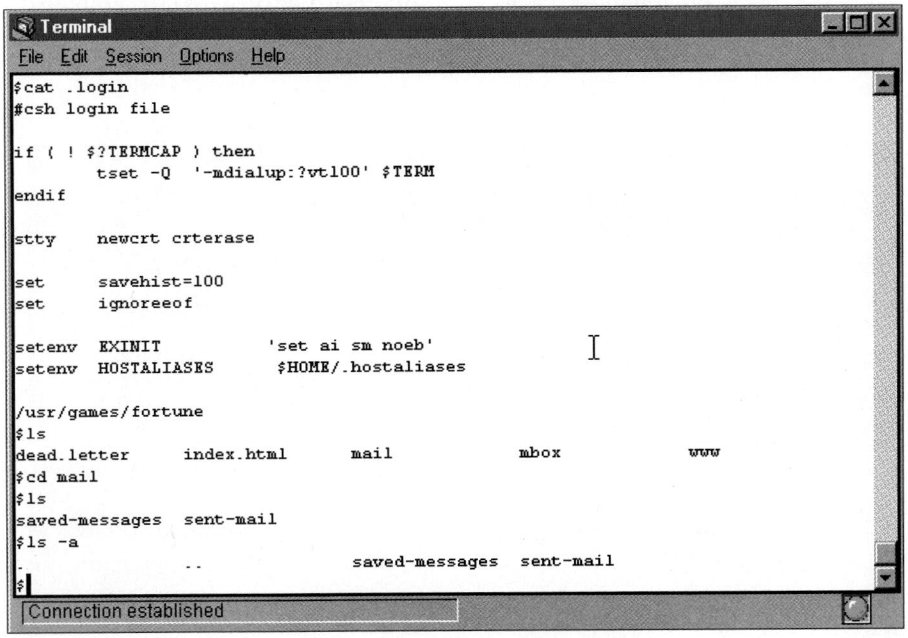

Figure 8-24 Many versions of UNIX have a command-line interface.

APPLY IT!
Desktop Shortcuts

Do you use specific programs or files frequently? If so, you may want to consider a desktop shortcut. A shortcut, which displays as an icon on your desktop, is a special type of file that points to a program or file. Shortcuts allow you to open quickly a Windows object without accessing its permanent location within Windows Explorer. Double-click the icon the same as you double-click a file name.

Follow these steps to create a desktop shortcut to a program or file:

1. Point to an open area on the desktop and then right-click to display a shortcut menu.
2. Point to New and then click Shortcut to display the Create Shortcut wizard.
3. Click the Browse button and then locate the program or file to which you want to create a shortcut.
4. Click the Open (or OK) button and then click the Next button.
5. Type a name for the shortcut and then click the Finish button.

To create a desktop shortcut to other objects (such as a folder), follow these steps:

1. Use My Computer or Windows Explorer to locate the object to which you want to create a shortcut.
2. Right-click the object, and then point to Send To.
3. Click Desktop (create shortcut).

To change the shortcut's name, right-click the shortcut and then click Rename. To delete a shortcut, drag it to the Recycle Bin. This deletes the shortcut, but the original item still exists on the computer.

For more information on creating shortcuts and links to Windows operating systems, visit the Discovering Computers 2002 Apply It Web page (**scsite.com/dc2002/apply.htm**) and click Chapter 8 Apply It #1.

Web Link

For more information on Novell, visit the Discovering Computers 2002 Chapter 8 WEB LINK page (**scsite.com/dc2002/ch8/weblink.htm**) and click Novell.

Many of the UNIX commands are difficult to remember and use. To help reduce this problem, some versions of UNIX offer a GUI.

Today, a version of UNIX is available for most computers of all sizes. Power users often work with UNIX because of its flexibility and power. In addition to being a stand-alone operating system, UNIX also is a network operating system. That is, UNIX is capable of handling a high volume of transactions in a multiuser environment and working with multiple processors using multiprocessing. Some call UNIX a **multipurpose operating system** because it is both a stand-alone and network operating system.

Linux

Linux is one of the fastest growing operating systems. **Linux** (pronounced LINN-uks) is a popular, free, multitasking UNIX-type operating system. In addition to the basic operating system, Linux also includes many programming languages — all for free.

Linux is not proprietary software like the operating systems discussed thus far. Instead, Linux is **open-source software**, which means its code is available to the public. Based on UNIX, many programmers have donated time to make Linux the best possible version of UNIX. Promoters of open-source software state two main advantages: users that modify the software share their improvements with others, and customers can personalize the software to meet their needs.

Some versions of Linux are command-line. Others are GUI. The two most popular GUIs available for Linux are GNOME and KDE.

You can obtain Linux in a variety of ways. You can download it from the Web free of charge. Many Linux books include a CD-ROM containing Linux. Some vendors sell a CD-ROM version of Linux. If you are purchasing a new computer, some retailers will pre-install Linux on the hard disk. Some companies market software applications that run on their own version of Linux. Figure 8-25 shows Red Hat Linux's GNOME graphical user interface.

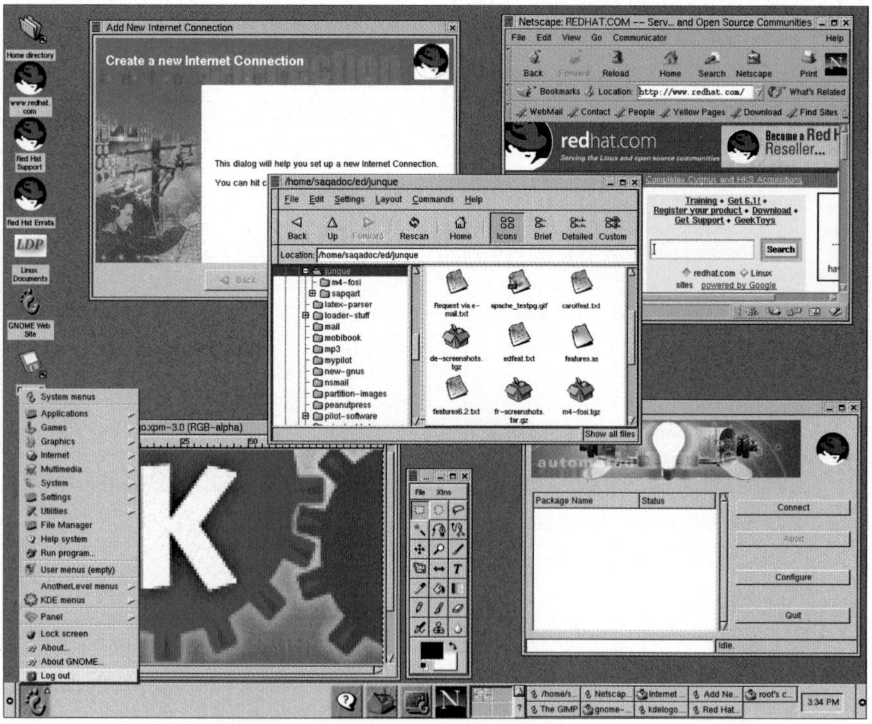

Figure 8-25 Red Hat provides a version of Linux called Red Hat Linux. Shown here is the GNOME graphical user interface.

PRODUCT ON THE CUTTING EDGE

LiNUX.

Users Embrace Free Operating System

Linux belongs to everybody, according to its creator, Linus Torvalds. Although he owns the trademark for the name and is in charge of development, a large, friendly community distributes the operating system. These individuals are driven to offer an alternative to Microsoft Windows and Apple Mac OS, and they have an extensive number of user groups, mailing lists, newsletters, and forums.

Linux' GNU General Public License allows anyone to obtain and modify the source code and then redistribute the revised product. Torvalds encourages this creativity and productivity, believing that the refinements ultimately stimulate more interest in the product and increase its popularity.

He admits he is not opposed to commercial software because the revenue it generates helps support the development of new incentives that help create a polished product, which most free software does not have. For example, commercial software packages — especially word processing — usually have a better user interface than free software does. But many Linux applications and games are available.

For more information on Linux, visit the Discovering Computers 2002 Companies Web page (**scsite.com/dc2002/companies.htm**) and click Linux.

Solaris

Solaris™, a version of UNIX developed by Sun Microsystems, is a network operating system designed specifically for e-commerce applications. Solaris™ can manage high-traffic accounts and incorporate security necessary for Web transactions. Client computers use a version of Solaris™, called CDE (Common Desktop Environment), that specifically works with the Solaris™ operating system.

EMBEDDED OPERATING SYSTEMS

The operating system on most handheld computers and small devices, called an **embedded operating system**, resides on a ROM chip. Popular embedded operating systems include Windows CE, Pocket PC OS, and Palm OS. The following pages discuss these operating systems.

Windows CE

Windows CE is a scaled-down Windows operating system designed for use on wireless communications devices and smaller computers such as handheld computers, in-vehicle devices, and Web-enabled devices. On most of these devices, the Windows CE interface incorporates many elements of the Windows GUI. The operating system also supports color, sound, multitasking, e-mail, and Internet capabilities. Many applications, such as Microsoft Word and Microsoft Excel, have scaled-down versions that run with Windows CE.

Web Link

For more information on UNIX, visit the Discovering Computers 2002 Chapter 8 WEB LINK page (**scsite.com/dc2002/ch8/weblink.htm**) and click UNIX.

TECHNOLOGY TRAILBLAZER

LINUS **TORVALDS**

Free is good, in the mind of Linus Torvalds and the millions of people who benefit from his free operating system, Linux.

The software's roots began when Torvalds was a student in Finland and began writing an operating system for a study he was performing. He believes that Finland's high level of technology and superior educational system gave him the advantages of being able to concentrate on his brainstorm instead of worrying about economic issues.

Today he considers himself the operating system's lead technical developer and still spends time writing code. Due to Linux' success, however, he now has to delegate tasks and spend more time answering e-mail messages and coordinating work efforts. He knows that everyone agrees that he is in charge and is solely responsible for project management, setting milestones, and making radical decisions.

Torvalds states that he does not worry about the future of Linux and that it will continue to be refined. His sole long-range plan is to improve the software.

For more information on Linus Torvalds, visit the Discovering Computers 2002 People Web page (**scsite.com/dc2002/people.htm**) and click Linus Torvalds.

ISSUE

UNIX versus Windows

Choosing an Operating System

A question that confronts the IT management, individuals, and companies worldwide when upgrading computers is "What operating system should we select?" Price is certainly a consideration. Determining price, however, includes the original operating system cost, maintenance, and upgrade. Microsoft Windows definitely has the edge as far as the most widely used and popular operating system. UNIX, which includes a family of operating systems such as Linux, AIX, OpenBSD, and others, is a free open-source program. UNIX is a mature system, developed in the early 1970s, long before Microsoft even existed. Why then, would a company select Microsoft instead of UNIX or one of the operating systems from the UNIX family? Which one would you select? Why? Is Microsoft a better operating system than UNIX? What operating system factors would you consider when purchasing a new personal computer? Would you buy a computer with a UNIX-based operating system?

For more information on operating systems and upgrading operating systems, visit the Discovering Computers 2002 Issues Web page (**scsite.com/dc2002/issues.htm**) and click Chapter 8 Issue #4.

The **Auto PC** is a device mounted onto a vehicle's dashboard that is powered by Windows CE (Figure 8-26). Using an automobile equipped with Auto PC, the driver can obtain information such as driving directions, traffic conditions, weather, and stock quotes; access and listen to e-mail; listen to the radio or an audio CD; and share information with a handheld or notebook computer. The Auto PC is ideal for the mobile user because it is directed through voice commands.

Pocket PC OS

Pocket PC OS is a scaled-down operating system developed by Microsoft that works on a specific type of handheld computer, called a **Pocket PC** (Figure 8-27). With this operating system and a Pocket PC device, you have access to all the basic PIM functions such as contact lists, schedules, tasks, calendars, and notes. These devices also provide many other features. For example, you can check e-mail, browse the Web, listen to music, send and receive instant messages, record a voice message, manage your finances, read an e-book, or create a word processing document or spreadsheet. These devices also support handwriting recognition.

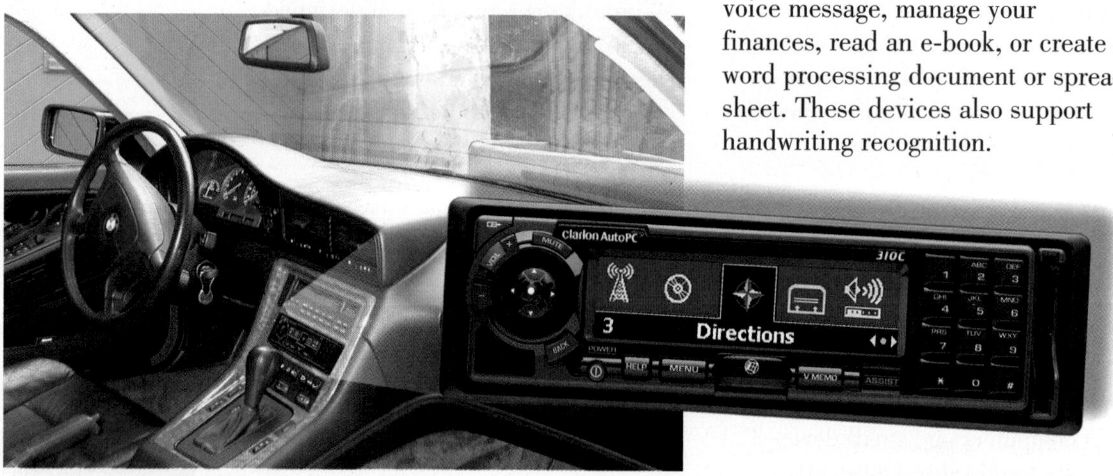

Figure 8-26 Auto PC is powered by Windows CE.

APPLY IT!

Pocket PC OS versus Palm OS

You are ready to purchase a handheld computer. Next is the difficult part — which operating system to choose. The Palm OS® currently runs on many handheld computers, including all Palms, PalmPilots, and Handspring™ Visors. Microsoft's Pocket PC, however, is creating stiff competition. To make a decision, you first must evaluate your own personal needs and then determine which OS is for you. Some features you may want to consider are as follows:

- Your use as a student may be to take notes, keep track of your class schedule, play music, and play games.
- For business needs, you may need to keep a contact list, an appointment schedule, and keep in touch with clients via e-mail.
- For personal use, you may want to keep track of birthdays, maintain a list of addresses, keep a calendar, and access news.

After establishing your goals, your next step is to compare the two operating systems and determine which one has the features that best meet your needs. Some features to consider in your comparison are as follows:

- Ease of use
- Synchronizing with your personal computer
- Application availability (calendar, games, notes, appointments, music, e-mail, contacts, and so on.)
- Price
- Color display
- Battery life

For more information and links to Palm OS and Pocket PC, visit the Discovering Computers 2002 Apply It Web page (**scsite.com/dc2002/apply.htm**) and click Chapter 8 Apply It #2.

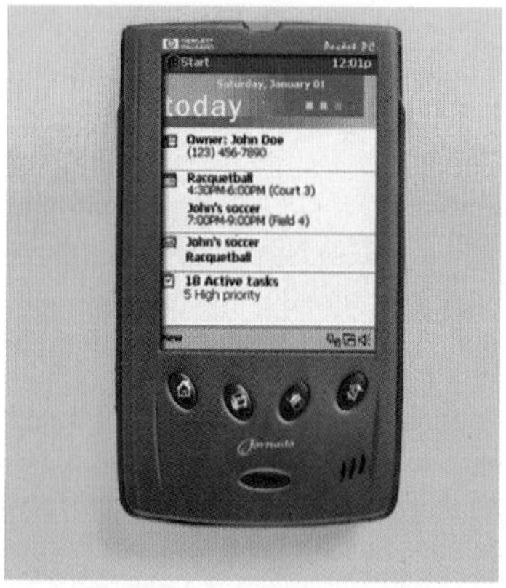

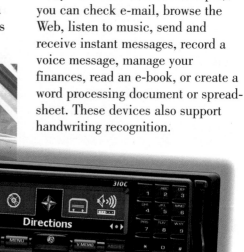

Figure 8-27 The Pocket PC OS runs on any Pocket PC device.

Palm OS

The Palm handheld computers from Palm, Inc., and Visor handheld computers from Handspring™ use an operating system called **Palm OS®**. With this operating system and a compatible handheld computer, you can manage schedules and contacts and easily synchronize this information with a desktop computer. With some handheld computers, you also have wireless access to the Internet and your e-mail. These handheld computers contain handwriting recognition software, called Graffiti®. They also have software that allows you to manage many different types of information such as telephone messages, project notes, reminders, task and address lists, and important dates and appointments.

UTILITY PROGRAMS

A **utility program**, also called a **utility**, is a type of system software that performs a specific task, usually related to managing a computer, its devices, or its programs. Most operating systems include several utility programs. You also can buy stand-alone utilities that offer improvements over those included with the operating system.

Some vendors offer **utility suites** that combine several utility programs into a single package. Others offer Web-based utility services. To use a **Web-based utility service**, you usually pay an annual fee that allows you to access and use the vendor's utility programs on the Web. McAfee and Norton offer utility suites and Web-based utility services.

Popular utility programs offer these functions: viewing files, compressing files, diagnosing problems, uninstalling software, scanning disks, defragmenting disks, backing up files and disks, and displaying screen savers. The following paragraphs briefly discuss each of these utilities.

File Viewer

A **file viewer** is a utility that allows you to display and copy the contents of a file. An operating system's file manager often includes a file viewer. For example, Windows Explorer has a viewer called **Imaging Preview** that displays the contents of graphics files (Figure 8-28). The title bar of the file viewer window displays the name of the file being viewed.

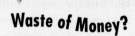

ISSUE

Waste of Money?

Utility Programs

Most operating systems include a number of utility programs. On the other hand, private companies have developed utility programs to meet user needs. One new utility helps guard against computer theft by making a weekly silent call to a control center. If the call emanates from an appropriate number, the call is logged. If the computer has been reported stolen, however, the center traces the call to locate the missing computer. Should operating systems include these types of features? Many popular operating systems include basic utilities. Why then is there a proliferation of utility programs such as PC Tools and Norton Utilities? Is purchasing one of these utilities a waste of money? Should they be sold separately or be part of the operating system? What other needs could be addressed by a utility program? If you marketed the utility program, what would you call it?

For more information on utility programs and operating systems, visit the Discovering Computers 2002 Issues Web page (**scsite.com/dc2002/issues.htm**) and click Chapter 8 Issue #5.

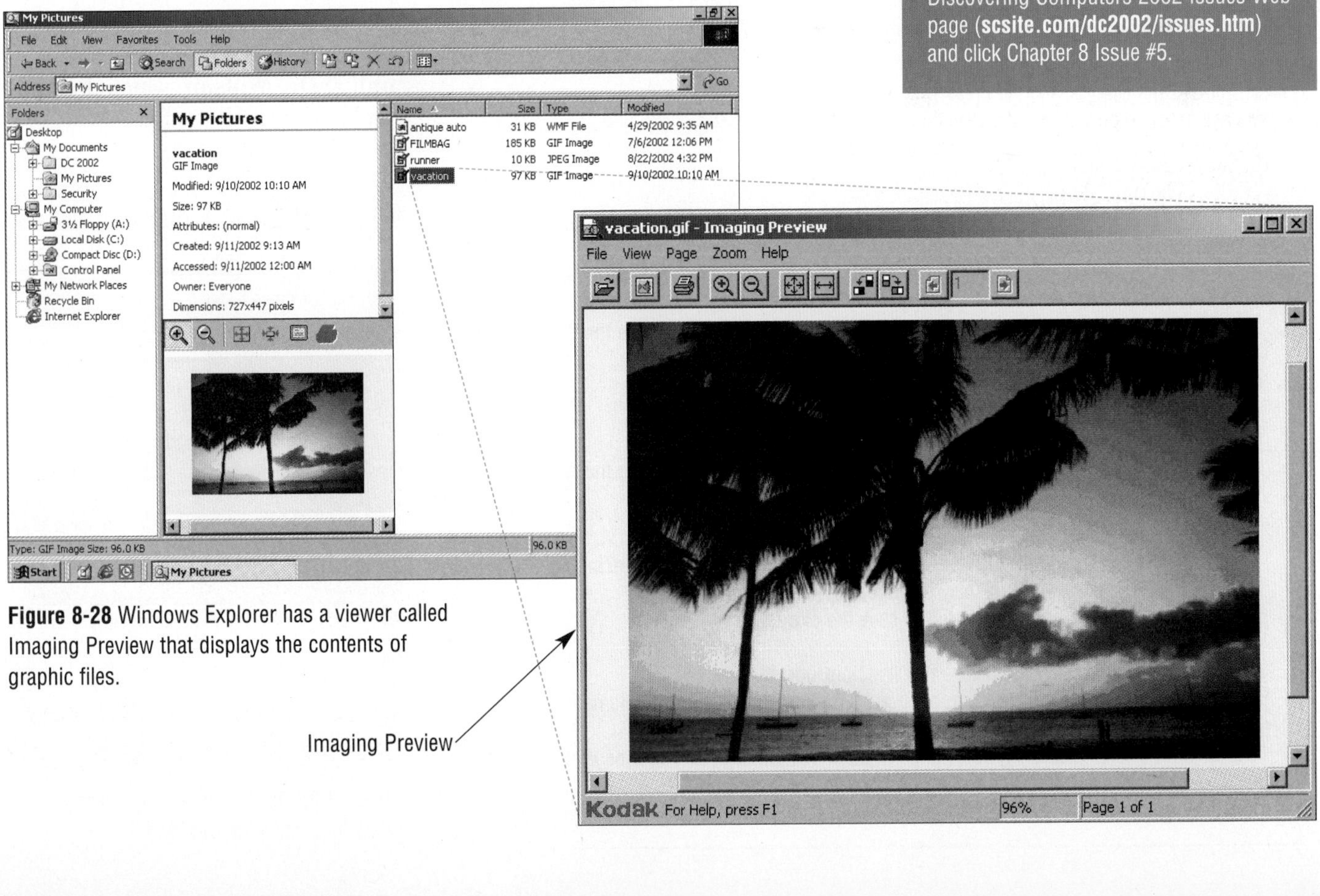

Figure 8-28 Windows Explorer has a viewer called Imaging Preview that displays the contents of graphic files.

File Compression

A **file compression utility** shrinks the size of a file. A compressed file takes up less storage space than the original file. Compressing files frees up room on the storage media and improves system performance. Attaching a compressed file to an e-mail message reduces the time needed for file transmission. Uploading and downloading compressed files to and from the Internet reduces the file transmission time.

Compressed files, sometimes called **zipped files**, usually have a .zip extension. When you receive or download a compressed file, you must uncompress it. To **uncompress**, or **unzip**, a file, you restore it to its original form. Two popular stand-alone file compression utilities are PKZIP™ and WinZip® (Figure 8-29).

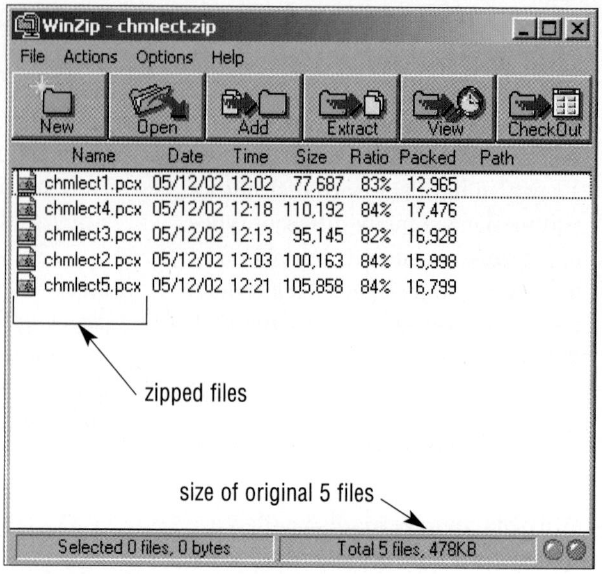

Figure 8-29 WinZip® is a popular stand-alone file compression utility. This zipped file (chmlect) contains 5 files. Without being zipped, these files consume 478 KB. Zipping the files reduced the amount of storage to 79 KB.

APPLY IT!

File Compression – Zipped Files

You may have received an e-mail file attachment or downloaded a file with a .zip extension. The .zip extension indicates the file has been compressed. People use file compression to reduce the size of a file, to combine several files and/or folders into a single file, and to reduce Internet download/upload time.

One of the most popular Windows file compression programs is WinZip. Because WinZip is shareware, you can download an evaluation copy.

Downloading and installing WinZip:
1. Access the WinZip Web site (see URL below).
2. Follow the instructions at the WinZip Web site to download and install the program.

Compressing a group of files:
1. Start WinZip.
2. Click I Agree when the Licensing Agreement displays.
3. Click the New button to display the New Archive dialog box.
4. Click the box arrow to the right of the Create text box and then select the folder in which you wish to save the zipped file.
5. In the File name text box, type the name of the zipped file. Do not type the extension .zip.
6. Click the OK button to display the Add dialog box.
7. If necessary, change folders and then select the files you wish to add.
8. Click the Add button.
9. You can add additional files from the same or other folders by clicking the Add button again.

To unzip or decompress a zipped file:
1. Start Windows Explorer and double-click the file name. This starts WinZip.
2. Click the Extract button to display the Extract dialog box.
3. Select the folder in which you wish to save the extracted file(s).
4. Click the Extract button.
5. After the files are extracted, close the WinZip program.

Note: After Step 1, if you want to open a single file, double-click the file name instead of clicking the Extract button.

For more information on WinZip, links to other WinZip tutorials, and the Web site mentioned above, visit the Discovering Computers 2002 Apply It Web page (**scsite.com/dc2002/apply.htm**) and click Chapter 8 Apply It #3.

Diagnostic Utility

A **diagnostic utility** compiles technical information about your computer's hardware and certain system software programs and then prepares a report outlining any identified problems. For example, Windows includes the diagnostic utility, **Dr. Watson**, which diagnoses problems as well as suggests courses of action (Figure 8-30).

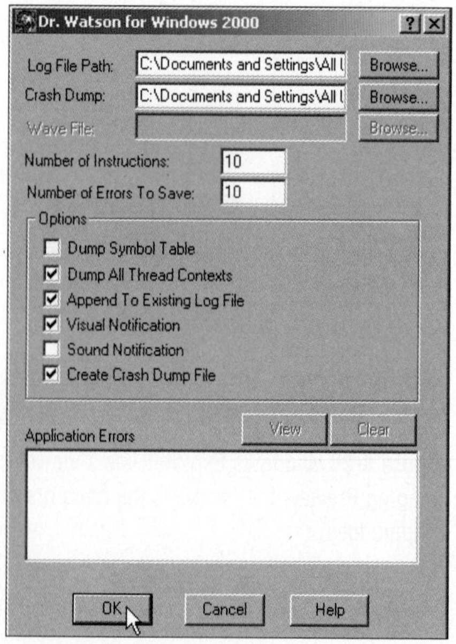

Figure 8-30 Dr. Watson is a diagnostic utility included with Windows.

Uninstaller

An **uninstaller** is a utility that removes an application, as well as any associated entries in the system files (Figure 8-31). When you install an application, the operating system records the information it uses to run the software in the system files. The system file entries will remain, if you attempt to remove the application from your computer by deleting the files and folders associated with the program without running the uninstaller. Most operating systems include an uninstaller. You also can purchase a stand-alone program, such as McAfee's UnInstaller.

Disk Scanner

A **disk scanner** is a utility that (1) detects and corrects both physical and logical problems on a hard disk or floppy disk and (2) searches for and removes unnecessary files. A physical problem is one with the media such as a scratch on the surface of the disk. A logical problem is one with the data, such as a corrupted file allocation table (FAT). Windows includes two disk scanner utilities. One detects problems and the other searches for and removes unnecessary files such as temporary files (Figure 8-32).

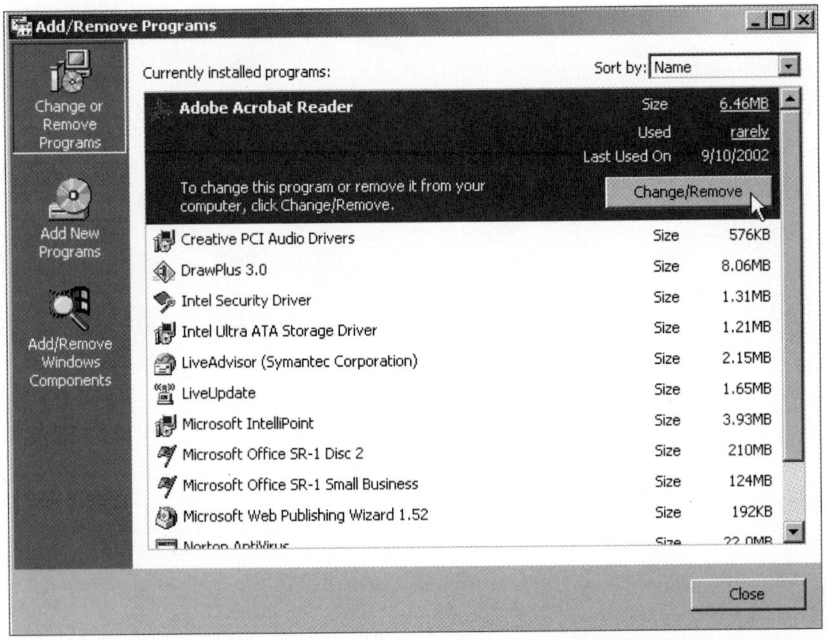

Figure 8-31 An uninstaller removes software applications and associated system file entries from your hard disk.

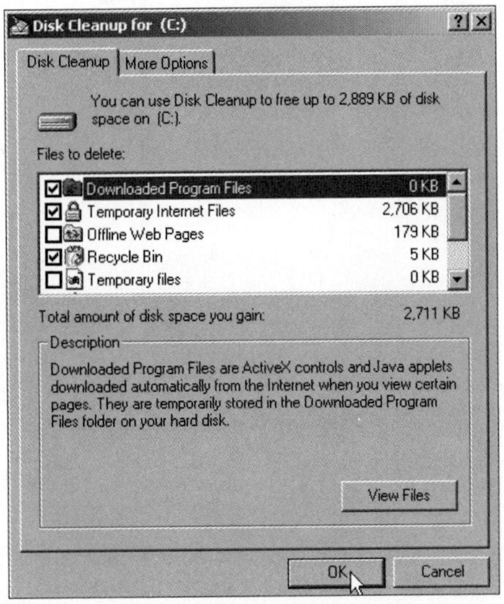

Figure 8-32 Disk Cleanup searches for and removes unnecessary files.

TECHNOLOGY TRAILBLAZER

PHILLIP **KATZ**

It happens every time you are packing for your vacation: you have too much stuff crammed in your suitcase, and you cannot close the zipper. Phillip Katz had a similar problem: too much stuff to cram onto a floppy disk. He decided to do something about this situation and developed PKZIP, using his initials as the first letters in the software's name.

As a high school student in suburban Milwaukee, Katz was brilliant and creative. He was enrolled in advanced math and physics classes and participated on the math team.

Six years after graduation, he quit his job as a software design engineer and started his business, PKWARE, with his mother at their kitchen table.

The innovative PKZIP shareware cornered the data compression market, and PKWARE has steady annual sales of $5 million. This success, however, was not enough to fulfill Katz' life. He lived his life alone and as a transient, never attending computer conferences or lectures and losing contact with his mother. He died unexpectedly in 2000 at the young age of 37.

For more information on Phillip Katz, visit the Discovering Computers 2002 People Web page (**scsite.com/dc2002/people.htm**) and click Phillip Katz.

Disk Defragmenter

A **disk defragmenter** is a utility that reorganizes the files and unused space on a computer's hard disk so the operating system can access data more quickly and programs can run faster. When an operating system stores data on a disk, it places the data in the first available sector on the disk. Although it attempts to place data in sectors that are contiguous (next to each other), this is not always possible. When the contents of a file are scattered across two or more noncontiguous sectors, the file is **fragmented**. Fragmentation slows down disk access and thus the performance of the entire computer. **Defragmenting** the disk, or reorganizing it so the files are stored in contiguous sectors, solves this problem (Figure 8-33). Windows includes a disk defragmenter, called **Disk Defragmenter**.

Backup Utility

A **backup utility** allows you to copy, or backup, selected files or your entire hard disk onto another disk or tape. During the backup process, the backup utility monitors progress and alerts you if it needs additional disks or tapes. Many backup programs will compress files during this process, so the backup files require less storage space than the original files.

For this reason, you usually cannot use backup files in their backed up form. In the event you need to use one of these files, a **restore program** reverses the process and returns backed up files to their original form. Backup utilities include restore programs.

You should back up files and disks regularly in the event your originals are lost, damaged, or destroyed. Windows includes a backup utility (Figure 8-34). Some users opt to back up their files to an Internet hard drive. As described in Chapter 7, an Internet hard drive, sometimes called online storage, is a service on the Web that provides storage to computer users.

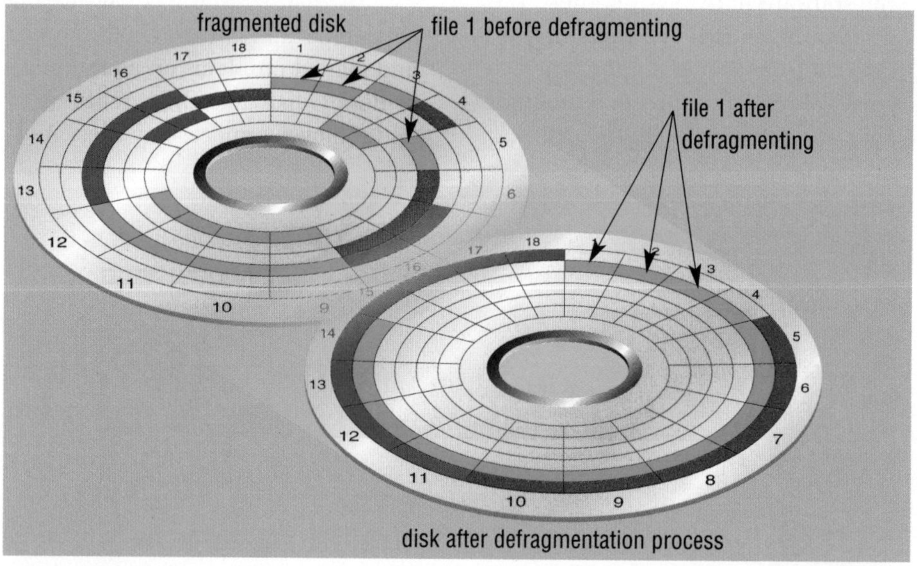

Figure 8-33 A fragmented disk has many files stored in noncontiguous sectors. Defragmenting reorganizes the files, so they are located in contiguous sectors, which speeds access time.

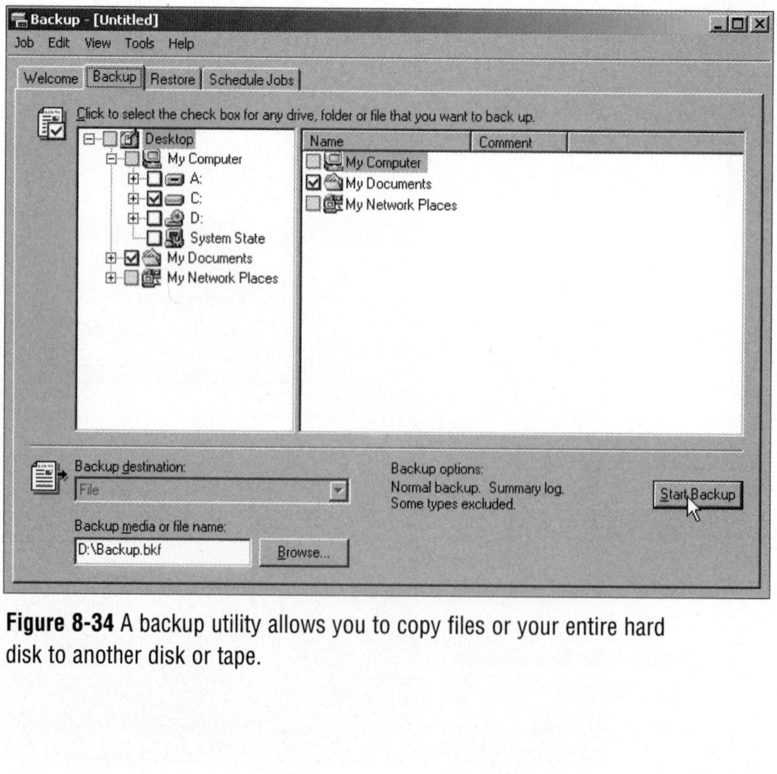

Figure 8-34 A backup utility allows you to copy files or your entire hard disk to another disk or tape.

Screen Saver

A **screen saver** is a utility that causes a monitor's screen to display a moving image or blank screen if no keyboard or mouse activity occurs for a specified time period (Figure 8-35). When you press a key on the keyboard or move the mouse, the screen returns to the previously displayed image.

Screen savers originally were developed to prevent a problem called **ghosting**, in which images could be permanently etched on a monitor's screen. Ghosting is not a problem with today's monitors. Still, screen savers are popular for security, business, or entertainment purposes. To secure a computer, you can configure your screen saver so a user must enter a password to stop the screen saver and redisplay the previous image. Some screen savers use push technology, enabling you to receive updated and new information each time the screen saver displays. As described in Chapter 2, push technology occurs when Web-based content downloads automatically to your computer at a regular interval or whenever the Web site updates.

An operating system often includes several screen savers. You also can purchase screen savers or download them from the Web.

CHAPTER SUMMARY

This chapter defined an operating system and then discussed the functions common to most operating systems. The chapter also presented a variety of stand-alone operating systems, network operating systems, and embedded operating systems. Finally, the chapter discussed several utility programs used with today's personal computers.

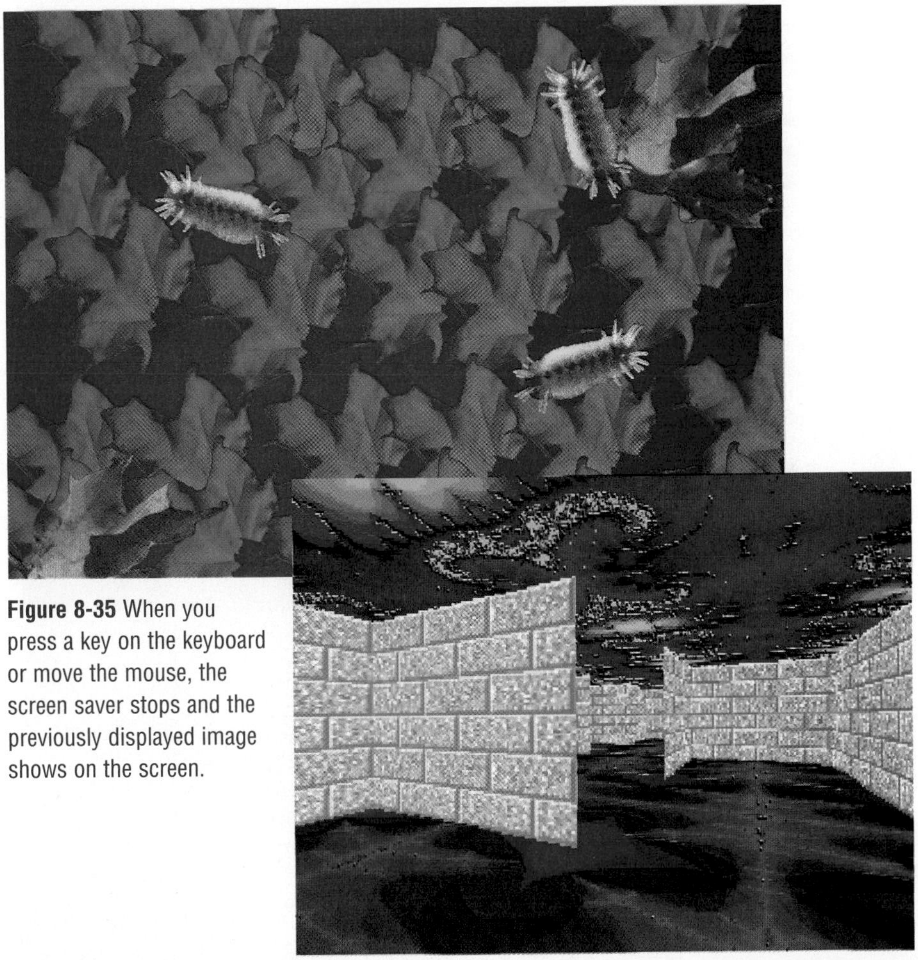

Figure 8-35 When you press a key on the keyboard or move the mouse, the screen saver stops and the previously displayed image shows on the screen.

Network Administrator

Networking professionals are in high demand. A network administrator (NA) must have a thorough knowledge of operating system software and generally has a multi-function position. Some of the tasks an NA may be asked to complete are as follows:

- Ensure servers and workstations function properly
- Implement system backups, upgrades, and security policies
- Identify and resolve connectivity issues
- Install and maintain software on clients and servers
- Perform support of network hardware components such as terminals, servers, hubs, and routers
- Participate in technical group projects to provide networking related support and keep abreast of new developments in networking, systems, and office automation technologies
- Suggest new solutions to increase network productivity

Many network administrators have some type of networking certification, which is the first step in establishing a career as a networking professional. Some of the more popular of these certifications include Microsoft Certified System Engineer (MCSE) (see URL below), Certified Novell Engineer (CNE) (see URL below), and Cisco Certified Network Associate (CCNA) (see URL below).

Salaries within these positions vary greatly and are based on job responsibilities. Those individuals with certifications, however, can expect an approximate starting salary between $35,000 to $75,000.

To learn more about the field of a network administrator as a career and the Web sites mentioned above, visit the Discovering Computers 2002 Careers Web page (**scsite.com/dc2002/careers.htm**) and click Network Administrator.

E-WEATHER E-SPORTS E-NEWS

WHAT'S NEWS?

Weather, Sports, and News Web Sites Score Big Hits

Rain or sun? Hot or cold? Do you toss a coin to determine tomorrow's forecast? Or, do you study weather maps displayed on television and Internet sites? The world seems neatly divided into these two camps, with Web sites such as The Weather Channel (Figure 8-36) receiving more than 10 million hits each day. Weather is the leading online news item, with at least 10,000 Web sites devoted to this field. A few of the more popular Web sites are listed in Figure 8-37. A multitude of news, sports, and weather Web sites resides on the Internet.

Baseball may be the national pastime, but sports aficionados yearn for major league football, basketball, and hockey along with everything from auto racing to cricket. Although television has four major networks and two live, 24-hour all-sports channels, these media outlets do not provide enough action to quench the thirst of fans across the globe. The Internet fills this void with such Web sites as CBS SportsLine.com (Figure 8-38), with more than one million pages of multimedia sports news, entertainment, and merchandise, and Sports.com, which covers rugby, cricket, Formula One racing, tennis, and golf. CBS SportsLine.com creates the official Major League Football and the PGA Tour Web sites and provides content for America Online, Netscape, and Excite.

Olympics fans are hungry for sports action, results, and athlete profiles. The biggest event ever delivered on the Internet was the 2000 Olympic Games in Sydney, Australia. The official Olympics Web site received more than 6.5 billion hits during the 17-day event. That number is 10 times the number of Internet visitors at the 1998 Nagano Winter Olympic Games Web site.

Figure 8-36 Local, national, and international weather conditions, along with details on breaking weather stories, are available on The Weather Channel Web pages.

REPORTING WEB SITES	URL
Weather	
Information Please Weather Page	infoplease.com/weather.html
STORMFax®	stormfax.com
The Weather Channel	weather.com
Weatherplanner	weatherplanner.com
Wx.com	wx.com
Sports	
Athletes Direct	athletesdirect.com
CBS SportsLine	cbs.sportsline.com
ESPN.com	espn.com
Halife E-Sports	halife.com/sports/esports.html
Live Internet Sports Radio Stations	www.csi.ukns.com/radios.html
Todays Sports	todayssports.com
Sports.com	sports.com
News	
APBnews	apbnews.com
MSNBC	msnbc.com
New York Post	newyorkpost.com
Online Newspapers	onlinenewspapers.com
Silicon Valley News	mercurycenter.com/svtech/news
Starting Page Best News Sites	startingpage.com/html/news.html
The Washington Post	washingtonpost.com
The Web Cowboy	thewebcowboy.com

For an updated list of reporting Web sites, visit scsite.com/dc2002/e-rev.htm.

Figure 8-37 Numerous weather, sports, and news Web sites reside on the Internet.

The IBM-run Web site also permitted fans to send e-mail to the 10,500 competitors.

The Internet has emerged as a major source for news, with one-third of Americans going online at least once a week and 15 percent going online daily for reports of major news events. These viewers, who tend to be under the age of 50 and college graduates, are attracted to the Internet's flashy headline format, immediacy, and in-depth reports.

Users are attracted to Web news sites that have a corresponding print or television presence. MSNBC, CNN, ABC News, *USA TODAY*, *The Washington Post*, and *The New York Times* are among the more popular Internet news destinations. The technology content in the Silicon Valley News Web site (Figure 8-39) and crime, justice, and safety news in APBnews.com appeal to users.

For more information on weather, sports, and news sites, visit the Discovering Computers 2002 E-Revolution Web page (scsite.com/dc2002/e-rev.htm) and click Weather, Sports, and News.

Figure 8-38 Sports fans can catch the latest scores and player profiles on sports Web sites.

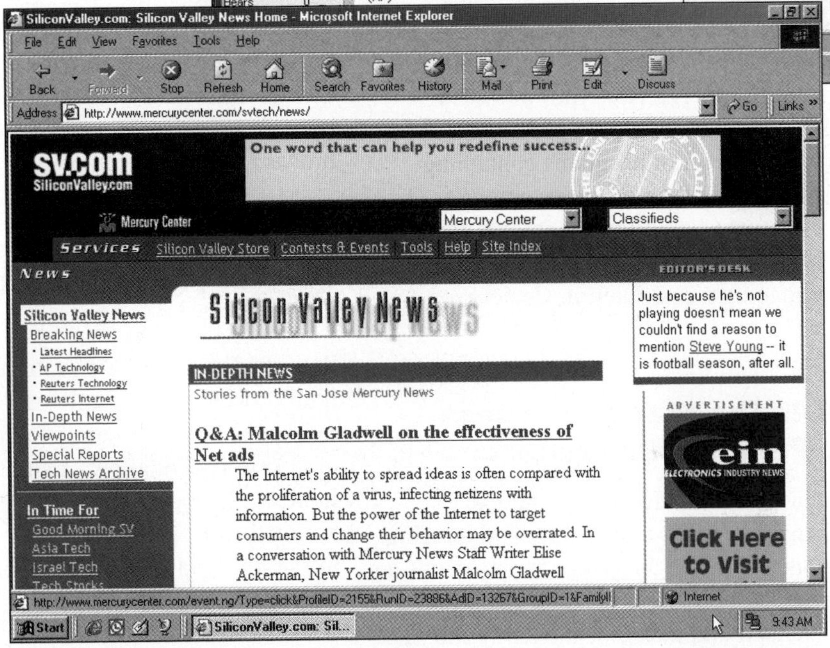

Figure 8-39 The Silicon Valley News Web site posts feature stories with details on the ever-changing world of technology.

e-REVOLUTION E-WEATHER E-SPORTS E-NEWS *applied:*

1. Visit two of the weather Web sites listed in the table in Figure 8-37. Do they contain the same local and five-day forecasts for your city? What similarities and differences do they have in coverage of a national weather story? Next visit two of the sports Web sites in the table and write a paragraph describing the content these Web sites provide concerning your favorite sport.

2. Visit the Online Newspapers and Starting Page Best News Sites Web sites listed in Figure 8-37 and select two newspapers from each site. Write a paragraph describing the top national news story featured in each of these four Web pages. Then, write another paragraph describing the top international news story displayed at each Web site. In the third paragraph, discuss which of the four Web sites is the most interesting in terms of story selection, photographs, and Web page design.

In Summary

Web Instructions: To display this page from the Web, start your browser and enter the URL scsite.com/dc2002/ch8/summary.htm. Click the links for current and additional information. To listen to an audio version of this In Summary, click the Audio button. To play the audio, RealPlayer must be installed on your computer (download by clicking here).

1 What Are the Two Types of System Software?

System software consists of the programs that control the operations of the computer and its devices. System software performs a variety of functions, such as running applications and storing files, and serves as the interface between a user, the application software, and the computer's hardware. The two types of system software are operating systems and utility programs. An operating system (OS) is a set of programs containing instructions to coordinate all of the activities among computer hardware resources. A utility program is a type of system software that performs a specific task, usually related to managing a computer, its devices, or its programs.

2 What Is the Startup Process for a Personal Computer?

Starting a computer involves loading an operating system into memory — a process called **booting**. When the computer is turned on, the power supply sends an electrical signal to devices located in the system unit. The processor chip resets itself and looks for the ROM chip that contains the **BIOS (basic input/output system)**, which is firmware that holds the startup instructions. The BIOS executes the power-on self test (POST) to make sure hardware is connected properly and operating correctly. Results of the POST are compared with data in a CMOS chip on the motherboard. If the POST is completed successfully, the BIOS looks for **system files**. Once located, the system files load into memory and execute. The boot program next loads the **kernel** of the operating system into memory. The operating system loads system configuration information from the **registry** for each device. The remainder of the operating system is loaded into RAM, the desktop and icons display on the screen, and programs in the **StartUp folder** are executed.

3 What Is a User Interface?

The part of the OS software with which you interact is the **user interface**. Two types of user interfaces are command-line and graphical. With a **command-line interface**, you type keywords or press special keys on the keyboard to enter data and instructions. A graphical user interface (GUI) allows you to use **menus** and visual images such as **icons** and buttons to issue commands. Many of today's GUIs incorporate Web browser-like features.

4 What Are the More Common Features of Operating Systems?

Various capabilities of operating systems are described as single user, multitasking, multiuser, and multiprocessing. A **single user** operating system allows only one user to run one program at a time. A **multitasking** operating system allows a single user to work on two or more applications that reside in memory at the same time. A **multiuser** operating system enables two or more users to run a program simultaneously. A **multiprocessing** operating system can support two or more processors running programs at the same time.

Operating systems manage memory, schedule jobs, configure devices, establish Web connections, monitor system performance, control networks, administer security, and manage storage media and files. **Memory management** optimizes use of random access memory (RAM). Spooling increases efficiency by placing print jobs in a buffer until the printer is ready, freeing the processor for other tasks. A **device driver** is a small program that configures devices by accepting commands and converting them into commands the device understands. **Plug and Play** is the computer's capability of recognizing any new device and assisting in the installation of the device. A **performance monitor** assesses and reports information about various system resources and devices. A type of program called a **file manager** performs functions related to storage and file management.

5 What Is the Difference between Stand-Alone Operating Systems and Network Operating Systems?

A stand-alone operating system is an operating system that works on a desktop or notebook computer. Some stand-alone operating systems, called **client operating systems**, also work in conjunction with a network operating system. A **network operating system** (**NOS**) supports a **network**. In some networks, the **server** controls access to the network hardware and software. **Clients**, which are other computers on the network, rely on the server for resources. The network OS organizes and coordinates how multiple users access and share resources on the network. Most multiuser operating systems administer security by allowing each user to **log on**, which is the process of entering a **user name** and **password**.

6 What Are Some Stand-Alone Operating Systems?

DOS (**Disk Operating System**) refers to several single user, command-line and menu-driven operating systems developed in the early 1980s for personal computers. **Windows 3.x** refers to three early **operating environments** that provided a graphical user interface to work in combination with DOS and simplify its use. **Windows 95** is a true multitasking operating system — not an operating environment. The **Windows 98** operating system is easier to use than Windows 95 and is more integrated with the Internet. Windows 2000 Professional is an upgrade to **Windows NT**, which is an operating system designed for client-server networks. **Windows Millennium Edition** is an updated version of Windows 98 that contains features specifically designed for home computer users. The **Macintosh OS**, a descendant of the first commercially successful graphical user interface, is available only on Macintosh computers. **OS/2 Warp** is IBM's network operating system. **UNIX** is a multitasking operating system developed by scientists at Bell Laboratories. **Linux** is a popular, free, multitasking, UNIX-like operating system.

7 What Are Some Network Operating Systems?

A network OS supports a network and generally resides on a server. Examples of network operating systems include Novel **Netware**; Microsoft **Windows NT Server** and **Windows 2000 Server family**; IBM **OS/2 Warp** and **OS/2Warp Server; UNIX**, which is a **multipurpose operating system**; Linux, which is a multitasking, UNIX-type operating system; and **Solaris™**, a version of UNIX developed by Sun Microsystems specifically for e-commerce applications.

8 What Devices Use Embedded Operating Systems?

Most handheld computers and small devices use an embedded operating system. **Windows CE** is a scaled-down Windows operating system designed for use on wireless communications devices and smaller computers. **Pocket PC OS** is a scaled-down Microsoft operating system that works on a specific type of handheld computer, called a **Pocket PC**. **Palm OS®** is a popular operating system used with handheld computers from Palm, Inc. and Handspring™.

9 What Are Some Common Utility Programs?

A **file viewer** displays the contents of a file. A **file compression utility** reduces the size of a file. A **diagnostic utility** compiles technical information about a computer's hardware and certain system software programs and then prepares a report outlining any identified problems. An **uninstaller** removes an application, as well as any associated entries in the system files. A **disk scanner** detects and corrects problems on a disk and searches for and removes unwanted files. A disk defragmenter reorganizes files and unused space on a computer's hard disk so data can be accessed more quickly and programs can run faster. A **backup utility** copies or backs up selected files or the entire hard drive onto another disk or tape. A **screen saver** causes the monitor's screen to display a moving image on a blank screen if no keyboard or mouse activity occurs for a specific time.

Key Terms

Web Instructions: To display this page from the Web, start your browser and enter the URL scsite.com/dc2002/ch8/terms.htm. Scroll through the list of terms. Click a term to display its definition and a picture. Click the To WEB button for current and additional information about the term from the Web. To see animations, Shockwave and Flash Player must be installed on your computer (download by clicking here).

PALM OS®

An operating system used with handheld computers such as Palm and Visor. (8.26)

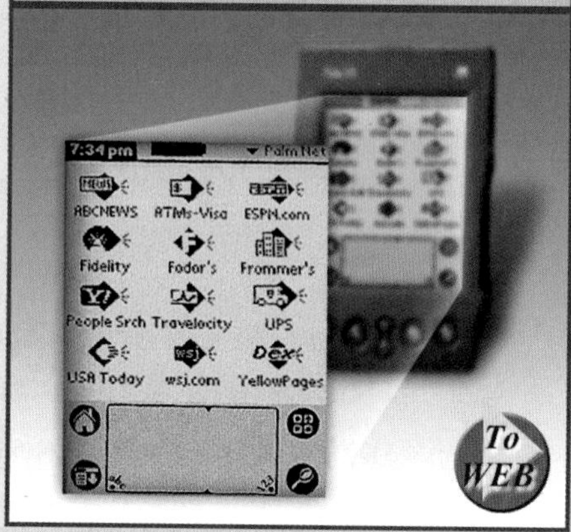

Learn It Online

Web Instructions: To display this page from the Web, start your browser and enter the URL scsite.com/dc2002/ch8/learn.htm.

1. Web Guide

Click Web Guide to display the Guide to World Wide Web Sites and Searching Techniques Web page. Click Reference and then click Webopedia. Search for operating systems. Click one of the operating system links. Prepare a brief report on your findings and submit your assignment to your instructor.

2. Scavenger Hunt

Click Scavenger Hunt. Print a copy of the Scavenger Hunt page; use this page to write down your answers as you search the Web. Submit your completed page to your instructor.

3. Who Wants to Be a Computer Genius?

Click Computer Genius to find out if you are a computer genius. Directions on how to play the game will display. When you are ready to play, click the PLAY button. Submit your score to your instructor.

4. Wheel of Terms

Click Wheel of Terms to reinforce important terms you learned in this chapter by playing the Shelly Cashman Series version of this popular game. Directions on how to play the game will display. When you are ready to play, click the PLAY button. Submit your score to your instructor.

5. Career Corner

Click Career Corner to display the QuintEssential Careers page. Click one of the tutorial links and complete the tutorial. Prepare a brief report describing what you learned. Submit the report to your instructor.

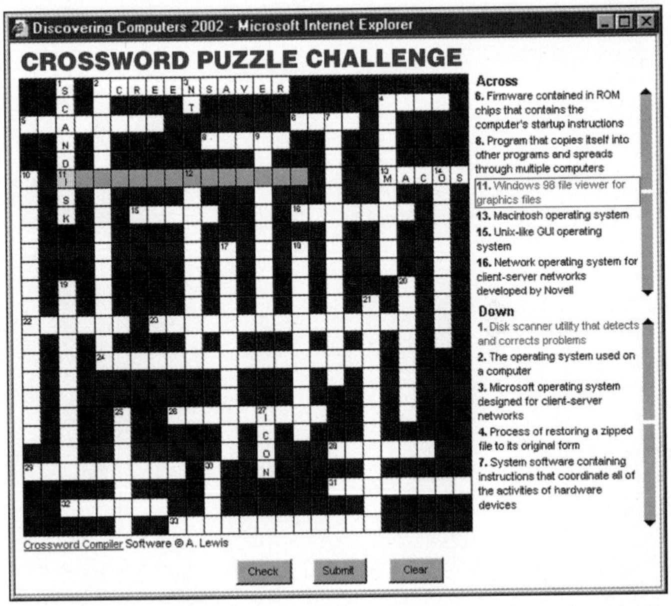

6. Search Sleuth

Click Search Sleuth to learn search techniques that will help make you a research expert. Submit the completed assignment to your instructor.

7. Crossword Puzzle Challenge

Click Crossword Puzzle Challenge. Complete the puzzle to reinforce skills you learned in this chapter. Directions on how to play the game will display. When you are ready to play, click the PLAY button. Submit the completed puzzle to your instructor.

8. Practice Test

Click Practice Test. Answer each question. When completed, enter your name and click the Grade Test button to submit the quiz for grading. Make a note of any missed questions. If required, print a copy to submit to your instructor.

Checkpoint

Web Instructions: To display this page from the Web, start your browser and enter the URL scsite.com/dc2002/ch8/check.htm. Click the links for current and additional information. To experience the animation and interactivity, Shockwave and Flash Player must be installed on your computer (download by clicking here).

LABEL THE FIGURE

Instructions: Identify each step of how a personal computer boots up.

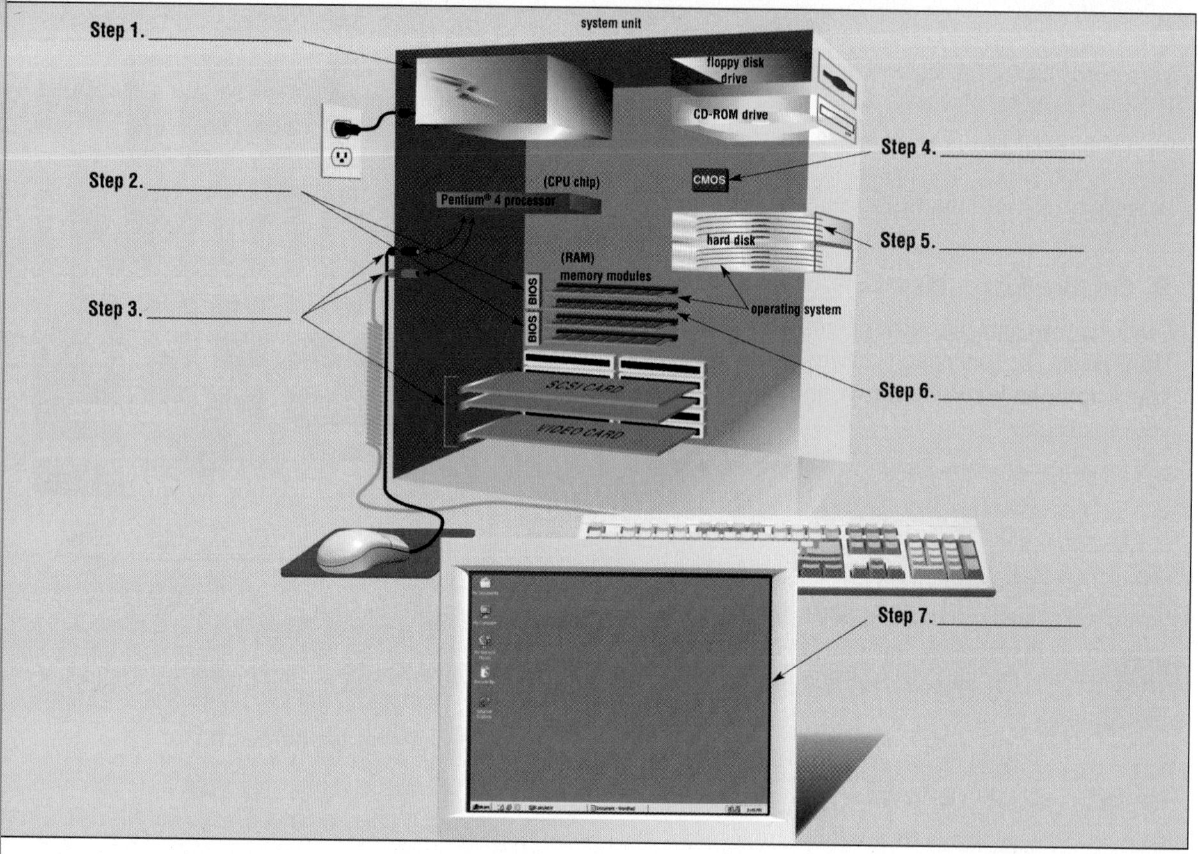

MATCHING

Instructions: Match each term from the column on the left with the best description from the column on the right.

_______ 1. OS/2 Warp
_______ 2. Windows 2000 Professional
_______ 3. Windows NT
_______ 4. Linux
_______ 5. Windows Me

a. Operating environment that works in combination with an operating system to simplify its use.
b. An operating system designed for client/server networks.
c. An upgrade to Windows 98 that has features specifically for the home user.
d. A complete multitasking client operating system for desktop and notebook business computers.
e. IBM's multitasking client operating system that supports networking, the Internet, Java, and speech recognition.
f. An open-source operating system.

MULTIPLE CHOICE

Instructions: Select the letter of the correct answer for each of the following questions.

1. The two types of system software include operating systems and ___________ .
   a. file viewers
   b. utility services
   c. utility programs
   d. compression programs
2. Stand-alone operating systems that work in conjunction with a network operating system are called ___________ .
   a. client operation systems
   b. DOS
   c. Linux
   d. operating environments
3. One weakness of the ___________ operating system is its command-line interface.
   a. Mac OS
   b. OS/2 Warp
   c. UNIX
   d. Windows 2000 Professional
4. An embedded operating system usually resides on a ___________ .
   a. hard drive
   b. ROM chip
   c. RAM chip
   d. removable disk
5. A ___________ combines several utility programs into a single package.
   a. utility service
   b. zipped file
   c. disk scanner
   d. utility suite

SHORT ANSWER

Instructions: Write a brief answer to each of the following questions.

1. How is a command-line interface different from a graphical user interface? ___________ Why is a graphical user interface described as user-friendly? ___________ List two operating systems with graphical user interfaces and two with command-line interfaces. ___________
2. What are networking operating systems? ___________ How are networking operating systems different from stand-alone operating systems? ___________
3. How is a single user operating system different from a multiuser operating system? ___________ How is a multitasking operating system different from a multiprocessing operating system? ___________
4. What is a boot disk? ___________ Why is it important to have a boot disk available? ___________
5. What is a file compression utility? ___________ When and why would you use a file compression utility program? ___________ What are some other utility programs you would find useful? ___________

WORKING TOGETHER

Instructions: Working with a group of your classmates, complete the following team exercise.

You and your group have been hired as consultants for ABC Importing. ABC has offices throughout the world — each using a multitude of different operating systems. Many times, it is very difficult to transfer data and information among these systems. ABC's CEO would like your consulting group to recommend a solution for this problem. Prepare a written report and a PowerPoint presentation explaining your solution. Share your report and presentation with your class.

Web Instructions: To display this page from the Web, start your browser and enter the URL scsite.com/dc2002/ch8/lab.htm. Click the links for current and additional information.

1 About Windows

This exercise uses Windows 98 procedures. Double-click the My Computer icon on the desktop. When the My Computer window displays, click Help on the menu bar and then click About Windows 98. Answer the following questions:

- To whom is Windows licensed?
- How much physical memory is available to Windows?
- What percent of the system resources are free?

Click the OK button in the About Windows dialog box. Close the My Computer window.

2 Using a Screen Saver

Right-click an empty area on the desktop and then click Properties on the shortcut menu. When the Display Properties dialog box displays, click the Screen Saver tab. Click the Screen Saver box arrow and then click Mystify Your Mind or any other selection. Click the Preview button to display the actual screen saver. Move the mouse to make the screen saver disappear. Answer the following questions:

- How many screen savers are available in your Screen Saver list?
- How many minutes does your system wait before activating a screen saver?

Click the Cancel button in the Display Properties dialog box.

3 Changing Desktop Colors

Right-click an empty area on the desktop and then click Properties on the shortcut menu. When the Display Properties dialog box displays, click the Appearance tab. Perform the following tasks: (1) Click the Question Mark button on the title bar and then click the Scheme box. When the pop-up window displays, right-click it. Click Print Topic on the shortcut menu and then click the OK button in the Print dialog box. Click anywhere to remove the pop-up window. (2) Click the Scheme box arrow and then click Rose to display the Rose color scheme shown in Figure 8.40. Select a color scheme you like. Click the Cancel button in the Display Properties dialog box.

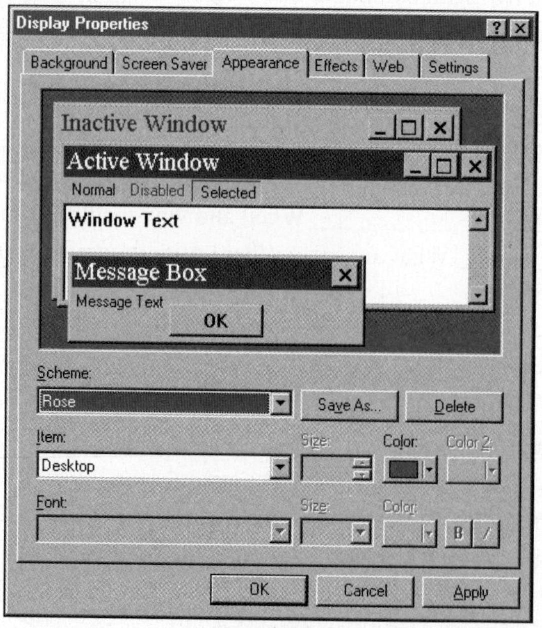

Figure 8-40

4 Customizing the Desktop for Multiple Users

This exercise uses Windows 98 procedures. If more than one person uses a computer, how can you customize the desktop for each user? Click the Start button on the taskbar and then click Help on the Start menu. Click the Contents tab. Click the Exploring Your Computer book. Click The Windows Desktop book. Click the Customizing for Multiple Users book. Click an appropriate Help topic and read the information to answer each of the following questions:

- How can you display a list of users at startup?
- How can you add personalized settings for a new user?
- How can you change desktop settings for multiple users?

Click the Close button to close the Windows Help window.

Web Work

Web Instructions: To display this page from the Web, start your browser and enter the URL scsite.com/dc2002/ch8/web.htm. To view At The Movies in exercise 1, RealPlayer must be installed on your computer (download by clicking here). To use the Shelly Cashman Series Evaluating Operating Systems Lab and Working at Your Computer Lab from the Web, Shockwave and Flash Player must be installed on your computer (download by clicking here).

Linux Gets Personal

To view the Linux Gets Personal movie, click the button to the left or click the Play button to the right. Watch the movie, and then complete the exercise by answering the question below. It looks like Microsoft Windows has some meaningful competition. The Linux operating system has shown itself to be easy to transition to from Windows, apparently more reliable in networking situations, and, at the price of free, it decidedly is less expensive. Though Linux is free, aligned companies make their money by providing customization services and selling new applications. Major companies, including IBM, Compaq, and HP, have formed an alliance to develop desktop office software that competes with Microsoft. Is Linux a boon to, or will it just complicate things for, computer users?

Shelly Cashman Series Evaluating Operating Systems Lab

Follow the instructions in Web Work 2 on page 1.47 to start and use the Shelly Cashman Series Evaluating Operating Systems Lab. If you are running from the Web, enter the URL, www.scsite.com/ sclabs/menu.htm; or display the Web Work Web page (see instructions at the top of this page) and then click the button to the left.

Shelly Cashman Series Working at Your Computer Lab

Follow the instructions in Web Work 2 on page 1.47 to start and use the Shelly Cashman Series Working at Your Computer Lab. If you are running from the Web, enter the URL, www.scsite.com/sclabs/menu.htm; or display the Web Work Web page (see instructions at the top of this page) and then click the button to the left.

A Picture's Worth a Thousand Words

Although she is not a programmer, Susan Kare's impact on the modern graphical user interface has been substantial. Kare is the person responsible for many of the icons used in modern graphical interfaces. According to Forbes magazine, "When it comes to giving personality to what otherwise might be cold and uncaring office machines, Kare is the queen of look and feel." Click the button to the left to learn more about Susan Kare and her approach to developing icons.

In the News

When Windows 2000 was launched in March 2000, hundreds queued up at computer outlets. It is unclear, however, whether the anticipation was caused by the new operating system or by the promotions many dealers offered — one vendor gave computer buyers the chance also to purchase a computer for $20. Click the button to the left and read a news article about the impact, quality, or promotion of an operating system. What operating system was it? What was done to sell the operating system? Is the operating system recommended? Why or why not?

The decision to buy a personal computer is an important one — and finding and purchasing a personal computer suited to your needs will require an investment of both time and money. As with many buyers, you may have little computer experience and find yourself unsure of how to proceed. The following guidelines are presented to help you purchase, install, and maintain a desktop computer. These guidelines also apply to the purchase of a notebook computer or handheld computer. Purchasing a notebook computer or handheld computer also involves some additional considerations, which are addressed later in this special feature.

Buyer's Guide 2002

How to Purchase, Install, and Maintain a Personal Computer

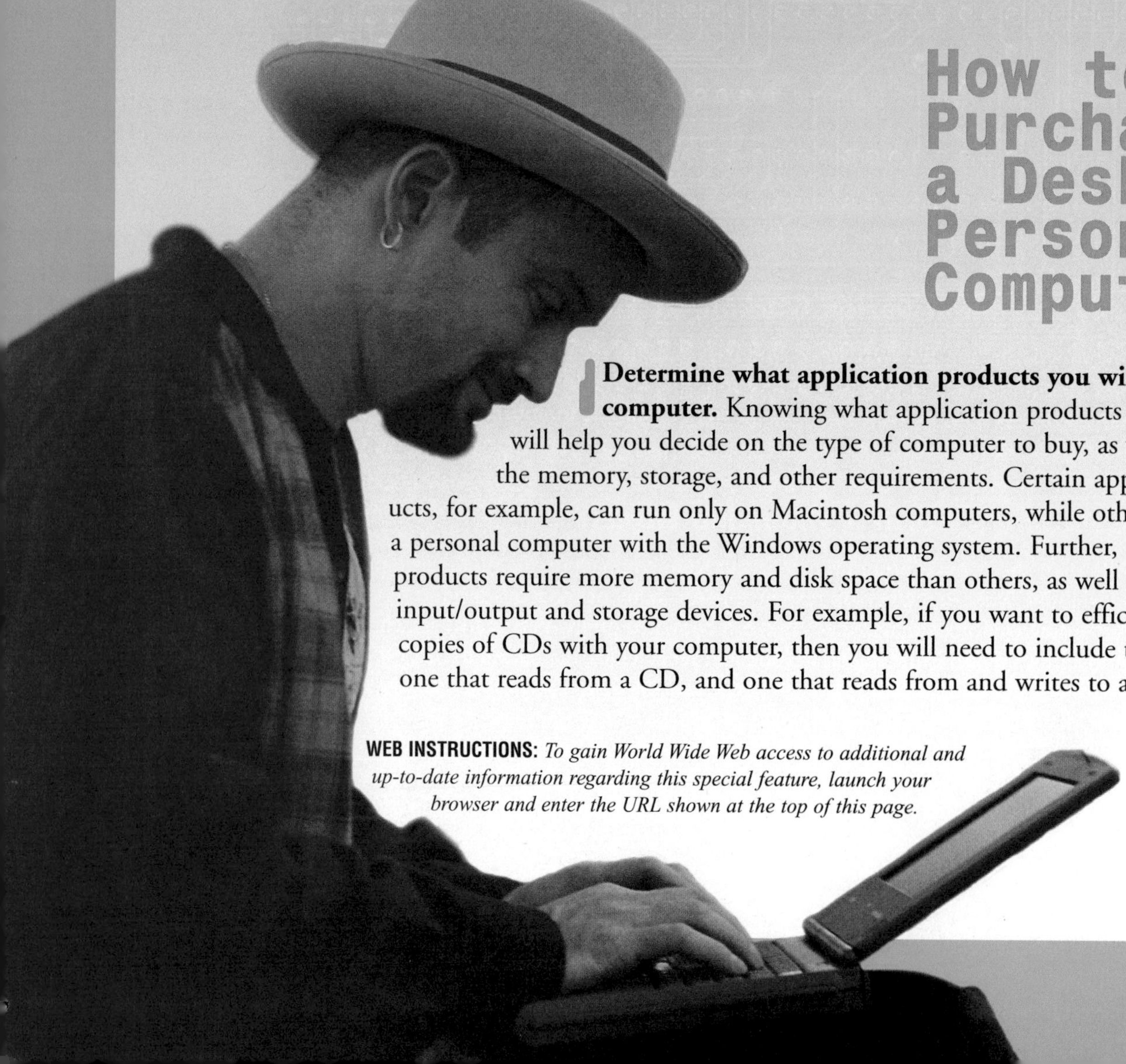

How to Purchase a Desktop Personal Computer

1 **Determine what application products you will use on your computer.** Knowing what application products you plan to use will help you decide on the type of computer to buy, as well as to define the memory, storage, and other requirements. Certain application products, for example, can run only on Macintosh computers, while others run only on a personal computer with the Windows operating system. Further, some application products require more memory and disk space than others, as well as additional input/output and storage devices. For example, if you want to efficiently create copies of CDs with your computer, then you will need to include two CD drives: one that reads from a CD, and one that reads from and writes to a CD.

WEB INSTRUCTIONS: *To gain World Wide Web access to additional and up-to-date information regarding this special feature, launch your browser and enter the URL shown at the top of this page.*

When you purchase a computer, it may come bundled with several software products. At the very least, you probably will want software for word processing and a browser to access the World Wide Web. If you need additional applications, such as a spreadsheet, a database, or presentation graphics, consider purchasing a software suite that offers reduced pricing on several applications, such as Microsoft Works or Microsoft Office.

Before selecting a specific package, be sure the software contains the features necessary for the tasks you want to perform. Many Web sites and magazines, such as those listed in Figure 1, provide reviews of software products. These Web sites frequently have articles that rate computers and software on cost, performance, and support.

Type of Computer	Web Site	URL
PC	Computer Shopper	zdnet.com/computershopper/edit/howtobuy
	PC World Magazine	pcworld.com
	Byte Magazine	byte.com
	Smart Business for New Economy	zdnet.com/smartbusinessmag/
	PC Magazine	zdnet.com/pcmag
	Yahoo! Computers	computers.yahoo.com
	FamilyPC Magazine	familypc.zdnet.com
	Microsoft Network	eshop.msn.com
	Dave's Guide to Buying a PC	css.msu.edu/pc-guide.html
Macintosh	TechWeb News	www.techweb.com/wire/apple
	ZDNet News	zdnet.com/mac
	Macworld Magazine	macworld.zdnet.com
	Apple	apple.com

For an updated list of hardware and software reviews and their Web sites, visit scsite.com/dc2002/ch8/buyers.htm.

Figure 1 Hardware and software reviews.

2 **Before buying a computer, do some research.** Talk to friends, coworkers, and instructors about prospective computers. What type of computers did they buy? Why? Would they recommend their computer and the company from which they bought it? You also should visit the Web sites or read reviews in the magazines listed in Figure 1. As you conduct your research, consider the following important criteria:

- Speed of the processor
- Size and types of memory (RAM) and storage (hard disk, floppy disk, CD-ROM, CD-RW, DVD-ROM, Zip® drive)
- Input/output devices included with the computer (e.g., mouse, keyboard, monitor, printer, sound card, video card)
- Communications devices included with the computer (modem, network interface card)
- Any software included with the computer

3 **Look for free software.** Many computer vendors include free software with their systems. Some sellers even let you choose which software you want. Remember, however, that free software has value only if you would have purchased the software even if it had not come with the computer.

4 **If you are buying a new computer, you have several purchasing options: buying from your school bookstore, a local computer dealer, a local large retail store, or ordering by mail via telephone or the World Wide Web.** Each purchasing option has certain advantages. Many college bookstores, for example, sign exclusive pricing agreements with computer manufacturers and, thus, can offer student discounts. Local dealers and local large retail stores, however, more easily can provide hands-on support. Mail-order companies

that sell computers by telephone or online via the Web (Figure 2) often provide the lowest prices but extend less personal service. Some major mail-order companies, however, have started to provide next-business-day, onsite services. A credit card usually is required to buy from a mail-order company. Figure 3 lists some of the more popular mail-order companies and their Web site addresses.

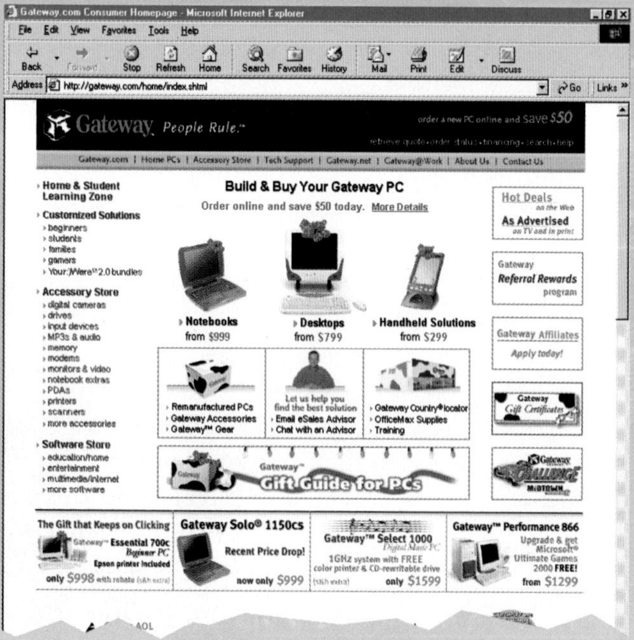

Figure 2 Some mail-order companies, like Gateway, sell computers online.

Type of Computer	Company	URL	Telephone Number
PC	Computer Shopper	computershopper.com	Not Available
	Compaq	compaq.com	1-800-888-0220
	CompUSA	compusa.com	1-800-266-7872
	dartek.com	dartek.com	1-800-531-4622
	Dell	dell.com	1-800-678-1626
	Gateway	gateway.com	1-800-846-4208
	Micron	micron.com	1-800-964-2766
Macintosh	Apple Computer	store.apple.com	1-800-795-1000
	Club Mac	www.clubmac.com	1-800-258-2622
	MacConnection	macconnection.com	1-888-213-0260
	MacExchange	macx.com	1-888-650-4488

For an updated list of new computer mail-order companies and their Web sites, visit scsite.com/dc2002/ch8/buyers.htm.

Figure 3 New computer mail-order companies.

5 If you are buying a used computer, stick with name brands. Although brand-name equipment can cost more, most brand-name computers have longer, more comprehensive warranties, are better supported, and have more authorized centers for repair services. As with new computers, you can purchase a used computer from local computer dealers, local large retail stores, or mail order via the telephone or the Web. Classified ads and used computer brokers offer additional outlets for purchasing used computers. Figure 4 lists several major used computer brokers and their Web site addresses.

Company	URL	Telephone Number
American Computer Exchange	www.amcoex.com	1-800-786-0717
Custom Edge, Inc.	bocoex.com	1-617-625-7722
U.S. Computer Exchange, Inc.	www.uscomputerexchange.com	1-800-711-9000
eBay	ebay.com	Not Available

For an updated list of used computer mail-order companies and their Web sites, visit *scsite.com/dc2002/ch8/buyers.htm*.

Figure 4 Used computer mail-order companies.

6 Use a worksheet to compare computers, services, and other considerations. You can use a separate sheet of paper to take notes on each vendor's computer and then summarize the information on a spreadsheet, such as the one shown in Figure 5. Most companies advertise a price for a base computer that includes components housed in the system unit (processor, RAM, sound card, video card), disk drives (floppy disk, hard disk, CD-ROM, CD-RW, and DVD-ROM), a keyboard, mouse, monitor, printer, speakers, and modem. Be aware, however, that some advertisements list prices for computers with only some of these components. Monitors, printers, and modems, for example, often are not included in a base computers price. Depending on how you plan to use the computers, you may want to invest in additional or more powerful components. When you are comparing the prices of computers, make sure you are comparing identical or similar configurations.

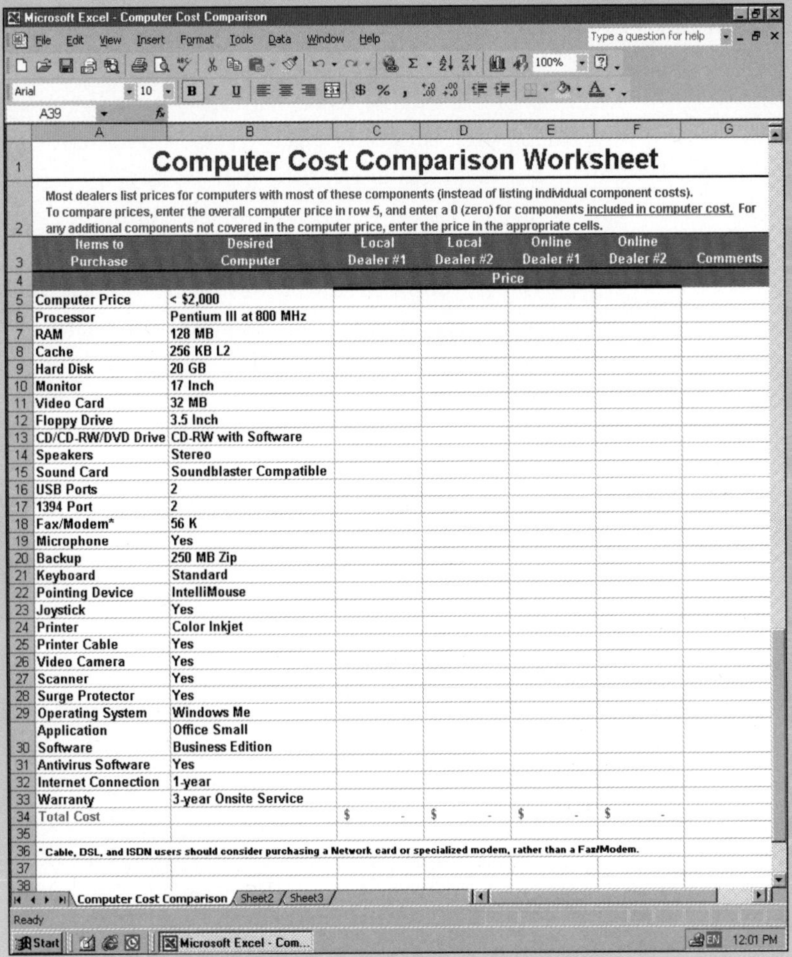

	A	B	C	D	E	F	G
1	Computer Cost Comparison Worksheet						
2	Most dealers list prices for computers with most of these components (instead of listing individual component costs). To compare prices, enter the overall computer price in row 5, and enter a 0 (zero) for components included in computer cost. For any additional components not covered in the computer price, enter the price in the appropriate cells.						
3	Items to Purchase	Desired Computer	Local Dealer #1	Local Dealer #2	Online Dealer #1	Online Dealer #2	Comments
4			Price				
5	Computer Price	< $2,000					
6	Processor	Pentium III at 800 MHz					
7	RAM	128 MB					
8	Cache	256 KB L2					
9	Hard Disk	20 GB					
10	Monitor	17 Inch					
11	Video Card	32 MB					
12	Floppy Drive	3.5 Inch					
13	CD/CD-RW/DVD Drive	CD-RW with Software					
14	Speakers	Stereo					
15	Sound Card	Soundblaster Compatible					
16	USB Ports	2					
17	1394 Port	2					
18	Fax/Modem*	56 K					
19	Microphone	Yes					
20	Backup	250 MB Zip					
21	Keyboard	Standard					
22	Pointing Device	IntelliMouse					
23	Joystick	Yes					
24	Printer	Color Inkjet					
25	Printer Cable	Yes					
26	Video Camera	Yes					
27	Scanner	Yes					
28	Surge Protector	Yes					
29	Operating System	Windows Me					
30	Application Software	Office Small Business Edition					
31	Antivirus Software	Yes					
32	Internet Connection	1-year					
33	Warranty	3-year Onsite Service					
34	Total Cost		$ -	$ -	$ -	$ -	
35							
36	* Cable, DSL, and ISDN users should consider purchasing a Network card or specialized modem, rather than a Fax/Modem.						
37							
38							

Figure 5 A spreadsheet is an effective tool for summarizing and comparing the prices and components of different computer vendors. A copy of the Computer Cost Comparison Worksheet is on the Discover Data Disk. To obtain a copy of the Discover Data Disk, see the inside back cover of this book for instructions.

8 Consider more than just price. The lowest cost computer may not be the best buy. Consider such intangibles as the vendor's time in business, the vendor's regard for quality, and the vendor's reputation for support. If you need to upgrade your computer often, you may want to consider a leasing arrangement, in which you pay monthly lease fees but upgrade or add on to your computer as your equipment needs change. If you are a replacement buyer, ask if the vendor will buy your old computer; an increasing number of companies are taking trade-ins. No matter what type of buyer you are, insist on a 30-day, no questions-asked return policy on your computer.

7 Be aware of hidden costs. Before purchasing, be sure to consider any additional costs associated with buying a computer, such as an additional telephone line, an uninterruptible power supply (UPS), computer furniture, floppy disks and paper, or computer training classes you may want to take. Depending on where you buy your computer, the seller may be willing to include some or all of these in the computer purchase price.

9 Avoid restocking fees. Some companies charge a restocking fee of 10 to 20 percent as part of their money-back return policy. In some cases, there is no restocking fee for hardware, but there is for software. Ask about the existence and terms of any restocking policies before you buy.

10 Select an Internet service provider (ISP) or online service provider (OSP). You can access the Internet in one of two ways: via an ISP or an OSP. Both provide Internet access for a monthly fee that ranges from $5 to $20. Some OSPs offer free Internet access. Local ISPs offer Internet access through local telephone numbers to users in a limited geographic region. National ISPs provide access for users nationwide (including mobile users), through local and toll-free telephone numbers and cable. Because of their size, national ISPs offer more services and generally have a larger technical support staff than local ISPs. OSPs furnish Internet access as well as members-only features for users nationwide. Figure 6 lists several national ISPs and OSPs. Before you choose an Internet access provider, compare such features as the number of access hours, monthly fees, available services (e-mail, Web page hosting, chat), and reliability.

Company	Service	URL	Telephone Number
America Online	OSP	aol.com	1-800-827-6364
AT&T Data and IP Services	ISP	att.com/wss	1-800-288-3199
CompuServe	OSP	compuserve.com	1-800-848-8990
Earthlink Network	ISP	www.earthlink.com	1-800-395-8425
Juno	Free OSP	juno.com	1-888-829-5866
MCI	ISP	mciworldcom.com	1-800-888-0800
Microsoft Network	OSP	msn.com	1-800-386-5550
NetZero	Free OSP	netzero.com	Not Available
Prodigy	ISP/OSP	prodigy.com	1-800-776-3449

For information on local ISPs or to learn more on any ISPs and OSPs listed here, visit The List™ at thelist.internet.com. The List™ — the most comprehensive and accurate directory of ISPs and OSPs on the Web — compares dial-up services, access hours, and fees for over 9,000 access providers.

For an updated list of ISPs and OSPs, visit *scsite.com/dc2002/ ch8/buyers.htm*.

Figure 6 National ISPs and OSPs.

11 Buy a computer compatible with the ones you use elsewhere. If you use a personal computer at work or in some other capacity, make sure the computer you buy is compatible. For example, if you use a PC at work, you may not want to purchase a Macintosh for home use. Having a computer compatible with the ones at work or school will allow you to transfer files and spend time at home on work- or school-related projects.

12 Consider purchasing an onsite service agreement. If you use your computer for business or are unable to be without your computer, consider purchasing an onsite service agreement through a local dealer or third-party company. Most onsite service agreements state that a technician will come to your home, work, or school within 24 hours. If your computer includes onsite service only for the first year, think about extending the service for two or three years when you buy the computer.

13 Use a credit card to purchase your new computer. Many credit cards now offer purchase protection and extended warranty benefits that cover you in case of loss of or damage to purchased goods. Paying by credit card also gives you time to install and use the computer before you have to pay for it. Finally, if you are dissatisfied with the computer and are unable to reach an agreement with the seller, paying by credit card gives you certain rights regarding withholding payment until the dispute is resolved. Check your credit card for specific details.

19 Avoid buying the smallest computer available. Computer technology changes rapidly, meaning a computer that seems powerful enough today may not serve your computing needs in a few years. In fact, studies show that many users regret they did not buy a more powerful computer. Plan to buy a computer that will last you for two to three years. You can help delay obsolescence by purchasing the fastest processor, most memory, and largest hard drive you can afford. If you must buy a smaller computer, be sure you can upgrade it with additional memory and auxiliary devices as your computer requirements grow. Figure 7 includes minimum recommendations for each category of user discussed in this book: Home User, Small Business User, Mobile User, Large Business User, and Power User. The Home User category is divided into two groups: Application Home User and Game Home User.

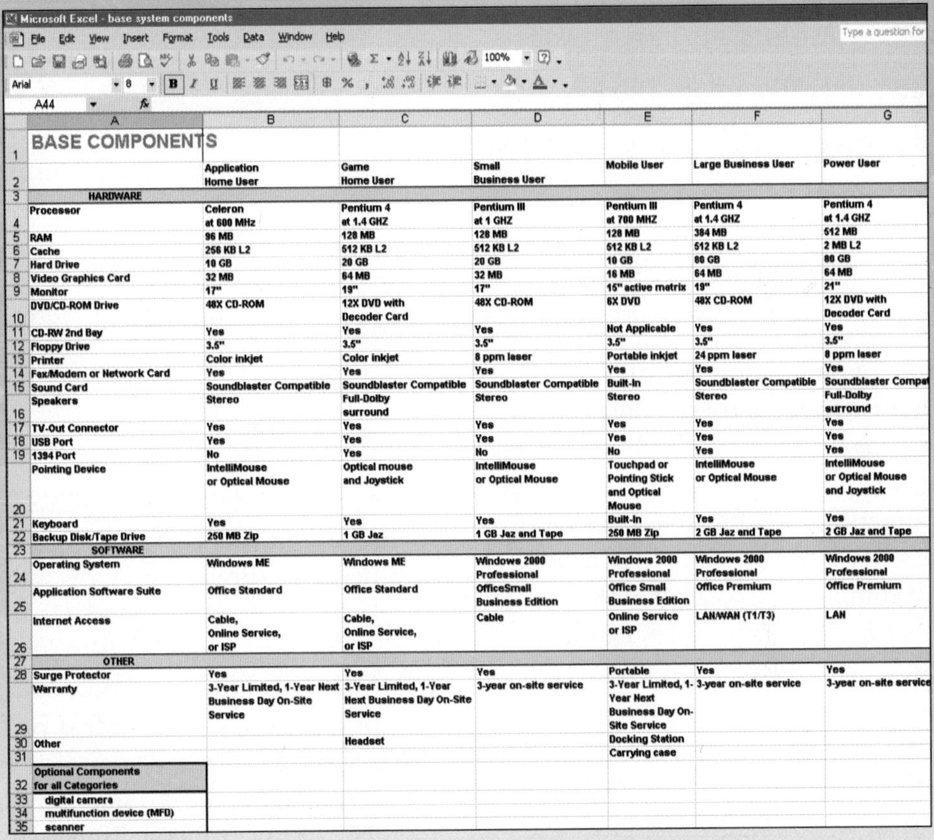

BASE COMPONENTS	Application Home User	Game Home User	Small Business User	Mobile User	Large Business User	Power User
HARDWARE						
Processor	Celeron at 600 MHz	Pentium 4 at 1.4 GHZ	Pentium III at 1 GHZ	Pentium III at 700 MHZ	Pentium 4 at 1.4 GHZ	Pentium 4 at 1.4 GHZ
RAM	96 MB	128 MB	128 MB	128 MB	384 MB	512 MB
Cache	256 KB L2	512 KB L2	512 KB L2	512 KB L2	512 KB L2	2 MB L2
Hard Drive	10 GB	20 GB	20 GB	10 GB	80 GB	80 GB
Video Graphics Card	32 MB	64 MB	32 MB	16 MB	64 MB	64 MB
Monitor	17"	19"	17"	15" active matrix	19"	21"
DVD/CD-ROM Drive	48X CD-ROM	12X DVD with Decoder Card	48X CD-ROM	6X DVD	48X CD-ROM	12X DVD with Decoder Card
CD-RW 2nd Bay	Yes	Yes	Yes	Not Applicable	Yes	Yes
Floppy Drive	3.5"	3.5"	3.5"	3.5"	3.5"	3.5"
Printer	Color inkjet	Color inkjet	8 ppm laser	Portable inkjet	24 ppm laser	8 ppm laser
Fax/Modem or Network Card	Yes	Yes	Yes	Yes	Yes	Yes
Sound Card	Soundblaster Compatible	Soundblaster Compatible	Soundblaster Compatible	Built-In	Soundblaster Compatible	Soundblaster Compat
Speakers	Stereo	Full-Dolby surround	Stereo	Stereo	Stereo	Full-Dolby surround
TV-Out Connector	Yes	Yes	Yes	Yes	Yes	Yes
USB Port	Yes	Yes	Yes	Yes	Yes	Yes
1394 Port	No	Yes	No	No	Yes	Yes
Pointing Device	IntelliMouse or Optical Mouse	Optical mouse and Joystick	IntelliMouse or Optical Mouse	Touchpad or Pointing Stick and Optical Mouse	IntelliMouse or Optical Mouse	IntelliMouse or Optical Mouse and Joystick
Keyboard	Yes	Yes	Yes	Built-In	Yes	Yes
Backup Disk/Tape Drive	250 MB Zip	1 GB Jaz	1 GB Jaz and Tape	250 MB Zip	2 GB Jaz and Tape	2 GB Jaz and Tape
SOFTWARE						
Operating System	Windows ME	Windows ME	Windows 2000 Professional	Windows 2000 Professional	Windows 2000 Professional	Windows 2000 Professional
Application Software Suite	Office Standard	Office Standard	OfficeSmall Business Edition	Office Small Business Edition	Office Premium	Office Premium
Internet Access	Cable, Online Service, or ISP	Cable, Online Service, or ISP	Cable	Online Service or ISP	LAN/WAN (T1/T3)	LAN
OTHER						
Surge Protector	Yes	Yes	Yes	Portable	Yes	Yes
Warranty	3-Year Limited, 1-Year Next Business Day On-Site Service	3-Year Limited, 1-Year Next Business Day On-Site Service	3-year on-site service	3-Year Limited, 1-Year Next Business Day On-Site Service	3-year on-site service	3-year on-site service
Other		Headset		Docking Station		
				Carrying case		
Optional Components for all Categories						
digital camera						
multifunction device (MFD)						
scanner						

Figure 7 Base computer components and optional components. A copy of the BASE COMPONENTS worksheet is on the Discover Data Disk. To obtain a copy of the Discover Data Disk, see the inside back cover of this book for instructions.

How to Purchase a Notebook Computer

If you need computing capability when you travel, you may find a notebook computer to be an appropriate choice. The guidelines mentioned in the previous section also apply to the purchase of a notebook computer (Figure 8). The following are additional considerations unique to notebook computers.

Figure 8 A notebook computer.

1 Purchase a notebook computer with a sufficiently large active-matrix screen. Active-matrix screens display high-quality color that is viewable from all angles. Less expensive, passive-matrix screens sometimes are difficult to see in low-light conditions and cannot be viewed from an angle. Notebook computers typically come with a 12.1-inch, 13.3-inch, 14.1-inch, or 15.4-inch display. For most users, a 14.1-inch display is satisfactory. If you intend to use your notebook computer as a desktop replacement, however, you may opt for a 15.4-inch display. If you travel a lot and portability is essential, consider that most of the lightest machines are equipped with a 13.3-inch display. Regardless of size, the resolution of the display should be at least 800 x 600 pixels.

2 Experiment with different pointing devices and keyboards. Notebook computer keyboards are far less standardized than those for desktop computers. Some notebook computers, for example, have wide wrist rests, while others have none. Notebook computers also use a range of pointing devices, including pointing sticks, touchpads, and trackballs. Before you purchase a notebook computer, try various types of keyboard and pointing devices to determine which is easiest for you to use. Regardless of the pointing device you select, you also may want to purchase a regular mouse unit to use when you are working at a desk or other large surface.

3 Make sure the notebook computer you purchase has a CD-ROM or DVD-ROM drive. Loading software, especially large software suites, is much faster if done from a CD-ROM, CD-RW, or DVD-ROM. Today, most notebook computers come with an internal CD-ROM drive. Some notebook computers even come with a CD-ROM drive and a CD-RW drive or both a DVD-ROM drive and a CD-RW drive. Some users prefer a DVD-ROM drive to a CD-ROM drive. Although DVD-ROM drives are more expensive, they allow you to read CD-ROMs and to play movies using your notebook computer.

4 If necessary, upgrade memory and disk storage at the time of purchase. As with a desktop computer, upgrading your notebook computer's memory and disk storage usually is less expensive at the time of initial purchase. Some disk storage is custom designed for notebook computer manufacturers, meaning an upgrade might not be available a year or two after you purchase your notebook computer.

5 If you are going to use your notebook computer on an airplane, purchase a second battery. Two batteries should provide enough power to last through most airplane flights. If you anticipate running your notebook computer on batteries frequently, choose a computer that uses lithium-ion batteries (they last longer than nickel cadmium or nickel hydride batteries).

6 Purchase a well-padded and well-designed carrying case. An amply padded carrying case will protect your notebook computer from the bumps it will receive while traveling. A well-designed carrying case will have room for accessories such as spare floppy disks, CD-ROMs, a user manual, pens, and paperwork (Figure 9).

Figure 9 Well-designed carrying case.

7 If you travel overseas, obtain a set of electrical and telephone adapters. Different countries use different outlets for electrical and telephone connections. Several manufacturers sell sets of adapters that will work in most countries (Figure 10).

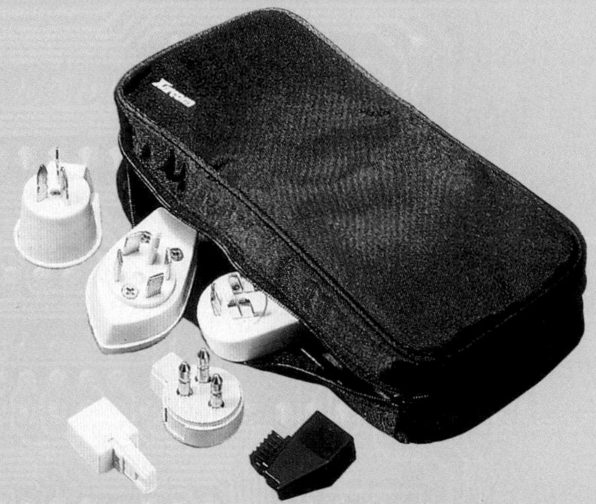

Figure 10 Set of electrical and telephone adapters.

8 If you plan to connect your notebook computer to a video projector, make sure the notebook computer is compatible with the video projector. Some notebook computers will not allow you to display an image on the notebook computer and projection device at the same time (Figure 11). Either of these factors can affect your presentation negatively.

Figure 11 Video projector.

How to Purchase a Handheld Computer

If you need to stay organized when you are on the go, then a lightweight, palm-size or pocketsize computer, called a handheld computer, may be the right choice. Handheld computers typically are categorized by the operating system they run. Although several are available, the two primary operating systems are Palm OS (Figure 12) and Pocket PC (Figure 13). Listed in this section are a few points you will want to consider when purchasing a handheld computer. You also should visit the Web sites listed in Figure 14.

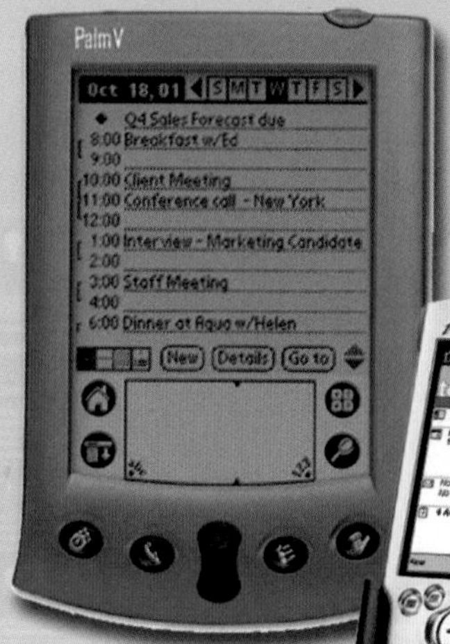

Figure 12 Palm V with Palm OS.

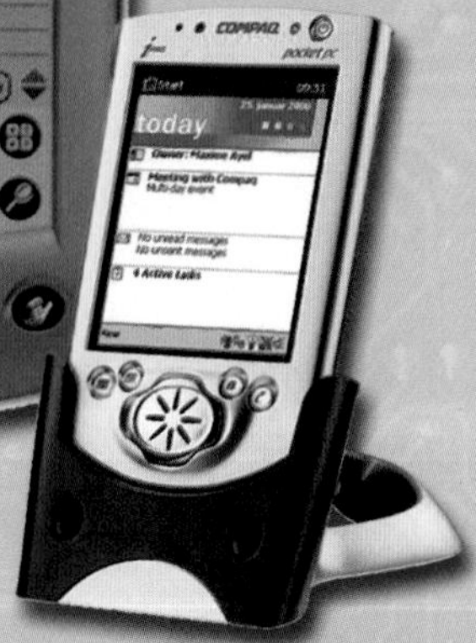

Figure 13 Compaq iPaq Pocket PC.

1 Determine the applications you plan to run on your handheld computer. All handheld computers can handle basic organizer-type applications, such as calendar, address book, and notepad. The availability of other applications is dependent on the operating system you choose. With more than 5,000 applications, the depth of software applications for the Palm OS is unmatched. Handheld computers that run Pocket PC have fewer applications available, but they do run a Windows-like operating system and applications you probably are familiar with, such as Word and Excel.

2 What do you want to pay? The price of handheld computers runs from $100 to $1,000, depending on their capabilities. In general, Palm OS devices are at the lower end of the cost spectrum and Pocket PC devices are at the higher end. The average selling price for handheld computers is in the $300 to $500 range. For the latest handheld computer prices, capabilities, and accessories, visit the Web sites listed in Figure 14.

Web Site	URL
Compaq	compaq.com/products/handhelds
Computer Shopper	computershopper.com
Handspring	handspring.com
Microsoft	pocketpc.com
Mobile Computing	mobilecomputing.com
Palm	palm.com
PDA Buyers Guide	pdabuyersguide.com
smaller.com	smaller.com
Wireless Developer Network	wirelessdevnet.com

For an updated list of handheld computer Web sites, visit scsite.com/dc2002/ch8/buyers.htm.

Figure 14 Reviews and information on handheld computers.

3 Practice with the touch screen and handwriting recognition before deciding on a model. You use a pen-like stylus to handwrite on the screen. The handheld computer then translates the handwriting into a computerized font. You also can use the stylus as a pointing device to select items on the screen and enter data using a transparent on-screen key board. Some handheld computers are easier to use than others. You can buy third-party software to improve a handheld computer's handwriting recognition.

4 Decide if you want a color screen. Pocket PC devices have color screens (as many as 65,536 colors), while most Palm OS devices have monochrome screens (4 to 16 shades of gray). More colors result in greater detail. Resolution also influences the quality of the display.

5 Compare battery life. Any mobile device is good only if it has the power to run. Palm OS devices with black-and-white screens tend to have a much longer battery life than Pocket PC devices with color screens. To help alleviate this problem, both Palm OS and Pocket PC devices have incorporated rechargeable batteries, but this only works if you are near a recharger.

6 Check out the accessories. You need to consider what accessories you want for your handheld computer. Handheld computer accessories include carrying cases, portable keyboards, removable storage, car chargers, GPS systems, dashboard mounts, replacement styli, synchronization cradles and cables, and more.

7 Decide if you want additional functionality. You will find that off-the-shelf Pocket PC devices have broader functionality than Palm OS devices. For example, voice-recording capability, e-book player, MP3 (music) player, and video player are standard on most Pocket PC devices. If you are leaning towards a Palm OS device and still want these additional functions, they can be added later if you find you really need them.

8 Is synchronization of data with other handheld computers, personal computers, or printers important? Most handheld computers come with a cradle that connects to the USB or serial port on your computer so that you can synchronize data. An infrared port, however, allows you to synchronize data with any device, including other handheld computers that have a similar infrared port.

9 If you travel often, then consider e-mail and Web access from your handheld computer. Some handheld computers come with a modem that can send and receive data across telephone lines. Other handheld computers allow you to connect to your cellular telephone and use it as a modem. More expensive handheld computers have wireless capabilities built in. In either case, for a monthly network connection fee you can access your e-mail, company Web sites, and any other information on the World Wide Web from anywhere.

WEB SITE	URL
Getting Started/Installation	
Computers 101	newsday.com/plugin/c101main.htm
HelpTalk Online	helptalk.com
Ergonomics	
Ergonomic Computing	cobweb.creighton.edu/training/ergo.htm
Healthy Choices for Computer Users	www-ehs.ucsd.edu/ergo/ergobk/vdt.htm
Video Display Terminal Health and Safety Guidelines	uhs.berkeley.edu/Facstaff/Ergonomics

For an updated list of reference materials, visit *scsite.com/dc2002/ch8/buyers.htm*.

Figure 15 Web references on setting up and using your computer.

How to Install a Personal Computer

It is important that you spend time planning for the installation of your computer. Follow these steps to ensure your installation experience will be a pleasant one and that your work area is safe, healthy, and efficient.

1 **Read the installation manuals before you start to install your equipment.** Many manufacturers include separate installation instructions with their equipment that contain important information. You can save a great deal of time and frustration if you make an effort to read the manuals.

2 **Do some research.** To locate additional instructions on installing your computer, review the computer magazines or Web sites listed in Figure 15 to search for articles on installing a computer.

3 **Set up your computer in a well-designed work area, with adequate workspace around the computer.** Ergonomics is an applied science devoted to making the equipment and its surrounding work area safer and more efficient. Ergonomic studies have shown that using the correct type and configuration of chair, keyboard, monitor, and work surface will help you work comfortably and efficiently, and help protect your health. For your computer workspace, experts recommend an area of at least two feet by four feet. Figure 16 illustrates additional guidelines for setting up your work area.

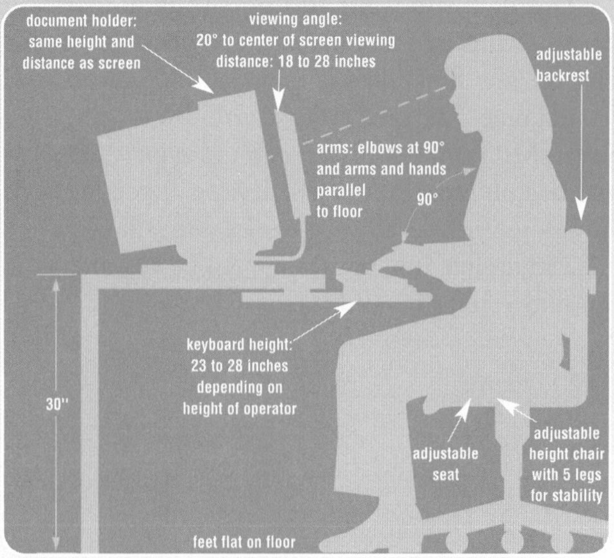

Figure 16 A well-designed work area should be flexible to allow adjustments to the height and build of different individuals. Good lighting and air quality also are important considerations.

4 Install bookshelves. Bookshelves above and/or to the side of your computer area are useful for keeping manuals and other reference materials handy.

5 Have a telephone outlet and telephone or cable connection near your workspace so you can connect your modem and/or place calls while using your computer. To plug in your modem to dial up and access the World Wide Web, you will need a telephone outlet or cable connection close to your computer. Having a telephone nearby also helps if you need to place business or technical support calls while you are working on your computer. Often, if you call a vendor about a hardware or software problem, the support person can talk you through a correction while you are on the telephone. To avoid data loss, however, do not place floppy disks on the telephone or near any other electrical or electronic equipment.

6 While working at your computer, be aware of health issues. Working safely at your computer requires that you consider several health issues. To minimize neck and eye discomfort, for instance, obtain a document holder that keeps documents at the same height and distance as your computer screen. To provide adequate lighting that reduces eye strain, use non-glare light bulbs that illuminate your entire work area. Figure 17 lists additional computer user health guidelines.

Computer User Health Guidelines

1. Work in a well-designed work area. See Figure 16 on the previous page.
2. Alternate work activities to prevent physical and mental fatigue. If possible, change the order of your work to provide some variety.
3. Take frequent breaks. Every fifteen minutes, look away from the screen to give your eyes a break. At least once per hour, get out of your chair and move around. Every two hours, take at least a fifteen-minute break.
4. Incorporate hand, arm, and body stretching exercises into your breaks. At lunch, try to get outside and walk.
5. Make sure your computer monitor is designed to minimize electromagnetic radiation (EMR). If it is an older model, consider adding EMR reducing accessories.
6. Try to eliminate or minimize surrounding noise. Noisy environments contribute to stress and tension.
7. If you frequently use the telephone and the computer at the same time, consider using a telephone headset. Cradling the telephone between your head and shoulder can cause muscle strain.
8. Be aware of symptoms of repetitive strain injuries: soreness, pain, numbness, or weakness in neck, shoulders, arms, wrists, and hands. Do not ignore early signs; seek medical advice.

Figure 17 Following these health guidelines will help computer users maintain their health.

7 Obtain a computer tool set. Computer tool sets include any screwdrivers and other tools you might need to work on your computer. Computer dealers, office supply stores, and mail-order companies sell these tool sets. To keep all the tools together, get a tool set that comes in a zippered carrying case.

8 Save all the paperwork that comes with your computer. Keep the documents that come with your computer in an accessible place, along with the paperwork from your other computer-related purchases. To keep different-sized documents together, consider putting them in a manila file folder, large envelope, or sealable plastic bag.

9 **Record the serial numbers of all your equipment and software.** Write the serial numbers of your equipment and software on the outside of the manuals packaged with these items. As noted in the next section, you also should create a single, comprehensive list that contains the serial numbers of all your equipment and software.

10 **Complete and send in your equipment and software registration cards.** When you register your equipment and software, the vendor usually enters you in its user database. Being a registered user not only can save you time when you call with a support question, it also makes you eligible for special pricing on software upgrades.

11 **Keep the shipping containers and packing materials for all your equipment.** Shipping containers and packing materials will come in handy if you have to return your equipment for servicing or must move it to another location.

12 **Identify device connectors.** At the back of your computer, you will find a number of connectors for your printer, monitor, mouse, telephone line, and so forth (Figure 18). If the manufacturer has not identified them for you, use a marking pen to write the purpose of each connector on the back of the computer case.

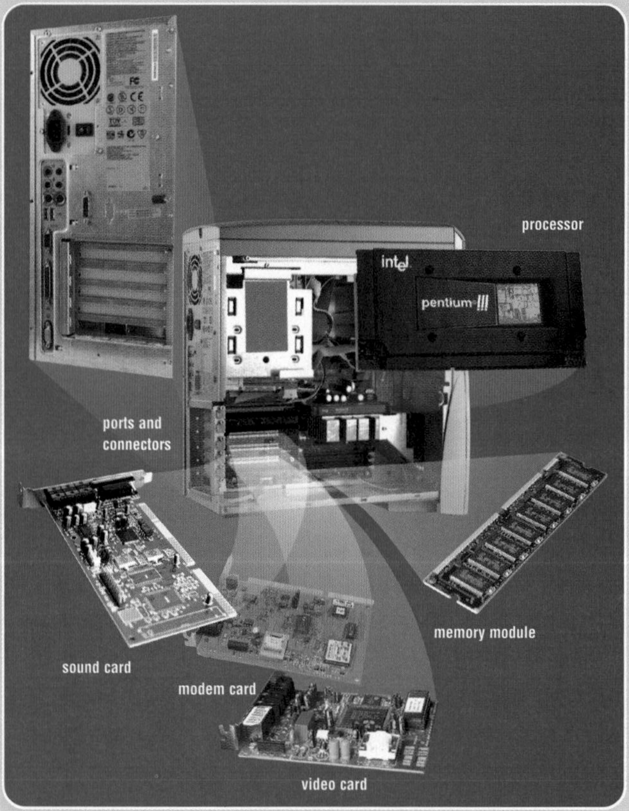

Figure 18 Inside the system unit and the connectors at the back.

13 **Install your computer in an area where you can maintain the temperature and humidity.** You should keep the computer in an area with a constant temperature between 60°F and 80°F. High temperatures and humidity can damage electronic components. Be careful when using space heaters, for example, as the hot, dry air they generate can cause disk problems.

14 **Keep your computer area clean.** Avoid eating and drinking around your computer. Also, avoid smoking. Cigarette smoke can damage the floppy disk drives and floppy disk surfaces.

15 **Check your home or renter's insurance policy.** Some renter's insurance policies have limits on the amount of computer equipment they cover. Other policies do not cover computer equipment at all if it is used for business. In this instance, you may want to obtain a separate insurance policy.

How to Maintain Your Computer

Even with the most sophisticated hardware and software, you will need to do some type of maintenance to keep everything working properly. You can simplify and minimize the maintenance by following the steps listed below.

1 Start a notebook that includes information on your computer. Keep a notebook that provides a single source of information about your entire computer, both hardware and software. Each time you make a change to your computer, such as adding or removing hardware or software or altering computer parameters, record the change in your notebook. Include the following items in your notebook:

- Vendor support numbers from your user manuals
- Serial numbers of all equipment and software
- User IDs, passwords, and nicknames for your ISP or OSP, network access, Web sites, and so on
- Vendor and date of purchase for all software and equipment
- Trouble log that provides a chronological history of equipment or software problems
- Notes on any discussions with vendor support personnel

Figure 19 provides a suggested outline for the contents of your notebook.

PC OWNER'S NOTEBOOK OUTLINE

1. Vendors
   Vendor
   City/State
   Product
   Telephone #
   URL
2. Internet and online services information
   Service provider name
   Logon telephone number
   Alternate logon telephone number
   Technical support telephone number
   User ID
   Password
3. Web site information
   Web site name
   URL
   User ID
   Password
   Nickname
4. Serial numbers
   Product
   Manufacturer
   Serial #
5. Purchase history
   Date
   Product
   Manufacturer
   Vendor
   Cost
6. Software log
   Date installed/uninstalled
7. Trouble log
   Date
   Time
   Problem
   Resolution
8. Support calls
   Date
   Time
   Company
   Contact
   Problem
   Comments
9. Vendor paperwork

Figure 19 To keep important information about your computer on hand and organized, use an outline such as this sample outline.

2 Before you work inside your computer, turn off the power and disconnect the equipment from the power source. Working inside your computer with the power on can affect both you and the computer adversely. Thus, you should turn off the power and disconnect the equipment from the power source before you open a computer to work inside. In addition, before you touch anything inside the computer, you should touch an unpainted metal surface such as the power supply. Doing so will help discharge any static electricity that could damage internal components.

3 **Keep the area surrounding your computer dirt and dust free.** Reducing the dirt and dust around your computer will reduce the need to clean the inside of your computer. If dust builds up inside the computer, remove it carefully with compressed air and a small vacuum. Do not touch the components with the vacuum.

4 **Back up important files and data.** Use the operating system or utility program to create an emergency or rescue disk to help you restart your computer if it crashes. You also regularly should copy important data files to disks, tape, or another computer.

5 **Protect your computer from viruses.** A computer virus is a potentially damaging computer program designed to infect other software or files by attaching itself to the software or files with which it comes in contact. Virus programs are dangerous because often they destroy or corrupt data stored on the infected computer. You can protect your computer from viruses by installing an antivirus program.

6 **Keep your computer tuned.** Most operating systems include several computer tools that provide basic maintenance functions. One important tool is the disk defragmenter. Defragmenting your hard disk reorganizes files so they are in contiguous (adjacent) clusters, making disk operations faster. Some programs allow you to schedule maintenance tasks for times when you are not using your computer. If necessary, leave your computer on at night so it can run the required maintenance programs. If your operating system does not provide the tools, you can purchase a stand-alone utility program to perform basic maintenance functions.

7 **Learn to use diagnostic tools.** Diagnostic tools help you identify and resolve problems, thereby helping to reduce your need for technical assistance. Diagnostic tools help you test components, monitor resources such as memory and processing power, undo changes made to files, and more. As with basic maintenance tools, most operating systems include diagnostic tools; you also can purchase or download many stand-alone diagnostic tools.

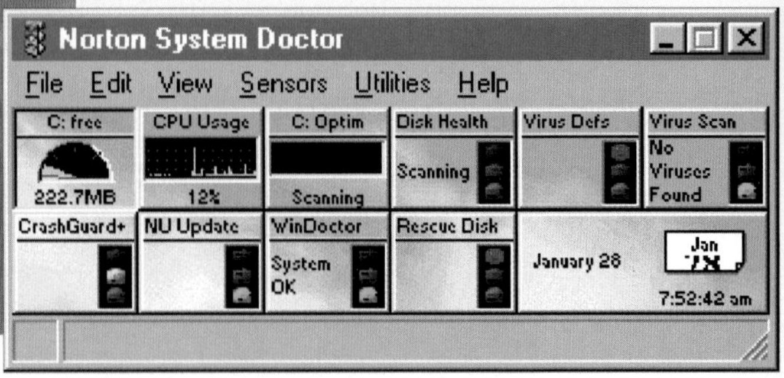

CHAPTER 9

Communications and Networks

You sleep with it on, eat with it on, even shower with it on. You have worn it since birth. It actually looks quite fashionable. You have the bracelet model. Your sister has the earring model. Fido has a choker model.

How did prior generations manage without it? Last week, a neighbor fell down the stairs and was knocked unconscious. The computer chip set in her ring sensed a change in her biological chemistry and signaled for help. Rescue workers arrived at her side in ten minutes. While this computer chip is capable of summoning medical assistance, it also can help law enforcement officials immediately locate missing children. Pets no longer are lost. Stolen valuables embedded with these chips instantly are recovered.

Now these chips even communicate with the electronics and devices around you. This is so cool! As you drive toward a subdivision, from the car speakers you hear an announcer say, "John's house is around the corner." When you walk by an ice cream shop, your Web-enabled cellular telephone beeps and displays a coupon for a 30 percent discount on a hot fudge sundae. While strolling through aisles of the local department store, your handheld computer displays sales and manufacturer's rebates. Life is good.

OBJECTIVES

After completing this chapter, you will be able to:

- Define the components required for successful communications
- Identify various sending and receiving devices
- Explain communications applications
- List advantages of using a network
- Differentiate between a local area network and a wide area network
- Understand the various communications technologies
- Identify uses of intranets and extranets
- Explain the purpose of communications software
- Understand the telephone network
- Describe commonly used communications devices
- Identify various physical and wireless transmission media

COMMUNICATIONS

Computers were stand-alone devices when first introduced. As they became more widely used, manufacturers designed hardware and software, so one computer could communicate with another. Computer **communications** describes a process in which one computer transfers data, instructions, and information to another computer(s). Originally, only large computers had communications capabilities. Today, even the smallest computers and devices can communicate with one another. Figure 9-1 shows a sample communications system. As illustrated in this figure, communications systems contain all types of devices.

For successful communications, you need the following:

- A **sending device** that initiates an instruction to transmit data, instructions, or information
- A communications device that converts or formats the data, instructions, or information from the sending device into signals carried by a communications channel
- A communications channel, or path, on which the signals travel
- A communications device that receives the signals from the communications channel and converts or formats them so the receiving device can understand the signals
- A **receiving device** that accepts the data, instructions, or information

Figure 9-1 An example of a communications system. Some devices that can serve as sending and receiving devices are (a) personal computers, (b) notebook computers, (c) Web-enabled cellular telephones, (d) Web-enabled handheld computers, (e) WebTV™, and (f) GPS receivers. The communications channel consists of telephone lines, underground cables, microwave stations, and satellites.

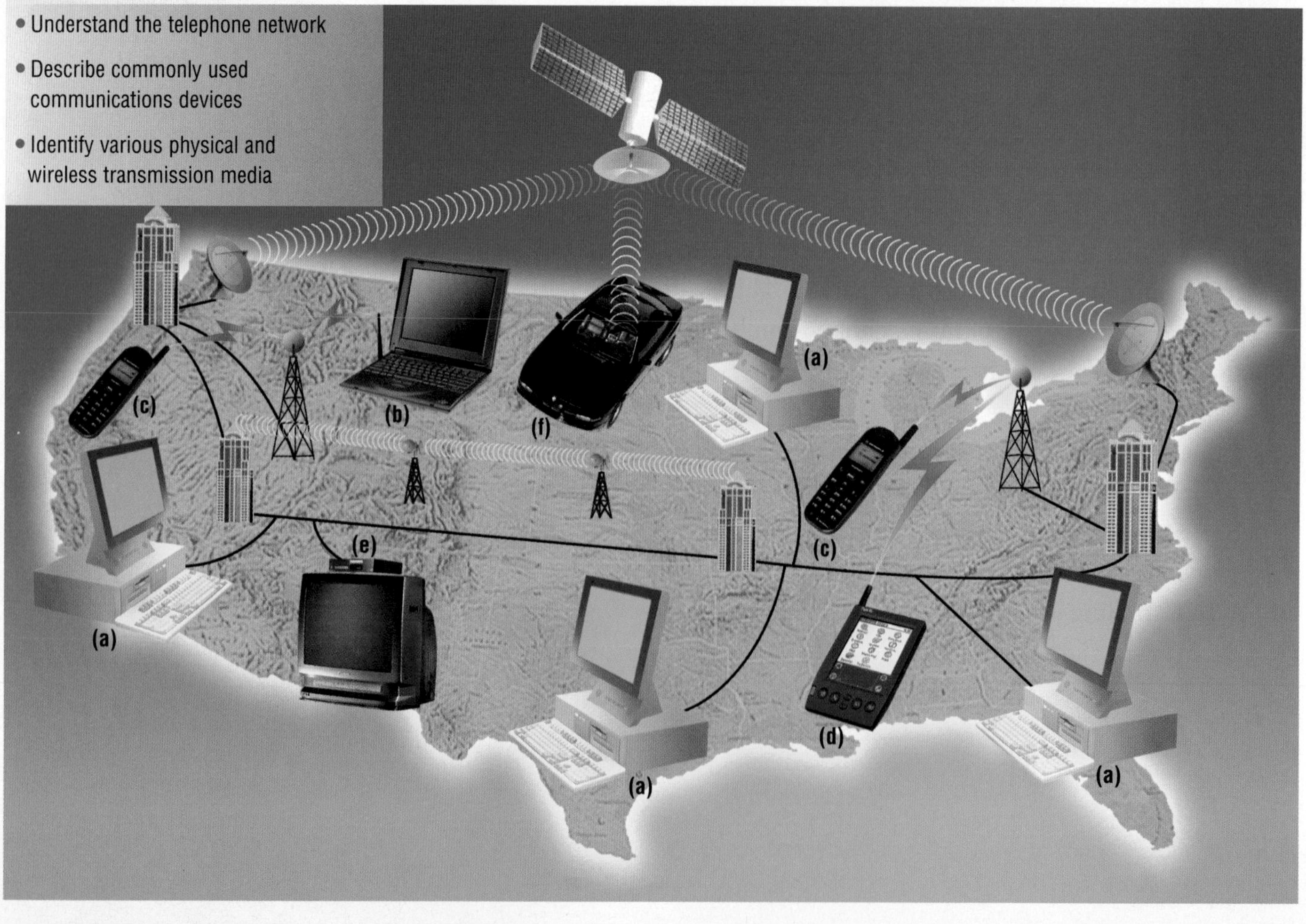

The primary function of a communications device, such as a modem, is to convert or format signals so they are suitable for the communications channel or a receiving device. When using a telephone line as the communications channel, you need a modem to convert between analog and digital signals (Figure 9-2). An **analog signal** consists of a continuous electrical wave. Computers, however, process data as digital signals. A **digital signal** consists of individual electrical pulses that represent the bits grouped together into bytes.

For instance, a modem connected to a sending computer converts the computer's digital signals into analog signals. The analog signals then travel over a communications channel, such as a standard telephone line. At the receiving end, another modem converts the analog signals back into digital signals that a receiving computer can understand.

SENDING AND RECEIVING DEVICES

Sending and receiving devices initiate or accept transmission of data, instructions, and information. Notebook computers, desktop computers, mid-range servers, and mainframe computers all can serve as sending and receiving devices. These computers can communicate directly with another computer, with hundreds of computers on a company network, or with millions of other computers on the Internet.

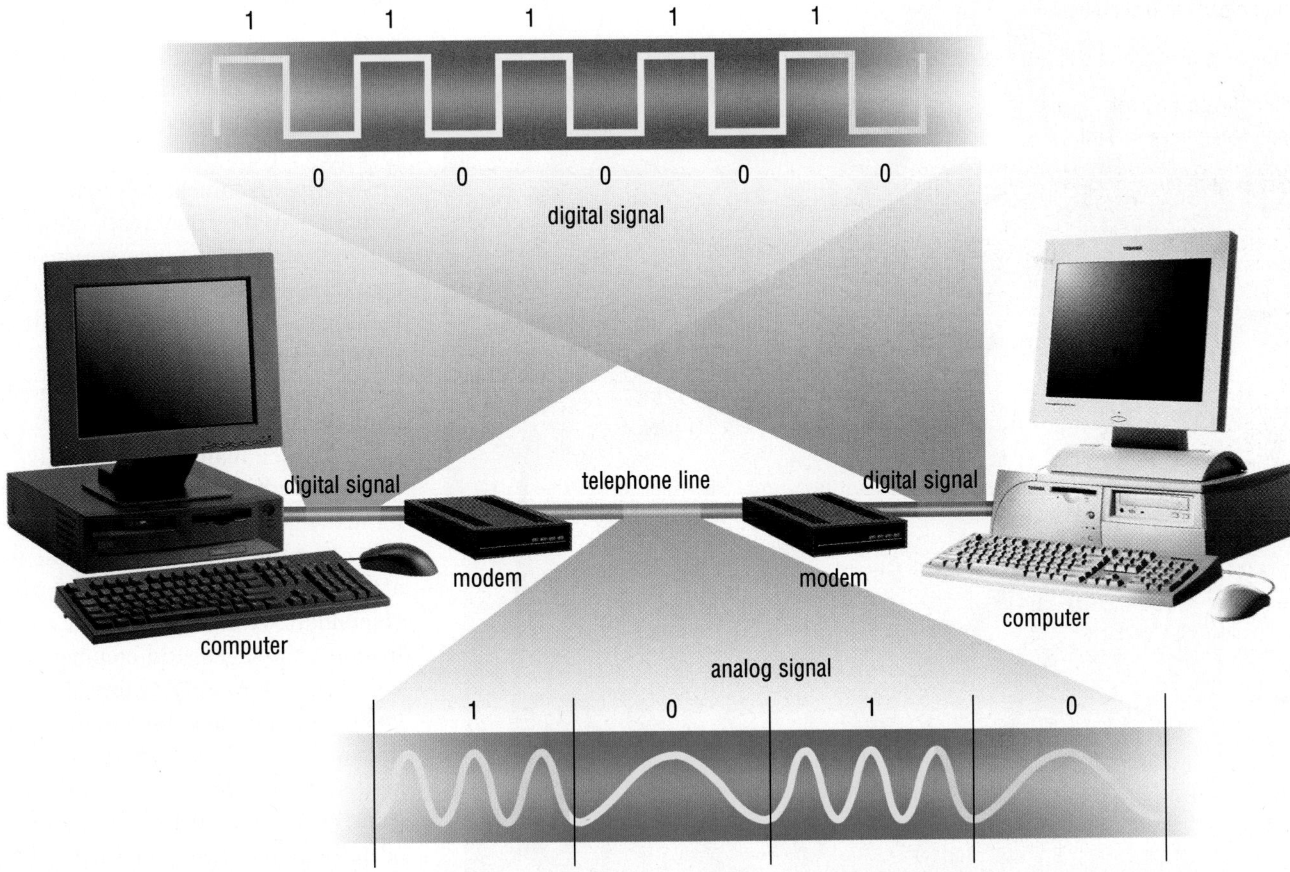

Figure 9-2 A modem converts individual electrical pulses of a digital signal into analog signals for data transmission over some telephone lines. At the receiving computer, another modem converts the analog signals back into digital signals that the computer can process.

Internet appliances and Web-enabled handheld computers and devices also serve as sending and receiving devices (Figure 9-3). An **Internet appliance**, sometimes called a **Web appliance**, is a computer with limited functionality whose main purpose is to connect to the Internet from home. A **Web-enabled device** is a handheld device that provides access to the Internet and e-mail from any location. Cellular telephones and pagers are examples of wireless devices that can be Web enabled.

Internet appliances typically sit on a countertop in the home. With these appliances, you can connect to the Internet in any room of the house. A set-top box, such as WebTV™, sits on top of or next to a television set. You communicate with a set-top box using a remote control or wireless keyboard.

A Web-enabled handheld computer provides Internet access, in addition to the other features normally provided by the computer. A Web-enabled cellular telephone, sometimes called a smart phone, allows you to send and receive messages on the Internet and browse Web sites specifically configured for display on the telephone. A Web-enabled pager, also called a smart pager, is a two-way radio that allows you to send and receive messages using the Internet.

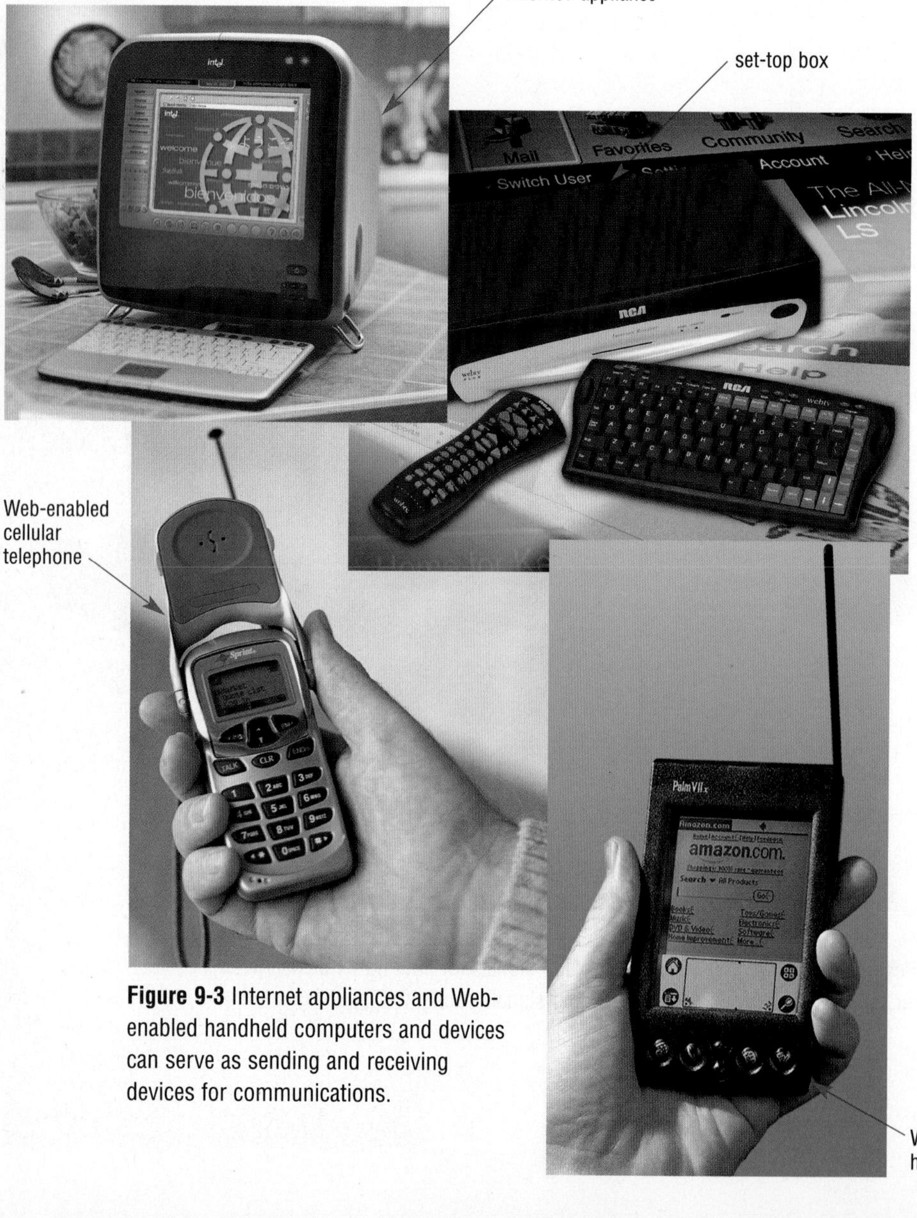

Figure 9-3 Internet appliances and Web-enabled handheld computers and devices can serve as sending and receiving devices for communications.

USES OF COMMUNICATIONS TECHNOLOGIES

Communications technology use is all around you. In the course of a day, for example, you might use, or use information generated by, one or more of the following communications technologies: voice mail, fax, e-mail, instant messaging, chat rooms, newsgroups, telephony, videoconferencing, collaboration, groupware, and a global positioning system (GPS). Previous chapters have presented most of these communications technologies, as they related to a particular topic. The following sections review these technologies and discuss how they specifically relate to communications.

Voice Mail

Voice mail, which functions much like an answering machine, allows callers to leave a voice message for the called party. Unlike answering machines, however, a computer in the voice mail system converts an analog voice message into digital form. Once digitized, the message is stored in a voice mailbox. A **voice mailbox** is a storage location on a computer in the voice mail system.

A voice mail system usually provides individual voice mailboxes for many users (for example, employees in a company or students and faculty at a college). By accessing his or her voice mailbox, a called party can listen to messages, add comments to a message, and reply or forward a message to another voice mailbox in the voice mail system. Some voice mail systems allow you to send the same message to a specific group of individuals or everyone listed in the system's database. Colleges, for example, can use voice mail to notify every student of registration deadlines and weather-related school closings.

Fax

A **fax** can contain handwritten or typed text, illustrations, photographs, or other graphics. As discussed in Chapter 6, you can send or receive a fax using a stand-alone fax machine or a computer fax modem.

Using a computer fax modem is more economical and efficient than a stand-alone fax machine. Not only does it save paper, a computer fax modem allows you to store received faxes on your computer. You then can use an e-mail program to send the fax to others. Many larger companies, such as insurance companies, route all incoming faxes to computer fax modems.

E-Mail

E-mail (electronic mail) is the exchange of text messages and computer files transmitted via a communications network such as a local area network or the Internet. Communications devices transfer the e-mail messages to and from computers or terminals on the same network or a separate network. To send and receive e-mail messages, you use e-mail software installed on your computer.

APPLY IT!

Send and Receive Faxes from Your Computer

Throw away the fax machine and use the Internet to send your fax document! Several options are available for receiving and sending fax documents to and from your computer. You can use a fax modem, or you can use one of many Internet services to send a fax. Some are free while others are pay services. Some services require you install special software on your computer.

To use a fax modem requires that you have fax software. Many fax software programs exist — from freeware to shareware to full priced, full featured communications packages. Most of these programs operate similarly. The software installs a specialized driver on your computer. This driver converts electronic documents into the proper format for faxing. You use your modem to transmit the converted documents to a remote fax machine. You can fax any document created in a Windows application or saved in a Windows-compatible format to a remote fax machine or another fax modem.

To send the fax, click File on the menu bar and then click Print to display the Print dialog box. Select your fax software, which displays in the list of printers, and follow the online instructions to send your document. Most of these software programs also support sending copies of paper documents directly from a scanner.

Another option is paperless Internet faxing, which has become popular because it is less expensive to fax through the Internet — no long distance telephone call charges. Receiving faxes through the Internet is convenient. You usually can receive the documents either through an e-mail address or through a Web site. Several companies on the Internet provide this service. One of the more popular is eFax.com (see URL below). To use this free service requires the following steps:

1. Sign up for the free service, which is available for Windows, Linux, UNIX, and Mac users.
2. An e-mail message is sent to you with your fax number and personal identification number (PIN).
3. Download and install the free software that allows you to create, annotate, and send faxes and e-mail messages, in addition to viewing faxes and listening to voice mail messages.
4. For a small monthly fee, you can add other services such as wireless messaging notification and forwarding.

For more information on sending faxes from your computer and the Web site mentioned above, visit the Discovering Computers 2002 Apply It Web page (**scsite.com/dc2002/apply.htm**) and click Chapter 9 Apply It #1.

ISSUE

The Nature of E-Mail

E-Mail

E-mail may be today's most popular, and influential, communications technology. It is permeating our writing lives. Millions of people around the world send and receive e-mail messages. E-mail links the geographically separated, connects the socially stratified, enables the physically limited, and encourages the publicly timid. Because of e-mail, people are writing more than ever before — but is it *good* writing? Our grandparents' carefully crafted letters have been replaced by e-mail messages stylistically equivalent to notes on the refrigerator. E-mail's immediacy often results in messages that are ill conceived, casually spelled, poorly worded, grammatically flawed, and tritely expressed (some trite phrases, such as *in my humble opinion*, are used so routinely they are replaced by abbreviations — IMHO). In general, has e-mail's impact on communications been positive or negative? Why? Should the quality of e-mail communications be a reason for concern? Why? Could someone's professional reputation be enhanced or hindered by the quality and effectiveness of their e-mail messages?

For more information on e-mail and the writing process, visit the Discovering Computers 2002 Issues Web page (**scsite.com/dc2002/issues.htm**) and click Chapter 9 Issue #1.

Instant Messaging

Instant messaging (IM) is a real-time Internet communications service that notifies you when one or more people are online and then allows you to exchange messages or files with them or join a private chat room. Figure 9-4 shows how to use one IM service. Many IM services also can alert you to information such as calendar appointments, stock quotes, weather, or sports scores. People use IM on all types of computers, including desktop computers, notebook computers, and Web-enabled handheld computers and devices.

Chat Rooms

A **chat room** permits users to converse in real time with each other via the computer while connected to the Internet. To participate in a chat, you and others connect to a server on the Internet. As you type on your

Figure 9-4 AN EXAMPLE OF INSTANT MESSAGING

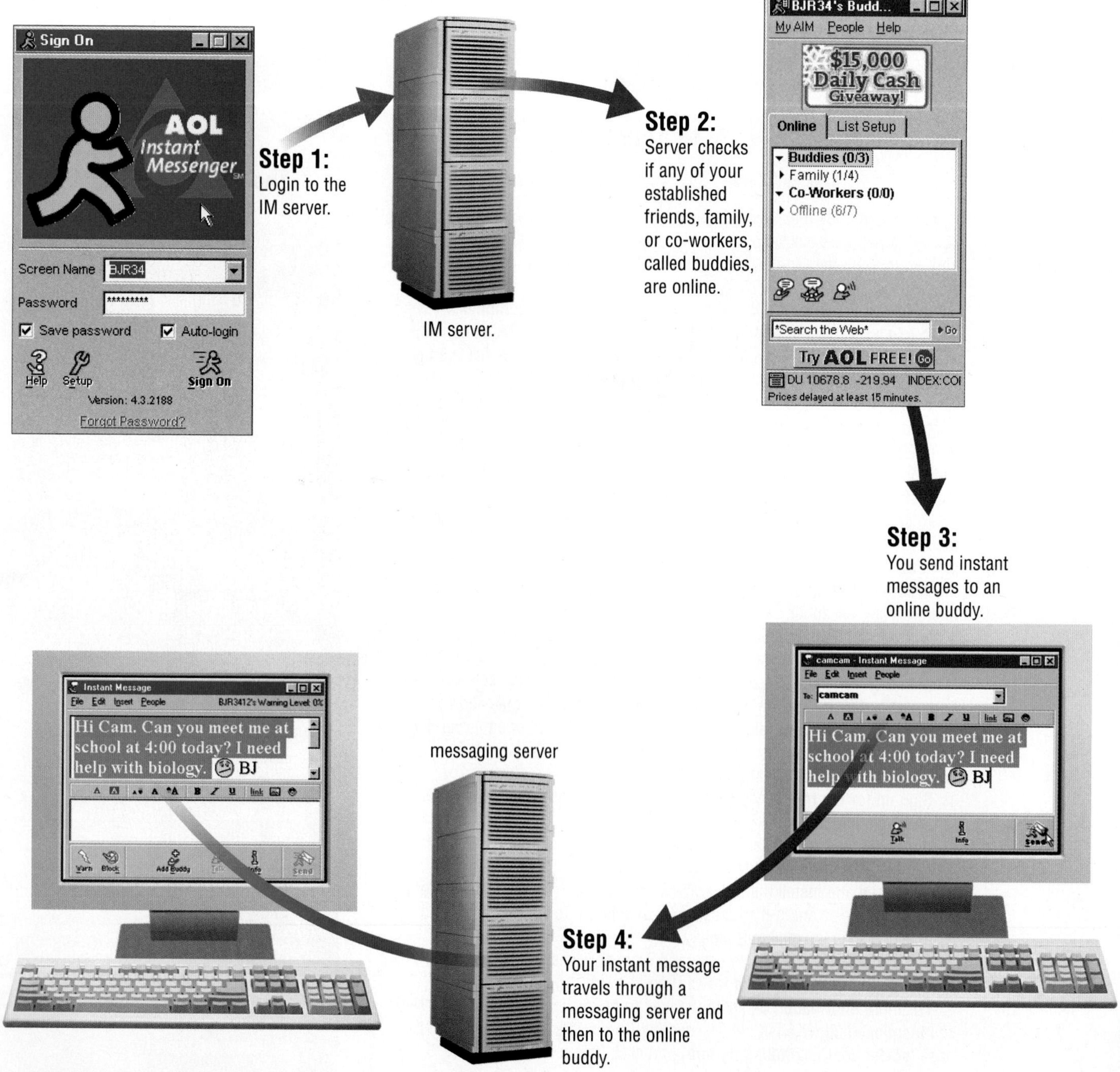

keyboard, a line of characters and symbols display on the computer screen. Others connected to the same chat room server also can see what you have typed (Figure 9-5). In some chat rooms, you can click a button to see a personal profile of someone in the chat room.

Chats typically are specific to a certain topic such as computers or cooking. Some chat rooms support **voice chats** and **video chats**, where you hear and see others and they can hear or see you while in the chat room. **Radio chats** play music while you chat.

Newsgroups

A **newsgroup**, also called a **threaded discussion**, is an area on the Web where users conduct written discussions about a particular subject. The difference between a chat room and a newsgroup is that a chat room is a live conversation. The newsgroup is not. Some people use the term **synchronous** to refer to real-time live communications and the term **asynchronous** to refer to communications that are not real time. Using this terminology, a chat room is synchronous, and a newsgroup is asynchronous.

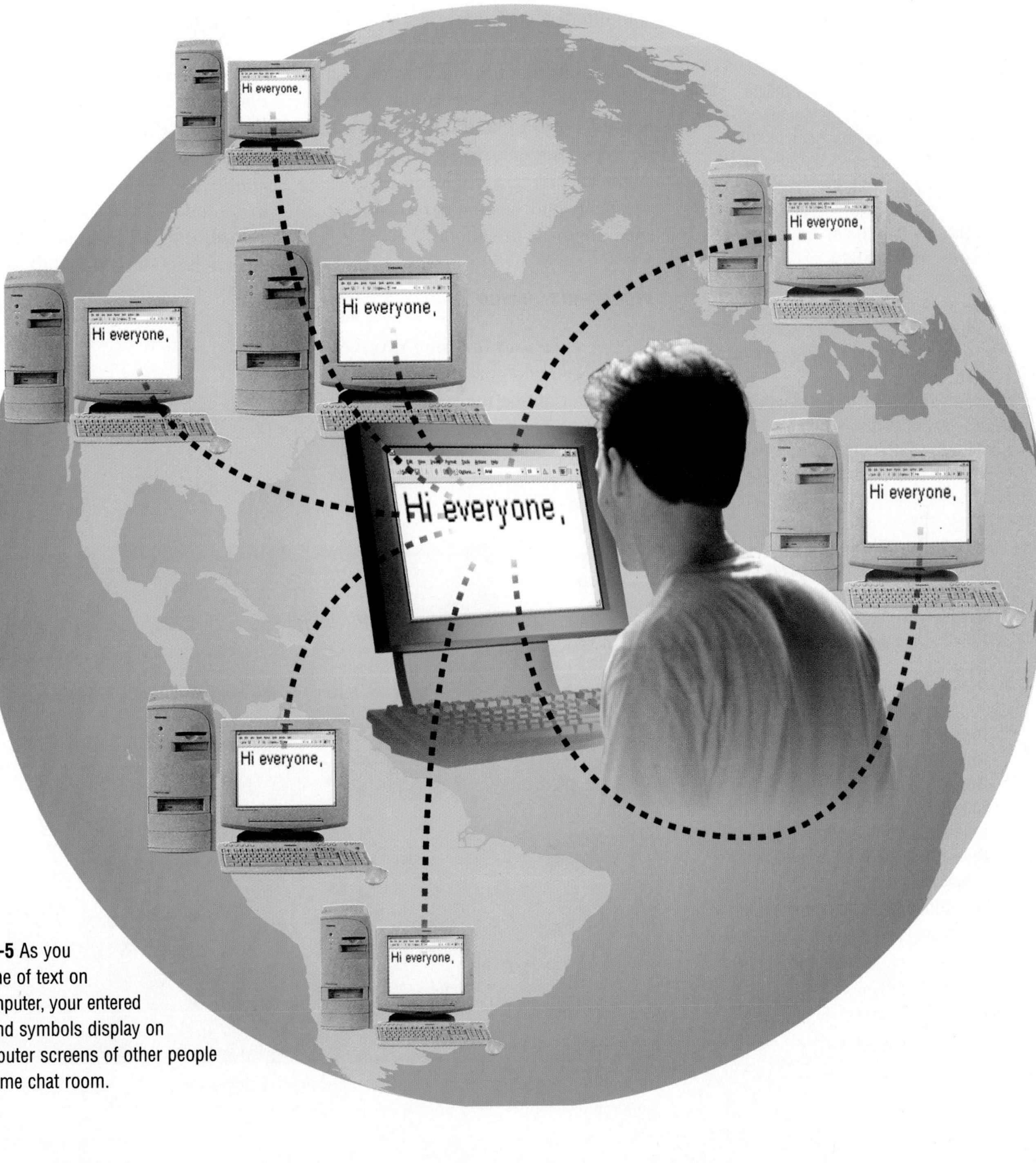

Figure 9-5 As you type a line of text on your computer, your entered words and symbols display on the computer screens of other people in the same chat room.

APPLY IT!

Chat Attack!

Looking for someone to talk to? If so, you can find a chat room to discuss just about any topic. Chat rooms are similar to conference calls; everyone is online at the same time. You can watch the chat without joining it, or you can join the conversation at any time. Some chat sessions are open discussions, while others are moderated by hosts. One of the most popular chat sites on the Web is Yahoo Chat (see URL below).

Before chatting, you should understand how chat rooms work. Chat rooms have their own special cyberlingo and a set of rules (netiquette) for online behavior. In a chat room, you will see many abbreviations, such as the following:

- **AFK** - **A**way **F**rom **K**eyboard
- **BAK** - **B**ack **A**t **K**eyboard
- **BBS** - **B**e **B**ack **S**oon
- **BRB** - **B**e **R**ight **B**ack
- **BBIAB** - **B**e **B**ack **I**n **A** **B**it
- **c-ya** - A quick way to say "see you"
- **<g>** - Grin
- **j/k** - **J**ust **K**idding
- **WB** - **W**elcome **B**ack

How you act and treat others online also is very important. The following Core Rules are from the book ***Netiquette*** by Virginia Shea, also known as Ms. Manners of the Internet (see URL below).

Rule 1: Be polite and courteous
Rule 2: Adhere to the same standards of behavior online that you follow in real life
Rule 3: Monitor postings before you participate
Rule 4: Respect other people's time and bandwidth
Rule 5: Spelling and grammar count
Rule 6: Share expert knowledge
Rule 7: Control your responses
Rule 8: Respect other people's privacy
Rule 9: Don't abuse your power
Rule 10: Be forgiving of other people's mistakes

For more information on chat rooms and netiquette and the Web sites mentioned above, visit the Discovering Computers 2002 Apply It Web page (**scsite.com/dc2002/apply.htm**) and click Chapter 9 Apply It #2.

Telephony

Internet telephony enables you to talk to other people over the Internet. Internet telephony uses the Internet (instead of the public switched telephone network) to connect a calling party and one or more called parties. To place an Internet telephone call, you need Internet telephone software. As you speak into a computer microphone, **Internet telephone software** and your computer's sound card digitize and compress your conversation (the audio) and then transmit the digitized audio over the Internet to the called parties. Software and equipment at the receiving end reverse the process so the receiving parties can hear what you have said, just as if you were speaking on a telephone.

Videoconferencing

A **videoconference** involves using video and computer technology to conduct a meeting between participants at two or more geographically separate locations (Figure 9-6). Videoconferencing allows participants to collaborate as if they were in the same room. Popular uses of videoconferencing include technical support, distance learning, job recruiting interviews, and telecommuting.

Conducting a videoconference requires computers with microphones, speakers, video cameras, and communications devices and software. The communications devices and software digitize and compress the video and audio data and then transmit it over a communications channel, such as a standard telephone line.

A **Web conference** is a conferencing system that uses the Internet, Web browsers, and Web servers to deliver this service. Using a technology similar to a Web conference, home users today can make a **video telephone call**, where both parties see each other as they talk on the Internet.

Figure 9-6 Videoconferencing allows participants to collaborate as if they were in the same room.

Collaboration

Many software products provide a means to **collaborate**, or work with other users connected to a server. With Microsoft Office, you can conduct online meetings (Figure 9-7). An **online meeting** allows you to share documents with others in real time. All participants see the document at the same time. As someone changes the document, everyone can see the changes being made. During the online meeting, participants can open a separate window and type messages to one another. Some products refer to this window as a chat room.

Instead of interacting in a live meeting, some users collaborate via e-mail. For example, if you want others to review a document, you can attach a routing slip to the document and send it via e-mail to everyone on the routing slip. When the first person on the routing slip receives the document, he or she can add comments to the document. As changes are made to the document, both the original text and the changes display. When each subsequent person on the routing slip receives the document via e-mail, they see all the previous people's changes and can make additional changes. Once everyone on the routing slip has reviewed the document, it automatically returns to the sender.

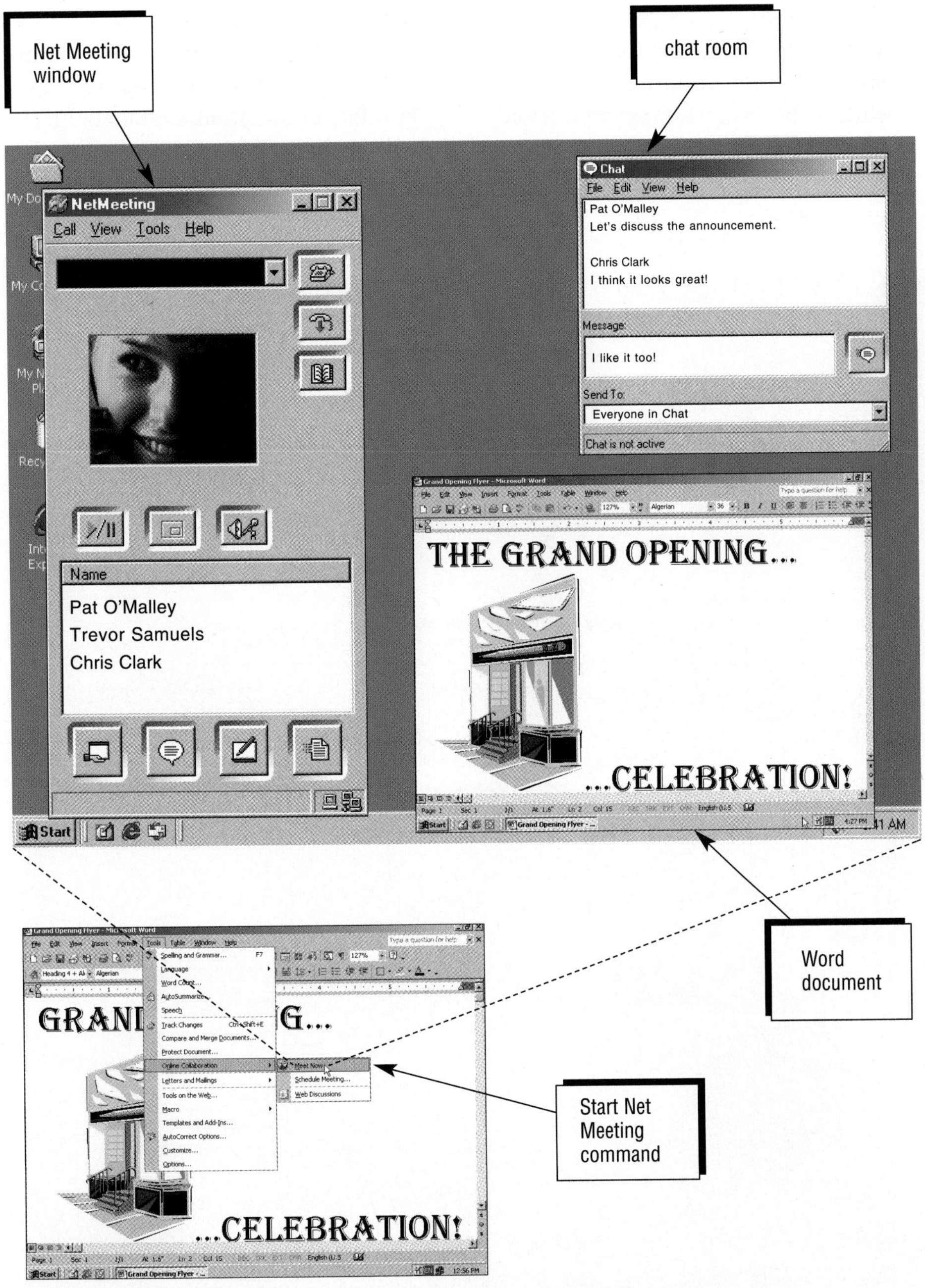

Figure 9-7 When you start an online meeting from a Microsoft Office product, the participants use NetMeeting to collaborate on the document.

ISSUE

Smile, You're on Video Camera

Public Video Surveillance

Cameras photographing real-time situations are everywhere — on street corners, in parking garages and daycare centers, public buildings, and more. Both public and private organizations use these cameras not only for security, but for a variety of other purposes. One of the most recent implementations of this technology by public agencies is as video watchdogs. On the New Jersey Turnpike, for example, a video system records a four second clip of the arm motion of every driver who pays the toll by tossing change into a basket. A second camera records pictures of the cars' license plates. In many cities, video cameras are installed at intersections to catch speeding motorists and those who run red lights. When someone violates a law, they automatically are sent a ticket. Is this a violation of privacy? Is this ethical? Alan Westin, a Columbia University professor who has studied privacy issues for 40 years, questions how long the tapes will be kept and what safeguards are in place to protect the government from misusing the information. Do you agree that the tapes could be misused? In what way? For how long should a governmental agency be able to keep these tapes?

For more information on video surveillance and privacy issues, visit the Discovering Computers 2002 Issues Web page (**scsite.com/dc 2002/issues.htm**) and click Chapter 9 Issue #2.

Groupware

Groupware is a software application that helps groups of people work together on projects and share information over a network. Groupware is a component of a broad concept called **workgroup computing**, which includes network hardware and software that enables group members to communicate, manage projects, schedule meetings, and make group decisions. To assist with these activities, most groupware provides personal information manager (PIM) functions, such as an electronic appointment calendar, an address book, and a notepad. A major feature of groupware is group scheduling, in which a group calendar tracks the schedules of multiple users and helps coordinate appointments and meeting times.

Global Positioning System

A **global positioning system** (**GPS**) consists of one or more earth-based receivers that accept and analyze signals sent by satellites in order to determine the receiver's geographic location. A GPS receiver is a handheld or mountable device, which can be secured to an automobile, boat, airplane, farm and construction equipment, or a computer. Some GPS receivers include a screen display that shows your position on a map. Other GPS receivers send location information to a base station, where humans can give you personal directions.

GPS has a variety of uses: to locate a person or object; ascertain the best route between two points; monitor the movement of a person or object (Figure 9-8); or create a map. GPSs help scientists, farmers, pilots, dispatchers, and rescue workers operate more productively and safely. A rescue worker, for example, might use a GPS to locate a motorist stranded in a blizzard. A surveyor might use a GPS to create design maps for construction projects.

GPSs also are popular in consumer products for travel and recreational activities. Many cars use GPSs to provide drivers with directions or other information, automatically call for help if the airbag deploys, dispatch roadside assistance, unlock

Figure 9-8 HOW GPS WORKS

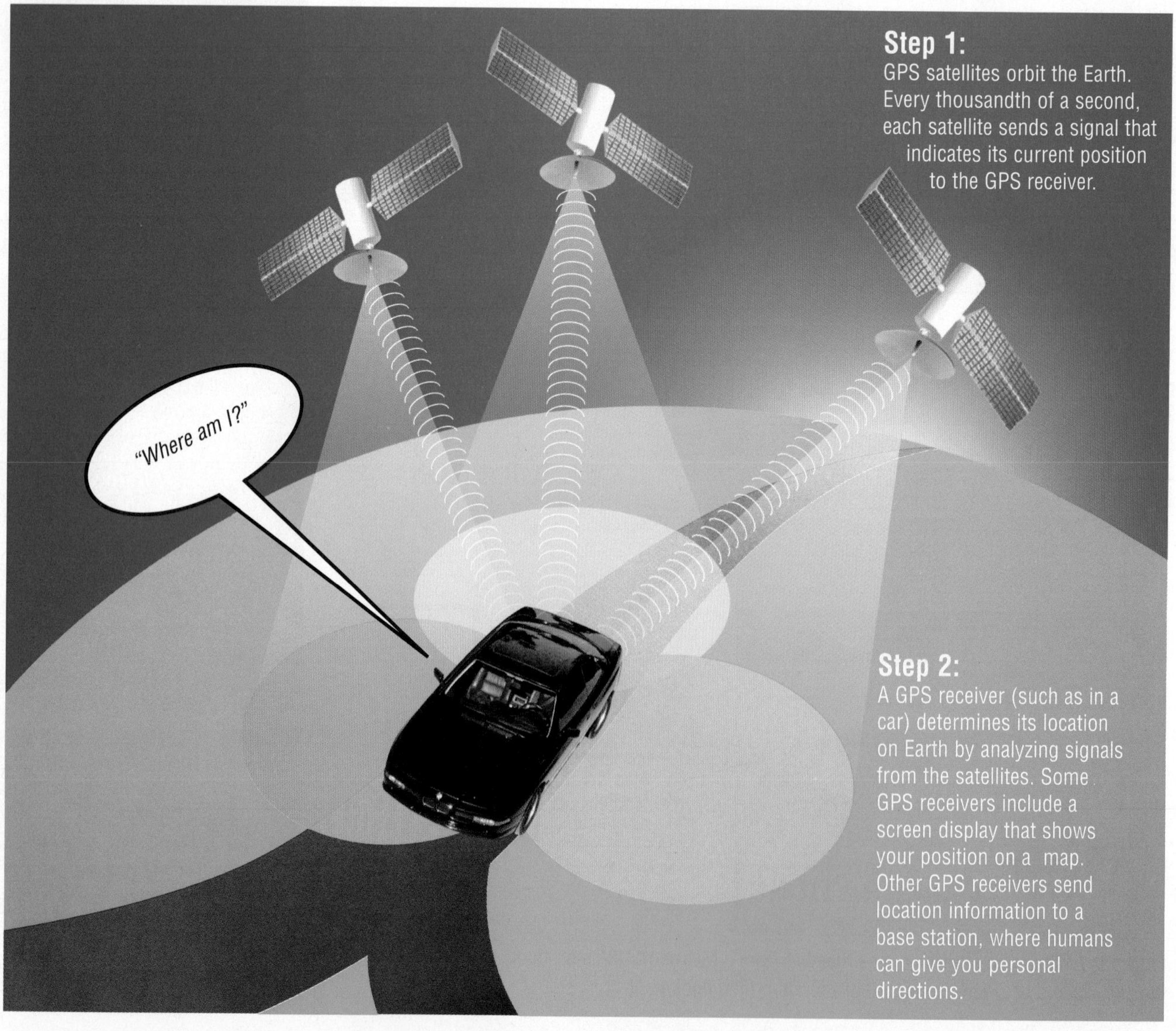
Step 1:
GPS satellites orbit the Earth. Every thousandth of a second, each satellite sends a signal that indicates its current position to the GPS receiver.
"Where am I?"
Step 2:
A GPS receiver (such as in a car) determines its location on Earth by analyzing signals from the satellites. Some GPS receivers include a screen display that shows your position on a map. Other GPS receivers send location information to a base station, where humans can give you personal directions.

the driver's side door if keys are locked in the car, and track the vehicle if it is stolen. For cars not equipped with a GPS, drivers can mount GPS receivers on the dashboard or place one in the glove compartment. Hikers and remote campers also carry GPS receivers in case they need emergency help or directions.

A new use of GPS places the device on a computer chip. The chip, called **Digital Angel™**, is worn as a bracelet or chain or woven into fabric and has an antenna that communicates with a GPS satellite. The chip measures and sends biological information to the GPS satellite. If information relayed indicates a person needs medical attention, dispatchers can send emergency medical help immediately. Other possible uses of Digital Angel™ include locating a missing person or pet, tracking parolees, and protecting valuables. Retailers take advantage of this technology, too. For example, a coffee shop could send a coupon into a handheld computer as the people walk by their store.

NETWORKS

A **network** is a collection of computers and devices connected by communications channels that facilitates communications among users and allows users to share resources with other users. Examples of resources are data, information, hardware, and software. The following paragraphs explain the advantages of using a network.

- Facilitating communications — Using a network, people can communicate efficiently and easily via e-mail, instant messaging, chat rooms, telephony, video telephone calls, and videoconferencing. Sometimes these communications occur within a business's network. Other times, they occur globally through the Internet. As discussed earlier in this chapter, users have a multitude of devices available for sending and receiving communications.
- Sharing hardware — In a networked environment, each computer on a network can access and use hardware on the network. Suppose several personal computers on a network each require the use of a laser printer. If the personal computers and a laser printer are connected into a network, the personal computer users each can access the laser printer on the network, as they need it.

  Businesses and home users network their hardware for one main reason. That is, it may be too costly to provide each user with the same piece of hardware such as a printer.
- Sharing data and information — In a networked environment, any authorized computer user can access data and information stored on other computers in the network. A large company, for example, might have a database of customer information. Any authorized person, including a mobile user using a handheld computer to connect to the network, can access this database. The capability of providing access to and storage of data and information on shared storage devices is an important feature of many networks.
- Sharing software — Users connected to a network can access software (programs) on the network. To support multiple user access of software, most software vendors sell network versions of their software. In this case, software vendors issue a site license. A **site license** is a legal agreement that allows multiple users to run the software package simultaneously. The site license fee usually is based on the number of users or the number of computers attached to the network. Sharing software via a network usually costs less than buying individual copies of the software package for each computer.

Web Link

For more information on GPSs, visit the Discovering Computers 2002 Chapter 9 WEB LINK page (**scsite.com/dc2002/ch9/weblink.htm**) and click GPS.

ISSUE

Implanting Computer Chips

A New Use for Global Positioning Systems

Twenty years ago, bar code technology revolutionized the way goods and merchandise were identified, priced, and inventoried. A new type of electronic identification is now on the horizon. Digital Angel™ (see URL below) is an implanted or worn device that uses miniaturized microchip technology for identification. Unlike the bar code, which requires physical contact between the reader and the bar code, Digital Angel™ uses Radio Frequency Identification (RFID). According to Applied Digital Systems (ADS) (see URL below), the company that manufactures Digital Angel, "The implantable transceiver sends and receives data and can be continuously tracked by GPS (Global Positioning Satellite) technology." The company further states, "When implanted within a body, the device is powered electromechanically through the movement of muscles, and it can be activated either by the 'wearer' or by the monitoring facility." What are the implications of chip implanting? Would you permit a chip to be implanted in your body? Why or why not? ADS promotes this technology as a method to track people on probation, eliminate kidnapping, or locate older people who may get lost. Do you agree? Is this a privacy invasion? What are the ethical issues surrounding this technology?

For more information on the microchip implant and the Web sites mentioned above, visit the Discovering Computers 2002 Issues Web page (**scsite.com/dc2002/issues.htm**) and click Chapter 9 Issue #3.

Local Area Network (LAN)

A **local area network (LAN)** is a network that connects computers and devices in a limited geographical area such as a home, school computer laboratory, office building (Figure 9-9), or closely positioned group of buildings. Each computer or device on the network is a **node**. Often, the nodes are connected to the LAN via cables. A **wireless LAN (WLAN)** is a LAN that uses no physical wires. Instead of wires, WLANs use wireless media such as radio waves.

A **network operating system**, also called a **network OS** or **NOS** (pronounced nauce), is the system software that organizes and coordinates the activities on a local area network. Some of the tasks performed by a NOS include the following:

- Administration – adding, deleting, and organizing users and performing maintenance tasks such as backup
- File management – locating and transferring files
- Printer management – prioritizing print jobs and reports sent to specific printers on the network
- Security – monitoring and, when necessary, restricting access to network resources

Many operating systems have network features built into them. In other cases, the network OS is a set of programs that works with another operating system(s). Figure 9-10 indicates which operating systems

Figure 9-9 An example of a local area network (LAN).

OPERATING SYSTEMS THAT SUPPORT NETWORKS

Operating System	Requires Separate Operating System	Network Type
IBM OS/2 Warp		Client/Server
Linux		Client/Server
Microsoft Windows 95, Windows 98, and Windows Me		Peer-to-Peer
Microsoft Windows NT and Windows 2000		Client/Server
Novell NetWare	DOS	Client/Server
SpartaCom LANtastic	Any PC operating system	Peer-to-Peer
Sun Solaris™		Client/Server
UNIX		Client/Server

Figure 9-10 A list of popular operating systems that support networks. Many operating systems have network features built into them. In other cases, it is a set of programs that works with another operating system(s).

Web Link

For more information on a LAN, visit the Discovering Computers 2002 Chapter 9 WEB LINK page (**scsite.com/dc2002/ch9/weblink.htm**) and click LAN.

have network features built into them. This figure also specifies the type of network the operating system supports, that is, peer-to-peer or client/server. The following paragraphs discuss peer-to-peer and client/server networks.

PEER-TO-PEER A **peer-to-peer** LAN is a simple, inexpensive network that typically connects less than 10 computers together. Each computer on a peer-to-peer network can share the hardware (such as a printer), data, or information located on any other computer in the network (Figure 9-11). Each computer stores files on its own storage devices. Thus, each computer in the network contains both the network operating system and application software. All computers on the network share any peripheral device attached to any computer. For example, one computer may have a laser printer and a scanner, while another has an ink-jet printer.

Peer-to-peer networks are ideal for very small businesses and home users. Some operating systems, such as Windows, include a peer-to-peer networking utility that allows you to set up a basic peer-to-peer network.

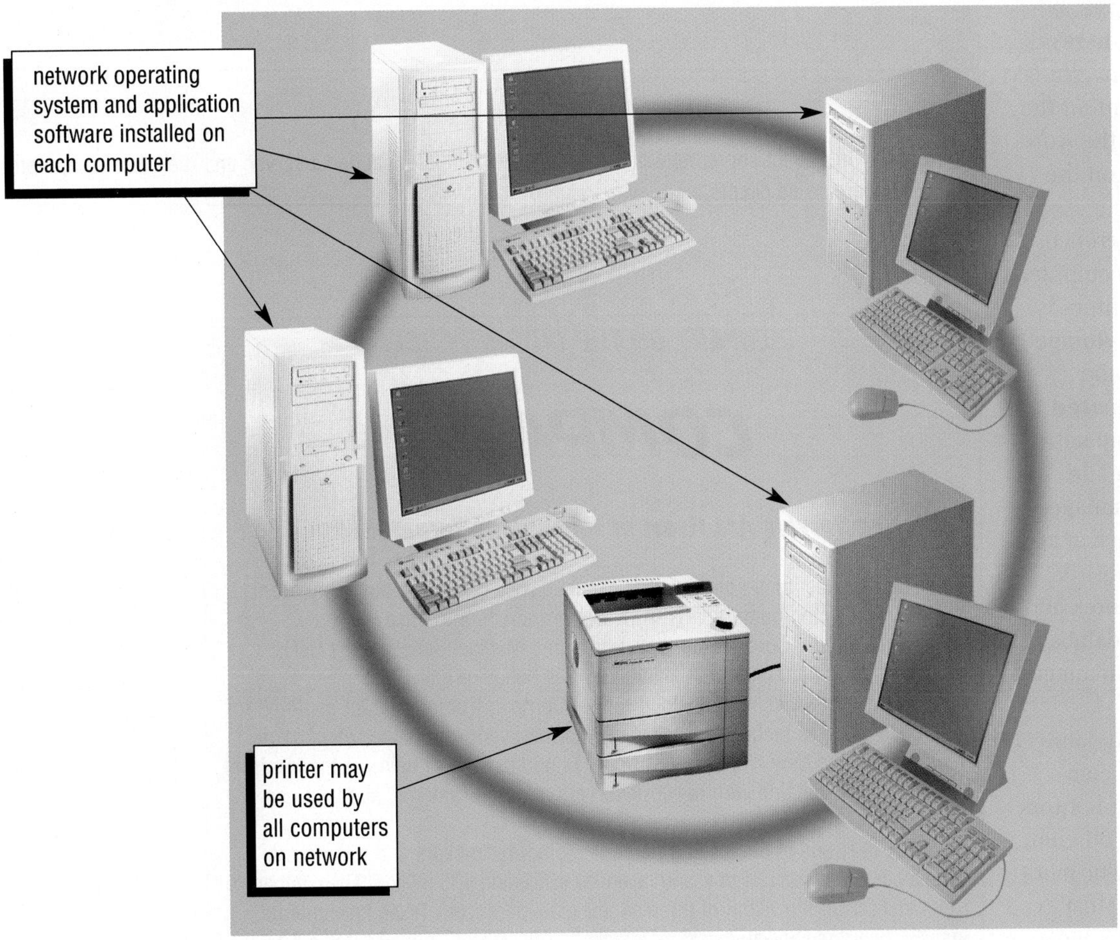

Figure 9-11 Each computer on a peer-to-peer network stores its own data and information.

CLIENT/SERVER A **client/server** LAN is a network in which one or more computers act as a server and the other computers on the network can request services from the server (Figure 9-12). A **server**, sometimes called the **host computer**, controls access to the hardware and software on the network and provides a centralized storage area for programs, data, and information. The other computers on the network, called **clients**, rely on the server for these resources. For example, a server might store a network version of a word processing program. Every client on the network can access the word processing program on the server.

The major difference between the server computer and the client computers is the server has more storage space and power. Some servers, called **dedicated servers**, perform a specific task. For example, a **file server** stores and manages files. A **print server** manages printers and print jobs. A **database server** stores and provides access to a database. A **network server** manages network traffic.

Although it can connect a smaller number of computers, a client/server network typically provides an efficient means to connect 10 or more computers together. Most client/server networks have a network administrator because of the larger size of a client/server network. The **network administrator** is the operations person in charge of the network.

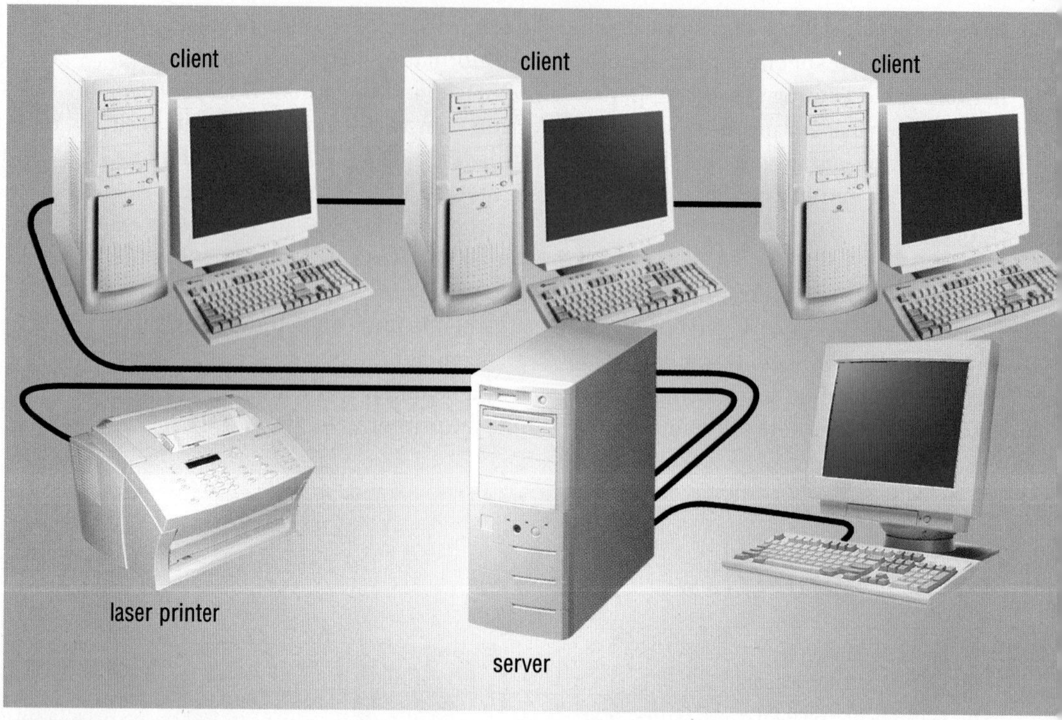

Figure 9-12 On a client/server network, one or more computers act as a server, and the other computers on the network are called clients.

COMPANY ON THE CUTTING EDGE

COMPAQ

Servers Are Heart of Technology Turnaround

When was the last time your boss lip-synched rock tunes at a company event and blasted electric-guitar songs from a boom box in the office? If you work at Compaq Computer Corporation, you would find Michael Capellas, the CEO, president, and board chairman, exhibiting this behavior daily.

Capellas' enthusiasm has helped reboot Compaq from a product-centered to a solution-oriented technology company. Its marketing campaign, *Inspiration Technology: The New IT*, reinforces Capellas' philosophy of being at the forefront of the digital revolution with network servers, storage systems, and wireless devices.

Compaq is one of the leading personal computer makers and the second-largest computer seller, with yearly revenues exceeding $38 million. The company's roots stem from the vision of three senior managers from Texas Instruments. In 1981, the three invested approximately $1,000 apiece and garnered a $2.5 million contribution from venture capitalist Ben Rosen.

Their initial success came from marketing IBM *clones*, look-alike computers that performed like IBMs, but were less costly. Compaq became the first company to achieve Fortune 500 status in less than four years. In 1988, the company acquired Digital Equipment Corporation, gaining that company's 25,000 field engineers and support staff.

For more information on Compaq, visit the Discovering Computers 2002 Companies Web page (**scsite.com/dc2002/companies.htm**) and click Compaq.

Wide Area Network (WAN)

A **wide area network (WAN)** is a network that covers a large geographic area (such as a city, country, or the world) using a communications channel that combines many types of media such as telephone lines, cables, and air waves (Figure 9-13). A WAN can be one large network or can consist of two or more LANs connected together. The Internet is the world's largest WAN.

Web Link
For more information on a wide area network, visit the Discovering Computers 2002 Chapter 9 WEB LINK page (**scsite.com/dc2002/ch9/weblink.htm**) and click Wide Area Network.

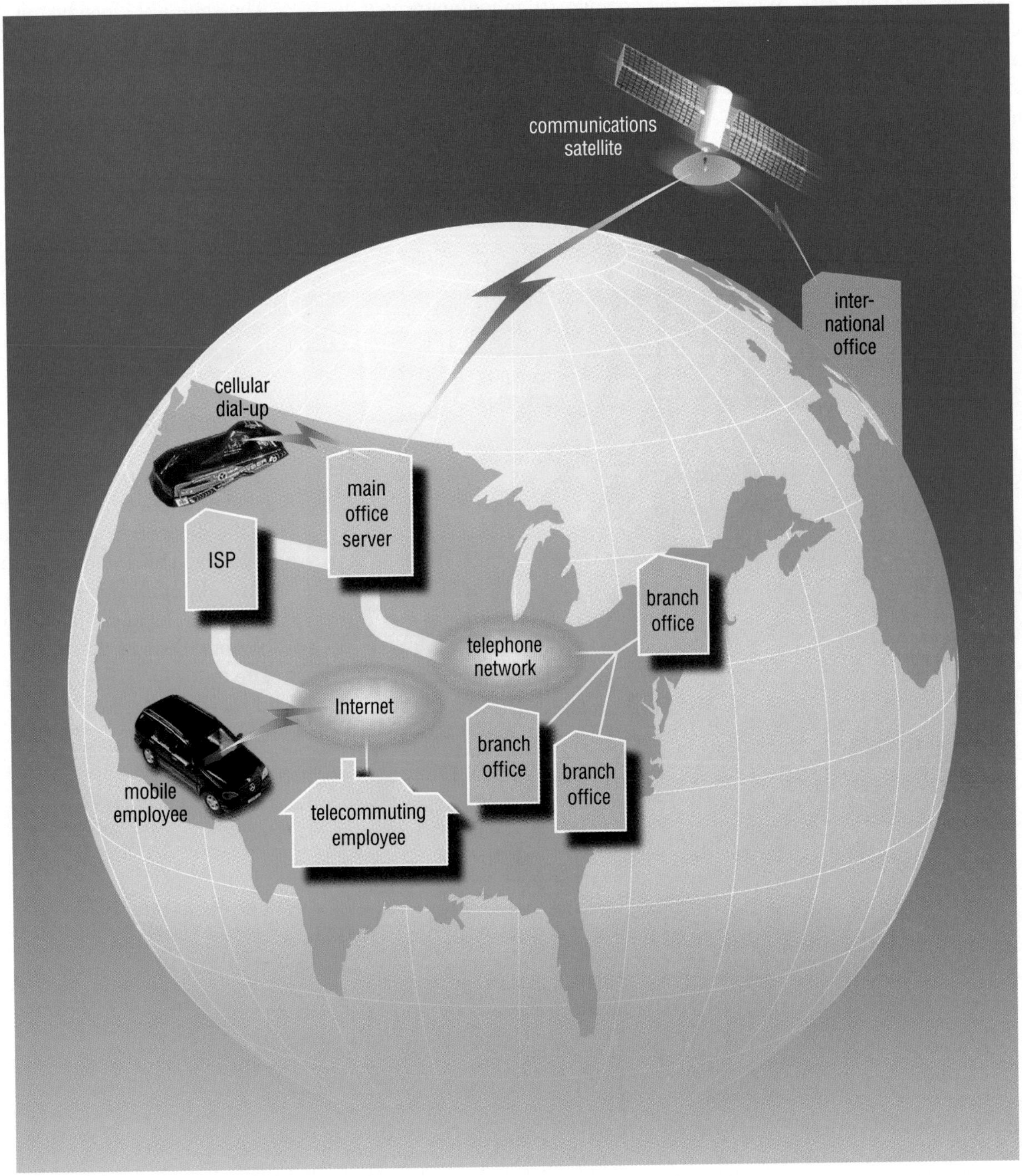

Figure 9-13 An example of a WAN.

INTERNET PEER-TO-PEER Another use of peer-to-peer, called **P2P**, describes an Internet network that enables users with the same networking software to connect to each other's hard disks and exchange files directly (Figure 9-14). With the appropriate software and an Internet connection, users can copy files from someone else's hard disk to their hard disk. As people connect to the network, you have access to their hard disk. When they log off, you no longer can access their hard disk. To maintain an acceptable speed for communications, most implementations of P2P limit the number of users.

Two examples of networking software that allow P2P are Napster and Gnutella. These programs have stirred much controversy with respect to copyright infringement of music because they allow users easily to copy MP3 music files from one computer to another. Many businesses, however, see an advantage to using P2P. That is, companies and employees can exchange files using P2P, freeing the company from maintaining a network for this purpose.

Figure 9-14 P2P describes an Internet network that enables users with the same networking software to connect to each other's hard disks and exchange files directly.

Metropolitan Area Network (MAN)

A **metropolitan area network** (**MAN**) is a backbone network that connects local area networks in a metropolitan area such as a city or town and handles the bulk of communications activity, or traffic, across that region. A MAN typically includes one or more LANs, but covers a smaller geographic area than a WAN. The state of Pennsylvania, for example, has a MAN that connects state agencies and individual users in the region around the state capital.

A MAN usually is managed by a consortium of users or by a single network provider who sells the service to the users. Local and state governments, for example, regulate some MANs. Telephone companies, cable television operators, and other organizations provide users with connections to the MAN.

Network Topologies

A **network topology** is the configuration, or physical arrangement, of the devices in a communications network. Three commonly used network topologies are bus, ring, and star. Networks usually use combinations of these topologies. The following pages discuss each of these topologies.

BUS NETWORK A **bus network** consists of a single central cable, to which all computers and other devices connect (Figure 9-15). The **bus**, also called the **backbone**, is the physical cable that connects the computers and other devices. The bus in a bus network can transmit data, instructions, and information in both directions. When a sending device transmits data, the address of the receiving device is included with the transmission so the data is routed to the appropriate receiving device.

Bus networks are very popular in LANs because they are inexpensive and easy to install. One advantage of the bus network is you can attach and detach computers and other devices at any point on the bus without disturbing the rest of the network. Another advantage is failure of one device usually does not affect the rest of the bus network. The transmission simply bypasses the failed device. The greatest risk to a bus network is that the bus itself might become inoperable. If that happens, the network remains inoperative until the bus is back in working order.

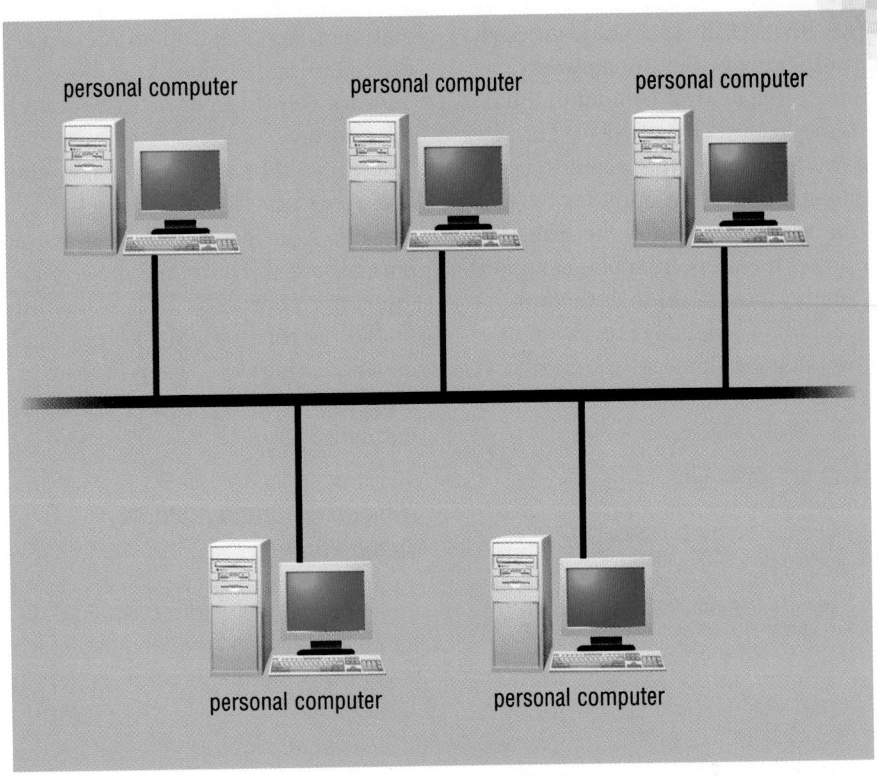

Figure 9-15 Devices in a bus network share a single data path.

RING NETWORK In a **ring network**, a cable forms a closed ring, or loop, with all computers and devices arranged along the ring (Figure 9-16). Data transmitted on a ring network travels from device to device around the entire ring, in one direction. When a computer sends data, the data travels to each computer on the ring until it reaches its destination.

If a device on a ring network fails, all devices before the failed device are unaffected, but those after the failed device cannot function. A ring network can span a larger distance than a bus network, but it is more difficult to install.

The ring topology primarily is used for LANs, but also is used to connect a mainframe to a WAN.

Figure 9-16 In a ring network, all connected devices form a continuous loop.

STAR NETWORK In a **star network**, all of the devices in the network connect to a central computer, thus forming a star (Figure 9-17). The central computer that provides a common connection point for devices in the network is called the **hub**. All data that transfers from one computer to another passes through the hub.

Similar to a bus network, star networks are fairly easy to install and maintain. You can add and remove computers and devices to and from the network with little or no disruption to the network.

In a star network, if one device fails, only that device is affected. The other devices continue to operate normally. If the hub fails, however, the entire network is inoperable until the hub is repaired. Most large star networks, therefore, keep backup hubs available in case the primary hub fails.

Web Link

For more information on Ethernet, visit the Discovering Computers 2002 Chapter 9 WEB LINK page (**scsite.com/dc2002/ch9/weblink.htm**) and click Ethernet.

Network Communications Technologies

Today's networks connect terminals, devices, and computers from many different manufacturers across many types of networks, such as wide area, local area, and wireless. For the different devices on several types of networks to be able to communicate, the network must use a specific combination of hardware and software. A variety of communications technologies exist for this purpose, as described in the following paragraphs.

ETHERNET **Ethernet** is a LAN technology that allows personal computers to contend for access to the network. If two computers on an Ethernet network attempt to send data at the same time, a collision occurs, and the computers must attempt to send their messages again.

Ethernet is based on a bus topology, but Ethernet networks can

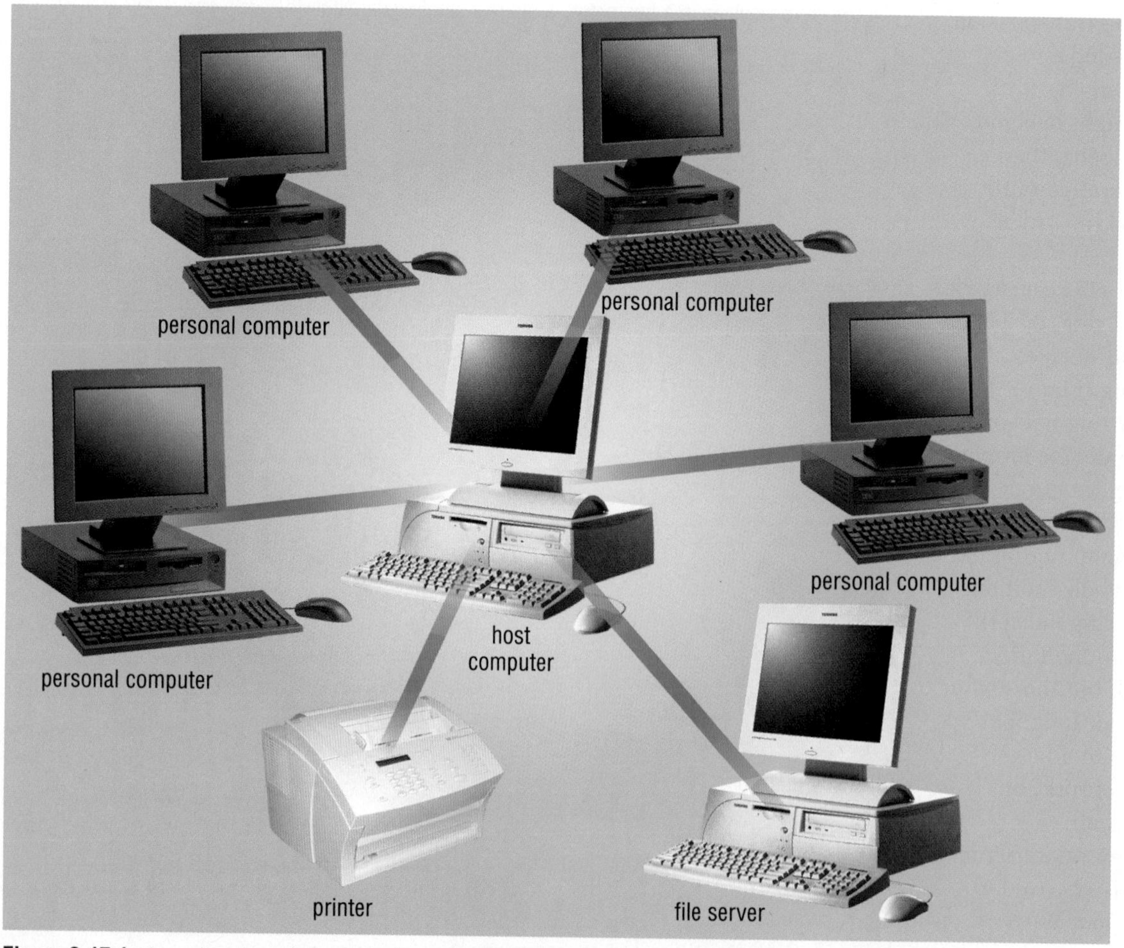

Figure 9-17 A star network contains a single, centralized host computer in which all the devices in the network communicate.

be wired in a star pattern. Today, Ethernet is the most popular LAN because it is relatively inexpensive and easy to install and maintain.

Ethernet networks often use cables to transmit data. The original Ethernet standard is not very fast by today's standards. For small to medium networks, however, Ethernet works quite well. A more recent Ethernet standard, called **Fast Ethernet**, transmits data and information at speeds up to 10 times faster than the original standard. **Gigabit Ethernet** provides an even higher speed of transmission, with speeds up to 10 times faster than Fast Ethernet.

TOKEN RING **Token ring**, another LAN technology, controls access to the network by requiring that network devices share or pass a special signal, called a token. A token is similar to a ticket. The device with the token can transmit data over the network. Only one token exists per network. This ensures that only one computer can transmit data at a time. Token ring is based on a ring topology (although it can use a star topology).

TCP/IP Short for **transmission control protocol/Internet protocol**, **TCP/IP** is a technology that manages the transmission of data by breaking it up into packets. Internet transmissions commonly use TCP/IP. When a computer sends data over the Internet, the data is divided into small pieces, or **packets**. Each packet contains the data, as well as the recipient (destination), origin (sender), and the sequence information used to reassemble the data at the destination. These packets travel along the fastest available path to the recipient's computer via devices called **routers**.

TECHNOLOGY TRAILBLAZER

ROBERT **METCALFE**

Communications is essential in today's digital world, and Robert Metcalfe is doing his part to enhance communications skills.

As the inventor of Ethernet, Metcalfe set the technology that allows personal computers to communicate across networks. As founder of California-based 3Com Corporation, he realizes the need for employees, especially engineers, to communicate their ideas clearly when they speak and write. To further this notion, he has funded a program at his alma mater, Massachusetts Institute of Technology, to support the faculty who teach writing to undergraduates. As a former publisher and a current *Infoworld* magazine columnist, he communicates in-depth technical analysis to hundreds of thousands of information technology professionals.

From age 10, Metcalfe wanted to be an electrical engineer. Graduating from MIT in 1969, he pursued a master's degree in applied mathematics and a Ph.D. in computer science at Harvard. While working on his dissertation at Xerox's Palo Alto Research Center, Metcalfe conducted research on packet switching for the ARPANET and AlohaNet computer networks. He started 3Com Corporation in 1979 to promote Ethernet.

For more information on Robert Metcalfe, visit the Discovering Computers 2002 People Web page (**scsite.com/dc2002/people.htm**) and click Robert Metcalfe.

COMPANY ON THE CUTTING EDGE

Sun microsystems

Networking First, Last, and Always

Despite the fact that one-half of the people on Earth never have made a telephone call, Sun Microsystems CEO and President Scott McNealy predicts every man, woman, and child always will be connected to a network. Chances are these people will be using technology developed by Sun.

McNealy and three friends started their company in 1982 with the goal of building engineering workstations in the network computer model. They were working closely with the Stanford University Network (SUN), which accounts for the name of their company. Their first workstation included TCP/IP, the Internet communications technology.

Networking increases employees' overall productivity, according to McNealy. His philosophy certainly holds true for his own company. By 1988, Sun had reached $1 billion in revenues, making it the fastest-growing company in history. Four years later, it had become the world's second most profitable company. Today, Sun has a presence in more than 170 countries and boasts $15.7 billion in annual revenues. Building industrial-strength hardware, software, and services around its vision, *The Network is the Computer*, Sun's technology powers the Internet and allows companies worldwide to become involved in e-commerce.

For more information on Sun Microsystems, visit the Discovering Computers 2002 Companies Web page (**scsite.com/dc2002/companies.htm**) and click Sun Microsystems.

This technique of breaking a message into individual packets, sending the packets along the best route available, and then reassembling the data is called **packet switching**.

WAP The **Wireless Application Protocol (WAP)** allows wireless mobile devices to access the Internet and its services such as the Web and e-mail. WAP uses a client/server network. The wireless device contains the client software, which connects to the Internet service provider's server. Devices that support WAP, called **WAP-enabled devices**, include Web-enabled telephones, pagers, and handheld computers. As the demand for wireless Internet access grows, the availability of WAP-enabled devices will increase.

Intranets

Recognizing the efficiency and power of the Internet, many organizations apply Internet and Web technologies to their own internal networks. An **intranet** (intra means inside) is an internal network that uses Internet technologies. Intranets generally make company information accessible to employees and facilitate working in groups. Simple intranet applications include electronic publishing of organizational materials such as telephone directories, event calendars, procedure manuals, employee benefits information, and job postings. An intranet typically also includes a connection to the Internet. More sophisticated uses of intranets include groupware applications such as project management, chat rooms, newsgroups, group scheduling, and videoconferencing.

An intranet essentially is a small version of the Internet that exists within an organization. It uses TCP/IP technologies, has a Web server, supports multimedia Web pages coded in HTML, and is accessible via a Web browser such as Microsoft Internet Explorer or Netscape Navigator. Users can post and update information on the intranet by creating and posting a Web page, using a method similar to that used on the Internet.

Sometimes a company uses an **extranet**, which allows customers or suppliers to access part of its intranet. Federal Express, for example, allows customers to access their intranet to print air bills, schedule pickups, and even track shipped packages as they travel to their destination (Figure 9-18).

FIREWALLS As a public network, anyone with the proper connection can access the Internet. A private corporate intranet or extranet, by contrast, restricts access to specific authorized users, usually employees, suppliers, vendors, and customers. To prevent unauthorized access to data and information, companies protect their intranet or extranet with a firewall. A **firewall** is a general term that refers to hardware and/or software that restricts access to data and information on a network (Figure 9-19). One use of firewalls is to deny network access to outsiders. Chapter 12 discusses firewalls in more depth.

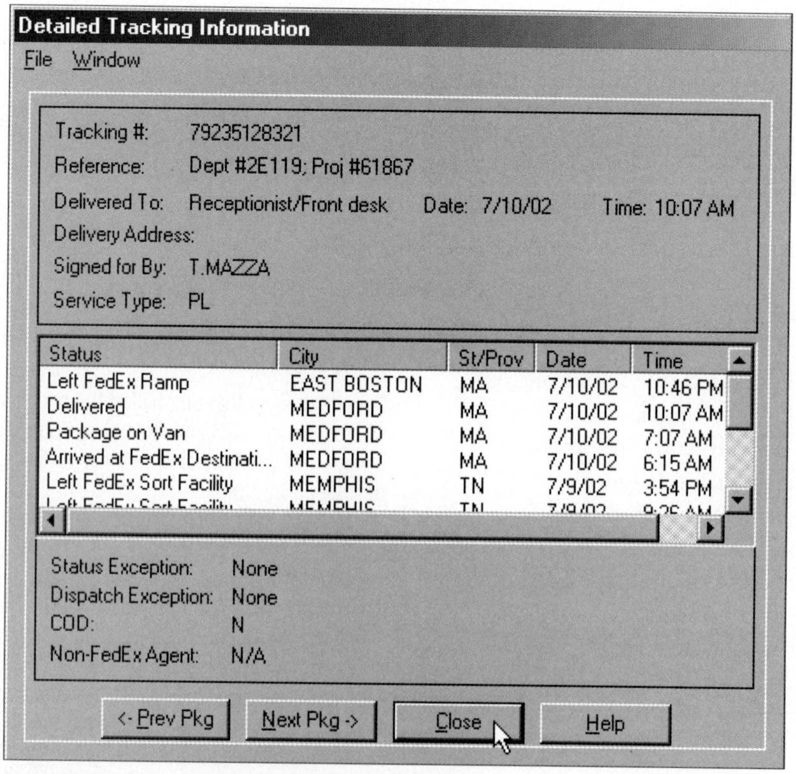

Figure 9-18 Federal Express uses an extranet to allow customers to ship and track packages. As shown in this figure, customers can track the progress of shipped packages as the packages travel to their destination.

Web Link

For more information on TCP/IP, visit the Discovering Computers 2002 Chapter 9 WEB LINK page (**scsite.com/dc2002/ch9/weblink.htm**) and click TCP/IP.

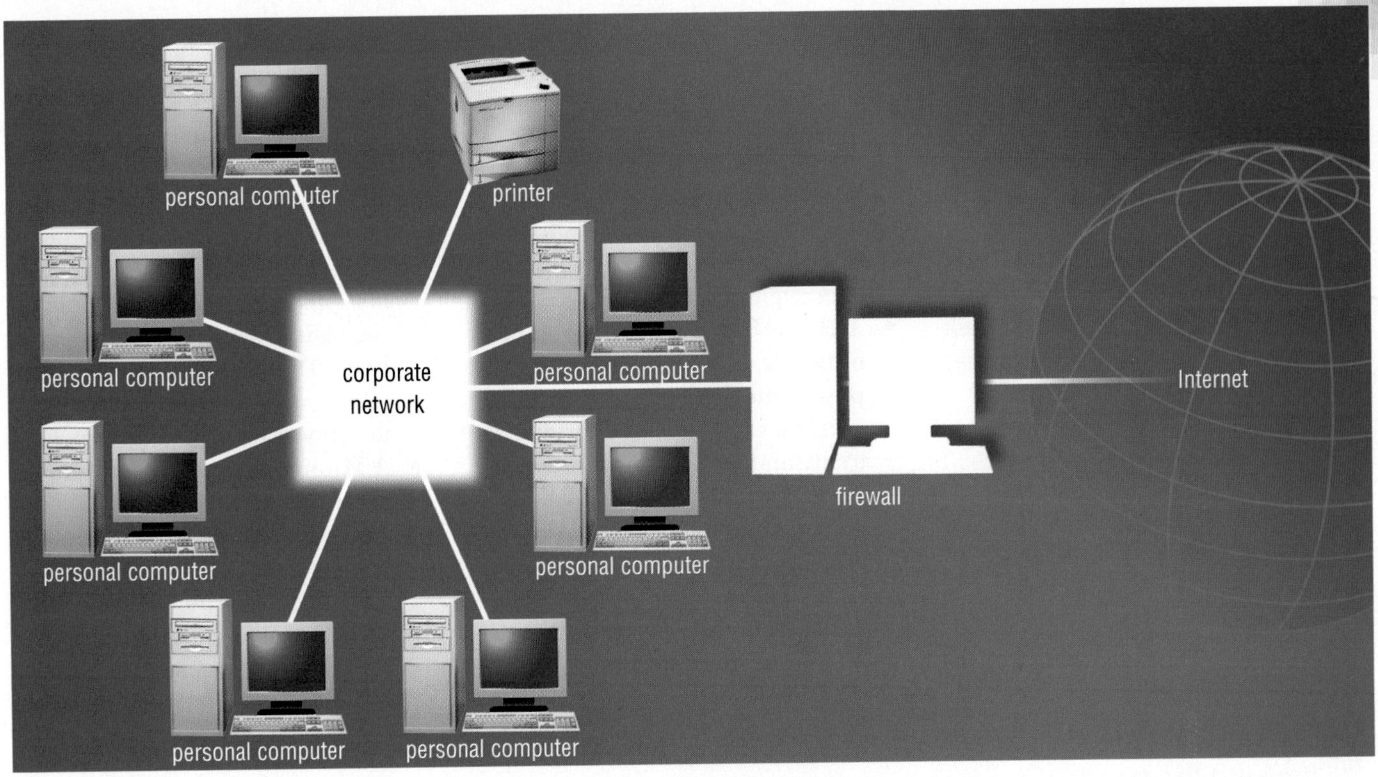

Figure 9-19 One use of a firewall is to restrict outsiders from accessing data and information on a network.

ISSUE

Spending Tax Money

Intranets

Some Florida law enforcement agencies have adopted an intranet to help solve crime. The internal network lets various bureaus access crime reports, rap sheets, mug shots, fingerprints, and other crime-related data stored by different agencies. Investigators can collect information in minutes that once might have taken days to gather. In addition, sophisticated search algorithms can pinpoint connections that may not have been recognized by human detectives. The intranet cost $1.5 million to establish, and future intranets will cost $300,000. Despite the intranet's success, some complain the money would be better spent putting more officers on the street. Do you think the intranet is worth the cost? Why or why not? If it were your tax dollars, how would you prefer to have the money spent? Why?

For more information on technology and law enforcement, visit the Discovering Computers 2002 Issues Web page (**scsite.com/dc2002/issues.htm**) and click Chapter 9 Issue #4.

Home Networks

If you have multiple computers in your home or home office, you can connect all of them together with a **home network** (Figure 9-20). The advantages of a home network are many. All computers in the house can be connected to the Internet at the same time. Each computer can access files and programs on the other computers in the home. All computers can share peripherals such as a scanner, printer, or a DVD drive.

Four types of home networks exist: Ethernet network, HomePLC network, Phoneline network, and HomeRF network.

Web Link
For more information on home networks, visit the Discovering Computers 2002 Chapter 9 WEB LINK page (**scsite.com/dc2002/ch9/weblink.htm**) and click Home Networks.

- As discussed earlier in this chapter, an Ethernet network requires you to connect a cable to each computer. This may involve running cable through walls, ceilings, and floors. For the average home user, the hardware and software of an Ethernet network can be difficult to configure.
- A **HomePLC (powerline cable) network**, sometimes called a **powerline LAN**, is a network that uses the same lines that bring electricity and power into your home. This network requires no additional wiring. You plug one end of a cable into the computer's parallel port and the other into a wall outlet. The data transmits through the existing power lines in the house.
- A **phoneline network** is an easy-to-install and inexpensive network that uses existing telephone lines in the home. With this network, you connect one end of a cable in the computer and the other end into a telephone jack. The phoneline network does not interfere with voice and data transmissions on the telephone lines. That is, you can talk on the telephone and use the same line to connect to the Internet.
- A **HomeRF (radio frequency) network** uses radio waves, instead of cables, to transmit data. A HomeRF network sends signals through the air. You connect one end of a cable to the special card in the computer and the other end to a transmitter/receiver that has an antenna to pick up signals.

Figure 9-20 An example of a home network.

Many vendors offer home networking packages that include all the necessary hardware and software to network your home using these techniques. Some also offer intelligent networking capabilities. An **intelligent home network** also extends the basic home network to include features such as lighting control, thermostat adjustment, and a security system.

COMMUNICATIONS SOFTWARE

Some communications devices are preprogrammed to accomplish communications tasks. Other communications devices require a separate communications software program to ensure proper transmission of data. **Communications software** consists of programs that help you establish a connection to another computer or network, and manage the transmission of data, instructions, and information. For two computers to communicate, they must have compatible communications software.

Often, separate communications programs on your computer each serve a different purpose. One type of communications software helps you establish a connection to another computer on the Internet using wizards, dialog boxes, and other on-screen messages (Figure 9-21).

Figure 9-21 HOW THE INTERNET CONNECTION WIZARD WORKS

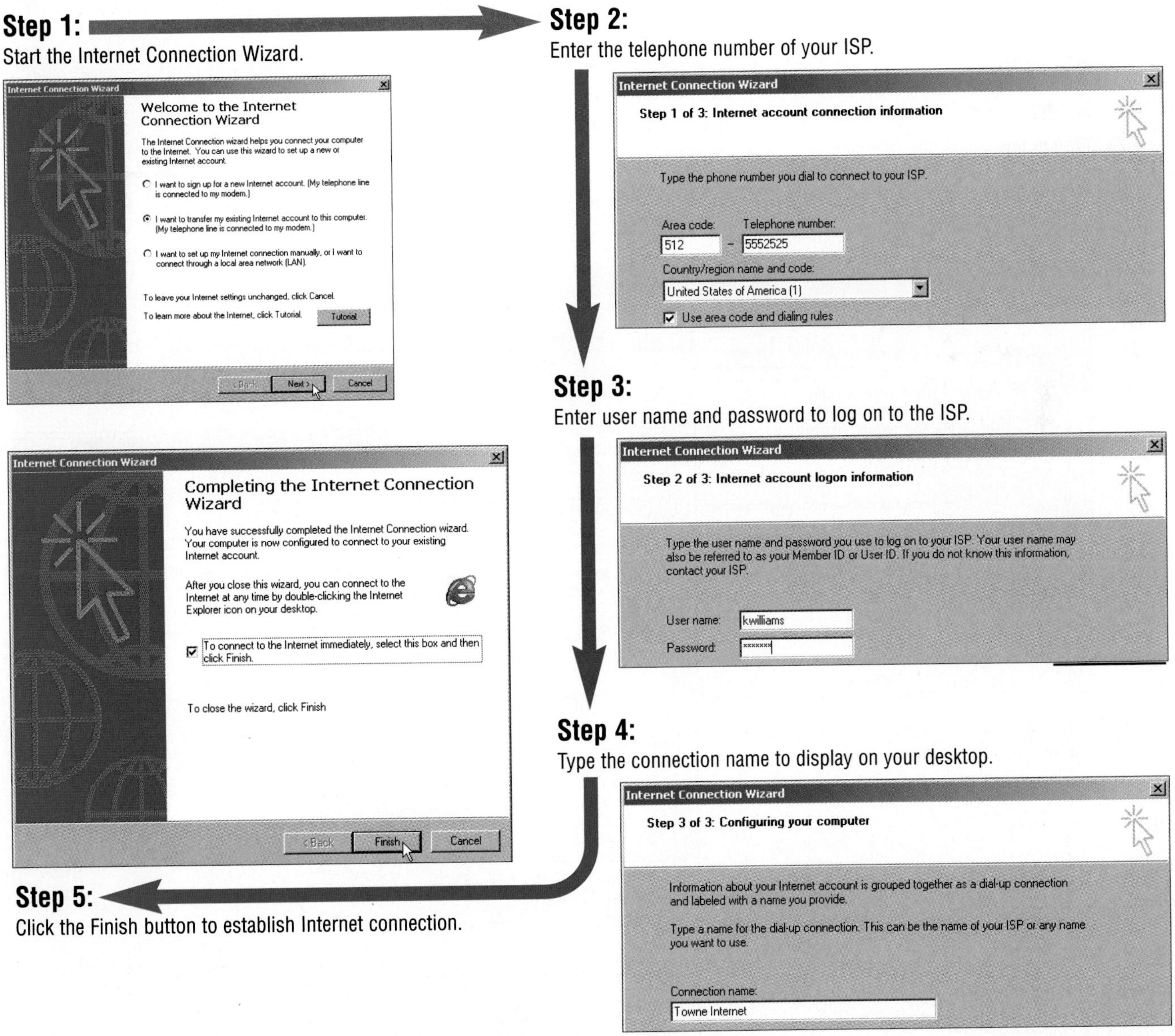

Once the Internet connection is established, communications software provides a means to access the Internet using an ISP (Figure 9-22).

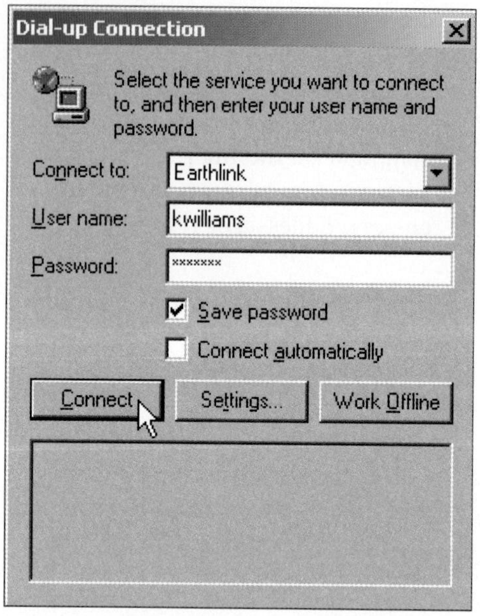

Figure 9-22 Through this dialog box, you can access the Internet using the Earthlink ISP.

Some communications software programs support file transfer protocol. **FTP** (**file transfer protocol**) is an Internet standard that allows you to upload and download files to and from a Web server, called the **FTP server**. To view or use a file on an FTP server, you can download the file from the server to your computer, or you can use an FTP program to access the file directly on the FTP server. Many FTP sites are public, called **anonymous FTP**, and allow anyone to transfer files using their FTP program. For these sites, you enter the word, anonymous, if prompted for a password. Other sites require a specific user name and password to access the FTP server.

Often, files on an FTP server are compressed to reduce their transfer time. As discussed in Chapter 8, you must decompress a compressed file before viewing it.

Sometimes, you want to upload files to an FTP server. For example, if you create a personal Web page, you will want to copy it from your computer to the Web server. To do this, you can use an FTP program (Figure 9-23). Many ISPs and OSPs provide an FTP program as part of their Internet access service. You also can download public-domain FTP programs from the Web.

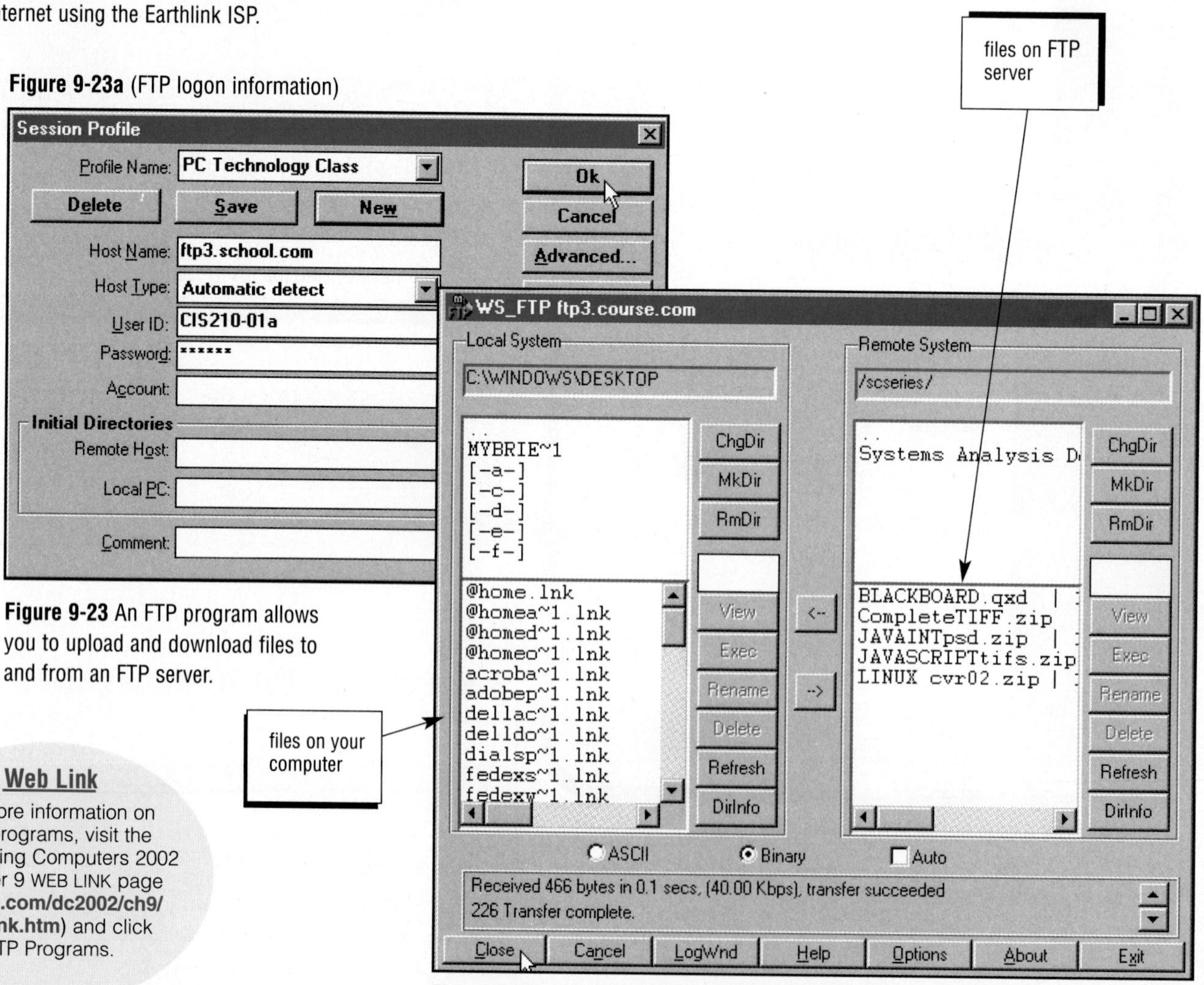

Figure 9-23a (FTP logon information)

Figure 9-23 An FTP program allows you to upload and download files to and from an FTP server.

Figure 9-23b (connection established to FTP server)

Web Link

For more information on FTP programs, visit the Discovering Computers 2002 Chapter 9 WEB LINK page (**scsite.com/dc2002/ch9/weblink.htm**) and click FTP Programs.

THE TELEPHONE NETWORK

The **public switched telephone network (PSTN)** is the worldwide telephone system that handles voice-oriented telephone calls (Figure 9-24). Nearly the entire telephone network today uses digital technology, with the exception of the final link from the local telephone company to a home, which usually is analog.

While initially it was built to handle voice communications, the telephone network also is an integral part of computer communications. Data, instructions, and information can be sent over the telephone network using dial-up lines or dedicated lines. The following sections discuss each of these types of connections.

Dial-Up Lines

A **dial-up line** is a temporary connection that uses one or more analog telephone lines for communications. A dial-up connection is not permanent. Using a dial-up line to transmit data is similar to using the telephone to make a call. A modem at the sending end dials the telephone number of a modem at the receiving end. When the modem at the receiving end answers the call, a connection is established and data can be transmitted. When either modem hangs up, the communications end.

One advantage of a dial-up line to connect computers is that it costs no more than making a regular telephone call. Another advantage is that computers at any two locations can establish a connection using modems and the telephone network. Mobile users, for example, often use dial-up lines to connect to their main office network so they can read e-mail messages, access the Internet, and upload files.

A disadvantage of dial-up lines is that you cannot control the quality of the connection because the telephone company's switching office randomly selects the line.

Dedicated Lines

A **dedicated line** is a connection that always is established between two communications devices (unlike a dial-up line where the connection is reestablished each time it is used). The quality and consistency of the connection on a dedicated line is better than a dial-up line because dedicated lines provide a constant connection.

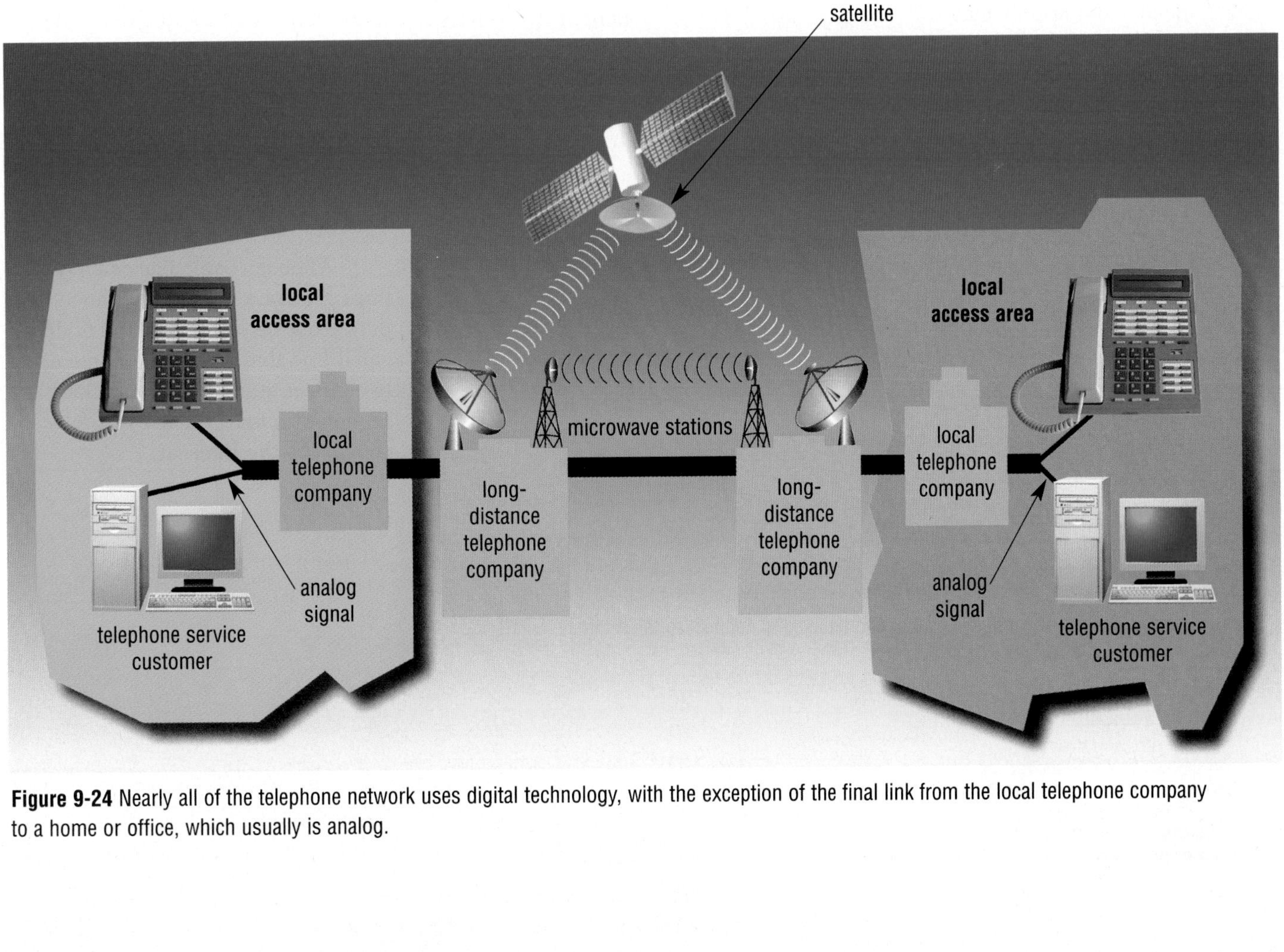

Figure 9-24 Nearly all of the telephone network uses digital technology, with the exception of the final link from the local telephone company to a home or office, which usually is analog.

Businesses often use dedicated lines to connect geographically distant offices. Dedicated lines either can be analog or digital. Digital lines increasingly are connecting home and business users to networks around the globe because they transmit data and information at faster rates than analog lines.

A **transfer rate** is the speed with which a line carries data and information. The faster the transfer rate, the faster you can send and receive data and information. Transfer rates usually are expressed as **bits per second (bps)** — that is, the number of bits the line can transmit in one second. Transfer rates range from thousands of bits per second, called **kilobits per second (Kbps)**, to millions of bits per second, called **megabits per second (Mbps)**, to billions of bits per second, called **gigabits per second (Gbps)**. The table in Figure 9-25 lists the transfer rates (speeds) and approximate monthly costs of various types of lines, as compared with dial-up lines.

Four popular types of digital dedicated lines are ISDN lines, digital subscriber lines, T-carrier lines, and ATM.

ISDN Lines

For the small business and home user, an ISDN line provides faster transfer rates than dial-up telephone lines. **ISDN (Integrated Services Digital Network)** is a set of standards for digital transmission of data over standard copper telephone lines. With ISDN, the same telephone line that could carry only one computer signal, now can carry three or more signals at once, through the same line, using a technique called **multiplexing**.

ISDN requires that both ends of the connection have an ISDN modem. This type of modem is different from the type used in dial-up connections. ISDN lines also require a special ISDN telephone for voice communications. Home and business users who choose ISDN lines benefit from faster Web page downloads and clearer videoconferencing. ISDN connections also produce voice conversations that are very clear.

DSL

DSL is another digital line alternative for the small business or home user. **DSL (digital subscriber line)** transmits at fast speeds on existing standard copper telephone wiring. Some of the DSL installations can provide a dial tone, so you can use the line for both voice and data.

To connect to DSL, a customer must have a special network card or DSL modem. Similar to ISDN modems, a DSL modem is different from the modem used for dial-up connections. Some experts predict that DSL eventually will replace ISDN because it is much easier to install and can provide much faster data transfer rates.

ADSL is one of the more popular types of DSLs. As shown in Figure 9-26, **ADSL (asymmetric digital subscriber line)** is a type of DSL that supports faster transfer rates when receiving data (the downstream rate) than when sending data (the upstream rate). ADSL is ideal for Internet access because most users download more information from the Internet than they upload.

Cable Television Lines

Although cable television (CATV) lines are not a type of telephone line, they are a very popular type of dedicated line that allows the home user to connect to the Internet. A later section discusses the use of CATV to connect to the Internet.

SPEEDS OF VARIOUS CONNECTIONS TO THE INTERNET

Type of Line	Transfer Rates	Approximate Monthly Cost
Dial-up	Up to 56 Kbps	Local or Long-Distance Rates
ISDN (BRI)	Up to 128 Kbps	\$10 to \$40
ADSL	128 Kbps – 8.45 Mbps	\$39 to \$110
Cable TV (CATV)	128 Kbps – 2.5 Mbps	\$30 to \$70
T1	1.544 Mbps	\$1,000 or more
T3	44 Mbps	\$10,000 or more
ATM	155 to 622 Mbps	\$8,000 or more

Figure 9-25 The speeds of various lines that can be used to connect to the Internet.

Web Link
For more information on DSL, visit the Discovering Computers 2002 Chapter 9 WEB LINK page (**scsite.com/dc2002/ch9/weblink.htm**) and click DSL.

T-carrier Lines

A **T-carrier line** is any of several types of digital lines that carry multiple signals over a single communications line. Whereas a standard dial-up telephone line carries only one signal, digital T-carrier lines use a technique called multiplexing so that multiple signals can share the telephone line. T-carrier lines provide extremely fast data transfer rates. Only medium to large companies usually can afford the investment in T-carrier lines because these lines also are so expensive.

The most popular T-carrier line is the **T1 line**. Businesses often use T1 lines to connect to the Internet. Many service providers also use T1 lines to connect to the Internet backbone. A **T3 line** is equal in speed to 28 T1 lines. T3 lines are quite expensive. Main users of T3 lines include large companies, telephone companies, and service providers connecting to the Internet backbone. The Internet backbone itself also uses T3 lines.

Asynchronous Transfer Mode

Asynchronous transfer mode (ATM) is a service that carries voice, data, video, and multimedia at extremely high speeds. Telephone networks, the Internet, and other networks with large amounts of traffic use ATM. Some experts predict that ATM eventually will become the Internet standard for data transmission, replacing T3 lines.

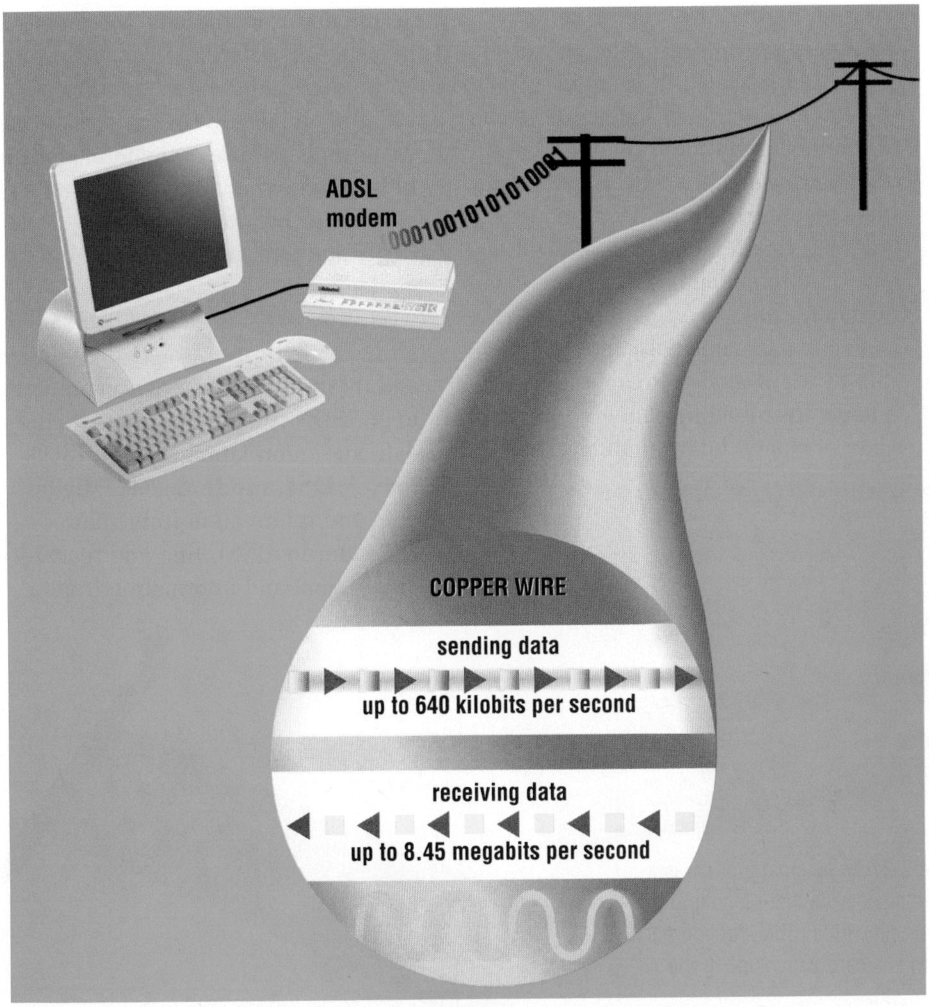

Figure 9-26 ADSL connections transmit data downstream at a much faster rate than upstream.

COMMUNICATIONS DEVICES

A **communications device** is any type of hardware capable of transmitting data, instructions, and information between a sending device and a receiving device. At the sending end, a communications device sends the data, instructions, or information from the sending device to a communications channel. At the receiving end, the communications device receives the signals from the communications channel. Sometimes, the communications device also must convert the data, instructions, and information from analog to digital signals or vice versa, depending on the devices and media involved.

Some of the more common types of communications devices are dial-up modems, ISDN and DSL modems, cable modems, and network interface cards. The following pages describe these devices.

Modems

As previously discussed, a computer's digital signals must be converted to analog signals before they are transmitted over standard telephone lines. The communications device that performs this conversion is a **modem**, sometimes called a **dial-up modem**. The word, modem, is derived from a combination of the words, **modulate**, to change into an analog signal and, **demodulate**, to convert an analog signal into a digital signal. Both the sending and receiving ends of a communications channel must have a modem for data transmission to occur.

Web Link
For more information on modems, visit the Discovering Computers 2002 Chapter 9 WEB LINK page (**scsite.com/dc2002/ch9/weblink.htm**) and click Modems.

Web Link
For more information on cable modems, visit the Discovering Computers 2002 Chapter 9 WEB LINK page (**scsite.com/dc2002/ch9/weblink.htm**) and click Cable Modems.

A modem can be an external or an internal device (Figure 9-27). An **external modem** is a stand-alone (separate) device that attaches to a special serial port, such as RS-232, on a computer with a standard telephone cord connected to a telephone outlet. You easily can move an external modem from one computer to another.

An **internal modem** is a card that you insert into an expansion slot on a computer's motherboard. One end of a standard telephone cord attaches to a port on the modem and the other end plugs into a telephone outlet. Devices other than computers use internal modems. A stand-alone fax machine, for example, has an internal modem that converts a scanned digitized image into an analog signal that can be sent to the recipient's fax machine. One advantage of internal modems over external modems is that they do not require desk space.

As discussed in Chapter 4, notebook and other mobile computers can use a modem in the form of a PC Card that you insert into a PC Card slot on the computer. The PC Card modem attaches to a telephone outlet with a standard telephone cord. Mobile users without access to a telephone outlet also can use a special cable to attach the PC Card modem to a cellular telephone, thus enabling them to transmit data over a cellular telephone. Some mobile users have a **wireless modem** that allows access to the Web wirelessly from notebook and handheld computers, cellular telephones, and other mobile devices. These wireless modems typically use the same waves used by cellular telephones.

ISDN and DSL Modems

If you access the Internet using ISDN or DSL, you need a communications device to send and receive the digital ISDN or DSL signals. A modem used for dial-up access will not work because it converts analog signals to digital signals and vice versa. In the case of ISDN and DSL, this conversion is not necessary. Both the computer and the ISDN or DSL already use digital signals.

A **digital modem** is one that sends and receives data and information to and from a digital telephone line such as ISDN or DSL. According to the definition of a modem (to convert from analog to digital signals and vice versa), the use of the term modem in this context is not correct. Industry manufacturers, however, still refer to ISDN and DSL modems as digital modems.

An **ISDN modem**, also called an **ISDN adapter**, sends digital data and information from your computer to an ISDN line and receives digital data and information from an ISDN line. A **DSL modem** sends digital data and information from your computer to a DSL line and receives digital data and information from a DSL line.

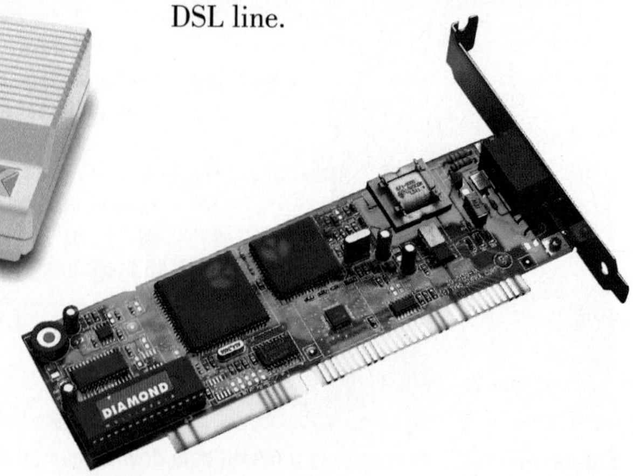

Figure 9-27 An external modem is a stand-alone device that plugs into the system unit with a cable. An internal modem is a card you install in the system unit.

Cable Modems

A **cable modem**, sometimes called a **broadband modem**, is a modem that sends and receives data over the cable television (CATV) network. With more than 100 million homes wired for cable television, cable modems provide a faster Internet access alternative to dial-up for the home user. Cable modems currently can transmit data at speeds much faster than either a dial-up modem or ISDN (see Figure 9-25 on page 9.26). Today, many home and business users are taking advantage of the resources available on the Internet and other networks with high-speed cable service.

As shown in Figure 9-28, CATV service enters your home through a single line. To access the Internet using the cable service, the cable company installs a splitter inside your house. From the splitter, one part of the cable runs to your televisions and the other part connects to the cable modem. A cable modem usually is a stand-alone (separate) device that you connect with a cable to a USB port or a port on a network interface card in your computer. The next section discusses network interface cards.

Network Interface Card

A **network interface card** (**NIC** pronounced nick), also called a **LAN adapter,** is a card you insert into an expansion slot of a personal computer or other device, such as a printer, enabling the device to connect to a network. Personal computers on a LAN typically contain a NIC. The NIC coordinates the transmission and receipt of data, instructions, and information to and from the computer or device containing the NIC.

A NIC works with a particular network technology, such as Ethernet or token ring. An Ethernet card is the most common type of NIC. Depending on the type of wiring used, the transfer rate on an Ethernet network is 10 Mbps, 100 Mbps, or 1,000 Mbps. Ethernet cards typically support one or more of these speeds. Some are called 10/100 because they support both 10 Mbps and 100 Mbps. Some NICs also are a combination Ethernet and dial-up modem card.

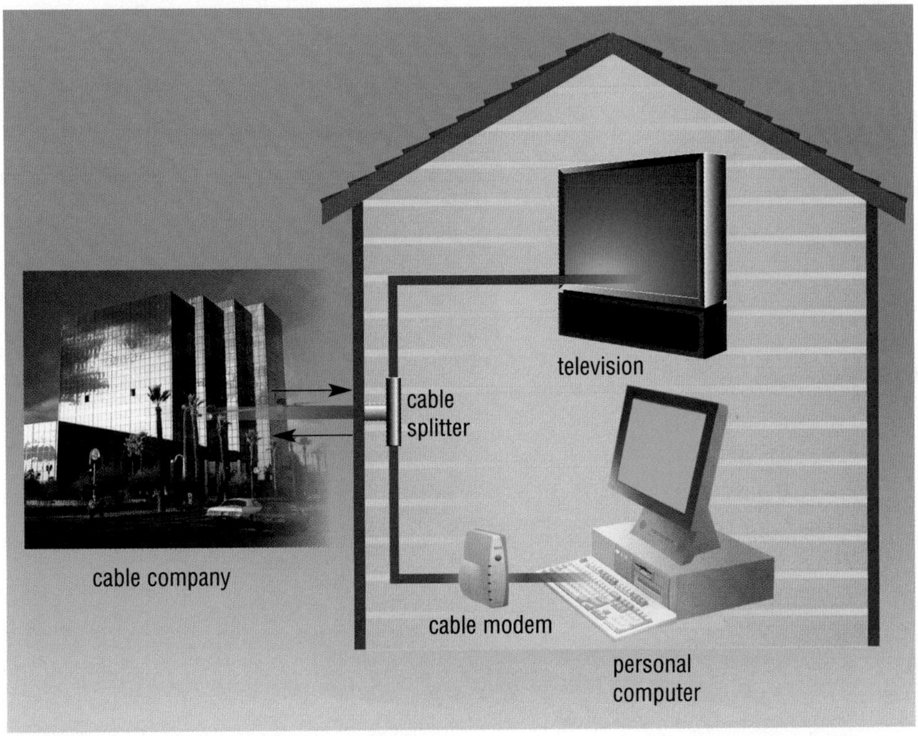

Figure 9-28 A typical cable modem installation.

APPLY IT!

Cable Modem versus DSL

So you are ready to move from the telephone line to a higher-speed Internet connection. Two options are cable modem and digital subscriber line (DSL). Cable modems piggyback on your local television cable connection. DSL uses existing telephone lines. Assuming you live in a geographic area where both options are available, how do you determine which is best for you?

First, DSL and cable share several common features. On the positive side, both approaches offer the benefits of constant connection. Instead of having to dial up every time you need to use the Internet, you are online 24 hours a day. On the negative side, "always on" creates a security issue. This makes your computer vulnerable to hackers who can gain access to your files and drop viruses on your hard disk. DSL is somewhat more secure than cable, but to be safe with either option, install antivirus and firewall software.

In making the decision of cable or DSL, consider several factors.

- Cable Modems
  - Speed – 1 to 2.5 Mbps download;128 to 384 Kbps upload
  - Security – Shared media with others in neighborhood
  - Installation – $75 to $100
  - Monthly Cost – rates vary from $30 to $70
  - Availability – limited to your local cable company
- DSL
  - Speed – 1.54 to 8.45 Mbps download; 128 to 640 Kbps upload
  - Security – dedicated line; no sharing
  - Installation – $100 to $200
  - Monthly Cost – $39 to $110
  - Availability – order service from your local ISP

For more information on cable modem versus DSL, visit the Discovering Computers 2002 Apply It Web page (**scsite.com/dc2002/apply.htm**) and click Chapter 9 Apply It #3.

NICs are available in a variety of styles (Figure 9-29). A NIC for a desktop computer has a port where a cable connects. A NIC for notebook and other mobile computers is in the form of a Type II PC Card. Many of these NICs have more than one type of port, enabling different types of cables to attach to the card. For example, some cable modems and DSL modems require that one end of a cable plug into the modem and the other end into a NIC. The NIC for a wireless transmission, by contrast, typically has an antenna.

Web Link

For more information on network interface cards, visit the Discovering Computers 2002 Chapter 9 WEB LINK page (**scsite.com/dc2002/ch9/weblink.htm**) and click Network Interface Cards.

Connecting Networks

Today, thousands of computer networks exist, ranging from small networks operated by home users to global networks operated by numerous telecommunications firms. To interconnect these many types of networks, various types of communications devices exist. For example, as shown in Figure 9-30, a **hub** is a device that provides a central point for cables in a network.

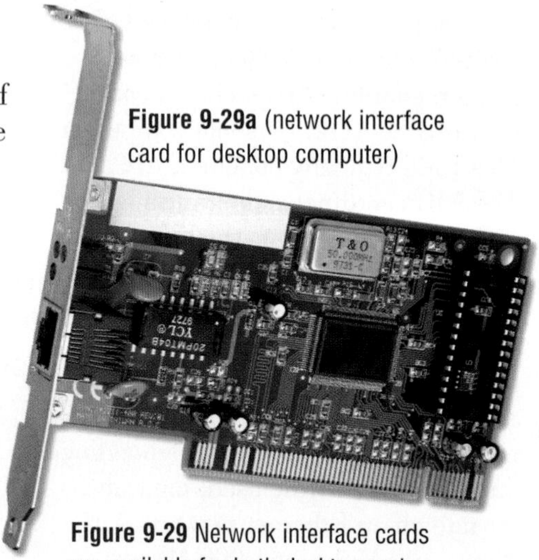

Figure 9-29a (network interface card for desktop computer)

Figure 9-29b (network interface card for notebook computer)

Figure 9-29 Network interface cards are available for both desktop and notebook computers.

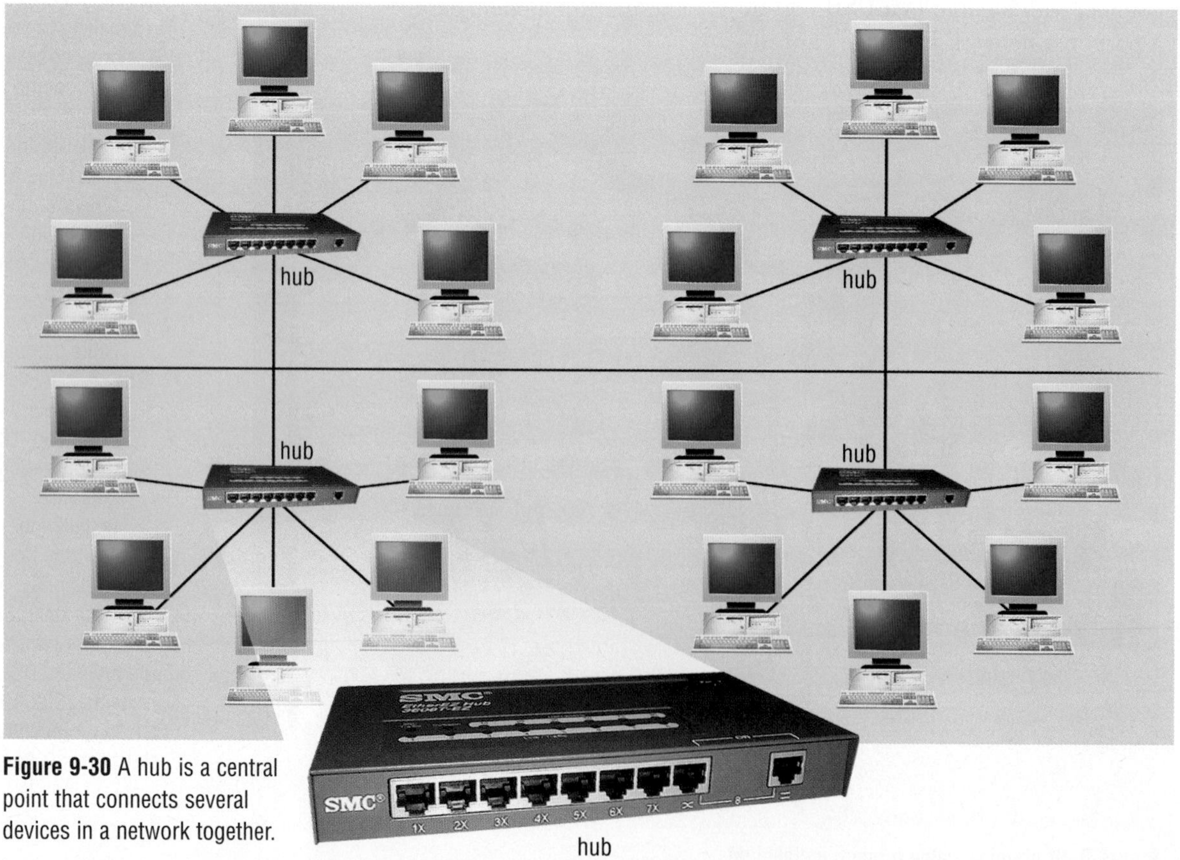

Figure 9-30 A hub is a central point that connects several devices in a network together.

COMMUNICATIONS CHANNEL

An important aspect of communications is the **channel**, which is the communications path between two devices. **Bandwidth** is the width of the communications channel. The higher the bandwidth, the more data and information the channel can transmit.

For transmission of text-based documents, a lower bandwidth delivers acceptable performance. If you transmit music, graphics, photographs, or work with virtual reality or 3-D games, you need a higher bandwidth. When the bandwidth is too low for the application, you will notice a considerable slow-down in system performance.

A communications channel consists of one or more transmission media. **Transmission media** consists of materials or techniques capable of carrying one or more signals. When you send data from your computer to another device, the signal carrying that data most likely travels over a variety of transmission media — especially when the transmission is sent a long distance. Figure 9-31 illustrates a typical communications channel — much like the one that connects a computer to the Internet — and shows the variety of transmission media used to complete the connection. The following pages discuss in depth the media shown

Figure 9-31 AN EXAMPLE OF A COMMUNICATIONS CHANNEL SENDING A REQUEST OVER THE INTERNET

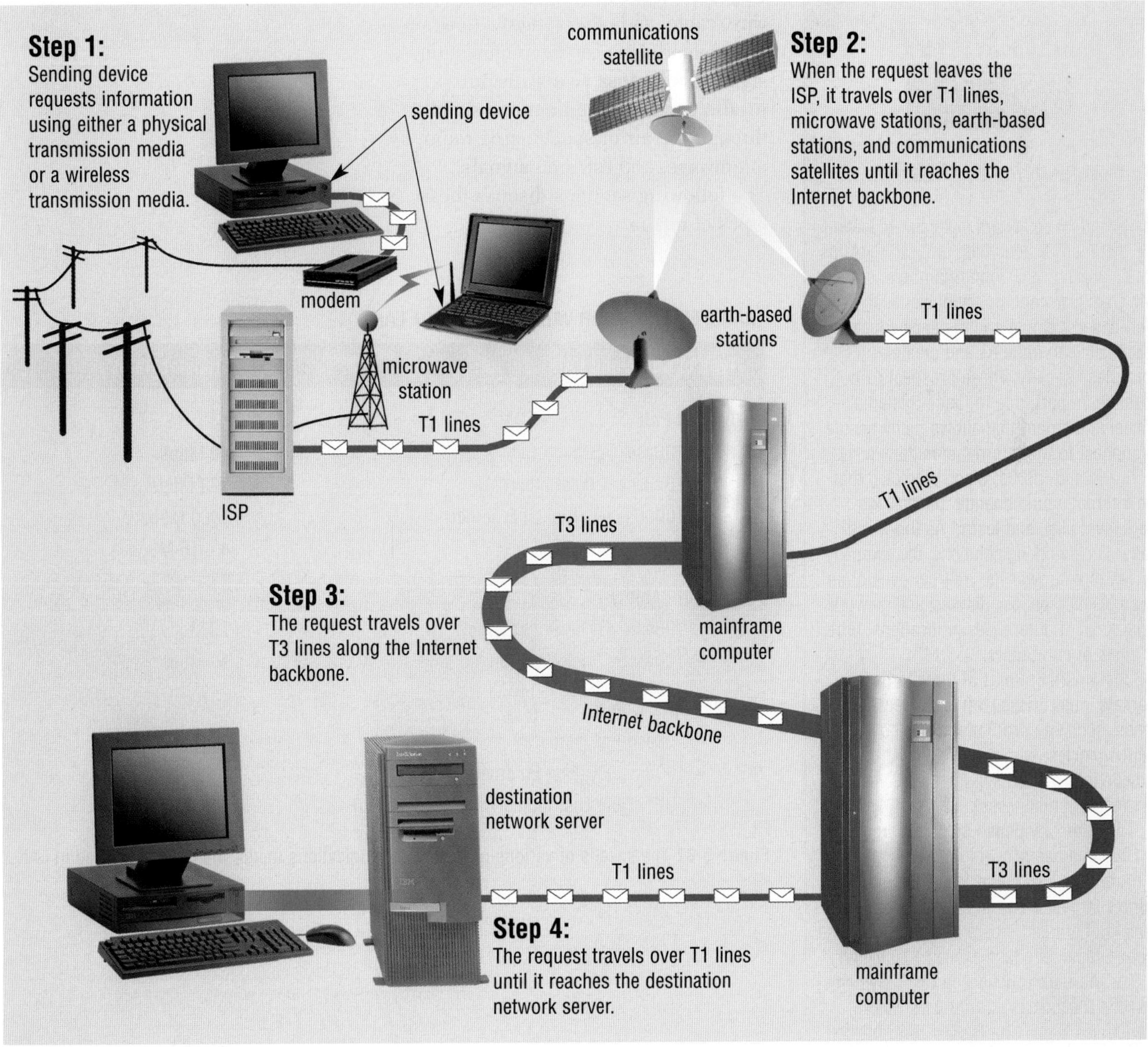
Step 1:
Sending device requests information using either a physical transmission media or a wireless transmission media.
sending device
communications satellite
Step 2:
When the request leaves the ISP, it travels over T1 lines, microwave stations, earth-based stations, and communications satellites until it reaches the Internet backbone.
modem
microwave station
T1 lines
earth-based stations
T1 lines
ISP
T1 lines
T3 lines
Step 3:
The request travels over T3 lines along the Internet backbone.
mainframe computer
Internet backbone
destination network server
T1 lines
T3 lines
Step 4:
The request travels over T1 lines until it reaches the destination network server.
mainframe computer

in the figure on the previous page. Although many media and devices are involved, the entire communications process could take less than one second.

Web Link

For more information on bandwidth, visit the Discovering Computers 2002 Chapter 9 WEB LINK page (**scsite.com/dc2002/ch9/weblink.htm**) and click Bandwidth.

COMPANY ON THE CUTTING EDGE

CISCO SYSTEMS

Networking the Internet

The two great equalizers in life are education and the Internet, according to Cisco Systems President and CEO John Chambers. Universal learning opportunities, such as Web-based training and distance education, potentially can unite us and create a borderless society. These prospects are possible, in part, due to Cisco Systems' critical equipment that allows many people to connect to the Internet simultaneously.

In the mid-1990s, Cisco predicted that the Internet would change "the way we work, live, play, and learn." As the world leader in networking solutions, the company strives to empower the Internet generation by connecting people, devices, and networks regardless of differences in locations, time, or types of computers.

Customers are part of three target markets: enterprises with large networking needs, such as corporations and government agencies; service providers that provide information services; and small and medium businesses.

The company began shipping products in 1986 and has grown into a market leader in more than 115 countries. It has the world's largest e-commerce site, with 90 percent of product orders transacted over the Web. Annual revenues exceed $18 billion.

For more information on Cisco Systems, visit the Discovering Computers 2002 Companies Web page (**scsite.com/dc2002/companies.htm**) and click Cisco Systems.

Baseband media can transmit only one signal at a time. **Broadband** media can transmit multiple signals simultaneously. Media that use broadband transmit signals at a much faster speed than those that use baseband. Home and business users today are opting for broadband Internet access because of the much faster transfer rates. Two previously discussed services that offer broadband transmission are DSL and the cable television network. Satellites also offer broadband transmission.

Transmission media are one of two types: physical or wireless. **Physical transmission media** use wire, cable, and other tangible (touchable) materials to send communications signals. **Wireless transmission media** send communications signals through the air or space using radio, microwave, and infrared signals. The following sections discuss these types of media.

PHYSICAL TRANSMISSION MEDIA

Physical transmission media used in communications include twisted-pair cable, coaxial cable, and fiber-optic cable. These cables typically are used within buildings or underground. Ethernet and token ring LANs often use physical transmission media. The table in Figure 9-32 lists the transfer rates of LANs using various physical transmission media. The following sections discuss each of these types of cables.

TRANSFER RATES FOR VARIOUS TYPES OF LANs

Type of Cable and LAN	Transfer Rates
Twisted Pair	
• 10Base-T (Ethernet)	10 Mbps
• 100Base-T (Fast Ethernet)	100 Mbps
• 1000Base-T (Gigabit Ethernet)	1000 Mbps
• Token ring	4 – 16 Mbps
Coaxial Cable	
• 10Base2 (ThinWire Ethernet)	10 Mbps
• 10Base5 (ThickWire Ethernet)	10 Mbps
Fiber-Optic Cable	
• 10Base-F (Ethernet)	10 Mbps
• 100Base-FX (Fast Ethernet)	100 Mbps
• FDDI (Fiber Distributed-Data Interface) token ring	100 Mbps

Figure 9-32 The speeds of various physical communications media when they are used in LANs.

Twisted-Pair Cable

One of the more commonly used transmission media for network cabling and telephone systems is twisted-pair cable. **Twisted-pair cable** consists of one or more twisted-pair wires bundled together (Figure 9-33). Each **twisted-pair wire** consists of two separate insulated copper wires that are twisted together. The wires are twisted together to reduce noise. **Noise** is an electrical disturbance that can degrade communications.

Coaxial Cable

A second type of physical transmission media is coaxial cable. **Coaxial cable**, often referred to as **coax** (pronounced CO-ax), consists of a single copper wire surrounded by at least three layers: (1) an insulating material, (2) a woven or braided metal, and (3) a plastic outer coating (Figure 9-34).

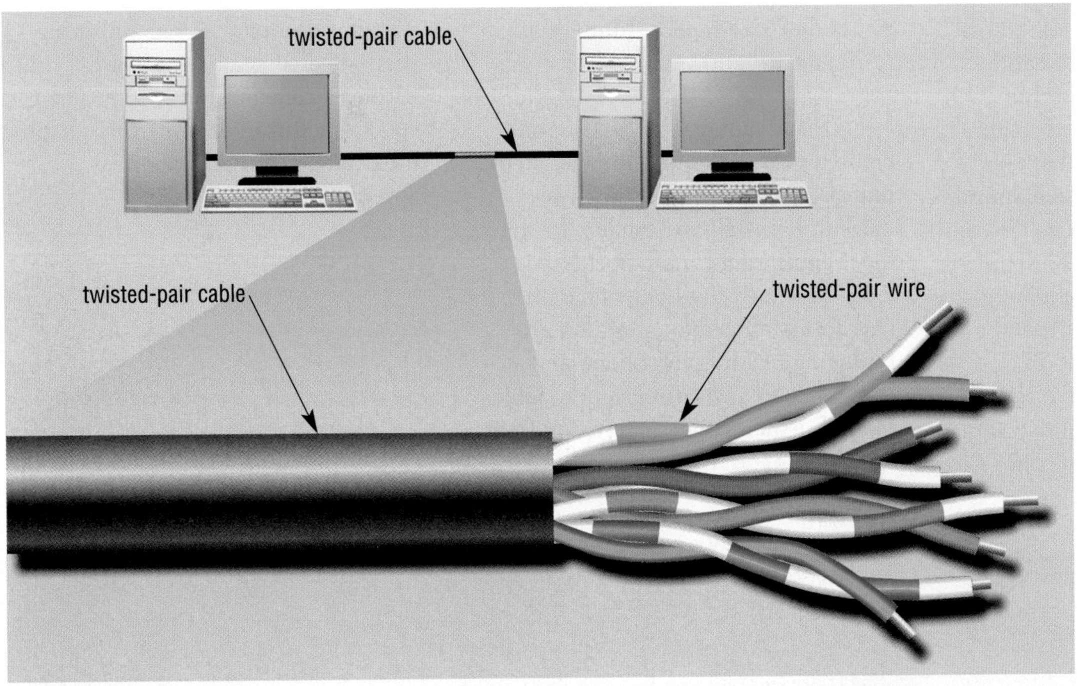

Figure 9-33 A twisted-pair cable consists of one or more twisted-pair wires. Each twisted-pair wire usually is color coded for identification. Telephone networks and local area networks often use twisted-pair cable.

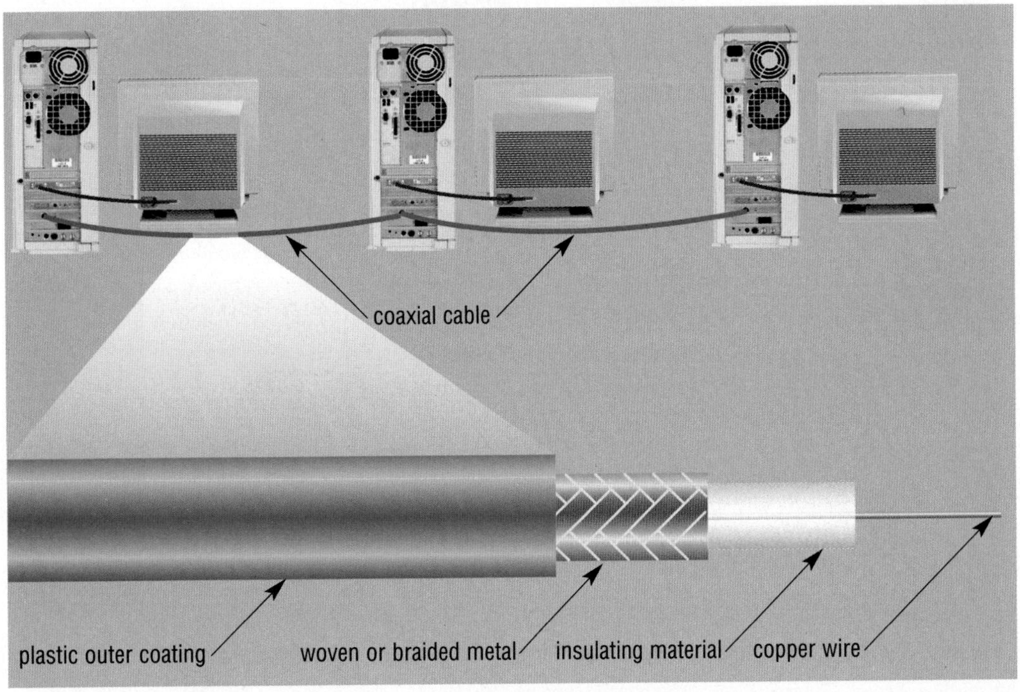

Figure 9-34 On a coaxial cable, data travels through the copper wire. This illustration shows computers networked together with coaxial cable.

Cable television (CATV) wiring often uses coaxial cable because it can be cabled over longer distances than twisted-pair cable. Most of today's computer networks, however, do not use coaxial cable because other transmission media such as fiber-optic cable transmit signals at faster rates.

Fiber-Optic Cable

Another type of physical transmission media is fiber-optic cable. The core of a **fiber-optic cable** consists of dozens or hundreds of thin strands of glass or plastic that use light to transmit signals. Each strand, called an **optical fiber**, is as thin as a human hair. Inside the fiber-optic cable, an insulating glass cladding and a protective coating surround each optical fiber (Figure 9-35).

Fiber-optic cables have several advantages over cables that use wire, such as twisted-pair and coaxial cables. These advantages include the following:

- Capability of carrying significantly more signals than wire cables
- Faster data transmission
- Less susceptible to noise (interference) from other devices such as a copy machine
- Better security for signals during transmission because they are less susceptible to noise
- Smaller size (much thinner and lighter weight)

Disadvantages of fiber-optic cable are it costs more than twisted-pair or coaxial cable and can be difficult to install and modify. Despite these limitations, many local and long-distance telephone companies and cable television operators are replacing existing telephone and coaxial cables with fiber-optic cables. Many businesses also are using fiber-optic cables in high-traffic networks or as the main cable in a network.

WIRELESS TRANSMISSION MEDIA

Wireless transmission media are used when it is inconvenient, impractical, or impossible to install cables. Wireless transmission media used in communications include broadcast radio, cellular radio, microwaves, communications satellites, and infrared. The table in Figure 9-36 lists transfer rates of various wireless transmission media. The following sections discuss these types of wireless transmission media. The special feature following this chapter illustrates a series of wireless applications.

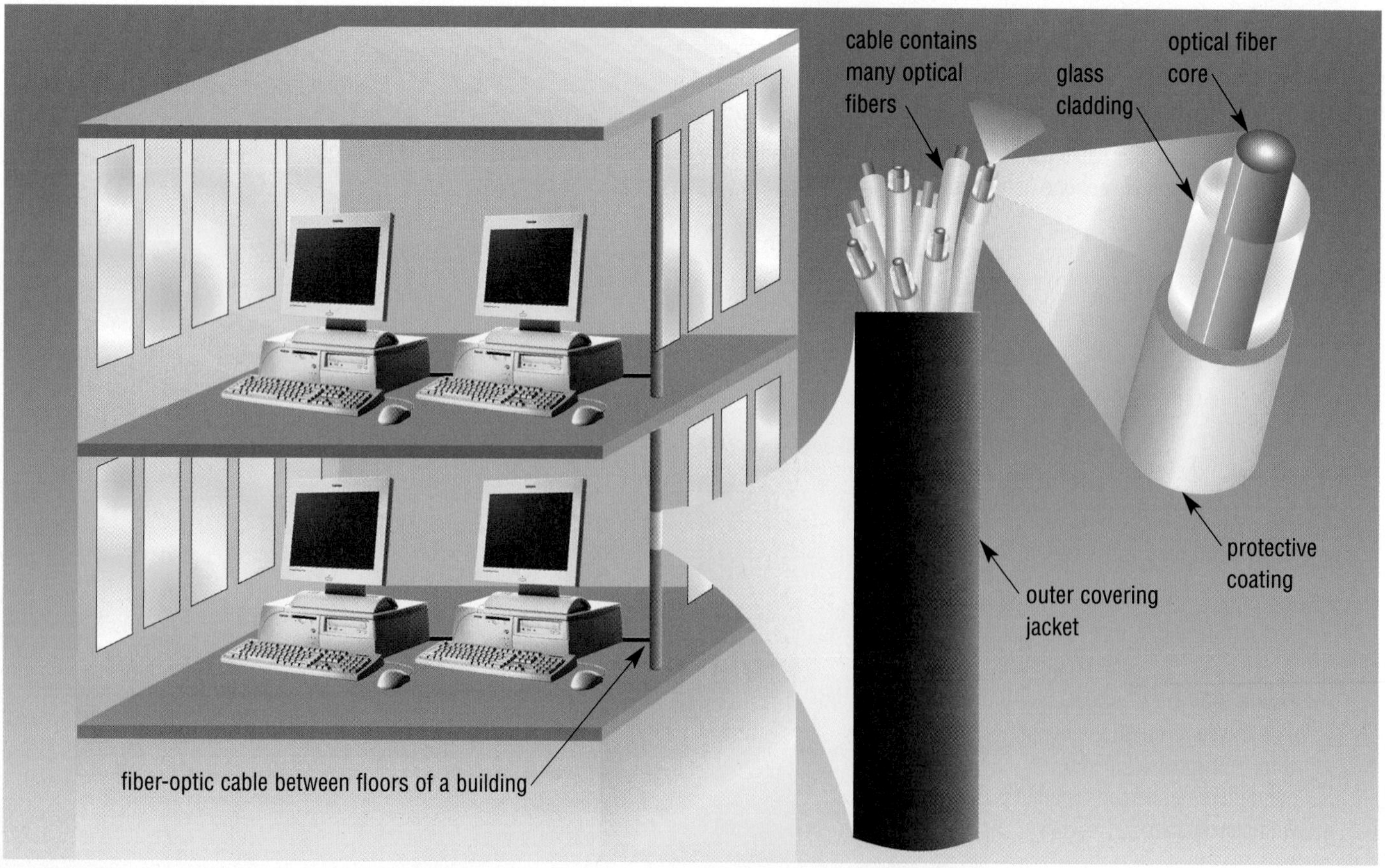

Figure 9-35 A fiber-optic cable consists of hair-thin strands of glass or plastic that carry data as pulses of light.

Broadcast Radio

Broadcast radio is a wireless transmission medium that distributes radio signals through the air over long distances such as between cities, regions, and countries and short distances such as within an office or home. For radio transmissions, you need a transmitter to send the broadcast radio signal and a receiver to accept it. To receive the broadcast radio signal, the receiver has an antenna that is located in the range of the signal. Some networks use a **transceiver,** which both sends and receives signals from wireless devices. Broadcast radio is slower and more susceptible to noise than physical transmission media but it provides flexibility and portability.

Home and small business users are finding many uses for short-range broadcast radio communications such as Bluetooth™. **Bluetooth™** uses short-range radio waves to transmit data among Bluetooth™-enabled devices. A Bluetooth™-enabled device contains a small chip that allows it to communicate with other Bluetooth™-enabled devices. Examples of these devices can include desktop personal computers, Internet appliances, notebook computers, handheld computers, cellular telephones, fax machines, and printers. To communicate with each other, these devices must be within a specified range (about 10 meters but can be extended to 100 meters with additional equipment).

Figure 9-37 illustrates how users can *buy* movie tickets on the

TRANSFER RATES FOR VARIOUS TYPES OF WIRELESS TRANSMISSION MEDIA

Channel	Transfer Rates
Broadcast radio	Up to 2 Mbps
Microwave radio	45 Mbps
Communications satellite	50 Mbps
Cellular radio	9,600 bps to 14.4 Kbps
Infrared	1 to 4 Mbps

Figure 9-36 The speeds of various wireless communications media.

Figure 9-37 AN EXAMPLE OF A BLUETOOTH™ USE FOR SHORT-RANGE RADIO TRANSMISSION

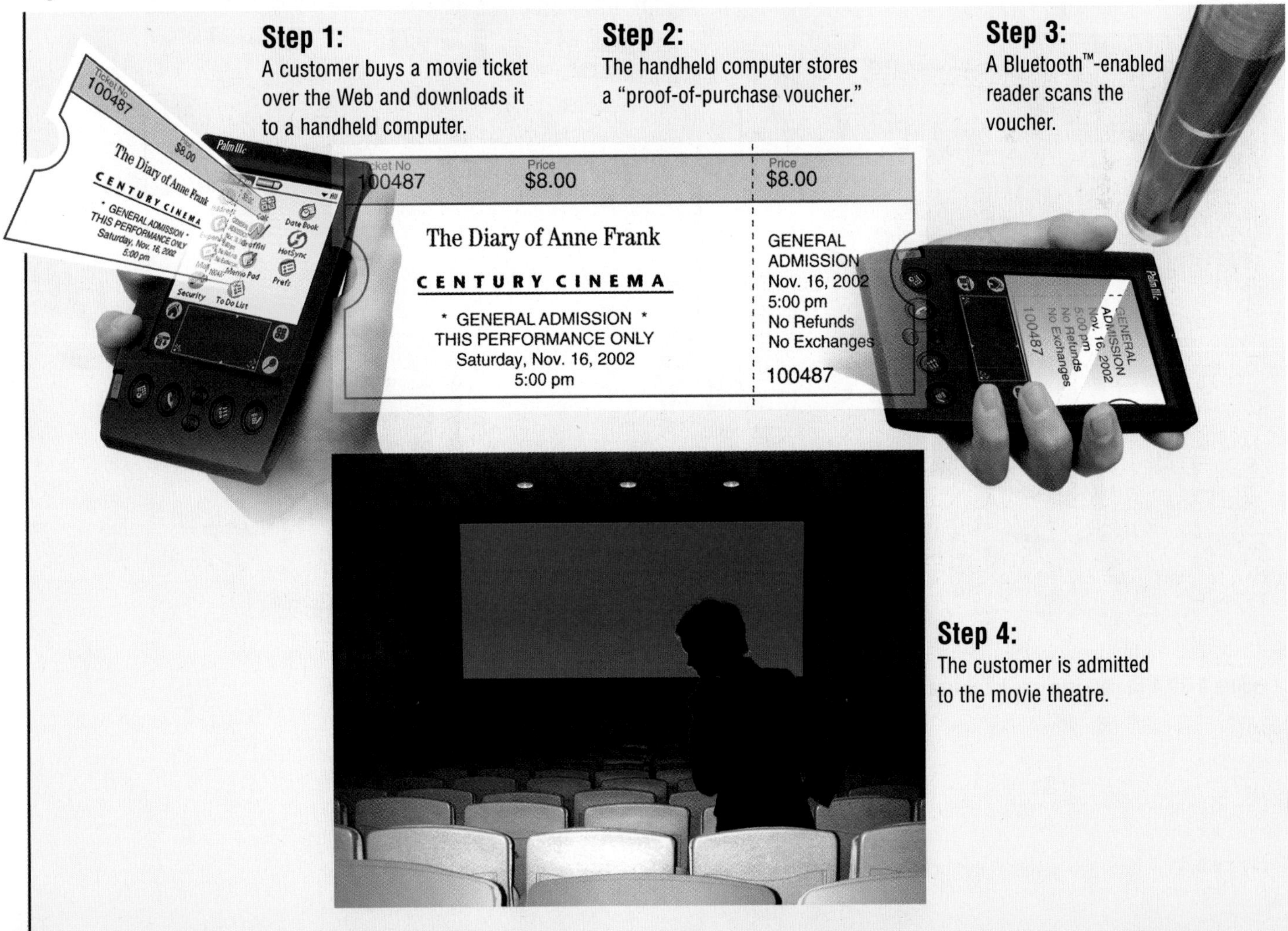
Step 1:
A customer buys a movie ticket over the Web and downloads it to a handheld computer.
Step 2:
The handheld computer stores a "proof-of-purchase voucher."
Step 3:
A Bluetooth™-enabled reader scans the voucher.
Step 4:
The customer is admitted to the movie theatre.
Price
$8.00
The Diary of Anne Frank
CENTURY CINEMA
* GENERAL ADMISSION *
THIS PERFORMANCE ONLY
Saturday, Nov. 16, 2002
5:00 pm
GENERAL
Nov. 16, 2002
5:00 pm
No Refunds
100487

Web, save the ticket on their handheld computer, and then transfer the ticket using short-range radio Bluetooth™ technology to a Bluetooth-reader at the movie theater when they wish to see the movie.

As discussed earlier in this chapter, many homes and businesses today are using broadcast radio to wirelessly network computers and other devices in the household or office. Figure 9-38 shows a sample wireless local area network. Wireless devices such as terminals, notebook computers, or handheld computers have an antenna so they can communicate with the network transceiver.

Cellular Radio

Cellular radio is a form of broadcast radio that is used widely for mobile communications, specifically wireless modems and cellular telephones (Figure 9-39). A **cellular telephone** is a telephone device that uses radio signals to transmit voice

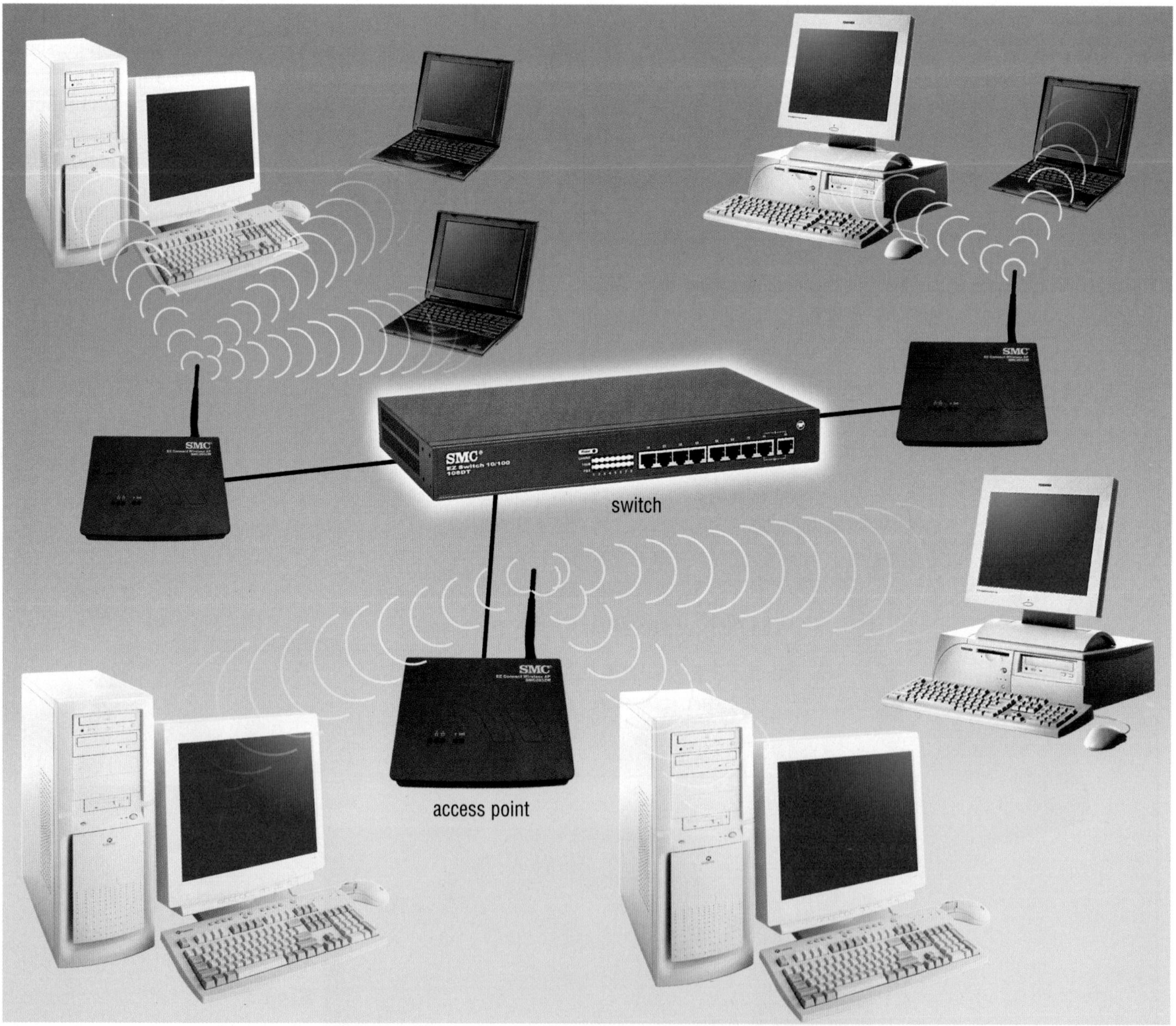

Figure 9-38 A sample wireless local area network.

and digital data messages. Some mobile users connect their notebook computer or other mobile computer to a cellular telephone to access the Web, send and receive e-mail, enter a chat room, or connect to an office or school network while away from a standard telephone line, for example, from a car or a park bench.

Personal Communications Services (PCS) is a set of technologies used for completely digital cellular devices. Devices that use PCS include handheld computers, cellular telephones, pagers, and fax machines. These devices have voice mail, call forwarding, fax capability, and caller ID. They also have wireless modems allowing you Internet access and e-mail capabilities.

Microwaves

Microwaves are radio waves that provide a high-speed signal transmission. Microwave transmission involves sending signals from one microwave station to another (Figure 9-40 on the next page). Microwaves can transmit data at rates up to 4,500 times faster than a dial-up modem.

A **microwave station** is an earth-based reflective dish that contains the antenna, transceivers, and other equipment necessary for microwave communications. Microwaves use **line-of-sight transmission**, which means that microwaves must transmit in a straight line with no obstructions between microwave antennas. To avoid possible obstructions, such as buildings or mountains, microwave stations often sit on the tops of buildings, towers, or mountains.

Microwave transmission is used in environments where installing physical transmission media is difficult or impossible and where line-of-sight transmission is available.

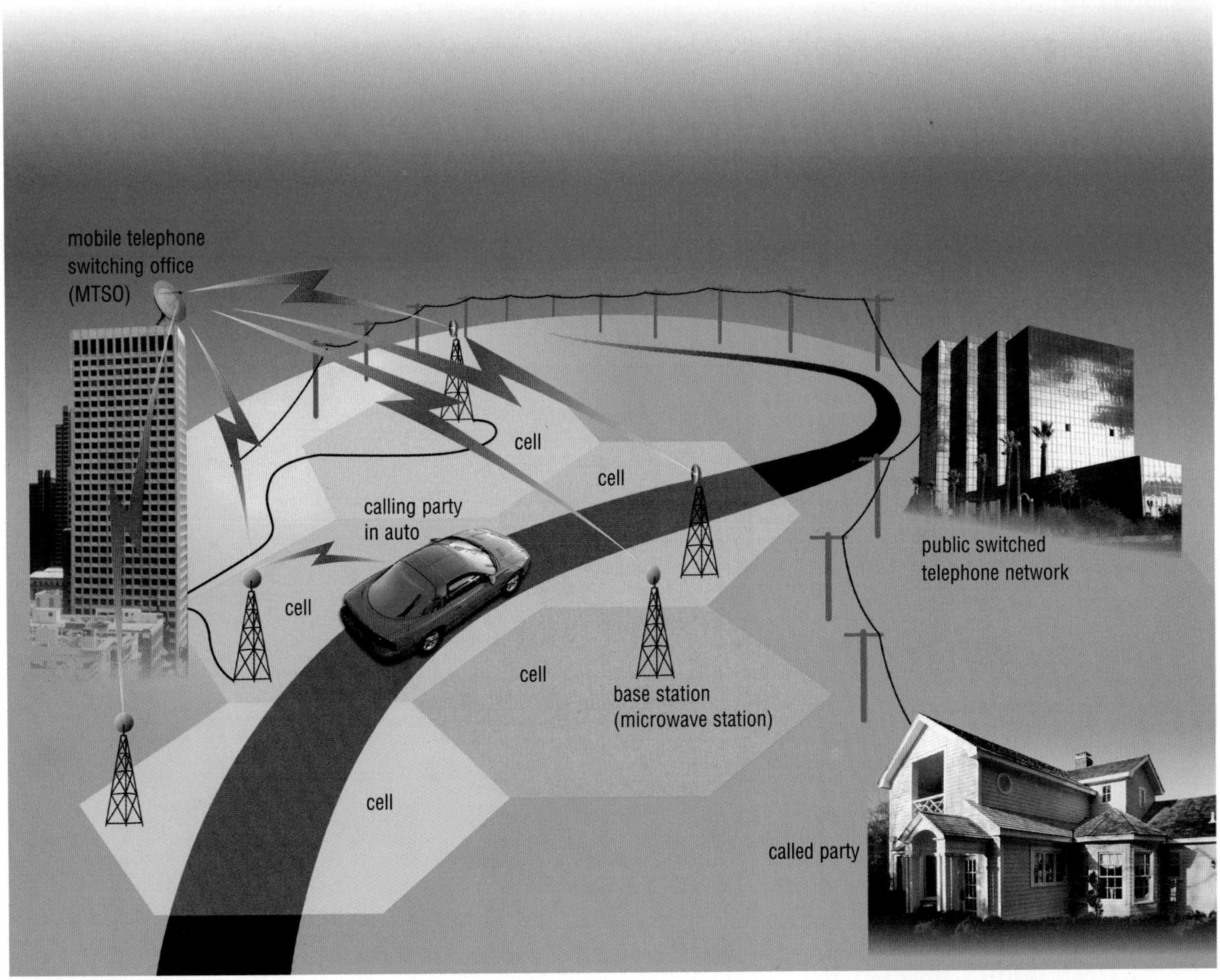

Figure 9-39 As a person with a cellular telephone drives from one cell to another, the radio signals transfer from the base station (microwave station) in one cell to a base station in another cell.

For example, microwave transmission is used in wide-open areas such as deserts or lakes; between buildings in a close geographic area; or to communicate with a satellite. Current users of microwave transmission include universities, hospitals, city governments, cable television providers, and telephone companies.

Communications Satellite

A **communications satellite** is a space station that receives microwave signals from an earth-based station, amplifies (strengthens) the signals, and broadcasts the signals back over a wide area to any number of earth-based stations (Figure 9-41).

Figure 9-40 A microwave station is an earth-based reflective dish that contains the antenna and other equipment necessary for microwave communications.

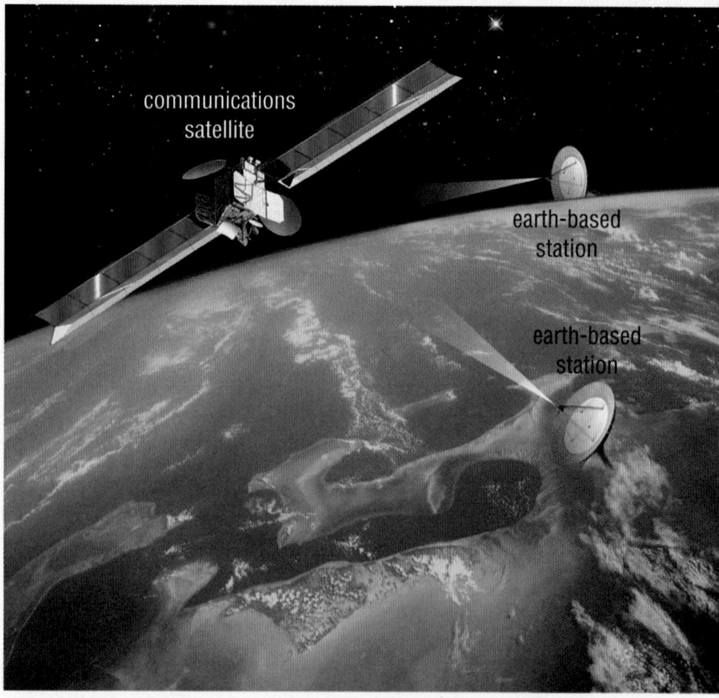

Figure 9-41 Communications satellites are placed about 22,300 miles above the Earth's equator.

ISSUE

Wireless Advertising

Cellular Radio

Are you ready for wireless advertising? You are on the road and need to call home. You dial your cellular telephone just as you pass a Pizza Hut. The first words you hear? "The Best Pizza Under One Roof." This scenario may seem a little futuristic, but today's technology makes it possible to deliver targeted advertising in all sorts of new ways. WindWire and DoubleClick (see URLs below), for example, both have wireless marketing and advertising networks that deliver targeted advertisements, coupons, and promotions to leading wireless Internet devices, including cellular telephones, handheld computers, and two-way pagers. Ericsson Telephone (see URL below) recently conducted a six-week wireless advertising study with 5,000 users. In return for the more than 100,000 targeted advertising messages, the users were given free text-messaging capabilities. The results of the study indicate more than 60 percent of the participants liked receiving targeted advertisements, and 20 percent asked for more information after viewing the advertising message. Will American users willingly accept wireless advertisements sent to them over cellular telephones and other mobile devices? What inducement would convince someone to accept the messages? Free air time? Free information such as the location of a restaurant? Would you accept the advertising in return for a free service? What if the advertisements were targeted at your personal profile? Would this make a difference in your willingness to accept the advertisements?

For more information on wireless devices and wireless advertising and the Web sites mentioned above, visit the Discovering Computers 2002 Issues Web page (**scsite.com/dc2002/issues.htm**) and click Chapter 9 Issue #5.

These earth-based stations often are microwave stations. Other devices, such as handheld computers and GPS receivers, also can function as an earth-based station. Transmission from an earth-based station to a satellite is an **uplink**. Transmission from a satellite to an earth-based station is a **downlink**.

Applications such as air navigation, television and radio broadcasts, videoconferencing, paging, and global positioning systems use communications satellites. With the proper satellite dish and a satellite modem card, consumers can access the Internet using satellite technology. Web satellites, however, only can transmit to your computer (one-way communications). For uplink transmissions, you more than likely will use a dial-up modem. This difference in speeds usually is acceptable to most Internet satellite users because they download much more data than they upload. Future satellite technology will allow for two-way communications.

Infrared

Infrared (**IR**) is a wireless transmission media that sends signals using infrared light waves. Similar to microwaves, infrared transmission requires a line-of-sight transmission. That is, the sending device and the receiving device must be in line with each other so that nothing obstructs the path of the infrared light wave.

As discussed in Chapter 4, many computers and devices, such as a mouse, printer, and digital camera, have an IrDA port that enables the transfer of data from one device to another using infrared light waves. If your notebook computer has an IrDA port, simply position the port in front of the IrDA port on a printer to print a document wirelessly. Many handheld computers also have IrDA ports, allowing you to transfer data to another handheld computer or a network wirelessly (Figure 9-42).

CHAPTER SUMMARY

This chapter provided an overview of communications terminology and applications. It also discussed how you can join computers together into a network, allowing them to communicate and share resources such as hardware, software, data, and information. It also explained various communications devices, media, and procedures as they relate to computers.

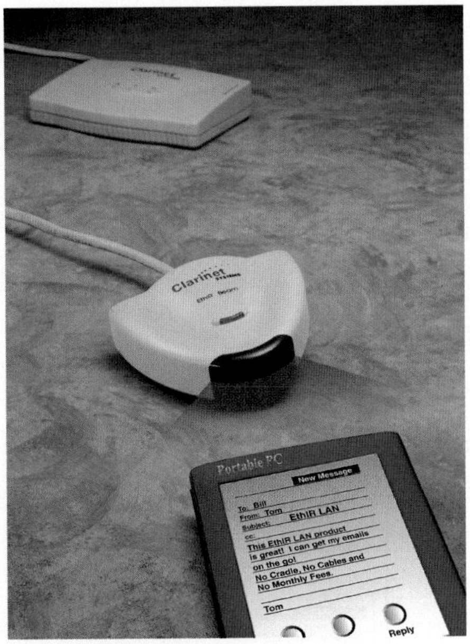

Figure 9-42 Many handheld computers have IrDA ports, allowing users to transmit business cards wirelessly to each other's handheld computer.

Data Communications Analyst

As a data communications analyst, you would aid in the research, design, installation, maintenance, and troubleshooting of data networks such as LANs and WANs. Common environments include voice, fiber optics, and TCP/IP. The analyst assists users with connectivity problems, analyzes data flow, configures modems, routers, and other devices. Experience with Cisco routers, switches, firewalls, and other data communications equipment is a plus. Someone who works in the field needs knowledge of various network operating systems and strong problem-solving skills.

Educational requirements vary widely from company to company. Some analysts have a two-year community college degree while others have a degree in electrical engineering. Similarly, a wide variation exists in salaries. Those with more education and experience earn more. Salaries range anywhere from $40,000 to $80,000.

To learn more about the field of data communications analyst as a career, visit the Discovering Computers 2002 Careers Web page (**scsite.com/dc2002/careers.htm**) and click Data Communications Analyst.

E-LEARNING

YEARN TO LEARN

Discover New Worlds Online

"To try and fail is at least to learn. To fail to try is to suffer the loss of what might have been." Benjamin Franklin's words bring home the point that despite setbacks encountered along the way, learning nurtures the creative spirit and helps people grow.

While you may believe your education ends when you finally graduate from college, learning is a lifelong process. Although much of this learning may occur on the job and through personal experiences, the Internet can fuel much of your desire and need to expand your mind. Many Web sites use streaming media and graphic-intense applications, so the high-speed Internet connections discussed in this chapter, such as cable modems and DSL, are ideal for these e-learning tools.

Learning to enhance your culinary skills can be a rewarding endeavor. No matter if you are a gourmet chef or a weekend cook, you will be cooking in style with the help of online resources. At the Betty Crocker Web site (Figure 9-43), you can learn how to prepare nutritious meals and bake for special occasions, almost as if Betty Crocker herself were guiding you along. If you find your kitchen familiar territory, The MasterCook's video tips can add flair and finesse to your style.

If you would rather sit in front of the computer than stand in front of the stove, you can learn to search the Internet skillfully and delve into its treasures by visiting several Web sites, including Learn the Net (Figure 9-45) and NetLearn. These learning Web sites offer tutorials on building your own Web sites, the latest news about the Internet, and resources for visually impaired users.

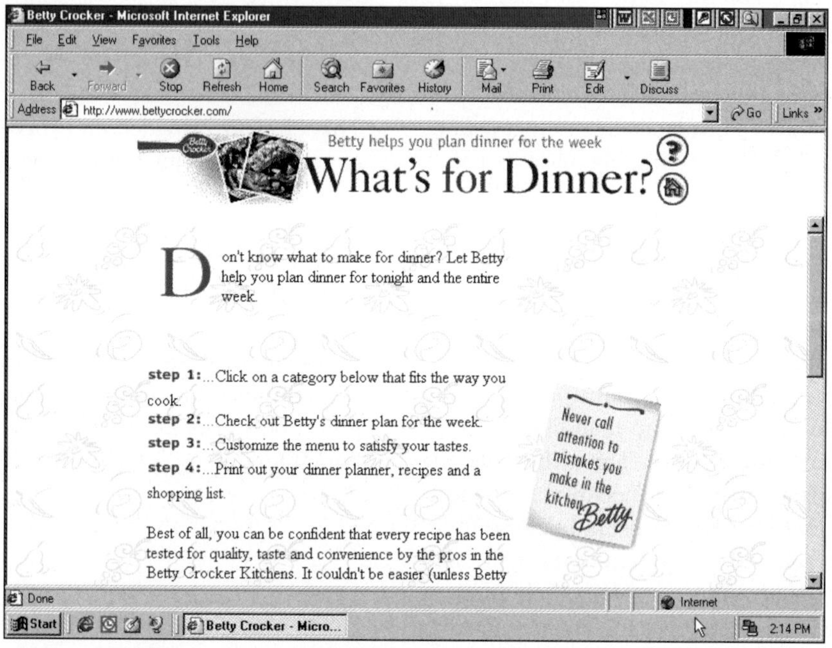

Figure 9-43 From soups to soufflés, cooking will be a piece of cake with tips from the Betty Crocker and other culinary Web sites.

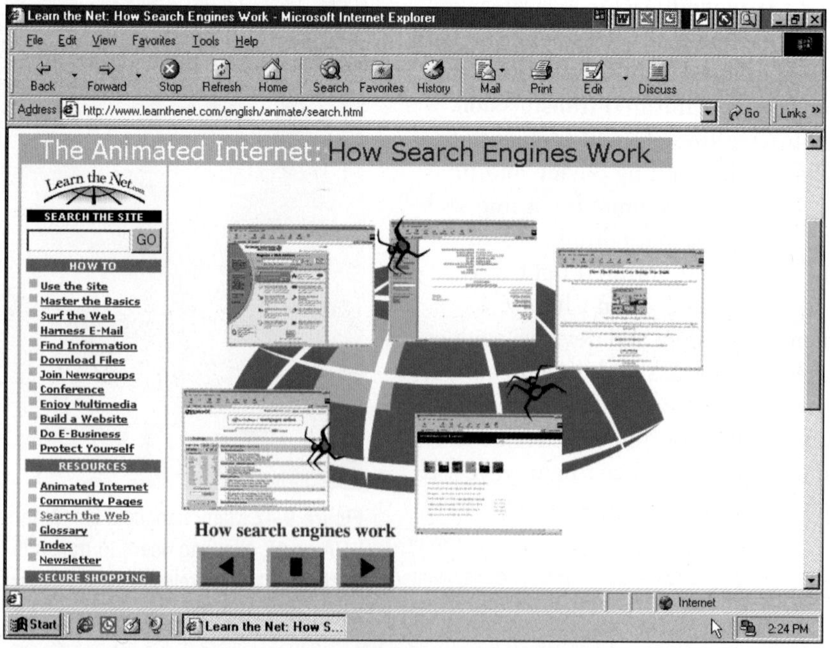

Figure 9-44 Web sites such as Learn the Net make navigating the Web a more rewarding experience.

Have you ever wondered how an airplane flies? Take a look at the See How it Flies Web site. You might be interested in finding out about how your car's catalytic converter reduces pollution or how the Electoral College functions? Marshall Brain's How Stuff Works Web site (Figure 9-45) is filled with articles and animations.

The table in Figure 9-46 lists some innovative and informative learning Web sites. Have a seat in this virtual classroom, and do not be afraid to fail along the way.

For more information on learning Web sites, visit the Discovering Computers 2002 E-Revolution Web page (scsite.com/dc2002/e-rev.htm) and click Learning.

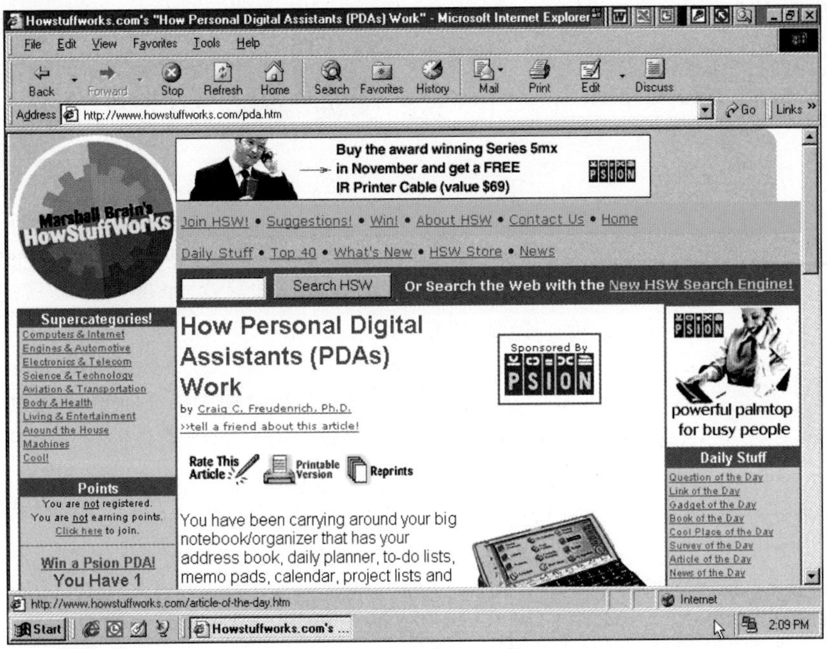

Figure 9-45 The Internet has something for everyone with numerous Web sites that help you find information quickly and easily about how technology works, the principles of flight, or educational adventures.

LEARNING WEB SITES	URL
Cooking	
Betty Crocker	bettycrocker.com
SierraHome Network MasterCook.com	mastercook.sierrahome.com
Internet	
Learn the Net	learnthenet.com
NetLearn	www.rgu.ac.uk/schools/sim/research/netlearn/callist.htm
Technology and Science	
Global Online Adventure Learning Site	goals.com/homebody.asp
How Stuff Works	howstuffworks.com/welcome.htm
General Learning	
Bartleby.com: Great Books Online	bartleby.com
Blue Web'n Learning Sites Library	www.kn.pacbell.com/wired/bluewebn

For an updated list of learning Web sites, visit scsite.com/dc2002/e-rev.htm.

Figure 9-46 These Web sites contain a variety of topics that can help you learn about all aspects of life.

e-REVOLUTION E-LEARNING *applied:*

1. Visit one of the three cooking Web sites listed in Figure 9-46 and find two recipes or cooking tips that you can use when preparing your next meal. Write a paragraph on each summarizing your discoveries. What are the advantages and disadvantages of accessing these Web sites on the new Web appliances that might someday be in your kitchen?

2. Using one of the technology and science Web sites and one of the Web sites in Figure 9-46, search for information about communications and networks that supplements the material discussed in this chapter. Write a paragraph about your findings. Then, review the material in the two general learning Web sites listed in Figure 9-46, and write a paragraph describing the content on each Web site that is pertinent to your major.

In Summary

Web Instructions: To display this page from the Web, start your browser and enter the URL scsite.com/dc2002/ch9/summary.htm. Click the links for current and additional information. To listen to an audio version of this In Summary, click the Audio button. To play the audio, RealPlayer must be installed on your computer (download by clicking here).

1 What Components Are Required for Successful Communications?

When referring to computers, **communications** describes a process in which one computer transfers data, instructions, and information to another computer(s). Communications requires a **sending device** that initiates the transfer; a communications device (such as a modem) that converts the sent material into signals capable of being carried by a communications channel; a communications channel over which the signals travel; a communications device that receives the signals and converts them into a form understood by the **receiving device**, which accepts the sent material.

2 What Are Some Sending and Receiving Devices?

Notebook computers, desktop computers, mid-range servers, and mainframe computers all can serve as sending and receiving devices. **Internet appliances** and Web-enabled devices also serve as sending and receiving devices. Cellular telephones and pagers are examples of wireless devices that can be Web enabled.

3 What Are Some Communications Applications?

Voice mail functions similarly to answering machine but converts an analog voice message into digital form. A **fax** sends and receives documents via telephone lines, and a fax modem sends and receives faxes using a computer. **E-mail (electronic mail)** is the exchange of text messages and computer files via a communications network. **Instant messaging (IM)** is a communications service that notifies you when people are online and allows you to exchange messages or files. In a **chat room**, participants use the computer to converse with each other in real time. **Internet telephony** uses the Internet instead of the telephone to enable you to talk to other people over the Web. **Videoconferencing** uses video and computer technology to conduct a meeting between participants at geographically separate locations. A **Web conference** uses the Internet, Web browsers, and Web servers. **Groupware** is a software application that helps people work together and share information over a network. A **global positioning system (GPS)** consists of earth-based receivers that analyze satellite signals to determine the receiver's geographic location.

4 What Are the Advantages of Using a Network?

A **network** is a collection of computers and devices connected by communications channels that facilitates communications among users and allows users to share resources with other users. Using a network enables people to communicate efficiently and easily, both internally and externally. Each user on a network can share hardware, software, data, and information.

5 What Is the Difference between a Local Area Network and a Wide Area Network?

A **local area network (LAN)** is a network that connects computers and devices in a limited geographical area such as a home, school computer laboratory, office building, or closely positioned group of buildings. Two popular types of LANs are **peer-to-peer** and **client/server**. A **wide area network (WAN)** covers a large geographical area (such as a city, country, or the world) using a communications channel that combines many types of media such as telephone lines, cables, and air waves.

6 What Are the Various Types of Communications Technologies?

To communicate effectively requires that a network uses a variety of communications technologies. **Ethernet**, the most poplar LAN, is based on a bus topology, but can be wired in a star pattern. This LAN technology enables personal computers to contend for access to the network. Variations of the Ethernet standard include **Fast Ethernet** and **Gigabit Ethernet**. **Token ring** controls access to the network by requiring that network devices share or pass a token or special signal to access the network. Internet transmissions commonly use **transmission control protocol/Internet protocol**, or **TCP/IP**, to manage data transmission by breaking it up into packets. The Wireless Application Protocol (WAP) uses a client/server network and allows wireless mobile devices to access the Internet and its services such as the Web and e-mail.

7 What Are Some Uses for Intranets and Extranets?

Intranets generally make company information accessible to employees and facilitate working in groups. Simple intranet applications include electronic publishing of organizational materials such as telephone directories, event calendars, procedure manuals, employee benefits information, and job postings. An **extranet** is a type of network that extends to authorized users outside the company. Extranets facilitate communications among a company's customers or suppliers. A firewall restricts access to data and information on a network.

8 What Is the Purpose of Communications Software?

Communications software establishes a connection to another computer or network, and manages the transmission of data, instructions, and information. For two computers to communicate, they must have compatible communications software. Once a connection is established, communications software provides a means to access the Internet. Some communications programs support **FTP (file transfer protocol)**, which is an Internet standard that enables the uploading and downloading of files to and from a Web server.

9 How Does the Telephone Network Work?

The public switched telephone network (PSTN) is the worldwide telephone system that handles voice-oriented telephone calls. With the exception of the final link from the local telephone company to the home, today's system is mostly digital. Data, instructions, and information are sent over the telephone network using a **dial-up line** or a **dedicated line**. The **transfer rate** is the speed with which a line carries data and information, and rates can range from thousands of **bits per second (bps)** to billions of bits per second. Four popular types of digital dedicated lines are **ISDN** (Integrated Services Digital Network), **DSL (digital subscriber line)**, **T-carrier line**, and **asynchronous transfer mode** (ATM).

10 What Are Commonly Used Communications Devices?

A **communications device** is any type of hardware capable of transmitting data, instructions, and information between a sending device and a receiving device. A modem converts a computer's digital signals into analog signals (**modulate**) so they can be transmitted over standard telephone lines, and then reconverts the analog signals into digital signals (**demodulate**) that a computer can understand. ISDN and DSL use a **digital modem** that sends and receives data and information to and from a digital telephone line. A **cable modem** sends and receives data over the cable television (CATV) network. A **network interface card** (NIC) is a card inserted into an expansion slot of a personal computer or other device, enabling the device to connect to a network.

11 What Are Various Types of Transmission Media?

Transmission media consists of materials or techniques capable of carrying signals. **Physical transmission media**, which use tangible (touchable) materials to send communications signals, include twisted-pair cable, coaxial cable, and fiber-optic cable. **Twisted-pair cable** consists of twisted-pair wires that are twisted together. **Coaxial cable** consists of a single copper wire surrounded by at least three layers (insulating material, woven or braided metal, and a plastic outer coating). **Fiber-optic cable** consists of dozens or hundreds of thin strands of glass or plastic that use light to transmit signals. Wireless transmission media, which send communications signals through air or space, include broadcast radio, cellular radio, microwaves, communications satellites, and infrared. **Broadcast radio** distributes radio signals through the air over long distances. **Cellular radio** is a form of broadcast radio used widely for mobile communications. **Microwaves** are radio waves that provide a high-speed signal transmission. A **communications satellite** is a space station that receives microwave signals from an earth-based station, amplifies the signals, and broadcasts the signals back over a wide area to any number of earth-based stations. **Infrared (IR)** sends signals using infrared light waves.

Key Terms

Web Instructions: To display this page from the Web, start your browser and enter the URL scsite.com/dc2002/ch9/terms.htm. Scroll through the list of terms. Click a term to display its definition and a picture. Click the To WEB button for current and additional information about the term from the Web. To see animations, Shockwave and Flash Player must be installed on your computer (download by clicking here).

ADSL (asymmetric digital subscriber line) (9.26)
analog signal (9.3)
anonymous FTP (9.24)
asynchronous (9.7)
asynchronous transfer mode (ATM) (9.27)
backbone (9.17)
bandwidth (9.31)
baseband (9.32)
bits per second (bps) (9.26)
Bluetooth™ (9.35)
broadband (9.32)
broadband modem (9.29)
broadcast radio (9.35)
bus (9.17)
bus network (9.17)
cable modem (9.29)
cellular radio (9.36)
cellular telephone (9.36)
channel (9.31)
chat room (9.6)
client/server (9.14)
clients (9.14)
coax (9.33)
coaxial cable (9.33)
collaborate (9.9)
communications (9.2)
communications device (9.27)
communications satellite (9.38)
communications software (9.23)
database server (9.14)
dedicated line (9.25)
dedicated servers (9.14)
demodulate (9.28)
dial-up line (9.25)
dial-up modem (9.28)
Digital Angel™ (9.11)
digital modem (9.28)
digital signal (9.3)
downlink (9.39)
DSL (digital subscriber line) (9.26)
DSL modem (9.28)
e-mail (electronic mail) (9.5)
Ethernet (9.18)
external modem (9.28)
extranet (9.20)
Fast Ethernet (9.19)
fax (9.5)
fiber-optic cable (9.34)
file server (9.14)
firewall (9.20)
FTP (file transfer protocol) (9.24)
FTP server (9.24)
Gigabit Ethernet (9.19)
gigabits per second (Gbps) (9.26)
global positioning system (GPS) (9.10)
groupware (9.10)
home network (9.22)
HomePLC (powerline cable) network (9.22)
HomeRF (radio frequency) network (9.22)
host computer (9.14)
hub (connecting networks) (9.30)
hub (star network) (9.18)
infrared (IR) (9.39)
instant messaging (IM) (9.6)
intelligent home network (9.23)
internal modem (9.28)

COMMUNICATIONS SATELLITE
Space station that receives microwave signals from an earth-based station, amplifies (strenghtens) the signals, and broadcasts the signals back over a earth-based stations. (9.38)

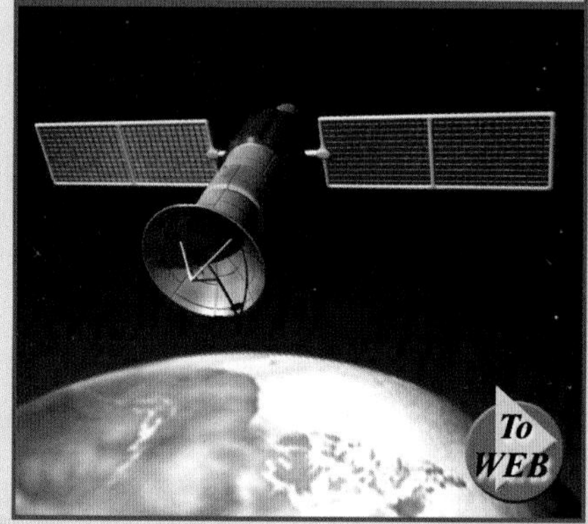

Internet appliance (9.4)
Internet telephone software (9.8)
Internet telephony (9.8)
intranet (9.20)
ISDN (Integrated Services Digital Network) (9.26)
ISDN adapter (9.28)
ISDN modem (9.28)
kilobits per second (Kbps) (9.26)
LAN adapter (9.29)
line-of-sight transmission (9.37)
local area network (LAN) (9.12)
megabits per second (Mbps) (9.26)
metropolitan area network (MAN) (9.16)
microwave station (9.37)
microwaves (9.37)
modem (9.28)
modulate (9.28)
multiplexing (9.26)
network (9.11)
network administrator (9.14)
network interface card (NIC) (9.29)
network operating system (9.12)
network OS (9.12)
network server (9.14)
network topology (9.16)
newsgroup (9.7)
noise (9.33)
NOS (9.12)
online meeting (9.9)
optical fiber (9.34)
P2P (9.16)
packet switching (9.20)
packets (9.19)
peer-to-peer (9.13)
Personal Communications Services (PCS) (9.37)
phoneline network (9.22)
physical transmission media (9.32)
powerline LAN (9.22)
print server (9.14)
public switched telephone network (PSTN) (9.25)
radio chats (9.7)
receiving device (9.2)
ring network (9.17)
routers (9.19)
sending device (9.2)
server (9.14)
site license (9.11)
star network (9.18)
synchronous (9.7)
T1 line (9.27)
T3 line (9.27)
T-carrier line (9.27)
threaded discussion (9.7)
token ring (9.19)
transceiver (9.35)
transfer rate (9.26)
transmission control protocol/Internet protocol TCP/IP (9.19)
transmission media (9.31)
twisted-pair cable (9.33)
twisted-pair wire (9.33)
uplink (9.39)
video chats (9.7)
video telephone call (9.8)
videoconference (9.8)
voice chats (9.7)
voice mail (9.4)
voice mailbox (9.4)
WAP-enabled devices (9.20)
Web appliance (9.4)
Web conference (9.8)
Web-enabled device (9.4)
wide area network (WAN) (9.15)
Wireless Application Protocol (WAP) (9.20)
wireless LAN (WLAN) (9.12)
wireless modem (9.28)
wireless transmission media (9.32)
workgroup computing (9.10)

Learn It Online

Web Instructions: To display this page from the Web, start your browser and enter the URL scsite.com/dc2002/ch9/learn.htm.

1. Web Guide

Click Web Guide to display the Guide to World Wide Web Sites and Searching Techniques Web page. Click Reference and then click Webopedia. Search for Networks. Click one of the Networks links. Use your word processing program to prepare a brief report on your findings and submit your assignment to your instructor.

2. Scavenger Hunt

Click Scavenger Hunt. Print a copy of the Scavenger Hunt page; use this page to write down your answers as you search the Web. Submit your completed page to your instructor.

3. Who Wants to Be a Computer Genius?

Click Computer Genius to find out if you are a computer genius. Directions on how to play the game will display. When you are ready to play, click the PLAY button. Submit your score to your instructor.

4. Wheel of Terms

Click Wheel of Terms to reinforce important terms you learned in this chapter by playing the Shelly Cashman Series version of this popular game. Directions on how to play the game will display. When you are ready to play, click the PLAY button. Submit your score to your instructor.

5. Career Corner

Click Career Corner to display the About.com page. In the Find It Now text box, type `distance learning`. Scroll through the results and then click a link related to technology learning online. Write a brief report on what you discovered. Submit the report to your instructor.

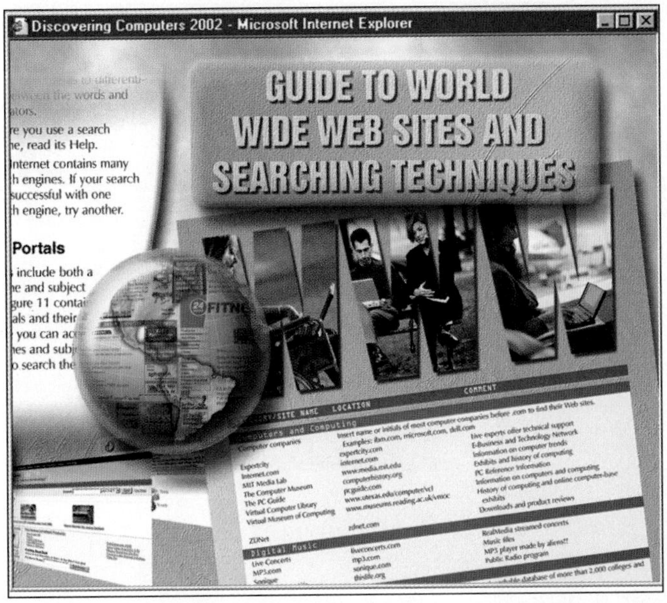

6. Search Sleuth:

Click Search Sleuth to learn search techniques that will help make you a research expert. Submit the completed assignment to your instructor.

7. Crossword Puzzle Challenge

Click Crossword Puzzle Challenge. Complete the puzzle to reinforce skills you learned in this chapter. Directions on how to play the game will display. When you are ready to play, click the PLAY button. Submit the completed puzzle to your instructor.

8. Practice Test

Click Practice Test. Answer each question. When completed enter your name and click the Grade Test button to submit the quiz for grading. Make a note of any missed questions. If required, print a copy to submit to your instructor.

Web Instructions: To display this page from the Web, start your browser and enter the URL scsite.com/dc2002/ch9/check.htm. Click the links for current and additional information. To experience the animation and interactivity, Shockwave and Flash Player must be installed on your computer (download by clicking here).

LABEL THE FIGURE

Instructions: Identify the steps in this example of instant messaging.

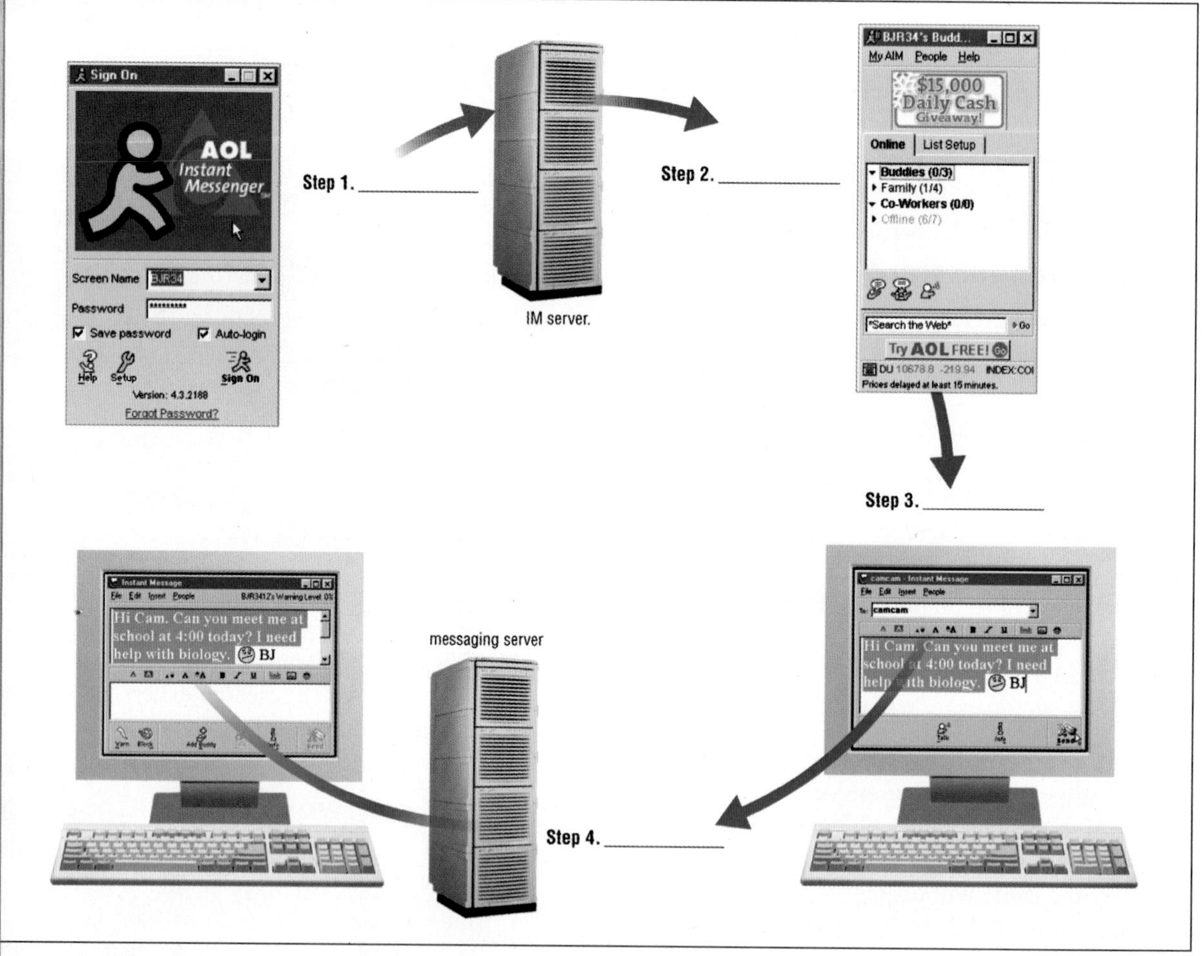

MATCHING

Instructions: Match each term from the column on the left with the best description from the column on the right.

_______ 1. coaxial cable
_______ 2. cellular radio
_______ 3. microwave
_______ 4. fiber-optic cable
_______ 5. twisted-pair cable

a. Two separate insulated copper wires that are twisted together.
b. A single copper wire surrounded by at least three layers.
c. A space station that receives microwave signals.
d. Radio waves that provide a high-speed signal transmission.
e. A form of broadcast radio that is used widely for mobile communications.
f. A wireless transmission media that sends signals using infrared light waves.
g. Consists of dozens or hundreds of thin strands of glass or plastic that use light to transmit signals.

MULTIPLE CHOICE

Instructions: Select the letter of the correct answer for each of the following questions.

1. A(n) __________ consists of a continuous electrical wave.
   a. digital signal
   b. analog signal
   c. GPS
   d. bus
2. A __________ network covers a large geographical area.
   a. local area
   b. metropolitan area network
   c. peer-to-peer
   d. wide area
3. In a __________ network, all of the devices in the network connect to a central computer.
   a. star
   b. bus
   c. ring
   d. peer-to-peer
4. A(n) __________ is an internal network that uses Internet technologies.
   a. extranet
   b. intranet
   c. wide area network
   d. metropolitan area network
5. __________ is an Internet standard that allows you to upload and download files to and from a Web server.
   a. FTP
   b. TCP/IP
   c. WAP
   d. PSTN

SHORT ANSWER

Instructions: Write a brief answer to each of the following questions.

1. What is noise? __________ Why do most of today's networks not use cable? __________
2. How are analog signals different from digital signals? __________ Why must both the sending and receiving ends of some communications channels have a modem for data transmission to occur? __________
3. What is a network operating system (NOS)? __________ What tasks does a network operating system perform? __________
4. How is a peer-to-peer network different from a client/server network? __________ What is the role of a network administrator? __________
5. What is network topology? __________ How are bus networks, ring networks, and star networks different? __________

WORKING TOGETHER

Instructions: Working with a group of your classmates, complete the following team exercise.

Assume you are part of a group hired as consultants to recommend a network plan for a small company of 20 employees. Using the Internet and other available resources, develop a network plan for the company. Include the following components in your plan: (1) the type of network — peer-to-peer or client/server; (2) the suggested topology; (3) the type and number of servers; (4) the peripheral devices; and (5) the communications media. Prepare a written report and a PowerPoint presentation to share with the class.

Web Instructions: To display this page from the Web, start your browser and enter the URL scsite.com/dc2002/ch9/lab.htm. Click the links for current and additional information.

Understanding Your Modem

1. This exercise uses Windows 95 or Windows 98 procedures and requires that you have a modem. Click the Start button on the taskbar, point to Settings on the Start menu, and then click Control Panel on the Settings submenu. Double-click the Modems icon in the Control Panel window. When the Modems Properties dialog box displays, click the General tab and then click the Properties button. Answer the following questions:

- What is the name of the modem?
- To which port is the modem connected?
- What is the maximum speed of the modem?
- Click the Connection tab and then answer the following questions:
- What is the number of data bits?
- What is the parity?
- What is the number of stop bits?
- Which call preferences (if any) are set on your modem?

Click the Cancel button to close each dialog box, and then click the Close button to close the Control Panel window.

Phone Dialer

2. This exercise uses Windows 98 or Windows 2000 procedures. Click the Start button on the taskbar and then click Help on the Start menu. When the Windows Help window opens, click the Index tab. Type `phone dialer` in the Type in a keyword to find text box and then click the Display button to learn about using Phone Dialer to dial from your computer. What is Phone Dialer? How do you start Phone Dialer after clicking the Start button? How can you obtain information about how to use Phone Dialer? Click the Close button to close the Windows Help window.

Network Access

3. This exercise uses Windows 95 or Windows 98 procedures. Double-click the My Computer icon on the desktop. Double-click the Control Panel icon in the My Computer window. Double-click the Network icon in the Control Panel window. When the Network dialog box displays, click the Identification tab. What is the Computer name? What is the Workgroup? What, if any, is the Computer Description? Click the Access Control tab. How is Share-level access control different from User-level access control? Click the Close button to close the Network dialog box and the Control Panel window.

Using Help to Understand Networks

4. This exercise uses Windows 98 procedures. Click the Start button on the taskbar and then click Help on the Start menu. Click the Contents tab. Click the Connecting to Networks book. Click the Connecting to a Network book. Click an appropriate Help topic to answer the following questions:

- How do you log on to a network?
- How do you connect to another computer on your network?
- How do you log off the network?

Click the Close button to close the Windows Help window.

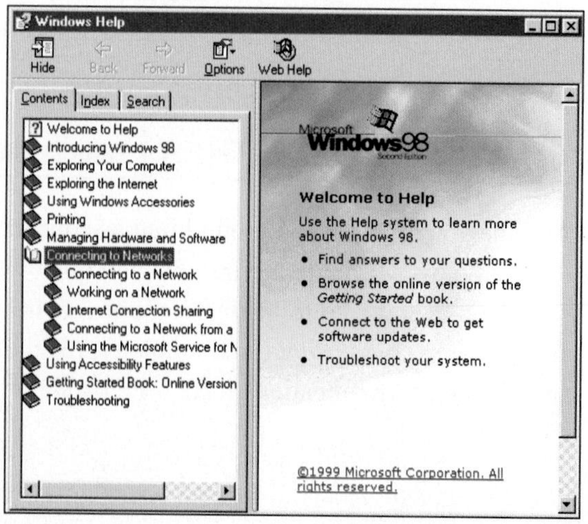

Web Work

Web Instructions: To display this page from the Web, start your browser and enter the URL scsite.com/dc2002/ch9/web.htm. To view At The Movies in exercise 1, RealPlayer must be installed on your computer (download by clicking here). To use the Shelly Cashman Series Exploring the Computers of the Future Lab from the Web, Shockwave and Flash Player must be installed on your computer (download by clicking here).

Distracted Drivers

To view the Distracted Drivers movie, click the button to the left or click the Play button to the right. Watch the movie, and then complete the exercise by answering the questions below. Technology-based driving distractions are responsible for 20 to 30 percent of the approximately six million accidents recorded each year. Radios, CD players, and especially cellular telephones have been the major culprits; however, new on-board navigational apparatus, many of them handheld devices, threaten to escalate the problem exponentially. Auto manufacturers are developing new safety features in response, but the growing convergence of technologies continues to spawn new systems and devices. Are strict laws against using these devices while driving the answer? Should laws be enacted that regulate carmakers or the device makers? What are other solutions?

Shelly Cashman Series Exploring the Computers of the Future Lab

Follow the instructions in Web Work 2 on page 1.47 to start and use the Shelly Cashman Series Exploring the Computers of the Future Lab. If you are running from the Web, enter the URL, scsite.com/sclabs/menu.htm or display the Web Work page (see instructions at the top of this page) and then click the button to the left.

Attachments

People often attach files to e-mail messages. To send an e-mail message with an attachment, click the button to the left to display your e-mail service. Enter your Login Name and Password. When the In-Box screen displays, click Compose. Type a classmate's e-mail address in the To text box and then type `Attachments` in the Subject text box. Click the Attachments button. Insert your floppy disk in drive A. Type `a:\h7-2.doc` in the Attach File text box. This is the document you create to complete Chapter 7 In the Lab 2. Click Attach to Message. Click the Done button. Click in the message box and then type a brief message about which E-Revolution applied question the attached document answers. When you are finished, click the Send button. Click the OK button on the Compose: sent Message Confirmation screen. Read any newly arrived mail. When you have read all of your messages, click Log Out to quit the e-mail service.

In the News

Theoretically, business travelers can access e-mail, fax documents, and transmit data from anywhere in the world. In practice, however, incompatible telephone standards and mismatched telephone jacks can frustrate even experienced globetrotters. 3Com's Megahertz International PC Card addresses this problem. The modem and accompanying software allow travelers to use computer communications with more than 250 telephone systems simply by selecting the appropriate country from a menu and attaching a suitable adapter plug. Click the button to the left and read a news article about a product that is changing computer communications. What is the product? What does it do? Who is more likely to use this product?

A World Without Wires

Not long ago, you used wired telephones and other devices to communicate with your friends, family, and employees. Today, wireless technology allows you to collaborate on projects and keep in touch with friends and family from anywhere in the world using a variety of gadgets: a smart pager, a cellular telephone, a handheld computer, and a notebook computer with high-speed Internet access. You also have the technology to check your e-mail as you travel throughout your town or the world.

Wireless networks are springing up everywhere, driven by convenience, cost, and access. Indeed, the wireless evolution is taking the world by storm. Even the casual observer notices dramatic changes in the way computer users send e-mail and communicate, access the Internet, and create and share files in the office. Your pockets and backpack may be overflowing with small electronic devices, but the wireless revolution is making headway to combine some of these products and simplify your life.

Today's wireless technology represents an evolution of products and standards. This special feature looks at a wide variety of these wireless products and illustrates how this technology is being used to simplify and expand your communication abilities.

Web Instructions: *To gain World Wide Web access to additional and up-to-date information regarding this special feature, start your browser and enter the URL shown at the top of this page.*

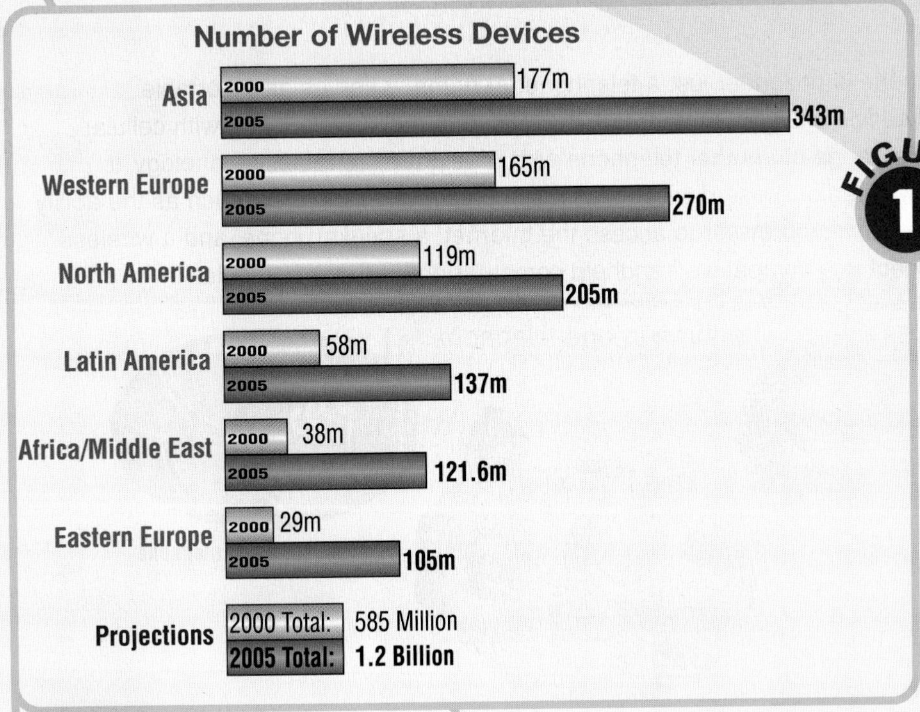

FIGURE 1

Today's technological changes are just the beginning of our fast-paced expansion into the wireless domain. Asia and Western Europe have emerged as world leaders in wireless device use. By 2005, more than 1.2 billion wireless devices will be in use, with millions of these products able to access the entire Web wirelessly.

FIGURE 2

Messaging is the foremost reason for the wireless market explosion. Wireless links to corporate networks allow employees to connect their cellular telephones, notebook computers with wireless Web modems, and handheld computers, and access their e-mail and key applications. Today, more than 170 million people worldwide send more than 3 billion messages per month. Analysts expect these numbers to surge by 2004, estimating that more than 1.3 billion people will send 244 billion messages monthly.

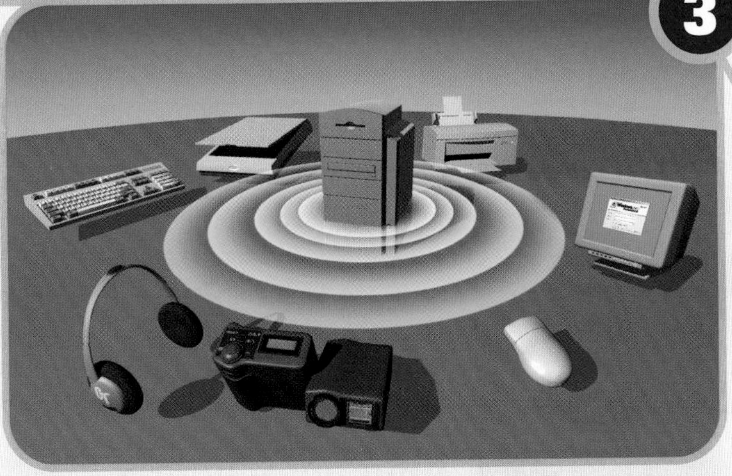

FIGURE 3

Wireless desktop computer components eliminate tangled cords and provide flexibility and freedom of movement. Digital radio technology allows peripherals, such as cordless pointing devices and keyboards, to work in a short range without being pointed at the computer.

FIGURE 4

Your wireless telephone is no longer just a telephone. At home, it serves as a portable telephone with a fixed line charge. On the road, it works as a mobile telephone with cellular charges. When it is in range of another telephone with Bluetooth™ wireless technology, it functions as a two-way radio. These devices also may contain other features, such as the ability to send text messages, a microbrowser to access the Internet, a speakerphone, and a wireless modem that can connect to a compatible handheld computer or notebook computer.

The three-in-one telephone

FIGURE 5

Compaq iPAQ BlackBerry users can access their e-mail at all times because they always are connected to a wireless network. They can watch e-mail messages scroll by while waiting for a bus, sitting in a meeting, taking coffee breaks, or studying with friends. Users also can compose, forward, and reply to messages.

FIGURE 6

Today's smart pagers are small and relatively inexpensive. Compared to cellular telephones, they have a longer battery life, lower access fee, and smaller size. Many provide instant messaging capability. Some computer experts consider Internet instant messaging (IM) the e-mail of the new millennium. Interactive pagers provide two-way messaging, information managers, and news, sports, and stock updates. Depending on the subscription service, some allow users to execute stock trades and make purchases, such as airline tickets.

FIGURE 7

Ericsson introduced the first Bluetooth™ product in 2000 — a headset that communicates with a wireless telephone, thus enabling users to talk hands-free. Wireless headsets also can connect to notebook computers and handheld computers.

FIGURE 8

United, American, and Delta airlines have set up high-speed wireless access at their main hubs and select international airports. This wireless infrastructure may improve productivity by having employees use the network while waiting for airplanes. The three airlines recognize that passengers travel with notebook computers, and with wireless access available, these customers can accomplish routine tasks such as accessing the Internet.

FIGURE 9

Wireless technology revolutionizes the way we learn and interact. During meetings, employees can use their wireless notebook computers, e-mail devices, and handheld computers to exchange electronic documents, business cards, schedules, and photos with all the people in the room or with selected participants. They even can transmit their documents to a data projector.

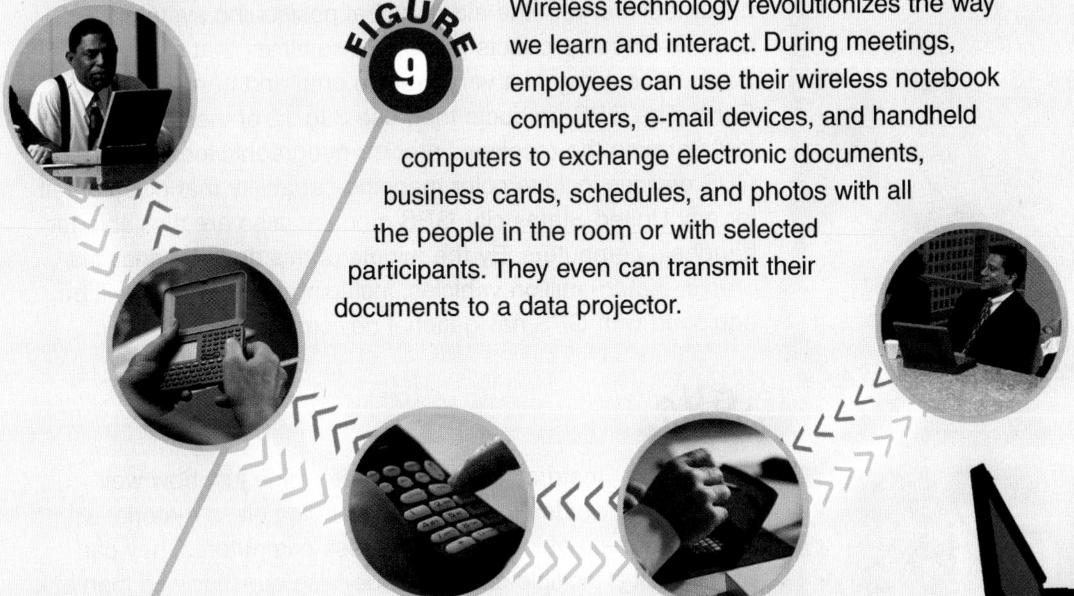

FIGURE 10

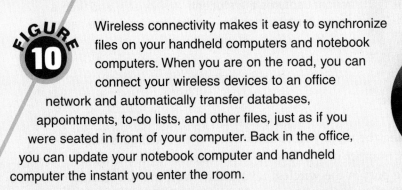

Wireless connectivity makes it easy to synchronize files on your handheld computers and notebook computers. When you are on the road, you can connect your wireless devices to an office network and automatically transfer databases, appointments, to-do lists, and other files, just as if you were seated in front of your computer. Back in the office, you can update your notebook computer and handheld computer the instant you enter the room.

FIGURE 11

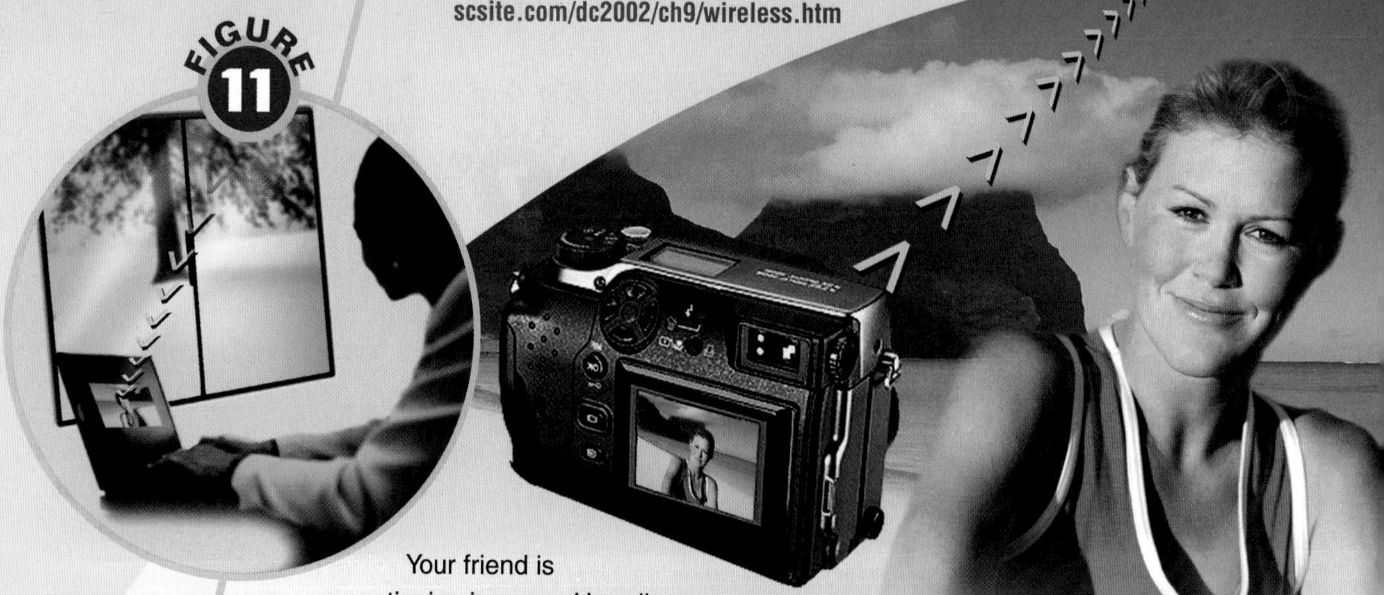

Your friend is vacationing in sunny Hawaii; you are shoveling snow in frigid Chicago. You can bask in your friend's warmth with instant postcards. All your friend needs to do is capture an image with a digital camera, connect the camera to a mobile telephone, and transmit the postcard to you. In seconds, you will receive the image on your notebook computer that is connected wirelessly to your mobile telephone.

FIGURE 12

Millions of hikers, boaters, pilots, drivers, and other navigators never feel lost with the aid of global positioning system (GPS) devices. These products rely on 24 satellites that circle the Earth twice a day in a very precise orbit and transmit data to Earth. The GPS products then use 3 to 12 of these satellites to determine the receivers' precise geographic locations. Some GPS devices include color mapping capability that gives detail for any United States city. GPS modules also are available for handheld computers. By the middle of this decade, analysts predict that 25 million vehicles, including all new cars, will be equipped with GPS navigational devices.

FIGURE 13

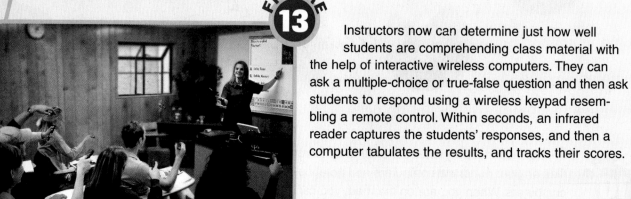

Instructors now can determine just how well students are comprehending class material with the help of interactive wireless computers. They can ask a multiple-choice or true-false question and then ask students to respond using a wireless keypad resembling a remote control. Within seconds, an infrared reader captures the students' responses, and then a computer tabulates the results, and tracks their scores.

Wireless technological changes are affecting the ways you communicate with colleagues and relatives throughout the world. Each day, the number of wireless devices increases as the price of connectivity decreases. Indeed, you are taking part in the wireless revolution sweeping the world.

CHAPTER 10

E-Commerce: A Revolution in the Way We Do Business

Ah, to drift along the shores of Lake Patanaomi. With the office closed for inventory, you and a co-worker both have Friday off. He invites you to spend a relaxing day on the lake aboard his boat. You meet him at the docks at 7:00 a.m. The weather is perfect … 80 degrees with a light breeze.

As you depart from the pier, you begin to talk about investments and your current portfolios of stocks, bonds, and mutual funds. He uses a stockbroker. You explain that you trade on the Internet because it saves a lot of money in transaction fees. Fascinated with the idea, your friend asks if he can watch you trade online sometime when the two of you are on dry land.

"No reason to wait," you say. Out of your pocket, you pull a handheld computer, extend the antenna, connect to the Internet, and display the online trading service Web page. You buy 100 shares of a stock your friend recommends. Within moments, the trade is complete. Your friend is amazed. He wonders what else you can do with that little computer. So, you display a Web site that sells electronics and show him how to order a handheld computer.

OBJECTIVES

After completing this chapter, you will be able to:

- Understand how e-commerce has changed the way we do business
- Discuss the positive impact of e-commerce on our society
- Differentiate between the various e-commerce business models: business-to-consumer, consumer-to-consumer, business-to-business, and business-to-employee
- Identify various e-commerce revenue streams
- Know how e-retailing works
- Identify e-commerce market sectors
- Discuss issues associated with building a storefront, accepting payment, managing product delivery, designing a site, managing the site, and promoting the site

WHAT IS E-COMMERCE?

Electronic commerce (e-commerce), sometimes called **e-business**, is a financial business transaction that occurs over an electronic network. Anyone with access to a computer, a network connection such as the Internet, and a means to pay for purchased goods or services can participate in e-commerce.

Two popular types of e-commerce are shopping and trading stocks (Figure 10-1). Recent studies indicate that nearly one half of Web users shop online and about one half of investors trade securities online. These results indicate a strong confidence in the Internet as a business transaction tool.

Figure 10-1 Anyone with access to a computer, an Internet connection, and a means to pay for purchased goods or services can participate in e-commerce.

From a business perspective, the Internet means opportunity. It provides companies and individuals with avenues to obtain information. Using the Internet can enhance communications among employees, customers, and vendors, and increase human resource productivity. E-commerce virtually eliminates the barriers of time and distance that can slow traditional business transactions. With e-commerce, transactions can occur instantaneously and globally. This saves time for participants on both ends.

At first, e-commerce transactions were conducted primarily through desktop computers. Today, many handheld computers and devices can access the Web wirelessly. Handheld Web-enabled devices include cellular telephones and pagers. Some people use the term **m-commerce** (**mobile commerce**) to identify e-commerce that takes place using mobile devices.

Since the introduction of e-commerce, many new terms have evolved to describe various types of businesses. For example, a **bricks-and-mortar** business, sometimes called a **brick-and-mortar** business, is a company that has a physical location (Figure 10-2). A **clicks-and-mortar** business is a company that has a bricks-and-mortar location as well as an online presence (Figure 10-3). Some companies, such as Amazon.com and E*TRADE, (see Figure 10-1), only have an online presence without physical locations.

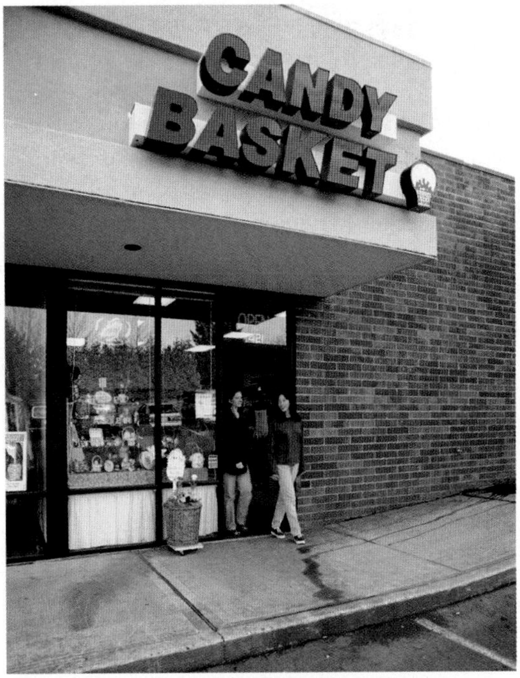

Figure 10-2 At a bricks-and-mortar company, you can make a purchase at a physical location.

Web Link

For more information on m-commerce, visit the Discovering Computers 2002 Chapter 10 WEB LINK page (**scsite.com/dc2002/ch10/weblink.htm**) and click M-Commerce.

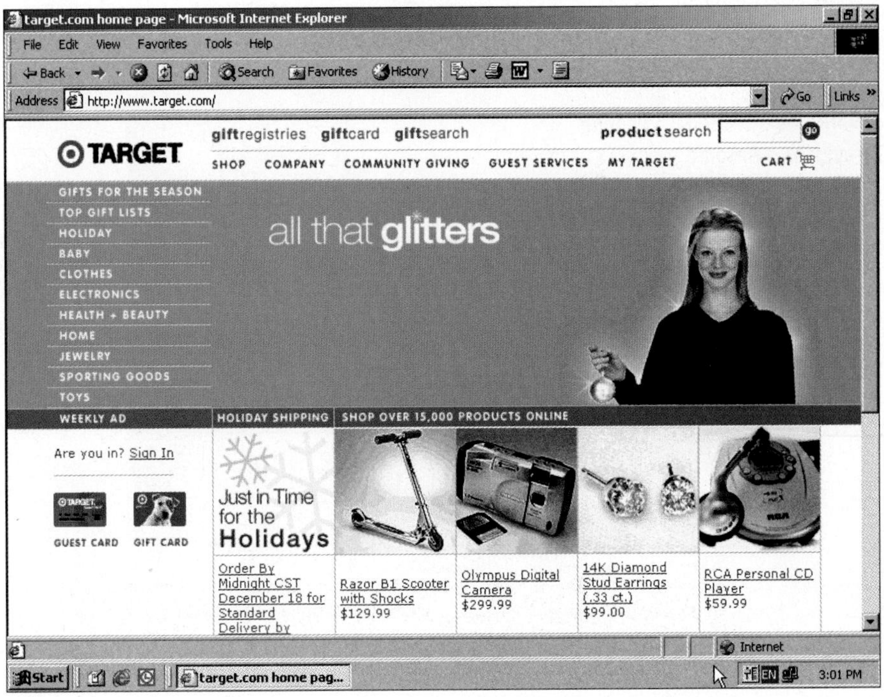

Figure 10-3 The Target department store chain is an example of a clicks-and-mortar business because it has physical locations throughout the country as well as an online presence.

The Growth of E-Commerce

One report from Forrester Research, a leading independent research firm, indicates that total worldwide e-commerce for 2000 exceeded $657 billion. As shown in Figure 10-4, Forrester Research estimates by 2004 this number will escalate to more than $6.7 trillion.

One of the first steps in the development of e-commerce was electronic data interchange, originally created to eliminate paperwork and increase response time in business interactions. **Electronic data interchange** (**EDI**) is a set of standards that control the transfer of business data and information among computers both within and among companies. Today businesses use these standards to communicate with industry partners on the Internet.

The automated teller machine (ATM) was another precursor to the present form of e-commerce. As discussed in Chapter 6, an ATM is a self-service banking machine that connects to a host computer through a telephone network.

When the Internet became available for commercial use in 1991, most consumers knew little about the Internet, much less imagined using it for profit. Now e-commerce almost is synonymous with the Web. The growth of one enhances the other. Improvements in communications technologies and computing hardware and software have been major contributing factors to the recent phenomenal growth of e-commerce.

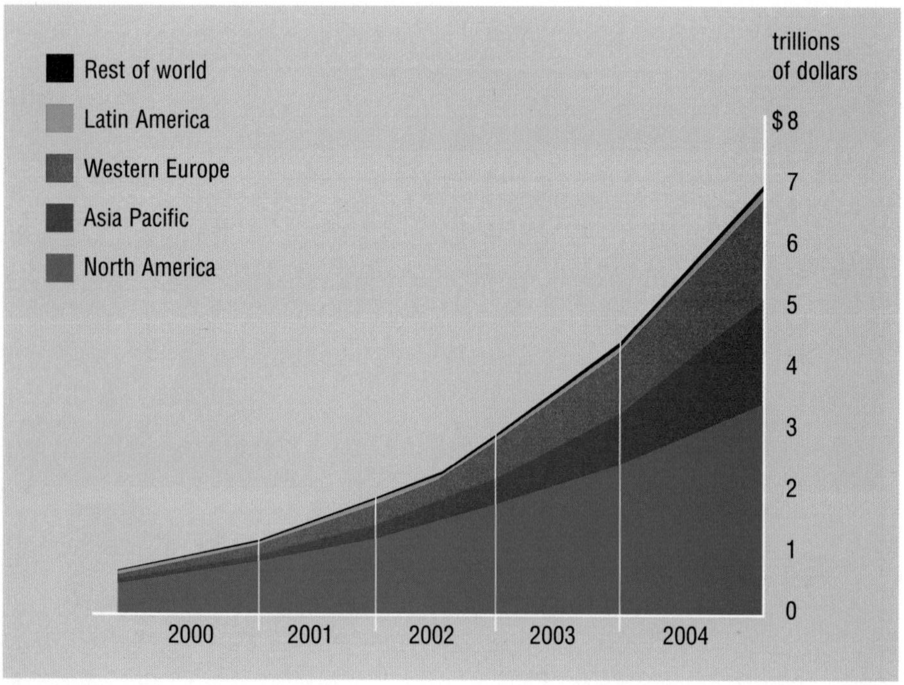

Figure 10-4 This graph illustrates historical and projected e-commerce growth from 2000 to 2004.

Web Link

For more information on business-to-consumer e-commerce, visit the Discovering Computers 2002 Chapter 10 WEB LINK page (**scsite.com/dc2002/ch10/weblink.htm**) and click Business-to-Consumer E-Commerce.

E-COMMERCE BUSINESS MODELS

E-commerce businesses can be grouped into four basic models: business-to-consumer, consumer-to-consumer, business-to-business, and business-to-employee. The following sections discuss each of these e-commerce business models.

Business-to-Consumer E-Commerce

Business-to-consumer (**B-to-C** or **B2C**) e-commerce consists of the sale of products or services from a business to the general public or end user (Figure 10-5). In this model, the seller is the business and the buyer is the consumer (public). Products for sale can be physical objects such as books, flowers, computers, groceries, prescription drugs, music, movies, and cars. They also can be intangible items. For example, you can subscribe to an online magazine or download software. Services offered by B2C businesses include online banking, stock trading, and airline reservations.

Sellers that use a B2C business model can maximize benefits by eliminating the middleman. Called **disintermediation**, businesses sell products directly to consumers without using traditional retail channels. This enables some B2C companies to sell products at a lower cost and with faster service than comparable bricks-and-mortar businesses.

Consumers also derive benefits from the B2C business model. They have access to a variety of products and services without the constraints of time or distance. Consumers easily can comparison shop to find the best buy. Many B2C Web sites provide consumer services such as access to product reviews, chat rooms, and other product-related information. These services often attract and retain customers.

Many B2C businesses personalize their sites to consumers by tracking visitors' preferences while they browse through the Web pages. This enables the B2C business to target advertisements, determine customer needs, and personalize offerings to a customer's profile.

ISSUE

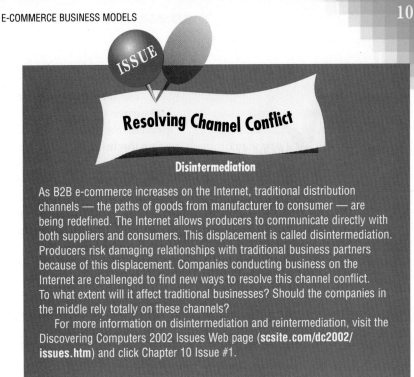

Resolving Channel Conflict

Disintermediation

As B2B e-commerce increases on the Internet, traditional distribution channels — the paths of goods from manufacturer to consumer — are being redefined. The Internet allows producers to communicate directly with both suppliers and consumers. This displacement is called disintermediation. Producers risk damaging relationships with traditional business partners because of this displacement. Companies conducting business on the Internet are challenged to find new ways to resolve this channel conflict. To what extent will it affect traditional businesses? Should the companies in the middle rely totally on these channels?

For more information on disintermediation and reintermediation, visit the Discovering Computers 2002 Issues Web page (**scsite.com/dc2002/issues.htm**) and click Chapter 10 Issue #1.

Figure 10-5 HOW A B2C E-COMMERCE BUSINESS MIGHT OPERATE

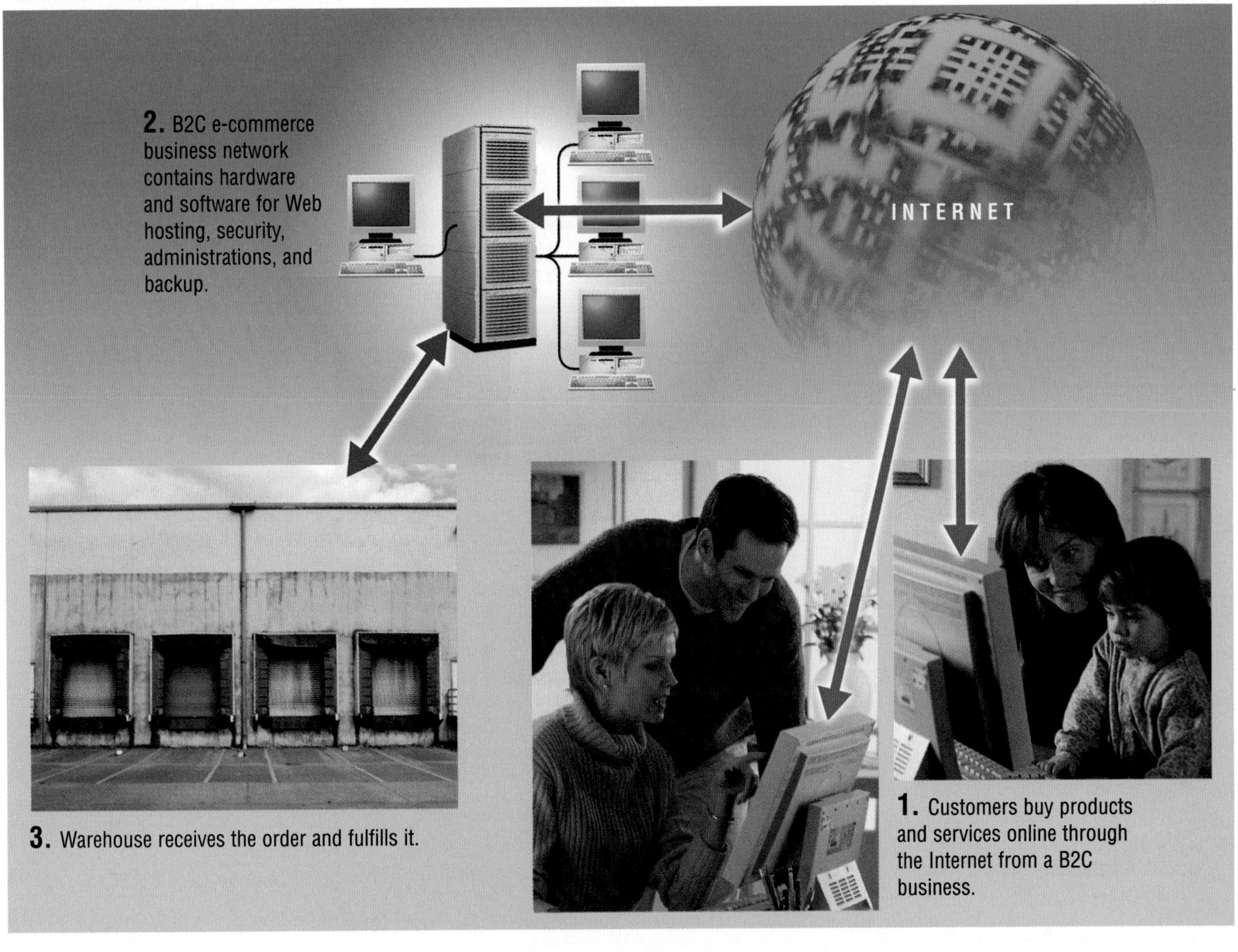

2. B2C e-commerce business network contains hardware and software for Web hosting, security, administrations, and backup.
INTERNET
3. Warehouse receives the order and fulfills it.
1. Customers buy products and services online through the Internet from a B2C business.

APPLY IT!

Look Before You Click

Have you considered purchasing products online? Many individuals are ready to engage in e-commerce but feel somewhat uncomfortable with legitimacy and privacy issues. The rules for purchasing online are very similar to those for purchasing offline — the best consumer is the best-informed consumer. Keep the following guidelines in mind while shopping online.

1. Use a secure browser that will encrypt or scramble purchase information.
2. The Web site from which you are making a purchase should be well designed and should provide a name, address, and telephone number.
3. Look for and read the privacy policy. How information is collected, how it will be used, who will have access, and what options you have in controlling the information should be disclosed clearly.
4. If the Web site requires you create an account, never use the same password you use with other accounts.
5. Do not supply personal information such as your Social Security number, bank account number, or mother's maiden name.
6. Check to verify the business uses a secure server. This generally is indicated by a graphical image such as a closed lock or key in the lower-right corner of your browser window.
7. Look for symbols such as the BBBOnline and TRUSTe (see URLs below). Click the symbols to confirm participation.
8. Use online payment networks such as DigiCash and PayPal (see URLs below).

To obtain a better understanding of Internet privacy, visit the Privacy.net site (see URL below) and complete the online demonstration of how you can be traced when using the Internet.

For more information on online shopping and the Web sites mentioned above, visit the Discovering Computers 2002 Apply It Web page (**scsite.com/dc2002/apply.htm**) and click Chapter 10 Apply It #1.

Consumer-to-Consumer E-Commerce

The term **consumer-to-consumer** (**C-to-C** or **C2C**) e-commerce consists of individuals using the Internet to sell products and services directly to other individuals. The most popular vehicle for C2C e-commerce is the online auction (Figure 10-6). An **online auction** is similar to negotiating, in which one consumer auctions goods to other consumers. If interested, you bid on an item. The highest bidder at the end of the bidding period purchases the item.

Another form of C2C e-commerce is Internet peer-to-peer (P2P). As described in Chapter 9, **P2P** describes an Internet network that enables users with the same networking software to connect to each other's hard disks and exchange files directly. With the appropriate software and an Internet connection, a consumer can pay another consumer to copy a file. That is, the buyer copies a file from the seller's hard disk. These programs have stirred controversy with respect to copyright infringement of music because they allow users easily to copy MP3 music files from one computer to another.

Business-to-Business E-Commerce

Although you probably are most familiar with B2C and C2C e-commerce Web sites, the major type of e-commerce interaction occurs among businesses. **Business-to-business** (**B-to-B** or **B2B**) e-commerce consists of the sale and exchange of products and service between businesses. For example, a company that manufactures bicycles might use the Internet to purchase tires from their supplier.

The B2B market is expanding at a much faster rate than the B2C market. Forrester Research predicts that B2B e-commerce will reach \$6.3 trillion by 2004, while B2C e-commerce only will reach \$454 billion.

Many businesses use the unique advantages of the Internet to communicate with business partners. For example, some companies provide

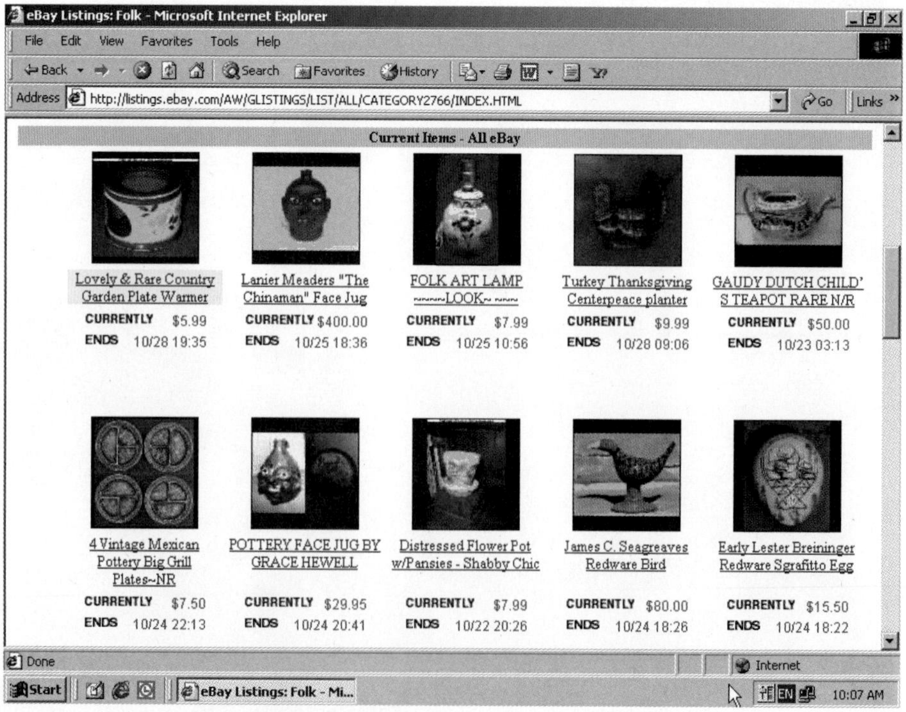

Figure 10-6 eBay is a popular online auction Web site.

services to help a manufacturer locate suppliers. The Internet enables all participants in a supply chain to relay information to each other. A **supply chain** is the interrelated network of facilities and distribution methods that obtains materials, transforms materials into finished products, and delivers the finished products to customers.

Most businesses that engage in B2C e-commerce also participate in B2B e-commerce. Thus, many company Web sites also provide goods and services to other businesses. Figure 10-7 illustrates the relationship of B2C and B2B e-commerce.

Four basic types of B2B e-commerce sites are vendor, service, broker, and infomediary sites. A **vendor B2B** site, also called an **e-procurement** site, is a product supplier that allows purchasing agents to use a network to shop, submit request for quotes (RFQs), and purchase items. A **service B2B** site uses a network to provide one or more services to business such as financing, warehousing, or shipping. A **brokering** B2B site acts as a middleman by negotiating the contract of a purchase and a sale. An **infomediary**, short for information intermediary, B2B site provides specialized information about suppliers and other businesses.

COMPANY ON THE CUTTING EDGE

Trading Practically Everything on Earth

Beanie Babies. Elian Gonzalez' raft. Kidneys. Just about everything imaginable has been auctioned on the world's largest online trading community: eBay. These items are among the more than 60 million objects offered for sale since the company's inception.

eBay's trading community consists of 10 million collectors, hobbyists, bargain hunters, sellers, and browsers in search of one-to-one trading in an auction format on the Web. Each day they can participate in more than 4 million auctions for items sorted in 4,320 categories ranging from automobiles to teddy bears. More than 450,000 objects are added daily, and 1,000 bids are placed every second. Sellers are charged a small fee to list their objects and then pay a variable commission ranging from one to five percent when the item is sold.

Founder Pierre Omidyar conceived the idea for eBay when his then-girlfriend, an avid Pez collector, commented that she would like to interact with other Pez collectors over the Internet. Living in the San Francisco Bay area, Omidyar paid homage to his hometown by naming his company "electronic Bay" and held the first auction on Labor Day, 1995.

For more information on eBay, visit the Discovering Computers 2002 Companies Web page (**scsite.com/dc2002/companies.htm**) and click eBay.

Web Link

For more information on business-to-business e-commerce, visit the Discovering Computers 2002 Chapter 10 WEB LINK page (**scsite.com/dc2002/ch10/weblink.htm**) and click Business-to-Business E-Commerce.

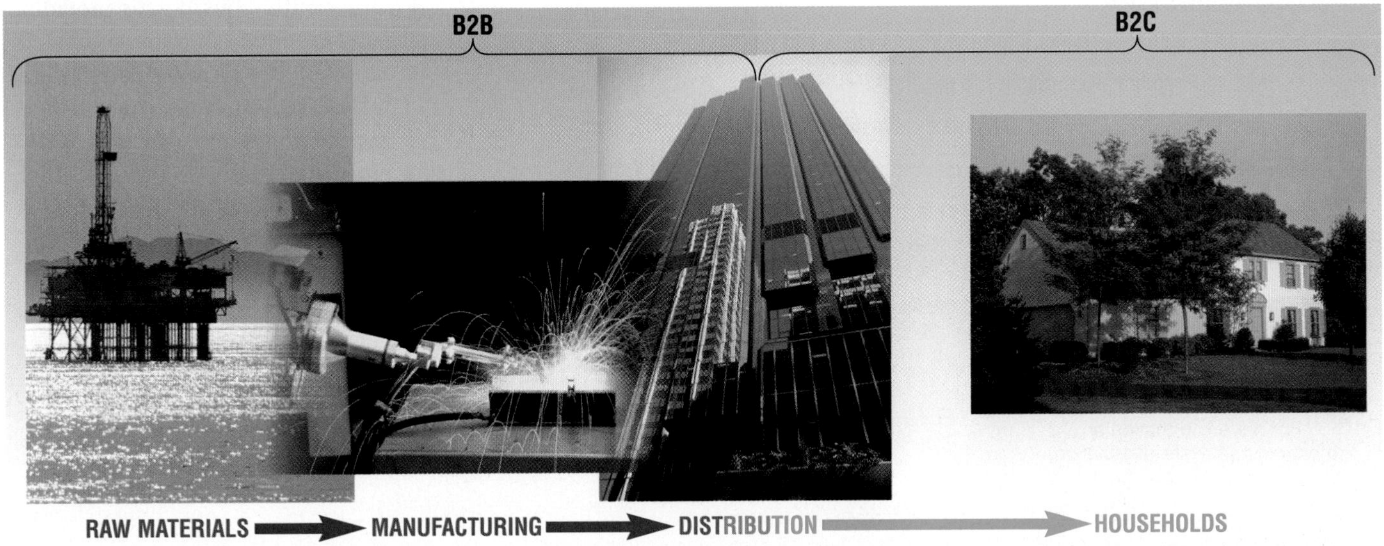

Figure 10-7 The relationship of B2B and B2C e-commerce. B2B e-commerce includes sales and exchange of products and services among businesses, while B2C e-commerce involves the sale and exchange of products and services between a business and a consumer.

Many B2B e-commerce sites fall into one or more of the previous categories. Some specialize in a particular industry; this type of specialized site sometimes is called **vertical B2B** e-commerce. Many also are portals that provide numerous additional features such as chat rooms and product comparisons.

Business-to-Employee E-Commerce

Business-to-employee (**B-to-E** or **B2E**) e-commerce, sometimes called **intrabusiness e-commerce**, refers to the use of intranet technology to handle activities that take place within a business. As discussed in Chapter 9, an **intranet** (intra means inside) is an internal network that uses Internet technologies.

B2E e-commerce does not generate revenue like the previously discussed types of e-commerce business models. Instead, it increases profits by reducing expenses within a company. For example, using B2E e-commerce employees collaborate with each other, exchange data and information, and access in-house databases, sales information, market news, and competitive analysis. By having instantaneous access to this type of technology, employees do not spend time manually looking up information.

Advantages of E-Commerce

Many businesses and individuals choose to enter the e-commerce arena for a variety of reasons. Figure 10-8 lists some of the advantages of e-commerce. Many e-commerce ventures realize more than one of these benefits.

Advantages of E-Commerce

- Global market 24 hours per day
- Businesses have access to 360 million people with Internet access
- Customers can conduct price comparisons easily
- Feedback can be immediate
- Changing information can be available quickly
- FAQ (frequently asked questions) pages can provide easy access to customer support
- Ability to gather customer information, analyze it, and react
- New and traditional approaches to generating revenue
- Manufacturers can buy and sell directly, avoiding the cost of the middleman
- Distribution costs for information reduced or eliminated
- Options to create a paperless environment

Figure 10-8 E-commerce has revolutionized the way we do business.

Web Link

For more information on electronic software distribution, visit the Discovering Computers 2002 Chapter 10 WEB LINK page (**scsite.com/dc2002/ch10/weblink.htm**) and click Electronic Software Distribution.

E-COMMERCE REVENUE STREAMS

E-commerce businesses generate revenues in many ways. A **revenue stream** is the method a business uses to generate income. Some of the more common e-commerce revenue streams include direct sales, electronic software distribution, software rental, advertising, subscriptions, Web site hosting, and Web storage. The following paragraphs briefly describe how Web sites generate these types of revenue streams. A single Web site may use more than one method of generating revenue.

- At many e-commerce sites, you purchase a product or service and the business arranges to deliver it to you (Figure 10-9). These sites generate revenue from sales of goods to consumers or to other businesses.
- Some online businesses do not ship their products; instead they use **electronic software distribution** (**ESD**) to sell digital products such as software, music, movies, books, and photographs. With ESD, a purchase entitles you to download one copy of the item (Figure 10-10). These businesses attempt to maximize their profits by eliminating expenses associated with shipping.
- Other online businesses provide software rental of applications on the Web. Recall from Chapter 3 that a **Web application** is a software application that exists on a Web site. To access a Web application, you simply visit the Web site that offers the program. For example, Microsoft's Web applications, called **.NET**, enable users to access Microsoft software on the Web from any type of device or computer that can connect to the Internet.

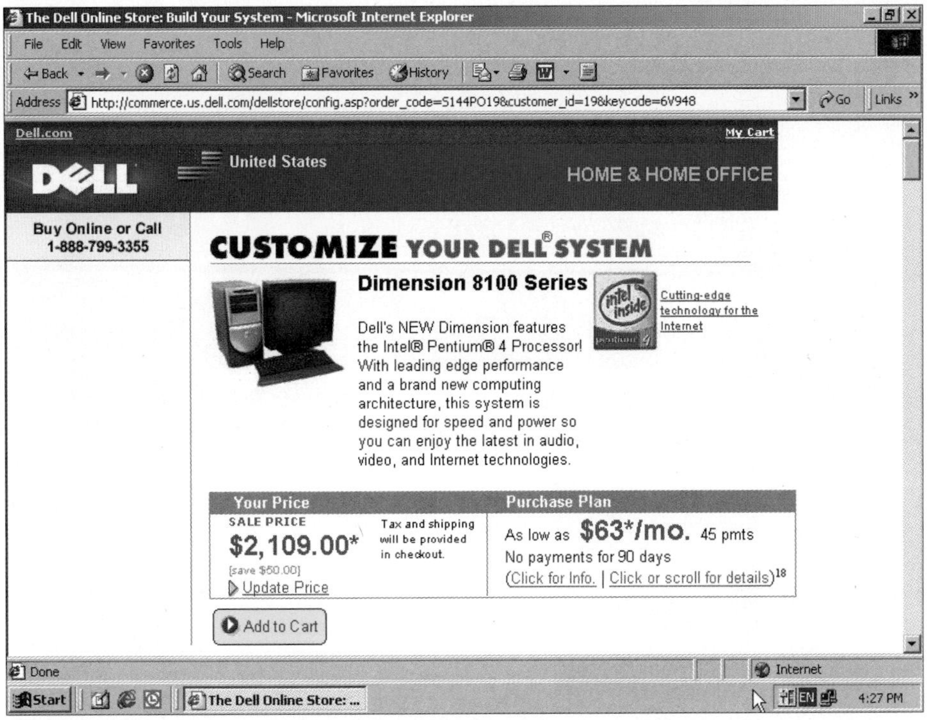

Figure 10-9 You can buy computers from Dell Computer Corporation online and have them shipped directly to your home or office.

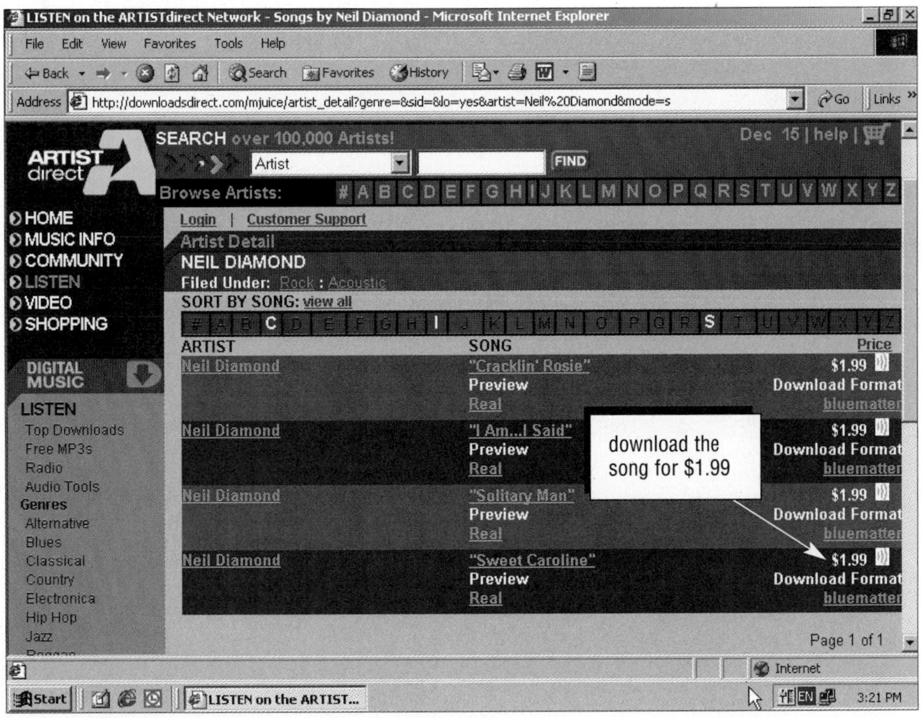

Figure 10-10 At this site, you can download songs from artists, such as Neil Diamond, for $1.99 per song.

TECHNOLOGY TRAILBLAZER

MICHAEL **DELL**

Sometimes it is a good thing not to listen to your parents. When Michael Dell was enrolled in the University of Texas at Austin in 1983, his parents urged him to give up his fledgling computer business and get serious with his biology major. After all, instead of going to class, the 18-year-old entrepreneur was building personal computers in his dorm and selling them via telephone orders.

Business grew astronomically, and Dell dropped out of college to nurture his operations. In 1984, Dell's first full year of business, sales reached $6 million. He used some of these profits to incorporate and, in 1987, formally changed the company name to Dell Computer Corporation. In 1992, he became the youngest CEO of a company named to the Fortune 500 list. Sales reached more than $25.3 billion in fiscal year 2000, with 50 percent of the orders transacted online.

Michael Dell's book, *Direct from Dell – Strategies that Revolutionized an Industry*, is a chronicle of the company's success in bypassing the middleman and selling custom-built personal computers directly to consumers.

For more information on Michael Dell, visit the Discovering Computers 2002 People Web page (**scsite.com/dc2002/people.htm**) and click Michael Dell.

Web Link

For more information on .NET, visit the Discovering Computers 2002 Chapter 10 WEB LINK page (**scsite.com/dc2002/ch10/weblink.htm**) and click .NET.

Some Web application sites, called application service providers (ASPs), charge a rental fee before you can access and use the software. Rental fee arrangements vary by vendor and application. Some rent use of the application on a monthly basis, some charge based on the number of user accesses, and others charge a one-time fee.

- Businesses that do not sell a product or service can generate revenues through advertisements. Web sites that provide news, for example, contain many advertisements (Figure 10-11). In many cases, these sites earn commissions from the advertising sponsors when visitors make purchases as a result of clicking the advertisement.
- Other informational Web sites generate revenues by requiring visitors to subscribe to their service (Figure 10-12). Subscription fees vary from one site to another, but most recur on a monthly or annual basis. These sites usually provide some information at no cost — to entice visitors to subscribe. Once you pay for the subscription, you have access to the content of the entire site.
- Some sites make money by assisting people and companies in hosting their Web site. A **Web hosting service** provides the hardware, software, and communications required for a Web server. A **Web server** is a computer that delivers Web pages to users. Other Web hosting services provide more sophisticated services that include managing payments and tracking inventory. The fees, usually paid monthly, vary depending on the level of service offered. A section later in this chapter discusses Web hosting sites in more depth.

Figure 10-11 Many news Web sites use advertisements for their revenue stream.

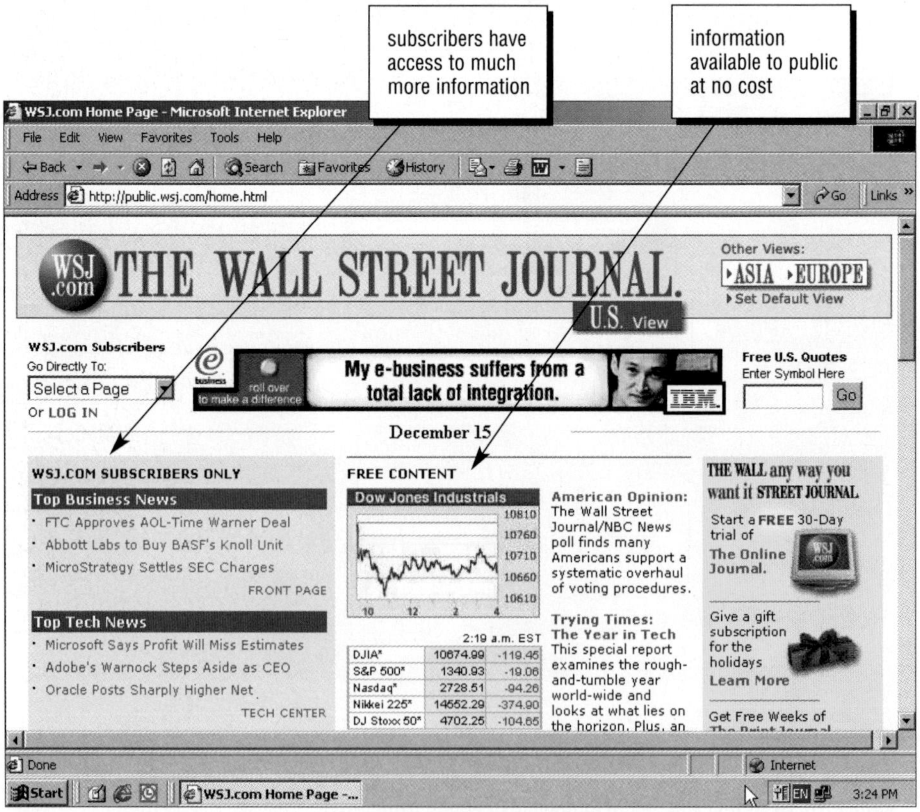

Figure 10-12 For about $60 per year, you have access to all the content at the Wall Street Journal Web site.

- Other sites on the Web, called **online storage services**, provide data storage to computer users (Figure 10-13). Many users take advantage of online storage services for the purpose of storing backup copies of data and information. Chapter 12 discusses backups and online storage in more depth.
- Some sites provide Internet access (Figure 10-14). Many of these sites have become portals offering many of the previously discussed services, as well.

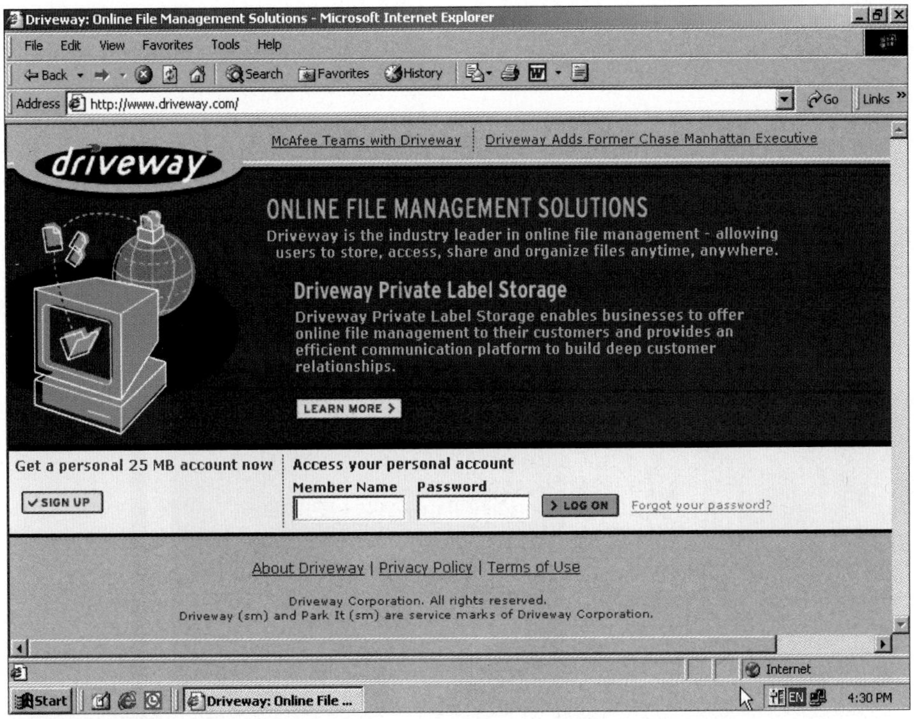

Figure 10-13 Driveway is an online storage service that allows users to store, access, organize, and share files.

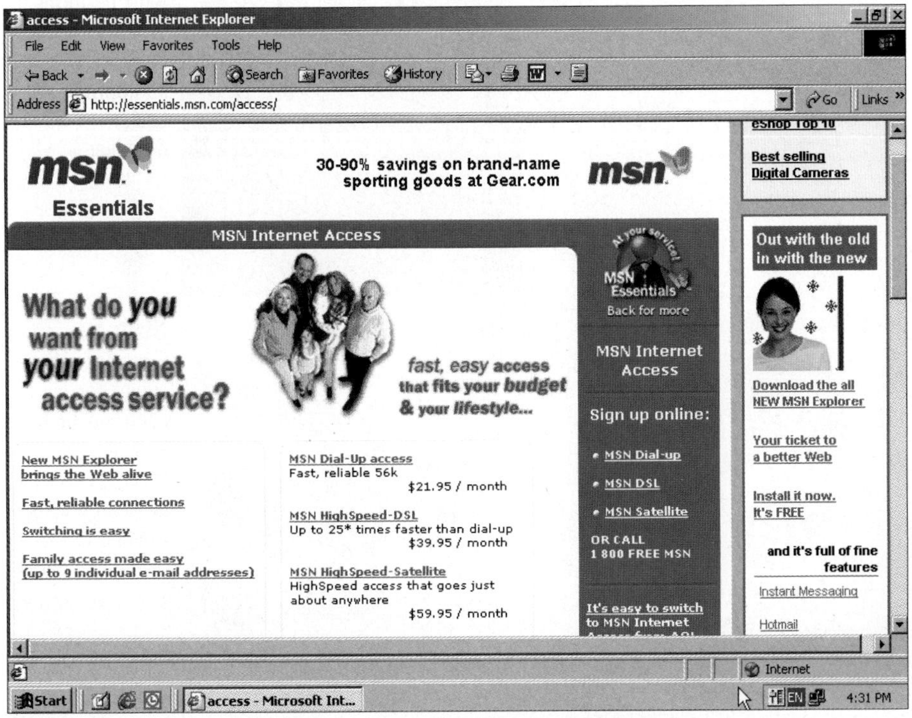

Figure 10-14 MSN provides three types of Internet access: dial-up, DSL, and satellite.

APPLY IT!

The Best Things in Life Are Free

Are you a coupon clipper? Do you enjoy a bargain? If so, check out the freebies on the Internet. You already may have heard you can find all kinds of free stuff online — and, to some extent, it is true. Before you jump into the world of freebies, you should keep some guidelines in mind. First, no one gives something for nothing. Many companies try to increase their customer base, create a mailing list, or sell you their products or services. Many free offers require you make a purchase first or pay shipping and handling. Some even resort to the old bait-and-switch trick and out-and-out scams.

It is a good idea to set up a free e-mail account such as HotMail or Yahoo! mail (see URLs below). This will protect your normal e-mail from an overload of unsolicited messages. If you plan to receive free offers through the postal service, use a post office box.

With these cautions in mind, you can explore and look for freebies. Instead of using search engines to locate sites, visit a master site. These sites organize, index, and rate freebie sites. The following is a list of some of the main indexes.

- The Cool Freebies Links (see URL below) site is one of the most comprehensive freebies guides on the Internet. It contains links to hundreds of topically arranged freebie Web sites. Subscribe to the newsletter for weekly updates.
- The Freebie Directory (see URL below) has a well-organized directory structure and also offers a free weekly newsletter.
- The Daily Freebie site (see URL below) includes new freebies daily.
- The My Jungle site (see URL below) updates its offers two to three times a day.

For more information on freebies online and the Web sites mentioned above, visit the Discovering Computers 2002 Apply It Web page (**scsite.com/dc2002/apply.htm**) and click Chapter 10 Apply It #2.

THE E-RETAILING MARKET SECTOR

Retailing is one of the most visible market sectors on the Web. In retail, merchants sell products and services directly to a buyer. **E-retail**, also called **e-tail**, occurs when retailers use the Web to sell their products and services. E-retailers constantly are challenging the old ways of conducting business as they bring new products and services to market. All e-retailers, however, operate in a similar way. Figure 10-15 illustrates how an e-retail transaction might occur.

A customer (consumer) visits an online business at the Web-equivalent of a showroom: the electronic storefront. An **electronic storefront**, also called an **online catalog**, is the Web site where an e-retailer displays its products (Figure 10-16a). It contains descriptions, graphics, and sometimes product reviews. After browsing through the merchandise, the customer makes a selection. This activates a second area of the store known as the shopping cart. The **shopping cart** is a software component on the Web that

Figure 10-15 THE PATH OF AN AUTHORIZED E-RETAIL TRANSACTION

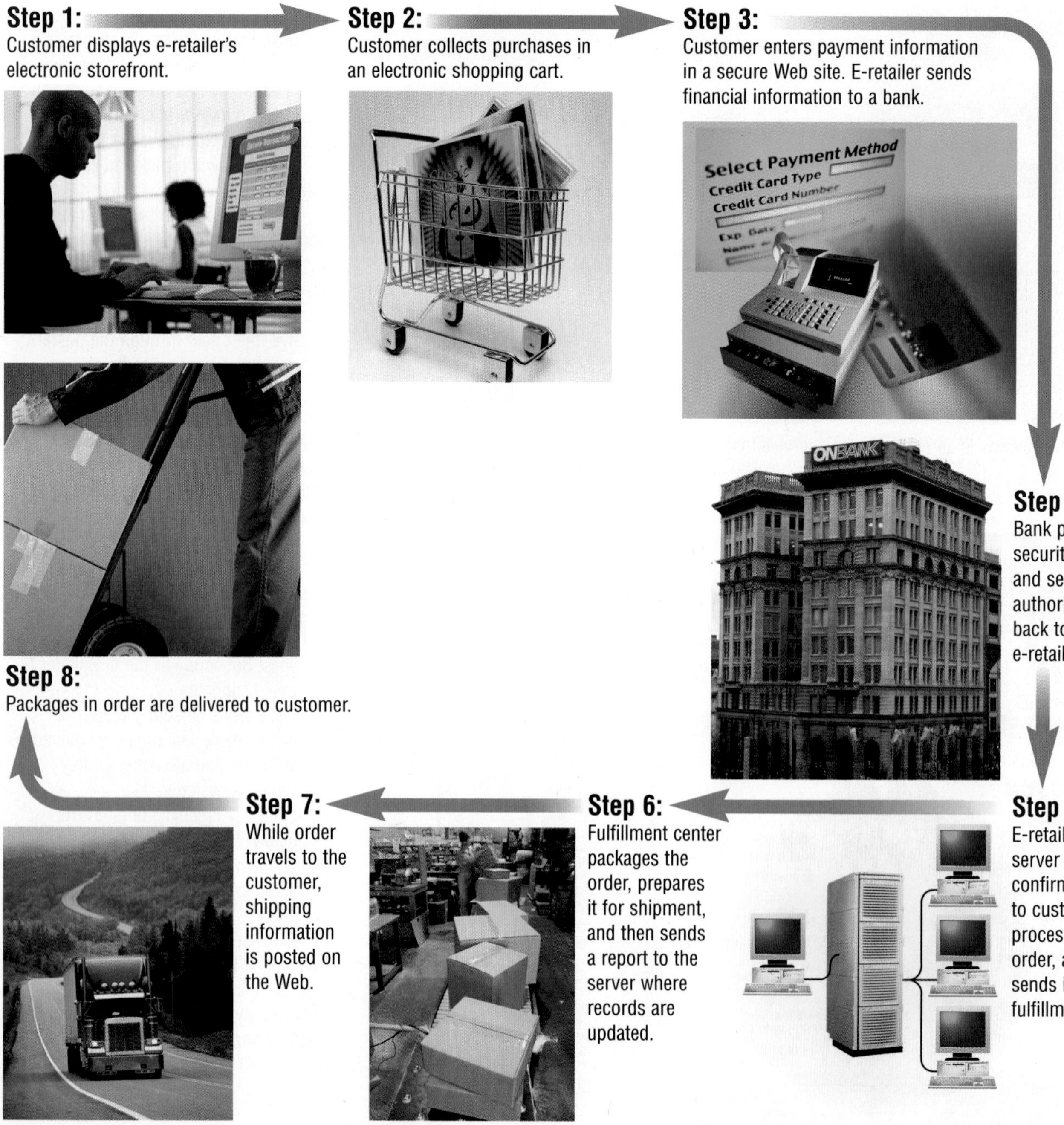
Step 1:
Customer displays e-retailer's electronic storefront.
Step 2:
Customer collects purchases in an electronic shopping cart.
Step 3:
Customer enters payment information in a secure Web site. E-retailer sends financial information to a bank.
Select Payment Method
Credit Card Type
Credit Card Number
ONBANK
Step 4:
Bank performs security checks and sends authorization back to e-retailer.
Step 5:
E-retailer's Web server sends confirmation to customer, processes the order, and then sends it to the fulfillment center.
Step 6:
Fulfillment center packages the order, prepares it for shipment, and then sends a report to the server where records are updated.
Step 7:
While order travels to the customer, shipping information is posted on the Web.
Step 8:
Packages in order are delivered to customer.

allows the customer to collect purchases (Figure 10-16b). Items in the cart can be added, deleted, or even saved for a future visit.

When ready to complete the sale, the customer proceeds to the checkout. At this time, the customer enters personal and financial data through a secure Web connection (Figure 10-16c). The transaction and financial data automatically are verified at a banking Web site. If the bank approves the transaction, the customer receives a confirmation notice of the purchase. Then, the e-retailer processes the order and sends it to the fulfillment center where it is packaged and shipped. Inventory systems are updated. The e-retailer notifies the bank of the shipment and payment is sent via electronic channels to the e-retailer. Shipping information is posted on the Internet, so the customer can track the order. The customer typically receives the order a few days after the purchase.

Figure 10-16a (storefront)

Figure 10-16b (shopping cart)

Figure 10-16c (secure checkout)

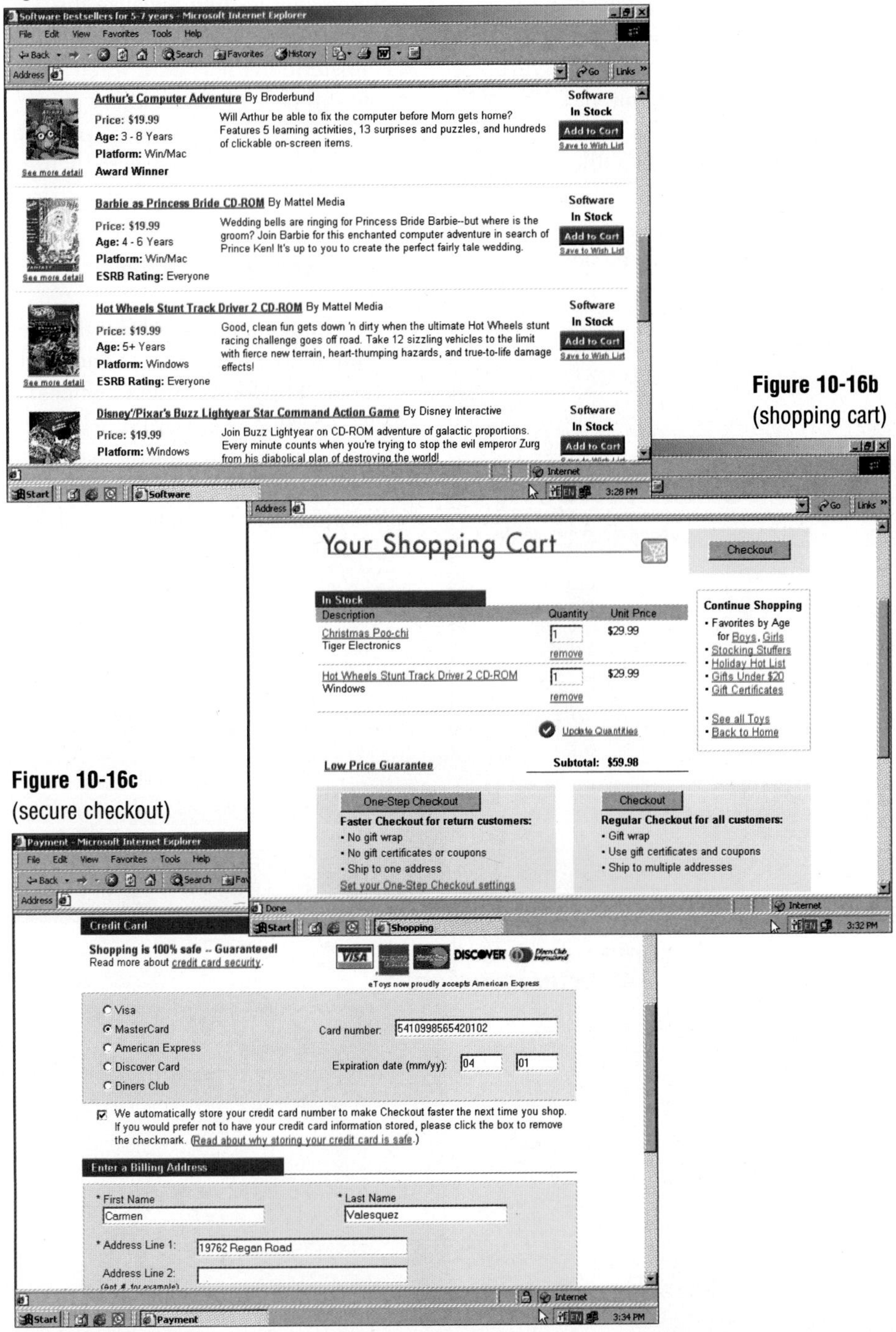

Figure 10-16 Storefront, shopping cart, and secure checkout at an online retailer.

COMPANY ON THE CUTTING EDGE

amazon.com.

Incredible Selection Propels Top Retailer

Earth's Biggest Selection™. Indeed, Amazon.com's 18 million unique items give Web shoppers an astonishing shopping extravaganza of books, CDs, videos, DVDs, toys, games, electronics, and free electronic greeting cards.

Founder Jeff Bezos spotted a business opportunity in 1994 when he learned that the Internet was experiencing a 2,300 percent growth rate. He studied 20 mail-order products and decided that books presented the most attractive retailing option. He named the company based on the world's largest river and opened the company's virtual doors in 1995 with the goal of making book buying a fast, easy, and enjoyable shopping experience.

Marketing was a family affair. Bezos simply told 300 family members and friends to spread the word. Within one month, people from all 50 states and 45 countries had placed orders. Since that time, Amazon.com has become the Internet's top retailer, with 20 million people in more than 160 countries spending approximately $600 million annually. Bezos was named *Time* magazine's Person of the Year in 1999, who at age 35 was the fourth youngest individual to receive this honor.

For more information on Amazon.com, visit the Discovering Computers 2002 Companies Web page (**scsite.com/dc2002/companies.htm**) and click Amazon.com.

OTHER E-COMMERCE MARKET SECTORS ON THE WEB

In addition to retail, several other market sectors have taken advantage of business opportunities on the Web. The more popular market segments include finance, entertainment and media, travel, and health. The following paragraphs describe how the general public interacts with each of these market sectors on the Web.

Web Link

For more information on online banking, visit the Discovering Computers 2002 Chapter 10 WEB LINK page (**scsite.com/dc2002/ch10/weblink.htm**) and click Online Banking.

Finance

Financial institutions include any business that manages the circulation of money, grants credit, makes investments, or meets banking needs. These include banks, mortgage companies, brokerage firms, and insurance companies. In the past, financial institutions were strictly traditional bricks-and-mortar institutions. Today, many also conduct business on the Internet. Figure 10-17a shows the home page for an online banking site and Figure 10-17b shows the home page for an online trading site.

Online banking allows you to pay bills from your computer, that is, transfer money electronically from your account to a payee's account such as the electric company or telephone company. At any time, you also can download monthly banking transactions such as cleared checks, ATM withdrawals, and deposits, which allows you always to have an up-to-date bank statement.

With **online trading,** you can invest in stocks, options, bonds, treasuries, CDs, money markets, annuities, and mutual funds — without using a broker. Many investors prefer online stock trading because the transaction fee for each trade usually is substantially less than when you trade through a broker. Many of these online businesses also provide other financial services such as life insurance and retirement plans.

Entertainment and Media

The technology behind the Web has enabled entertainment and media to take many forms. Music, videos, news, sporting events, and 3-D multiplayer games are a growing part of the Web's future. Newsprint on the Web is not replacing the newspaper, but enhancing it and reaching different

Figure 10-17a (online banking Web site home page)

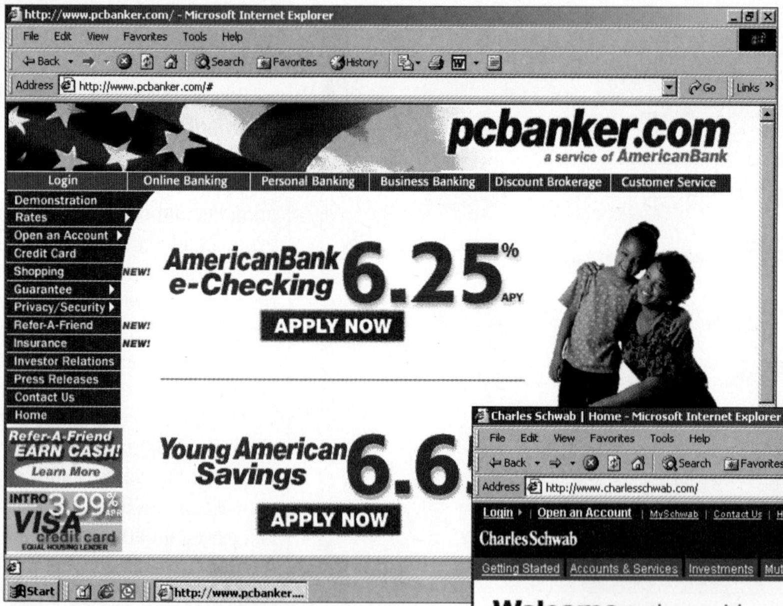

Figure 10-17b (online trading Web site home page)

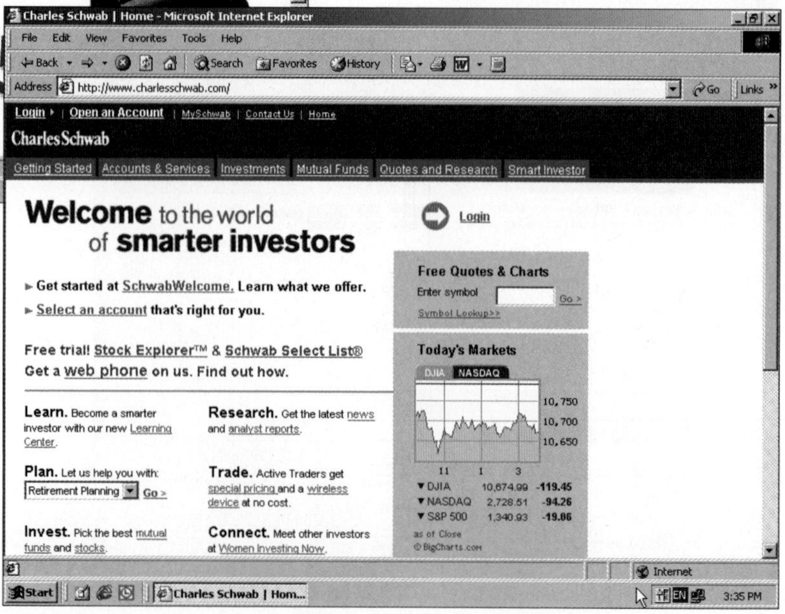

Figure 10-17 With online banking, you can pay bills from your computer. Online trading services allow you to manage your financial investments on the Web.

Web Link

For more information on online trading, visit the Discovering Computers 2002 Chapter 10 WEB LINK page (**scsite.com/dc2002/ch10/weblink.htm**) and click Online Trading.

populations. Current technology supports live radio broadcasting, live videos, and live concerts due to streaming technology. As discussed in Chapter 2, streaming allows users to access and use a file while it is transmitting. You can purchase music online and download MP3 files directly to your hard disk, allowing you to listen to the purchased music immediately from your computer or any MP3 player.

Travel

The Web provides many travel-related services. If you need directions, simply enter a starting point and destination and many Web sites will provide detailed directions along with a map. You can make airline reservations and reserve a hotel or car.

Some of these sites are shopping bots that save you much time by doing all the investigative cost-comparison work. A **shopping bot**, also called a **shopbot**, is a Web site that searches the Internet for the best price on a product or service in which you are interested (Figure 10-18).

TECHNOLOGY TRAILBLAZERS

DIETER **SEITZER** and HEINZ **GERHÄUSER**

MP3 is the term that Internet users search for most often. This popular technology is used to compress audio files so they transfer quickly from a Web page to a computer.

With more than one-half million MP3 files online, music lovers can thank Dieter Seitzer and Heinz Gerhäuser for saving them hours of downloading time. These two researchers began developing this format, formally called Moving Pictures Experts Group Audio Layer 3, in 1987 when Seitzer was managing director of the Applied Electronics division at the Fraunhofer Institute in Germany. At that time, a mainframe computer needed 10 hours to decode 1 minute of digitized music.

One of Seitzer's graduate students wrote a research paper proposing that compressed audio could be decoded in real time, making it sound realistic to the human ear. Engineers at the Institute began developing the Layer 3 algorithm that filters out sounds we cannot hear, thus shrinking the audio files to one-tenth their original size.

Gerhäuser became the Institute's co-director in 1993, and under his guidance the Institute released Winplay, the first player that could decode MP3 files on a personal computer in real time.

For more information on Dieter Seitzer and Heinz Gerhäuser, visit the Discovering Computers 2002 People Web page (**scsite.com/dc2002/people.htm**) and click Seitzer and Gerhäuser.

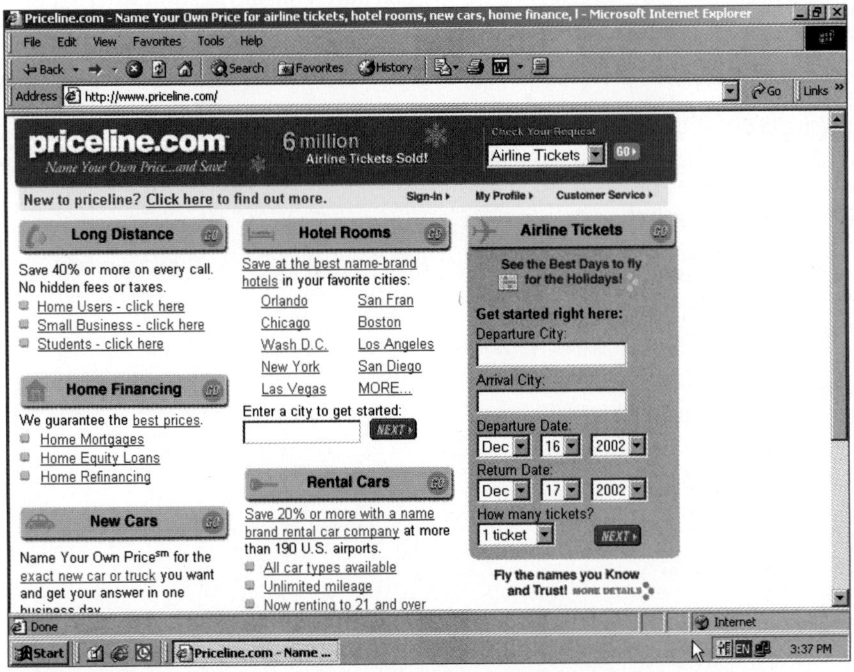

Figure 10-18 At Priceline.com, you name the price you are willing to pay and they find items such as flights, hotel rooms, and car rentals that meet your budget.

Web Link

For more information on shopping bots, visit the Discovering Computers 2002 Chapter 10 WEB LINK page (**scsite.com/dc2002/ch10/weblink.htm**) and click Shopping Bots.

With airline reservations, for example, simply name the price you are willing to pay per ticket, your travel dates, and the cities between which you are traveling. This service finds a flight arrangement that meets your budget.

Health

Many Web sites provide up-to-date medical, fitness, nutrition, or exercise information. As with any other information on the Web, you should verify the legitimacy of the site before relying on its information.

Some of these health-related Web sites maintain databases of doctors and dentists to help you find the one that suits your needs. They also may have chat rooms, so you can talk to others diagnosed with similar conditions.

Bricks-and-mortar pharmacies also exist on the Web, allowing customers to refill prescriptions and ask pharmacists questions. Some Web sites even allow you to order prescription drugs online and have them delivered directly to your door (Figure 10-19).

Other Business Services

Many businesses use the Web to provide services to consumers and other businesses. Public relations, online advertising, direct mail, recruiting, credit, sales, market research, technical support, training, software consulting, and Internet access represent a few of the areas of service.

APPLY IT!

Let the Bot Do the Walking

One of the advantages of shopping online is you can visit dozens of sites within a few minutes. In fact, when you start comparing prices, you can visit dozens of sites, which could take almost as much time as driving to the local shopping mall. A solution to this problem is a shopping bot (short for robot because of its automated features). These automated price-comparison services search dozens of online stores for the best prices on thousands of products.

Generally, to use one of these services, you visit their Web site and select the directory in which your product resides or type keywords for which to search. Within a few seconds, the shopping bot displays a list of sites where your product is located, along with product prices. Clicking a Buy button takes you to the site where you can purchase your selection. Some of the more popular comparison shopping sites are as follows:

- mySimon (see URL below) allows you to select a category and then narrow it to a subcategory. You also can narrow your search further by entering the manufacturer's name, model number, and so on.
- DealTime (see URL below) offers a lowest price guarantee and consumer advice, ratings, and reviews.
- BizRate (see URL below) includes a store rating section.
- Yahoo! (see URL below) is an all-encompassing Web site that also offers comparison shopping.
- Half.com (see URL below), which is owned by eBay (see URL below), allows you to compare prices for products sold by individuals as well as e-commerce sites.

Consider the following when comparing prices: a) some companies may not include shipping and handling; and b) an agreement between the shopping service and the online merchant may give certain companies a preferred placement in the search results.

Regardless of the site you select, keep these shopping tips in mind:

- Review the privacy policy and check that the site participates in one of the online privacy programs such as TRUSTe.
- Verify the site is secure by checking for a closed lock or key in the lower-right corner of your browser window.
- Read the return policy.
- Compare the price to advertisements in your local paper and look for a price guarantee.

For more information on comparison shopping online and the Web sites mentioned above, visit the Discovering Computers 2002 Apply It Web page (**scsite.com/dc2002/apply.htm**) and click Chapter 10 Apply It #3.

ISSUE

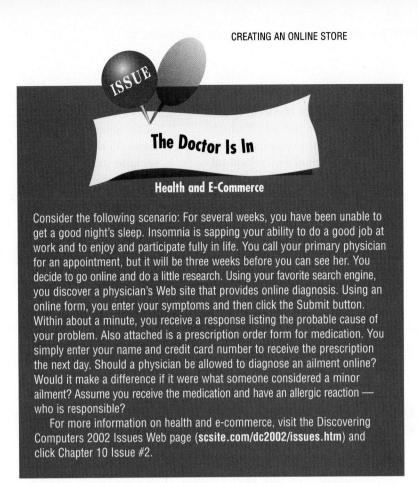

The Doctor Is In

Health and E-Commerce

Consider the following scenario: For several weeks, you have been unable to get a good night's sleep. Insomnia is sapping your ability to do a good job at work and to enjoy and participate fully in life. You call your primary physician for an appointment, but it will be three weeks before you can see her. You decide to go online and do a little research. Using your favorite search engine, you discover a physician's Web site that provides online diagnosis. Using an online form, you enter your symptoms and then click the Submit button. Within about a minute, you receive a response listing the probable cause of your problem. Also attached is a prescription order form for medication. You simply enter your name and credit card number to receive the prescription the next day. Should a physician be allowed to diagnose an ailment online? Would it make a difference if it were what someone considered a minor ailment? Assume you receive the medication and have an allergic reaction — who is responsible?

For more information on health and e-commerce, visit the Discovering Computers 2002 Issues Web page (**scsite.com/dc2002/issues.htm**) and click Chapter 10 Issue #2.

CREATING AN ONLINE STORE

With the Web offering such a tremendous business potential, many people and companies are venturing into this worldwide horizon. Depending on the nature of the existing business, the approach used to establish an online presence varies. The following discussion uses e-retail as an example.

Some merchants start an e-retail store without having a physical presence. Others establish an electronic storefront as an extension of an existing bricks-and-mortar business. Some expand an informational Web site into a full-featured e-commerce site.

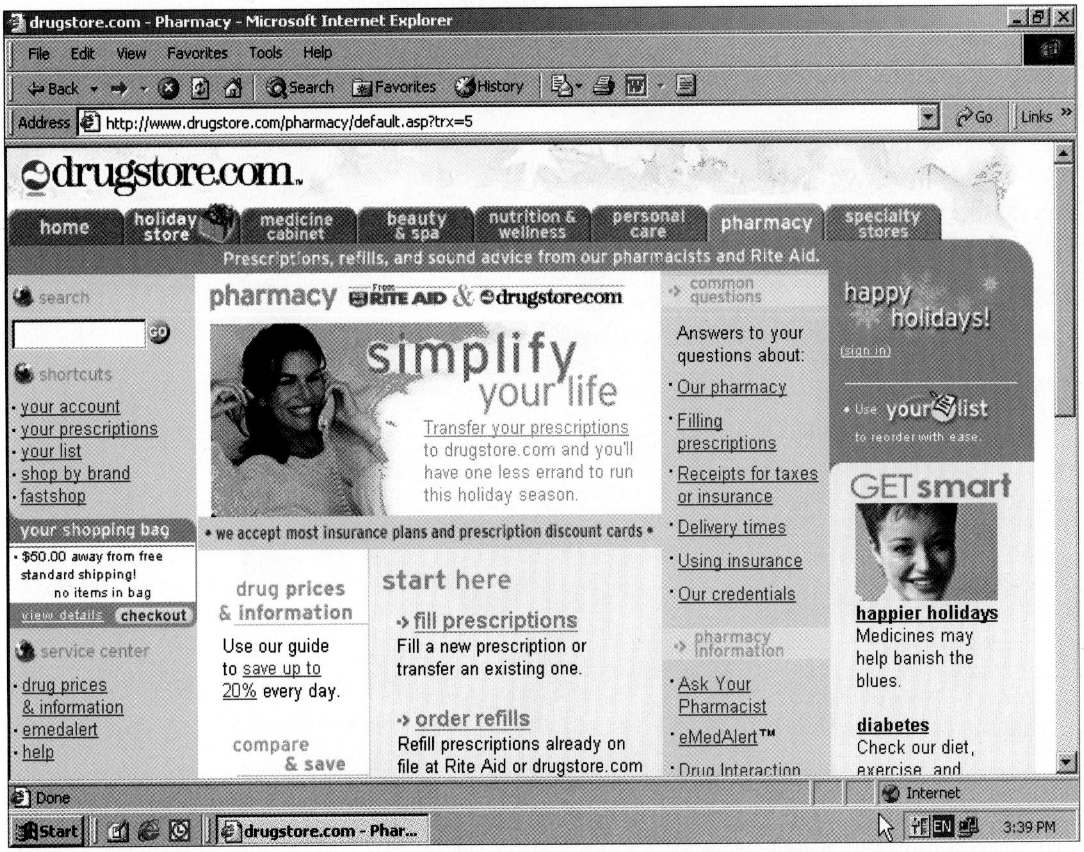

Figure 10-19 At drugstore.com, you can fill prescriptions online and have them delivered directly to your door.

Regardless of the scope or size of business, all e-commerce must address some common concerns. To provide for e-commerce, a company or individual must decide on the following items (Figure 10-20):

- Building a storefront
- Managing payment
- Managing product delivery
- Designing a site that attracts customers and keeps them returning
- Managing the site
- Promoting the site

Building a Storefront

One of the more important decisions facing e-retailers is the choice of the software and hardware to build a storefront. The e-retail storefront must inform potential customers about the business, its products, and its services. It must provide for purchases and supply feedback to the e-retailer.

The method a merchant takes to establish the storefront varies depending on the time and money available and the required complexity of the site. Some e-retailers develop and maintain the Web site in house, while others outsource all or part of the system. The following paragraphs describe each of these scenarios.

With the proper expertise and equipment, some e-retailers purchase their own hardware and e-commerce software to maintain their Web site in house. E-commerce software packages are available with a range of features. **E-commerce software** allows a merchant to set up a storefront with a product database, combined with a shopping cart. In addition, the software should provide a secure environment to process order transactions. More sophisticated packages include statistical tracking features and capability of integrating with a business' other systems such as billing and inventory management. Depending on the complexity of the e-commerce site, these packages can cost from a few hundred dollars to more than $20,000. Figure 10-21 lists some of the more popular e-commerce software packages.

Although this option requires a very large financial outlay, it gives the merchant total control over its e-retail site. E-retailers that develop a Web site in house usually hire an expert in Web design and development to assist in implementing the site.

Figure 10-20 You must make several decisions before developing an e-commerce site.

SOME E-COMMERCE APPLICATIONS

- Actinic
- Cat@log
- Ecware
- EasyMarketPlace.com
- eSalesSuite
- Freemerchant.com
- FrontHost
- IHTML Merchant Pro
- InterShop
- Maestro Commerce Online
- MerchandiZer
- Merchant Builder
- Net.Commerce
- ShopZone
- SoftCart
- Web+Shop

Figure 10-21 Some of the more common e-commerce software application packages.

Some e-retailers do not have all of the necessary hardware, software, or personnel to develop and maintain the e-commerce site in house. These businesses choose to lease all or a portion of the e-commerce Web site from a Web host. As discussed earlier in this chapter, a **Web host** is an outside company that provides the hardware, software, and communications required for a Web server. In e-commerce environments, this Web server is known as an **e-commerce server** or **commerce server**.

Figure 10-22 shows a Web hosting service. The hosting service charges a monthly fee, or may take a percentage of the sales income. Using a hosting service is less expensive than developing and maintaining the entire e-commerce site in house.

Web Link

For more information on e-commerce software, visit the Discovering Computers 2002 Chapter 10 WEB LINK page (**scsite.com/dc2002/ch10/weblink.htm**) and click E-Commerce Software.

Web Link

For more information on Web hosts, visit the Discovering Computers 2002 Chapter 10 WEB LINK page (**scsite.com/dc2002/ch10/weblink.htm**) and click Web Hosts.

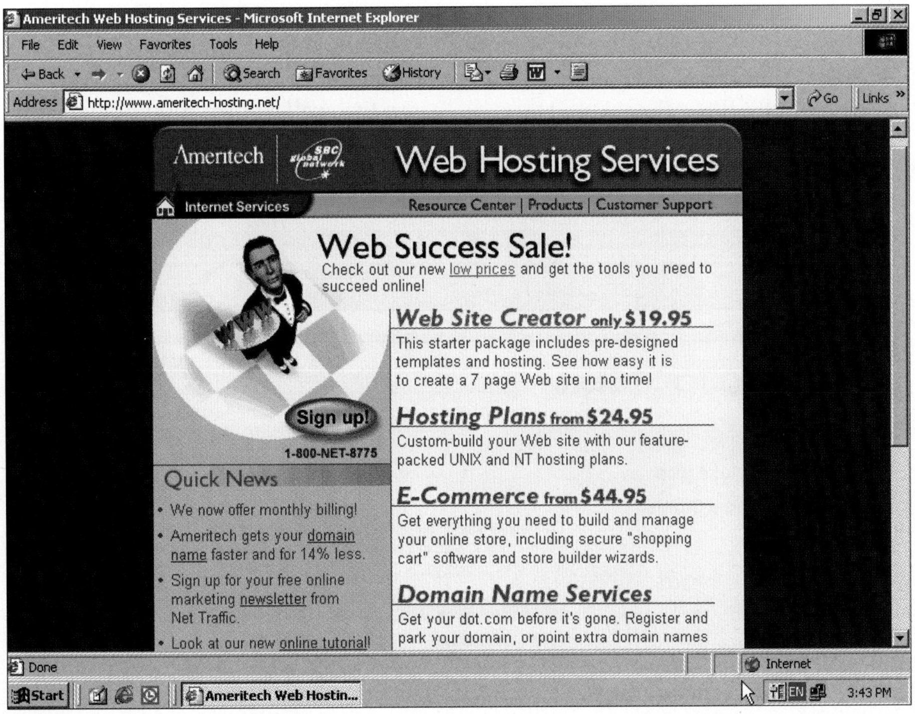

Figure 10-22 A Web hosting site.

ISSUE

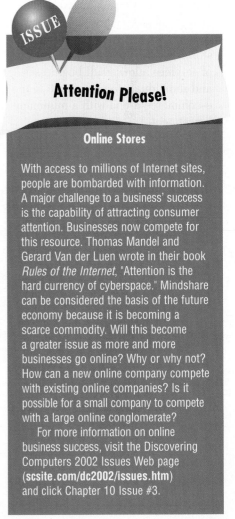

Attention Please!

Online Stores

With access to millions of Internet sites, people are bombarded with information. A major challenge to a business' success is the capability of attracting consumer attention. Businesses now compete for this resource. Thomas Mandel and Gerard Van der Luen wrote in their book *Rules of the Internet*, "Attention is the hard currency of cyberspace." Mindshare can be considered the basis of the future economy because it is becoming a scarce commodity. Will this become a greater issue as more and more businesses go online? Why or why not? How can a new online company compete with existing online companies? Is it possible for a small company to compete with a large online conglomerate?

For more information on online business success, visit the Discovering Computers 2002 Issues Web page (**scsite.com/dc2002/issues.htm**) and click Chapter 10 Issue #3.

An e-retailer may choose to outsource the entire e-commerce site to the Web hosting service. Or, it may use its own in-house server to store part of its Web site and use an outside host for other components. These companies usually outsource the transaction services that require a secure server. A **secure server** prevents access to the system by unauthorized users. The storefront and shopping cart connect to the transaction services through links. When ready to order, the customer clicks an order button and moves seamlessly to the transaction area on the outside hosting company's server. After placing the order on the secure system, the customer returns to the original business site.

Many Internet service providers (ISPs), online service providers (OSPs), content portals such as Yahoo!, and online malls provide Web hosting services. Most also offer Web site development services that assist you through the process of creating a storefront (Figure 10-23). These types of services allow small businesses and individuals to participate in the e-commerce arena with a minimum investment.

Storefront capabilities vary widely, depending on the host. Some solutions provide little more than a product billboard. Others allow merchants to set up elaborate, customized sites. The site developer must realize that some merchandise does not transfer equally well to the Web. For example, clothing sales often work better when customers physically can browse and try on items in a bricks-and-mortar store. You should research the solutions provided by a Web hosting service before spending the time and resources to establish your site.

Web Link

For more information on a merchant account, visit the Discovering Computers 2002 Chapter 10 WEB LINK page (**scsite.com/dc2002/ch10/weblink.htm**) and click Merchant Account.

Managing Payments

Before an e-business can operate efficiently as an e-retailer, it must be able to accept customer payments. Credit cards are the most popular payment method on the Web. To accept credit cards safely from consumers, a business must complete three steps: (1) obtain a merchant account, (2) provide a secure order form, and (3) use payment-processing software.

Potential e-retailers typically apply to a bank to obtain an e-commerce merchant account. The e-retailer (merchant) pays a one-time setup fee and an ongoing monthly fee to the bank to maintain the merchant account, along with a commission on each transaction. The **merchant account** thus establishes a relationship between the e-retailer and a bank, which allows the e-retailer to accept credit card payments.

E-retailers use an order form to collect orders and credit card information from the customer. The form is stored on a secure server, provided either by the hosting service or the merchant. Chapter 12 discusses techniques used to secure these financial transactions. Topics covered include user names, passwords, biometrics, encryption, digital certificates, Secure Sockets Layer (SSL), secure HTTP (S-HTTP), and Secure Electronics Transaction (SET).

Finally, the e-retailer must arrange to use a payment-processing service. These services provide software to manage the transaction between the e-retailer and the bank. The e-retailer pays a monthly fee for this service.

Often, Web hosting services provide some or all of the payment and security needs as part of the package to set up a storefront. In addition some companies' primary business is to provide secure and reliable management of the entire ordering and payment process. For example, First Data and Paymentech are two well-known reputable companies that provide complete

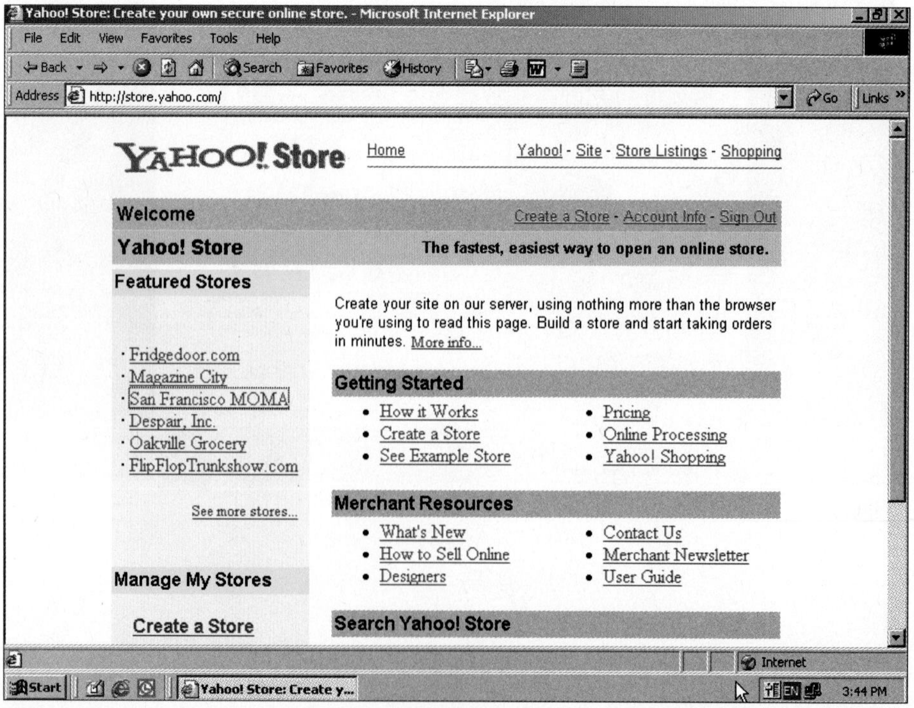

Figure 10-23 Through Yahoo! Store, you can build a storefront in minutes using your Web browser.

credit card transaction solutions for e-retailers from setting up merchant accounts to processing payments.

The entire payment process should be designed to protect against fraud. Most experts agree that with proper safeguards, a credit card is safer to use over the Internet than in many face-to-face transactions. Consumers should verify that a merchant provides secure transactions before using a credit card on the Internet. Secure sites have URLs that begin with https:// instead of http://. Chapter 12 discusses other techniques to protect against fraud on the Internet.

ISSUE

Scammed on the Web

Security

Complaints about fraud and scams have increased 600 percent since 1998, according to Internet Fraud Watch (see URL below), operated by the National Consumers League.

Just as in bricks-and-mortar businesses, both online merchants and consumers must guard against fraud. Online merchants are legally responsible for ensuring security at their sites. They should investigate thoroughly the security measures they use, whether installed in-house or outsourced. Consumers can protect themselves best by becoming educated about Internet fraud and avoiding unsafe practices. If a company is involved in a scam, should the people scammed be responsible for their own losses? Who should *police* the Internet for fraud and scams? What penalties should be imposed?

For more information on Internet security and fraud and the Web site mentioned above, visit the Discovering Computers 2002 Issues Web page (**scsite.com/dc2002/issues.htm**) and click Chapter 10 Issue #4.

APPLY IT!

Become an E-Commerce Merchant

One of the more popular Web hosting services is Yahoo! Store (see URL below). At this site, the potential e-retailer can find a convenient, easy-to-use, and inexpensive storefront solution. Yahoo! Store even offers the prospective merchant an opportunity for a 10-day test drive. You should have a store name in mind before you begin this process. In addition, be sure to read the Terms of Service and Privacy Policy documents.

To generate a Yahoo! storefront, perform the following steps:

1. Display the Yahoo! Store information page (see URL below).
2. Click the How it Works or Create a Store link to begin the sign up process.
3. Click the Sign me up link, complete the form, and then click the Submit button to complete your registration. Within a few seconds, you should receive an e-mail confirmation.
4. Choose an ID for your store and the full name of your site and then click the Create button. Your 10-day account is created. Click I Accept, and you are ready to build your store.
5. After completing the forms, you take a tour of the working area where you will develop the storefront. This tour is a tutorial that shows how to construct a storefront. Later you can use the program's editing features to modify the store's content and appearance. The first stop in the guided tour is the new home page, or storefront. The program automatically generates the left panel and its buttons. An Edit bar always is visible during storefront construction.
6. As you work your way through the tour, it shows how to build sections, or rooms, in the store, how to add buttons on the storefront panel, and how to enter sales items. Each item is identified with a name, price, graphic, code number, and description.
7. Each item has its own display case. Clicking an item enlarges its view and displays any pertinent information associated with it.
8. Yahoo!'s guided tour is not intended to be a comprehensive tutorial on how to use the program. It demonstrates how a few simple commands can build a rudimentary storefront in a few minutes. After completing the tutorial, your storefront displays.
9. Editing the site and making it more attractive requires time and planning. As with any retail store, a Web storefront ultimately must attract customers and provide reasons for a customer to return to the site.
10. After the store is completed, you must test it for accuracy before a public opening. To do this, enter the store as a customer, order some products, and verify the shopping cart and customer order form work properly.
11. You can verify the order was received by returning to the Store Management screen at the editing site. The Store Management screen accesses all of the back office operations necessary to maintain the site and communicate with customers. The Orders link in the Process category accesses the customer orders and related information. One type of automated feedback you can receive is through the Customer Order Status Form. It displays all of the pertinent information about a purchase including the shipping date and tracking number.
12. Sales and customer tracking statistics are generated immediately and are accessible through the Statistics option on Yahoo!'s Store Management screen. You receive instantaneous reports showing the number of customers visiting the site, the pages visited, repeat customers, and graphs.
13. Your store is accessible to the e-consumers visiting Yahoo! Shopping. A customer at Yahoo! Shopping can search for a product using the product category, the product name, or the company name. When a search is made for a product you sell, your store's name or product will be listed among all of the other stores selling similar products.

For more information on online retailing and the Web site mentioned above, visit the Discovering Computers 2002 Apply It Web page (**scsite.com/dc2002/apply.htm**) and click Chapter 10 Apply It #4.

For those customers uneasy with sending credit card information over the Internet, many e-commerce Web sites also add a toll-free telephone number through which customers can place an order.

Another option is to accept electronic money as a payment for goods or services. **Electronic money (e-money)**, also called **digital cash** or **e-cash**, is a payment system that allows an individual to pay for products or services by transmitting an identifying number to the e-retailer. The general concept is a bank issues a unique cash number that represents a specific sum of real money, such as $1, $5, and $10. When customers make a purchase with e-money, they enter the unique cash numbers. The e-retailer then deposits the cash numbers in a participating bank. Thus, paying with e-money is very similar to paying with regular cash. A major advantage is it is reusable and anonymous; that is, the e-retailer has no information about the buyer. Currently, no standard exists for e-money. Thus, several companies offer various e-money schemes.

Fulfillment

Fulfillment includes managing and storing inventory, packaging and shipping products, and maintaining records of all transactions. Existing bricks-and-mortar retailers already have a system to handle the fulfillment segment of the business. For larger e-retailers that wish to manage fulfillment operations in house, sophisticated e-commerce software packages can integrate and help automate existing business functions.

As with other aspects of the e-commerce world, the e-retailer can opt to outsource some or all areas of fulfillment. **Fulfillment companies**, also called **logistics companies**, can provide warehousing and inventory management, product assembly, order processing, packing, shipping, return processing, and online reporting.

Increased e-retail sales mean increased business for traditional delivery services such as Federal Express and UPS (Figure 10-24). These delivery services often handle the shipping of products from the e-retailer to the customer, as well as any returned merchandise. It is important that the Web site clearly state all shipping costs.

Attracting and Retaining Customers

A successful Web site attracts customers and keeps them returning to the site. Figure 10-25 lists factors that lead to e-commerce customer loyalty. The best storefronts plan for

Figure 10-24 Increased Internet sales mean increased business for package delivery services such as UPS.

Factors That Lead to E-Loyalty

- Price
- Selection
- Site appearance
- Ease of use/navigation
- Availability of information
- Ease of ordering
- Posted privacy policies
- Quality of storefront/product representation
- Shipping
- On-time delivery
- Quality of customer support

Figure 10-25 Factors that might affect whether an e-commerce customer will return for business.

convenience, are efficient, and easy to use. Studies indicate that Web customers will click to another site if they must wait more than eight seconds for a page to download. Consumers want to navigate easily through a site. Instructions should be clear and easy to follow. Too many special effects can slow downloading and clutter a site. In addition, the fewer clicks it takes for a customer to find a product and place an order, the more sales the store will make.

Successful businesses incorporate features to take advantage of the capabilities of the Internet. These features enhance a customer's experience and move the store beyond simply a catalog site. The features should coincide with the store's function. For example, a store selling music can provide audio previews. Discussion groups, newsletters, and informational articles related to the store's product could draw visitors to the site and generate goodwill.

Businesses need to consider carefully how to provide service after a sale. Surveys indicate that a large percentage of customers are dissatisfied with customer service at online businesses. Thus, many e-commerce sites now use an **electronic Customer Relationship Management** (**eCRM**) strategy to combine personalized touch and customized service to customers. E-retailers can improve communications by using automatic e-mail to confirm orders (Figure 10-26), displaying a list of frequently asked questions (FAQ), and sending surveys for customer feedback. E-retailers should answer customer queries quickly and accurately and offer live chat rooms for sales assistance.

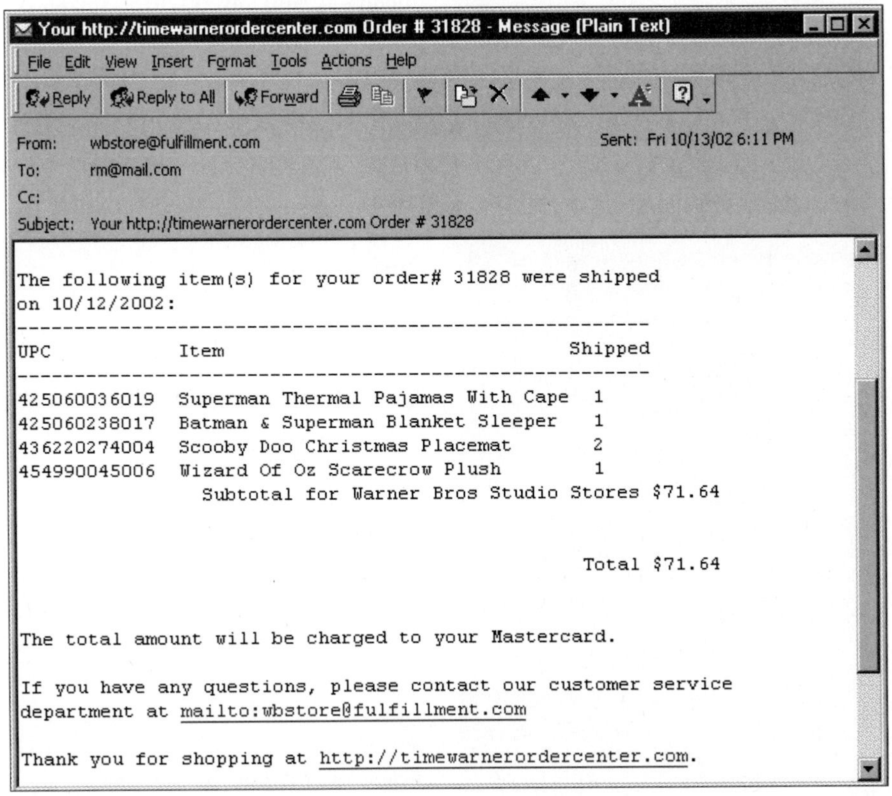

Your http://timewarnerordercenter.com Order # 31828 - Message (Plain Text)

File Edit View Insert Format Tools Actions Help

Reply | Reply to All | Forward

From: wbstore@fulfillment.com Sent: Fri 10/13/02 6:11 PM
To: rm@mail.com
Cc:
Subject: Your http://timewarnerordercenter.com Order # 31828

The following item(s) for your order# 31828 were shipped on 10/12/2002:

UPC	Item	Shipped
425060036019	Superman Thermal Pajamas With Cape	1
425060238017	Batman & Superman Blanket Sleeper	1
436220274004	Scooby Doo Christmas Placemat	2
454990045006	Wizard Of Oz Scarecrow Plush	1

Subtotal for Warner Bros Studio Stores $71.64

Total $71.64

The total amount will be charged to your Mastercard.

If you have any questions, please contact our customer service department at mailto:wbstore@fulfillment.com

Thank you for shopping at http://timewarnerordercenter.com.

Figure 10-26 An e-mail confirmation of an order from Warner Brothers online store.

ISSUE

Who Is *in* Charge?

Privacy Matters

Many people take privacy for granted. Trying to get the same level of privacy on the Internet as in a bricks-and-mortar establishment is a little less accepted and a bit more complicated. An enormous potential exists for abuse as companies increasingly collect data and profile customers. Who owns and has control over personal and collective data, the individual or the data collector, are unresolved questions courts may decide. Many online merchants have added privacy policies to their sites to notify customers how they will use collected information. Watchdog organizations such as TRUSTe, the Online Privacy Alliance, and the Federal Trade Commission (FTC) (see URLs below) monitor privacy issues. Should all online companies be required to post their privacy policy? Should Federal laws be passed to protect an individual's privacy online? Should it be legal for Internet companies to sell your personal data for marketing purposes? Why or why not?

For more information on online privacy and the Web sites mentioned above, visit the Discovering Computers 2002 Issues Web page (**scsite.com/dc2002/issues.htm**) and click Chapter 10 Issue #5.

Customers should be able to track shipments. Return policies should allow customers to make returns and exchanges conveniently.

Follow up after a sale can generate return business and recommendations. Many e-commerce sites use e-mail publishing to keep in touch with customers. **E-mail publishing** is the process of sending newsletters via e-mail messages to a large group of people with similar interests. For example, an e-retailer can use e-mail publishing to offer loyal customers special discounts and promotions, announce new products, or deliver industry news.

Site Management

By monitoring Web site use, e-retailers can collect data and use it to improve their Web sites. Most e-commerce software packages include features to monitor site use and collect statistics. These programs count the numbers of hits for each page. They also can track a customer's path taken through the site. Using tracking information, e-retailers can personalize the Web site or display customized advertisements to adapt a site to individual customers. To do this, these programs use cookies. Chapter 12 discusses cookies and their uses in more depth.

Promoting the Site

The first decision in promoting a site actually should be made before you set up the storefront: the company must have a name. Choosing a name for a site and an associated domain name can be a crucial decision. A company may use the bricks-and-mortar business name, create a Web variation of the name, or coin an entirely new title. As discussed in Chapter 2, a domain name is a unique registered name that identifies and locates a Web site (Figure 10-27). A customer types the domain name in the Web browser to display a Web page. Thus, domain names can have a great influence on the number of hits a Web page receives. Ideally, a domain name corresponds to the business name or the function of the business.

Sample Domain Names of E-Commerce Sites

scsite.com
amazon.com
etrade.com
ebay.com
dell.com

Figure 10-27 Sample domain names of some e-commerce Web sites.

Web Link

For more information on eCRM, visit the Discovering Computers 2002 Chapter 10 WEB LINK page (**scsite.com/dc2002/ch10/weblink.htm**) and click eCRM.

ISSUE

Who to Trust?

Internet Protection

Because Internet interactions are faceless, a business has to generate trust to turn window shoppers into customers. Displaying an actual address and telephone number is one indication a business is established and willing to be contacted. Online merchants can join an Internet protection group such as Netcheck, TRUSTe, or the Better Business Bureau Online (see URLs below) to show they are reputable and safe businesses. Stores often display a security or privacy statement to encourage customer confidence. Would you be comfortable purchasing a product from an online company that provides a security statement or privacy seal? Do these seals authenticate the businesses' legitimacy? Is it possible for an unreputable company to obtain one of these seals? Would you spend $100 or more for an online purchase? Why or why not?

For more information on Internet protection groups and the Web sites mentioned above, visit the Discovering Computers 2002 Issues Web page (**scsite.com/dc2002/issues.htm**) and click Chapter 10 Issue #6.

ISSUE

Cybersquatting

Domain Names

Cybersquatting is the practice of domain name speculation. Cybersquatters register domain names they think will become popular, and then attempt to resell the rights to each name to the highest bidder. Some organizations have paid millions of dollars for a single domain name. For example, the name business.com sold for $7.5 million and autos.com for $2.2 million. Alternately, the cybersquatter may use a name to divert Web surfers from legitimate sites with similar names. Cybersquatters have registered names of famous people, company names, and products. They also register modifications of these. The World Intellectual Property Organization (WIPO) and The Internet Corporation for Assigned Names and Numbers (ICANN) (see URLs below) are establishing guidelines to help regulate rights to domain names. Should there be guidelines or should this be on a first-come, first-served basis? Should anyone be able to purchase the name of a famous person? If a company has a name copyrighted, does it give the company the right to own the domain name?

For more information about cybersquatting and the Web sites mentioned above, visit the Discovering Computers 2002 Issues Web page (**scsite.com/dc2002/issues.htm**) and click Chapter 10 Issue #7.

The next step is to register the domain name with various search engines. Doing so ensures your site will appear in the hit lists for searches on related keywords. Online businesses can register domain names at each search engine individually. Registering your site with the various search engines, however, can be an extremely time-consuming task. Instead, you can use a submission service. As described in Chapter 2, a **submission service** is a Web-based business in which you typically pay a fee to register with hundreds of search engines (Figure 10-28).

Another method of promoting your site is to use online advertisements at another site, often called **banner ads**. The advertisements display a brief message and are linked to the advertiser's Web site. They can be personalized to match a customer's interests. The advertiser usually pays based on the number of click-throughs. A **click-through** occurs when a visitor clicks an advertisement to move to the advertiser's Web page.

Some e-commerce businesses also use unsolicited advertising through newsgroups and e-mail. These unsolicited e-mail messages or newsgroup postings, called **spam,** are sent to many recipients or newsgroups at once. Spam is Internet junk mail. Spam usually generates antagonism instead of sales. A better method is to promote goodwill by providing information or services for groups and individuals. They then may reciprocate by promoting the site.

CHAPTER SUMMARY

This chapter discussed how e-commerce has changed the way we do business. It presented various e-commerce business models and revenue streams. Then, the chapter discussed e-retailing and other market sectors. Finally, it presented issues associated with building a storefront, accepting payment, managing product delivery, designing a site, managing the site, and promoting the site.

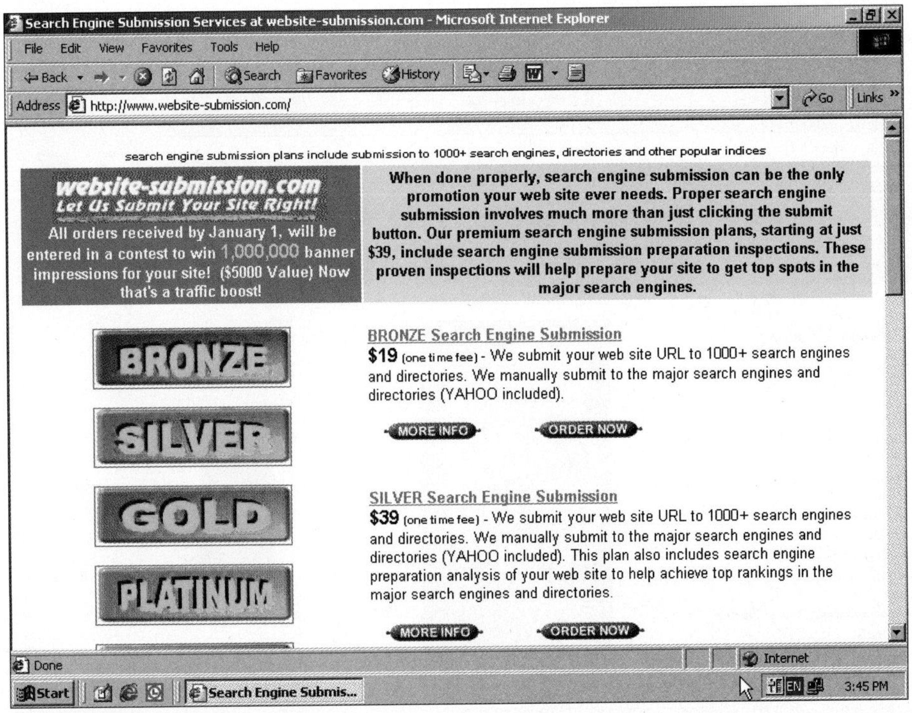

Figure 10-28 A submission service.

Web Developer

If you are looking for a job working with the latest Internet technology, then a Web developer could be the career for you. Generally, this type of employment requires specialized skills. Many Web developers analyze, design, develop, implement, and support Web applications and functionality. A Web developer may be responsible for supporting the presentation and marketing-related features of the Web site. Specialized scripting skills include HTML, JavaScript, Perl, and VBScript. Developers also may be required to have multimedia knowledge, including Adobe PhotoShop and Macromedia Flash and Director (see URLs below).

Educational requirements vary from company to company and can range from a high school education to a four-year degree. Many companies place heavy emphasis on certifications. Two of the most popular certifications are through the International Webmasters Association (IWA) and the World Organization of Webmasters (WOW) (see URLs below). These organizations team with many corporate and academic partners to provide the curriculum for this certification. A wide salary range exists — from $25,000 to $65,000 — depending on educational background and location.

To learn more about the field of Web developer as a career and for links to the Web sites mentioned above, visit the Discovering Computers 2002 Careers Web page (**scsite.com/dc2002/careers.htm**) and click Web Developer.

E-AUCTIONS

GOING ONCE, GOING TWICE

Rare, Common Items Flood Web Sites

Would you like to own the Ryder truck that made U.S. history during the 2000 presidential election? A 15-car motorcade, two sheriff's vehicles, and a helicopter accompanied the famous yellow truck on its 430-mile journey to take Palm Beach County's 462,644 ballots to a court hearing in Tallahassee, Florida. The spectacle was telecast throughout the world.

Days after what some people consider the most famous move in American history, that Ryder truck was auctioned on the Yahoo! Auctions Web site. An anonymous bidder paid $67,100 for the 1999 Ford F350 truck that had 31,297 miles on it and would have been worth $17,051 under normal circumstances. Budget, which owns Ryder truck rentals, donated the net profits to the American Red Cross.

Yahoo! Auctions (Figure 10-29) is one of an estimated 1,200 Internet auction Web sites. Traditional auction powerhouses, such as Christie's in London and Sotheby's (Figure 10-30) on Manhattan's Upper East Side, are known for their big-ticket items: Elton John's clothing sold for $615,000, a bottle of Italian red wine for $13,000, and a Tyrannosaurus Rex fossil for $8.4 million.

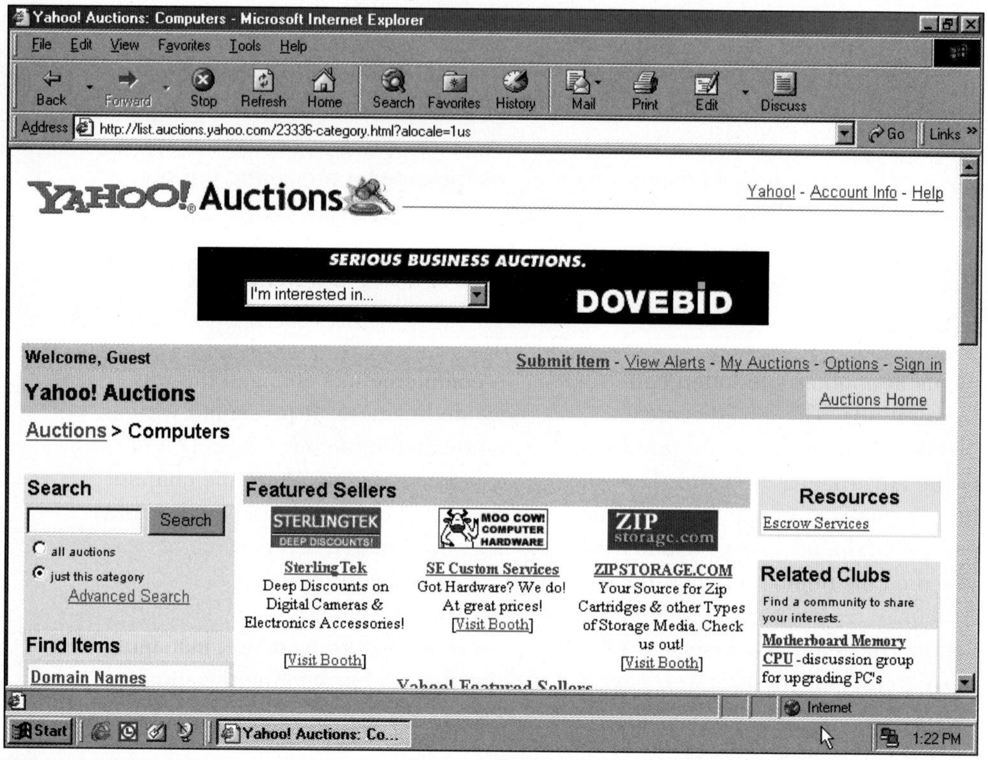

Figure 10-29 Computer equipment is among the many items up for bid on the Yahoo! auction Web site.

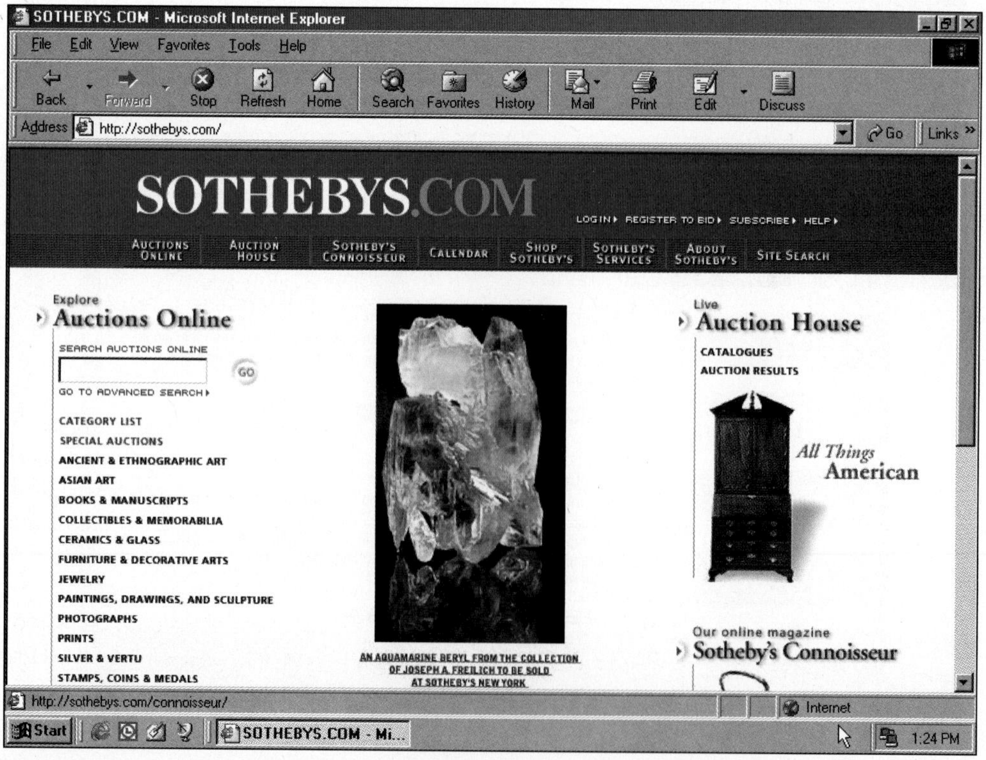

Figure 10-30 Rare and valuable art, jewelry, and furniture are featured on Sotheby's Web pages.

If those prices are a bit out of your league, you can turn to a wealth of other auction Web sites to find just the items you need — and maybe some you really do not — for as little as $1. Some of these auctions are listed in Figure 10-31. Categories include antiques and collectibles, automobiles, computers, electronics, sports, sports cards and memorabilia, and toys.

One of the most noted auction Web sites is eBay, the world's largest personal online trading community (Figure 10-32). As described in a Company on the Cutting Edge feature earlier in this chapter, the company's assortment of auctioned items has ranged from the usual to the unusual. Among the unusual, and perhaps a precursor to the Ryder truck auction, was the opportunity to bid to become the 43rd president of the United States. Bidding opened at one penny and soared to $100 million in four hours before eBay officials cancelled the auction.

For more information on auction Web sites, visit the Discovering Computers 2002 E-Revolution Web page (scsite.com/ dc2002/ e-rev.htm) and click Auctions.

AUCTION WEB SITES	URL
eBay	ebay.com
Yahoo! Auctions	auctions.yahoo.com
Sotheby's	sothebys.com
Christie's	christies.com
uBid	ubid.com
Egghead.com	egghead.com
Wolf's	ewolfs.com
Penbid	www.penbid.com
Auction Frenzy	cyber-auctions.com

For an updated list of auction Web sites, visit scsite.com/dc2002/e-rev.htm.

Figure 10-31 These auction Web sites feature a wide variety of items.

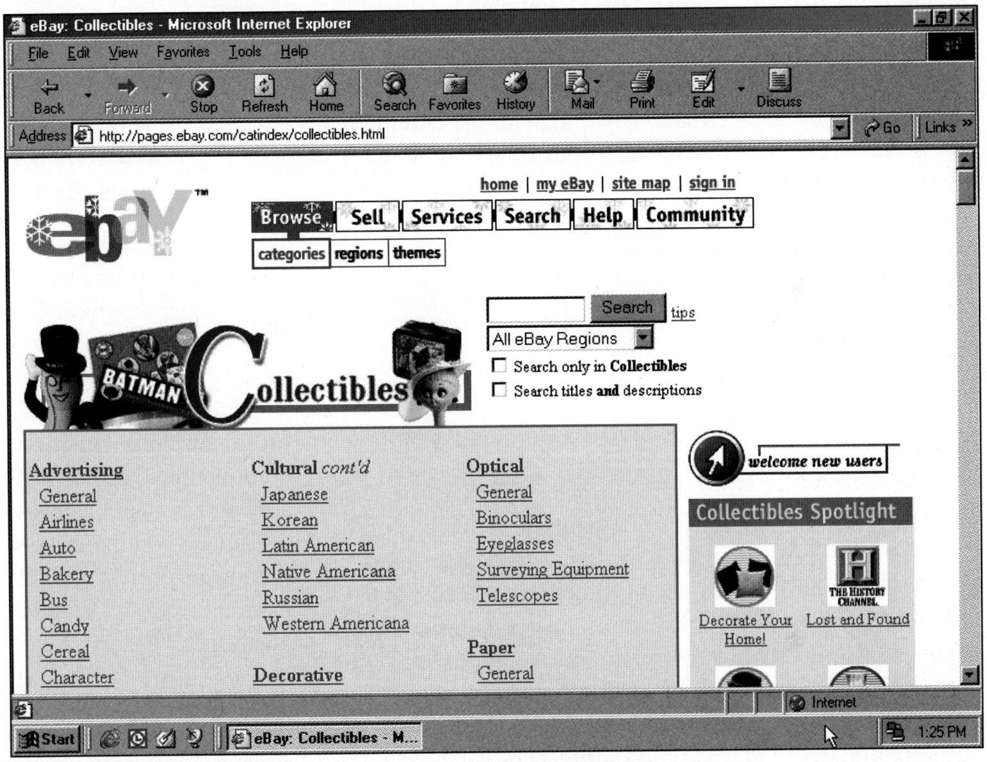

Figure 10-32 eBay is one of the world's most popular auction Web sites.

e-REVOLUTION E-AUCTIONS applied:

1. Visit the Christie's and Sotheby's Web sites and read about the items that have been sold recently. Find two unusual objects and write a paragraph on each auction item summarizing your discoveries. What were the opening and final bids on these objects? Then, review two of the upcoming auctions. When are the auctions' dates? What items are available? What are some of the opening bids? What are the advantages and disadvantages of bidding online?

2. Using one of the auction Web sites listed in Figure 10-31, search for two objects pertaining to your hobbies. For example, if you are a baseball fan, you can search for a complete set of Topps cards. If you are a car buff, search for your dream car. Describe these two items. How many people have bid on these items? Who are the sellers? What are the opening and current bids?

In Summary

Web Instructions: To display this page from the Web, start your browser and enter the URL scsite.com/dc2002/ch10/summary.htm. Click the links for current and additional information. To listen to an audio version of this In Summary, click the Audio button. To play the audio, RealPlayer must be installed on your computer (download by clicking here).

1 How Has E-commerce Changed the Way We Do Business?

Electronic commerce (e-commerce), sometimes called e-business, is a financial business transaction that occurs over an electronic network. With the elimination of the barriers of time and distance that slow traditional business dealings, transactions can occur instantaneously and globally. E-commerce has changed the way businesses do business. Many companies no longer have merely a physical **bricks-and-mortar** location but have both a physical and an online presence — **clicks-and-mortar** businesses.

2 What Is the Positive Impact of E-commerce on Our Society?

Some advantages of **e-commerce** include global markets have no geographic boundaries, businesses have access to 360 million people, customers have access to multiple suppliers and prices, stores are open all the time, feedback is immediate, turnaround time is short with changing information, FAQs provide customer support, companies have the ability to gather and analyze customer information, new and traditional approaches generate revenue, the middleman is eliminated, distribution costs are reduced or eliminated, and the cost of paperwork is reduced.

3 What Is the Difference between the Various E-commerce Business Models: Business-to-Consumer, Consumer-to-Consumer, Business-to-Business, and Business-to-Employee?

Business-to-consumer (**B-to-C** or **B2C**) e-commerce consists of the sale of products or services from a business to the general public. **Consumer-to-consumer (C-to-C or C2C)** e-commerce consists of individuals using the Internet to sell products and services directly to other individuals. The most popular vehicle for C2C e-commerce is the **online auction**. **Business-to-business** (**B-to-B** or **B2B**) e-commerce consists of the exchange of products and service between businesses. **Business-to-employee** (**B-to-E** or **B2E**) e-commerce, sometimes called **intrabusiness e-commerce**, refers to the use of intranet technology to handle electronic transactions that take place within a business.

4 What Are Various E-commerce Revenue Streams?

A **revenue stream** is the method a business uses to generate income. Some of the more common **e-commerce** revenue streams include direct sales which is the purchase of a product or service that is delivered to the customer; downloads of products such as software, music, movies, books and other items; software rental of an application that exists on a Web site; advertising; subscriptions to services; Web site hosting; and **online storage services** for storing backup copies of data and information.

In Summary

5 How Does E-retailing Work?

E-retail, also called **e-tail**, occurs when retailers use the Web to sell their products and services. A customer visits the **electronic storefront** of the online business. The customer collects purchases in an electronic shopping cart and then enters payment information. This financial information is sent to a bank for authorization and then sent back to the e-retailer. Confirmation is sent to the customer, the order is processed, and the package is prepared for shipment. Shipping information is posted on the Web, and the package is delivered to the customer.

6 What Are E-commerce Market Sectors?

In addition to retail, other market sectors include finance that supports **online banking** and online trading; entertainment and media, which includes music, videos, news, sporting events, and 3-D multiplayer games; travel, including driving directions and airline, car, and hotel reservations; and health issues, including databases of doctors, dentists, and online pharmacies.

7 What Are Issues Associated with Building a Storefront, Accepting Payment, Managing Product Delivery, and Designing, Managing and Promoting the Web Site?

Choosing the software and hardware to build an electronic storefront is one of the most important decisions facing e-retailers. Some e-retailers may choose to develop and maintain their Web site in-house, while others outsource all or part of the system. Using **E-commerce software,** a merchant can set up a storefront with a product database, combined with a shopping cart. Credit cards are the most popular payment method on the Web for the acceptance of customer payments. Another option is to use an **electronic money (e-money)**, also called digital cash or **e-cash**, payment system. Traditional delivery services such as Federal Express and UPS often handle the shipping of products. Web site navigation must be convenient, efficient, and easy to use. Fulfillment includes managing and storing inventory, packaging and shipping products, and maintaining records of all transactions. Some e-retailers manage in-house and others outsource. Selecting a Web site and domain name is a crucial decision and can have a great influence on the number of visitors a Web site receives. Submitting the name to search engines and purchasing banner ads are other promotional options.

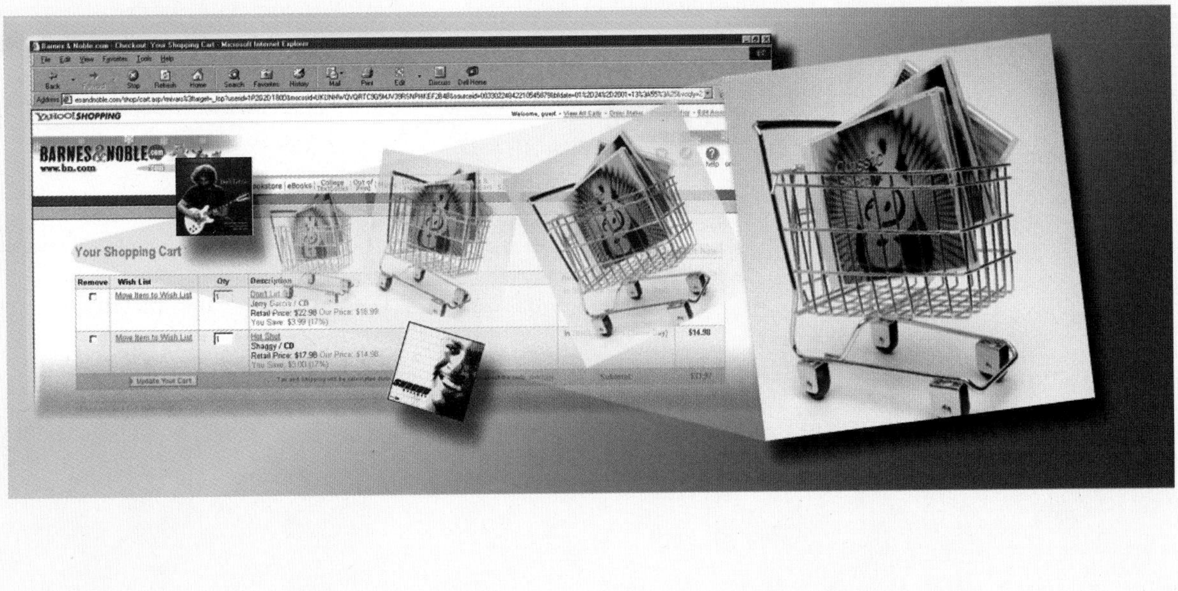

Key Terms

Web Instructions: To display this page from the Web, start your browser and enter the URL scsite.com/dc2002/ch10/terms.htm. Scroll through the list of terms. Click a term to display its definition and a picture. Click the To WEB button for current and additional information about the term from the Web. To see animations, Shockwave and Flash Player must be installed on your computer (download by clicking here).

banner ads (10.25)
bricks-and-mortar (10.3)
brokering (10.7)
business-to-business (B-to-B or B2B) (10.6)
business-to-consumer (B-to-C or B2C) (10.4)
business-to-employee (B-to-E or B2E) (10.8)
click-through (10.25)
clicks-and-mortar (10.3)
commerce server (10.19)
consumer-to-consumer (C-to-C or C2C) (10.6)
digital cash (10.22)

BRICKS-AND-MORTAR
This is a business where buyers make purchases at a physical location. Sometimes called a brick-and-mortar business. (10.3)

disintermediation (10.4)
e-business (10.2)
e-cash (10.22)
e-commerce server (10.19)
e-commerce software (10.18)
electronic commerce (e-commerce) (10.2)
electronic Customer Relationship Management (eCRM) (10.23)
electronic data interchange (EDI) (10.4)
electronic money (e-money) (10.22)
electronic software distribution (ESD) (10.8)
electronic storefront (10.12)
e-mail publishing (10.24)
e-procurement (10.7)
e-retail (10.12)
e-tail (10.12)
fulfillment companies (10.22)
infomediary (10.7)
intrabusiness e-commerce (10.8)
intranet (10.8)
logistics companies (10.22)
m-commerce (mobile commerce) (10.3)
merchant account (10.20)
.NET (10.8)
online auction (10.6)
online banking (10.14)
online catalog (10.12)
online storage services (10.11)
online trading (10.14)
P2P (10.6)
revenue stream (10.8)
secure server (10.20)
service B2B (10.7)

shopbot (10.15)
shopping bot (10.15)
shopping cart (10.12)

ONLINE BANKING
Online service that allows electronic money transfers for bill paying and provides up-to-date transaction data and bank statements. (10.14)

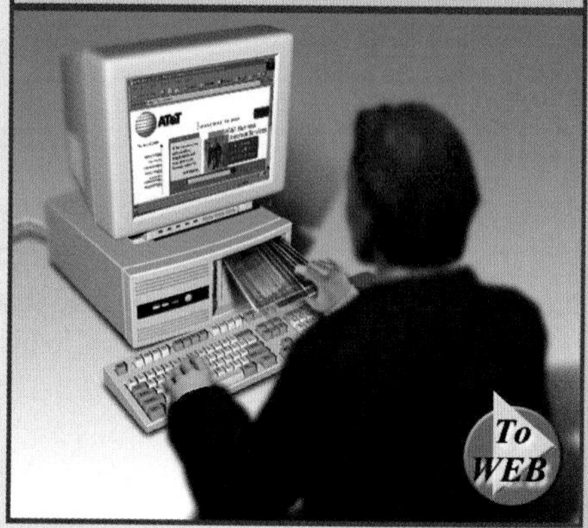

spam (10.25)
submission service (10.25)
supply chain (10.7)
vendor B2B (10.7)
vertical B2B (10.8)
Web application (10.8)
Web host (10.19)
Web hosting service (10.10)
Web server (10.10)

Learn It Online

Web Instructions: To display this page from the Web, start your browser, and then enter the URL scsite.com/dc2002/ch10/learn.htm.

1. Web Guide

Click Web Guide to display the Guide to World Wide Web Sites and Searching Techniques Web page. Click Reference and then click About.com. Search for electronic commerce. Click one of the electronic commerce links. Use your word processing program to prepare a brief report on your findings and submit your assignment to your instructor.

2. Scavenger Hunt

Click Scavenger Hunt. Print a copy of the Scavenger Hunt page; use this page to write down your answers as you search the Web. Submit your completed page to your instructor.

3. Who Wants to Be a Computer Genius?

Click Computer Genius to find out if you are a computer genius. Directions on how to play the game will display. When you are ready to play, click the PLAY button. Submit your score to your instructor.

4. Wheel of Terms

Click Wheel of Terms to reinforce important terms you learned in this chapter by playing the Shelly Cashman Series version of this popular game. Directions on how to play the game will display. When you are ready to play, click the PLAY button. Submit your score to your instructor.

5. Career Corner

Click Career Corner to display the BrainBuzz page. In the Job Search text box, type `Web developer`. Select your state and click the Go button. Scroll through the results until you find a link in which you are interested. Write a brief report on what you discovered by clicking this link. Submit the report to your instructor.

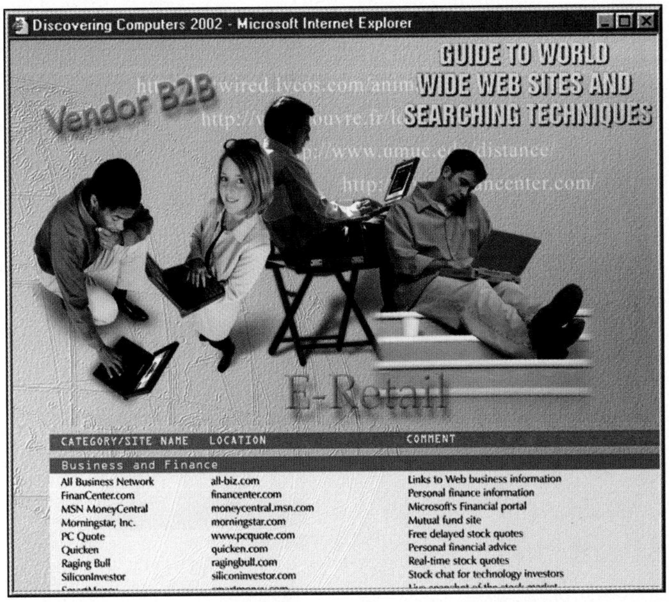

6. Search Sleuth

Click Search Sleuth to learn search techniques that will help make you a research expert. Submit the completed assignment to your instructor.

7. Crossword Puzzle Challenge

Click Crossword Puzzle Challenge. Complete the puzzle to reinforce skills you learned in this chapter. Directions on how to play the game will display. When you are ready to play, click the PLAY button. Submit the completed puzzle to your instructor.

8. Practice Test

Click Practice Test. Answer each question. When completed, enter your name and click the Grade Test button to submit the quiz for grading. Make a note of any missed questions. If required, print a copy to submit to your instructor.

Web Instructions: To display this page from the Web, start your browser and enter the URL scsite.com/dc2002/ch10/check.htm. Click the links for current and additional information. To experience the animation and interactivity, Shockwave and Flash Player must be installed on your computer (download by clicking here.)

LABEL THE FIGURE

Instructions: Identify each element of the path of an authorized e-retail transaction.

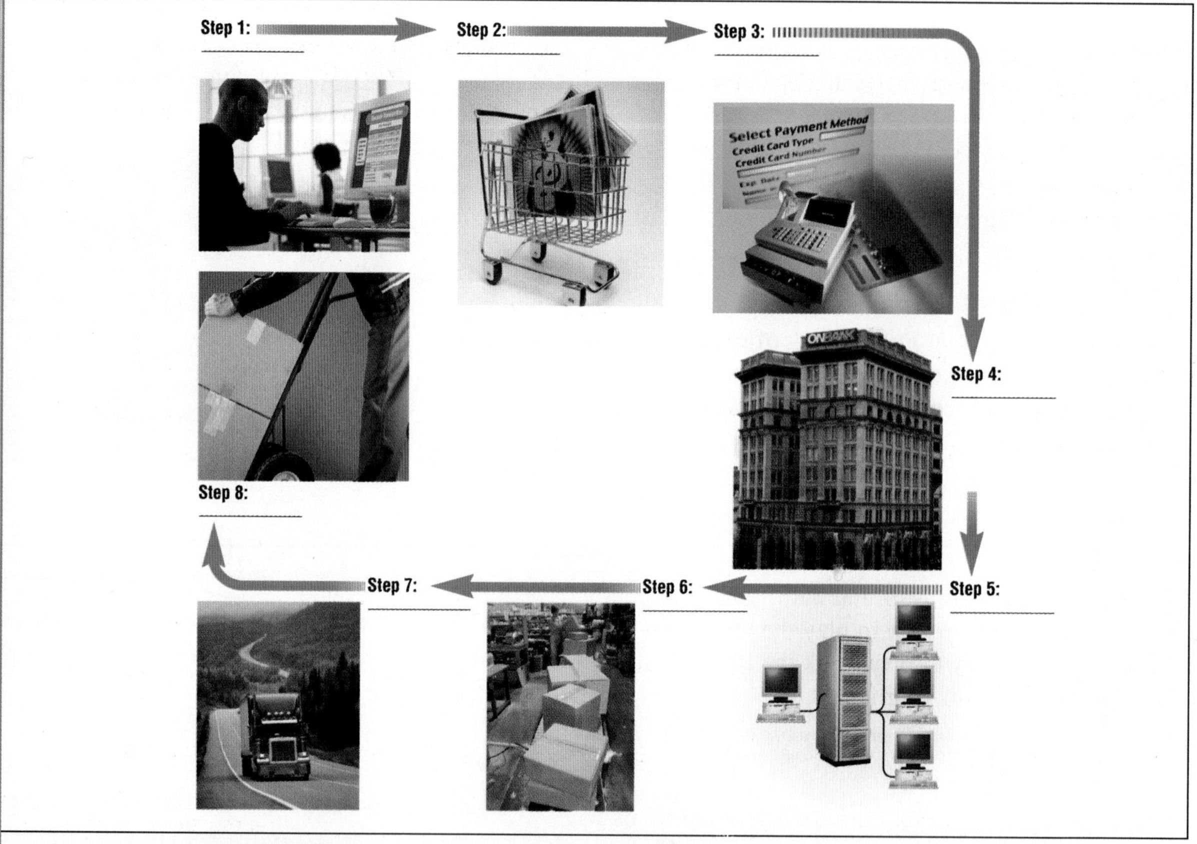

MATCHING

Instructions: Match each term from the column on the left with the best description from the column on the right.

_______ 1. B-to-B or B2B
_______ 2. Web application
_______ 3. Web hosting service
_______ 4. disintermediation
_______ 5. online auction

a. Provides the hardware, software, and communications required for a Web server.
b. A software application that exists on a Web site.
c. A Web site that provides specialized information about suppliers and other businesses.
d. E-commerce that consists of the exchange of products and service between businesses.
e. E-commerce that consists of individuals using the Internet to sell products and services directly to other individuals.
f. Enables a business to sell products directly to consumers without using traditional retail channels.
g. One consumer sells goods to other consumers.

MULTIPLE CHOICE

Instructions: Select the letter of the correct answer for each of the following questions.

1. __________ is e-commerce that uses handheld Web-enabled devices.
   a. M-commerce
   b. EDI
   c. B-to-C
   d. C-to-C
2. __________ is a set of standards that controls the transfer of business data and information among computers both within and among companies.
   a. Infomediary
   b. B2B
   c. EDI
   d. Brokering
3. __________ was precursor to the present form of e-commerce.
   a. The Intranet
   b. The ATM
   c. B-to-E
   d. E-retail
4. The most popular use for C2C e-commerce is __________ .
   a. peer-to-peer transactions
   b. online auctions
   c. individual to business transactions
   d. business to individual transactions
5. A(n) __________ B2B site provides one or more benefits to business such as financing, warehousing, or shipping.
   a. e-procurement
   b. vendor
   c. service
   d. brokering

SHORT ANSWER

Instructions: Write a brief answer to each of the following questions.

1. What is e-commerce? __________ What traditional barriers are almost eliminated by e-commerce? __________
2. How do B2C business models maximize their benefits? __________ What is disintermediation? __________
3. Describe business-to-business (B-to-B or B2B) e-commerce. __________ What is the supply chain and how it is integrated with the B2B model? __________
4. What is the difference between a Web hosting service and a Web server? __________ What are some services provided by Web hosting services? __________
5. In addition to retail, what are some other e-commerce market sectors? __________ Describe some of the ways in which the general public may interact with these market sectors? __________

WORKING TOGETHER

Instructions: Working with a group of your classmates, complete the following team exercise.

Assume that your team is going into the e-commerce business and your goal is to develop a Web site. Your textbook provides a list of six common concerns that a company must consider in the development of an e-commerce Web site. Review each of these six concerns and determine how you will address each. Your report should include the following information: the type of e-commerce model, the product or service, domain name, in-house hosting or outsourcing, payment type, and promotional techniques for the Web site. In addition to your report, create a PowerPoint presentation to share with the class.

Web Instructions: To display this page from the Web, start your browser and enter the URL scsite.com/dc2002/ch10/lab.htm. Click the links for current and additional information.

1 Changing Views in Windows Explorer

Windows Explorer provides four ways of viewing folders and files. Right-click the Start button on the taskbar and click Explore on the shortcut menu. When the Exploring window opens, click View on the menu bar and then click Large Icons on the View menu. Note the display in the right panel. Click View on the menu bar again and click Small Icons on the View menu. Again, note the display in the right panel. Repeat the above procedure, this time clicking List on the View menu. Lastly, click Details on the View menu. Answer the following questions:

- Which view option displays the type of file?
- Which view option displays the date the file or folder was modified?
- What is the difference between the List view and the Small Icon view?
- Which view is easiest to read?

Click the Close button to close the Exploring window.

2 Using Windows Update

This exercise uses Windows 98 procedures. You must be connected to the Internet to complete this activity. Click the Start button on the taskbar and then click Help on the Start menu. When the Windows Help window opens, click the Web Help button. Read the information in the right pane and then click the Support Online link to access the Microsoft Windows 98 Web site. Click the Using Windows 98 link and then click the Frequently Asked Questions link. Answer the following questions by clicking the appropriate links.

- What is device contention?
- How can you print a file list of Windows Explorer?
- How can you tell which version of Windows you are running?

Click the Close button to close each open window.

3 Create a Desktop Shortcut to the Printer

To create a desktop shortcut to a printer, click the Start button on the taskbar, point to Settings, and then click Printers. Right-click the icon of your default printer and click Create Shortcut. Windows will tell you that the shortcut has to go on the desktop. Click OK or Yes to place the shortcut on the desktop. After you create a shortcut to a printer, you can print documents by dragging them to the printer shortcut on the desktop. The program used to print the document will open briefly and then close. Right-click the printer desktop shortcut icon, click Properties, and then click the General tab. What information is contained in this dialog box? Click the Shortcut tab. What are the two settings that can be modified? Close the Properties dialog box. Right-click the Printer desktop shortcut icon and then click Delete on the shortcut menu. If necessary, click the Yes button in the Delete dialog box.

4 Determine the Brand and Model of Sound Cards or Devices in Your Computer

This exercise uses Windows 98 procedures. To determine the brand and model of any sound cards or audio devices installed in your computer, click the Start button on the taskbar, point to Settings, and then click Control Panel. Double-click the System icon to display the System Properties dialog box. Click the Devices Manager tab and double-click sound, video and game controllers to expand the branch. What sound devices are listed? What video devices are listed? What game controller devices are listed? Click the OK or Cancel button to close the System Properties dialog box. In the Control Panel window, double-click the Multimedia icon. Click the Devices tab and double-click Audio Devices to expand the branch. What audio devices are listed? Click the OK or Cancel button to close the dialog box. Click the Close button to close each open window.

Web Work

Veb Instructions: To display this page from the Web, start your browser and enter the URL scsite.com/dc2002/ch10/web.htm. To view At 'he Movies in exercise 1, RealPlayer must be installed on your computer (download by clicking here).

1 Yahoo!

To view the Yahoo! movie, click the button to the left or click the Play button to the right. Watch the movie, and then complete the exercise by answering the questions below. Basically it's a list — a list of Web sites and chat rooms. When Yahoo! went public in 1996, its two, 20-something founders became overnight billionaires. Yahoo! is a $200 million a year business, with a business model based on deriving revenue from advertising. Yahoo! gets over 235 million hits a day, a number used to calculate charges to advertisers. It has become a highly competitive business, but a business model under intense scrutiny. How secure is a business based on hits or clicks? Is it likely that emerging Internet technologies will solidify the rightness of Yahoo!'s business model … or not?

2 Online Banking

Online banking rapidly is becoming a standard offering in the United States. Online banking effectively transforms your personal computer into a bank teller. Using an online banking service, you can complete nearly all transactions, with the exception of cash withdrawal, you would take care of during a trip to the bank. Access to more detailed financial information allows you to better track where your money is going, as well as plan where you want it to go in the future. To determine if online banking is for you, click the button to the left and read Online Banking: The Basics.

3 E-Government

Will e-government revolutionize the way U. S. citizens interact with government? The increased use of Internet-based solutions to facilitate business-to-business and business-to-customer interactions has major implications for federal, state, and local governments. The ideal concept of e-government would be to provide services and information to citizens electronically, 24 hours a day, 7 days a week. Many government agencies have some of these services in place. Click the button to the left to find out more about what governmental agencies are doing. Download and review one of the PowerPoint presentations. Write a summary of your discoveries.

4 Online Sales

A recent Forrester Research report predicts that by the year 2005, U.S. online retail sales will total $269 billion, or 11% of US retail sales. The report further projects large increases in Web-researched offline sales, and factors that determine which items are purchased offline versus online. Click the button to the left to access a list of some of the more successful online e-tailers. Click one of the company links. Which company did you select? What products does it have available? Is the Web site easy to navigate? Does it have a product you would purchase online?

5 In the News

The Internet is predicted to be a driving force in both the new and used vehicle market over the next five years. A survey released by the National Automobile Dealers Association indicates that e-commerce is starting to pay off for car dealers that have a well-established Internet presence. As more dealerships recognize the Web's power as a sales tool, online sales are expected to continue to increase. Click the button to the left and read a news article about a recent e-commerce success story. What is the product or company? How has it been successful? Is this success predicted to continue?

CHAPTER 11

Computers and Society: Home, Work, and Ethical Issues

"Look, hands-free!" For years, your friend has told you that using the mobile telephone while driving is dangerous. Although you are aware of the risks, you accomplish a lot while in the car. Your Web-enabled cellular telephone allows you to return countless calls, as well as check stock prices. Someone out there agrees with your friend, however. The city in which you live just made it illegal to hold a cellular telephone while driving. City officials say you need both hands on the steering wheel. They suggest consumers look into hands-free Bluetooth™-enabled cellular devices.

You immediately visit a Bluetooth™ dealer and purchase a cellular telephone that uses radio waves to *connect* to a headset with a microphone. This is great! You speak into the microphone and, according to your verbal instructions, the telephone dials a telephone number, connects to the Internet, and checks stock prices. The telephone even has voice output that speaks information such as the stock prices, so you can keep your eyes on the road.

This new wireless technology is just what your friend has suggested. When you leave the store, you call your friend from the car and invite her to dinner. She will be glad to hear she was right.

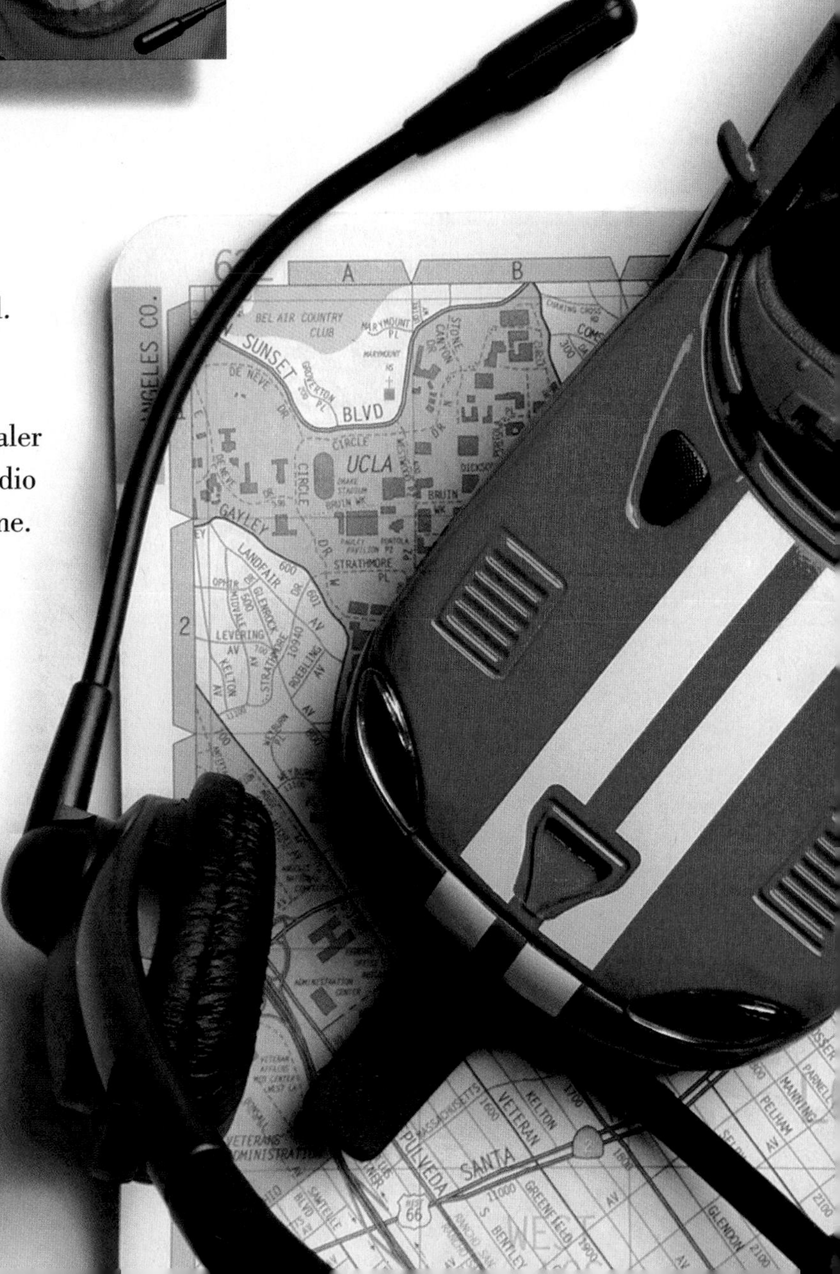

OBJECTIVES

After completing this chapter, you will be able to:

- Understand that computers have made a tremendous difference in daily living
- Explain how computers are used at home
- Describe how computers change the way society interacts with disciplines such as education, entertainment, finance, government, health care, science, publishing, and travel
- Recognize the issues associated with the digital divide
- Understand how e-commerce affects the way people conduct business
- Identify ways virtual reality, intelligent agents, and robots are being used in daily life
- Learn how to prevent health-related disorders and injuries due to computer use
- Understand how to design a workspace ergonomically
- Recognize symptoms of computer addiction
- Explain green computing
- Understand ethical issues surrounding computer use

LIVING WITH COMPUTERS

The computer has changed society today as much as the industrial revolution changed society in the eighteenth and nineteenth centuries. Computers are everywhere — at home, at work, and at school (Figure 11-1).

Society has benefited greatly from computers. In a recent report, the United States government attributed one-third of the country's economic growth to digital technologies, resulting in tremendous increases in productivity. Both business and home users can make well-informed

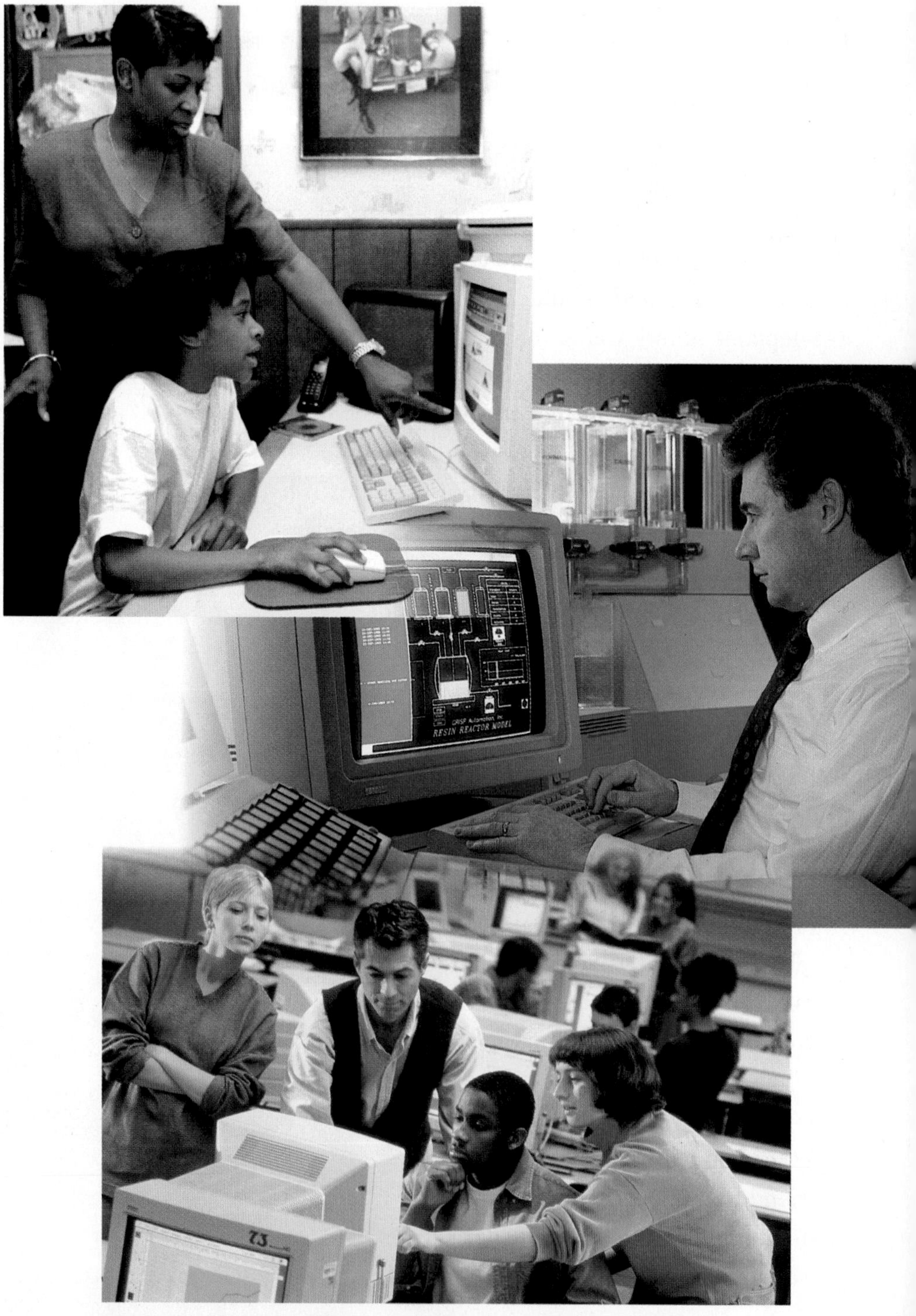

Figure 11-1 People use computers everywhere — at home, at work, and at school.

decisions because they have instant access to information from anywhere in the world. Students have more tools to assist them in the learning process. Homes have many more conveniences, which potentially could allow families to spend more quality time together.

Nearly every discipline uses computers. The use of computers in fields such as education, finance, government, health care, science, publishing, and travel has had a tremendous impact on society. The following pages describe how computers have made a difference in our lives at home, as well as in our interactions with these disciplines. You may interact directly with computers in these areas. Or, you may reap the benefits from breakthroughs and advances in these fields. The use of computers in each of these areas, however, raises some important issues. These issues are explored, as well.

At Home

In a growing number of homes, the computer no longer is a convenience. Instead, it has become a basic necessity. Each family member uses the computer for different purposes. These include entertainment, research and education, budgeting and personal financial management, home business management, personal and business communications, and Web access (Figure 11-2).

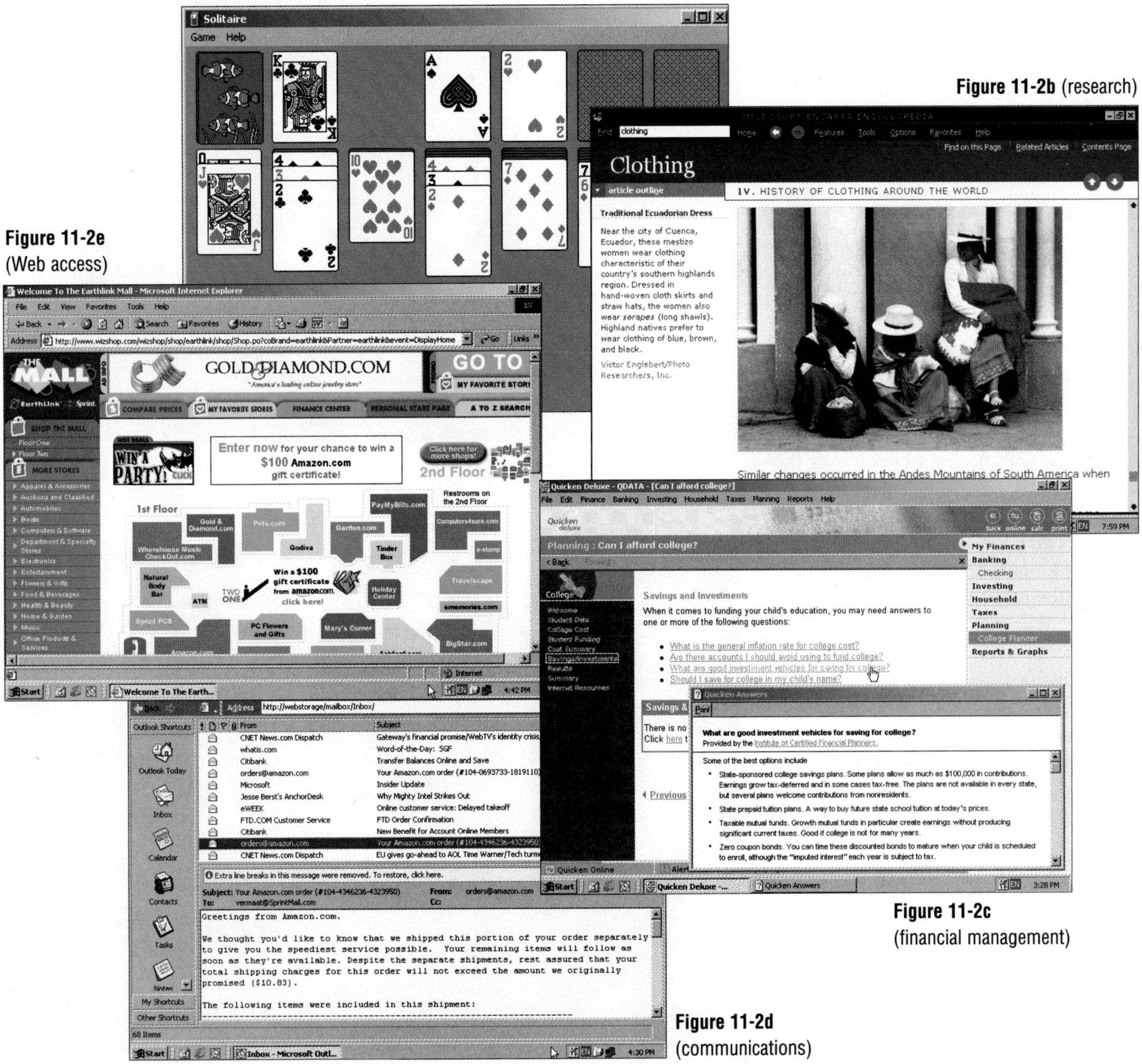

Figure 11-2a (entertainment)

Figure 11-2b (research)

Figure 11-2c (financial management)

Figure 11-2d (communications)

Figure 11-2e (Web access)

Figure 11-2 Family members each use computers for different reasons.

The main reason computers have infiltrated homes is because people want access to the Web. Home users connect to the Web for a variety of reasons.

- Access a wealth of information, news, research, and educational material
- Shop for goods and services
- Bank and invest
- Take a course or access other educational material
- Download and listen to music
- Download and watch movies
- Access sources of entertainment and leisure such as online games, magazines, and vacation planning guides
- Communicate with others around the world

Computers networked to the world via the Internet have become a primary means of communications for home users. E-mail messages fill inboxes. Instant messaging services alert you to calendar appointments, stock quotes, sports scores, weather, or when a certain person is online. While in chat rooms, you meet and converse with people from all over the globe. With the cost of PC cameras less than one hundred dollars, you easily can have a video conference with friends and family members.

Communications are not limited to text. With today's technology, you also can transmit voice, sounds, video, and graphics. As shown in Figure 11-3, you can take a photograph with a PC camera and send the digitized image to anyone. Figure 11-4 shows that you can have live conversations with others.

To meet the varying needs of consumers, today's homes have a variety of computers. These include desktop, notebook, and handheld computers; Web-enabled telephones and pagers; and Internet appliances. Some of these computers are available in a variety of stylish colors and sleek designs (Figure 11-5). This allows you to coordinate computers with room décor and lifestyle.

Figure 11-3 This user photographed her freshly picked flowers with her PC camera, saved the image on the computer, and e-mailed the image of the flowers to her mother.

Figure 11-4 Using videoconferencing software, you can have live conversations with others through your computer.

Internet appliances are ideal for the family that uses the computer only for Web access (Figure 11-6). Other more sophisticated home users network computers throughout the house, so family members can access each other's files, printers, and other devices.

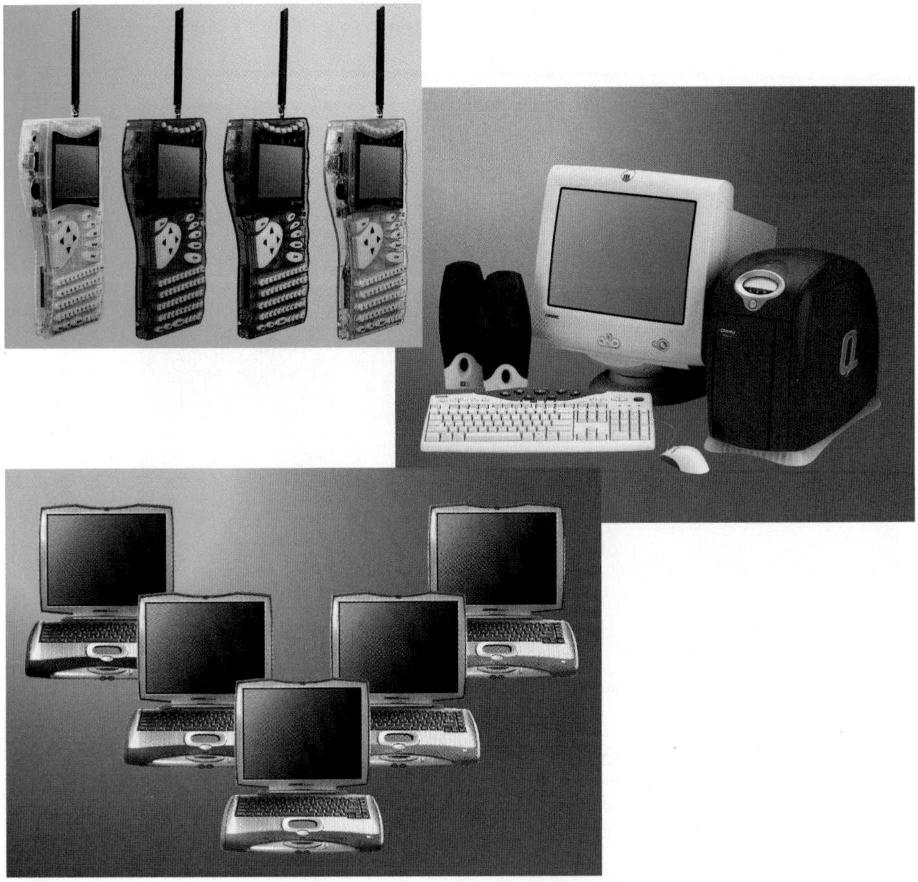

Figure 11-5 Many computers are available in a variety of sleek designs and colors.

Figure 11-6 This home user sits at the kitchen table and searches the Web using an Internet appliance.

TECHNOLOGY TRAILBLAZER

STEVE **WOZNIAK**

Steve Wozniak is such a Tetris fanatic that he plays even during the Superbowl. His high score is 710,000.

Wozniak was named to the National Inventors Hall of Fame in Akron, Ohio, for his $666 Apple II, which combined the central processing unit, keyboard, and disk drive into one unit. With an intense interest in computers, Wozniak devoted his spare time to designing and building machines. One of his projects was a *blue box* that contained a whistle from a Cap'n Crunch cereal box. The whistle could generate tones capable of making telephone calls.

Wozniak began working at Hewlett-Packard after dropping out of the University of California at Berkeley. At HP he met Steve Jobs, who was a summer employee. In 1976, these two creative visionaries developed the Apple I, and it was an instant success. It led to the Apple II in 1979, the first mass-marketed personal computer, and eventually to the Macintosh in 1984. Although Wozniak left Apple in 1985 to spend time with his family, work with community projects, and teach, he still serves as an adviser to the corporation.

For more information on Steve Wozniak, visit the Discovering Computers 2002 People Web page (**scsite.com/dc2002/people.htm**) and click Steve Wozniak.

Education

Education is the process of developing knowledge through instruction. Traditionally, this instruction came from people such as parents, teachers, and employers, and from printed material such as books, journals, and guides. Today, educators are turning to computers to assist with the learning process.

As the costs of personal computers drop, many schools and businesses can afford to equip labs and classrooms with computers (Figure 11-7). In these labs, students use software packages to complete assignments. Some educators also use computer-based training and Web-based training along with or as a replacement for their lecture presentations.

Computer-based training (CBT), also called **computer-aided instruction (CAI)**, helps students learn by using computers and completing exercises with instructional software (Figure 11-8). **Web-based training (WBT)** is a type of CBT that

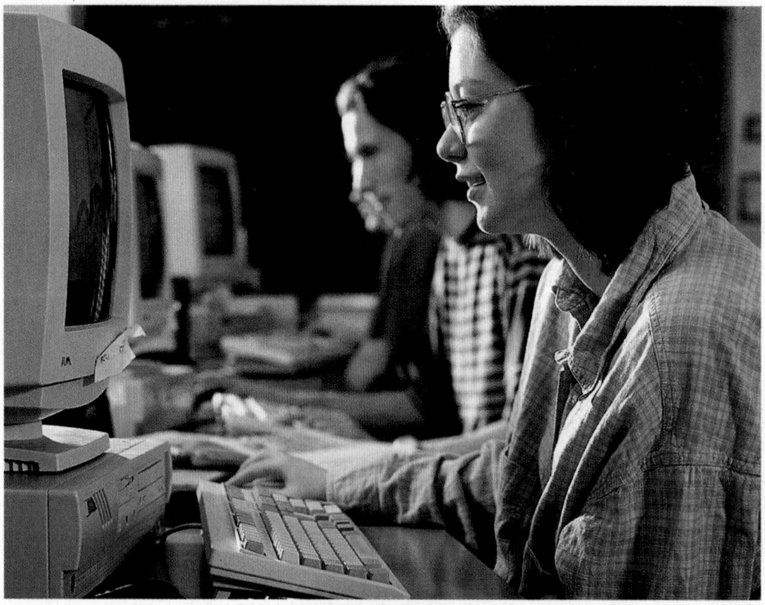

Figure 11-7 Many schools and businesses have computer labs to provide an environment conducive for students and employees to learn.

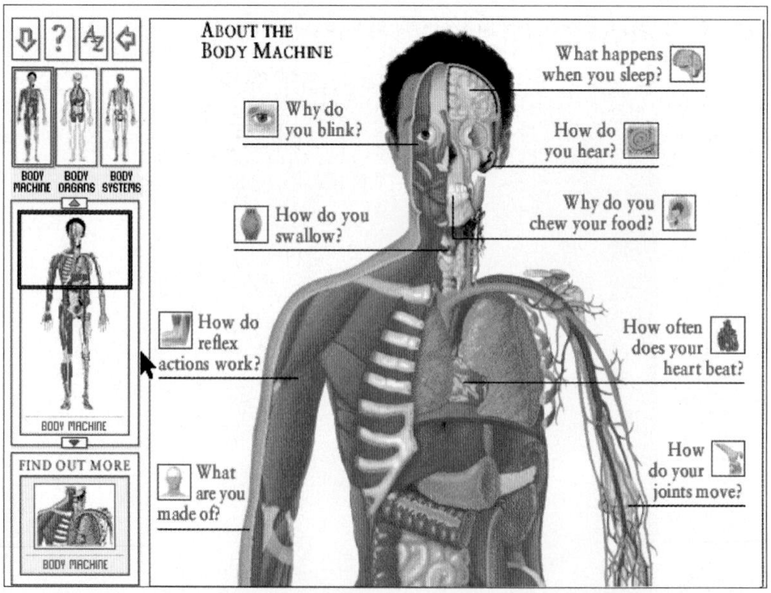

Figure 11-8 The Ultimate Human Body is a popular educational program that allows students to interact with and learn about the human body. For example, clicking the heart allows students to see and hear a human heart beat.

ISSUE

Books Versus Bytes

Electronic Books

In one county, the number of computers purchased by local school districts increased by 85 percent, while the supply of library books declined by almost 10 percent. School officials claim computers extend learning opportunities and satisfy computer literacy needed in today's technological world. Yet, some parents complain that computer purchases represent frivolous, status-seeking spending. How should a school district's money be spent? If you were an administrator, what percentage of your budget would you spend on computers? On library books and textbooks? Why? What factors would influence your decision? Do you think the availability of books in electronic form, such as CD-ROM, e-books, and the Internet, will cause books as we know them today to become obsolete?

For more information on books versus computers, visit the Discovering Computers 2002 Issues Web page (**scsite.com/dc 2002/issues.htm**) and click Chapter 11 Issue #1.

uses Internet technology (Figure 11-9). CBT and WBT typically consist of self-directed, self-paced instruction on a topic.

CBT and WBT are popular in business, industry, and schools for teaching new skills or enhancing existing skills of employees, teachers, or students. When using CBT or WBT, students become actively involved in the learning process instead of passive recipients of information. Some of the many advantages of CBT and WBT over traditional training include the following:

- Self-paced study – students can progress at their own pace, skipping strong areas to focus on areas of weakness.
- Unique content – multimedia content appeals to many types of learners and can help make difficult concepts simple.
- Unique instructional experience – **simulations**, or computer-based models of real-life situations, allow students to learn skills in hazardous, emergency, or other situations.
- Reduced training costs – elimination of travel expenses reduces training costs. Students can access training materials from home, work, or any location that has a computer.

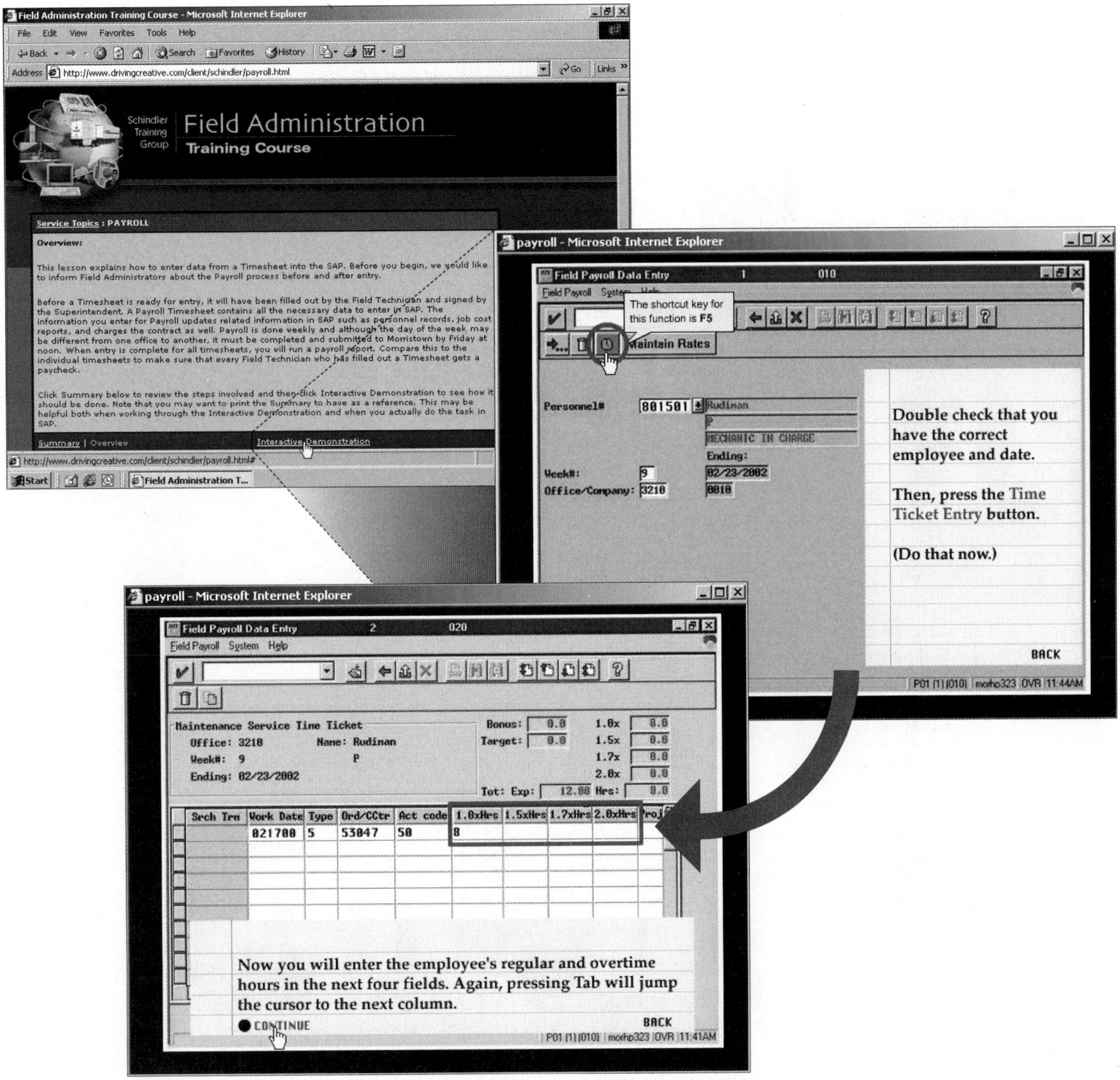

Figure 11-9 This instructional program teaches office personnel how to enter data from a timecard into the computer program.

In addition, WBT can provide up-to-date content on any type of computer platform. Many Web sites offer WBT to the general public. Such training covers a wide range of topics, from how to change a flat tire to creating documents in Word. Many of these Web sites are free. Others ask you to register and pay a fee to take the complete Web-based course.

WBT, CBT, and other materials often are combined as materials for distance learning courses. **Distance learning** (**DL**), also called **distance education** (**DE**) or **online learning**, is the delivery of education at one location while the learning takes place at other locations. DL courses provide many time, distance, and place advantages for students who live far from a college campus or work full time. These courses enable students to attend class from anywhere in the world and at times that fit their schedules.

Many national and international companies offer DL training. These training courses eliminate the costs of airfare, hotels, and meals for centralized training sessions. For example, a global oil company may use a distance learning format to keep its personnel trained, regardless of where they are working (Figure 11-10). More than 70 percent of colleges and universities offer some form of distance learning (Figure 11-11). A few even offer entire degrees online.

Another form of CBT is edutainment. **Edutainment** is a type of educational software that combines education with entertainment. Many CD-ROMs and DVD-ROMs, such as the *Reader Rabbit* and *Carmen Sandiego* series, teach children in a fun and exciting way (Figure 11-12). Others, such as *Nascar Racing* and *Mavis Beacon Teaches Typing*, provide edutainment for computer users of all ages.

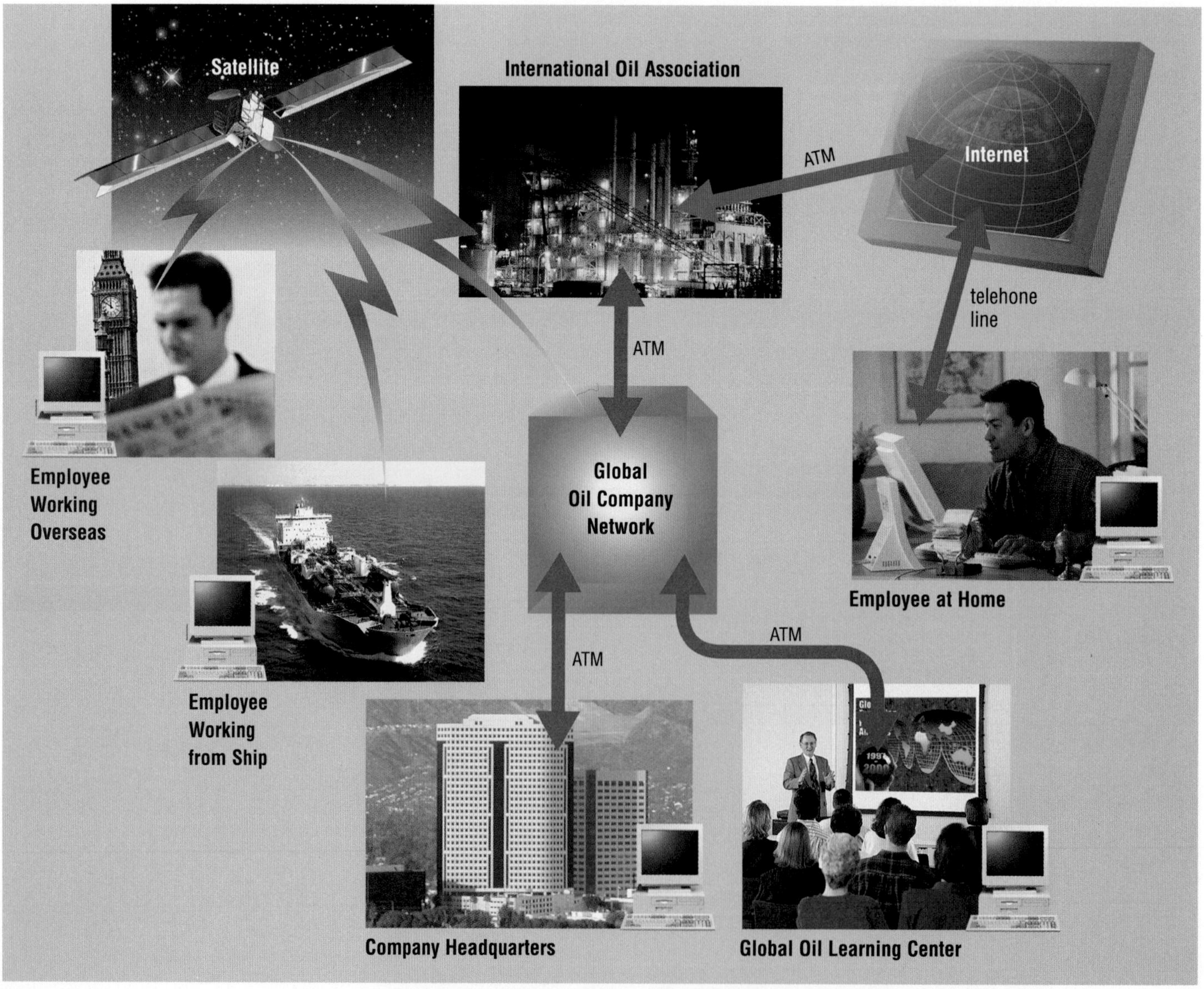

Figure 11-10 A global oil company may use the Internet and its own network to ensure that it can train personnel, regardless of where they are working.

Digital Divide

A major concern of the United States government and many citizens around the world is the digital divide. The digital divide is the idea that you can separate people of the world into two distinct groups: (1) those who have access to technology with the ability to use it and (2) those who do not have access to technology or are without the ability to use it. In this definition, technology includes items such as telephones, television, computers, and the Internet.

Some of the less fortunate people in the world are not able to take advantage of the very technology that makes much of our society prosper and grow. A recent study shows the 20 largest cities of the United States receive 86% of Internet delivery. Given this statistic, people living in cities have access to more technology than those living in rural areas. This is just one example of a digital divide.

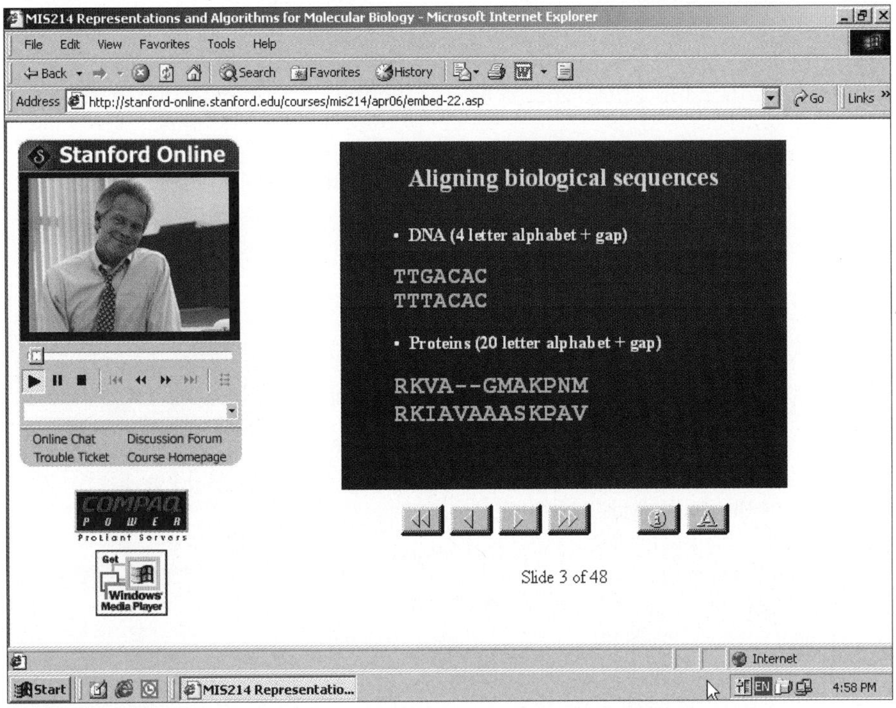

Figure 11-11 Many colleges offer courses in a distance learning format.

Figure 11-12 Many edutainment applications entertain children while they learn.

COMPANY ON THE CUTTING EDGE

WebCT™ courses · campus · community

Enriching Learning Experiences

If you have taken online courses, chances are you have encountered WebCT.

This tool helps teachers develop sophisticated Internet learning environments for their classes. WebCT features educational and administrative tools, such as conferencing systems, chat rooms, e-mail, and group presentation areas, and a design interface that includes color schemes and layouts. More than 7 million students in 57 countries have WebCT accounts.

Murray Goldberg developed WebCT for his own use during his first year teaching in the computer science department at the University of British Columbia. He had earned bachelor's and master's degrees in computer science and wanted to combine his passion for this discipline with his love of teaching. WebCT enabled him to prepare his Web-based courses effectively and allowed his students to experience the richness of the Web.

The software was a success, and Goldberg won the University Teaching Prize during his first year on staff. He currently studies how students use and react to the World Wide Web.

For more information on WebCT, visit the Discovering Computers 2002 Companies Web page (**scsite.com/dc2002/companies.htm**) and click WebCT.

Some people refer to the digital divide as separating the *haves* from the *have-nots*. As shown in the table in Figure 11-13, a variety of *have* and *have-not* categories exist.

To narrow the gap in the digital divide, the United States government and many organizations have efforts underway. Microsoft and Toshiba launched an **Anytime Anywhere Learning program** that provides teachers and students with notebook computers equipped with the Microsoft Office suite and the capability to access the Internet. Microsoft has distributed more than 125,000 notebook computers in this program.

Gateway launched a Teach America! program that provides online computer training to 75,000 teachers. Gateway also donated 50,000 computers to **PowerUp**, a nationwide industry partnership whose goal is to place technology in schools and community centers. AOL offered 100,000 free Internet access accounts at PowerUp sites. Hewlett-Packard is investing $5 million into a building dedicated to provide technology training to low-income Californians. The Federal Communications Commission offered telephone service to Native Americans for $1 per month. The list goes on (Figure 11-14).

Society is attempting to make technology accessible to everyone, including those with disabilities.

ISSUE

A Storm of Change

Education

Many educators praise the use of technology in education. We now see computers moving from computer labs to the classroom. Computer-based training (CBT) is all the rage and appears to be the answer for many students, especially those that need extra help. On the other hand, another group of educators vehemently disagree with CBT. They argue no evidence exists to support CBT, and this flood of technology into the classroom may be detracting from basic subjects. What is your opinion of CBT? Do you think it is effective? Why or why not?

Distance learning (DL) is another hotly debated educational topic. The following findings are from research reports comparing traditional learning with online learning: "There were no significant differences in the test scores for the classes measured and more than 85 percent of faculty felt that student learning outcomes in online education were comparable or better to those found in face-to-face classrooms." Do you agree with these findings? Does a college degree earned online have the same educational value as one earned in the classroom? Can one learn as much in an online course as in a traditional course?

For more information on education, computer-based training, and distance learning, visit the Discovering Computers 2002 Issues Web page (**scsite.com/dc2002/issues.htm**) and click Chapter 11 Issue #2.

SOCIETY'S GOAL: TO BRIDGE THE DIGITAL DIVIDE

Haves (have access to technology and have the ability to use it)
• Cities
• Educated people
• Upper income families
• More industrially developed nations
• Nonminority neighborhoods
• People without disabilities

Figure 11-13 The digital divide recognizes that some of the less fortunate people in the world are not able to take advantage of technology. Society's goal is to narrow the gap, or bridge the divide, between the haves and have-nots.

Figure 11-14 These junior high school students use handheld computers to take notes, download assignments, write papers, and relay information to and from each other's computers.

Due to the efforts of many public and private organizations, blind or visually impaired people can have Web pages read out loud. Web pages can display captions for deaf and hard-of-hearing individuals. Those with significant disabilities can type or control a pointer on the screen with eye movements and brain waves. These amazing technologies are becoming available in schools, work, and home environments so that people with disabilities may have equal access to computers and the Internet.

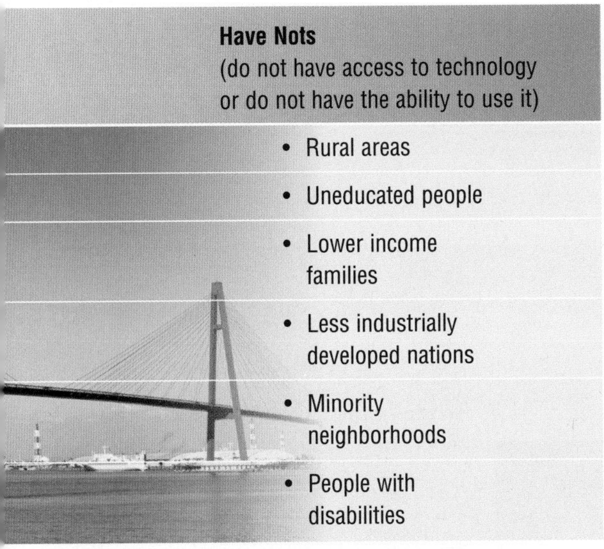

Entertainment

In the past, you played board games with friends and family members, viewed fine art in an art gallery, listened to music on your stereo, watched a movie at a theater or on television, and inserted pictures into sleeves of photo albums. Today, you can have a much more fulfilling experience in each of these areas of entertainment.

In addition to playing exciting, action-packed, 3-D multiplayer games, you can find hours of entertainment on the computer. For example, you can make a family tree, read a book or magazine online, listen to music on the computer, watch a video or movie on the computer, compose a video, edit photographs, plan a vacation, and countless other activities. These forms of entertainment are available on CD-ROM, DVD-ROM, and also on the Web.

On the Web, you can view images of fine art in online museums, galleries, and centers (Figure 11-15). Some artists sell their works online. Others display them for your viewing pleasure.

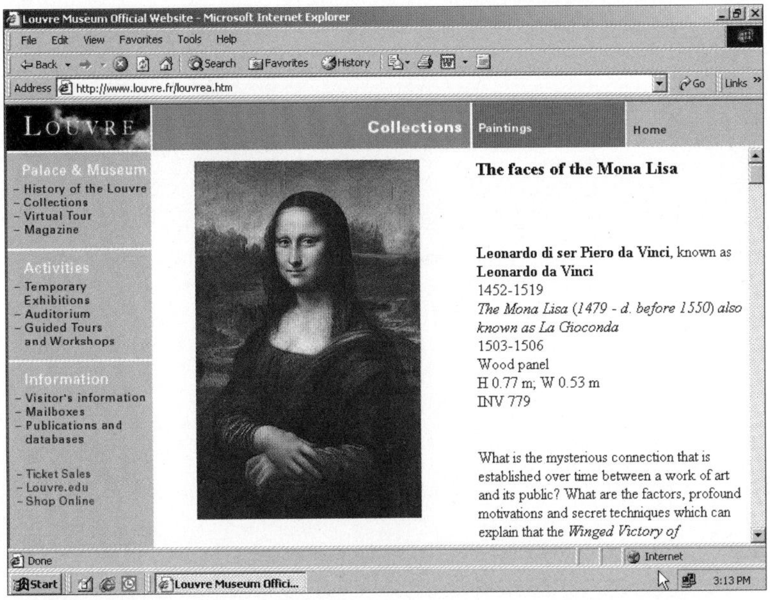

Figure 11-15 Fine art galleries, such as the Louvre, display works online for your enjoyment.

ISSUE

How Big Is the Gap?

Digital Divide

For many, the Internet has ushered in the greatest period of wealth creation in history. Those without Internet access are not quite so fortunate because they are on the other side of the digital divide. This group has less opportunity to take part in our new information-based economy in which many jobs are related to computers. These individuals also have less opportunity to participate in other online educational and online training activities. Does the digital divide exist? How big is the divide? What groups are most likely to be affected by the divide? What can be done to help individuals cross the divide? Is this problem confined to the United States or is it global? Will technology-rich countries continue to thrive even more because of the divide?

For more information on the digital divide, visit the Discovering Computers 2002 Issues Web page (**scsite.com/dc2002/issues.htm**) and click Chapter 11 Issue #3.

You have several options if you wish to listen to music while working on the computer. Insert your favorite music CD into the CD or DVD drive on your computer and listen while you work. Visit an online radio station to hear music (Figure 11-16), news, and sporting events. At some of these sites, you even can watch videos of artists as they sing or play their songs.

Instead of driving to the music store or video store to purchase music or movies, you can buy them on the Web. After paying for the music or movie online, you download it to your hard disk. Once on your hard disk, you listen to the music or watch the movie on the computer. Or, you can transfer it to a CD using a CD-RW and play the music on any audio CD player or the movie on a DVD player.

Some people prefer to create their own music or movies. You can compose music and other sound effects using external devices such as an electric piano keyboard or synthesizer. You also can transfer or create movies by connecting a video camera to the computer. Once on the computer, the music or movies are ready for editing, e-mailing, or posting to a Web page.

Instead of creating digital music or movies, you may wish to create digital photographs. A **digital camera** allows you to take pictures and store the photographed images digitally, instead of on traditional film. Digital cameras can save the expense of film developing, duplication, and postage. You can share digital images with family, friends, co-workers, and clients by posting the photographs on a Web site or e-mailing them. You also can add dazzling special effects and print multiple copies of an image from the comfort of your home or office.

ISSUE

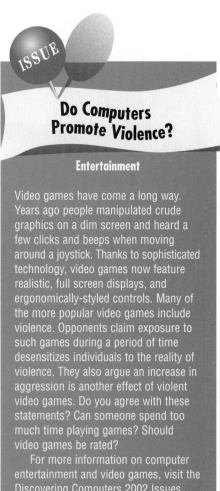

Do Computers Promote Violence?

Entertainment

Video games have come a long way. Years ago people manipulated crude graphics on a dim screen and heard a few clicks and beeps when moving around a joystick. Thanks to sophisticated technology, video games now feature realistic, full screen displays, and ergonomically-styled controls. Many of the more popular video games include violence. Opponents claim exposure to such games during a period of time desensitizes individuals to the reality of violence. They also argue an increase in aggression is another effect of violent video games. Do you agree with these statements? Can someone spend too much time playing games? Should video games be rated?

For more information on computer entertainment and video games, visit the Discovering Computers 2002 Issues Web page (**scsite.com/dc2002/issues.htm**) and click Chapter 11 Issue #4.

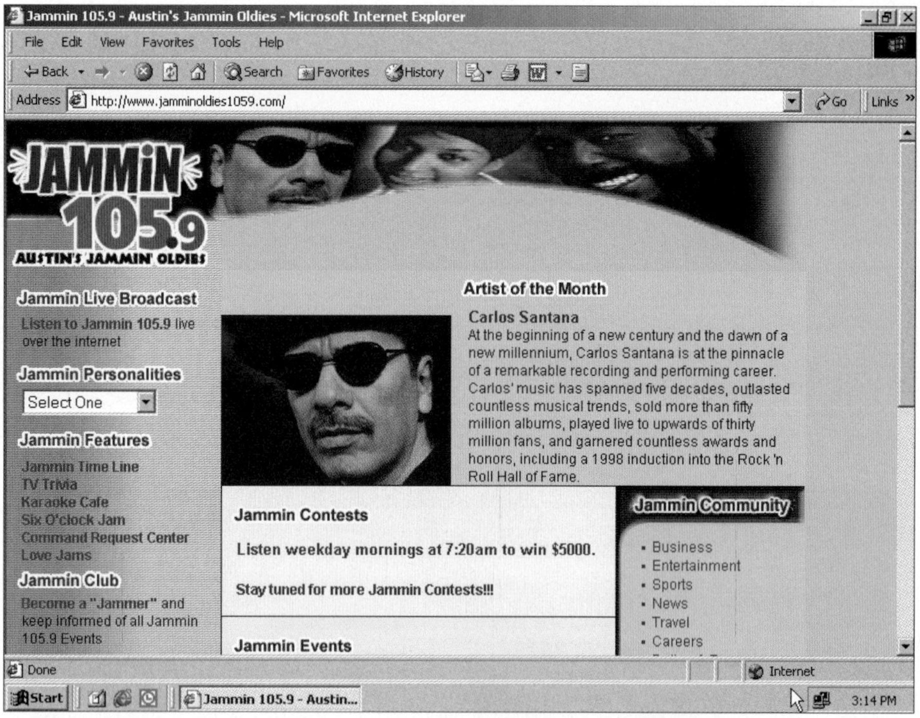

Figure 11-16 Many radio stations have online broadcasts for your listening pleasure.

E-Commerce

Electronic commerce, also know as **e-commerce**, is a financial business transaction that occurs over an electronic network such as the Internet. Anyone with access to a computer, an Internet connection, and a means to pay for purchased goods or services can participate in e-commerce (Figure 11-17). In the past, e-commerce transactions were conducted primarily through desktop computers. Today, many mobile computers and devices also can access the Web wirelessly. These include notebook computers, handheld computers, pagers, and cellular telephones.

E-commerce has changed the way businesses conduct business. It virtually eliminates the barriers of time and distance that slow traditional transactions. Now, with e-commerce, transactions can occur instantaneously and globally. This saves time for participants on both ends.

One of the most popular uses of e-commerce is shopping. You can purchase just about any good or service on the Web. Examples include flowers, books, groceries, computers, prescription drugs, music, movies, cars, airline tickets, and concert tickets.

Figure 11-17 To participate in e-commerce, you need a computer that has Internet access and a means to pay for purchased goods or services.

Users purchase items through an electronic storefront or an online auction. A customer visits the online business through its electronic storefront. An **electronic storefront** contains descriptions, graphics, and a shopping cart. A **shopping cart** allows you to collect purchases (Figure 11-18a). When ready to complete the sale, the customer enters personal and financial data through a secure Web connection. With an **online auction**, you bid on an item (Figure 11-18b). The highest bidder at the end of the bidding period purchases the item.

In the past, merchants shipped goods to a specified location such as your house. Today, merchants can deliver some items directly to your handheld computer or device such as a cellular telephone or pager. For example, you can purchase a movie ticket on the Web and store the ticket on your handheld computer. When you wish to see the movie, a device at the movie theater wirelessly collects the ticket from your handheld device. Airline tickets, event tickets, train tickets, and coupons are just a few other examples of uses of this short range wireless communications technology, called **Bluetooth**™.

Another popular e-commerce activity is managing finances. The next section discusses this activity.

Finance

Many people today use computers to help them manage their finances (Figure 11-19). Some use **personal finance software** to balance their checkbook, pay bills, track personal income and expenses, track investments, and evaluate financial plans. Most of these packages offer a variety of online services. For example, you can track investments online, compare insurance rates from leading insurance companies, and do online banking. With **online banking**, you transfer money electronically from your account to a payee's account or download monthly transactions from the Web right into your computer.

ISSUE

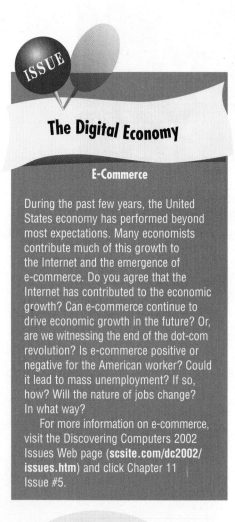

The Digital Economy

E-Commerce

During the past few years, the United States economy has performed beyond most expectations. Many economists contribute much of this growth to the Internet and the emergence of e-commerce. Do you agree that the Internet has contributed to the economic growth? Can e-commerce continue to drive economic growth in the future? Or, are we witnessing the end of the dot-com revolution? Is e-commerce positive or negative for the American worker? Could it lead to mass unemployment? If so, how? Will the nature of jobs change? In what way?

For more information on e-commerce, visit the Discovering Computers 2002 Issues Web page (**scsite.com/dc2002/issues.htm**) and click Chapter 11 Issue #5.

Web Link

For more information on Bluetooth™, visit the Discovering Computers 2002 Chapter 11 WEB LINK page (**scsite.com/dc2002/ch11/weblink.htm**) and click Bluetooth™.

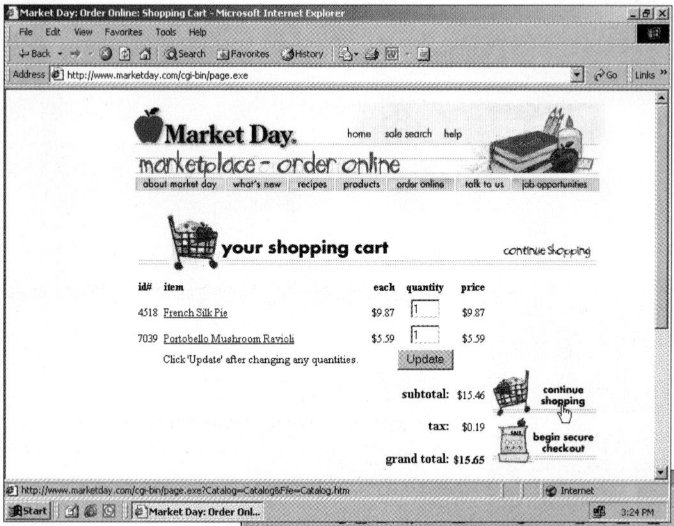

Figure 11-18a (shopping cart at electronic storefront)

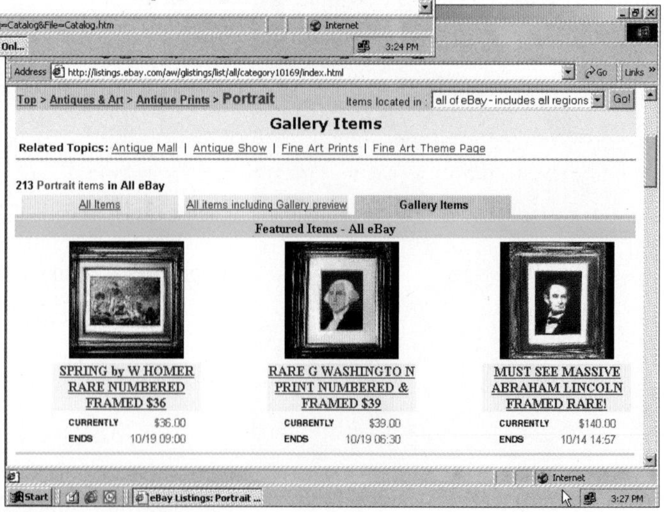

Figure 11-18b (online auction)

Figure 11-18 A shopping cart at an electronic storefront and an online auction.

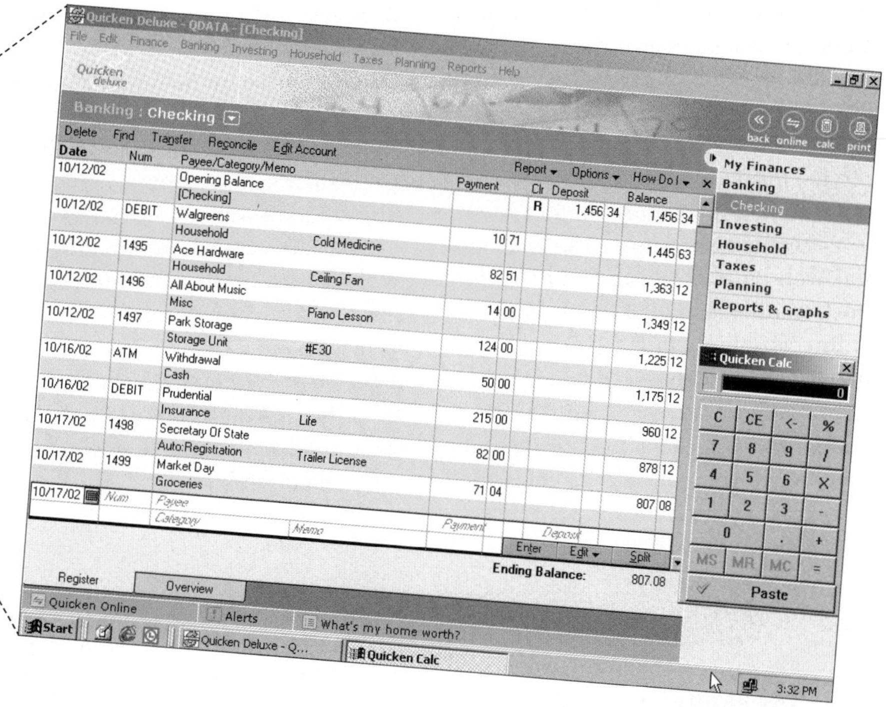

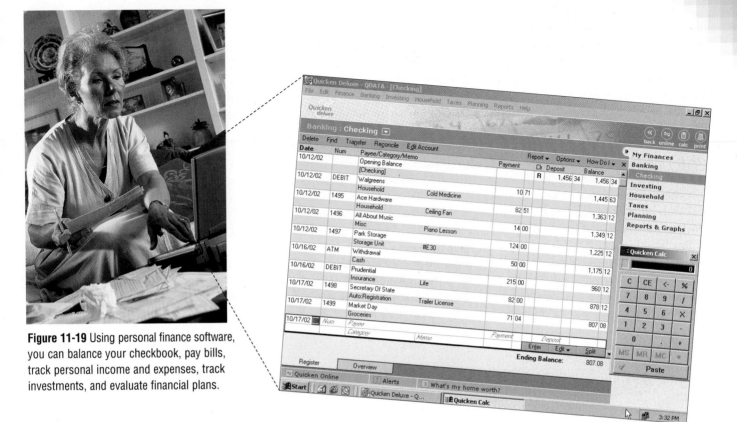

Figure 11-19 Using personal finance software, you can balance your checkbook, pay bills, track personal income and expenses, track investments, and evaluate financial plans.

Many financial institutions offer Web-based online banking. The difference between these Web sites and personal finance software is all your account information is stored on the bank's computer. The advantage is you can access your information from anywhere in the world. From these Web sites, you can transfer money electronically to payees' accounts and view current statements and account balances (Figure 11-20).

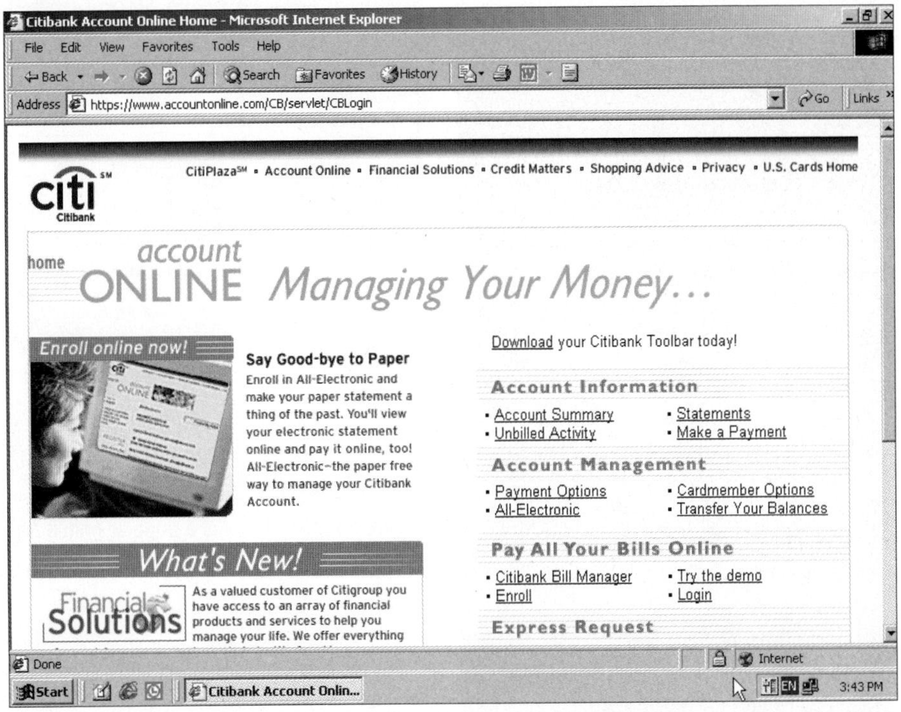

Figure 11-20 Many financial institutions offer Web-based online banking. For example, at Citibank Account Online, you can view credit card transactions, make a payment, view a statement, pay bills, and transfer balances.

Many of these Web-based financial institutions also allow you to transfer funds from one individual to another. Using a computer or Web-enabled cellular telephone, you can transfer money from your credit card, debit card, or checking account to another person's credit card or bank account. Individuals use this service for monetary gifts. Companies use it for rebates and refunds.

One of the fastest growing financial Web-based applications is online stock trading (Figure 11-21). With **online stock trading**, you can buy and sell stocks online — without using a broker. Many investors prefer online stock trading because the transaction fee for each trade usually is substantially less than when you trade through a broker.

Government

A government provides society with direction by making and administering policies. Many people associate government with executive, judicial, and legislative offices. The United States government also includes areas such as law enforcement, employment, military, national security, and taxes. To provide citizens with up-to-date information, most government offices have Web sites (Figure 11-22). A recent survey estimated that about 62 percent of people in the United States access online government Web sites.

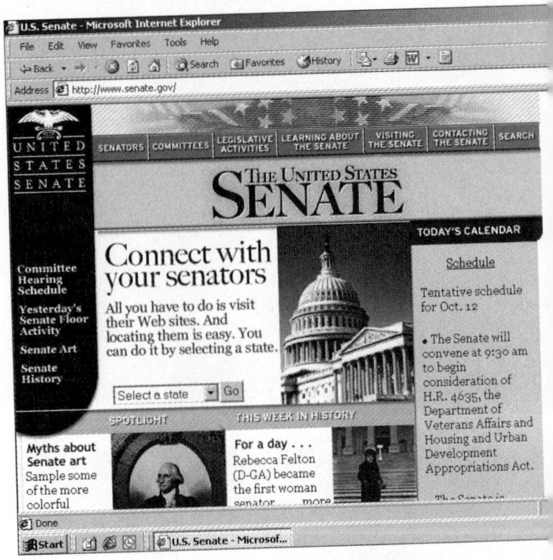

Figure 11-22 Most United States government offices have Web sites that provide you with information.

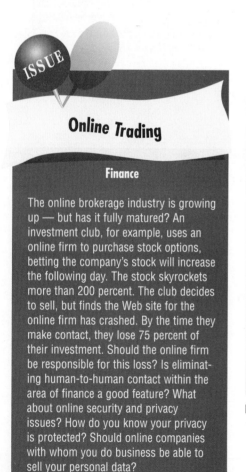

ISSUE

Online Trading

Finance

The online brokerage industry is growing up — but has it fully matured? An investment club, for example, uses an online firm to purchase stock options, betting the company's stock will increase the following day. The stock skyrockets more than 200 percent. The club decides to sell, but finds the Web site for the online firm has crashed. By the time they make contact, they lose 75 percent of their investment. Should the online firm be responsible for this loss? Is eliminating human-to-human contact within the area of finance a good feature? What about online security and privacy issues? How do you know your privacy is protected? Should online companies with whom you do business be able to sell your personal data?

For more information on finance and online trading, visit the Discovering Computers 2002 Issues Web page (**scsite.com/dc2002/issues.htm**) and click Chapter 11 Issue #6.

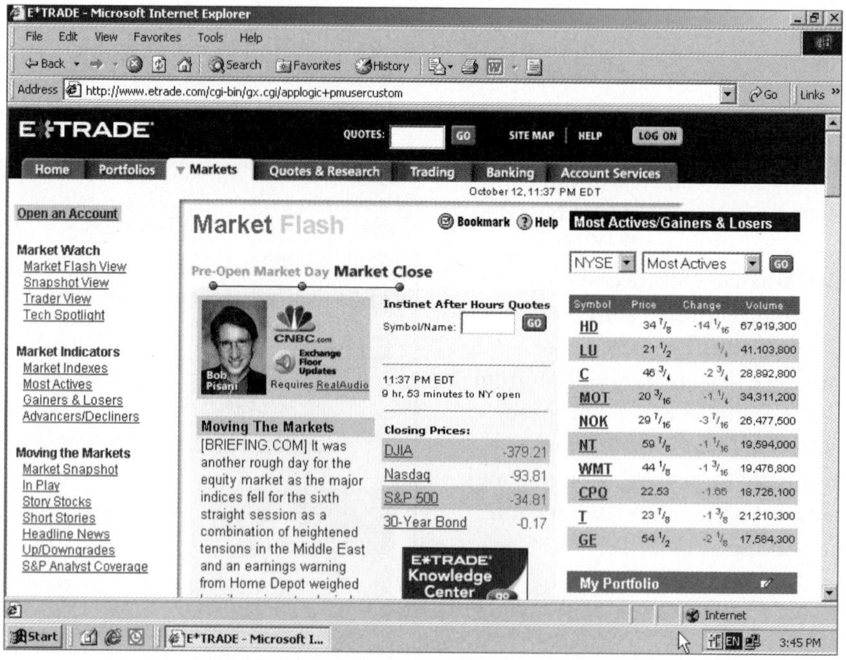

Figure 11-21 E*Trade is a popular online trading application.

APPLY IT!

Your Government

Are you interested in a particular piece of federal, state, or local legislation and would like to know the status or other information about this matter? Do you have a political issue on which you would like to express your opinion to a local or state government representative? Perhaps you would like to contact a member of Congress for your state. Or, maybe you want to go straight to the top and send a message to the President of the United States. Not too many years ago, these were somewhat difficult tasks. The Internet changed all that. Today, Web sites exist for most government agencies. They provide a gateway to legislation and other relevant information. Contacting a government official is as simple as sending an e-mail message. The key to all of this is knowing the Web sites, URLs, and the e-mail addresses of the officials whom you wish to contact.

- The National Political Index (see URL below) provides a comprehensive index and links to more than 3,500 local, state, and government Web sites.
- The Contacting the Congress site (see URL below) provides resources on Congress and other federal government agencies. You can find e-mail addresses for all members of Congress and other federal agencies.
- To contact a senator, or find more information about the Senate, try The United States Senate site (see URL below).
- The Thomas Legislative Information site (see URL below) provides up-to-date information on legislative activity.
- At the Whitehouse site (see URL below), you will find information on how to contact the President, Vice President, their spouses, and links to other federal agencies.
- The Library of Congress (see URL below) provides a meta index for state and local government information as well as links to the Library of Congress.

For more information on government agencies and the Web sites mentioned above, visit the Discovering Computers 2002 Apply It Web page (**scsite.com/dc2002/apply.htm**) and click Chapter 11 Apply It #1.

In addition to providing information via computers, employees of government agencies use computers as part of their daily routine (Figure 11-23). North American 911 call centers use computers to dispatch calls for fire, police, and medical assistance. Law enforcement officers have online access to the FBI's National Crime Information Center (NCIC) through the police cars equipped with computers and fingerprint scanners. The NCIC contains more than 10 million criminal records, including names, fingerprints, parole/probation records, mug shots, and other pertinent information.

More than 210 million Americans interact with the government every year. They file taxes, apply for permits and licenses, pay parking tickets, buy stamps, and renew automobile registrations and driver's licenses. Some companies provide these government services on the Web, allowing the public to complete these transactions online (Figure 11-24).

ISSUE

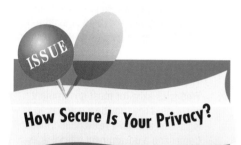

How Secure Is Your Privacy?

Government Records

Government records within a democratic society are public. Virtually every major change in life is recorded somewhere in a government document. Shortly after you are born, a birth certificate is issued; if you get married or divorced, buy a house, file a lawsuit, all of these events are recorded in public documents. Noncertified copies of these documents are available to anyone. Should there be a restriction on the release of these records? If so, what type of restriction? What about your Social Security number? This is the most frequently used record keeping number in the United States and often is used as your ID in a wide variety of databases. Should you be required to provide your Social Security number to companies? Federal law states that, unless certain circumstances prevail, you are not required to provide your Social Security number to private businesses. Should a private business have the right to refuse to provide you with service if you do not give them the number?

For more information on government records and privacy, visit the Discovering Computers 2002 Issues Web page (**scsite.com/dc2002/issues.htm**) and click Chapter 11 Issue #7.

Figure 11-23a (911 call center operators)

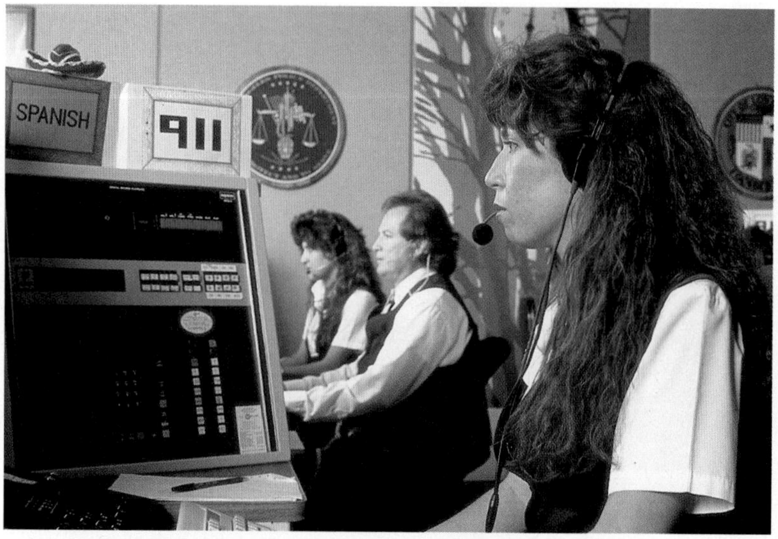

Figure 11-23b (law enforcement officer)

Figure 11-23 Many government employees use computers.

Health Care

Nearly every aspect of the medical field uses computers (Figure 11-25). Whether you are visiting a family physician for a regular checkup, having lab work or an outpatient test, or being rushed in for emergency surgery, the medical staff around you will be using computers for various purposes:

- Hospitals and doctors maintain patient records on computers.
- Computers monitor patients' vital signs in hospital rooms and at home.
- Doctors use the Web and specialized medical software to assist them in research and diagnosing medical conditions.
- Pharmacists use computers to file insurance claims.
- Computers and computerized devices assist doctors, nurses, and technicians with medical tests.
- Doctors use e-mail to communicate with patients.
- Surgeons implant computerized devices, such as pacemakers, that allow patients to live longer lives.
- Surgeons use computer-controlled devices to provide them with greater precision during operations, such as for laser eye surgery and robot-assisted heart surgery.

Another exciting development in the medical field is telemedicine. As a result of joint efforts of medical societies, the government, communications companies, and Internet service providers, **telemedicine** affords health-care professionals and consumers access to medical care through computers with videoconferencing capabilities.

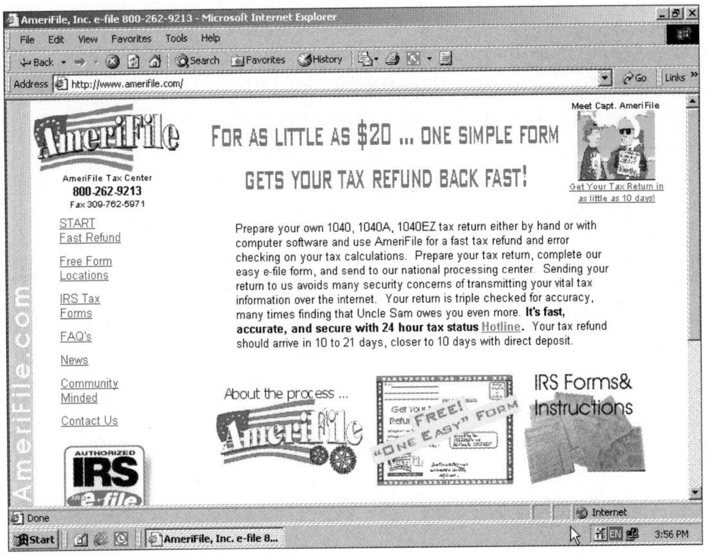

Figure 11-24 This Web site allows you to file income taxes.

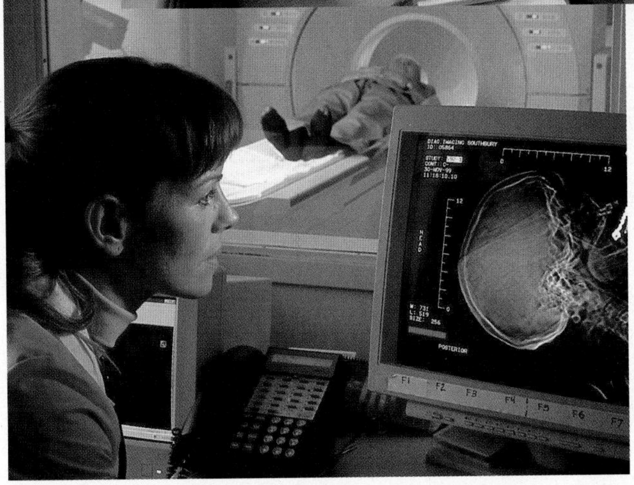

Figure 11-25 Nearly every aspect of the medical field uses computers. Shown here is a pharmacist checking patient records and a lab technician monitoring an MRI.

Web Link

For more information on telemedicine, visit the Discovering Computers 2002 Chapter 11 WEB LINK page (**scsite.com/dc2002/ch11/weblink.htm**) and click Telemedicine.

As shown in Figure 11-26, a doctor at one location can have a videoconference with a doctor at another location to discuss a bone x-ray, which also displays on the computer screen. In essence, telemedicine is long-distance health care. Areas such as medical training, research, collaboration, decision making, and treatment are using telemedicine.

Prior to performing surgery on live humans, many surgeons use computer-aided surgery while they are in training. **Computer-aided surgery** (**CAS**) involves using computer simulations to assist in learning surgical techniques. Other medical professionals, such as physicians and dentists, use some form of computer-aided learning (CAL) program during training. CAS and CAL programs allow professionals in the medical field to practice procedures before actually performing them on human patients.

Many times you leave a doctor's office or hospital with a diagnosis and a prescription in hand. On the way home, you stop at the pharmacy to have the prescription filled. If you would like more information about your diagnosis, you could read a medical dictionary or attend a seminar. You also can use the Web for these purposes (Figure 11-27). Many Web sites provide up-to-date medical, fitness, nutrition, or exercise information. These Web sites also maintain databases of doctors and dentists to help you find the one that suits your

ISSUE

Protecting Electronic Health Information

Health Care

Societies that value privacy, but keep records of transactions or activities, are concerned about possible invasions of privacy. Medical records are becoming fully computerized. Government and private forces are pushing for standardization on a single identifier, such as the Social Security number (SSN) to index all medical records. The American College of Medical Informatics concluded the most expedient way to identify patient records is the Social Security number. Opponents argue the more threatening consequence of large, insecure databases is the ability to search for groups of previously anonymous people with certain characteristics. Will the privacy and security of an individual's medical history be compromised through the use of the SSN? What preventative measures could be used to protect an individual's privacy? Should an identifier other than the SSN be used for medical records? Should federal regulations protect the privacy of electronically stored medical records?

For more information on health and privacy, visit the Discovering Computers 2002 Issues Web page (**scsite.com/dc2002/issues.htm**) and click Chapter 11 Issue #8.

Figure 11-26 Using the capabilities of the Internet, doctors can collaborate online while viewing x-rays and other patient information.

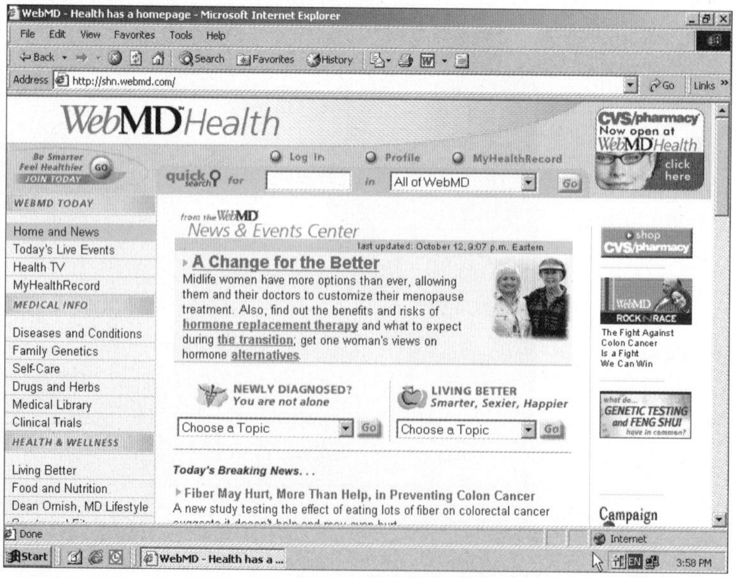

Figure 11-27 Many Web sites disseminate up-to-date health information.

needs. They have chat rooms, so you can talk to others diagnosed with similar conditions. Some Web sites even allow you to order prescription drugs online.

Much of society today is fitness conscious. Diet and exercise have become a part of daily life. Doctors often recommend some type of physical activity along with proper nutrition to maintain a healthy lifestyle. Whether you exercise at the local health club or at home in your basement, the equipment often has a computer built into it to track your progress (Figure 11-28). These computers monitor physical conditions, such as heart rate and pulse, to be sure you are exercising within safe limits.

Science

All branches of science, from biology to chemistry to physics, use computers to assist them with collecting, analyzing, and modeling data (Figure 11-29). Scientists also use the Internet to communicate with colleagues around the world.

Figure 11-28 Exercise equipment often uses computers to track progress and monitor physical conditions such as your heart rate and pulse.

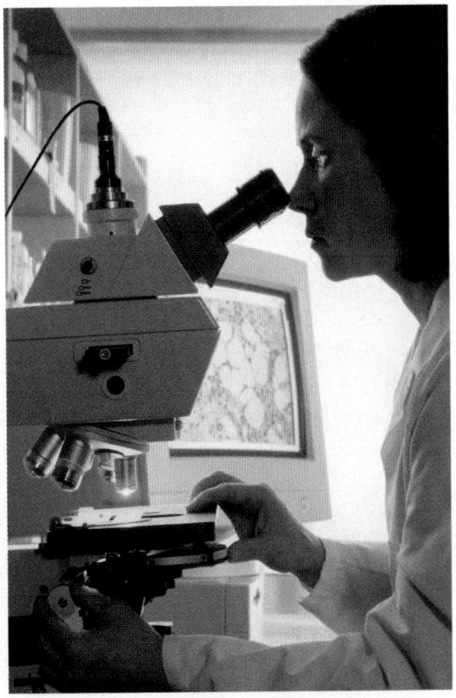

Figure 11-29 Scientists use computers to assist them with collecting, analyzing, and modeling data.

Much of the success related to computers in the medical field is a result of breakthroughs made by scientists. The creation of computer chips that imitate the functions of the retina of the eye, cochlea of the ear, and the central nervous system have led to innovations in surgery, medicine, and treatments. For example, a cochlear implant allows a deaf person to talk and listen (Figure 11-30). Electrodes implanted in the brain can stop tremors associated with Parkinson's disease.

The voice recognition software we use today to speak into the computer is a result of scientific experimentation using neural networks. A **neural network** is a system that attempts to simulate the behavior of the human brain. Scientists create neural networks by connecting thousands of processors together much like the neurons in the brain are connected.

Publishing

Publishing is the process of making a work available to the public. These works include books, magazines, and newspapers. Publishers use computers and associated equipment to perform their daily jobs. They use desktop publishing and graphics software to design pages that include text, graphics, and photographs. Journalists have notebook computers and digital cameras to capture and record news as it occurs.

Many publishers make the content of magazines and newspapers available online (Figure 11-31). Some Web sites allow you to download an entire book to your computer (Figure 11-32). The cost for the electronic book is about the same or less than the cost of purchasing the print version. You can download these **electronic books** (**e-books**) to your desktop, notebook, or handheld computer. Handheld devices specifically designed for reading these electronic books also are available.

ISSUE

Cloning – Are Humans Next?

Science

The successful cloning of Dolly, the sheep, and Millie, the Jersey cow, are dramatic examples of a scientific discovery becoming a public issue. A survey of British medical scientists by The Independent (see URL below) indicates more than 50 percent believe the birth of a cloned baby is inevitable, despite society's current aversion to the idea. Scientists now have stirred up more controversy with the idea of using cells and tissue from human embryos in medical research. Cloned stem cells removed from one-week-old human embryos can be developed into any type of cell such as liver cells, brain cells, or heart cells. These cells then could be inserted into these and other organs of the body to repair damage and treat disease. Do you support cloned cell technology? Should cloned cell technology be legal? Should there be a law against cloning a human? Could you justify cloning if it was the only way for a couple to experience having a child of their own? Will society be able to prevent human cloning?

For more information on science, cloning, and the Web site mentioned above, visit the Discovering Computers 2002 Issues Web page (**scsite.com/dc2002/issues.htm**) and click Chapter 11 Issue #9.

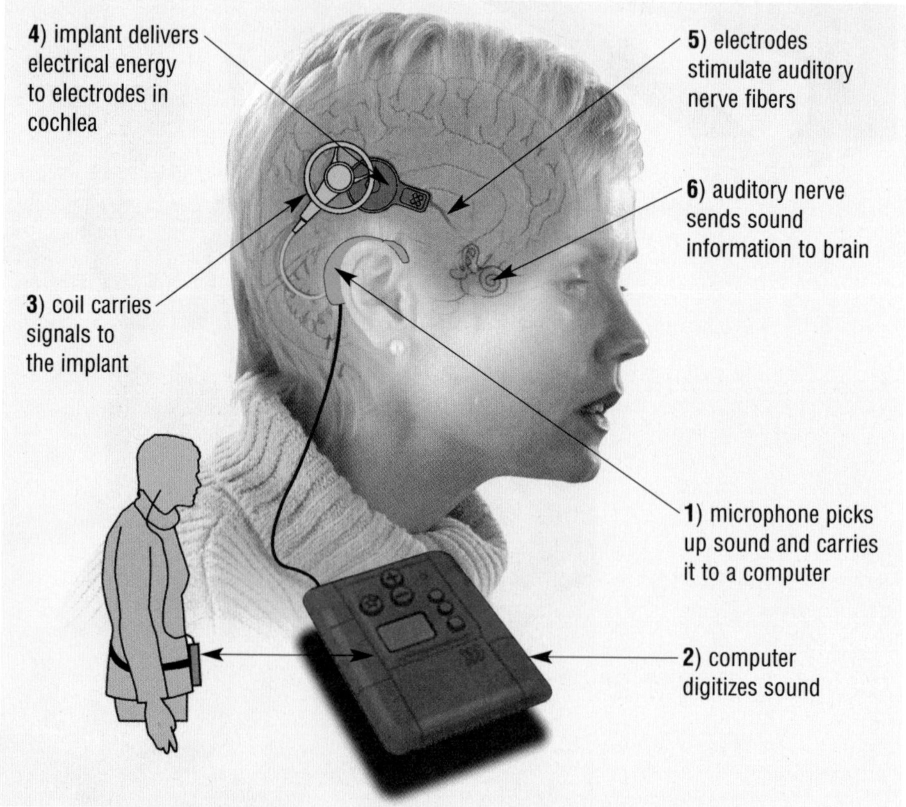
4) implant delivers electrical energy to electrodes in cochlea
5) electrodes stimulate auditory nerve fibers
6) auditory nerve sends sound information to brain
3) coil carries signals to the implant
1) microphone picks up sound and carries it to a computer
2) computer digitizes sound

Figure 11-30 Scientists developed an implant that when placed in the inner ear allows a deaf patient to hear.

Figure 11-31 Many publishers make the content of their magazines and newspapers available online.

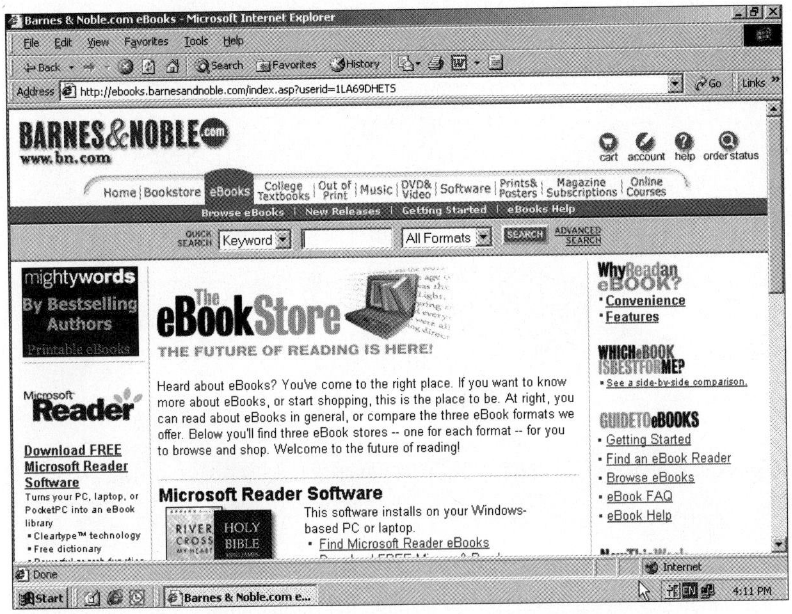

Figure 11-32 One study predicts electronic books will capture one third of the printed book market.

Web Link

For more information on e-books, visit the Discovering Computers 2002 Chapter 11 WEB LINK page (**scsite.com/dc2002/ch11/weblink.htm**) and click E-Books.

COMPANY ON THE CUTTING EDGE

britannica.com

Publishing Information Electronically

All men by nature desire to know, according to Aristotle. For more than two centuries, Britannica editors have been satisfying this quest for information.

In 1768, two men in Edinburgh, Scotland, hired an editor to capture the major developments occurring in the arts and sciences. Three years later, the three-volume *Encyclopædia Britannica* was born. The first printing sold out quickly, leading to subsequent editions. By 1809, the fourth edition of the publication had grown to 20 volumes. In 1974, the 15th edition blossomed to 30 volumes.

The 15th edition, revolutionary in many ways, had been edited and published completely in-house using computers. By creating the first CD-ROM multimedia encyclopedia in 1989 and by putting the entire print version on the Internet in 1993, Britannica has maximized the features of electronic publishing.

Today's Britannica.com contains databases that combine the text of the encyclopedia with more than 125,000 Web sites, 100 million Web pages, articles from the world's leading magazines, current news supplied by washingtonpost.com, stock market updates, weather forecasts, and links to related books that can be ordered online.

For more information on Britannica.com, visit the Discovering Computers 2002 Companies Web page (**scsite.com/dc2002/companies.htm**) and click Britannica.com.

Web bar codes are another recent development that link printed media to the Web. Newspapers, magazines, books, and postcards display these bar codes throughout the printed pages. Using a handheld scanner connected to your computer, you scan the bar code to display a related Web page on your computer screen.

Travel

Whether traveling by car or airplane, your goal is to arrive safely at your destination. As you make the journey, you may interact with some of the latest technology.

Many vehicles manufactured today include some type of onboard navigation facility (Figure 11-33). These cars have a **GPS (global positioning system)** receiver that reports your car's location via satellites. Depending on the one you choose, the onboard navigation systems offer the consumer many worthwhile features:

- Provide you with directions
- Automatically call for help if your airbag deploys and you do not respond to voice contact
- Provide emergency services as soon as you press the emergency button
- Dispatch roadside assistance
- Perform remote diagnostics if a warning light appears on the dashboard
- Unlock the driver's side door if you lock the keys in the car
- Make hotel and restaurant reservations
- Track the vehicle if it is stolen
- Honk the horn to help you locate the car in a parking lot

The fee for an onboard navigation system varies by manufacturer.

The search for a new or used car to meet your needs no longer has to involve driving from one car dealership to another. Instead, you

Figure 11-33 Many vehicles made by General Motors are equipped with an onboard safety, security, and information service called OnStar. By pushing the OnStar button, you immediately connect to an OnStar advisor.

ISSUE

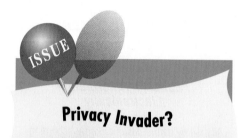

Privacy Invader?

Publishing

First the mouse and now the cat, CueCat that is! This free, handheld device attaches to your computer. Instead of typing in a Web site address, you use the Cat to scan bar codes in magazines and other marketing promotions. Using the CueCat involves a lengthy installation process requiring the user to submit personal information to receive an authentication code. Many people contend it is not consumer convenience driving this promotion, but rather marketing mania. On the Web, it is easy to track those who click the Web advertisements. Bar code scanning would provide the capability to track print advertisements. Do you agree the CueCat is more of a marketing gadget to track advertisement response? Is using Web bar codes to track people's Web behavior an invasion of privacy? Should you have to provide personal information before you can use a device such as the CueCat? Do you think the CueCat will become the biggest computer innovation since the mouse?

For more information on publishing, Web bar code tracking, and the CueCat, visit the Discovering Computers 2002 Issues Web page (**scsite.com/dc2002/issues.htm**) and click Chapter 11 Issue #10.

can shop online for your next car (Figure 11-34). In addition to locating and delivering cars for customers, these sites offer services such as loans, leases, insurance, and warranties. Many allow you to sell a used car as well.

If you plan to drive somewhere and are unsure of the path to take to your destination, you can print directions and a map from the Web. By entering the starting address and ending address, the Web site generates the best route for your trip.

Many vehicles today also include options such as screens with e-mail and Internet access, printers, and fax capability. Airlines also are joining the online forces. Airplanes equipped with Internet connections allow passengers to connect their notebook or handheld computer to the Web. Some airlines even provide passengers with Web surfing devices during their flight.

In preparing for an upcoming trip, you may need to reserve a car, hotel, or flight. Many Web sites offer these services to the public. For example, you can order airline tickets from any computer connected to the Web through an online travel reservation service and have the tickets waiting for you at the airport or delivered directly to your door (Figure 11-35).

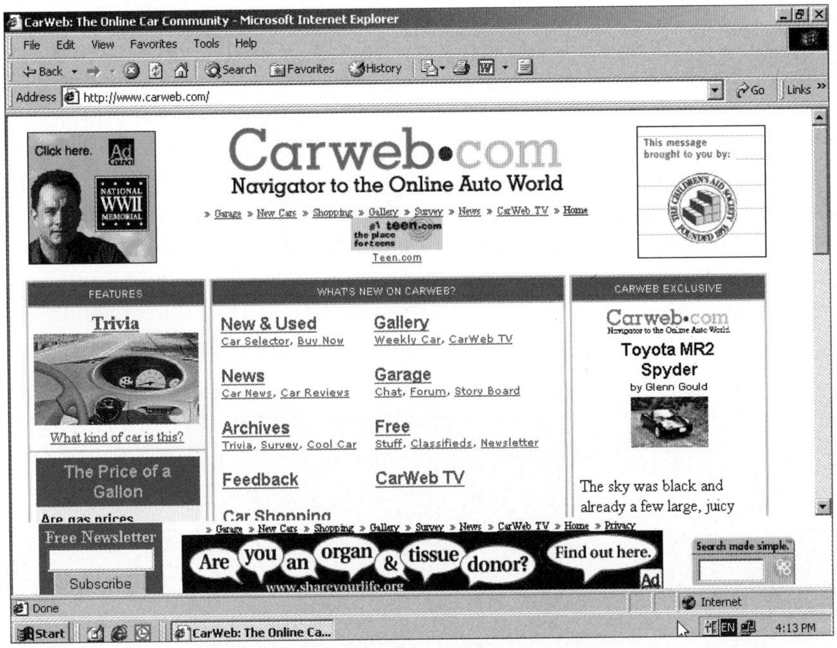

Figure 11-34 You can buy a new or used car online at Web sites such as the one shown in this figure.

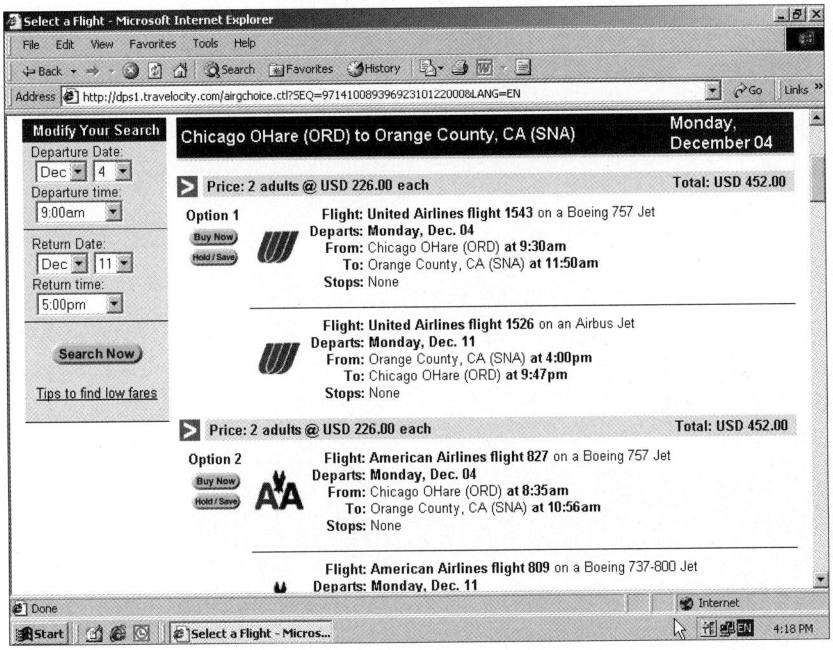

Figure 11-35 You can make car, hotel, and airline reservations directly from the Web.

ISSUE

Online Travel Travails

Travel

A recent study from the Travel Industry Association of America (see URL below) says eight million Americans booked travel on the Web last year. Buying tickets on the Web does have an advantage; the store is open 24 hours a day. What about disadvantages? Some travelers report their ticket price was as high or higher than from a travel agency. Others report with some services they can book a seat online, but when they arrive at the gate, the seat is not valid. Or, the fabulous vacation was not so fabulous, and the five star hotel accommodations were three star. Which is the better option — to use a travel agent or to be your own travel agent via the Web? When using the Web, are people tempted to purchase a trip beyond their budget? Should the online travel agency be responsible if the accommodations are less than advertised? Some online agencies sell your personal data. Should you be concerned about privacy issues?

For more information on online travel and the Web site mentioned above, visit the Discovering Computers 2002 Issues Web page (**scsite.com/ dc2002/ issues.htm**) and click Chapter 11 Issue #11.

ISSUE

The Good Life

Telecommuting

More than 20 million Americans telecommute to work today, up from just 4 million in 1990. Predictions are that number will grow during this decade as advances in technology and more jobs in the digital economy make it possible for more people to work at home. Telecommuting definitely has advantages — but what about disadvantages? For example, out of sight, out of mind. If you are not in the office every day, could you be passed over for a promotion? Where is a worker more productive, at home or in the office? Are there benefits to working at home? If so, what are they?

For more information on telecommuting, visit the Discovering Computers 2002 Issues Web page (**scsite.com/dc2002/issues.htm**) and click Chapter 11 Issue #12.

Web Link

For more information on telecommuting, visit the Discovering Computers 2002 Chapter 11 WEB LINK page (**scsite.com/dc2002/ch11/weblink.htm**) and click Telecommuting.

Telecommuting

Telecommuting is a work arrangement in which employees work away from a company's standard workplace, and often communicate with the office using some communications technology (Figure 11-36). The amount of people that telecommute has exploded in recent years. The number has risen from 4 million in 1990 to more than 20 million today.

Workers telecommute for a variety of reasons:

1. Reduce time and expense spent traveling to the office.
2. Eliminate travel during unsafe weather conditions.
3. Allow a flexible work schedule so that employees can combine work and personal responsibilities, such as childcare.
4. Provide a convenient, comfortable work environment for disabled employees or those recovering from injury or illness.

Employees that telecommute tend to have higher job satisfaction rates and are more productive. Employers benefit from this increase in productivity. Employers also realize a reduction in overhead because telecommuting employees require less office space, furniture, and so on.

Another added benefit of telecommuting is it reduces air pollution caused by vehicles traveling to and from an office. Thus, telecommuting is healthy for the environment.

Figure 11-36 Telecommuting allows you to work from home or some other location away from a main office.

EMERGING TECHNOLOGIES

The previous sections discussed how society uses computers in everyday life. Other specialized applications of computers include virtual reality, intelligent agents, and robotics. In the past, these areas of computer usage were considered *high tech* and not to be used by the average consumer. Today, these amazing technologies are emerging in everyday applications. The following sections discuss each of these emerging technologies.

Virtual Reality

Virtual reality (VR) is the use of computers to simulate a real or imagined environment that appears as a three-dimensional (3-D) space. VR allows you to explore and manipulate controls to experience the 3-D space fully.

On the Web, VR involves the display of 3-D images you can explore and manipulate interactively. Using special VR software, a Web developer creates an entire 3-D site that contains infinite space and depth, called a **VR world**. Many of these worlds provide 360-degree tours of locations such as automobiles, buildings, colleges, sites of interest, and cities (Figure 11-37).

When many people think of virtual reality, they focus on the thrilling aspects of VR games. Virtual reality, however, does have numerous practical applications. Training, engineering, e-commerce, science, and medicine use virtual reality. Many companies use VR simulations to train people that operate expensive and complicated equipment such as airplanes and ships.

Figure 11-37 This virtual reality (VR) tour gives you a 360-degree view of the Kishibo Shrine in Ikebukuro, Tokyo.

In recent years, developers also have created VR simulations for less expensive, simpler equipment such as trucks and construction machinery. Architects use VR to show clients previews of buildings and landscapes. Automobile dealers use VR to create a virtual showroom in which customers can view the exterior and interior of available vehicles. Medical schools also use VR for training — most often to simulate surgery. Several schools even use VR to allow parents and prospective students to take a virtual tour of the school from their home.

Web Link

For more information on virtual reality, visit the Discovering Computers 2002 Chapter 11 WEB LINK page (**scsite.com/dc2002/ch11/weblink.htm**) and click Virtual Reality.

In more advanced forms, VR software requires you to wear specialized headgear, body suits, and gloves to enhance the experience of the simulated environment (Figure 11-38). The headgear displays the artificial environment in front of both of your eyes. As the headgear moves, so do the views on the screens.

A body suit and gloves sense your motion and direction, allowing you to move through and pick up and hold items displayed in the virtual environment. Experts predict that eventually the body suits will provide tactile feedback, enabling people to experience the touch and feel of the virtual world.

Intelligent Agents

Artificial intelligence (AI) is the application of human intelligence to computers. AI technology can sense your actions and, based on logical assumptions and prior experience, take the appropriate action to complete a task. For more than 40 years, AI experts promoted the advantages of **smart software**, or software with built-in intelligence. In recent years, this concept has become a reality in the form of intelligent agents.

Figure 11-38 As this pool player looks through virtual reality (VR) goggles at the pool table, a miniature video recorder on the VR goggles sends an image of the pool table to a computer that is in a backpack worn by the pool player. The computer determines the best shot and shows the player exactly how to hit the cue ball by projecting a white line onto the VR goggles that leads from the cue ball to the target ball. A second white line shows the pool player which pocket the ball will drop in if he hits the cue ball along the first white line.

An **intelligent agent** is any software program that independently asks questions, pays attention to work patterns, and carries out tasks on behalf of a user. Many software packages today include intelligent agents. Some e-mail programs allow you to filter incoming messages and request immediate notification if messages arrive with a particular subject or from a certain person. Microsoft Office has IntelliSense™ technology that corrects text as you enter it, organizes and updates your menus and toolbars to display frequently used commands and buttons, and suggests more efficient ways to complete tasks (Figure 11-39).

A **network agent** is a sophisticated type of intelligent agent that performs tasks on remote computers before bringing the results back to the user. You often use a network agent, sometimes called a **bot**, when you search the Web or other networks for information. You could direct a network agent to research all references to Civil War battles in the state of Virginia. Some network agents can learn a user's interests, develop a user profile, search the entire Internet to find relevant documents, and deliver the information to your desktop automatically. For example, you could request to receive an e-mail message whenever a stock alert occurs, the market closes, or a stock price varies greatly.

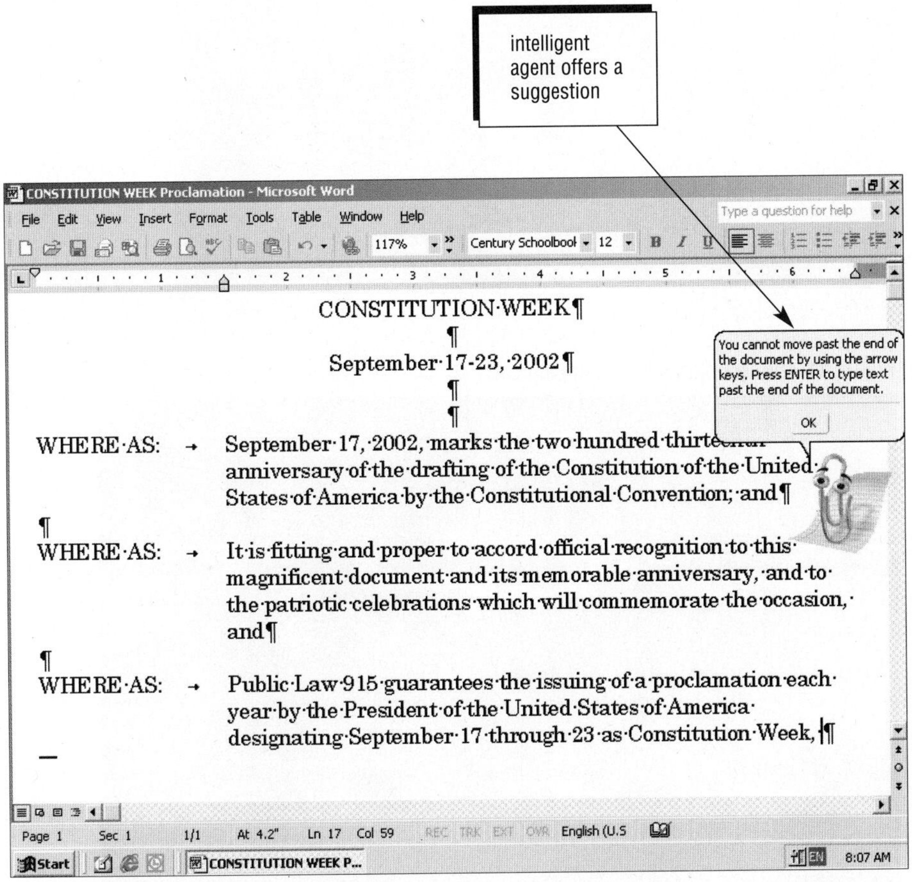

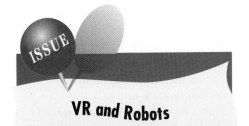

Figure 11-39 Shown here is the Microsoft Office intelligent agent offering a suggestion for a more efficient way to complete a task.

Web Link

For more information on intelligent agents, visit the Discovering Computers 2002 Chapter 11 WEB LINK page (**scsite.com/dc2002/ch11/weblink.htm**) and click Intelligent Agents.

ISSUE

VR and Robots

Emerging Technologies

Manipulation of objects in virtual environments is awkward. The simple task of grabbing and moving a virtual object is difficult because of the lack of tactile feedback and other factors. At the University of Washington (see URL below), the Human Interface Technology Research Lab focuses on human computer interfaces and virtual interface technology. One research project uses virtual reality technology as applied to the design and implementation of medical robotic interfaces. One element of this project is human-controlled robotic surgery. This system contains two components: a master and a slave. The slave is a robotic device that performs the surgery. The master is the human interface that controls the slave. One advantage is in microsurgery where robots perform small, delicate operations that the human hand cannot perform. How practical is this type of research? What are the advantages? Disadvantages? Will microsurgery soon be possible? Would you be willing to be a microsurgery patient? Why or why not?

For more information on emerging technologies and the Web site mentioned above, visit the Discovering Computers 2002 Issues Web page (**scsite.com/dc2002/issues.htm**) and click Chapter 11 Issue #13.

Robots

A **robot** is a computer-controlled device that can move and react to feedback from the outside world (Figure 11-40). In the past, robots were used only in specialized areas. For example, factories have used robots to perform jobs requiring repetitive tasks, lifting heavy equipment, or high degrees of precision.

As the cost of robots drops, more and more homes will be using them as well. For example, AIBO is a dog that has the ability to learn and mature. You send commands to AIBO, such as sit and roll over, through a remote control. AIBO also can play games that other dogs play, such as fetching a stick or a ball.

A more sophisticated robot is the CareBot, which is a mechanical servant on wheels. A personal computer controls the CareBot via radio frequency signals. This advanced technology robot can baby-sit, help older children with homework such as learning Spanish, fetch items such as cans of soda, remind you to take medicine, alert medical authorities if its microphone does not hear a heartbeat, monitor the security system in your home, adjust room temperature, and yes, vacuum. Depending on features, the cost of the CareBot ranges from $2,500 to $4,500.

Web Link

For more information on robotics, visit the Discovering Computers 2002 Chapter 11 WEB LINK page (**scsite.com/dc2002/ch11/weblink.htm**) and click Robotics.

A HEALTHY WORK ENVIRONMENT

This widespread computer use also has led to some important concerns. Long-term computer use can lead to health complications. Be proactive and minimize your chance of risk. The following sections discuss health risks and preventions, along with measures you can take to keep our environment healthy.

Computers and Health Risks

The Bureau of Labor Statistics reports that work-related musculoskeletal disorders account for one-third of all job-related injuries and illnesses. A **musculoskeletal disorder** (**MSD**), also called a **repetitive stress injury** (**RSI**), is an injury or disorder of the muscles, nerves, tendons, ligaments, and joints. Computer-related RSIs include tendonitis and carpal tunnel syndrome.

Figure 11-40a (SR2 security robot)

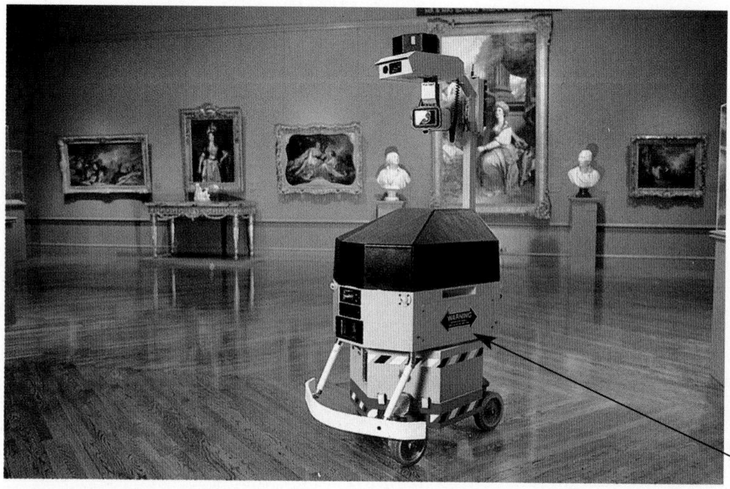

Figure 11-40b (robot pushing shopping cart)

Figure 11-40 Some robots operate by remote control, such as the one shown immediately above that pushes shopping carts. Others use more advanced technology. For example, the SR2 security robot shown in the top photo guards art objects in the Los Angeles County Museum of Art. The SR2 detects motion and warns of intruders. It also detects smoke, fire, and increases in humidity or gases.

RSIs are the largest job-related injury and illness problem in the United States today. For this reason, OSHA (Occupational Safety and Health Administration) has proposed standards whereby employers must establish programs that prevent workplace injuries with respect to computer usage.

Tendonitis is inflammation of a tendon due to some repeated motion or stress on that tendon. **Carpal tunnel syndrome** (**CTS**) is inflammation of the nerve that connects your forearm to the palm of your wrist. Repeated or forceful bending of the wrist can cause CTS or tendonitis of the wrist. Symptoms of tendonitis of the wrist include extreme pain that extends from the forearm to the hand, along with tingling in the fingers. Symptoms of CTS include burning pain when the nerve is compressed, along with numbness and tingling in the thumb and first two fingers.

Long-term computer work can lead to tendonitis or CTS. Factors that cause these disorders include prolonged typing, prolonged mouse usage, or continual shifting between the mouse and the keyboard. If untreated, these disorders can lead to permanent damage to your body.

You can take many precautions to prevent these types of injuries. Take frequent breaks during the computer session to exercise your hands and arms (Figure 11-41). To prevent injury due to typing, place a wrist rest between the keyboard and the edge of your desk. The wrist rest reduces strain on your wrist while typing. To prevent injury while using a mouse, place the mouse at least six inches from the edge of the desk. In this position, your wrist is flat on the desk, which causes bending to occur at the elbow when you move the mouse. Finally, minimize the number of times you switch between the mouse and the keyboard.

Another type of health-related condition due to computer usage is **computer vision syndrome** (**CVS**). You may have CVS if you have any of these conditions: sore, tired, burning, itching, or dry eyes; blurred or double vision; distance vision blurred after prolonged staring at monitor; headache or sore neck; difficulty shifting focus between monitor and documents; difficulty focusing on the screen image; color fringes or afterimages when you look away from the monitor; and increased sensitivity to light. Although eyestrain associated with CVS is not thought to have serious or long-term consequences, it is disruptive and unpleasant. Figure 11-42 outlines some techniques you can follow to ease the eyestrain.

Computer workers also sometimes complain of lower back pain, muscle fatigue, and emotional fatigue. Lower back pain sometimes is caused from poor posture. Always sit properly in the chair while working. Take a break every 30 to 60 minutes — stand up, walk around, or stretch. Another way to help prevent these injuries is to be sure your workplace is designed ergonomically.

HAND EXERCISES

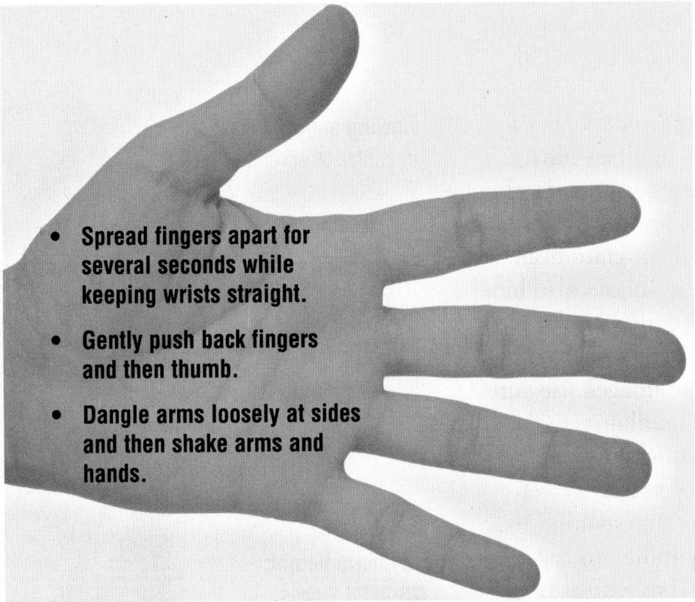
Spread fingers apart for several seconds while keeping wrists straight.
Gently push back fingers and then thumb.
Dangle arms loosely at sides and then shake arms and hands.

Figure 11-41 To reduce the chance of developing tendonitis or carpal tunnel syndrome, take frequent breaks during computer sessions to exercise your hands and arms.

TECHNIQUES TO EASE EYESTRAIN

- Every 10 to 15 minutes, take an eye break.
    - Look into the distance and focus on an object for 20 to 30 seconds.
    - Roll your eyes in a complete circle.
    - Close your eyes and rest them for at least a minute.
- Blink your eyes every five seconds.
- Place your monitor about an arm's length away from your eyes with the top of the screen at eye level or below.
- Use a glare screen.
- Use large fonts.
- If you wear glasses, ask your doctor for computer glasses.
- Adjust the lighting.

Figure 11-42 Following these tips may help to reduce eyestrain while working on the computer.

Ergonomics and Workplace Design

Ergonomics is an applied science devoted to incorporate comfort, efficiency, and safety into the design of items in the workplace. Ergonomic studies have shown that using the correct type and configuration of chair, keyboard, monitor, and work surface will help you work comfortably and efficiently, and help protect your health. For the computer workspace, experts recommend an area of at least two feet by four feet. Figure 11-43 illustrates additional guidelines for setting up the work area.

Many monitors and keyboards have features that help address ergonomic issues. Some keyboards have built-in wrist rests. Others have an ergonomic design specifically to prevent RSI. Most monitors have a tilt-and-swivel base, so you can adjust the angle of the screen to minimize neck strain and reduce glare from overhead lighting. Monitors also have controls that allow you to adjust the brightness, contrast, positioning, height, and width of images. Be sure the monitor you use adheres to the **MPR II standard**, which defines acceptable levels of radiation. Sit at arm's length from the monitor to reduce further any radiation risk, because radiation levels drop dramatically with distance.

Web Link

For more information on ergonomics, visit the Discovering Computers 2002 Chapter 11 WEB LINK page (**scsite.com/dc2002/ch11/weblink.htm**) and click Ergonomics.

Computer Addiction

Computers can provide hours of entertainment and enjoyment. Some people, however, are obsessed with the computer and the Internet. Computer addiction is a growing health problem. **Computer addiction** occurs when the computer consumes someone's entire social life. Users addicted to the Internet are said to have an **Internet addiction disorder** (**IAD**).

Symptoms of computer addiction include the following:

- Craves computer time
- Overjoyed when at the computer
- Unable to stop computer activity
- Irritable when not at the computer
- Neglects family and friends
- Problems at work or school

Computer addiction is a treatable illness through therapy and support groups.

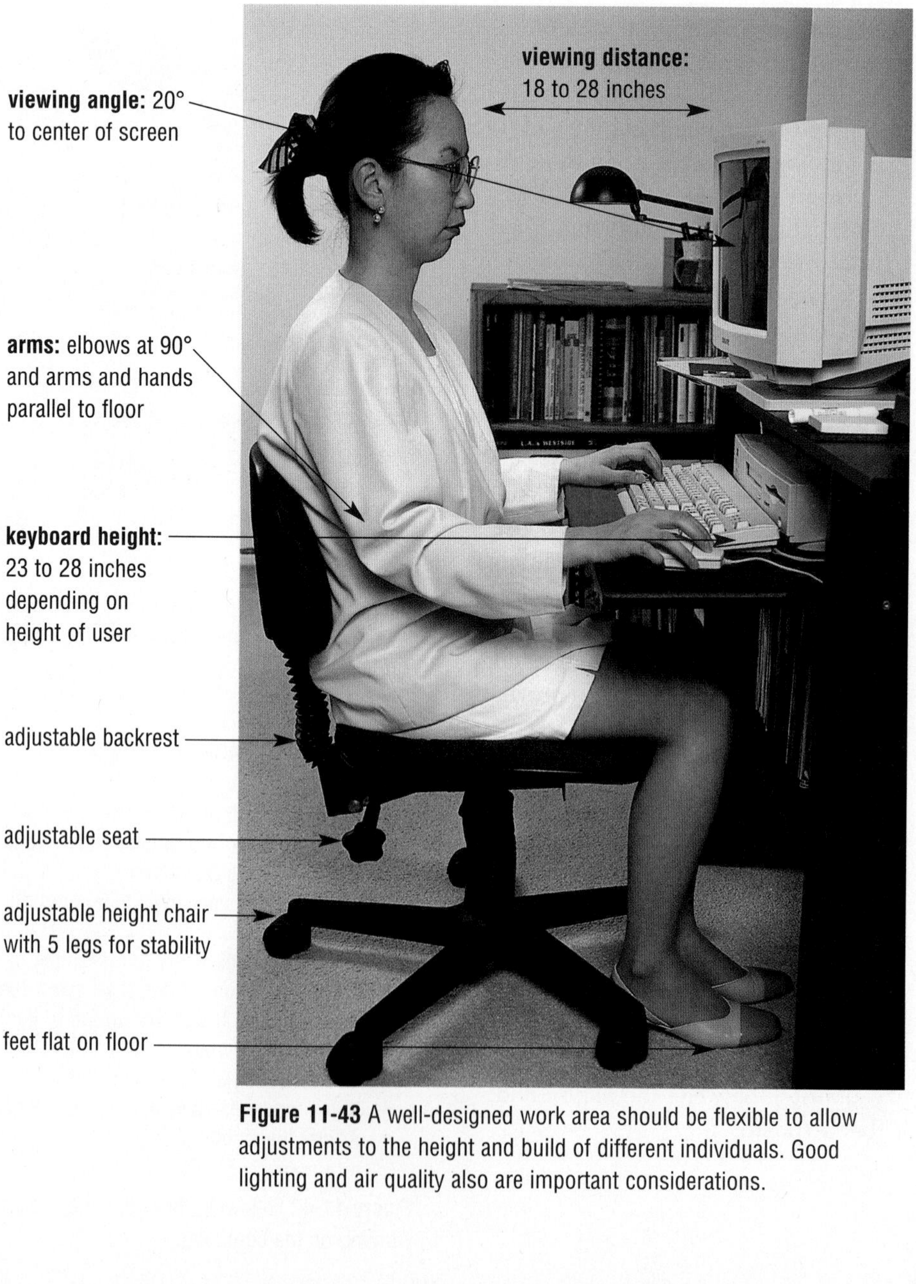

Figure 11-43 A well-designed work area should be flexible to allow adjustments to the height and build of different individuals. Good lighting and air quality also are important considerations.

Green Computing

Green computing involves reducing the electricity and environmental waste while using a computer. Computers use, and often waste, resources such as electricity and paper. Society has become aware of this waste and is taking measures to combat it.

Personal computers, monitors, and printers should comply with the **ENERGY STAR program**, which was developed by the United States Department of Energy (DOE) and the United States Environmental Protection Agency (EPA). This program encourages manufacturers to create energy-efficient devices that require little power when they are not in use. For example, many devices switch to standby mode after a specified number of inactive minutes. Computers and devices that meet ENERGY STAR guidelines display an ENERGY STAR® label.

Do not store obsolete computers and devices in your basement, storage room, attic, warehouse, or any other location. Computers, monitors, and other equipment contain toxic materials and potentially dangerous elements including lead, mercury, and flame retardants. In a landfill, these materials release into the environment. Experts recommend refurbishing or recycling the equipment. For this reason, local governments are working on methods to make it easy for the consumer to recycle this type of equipment. Manufacturers can use the millions of pounds of recycled raw material in products such as outdoor furniture and automotive parts.

To reduce further the environmental impact of computing, simply alter a few habits. Figure 11-44 lists the ways you can contribute to green computing.

Web Link

For more information on green computing, visit the Discovering Computers 2002 Chapter 11 WEB LINK page (**scsite.com/dc2002/ch11/weblink.htm**) and click Green Computing.

GREEN COMPUTING SUGGESTIONS

1. **Use computers and devices that comply with the ENERGY STAR program.**
2. **Do not leave the computer and devices running overnight.**
3. **Turn off your monitor, printer, and other devices when not in use.**
4. **Use paperless methods to communicate.**
5. **Recycle paper.**
6. **Buy recycled paper.**
7. **Recycle toner cartridges.**
8. **Recycle old computers and printers.**
9. **Shop online (saves gas).**
10. **Telecommute (saves gas).**

Figure 11-44 A list of suggestions to make computing healthy for the environment.

ISSUE

Cyberspace Addiction

Internet Addiction Disorder

USA TODAY recently reported on a study that indicates more than six percent of Internet users suffer from Internet addiction disorder (IAD). Researcher David Greenfield, who conducted the study, says marriages are being disrupted, kids are getting into trouble, people are committing illegal acts, and are spending too much money for online purchases. Do you agree that IAD exists? Is someone in your family suffering from IAD? Do families spend more quality time together because of all the electronic conveniences in the home? Or, do family members spend more time using these devices and less time with the family? Can one partner spending time in a chat room be a problem for married couples? Can chat rooms be a problem for children?

For more information on Internet addiction disorder, visit the Discovering Computers 2002 Issues Web page (**scsite.com/dc2002/issues.htm**) and click Chapter 11 Issue #14.

ETHICS AND SOCIETY

As with any powerful technology, computers can be used for both good and bad actions. The standards that determine whether an action is good or bad are known as ethics. **Computer ethics** are the moral guidelines that govern the use of computers and information systems. Six frequently discussed areas of computer ethics are unauthorized use of computer systems, software theft (piracy), information privacy, information accuracy, intellectual property rights, and codes of conduct. The questionnaire in Figure 11-45 raises issues in each of these areas.

The next chapter discusses issues related to unauthorized use, software piracy, and information privacy. The following section deals with the accuracy of computer information, intellectual property rights, and codes of conduct.

Information Accuracy

People need to be aware of issues associated with the accuracy of computer input. Inaccurate input can result in erroneous information and incorrect decisions based on that information.

Information accuracy today is even more of an issue because many users access information maintained by other people or companies, such as on the Internet. Do not assume that because the information is on the Web that it is right. You should evaluate the value of a Web page before relying on its content (Figure 11-46).

Be aware the company providing access to the information may not be the creator of the information. For example, airline flight schedules are available through several Web sites. The question that arises is who is responsible for the accuracy of this information? Does the responsibility rest solely with the original creator of the information, or does the service that passes along the information also have some responsibility to verify its accuracy? Legally, these questions have not been resolved.

	ETHICAL	UNETHICAL
1. A company requires employees to wear badges that track their whereabouts while at work.	☐	☐
2. A supervisor reads an employee's e-mail.	☐	☐
3. An employee uses his computer at work to send e-mail messages to a friend.	☐	☐
4. An employee sends an e-mail message to several co-workers and blind copies his supervisor.	☐	☐
5. An employee forwards an e-mail message to a third party without permission from the sender of the message.	☐	☐
6. An employee uses her computer at work to complete a homework assignment for school.	☐	☐
7. The vice president of your Student Government Association (SGA) downloads a photograph from the Web and uses it in a flier recruiting SGA members.	☐	☐
8. A student copies text from the Web and uses it in a research paper for his English Composition class.	☐	☐
9. An employee sends political campaign material to individuals on her employer's mailing list.	☐	☐
10. As an employee in the registration office, you have access to student grades. You look up grades for your friends so they do not have to wait for delivery of grade reports from the postal service.	☐	☐
11. An employee makes a copy of software and installs it on her computer at home. No one uses her computer at home while she is at work, and she uses her computer at home only to finish projects from work.	☐	☐
12. An employee that has been laid off installs a computer virus on his employer's computer.	☐	☐
13. A person designing a Web page finds one on the Web similar to his requirements, copies it, modifies it, and publishes it as his own Web page.	☐	☐
14. A student researches solely using the Web to write a report.	☐	☐
15. In a society in which all transactions occur online (a cashless society), the government tracks every transaction you make and automatically deducts taxes from your bank account.	☐	☐
16. Someone copies a well-known novel to the Web and encourages others to read it.	☐	☐

Figure 11-45 Indicate whether you think the situation described is ethical or unethical. Discuss your answers with your instructor and other students.

GUIDELINES FOR EVALUATING THE VALUE OF A WEB SITE

Evaluation Criteria	Reliable Web Pages
Audience	The Web page should be written at an appropriate level.
Authority	The Web page should list the author and the appropriate credentials.
Affiliation	A reputable institution should support the Web site without bias in the information.
Content	The Web page should be well organized and the links should work.
Currency	The information on the Web page should be current.
Design	The Web site should load quickly, and be pleasing visually and easy to navigate.
Objectivity	The Web page should contain little advertising and be free of bias.

Figure 11-46 Criteria for evaluating a Web site's content.

APPLY IT!

Check Your Credit Report

If you are applying for a loan or credit card, records of your previous financial history are vital. Whether or not you are given the loan or credit card may depend on a network of credit reporting agencies that either share information with, or are owned by, three major credit bureaus. A credit scoring system is applied to your credit report. Lenders rely on the numbers generated by this scoring system to determine whether to offer someone credit. Check your credit report periodically to determine your score and to ensure that your report is in good standing. The following list provides information on how to obtain a copy of your credit report.

1. You can request a copy from one of the three credit bureaus (see URL below). Depending on the state in which you live, you may have to pay a small fee. Call the appropriate agency and follow its instructions.
2. If you applied for and were denied a loan, you are entitled to a free copy of your credit report. Submit a request in writing within 30 days of the rejection.
3. If you are unemployed and looking for employment, receive public welfare assistance, or believe that your credit file contains fraudulent statements, you are entitled to a free copy of your credit report.

After receiving the report, verify the following is correct: name, Social Security number, date of birth, residential addresses, past employment addresses, and closed accounts. Your report should not contain records of any bankruptcies more than 10 years old or lawsuits, judgments, and other unfavorable information more than 7 years old. If you find errors, ask to have those errors corrected. You are protected under the Fair Credit Billing Act (see URL below).

For more information on societal issues, credit reports, and the Web sites mentioned above, visit the Discovering Computers 2002 Apply It Web page (**scsite.com/dc2002/apply.htm**) and click Chapter 11 Apply It #3.

TECHNOLOGY TRAILBLAZER

MITCH **KAPOR**

Experience as a disc jockey and stand-up comic generally are not prerequisites for a multi-million-dollar career as a software programmer. For Mitch Kapor, however, these jobs led to founding the Lotus Development Company, creating Lotus 1-2-3, and co-founding the Electronic Frontier Foundation, a not-for-profit organization dedicated to protecting online privacy, free expression, and access to public resources.

Kapor studied linguistics and psychology at Yale University. After graduating in 1971, he worked as a disc jockey, a Transcendental Meditation teacher, and an entry-level computer programmer. Kapor developed the Apple II's first graphics and statistics program and then became product manager for the company that created VisiCalc, the first electronic spreadsheet. Completing all but his final semester at MIT's Sloan School of Management, Kapor left MIT to take a job in Silicon Valley, where he founded Lotus Development Corporation in 1982 and created Lotus 1-2-3.

Today, Kapor is active in running a leading venture capital firm, overseeing his Mitchell Kapor Foundation, which helps people attempt to balance humanitarian and environmental concerns. He also writes numerous articles analyzing computers' effects on society.

For more information on Mitch Kapor, visit the Discovering Computers 2002 People Web page (**scsite.com/dc2002/people.htm**) and click Mitch Kapor.

In addition to concerns about the accuracy of computer input, some people raise questions about the ethics of using computers to alter output, primarily graphic output such as retouched photographs. Using graphics equipment and software, you can digitize photographs and then add, change, or remove images (Figure 11-47). One group that opposes any manipulation of an image is the National Press Photographers Association. It believes that allowing even the slightest alteration eventually could lead to deliberately misleading photographs. Others believe that digital photograph retouching is acceptable as long as the significant content or meaning of the photograph does not change. Digital retouching is another area where legal precedents have not been established yet.

ISSUE

Digital Dilemma

Ethics and Society

The Web is one of the world's largest libraries and surely the world's largest copy machine. The global reach of the Web has added substantially to the production of an astonishing abundance of information in digital form, as well as offering unprecedented ease of access. Creating, publishing, distributing, and using information is easier and faster. The good news is the explosive growth and the wealth of knowledge brought by the Web enriches society. The bad news is people easily can obtain illegal copies of information or intellectual property available on the Web without the consent of the originator. Copyright laws have been in place for more than 200 years, but protecting intellectual property never has been an easy task. Now, the capability to convert information into digital format easily makes it even more difficult. Will copyright laws be changed? Should copyright laws be changed? Is it ethical to download copyrighted music to your computer for personal use? Is it legal? Can governments enforce copyright laws? What rights should the individual have who created the original work?

For more information on ethics and society and intellectual copyright issues, visit the Discovering Computers 2002 Issues Web page (**scsite.com/dc2002/issues.htm**) and click Chapter 11 Issue #15.

Intellectual Property Rights

Intellectual property (**IP**) refers to work created by inventors, authors, and artists. **Intellectual property rights** are the rights to which creators are entitled for their inventions, writings, and works of art. Certain issues arise surrounding IP today because many of these works are available digitally. These include copyright and trademark infringement.

A **copyright** gives authors and artists exclusive rights to duplicate, publish, and sell their material. A copyright protects any tangible form of expression. A common infringement of copyright is software piracy. **Software piracy** is the unauthorized and illegal duplication of copyrighted software. Pirating software, which is discussed in the next chapter in more depth, is illegal.

Other areas are not so clear-cut, with respect to the law because copyright law also gives the public fair use to copyrighted material. The issues surround the phrase, fair use, which allows use for educational and critical purposes. This vague definition is subject to widespread interpretation.

- Should an individual be able to download contents of your Web site, modify it, and then put it on the Web again as their own?
- Should a faculty member have the right to print material from the Web and distribute it to all members of the class for teaching purposes only?
- Should someone be able to scan photographs or pages from a book, publish them to the Web, and allow others to download them?
- Should someone be able to put the lyrics to a song on the Web?
- Should students be able to post term papers they have written on the Web, making it tempting for other students to download and submit it as their own work?

These and many more issues are being debated strongly by members of society. Similar issues surround trademarks. A **trademark** protects a company's logos and brand names. The controversy with trademarks relates to Web addresses. When creating a Web site, some people and smaller companies purposely acquire a Web address that uses the exact trademarked name of their competition. For example,

Figure 11-47 President John F. Kennedy seen with Tom Hanks portraying Forrest Gump in this digitally altered photograph.

Macromedia has trademarked the name Flash™. Someone that develops a product similar to Flash™ might acquire a Web address of www.flash.com. A person or company that uses this sneaky technique hopes the public will not know the correct address and end up at their Web site instead.

Codes of Conduct

Recognizing that individuals need specific standards for the ethical use of computers, a number of computer-related organizations have established an IT (information technology) code of conduct (Figure 11-48). An IT **code of conduct** is a written guideline that helps determine whether a specific computer action is ethical or unethical.

IT CODE OF CONDUCT

1. Computers may not be used to harm other people.
2. Employees may not interfere with other's computer work.
3. Employees may not meddle in other's computer files.
4. Computers may not be used to steal.
5. Computers may not be used to bear false witness.
6. Employees may not copy or use software illegally.
7. Employees may not use other's computer resources without authorization.
8. Employees may not use other's output.
9. Employees shall consider the social impact of programs and systems they design.
10. Employees always should use computers in a way that demonstrates consideration and respect for fellow humans.

Figure 11-48 Sample IT code of conduct employers may distribute to employees.

CHAPTER SUMMARY

This chapter presented ways in which the computer has changed society. It discussed ways computers are used at home and in many fields such as education, entertainment, finance, government, health care, science, publishing, and travel. Next, it addressed how emerging technologies are being used in everyday life. Health issues and preventions related to computers also were presented. The chapter ended with a discussion of ethical issues surrounding computer use.

Who Is Responsible?

Ethical Conduct

Many computer-related organizations and professional associations have published guidelines pertaining to computer-related ethical conduct. These codes of conduct help determine if a specific computer action is ethical or unethical. The adherence to and enforcement of these guidelines is, however, an issue in many companies. Consider the following scenario: A programmer is working on a software project for his company. The deadline for the project is approaching quickly, and the programmer realizes he will not be able to meet the deadline. He makes a decision to omit one of the modules he considers non-essential without informing management. The program is released and sold to the public. It immediately crashes. Who is responsible — the programmer or the company? Should the company have a verification policy before releasing the product? If an IT professional violates a code of conduct, what action should a company take? Termination? Leave of absence without pay? Legal action?

For more information on code of ethics and ethical responsibility, visit the Discovering Computers 2002 Issues Web page (**scsite.com/dc2002/issues.htm**) and click Chapter 11 Issue #16.

IT Consultant

Many people would like to be their own boss. Working as a consultant can help you achieve this goal. As the business environment becomes more complex, firms increasingly will rely on outside consultants to help them remain current and competitive. One of the most in-demand types of consultant is for someone in the field of IT (information technology). To become a successful IT consultant, you need to specialize. Specialties within the field can vary from general to networking, systems analysis to programming, and technical writing to Internet development. Your area of specialty will determine educational requirements, certifications, and work experience. The Occupational Outlook Handbook (see URL below) indicates that more than 55 percent of consultants are self-employed, which is about 4 times the average for other executive, administrative, and managerial occupations. The industry is one of the highest paying, but most of the self-employed have worked previously in the private or public sector.

To be a successful consultant requires at least a bachelor's degree and possibly a master's, depending on the area of specialization. Many consultants travel extensively. Salaries range anywhere from $25,000 to more than $250,000 per year.

To learn more about the field of IT consulting as a career and for links to the Web site mentioned above, visit the Discovering Computers 2002 Careers Web page (**scsite.com/dc2002/careers.htm**) and click IT Consultant.

E-SCIENCE

E = MC²

Rocket Science on the Web

For some people, space exploration is a hobby. Building and launching model rockets allow these scientists to participate in exploring the great frontier of space. For others, space exploration is their life. For one such person, building rocket engines is his full-time job. Dennis K. Van Gemert is an engineer and scientist with the Boeing Company. Because of his passion for science, he created a Web site, shown in Figure 11-49, where curious individuals can write and ask him questions.

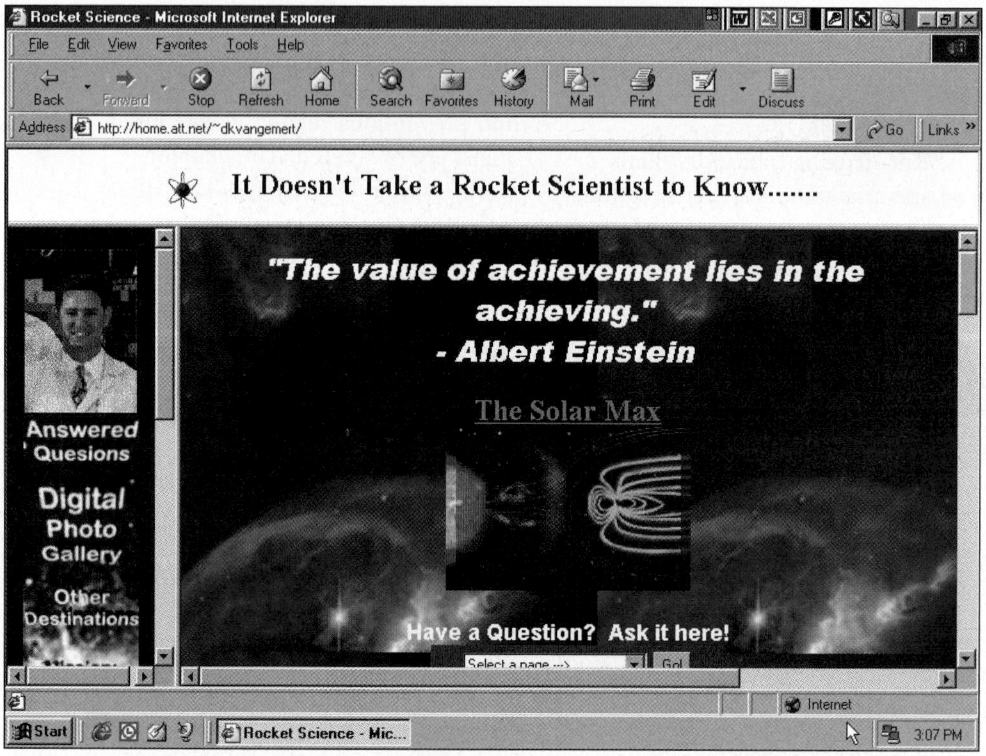

Figure 11-49 The Dennis K. Van Gemert extensive Rocket Science Web site takes space exploration to new heights.

The main page of Van Gemert's Web site contains links to rocket history, a virtual tour of Cape Canaveral in Florida, Mark Wade's Encyclopedia Astronautica, and such aeronautical sites as NASA, Boeing, and the American Institute of Aeronautics and Astronautics.

Rockets and space are not the only areas to explore in the world of science. Where can you find the latest pictures taken with the Hubble telescope? Do you know which cities experienced an earthquake today? Have you ever wondered what a 3-D model of the amino acid glutamine looks like? You can find the answer to these questions and many others through the Librarians' Index to the Internet (lii.org) shown in Figure 11-50.

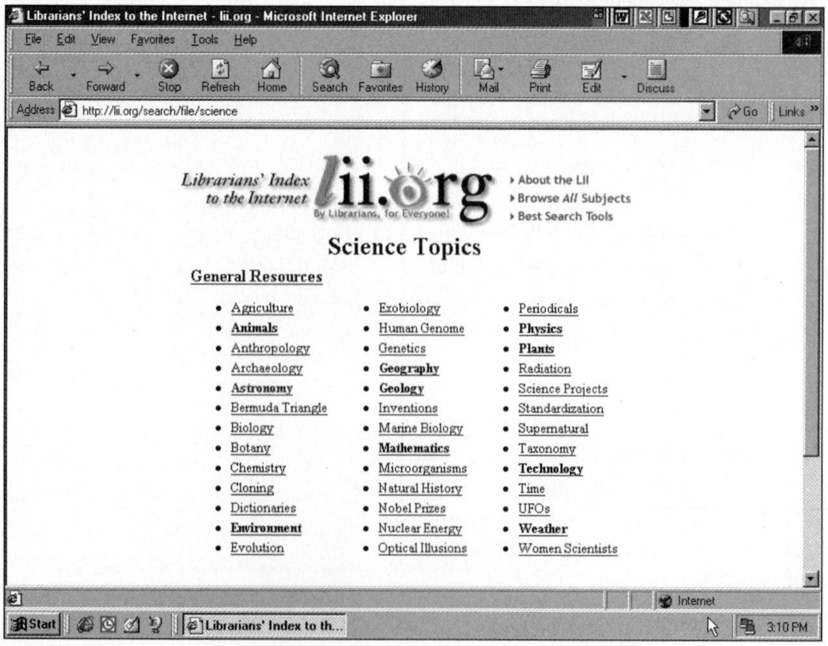

Figure 11-50 Numerous science resources are organized clearly in the Librarians' Index to the Internet.

Figure 11-51 The Yuckiest Site on the Internet Web site makes learning science fun for children.

This index can take you to the Hurricane Center so you can track a hurricane or fly through the eye of a hurricane with the Hurricane Hunters. It also provides a link to the National Earthquake Information Center where you can learn the locations and the intensities of earthquakes that have occurred in the past few days.

The Yuckiest Site on the Internet Web site (Figure 11-51) from Discovery Communications entertains as it teaches; especially when children are involved. Combined with Discovery Kids TV, the Web site features fun and games, crafts, recipes, and other activities that capture kids' imaginations as they learn science through adventure and experiments.

The Web offers a wide variety of science resources designed for all ages. Professional scientists, students, hobbyists, and children can find information with a few clicks of the mouse. The Web sites can answer technical questions and discuss the latest research to help students or merely satisfy a thirst for knowledge.

For more information on science resource Web sites, visit the Discovering Computers 2002 E-Revolution Web page (scsite.com/ dc2002/e-rev.htm) and click Science.

SCIENCE RESOURCE WEB SITES	URL
Periodicals	
Astronomy.com	astronomy.com
Discovering Archaeology	discoveringarchaeology.com
New Scientist	newscientist.com
OceanLink	oceanlink.island.net
Science Magazine	sciencemag.org
Scientific American	sciam.com
Resources	
National Science Foundation (NSF)	nsf.gov
SOFWEB Useful Internet Resources	www.sofweb.vic.edu.au/resource/ressci.htm
To Science Databases	www.internets.com/sscilink.htm
Science Community	
Federation of American Scientists	fas.org
Sigma XI, The Scientific Research Society	amsci.org or sigmaxi.org

For an updated list of science resource Web sites, visit scsite.com/dc2002/e-rev.htm.

Figure 11-52 Resources available on the Internet offer a wide range of subjects for enthusiasts who want to delve into familiar and unknown territories in the world of science.

eREVOLUTION E-SCIENCE *applied:*

1. Visit Dennis Van Gemert's Rocket Science Web site shown in Figure 11-49. View A Brief History of Rocketry and draw a time line showing the development of the rocket. Then, view the Astronomy.com Web site listed in Figure 11-52, read two topics in the Discussion Forums and two articles in the Feature Stories section, and write a summary of the astronomy subjects covered.

2. Visit the Librarians' Index to the Internet shown in Figure 11-50. Click the Inventions topic. View the Web site for the Greatest Engineering Achievements of the 20th Century. Pick two achievements, read their history, and write a paragraph summarizing each of these accomplishments. Then, view two of the science resources Web Sites listed in Figure 11-52 and write a paragraph on each of these Web sites describing the information each contains.

In Summary

Web Instructions: To display this page from the Web, start your browser and enter the URL scsite.com/dc2002/ch11/summary.htm. Click the links for current and additional information. To listen to an audio version of this In Summary, click the Audio button. To play the audio, RealPlayer must be installed on your computer (download by clicking here).

1 How Have Computers Made a Difference in Daily Living?

Computers are everywhere in society today — at home, at work, and at play. Both business and home users have benefited greatly. Instant access to information from anywhere in the world has contributed to tremendous increases in productivity. Nearly every discipline uses computers. Most daily activities either involve the use of or depend on information from a computer.

2 How Are Computers Used at Home?

The computer has become a necessity in many homes. Some uses for a family computer include entertainment, research and education, budgeting and personal financial management, home business management, personal and business communications, and Web access. Each family member may use the computer for some or all of these purpose.

3 How Have Computers Changed the Way Society Interacts with Disciplines Such as Education, Entertainment, Finance, Government, Health Care, Science, Publishing, and Travel?

Educators today are using computers to assist with the learning process, including **computer-based training (CBT)** and **Web-based training (WBT)**. Simulations, or computer-based models of real-life situations, allow students to learn skills in hazardous, emergency, or other situations. **Distance learning (DL)**, also called **distance education (DE)** or **online learning**, is the delivery of education at one location while the learning takes place at other locations. The computer provides several entertainment options, including games, listening to music, and creating digital photographs. Using **personal finance software**, you can pay bills and track expenses. With **online banking**, you transfer money electronically from one account to another. Multiple Web sites provide government and health-related information. All branches of science use computers to assist with collecting, analyzing, and modeling data. Publishers use computers to perform their daily jobs, and on many Web sites, you can download **electronic books (e-books)**. When traveling, your vehicle may have a **GPS (global positioning system)** to help provide you with directions.

4 What Are the Issues Associated with the Digital Divide?

The digital divide is the idea that you can separate people of the world into two distinct groups: (1) those who have access to technology with the ability to use it, and (2) those who do not have access to technology or are unable to use it. Several programs are underway to narrow the gap, including the Microsoft/Toshiba **Anytime Anywhere Learning program**. **PowerUp** is a nationwide industry partnership whose goal is to place technology in schools and community centers.

5 How Does E-Commerce Affect the Way People Conduct Business?

E-commerce is financial business transactions that occur over an electronic network such as the Internet. E-commerce has changed the way people conduct business by virtually eliminating the barriers of time and distance. Transactions can occur instantaneously and globally. You can purchase just about any good or service on the Web through an **electronic storefront** or **online auction**. Some items, such as a movie ticket, can be delivered directly to a handheld computer. A reader at the movie theater wirelessly collects the ticket from your handheld computer. Airline tickets, event tickets, train tickets, and coupons are just a few other examples of uses of the short-range wireless communications technology, called **Bluetooth™**.

In Summary

6 What Are the Ways in Which Virtual Reality, Intelligent Agents, and Robots Are Being Used in Everyday Life?

Virtual reality (**VR**) is the use of computers to simulate a real or imagined environment that appears as a three-dimensional (3-D) space. VR is being used in training, engineering, e-commerce, science, and medicine. An intelligent agent is a software program that carries out tasks on behalf of a user, such as correcting spelling. A **robot** is a computer-controlled device that moves and reacts to feedback from the outside world. Robots have been used mostly in industry, but the cost is dropping. As a result, some manufacturers are making entertainment and personal servant robots.

7 How Can You Prevent Health-Related Disorders and Injuries Due to Computer Use?

Long-term computer use can lead to health complications. Some examples of computer health-related problems are **musculoskeletal disorder** (**MSD**), also called **repetitive stress injury** (**RSI**), **tendonitis**, **carpal tunnel syndrome** (**CTS**), and **computer vision syndrome** (**CVS**). Taking frequent breaks and exercising your hands and arms may help prevent some of these injuries.

8 What Is an Ergonomically Designed Workspace?

Ergonomics is an applied science devoted to incorporate comfort, efficiency, and safety into the design of items in the workplace. The work area should be at least two feet by four feet. Some keyboards have built-in wrist rests. Monitors have a tilt-and-swivel base and controls that allow you to adjust the brightness, contrast, positioning, height, and width of images. Monitors should meet the **MPR II standard**, which defines acceptable levels of radiation.

9 What Are the Symptoms of Computer Addiction?

Computer addiction is a growing health problem and occurs when the computer consumes someone's entire social life. Users addicted to the Internet are said to have an Internet addiction disorder (IAD). Symptoms of this addiction include inability to stop computer activity, irritability when not at a computer, neglecting family and friends, and problems at work or school.

10 What Is Green Computing?

Green computing involves reducing the electricity and environmental waste while using a computer. Personal computers, monitors, and printers should comply with the ENERGY STAR program, which was developed by the United States Department of Energy (DOE) and the United States Environmental Protection Agency (EPA). All obsolete computer equipment should be recycled or disposed of properly.

11 What Are the Ethical Issues Surrounding Computer Use?

Computer ethics are the moral guidelines that govern the use of computers and information systems. The six areas of computer ethics include unauthorized use of computer systems, software theft (piracy), information privacy, information accuracy, intellectual property rights, and codes of conduct. **Intellectual property** (**IP**) is the work created by inventors, authors, and artists, and **intellectual property rights** are the rights to which these creators are entitled for their inventions, writings, and works of art. **Software piracy** is the illegal duplication of **copyrighted** software.

Key Terms

Web Instructions: To display this page from the Web, start your browser and enter the URL scsite.com/dc2002/ch11/terms.htm. Scroll through the list of terms. Click a term to display its definition and a picture. Click the To WEB button for current and additional information about the term from the Web. To see animations, Shockwave and Flash Player must be installed on your computer (download by clicking here).

DIGITAL CAMERA
Camera used to take pictures and store the photographed images digitally instead of on traditional film. Some digital cameras allow a download of the stored pictures to a computer. (11.12)

INTERNET APPLIANCE
Device designed specifically to connect to the Internet; the most popular are set-top boxes, smart phones, smart pagers, and Web-enabled PDAs. Also called Web appliance. (11.5)

Learn It Online

Web Instructions: To display this page from the Web, start your browser, enter the URL scsite.com/dc2002/ch11/learn.htm.

1. Web Guide

Click Web Guide to display the Guide to World Wide Web Sites and Searching Techniques Web page. Click Shopping and then click Consumer World. Scroll down the page and locate an article of interest. Prepare a brief report of your findings and submit your assignment to your instructor.

2. Scavenger Hunt

Click Scavenger Hunt. Print a copy of the Scavenger Hunt page; use this page to write down your answers as you search the Web. Submit your completed page to your instructor.

3. Who Wants to Be a Computer Genius?

Click Computer Genius to find out if you are a computer genius. Directions on how to play the game will display. When you are ready to play, click the Play button. Submit your score to your instructor.

4. Wheel of Terms

Click Wheel of Terms to reinforce important terms you learned in this chapter by playing the Shelly Cashman Series version of this popular game. Directions on how to play the game will display. When you are ready to play, click the PLAY button. Submit your score to your instructor.

5. Career Corner

Click Career Corner to display the Career Magazine page. Click the Feature of the Week link. Review this page, clicking any links within the page. Write a brief report on what you discovered in this feature. Submit the report to your instructor.

6. Search Sleuth

Click Search Sleuth to learn search techniques that will help make you a research expert. Submit the completed assignment to your instructor.

7. Crossword Puzzle Challenge

Click Crossword Puzzle Challenge. Complete the puzzle to reinforce skills you learned in this chapter. Directions on how to play the game will display. When you are ready to play, click the PLAY button. Submit the completed puzzle to your instructor.

8. Practice Test

Click Practice Test. Answer each question. When completed, enter your name and click the Grade Test button to submit the quiz for grading. Make a note of any missed questions. If required, print a copy to submit to your instructor.

Checkpoint

Web Instructions: To display this page from the Web, start your browser and enter the URL scsite.com/dc2002/ch11/check.htm. Click the links for current and additional information. To experience the animation and interactivity, Shockwave and Flash Player must be installed on your computer (download by clicking here.)

LABEL THE FIGURE

Instructions: Complete the Evaluation Criteria column in this guideline document.

GUIDELINES FOR EVALUATING THE VALUE OF A WEB SITE

Evaluation Criteria	Reliable Web Pages
1. ____________	The Web page should be written at an appropriate level.
2. ____________	The Web page should list the author and the appropriate credentials.
3. ____________	A reputable institution should support the Web site without bias in the information.
4. ____________	The Web page should be well organized and the links should work.
5. ____________	The information on the Web page should be current.
6. ____________	The Web site should load quickly, and be pleasing visually and easy to navigate.
7. ____________	The Web page should contain little advertising and be free of bias.

MATCHING

Instructions: Match each term from the column on the left with the best description from the column on the right.

_______ 1. intellectual property rights
_______ 2. edutainment
_______ 3. virtual reality
_______ 4. distance learning
_______ 5. ergonomics

a. A type of educational software that combines education with entertainment.
b. A financial business transaction that occurs over an electronic network such as the Internet.
c. The rights to which creators are entitled for their inventions, writings, and works of art.
d. The use of computers to simulate a real or imagined environment.
e. The delivery of education at one location while the learning takes place at other locations.
f. The incorporation of comfort, efficiency, and safety into the design of workplace items.
g. A work arrangement in which employees work away from a company's standard workplace.

MULTIPLE CHOICE

Instructions: Select the letter of the correct answer for each of the following questions.

1. __________ is a type of training that uses Internet technology.
   a. Computer-based training
   b. Computer-aided instruction
   c. Web-based training
   d. Edutainment
2. __________ involves using computer simulations to assist in learning surgical techniques.
   a. Computer-aided surgery
   b. Telemedicine
   c. Robotics
   d. Intelligent agents
3. A recent development that links printed media to the Web is called __________ .
   a. electronic books
   b. Web bar codes
   c. CBT
   d. AI
4. A book published online is called a(n) __________ book.
   a. Web
   b. online
   c. electronic
   d. published
5. __________ is the application of human intelligence to computers.
   a. Green computing
   b. AI
   c. Networking
   d. Neural networks

SHORT ANSWER

Instructions: Write a brief answer to each of the following questions.

1. What is an Internet appliance? __________ Why would someone want to use one of these devices? __________
2. What is CBT? __________ What are some advantages of CBT? __________ How do simulations help someone learn? __________
3. What is e-commerce? __________ How has it changed the way in which an organization does business? __________ What are some examples of e-commerce transactions? __________
4. What is a global positioning system (GPS)? __________ What are some advantages of a GPS? __________
5. What is the digital divide? __________ What agencies and companies are working to eliminate the divide? __________ What programs have been launched in an effort to eliminate the digital divide? __________

WORKING TOGETHER

Instructions: Working with a group of your classmates, complete the following team exercise.

Create a report on the digital divide. Within the report, give a brief overview of the following: (1) an explanation of the digital divide and why it exists; (2) an overview of how the divide affects the United States and the world; (3) what efforts are underway to eliminate the divide; and (4) pros and cons of these efforts. Use your word processing program to prepare a written report and PowerPoint to present the report to your class. Include links to at least three Web sites that your group used as reference sources.

Web Instructions: To display this page from the Web, launch your browser and enter the URL scsite.com/dc2002/ch11/lab.htm. Click the links for current and additional information.

1 Playing Audio Compact Disks

This exercise uses Windows 2000 procedures. Click the Start button on the taskbar, point to Programs on the Start menu, and then point to Accessories on the Programs submenu. Point to Entertainment on the Accessories submenu, and then click CD Player on the Entertainment submenu. When the CD Player displays, click the Options button and then click CD Player Help on the Options button menu. When the CD Player window opens read the Help information and answer the following questions:

- How do you play a CD?
- How do you stop a CD?
- How do you eject a CD from the drive?

Close the CD Player window. If your system has a CD-ROM drive and a sound card, insert a CD into the CD-ROM drive and then play it. Close the CD Player.

2 Understanding Multimedia Properties

This exercise uses Windows 95 or Windows 98 procedures. Click the Start button on the taskbar, point to Settings on the Start menu, and then click Control Panel on the Settings submenu. When the Control Panel window opens, double-click the Multimedia icon. When the Multimedia Properties dialog box displays, if necessary, click the Audio tab and then answer the following questions:

- What is the Playback Preferred device?
- Will the volume control display on the taskbar of your computer?

Click the Advanced or Devices tab. For each multimedia device listed, if a plus sign (+) displays in the box to its left, click the plus sign to change it to a minus sign (–). For each device driver listed, write down the name(s) of the hardware device(s) installed on your system. Close the Multimedia Properties dialog box and the Control Panel window.

3 Dragging and Dropping Windows Objects

This exercise uses Windows 98 procedures. Dragging and dropping objects in Windows 98 causes different things to happen. For example, if you drag a program icon from one folder to another or to the desktop, Windows assumes you want to create a shortcut. If you drag a file from one folder to another or to the desktop, Windows assumes you want to move it. Or, if you drag an object from one drive to another, Windows assumes you want to copy it. You can specify the kind of drag-and-drop operation you want to perform by holding down the right mouse button and dragging the object (right-dragging). Insert the Discover Data Disk into drive A. See the inside back cover of this book for instructions for downloading the Data Disk or see your instructor for information on accessing the files required in this book. Right-click the Start button on the taskbar and then click Explore on the shortcut menu. Click the 3½ Floppy (A:) icon in the Folders pane of the Exploring - Start Menu window. When the Exploring - 3½ Floppy (A:) window displays, right-click and drag the file name h7-2 in the right pane to the desktop. Release the right mouse button. What are the three commands on the shortcut menu that allow you to perform drag and drop operations? What is a shortcut? Click Cancel on the shortcut menu. Close the Exploring - 3½ Floppy (A:) window.

4 System Sounds

Double-click the My Computer icon on the Desktop. Double-click the Control Panel icon in the My Computer window. Double-click the Sounds icon in the Control Panel window. In the Sounds Properties dialog box, some of the items in the Events list have an associated sound. To hear the sound for an event, click the event in the Events list and then click the right arrow button in the Sound area.

- What events have the same sound?
- Do any events listed have no sound?

Close the Sounds Properties dialog box and the Control Panel window.

Web Work

Web Instructions: To display this page from the Web, start your browser and enter the URL scsite.com/dc2002/ch11/web.htm. To view At The Movies in exercise 1, RealPlayer must be installed on your computer (download by clicking here). To use the Shelly Cashman Series Understanding Multimedia Lab from the Web, Shockwave and Flash Player must be installed on your computer (download by clicking here).

1 Online Organizations

To view the Online Organizations movie, click the button to the left or click the Play button to the right. Watch the movie, and then complete the exercise by answering the questions below. The Internet has become The Place to organize, whether to rally for a worthy cause or launch a revolution. More than that, new technologies have taken the Internet beyond providing a convenient, efficient meeting place. It also is a means of planning and digitally documenting (audio/video) major events. Organizations around the world use the Web to gather information, plan logistics, arrange transportation, and educate members. Does this make the world safer or more dangerous? Are surveillance and safeguards necessary? What agency, if any, should impose regulations?

2 Shelly Cashman Series Understanding Multimedia Lab

Follow the instructions in Web Work 2 on page 1.47 to start and use the Shelly Cashman Series Understanding Multimedia Lab. If you are running from the Web, enter the URL, www.scsite.com/sclabs/menu.htm, or display the Web Work page (see instructions at the top of this page) and then click the button to the left.

3 Digital Cameras

The Creative Web Cam Go is a digital camera that not only takes photographs but, when folded in half and placed on a monitor, can serve as a Web cam. Other digital camera innovations include a digital camera that downloads pictures simply by placing it in a cradle attached to a computer; a digital camera that boasts a 3x optical zoom; and a digital camera that packs auto focus, auto flash, and auto exposure into a package smaller than most conventional cameras. Click the button to the left to learn more about digital cameras and complete this exercise.

4 Animation and Graphics

Animation and graphics add interest to games and to educational applications. Recent multimedia games have used detailed animation and graphics to add verisimilitude to Louis XIV's Versailles, provide integrity to the shah's Istanbul, and offer substance to Scottish golf courses. Graphics and animation also are used to reinforce Web page content. Click the button to the left to complete this exercise to visit a Web page with hundreds of free animations and graphics you can download on your Web pages.

5 In the News

Why own the latest video game when you can rent it from the comfort of your personal computer? Yummy Interactive has agreements with leading video-game publishers — Infogrames, Activision, Ripcord Games, and Eidos — that will allow broadband users to download files from Yummy's site to play stand-alone or multi-player games. Yummy's Web site sends users all they need to get started playing the games, and as more bytes are needed, they are sent from the server to the users. Click the button to the left and read a news article about online games and edutainment applications. What applications have been developed? Do you think the applications will be successful? Why or why not? Do you think online games will replace the traditional, local CD-ROM game?

CHAPTER 12

Computers and Society: Security and Privacy

While enjoying your breakfast, you read an offer for a crossword puzzle CD-ROM on the back of your cereal box. All you have to do is send two UPC labels and $1 for processing and handling. You immediately cut out the order form and fill in your name, home address, e-mail address, and telephone number. Crossword puzzles are your favorite pastime!

Three weeks later the software arrives. While installing the software, you register the product online. The next day, the manufacturer sends you an e-mail message with a list of other entertainment software in which you might be interested. As time passes, you begin to receive increasingly more e-mail messages from vendors of game and entertainment software. In addition, you begin to receive brochures in the U.S. mail from various related sources. Then, you receive a call from one of the vendors. How did all these companies obtain your name, e-mail address, and telephone number?

With school starting soon, you decide to buy your semester books from the campus online bookstore. While placing your order, the advertisement banner on the bookstore's Web page reads, Click here for a 50 percent discount on entertainment software. Is the content of this message a coincidence?

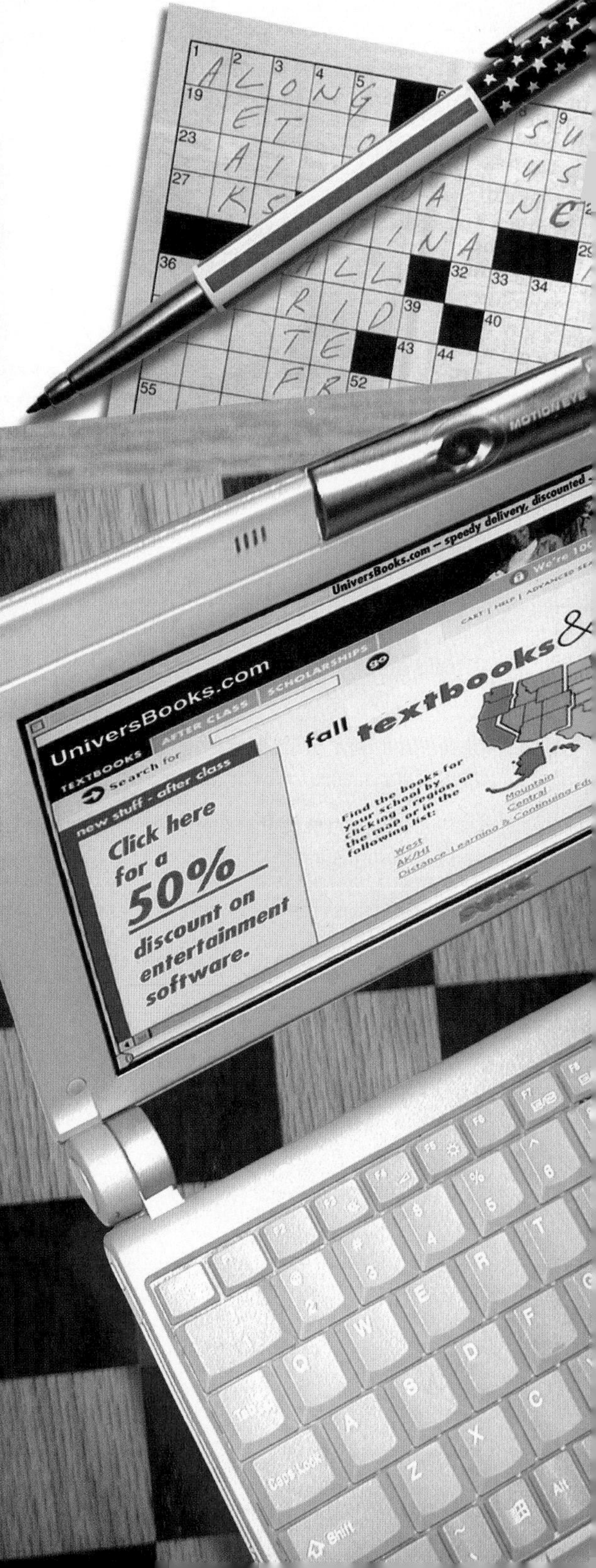

OBJECTIVES

After completing this chapter, you will be able to:

- Identify the various types of security risks that can threaten computers
- Describe ways to safeguard a computer
- Know how a computer virus works and the steps individuals can take to prevent viruses
- Understand how to create a good password
- Identify various biometric devices
- Recognize that software piracy is illegal
- Explain why encryption is necessary
- Know why computer backup is important and how it is accomplished
- Discuss the steps in a disaster recovery plan
- Understand ways to secure an Internet transaction
- List ways to protect your personal information

COMPUTER SECURITY: RISKS AND SAFEGUARDS

Today, more and more people rely on computers to create, store, and manage critical information. Thus, it is important that computers and the data they store are accessible and available when needed. It also is crucial that users take measures to protect their computers and data from loss, damage, and misuse. For example, businesses must ensure that information such as credit records, employee and customer data, and purchase information are secure and confidential.

A **computer security risk** is any event or action that could cause a loss of or damage to computer hardware, software, data, information, or processing capability. Some breaches to computer security are accidental. Others are planned. An intentional breach of computer security often involves a deliberate act that is against the law. Any illegal act involving a computer generally is referred to as a **computer crime**. The term **cybercrime** refers to online or Internet-based illegal acts.

The following sections describe some of the more common computer security risks and protective measures, or **safeguards**, you can take to minimize or prevent their consequences. This section concludes with a discussion of how to develop an overall computer security plan.

Computer Viruses

A computer **virus** is a potentially damaging computer program that affects, or *infects*, your computer negatively by altering the way the computer works without your knowledge or permission. More specifically, a computer virus is a segment of program code from some outside source that implants itself in a computer. Once the virus is in your computer, it can spread throughout and may damage your files and operating system.

The increased use of networks, the Internet, and e-mail has accelerated the spread of computer viruses. With these technologies, computer users easily can share files and any related viruses. Viruses are activated on your computer in three basic ways: (1) opening an infected file, (2) running an infected program, or (3) booting the computer with an infected floppy disk in the disk drive.

Today, the most common way that computers become infected with viruses is through e-mail attachments. Figure 12-1 shows how a virus can spread from one computer to another through an infected e-mail attachment. Before you open or execute any e-mail attachment, you should ensure that the e-mail message is from a trusted source. A **trusted source** is a company or person you believe will not send you a virus-infected file knowingly. If the e-mail is from an unknown source, you should delete it without opening or executing any attachments. Following this precautionary measure will help protect your computer from virus infection.

Computer viruses do not generate by chance. The programmer of a virus, known as a **virus author**, intentionally writes a virus program. Some virus authors find writing viruses a challenge. Others write them to cause destruction. Writing a virus program usually requires significant programming skills. If virus authors would devote their time, energy, and skills to more productive activities, they most certainly could earn a substantial amount of honest money.

Web Link
For more information on computer viruses, visit the Discovering Computers 2002 Chapter 12 WEB LINK page (**scsite.com/dc2002/ch12/weblink.htm**) and click Computer Viruses.

Figure 12-1 HOW A VIRUS CAN SPREAD THROUGH AN E-MAIL MESSAGE

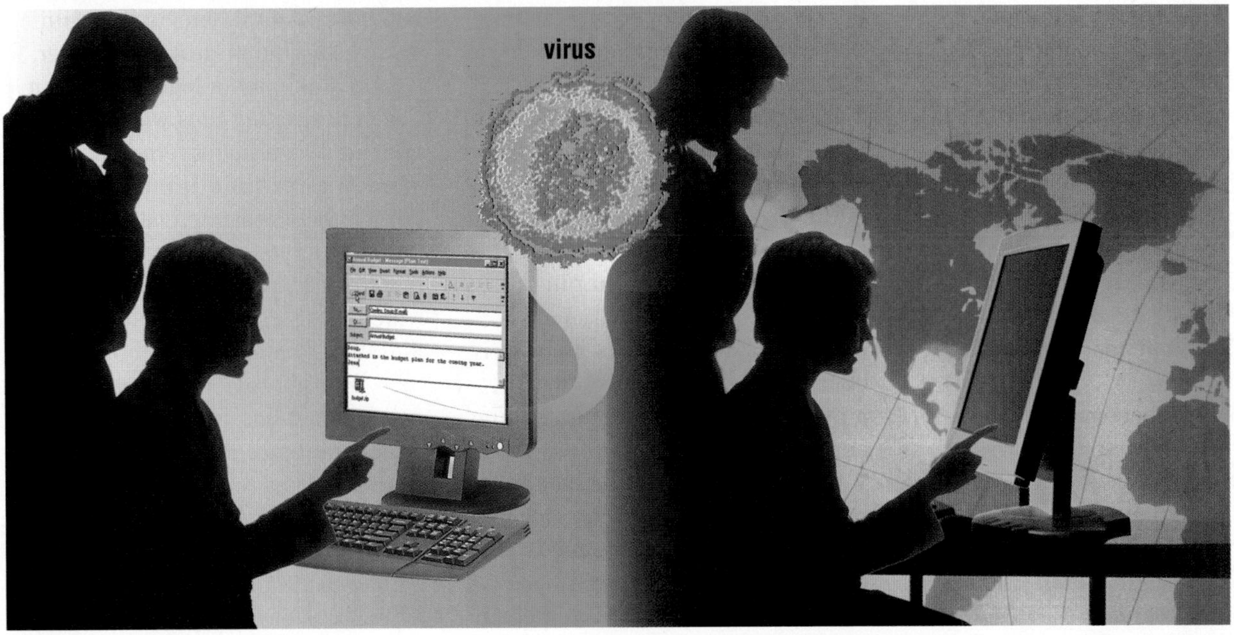

Step 1:
Unscrupulous programmers create a virus program. They hide the virus in a Word document and attach the Word document to an e-mail message.

Step 2:
They use the Internet to send the e-mail message to thousands of users around the world.

Step 3b:
Other users do not recognize the name of the sender of the e-mail message. These users do not open the e-mail message — instead they immediately delete the e-mail message. These users' computers are not infected with the virus.

Step 3a:
Some users open the attachment and their computers become infected with the virus.

Some viruses are harmless pranks that simply freeze a computer temporarily or display sounds or messages. The Music Bug virus, for example, instructs the computer to play a few chords of music. Other viruses destroy or corrupt data stored on the hard disk of the infected computer. If your computer acts differently from usual, it may be infected with a virus. Figure 12-2 outlines some common symptoms of virus infection.

Viruses have become a serious problem in recent years. Currently, more than 53,000 known virus programs exist with an estimated 6 new virus programs discovered each day. Many Web sites maintain lists of all known virus programs.

Although numerous variations are known, three main types of viruses exist: boot sector, file, and macro.

- A **boot sector virus**, sometimes called a **system virus**, executes when a computer boots up because it resides in the boot sector of a floppy disk or the master boot record of a hard disk. When you leave a floppy disk in the floppy disk drive and boot up the computer, the computer attempts to execute the boot sector on the disk in drive A. Even if the disk is not a boot disk, any virus on the floppy disk's boot sector can infect the computer's hard disk.
- A **file virus**, sometimes called a **program virus**, attaches itself to program files. When you run the infected program, the virus loads into memory. Most users innocently obtain a file virus by downloading a program from the Web or opening an e-mail attachment.
- A **macro virus** uses the macro language of an application, such as word processing or spreadsheet, to hide virus code. When you open a document that contains an infected macro, the virus loads into memory. The creators of macro viruses often hide them in templates, so the virus infects any document that uses the template.

Many viruses activate as soon as a computer accesses an infected file or runs an infected program. Other viruses, called logic bombs or time bombs, activate based on specific criterion. A **logic bomb** is a virus that activates when it detects a certain condition. One disgruntled worker, for example, planted a logic bomb that began destroying files when his name appeared on a list of terminated employees. A **time bomb** is a type of logic bomb that activates on a particular date. A well-known time bomb is the Michelangelo virus, which destroys data on a hard disk on March 6, Michelangelo's birthday.

Viruses sometimes are called malicious-logic programs. A **malicious-logic program**, or **malware**, is a program that acts without a user's knowledge and deliberately alters the computer's operations. In addition to viruses, other types of malware are worms and Trojan horses.

- A **worm** is a malicious-logic program that copies itself repeatedly in memory or on a disk drive until no memory or disk space remains. When no memory or disk space remains, the computer stops working. Some worm programs even copy themselves to other computers on a network.
- A **Trojan horse** (named after the Greek myth) is a malicious-logic program that hides within or looks like a legitimate program. A certain condition or action usually triggers the Trojan horse. Unlike a virus or worm, a Trojan horse does not replicate itself to other computers.

SIGNS OF VIRUS INFECTION

- An unusual message or graphical image displays on the computer monitor
- An unusual sound or music plays randomly
- The available memory is less than what should be available
- A program or file suddenly is missing
- An unknown program or file mysteriously appears
- The size of a file changes without explanation
- A file becomes corrupted
- A program or file does not work properly

Figure 12-2 Viruses attack computers in a variety of ways. Listed here are some of the more common signs of virus infection.

Virus Detection and Removal

No completely effective methods exist to ensure a computer or network is safe from computer viruses and other malware. You can take precautions, however, to protect your home and work computers from these infections. The following paragraphs discuss these precautions.

To reduce the chance of infecting your computer with a boot sector virus, never start your computer with a floppy disk in drive A — unless you are certain the disk is an uninfected boot disk. All floppy disks contain a boot sector. During the startup process, the computer attempts to execute the boot sector on a disk in drive A. Even if the attempt is unsuccessful, any virus on the floppy disk's boot sector can infect the computer's hard disk.

To protect your computer from a macro virus, you can set a macro's security level in all applications that allow you to write macros. With a medium security level, for example, Microsoft Word will warn you that a document you are attempting to open contains a macro (Figure 12-3). From this warning, you can choose to disable or enable the macro. If the document is from a trusted source, you can enable the macro. Otherwise, you should disable it.

To safeguard your computer from virus attacks, install an antivirus program and update it frequently. An **antivirus program** protects a computer against viruses by identifying and removing any computer viruses found in memory, on storage media, or on incoming files. Most antivirus programs also protect against worms and Trojan horses. When you purchase a new computer, it often includes an antivirus software package. The table in Figure 12-4 lists popular antivirus software packages.

POPULAR ANTIVIRUS SOFTWARE PACKAGES

- AVG Anti-Virus
- Command AntiVirus
- eSafe Desktop
- F-Secure Anti-Virus
- InoculateIT
- McAfee VirusScan
- Norton AntiVirus
- PC-cillin
- RAV AntiVirus Desktop

Figure 12-4 Popular antivirus software packages.

Figure 12-3a (dialog box to set macro security)

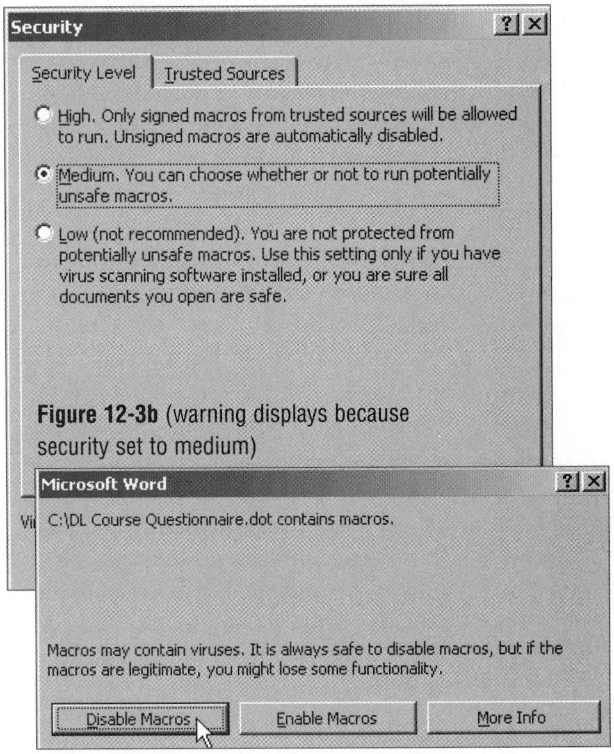

Figure 12-3b (warning displays because security set to medium)

Figure 12-3 Many application software products, such as Microsoft Word, allow you to set security levels for macros. To display the dialog box shown in Figure 12-3a in Word, click Tools on the menu bar, point to Macro, and then click Security.

COMPANY ON THE CUTTING EDGE

network ASSOCIATES

Antivirus Program Provides Personal Computer Protection

Some people take megadoses of Vitamin C to fight a cold. Others rely on homemade chicken soup to eliminate viral infections. But how can they protect their computers from viral attacks? Their best bet is to use a combination of an antivirus program and a personal firewall, such as McAfee VirusScan and Firewall, developed by Network Associates.

More than 53,000 strains of viruses are on the rampage to infect your system with Trojan horses, worms, and bugs. But Network Associates' cybersleuths are on the lookout for these malicious programs, sometimes finding as many as six new viruses each day. They are part of the company's 2,800 worldwide employees and the largest independent network security and management software corporation.

VirusScan has been named the top antivirus product in independent testing performed by the University of Hamburg's Virus Test Center and by the West Coast Labs for Secure Computing. This software, along with Network Associates' other e-business products, is used by more than 60 million people worldwide.

For more information on Network Associates, Inc., visit the Discovering Computers 2002 Companies Web page (**scsite.com/dc2002/companies.htm**) and click Network Associates.

An antivirus program scans for programs that attempt to modify the boot program, the operating system, and other programs that normally are read from but not modified. Many antivirus programs also automatically scan files you download from the Web, e-mail attachments, files you open, and all removable media you insert into the computer such as floppy disks and Zip® disks.

One technique that antivirus programs use to identify a virus is to look for virus signatures. A **virus signature**, also called a **virus definition**, is a known specific pattern of virus code. You should update your antivirus program's signature files as often as necessary to ensure these files contain patterns for newly discovered viruses. This extremely important activity allows your antivirus software to protect against viruses written since the antivirus program was released. Most antivirus programs contain an auto-update feature that regularly prompts you to download the virus signature (Figure 12-5). The vendor usually provides this service at no cost for a specified time period.

Even with an updated virus signature file, antivirus programs can have difficulty detecting some viruses. For example, a **polymorphic virus** modifies its program code each time it attaches itself to another program or file. An antivirus program cannot detect a polymorphic virus by its virus signature because the code pattern in the virus never looks the same.

Another technique that antivirus programs use to detect viruses is to inoculate existing program files. To **inoculate** a program file, the antivirus program records information such as the file size and file creation date in a separate inoculation file. The antivirus program then can use this information to detect if a virus tampers with the inoculated program file. Again, some sophisticated viruses take steps to avoid detection. A **stealth virus** infects a program file, but still reports the size and creation date of the original, uninfected program.

Once an antivirus program identifies an infected file, it attempts to remove its virus. If the antivirus program cannot remove the virus, it often quarantines the infected file. A **quarantine** is a separate area of a hard disk that holds the infected file until you can remove its virus. This step ensures other files will not become infected. You also can quarantine suspicious files yourself.

In addition to detecting and inoculating against viruses, most antivirus programs have utilities that create a rescue disk and remove or repair infected programs and files. For boot sector viruses, the antivirus program requires you to restart the computer with a rescue disk. The **rescue disk**, or **emergency disk**, is a removable disk that contains an uninfected copy of key operating system commands and startup information that enables the computer to restart correctly. Upon startup, the rescue disk finds and removes the boot sector virus. Floppy disks and Zip® disks often serve as rescue disks. Once you have restarted the computer using the rescue disk, the antivirus program can attempt to repair damaged files. If it cannot repair the damaged files, you may have to replace, or *restore*, them with uninfected backup copies of the files.

In extreme cases, you may need to reformat your hard disk to remove a virus. Having uninfected, or clean, backups of all files is important. A later section in this chapter covers backup and restore procedures in detail.

If a virus has infected your computer, you should remove the virus. If you share data with other users, such as via e-mail attachments, floppy disks, or Zip® disks, then you should inform these users of your virus infection. This courteous gesture allows fellow users to check their system for the same virus infection.

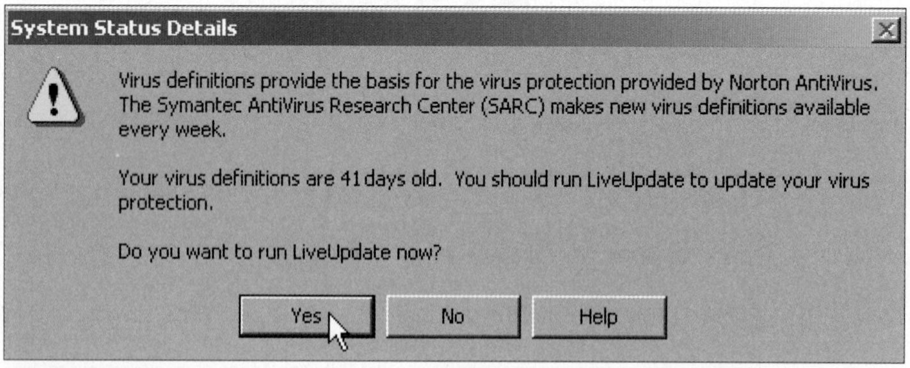

Figure 12-5 Many vendors of antivirus programs allow you to update virus signature files automatically from the Web at no cost for a specified time period.

Finally, stay informed about new virus alerts and virus hoaxes. A **virus hoax** is an e-mail message that warns you of a non-existent virus. Often, these virus hoaxes are in the form of a chain letter that requests you send a copy of the e-mail to as many people as possible. Instead of forwarding the e-mail, visit a Web site that publishes a list of virus alerts and virus hoaxes (Figure 12-6).

The list in Figure 12-7 summarizes important tips discussed in this section for protecting your computer from virus infection.

Unauthorized Access and Use

Unauthorized access is the use of a computer or network without permission. A **cracker** is someone who tries to access a computer or network illegally. The term **hacker**, although originally a complimentary word for a computer enthusiast, now has a derogatory connotation with the same definition as cracker. Some hackers break into a computer for the challenge. Other hackers use or steal computer resources or corrupt a computer's data.

Hackers typically break into a computer by connecting to it and then logging in as a legitimate user. Some intruders do no damage. They merely access data, information, or programs on the computer before logging off. Other intruders leave some evidence of their presence either by leaving a message or deliberately altering data.

Unauthorized use is the use of a computer or its data for unapproved or possibly illegal activities. Unauthorized use includes a variety of activities: an employee using a company computer to send personal e-mail, an employee using the company's word processing software to track his or her child's soccer league scores, or someone gaining access to a bank computer and performing an unauthorized transfer.

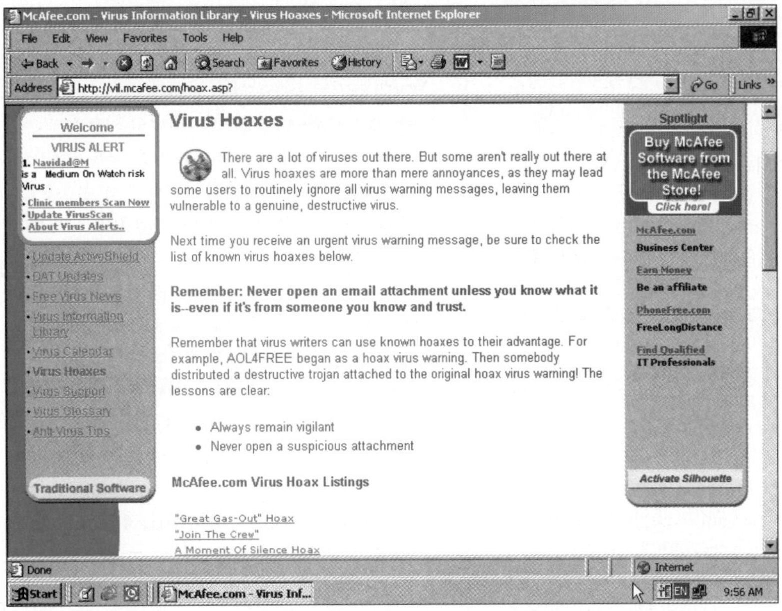

Figure 12-6 Stay informed of virus alerts and hoaxes by regularly visiting a Web site such as the one shown here.

TIPS FOR PREVENTING VIRUS INFECTIONS

1. Never start your computer with a floppy disk in drive A, unless it is an uninfected rescue disk.
2. Set the macro security in programs so you can enable or disable macros. Only enable macros if the document is from a trusted source.
3. Install an antivirus program on all of your computers. Obtain updates to the antivirus signature files. The cost of antivirus software is much less than the cost of rebuilding damaged files. As a result, most businesses and large organizations have adopted this policy.
4. If your antivirus program flags an e-mail attachment as virus infected, delete the attachment immediately. Never open an e-mail attachment unless it is from a trusted source. Scan all e-mail attachments you intend to open.
5. Check all downloaded programs for viruses. Viruses often are placed in seemingly innocent programs so they will affect a large number of users.
6. Before using any floppy disk or Zip® disk, use the antivirus scan program to check the disk for viruses. This holds true even for shrink-wrapped software from major developers. Even commercial software has been infected and distributed to unsuspecting users.
7. Write-protect your rescue disk by sliding the write-protect tab into the write-protect position.
8. Back up your files regularly. Scan the backup program prior to backing up disks and files to ensure the backup program is virus free.

Figure 12-7 With the growing number of new viruses, it is crucial you take steps to protect your computer. Experts recommend the precautions listed here.

TECHNOLOGY TRAILBLAZER

CLIFFORD **STOLL**

Technology Trailblazers have invented computer hardware, developed computer software, changed the way individuals and organizations use computers, and led prominent companies in the computer industry. Clifford Stoll, however, does not create computer technology. Instead, Stoll provokes people to *think* about how they use computer technology.

Stoll first gained fame working as a systems manager at Lawrence Berkeley National Laboratory, managed by the University of California for the U.S. Department of Energy. While tracking the source of a 75-cent accounting error in his company's billing logs, he noticed something awry. After a year of thorough investigation — done solely from his computer — Stoll finally tracked the hacker to Hanover, West Germany. The hacker turned out to be part of a spy ring selling computer secrets to the Soviet Union's KGB for money and drugs. The details of this pursuit are revealed in Stoll's 1989 book, *The Cuckoo's Egg*, which made *The New York Times*' bestseller list.

He also wrote two other books, *Silicon Snake Oil — Second Thoughts on the Information Highway* and *High Tech Heretic: Why Computers Don't Belong in the Classroom.* As these titles suggest, Stoll is highly critical of the benefits computers and the Internet presumably provide. He questions why computers are so bland looking and why hardware has such a short useful life, and he proclaims that schools should spend money on teachers, librarians, and books rather than on technology because computers tend to isolate and weaken people.

For more information on Clifford Stoll, visit the Discovering Computers 2002 People Web page (**scsite.com/dc2002/people.htm**) and click Clifford Stoll.

One way to prevent unauthorized access and unauthorized use of computers is to utilize access controls. An **access control** is a security measure that defines who can access a computer, when they can access it, and what actions they can take while accessing the computer. Many commercial software packages implement access controls using a two-phase process called identification and authentication. **Identification** verifies that you are a valid user. **Authentication** verifies that you are whom you claim to be. Four methods of identification and authentication exist: user names and passwords, possessed objects, biometric devices, and callback systems. The following pages discuss these methods of identification and authentication.

USER NAMES AND PASSWORDS A **user name**, or **user ID**, is a unique combination of characters, such as letters of the alphabet or numbers, that identifies one specific user. A **password** is a secret combination of characters associated with the user name that allows access to certain computer resources.

As discussed in Chapter 8, most multiuser (networked) operating systems require that you correctly enter a user name and a password before you can access the data, information, and programs stored on a computer or network. Many other systems that maintain financial, personal, and other confidential information also require a user name and password as part of their logon procedure (Figure 12-8).

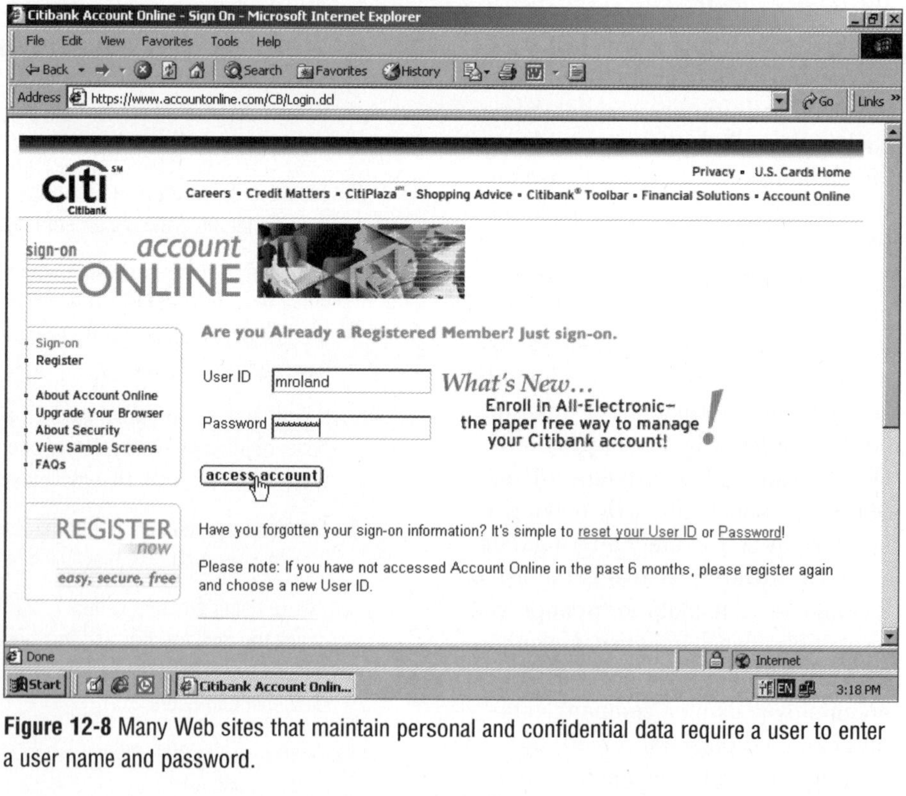

Figure 12-8 Many Web sites that maintain personal and confidential data require a user to enter a user name and password.

Some systems assign your user name or user identification (ID). For example, a school may use your student identification number as your user ID. With other systems, you select your own user name. Many users select a mixture of their first and last names. A user named Michael Roland might choose mroland as his user name.

Most systems require you to select your own password. Users typically choose an easy-to-remember word or series of characters for passwords. If your password is too obvious, however, such as your initials or birthday, others can guess it easily. Easy passwords make it simple for hackers to break into a system. Thus, you should select a password carefully.

Longer passwords provide greater security than shorter ones. Each character you add to a password significantly increases the number of possible combinations and the length of time it might take for someone to guess the password (Figure 12-9).

Generally, the more creative you are when selecting a password, the more difficult it is for someone to figure out.

APPLY IT!

The Perfect Password

Accessing your computer account online, at school, or at work generally requires that you have a user name and password. Passwords are effective, however, only if they are chosen carefully. Ideally, the password should be one that nobody could guess. In practice, most people select passwords that are easy to guess: their name or their initials, or names of their children, spouse, or pets.

Below are some tips on selecting a password.

Do not use:
- Your name in any form.
- The name of a family member.
- A password of all digits or all the same letter.
- A password contained in an English or foreign language dictionary.

Do use:
- At least eight characters (if supported by the software).
- Mixed case letters.
- A combination of letters, digits, words, initials, and dates.
- The license plate rule (characters you would use to create a personal license plate).
- A password you can type easily without looking at the keyboard.
- Something that no one but you would know.
- A line or two from a song, using the first letter of each word.

Below are some tips on safeguarding your password:
- Do not share your password with anyone.
- Do not write down your password.
- Change your password frequently.
- Do not fall for e-mail or telephone scams and share your password.

For more information on password protection, visit the Discovering Computers 2002 Apply It Web page (**scsite.com/dc2002/apply.htm**) and click Chapter 12 Apply It #1.

PASSWORD PROTECTION

NUMBER OF CHARACTERS	POSSIBLE COMBINATIONS	AVERAGE TIME TO DISCOVER: HUMAN	AVERAGE TIME TO DISCOVER: COMPUTER
1	36	3 minutes	.000018 second
2	1,300	2 hours	.00065 second
3	47,000	3 days	.02 second
4	1,700,000	3 months	1 second
5	60,000,000	10 years	30 seconds
10	3,700,000,000,000,000	580 million years	59 years

- *Possible characters include the letters A-Z and numbers 0-9*
- *Human discovery assumes 1 try every 10 seconds*
- *Computer discovery assumes one million tries per second*
- *Average time assumes the password would be discovered in approximately half the time it would take to try all possible combinations*

Figure 12-9 This table shows the effect of increasing the length of a password that consists of letters and numbers. The longer the password, the more effort required to discover it. Long passwords, however, are more difficult for users to remember.

Many software programs have guidelines you must follow when you create your password. One system may require your password be at least six characters long and use a mixture of numbers and letters. Following these guidelines, the password IAWL is invalid (it is too short), but IAWL0901 is valid. This password also is easy for you to remember because the letters IAWL are the first letter of each word in your favorite movie, It's a Wonderful Life, and September 1 is your anniversary (09/01). Although easy for you to remember, this password is difficult for a hacker to guess easily.

To provide even more protection, some systems ask users to enter one of several pieces of personal information. The question is chosen randomly from information on file. Such items can include a spouse's first name, a birth date, a place of birth, or a mother's maiden name. As with a password, if the user's response does not match the information on file, the system denies access.

Web Link

For more information on personal identification numbers, visit the Discovering Computers 2002 Chapter 12 WEB LINK page (**scsite.com/dc2002/ch12/weblink.htm**) and click Personal Identification Numbers.

POSSESSED OBJECTS A **possessed object** is any item that you must carry to gain access to a computer or computer facility. Examples of possessed objects are badges, cards, and keys. The card you use in an automated teller machine (ATM) is a possessed object that allows access to your bank account (Figure 12-10).

Possessed objects often are used in combination with personal identification numbers. A **personal identification number (PIN)** is a numeric password, either assigned by a company or selected by you. PINs provide an additional level of security. An ATM card typically requires a four-digit PIN. If someone steals your ATM card, the thief must enter your PIN to access your bank account. PINs are passwords. Select them carefully and protect them as you do any other password.

BIOMETRIC DEVICES A **biometric device** authenticates a person's identity by verifying personal characteristics. These devices grant access to programs, systems, or rooms using computer analysis of some biometric identifier. A **biometric identifier** is a physical or behavioral characteristic. Examples include fingerprints, hand geometry, facial features, voice, signatures, and retinal (eye) patterns.

A biometric device translates a personal characteristic into a digital code that is compared to a digital code stored in the computer. If the digital code in the computer does not match the personal characteristics code, the computer denies access to the individual. Many types of biometric devices exist for computer security purposes.

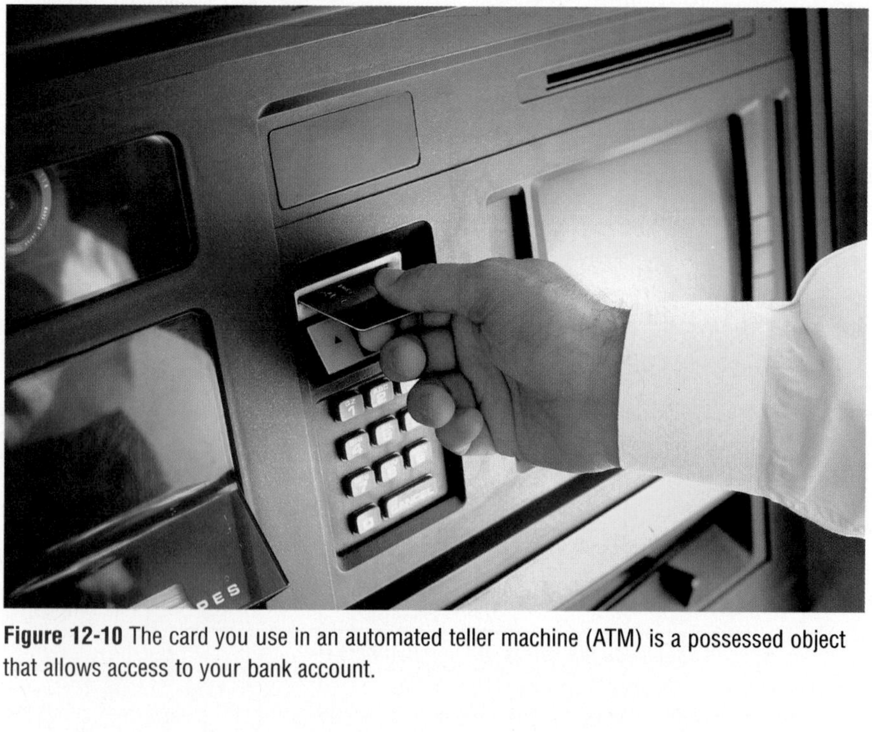

Figure 12-10 The card you use in an automated teller machine (ATM) is a possessed object that allows access to your bank account.

The most widely used biometric device today is a fingerprint scanner. A **fingerprint scanner** captures curves and indentations of a fingerprint (Figure 12-11). With the cost of fingerprint scanners dropping to less than $100, many believe this will become the home user's authentication device for e-commerce transactions.

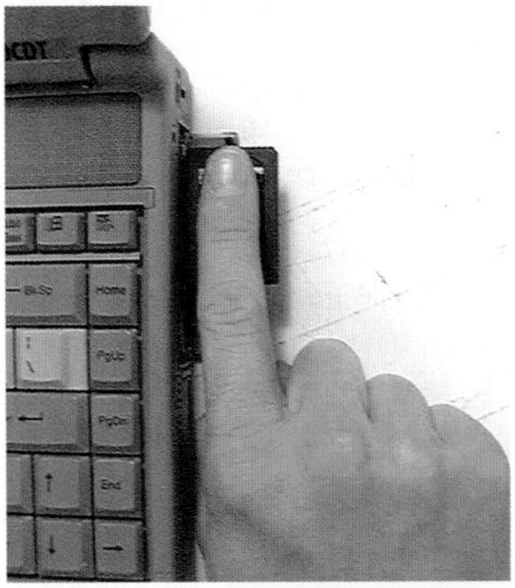

Figure 12-11 Many people believe fingerprint scanners will become the home user's authentication device for e-commerce transactions.

To make a credit-card transaction, the Web site would require you hold your finger on the scanner. These devices usually plug into a parallel or USB port. To save on desk space, some newer keyboards and notebook computers have a fingerprint scanner built into them.

Biometric devices also can measure the shape and size of a person's hand using a **hand geometry system** (Figure 12-12). Costing more than $1,000, larger companies typically use these systems as time and attendance devices. One university cafeteria uses a hand geometry system to verify students when they use their meal card. A day care center uses a hand geometry system to verify parents that pick up their children.

A **face recognition system** captures a live face image and compares it to a stored image to determine if the person is a legitimate user (Figure 12-13). Some notebook computers use this security technique to safeguard the computer. The computer will not boot up unless the user is legitimate. These programs are becoming more sophisticated and can recognize people with or without glasses, makeup, or jewelry, and with new hairstyles.

Web Link

For more information on biometric devices, visit the Discovering Computers 2002 Chapter 12 WEB LINK page (**scsite.com/dc2002/ch12/weblink.htm**) and click Biometric Devices.

Figure 12-12 A user's identity can be verified by his or her hand with a hand geometry system.

Figure 12-13 A face recognition system captures a live face image and compares it to a stored image to determine if the person is a legitimate user.

A **voice verification system** compares a person's live speech to their stored voice pattern. Larger organizations sometimes use voice verification systems as time and attendance devices. Many companies also use this technology for access to sensitive files and networks. Some financial services use voice verification systems to secure telephone banking transactions. These systems use speaker dependent voice recognition software. As discussed in Chapter 5, this type of software requires the computer to make a profile of your voice. That is, you train the computer to recognize your inflection patterns.

A **signature verification system** recognizes the shape of your handwritten signature, as well as measuring the pressure exerted and the motion used to write the signature. Signature verification systems use a specialized pen and tablet.

Extremely high-security areas use retinal scanners (Figure 12-14). An **iris recognition system** reads patterns in the tiny blood vessels in the back of the eye, which are as unique as a fingerprint. These systems are very expensive and are used by government security organizations, the military, and financial institutions that deal with highly sensitive data.

Biometric devices are gaining popularity as a security precaution because they are a virtually foolproof method of identification and authentication. Users can forget their user names and passwords. Possessed objects can be lost, copied, duplicated, or stolen. Personal characteristics, by contrast, are unique and cannot be forgotten or misplaced.

Biometric devices do have some disadvantages. If you cut your finger, a fingerprint scanner might reject you as a legitimate user. Hand geometry readers can transmit germs. If you are nervous, a signature might not match the one on file. If you have a sore throat, a voice recognition system might reject you. Many people are uncomfortable with the thought of using an iris scanner.

CALLBACK SYSTEM A callback system is an access control method that some systems utilize to authenticate remote users. With a **callback system**, you can connect to a computer only after the computer calls you back at a previously established telephone number.

To initiate the callback system, you call the computer and enter a user name and password. If these entries are valid, the computer instructs you to hang up and then calls you back. A callback system provides an additional layer of security. Even if a person steals or guesses a user name and password, that person also must be at the authorized telephone number to access the computer.

Callback systems work best for users who regularly work at the same remote location such as from home or a branch office. Mobile users that need to access a computer from different locations and telephone numbers can use a callback system, but they have to change the callback number stored by the callback system each time they move to a different location.

Figure 12-14 As this customer looks into the camera, an iris recognition system verifies her identity by comparing her iris structure with one stored in the computer. She only will be allowed to make a transaction if the system authenticates her as a valid user.

The authentication technique a company uses should correspond to the degree of risk associated with the unauthorized access. In addition, a company regularly should review users' authorization levels to determine if they still are appropriate.

No matter what type of identification and authentication techniques a company uses, the computer should maintain an **audit trail** or **log** that records in a file both successful and unsuccessful access attempts. Companies should investigate unsuccessful access attempts immediately to ensure they were not intentional breaches of security. They also should review successful access for irregularities, such as use of the computer after normal working hours or from remote computers.

In addition, companies should have written policies regarding the use of computers by employees for personal reasons. Some companies prohibit such use entirely. Others allow personal use on the employee's own time such as a lunch hour. Whatever the policy, a company should document and explain it to employees.

Hardware Theft

Hardware theft is the act of stealing computer equipment. **Hardware vandalism** is the act of defacing or destroying computer equipment. For the desktop computer at home, hardware theft and vandalism usually are not a problem. Companies, however, must protect their computers and associated equipment from theft or vandalism.

To help reduce the chances of theft, companies can use a variety of security measures. Physical access controls, such as locked doors and windows, usually are adequate to protect the equipment. Many businesses, schools, and some homeowners also install alarm systems for additional security. School computer labs and other areas with a large number of semi-frequent users often utilize additional physical security devices such as cables that lock the equipment to a desk, cabinet, or floor (Figure 12-15).

With mobile equipment such as notebook and handheld computers, hardware theft poses a more serious risk. Increasingly, businesses and schools provide notebook computers to employees and students, in addition to loaning them out for short periods. Mobile computer users must take special care to protect their equipment. High-end notebook computers, some of which cost more than $5,000, are particularly at risk. Their size and weight make them easy to steal, and their value makes them tempting targets for thieves.

Common sense and a constant awareness of the risk are the best preventive measures against theft of notebook computers and other mobile equipment. For example, you should never leave a notebook computer unattended in a public place such as an airport or a restaurant or out in the open such as on the seat of a car. You also may want to use a physical device such as a cable to lock a mobile computer temporarily to a desk or table.

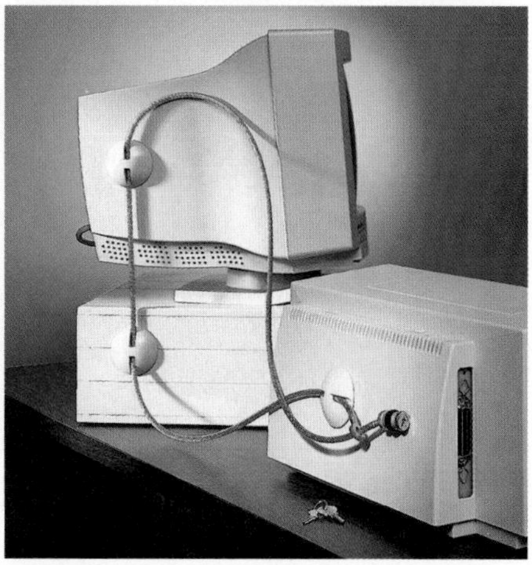

Figure 12-15 Using cables to lock computers can help prevent the theft of desktop and mobile computer equipment.

Some notebook computers use passwords, possessed objects, and biometrics as a method of security. When you boot up these computers, users must authenticate themselves before the password-protected hard disk unlocks. As discussed earlier, some use a face recognition system. Others use a fingerprint scanner, card, or other device. This type of security will not prevent theft, but it will render the computer useless if it is stolen. As a precaution in case of theft, you should back up the files stored on your notebook computer regularly.

For handheld computers, you also can password protect the device. This allows only authorized users access to its data. You usually can instruct the password screen to display your name and telephone number, so a Good Samaritan can return it to you if lost. Several models allow you to encrypt data in the device. A later section in this chapter discusses encryption.

In addition to hardware theft, another area of concern for businesses and schools is vandalism. Computer vandalism takes many forms, from someone cutting a computer cable or deleting important files, to individuals breaking in a business or school computer lab and randomly smashing computers. Most organizations have written policies and procedures for dealing with the various types of vandalism.

Software Theft

As with hardware theft and vandalism, software theft can take many forms — from someone physically stealing media that contains software, such as a DVD-ROM, CD-ROM, Zip® disk, or floppy disk, to intentional piracy of software. **Software piracy** is the unauthorized and illegal duplication of copyrighted software. Software piracy is by far the most common form of software theft.

When you purchase software, you do not *own* the software. Instead, you become a licensed user. You obtain a **license agreement**, or the right to use the software. The license agreement provides specific conditions for use of the software, which a user must accept before using the software (Figure 12-16). You often can see the terms of a license agreement through the shrink wrap surrounding purchased software. In addition, these terms usually display when you install the software. In the case of software on the Web, the terms display on a page at the manufacturer's Web site. Use of the software constitutes acceptance of the terms on the user's part.

Web Link
For more information on software piracy, visit the Discovering Computers 2002 Chapter 12 WEB LINK page (**scsite.com/dc2002/ch12/weblink.htm**) and click Software Piracy.

The most common type of license included with software packages purchased by individual users is a **single-user license agreement**, also called an **end-user license agreement** (**EULA**). A single-user license agreement typically includes many of the following conditions that specify a user's responsibility upon acceptance of the agreement.

Users are permitted to:

- Install the software on only one computer.
- Make one copy for backup.
- Give or sell the software to another individual, but only if they remove the software from their computer first.

Users are not permitted to:

- Install the software on a network, such a school computer lab.
- Give copies to friends and colleagues.
- Export the software.
- Rent or lease the software.

Unless otherwise specified by a license agreement, you do not have the right to copy, loan, rent, or in any way distribute the software. Doing so is a violation of copyright law. It also is a federal crime. Despite this, experts estimate for every authorized copy of software in use, at least one unauthorized copy exists. One study reported software piracy results in worldwide sales losses of more than $11 billion per year.

Software piracy continues for several reasons. In some countries, legal protection for software does not exist. In other countries, laws rarely are enforced. In addition, many buyers believe they have the right to copy the software for which they pay hundreds, even thousands of dollars. Finally, particularly in the case of removable media such as Zip® disks and floppy disks, software piracy is a simple crime to commit.

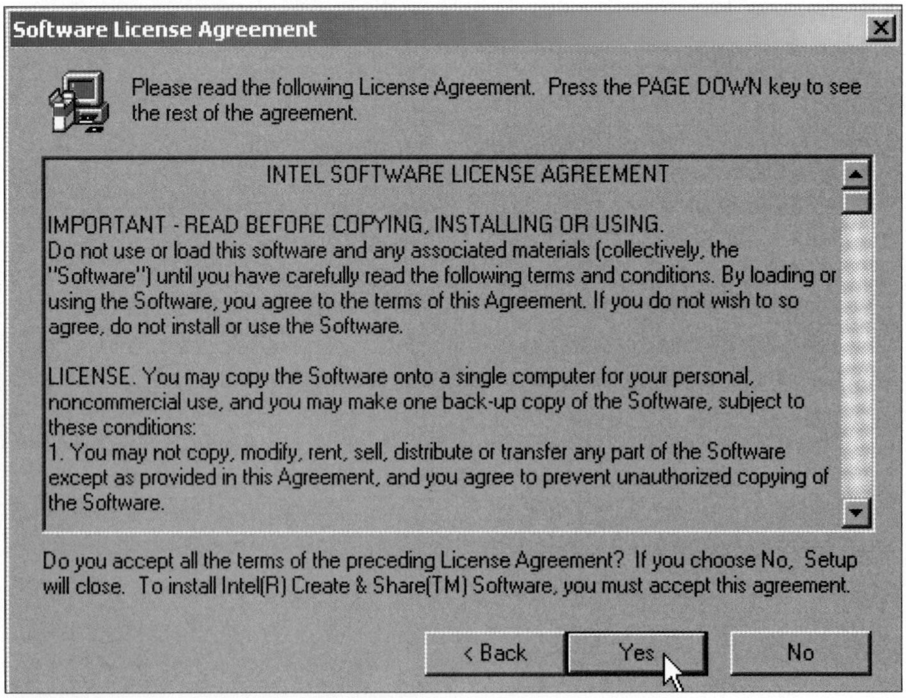

Figure 12-16 You must accept the terms in the license agreement before using the software.

Software piracy, however, is a serious offense. For one, it introduces a number of risks into the software market. It increases the chance of viruses, reduces your ability to receive technical support, and significantly drives up the price of software for all users. Further, software companies take illegal copying seriously. In some cases, offenders have been prosecuted to the fullest extent of the law with penalties including fines up to $250,000 and five years in jail.

To promote a better understanding of software piracy problems and, if necessary, to take legal action, a number of major U.S. software companies formed the **Business Software Alliance** (**BSA**). BSA operates a Web site (Figure 12-17) and antipiracy hotlines in the United States and more than 60 other countries.

Many organizations and businesses also have strict written policies governing the installation and use of software and enforce their rules by periodically checking networked or online computers to ensure that all software is licensed properly. If you are not completely familiar with your school or employer's policies governing installation of software, you always should check with the information technology department or your school's technology coordinator.

To help reduce the software costs for companies with large numbers of users, software vendors often offer them special discount pricing. The more copies of a program a company purchases, the greater the discount. A software **site license** gives the buyer the right to install the software on multiple computers at a single site. Site license fees usually cost significantly less than purchasing individual copies of software for each computer.

Many software packages also have network versions. A **network site license** allows network users to share a single copy of the software, which resides on the network server. Software companies typically price network software site licenses based either on a fixed fee for an unlimited number of users, a maximum number of users, or on a per-user basis.

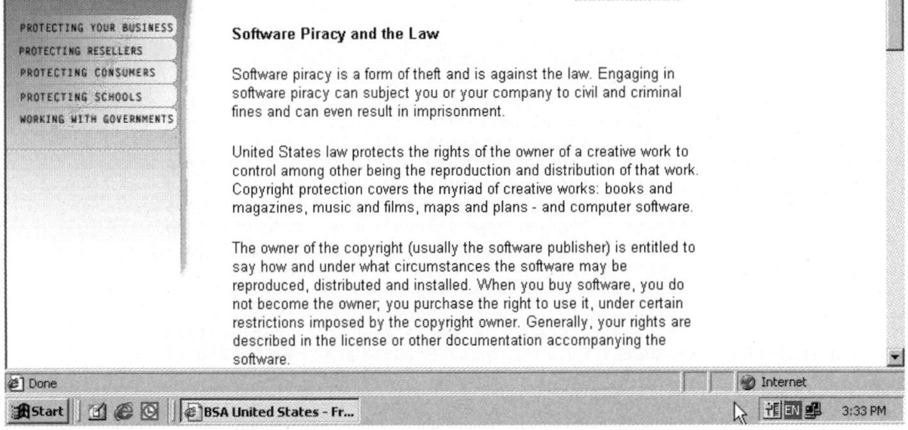

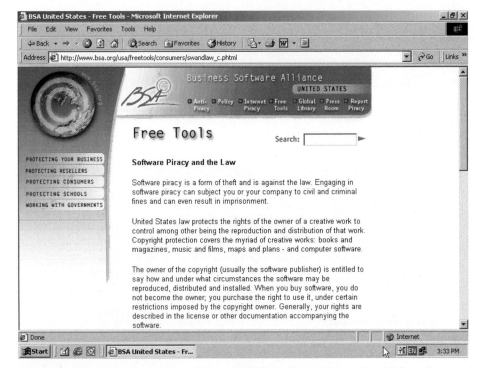

Figure 12-17 The Business Software Alliance (BSA) Web site provides the latest information about software piracy.

Information Theft

Information is a valuable asset to a company. **Information theft** occurs when someone steals personal or confidential information. If stolen, the loss of information can cause as much damage as (if not more than) the theft of hardware or software.

Both business and home users can fall victim to information theft. A company may steal or buy stolen information to learn about a competitor. An individual may steal credit card numbers to make fraudulent purchases. Information theft often is linked to other types of computer crime. An individual might first gain unauthorized access to a computer and then steal credit card numbers stored in a firm's accounting department.

Most companies attempt to prevent information theft by implementing the user identification and authentication controls discussed earlier in this chapter. These controls are best suited for protecting information on computers located on a company's premises. Information transmitted over networks offers a higher degree of risk because unscrupulous users can intercept it during transmission.

One way to protect sensitive data is to encrypt it. The following section discusses encryption techniques.

Web Link

For more information on the Business Software Alliance, visit the Discovering Computers 2002 Chapter 12 WEB LINK page (**scsite.com/dc2002/ch12/weblink.htm**) and click Business Software Alliance.

ENCRYPTION **Encryption** is the process of converting readable data into unreadable characters to prevent unauthorized access. You treat encrypted data just like any other data. That is, you can store it or send it in an e-mail message. To read the data, the recipient must **decrypt** it, or decipher it into a readable form.

In the encryption process, the unencrypted, readable data is called **plaintext**. The encrypted (scrambled) data is called **ciphertext**. To encrypt the data, the originator of the data converts the plaintext into ciphertext using a password or an encryption key. In its simplest form, an **encryption key** is a formula that the recipient of the data uses to decrypt ciphertext.

Many data encryption methods exist. Figure 12-18 shows examples of some simple encryption methods. Figure 12-19 shows a sample encrypted file. An encryption key (formula) often uses more than one of these methods, such as a combination of transposition and substitution. Most organizations use available software packages for encryption. Others develop their own encryption programs.

The two basic types of encryption are private key and public key. With **private key encryption**, also called a **symmetric key encryption**, both the originator and recipient use the same secret key to encrypt and decrypt the data. The most popular private key encryption system is the **data encryption standard (DES)**. The U.S. government is a primary user of the DES.

SIMPLE ENCRYPTION METHODS

NAME	METHOD	PLAINTEXT	CIPHERTEXT	EXPLANATION
Transposition	Switch the order of characters	WIRELESS	IWERELSS	Adjacent characters swapped
Substitution	Replace characters with other characters	LAPTOP	XDQORQ	Each letter replaced with another
Expansion	Insert characters between existing characters	MOUSE	MDODUDSDED	Letter D inserted after each character
Compaction	Remove characters and store elsewhere	COMMUNICATION	COMUICTIN	Every third letter removed (M, N, A, O)

Figure 12-18 This table shows four simple methods of encryption, the process of translating plaintext into ciphertext. Most encryption programs use a combination of these four methods.

Web Link

For more information on encryption, visit the Discovering Computers 2002 Chapter 12 WEB LINK page (**scsite.com/dc2002/ch12/weblink.htm**) and click Encryption.

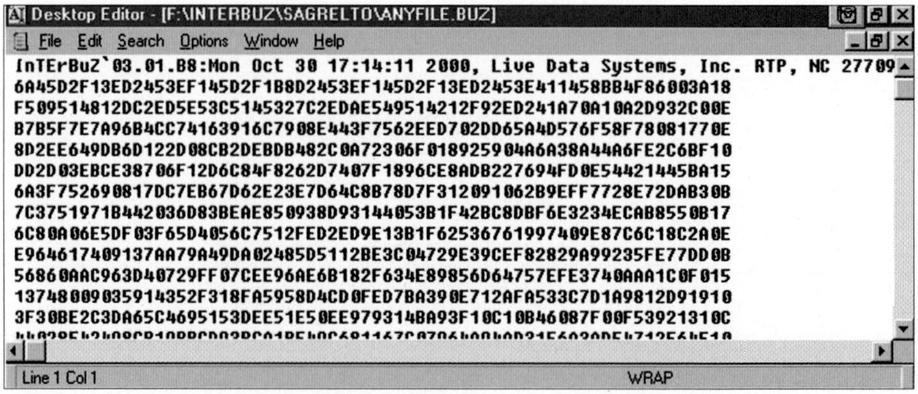

Figure 12-19 A sample encrypted file.

Public key encryption, also called **asymmetric key encryption**, uses two encryption keys: a public key and a private key. Public key encryption software generates both your private key and public key. A message encrypted with your public key only can be decrypted with your private key, and vice-versa.

The public key is made known to those with which you communicate. For example, public keys are posted on a Web page or e-mailed. In other cases, a central administrator publishes a list of public keys on a public-key server. The private key, by contrast, is kept confidential. Never share your private key with anyone nor send it over the Internet for any reason.

To send an encrypted e-mail message with public key encryption, the sender uses the receiver's public key to encrypt the message. Then the receiver uses his or her private key to decrypt the message (Figure 12-20). For example, if Joan wants to send Mohammed an encrypted message, she would use Mohammed's public key to encrypt the message. When Mohammed receives the encrypted message, he would use his private key to decrypt it. Mohammed's encryption software generated his public and private keys. Joan used Mohammed's public key to encrypt the message. Thus, only Mohammed will be able to decrypt the message with his private key.

RSA encryption, named from its inventors, Rivest, Shamir, and Adleman, is a powerful public key encryption technology used to encrypt data transmitted over the Internet. Many software and public key encryption programs use RSA technology. Examples include Pretty Good Privacy (PGP) and newer versions of Netscape Navigator and Microsoft Internet Explorer.

Fortezza is another public key encryption technology that stores the user's private key and other information on a PC Card.

Since 1993, the United States government has proposed several ideas for developing a standard for voice and data encryption that would enable government agencies, such as the National Security Agency (NSA) and the Federal Bureau of Investigation (FBI), to monitor private communications as ordered through court decree. An early government proposal used an encryption formula in a tamper-resistant personal computer processor called the **Clipper chip**. Widespread opposition to this hardware approach caused the idea to be abandoned. In its place, the government proposed a key escrow plan, similar to the public key encryption method. The government's **key escrow** plan proposed using independent escrow organizations that would have custody of private keys that could decode encrypted messages. If necessary, authorized government agencies could obtain the necessary key. This plan also has been opposed and has not yet been implemented.

Figure 12-20 AN EXAMPLE OF PUBLIC KEY ENCRYPTION

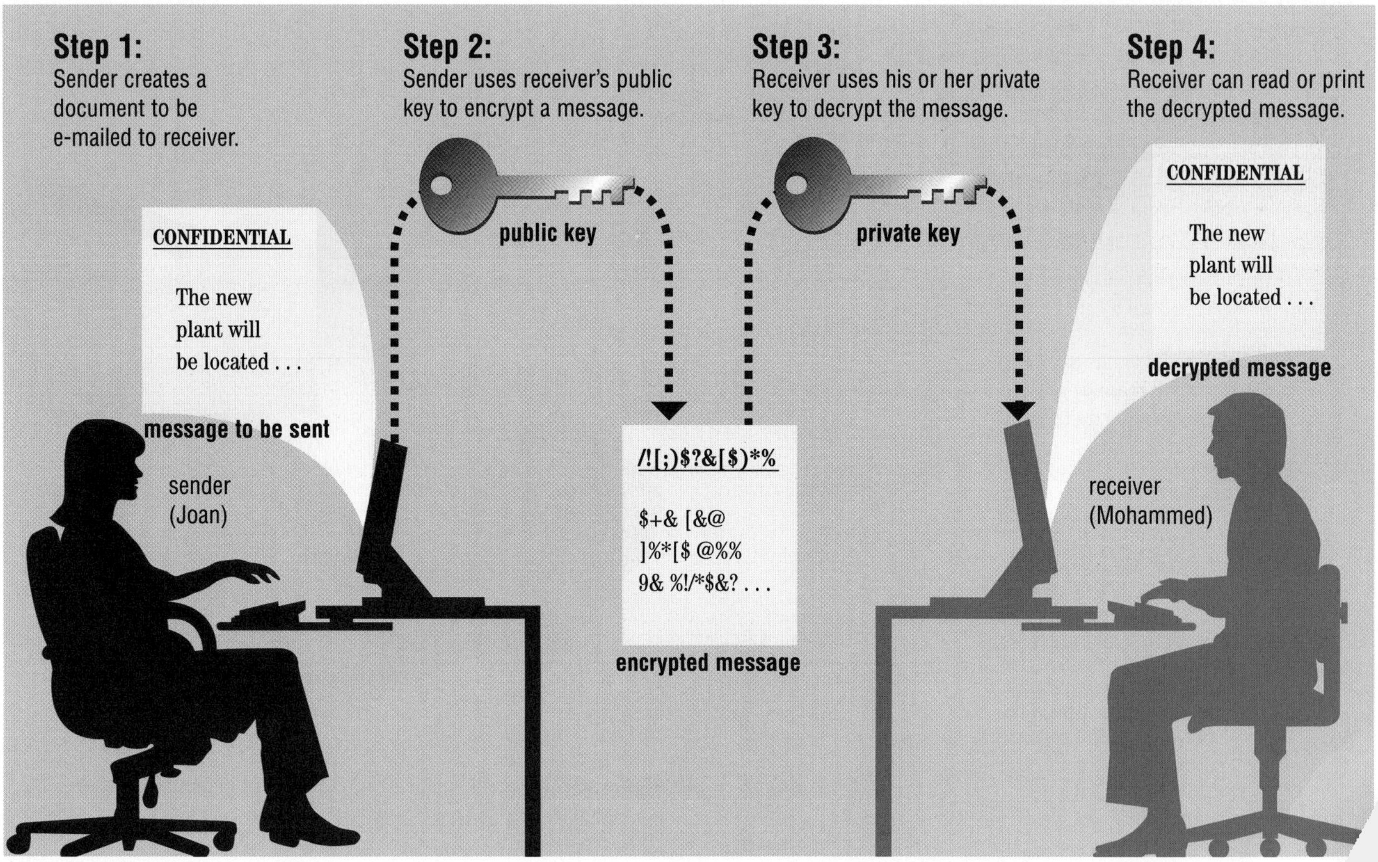

System Failure

Theft is not the only cause of hardware, software, data, or information loss. A **system failure**, which is the prolonged malfunction of a computer, also can cause loss of hardware, software, data, or information. A variety of causes can lead to system failure. These include aging hardware; natural disasters such as fires, floods, or storms; and random events such as electrical power problems.

One of the more common causes of system failure is an electrical power variation. Electrical power variations can cause loss of data or loss of equipment. If the computer equipment is networked, a single power disturbance can damage multiple systems. Electrical disturbances include noise, undervoltages, and overvoltages.

Noise is any unwanted signal, usually varying quickly, that is mixed with the normal voltage entering the computer. Noise is caused by external devices such as fluorescent lighting, radios, and televisions, as well as from components within the computer itself. Noise generally is not a risk to hardware, software, or data. Computer power supplies, however, do filter out noise.

An **undervoltage** occurs when the electrical supply drops. In North America, electricity normally flows from the wall plug at approximately 120 volts. Any significant drop below 120 volts is an undervoltage. A **brownout** is a prolonged undervoltage. A **blackout** is a complete power failure. Undervoltages can cause data loss but generally do not cause equipment damage.

An **overvoltage**, or **power surge**, occurs when the incoming electrical power increases significantly above the normal 120 volts. A momentary overvoltage, called a **spike**, occurs when the power increase lasts for less than one millisecond (one thousandth of a second). Uncontrollable disturbances such as lightning bolts cause spikes. Overvoltages can cause immediate and permanent damage to hardware.

To protect against overvoltages and undervoltages, use a surge protector. A **surge protector**, also called a **surge suppressor**, uses special electrical components to smooth out minor noise, provide a stable current flow, and keep an overvoltage from reaching the computer and other electronic equipment (Figure 12-21).

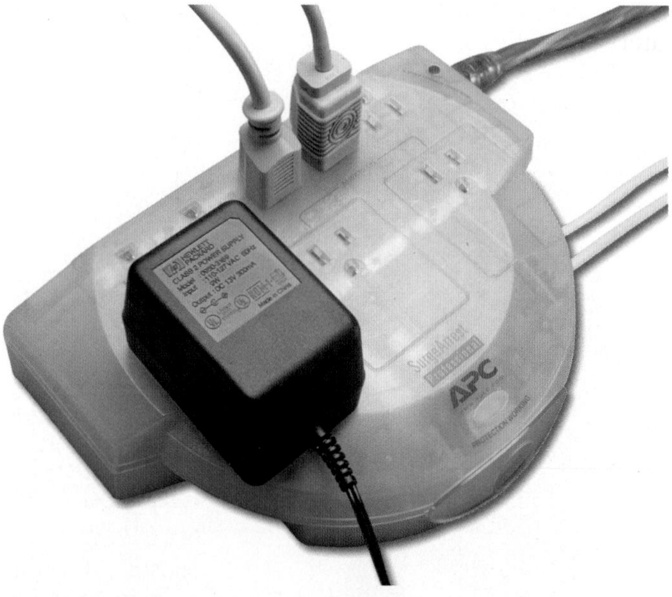

Figure 12-21 Circuits inside a surge protector safeguard against overvoltages and undervoltages.

ISSUE

Secret Code on the Internet?

Data Encryption

Encryption is technology that encodes computer files and communications, much as a combination lock secures a filing cabinet. Internationally, encryption products are widely available. The Freedom system, a new product from Zero-Knowledge Systems (see URL below), strips identifying information from e-mail and makes it impossible to track Web surfing habits. Consumer advocates and civil libertarians praise the new product, but police officers and Internet lawyers are wary. Freedom's encryption techniques can camouflage people participating in illegal activities on the Internet, such as child pornography or software piracy. Law enforcement officials insist that Freedom should allow them, when they have proof a crime has been committed, to trace Freedom users. To what extent is online anonymity a desirable trait? Why? Should there be limits to online anonymity? Why or why not? Should data encryption techniques be available without limit around the world? What about their antisocial uses by criminals?

For more information on encryption and privacy and the Web site mentioned above, visit the Discovering Computers 2002 Issues Web page (**scsite.com/dc2002/issues.htm**) and click Chapter 12 Issue #1.

Web Link

For more information on surge protectors, visit the Discovering Computers 2002 Chapter 12 WEB LINK page (**scsite.com/dc2002/ch12/weblink.htm**) and click Surge Protectors.

Resembling a power strip, the computer and other devices plug into the surge protector, which plugs into the power source. The surge protector absorbs small overvoltages — generally without damage to the computer and equipment. Large overvoltages, such as those caused by a lightning strike, often cause the surge protector to fail in order to protect the computer and other equipment.

Surge protectors are not 100 percent effective. Large power surges can bypass the protector. Repeated small overvoltages can weaken a surge protector permanently. Some experts recommend replacing a surge protector every two to three years. Typically, the amount of protection offered by a surge protector is proportional to its cost. That is, the more expensive, the more protection the protector offers.

The surge protector you purchase should meet the safety specification for surge suppression products. This specification, called the **Underwriters Laboratories (UL) 1449 standard**, allows no more than 500 maximum volts to pass through the line. The surge protector also should have a Joule rating of at least 200. A **Joule** is the unit of energy a surge protection device can absorb before it can be damaged. The higher the Joule rating, the better the protection.

If your computer connects to a network or the Internet, be sure also to have protection for your modem, telephone lines, and network lines. Many surge protectors include plug-ins for telephone lines and other cables. If yours does not, you can purchase separate devices to protect these lines.

For additional electrical protection, many users connect an uninterruptible power supply to the computer. An **uninterruptible power supply (UPS)** is a device that contains surge protection circuits and one or more batteries that can provide power during a temporary or permanent loss of power (Figure 12-22). A UPS connects between your computer and a power source.

Two types of UPS devices are standby and online. A standby UPS, sometimes called an offline UPS, switches to battery power when a problem occurs in the power line. The amount of time a standby UPS allows you to continue working depends on the electrical requirements of the computer and the size of the batteries in the UPS. A UPS for a personal computer should provide from 10 to 30 minutes of use in the case of a total power loss. This should be enough time to save current work and shut down the computer properly.

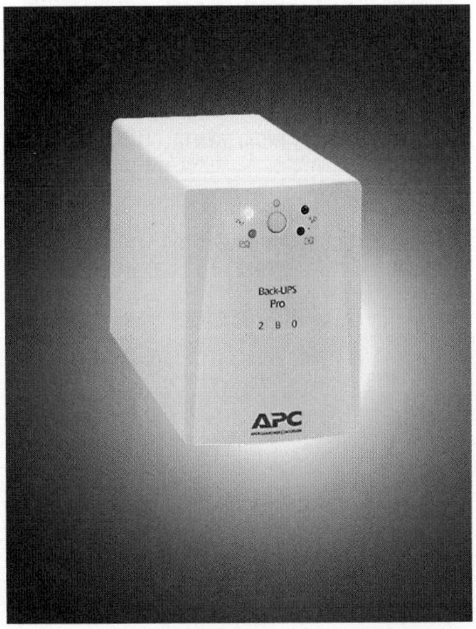

Figure 12-22 If power fails, an uninterruptable power supply (UPS) uses batteries to provide electricity for a limited amount of time.

An online UPS always runs off the battery, which provides continuous protection. An online UPS is much more expensive than a standby UPS.

Backup Procedures

To prevent against data loss caused by a system failure, computer users should back up files regularly. A **backup** is a duplicate of a file, program, or disk that can be used if the original is lost, damaged, or destroyed. Thus, to **back up** a file means to make a copy of it. In the case of a system failure or the discovery of corrupted files, you **restore** the files by copying the backed up files to their original location on the computer.

You can use just about any media to store backups. Be sure to use high-quality media. Losing data is expensive. High-quality media is worth the investment. A good choice for a home user might be Zip® disks or CD-RWs.

Keep backup copies in a fireproof and heatproof safe or vault, or offsite. **Offsite** means in a location separate from the computer site. Home and business users utilize offsite storage so that a single disaster, such as a fire, does not destroy both the original and the backup copy of the data. One type of offsite location is a safe deposit box at a bank. A growing trend is to use an Internet hard drive as an offsite location. As discussed in Chapter 7, an Internet hard drive or online storage is a service on the Web that provides storage to computer users.

Business and home users can perform three types of backup: full, differential, or incremental. A **full backup**, sometimes called an **archival backup**, copies all of the files in the computer. A full backup provides the best protection against data loss because it copies all program and data files. Performing a full backup can be time consuming. Users often combine full backups with differential and incremental backups. A **differential backup** copies only the files that have changed since the last full backup. An **incremental backup** copies only the files that have changed since the last full *or* last incremental backup.

The main difference between a differential backup and an incremental backup is the number of backup files and the time required for backup. With a differential backup, you always have two backups: the full backup and the differential backup that contains all changes since the last full backup.

With incremental backups, you have the full backup and one or more incremental backups. The first incremental backup contains changes since the last full backup. Each incremental backup contains changes only since the previous incremental backup. For files that contain many changes and comprise a large portion of the total data, incremental backup usually is fastest. If files contain only a few changes, differential backups may be appropriate. Figure 12-23 outlines the advantages and disadvantages of each type of backup.

Backup procedures specify a regular plan of copying and storing important data and program files. Generally, users should perform a full backup at regular intervals, such as at the end of each week and at the end of the month. Between full backups, you can perform differential or incremental backups. Figure 12-24 shows a sample approach a company might follow for backing up a system for one month. This combination of full and incremental backups provides an efficient way to protect data. Whatever backup procedures a company adopts, they should be stated clearly, documented in writing, and followed consistently.

August 2002

MONDAY	TUESDAY	WEDNESDAY	THURSDAY	FRIDAY	SAT/SUN
29 DAILY INCREMENTAL	30 DAILY INCREMENTAL	31 END OF MONTH FULL BACKUP	1 DAILY INCREMENTAL	2 WEEKLY FULL BACKUP	3/4
5 DAILY INCREMENTAL	6 DAILY INCREMENTAL	7 DAILY INCREMENTAL	8 DAILY INCREMENTAL	9 WEEKLY FULL BACKUP	10/11
12 DAILY INCREMENTAL	13 DAILY INCREMENTAL	14 DAILY INCREMENTAL	15 DAILY INCREMENTAL	16 WEEKLY FULL BACKUP	17/18
19 DAILY INCREMENTAL	20 DAILY INCREMENTAL	21 DAILY INCREMENTAL	22 DAILY INCREMENTAL	23 WEEKLY FULL BACKUP	24/25
26 DAILY INCREMENTAL	27 DAILY INCREMENTAL	28 DAILY INCREMENTAL	29 DAILY INCREMENTAL	30 END OF MONTH FULL BACKUP	31/1

Figure 12-24 This calendar shows a backup strategy for a month. End-of-month backups usually are kept for at least one year.

VARIOUS BACKUP METHODS

TYPE OF BACKUP	ADVANTAGES	DISADVANTAGES
Full	Fastest recovery method. All files are saved.	Longest backup time.
Differential	Fast backup method. Requires minimal space to back up.	Recovery is time consuming because need last full backup plus the differential backup.
Incremental	Fastest backup method. Requires minimal space to back up. Only most recent changes saved.	Recovery is most time consuming because need last full backup and all incremental backups since last full backup.

Figure 12-23 The advantages and disadvantages of various backup methods.

Some users implement a **three-generation backup** policy to preserve three copies of important files. The **grandparent** is the oldest copy of the file. The **parent** is the second oldest copy of the file. The **child** is the most recent copy of the file.

Backup programs are available from many sources. Most operating systems include a backup program. Backup devices, such as tape and removable disk drives, also include backup programs. Numerous stand-alone backup utilities exist. Many of these can be downloaded from the Web at no cost. As discussed in Chapter 8, some vendors offer utility suites that combine several utility programs into a single package or make them available on the Web. These suites typically include a backup utility.

Some companies opt to use an online backup service to handle their backup needs. An **online backup service** is a Web site that automatically backs up your files to their online location. These sites usually charge a monthly or annual fee. If your system crashes, the online backup service typically sends you a CD-ROM that contains all your backed up data. Users with high-speed Internet connections opt for online backup services. For slower connections, these services are not practical.

Disaster Recovery Plan

Every company should develop a disaster recovery plan. A **disaster recovery plan** is a written plan describing the steps a company would take to restore computer operations in the event of a disaster. A disaster recovery plan contains four major components: the emergency plan, the backup plan, the recovery plan, and the test plan.

THE EMERGENCY PLAN An **emergency plan** specifies the steps to be taken immediately after a disaster strikes. The emergency plan usually is organized by type of disaster, such as fire, flood, or earthquake. Depending on the nature and extent of the disaster, emergency procedures will differ. All emergency plans should contain the following information:

1. Names and telephone numbers of people and organizations to notify (e.g., management, fire department, police department)
2. Procedures to follow with the computer equipment (e.g., equipment shutdown, power shutoff, file removal)
3. Employee evacuation procedures
4. Return procedures; that is, who can re-enter the facility and what actions they are to perform

THE BACKUP PLAN Once the procedures in the emergency plan have been executed, the next step is to follow the backup plan. The **backup plan** specifies how a company uses backup files and equipment to resume information processing. The backup plan should specify the location of an alternate computer facility in the event the company's normal location is destroyed or unusable. The backup plan identifies these items:

1. The location of backup data, supplies, and equipment
2. The personnel responsible for gathering backup resources and transporting them to the alternate computer facility
3. A schedule indicating the order and approximate time each application should be up and running

For a backup plan to be successful, it is crucial the company backs up all critical resources. It also is crucial that additional people, including possibly non-employees, are trained in the backup and recovery procedures because company personnel could be injured in a disaster.

The location of the alternate computer facility is important. It should be close enough to be convenient, yet not too close that a single disaster, such as an earthquake, could destroy both the main and alternate computer facilities. Some companies pre-install all the necessary hardware, software, and communications devices at the alternate computer facility. These facilities immediately are ready in the event of a disaster. In other cases, the alternate computer facility is simply an empty facility that can accommodate the necessary computer resources, if necessary. Another alternative is to enter into a **reciprocal backup relationship** with another firm, where one firm provides space and sometimes equipment to the other in case of a disaster.

THE RECOVERY PLAN The **recovery plan** specifies the actions to be taken to restore full information processing operations. As with the emergency plan, the recovery plan differs for each type of disaster. To prepare for disaster recovery, a company should establish planning committees, with each one responsible for different forms of recovery. For example, one committee is in charge of hardware replacement. Another is responsible for software replacement.

THE TEST PLAN To provide assurance that the disaster plan is complete, it should be tested. A disaster recovery **test plan** contains information for simulating various levels of disasters and recording an organization's ability to recover. In a simulation, all personnel follow the steps in the disaster recovery plan. Any needed recovery actions that are not specified in the plan should be added. Although simulations can be scheduled, the best test of the plan is to simulate a disaster without advance notice.

Developing a Computer Security Plan

A company should incorporate the individual risks and safeguards previously mentioned and the disaster recovery into an overall computer security plan. A **computer security plan** summarizes in writing all of the safeguards that are in place to protect a company's information assets. A computer security plan should do the following:

1. Identify all information assets of an organization, including hardware, software, documentation, procedures, people, data, facilities, and supplies.
2. Identify all security risks that may cause an information asset loss. Rank risks from most likely to occur to least likely to occur. Place an estimated value on each risk, including the value of lost business. For example, what is the estimated loss if customers cannot place orders for one hour, one day, or one week?
3. For each risk, identify the safeguards that exist to detect, prevent, and recover from a loss.

The company should evaluate the computer security plan annually or more frequently for major changes in information assets, such as the addition of a new computer or the implementation of a new application. In developing the plan, keep in mind that some degree of risk is unavoidable. The more secure a system is, the more difficult it is for everyone to use. The goal of a computer security plan is to match an appropriate level of safeguards against the identified risks. Fortunately, most organizations will never experience a major information system disaster.

Companies and individuals who need help with computer security plans can contact the **International Computer Security Association** (**ICSA**) via the telephone or on the Web for assistance (Figure 12-25).

INTERNET AND NETWORK SECURITY

Information transmitted over networks has a higher degree of security risk than information kept on a company's premises. The Internet and networks employ many security techniques discussed thus far such as user names, passwords, biometrics, and callback systems. Network administrators usually take measures to protect a network from security risks. On a vast network such as the Internet with no central administrator, the risk is even greater. Every computer along the path of your data can see what you send and receive. Fortunately, most Web browsers and many Web sites use techniques to keep data secure and private.

Web Link

For more information on the International Computer Security Association, visit the Discovering Computers 2002 Chapter 12 WEB LINK page (**scsite.com/dc2002/ch12/weblink.htm**) and click International Computer Security Association.

Figure 12-25 The ICSA is available for companies or individuals that need assistance with computer security plans.

The following pages address the increased risks associated with networks and the measures you can take to protect your systems while online. Most businesses use more than one of these security techniques.

Securing Internet Transactions

To provide secure data transmission, many Web browsers use encryption. Newer versions of Netscape Navigator and Microsoft Internet Explorer use RSA. Recall that RSA is a very popular public key encryption technology. Some browsers offer a protection level known as 40-bit encryption. Many offer 128-bit encryption, which is an even higher level of protection. Applications requiring more security, such as banks, brokerage firms, or online retailers that use credit card or other financial information, use 128-bit encryption.

A Web site that uses encryption techniques to secure its data is known as a **secure site**. Secure sites use digital certificates along with a security protocol. Two popular security protocols are Secure Sockets Layer and Secure HTTP. Credit card transactions sometimes use the Secure Electronics Transaction specification. The following paragraphs discuss each of these encryption techniques.

DIGITAL CERTIFICATES A **digital certificate**, also called a **public-key certificate**, is a notice that guarantees a user or a Web site is legitimate. E-commerce applications commonly use digital certificates.

A **certificate authority** (**CA**) or **issuing authority** (**IA**) is an authorized company or person that issues and verifies digital certificates. You apply for a digital certificate from a CA (Figure 12-26). A digital certificate typically contains your name, your public key and its expiration date, the issuing CA's name and signature, and the serial number of the certificate. The information in a digital certificate is encrypted using the CA's private key.

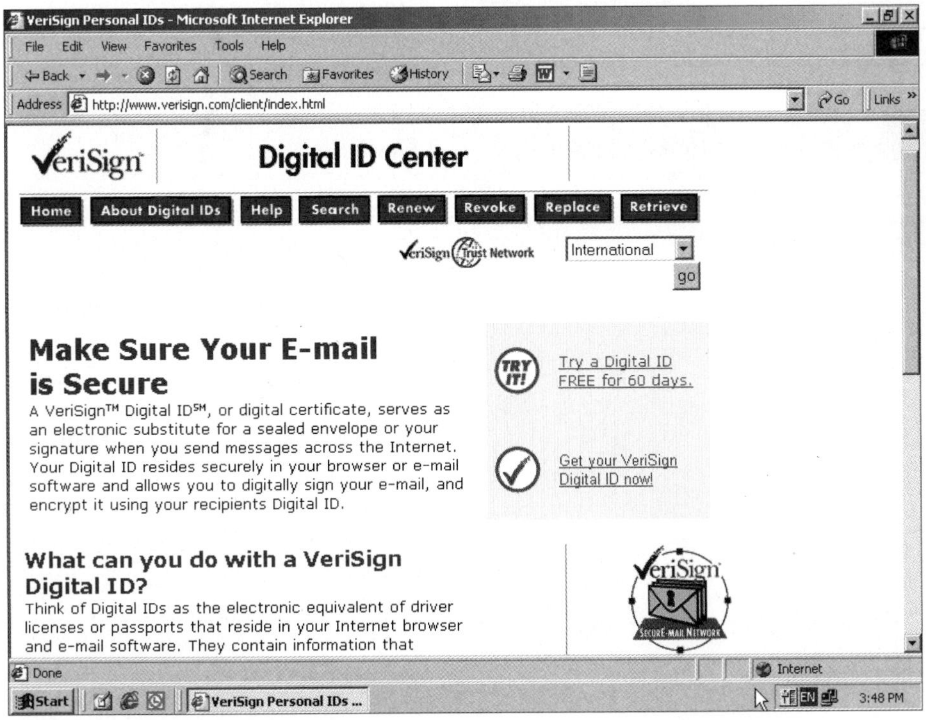

Figure 12-26 VeriSign is a certificate authority that issues and verifies digital certificates.

Web Link

For more information on digital certificates, visit the Discovering Computers 2002 Chapter 12 WEB LINK page (**scsite.com/dc2002/ch12/weblink.htm**) and click Digital Certificates.

COMPANY ON THE CUTTING EDGE

SYMANTEC.

Internet Security

You lock the door to your apartment and exercise extra caution when walking alone at night. But do you protect your computer from hacker attacks or theft of your personal and financial data? Probably not, according to a survey conducted by Applied Marketing Research, Inc. Only about one in five personal computer users has some sort of personal firewall to deter cybercriminals.

Although nearly 90 percent of these users have installed an antivirus program, they are leaving their computers open to attack each time they surf the Internet or buy products online.

Symantec is one of the world's premier Internet security technology companies with operations in more than 33 countries. Its more than 2,600 employees develop mobile code protection and e-mail and Internet content filtering programs, along with antivirus and risk management software to protect 60 million users against malicious threats. Ninety-eight of the Fortune 100 companies use one or more of these products daily.

For more information on Symantec, visit the Discovering Computers 2002 Companies Web page (**scsite.com/dc2002/companies.htm**) and click Symantec.

SECURE SOCKETS LAYER **Secure Sockets Layer** (**SSL**) provides private-key encryption of all data that passes between a client and a server. SSL requires the client has a digital certificate. Once the server has a digital certificate, the Web browser communicates securely with the client. Web pages that use SSL typically begin with https, instead of http (Figure 12-27).

SECURE HTTP **Secure HTTP** (**S-HTTP**) allows you to choose an encryption scheme for data that passes between a client and a server. With S-HTTP, the client and server both must have digital certificates. S-HTTP is more difficult to use than SSL, but it is more secure. Applications that must verify the authenticity of a client, such as for online banking, use S-HTTP.

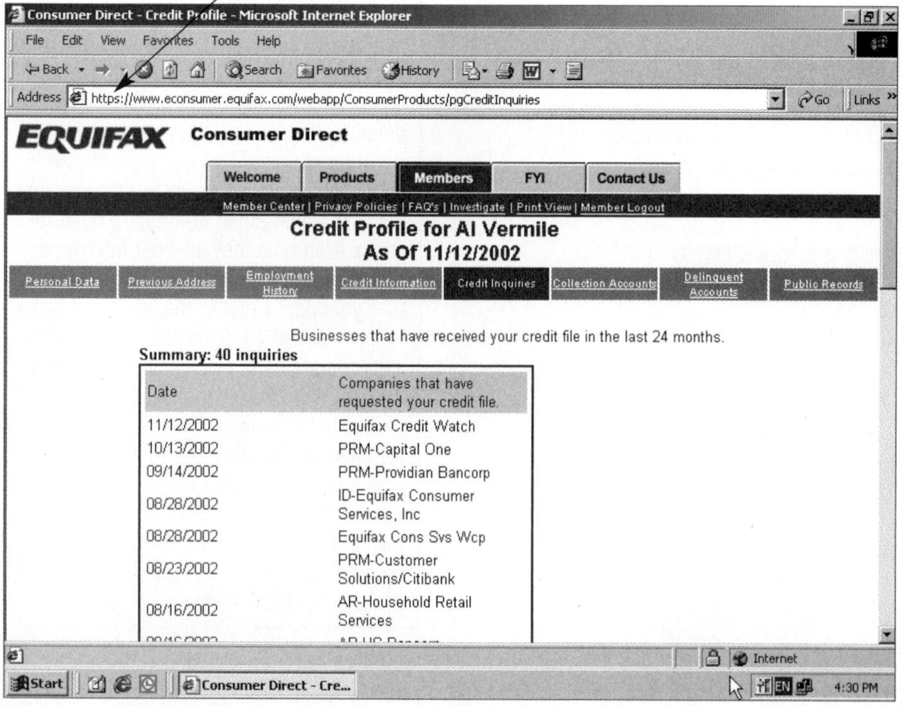

Figure 12-27 Secure Web pages often begin with https instead of http.

SECURE ELECTRONIC TRANSACTION The **Secure Electronic Transaction** (**SET**) specification uses a public-key encryption to secure credit-card transaction systems. The SET specification is quite complex, making it slow on some systems.

Securing E-mail Messages

When you send an e-mail message over the Internet, just about anyone can read it. If you are sending personal or confidential information in the message, you should protect the message from prying eyes. An unprotected e-mail sent through the Internet is similar to sending a post-card through the United States mail. Two ways to protect an e-mail message are to encrypt it and to sign it digitally.

One of the most popular e-mail encryption programs is **Pretty Good Privacy** (**PGP**). PGP is freeware for personal, non-commercial users. Home users can download PGP from the Web at no cost. PGP uses a public-key encryption scheme. As shown in Figure 12-20 on page 12.17, when you receive an e-mail message encrypted with your public key, you use your private key to decrypt the message.

A **digital signature**, also called a **digital ID**, is an encrypted code that a person, Web site, or company attaches to an electronic message to verify the identity of the message sender. The code usually consists of the user's name and a hash of all or part of the message. A **hash** is a mathematical formula that generates a code from the contents of the message. Thus, the hash differs for each message.

Digital signatures use a public key method. Senders use their private key to encrypt their digital signature. Receivers of the message use the sender's public key to decrypt the digital signature. The recipient then generates a new hash of the received message and compares it to one in the digital signature to ensure they match.

Digital signatures often are used to ensure that an impostor is not participating in an Internet transaction. That is, digital signatures help to prevent e-mail forgery. A digital signature also can verify that the content of a message has not changed.

Firewalls

Despite efforts to protect the data on your computer's hard disk, it still is vulnerable to attacks from a hacker. A **firewall** is a security system consisting of hardware and/or software that prevents unauthorized access to data and information on a network. Companies use firewalls to deny network access to outsiders and to restrict employees' access to sensitive data such as payroll or personnel records.

To implement a firewall, many large companies route all communications through a proxy server. A **proxy server** is a server outside the company's network that controls which communications pass into the company's network. That is, the firewall carefully screens all incoming and outgoing messages.

Firewalls use a variety of screening techniques. Some check the domain name or IP address of the message for legitimacy. Others require the messages have digital signatures.

All networked or online computer users should have a firewall. Businesses can implement a firewall solution themselves or outsource their needs to a company that specializes in providing firewall protection. Home and small office/home office users should install personal firewalls.

A **personal firewall** is a software program that detects and protects your personal computer and its data from unauthorized intrusions. These products constantly monitor all transmissions to and from your computer and inform you of any attempted intrusion (Figure 12-28). These easy-to-use products are definitely worth their expense, which usually is less than $50. The table in Figure 12-29 lists popular personal firewall products.

APPLY IT!

Personal Firewall

When you think about a firewall, you might think about a business network. Firewalls keep out hackers and others who attempt to steal data or crash your system. Traditionally, firewall software for the home user was too expensive, difficult to install, and rarely needed when most individuals used slow dial-up modems. Enter broadband access and personal computers with new high-speed always on DSL or cable modem connections and the personal firewall moves into the mainstream. Today, a variety of inexpensive and even almost free shareware programs exists for the home user. This new class of host-based firewalls typically protects a single personal computer against network threats. These programs are easy to use and easy to install.

If you have a home network connecting several computers that share a broadband link to the Internet, you should consider installing a network firewall. Unlike a personal firewall, which usually is software only, a network firewall often is a combination of software and hardware that creates a secure barrier between your network and the Internet.

You probably would benefit from a home network or personal firewall if your computing practices include any of the following:

- Your computer files need to be accessed remotely across the network
- You use any sort of Internet-based remote control or remote access program such as PC Anywhere, Laplink, or Wingate
- You want to monitor your Internet connection for intrusion attempts
- You operate an Internet server such as Personal Web Server
- You want to protect your system from Trojan horse virus programs

For more information on personal firewalls and home network firewalls, visit the Discovering Computers 2002 Apply It Web page (**scsite.com/dc2002/apply.htm**) and click Chapter 12 Apply It #2.

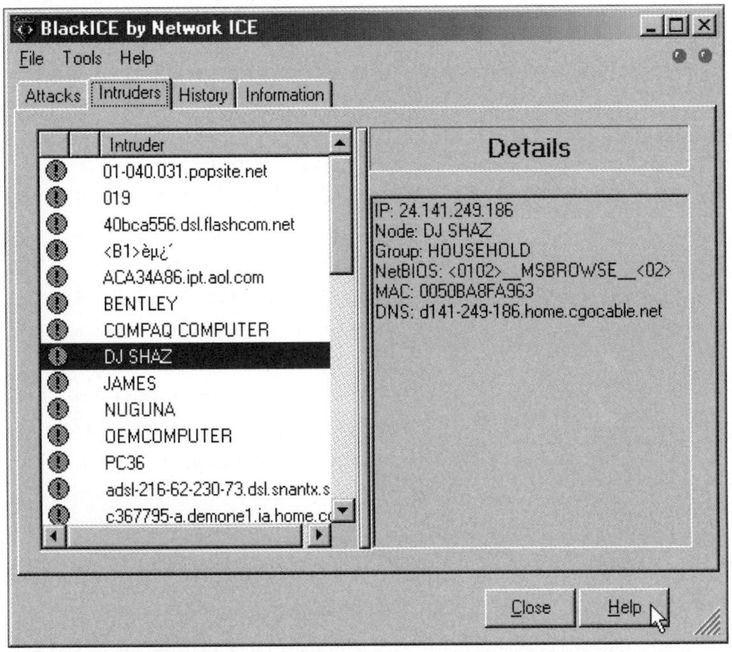

Figure 12-28 Personal firewall packages detect and protect your personal computer from hackers.

POPULAR PERSONAL FIREWALL PRODUCTS

- BlackICE Defender
- Internet Guard Dog
- McAfee Firewall
- Norton Internet Security
- ZoneAlarm

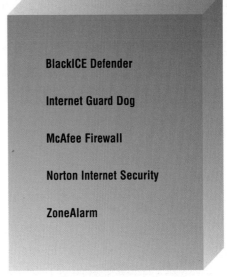

Figure 12-29 Popular personal firewall products.

Web Link

For more information on online security services, visit the Discovering Computers 2002 Chapter 12 WEB LINK page (**scsite.com/dc2002/ch12/weblink.htm**) and click Online Security Services.

TECHNOLOGY TRAILBLAZER

DONN **PARKER**

Computer crime cannot be predicted, according to the Parker Philosophy. Consequently, companies cannot prepare for future threats based on previous attacks. Donn Parker ought to know — he is one of the world's leading authorities on cybercrime.

For the past 30 years, Parker has been interviewing more than 200 computer criminals and reviewing thousands of cases of reported security crimes. He has learned that these crooks are unpredictable and irrational. They generally believe they are acting ethically and that violating the law is the best method of solving deep personal problems.

Companies can fight cybercrime by using Parker's Peer Principle: Share information about the vulnerability of attacks, develop security methods, and then apply and practice these models.

With six books published on computer security, Parker has participated in more than 250 security reviews for major corporations. His most recent book is *Fighting Computer Crime, a New Framework for Protecting Information.* He has appeared on *60 Minutes*, *20/20*, and *NOVA* and has been featured in *People* and the *Los Angeles Times*. He earned bachelor's and master's degrees from the University of California at Berkeley.

For more information on Donn Parker, visit the Discovering Computers 2002 People Web page (**scsite.com/dc2002/people.htm**) and click Donn Parker.

To further protect your personal computer from unauthorized intrusions, you should disable File and Print Sharing on your Internet connection (Figure 12-30). This security measure attempts to ensure that others cannot access your files or your printer.

To determine if your computer is vulnerable to a hacker attack, you could use an online security service. An **online security service** is a Web site that evaluates your computer to check for Web and e-mail vulnerabilities. The service then provides recommendations of how to deal with the vulnerabilities.

INFORMATION PRIVACY

Information privacy refers to the right of individuals and companies to deny or restrict the collection and use of information about them. In the past, information privacy was easier to maintain because information was kept in separate locations. Retail stores each had their own credit files. Each government agency maintained separate records. Doctors had their own patient files.

Today, huge databases store this data in online databases. Much of the data is personal and confidential and should be accessible to only authorized users. Many individuals and organizations, however, question whether this data really is private. That is, some companies and individuals collect and use this information without your authorization. Many Web sites collect data about you so they can customize advertisements and send you personalized e-mail messages. Some employers monitor your computer usage and e-mail messages.

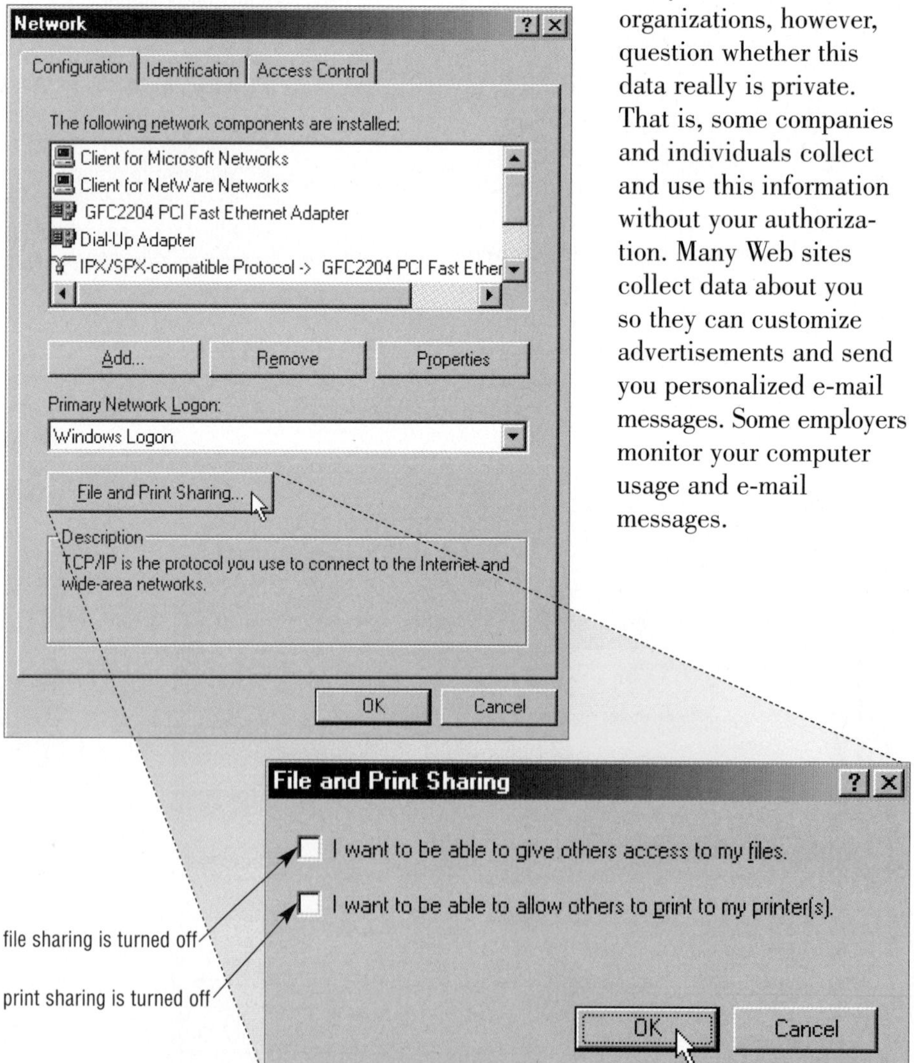

Figure 12-30 To protect files on your local hard disk from hackers, turn off File and Print Sharing on your Internet connection.

The following sections address techniques companies and employers use to collect your personal data. Figure 12-31 lists actions you can take to make your personal data more private.

Electronic Profiles

When you fill out a form such as a magazine subscription, product warranty registration card, or contest entry form, the merchant that receives the form usually enters it into a database. Likewise, every time you click an advertisement on the Web or register a software product online, your information and preferences enter a database. Merchants then sell the contents of their databases to national marketing firms and Internet advertising firms. By combining this data with information from public sources such as driver's license and vehicle registrations, these firms create an electronic profile of individuals.

The marketing and advertising firms pride themselves on being able to collect accurate, in depth information about people. The information in an electronic profile includes very personal details such as your age, address, telephone number, spending habits, marital status, number of dependents, ages of dependents, and so on.

These firms then sell your electronic profile to any company that requests it. A car dealership may

How to Safeguard Personal Information
1. Fill in only necessary information on rebate, warranty, and registration forms.
2. Do not preprint your telephone number or Social Security number on personal checks.
3. Have an unlisted or unpublished telephone number.
4. If Caller ID is available in your area, find out how to block your number from displaying on the receiver's system.
5. Do not write your telephone number on charge or credit receipts.
6. Ask merchants to not write credit card numbers, telephone numbers, Social Security numbers, and driver's license numbers on the back of your personal checks.
7. Purchase goods with cash, rather than credit or checks.
8. Avoid shopping clubs and buyers' cards.
9. If a merchant asks personal questions, find out why they want to know before releasing the information.
10. Inform merchants that you do not want them to distribute your personal information.
11. Ask, in writing, to be removed from mailing lists.
12. Obtain your credit report once a year from each of the three major credit reporting agencies (Equifax, Experian, and TransUnion) and correct any errors.
13. Request a free copy of your medical records once a year from the Medical Information Bureau.
14. Limit the amount of information you provide to Web sites. Just fill in required information.
15. Install a cookie manager to filter cookies.
16. Clear your history file when you are finished browsing.
17. Set up a free e-mail account. Use this e-mail address for merchant forms.
18. Turn off File and Print Sharing on your Internet connection.
19. Install a personal firewall.
20. Sign-up for e-mail filtering through your Internet service provider or use an anti-spam program such as Brightmail.
21. Do not reply to spam for any reason.
22. Surf the Web anonymously with programs such as Freedom or through an anonymous Web site such as Anonymizer.

Figure 12-31 Techniques to keep personal data private.

Web Link

For more information on cookies, visit the Discovering Computers 2002 Chapter 12 WEB LINK page (**scsite.com/dc2002/ch12/weblink.htm**) and click Cookies.

ISSUE

Personal Information for Sale

Privacy Invasion

The State of Virginia has a law that declares that "Any person whose name, portrait, or picture is used without having first obtained the written consent of such person … for advertising purposes or for the purposes of trade, such persons may maintain a suit in equity against the person, firm…" Citing this law, a Virginia resident recently filed a claim against a national magazine challenging the right of the magazine to sell or rent his name and other personal information to another publication without his express written consent. The company obtained the personal information when the Virginia resident filled out an online registration form to obtain a free sample copy of a magazine. When you fill out online forms or purchase an item online, the retailer has your e-mail address and other personal information. Should these retailers be allowed to send you marketing pieces? Should they be allowed to sell your e-mail address to others? Is this an ethical practice? Should there be a Federal law prohibiting companies from selling your personal information? Why or why not?

For more information on personal information and privacy issues, visit the Discovering Computers 2002 Issues Web page (**scsite.com/dc2002/issues.htm**) and click Chapter 12 Issue #2.

want to send an advertisement piece or e-mail message to all sports car owners in its vicinity. Thus, the dealership may request a list of all sports car owners living in the southeastern United States.

Direct marketing supporters say that using information in this way lowers overall selling costs, which lowers product prices. Critics contend that the information in an electronic profile can reveal more about an individual than anyone has a right to know. They claim that companies should inform people if they plan to provide personal information to others. Further, people should have the right to deny such use. Many companies today allow you to specify whether you want them to distribute your personal information (Figure 12-32).

Cookies

Webcasting, e-commerce, and other Web applications often rely on cookies to identify users and customize Web pages. A **cookie** is a small file that a Web server stores on *your* computer. Cookie files typically contain data about you, such as your user name or viewing preferences. Many commercial Web sites send a cookie to your browser, and then your computer's hard disk stores the cookie. The next time you visit the Web site, your browser retrieves the cookie from your hard disk and sends the data in the cookie to the Web site. Web sites use cookies for a variety of purposes.

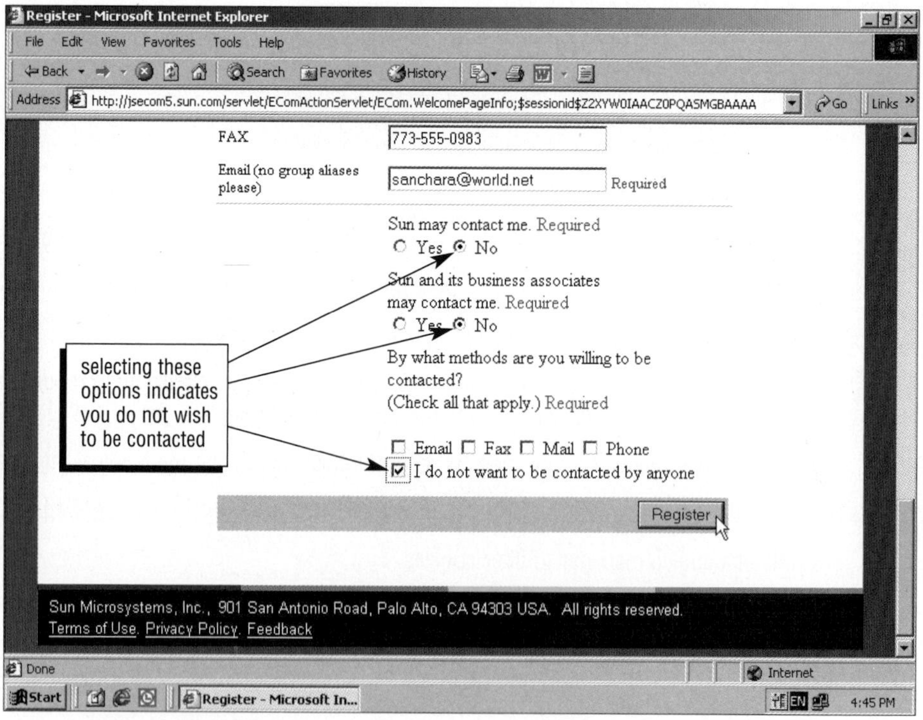

Figure 12-32 Many companies today allow you to specify whether you want them to distribute your personal information.

- Web sites that allow for personalization often use cookies to track user preferences (Figure 12-33). On such sites, you may be asked to fill in a form requesting personal information, such as your name, zip code, or site preferences. A news site, for example, might allow you to customize your viewing preferences to display certain stock quotes. The site stores your preferences in a cookie on your hard disk.
- Some Web sites use cookies to store your password so that you do not need to enter it every time you log in to their site.
- Online shopping sites generally use a **session cookie** to keep track of items in your shopping cart. This way, you can start an order during one Web session and finish it on another day in another session. Session cookies usually expire after a certain time period, such as a week or a month.
- Some Web sites use cookies to track how regularly you visit a site and the Web pages you visit while at the site.
- Web sites may use cookies to target advertisements. These sites store your interests and browsing habits in the cookie.

A Web site can read data only from its own cookie file. It cannot access or view any other data on your hard disk — including another cookie file. Some Web sites do sell or trade information stored in your cookie to advertisers — a practice many believe to be unethical. If you do not want your personal information to be distributed, you should limit the amount of information you provide to a Web site.

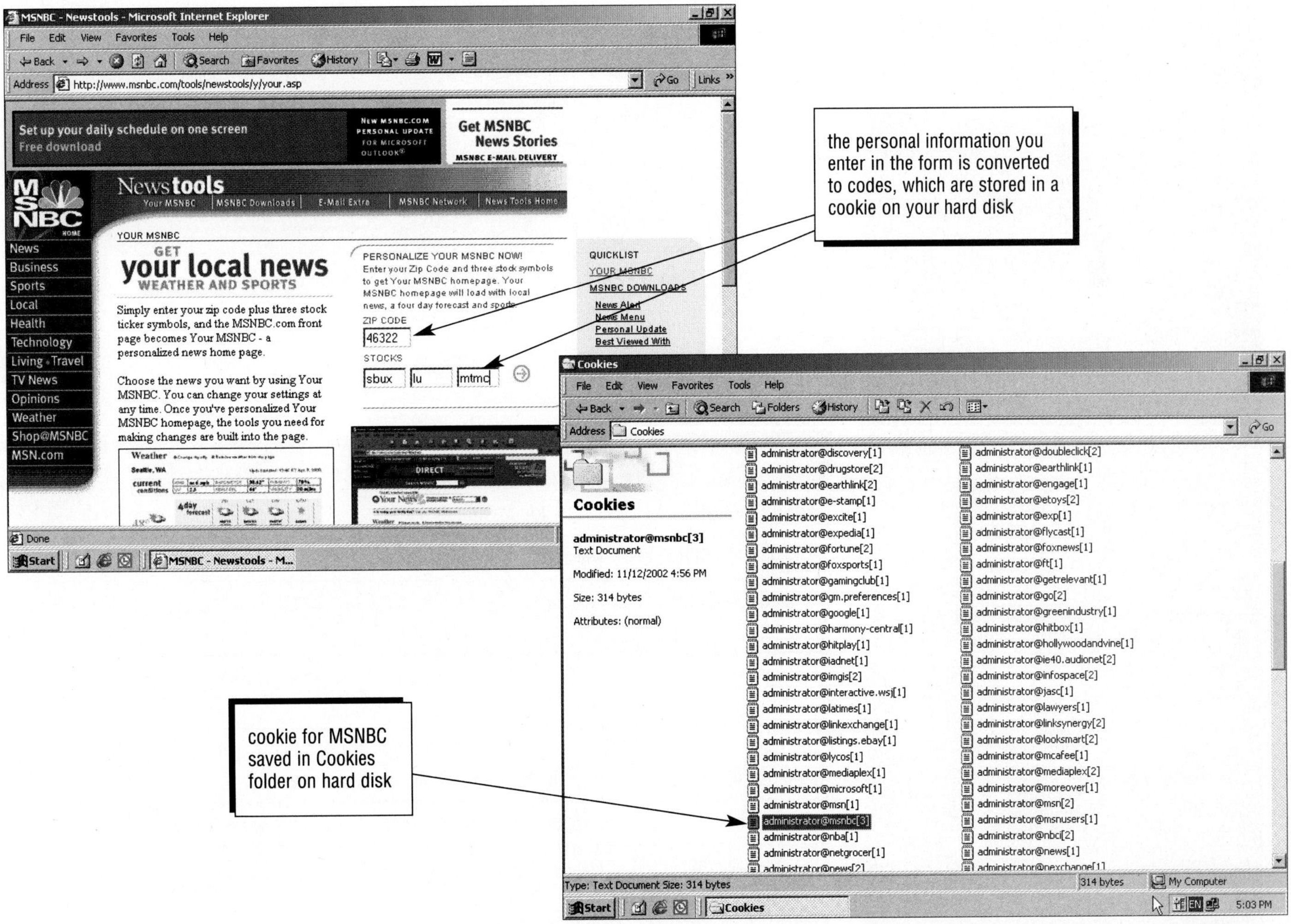

Figure 12-33 Some Web sites store user preferences in a cookie on your hard disk.

ISSUE

Cookie Anyone?

Web Server Cookies – Do They Threaten Your Privacy?

Cookies are small files that online companies transfer to your computer's hard disk through your Web browser. These files enable a company's system to track your online activities. Examples of information that a cookie can collect from a user includes the computer's IP address; login name and password; e-mail address; the computer's operating system and platform; the type of and version number of the user's browser; the date, time, and length of time the host system was accessed; and the pages visited while the user was online. Many consumer groups and privacy advocates are taking legal action because of this collection of information. They contend that companies are not doing enough to protect the privacy of Web users. As a result of several of these class-action lawsuits, the giant online retailer Amazon.com (see URL below) has revamped its privacy policy. An overview of the new policy is contained on their Web site and explains what information the company gathers, why it gathers that information, and by what means it gathers that information. Do you think that all online companies should be required to post their policies and explain what information they collect and how it is used? Should this be enforced by the Federal government? Should you, as a private citizen, have the right to sue companies who collect this information for privacy invasion? Why or why not?

For more information on cookies and privacy issues and the Web site mentioned above, visit the Discovering Computers 2002 Issues Web page (**scsite.com/dc2002/issues.htm**) and click Chapter 12 Issue #3.

You can set your browser to accept cookies automatically, prompt you if you wish to accept a cookie, or disable cookie use altogether (Figure 12-34). Keep in mind if you disable cookie use, you will not be able to use many of the e-commerce Web sites. As an alternative, you can purchase a software program that selectively blocks cookies. Figure 12-35 outlines these and other types of cookie managers.

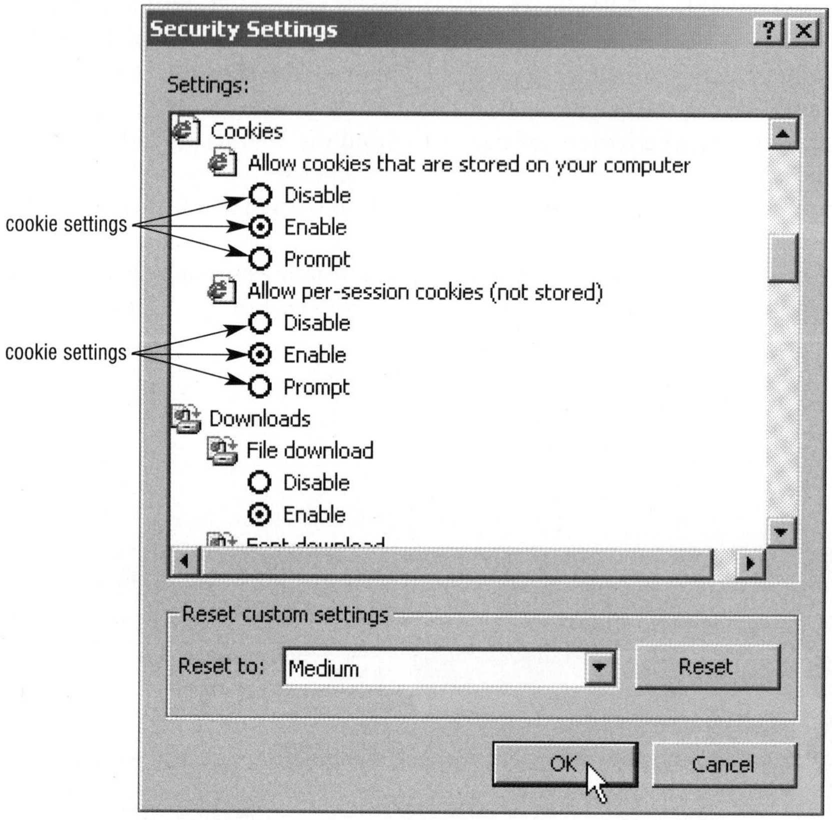

Figure 12-34 You can change cookie settings through Windows.

COOKIE MANAGERS

Program Name	Function
AdSubtract SE	Block advertising and cookies
Cookie Cruncher	View, edit, and delete cookies
Cookie Crusher	Accept or reject cookies by Web site – tells you purpose of cookie (tracking, shopping cart, etc.)
IEClean, NSClean	Delete cookies; also can delete cache, history files, and other browsing files
Internet Junkbuster Proxy	Advertising and cookie blocker that allows you to block or allow cookies based on their domain name
WebWasher	Blocks advertising banners and associated cookies
Window Washer	Delete cache, history, and cookie files

Figure 12-35 Popular cookie manager programs.

Spyware

Spyware is a program placed on a computer without the user's knowledge that secretly collects information about the user. Spyware can enter your computer as a virus or as a result of installing a new program. The spyware program communicates information it collects to some outside source while you are online.

Some Internet advertising firms use spyware, which in this case is called **adware**, to collect information about user's Web browsing habits. (Cookies are not considered spyware because you know they exist; otherwise they operate in a manner similar to spyware.)

If you download software from the Web, pay careful attention to the license agreement and registration information requested during installation. The software provider, in principle, should notify you that your information may be communicated to advertisers. To remove spyware, you need to purchase a special program that can detect and delete it.

Spam

Spam is an unsolicited e-mail message or newsgroup posting sent to many recipients or newsgroups at once. Spam is Internet junk mail (Figure 12-36). The content of spam ranges from selling a product or service, to promoting a business opportunity, to advertising offensive material.

You can reduce the amount of spam you receive by signing up for e-mail filtering from your Internet service provider. **E-mail filtering** is a service that blocks e-mail messages from designated sources. These services typically collect the spam in a central location that you can view at any time. An alternative to e-mail filtering is to purchase an **anti-spam program** that attempts to remove spam. Sometimes, though, these programs remove valid e-mail messages.

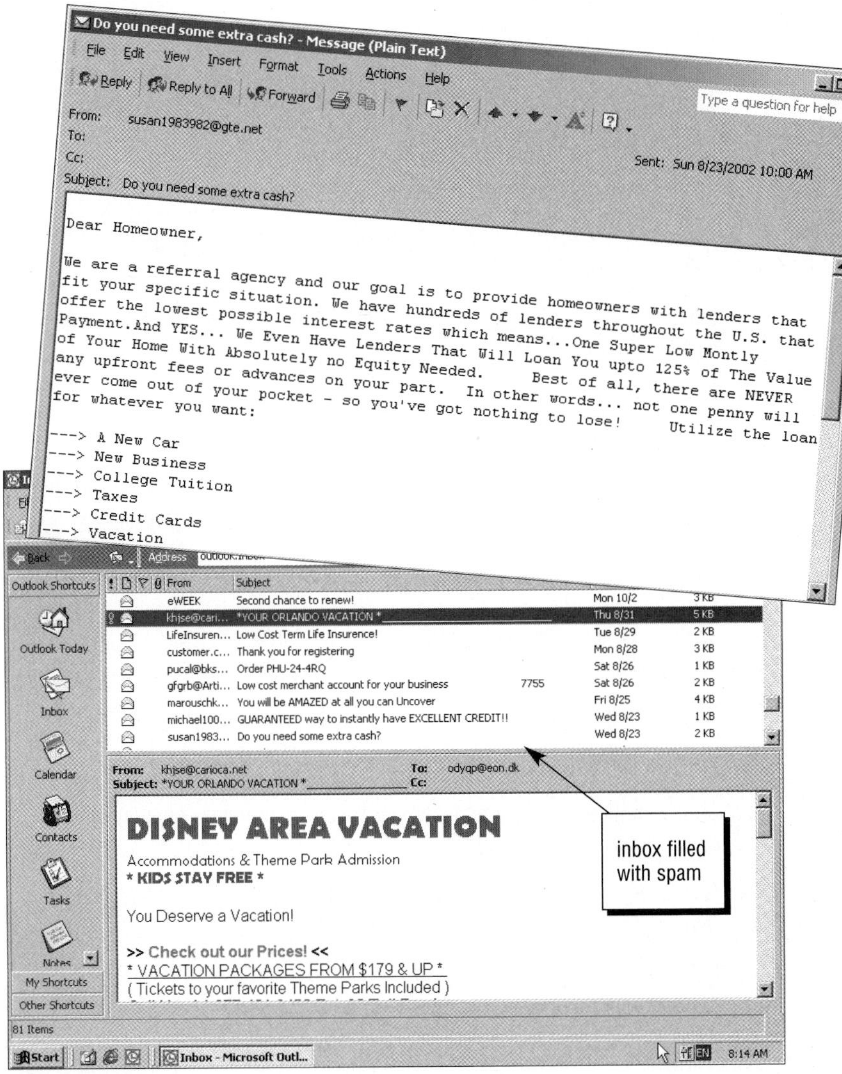

Figure 12-36 Spam is Internet junk mail.

ISSUE

Cybersleuths to the Rescue

Catching Unauthorized Intruders

Companies do not like to publicize breaches to their security systems. A recent survey, however, uncovered that more than 60 percent of organizations have fallen victim to cybercrime. Online intruders range from curiosity seekers to pranksters to criminals to terrorists. Their crimes range from accessing and erasing confidential records, to causing airport computers to malfunction, to paralyzing a hospital information system, to attaching a virus to an e-mail message and sending it across the Internet. In response to these cybercrimes, a new type of detective, called a cybersleuth, has emerged. Instead of footprints, cybersleuths use clues on hard disks to solve a cybercrime. Fighting computer crime is challenging because it is a relatively new phenomenon. Cybersleuths cannot use the proven crime-fighting techniques that have been used for centuries to solve other non-computer crimes. What skills and abilities do you think a cybersleuth must possess? Why? Would you be a good cybersleuth? Why or why not?

For more information on cybercrime and cybersleuths, visit the Discovering Computers 2002 Issues Web page (**scsite.com/dc2002/issues.htm**) and click Chapter 12 Issue #4.

Privacy Laws

The concern about privacy has led to federal and state laws regarding the storage and disclosure of personal data (Figure 12-37). Common points in some of these laws include the following:

1. Information collected and stored about individuals should be limited to what is necessary to carry out the function of the business or government agency collecting the data.
2. Once collected, provisions should be made to restrict access to the data to those employees within the organization who need access to it to perform their job duties.
3. Personal information should be released outside the organization collecting the data only when the person has agreed to its disclosure.
4. When information is collected about an individual, the individual should know that the data is being collected and have the opportunity to determine the accuracy of the data.

Several federal laws deal specifically with computers. The 1986 **Electronic Communications Privacy Act (ECPA)** provides the same protection that covers mail and telephone communications to electronic communications such as voice mail. The 1988 **Computer Matching and Privacy Protection Act** regulates the use of government data to determine the eligibility of individuals for federal benefits. The 1984 and 1994 **Computer Fraud and Abuse Acts** outlaw unauthorized

DATE	LAW	PURPOSE
1998	**Child Online Protection Act (COPA)**	Penalizes online commercial entities that knowingly distribute material deemed harmful to minors.
1997	**No Electronic Theft (NET) Act**	Closed a narrow loophole in the law that allowed people to give away copyrighted material (such as software) on the Internet without legal repercussions.
1996	**National Information Infrastructure Protection Act**	Penalizes theft of information across state lines, threats against networks, and computer system trespassing.
1994	**Computer Abuse Amendments Act**	Amends 1984 act to outlaw transmission of harmful computer code such as viruses.
1992	**Cable Act**	Extends privacy of Cable Communications Policy Act of 1984 to include cellular and other wireless services.
1991	**Telephone Consumer Protection Act**	Restricts activities of telemarketers.
1988	**Computer Matching and Privacy Protection Act**	Regulates the use of government data to determine the eligibility of individuals for federal benefits.
1988	**Video Privacy Protection Act**	Forbids retailers from releasing or selling video-rental records without customer consent or a court order.
1986	**Electronic Communications Privacy Act (ECPA)**	Provides the same right of privacy protection for the postal delivery service and telephone companies to the new forms of electronic communications, such as voice mail, e-mail, and cellular telephones.
1984	**Cable Communications Policy Act**	Regulates disclosure of cable television subscriber records.
1984	**Computer Fraud and Abuse Act**	Outlaws unauthorized access of federal government computers.
1978	**Right to Financial Privacy Act**	Strictly outlines procedures federal agencies must follow when looking at customer records in banks.
1974	**Privacy Act**	Forbids federal agencies from allowing information to be used for a reason other than for which it was collected.
1974	**Family Educational Rights and Privacy Act**	Gives students and parents access to school records and limits disclosure of records to unauthorized parties.
1970	**Fair Credit Reporting Act**	Prohibits credit reporting agencies from releasing credit information to unauthorized people and allows consumers to review their own credit records.

Figure 12-37 Summary of the major U.S. government laws concerning privacy.

access to federal government computers and the transmission of harmful computer code such as viruses.

One law with an apparent legal loophole is in the 1970 **Fair Credit Reporting Act**. The act limits the rights of others viewing a credit report to those with a legitimate business need. The problem is that it does not define a legitimate business need. The result is that just about anyone can say they have a legitimate business need and gain access to your credit report.

Credit reports contain much more than just balance and payment information on mortgages and credit cards. The largest credit bureaus maintain information on family income, number of dependents, employment history, bank balances, driving records, lawsuits, and Social Security numbers. In total, these credit bureaus have more than 400 million records on more than 160 million people. Some credit bureaus sell combinations of the data they have in their databases to direct marketing organizations. The U.S. Congress is considering a major revision of the Fair Credit Reporting Act because of continuing complaints about credit report errors and the invasion of privacy.

Employee Monitoring

Employee monitoring involves the use of computers to observe, record, and review an individual's use of a computer, including communications such as e-mail, keyboard activity (used to measure productivity), and Web sites visited. Many software programs exist that easily allow employers to monitor employees. Further, it is legal for employers to use these software programs.

A frequently debated issue is whether an employer has the right to read employee e-mail messages. Actual policies vary widely. Some companies declare that they will review e-mail messages regularly and others state that e-mail is private. If a company does not have a formal e-mail policy, it can read e-mail without employee notification. One survey discovered that more than 73 percent of companies search and/or read employee files, voice mail, e-mail, Web connections, and other networking communications. Another claimed that 25 percent of companies have fired employees for misusing communications technology.

At present, no laws exist relating to e-mail. The 1986 Electronic Communications Privacy Act does not cover communications within a company because any piece of mail sent from an employer's computer is considered company property. Several lawsuits have been filed against employers because many believe that such internal communications should be private. In response to the issue of workplace privacy, the U.S. Congress proposed the **Privacy for Consumers and Workers Act**, which states that employers must notify employees if they are monitoring electronic communications. Supporters of the legislation hope that it also will restrict the types and amount of monitoring that employers can conduct legally.

ISSUE

How Private Is Your Credit Report?

Information Privacy

Your credit report is a gold mine of information. It contains your Social Security number, home address, employment data, credit history, payment status, and even legal information. Federal and state laws restrict who has access to this sensitive information and what uses can be made of it. Anyone with a legitimate business need, however, can gain access to your credit report. In some states, companies known as information vendors can obtain and resell credit reports. Alternatively, credit bureaus frequently provide lists of individuals who meet certain credit criteria to companies that offer pre-approved credit cards or other lines of credit. Can information collected by a credit bureau present a privacy threat? How carefully should credit bureaus be required to monitor the requests for your credit report? Should credit bureaus be able to sell your report to information vendors? Should Federal law require that they first have your permission before they distribute your credit history?

For more information on privacy and credit reports, visit the Discovering Computers 2002 Issues Web page (**scsite.com/dc2002/issues.htm**) and click Chapter 12 Issue #5.

Protecting Children from Objectionable Material

One of the most controversial issues surrounding the Internet is the availability of objectionable material, such as racist literature and obscene pictures. Some believe that such materials should be banned. Others believe that the materials should be filtered; that is, restricted and unavailable to minors. Internet filtering opponents argue that banning any materials violates constitutional guarantees of free speech and personal rights.

Responding to pressure for restrictions, in February 1996, President Clinton signed the **Communications Decency Act**, which made it a criminal offense to distribute indecent or patently offensive material online. In June 1997, the Supreme Court declared the law unconstitutional because it violated the guarantee of free speech.

One approach to restricting access to certain material is a rating system similar to those used for movies and videos (Figure 12-38). If content at the Web site goes beyond the rating limits set in the Web browser software, a user cannot access the

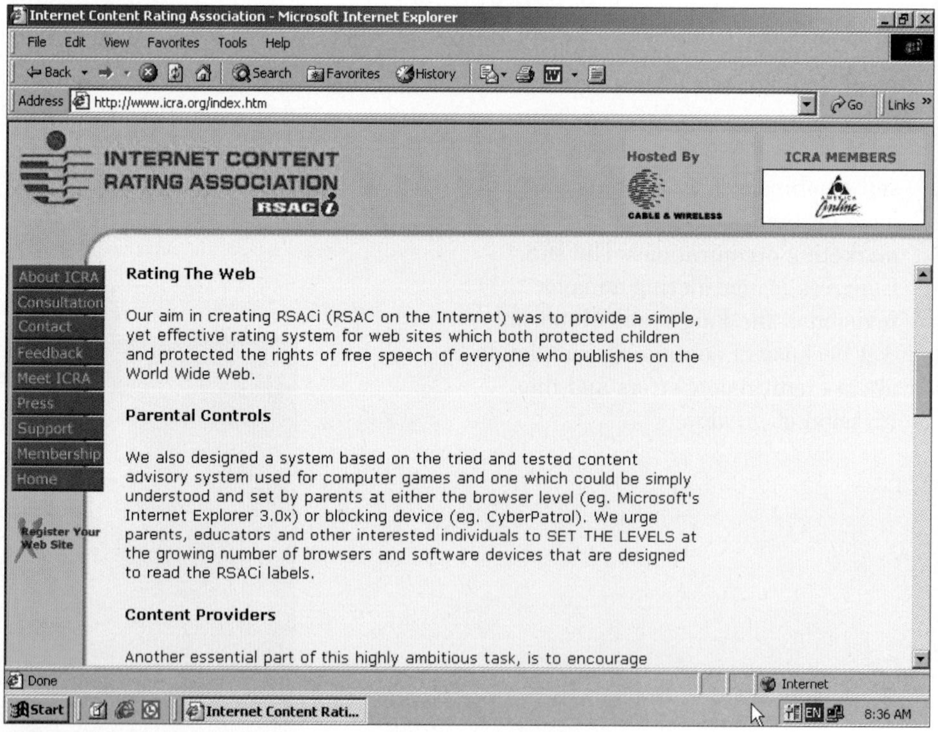

Figure 12-38 Many Web browsers use the ratings of the RSACi (Recreational Software Advisory Council for the Internet), which allows you to specify a rating level for material unsuitable for minors.

ISSUE

Freedom Challenge?

Web Filtering and Censorship

An issue heavily debated in the United States and around the world is Internet censorship. In many states and within the Federal government, politicians are attempting to pass laws and legislation that would permit the government and other agencies to regulate Internet content. The public libraries and schools are the main focus of many of these proposed laws. In general, these laws would require that these public institutions use filtering software. This type of software prevents users from accessing a wide range of information, including such topics as art, literature, politics, religion, and free speech. The American Civil Liberties Union (see URL below) and other similar organizations vehemently oppose any type of legislative censorship. Instead, they argue, it is the responsibility of the parent to control what content their child accesses at a library. They suggest that schools have acceptable use policies and that the schools be responsible for enforcing those policies. They further contend that without free and unregulated access to the Internet, this exciting new medium could become, for many Americans, little more than a G-rated television network. Do you agree or disagree that the government should control Internet content? Is control even possible? Should a college or university use filtering software? Should college students be able to use school computers to access any Web site of their choice or should the school use filtering software?

For more information on censorship and filtering software and the Web site mentioned above, visit the Discovering Computers 2002 Issues Web page (**scsite.com/dc2002/issues.htm**) and click Chapter 12 Issue #6.

Web site. Concerned parents can set the rating limits and prevent these limits from being changed by using a password.

Another approach is to use Web filtering software. **Web filtering software**, also called an **Internet filtering program**, is software that can restrict access to specified Web sites. Some also filter sites that use specific words. Others allow you to filter e-mail messages and chat rooms.

CHAPTER SUMMARY

This chapter identified some potential risks to computers and software and the safeguards that schools, businesses, and individuals can implement to minimize these risks. Internet security risks and safeguards also were discussed. The chapter also presented actions you can take to keep your personal data private.

APPLY IT!

Privacy Online

The loss of personal privacy is a major concern of many Americans. Concerns about loss of privacy are not new, but the computer's ability to gather and sort vast amounts of data — and the Internet's ability to distribute it globally — magnifies those concerns. It is difficult to be anonymous once you have ventured onto the Internet. You can expect to receive unsolicited advertising via e-mail and even personalized ads that seem to know you. This so-called junk e-mail can be a nuisance, even a scam. The Online Privacy Organization (see URL below) guidelines for Web sites are as follows: "The policy should clearly state what information is being collected; the use of that information; possible third party distribution of that information; the choices available to an individual regarding collection, use and distribution of the collected information; a statement of the organization's commitment to data security; and what steps the organization takes to ensure data quality and access." So how do you protect yourself online?

- If you are going to provide personal information through an online form, verify that the Web site has a privacy policy. The policy should be easy to find and should follow the guidelines of the Online Privacy Organization.
- If you are providing information to one of the three major credit bureaus, request that your personal information not be shared with others or used for promotional purposes.
- Some state Department of Motor Vehicles (DMV) distribute your personal information for direct marketing. The Federal Drivers Protection Act (see URL below) gives you privacy rights concerning your personal information. Contact the DMV in your state to find out if your personal information is sold for direct marketing purposes.
- The Direct Marketing Association (DMA) (see URL below) offers services that allow you to opt-out of direct marketing from many national companies. This includes e-mail advertising. Fill out the forms online at the DMA Web site.
- Use filtering software for children.
- Look for third party seals, such as the TRUSTe trustmarks.
- Some other tips are as follows:
  - Use a screen name when participating in chat rooms.
  - Set your browser to let you make the decision regarding cookie files being saved to your computer.
  - Do not send your credit card number or other sensitive, personal data by e-mail unless you are assured that the data is encrypted with the latest software technology.
  - Be cautious about giving out your Social Security number or credit card number.

For more information on protecting yourself online, privacy issues, and the Web sites mentioned above, visit the Discovering Computers 2002 Apply It Web page (**scsite.com/dc2002/apply.htm**) and click Chapter 12 Apply It #3.

Network Security Specialist

Employment as a network security specialist requires a technical background, including a thorough understanding of industry-standard network design practices and tools. Hands-on experience configuring routers and firewalls is a necessity. Many companies require a strong knowledge of Web protocols and enterprise technologies.

Certification within the networking security field is not as defined and as well known as other IT certifications. The following includes some certification examples:

- Checkpoint – offers certification in three different categories, including Certified Security Administrator (CSA), Certified Security Engineer (CSE), and Certified Senior Security Specialist (CSSS) (see URL below).
- IBM – provides certification opportunities for their IBM SecureWay Firewall for Windows (see URL below).
- The International Information Systems Security Certification Consortium, Inc. – developed a Certified Information Systems Security Professional examination (see URL below).
- Learning Tree – provides three courses in System and Network Security (see URL below).

Salaries for network security specialists are generally in the $75,000 and up range. To work within this technical field requires prior network knowledge and experience. Certification is a plus, although most of the existing certification programs are very specialized.

To learn more about the field of network security as a career and for links to the Web sites mentioned above, visit the Discovering Computers 2002 Careers Web page (**scsite.com/dc2002/careers.htm**) and click Network Security Specialist.

E-ENVIRONMENT

THE FATE OF THE ENVIRONMENT

Protecting the Planet's Ecosystem

The figures are startling: Each year Americans consume 1.4 trillion sheets of paper, an increase of 76 percent since 1980. In the past 50 years, people have consumed as many natural resources as every human who has ever lived. According to The Center for a New American Dream (Figure 12-39), the U.S. Postal Service's letter carriers deliver an average of 17.8 tons of junk mail each year, which is the weight of four male elephants.

From the rain forests of Africa to the marine life in the Pacific Ocean, the fragile ecosystem is under extreme stress. Many environmental groups have developed Internet sites in attempts to educate worldwide populations and to increase resource conservation.

The U.S. Government has a number of Web sites devoted to specific environmental concerns. For example, the U.S. Geological Survey monitors the chemicals found in acid rain and conducts research to analyze the effects of these atmospheric deposits on aquatic and terrestrial ecosystems. Figure 12-40 shows the home page for the Central African Regional Program for the Environment (CARPE). This continuing project of the U.S. Agency for International Development protects the Congo Basin's tropical forests from population growth, deforestation, and other economic and political problems. In another Web site, the U.S. Environmental Protection Agency (EPA) provides pollution data, including ozone levels and air pollutants, for specific

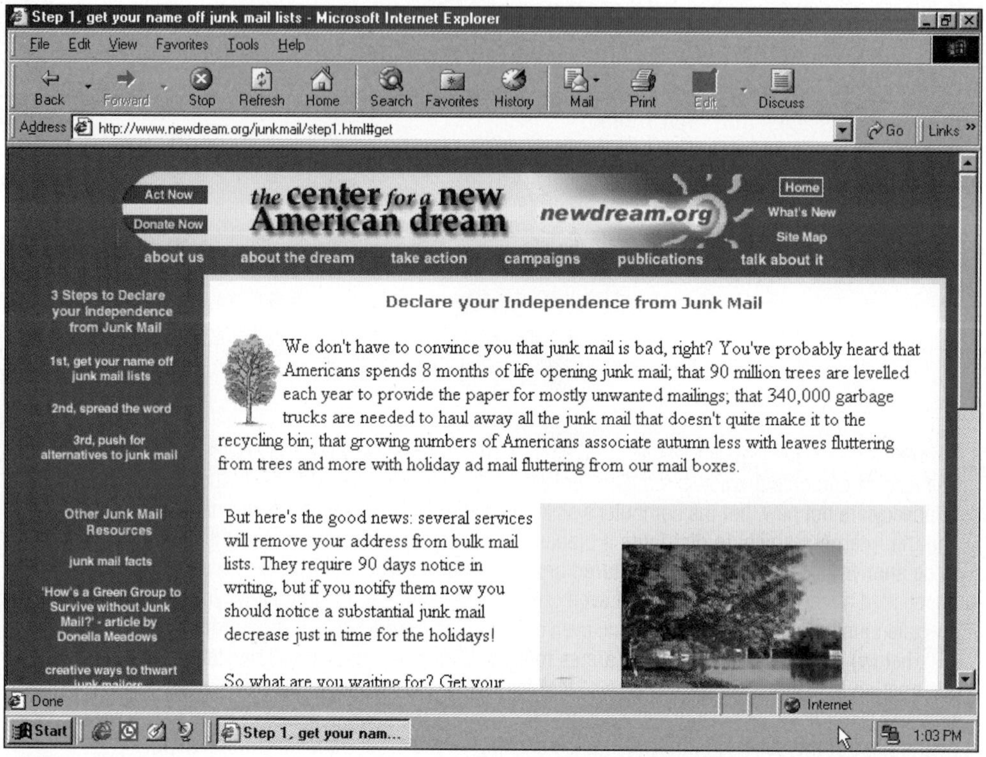

Figure 12-39 The Center for a New American Dream Web site provides an area where you can declare your independence from junk mail and get your address removed from bulk mail lists.

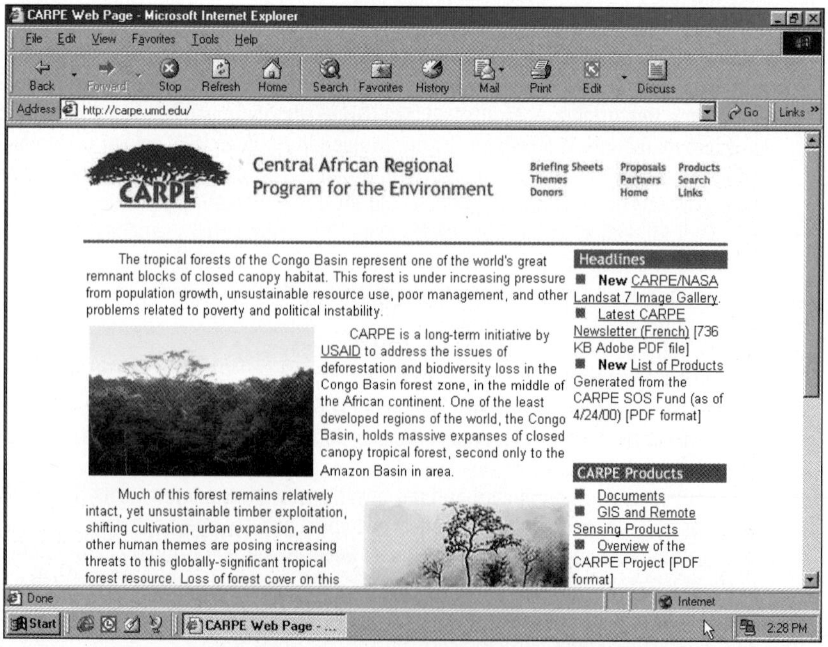

Figure 12-40 The Congo Basin's ecological, economic, and political issues are discussed in the CARPE Web site.

areas. Its Aerometric Information Retrieval System (AIRS) database, shown in Figure 12-41, is the world's most extensive collection of air pollution data.

On an international scale, the Environmental Sites on the Internet (Figure 12-42) Web page developed by the Royal Institute of Technology in Stockholm, Sweden, has been rated as one of the best ecological sites. Its comprehensive listing of environmental concerns range from aquatic ecology to wetlands.

For more information on environment Web sites, visit the Discovering Computers 2002 E-Revolution Web page (scsite.com/dc2002/e-rev.htm) and click Environment.

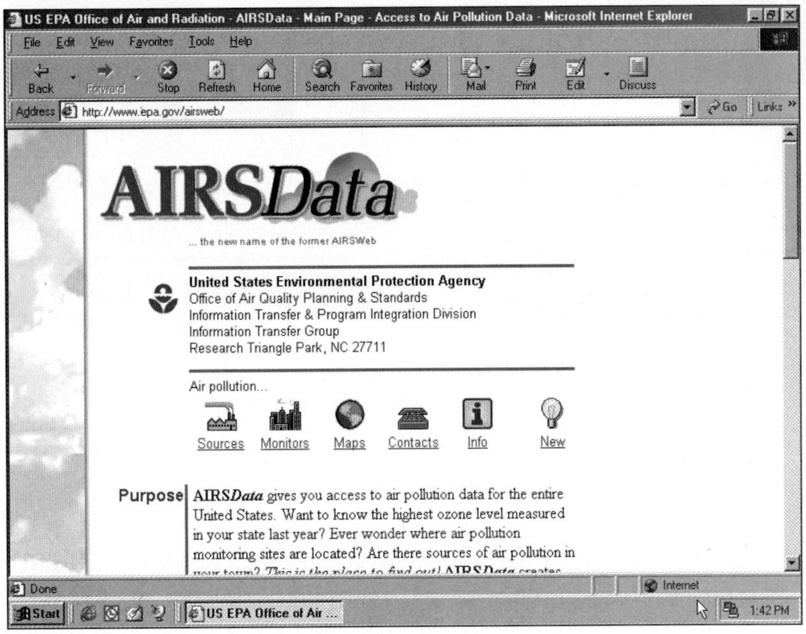

Figure 12-41 A visit to the AIRSData Web site, with its extensive database, can assist you in checking your community's ozone and air pollutant levels.

ENVIRONMENT WEB SITES	URL
Central African Regional Program for the Environment (CARPE)	carpe.umd.edu
EarthJustice Legal Defense Fund	www.earthjustice.org
Environmental Defense	edf.org
Environmental Sites on the Internet	www.lib.kth.se/~lg/envsite.htm
Green Solitaire	greensolitaire.bizland.com
GreenNet	www.gn.apc.org
Lycos Environment News	ens-news.com
The Center for a New American Dream	newdream.org
The World Wide Web Virtual Library of Ecology & Biodiversity	conbio.rice.edu/vl
U.S. EPA, Office of Air and Radiation	www.epa.gov/airsweb
U.S. Geological Survey (USGA), Acid Rain Data and Reports	btdqs.usgs.gov/acidrain
UWM Environmental Health, Safety, & Risk Management	www.uwm.edu/Dept/EHSRM/EHSLINKS

For an updated list of environment Web sites, visit scsite.com/dc2002/e-rev.htm.

Figure 12-42 Environmental Web sites provide vast resources for ecological data and action groups.

eREVOLUTION E-ENVIRONMENT *applied:*

1. The Center for a New American Dream Web site encourages consumers to reduce the amount of junk mail sent to their homes. Using the table in Figure 12-42, visit the Web site and write a paragraph stating how many trees are leveled each year to provide paper for these mailings, how many garbage trucks are needed to haul this waste, and other statistics. Read the letters that you can use to eliminate your name from bulk mail lists. To whom would you mail these letters? How long does it take to stop these unsolicited letters?

2. Visit the AIRSData Web site. What is the highest ozone level recorded in your state this past year? Where are the nearest air pollution monitoring Web sites, and what are their levels? Where are the nearest sources of air pollution? Read two reports on two different topics, such as acid rain and air quality, and summarize their findings. Include information on who sponsored the research, who conducted the studies, when the data was collected, and the impact of this pollution on the atmosphere, water, forests, and human health. Whom would you contact for further information regarding the data and studies?

In Summary

Web Instructions: To display this page from the Web, start your browser and enter the URL scsite.com/dc2002/ch12/summary.htm. Click the links for current and additional information. To listen to an audio version of this In Summary, click the Audio button. To play the audio, RealPlayer must be installed on your computer (download by clicking here).

1 What Are the Various Types of Security Risks that Can Threaten Computers?

A **computer security risk** is any event or action that could cause a loss of or damage to computer hardware, software, data, information, or processing capability. Computer security risks include computer viruses, unauthorized access and use, hardware theft, software theft, information theft, and system failure. A computer **virus** is a potentially damaging computer program designed to affect or infect a computer negatively by altering the way it works. **Unauthorized access** is the use of a computer or network without permission; **unauthorized use** is the use of a computer or its data for unapproved or possibly illegal activities. An individual who tries to access a computer or network illegally is called a **cracker** or a **hacker**. **Hardware theft**, software theft, and **information theft** present difficult security challenges. The most common form of software theft is **software piracy**, which is the unauthorized and illegal duplication of copyrighted software. A **system failure** is the prolonged malfunction of a computer.

2 How Can a Computer Be Safeguarded?

Safeguards are protective measures that can be taken to minimize or prevent the consequences of computer security risks. An **antivirus program** protects a computer against viruses by identifying and removing any computer viruses found in memory. An **access control** prevents unauthorized access and use by defining who can access a computer, when they can access it, and what actions they can take. Physical access controls and common sense can minimize hardware theft. For an organization, a **site license** addresses software piracy by giving the buyer the right to install the software on multiple computers at a single site. **Encryption** reduces information theft by converting readable data into unreadable characters. A **surge protector** and an **uninterruptible power supply** guard against system failure by controlling power irregularities.

3 How Does a Computer Virus Work and What Steps Can Be Taken to Prevent Viruses?

A **virus** is a potentially damaging computer program that affect, or infects, a computer negatively by altering the way the computer works. A virus can replace the boot program with an infected version (**boot sector virus**), attach itself to a file (**file virus**), or use an application's macro language to hide virus code (**macro virus**). Other viruses are activated when a certain action takes place or condition is met (**a logic bomb**) or on a specific date (**a time bomb**). A **malicious-logic program**, or **malware**, is a program that acts without a user's knowledge and deliberately alters the computer's operations. These include programs that copy themselves repeatedly in memory (**worm**), or viruses that hide within a legitimate program (**Trojan horse**). Viruses can be prevented by installing an antivirus program, setting the macro security level in all applications, write-protecting a **rescue disk** or **emergency disk**, never starting a computer with a disk in drive A, scanning floppy disks for viruses, checking downloaded programs, and regularly backing up files.

4 How Can an Individual Create a Good Password?

A **password** is a secret combination of characters associated with the **user name** that allows access to certain computer resources. With most systems, you can select your own password. Passwords are effective only if they are chosen carefully and are impossible to guess. Guidelines to ensure secure passwords include using at least eight characters; using a combination of numbers, letters, words, initials, and dates; and choosing a combination that only you would know. To safeguard your password, do not write it down or share it. Choose a password that you can type easily without looking at the keyboard, and change your password frequently.

In Summary

5 What Are Various Biometric Devices?

A biometric device authenticates a person's identity by verifying personal characteristics. They are used to access programs, systems, or rooms using computer analysis of some **biometric identifier**. Examples of biometric identifiers include a **fingerprint scanner**, a **hand geometry system**, and a **face recognition system**, a **voice verification system**, a **signature verification system**, and an **iris recognition system**.

6 What Is Software Piracy?

Software piracy is the unauthorized and illegal duplication of copyrighted software and is the most common form of software theft. When people purchase software, they purchase a license agreement for the right to use the software. Users are permitted to install the software on only one computer, make one backup copy, and give or sell the software to another person if they remove it from their computers.

7 Why Is Encryption Necessary?

Encryption converts readable data into unreadable characters to prevent unauthorized access. The two basic types of encryption are **private key encryption**, where both the originator and recipient use the same secret key; and **public key encryption**, where a public key is known to everyone and a private key is known only by the sender or receiver. **RSA encryption** is a public key encryption technology used to encrypt data transmitted over the Internet, and Fortezza is a public key encryption technology that stores user information on a PC Card.

8 Why Is Computer Backup Important and How Is It Accomplished?

A **backup** is a duplicate of a file, program, or disk that can be used if the original is lost, damaged, or destroyed. In case of **system failure** or the discovery of corrupted files, the backup can be used to **restore** the files by copying the backed up files to their original location on the computer. Backup procedures specify a regular plan of copying and storing important data and program files. Three methods of backup are: a **full backup**, a **differential backup**, and an **incremental backup**.

9 What Are the Steps in a Disaster Recovery Plan?

A disaster recovery plan describes the steps an organization would take to restore computer operations in the event of a disaster and has four major components: the **emergency plan**, the **backup plan**, the **recovery plan**, and the **test plan**.

10 What Are the Ways to Secure an Internet Transaction?

Information transmitted over the Internet has a high degree of security risk. **Secure sites** use encryption techniques to secure data. To provide secure data transmission, Web browsers use encryption technology such as **Secure Socket Layers** (**SSL**) and digital signatures. Netscape Navigator and Microsoft Internet Explorer use RSA. The **Secure Electronic Transaction** (**SET**) uses a public key encryption to secure credit card transaction systems.

11 What Are Issues Pertaining to Personal Information?

Information privacy refers to the right of individuals and organizations to deny or restrict the collection and use of information about them. Information privacy issues include unauthorized collection and use of information and employee monitoring. Unauthorized collection and use of information involves the compilation of data about an individual from a variety of sources. A **cookie** is a small file that a Web server stores on your computer that contains data about you. Web sites use cookies to track user preferences, how often you visit a Web site and Web pages visited; to store your password; to keep track of items you purchase (**session cookie**); and to target advertisements. **Spyware** is a program that communicates information to some outside source while you are online. It is placed on your computer without your knowledge and can enter your computer as a virus or as a result of installing a new program. **Employee monitoring** involves the use of computers to observe, record, and review an individual's use of a computer, including communications, keyboard activity, and Internet sites visited.

Key Terms

Web Instructions: To display this page from the Web, start your browser and enter the URL scsite.com/dc2002/ch1/terms.htm. Scroll through the list of terms. Click a term to display its definition and a picture. Click the To WEB button for current and additional information about the term from the Web. To see animations, Shockwave and Flash Player must be installed on your computer (download by clicking here).

access control (12.8)
adware (12.31)
anti-spam program (12.31)
antivirus program (12.5)
archival backup (12.20)
asymmetric key encryption (12.17)
audit trail (12.13)
authentication (12.8)
back up (12.19)
backup (12.19)
backup plan (12.21)
backup procedures (12.20)
biometric device (12.10)
biometric identifier (12.10)
blackout (12.18)
boot sector virus (12.4)
brownout (12.18)
Business Software Alliance (BSA) (12.15)
callback system (12.12)
certificate authority (CA) (12.23)
child (12.21)
ciphertext (12.16)
Clipper chip (12.17)
Communications Decency Act (12.34)
computer crime (12.2)
Computer Fraud and Abuse Acts (12.32)
Computer Matching and Privacy Protection Act (12.32)
computer security plan (12.22)
computer security risk (12.2)
cookie (12.28)
cracker (12.7)
cybercrime (12.2)
data encryption standard (DES) (12.16)
decrypt (12.16)
differential backup (12.20)
digital certificate (12.23)
digital ID (12.24)
digital signature (12.24)
disaster recovery plan (12.21)
Electronic Communications Privacy Act (ECPA) (12.32)
e-mail filtering (12.31)
emergency disk (12.6)
emergency plan (12.21)
employee monitoring (12.33)
encryption (12.16)
encryption key (12.16)
end-user license agreement (EULA) (12.14)
face recognition system (12.11)
Fair Credit Reporting Act (12.33)
file virus (12.4)
fingerprint scanner (12.11)
firewall (12.24)
Fortezza (12.17)
full backup (12.20)
grandparent (12.21)
hacker (12.7)
hand geometry system (12.11)
hardware theft (12.13)
hardware vandalism (12.13)
hash (12.24)
identification (12.8)
incremental backup (12.20)
information privacy (12.26)
information theft (12.15)
inoculate (12.6)

POSSESSED OBJECT
An item, such as a badge, card, or key, that must be carried to gain access to a computer or computer facility. The card that allows access to an ATM is an example of a possessed object. (12.10)

International Computer Security Association (ICSA) (12.22)
Internet filtering program (12.35)
iris recognition system (12.12)
issuing authority (IA) (12.23)
Joule (12.19)
key escrow (12.17)
license agreement (12.14)
log (12.13)
logic bomb (12.4)
macro virus (12.4)
malicious-logic program (12.4)
malware (12.4)
network site license (12.15)
noise (12.18)
offsite (12.19)
online backup service (12.21)
online security service (12.26)
overvoltage (12.18)
parent (12.21)
password (12.8)
personal firewall (12.25)
personal identification number (PIN) (12.10)
plaintext (12.16)
polymorphic virus (12.6)
possessed object (12.10)
power surge (12.18)
Pretty Good Privacy (PGP) (12.24)
Privacy for Consumers and Workers Act (12.33)
private key encryption (12.16)
program virus (12.4)
proxy server (12.25)
public key encryption (12.17)
public-key certificate (12.23)
quarantine (12.6)
reciprocal backup relationship (12.21)
recovery plan (12.21)
rescue disk (12.6)
restore (12.19)
RSA encryption (12.17)
safeguards (12.2)
Secure Electronic Transaction (SET) (12.24)
Secure HTTP (S-HTTP) (12.24)
secure site (12.23)
Secure Sockets Layer (SSL) (12.24)
session cookie (12.29)
signature verification system (12.12)
single-user license agreement (12.14)
site license (12.15)
software piracy (12.14)
spam (12.31)
spike (12.18)
spyware (12.31)
stealth virus (12.6)
surge protector (12.18)
surge suppressor (12.18)
symmetric key encryption (12.16)
system failure (12.18)
system virus (12.4)
test plan (12.21)
three-generation backup (12.21)
time bomb (12.4)
Trojan horse (12.4)
trusted source (12.2)
unauthorized access (12.7)
unauthorized use (12.7)
undervoltage (12.18)
Underwriters Laboratories (UL) 1449 standard (12.19)
uninterruptible power supply (UPS) (12.19)
user ID (12.8)
user name (12.8)
virus (12.2)
virus author (12.2)
virus definition (12.6)
virus hoax (12.7)
virus signature (12.6)
voice verification system (12.12)
Web filtering software (12.35)
worm (12.4)

Learn It Online

Web Instructions: To display this page from the Web, start your browser, and then enter the URL scsite.com/dc2002/ch12/learn.htm.

1. Web Guide

Click Web Guide to display the Guide to World Wide Web Sites and Searching Techniques Web page. Click Computers and Computing. Click Government and Politics and then click Electronic Frontier. Click one of the Recent News links and review the information. Use your word processing program to prepare a brief report on what you learned and submit your assignment to your instructor.

2. Scavenger Hunt

Click Scavenger Hunt. Print a copy of the Scavenger Hunt page; use this page to write down your answers as you search the Web. Submit your completed page to your instructor.

3. Who Wants to Be a Computer Genius?

Click Computer Genius to find out if you are a computer genius. Directions on how to play the game will display. When you are ready to play, click the PLAY button. Submit your score to your instructor.

4. Wheel of Terms

Click Wheel of Terms to reinforce important terms you learned in this chapter by playing the Shelly Cashman Series version of this popular game. Directions on how to play the game will display. When you are ready to play, click the PLAY button. Submit your score to your instructor.

5. Career Corner

Click Career Corner to display the Career Center page. Review this page. Click one of the Online Job Bank links. Write a brief report on what you discovered. Submit the report to your instructor.

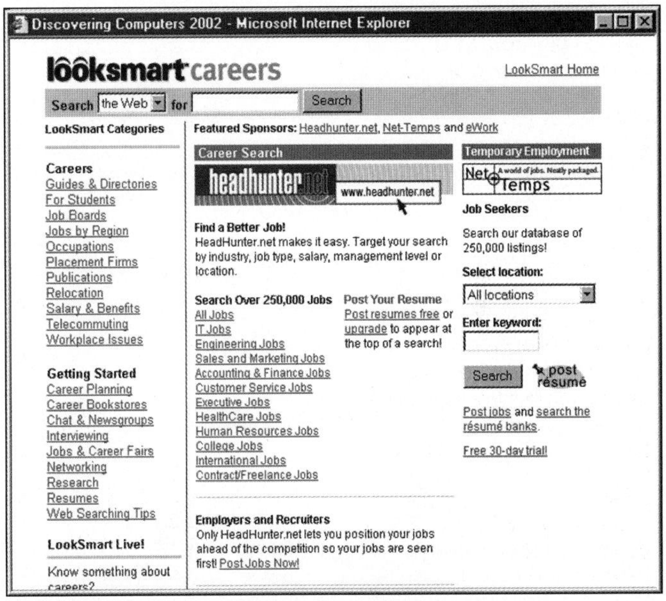

6. Search Sleuth

Click Search Sleuth to learn search techniques that will help make you a research expert. Submit the completed assignment to your instructor.

7. Crossword Puzzle Challenge

Click Crossword Puzzle Challenge. Complete the puzzle to reinforce skills you learned in this chapter. Directions on how to play the game will display. When you are ready to play, click the PLAY button. Submit the completed puzzle to your instructor.

8. Practice Test

Click Practice Test. Answer each question. When completed, enter your name and click the Grade Test button to submit the quiz for grading. Make a note of any missed questions. If required, print a copy to submit to your instructor.

Checkpoint

Web Instructions: To display this page from the Web, start your browser and enter the URL scsite.com/dc2002/ch12/check.htm. Click the links for current and additional information. To experience the animation and interactivity, Shockwave and Flash Player must be installed on your computer (download by clicking here).

LABEL THE FIGURE

Instructions: Identify the steps showing how public key encryption works.

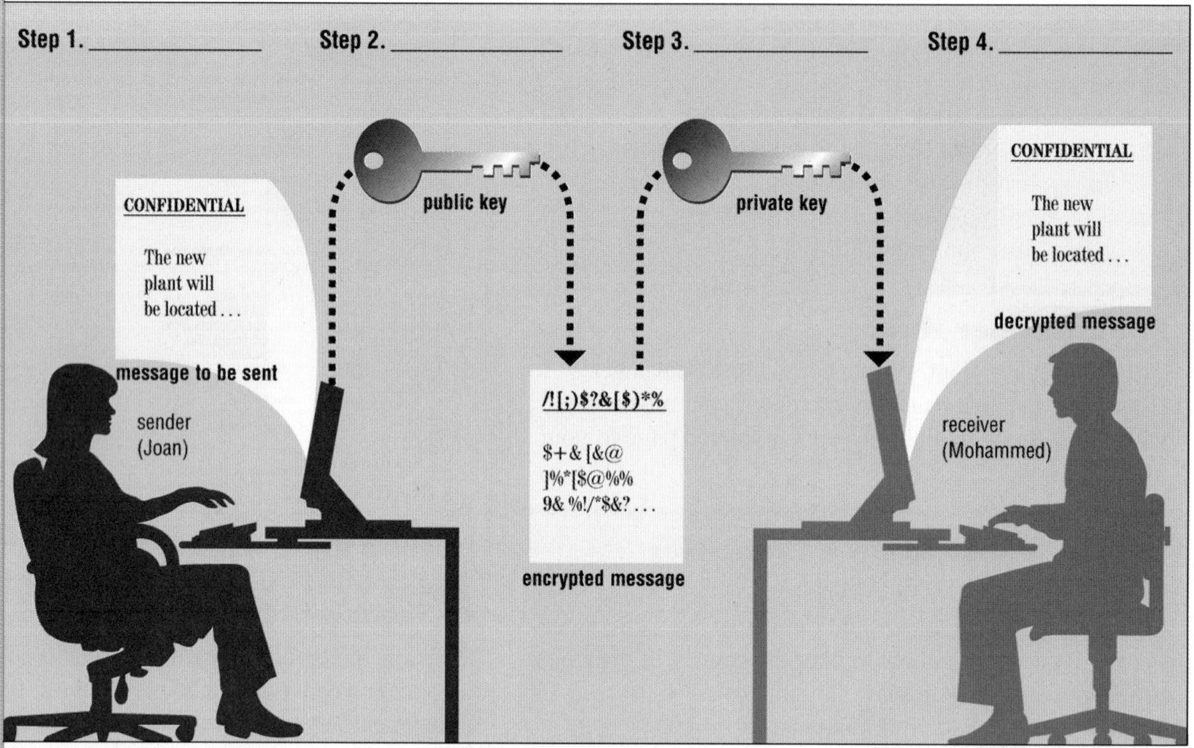

MATCHING

Instructions: Match each term from the column on the left with the best description from the column on the right.

_______ 1. digital certificate
_______ 2. possessed object
_______ 3. voice verification system
_______ 4. password
_______ 5. callback system

a. Compares a person's live speech to his or her stored voice pattern.
b. Encrypted code that a person, Web site, or company attaches to an electronic number (PIN) message.
c. Connects to a computer only after the computer calls back at a previously established number.
d. A notice that guarantees a user or a Web site is legitimate.
e. A secret combination of characters associated with the user name that allows access to certain computer resources.
f. Item that must be carried to gain access to a computer or computer facility.
g. Uses special electrical components to smooth out minor noise and provide a stable flow.

Checkpoint

MULTIPLE CHOICE

Instructions: Select the letter of the correct answer for each of the following questions.

1. A(n) ___________ is a company or person you believe will not send you a virus-infected file knowingly.
   a. trusted source
   b. antivirus author
   c. certificate authority
   d. grandparent
2. A security option that authenticates someone's identity by verifying personal characteristics is called a ___________ .
   a. digital signature
   b. PIN
   c. possessed object
   d. biometric device
3. Illegal duplication of copyrighted software is referred to as ___________ .
   a. software piracy
   b. software vandalism
   c. information theft
   d. site license removal
4. A ___________ virus executes when you turn on the computer.
   a. file
   b. boot
   c. macro
   d. time bomb
5. A(n) ___________ tries to access a computer or computer network illegally.
   a. hacker
   b. unidentified user
   c. auditor
   d. software tester

SHORT ANSWER

Instructions: Write a brief answer to each of the following questions.

1. In terms of computer viruses, how is a logic bomb different from a time bomb? ___________ What is a worm? ___________ What are some other types of viruses? ___________
2. What is an Internet security risk? ___________ What are some security techniques? ___________
3. What is a computer security plan? ___________ What are the three steps for a security plan? ___________
4. How is private key encryption different from public key encryption? ___________ What is the government's key escrow plan? ___________ What are two types of public key encryption? ___________
5. What is a password? ___________ How can you create a good password? ___________ What are some password precautions? ___________

WORKING TOGETHER

Instructions: Working with a group of your classmates, complete the following team exercise.

Your group has been hired by XYZ Corporation to create a privacy information policy for an online Web site for the company. Directions include putting together a policy that not only will respect an individual's privacy rights, but also will enable the company to collect data that can be used in targeted marketing. The company would like to know who visits the Web site, how often they visit, what pages are viewed, and how long someone stays on a particular page. Create a privacy policy that will include all of the above. Justify each component within the policy and explain how the policy will not violate the individual's right to privacy. Share your report and/or a PowerPoint presentation with the class.

Web Instructions: To display this page from the Web, start your browser and enter the URL scsite.com/dc2002/ch12/lab.htm. Click the links for current and additional information.

Understanding Backup

1

This exercise uses Windows 98 or Windows 2000 procedures. Click the Start button on the taskbar, point to Programs on the Start menu, and then point to Accessories on the Programs submenu. Point to System Tools on the Accessories submenu, and then click Backup on the System Tools submenu. If a Welcome screen displays, click the Close button. When the Microsoft Backup - [Untitled] window displays, maximize it and then click the Backup tab. Click Help on the menu bar and then click Help Topics. If necessary, click the Contents tab. Click Back Up, and then click Backing Up Everything On Your Computer. How can you backup your system? Close the Backup Help window. Close the Microsoft Backup - [Untitled] window.

License Agreements

2

This exercise uses Windows 98 or Windows 2000 procedures. Click the Start button on the taskbar. Click Help on the Start menu. If necessary, click the Contents tab. Click the Introducing Windows 98 or Windows 2000 book. Click the Register Your Software book. Click the License Agreement questions and answers topic. Click an appropriate link to answer each of the following questions:

- Where do you find your End User License Agreement?
- Is it legal to sell software you have bought and used?
- Can you make a second copy of software for a home or notebook computer?
- Can you transfer or give away old versions of products when you buy an upgrade?

Click the Close button to close Windows Help.

Scanning a Disk

3

This exercise uses Windows 98 procedures. ScanDisk is a Windows utility that checks a disk for physical and logical errors. To run ScanDisk, click the Start button on the taskbar, point to Programs on the Start menu, and then point to Accessories on the Programs submenu. Point to System Tools on the Accessories submenu, and then click ScanDisk on the System Tools submenu. Click the Advanced button in the ScanDisk window. When the ScanDisk Advanced Options dialog box displays, if necessary click Always in the Display summary area and then click the OK button. Insert your floppy disk into drive A. Click 3½ Floppy (A:) in the Select the drive(s) you want to check for errors list. Click the Thorough option button in the Type of test area. Click the Start button in the ScanDisk - 3½ Floppy (A:) window. What errors, if any, are detected? In bytes, what is the total disk space? How many folders are on the floppy disk? How many user files are on the floppy disk? Close the ScanDisk Results dialog box and the ScanDisk - 3½ Floppy (A:) window.

Checking System Resources

4

This exercise uses Windows 98 procedures. Resource Meter monitors the system resources your programs are using. To run Resource Meter, click the Start button on the taskbar, point to Programs on the Start menu, and then point to Accessories on the Programs submenu. Point to System Tools on the Accessories submenu, and then click Resource Meter on the System Tools submenu. If a Resource Meter dialog box displays, read the information and then click the OK button. Double-click the Resource Meter icon that displays to the left of the time on the taskbar. What percentage of system resources is free? What percentage of user resources is free? Click the OK button. Right-click the Resource Meter icon on the taskbar and then click Exit on the shortcut menu.

Web Work

Web Instructions: To display this page from the Web, start your browser and enter the URL scsite.com/dc2002/ch12/web.htm. To view At The Movies in exercise 1, RealPlayer must be installed on your computer (download by clicking here). To use the Shelly Cashman Series Keeping Your Computer Virus Free Lab from the Web, Shockwave and Flash Player must be installed on your computer (download by clicking here).

Workplace Watchdog

To view the Workplace Watchdog movie, click the button to the left or click the Play button to the right. Watch the movie, and then complete the exercise by answering the questions below. Increasingly, companies are installing computer surveillance software to monitor and record all employee activities on the computer. One employer discovered that several employees were spending 50 to 70 percent of their time playing games, sending personal e-mail, and surfing the Web. So far the courts have said that, because the employer owns the computers, workplace surveillance is okay, provided employees are forewarned of the policy. Does the employee have any right to privacy on the company's computer? Can the employer record employee telephone calls? Do employees have the right make private cellular telephone calls on company property? Can a company use video surveillance in the factory, lunchroom, or rest rooms?

Shelly Cashman Series Keeping Your Computer Virus Free Lab

Follow the instructions in Web Work 2 on page 1.47 to start and use the Shelly Cashman Series Keeping Your Computer Virus Free Lab. If you are running from the Web, enter the URL www.scsite.com/sclabs/menu.htm; or display the Web Work page (see instructions at the top of this page) and then click the button to the left.

Software Piracy

Hong Kong once was the pirated software capital of the world. The availability of stolen software manufactured in China and smuggled across the border led to the use of pirated software by almost 65 percent of Hong Kong firms. To date, the impact of China's takeover of Hong Kong on the pirated software market is unknown. The Business Software Alliance (BSA) Web site provides the latest information about software piracy. To learn more, click the button to the left and complete this exercise.

Computer Crime

The Federal Bureau of Investigation is taking computer crime seriously. The FBI has computer crime units in several cities, and a team of 125 agents is responsible for coordinating investigations around the country. Part of their job is to anticipate, and prevent, the most catastrophic crimes computer crackers could commit. Many computer crimes fall under the jurisdiction of the FBI. To learn more about the computer crimes the FBI investigates, click the button to the left and complete this exercise.

In the News

Carnivore is the name of an electronic surveillance tool used by the FBI to monitor the e-mail communications of suspected criminals and other people under investigation. Many consider this Internet wiretapping because the program must read all e-mail address information that passes through an ISP in order to work. Click the button to the left and read a news story about a security, ethics, or privacy issue related to computers. What is the issue? Who does it affect? How do you think the issue can, or should, be resolved?

CHAPTER 13

Databases and Information Management

Your Grand Canyon vacation ends tomorrow. As you relax by the fire in your cabin, you think about the spectacular views and natural wonders you experienced throughout the past two weeks. Then your thoughts drift to home and work and the dozens of e-mail and voice mail messages you likely have received.

That is only the beginning. The front and back lawns will need mowing, the laundry will be monumental, and the refrigerator is empty. Wait! You usually order groceries on the Web. Your cellular telephone is in your suitcase, which means you have wireless access to the Web. Why not go online and place your order right now? You immediately shop at your Web grocer and schedule a delivery for tomorrow night.

Online shopping no doubt has been a timesaver for you and millions of other shoppers worldwide. When ordering online, you access the retailer's huge inventory database. These databases store thousands of products. You certainly are grateful to the people who design those product databases for the Web. Now, you can relax again. At least you will have something to eat when you get home.

OBJECTIVES

After completing this chapter, you will be able to:

- Explain why data and information are important to an organization
- Identify file maintenance techniques
- Differentiate between the file processing and database approaches
- Discuss the advantages of using a database management system (DBMS)
- Describe characteristics of relational and object-oriented databases
- Explain how to use a query language
- Understand how Web databases work
- Discuss the responsibilities of the database analysts and administrators
- Identify the qualities of valuable information
- Describe the various types of information systems
- Understand the concept of a data warehouse

DATA AND INFORMATION

Data is a collection of raw unprocessed facts, figures, and symbols. In the past, data was limited to words and numbers. Today, data is much more interesting because it includes sounds, images, and video. For example, you can talk into a computer's microphone. A digital camera can send your pictures directly into the computer. You can attach a video camera to capture movements and sounds.

Information is data that is organized, meaningful, and useful. Your voice communication can be sent in an e-mail message for a friend or co-worker to hear. You can post a photograph from your digital camera on a personal Web page. Using a PC camera, others can view you in real-time during a conference call.

Computers process data into information. A computer in a video rental store, for example, processes customer and movie data and then prints information on a rental receipt. As shown in Figure 13-1, a clerk enters several data items into the computer. The clerk also uses a digital camera to photograph the customer. This picture, along with the other entered data, is stored in the database on disk.

As presented in Chapter 3, a **database** includes a collection of data organized so you can access, retrieve, and use the data. A database at a video rental store contains data about customers and movies.

With database software, also called a database management system (DBMS), you can create a computerized database; add, change, and delete data; sort and retrieve data from the database; and create forms and reports from the data in the database. A video rental store might use Microsoft Access as its DBMS. When a customer wishes to rent a movie, a checkout clerk enters the customer and movie data. Then, the database software creates and prints the rental receipt. Database software includes these and many other powerful features, as you will discover later in this chapter.

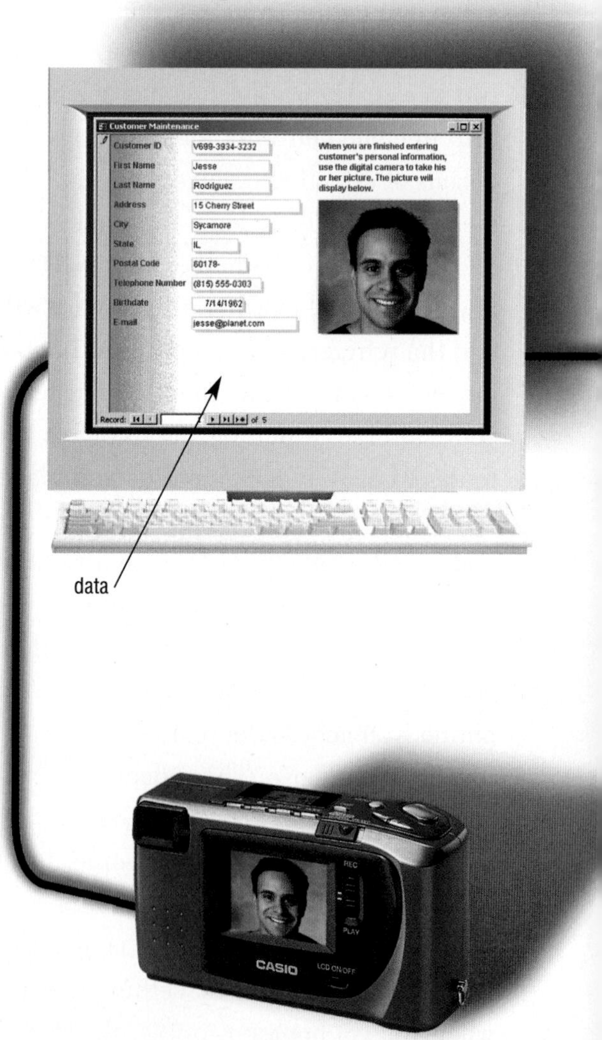

Figure 13-1 A computer processes data into information. In this example, a clerk enters several data items into the computer. The clerk also uses a digital camera to take a picture of the customer.

Most companies realize that data is one of their more valuable assets. Many business transactions take less time when employees have instant access to data. If checkout clerks in a video rental store have instant access to movie rental data, they can determine which movies are in stock upon customer request. An increase in employee productivity often leads to an increase in customer satisfaction. When customers are happy, they typically become loyal to that business. Loyal customers can lead to an increase in profits.

Managers in a company make decisions using all types of information such as sales trends, competitors' products and services, production processes, and even employee skills. This information would be difficult, if not impossible, to replace. Because information is created from data, a company must manage and protect its data just as it would any other resource. It is extremely important the data has integrity and is kept secure. Chapter 12 presented a variety of methods to secure data. The next section discusses data integrity.

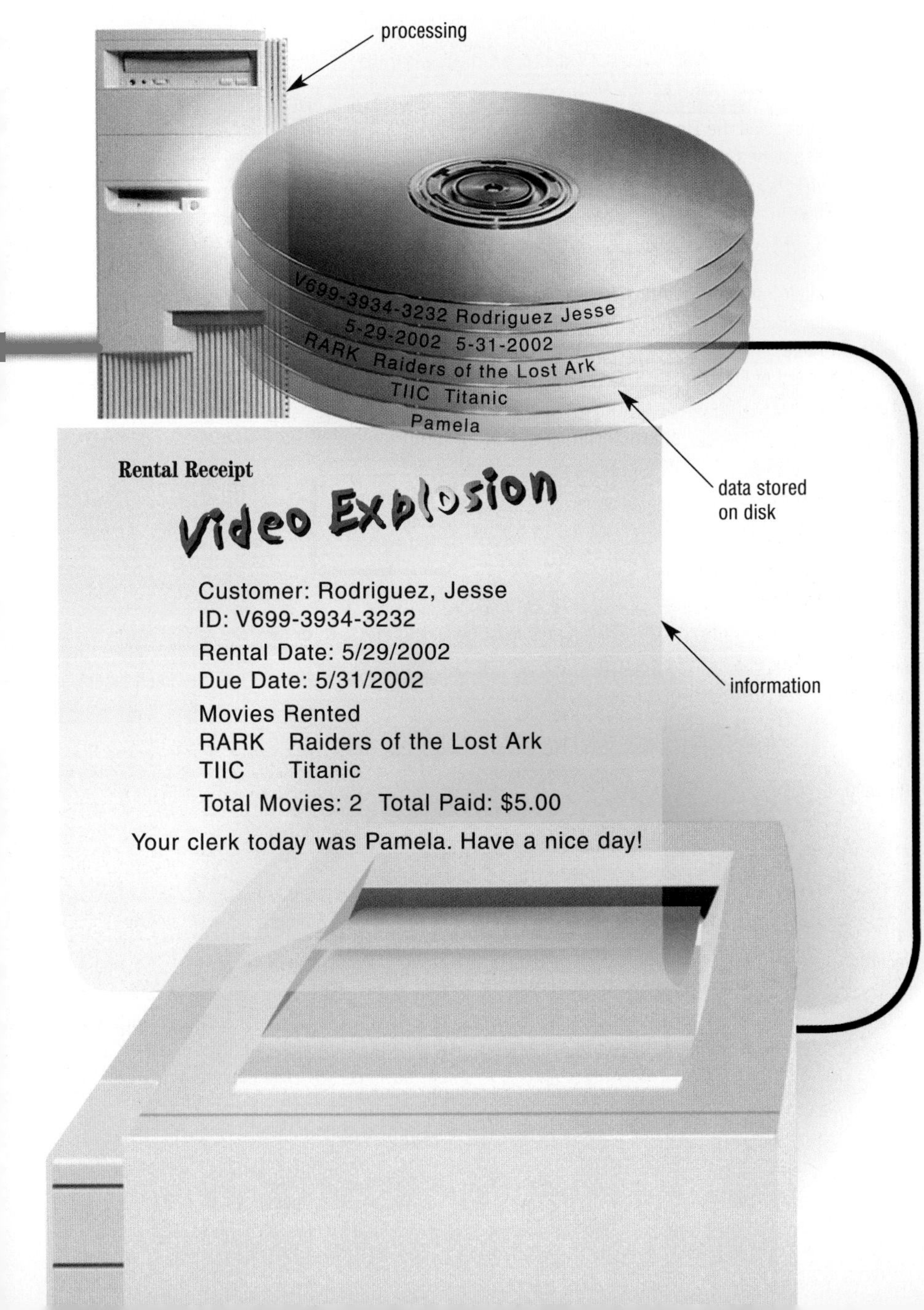

processing
V699-3934-3232 Rodriguez Jesse
5-29-2002 5-31-2002
RARK Raiders of the Lost Ark
TIIC Titanic
Pamela
data stored on disk
Rental Receipt
Video Explosion
Customer: Rodriguez, Jesse
ID: V699-3934-3232
Rental Date: 5/29/2002
Due Date: 5/31/2002
Movies Rented
RARK Raiders of the Lost Ark
TIIC Titanic
Total Movies: 2 Total Paid: $5.00
Your clerk today was Pamela. Have a nice day!
information

Data Integrity

For a computer to produce correct information, the data that is input into a database must have integrity. **Data integrity** is the degree to which data is correct. A misspelled movie title in a movie database is an example of incorrect data. When a database contains these types of errors, it loses integrity. The more errors the data contains, the less its integrity. Users will not rely on data that has little or no integrity.

Garbage in, garbage out (**GIGO** pronounced ghee-go) is a computer phrase that states you cannot create correct information from data that is incorrect. If you enter incorrect data into a computer (garbage in), the computer will produce incorrect information (garbage out). Correct data does not guarantee the information is correct, but it does increase the chances.

Data integrity is very important because computers and people use information to make decisions and take actions. When you order a product, such as a book about gardening, a process begins that eventually delivers you the book. Before you receive the book, the retailer usually charges the order to your credit card. The retailer will bill an incorrect amount to your credit card if the book's price is not correct in its database. This type of error causes both you and the retailer extra time and effort to remedy.

THE HIERARCHY OF DATA

Data is built in layers. In the computer field, data is classified in a hierarchy. Each higher level of data consists of one or more items from the prior level. For example, a customer has an address, and an address consists of letters and numbers. Depending on the application and the user, different terms describe the various levels of the hierarchy. While using database software, you will see one or more of these terms. Thus, it is important to understand their usages and meanings.

Commonly used terms are character, field, record, file, and database. As shown in Figure 13-2, a database contains files, a file contains records, a record contains fields, and a field is made up of characters. As discussed in Chapter 4, a bit is the smallest unit of data the computer can recognize. Eight bits grouped together in a unit comprise a byte. Each byte represents a single **character**, such as a number (4), letter (R), punctuation mark (?), or other symbol (&).

A **field** is a combination of one or more characters and is the smallest unit of data a user accesses. A **field name** uniquely identifies each field. When you search for data in a database, you enter the field name. Field names for the records in the Movie file are Movie ID, Title, and Rating.

A database uses a variety of characteristics, such as data type and

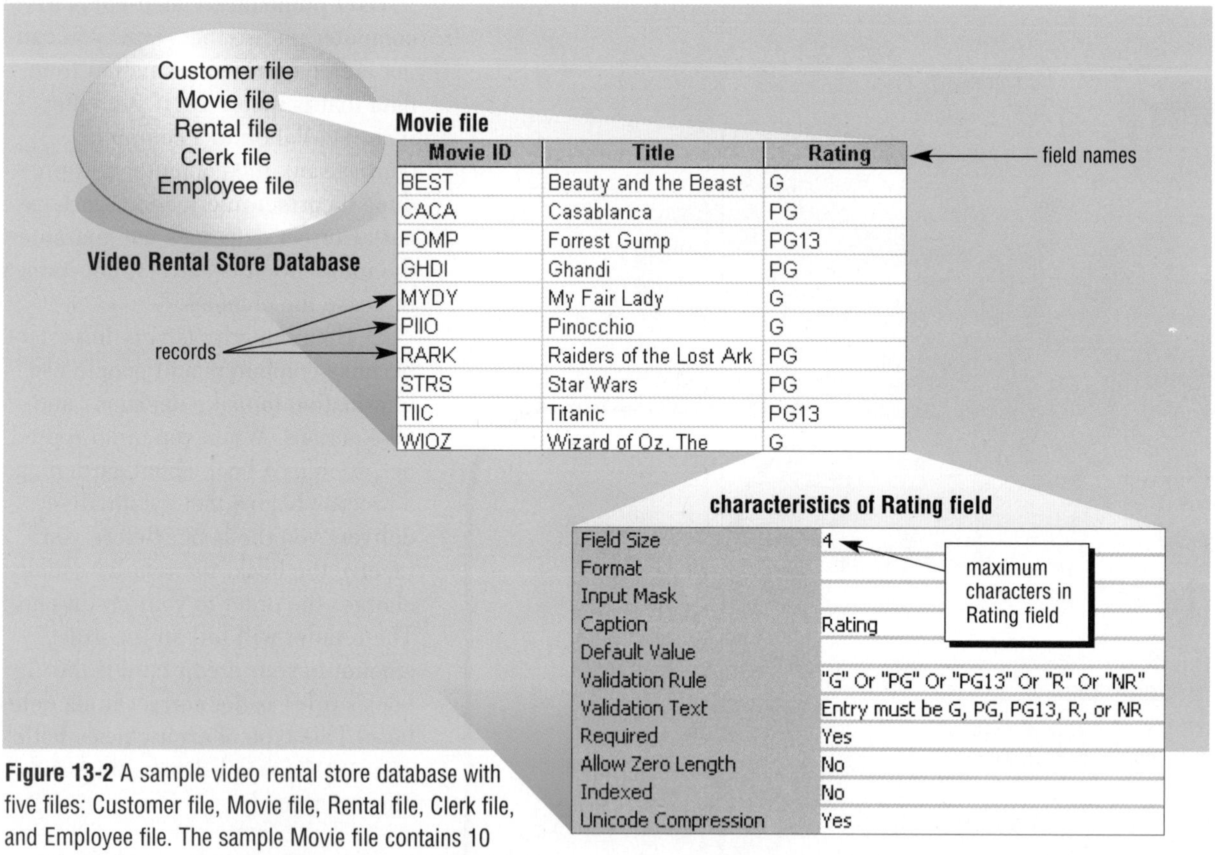

Movie file

Movie ID	Title	Rating
BEST	Beauty and the Beast	G
CACA	Casablanca	PG
FOMP	Forrest Gump	PG13
GHDI	Ghandi	PG
MYDY	My Fair Lady	G
PIIO	Pinocchio	G
RARK	Raiders of the Lost Ark	PG
STRS	Star Wars	PG
TIIC	Titanic	PG13
WIOZ	Wizard of Oz, The	G

characteristics of Rating field

Field Size	4
Format	
Input Mask	
Caption	Rating
Default Value	
Validation Rule	"G" Or "PG" Or "PG13" Or "R" Or "NR"
Validation Text	Entry must be G, PG, PG13, R, or NR
Required	Yes
Allow Zero Length	No
Indexed	No
Unicode Compression	Yes

Figure 13-2 A sample video rental store database with five files: Customer file, Movie file, Rental file, Clerk file, and Employee file. The sample Movie file contains 10 records. Each record contains three fields. The Rating field can contain a maximum of four characters (bytes).

Sample Customer File

Customer ID	First Name	Last Name	Address	City	State
V799-0092-5722	Elizabeth	Martin	983 Haines Street	Courtland	IL
V699-3934-3232	Jesse	Rodriguez	15 Cherry Street	Sycamore	IL
V799-3387-0923	Mae	Li	1437 Tenth Avenue	Sycamore	IL
V999-2003-9938	Tina	Popovich	154 Reckitt Street	Dekalb	IL
V999-2938-7766	Alex	Renwoeld	78 West Boulevard	Dekalb	IL

records

fields

field size, to define each field. As described in Chapter 3, the **data type** specifies the kind of data a field can contain and how the field is used. Common data types include:

- **Text** – letters, numbers, or special characters
- **Numeric** – numbers only
- **Currency** – dollar and cent amounts or numbers containing decimal values
- **Date** – month, day, year, and sometimes time information
- **Memo** – lengthy text entries
- **Yes/No** – only the values Yes or No
- **Hyperlink** – Web address that links to a document or a Web page
- **Object** – picture, audio, video, or a document created in other applications such as word processing or spreadsheet

The **field size** defines the maximum number of characters a field can contain. A State field may contain the two-character postal code. A Rating field for a movie, by contrast, may contain up to four characters. Some movies have a G rating (one character), some have a PG rating (two characters), and some have a PG13 rating (four characters).

A **record** is a group of related fields. A movie record includes a set of fields about one movie. This record might contain field names such as Movie ID, Title, and Rating.

A **key field**, or **primary key**, is a field that uniquely identifies each record in a file. The data in a key field is unique to a specific record. For example, the Movie ID field uniquely identifies each movie because no two movies have the same Movie ID.

A **data file**, also often called a **file**, is a collection of related records stored on a disk such as a hard disk or CD-ROM. A video rental store's Customer file would consist of hundreds of individual customer records. Each customer record in the file contains the same fields. Each field, however, contains different data. Figure 13-3 shows a small sample Customer file that contains 5 customer records, each with 11 fields. Typical fields about people often include First Name, Last Name, Address, City, State, Postal Code, Telephone Number, and E-mail Address.

As defined in previous chapters, the term file also can refer to word processing, spreadsheet, or other executable application files. These types of files, sometimes known as **program files**, may or may not use data files.

A database includes a group of related data files. A video rental store's database, for example, might have many individual files such as a Customer file, a Movie file, and a Rental file. With a DBMS, you can access and relate the data in data files.

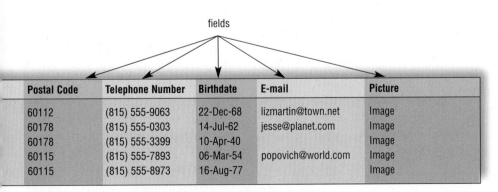

fields

Postal Code	Telephone Number	Birthdate	E-mail	Picture
60112	(815) 555-9063	22-Dec-68	lizmartin@town.net	Image
60178	(815) 555-0303	14-Jul-62	jesse@planet.com	Image
60178	(815) 555-3399	10-Apr-40		Image
60115	(815) 555-7893	06-Mar-54	popovich@world.com	Image
60115	(815) 555-8973	16-Aug-77		Image

Figure 13-3 A sample data file stored on a hard disk that contains 5 records, each with 11 fields.

APPLY IT!

What's in a Home Inventory List?

Everyone should have a home inventory list of his or her possessions for insurance and personal use. A database program is the perfect tool for creating such a list.

Follow these instructions to plan your home inventory database:

1. Categorize your personal property into tables using meaningful names such as appliances, artwork, collectibles, china, electronics, furniture, jewelry, and silver.
2. Determine the fields within each table. Use the Text data type for the item name, manufacturer name, and location. Use the Currency data type for price and the Date data type for the purchase date. If you intend to add pictures, use the Object data type. You also may want to add a Memo field for notes.
3. For electronics and appliances, most likely you would use serial numbers or the model number for the primary key. For categories that may not have identifying numbers, you can number each item sequentially, or use your own unique combination of numbers and/or letters.

To create a home inventory database, you have several options. You can use a database program such as Microsoft Access. With this type of software, you can create reports and query your database. If you choose to use Access, you can download a Home Inventory template (see URL below). Modify the template to meet your personal needs and then add your data.

You also may use a spreadsheet program such as Microsoft Excel, which is easier and faster, though not as powerful as a database program. Using the Excel Help Answer Wizard, type `how do I manage lists` to view instructions on setting up your data.

Finally, use a software program designed specifically for home inventory purposes. Several free and shareware inventory programs are available online.

For more information on shareware and databases, visit the Discovering Computers 2002 Apply It Web page (**scsite.com/dc2002/apply.htm**) and click Chapter 13 Apply It #1.

MAINTAINING DATA

File maintenance, also called **data maintenance**, refers to the procedures that keep data current. File maintenance procedures include adding records to, changing records in, and deleting records from a file.

Adding Records

You add new records to a file when you have new data. If a new customer wishes to rent a movie from a video store, the checkout clerk would add a new record to the store's Customer database file. The process required to add this record to the file might include the following steps:

1. A checkout clerk starts a Customer Maintenance program that gives him or her access to the file. The clerk then clicks the New Record button, which begins the process of adding a record to the Customer file.
2. The clerk enters the customer's driver's license number into the Customer ID field. This number serves as the primary key for the new customer record. Every person's driver's license number is unique.
3. The clerk fills in the fields of the customer record with data. In this example, the data entered is kept to a minimum.
4. The clerk takes a picture of the customer using a digital camera. The DBMS stores this picture in the Customer file and prints it on the customer's ID card.
5. The checkout clerk verifies the data on the screen and then presses the TAB key on the keyboard to add the new customer record to the Customer file. The system software that manages the disk determines where to write the record on the disk. In some cases, it writes the new record at the end of the file. In other cases, such as illustrated in Figure 13-4, it writes the new record between existing records in the file.

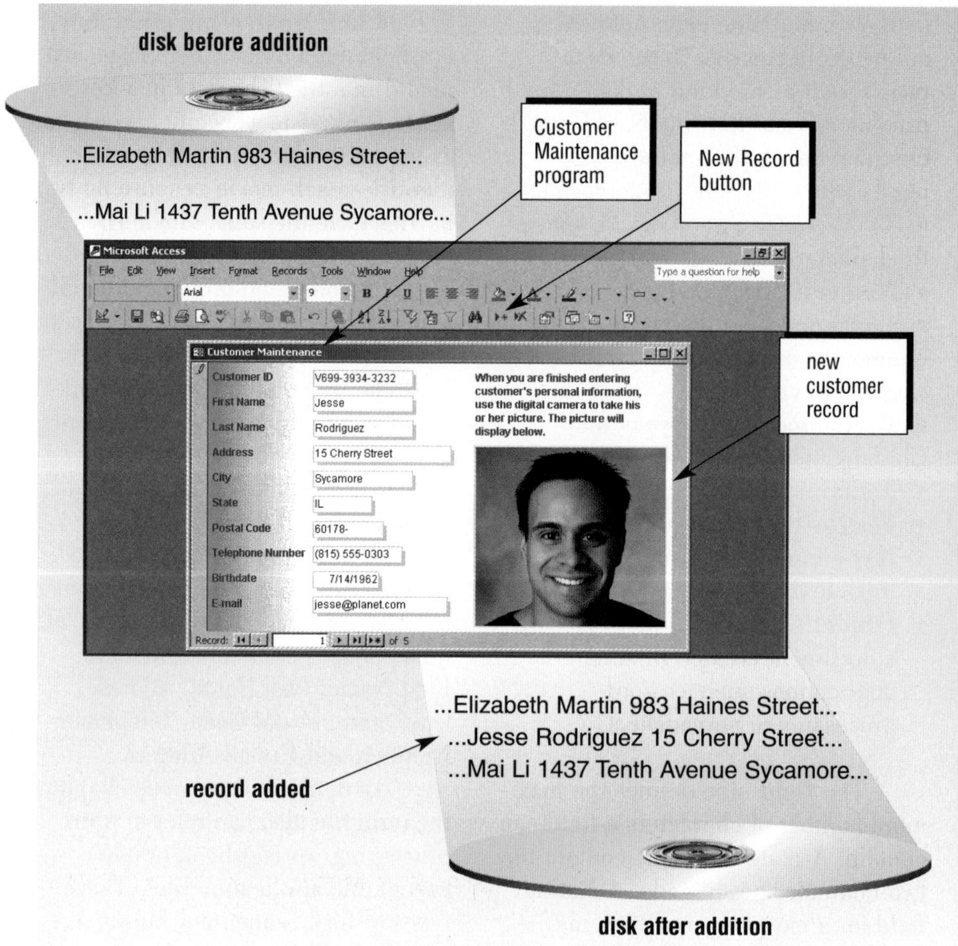

Figure 13-4 Using the Customer Maintenance program, a checkout clerk adds a new customer record. After the clerk takes the photograph with the digital camera and confirms the data is correct, he or she adds the record to the database file.

Changing Records

Generally, you change a record in a file for two reasons: (1) to correct inaccurate data or (2) to update old data with new data.

As an example of the first type of change, assume that a checkout clerk enters a customer's home telephone number as (815) 555-0909, instead of (815) 555-0303. The customer notices the error when he reviews his video rental agreement at home. The next time he rents a movie, he requests the clerk correct his telephone number.

To do this, a video store checkout clerk displays the customer's record on the screen by entering the primary key value. Next, the clerk changes this customer's telephone number from (815) 555-0909 to (815) 555-0303. The change corrects the inaccurate data and replaces it with accurate data.

A more common reason to change a record is to update old data with new data. Suppose, for example, that Jesse Rodriguez moves from 15 Cherry Street to 1126 Johnston Street. The process to change the address and update Jesse Rodriguez's record might include the following steps:

1. The checkout clerk starts the Customer Maintenance program.
2. The clerk scans Jesse Rodriguez's customer ID card to display his customer record on the screen. If Jesse did not have his ID card, the clerk could enter Jesse's driver's license number in the Customer ID field. The clerk also could enter Rodriguez in the Last Name field, which would retrieve all customers with that same last name. The clerk then would scroll through all of the retrieved records to determine which one is Jesse's.
3. The program displays data about Jesse Rodriguez. By looking at Jesse's picture on the screen, the clerk can confirm that the correct customer record displays.
4. The clerk enters the new street address of 1126 Johnston Street.
5. The checkout clerk verifies the data on the screen and then clicks the Save button to change the record in the Customer file. The program changes the record on the disk (Figure 13-5).

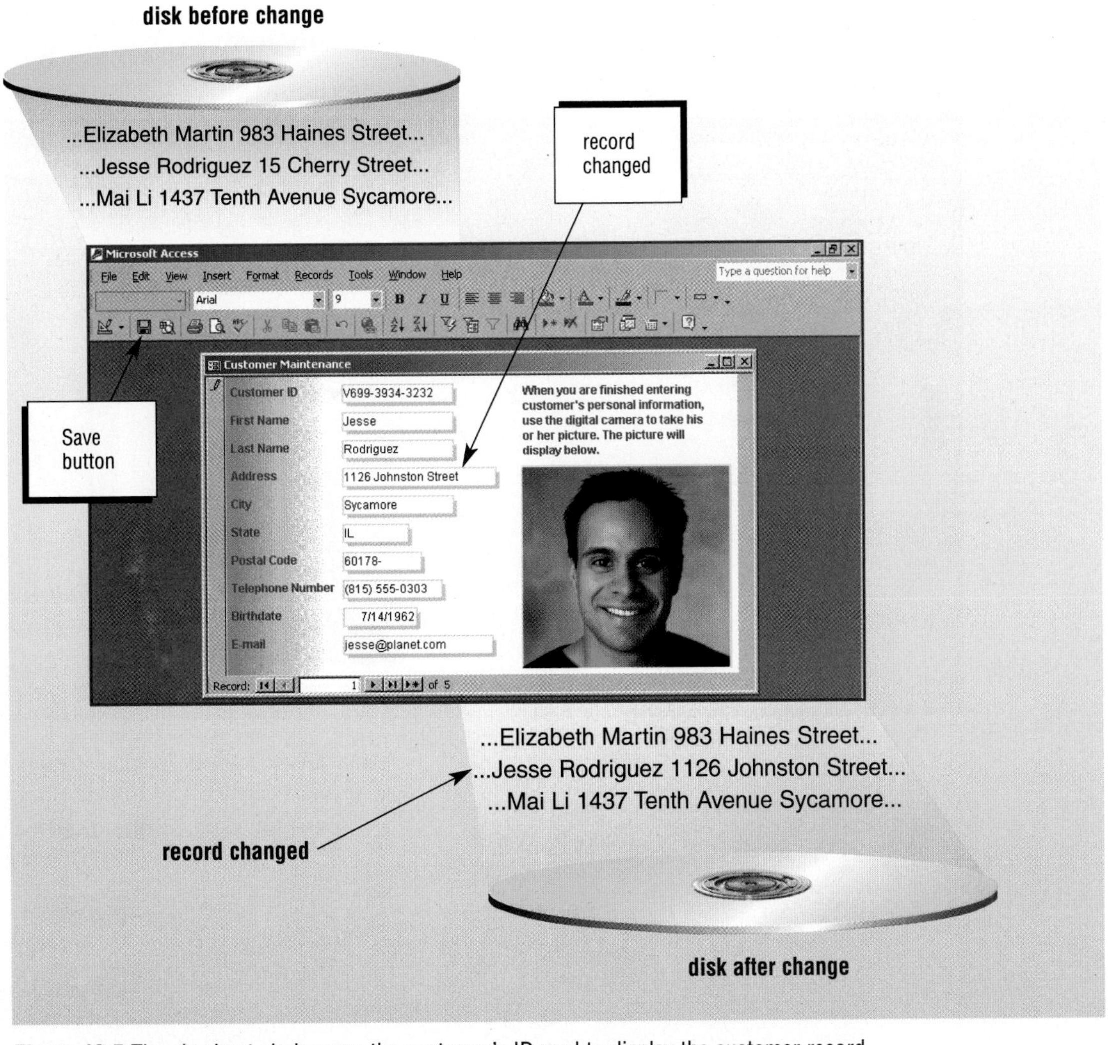

Figure 13-5 The checkout clerk scans the customer's ID card to display the customer record. After looking at the photograph on the screen to confirm the correct customer record displays, the clerk changes the customer's address.

Deleting Records

When you no longer need a record, you delete it from a file. Assume a customer named Tina Popovich is moving out of state. The process required to delete a record from a file includes the following steps:

1. The checkout clerk starts the Customer Maintenance program.
2. The clerk scans Tina's customer ID card to display her customer record on the screen.
3. The program displays Tina Popovich's name and other data about Tina on the screen.
4. By looking at Tina's picture on the screen, the clerk can confirm the correct customer record displays. Then, the clerk clicks the Delete Record button to delete the record from the Customer file.

Applications use a variety of techniques to manage deleted records. Sometimes, the program removes the record from the file immediately. Other times, the program does not remove the record from the file. Instead, the record is *flagged* or marked, so the program will not process it again. In this case, the program places an asterisk (*) at the beginning of the record (Figure 13-6).

Applications that maintain inactive data for a period of time commonly flag records. A video rental store might flag closed accounts. When a program flags a deleted record, the record remains physically on the disk. The record, however, is *logically* deleted because the program will not process it. Programs ignore flagged records unless they are instructed to process them.

From time to time, you should run a utility program that removes flagged records and reorganizes current records. For example, the video rental store may remove from disk any accounts that have been closed for more than one year. Deleting unneeded records reduces the size of files and creates additional storage space.

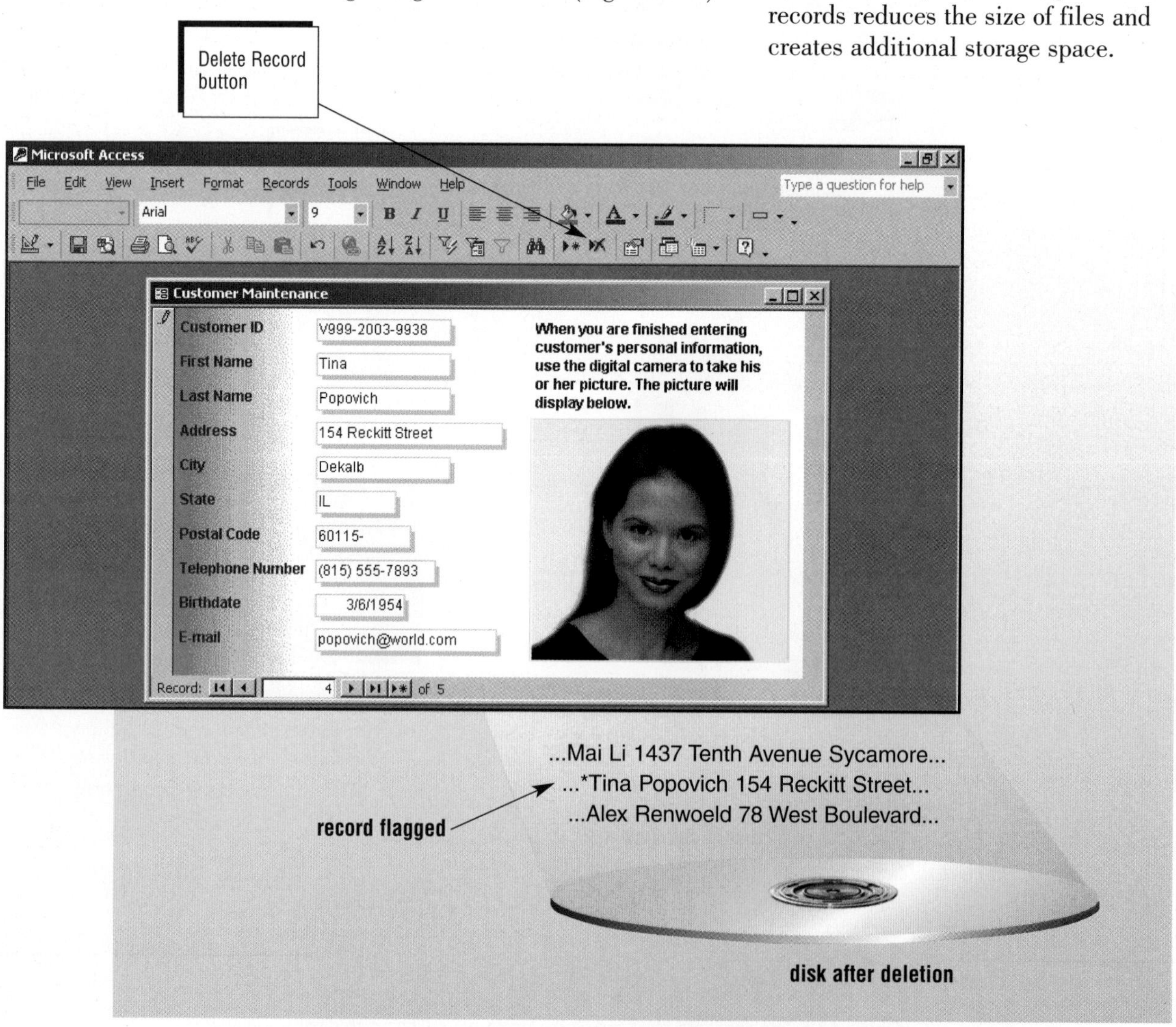

Figure 13-6 The checkout clerk displays the customer's record on the screen. After the clerk verifies the correct customer record displays, he or she clicks the Delete Record button to delete the record. The program flags the customer record on disk by placing an asterisk in the first position of the record.

Data Validation

As discussed in Chapter 3, **validation** is the process of comparing data to a set of rules or values to find out if the data is correct. Many programs perform a **validity check** that analyzes entered data to help ensure that it is correct. For instance, when a checkout clerk adds or changes data in a customer record, the DBMS tests the entered data.

With a telephone number, you would expect to see numbers inside the parenthesis and also before and after the hyphen. A valid telephone number is (815) 555-6753. An entry of (SED) ERK-URID clearly is not correct. If the entered data fails a validity check, the computer usually displays an error message and asks you to enter the data again. Validity checks, also called **validation rules**, reduce data entry errors. Validating data enhances its integrity before the program writes the data on disk. Validation reduces the possibility of GIGO (garbage in, garbage out).

Various types of validity checks include alphabetic checks, numeric checks, range checks, consistency checks, completeness checks, and check digits. The table in Figure 13-7 illustrates several validity checks and shows valid data that passes the check and invalid data that fails the check. The following paragraphs describe the purpose of these validity checks.

ALPHABETIC/NUMERIC CHECK An **alphabetic check** ensures that you enter only alphabetic data into a field. A **numeric check** ensures that you enter only numeric data into a field. For example, data in a First Name field should contain only characters from the alphabet. Data in a Telephone Number field should contain numbers (with the exception of the special characters such as the parenthesis and the dash).

RANGE CHECK A **range check** determines whether a number is within a specified range. Assume a video rental store limits a customer to five rentals per day. A range check on the Total Rentals data item ensures it is a value between 1 and 5.

CONSISTENCY CHECK A **consistency check** tests if the data in two or more associated fields is logical. For example, a Due Date cannot occur earlier in time than a Rental Date.

Sample Valid and Invalid Data

Validity Check	Field Being Checked	Valid Data	Invalid Data
Alphabetic Check	First Name	Jesse	Je33e
Numeric Check	Telephone Number	(815) 555-0303	(815) rrr-0303
Range Check	Total Rentals	4	18
Consistency Check	Rental Date	07-15-2002	07-18-2002
	Due Date	07-18-2002	07-15-2002
Completeness Check	Last Name	Rodriguez	

Figure 13-7 In this table of sample valid and invalid data, the first column lists commonly used validity checks. The second column lists the name of the field that contains data being tested. The third column shows valid data that passes the validity tests. The fourth column shows invalid data that fails the validity tests.

Web Link

For more information on validity checks, visit the Discovering Computers 2002 Chapter 13 WEB LINK page (**scsite.com/dc2002/ch13/weblink.htm**) and click Validity Checks.

COMPLETENESS CHECK A **completeness check** verifies a required field contains data. In many application programs, you cannot leave the Last Name field blank. The completeness check ensures data exists in the Last Name field (Figure 13-8).

CHECK DIGIT A check digit confirms the accuracy of a primary key value. Bank account, credit card, and other identification numbers often include one or more check digits. A **check digit** is a number(s) or character(s) that is appended to or inserted into a primary key value.

A program determines the check digit by applying a formula to the numbers in the primary key value. An oversimplified illustration of a check digit formula is to add together the numbers in the primary key. For example, if the primary key is 1367, this formula would add together these numbers (1 + 3 + 6 + 7) for a sum of 17. Next, the formula would add together the numbers in the result (1 + 7) to generate a check digit of 8. The primary key then is 13678. This example began with the original primary key value, 1367, then the check digit, 8, was appended.

When a data entry clerk enters the primary key of 13678, the program determines if the check digit is valid. The program applies the check digit formula to the first four digits of the primary key. If the computed check digit matches the entered check digit (8, in this example), the program assumes the entered primary key is valid. If the clerk enters an incorrect primary key, such as 13778, the check digit entered (8) will not match the computed check digit (9). In this case, the program displays an error message and asks the user to enter the primary key value again.

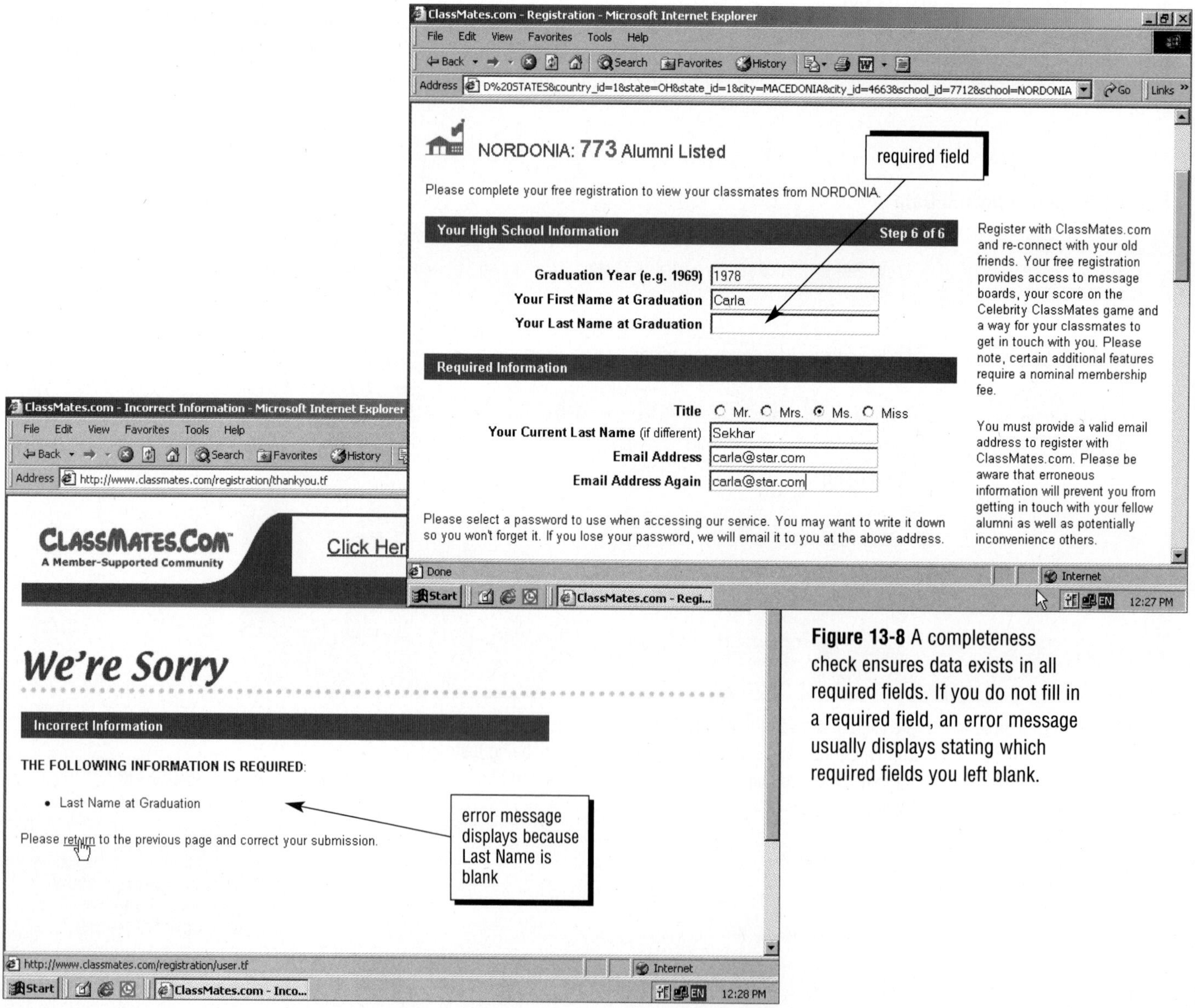

Figure 13-8 A completeness check ensures data exists in all required fields. If you do not fill in a required field, an error message usually displays stating which required fields you left blank.

FILE PROCESSING VERSUS DATABASES

Almost all application programs use either the file processing approach or the database approach to store and manage data. The following sections discuss these two approaches.

File Processing Systems

In the past, many organizations used file processing systems to store and manage data. In a typical **file processing system**, each department or area within an organization has its own set of files. These files often are designed specifically for their own applications. The records in one file often do not relate to the records in any other file.

Figure 13-9 shows how a video rental store might use a file processing system. The computers at the checkout counter might have their own files containing customers' rented movie records. The computer in the store manager's office may have its own set of files for sending promotional mailings to customers.

Companies have used file processing systems for many years. A lot of these systems, however, have two major weaknesses: they have redundant data, and they isolate data.

- **Data Redundancy** – Because each department or area in a company has its own files in a file processing system, the files often store the same fields in multiple files. At the video rental store, for example, the files in the checkout area and the store manager's office store the same customers' names and addresses.

Duplicating data in this manner wastes resources such as storage space and people's time. Storing the same data in more than one file requires a larger storage capacity. When you add or change data, file maintenance takes additional time because people must update more than one file.

Data redundancy also compromises data integrity. If customers change their address, the video rental store must update their address wherever it appears. In this example, the Address field is in the files at the checkout counter and also in the store manager's files. The Address field also may be stored in other areas. If the Address field is not changed in all the files where it is stored, then discrepancies among the files exist.

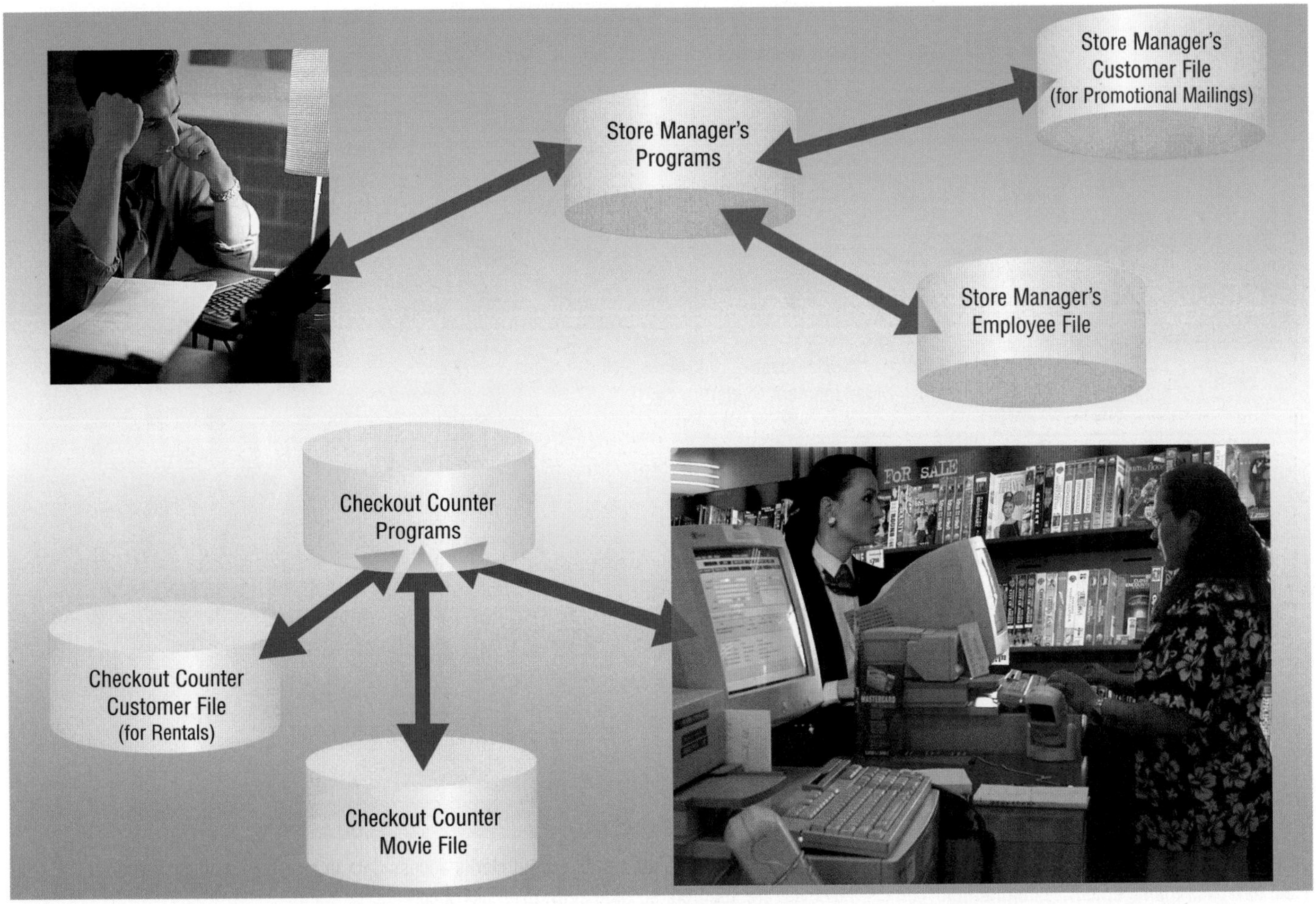

Figure 13-9 In a video rental store that uses file processing, the checkout counter area and store manager's computers have their own files that are designed specifically for their applications.

- **Isolated Data** – Often it is difficult to access data stored in many files across several departments. Assume that the customer e-mail addresses are only in the store manager's files, and customer rental information is only in the checkout area files. To send an e-mail message informing a customer that a movie is overdue, you need data from both the checkout area files and the store manager's files. Sharing data from multiple, separate files to generate such a list often is a complicated procedure and typically requires the experience of a computer programmer.

The Database Approach

When a company uses the **database approach**, many programs and users can share the data in the database. A video rental store's database most likely contains data about customers, rentals, movies, and employees. As shown in Figure 13-10, various areas within the store share and interact with the data in this database. The database, however, does secure its data so only authorized users can access certain data items. For example, only the store manager can view an employee's hourly pay rate.

As described in Chapter 3, users can access the data in the database using database software, also called a database management system (DBMS). While a user is working with the database, the DBMS resides in the memory of the computer.

Instead of working with the DBMS, some users interact with a front end. A **front end** is a program that typically has a more user-friendly interface than the DBMS. For example, a checkout clerk interacts with the Movie Rental program. This front-end program interacts with the DBMS, which in turn, interacts with the database. The application that supports the front end sometimes is called the **back end.** In this case, the DBMS is the back-end application.

The database approach addresses many of the weaknesses connected with file processing systems. The following paragraphs present some strengths of the database approach.

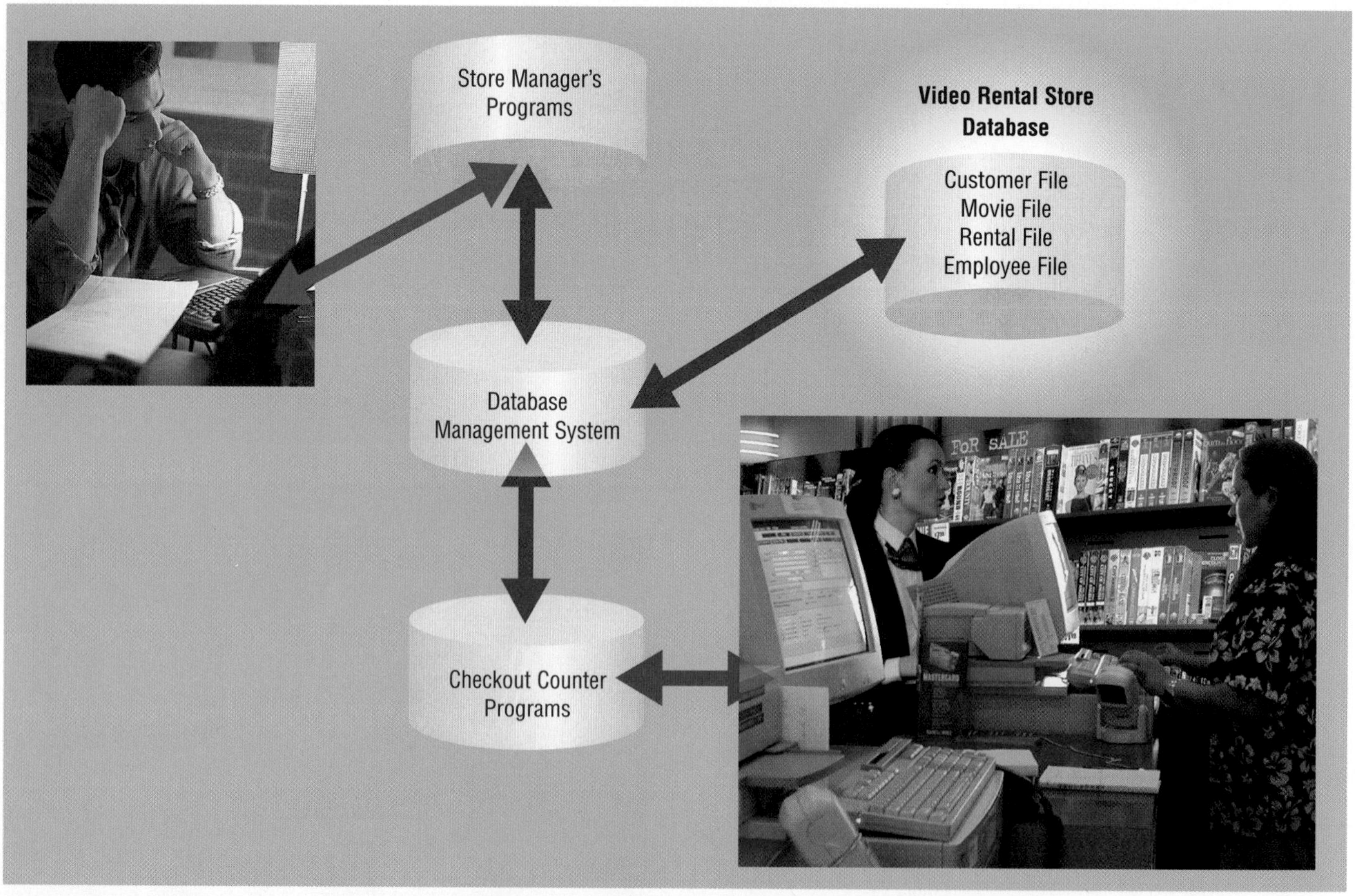

Figure 13-10 In a video rental store that uses a database, the store manager and checkout clerks access data in a single database through the database management system. Employee files, however, are secured, so only authorized users can access them.

- **Reduced Data Redundancy** – A centralized database stores all related data in one location, which greatly reduces duplicate data. A video store database would record a customer's name and address only once. When customer data is entered or changed, one employee makes the change once. Figure 13-11 demonstrates the differences between how a database application and a file processing application might store data.
- **Improved Data Integrity** – When users modify data in the database, they make changes to one file instead of multiple files. Thus, the database approach increases the data's integrity by reducing the chances of introducing inconsistencies.
- **Shared Data** – Each application in a file processing environment often has its own set of files. The data in a database environment, by contrast, belongs to and is shared by the entire organization. This data is independent, or separate from, the programs that access the data. Companies that use databases typically have security settings to define who can access, add, change, and delete the data in a database.
- **Reduced Development Time** – It often is easier and faster to develop programs that use the database approach. Many DBMSs also provide several tools to assist in developing programs, which further reduces the development time. The next section discusses these tools and other DBMS features.
- **Easier Reporting** – The database approach allows nontechnical users to access and maintain data. Many computer users also develop smaller databases themselves, without professional assistance.

Databases have many advantages as well as some disadvantages. A large database can be more complex than a file processing system. People with special training usually develop larger databases and their applications. Larger databases also require more memory, storage, and processing power than file processing systems.

Data in a database is more vulnerable than data in file processing systems. A database stores all data in a single location. Many users and programs share and depend on this data. If the database is not operating properly or is damaged or destroyed, users may not be able to perform their jobs. In some cases, certain application programs may stop working. To protect their valuable database resource, individuals and companies should establish and follow security procedures. Chapter 12 discussed a variety of security methods.

Despite these limitations, many business and home users work with databases because of their tremendous advantages. Although the hardware and software costs to set up a database may seem expensive, long-term benefits exceed the initial costs.

File Processing Example

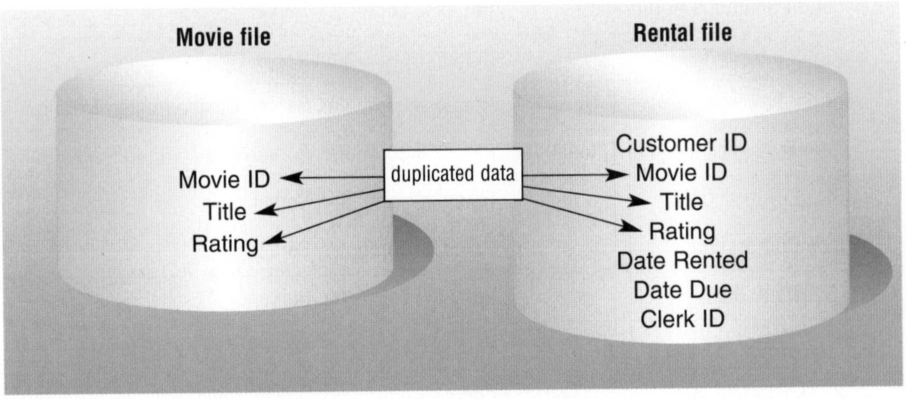

Figure 13-11 In the file processing environment, both files contain the Movie ID, Title, and Rating fields. In a database environment, only the Movie file contains the Title and Rating fields. Other files, such as the Rental file, contain the Movie ID, which is used to retrieve the title and rating data about the movie when it is needed.

Database Example

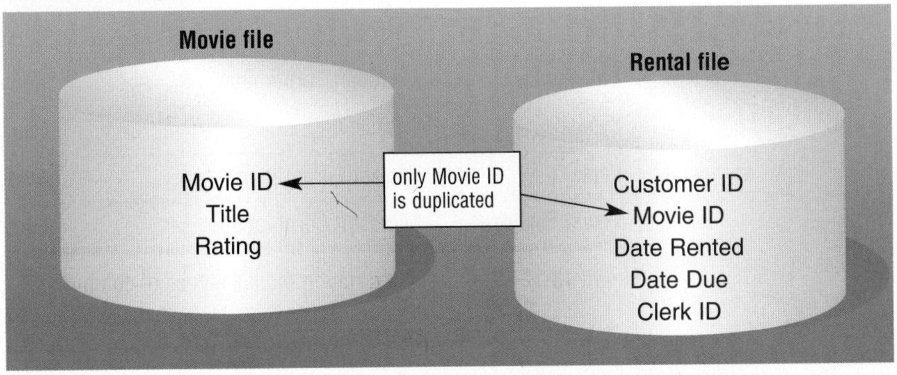

Web Link
For more information on database management systems, visit the Discovering Computers 2002 Chapter 13 WEB LINK page (**scsite.com/dc2002/ch13/weblink.htm**) and click Database Management Systems.

Web Link
For more information on the data dictionary, visit the Discovering Computers 2002 Chapter 13 WEB LINK page (**scsite.com/dc2002/ch13/weblink.htm**) and click Data Dictionary.

DATABASE MANAGEMENT SYSTEMS

As previously discussed, a **database management system (DBMS)**, or database program, is software that allows you to create, access, and manage a database. DBMSs are available for many sizes and types of computers (Figure 13-12). Whether designed for a small or large computer, most DBMSs have common features and functions. The following pages discuss these common elements of a DBMS.

Data Dictionary

A **data dictionary**, sometimes called a **repository**, contains data about each file in the database and each field within those files. For each file, it stores details such as the file name, description, the file's relationship to other files, and the number of records in the file. For each field, it stores details such as the field name, description, field type, field size, default value, validation rules, and the field's relationship to other fields. Figure 13-13 shows how a data dictionary might list data for a Customer file.

Popular Database Management Systems

Database	Manufacturer	Computer Type
Access	Microsoft Corporation	Personal computer, Server
Adabas	Software AG	Server, Minicomputer, Mainframe
Approach	Lotus Development Corporation	Personal computer, Server
D^3	Pick Systems	Personal computer, Server, Minicomputer
DB2	IBM Corporation	Personal computer, Server, Minicomputer, Mainframe
Essbase	Hyperion Solutions Corporation	Personal computer, Server
GemStone	GemStone Systems, Inc.	Server, Minicomputer
Informix	Informix Software	Personal computer, Server, Minicomputer, Mainframe
Ingres	Computer Associates International, Inc.	Personal computer, Server, Minicomputer, Mainframe
InterBase	Inprise Corporation	Personal computer, Server
JDataStore	Inprise Corporation	Personal computer, Server
KE Texpress	KE Software, Inc.	Personal computer, Server
Objectivity	Object Design, Inc.	Personal computer, Server, Minicomputer
Oracle	Oracle Corporation	Personal computer, Server, Minicomputer, Mainframe
Paradox	Corel Corporation	Personal computer, Server
POET	POET Software Corporation	Personal computer, Server, Minicomputer
SQL Server	Microsoft Corporation	Server
Sybase	Sybase, Inc.	Handheld and desktop computers, Server, Minicomputer
Versant	Versant Corporation	Personal computer, Server, Minicomputer
Visual FoxPro	Microsoft Corporation	Personal computer, Server

Figure 13-12 Many databases run on multiple types of computers.

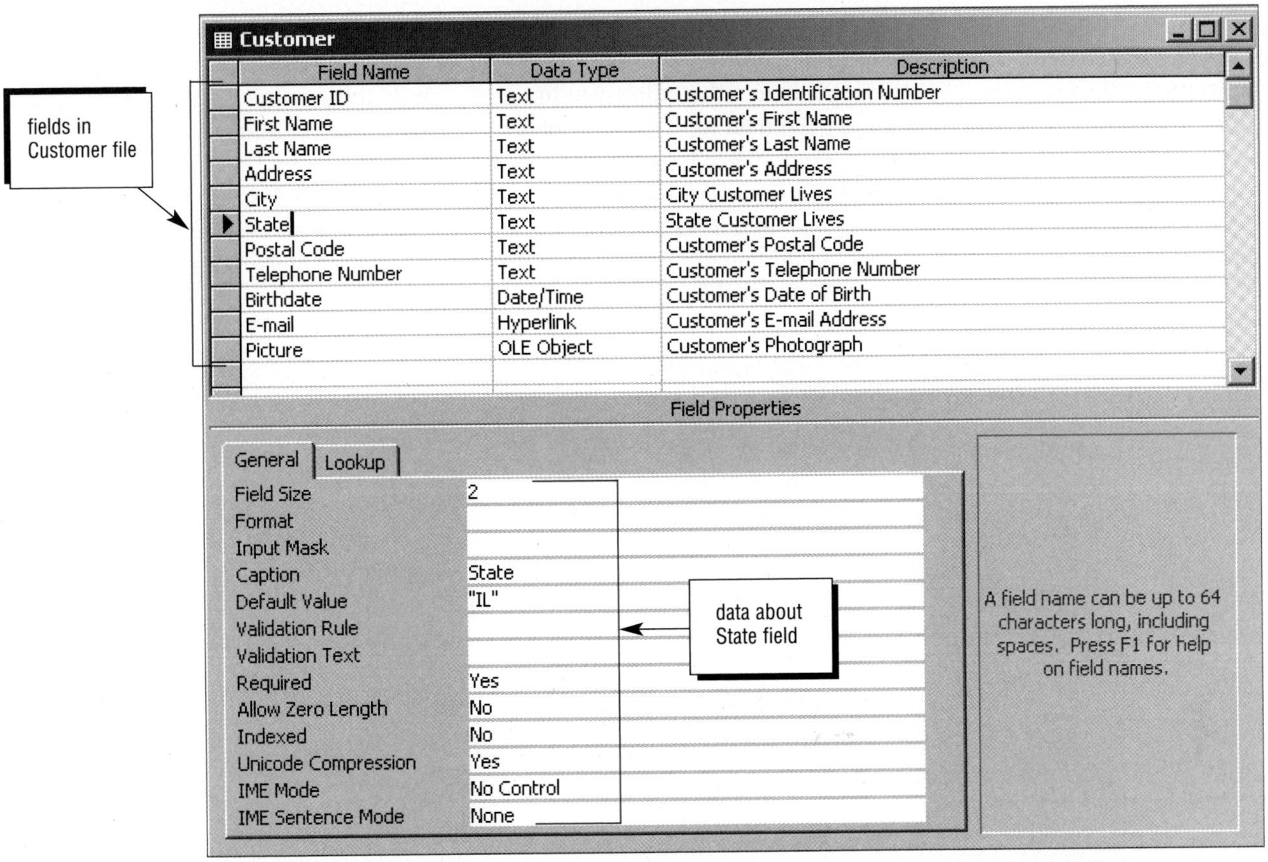

Figure 13-13 A sample data dictionary entry showing the fields in the Customer file and the properties of the State field.

Because the data dictionary contains data about data, some call it **metadata**. A data dictionary also sometimes contains data about programs and users. It might keep track of who accessed data and when they accessed it. The data dictionary is a crucial backbone to a DBMS, thus only skilled professionals should update its contents.

A DBMS uses the data dictionary to perform validation checks. When you enter data, the data dictionary verifies that the entered data matches the field's data type. The State field must contain a valid state code such as "IL". By validating data, the data dictionary helps to maintain the integrity of the data.

A data dictionary allows you to specify a default value for a field. A **default value** is a value that the DBMS initially displays in a field. If most customers who rent videos from your store live in Illinois, then the DBMS initially could display IL in the State field. The user does not have to type in a default value. Displaying a default value reduces the possibility of errors. Usually, a user can override a default value if it does not apply for a certain record. For example, you can change the value from IL to WI if the customer lives in Wisconsin.

File Maintenance and Retrieval

A DBMS provides several tools that allow users and programs to maintain and retrieve data in the database. As discussed earlier in this chapter, file maintenance involves adding new records, changing data in existing records, and removing unwanted records from the database.

To retrieve or select data in a database, you query it. A **query** is a request for specific data from the database. You can instruct the DBMS to display, print, or store the results of a query. As described in Chapter 3, the capability of querying a database is one of the more powerful database features.

All skill levels of users, from trained experts to nontechnical, maintain and retrieve the data in a database. To deal with this variety of database users, a DBMS offers several methods to access its data. The four most commonly used are query languages, query-by-example, forms, and report generators. The following paragraphs describe each of these methods.

QUERY LANGUAGE A **query language** consists of simple, English-like statements that allow you to specify the data to display, print, or store. Each query language has its own grammar and vocabulary. A person without a programming background usually can learn these languages in a short time.

Although you can use a query language to maintain data, most users only retrieve (query) data with a query language. To simplify the query process, many DBMSs provide wizards to guide you through the steps of creating a query. Figure 13-14 shows a Simple Query Wizard and the query it creates.

Figure 13-14a (wizard for querying the database)

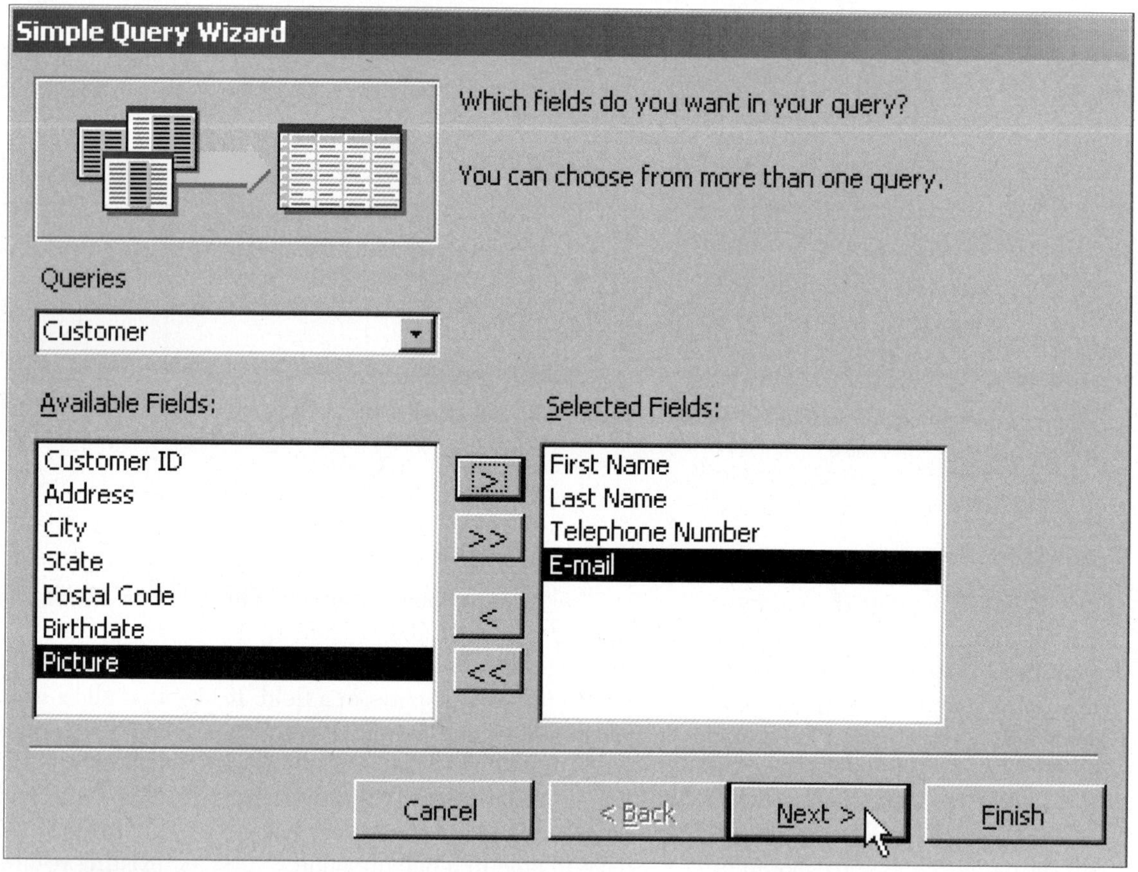

Figure 13-14b (query results)

First Name	Last Name	Telephone Number	E-mail
Mae	Li	(815) 555-3399	
Elizabeth	Martin	(815) 555-9063	lizmartin@town.net
Tina	Popovich	(815) 555-7893	popovich@world.com
Alex	Renwoeld	(815) 555-8973	
Jesse	Rodriguez	(815) 555-0303	jesse@planet.com

Figure 13-14 In the Simple Query Wizard, you indicate which fields to display in the query results. The query shown displays the First Name, Last Name, Telephone Number, and E-mail fields for customers in the Customer file. The list is sorted alphabetically by Last Name. For a list of all fields in the Customer file, see Figure 13-3 on page 13.5.

QUERY BY EXAMPLE Instead of learning the grammar and vocabulary associated with a query language, you can use a **query by example (QBE)** to request data from the database. Most DBMSs include a QBE feature. QBEs have a graphical user interface that assists you with retrieving data. Figure 13-15 shows a sample QBE screen for a query that searches for and lists movies with a "PG" rating. Later in the chapter, specific query languages are presented in more depth.

FORM A **form**, sometimes called a **data entry form**, is a window on the screen that provides areas for entering or changing data in a database. You use forms to retrieve (see Figure 13-15) and maintain (Figure 13-16) the data in a database.

Figure 13-15a (query by example screen)

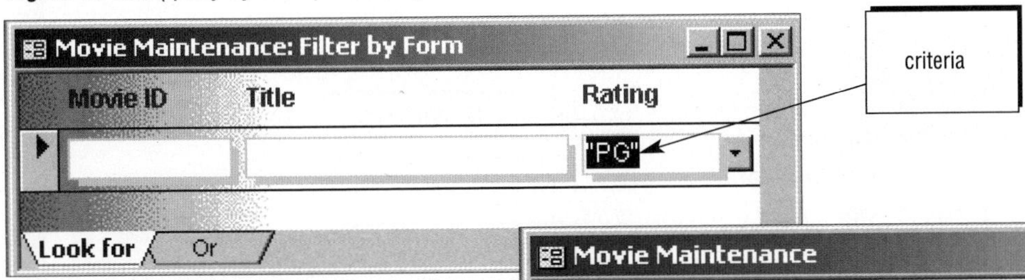

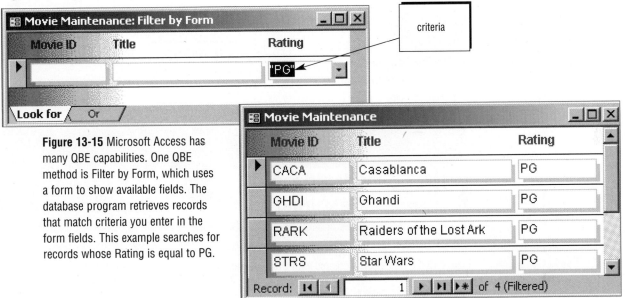

Figure 13-15 Microsoft Access has many QBE capabilities. One QBE method is Filter by Form, which uses a form to show available fields. The database program retrieves records that match criteria you enter in the form fields. This example searches for records whose Rating is equal to PG.

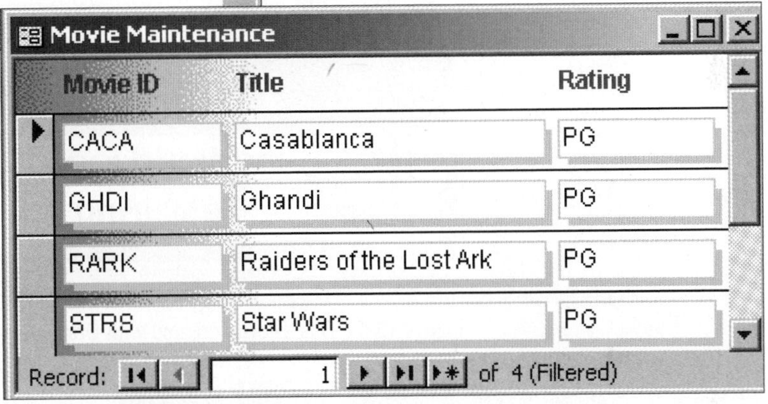

Figure 13-15b (query results)

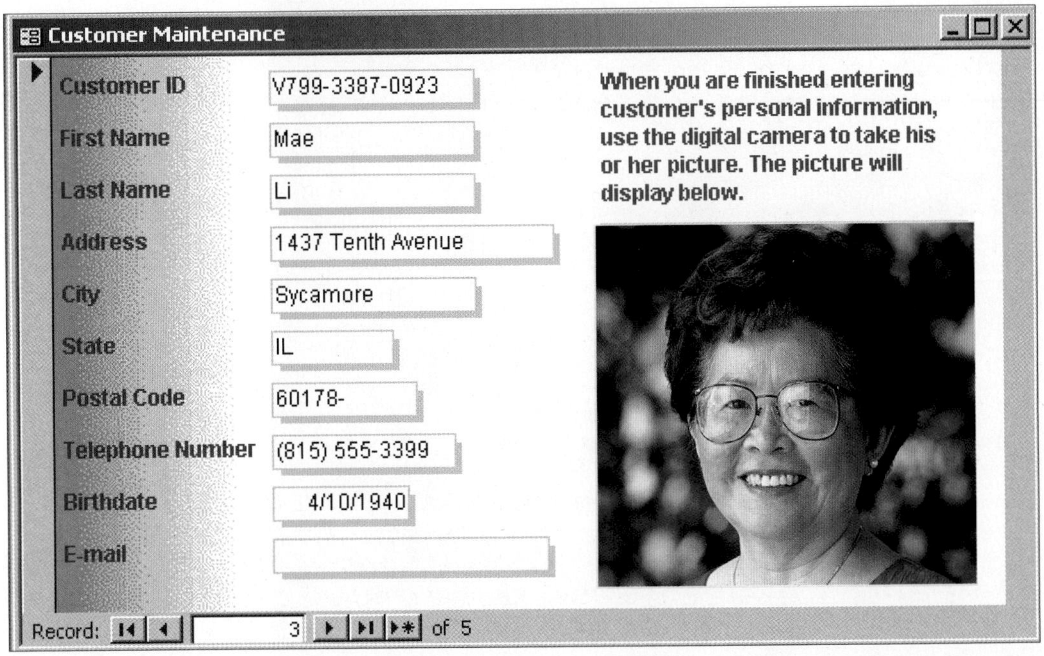

Figure 13-16 This form, created in Microsoft Access, is used to add customers to the Customer file.

To reduce data entry errors, well-designed forms validate data as it is input. When designing a form using a DBMS, you can make the form attractive and easy to use by incorporating color, shading, lines, boxes, and graphics; varying the fonts and font styles; and using other formatting features.

A form that sends entered data across a network or the Internet is called an **electronic form**, or **e-form** (Figure 13-17). E-forms typically use a means to secure the data while it is transported across the network. Often, the data in the e-form automatically updates data in a database on the network or the Internet. Thus, many DBMSs include the capability to create e-forms.

Figure 13-17 This e-form, created with Oracle, sends your registration information to a database at CNN.

ISSUE

Who Can You Trust?

E-Forms and Your Personal Information

Who can you trust? While surfing the Internet you come across an interesting site. The headline invites you to take a minute to enroll. In return for your time, the Web site states you will receive a lifetime of savings. The offer seems too good to pass up, so you type in your name, e-mail, home address, and telephone number. As soon as you click the Submit button, the information is whisked away, where it is added to a huge database. Within seconds, the information you entered is most likely traveling via high-speed networks halfway around the world. The company now has your personal information and can sell your name, address, and telephone number to dozens of marketing firms, without your knowledge or consent. How do you feel about this? Do you think a company should have the option to sell your personal information? Some sites post privacy statements and a TRUSTe seal. Would you feel confident leaving your information at one of these sites? How do you know that you can trust this company and that the seal is legitimate?

For more information on privacy, visit the Discovering Computers 2002 Issues Web page (**scsite.com/dc2002/issues.htm**) and click Chapter 13 Issue #1.

REPORT GENERATOR A **report generator**, also called a **report writer**, allows you to design a report on the screen, retrieve data into the report design, and then display or print the report (Figure 13-18). Unlike a form, you use a report generator only to retrieve data. Report generators usually allow you to format page numbers and dates; titles and column headings; subtotals and totals; and fonts, font sizes, color, and shading.

Data Security

Sometimes, users accidentally delete the data from a database; others misuse the data intentionally. Thus, a DBMS provides means to make certain only authorized users can access data at permitted times. In addition, most DBMSs allow you to identify different levels of access privileges for each field in the database. These **access privileges** define the activities that a specific user or group of users can perform.

Access privileges for data involve establishing who can enter new data, change existing data, delete unwanted data, and retrieve data. In the movie database, a checkout clerk might have **read-only privileges** for movie ratings. The clerk could retrieve the movie rating data, but cannot change it. The store manager, by contrast, would have **full-update privileges** to movie data, meaning they can retrieve and change the data. Finally, a customer would have no access privileges to the movie data. Customers can neither retrieve nor change the data. Chapter 12 discussed access privileges and other security techniques in more depth.

Movie Listing by Rating

Rating	Title	Movie ID
G		
	Beauty and the Beast	BEST
	My Fair Lady	MYDY
	Pinocchio	PIIO
	Wizard of Oz, The	WIOZ
PG		
	Casablanca	CACA
	Ghandi	GHDI
	Raiders of the Lost Ark	RARK
	Star Wars	STRS
PG13		
	Forrest Gump	FOMP
	Titanic	TIIC

Figure 13-18 This report, created in Microsoft Access, displays movie titles by movie ratings.

Background Checks

Retrieving Personal Information from the Internet

If you are concerned about your privacy on the Internet, you should be. In fact, you may be shocked to learn what type of personal information is available about anyone and how easy it is to purchase. Much of this information is available through public records and has been freely available for years. Before the Internet, however, it was difficult to locate and search the databases. Now much of it is there — most of it is free for the asking, and some for a small price. Are you curious about your new neighbors and how much they paid for the house next door? What about the misfit on the next block? Does he have a tainted background? The company where you work just hired a new manager, who claims to have a degree in MIS. You have your doubts, based on your observations. Does she really have that degree? You can find the answers to these questions and many more by searching public records or using an online search company. What privacy issues do you see here? Is this a good or bad practice? How could this affect you personally? Would you use one of these online search services?

For more information on public records, visit the Discovering Computers 2002 Issues Web page (**scsite.com/dc 2002/issues.htm**) and click Chapter 13 Issue #2.

Backup and Recovery

Occasionally a database is damaged or destroyed because of hardware failure, a problem with the software, human error, or a catastrophe such as fire or flood. A DBMS provides a variety of techniques to restore the database to a usable form in case it is damaged or destroyed.

- On a regular basis, you should make a **backup**, or copy, of the entire database. Some DBMSs have their own backup utilities. Others require you to purchase a separate backup utility, or use one included with your operating system.
- More complex DBMSs maintain a **log**, which is a listing of activities that change the contents of the database. If you modify a customer address, for example, the change appears in the log. The DBMS places the following in the log: (1) a copy of the customer record prior to the change, called the **before image**; (2) the actual change of address data; and (3) a copy of the customer record after the change, called the **after image** (Figure 13-19).
- A DBMS that creates a log usually provides a recovery utility. A **recovery utility** uses the logs and/or backups to restore a database when it is damaged or destroyed. The recovery utility restores the database using rollback and rollforward techniques. In a **rollforward**, also called **forward recovery**, the DBMS uses the log to re-enter changes made to the database since the last save or backup. In a **rollback**, also called **backward recovery**, the DBMS uses the log to undo any changes made to the database during a certain period of time, such as an hour. The rollback restores the database to its condition prior to the failure. Then, you must re-enter any transactions entered after the failure.

Depending on the type of failure, the DBMS determines which type of recovery technique to use. For example, if the database is destroyed by a lightning strike, the DBMS would rollforward from the last backup. Assume, however, that a power failure happens at 3:15 p.m. and shuts down all computers, but does not destroy any data. Because some users may have been in the middle of entering transactions, the DBMS needs to undo any partial transactions. Thus, it would rollback to 3:00 p.m. and send a message to all users that they need to re-enter any transactions made after that time.

Figure 13-19a (before image)

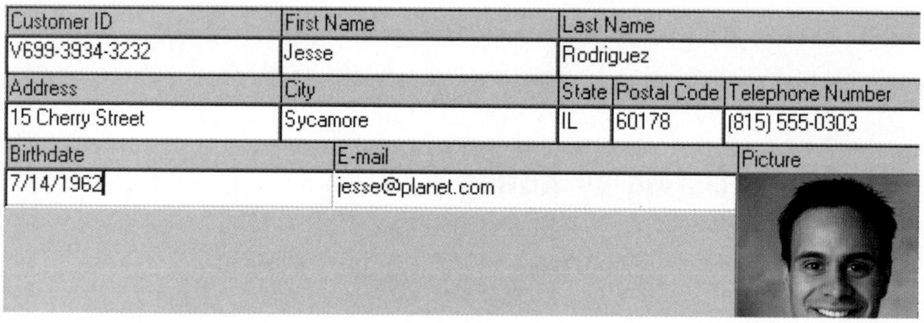

Customer ID
V699-3934-3232
First Name
Jesse
Last Name
Rodriguez
Address
15 Cherry Street
City
Sycamore
State
IL
Postal Code
60178
Telephone Number
(815) 555-0303
Birthdate
7/14/1962
E-mail
jesse@planet.com
Picture

Figure 13-19b (change)

Figure 13-19c (after image)

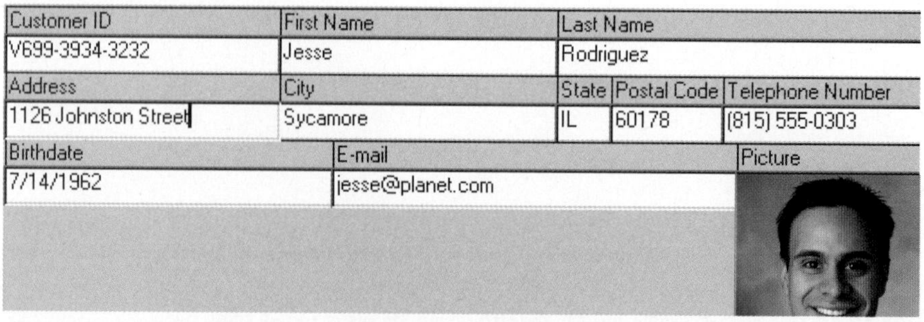

Figure 13-19 If you change the contents of a record, the DBMS places three items in the log: before image of the record; the actual change; and the after image of the record.

RELATIONAL, OBJECT-ORIENTED, AND MULTIDIMENSIONAL DATABASES

Every database and DBMS is based on a specific data model. A **data model** consists of rules and standards that define how the database organizes data. A data model defines how users view the organization of the data. It does not define how the operating system actually arranges the data on the disk.

Three popular data models in use today are relational, object-oriented, and multidimensional. A database typically is based on one data model. For example, when using a relational database, you work with the relational data model. Some databases are **object-relational databases** and combine features of the relational and object-oriented data models.

The table in Figure 13-20 lists some popular DBMSs and the data model on which they are based. The following sections discuss the features of relational, object-oriented, and multidimensional databases.

Data Models and Associated DBMSs

Data Model	Popular DBMSs
Relational Databases	Access
	Adabas
	Approach
	Informix
	Ingres
	InterBase
	Paradox
	SQL Server
	Sybase
	Visual FoxPro
Object-oriented Databases	GemStone
	KE Texpress
	Objectivity
	Objectstore
	POET
	Versant
Object-relational Databases	DB2
	JDataStore
	Oracle
	Polyhedra
	PostgreSQL
Multidimensional Databases	D^3
	Essbase
	Oracle Express

Figure 13-20 Four popular data models are relational, object-oriented, object-relational, and multidimensional. Most DBMSs are based on one of these models.

COMPANY ON THE CUTTING EDGE

ORACLE®

Supplying the World with E-Business Solutions

When 96 percent of the Fortune 500 companies use software produced by one company, that company must be flexible, accountable, and effective. Indeed, Oracle Corporation fits those requirements, for its products are available in nearly 30 languages and used by customers in more than 145 countries.

These corporations range from Xerox, which uses Oracle products to purchase and manage goods and services, to UPS, which uses the software to coordinate shipping activities to ensure that packages arrive at the customers' locations on time.

In 1977, Larry Ellison co-founded Oracle. Today, the company, based in Redwood Shores, CA, is the world's leading supplier of software for e-business. The software runs on computers as large as parallel systems to as small as PDAs. Its database product, aptly named Oracle, is the world's leading database software.

For more information on Oracle Corporation, visit the Discovering Computers 2002 Companies Web page (**scsite.com/dc2002/companies.htm**) and click Oracle Corporation.

Relational Databases

Today, a relational database is a widely used type of database. A **relational database** stores data in tables that consist of rows and columns. Each row has a primary key and each column has a unique name.

As discussed earlier in this chapter, a file processing environment uses the terms file, record, and field to represent data. A relational database uses terms different from a file processing environment. A developer of a relational database refers to a file as a **relation**, a record as a **tuple**, and a field as an **attribute**. A user of a relational database, by contrast, refers to a file as a **table**, a record as a **row**, and a field as a **column**. Figure 13-21 shows this varied terminology.

In addition to storing data, a relational database also stores data relationships. A **relationship** is a connection within the data. In a relational database, you can set up a relationship between tables at any time. The tables must have a common column (field). For example, you would relate the Movie table and the Rental table using the Movie ID column. Figure 13-22 illustrates these relational database concepts. In a relational database, the only data redundancy (duplication) exists in the common columns (fields). The database uses these common columns for relationships.

A developer of relational databases uses normalization to organize the data. **Normalization** is a process designed to make sure the data within the relations (tables) contains the least amount of duplication.

Web Link

For more information on relational databases, visit the Discovering Computers 2002 Chapter 13 WEB LINK page (**scsite.com/dc2002/ch13/weblink.htm**) and click Relational Databases.

TECHNOLOGY TRAILBLAZER

E.F. CODD

Known as the liberator of information from the computer, Dr. Edgar F. Codd has had a profound effect on data access. In 1970, he created the relational approach to database management in a series of research papers that quickly became the standard for database development.

Codd's model continues to serve as the de facto standard on which large and small databases are structured. In the 1950s, Codd participated in the development of several important IBM products. He then turned his focus to large commercial databases and developed his relational model as a foundation. Codd's widely published 12 rules are based on a single foundation principle, called Rule Zero, mandating that any system identified as a relational database management system must be able to manage databases entirely through its relational capabilities. In essence, Codd followed Einstein's advice; "Make it as simple as possible, but no simpler."

In 1981, Dr. Codd received the prestigious ACM A.M. Turing Award for Relational Database Management Theory, the highest technical achievement honor given to an individual by the Association for Computing Machinery for contributions that are lasting and of major technical importance to the computer community.

In 1993, Codd published a paper defining online analytical processing (OLAP) which has resulted in significant growth in the OLAP market. Data warehouses and multidimensional databases such as Oracle Express use the OLAP concept.

For more information on E. F. Codd, visit the Discovering Computers 2002 People Web page (**scsite.com/dc2002/people.htm**) and click E. F. Codd.

Data Terminology

File Processing Developer	Relational Database Developer	Relational Database User
File	Relation	Table
Record	Tuple	Row
Field	Attribute	Column

Figure 13-21 In this data terminology table, the first column identifies the terms used in a file processing environment. The second column presents the terms used by developers of a relational database. The third column indicates terms to which the users of a relational database refer.

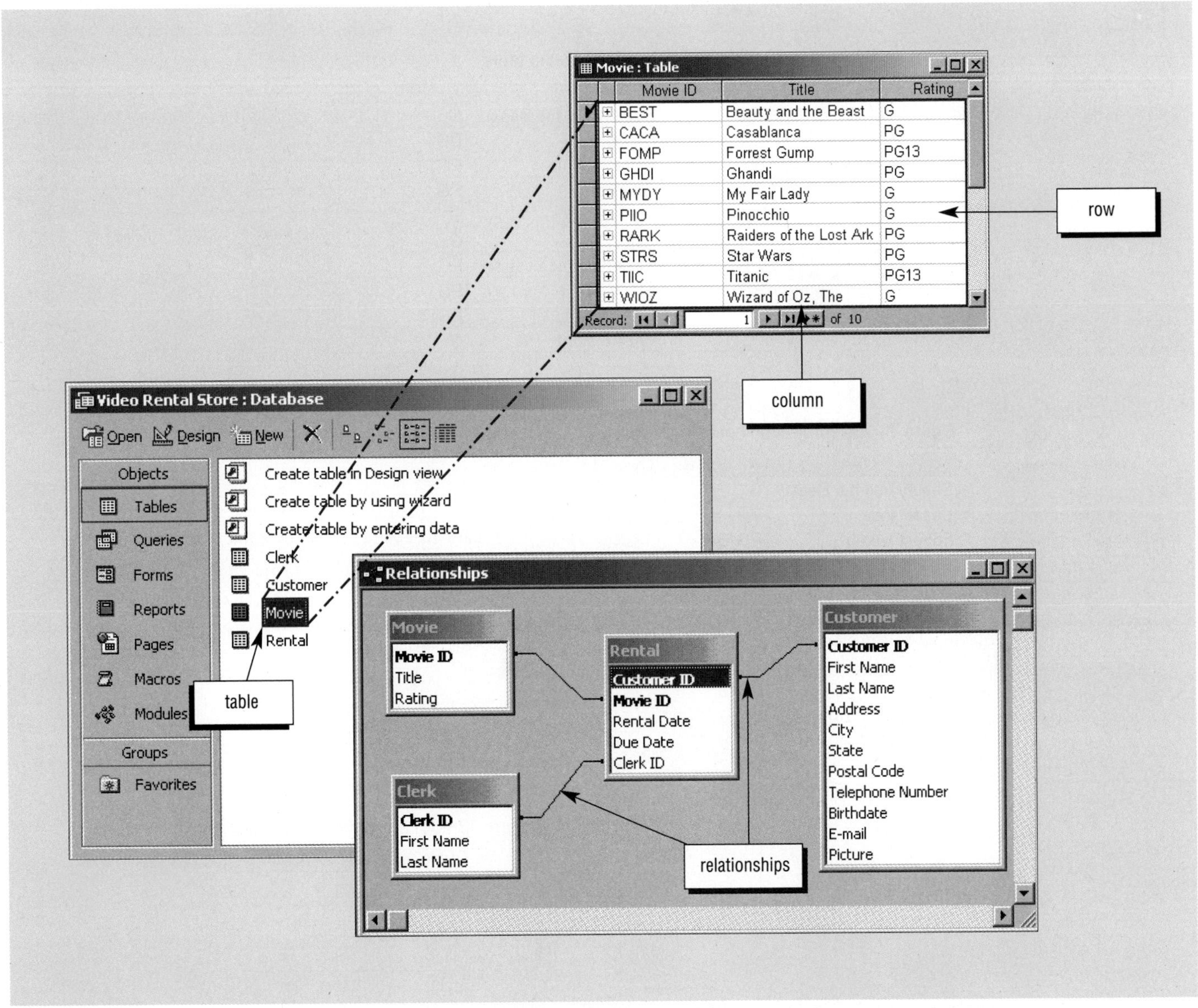

Figure 13-22 The Movie table is linked to the Rental table through the Movie ID column. The Rental table is linked to the Customer table through the Customer ID column. The Clerk table is linked to the Rental table through the Clerk ID column.

RELATIONAL ALGEBRA Relational databases often manipulate and retrieve data with relational algebra. **Relational algebra** uses variables and operations to build new relations. The variables typically are the tables, rows, and columns of the database. Three of the more common operations are projection, selection, and join.

The **projection operation** retrieves data from columns (fields). That is, it extracts a vertical subset from a table. Figure 13-23a shows the result of a projection operation that retrieves the Title and Rating columns from the Movie table.

The **selection operation** retrieves data from certain rows (records) using the criteria you specify. That is, it extracts a horizontal subset of a table. The selection operation in Figure 13-23b retrieves all rows containing PG in the Rating column of the Movie table.

Users often combine the projection and selection operations. Figure 13-23c shows a projection and selection that lists titles of movies with a PG rating.

The **join operation** combines the data from the two or more tables using a common column. For example, to list the movies due today, you need data from the Rental and Movie tables. The Rental table contains the Due Date and Movie ID columns, and the Movie table contains the Movie ID and Title columns. The join operation uses the Movie ID column to combine

All rows and columns in Movie table

Movie ID	Title	Rating
BEST	Beauty and the Beast	G
CACA	Casablanca	PG
FOMP	Forrest Gump	PG13
GHDI	Ghandi	PG
MYDY	My Fair Lady	G
PIIO	Pinocchio	G
RARK	Raiders of the Lost Ark	PG
STRS	Star Wars	PG
TIIC	Titanic	PG13
WIOZ	Wizard of Oz, The	G

Figure 13-23a (projection operation results)

Title	Rating
Beauty and the Beast	G
Casablanca	PG
Forrest Gump	PG13
Ghandi	PG
My Fair Lady	G
Pinocchio	G
Raiders of the Lost Ark	PG
Star Wars	PG
Titanic	PG13
Wizard of Oz, The	G

Figure 13-23b (selection operation results)

Movie ID	Title	Rating
CACA	Casablanca	PG
GHDI	Ghandi	PG
RARK	Raiders of the Lost Ark	PG
STRS	Star Wars	PG

Figure 13-23c (projection and selection operation results)

Title	Rating
Casablanca	PG
Ghandi	PG
Raiders of the Lost Ark	PG
Star Wars	PG

Figure 13-23 The projection and selection operations extract columns and rows from a table respectively.

data from the Rental and the Movie tables. Figure 13-24 shows the results of joining the two tables.

STRUCTURED QUERY LANGUAGE

Structured Query Language (SQL) is a query language that allows you to manage, update, and retrieve data. To use relational algebra, SQL has special keywords and rules that you include in SQL statements.

For example, the SQL statement in Figure 13-25 shows how to write the join operation that creates the relation shown at the bottom of Figure 13-24. The statement displays the Movie ID, Title, and Due Date fields for all movies due today (05/31/2002).

Most relational database products for minicomputers and mainframes include SQL. Many personal computer databases also include SQL. Chapter 15 covers SQL in more depth.

Cybersnooping

Are you considering purchasing or selling your home? Would you like to know how much a neighbor paid for her house or obtain details about the floor plan? This information and much more is public record. Until recently, accessing this data meant a trip to the courthouse and laboriously searching through a mountain of records. The Internet is changing this; and in many cities and counties, public records are available online.

Depending on the Web site, you can search by name, address (full address or just the street name), map ID numbers, parcel number, and township range section numbers. Your search may return information such as legal description; date and sales amount; value summary, including market value and assessed value; building information, including year built, square feet, number of bedrooms and baths; and other building structural elements.

Use a natural language search engine, such as AskJeeves, to discover if your city or county public records are available online (see URL below). Your question for AskJeeves may be, Where can I find public records for (name of your county or city)? If this does not work, try substituting property appraiser records for public records. Another resource is BRB Publications. This Web site consists of hundreds of links to county, city, federal, and state Web sites where you can access public record information without charge.

For more information on public records and the Web sites mentioned above, visit the Discovering Computers 2002 Apply It Web page (**scsite.com/dc2002/apply.htm**) and click Chapter 13 Apply It #2.

Rental Table

Customer ID	Movie ID	Rental Date	Due Date	Clerk ID
V999-2003-9938	RARK	05/29/2002	05/31/2002	S1
V699-3934-3232	TIIC	05/29/2002	05/31/2002	D1
V699-3934-3232	FOMP	05/29/2002	05/31/2002	D2
V999-2938-7766	GHDI	05/30/2002	06/01/2002	M1
V799-0092-5722	STRS	05/30/2002	06/01/2002	S1
V799-3387-0923	CACA	05/30/2002	06/01/2002	D1
V799-3387-0923	MYDY	05/31/2002	06/02/2002	D2

Movie Table

Movie ID	Title	Rating
BEST	Beauty and the Beast	G
CACA	Casablanca	PG
FOMP	Forrest Gump	PG13
GHDI	Ghandi	PG
MYDY	My Fair Lady	G
PIIO	Pinocchio	G
RARK	Raiders of the Lost Ark	PG
STRS	Star Wars	PG
TIIC	Titanic	PG13
WIOZ	Wizard of Oz, The	G

Rental Table and Movie Table Joined on Movie ID Column

Movie ID	Title	Due Date
FOMP	Forrest Gump	05/31/2002
RARK	Raiders of the Lost Ark	05/31/2002
TIIC	Titanic	05/31/2002

Figure 13-24 This join operation displays all movie titles that are due today (05/31/2002).

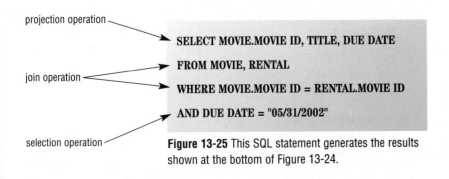

projection operation → SELECT MOVIE.MOVIE ID, TITLE, DUE DATE

join operation → FROM MOVIE, RENTAL
join operation → WHERE MOVIE.MOVIE ID = RENTAL.MOVIE ID

selection operation → AND DUE DATE = "05/31/2002"

```
SELECT MOVIE.MOVIE ID, TITLE, DUE DATE
FROM MOVIE, RENTAL
WHERE MOVIE.MOVIE ID = RENTAL.MOVIE ID
AND DUE DATE = "05/31/2002"
```

Figure 13-25 This SQL statement generates the results shown at the bottom of Figure 13-24.

Web Link

For more information on SQL, visit the Discovering Computers 2002 Chapter 13 WEB LINK page (**scsite.com/dc2002/ch13/weblink.htm**) and click SQL.

Object-Oriented Databases

An **object-oriented database** (**OODB**) stores data in objects. An **object** is an item that can contain both data *and* the activities that read or process the data. A Customer object, for example, might contain data about a customer such as Customer ID, First Name, Last Name, Address, and so on. It also could contain instructions on how to print the customer record or the formula required to calculate a customer's balance due. A record in a relational database, by contrast, would contain *only* data about a customer. Chapter 15 provides a more detailed discussion of object-oriented concepts.

Object-oriented databases have two advantages relative to relational databases: they can store more types of data and access this data faster. With an object-oriented database, you can store unstructured data more efficiently than in a relational database. Unstructured data includes photographs, video clips, audio clips, and documents. When you query an object-oriented database, the results often display more quickly than the same query of a relational database.

Examples of applications appropriate for an object-oriented database include the following:

- **Multimedia databases** store images, audio clips, and/or video clips. For example, a geographic information system (GIS) database stores maps. A voice mail system stores audio messages. A television news station database stores audio and video clips.
- **Groupware databases** store documents such as schedules, calendars, manuals, memos, and reports. Users can perform queries to search the document contents. For example, you can search people's schedules for available meeting times.
- **Computer-aided design (CAD) databases** store data about engineering, architectural, and scientific designs. Data in the database includes a list of components of the item being designed, the relationship among the components, and previous versions of the design drafts.
- **Hypertext databases** contain text links to other documents. **Hypermedia databases** contain text, graphics, video, and sound. The Web contains a variety of hypertext and hypermedia databases. You can search these databases for items such as documents, graphics, audio and video clips, and links to Web pages (Figure 13-26).

Web Link

For more information on object-oriented databases, visit the Discovering Computers 2002 Chapter 13 WEB LINK page (**scsite.com/dc2002/ch13/weblink.htm**) and click Object-Oriented Databases.

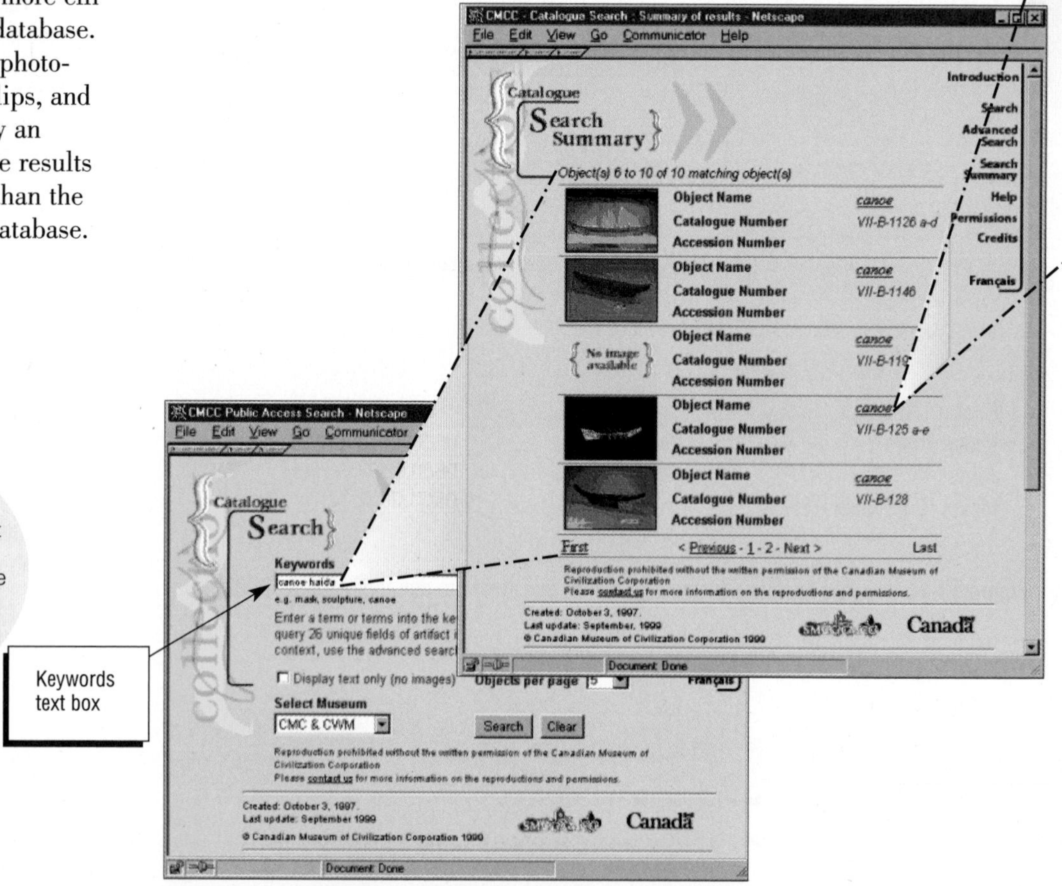

Figure 13-26 This hypermedia database stores museum collections. To display information about a particular artifact, you enter its description in the Keywords text box.

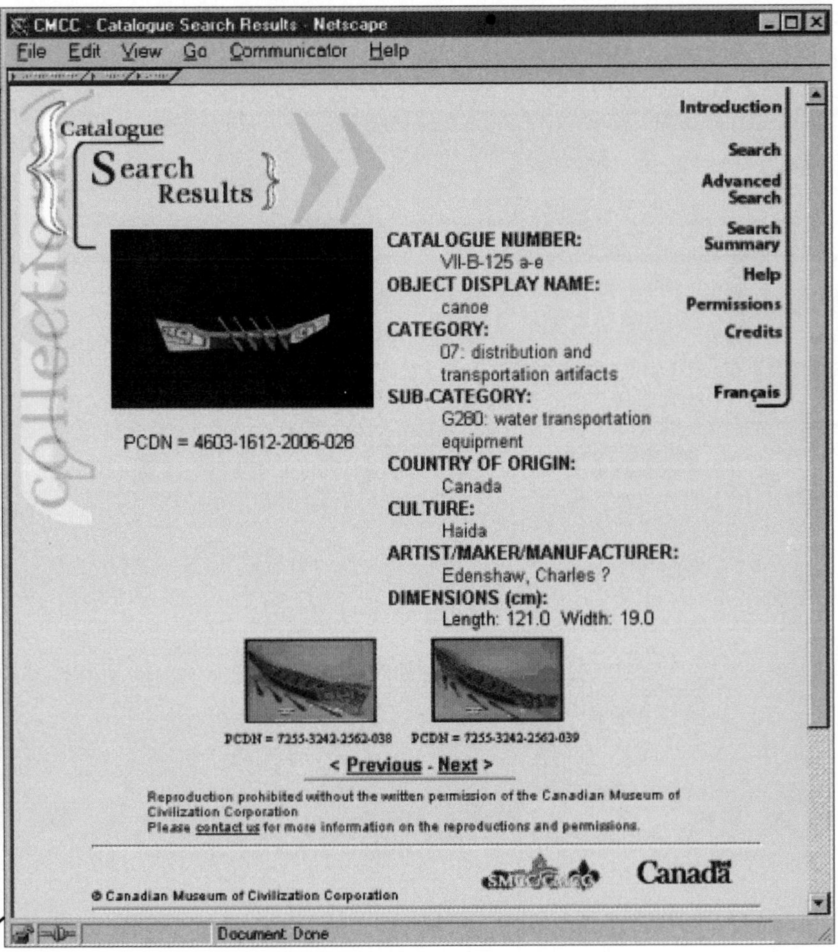

- **Web databases** link to an e-form on a Web page. The Web browser sends and receives data between the form and the database. The next page discusses Web databases in more depth.

OBJECT QUERY LANGUAGE Object-oriented and object-relational databases often use a query language called **object query language** (**OQL**) to manipulate and retrieve data. OQL is similar to SQL. OQL and SQL use many of the same rules, grammar, and keywords. Because OQL is a relatively new query language, not all object databases support it.

Multidimensional Databases

A **multidimensional database** (**MDDB**) stores data in dimensions. Whereas a relational database is a two-dimensional table, an MDDB can store more than two dimensions of data. These multiple dimensions, sometimes known as a hypercube, allow users to access and analyze any view of the database data.

A Webmaster at a retailing business may want information on product sales and customer sales for each region spanning a given time period. A manager at the same business may want information on product sales by department for each sales representative spanning a given time period.

An MDDB can consolidate this type of data from multiple dimensions at very high rates of speed. The number of dimensions in an MDDB varies. A retailing business might have four dimensions: products, customers, regions, and time. An MDDB for a hospital procedure could have six dimensions: time, procedure type, patient, hospital, physician, and diagnosis. An MDDB for an insurance policy may include five dimensions: time, policy type, agent, customer, and coverage. Nearly every multidimensional database has a dimension of time. The content of other dimensions varies depending on the subject.

The key advantage of the multidimensional database is that it can consolidate data much faster than a relational database. A relational database typically does not process and summarize large numbers of records efficiently. With a multidimensional database you can obtain summarized results very quickly. For example, a query that takes minutes or hours to execute in a relational database will take only seconds to execute in a multidimensional database.

No standard query language exists for multidimensional databases. Each database uses its own language. Most are similar to SQL.

Web Link

For more information on multidimensional databases, visit the Discovering Computers 2002 Chapter 13 WEB LINK page (**scsite.com/dc2002/ch13/weblink.htm**) and click Multidimensional Databases.

WEB DATABASES

One of the most profound features of the World Wide Web is the vast amount of information it provides. The Web offers information on jobs, travel destinations, television programming, movies and videos at the box office, local and national weather, sporting events, and legislative information (Figure 13-27). You can shop for just about any product or service, buy or sell stocks, search for a job, and make airline reservations. Much of this and other information on the Web exists in databases.

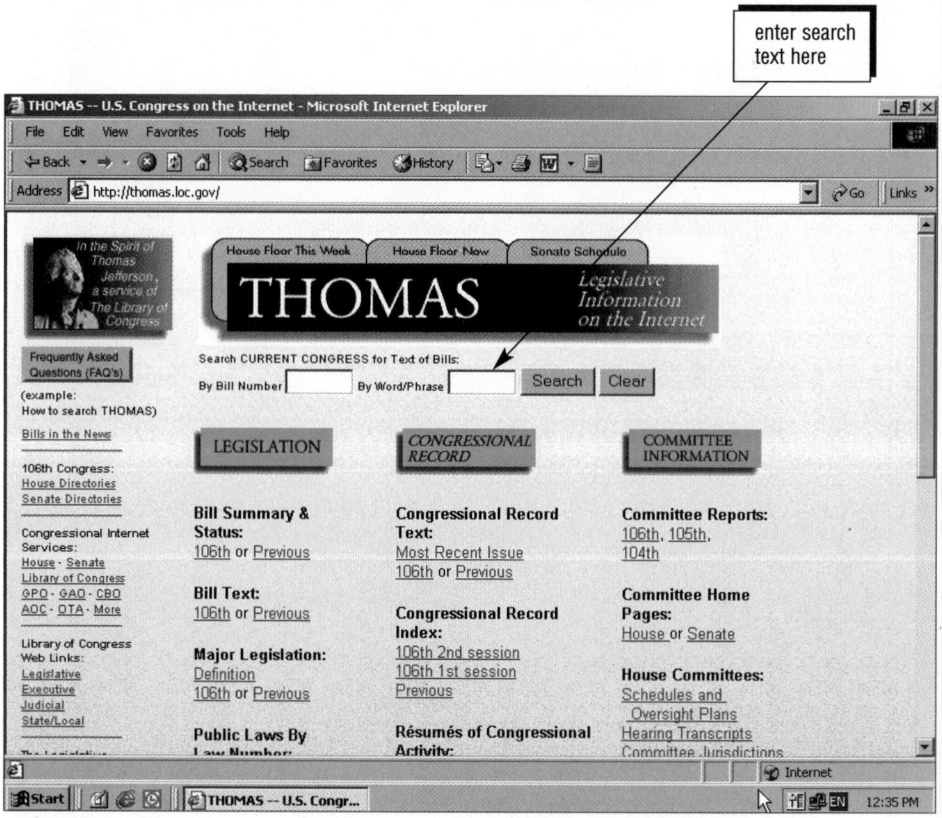

Figure 13-27 Through the THOMAS Web site, you can access a huge database containing congressional bills. To display a list of past and present Congressional bills that deal with Internet privacy, simply enter the text Internet privacy in the By Word/Phrase text box.

COMPANY ON THE CUTTING EDGE

Switchboard.com

100 Million Addresses at Your Fingertips

When your To-Do list is longer than your homework list for your algebra final exam, you need help. One Internet site may streamline your life: Switchboard.com. From finding the telephone number for the video store down the street to comparison shopping for a new digital camera or getting directions to the company where you have tomorrow's job interview, Switchboard.com connects you to a plethora of consumers, merchants, and advertisers.

Switchboard is among the 50 most popular Internet sites. The site receives more than 50-million hits monthly from people querying its telephone number and address directories of the nearly 100-million people, 12-million businesses, and 4-million U.S. e-mail addresses.

Founded in 1995, Switchboard rapidly became successful by being the first to market a free, national directory of U.S. residential information. Previously, most people had access only to their local telephone directories. Switchboard continued to connect people, helping organize busy lives. In 1998, Switchboard acquired Maps On Us, an award-winning site providing interactive maps and driving directions.

For more information on Switchboard, visit the Discovering Computers 2002 Companies Web page (**scsite.com/dc2002/companies.htm**) and click Switchboard.

To access one of these Web databases, you enter data into a form on a Web page. The Web page is the front end to the database. Many search engines such as Yahoo! use databases to store Web site descriptions. Thus, the search engine's home page is the front end to the database. To access the database, you enter search text into the search engine. The steps in Figure 13-28 illustrate how a search engine might interact with a Web database.

In addition to accessing information, users provide information to Web databases. Many Web sites request you to enter personal information such as your name, address, telephone number, and preferences into an e-form. The database then stores your personal information for future use. A company, for example, may send e-mail messages to certain groups of customers. If you are a frequent flyer, you may receive travel information.

A Web database typically resides on a database server. A **database server** is a computer that stores and provides access to the database. One type of program that manages the sending and receiving of data between the front end and the database server is a **CGI (Common Gateway Interface) script**. CGI scripts run automatically — as soon as you click the button to send or receive information. Writing a CGI script requires computer programming skills. Chapter 15 discusses CGI scripts in more detail.

For smaller databases, many personal computer database products provide Web publishing tools. Microsoft FrontPage 2000, for example, has a Database Results Wizard that requires no computer programming. The Wizard publishes a Web page that links to your existing database such as a Microsoft Access or Oracle database.

Figure 13-28 HOW A SEARCH ENGINE MIGHT INTERACT WITH A WEB DATABASE

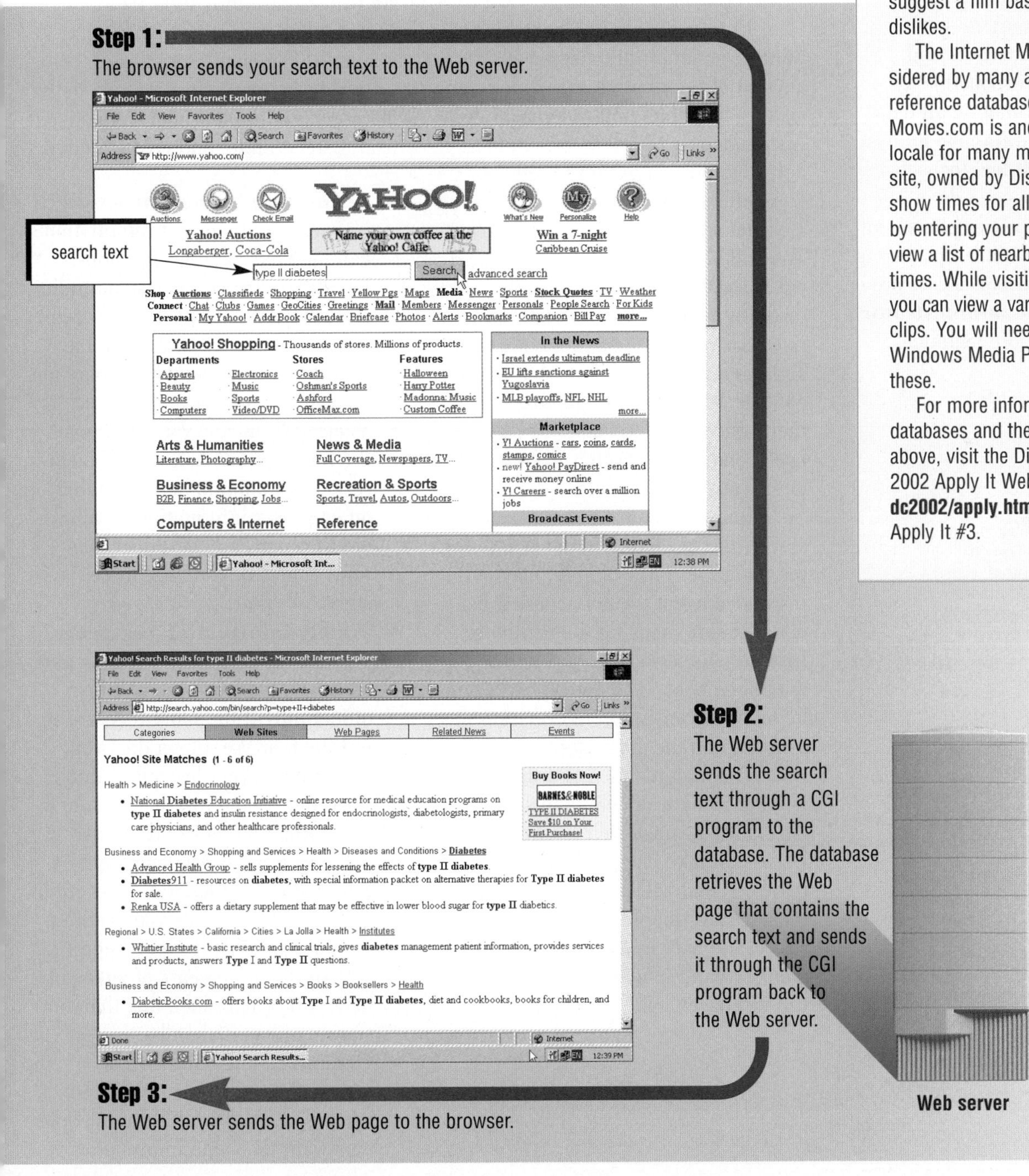
Step 1:
The browser sends your search text to the Web server.
search text
type II diabetes
Step 2:
The Web server sends the search text through a CGI program to the database. The database retrieves the Web page that contains the search text and sends it through the CGI program back to the Web server.
Web server
Step 3:
The Web server sends the Web page to the browser.

APPLY IT!

The Ultimate Movie Web Database

The Internet has a wealth of data for the movie enthusiast — literally hundreds of thousands of Web sites devoted to this industry. These Web sites provide an entertaining setting with links to movies of the week, reviews by critics and other movie-goers, celebrity information, and just about any other movie facts or trivia you may want to know. Not only do many of these Web sites tell you the plot of a movie, some even can suggest a film based on your likes and dislikes.

The Internet Movie Database is considered by many as the ultimate movie reference database (see URL below). Movies.com is another favorite online locale for many movie buffs. This Web site, owned by Disney, provides movie show times for all major cities. Usually by entering your postal code, you can view a list of nearby theaters and movie times. While visiting these Web sites, you can view a variety of trailers or movie clips. You will need the RealPlayer or Windows Media Player plug-ins to enjoy these.

For more information on movie databases and the Web sites mentioned above, visit the Discovering Computers 2002 Apply It Web page (**scsite.com/dc2002/apply.htm**) and click Chapter 13 Apply It #3.

DATABASE ADMINISTRATION

Managing a company's database requires a great deal of coordination. The role of coordinating the use of the database belongs to the database analysts and administrators. To carry out their responsibilities, these IT professionals need cooperation from all database users.

Role of the Database Analysts and Administrators

The database analysts and administrators are responsible for managing and coordinating all database activities. The **database analyst (DA)**, or **data modeler**, focuses on the meaning and usage of data. The DA decides on the proper placement of fields, defines relationships among data, and identifies users' access privileges. The **database administrator (DBA)** requires a more technical inside view of the data. The DBA creates and maintains the data dictionary, manages security of the database, monitors the performance of the database, and checks backup and recovery procedures.

In small companies, one person often is both the database analyst and administrator. In larger companies, the responsibilities of the database analyst and administrator are split among two or more persons.

Web Link

For more information on database administrators, visit the Discovering Computers 2002 Chapter 13 WEB LINK page (**scsite.com/dc2002/ch13/weblink.htm**) and click Database Administrators.

Role of the Employee as a User

Employees should learn how to utilize the data in the database. The amount of information available often amazes first-time database users. Instant access to this information helps employees perform their jobs more effectively. For example, assume a car backed into your parked car. You call your insurance agent to find out where to repair your car. She instantly reads to you a list of authorized car repair shops in your area. Today, employees such as the insurance agent can access databases from their office desktop computer, a notebook computer, or even a Web-enabled device such as a cellular telephone.

Employees also must take an active role in identifying new data for the database. For example, maybe the insurance agent cannot access a list of car repair shops on the computer. Instead, she looks them up in the telephone book. The agent's job would be much easier if this information was available on the computer.

The maintenance of a database is an ongoing task companies measure constantly against their overall goals. Users can take part in designing the database that will help them achieve those goals. Chapter 14 discusses the role of the user in system development, which includes the design of the database.

Database Design Guidelines

A carefully designed database makes it easier for a user to query the database, modify the data, and create reports. The guidelines shown in Figure 13-29 apply to databases of all sizes.

QUALITIES OF VALUABLE INFORMATION

As with data, information includes certain characteristics to make it valuable. The characteristics of **valuable information** include being accurate, verifiable, timely, organized, useful, accessible, and cost effective.

- **Accurate information** is correct information. Incorrect information can lead to incorrect decisions. People, for example, assume their credit report is right. If your credit report incorrectly shows you have past due payments, a bank may not give you a car loan.
- **Verifiable** means you can prove the information is correct or incorrect. For example, before relying on employer information in your credit report, a loan officer may want copies of your last three pay stubs.
- **Timely information** has an age suited to its use. Your credit report, for example, has value to a loan officer only if the bank receives it in time to make a loan decision. Most information loses its value with time. Some information, such as information on trends, gains value as time passes and more information is obtained. Your credit report gains value as you accumulate more credit. A credit report that shows three years of payment history has more meaning than one showing just six months.
- **Organized information** is arranged to suit your needs and requirements. Two different people may want the same information

Database Design Guidelines

1. Determine the purpose of the database.
2. Design the tables.
   - Design the tables on paper first.
   - Each table should contain data about one subject. The Customer table, for example, contains data about customers.
3. Design the fields for each table.
   - Be sure every field has a unique primary key.
   - Use separate fields for logically distinct items. For example, a name could be stored in six fields: Salutation (Mr., Mrs., Dr., etc.), First Name, Middle Name, Last Name, Suffix (Jr., Sr., etc.), and Nickname.
   - Do not create fields for information that can be derived from entries in other fields. For example, do not include a field for Age. Instead, store the birthdate and compute the age.
   - Allow enough space for each field.
   - Set default values for frequently entered data.
4. Determine the relationships among the tables.

Figure 13-29 Guidelines for developing a database.

presented in a different manner. For example, a loan officer may want a credit report to list most recent debts first. You may want your credit report alphabetized by creditor name.

- **Useful information** has meaning to the person who receives it. Most information is important only to certain people or groups of people. Thus, always consider the audience when you are collecting and reporting information. Avoid distributing useless information. A loan officer probably does not need information about your high school grades.
- **Accessible information** is available when you need it. Waiting for information may delay important decisions. If information is not available, people may make incorrect decisions because they are unaware of certain facts. The longer it takes your credit report to arrive, the longer you have to wait for a loan.
- **Cost-effective information** costs less to produce than the value of the resulting information. A company occasionally should review the information it produces. Is it still useful? Based on the answer, the company determines whether to continue, scale back, or even stop distributing the information.

Sometimes, it is not easy to place a value on information. For this reason, some companies create information only as people request it, instead of on a regular basis. Many companies make the information available online. Users then can access and print online information as they need it.

ISSUE

Free Online Service

Accessibility of College Scholarship Information

If you need help with college costs, consider scholarships. Many students think scholarships are available only for financial aid or high grade point averages, so they do not consider this option. You may be surprised to know that thousands of scholarships are available within many other categories. Free online services may be able to help you locate those that match your qualifications, plans, and chosen schools. When you register, the online service queries a database containing thousands of suitable scholarships and then returns the results. Ironically, those least likely to benefit from this service may be those who need it most. Because students from less affluent backgrounds usually have less computer experience, they may be unaware of, or unable to access, the scholarship search services. How can these free Web services be made more universally available? Who do you think should assume the leading role in extending access to these services, and why? Not all services may be legitimate, so how can you avoid scholarship scams?

For more information on scholarships, visit the Discovering Computers 2002 Issues Web page (**scsite.com/dc2002/issues.htm**) and click Chapter 13 Issue #3.

How Managers Use Information

All employees, including managers, in a company need correct information to perform their jobs effectively. **Managers** are responsible for coordinating the use of resources. Resources include people, money, materials, and information. Managers coordinate these resources by performing four activities: planning, organizing, leading, and controlling.

- **Planning** involves establishing goals and objectives. It also includes deciding on the strategies needed to meet these goals and objectives.
- **Organizing** includes identifying and combining resources so that the company can reach its goals and objectives. Organizing also involves setting up the management structure of a company, such as the departments and reporting relationships.
- **Leading**, sometimes referred to as directing, involves instructing and authorizing others to perform the necessary work.
- **Controlling** involves measuring performance and, if necessary, taking corrective action.

Figure 13-30 shows how these four management activities usually occur in an order that forms an endless cycle. During the controlling activity, managers measure actual performance against a previously established plan. Following this measurement, they may revise the plan. Revised plans may result in additional organizational and leadership activities. Managers then measure performance against the revised plan, and the cycle repeats itself. The four tasks are linked. A change in one task usually affects one or more of the other tasks.

Levels of Users

The types of information you need often depend on your employee level in the company. Users typically fall into one of four categories: executive management, middle management, operational management, and nonmanagement employees (Figure 13-31).

EXECUTIVE MANAGEMENT

Executive management, also referred to as senior management or top management, includes the highest management positions in a company. These managers focus on the long-range direction of the company. They primarily are responsible for **strategic decisions** that focus on the company's overall goals and objectives. Executive management oversees middle management.

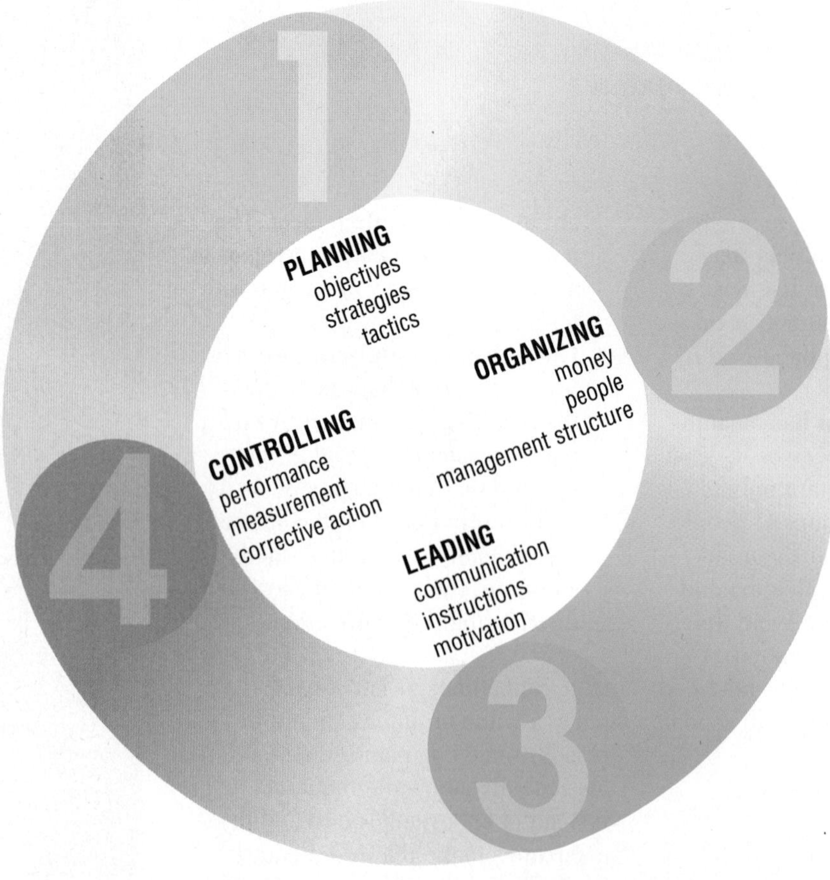

Figure 13-30 The four management activities include planning, organizing, leading, and controlling. They usually are performed in a continuous sequence.

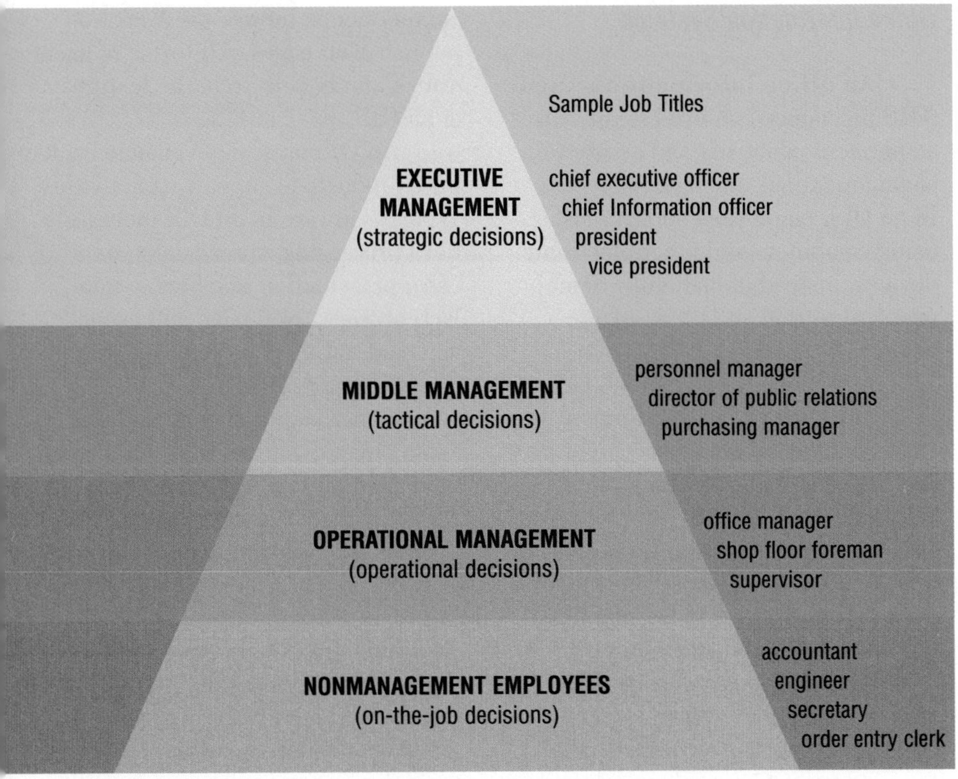

Figure 13-31 The information requirements of a user often depend on the user's level in the company. This pyramid illustrates the levels of users, sample job titles of each level of user, and the types of decisions these users make.

MIDDLE MANAGEMENT **Middle management** is responsible for implementing the strategic decisions of executive management. Middle managers do this by making tactical decisions. A **tactical decision**, also called a **short-range decision**, applies specific programs and plans necessary to meet the stated objectives. Middle management oversees operational management.

OPERATIONAL MANAGEMENT
Operational management supervises the production, clerical, and other nonmanagement employees of a company. In performing their duties, operational managers make operational decisions. An **operational decision** involves day-to-day activities within the company. These decisions should be consistent with and support the tactical decisions made by middle management.

NONMANAGEMENT EMPLOYEES
Nonmanagement employees include production, clerical, and staff personnel. Nonmanagement employees also frequently need information to perform their jobs. Today, these employees have more information available to them than in the past. They have access to the information necessary to make decisions that previously were made by managers — a trend called **empowering** users.

TECHNOLOGY TRAILBLAZER

LARRY **ELLISON**

Oracle chairman and co-founder Larry Ellison is a larger-than-life presence in today's software industry. His strong point is his uncanny ability to motivate his employees and partners toward a common vision.

As a young man, Ellison was interested in science and mathematics but lacked enthusiasm for school. Difficult technical problems, however, sparked his interest and motivated him. In 1976, he learned about relational database theory. Relational databases were powerful and easy to use, but industry experts believed they were too slow to be commercially feasible.

Ellison accepted the challenge. He set out to develop a commercially viable relational database. Then, in 1977, with three co-founders, Ellison started Oracle Corporation. When the Oracle relational database was released, it was an immediate success.

Today, Oracle is the world's leading provider of software for e-business. With a passion to become the new custodian of cyberspace, Ellison's goal is to grow Oracle into the largest software company in the world. Although eccentric and flamboyant, he never has been called boring.

For more information on Larry Ellison, visit the Discovering Computers 2002 People Web page (**scsite .com/dc2002/ people.htm**) and click Larry Ellison.

TYPES OF INFORMATION SYSTEMS

An **information system** is a set of hardware, software, data, people, and procedures that work together to produce information (Figure 13-32). A **procedure** is an instruction, or set of instructions, a user follows to accomplish an activity. An information system supports daily, short-term, and long-range activities of users in a company.

Information systems generally fall into one of five categories: office information systems, transaction processing systems, management information systems, decision support systems, and expert systems. The following sections present each type of information system.

Office Information Systems

An **office information system** (**OIS** pronounced oh-eye-ess) increases employee productivity and assists with communications among employees. In an OIS, employees perform tasks using computers and other electronic devices, instead of manually. Some people describe an OIS as **office automation.**

Just about every type of business or organization uses some form of OIS. For example, a school might post its class schedules on the Internet. When the school updates the schedule, students receive an e-mail notification. In a manual system, the school would photocopy the schedule and mail it to each student's house.

An OIS supports many office activities. With an OIS, you can create and distribute graphics and documents, send messages, schedule appointments, browse the Web, and publish Web pages. All levels of users utilize and benefit from the features of an OIS.

An OIS uses many common software products to support its activities. Typical software in an OIS includes word processing, spreadsheet, database, presentation graphics, e-mail, Web browser, Web page authoring, personal information management, and groupware. To send text, graphics, audio, and video to others, an OIS uses communications technology such as voice mail, fax, videoconferencing, and electronic data interchange (EDI).

In an OIS, computers have modems, video cameras, speakers, and microphones. Scanners, fax machines, digital cameras, and Web-enabled devices such as cellular telephones are other types of hardware often found in an OIS.

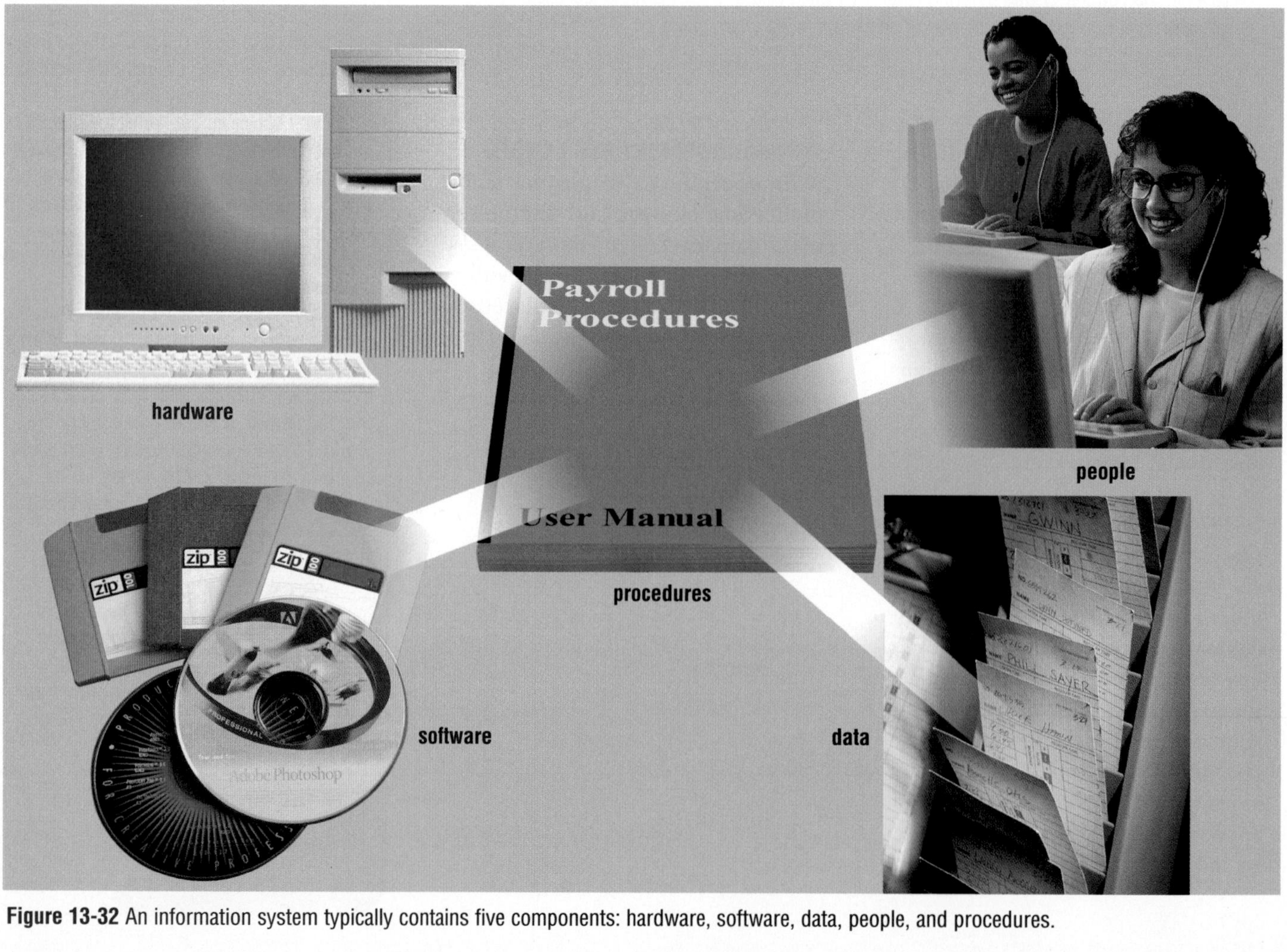

Figure 13-32 An information system typically contains five components: hardware, software, data, people, and procedures.

Transaction Processing Systems

A **transaction processing system (TPS)** captures and processes data from day-to-day business activities. When you use an automated teller machine to withdraw cash, you are using a TPS (Figure 13-33). Examples of transactions are deposits, payments, orders, and reservations. In a company, clerical staff typically perform the activities associated with a TPS, which include the following:

1. Recording a business activity such as a student's registration, a customer's order, an employee's timecard, or a car owner's payment
2. Confirming an action or causing a response, such as printing a student's schedule, sending a thank-you note to a customer, printing an employee's paycheck, or issuing a receipt to a car owner
3. Maintaining data, which involves adding new data, changing existing data, or removing unwanted data

Transaction processing systems were among the first computerized systems that processed business data. Many people initially referred to the functions of a TPS as **data processing**. The first TPSs computerized an existing manual system. The intent of these TPSs was to process faster, reduce clerical costs, and improve customer service.

The first TPSs mostly used batch processing. With **batch processing**, the computer collects data over a period of time and processes all transactions later, as a group. As computers became more powerful, system developers created online transaction processing systems. With **online transaction processing (OLTP)**, the computer processes each transaction as it is entered.

When you register for classes, your school probably uses OLTP. The registration clerk enters your desired schedule. The computer immediately prints your statement of classes. The invoices often are printed using batch processing. That is, the computer prints and mails all student invoices at a later date.

Today, most transaction processing systems use OLTP. For some routine processing tasks, they also use batch processing. Many organizations use batch processing to calculate paychecks and print invoices.

Figure 13-33 When you use an ATM to deposit or withdraw money, you are using a transaction processing system.

Management Information Systems

A **management information system** (**MIS** pronounced em-eye-ess) generates accurate, timely, and organized information, so managers and other users can make decisions, solve problems, supervise activities, and track progress. Management information systems evolved from transaction processing systems. Managers realized the computer had more potential than just supporting a TPS. Its capability of quick computing and data comparisons could produce meaningful information for managers.

MISs often are integrated with transaction processing systems. To process a sales order the TPS records the sale, updates the customer's account balance, and reduces the inventory count. Using this information, the related MIS can produce reports that recap daily sales activities; summarize weekly and monthly sales activities; list customers with past due account balances; graph slow or fast selling products; and highlight inventory items that need reordering. An MIS focuses on creating information that managers and other users need to perform their jobs.

An MIS creates three basic types of information: detailed, summary, and exception (Figure 13-34). A **detailed report** usually just lists transactions. For example, a Detailed Order Report lists orders taken during a given time period. A **summary report** consolidates data, so you can review it quickly and easily. A summary report usually has totals, tables, or graphs.

Figure 13-34a (detailed report)

DETAILED ORDER REPORT for May 21, 2002

Part Number	Part Description	Customer	Quantity Purchased
1788	stapler	Starlight Foods	15
		Wilson Automotive	40
		Victor Lighting	13
2372	postage scale	Regal Camera	1
		Wilson Automotive	4
3029	letter opener	AAA Rentals	25
		Starlight Foods	10
8942	bulletin board	Wilson Automotive	8

Figure 13-34b (summary report)

DETAILED SUMMARY REPORT for May 21, 2002
by Part Number

Part Number	Part Description	Total Quantity Sold	Vendor
1788	stapler	68	Geo Supplies
2372	postage scale	5	Marham Industries
3029	letter opener	35	Geo Supplies
8942	bulletin board	8	Geo Supplies

Inventory Summary

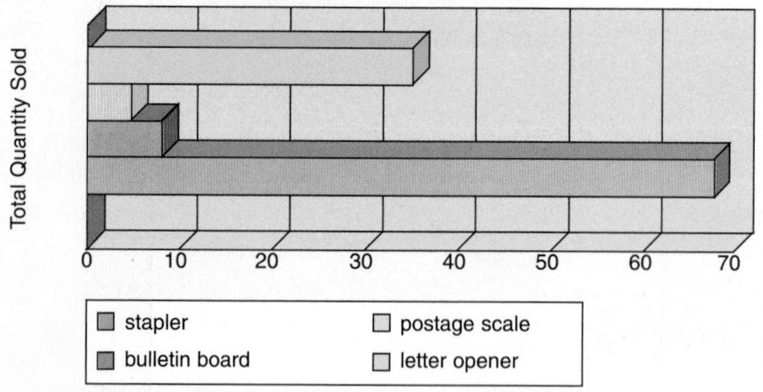

Figure 13-34c (exception report)

INVENTORY EXCEPTION REPORT for May 21, 2002

Part Number	Part Description	Total Quantity on Hand	Reorder Point
8942	bulletin board	228	240
3029	letter opener	558	560

Figure 13-34 Three basic types of information generated in an MIS are detailed, summary, and exception.

An **exception report** identifies data outside of a normal condition. These conditions, called the **exception criteria**, define the normal activity or status range. For example, an Inventory Exception Report notifies the purchasing department of items it needs to reorder.

Exception reports save managers time. Instead of searching through a detailed report, managers simply review the exception report. These reports help managers focus on situations that require immediate decisions or actions.

Decision Support Systems

A **decision support system** (**DSS**) helps you analyze data and make decisions. Often, a TPS or MIS does not generate the type of report a manager needs to make a decision. Different managers need various types of information. A marketing manager might need to know how much he or she has spent on Internet advertising in the past three months. Whereas an office manager might need to know how many pads of paper were used.

A variety of DSSs exist. Some are company specific and used by managers. Others are available to everyone on the Web. Programs that analyze data, such as those in a DSS, sometimes are called **online analytical processing** (**OLAP**) applications. Because they summarize information, these applications process many records at a time. This is different from OLTP applications, which process individual records at one time and typically use relational databases.

Some OLAP applications are called **MOLAP** because they use multidimensional databases. Those that use relational databases are known as **ROLAP**. Others blend the two database types. These hybrid OLAPs may use an ROLAP as the back end and an MOLAP as the front end.

A DSS uses data from internal and external sources. **Internal sources** of data might include sales, manufacturing, inventory, or financial data from a company's database. Data from **external sources** could include interest rates, population trends, costs of new housing construction, or raw material pricing.

Some DSSs have their own query languages, statistical analysis, spreadsheets, and graphics that help you retrieve data and analyze the results. Some also allow you to create a model of the factors affecting a decision. A product manager might need to decide on a price for a new product. A simple model for finding the best price would include factors for the expected sales volume at various price levels. The model allows you to ask what-if questions and view the expected results.

Instead of buying a DSS, many people use their application software to perform DSS functions. With Microsoft Excel, for example, you can model data and create what-if scenarios.

ISSUE

Tracking Buyers' Habits

Reporting Music and Book Sales Information

SoundScan turned the music world upside down — now we have BookScan. SoundScan is a database that tracks sales of music and music video products throughout the United States. When the sales clerk scanned the barcode on the new CD you just purchased, that data went directly into the SoundScan database. Sales data from the Billboard 200 Chart is compiled using SoundScan. CMT, MTV, and VH1 all use SoundScan data. The publishing industry now is applying this same technique by using BookScan. The goal is to make a similar impact on the publishing industry. If publishers and vendors use BookScan, will they base all decisions on sales figures? Book titles that slowly gain recognition through time may never be given a chance and new artists and authors may be ignored. Overall, do you think these databases have a positive or negative effect on publishers? Do they have an effect on authors and readers or retailers and musicians? Why or why not? What are potential disadvantages and how do you think they could be addressed?

For more information on SoundScan and BookScan, visit the Discovering Computers 2002 Issues Web page (**scsite.com/dc2002/issues.htm**) and click Chapter 13 Issue #4.

Web Link

For more information on decision support systems, visit the Discovering Computers 2002 Chapter 13 WEB LINK page (**scsite.com/dc2002/ch13/weblink.htm**) and click Decision Support Systems.

Web Link
For more information on data warehouses, visit the Discovering Computers 2002 Chapter 13 WEB LINK page (**scsite.com/dc2002/ch13/weblink.htm**) and click Data Warehouses.

A special type of DSS, called an **executive information system (EIS)**, supports the strategic information needs of executive management. An EIS presents information as charts and tables that show trends, ratios, and statistics (Figure 13-35). EISs typically use external data sources such as the Dow Jones News/Retrieval Service or the Internet. These external data sources can provide current information on interest rates, commodity prices, and other leading economic indicators.

Data Warehouses

A **data warehouse** is a huge database system that stores and manages the data required to analyze historical and current transactions. Through a data warehouse, managers and other users can access transactions and summaries of transactions quickly and efficiently. Some major credit card companies monitor and manage customers' credit card transactions using a data warehouse. Additionally, consumers can access their own transactions in the data warehouse via the Web. A data warehouse typically has a user-friendly interface, so users easily can interact with its data.

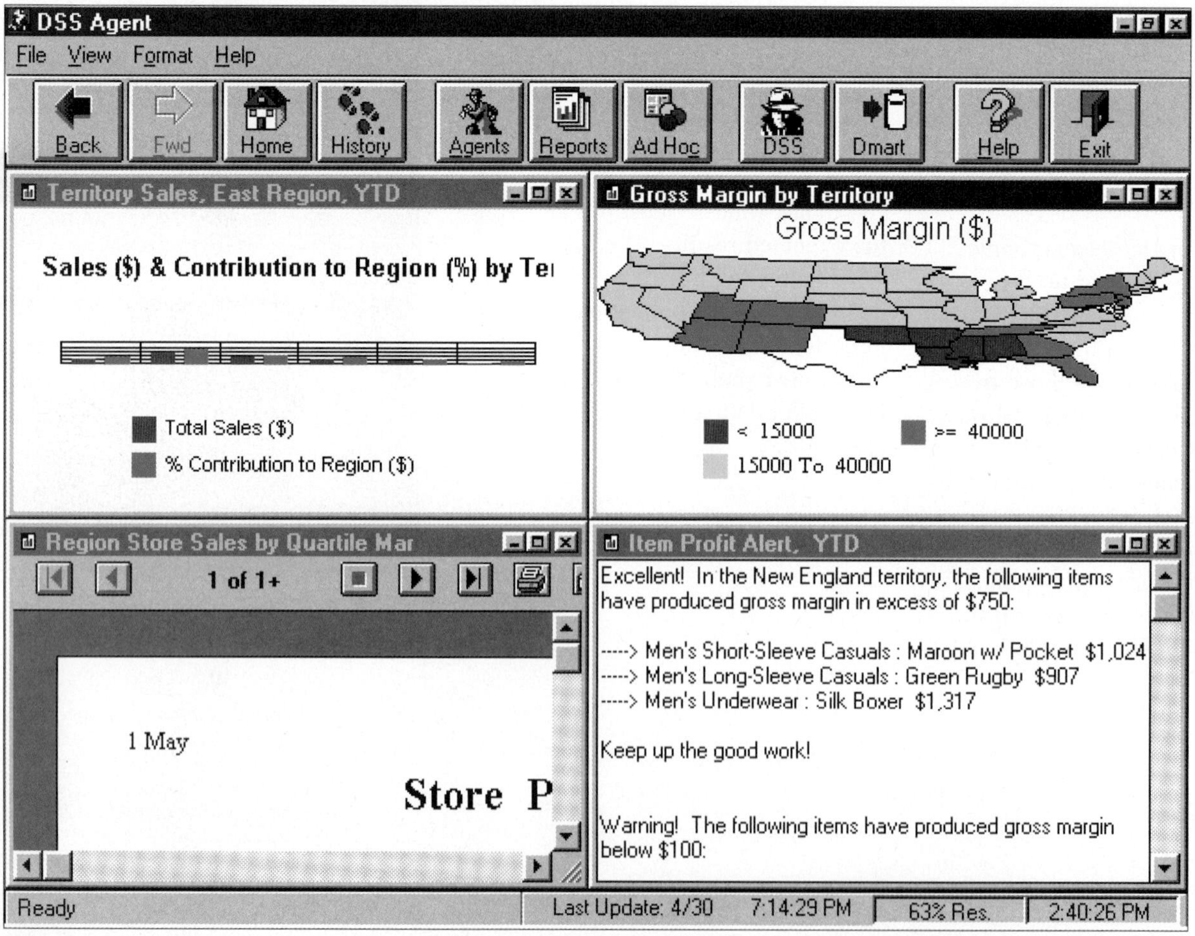

Figure 13-35 This EIS from MicroStrategy presents information to senior management in the form of graphics and reports.

Most data warehouses include one or more databases and one or more sources. The data in the databases consists of transaction data required for decision making. This data may come from internal or external sources (Figure 13-36). Some data warehouses use Web farming for their external data. **Web farming** is the process of collecting data from the Internet as a source for the data warehouse. With Web resources, the company must convert the data to a form suitable for the data warehouse.

Another growing external source of information is a click stream. A **click stream** is a collection of every action that users make as they move through a Web site. By analyzing visitors' click streams, companies can identify consumer preferences and determine which Web pages are most attractive to visitors.

The data in a data warehouse is accurate as of a moment in time. It contains *snapshots* of current and historical transactions. Thus, you usually do not change the content of existing data in a data warehouse. As time passes, you simply add new data. The data warehouse also contains summarizations of this data.

The databases in a data warehouse usually are quite large. Often, the database is distributed. The data in a **distributed database** exists in many separate locations throughout a network or the Internet. The data is accessible through a single server. The data's location is transparent to the user, who usually is unaware the data is stored in multiple servers.

A smaller version of a data warehouse is the data mart. A **data mart** contains a database that helps a specific group or department make decisions. Marketing and sales departments may have their own separate data marts. Individual groups or departments often extract data from the data warehouse to create their data marts.

Many DSS, EIS, and data mining applications use data warehouses. **Data mining** is the process of finding patterns and relationships among data. A state government could *mine* through data to check if the number of births has a relationship to income level. Many e-commerce sites use data mining to determine customer preferences.

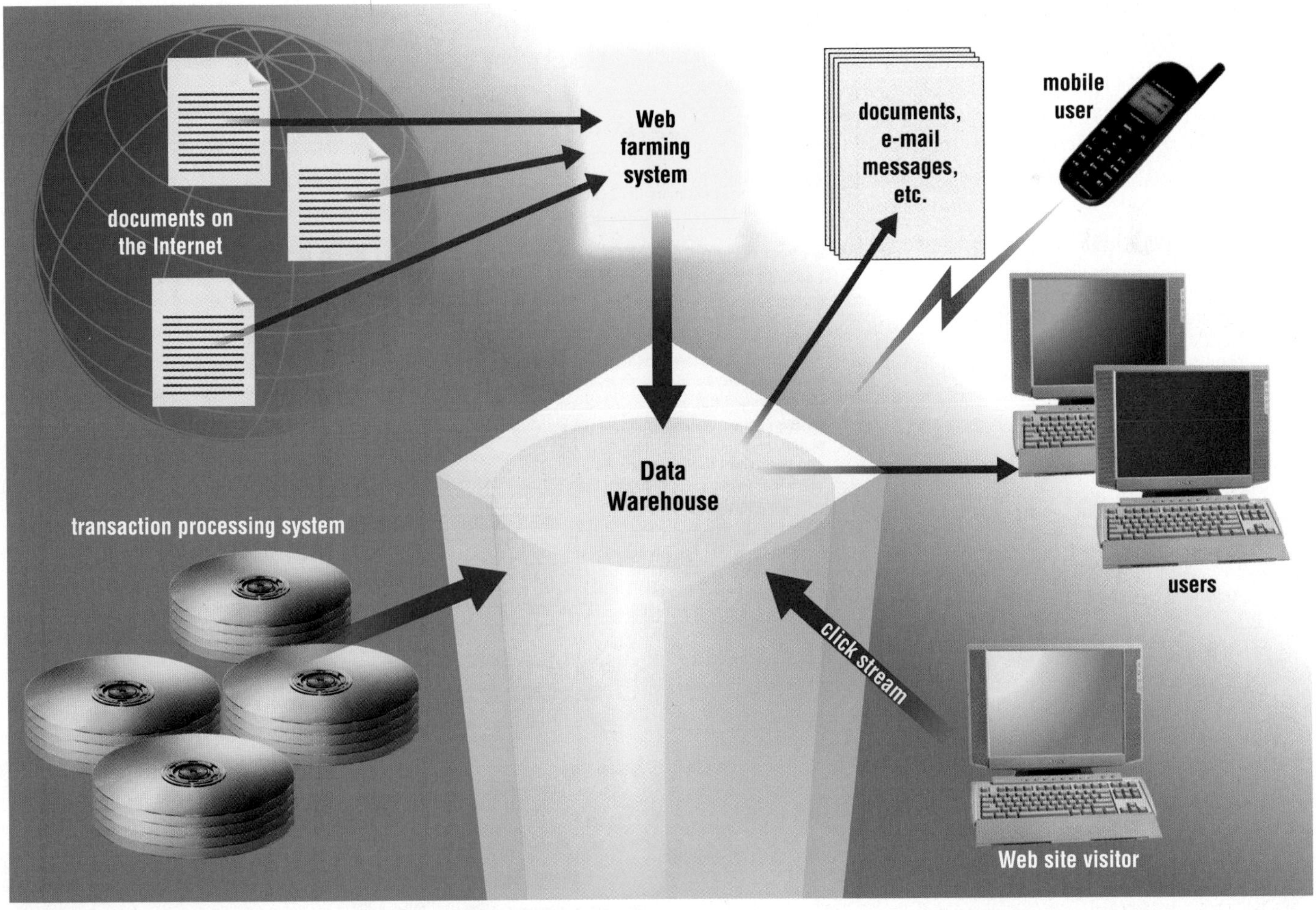

Figure 13-36 A data warehouse can receive inputs from a variety of sources, including company transactions, the Internet, and Web site visitor click streams.

Expert Systems

An **expert system** captures and stores the knowledge of human experts and then imitates human reasoning and decision making. Figure 13-37 shows how one expert system assists you with purchases of electronics.

Expert systems consist of two main components: a knowledge base and inference rules. A **knowledge base** is the combined subject knowledge and experiences of the human experts. The **inference rules** are a set of logical judgments that are applied to the knowledge base each time a user describes a situation to the expert system.

Expert systems help all levels of users make decisions. Nonmanagement employees use them to help with job-related decisions. Expert systems also successfully have resolved such diverse problems as diagnosing illnesses, searching for oil, and making soup.

Web Link

For more information on expert systems, visit the Discovering Computers 2002 Chapter 13 WEB LINK page (**scsite.com/dc2002/ch13/weblink.htm**) and click Expert Systems.

Figure 13-37 A SAMPLE EXPERT SYSTEM

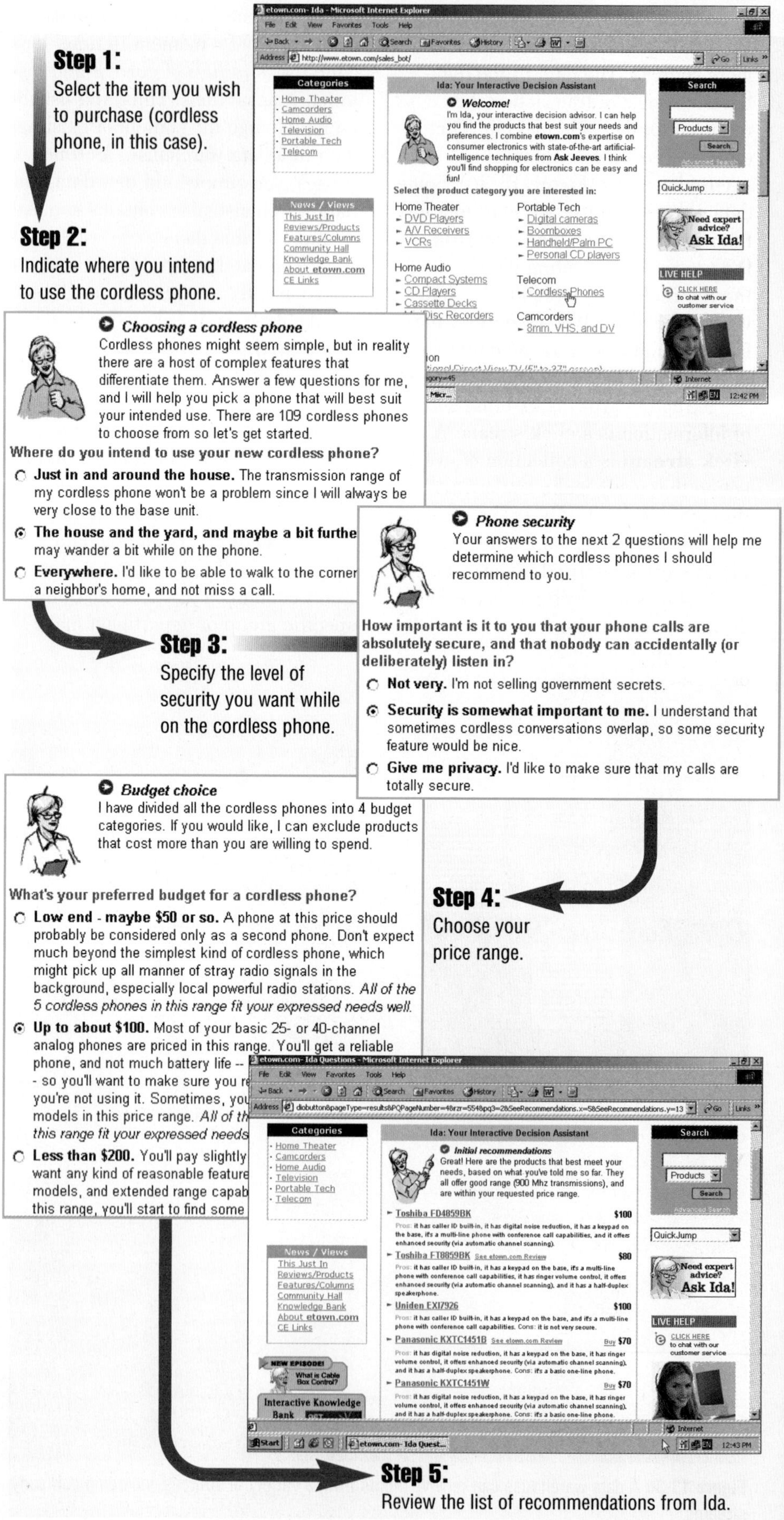
Step 1:
Select the item you wish to purchase (cordless phone, in this case).
Step 2:
Indicate where you intend to use the cordless phone.
Step 3:
Specify the level of security you want while on the cordless phone.
Step 4:
Choose your price range.
Step 5:
Review the list of recommendations from Ida.
Ida: Your Interactive Decision Assistant
Choosing a cordless phone
Cordless phones might seem simple, but in reality there are a host of complex features that differentiate them. Answer a few questions for me, and I will help you pick a phone that will best suit your intended use. There are 109 cordless phones to choose from so let's get started.
Where do you intend to use your new cordless phone?
Just in and around the house. The transmission range of my cordless phone won't be a problem since I will always be very close to the base unit.
Everywhere. I'd like to be able to walk to the corner a neighbor's home, and not miss a call.
Phone security
Your answers to the next 2 questions will help me determine which cordless phones I should recommend to you.
How important is it to you that your phone calls are absolutely secure, and that nobody can accidentally (or deliberately) listen in?
Not very. I'm not selling government secrets.
Security is somewhat important to me. I understand that sometimes cordless conversations overlap, so some security feature would be nice.
Give me privacy. I'd like to make sure that my calls are totally secure.
Budget choice
I have divided all the cordless phones into 4 budget categories. If you would like, I can exclude products that cost more than you are willing to spend.
What's your preferred budget for a cordless phone?
Low end - maybe $50 or so. A phone at this price should probably be considered only as a second phone. Don't expect much beyond the simplest kind of cordless phone, which might pick up all manner of stray radio signals in the background, especially local powerful radio stations. All of the 5 cordless phones in this range fit your expressed needs well.
Up to about $100. Most of your basic 25- or 40-channel analog phones are priced in this range. You'll get a reliable
Initial recommendations
Toshiba FD4859BK $100
Toshiba FT8859BK $80
Uniden EXI7926 $100
Panasonic KXTC1451B $70
Panasonic KXTC1451W $70

Expert systems are one part of an exciting branch of computer science called artificial intelligence. **Artificial intelligence (AI)** is the application of human intelligence to computers. AI technology can sense your actions and, based on logical assumptions and prior experience, will take the appropriate action to complete the task. AI has a variety of capabilities, including speech recognition, logical reasoning, and creative responses.

Computer professionals predict that AI features someday will be built into most computers and software applications. Even today, many word processing programs support speech recognition.

Integrated Information Systems

It often is difficult to classify an information system as belonging to only one of the five types just discussed. Much of today's application software supports transaction processing and creates MIS reports. Other applications provide transaction processing, management information, and decision support.

CHAPTER SUMMARY

This chapter reviewed data and information concepts and presented methods for maintaining high-quality data. It then discussed the advantages of organizing data in a database and described various types of databases. You learned about the role of the database analysts and administrators. Finally, the chapter outlined the qualities of valuable information and presented various types of information systems.

Web Link

For more information on artificial intelligence, visit the Discovering Computers 2002 Chapter 13 WEB LINK page (**scsite.com/dc2002/ch13/weblink.htm**) and click Artificial Intelligence.

HAL: "Checkmate! I win again."

Computers Imitate Human Thinking

A few years ago, Deep Blue, an IBM supercomputer, defeated world chess champion Gary Kasparov in a chess match. Does this victory mean a computer can think? Does it mean in the next few years computers such as HAL from the movie *2001: A Space Odyssey* will be commonplace? Deep Blue used a type of expert system to win the chess match, which is a branch of artificial intelligence (AI) that uses a knowledge base. Other branches include programming computers to understand natural human languages, robotics, and neural networks. A neural network attempts to imitate the human brain. Which of these branches of AI do you think can be the most beneficial to society? In what way? What are some of the negative aspects? List one or two applications you think would benefit from AI and explain why you think this is so. Will machines eventually have the intelligence to think for themselves?

For more information on artificial intelligence, visit the Discovering Computers 2002 Issues Web page (**scsite.com/dc2002/issues.htm**) and click Chapter 13 Issue #5.

Database Management

An information and database manager is a company's major asset. The majority of businesses and organizations are built around databases. Having access to timely, accurate, and relevant information is the company's lifeline. Individuals who have database skills and can provide this information are in high demand. A diversity of career opportunities exists within the IT industry. The more common job titles and descriptions within the database field are as follows:

- **Database administrator** administers and controls an organization's resources; works with system administrator and with applications development teams.
- **Database analyst or data modeler** uses data modeling techniques and tools to analyze, tune, and specify data usage within an application area.
- **Data warehousing specialist** develops and designs enterprise-wide applications for data mining (knowledge discovery).

Database jobs require a lot of mental work and the ability to focus on finite details. Being proficient with a database application such as Oracle, Informix, or SQL Server is a plus. The real key, however, is understanding, learning, and becoming an expert in database design.

For more information on database careers, visit the Discovering Computers 2002 Careers Web page (**scsite.com/dc2002/careers.htm**) and click Database Management.

E-HEALTH

NO PAIN

Store Personal Health Records Online

HEALTH WEB SITES	URL
WellMed	wellmed.com
IntelliHealth	intellihealth.com
Care Compass Solutions	carecompass.com
MedicalLogic/Medscape	aboutmyhealth.com
PersonalMD	personalmd.com
GlobalMedic	globalmedic.com

For an updated list of health Web sites, visit scsite.com/dc2002/e-rev.htm.

Figure 13-38 These Internet-based health database management systems Web sites allow you to organize your medical information and store it in an online database.

Ouch! You stepped on a rusty nail with your bare foot and made your way to the local hospital's emergency room. The admitting nurse asks when you had your last tetanus shot. You give her a sheepish grin and shrug your shoulders.

You might have been able to eliminate the pain and expense of an immunization if you had tracked your shots using an online database management system. Figure 13-38 shows some of the more than 25 Internet health services and portals available online to store your personal health history, including prescriptions, lab test results, doctor visits, allergies, and immunizations. Web sites such as WellMed (Figure 13-39) are free to consumers; revenue is generated in many ways, including charging insurance companies, physicians, and employers who offer this service.

In minutes, you can register with an e-health Web site by choosing a user name and password. Then you create a record to enter your medical history. You also can store data for your emergency contacts, primary care physicians, specialists, blood type, cholesterol levels, blood pressure, and insurance plan.

Similar to the records stored in the video database discussed in this chapter, you can access, retrieve, add, change, delete, and use these online records in a variety of ways. You can decide what data to include. You also can determine who

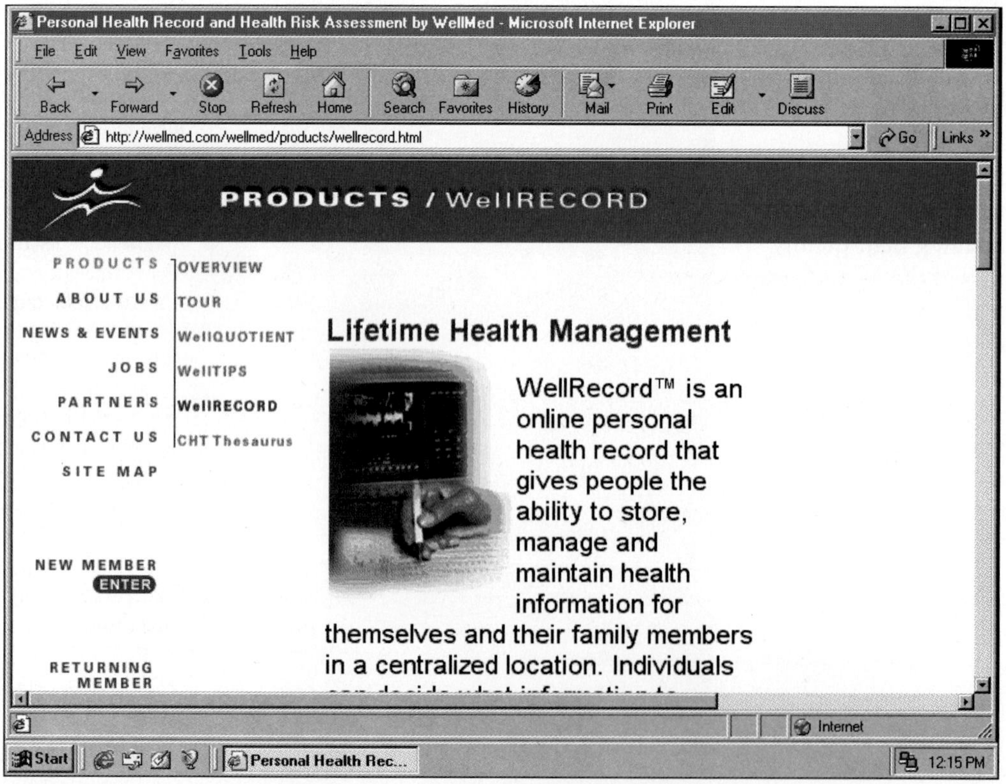

Figure 13-39 You can store health records for you and your family in WellMed's database.

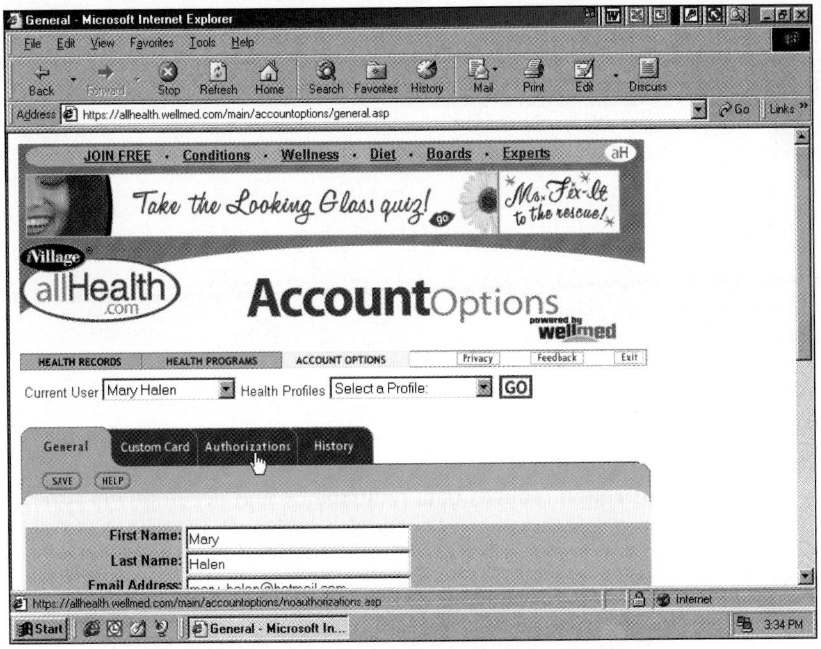

Figure 13-40 You can authorize physicians and medical personnel to access your health record stored in the allHealth.com database.

can access this medical data under specific circumstances. No matter where you are in the world, you and medical personnel can obtain these records via the Internet or fax machine (Figure 13-40). Some Web sites offer an audit log that displays the names of people who have accessed your record and when this action occurred.

Some Web sites issue a wallet-size emergency medical card with instructions for paramedics and other emergency medical personnel on how they can access your vital data (Figure 13-41). Other Web sites can import data directly from pharmacies, hospitals, and physicians' offices.

More than 70-million consumers use the Internet yearly to search for health information, so using the Web to store personal medical data is a natural extension of the Internet's capabilities. Health-care reformers strongly support comprehensive online databases. They explain that using the Internet as a health-history database helps eliminate administrative inefficiencies by automatically transferring data among patients, doctors, and insurance providers. The net results are improved health care overall.

For more information on online health database management systems and for an updated list of health Web sites, visit the Discovering Computers 2002 E-Revolution Web page (scsite.com/dc2002/e-rev.htm) and click Health.

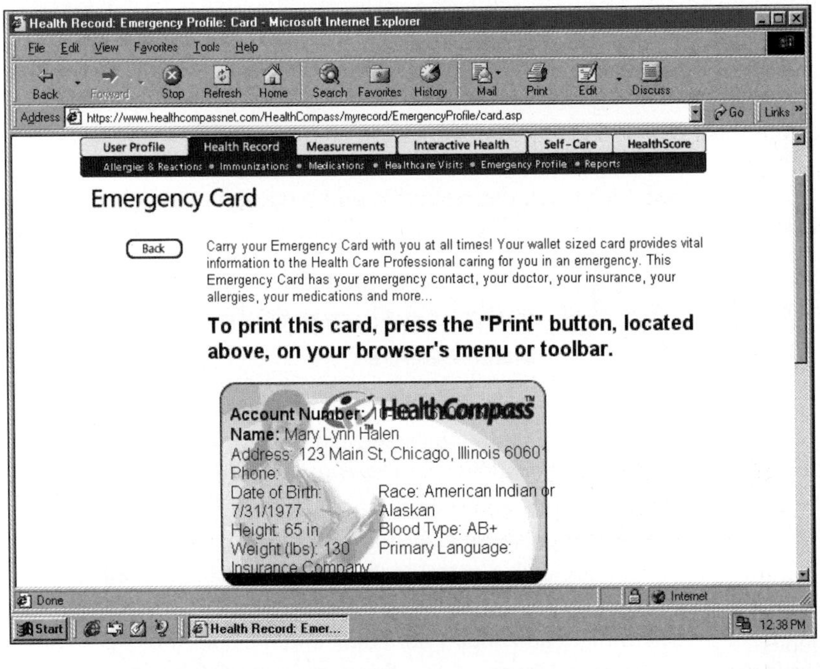

Figure 13-41 In an emergency, a HealthCompass card alerts health-care providers that your medical records are stored online.

eREVOLUTION E-HEALTH *applied:*

1. Access one of the health Web sites listed in Figure 13-38. Register yourself or a family member, and then enter the full health history. Create an emergency medical card if the site provides the card option. Print this record and emergency card.

2. Visit three of the health Web sites listed in Figure 13-38. Describe the features of each. Which of the three is the most user-friendly? Why? Describe the privacy policies of these three Web sites. Print your analysis of these Web sites.

Web Instructions: To display this page from the Web, start your browser and enter the URL scsite.com/dc2002/ch13/summary.htm. Click the links for current and additional information. To listen to an audio version of this In Summary, click the Audio button. To play the audio, RealPlayer must be installed on your computer (download by clicking here).

1 Why Are Data and Information Important to an Organization?

Data is a collection of items such as words, numbers, images, and sounds that are not organized and have little meaning individually. Data is processed into information. **Information** is data that is organized, has meaning, and therefore, is useful. A **database** is a collection of data organized in a manner that allows access, retrieval, and use of that data. Organizations need data and information to complete many business activities. Information allows a company to make decisions and develop, create, and distribute products and services. Because information is generated with data, an organization must manage, maintain, and protect its data resources.

2 What Are File Maintenance Techniques?

Data is organized in a hierarchy (ranking) in which each higher level is composed of elements from the level preceding it. Different terms describe the various levels. A byte represents a **character**, such as a number, a letter, a punctuation mark, or other symbol. A **field** is a combination of one or more characters and is the smallest unit of data that can be accessed. A **record** is a group of related fields. A **data file**, also called a **file**, is a collection of related records stored on a disk. A database is a group of related data files. Data maintenance refers to procedures used to keep data current. **Data maintenance** includes adding records, changing records to correct inaccurate data or update older data, deleting records when they no longer are needed, and validating data to determine its accuracy.

3 How Is a File Processing System Different from a Database Approach?

In a **file processing system**, each department within an organization has its own set of files, designed specifically for their own applications, and the records in one file often are not related to the records in another file. Disadvantages of file processing are data redundancy (duplication of data) and isolated data (data that is difficult to access). A database is a single, shared collection of data used by many application programs in an organization. The **database approach** reduces data redundancy and development time, improves data integrity, facilitates data sharing, and makes reporting easier.

4 What Are the Advantages of Using a Database Management System (DBMS)?

A **database management system** (**DBMS**) is a software program designed to control access to the database and manage data resources efficiently. Database management systems include a **data dictionary** that stores data about each file, and provides functions such as data maintenance and retrieval, data security, and **backup** and recovery.

5 What Are the Characteristics of Relational and Object-Oriented Databases?

A **relational database** is based on the relational data model and stores data in tables consisting of rows and columns. A file is referred to as a **relation** or **table**, a record as a **tuple** or **row**, and a field as an **attribute** or **column**. A relational database also stores associations among data, which are called **relationships**. An **object-oriented database** (**OODB**) stores data in objects. An **object** is an item that can contain both data and the activities that read or manipulate the data. Object-oriented databases can store more types of data and access the data faster than relational databases.

6 How Is a Query Language Used?

A **query language** consists of English-like statements used to specify exact data. **Structured Query Language (SQL)** is used to manipulate and retrieve data in relational databases. SQL includes keywords and rules used to implement **relational algebra** operations. **Object query language**

(**OQL**) is a query language often used to manipulate and retrieve data in object-oriented and object-relational databases. SQL and OQL use many of the same rules, grammar, and vocabulary.

7 How Do Web Databases Work?

Forms are used to access and input data into a Web database. A Web database resides on a **database server**. A **CGI (Common Gateway Interface) script** is a type of program that manages data transmission via the form from the user to the server. Personal computer products, such as Microsoft FrontPage, provide Web publishing tools for smaller databases.

8 What Are the Responsibilities of Database Analysts and Administrators?

The **database analyst** (**DA**) or **data modeler** focuses on the data use. The database administrator (DBA) creates and maintains the data dictionary, establishes and monitors database security and database performance, and implements and tests backup and recovery procedures.

9 What Are the Qualities of Valuable Information?

Valuable information is **accurate** (correct), **verifiable** (capable of being confirmed), **timely** (of an age suited to its use), **organized** (arranged to meet user requirements), **useful** (relevant to the person who receives it), **accessible** (available when needed), and **cost-effective** (less expensive to produce than its ultimate value).

10 What Are the Various Types of Information Systems?

An **information system** is a set of hardware, software, data, people, and procedures designed to produce information that supports the activities of users in an organization. An **office information system** (**OIS**) uses hardware, software, and networks to enhance work flow and facilitate communications among employees. A **transaction processing system** (**TPS**) is an information system that captures and processes data from day-to-day business activities. A management information system (MIS) generates accurate, timely, and organized information, so managers can make decisions, solve problems, supervise activities, and track progress. A **decision support system** (**DSS**) helps users analyze data and make decisions.

11 What Is a Data Warehouse?

A data warehouse stores and manages the data required to analyze historical and current transactions. **Web farming** is the process of collecting data from the Internet as a source for the data warehouse. Many data warehouses use **data mining**, which is the process of finding patterns and relationships among data.

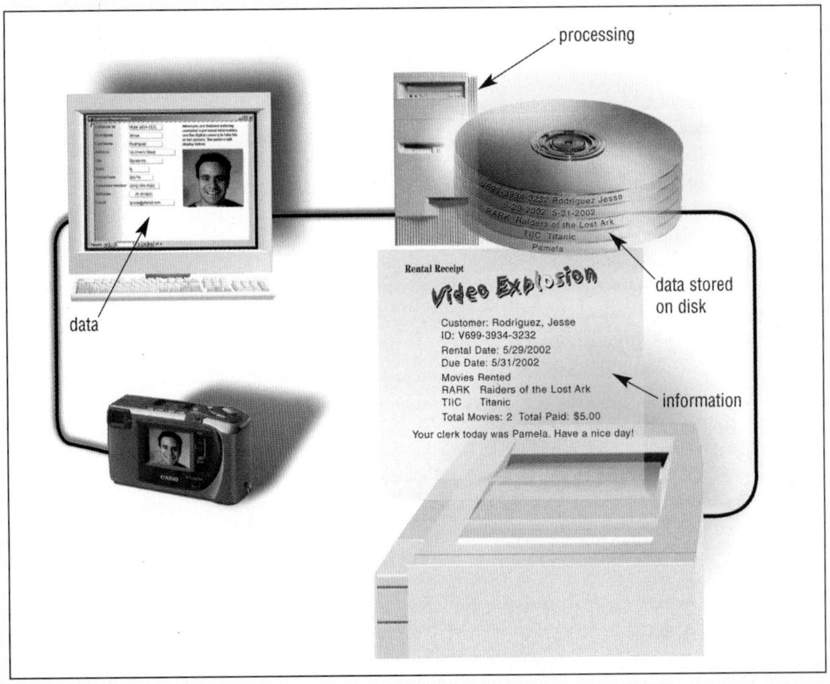

Key Terms

Web Instructions: To display this page from the Web, start your browser and enter the URL scsite.com/dc2002/ch13/terms.htm. Scroll through the list of terms. Click a term to display its definition and a picture. Click the To WEB button for current and additional information about the term from the Web. To see animations, Shockwave and Flash Player must be installed on your computer (download by clicking here).

access privileges (13.19)
accessible information (13.31)
accurate information (13.30)
after image (13.20)
alphabetic check (13.9)
artificial intelligence (AI) (13.41)
attribute (13.22)
back end (13.12)
backup (13.20)
backward recovery (13.20)
batch processing (13.35)
before image (13.20)
CGI (common gateway interface) script (13.29)
character (13.4)
check digit (13.10)
click stream (13.39)
column (13.22)
completeness check (13.10)
computer-aided design (CAD) database (13.26)
consistency check (13.9)
controlling (13.32)
cost-effective information (13.31)
data (13.2)
data dictionary (13.14)
data entry form (13.17)
data file (13.5)
data integrity (13.3)
data maintenance (13.6)
data mart (13.39)
data mining (13.39)
data model (13.21)
data modeler (13.30)
data processing (13.35)
data redundancy (13.11)
data type (13.5)
data warehouse (13.38)
database (13.2)
database administrator (DBA) (13.30)
database analyst (DA) (13.30)
database approach (13.12)
database management system (DBMS) (13.14)
database server (13.29)
decision support system (DSS) (13.37)
default value (13.15)
detailed report (13.36)
distributed database (13.39)
e-form (13.18)
electronic form (13.18)
empowering (13.33)
exception criteria (13.37)
exception report (13.37)
executive information system (EIS) (13.38)
executive management (13.32)
expert system (13.40)
external sources (13.37)
field (13.4)
field name (13.4)
field size (13.5)
file (13.5)
file maintenance (13.6)
file processing system (13.11)
form (13.17)
forward recovery (13.20)
front end (13.12)
full-update privileges (13.19)
garbage in, garbage out (GIGO) (13.3)

ARTIFICIAL INTELLIGENCE (AI)
Application of human intelligence to computers. AI technology can sense a user's actions and, based on logical assumptions and prior experience, will take the appropriate action to complete a task. (13.41)

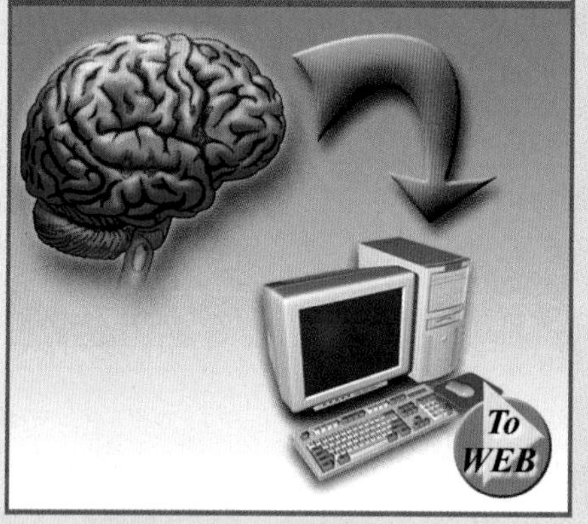

groupware database (13.26)
hypermedia database (13.26)
hypertext database (13.26)
inference rules (13.40)
information (13.2)
information system (13.34)
internal sources (13.37)
isolated data (13.12)
join operation (13.24)
key field (13.5)
knowledge base (13.40)
leading (13.32)
log (13.20)
management information system (MIS) (13.36)
managers (13.32)
metadata (13.15)
middle management (13.33)
MOLAP (13.37)
multidimensional database (MDDB) (13.27)
multimedia database (13.26)
nonmanagement employees (13.33)
normalization (13.22)
numeric check (13.9)
object (13.26)
object query language (OQL) (13.27)
object-oriented database (OODB) (13.26)
object-relational databases (13.21)
office automation (13.34)
office information system (OIS) (13.34)
online analytical processing (OLAP) (13.37)
online transaction processing (OLTP) (13.35)
operational decision (13.33)
operational management (13.33)
organized information (13.30)
organizing (13.32)
planning (13.32)
primary key (13.5)
procedure (13.34)
program files (13.5)
projection operation (13.24)
query (13.15)
query language (13.16)
query-by-example (QBE) (13.17)
range check (13.9)
read-only privileges (13.19)
record (13.5)
recovery utility (13.20)
relation (13.22)
relational algebra (13.24)
relational database (13.22)
relationship (13.22)
report generator (13.19)
report writer (13.19)
repository (13.14)
ROLAP (13.37)
rollback (13.20)
rollforward (13.20)
row (13.22)
selection operation (13.24)
short-range decision (13.33)
strategic decisions (13.32)
Structured Query Language (SQL) (13.25)
summary report (13.36)
table (13.22)
tactical decision (13.33)
timely information (13.30)
transaction processing system (TPS) (13.35)
tuple (13.22)
useful information (13.31)
validation (13.9)
validation rules (13.9)
validity check (13.9)
valuable information (13.30)
verifiable (13.30)
Web database (13.27)
Web farming (13.39)

Learn It Online

Web Instructions: To display this page from the Web, start your browser, and then enter the URL scsite.com/dc2002/ch13/learn.htm.

1. Web Guide

Click Web Guide to display the Guide to World Wide Web Sites and Searching Techniques Web page. Click Reference and then click Webopedia. Search for data dictionary. Click one of the data dictionary links. Use your word processing program to prepare a brief report on your findings and submit your assignment to your instructor.

2. Scavenger Hunt

Click Scavenger Hunt. Print a copy of the Scavenger Hunt page; use this page to write down your answers as you search the Web. Submit your completed page to your instructor.

3. Who Wants to Be a Computer Genius?

Click Computer Genius to find out if you are a computer genius. Directions on how to play the game will display. When you are ready to play, click the PLAY button. Submit your score to your instructor.

4. Wheel of Terms

Click Wheel of Terms to reinforce important terms you learned in this chapter by playing the Shelly Cashman Series version of this popular game. Directions on how to play the game will display. When you are ready to play, click the PLAY button. Submit your score to your instructor.

5. Career Corner

Click Career Corner to display the JobStarCalifornia page. Click one of the Facts and Information links and then review the information. Write a brief report describing what you learned. Submit the report to your instructor.

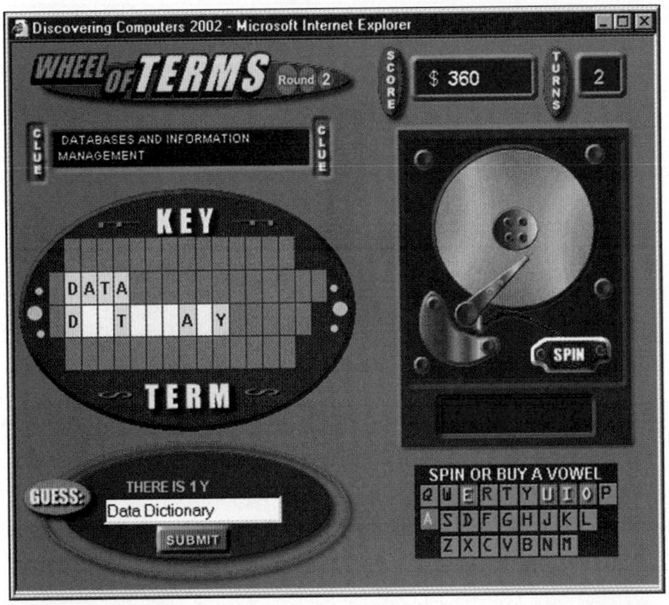

6. Search Sleuth

Click Search Sleuth to learn search techniques that will help make you a research expert. Submit the completed assignment to your instructor.

7. Crossword Puzzle Challenge

Click Crossword Puzzle Challenge. Complete the puzzle to reinforce skills you learned in this chapter. Directions on how to play the game will display. When you are ready to play, click the PLAY button. Submit the completed puzzle to your instructor.

8. Practice Test

Click Practice Test. Answer each question. When completed, enter your name and click the Grade Test button to submit the quiz for grading. Make a note of any missed questions. If required, print a copy to submit to your instructor.

Checkpoint

Web Instructions: To display this page from the Web, start your browser and enter the URL scsite.com/dc2002/ch13/check.htm. Click the links for current and additional information. To experience the animation and interactivity, Shockwave and Flash Player must be installed on your computer (download by clicking here.)

LABEL THE FIGURE

Instructions: Identify each component of a relational database.

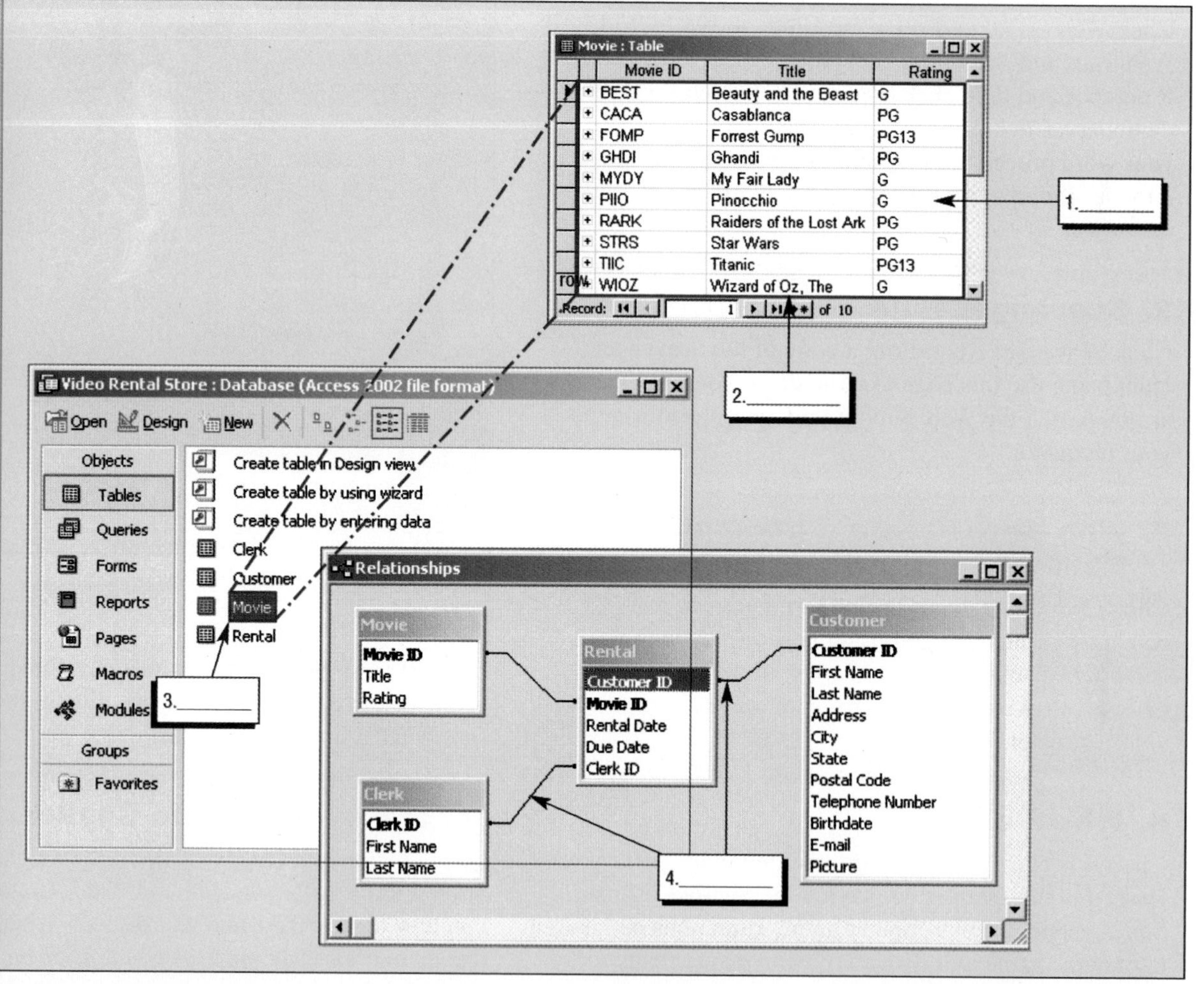

MATCHING

Instructions: Match each term from the column on the left with the best description from the column on the right.

_______ 1. relational database
_______ 2. database approach
_______ 3. validity
_______ 4. data dictionary
_______ 5. query

a. The process of comparing data to a set of rules or values to find out if the data is correct.
b. Verifies the accuracy of a primary key.
c. Many programs and users share the data in the database.
d. Contains data about each file in the database.
e. A value that the DBMS initially displays in a field.
f. A request for specific data from the database.
g. Stores data in tables that consist of rows and columns.

MULTIPLE CHOICE

Instructions: Select the letter of the correct answer for each of the following questions.

1. A user of a relational database refers to a file as a ___________.
   a. row
   b. column
   c. table
   d. tuple
2. ___________ is a process designed to make sure the data within the relations (tables) contains the least amount of duplication.
   a. Normalization
   b. Projection
   c. GI
   d. Dimension
3. ___________ is a query language that allows you to manage, update, and retrieve data.
   a. OQL
   b. SQL
   c. MQL
   d. CGI
4. A ___________ database contains text links to other documents.
   a. groupware
   b. multimedia
   c. Web
   d. hypertext
5. ___________ information is information that is correct.
   a. Verifiable
   b. Timely
   c. Accurate
   d. Organized

SHORT ANSWER

Instructions: Write a brief answer to each of the following questions.

1. What is the difference between a file processing system and the database approach? ___________ Which is most widely used in business? ___________
2. What is a data dictionary? ___________ How is it used within a database?___________
3. Why are data integrity and data security important? ___________ What is GIGO? ___________
4. How is a hypertext database different from a Web database? ___________ How is a hypermedia database different from a hypertext database? ___________
5. What is relational algebra? ___________ How are the projection operator, selection operator, and join operator different? ___________

WORKING TOGETHER

Instructions: Working with a group of your classmates, complete the following team exercise.

The ability to create intelligent machines has intrigued humans since ancient times. Many see the computer as the answer and the means to create artificial intelligence (AI). An investigation of AI shows there are several categories within this topic. These include neural networks, artificial life, expert systems, fuzzy logic, natural language processing, and robotics. Select one of these categories to explore. Prepare a report to share with the class. Include within your report information explaining the relationship of AI to databases. To learn more about AI, visit scsite.com/dc2002/ch13/check.htm.

Web Instructions: To display this page from the Web, start your browser and enter the URL scsite.com/dc2002/ch13/lab.htm. Click the links for current and additional information.

1 Managing Files and Folders

This exercise uses Windows 98 procedures. Click the Start button on the taskbar and then click Help on the Start menu. Click the Contents tab. Click the Exploring Your Computer book. Click the Files and Folders book. Click the Managing Files book. Click an appropriate Help topic to answer the following questions:

- How do you create a folder?
- How do you move a file or folder?
- How do you delete a file or folder?

Click the Close button to close the Windows Help window.

2 Working with Folders

Right-click the My Computer icon on the desktop. Click Explore on the shortcut menu to open the Exploring — My Computer window and then maximize it. Click View on the menu bar and then click Large Icons. Insert the Discover Data Disk into drive A. See the inside back cover of this book for instructions for downloading the Discover Data Disk or see your instructor for information on accessing the files required in this book. If necessary, drag the vertical scroll box to the top of the scroll bar in the Folders area. Click 3½ Floppy (A:) in the Folders area to display the contents of drive A. Click File on the menu bar, point to New, and then click Folder on the New submenu. When the new folder displays, type `In The Lab` and then press the ENTER key. Click View on the menu bar, point to Arrange Icons, and then click by Name. Click the plus sign next to 3½ Floppy (A:) in the All Folders area to display the In The Lab folder in the Folders area. Click the In The Lab folder in the Folders area to display its contents. What is in the In The Lab folder?

Click the Close button to close Windows Explorer.

3 Working with Files in Folders

To complete this exercise, you first must complete In The Lab 2 in Chapter 3 on page 3.54. Complete In The Lab 2 above before proceeding with this lab. Open Windows Explorer and then maximize the Exploring — My Computer window. Insert your floppy disk into drive A. Click 3½ Floppy (A:) in the Folders area to display the contents of drive A. Click the plus sign next to 3½ Floppy (A:) in the All Folders area to display the In The Lab folder in the All Folders area. To move the file you created in Chapter 3 (h3-2) into the In The Lab folder, follow the procedure suggested in Help In The Lab or perform the following steps:

- Click the h3-2 icon to select the file.
- Right-drag the h3-2 icon to the In The Lab folder.
- When the In The Lab folder is highlighted, release the right mouse button.

Click Move Here on the shortcut menu. To delete file h7-2 (the copy of file h3-2 that you created in Chapter 7), follow the procedure suggested in Help or perform the following steps:

- Right-click the h7-2 icon.
- Click Delete on the shortcut menu.
- Click the Yes button in the Confirm File Delete dialog box.
- Click the In The Lab folder in the All Folders area. What is in the In The Lab folder?
- Click 3½ Floppy (A:) in the All Folders area. What displays in the window?

Click the Close button to close Windows Explorer.

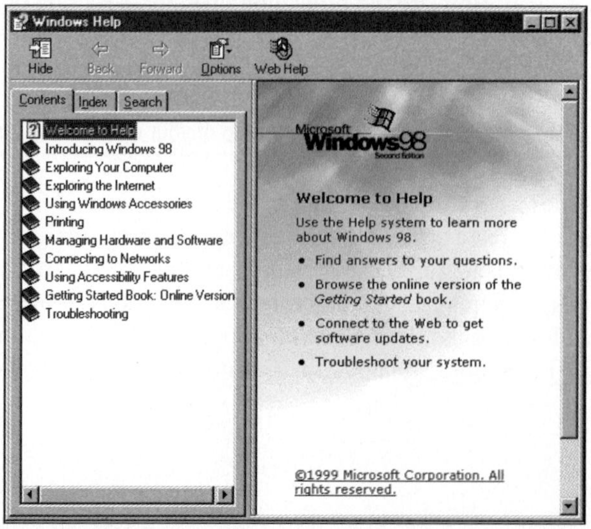

Web Work

Web Instructions: To display this page from the Web, start your browser and enter the URL scsite.com/dc2002/ch13/web.htm. To view At The Movies in exercise 1, RealPlayer must be installed on your computer (download by clicking here). To use the Shelly Cashman Series Designing a Database Lab from the Web, Shockwave and Flash Player must be installed on your computer (download by clicking here).

1 ToySmart.Com

ToySmart.Com was an e-tailer of children's toys that went belly up — bankrupt. In its final throes, the company began selling remaining inventory, office furniture, the Web site address itself ... and its customer list. Originally, the company had promised, via notice on its Web site, that it would not share mailing lists and other customer information with other companies. Obviously, information about families, children, and their consumer choices are very valuable assets. Should the company have been allowed to sell these assets to pay off creditors? Would a company have the right to transfer these asset if it were merely acquired by another company, rather than going out of business?

2 Shelly Cashman Series Designing a Database Lab

Follow the instructions in Web Work 2 on page 1.47 to start and use the Designing a Database Lab. If you are running from the Web, enter the URL, scsite.com/sclabs/menu.htm, or display the Web Work page (see instructions at the top of this page) and then click the button to the left.

3 Shopping Online

Online shopping is an increasingly prevalent Internet activity. Buying on the Web is especially popular among busy people who are financially secure. During a recent holiday season, a survey found that almost 75 percent of upper-income families made at least one purchase online. Web sites that offer products for sale must provide database search capability as well as online order entry. Click the button to the left and complete this exercise to learn more about database query and order entry in a large online music store.

4 Newsgroup FAQs

Redundancy in data wastes storage space. Redundant questions demand valuable employee time. Frequently asked questions (FAQs) help reduce the need for experienced newsgroup participants from having to read and answer the same questions more than once. Click the button to the left for a listing of newsgroups with FAQs. Click a newsgroup folder link in which you are interested. Continue clicking folder links until you see a file link called faq.html. Click the faq.html link to see the newsgroup's FAQs. Read the frequently asked questions. What question (or answer) is most surprising to you? Why?

5 In the News

To spare harried dispatchers, police officers used to request suspect information only when it was urgent. Now, IBM's eNetwork Law Enforcement Express lets officers directly access real-time databases of stolen cars, mug shots, and warrants. With a few taps on a notebook keyboard, police officers can search a database to see if a suspect in custody has a past criminal record. They also can find out if a suspect stopped for speeding is wanted for any more serious infractions. Click the button to the left and read a news article about a database that is being used in a new way. Who is using the database? How is it being used? How will the database benefit the user?

CHAPTER 14

Information Systems Development

It never fails. The telephone rings just as you sit down to dinner. Tonight, you decide to let the answering machine take the call. As you eat your salad, the caller begins to leave her message. She identifies herself as the vice president where you do your banking. You panic. Did you forget to deposit your last paycheck? Have you lost your checkbook or ATM card? Has someone illegally accessed your online bank account and transferred money from your account to theirs? You decide to take the call. Dinner can wait this time.

Her reason for calling amazes you. The bank is going to re-design its entire Web site. For this project, they are forming a customer advisory board. The board will work with the bank's computer professionals. Advisory board members will participate in all aspects of the project: make design suggestions, review work in progress, and test the new Web site.

The vice president asks if you would be willing to be on the customer advisory board. It will require your attention for about two hours per week during the next six months. As a thank you for your time, your online banking will be free for the next three years. Are you interested?

OBJECTIVES

After completing this chapter, you will be able to:

- Explain the phases in the system development life cycle
- Identify the guidelines for system development
- Recognize the responsibilities of various IT professionals
- Discuss the importance of project management, feasibility assessment, data and information gathering techniques, and documentation
- Describe how structured tools such as entity-relationship diagrams and data flow diagrams are used in analysis and design
- Differentiate between packaged software and custom software
- Identify program development as part of the system development life cycle
- Discuss techniques used to convert to a new system
- Understand how IT professionals support an information system

Web Link

For more information on software engineering, visit the Discovering Computers 2002 Chapter 14 WEB LINK page (**scsite.com/dc2002/ch14/weblink.htm**) and click Software Engineering.

WHAT IS THE SYSTEM DEVELOPMENT LIFE CYCLE?

A **system** is a set of components that interact to achieve a common goal. Your body, for example, contains many systems. The digestive system consists of organs that allow your body to process food. The immune system includes the elements that protect your body from disease. The respiratory system has many parts that work together, so you can breathe.

You use, observe, and interact with systems during daily activities. You drive a highway system to reach a destination. Your home maintains a comfortable temperature with its heating and cooling systems. You use the decimal number system to calculate an amount due. You watch the stars in the solar system.

Businesses also use many types of systems. A billing system allows a company to send invoices and receive payments from customers. Through a payroll system, employees receive paychecks. A manufacturing system produces the goods that customers order. The inventory system keeps track of the items in the warehouse. Very often, these systems also are information systems.

An **information system (IS)** is a set of hardware, software, data, people, and procedures that work together to produce information. You play an important role in many information systems. You provide information to some information systems. For example, many sytems display forms that ask you to enter personal information such as your name, address, telephone number, and interests. With other information systems, you use their information. When you receive a deposit slip from the bank, you verify the deposit amount is correct.

An information system supports daily, short-term, and long-range activities of users. Users include clerks, sales representatives, accountants, supervisors, managers, executives, and customers. As time passes, the kinds and types of information that users need often change. A sales manager may want the weekly summary report grouped by district instead of by product. When information requirements change, the information system must meet the new requirements. In some cases, the developers modify the current information system. In other cases, they develop an entirely new information system.

As a computer user in a business, you someday may participate in the modification of an existing system or the development of a new system. Thus, it is important you understand the development process. The **system development life cycle (SDLC)** is a set of activities developers use to build an information system. System developers should use an SDLC to guide them through system development. They also should use an SDLC to maintain and monitor ongoing activities.

Some IT professionals refer to the entire system development process as **software engineering**. The meaning of this term varies. For example, it can describe the programming process.

Some activities in the SDLC may be performed concurrently. Others are performed sequentially. Depending on the type and complexity of the information system, the length of each activity varies from one system to the next. In some cases, a developer skips an activity entirely.

Phases in the SDLC

To help organize the process, SDLCs often group many activities into larger categories called **phases**. Most SDLCs contain five phases:

1. Planning
2. Analysis
3. Design
4. Implementation
5. Support

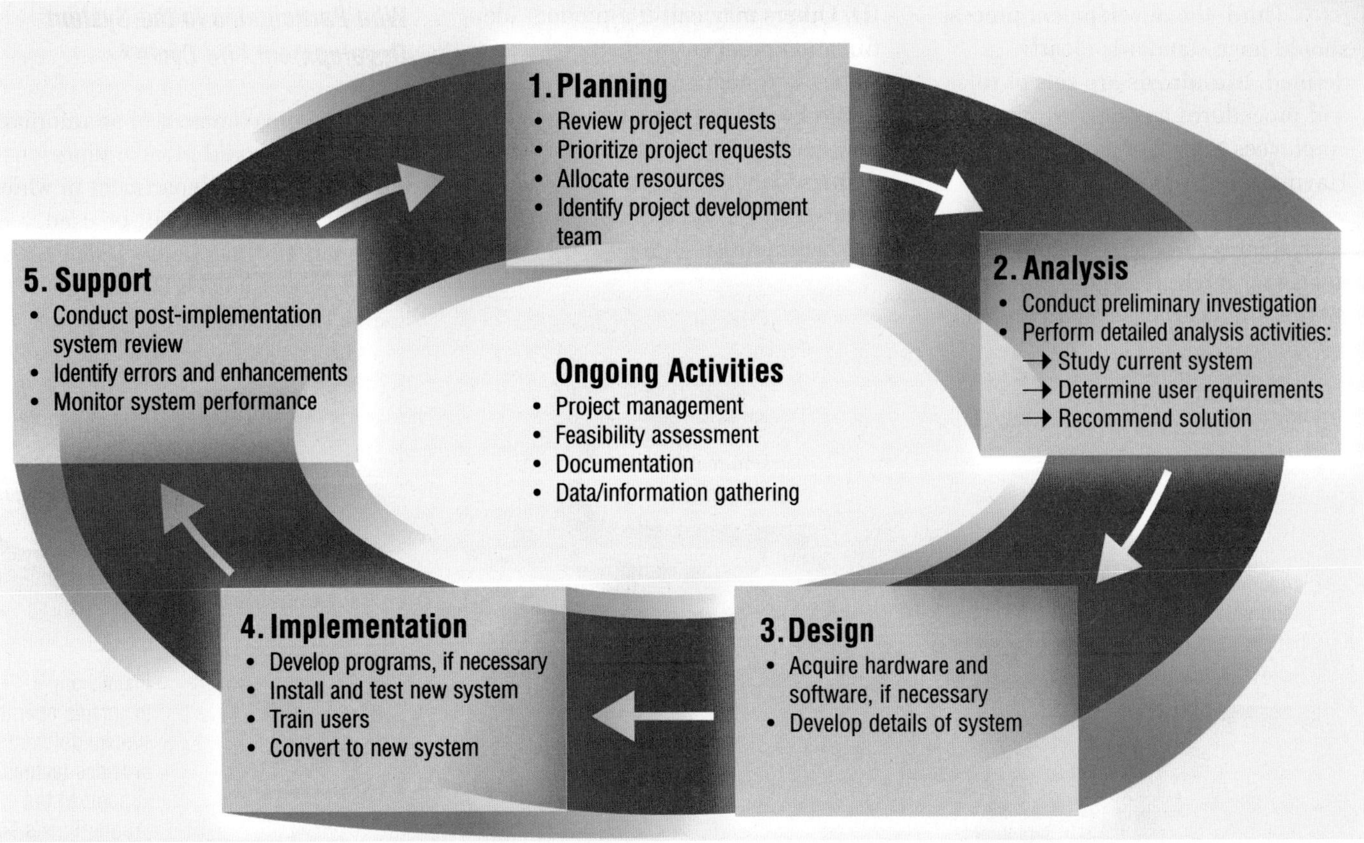

Figure 14-1 The system development life cycle consists of five phases that form a loop. Several ongoing activities also take place throughout the entire system development life cycle.

As shown in Figure 14-1, the phases in the SDLC form a loop. That is, information system development is an ongoing process. The cycle forms when the support phase points to the planning phase, thus creating a loop. This connection occurs when the information system requires changing. A variety of situations can lead to a change in the information system. A report might generate an incorrect total. Users may want information in a different format. A vendor may release a new version of software. Hardware might become obsolete. When change occurs, the planning phase for a new or modified system begins and the SDLC process starts again.

Developers follow established guidelines during the entire SDLC process. These developers also interact with a variety of IT professionals and others during the SDLC. Although the SDLC contains a set of five phases, several ongoing activities take place during the entire process. The following sections discuss each of these issues.

Guidelines for System Development

The development of an information system should follow three general guidelines: (1) use phases, (2) involve the users, and (3) develop standards.

First, the SDLC should group activities or tasks into phases. Many SDLCs contain the five major phases that are shown in Figure 14-1. Others have more or fewer phases. Regardless, all SDLCs have similar activities and tasks. Figure 14-1 shows the Develop Programs activity as part of the Implementation phase. Some SDLCs add a sixth phase called Construction or Development, which includes the Develop Programs activity. Other differences among SDLCs are the terminology they use, the order of their activities, and the level of detail within each phase.

Second, system developers must involve users throughout the entire system development process. **Users** include anyone for whom the system is being built. Customers, data entry clerks, accountants, sales managers, and owners are all examples of users. You are a user of many information systems. You, as a user, might interact with an information system at your bank, library, grocery store, video rental store, work, and school. System developers must remember they ultimately deliver the system to the user. If the system is to be successful, the user must be included in all stages of development. Users are more apt to accept a new system if they contribute to its design.

Third, the development process should have standards clearly defined. **Standards** are sets of rules and procedures a company expects employees to accept and follow. Having standards helps people working on the same project produce consistent results. For example, one developer might refer to a product number in a database as a Product ID. Others may call it a product identification number, product code, and so on. A system created in this way would be so confusing that it could never function correctly! If the SDLC defines standards, then everyone involved uses one term, such as product number.

Who Participates in the System Development Life Cycle?

The development of an information system should involve representatives from each department in which the proposed system will be used. This includes both nontechnical users and IT professionals. During the course of the SDLC, the systems

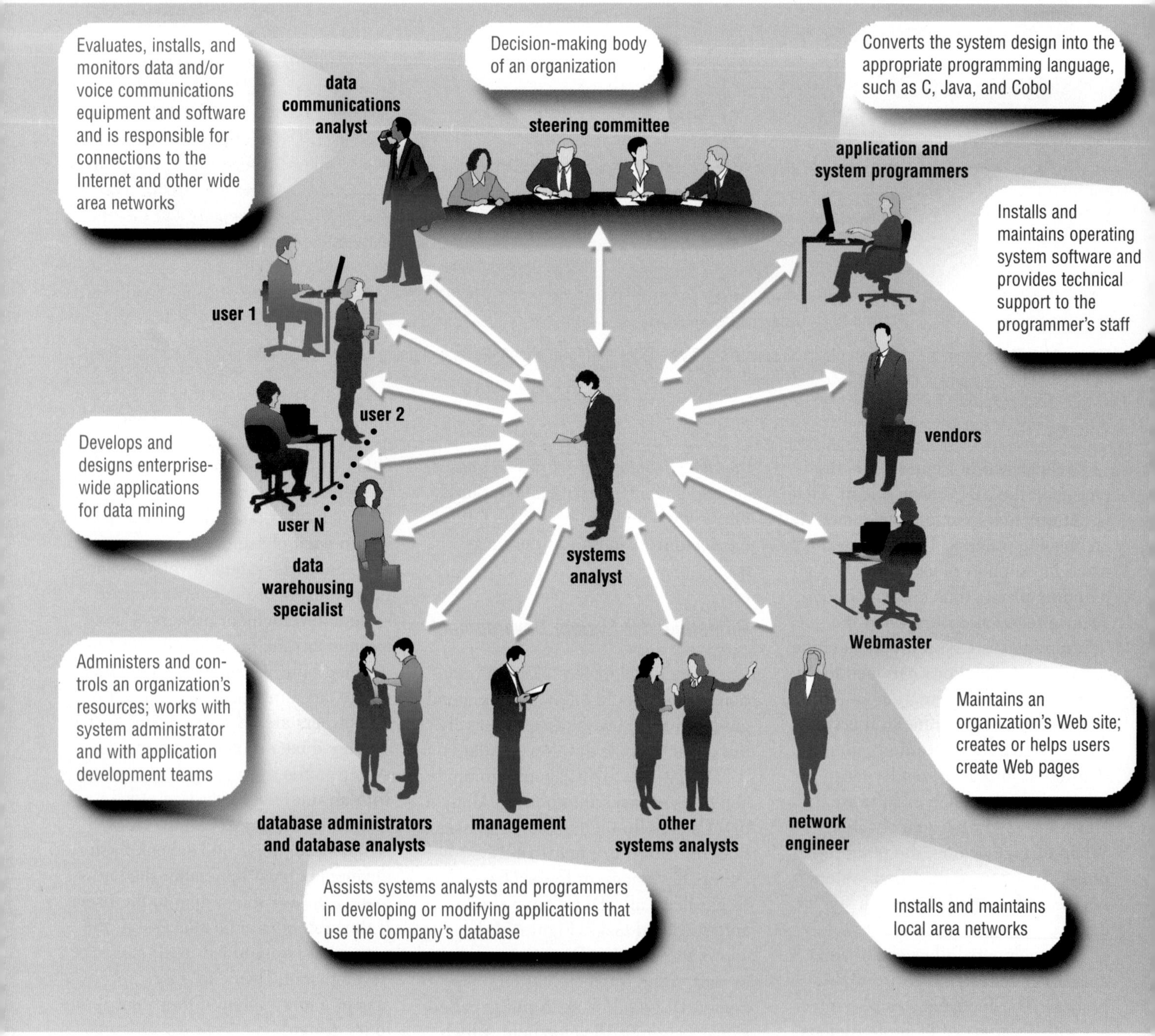
Evaluates, installs, and monitors data and/or voice communications equipment and software and is responsible for connections to the Internet and other wide area networks
data communications analyst
Decision-making body of an organization
steering committee
Converts the system design into the appropriate programming language, such as C, Java, and Cobol
application and system programmers
Installs and maintains operating system software and provides technical support to the programmer's staff
user 1
user 2
user N
Develops and designs enterprise-wide applications for data mining
vendors
data warehousing specialist
systems analyst
Webmaster
Administers and controls an organization's resources; works with system administrator and with application development teams
Maintains an organization's Web site; creates or helps users create Web pages
database administrators and database analysts
management
other systems analysts
network engineer
Assists systems analysts and programmers in developing or modifying applications that use the company's database
Installs and maintains local area networks

Figure 14-2 A systems analyst meets with a variety of people during a system development project.

analyst meets and works with a variety of people (Figure 14-2). The systems analyst is the users' primary contact person. A **systems analyst** is responsible for designing and developing an information system.

A systems analyst is the liaison between the users and the IT professionals. They convert user requests into technical specifications. Thus, a systems analyst must have some technical skills. They also must be familiar with business operations and have excellent communication and interpersonal skills. Systems analysts prepare many reports, drawings, and diagrams. They discuss various aspects of the development project with users, management, other analysts, database analysts, database administrators, network administrators, the Webmaster, programmers, vendors, and the steering committee. The **steering committee** is a decision-making body in a company.

For each system development project, a company usually forms a **project team** to work on the project from beginning to end. The project team consists of users, the systems analyst, and other IT professionals. One member of the team is the **project leader**, who manages and controls the budget and schedule of the project. The systems analyst may or may not be selected as the project leader of the project.

Project Management

Project management is the process of planning, scheduling, and then controlling the activities during the SDLC. The goal of project management is to deliver an acceptable system to the user in an agreed-upon time frame, while maintaining costs.

To plan and schedule a project effectively, the project leader identifies the following for the project:

- Goal, objectives, and expectations of the project, called the **scope**
- Required activities
- Time estimates for each activity
- Cost estimates for each activity
- Order of activities
- Activities that can take place at the same time

Once identified, the project leader usually records these items in a **project plan**. A popular tool used to plan and schedule the time relationships among project activities is called a Gantt chart (Figure 14-3). A **Gantt chart**, developed by Henry L. Gantt, is a bar chart that uses horizontal bars to show project phases or activities. The left side, or vertical axis, displays the list of required activities. A horizontal axis across the top or bottom of the chart represents time.

Time estimates assigned to activities should be realistic. If they are not realistic, the success of a project is in jeopardy from the beginning. When project members do not believe a schedule is reasonable, they may not participate to the full extent of their abilities. This could lead to missed deadlines and delivery dates.

Once a project begins, the project leader monitors and controls the project. Some activities will take less time than originally planned. Others will take longer. The project leader may realize that excessive time has been devoted to a particular activity. Thus, the team will not be able to meet the original deadline of the project. In these cases, the project leader may extend the deadline or may reduce the scope of the system development. If the latter occurs, the users will receive a less comprehensive system at the original deadline. In either case, the project leader revises the first project plan and presents the new plan to users for approval. It is crucial that everyone is aware of and agrees on any changes made to the project plan.

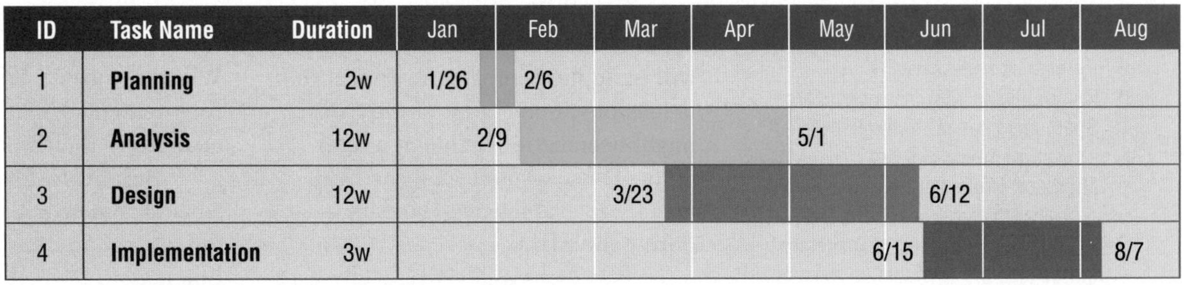
ID
Task Name
Duration
Jan
Feb
Mar
Apr
May
Jun
Jul
Aug
1
Planning
2w
1/26
2/6
2
Analysis
12w
2/9
5/1
3
Design
12w
3/23
6/12
4
Implementation
3w
6/15
8/7

Figure 14-3 A Gantt chart is an effective way to show the time relationships of a project's activities.

One aspect of managing projects is making sure everyone submits deliverables on time and according to plan. A **deliverable** is any tangible item such as a chart, diagram, report, or program file. Project leaders can use **project management software** such as Microsoft Project, to assist them in planning, scheduling, and controlling development projects (Figure 14-4).

Figure 14-4a (Gantt chart)

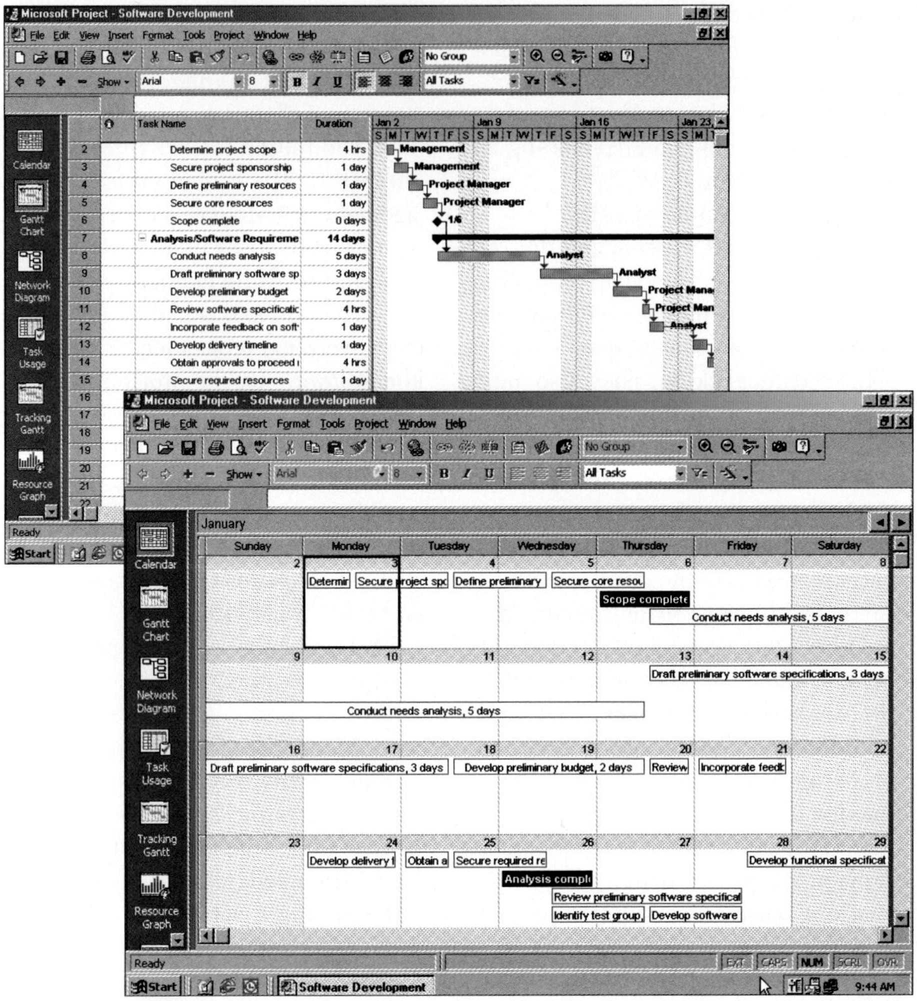

Figure 14-4b (calendar of activities)

Figure 14-4 Microsoft Project is a popular project management software package. Shown here is a Gantt chart and calendar for a software development project.

APPLY IT!

Project Management for Your Personal Life

Project management software is not limited to workplace situations. You can use this software to manage projects within your personal life as well. Consider some of these examples: planning a fund-raising project, building a new home, or preparing for a party or wedding. Any project that requires planning and coordination and is dynamic in nature can benefit from this application.

Suppose you are planning a wedding or one of the other above examples. To begin this process and build your project plan, you first determine baseline tasks.

1. Set specific dates for all tasks
2. Define roles and responsibilities
3. Enter all data into your project management program
4. Generate a Gantt chart to show the time relationships of your project
5. Continue to monitor your project and manage your tasks
6. Add unscheduled events
7. Track your budget and schedule
8. Re-plan as necessary
9. Communicate with team members
10. Share any changes with all involved project members

Microsoft Project is the most widely used project management software. Several shareware project management programs also are available or you can use Excel to create a Gantt chart.

For links to shareware programs and other helpful links, visit the Discovering Computers 2002 Apply It Web page (**scsite.com/dc2002/apply.htm**) and click Chapter 14 Apply It #1.

Feasibility Assessment

Feasibility is a measure of how suitable the development of a system will be to the company. A project that is feasible at one point of the SDLC might become infeasible at a later point. Thus, systems analysts frequently re-evaluate feasibility during the SDLC.

A systems analyst typically uses four tests to evaluate feasibility of a project: operational feasibility, schedule feasibility, technical feasibility, and economic feasibility.

Operational feasibility measures how well the proposed information system will work. Will the users like the new system? Will they use it? Will it meet their requirements? Will it cause any changes to their work environment?

Schedule feasibility measures whether the established deadlines for the project are reasonable. If a deadline is not reasonable, the project leader might make a new schedule. If a deadline cannot be extended, then the scope of the project might be reduced to meet the mandatory deadline.

Technical feasibility measures whether the company has or can obtain the hardware, software, and people needed to deliver and then support the proposed information system. For most system projects, the technology exists. Hardware, software, and people typically are available to support an information system. The challenge is obtaining funds to pay for these resources. Economic feasibility addresses funding.

Economic feasibility, also called **cost/benefit feasibility**, measures whether the lifetime benefits of the proposed information system will be greater than its lifetime costs. A systems analyst uses many financial techniques, such as return on investment and payback analysis, to perform the cost/benefit analysis. If systems analysts are not familiar with these financial techniques, they can ask for assistance from a financial analyst.

Documentation

During the entire SDLC, project team members produce much documentation. **Documentation** is the collection and summarization of data and information. It includes reports, diagrams, programs, or any other deliverable generated during the SDLC.

A **project notebook** contains all documentation for a single project. The project notebook might be a simple three-ring binder. Many companies, however, have analysis and design software packages that allow you to create an automated project notebook.

Users and IT professionals refer to existing documentation when working with and modifying existing systems. It is important that all documentation is well written, thorough, and understandable. Documentation should be an ongoing part of the SDLC. Too often, project team members put off documentation because it is time consuming. They mistakenly regard it as an unimportant or unproductive part of the SDLC.

Data and Information Gathering Techniques

Throughout the SDLC, members of the project team gather data and information. They need accurate and timely data and information for many reasons. They must keep a project on schedule, evaluate feasibility, and be sure the system meets requirements. Systems analysts and other IT professionals use several techniques to gather data and information. They review documentation, observe, send questionnaires, interview, conduct joint-application design sessions, and research. The following paragraphs discuss these techniques.

- **Review documentation** – By reviewing documentation such as a company's organization chart, memos, and meeting minutes, you can learn the history of a project. Documentation also provides information about the company such as its operations, weaknesses, and strengths.
- **Observe** – Observing people helps you understand exactly how they perform a task. Likewise, observing a machine allows you to see how it works.
- **Questionnaire** – To obtain data and information from a large number of people, you could send a questionnaire.
- **Interview** – The interview is the most important data and information gathering technique. It allows you to clarify responses and probe for feedback face to face.

Web Link

For more information on project management software, visit the Discovering Computers 2002 Chapter 14 WEB LINK page (**scsite.com/dc2002/ch14/weblink.htm**) and click Project Management Software.

ISSUE

Above and Beyond

Human Behavior While Being Observed

During the data and information gathering stage of the SLDC, employees are involved actively in the process. They complete questionnaires, participate in interviews, and are observed while performing their jobs. Many researchers suggest that during this process the employees may not exhibit everyday behavior and may perform above and beyond their normal workday activities. They base this premise on the Hawthorne Effect, the result of a study performed in the 1930s in Hawthorne, Illinois, in which it was discovered that the act of merely observing individual behavior could impact one's behavior. What is your opinion of the Hawthorne Effect? Do you agree with the research? If someone is observing you at work or you were receiving more attention than normally, would this influence you to alter your behavior? Why or why not?

For more information on the Hawthorne Effect, visit the Discovering Computers 2002 Issues Web page (**scsite.com/dc2002/issues.htm**) and click Chapter 14 Issue #1.

Web Link

For more information on JAD sessions, visit the Discovering Computers 2002 Chapter 14 WEB LINK page (**scsite.com/dc2002/ch14/weblink.htm**) and click JAD Sessions.

- **JAD session** – An alternative to the one-on-one interview is a joint-application design session. A **joint-application design (JAD) session** is a lengthy, structured, group work meeting where users and IT professionals discuss an aspect of the project (Figure 14-5). The goal of a JAD session is to obtain group agreement on an issue. For example, the participants may try to identify problems associated with an existing system.
- **Research** – Newspapers, computer magazines, reference books, and the Web are excellent sources of information (Figure 14-6). These sources can provide you with information such as the latest hardware and software products and explanations of new processes and procedures.

Figure 14-5 During a JAD session, the systems analyst is the moderator, or leader, of the discussion. Another member, called the scribe, records facts and action items assigned during the session.

Figure 14-6a (reference book)

Figure 14-6b (computer magazine)

Figure 14-6c (Web site)

Figure 14-6 Reference books, computer magazines, and the Web are resources that can provide the systems analyst with a variety of valuable information.

COMPANY ON THE CUTTING EDGE

ZIFF DAVIS MEDIA™

Tech Magazines Publisher

Shopping for a new computer? Looking for winning strategies for your video games? Wanting to start an innovative e-commerce site? Chances are one of the publications produced by Ziff Davis Media is just what you need.

Ziff Davis is the leading information authority for buying, using, and experiencing technology and the Internet. It is the largest technology and Internet magazine publisher and the sixth largest magazine publisher in the United States. The company also is at the forefront in creating a new generation of consumer and business media that educate, entertain, and empower people.

In the United States, Ziff Davis Media publishes industry-leading consumer and business publications: *PC Magazine, Ziff Davis SMART BUSINESS for the New Economy, Yahoo! Internet Life, Family PC, Expedia Travels, Electronic Gaming Monthly, Official U.S. PlayStation Magazine, Computer Gaming World, Expert Gamer, eWEEK, Inter@ctive Week, Sm@rt Partner,* and *The Net Economy.* Through a joint venture with International Data Group, the company also publishes *Macworld.*

For more information on Ziff Davis Media, visit the Discovering Computers 2002 Companies Web page (**scsite.com/dc2002/companies.htm**) and click Ziff Davis.

WHAT INITIATES THE SYSTEM DEVELOPMENT LIFE CYCLE?

A user may request a new or modified information system for a variety of reasons. The most obvious reason is to correct a problem. The total salaries on a report may be incorrect. Another reason is to improve the information system. For example, if a school wants to allow students to register for classes online, it would have to modify the existing registration system to include this new feature.

Sometimes situations outside your control cause you to modify an information system. Corporate management or some other governing body may mandate a change. For example, a nationwide insurance company might require all offices to use the same calendar software. Competition also can lead to change. Once one grocery store offers online shopping, others will follow for fear of losing customers.

A user may request a new or modified information system verbally in a telephone conversation or written as an e-mail message (Figure 14-7a). In larger companies, users write a formal request for a new or modified information system, which is called a **request for system services** or **project request** (Figure 14-7b). This document becomes the first item in the project notebook. It also triggers the first phase of the SDLC: planning.

Figure 14-7a (informal project request)

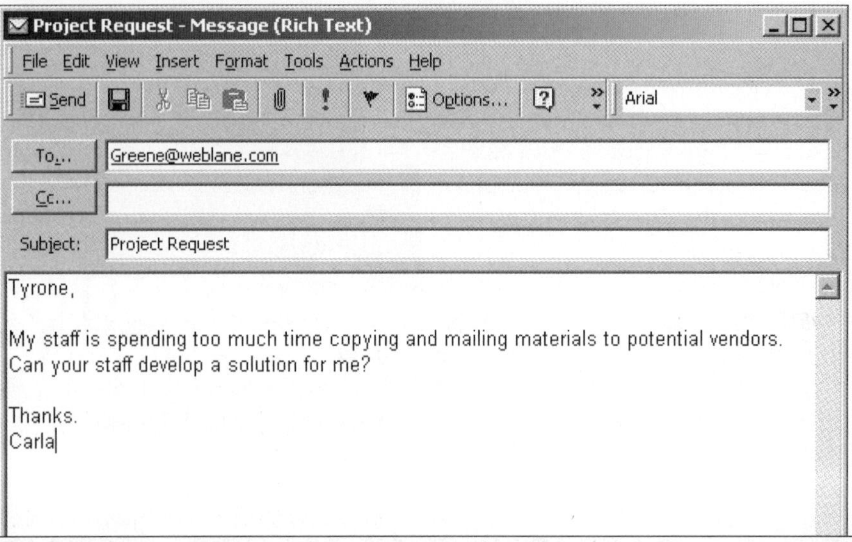

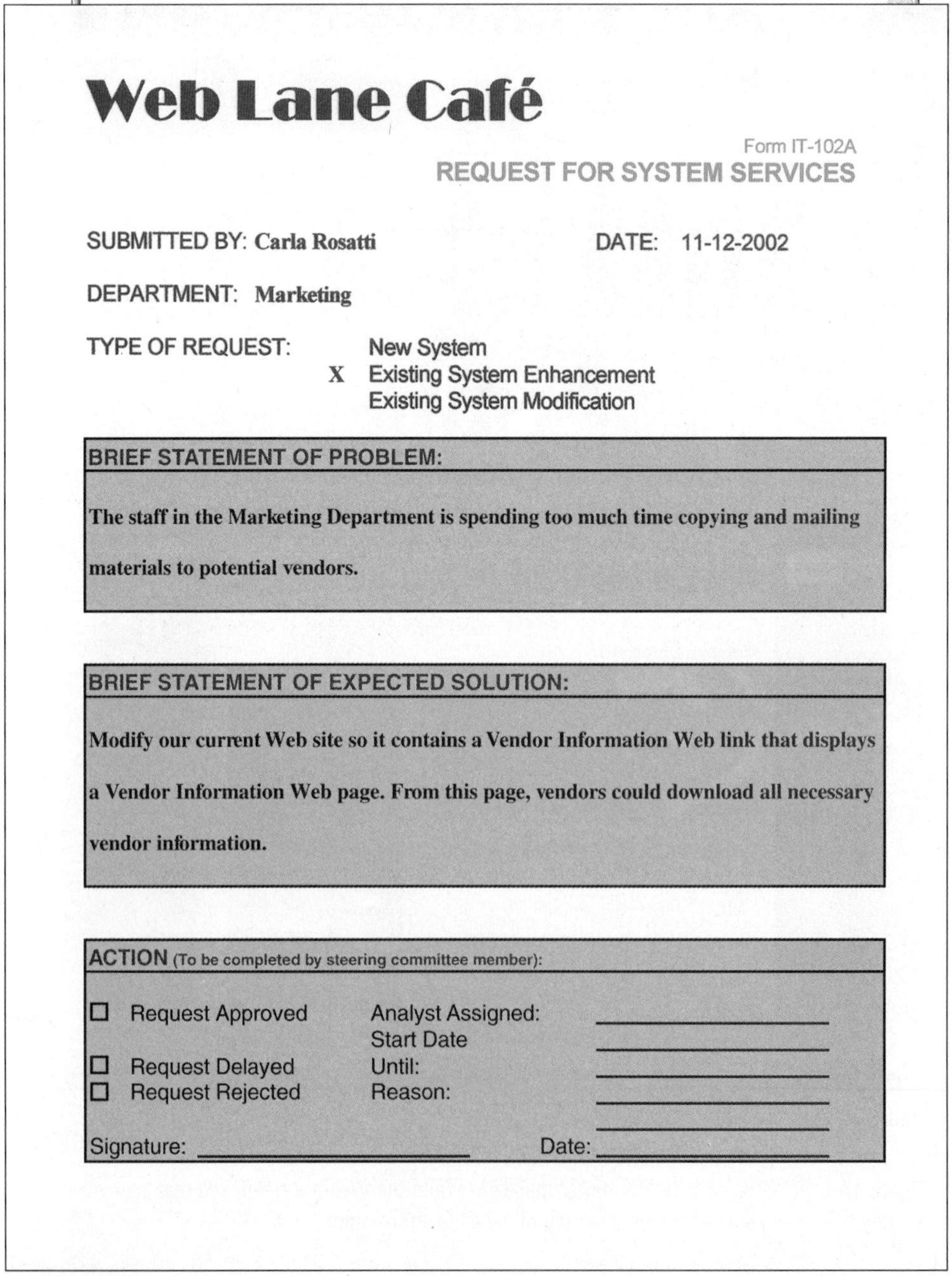

Web Lane Café

Form IT-102A

REQUEST FOR SYSTEM SERVICES

SUBMITTED BY: **Carla Rosatti** DATE: 11-12-2002

DEPARTMENT: **Marketing**

TYPE OF REQUEST:
- New System
- X Existing System Enhancement
- Existing System Modification

BRIEF STATEMENT OF PROBLEM:

The staff in the Marketing Department is spending too much time copying and mailing materials to potential vendors.

BRIEF STATEMENT OF EXPECTED SOLUTION:

Modify our current Web site so it contains a Vendor Information Web link that displays a Vendor Information Web page. From this page, vendors could download all necessary vendor information.

ACTION (To be completed by steering committee member):

☐ Request Approved — Analyst Assigned: ______ Start Date ______
☐ Request Delayed — Until: ______
☐ Request Rejected — Reason: ______

Signature: ______ Date: ______

Figure 14-7b (formal project request)

Figure 14-7 Sometimes users informally communicate a project request verbally or as an e-mail message. In larger companies, requests often are documented on a form such as this Request for System Services.

Web Lane Café — A Case Study

This chapter includes a case study to help you understand real-world SDLC applications. The case study appears shaded in yellow immediately after the discussion of each phase in the SDLC. The case is based on a fictitious company. The following paragraphs present a background on the Web Lane Café, a cybercafé. A **cybercafé** is a coffee house or restaurant that provides Web access to its customers.

Web Lane Café is a worldwide chain of cybercafés. With locations in 40 cities around the world, Web Lane Café is one of the most technologically advanced cybercafés on the planet.

At these cafés, you can do the following: connect to the Web while drinking your favorite specialty coffee or tea and eating a snack; chat with or send e-mail to co-workers, friends, and family; use Internet Explorer, Netscape, or AOL to browse the Web; and play online games or read an online book.

If customers have questions while using the computer, any staff member can provide assistance. Each café also offers training courses for beginning computer users.

Through high-speed T1 lines, customers have fast Internet access. Monitors are 19". Each café has a minimum of 15 computers, along with a color printer, a laser printer, a digital camera, and a scanner. All computers have popular productivity software such as Microsoft Office and Adobe PhotoShop. For each beverage or snack purchased, customers receive 30 minutes of free computer use — including Web access. If they would like additional computer time, the fee is $5.00 per hour.

Since Web Lane Café started operations in 1995, business has been thriving. The cafés serve thousands of customers around the world. The Web site (Figure 14-8) has hundreds of hits a day. John Simmons, chief information officer (CIO) for Web Lane Café, offers one suggestion for the company's financial success. "We do not pay for the computers

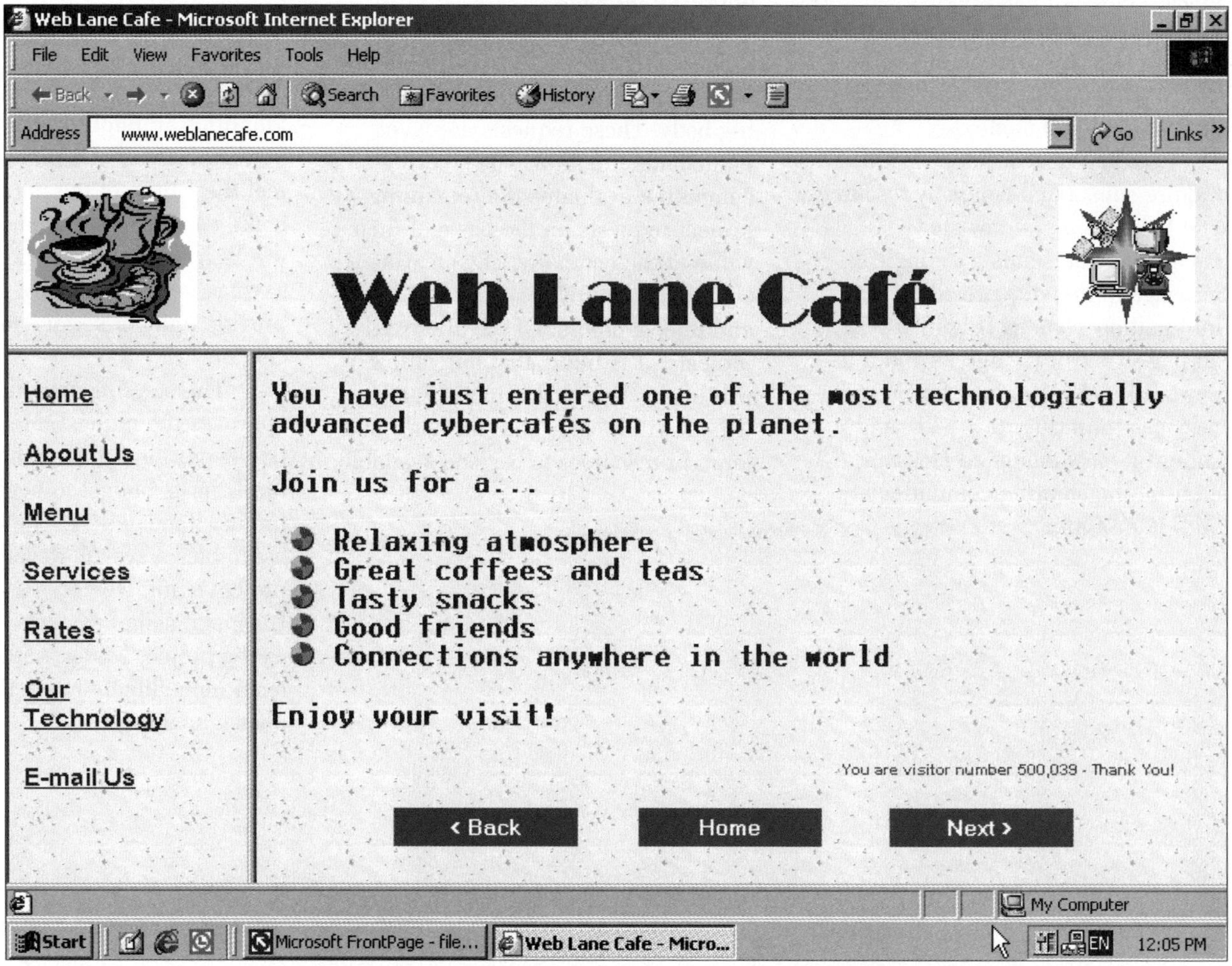

Figure 14-8 To help you better understand real-world applications of the SDLC, this chapter presents a case study about Web Lane Café. At this cybercafé, you can connect to the Web while eating a snack and drinking your favorite specialty coffee or tea.

and equipment in our cafés. Instead, we allow computer vendors to use our café as a storefront for their products. This provides customers with the opportunity to try out the hardware and software before making a purchase. When customers wish to purchase computers, we direct them to the vendor's online storefront for discount pricing."

To showcase their hardware and software in the cafés, computer vendors request information from Carla Rosatti, the marketing manager. The number of these requests is rising quickly. The cost of copying and mailing this material is becoming excessive. For this reason, Carla would like this vendor information made available on the Web. Vendors could download information sheets, press releases, photographs, and other information from the Web site. Placing this information on the Web would save Carla and her staff a great deal of time and money.

Carla realizes this task will require substantial company resources. She believes a systems study is necessary. She sends an e-mail message to the vice president of information systems (Figure 14-7a on page 14.10). He agrees and tells her to fill out a Request for System Services form (Figure 14-7b) and submit it to Mohammed Hossain, chair of the steering committee at Web Lane Café.

PLANNING PHASE

The **planning phase** for a project begins when the steering committee receives a project request. As mentioned earlier in this chapter, the steering committee is a decision-making body for a company. This committee usually consists of five to nine people. It typically includes a mix of vice presidents, managers, nonmanagement users, and IT personnel.

During the planning phase, four major activities are performed: (1) review and approve the project requests, (2) prioritize the project requests, (3) allocate resources such as money, people, and equipment to approved projects, and (4) form a project development team for each approved project.

The projects that receive the highest priority are those mandated by management or some other governing body. These requests are given immediate attention. The steering committee evaluates the remaining project requests on the basis of their value to the company. The steering committee approves some projects and rejects others. Of the approved projects, it is likely that only a few will begin their SDLC immediately. Others will have to wait for additional funds or resources to become available.

Planning at Web Lane Café

After receiving the project request (Figure 14-7b on page 14.10) from Carla, Mohammed Hossain distributes it to all members of the steering committee. They will discuss the request at their next meeting. The steering committee members of Web Lane Café are as follows: Mohammed Hossain, controller and chair of the steering committee; Tracy Houck, vice president of operations; Jesse Martinez, Webmaster; Mae Ling, training specialist; Sadie Lapinski, senior systems analyst; and Tyrone Greene, vice president of information systems. Mohammed also invites Carla Rosatti to the next steering committee meeting. Because she originated the project request, Carla will have the knowledge to answer questions.

During the meeting, the committee decides the project request identifies an improvement to the system, instead of a problem. They feel the nature of the improvement (to make vendor information available on the Web) could lead to considerable savings for the company. It also will provide quicker service to potential vendors.

The steering committee approves the request. Mohammed points out the company has enough funds in its budget to begin the project immediately. Thus, Tyrone assembles a system development project team. He assigns Sadie Lapinski, senior systems analyst, as the project leader. Sadie and her team immediately begin the next phase: analysis.

ANALYSIS PHASE

The **analysis phase** consists of two major tasks: (1) conduct a preliminary investigation and (2) perform detailed analysis. Detailed analysis has three activities: (1) study how the current system works; (2) determine the user's wants, needs, and requirements; and (3) recommend a solution.

In this phase the systems analyst must define the problem or improvement accurately. The actual problem may be different from the one suggested in the project request. For example, suppose vendors complain that the marketing department takes too long to send customer names and addresses. An investigation might reveal the marketing department is not the problem. The problem exists because some cafés wait three weeks before sending customer names and addresses to the marketing department. Thus, the preliminary investigation determines the real problem,

The Preliminary Investigation

The purpose of the **preliminary investigation**, sometimes called the **feasibility study**, is to decide whether the problem or improvement in a project request is worth pursuing. Should the company continue to assign resources to this project? To answer this question, the systems analyst conducts a very general study of the project. Then the systems analyst presents his or her findings in a report. Figure 14-9 to the right and on the next page shows a sample feasibility report, also sometimes known as the feasibility study.

WEB LANE CAFÉ

MEMORANDUM

To: **Steering Committee**
From: **Sadie Lapinski, Project Leader**
Date: **December 5, 2002**
Subject: **Feasibility Study of Vendor Web System**

Following is the feasibility study in response to the request for a modification to our Web site. Your approval is necessary before the next phase of the project will begin.

Introduction

The purpose of this feasibility report is to determine whether it is beneficial for Web Lane Café to continue studying the Vendor Web System. The marketing department manager has indicated her staff spends a considerable amount of time duplicating and distributing materials to potential vendors. This project would affect the marketing department and customer service. Also, any person that uses the Web site would notice a change.

Existing System

Background

One of the reasons for our financial success at Web Lane Café is we do not pay for the computers and equipment in our cafés. Instead, we allow computer vendors to use our café as a storefront for their products. This provides customers with the opportunity to try the hardware and software before making a purchase. When customers wish to purchase computers, we direct them to the vendor's online storefront for discount pricing.

To showcase their hardware and software in the cafés, computer vendors request information from our marketing manager. The number of these requests is rising quickly. The cost of copying and mailing this material is becoming excessive.

Problems

The following problems have been identified with the current information system at Web Lane Café:

- The time employees spend copying and duplicating vendor material is rising quickly
- Potential vendors do not receive material as quickly as in the past, which possibly could cause poor relations
- Resources are wasted including employee time, equipment usage, and supplies

Figure 14-9 A feasibility report presents the results of the preliminary investigation. The report must be prepared professionally and be well organized to be effective. *(continued on the next page)*

which is the marketing department does not have instant access to the customer names and addresses.

The first step in the preliminary investigation is to interview the user who submitted the project request. In the case of the cybercafé, the marketing manager submitted the request. Depending on the nature of the request, project team members may interview other users too. A request, for example, might involve data or a process that affects more than one department. In the case of the cybercafé, members of the team might interview the controller for costs of copying and mailing materials. They also might interview one or two vendors.

In addition to interviewing, members of the project team may use other data gathering techniques such as reviewing existing documentation. The time spent on this phase of the SDLC is quite short when compared to the remainder of the project. Often, the preliminary investigation takes just a few days.

Upon completion of the preliminary investigation, the systems analyst writes the feasibility report. This report presents the team's findings to the steering committee. The feasibility report contains these major sections: introduction, existing system, benefits of a new system, feasibility of a new system, and the recommendation.

FEASIBILITY STUDY
Page 2

Benefits of a New System

The following benefits are feasible if the Web site at Web Lane Café were modified:

- Potential vendors would be more satisfied, leading to possible long-term relations
- Supplies expenses would be reduced by 30%
- Through a more efficient use of employees' time, the company could realize a 20% reduction in temporary clerks in the marketing department
- Printers would last 50% longer, due to a much lower usage rate

Feasibility of a New System

Operational

A new system will decrease the amount of equipment use and paperwork. Vendor information will be available in an easily accessible form to any vendor. Employees will have time to complete meaningful job duties, alleviating the need to hire some temporary clerks.

Technical

Web Lane Café already has a functional Web site. To handle the increased volume of data, however, it will need to purchase a database server.

Economic

A detailed summary of the costs and benefits, including all assumptions, is attached. The potential costs of the proposed solution could range from $15,000 to $20,000. The estimated savings in supplies and postage alone will exceed $20,000.

If you have any questions on the attached detailed cost/benefit summary or require further information, please contact me.

Recommendation

Based on the findings presented in this report, we recommend a continued study of the Vendor Web System.

Figure 14-9 *(continued)*

The introduction states the purpose of the report, the problem or improvement, and the scope of the project. The existing system section describes the background of the request and the problems or limitations of the current system. The next section identifies the benefits the company will realize from the proposed solution. The feasibility section assesses operational, schedule, technical, and economic feasibility of the proposed solution. The last section recommends whether the company should continue the project.

In some cases, the project team may recommend not to continue the project. In other words, the team considers the project infeasible. If the steering committee agrees, the project ends at this point. If, however, the project team recommends continuing and the steering committee approves this recommendation, then detailed analysis begins.

Analysis: Preliminary Investigation at Web Lane Café

Sadie Lapinski, senior systems analyst and project leader, meets with Carla Rosatti to discuss the project request. During the interview, Sadie looks at the material that Carla's staff sends to a potential vendor. She asks Carla how many vendor requests she receives in a month. Then Sadie interviews the controller, Mohammed Hossain, to obtain some general cost and benefit figures for the feasibility report. She also calls a vendor. She wants to know if the material Carla's department sends is helpful.

Next, Sadie prepares the feasibility report (Figure 14-9 on pages 14.13 and 14.14). After the project team members review it, Sadie submits it to the steering committee. The report recommends continuing into the detailed analysis phase for this project. The steering committee agrees. Sadie and her team begin detailed analysis.

Detailed Analysis

Detailed analysis involves three major activities: (1) study how the current system works, (2) determine the users' wants, needs, and requirements, and (3) recommend a solution. Detailed analysis sometimes is called **logical design** because the systems analysts develop the proposed solution without regard to any specific hardware or software. That is, they make no attempt to identify the procedures that should be automated and those that should be manual.

During these activities, systems analysts use all of the data and information gathering techniques. They review documentation, observe employees and machines, send questionnaires, interview employees, conduct joint-application design (JAD) sessions, and do research. An important benefit from these activities is they build valuable relationships among the systems analysts and users. The systems analyst has much more credibility with users if he or she understands their concerns. This point may seem obvious, but some developers create or modify systems with little or no user participation.

Structured Analysis and Design Tools

While studying the current system and identifying user requirements, the systems analyst collects a lot of data and information. A major task for the systems analyst is to document these findings in a way that can be understood by everyone. Both users and IT professionals will refer to this documentation.

Structured analysis and design is a technique that attempts to address this problem by using graphics and other tools. Structured analysis and design tools include entity-relationship diagrams, data flow diagrams, and the project dictionary. The following pages discuss these tools.

TECHNOLOGY TRAILBLAZER

ED **YOURDON**

Ed Yourdon is a self-proclaimed alligator trainer, daredevil parachutist, and Himalayan mountain climber. He is recognized in the Computer Hall of Fame and by CrossTalk as one of the 10 Influential Men and Women of Software. Yourdon also is noted for developing the method of object-oriented systems analysis and design.

Yourdon is the author of more than two-dozen computer books and 200 technical articles and the publisher of *American Programmer.* As chairman of the Cutter Consortium, he helps companies build and implement successful information technology strategies.

Subscribers to his weekly e-zine, *The Yourdon Report*, can read about the latest business trends and products in the software field. His Web site contains specific "community" pages for students, software professionals and managers, and book lovers, and it contains drafts of the second edition of his classic text, *Modern Structured Analysis.*

For more information on Ed Yourdon, visit the Discovering Computers 2002 People Web page (**scsite.com/dc2002/people.htm**) and click Ed Yourdon.

Web Link

For more information on entity-relationship diagrams, visit the Discovering Computers 2002 Chapter 14 WEB LINK page (**scsite.com/dc2002/ch14/weblink.htm**) and click Entity-Relationship Diagrams.

Web Link

For more information on data flow diagrams, visit the Discovering Computers 2002 Chapter 14 WEB LINK page (**scsite.com/dc2002/ch14/weblink.htm**) and click Data Flow Diagrams.

ENTITY-RELATIONSHIP DIAGRAMS

An **entity-relationship diagram** (**ERD** or **E-R diagram**) is a tool that graphically shows the connections between entities in a system (Figure 14-10). An **entity** is an object in the system that has data. For example, a cybercafé might have customer, order, menu item, computer, and vendor entities.

On the ERD, entity names usually are nouns. You write the entity name in all capital letters. Each relationship describes a connection between two entities. In Figure 14-10 a vendor supplies one or more computers to the cafés. A computer is supplied by a single vendor. A customer may or may not sit down and use one of these computers during a visit to the café. A customer, however, places an order. Some customers place multiple orders. Each order contains one or more items from the menu.

It is important the systems analyst has an accurate understanding of the system. The systems analyst reviews the ERD with the user. Once users approve the ERD, the systems analyst identifies data items associated with an entity. For example, the VENDOR entity might have these data items: Vendor Number, Vendor Name, Vendor Contact Name, Address, City, State, Postal Code, Telephone Number, and E-mail Address.

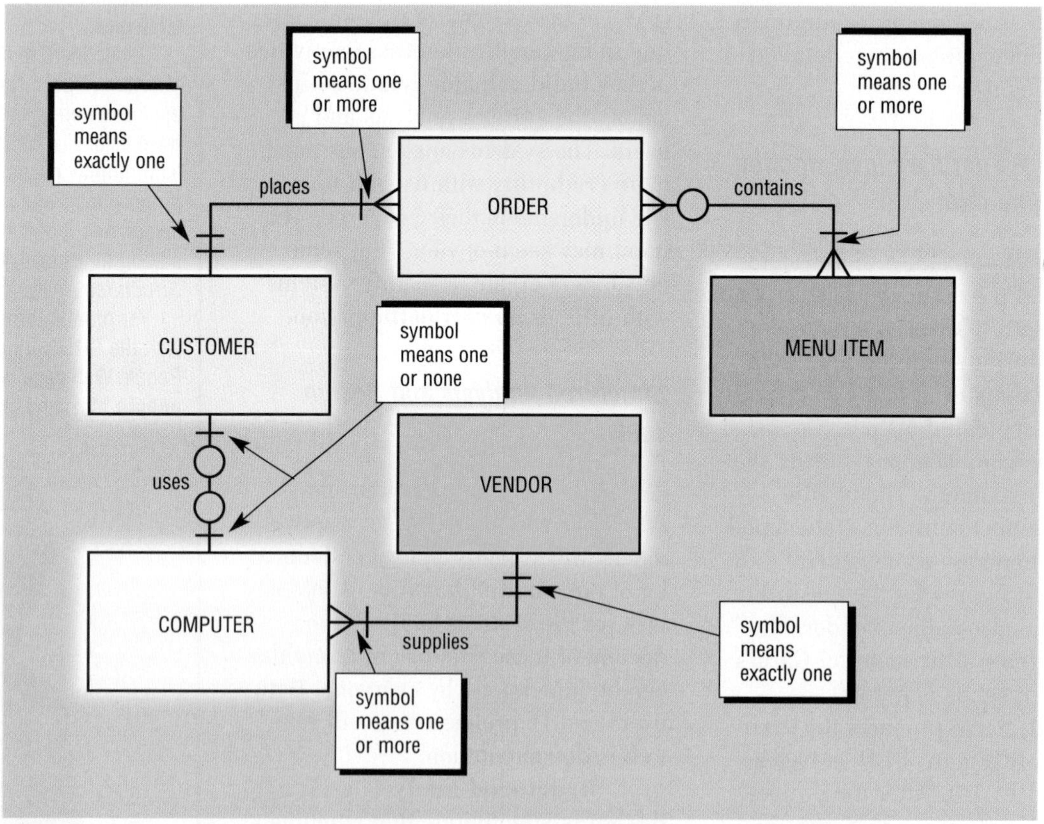

Figure 14-10 This ERD shows the relationships among entities in the Vendor Web System at Web Lane Café. A vendor supplies one or more computers to the cafés. A computer is supplied by a single vendor. A customer may or may not sit down and use one of these computers during a visit to the café. A customer, however, places an order. Some customers place multiple orders. Each order contains one or more items from the menu.

DATA FLOW DIAGRAMS A **data flow diagram (DFD)** is a tool that graphically shows the flow of data in a system. The key elements of a DFD are the data flows, the processes, the data stores, and the sources (Figure 14-11). A line with an arrow indicates a data flow. A **data flow** shows the input or output of data or information into or out from a process. A **process**, which is drawn as a circle, transforms an input data flow into an output data flow. A rectangle with no sides is a data store. A **data store** is a holding place for data and information. Examples of data stores are filing cabinets, checkbook registers, or electronic files in a computer. The squares on the DFD are sources. A **source**, or **agent**, identifies an entity outside the scope of the system. Sources send data into the system or receive information from the system.

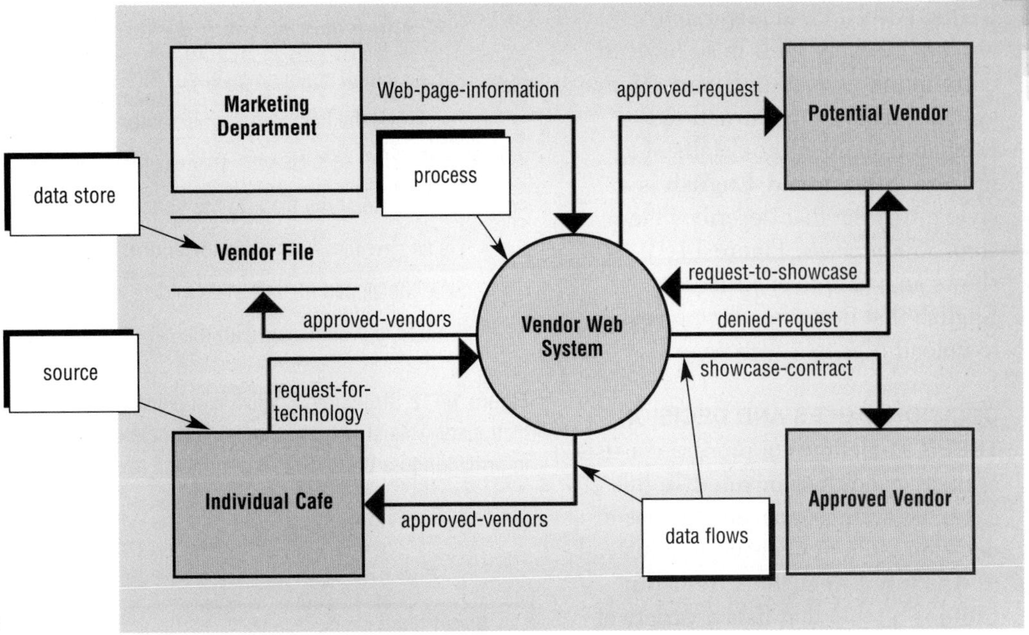

Figure 14-11 This data flow diagram, called the context diagram, has one process — the Vendor Web System being studied at Web Lane Café. The Vendor File is a data store. Sources both send and receive data and information to and from the system. For example, a café sends a request for technology (hardware and/or software) into the Vendor Web System. The Vendor Web System sends out a list of approved vendors for that technology. The list of approved vendors also is stored in the Vendor File.

Like ERDs, systems analysts often use DFDs to review processes with users. Systems analysts prepare DFDs on a level-by-level basis. The top level DFD, known as a **context diagram**, identifies only the major process. The context diagram shows the system being studied. Lower-level DFDs add detail and definition to the higher levels, similarly to zooming in on a computer screen. The lower-level DFDs then contain subprocesses. For example, Figure 14-11 shows a context diagram that contains the Vendor Web System process. This process might be split into three subprocesses: (1) gathering and organizing vendor information, (2) converting vendor information into electronic format, and (3) uploading the files to the Web page.

PROJECT DICTIONARY The **project dictionary**, sometimes called the **repository**, contains all the documentation and deliverables of a project. The project dictionary helps everyone keep track of the huge amount of details in a system. The dictionary begins with the project request and includes diagrams such as the ERD and DFDs.

Another section of the dictionary explains every item found on these diagrams. Each process, data store, data flow, and source on every DFD has an entry in the project dictionary. Every entity on the ERD has an entry in the project dictionary. The dictionary also contains an entry for each data item associated with the entities. Some systems can be represented with 25 or more DFDs and have hundreds of data items.

The number of entries added to the dictionary at this point can be enormous. As you might imagine, this activity requires a tremendous amount of time.

The system analyst uses a variety of techniques to enter these items in the project dictionary. Some of these include structured English, decision tables and decision trees, and the data dictionary.

Web Link

For more information on the project dictionary, visit the Discovering Computers 2002 Chapter 14 WEB LINK page (**scsite.com/dc2002/ch14/weblink.htm**) and click Project Dictionary.

STRUCTURED ENGLISH Each process on every DFD must have an entry in the project dictionary. Many systems analysts use structured English to explain the details of a process. **Structured English** is a style of writing that describes the steps in a process. Figure 14-12 shows an example of structured English that describes the process to upload files to a Web page.

UPLOADING VENDOR INFORMATION

For each item containing vendor information, perform the following steps:

 If the item is not a computer file then

  Use the scanner to convert it into a file format.

 Copy the file into the Vendor Information folder on your hard disk.

Zip all new files in the Vendor Information folder into a single file.

Save the zipped file in a Web folder.

E-mail the Webmaster with the name of the zipped file.

Figure 14-12 Structured English is a technique used to describe a process in the project dictionary. This structured English example describes the process of uploading vendor information to a Web page. The indented text is part of the loop.

DECISION TABLES AND DECISION TREES Sometimes, a process consists of many conditions or rules. In this case, the systems analyst may use a decision table or decision tree instead of structured English. A **decision table** is a table that lists a variety of conditions and the actions that correspond to each condition. A **decision tree** also shows conditions and actions, but it shows them graphically. Figures 14-13 and 14-14 show a decision table and decision tree for the same process: determining how to package files so the vendor can download them.

		RULES							
		1	2	3	4	5	6	7	8
CONDITIONS	Background check results (S = Satisfactory, U = Unsatisfactory)	S	S	S	S	U	U	U	U
	References furnished?	Y	Y	N	N	Y	Y	N	N
	Passed credit check?	Y	N	Y	N	Y	N	Y	N
ACTIONS	Vendor approved	X							
	Vendor not approved					X	X	X	X
	Waiting for additional information		X	X	X				

Figure 14-13 This decision table describes the policy for determining whether vendors are approved to showcase their products at Web Lane Café. A vendor is approved if they meet all conditions in Rule #1. For example, vendors are approved if their background check results are satisfactory, they have furnished all of their references, and have passed a credit check.

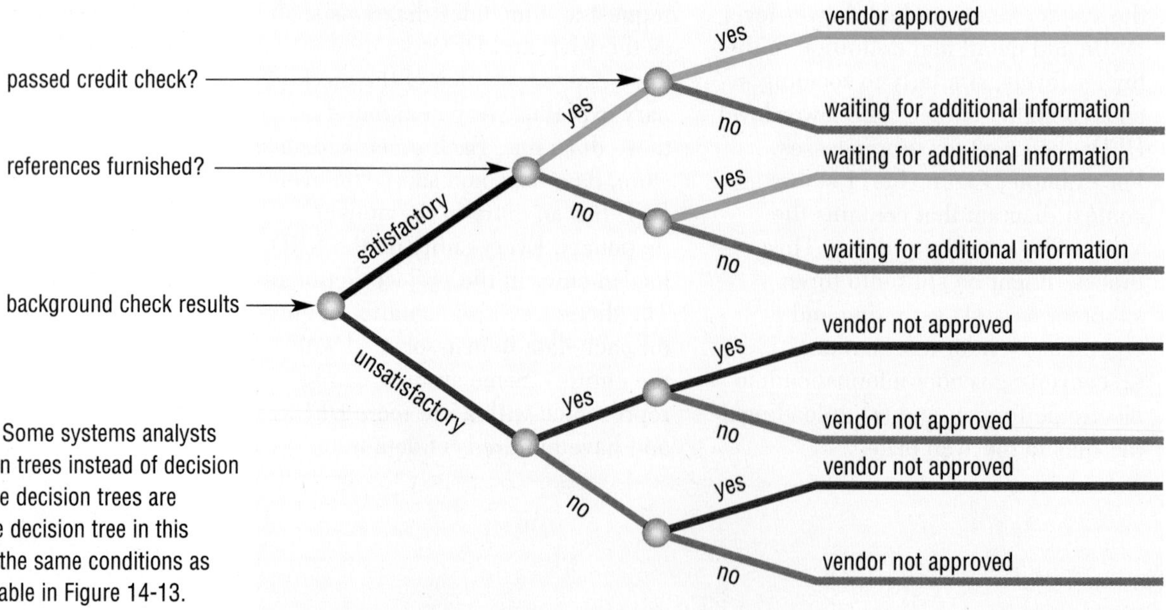

Figure 14-14 Some systems analysts prefer decision trees instead of decision tables because decision trees are graphical. The decision tree in this figure shows the same conditions as the decision table in Figure 14-13.

DATA DICTIONARY Each data item has an entry in the data dictionary section of the project dictionary (Figure 14-15). As discussed earlier in this chapter, the **data dictionary** stores the data item's name, description, and other details about each data item. The systems analyst creates the data dictionary during detailed analysis. In later phases of the SDLC, the systems analyst refers to and updates the data dictionary.

The System Proposal

At this point, the systems analyst has studied the current system and determined all user requirements. The next step is to communicate possible solutions for the project in a system proposal. The purpose of the **system proposal** is to assess the feasibility of each alternative solution and then recommend the most feasible solution for the project. The systems analyst re-evaluates feasibility at this point in the SDLC, especially economic feasibility. The systems analyst presents the system proposal to the steering committee. If the steering committee approves a solution, the project enters the design phase.

When the steering committee discusses the system proposal and decides which alternative to pursue, it often is deciding whether to buy packaged software from an outside source, build its own custom software, or hire an outside firm to handle more or all of its IT needs.

PACKAGED SOFTWARE **Packaged software**, sometimes called **commercial off-the-shelf software**, is pre-written software available for purchase. Packaged software is available for different types of computers. Chapter 3 presented

Date: 12/19/2002 *Project:* WEB LANE CAFE *Page:* 11
Time: 10:36:28 AM

Detailed Listing -- Alphabetically
All Entries -- Data Flow Diagrams

Vendor-ID Data Element
Vendor File::Vendor-ID
Description:
A unique identification number assigned to each vendor.
Alias:
Vendor Code
Values & Meanings:
Required element
Cannot be blank
May not be duplicated
Data element attributes
Storage Type: Char
Length: 4
Display Format: AAAA
Null Type: NotNull
Location:
File --> Vendor File
Date Last Altered: 12/19/2002 *Date Created:* 12/19/2002

Figure 14-15 The data dictionary records information about each of the data items that make up the data flows and entities in the system. This is a dictionary entry for the Vendor ID data element.

ISSUE

Why Should We Change?

The System Proposal and Changing Requirements

Following completion of the analysis phase of the SDLC, the systems analyst submits a written report. This report explains why an investigation of the current system was performed, describes the problems that were found, outlines possible solutions, and the actions recommended. Some authorities find that after the report is completed, the analysts resist any changes suggested by the user. Why do you think this is true? Under what circumstances should an analyst consider changes recommended by a user? Why? Should suggested changes ever be ignored? Why or why not?

For more information on the system proposal, visit the Discovering Computers 2002 Issues Web page (**scsite.com/dc2002/issues.htm**) and click Chapter 14 Issue #2.

numerous application packages available for personal computers. These include word processing, spreadsheet, database, desktop publishing, paint/image editing, Web page authoring, personal finance, legal, tax preparation, educational/reference, e-mail, and Web browser software.

Vendors offer two types of packaged software: horizontal and vertical. **Horizontal market software** is software that meets the needs of many different types of companies. The applications presented in Chapter 3 were horizontal. If a company has a unique way of accomplishing activities, then it also may require vertical market software. **Vertical market software** is software specifically designed for a particular business or industry. Examples of companies that use vertical market software include real estate offices, libraries, dental offices, insurance companies, and construction firms. Each of these industries has unique information processing requirements.

Horizontal market software packages tend to be widely available because a large number of companies use them. Thus, they typically are less expensive than vertical market software packages. You can search for names and vendors of vertical and horizontal market packages on the Web simply by entering your requirement as the search criteria (Figure 14-16). Other sources for names of vendors include computer magazines and trade publications. A **trade publication** is a magazine written for a specific business or industry. Companies and individuals who have written software for these industries often advertise in trade publications.

CUSTOM SOFTWARE Instead of buying packaged software, some companies opt to write their own applications. Application software developed by the user or at the user's request is called **custom software**. With so many software packages

Web Link

For more information on vertical market software, visit the Discovering Computers 2002 Chapter 14 WEB LINK page (**scsite.com/dc2002/ch14/weblink.htm**) and click Vertical Market Software.

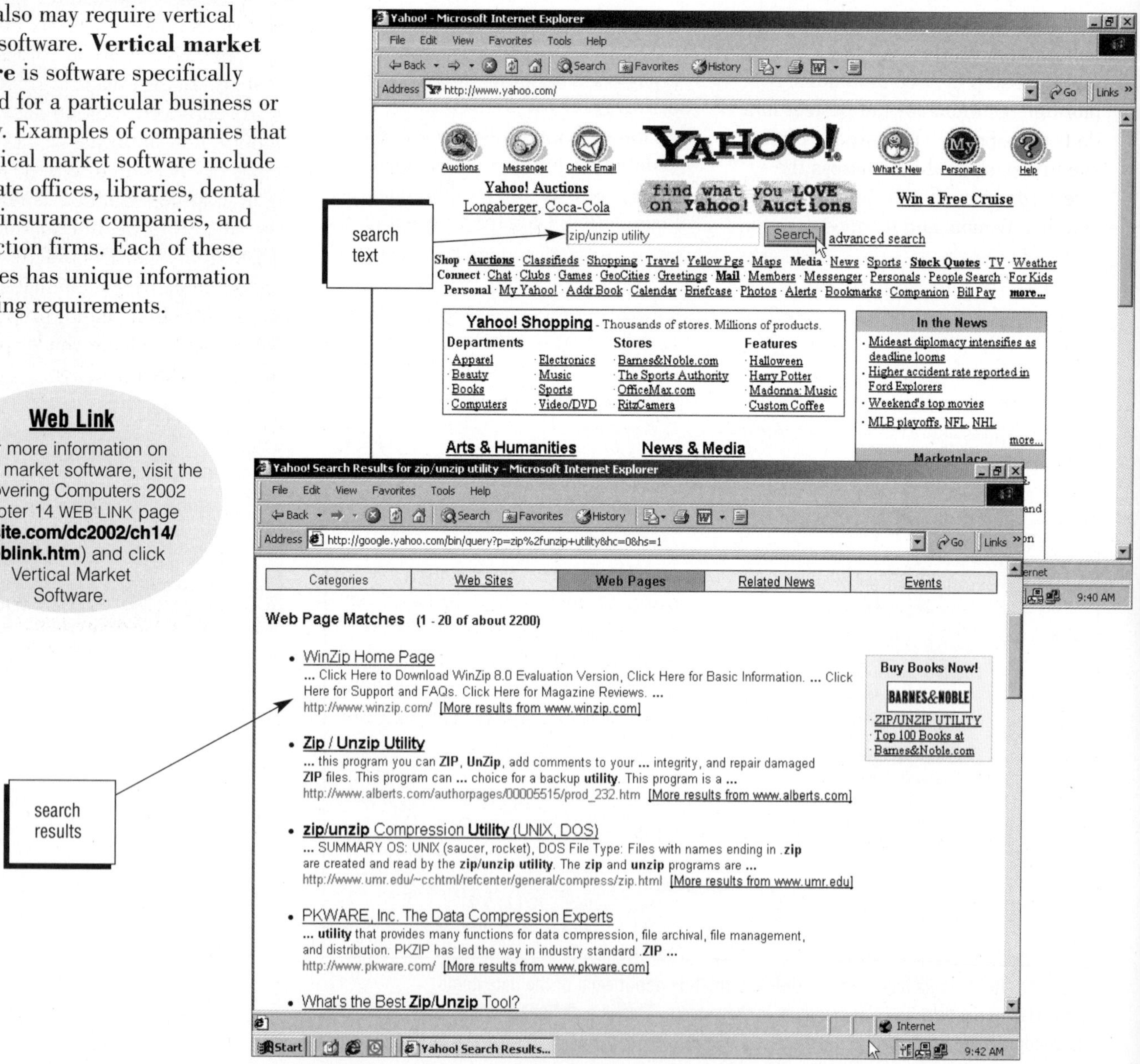

Figure 14-16 You can use Yahoo! or any other search engine on the Internet to locate vendors of application software packages. This search of zip/unzip utilities returned thousands of matches.

available, why would a company choose to write its own application software? Sometimes a company cannot find a package that meets all its needs because its software requirements are so unique. The company can develop the software in-house using its own IT personnel or have an outside source develop it for them.

The main advantage of custom software is it matches the company's requirements exactly. The disadvantages are usually it is more expensive and takes longer to design and implement than packaged software.

SOLUTIONS PROVIDERS Instead of outsourcing just the software portion of a project, some companies outsource more or all of their IT operation. They do this to remain competitive in this age of constantly changing technology. Every company should have a Web site that includes the latest technology. Many IT departments do not have the expertise to manage an entire Web operation, so they hire a firm that dedicates themselves to providing these special services.

Depending on your needs, solutions providers can handle as much or as little of your IT requirements as you desire. They can provide hardware and software. Some provide office space. Others provide a variety of services such as Web design and development, Web hosting, sales, marketing, billing, customer service, and legal assistance. A solutions provider that specializes in assisting Web-based companies with starting business operations often is called an **incubator**.

Detailed Analysis at Web Lane Café

Sadie and her team begin performing the activities in the detailed analysis phase of the Vendor Web System. As part of the study and requirements activities, they use several of the data and information gathering techniques available to them. They interview employees throughout the company and meet with some vendors. They observe the marketing staff copy and mail vendor information. They prepare many documents to record their findings: an entity-relationship diagram (see Figure 14-10 on page 14.16), a data flow diagram (see Figure 14-11 on page 14.17), a process specification using structured English (see Figure 14-12 on page 14.18), a process specification using a decision table (see Figure 14-13 on page 14.18), and a data dictionary entry for the Vendor-ID data item (see Figure 14-15 on page 14.19). These documents all become part of the project notebook. Members of the project team refer to these documents during the remainder of the SDLC.

After two months of studying the existing system and obtaining user requirements, Sadie discusses her findings with her supervisor, Tyrone Green. Sadie recommends their current Web site now include a link to Vendor Information. When someone clicks this link, a Vendor Information page will display. This Web page should contain all information that the marketing department usually sends to a vendor.

Based on Sadie's findings, Tyrone writes a system proposal for the steering committee to review. Jesse Martinez, Webmaster at Web Lane Café, developed the current Web site. Thus, Tyrone recommends that Jesse's staff modify the Web site in house. Tyrone also recommends Web Lane Café invest in a larger database server to handle the additional vendor information.

The steering committee agrees with Tyrone's proposal. Sadie and her team begin the design phase of the project.

DESIGN PHASE

The **design phase** consists of two major activities: (1) if necessary, acquire hardware and software and (2) develop all of the details of the new or modified information system. The systems analyst often performs these two activities at the same time instead of sequentially.

Acquiring Necessary Hardware and Software

Once the steering committee approves a solution, the systems analyst begins the activity to obtain additional hardware or software. The systems analyst may skip this activity if the approved solution does not require new hardware or software. If this activity is required, the selection of appropriate products is crucial for the success of the information system. The activity consists of four major tasks: (1) identify technical specifications, (2) solicit vendor proposals, (3) test and evaluate vendor proposals, and (4) make a decision.

Web Link

For more information on incubators, visit the Discovering Computers 2002 Chapter 14 WEB LINK page (**scsite.com/dc2002/ch14/weblink.htm**) and click Incubators.

Identifying Technical Specifications

The first step in acquiring necessary hardware and software is to identify all the hardware and software requirements of the new or modified system. To do this, the systems analysts use a variety of research techniques. They talk with other systems analysts, visit vendors' stores, and surf the Web. Many printed trade journals, newspapers, and magazines provide some or all of their printed content as e-zines (Figure 14-17). An **e-zine** (pronounced ee-zeen), or **electronic magazine**, is a publication available on the Web. By using the Web, the systems analyst can locate information more quickly and easily than in the past.

Once the systems analyst defines the technical requirements, the next step is to summarize these requirements for potential vendors. The systems analyst can use three basic types of documents for this purpose. A **request for quotation** (**RFQ**) identifies the product(s) you want. With an RFQ, the vendor quotes a price for the listed product(s).

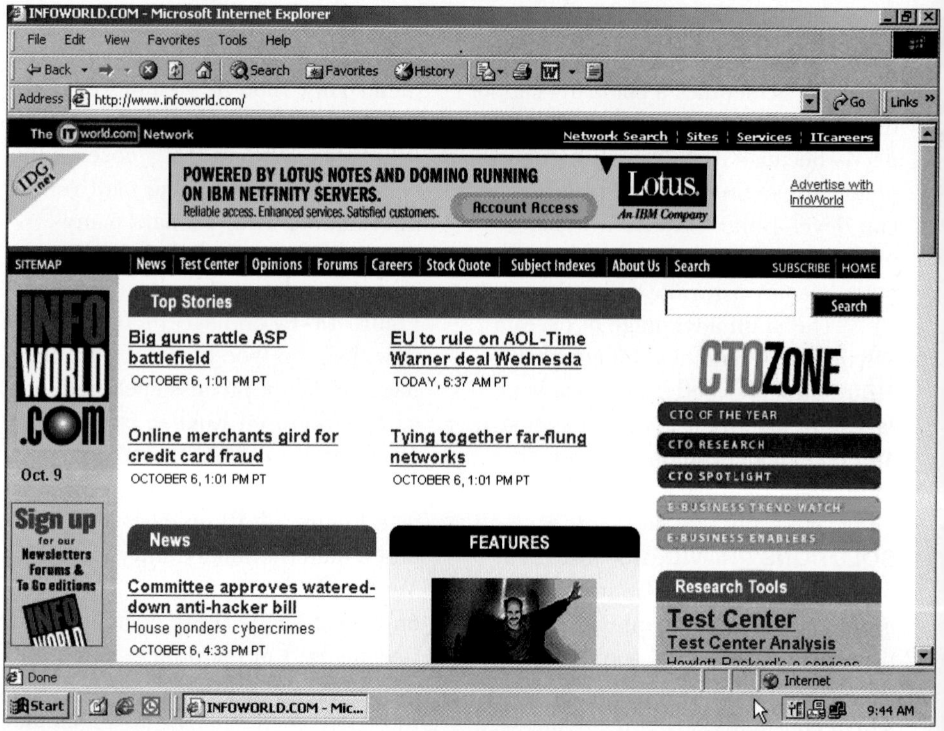

Figure 14-17 The systems analyst can save much time by researching on the Internet. Many printed trade journals and magazines, such as the one shown in this figure, provide some or all of their content as e-zines on the Web.

Web Link

For more information on e-zines, visit the Discovering Computers 2002 Chapter 14 WEB LINK page (**scsite.com/dc2002/ch14/weblink.htm**) and click E-Zines.

APPLY IT!

Searching for Magazines, Newspapers, and Companies

As you progress through your educational pursuits, you will encounter many instances where your instructor will require you to do some research for a term paper or other project. Or, perhaps you have a personal project for which you need some information. You may be familiar with and use popular search engines such as Yahoo!, Alta Vista, and others. You may be unaware, however, that many specialty search sites also exist. The three following described specialty sites provide links to current articles and may be useful especially if your topic is business or information technology.

- **InfoJump** (see URL below) – A search engine for magazines and newspapers; contains links to more than five million newspaper/magazine articles and a database of more than 4,000 electronic periodicals.
- **1st Headlines** (see URL below) – A site that links to thousands of headline news stories each day from more than 300 newspapers, broadcasts, and online sources; users also can browse current stories in any other topic area.
- **WorldWide Business Exchange** (see URL below) – A site that contains links to more than 60,000 companies listed by name, city, state, postal code, area code, county, and by SIC code; includes e-mail address and products and services offered by each company.

For more information on search engines and the Web sites mentioned above, visit the Discovering Computers 2002 Apply It Web page (**scsite.com/dc2002/apply.htm**) and click Chapter 14 Apply It #2.

With a **request for proposal (RFP)**, the vendor selects the product(s) that meets your requirements and then quotes the price(s). Several software packages exist that assist you in creating a professional RFP. Just as the depth of an information system varies, so does the length of an RFQ or RFP. Some can be as short as a couple of pages. Others consist of more than one hundred pages. Instead of an RFQ or RFP, some companies prefer to use a request for information. A **request for information (RFI)** is a less formal method that uses a standard form to request information about a product or service.

Soliciting Vendor Proposals

You send the RFQ, RFP, or RFI to potential hardware and software vendors. The systems analyst has a variety of ways to locate vendors. Many vendors publish their product catalogs on the Internet. These online catalogs provide you with up-to-date and easy access to products, prices, technical specifications, and ordering information (Figure 14-18). If you are unable to locate a vendor on the Internet, you could visit local computer stores or contact computer manufacturers.

Another source for hardware and software products is a value-added reseller. A **value-added reseller (VAR)** is a company that purchases products from manufacturers and then resells these products to the public – offering additional services with the product. Examples of additional services include user support, equipment maintenance, training, installation, and warranties. A **warranty** is a guarantee that a product will function properly for a specified time period. If the product is defective or does not function properly, the warranty specifies how it will be repaired or replaced. Warranties from VARs generally are better than those provided by individual vendors.

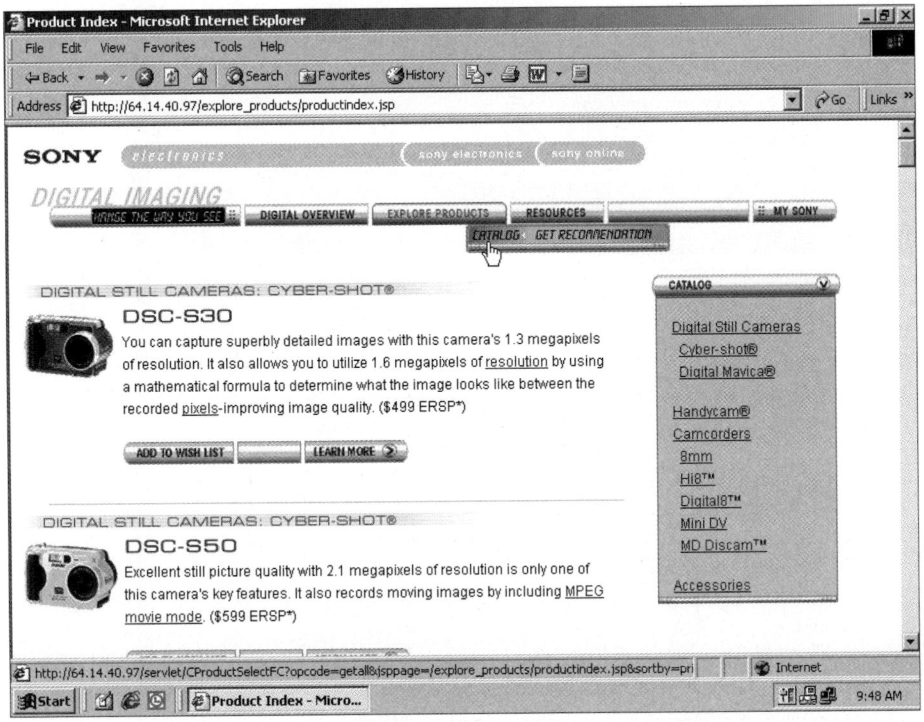

Figure 14-18 Many hardware and software vendors post their product and services catalogs on the Web. This figure shows Sony's digital imaging catalog.

Web Link

For more information on a request for proposal, visit the Discovering Computers 2002 Chapter 14 WEB LINK page (**scsite.com/dc2002/ch14/weblink.htm**) and click Request for Proposal.

APPLY IT!

Evaluating Warranties

When a company makes a large hardware purchase, they solicit and evaluate proposals. A warranty is an important element within the proposal and is one of the main considerations a company uses to judge which proposal to accept. You can use and apply this same process. Suppose you are ready to purchase a computer. You have made some basic decisions about the amount of memory, the speed of the processor, the monitor size, and more. The three vendors you are considering include Compaq, Dell, and Gateway. Your next step is a comparison of the warranties. Think about the following items before you make your final decision:

- **Time limit** – Does the vendor offer a one-year, two-year, or other extended warranty? Can you purchase additional time?
- **Effective date** – When does the warranty become effective? From the date of purchase? From the date of receipt?
- **Coverage** – What specifically does the warranty cover? Software? Additional hardware that you may have purchased?
- **Return** – If you return the computer for repair, for what arrangements and costs are you responsible? Can you return equipment to a local store? If you must ship it, who pays the shipping charges? What about insurance? If required, who is responsible for this cost?
- **Used parts** – Does the vendor replace defective parts with reconditioned parts?

For more information on warranties, visit the Discovering Computers 2002 Apply It Web page (**scsite.com/dc2002/apply.htm**) and click Chapter 14 Apply It #3.

To be an authorized VAR, most manufacturers have requirements the VAR must meet. Various terms that identify a VAR's relationship with a manufacturer are strategic partner, business partner, authorized reseller, or solutions provider. Some VARs offer one product or service. Others provide complete systems, also known as a **turnkey solution** (Figure 14-19). The advantage of a full-service VAR is you deal with only one company for an entire system.

Instead of dealing with the vendor, some companies hire a computer consultant. Many consultants specialize in configuring hardware and software for businesses of all sizes. For a reliable consultant reference, contact a professional organization in your industry, a local university, the yellow pages, the Web, or a local newspaper.

Testing and Evaluating Vendor Proposals

After sending RFQs and RFPs to potential vendors, you will receive completed quotations and proposals. A difficult task is to evaluate the proposals and then select the best one. Many systems analysts use a scoring system to rate each proposal. It is important to be as objective as possible while rating each proposal.

You can use many techniques to test the various software products from vendors. Obtain a list of user references from the software vendors. Talk to current users of the software for their opinions. Ask the vendor for a demonstration of the product(s) specified. If you wish to test the software yourself, ask the vendor if they have a demonstration copy. Some

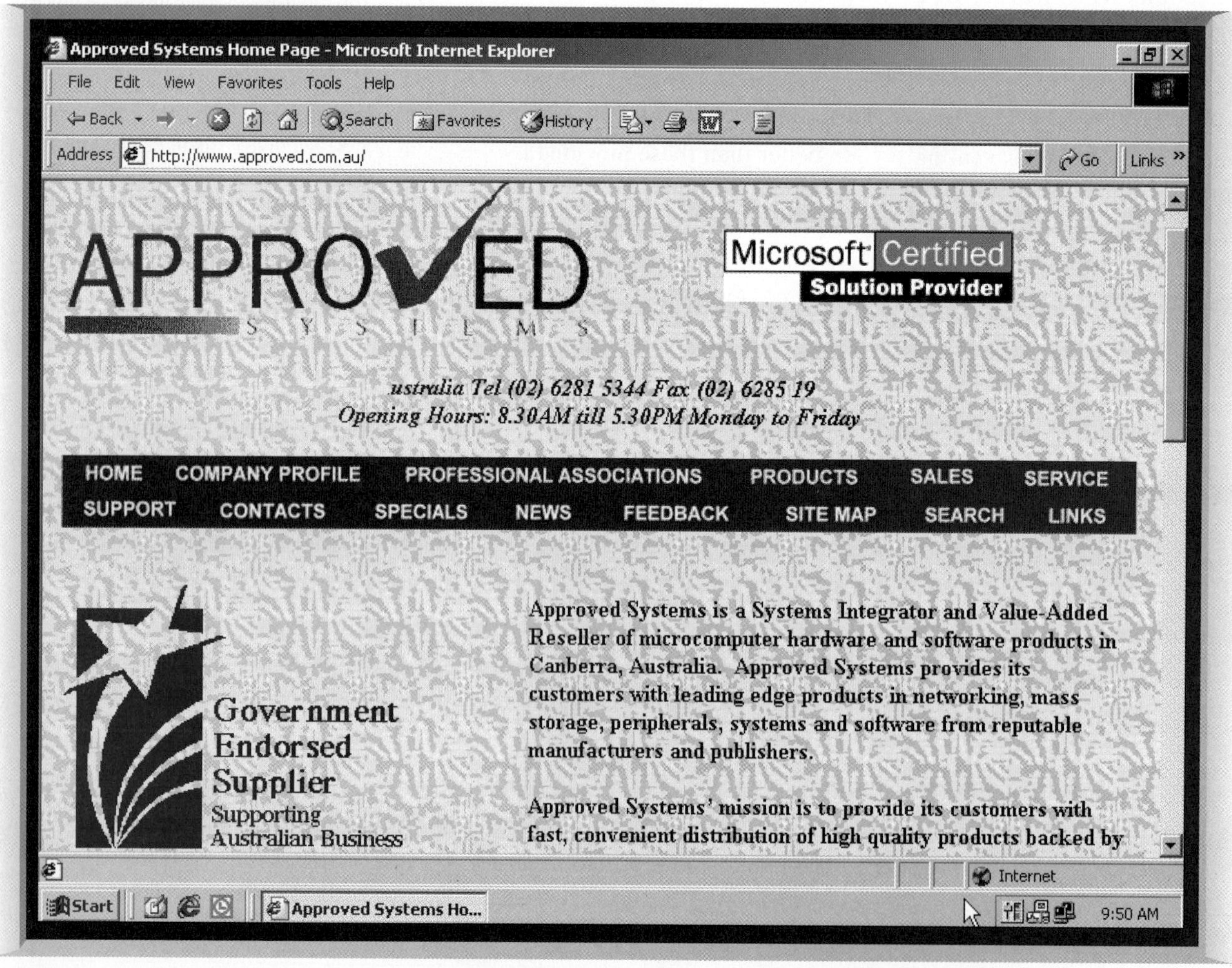

Figure 14-19 When searching for hardware and software vendors, the Internet is an excellent resource. Many VARs advertise their services on the Internet. This figure shows the home page for Approved Systems, which provides complete systems to Australian businesses.

vendors even allow you to download or run a demonstration copy directly from their Web site (Figure 14-20).

You may be concerned about whether the software can handle a certain volume of transactions efficiently. In this case, you can conduct a benchmark test. A **benchmark test** measures the performance of hardware or software. For example, a benchmark test could measure the time it takes a payroll package to print 50 paychecks. Comparing the time it takes various accounting packages to print the same 50 paychecks is one way of measuring each package's performance. Some computer magazines conduct benchmark tests while evaluating hardware and software and then publish these results for consumers to review.

Making a Decision

Having rated the proposals, the systems analyst presents a recommendation to the steering committee. The recommendation could be to award a contract to a vendor or to not make any purchases at this time.

Web Link

For more information on benchmark tests, visit the Discovering Computers 2002 Chapter 14 WEB LINK page (**scsite.com/dc2002/ch14/weblink.htm**) and click Benchmark Tests.

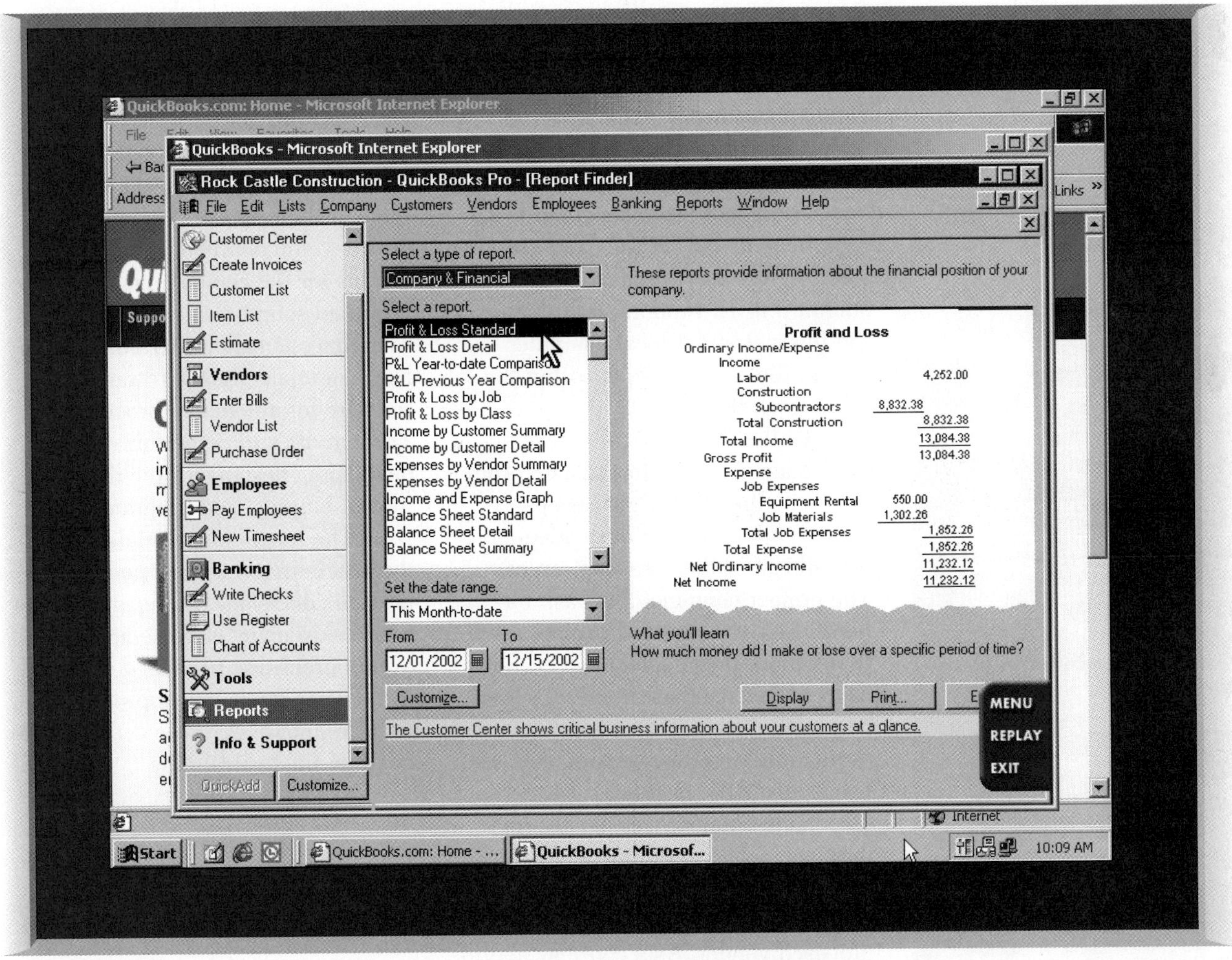

Figure 14-20 Many times, you will want to test software. Some vendors allow you to run a demonstration copy directly from their Web site. For example, Intuit has a demo of QuickBooks.

When you purchase hardware, you own it. When you purchase software, you do not. With software, you purchase an end-user license agreement. An **end-user license agreement (EULA)** gives you the legal right to use the software under certain terms and conditions (Figure 14-21). Most license agreements state the software may not be used on more than one computer or by more than one user. Other license restrictions include copying the software, modifying it, or translating it to another language. These restrictions protect the rights of software developers, who do not want someone else to benefit unfairly from their work.

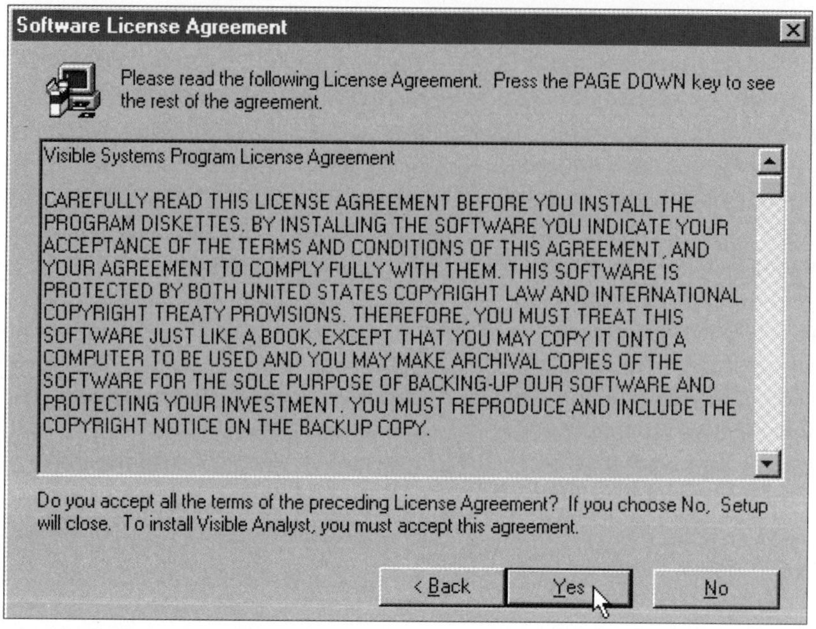

Figure 14-21 When you install software, you must accept the terms of the end-user license agreement.

ISSUE

Software Piracy

Software Licenses and the Law

Software piracy occurs whenever a software program is installed, downloaded from the Internet or another computer, or copied without a proper license from the software manufacturer. If you purchase a license for a software program, you have the right to install that software on one computer and to make a backup copy for archival purposes. In the workplace, two types of software piracy exist: installing a single purchased copy onto several computers and making an extra copy to take home. Do you think this is a fair law? Why or why not? Do you think that software piracy within the workplace is a common practice? How can companies prevent software piracy?

For more information on software piracy, visit the Discovering Computers 2002 Issues Web page (**scsite.com/dc2002/issues.htm**) and click Chapter 14 Issue #3.

Design: Hardware Acquisition at Web Lane Café

Sadie and her team compile a requirements list for the database server. They prepare an RFP and submit it to 12 vendors: 8 through the Internet and 4 local computer stores. Ten vendors reply within the three-week deadline.

Of the 10 replies, the development team selects 2 to evaluate. They eliminate the other eight because these vendors did not offer adequate warranties for the database server. The project team members ask for benchmark test results for each server. In addition, they contact two current users of this database server for their opinions on its performance. After evaluating these two servers, the team selects the best one.

Sadie summarizes her team's findings in a report to the steering committee. The committee gives Sadie authorization to award a contract to the proposed vendor. As a courtesy and to maintain good working relationships, Sadie sends a letter to all 12 vendors informing them of their decision.

Detailed Design

Once you identify the data and process requirements, the next step is to develop detailed design specifications for the components in the proposed solution. A detailed design sometimes is called **physical design** because it specifies hardware and software for automated procedures. The activities to be performed include developing designs for the databases, inputs, outputs, and programs.

The length and complexity of these activities varies depending on previous decisions. For example, you would skip many of these activities when purchasing packaged software. If the company is developing custom software, however, these activities can be quite time consuming.

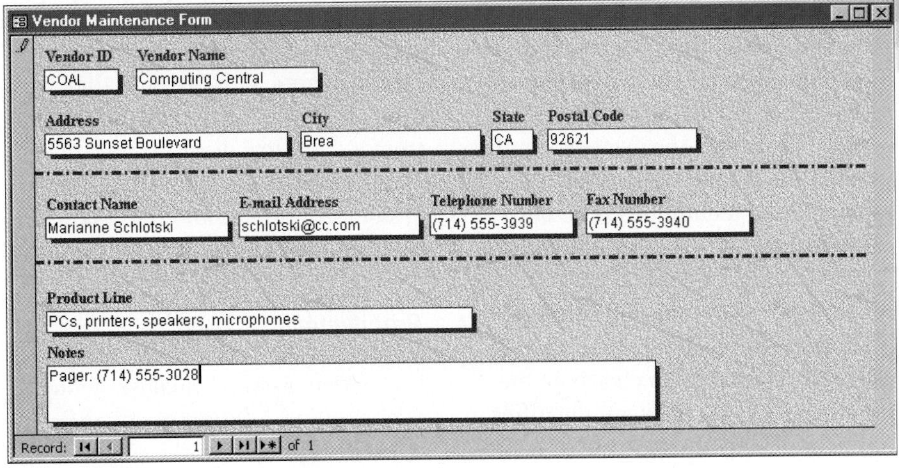

Figure 14-22 Users must give their approval on all inputs and outputs. This input screen is a mockup (containing actual data) for the user to review.

DATABASE DESIGN Data is one of the most valuable resources in an information system. Thus, it is crucial the content of the data dictionary be current, consistent, and correct. During database design, the systems analyst builds upon the data dictionary developed during the analysis phase. The dictionary should represent accurately the data requirements of the company. The systems analyst works closely with the database analysts and administrators to identify those data elements that currently exist within the company and those that are new.

With relational database systems, the systems analyst defines the structure of each table in the system, as well as relationships among the tables. The systems analyst also addresses user access privileges. This means the systems analyst defines which data elements each user can access, when they can access the data elements, what actions they can perform on the data elements, and under what circumstances they can access the elements. The systems analyst also considers the volume of database activity. For example, large, frequently accessed tables may be organized in a manner so that the database processes requests in an acceptable time frame.

INPUT AND OUTPUT DESIGN Because users will work with the inputs and outputs of the system, it is crucial to involve users during input and output design. During this activity, the systems analyst carefully designs every menu, screen, and report specified in the requirements. The outputs usually are designed first because they help define the requirements for the inputs.

The systems analyst typically develops two types of designs for each input and output: a mockup and a layout chart. A **mockup** is a sample of the input or output that contains actual data (Figure 14-22). The systems analyst shows mockups to users for their approval. Once users approve the mockup, the systems analyst develops a **layout chart** for the programmer. Layout charts are more technical and contain programming-like notations for the data items (Figure 14-23). Other issues that must be addressed during input and output design include the types of media to use (paper, video, audio); formats (graphical or narrative); and data entry validation techniques, which include making sure the inputted data is correct (for example, a pay rate cannot be less than 0).

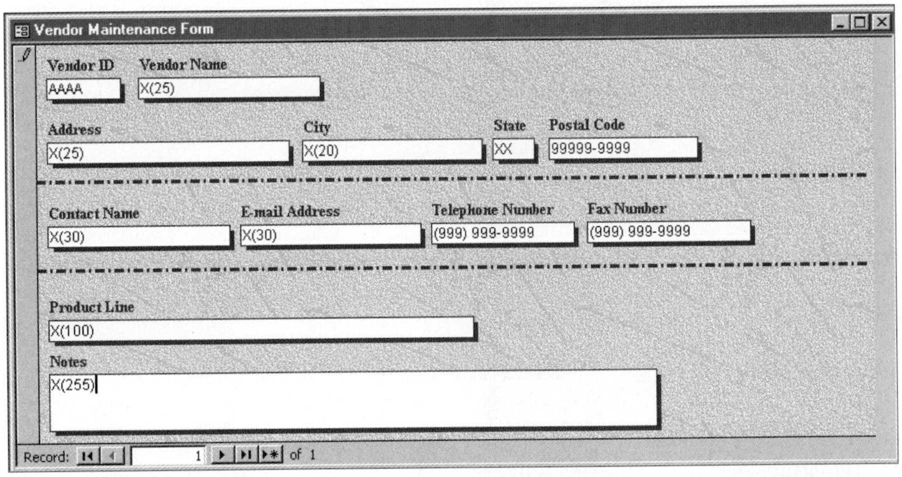

Figure 14-23 Once users approve a mockup, the layout chart (with technical specifications) is given to the programmer. This layout chart is for the mockup in Figure 14-22.

PROGRAM DESIGN During program design, the systems analyst identifies the processing requirements, or the **logic**, for each program in the system. To do this the systems analyst uses top-down and structured programming techniques. The next chapter discusses these techniques.

Next, the systems analyst prepares the **program specification package**, which communicates program requirements clearly to the programmer. This package identifies the relationship among each program in a process, as well as the input, output, processing, and database specifications.

The systems analyst sometimes uses a **systems flowchart** to document relationships among programs in a process (Figure 14-24). A systems flowchart shows how other elements of the system interact with a major process. The elements include programs, inputs, outputs, and files. A systems flowchart is very different from a data flow diagram. A DFD shows the flow of data through the system. A system flowchart shows methods and procedures for the data.

Prototyping

Many systems analysts today use prototypes during detailed design. A **prototype** is a working model of the proposed system. The systems analyst actually builds a functional form of the solution during design. The main advantage of a prototype is users can work with the system before it is completed — to make sure it meets their needs.

The Vendor Maintenance Screen shown in Figure 14-23 on the previous page is a prototype. Once users approve a prototype, system developers can implement a solution more quickly than without a prototype. In many cases, prototyped systems do not require a programmer for implementation. The systems analyst can convert the working model to the actual solution. The process of developing applications with prototypes is a part of **rapid application development** (**RAD**). The next chapter discusses RAD.

Some systems analysts use prototyping during the design phase. Others begin earlier in the SDLC — during analysis or even planning. Beginning a prototype too early, however, might lead to problems. When the development team sees a working model so early in the SDLC, they tend to skip critical analysis and design steps and overlook key features in the proposed solution.

A common problem with prototypes is they have inadequate documentation, or worse, none at all. Prototyping can be an effective tool if the development team and the users discipline themselves to follow all activities within the SDLC. Prototyping should not eliminate or replace activities — just improve the quality of these activities.

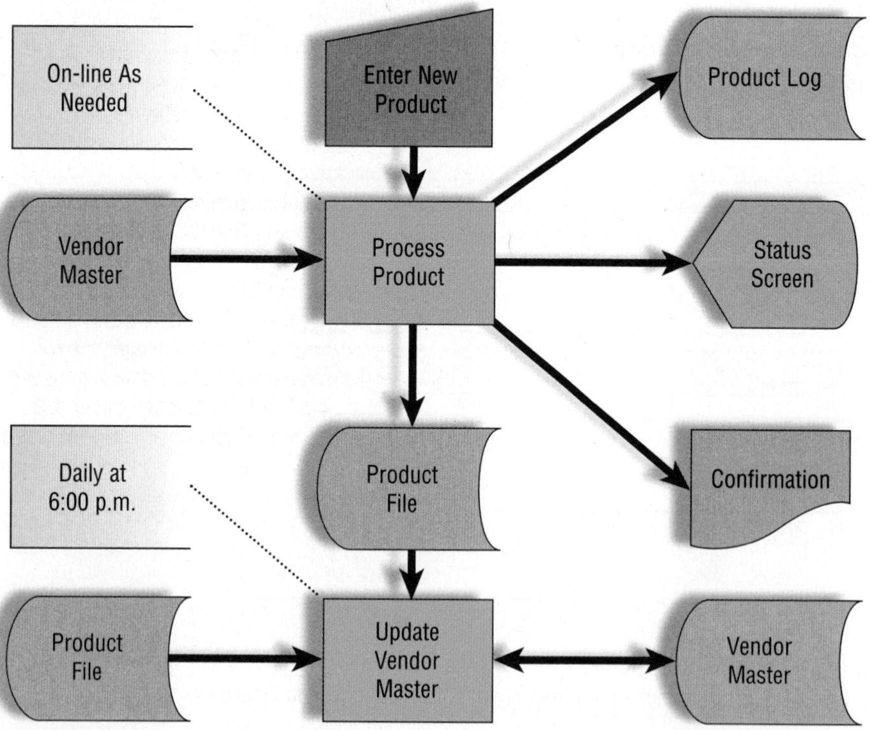

Figure 14-24 This systems flowchart describes the process of a transaction being entered such as entering a new product into the system. This chart contains six symbols, which are color coded so you can identify them: data entry, program, file, hard copy, comment, screen display. Comments are connected to the chart with dotted lines because they represent timing, not sequence.

CASE Tools

Many systems analysts use computer software to assist in the SDLC. **Computer-aided software engineering** (**CASE**) products are software tools designed to support one or more activities of the SDLC. The purpose of these products is to increase the efficiency and productivity of the project development team.

Some CASE tools exist separately. One package might be a dictionary and another allows you to create drawings. The most effective tools, however, are integrated (Figure 14-25). Integrated case products, sometimes called I-CASE or a CASE workbench include the following capabilities.

- Project repository – stores diagrams, specifications, descriptions, programs, and any other deliverable generated during the SDLC.
- Graphics – enables the drawing of diagrams, such as DFDs and ERDs.
- Prototyping – creates models of the proposed system.
- Quality assurance – analyzes deliverables, such as graphs and the data dictionary for accuracy.
- Code generators – create actual computer programs from design specifications.
- Housekeeping – establishes user accounts and provides backup and recovery functions.

CASE tools support a variety of SDLCs. Depending on the one your company uses, you can customize the CASE tools so all deliverables such as DFDs and ERDs use consistent terms.

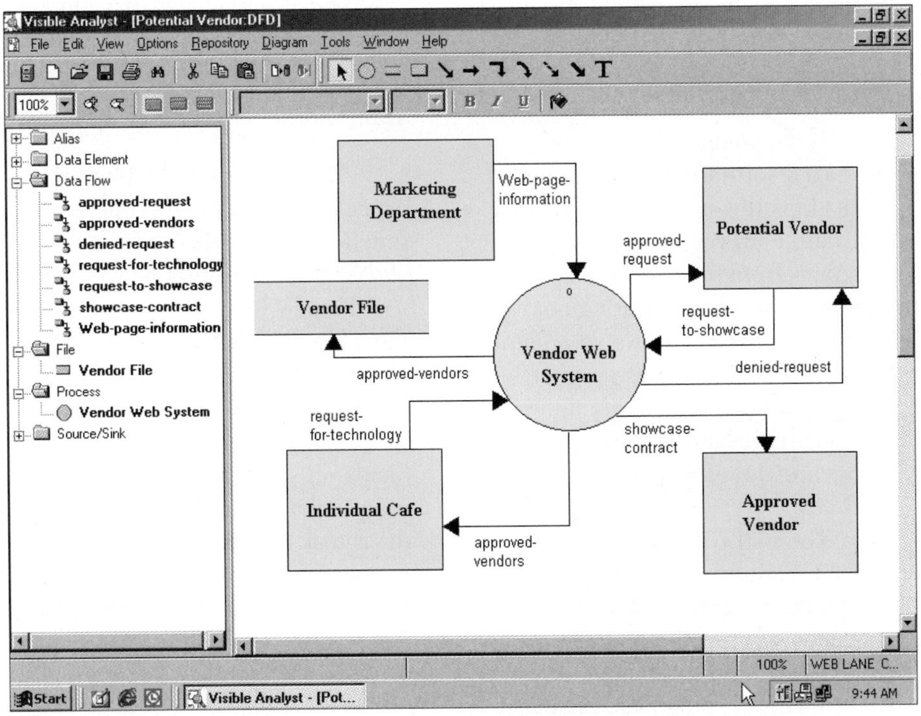

Figure 14-25 Integrated computer-aided software engineering (I-CASE) packages assist analysts in the development of an information system. Visible Analyst by Visible Systems Corporation enables analysts to create structured diagrams, as well as build the project dictionary. Figures 14-10 on page 14.16, 14-11 on page 14.17, and 14-15 on page 14.19 were created using Visible Analyst.

Web Link

For more information on CASE products, visit the Discovering Computers 2002 Chapter 14 WEB LINK page (**scsite.com/dc2002/ch14/weblink.htm**) and click CASE Products.

COMPANY ON THE CUTTING EDGE

Visible
SYSTEMS CORPORATION

Making a Case for CASE Tools

Donning night vision goggles and special clothing, National Guard members take their posts. Others climb into helicopters equipped with infrared devices and videotaping machines. These personnel are helping federal, state, and local law enforcement agencies intercept and eradicate illegal drugs in 54 states and territories.

As they plan, conduct, and evaluate their missions, they capture data on their activities and then enter these counterdrug facts and figures in a sophisticated information system developed with the Visible Systems Corporation's Visible Advantage™. This enterprise architecture and data warehouse development CASE (computer-aided software engineering) tool helps National Guard executives evaluate their activities and set thresholds for their future actions.

Another one of Visible Systems' popular software products is Visible Analyst®. This I-CASE tool provides graphical analysis and design resources for applications and database design. This software and other engineering tools help clients worldwide improve their processes and procedures, thus helping them become efficient and productive.

For more information on Visible, including case studies of actual projects, visit the Discovering Computers 2002 Companies Web page (**scsite.com/dc2002/companies.htm**) and click Visible Systems.

Quality Review Techniques

Several people should review the detailed design specifications before they are given to the programming team. The review process should include users, the senior systems analyst, and members of the project team.

One popular review technique is a structured walkthrough. A **structured walkthrough** is a step-by-step review of any SDLC deliverable. You can walk through items such as reports, diagrams, mockups, layout charts, and dictionary entries. The purpose of a walkthrough is to identify errors in the item being reviewed. If any errors are identified, the IT personnel must correct them. Developers use structured walkthroughs throughout the entire SDLC to review a variety of deliverables.

Once again, the systems analyst re-evaluates feasibility to determine if it still is beneficial to proceed with the proposed solution. It does not happen often, but companies cancel some projects at this point because they become infeasible. Although much time and money may have been spent, it is less costly to cancel the project than to proceed with an inadequate or incorrect solution. If the steering committee decides the project still is feasible, the project enters the implementation phase.

Detailed Design at Web Lane Café

As approved by the steering committee, Sadie and her team begin designing the Vendor Web System. After studying current vendor information and interviewing more users and vendors, the team designs changes to the company's database, Web site, and the associated programs. They prepare several documents including a mockup (see Figure 14-22 on page 14.27), a layout chart (see Figure 14-23 on page 14.27), and a systems flowchart (see Figure 14-24 on page 14.28).

After completing the detailed design, Sadie meets with several users and IT personnel to walk through the deliverables. They locate two errors. She corrects the errors and then presents the design to the steering committee. The committee agrees with the design solution and consents to implement it.

IMPLEMENTATION PHASE

Once you complete the design, the project enters the implementation phase. The purpose of the **implementation phase** is to construct, or build, the new or modified system and then deliver it to the users. System developers perform four major activities in this phase: (1) develop programs; (2) install and test the new system; (3) train users; and (4) convert to the new system. The following sections discuss each of these activities.

Develop Programs

If the company purchases packaged software, the development team skips this activity. For custom software, however, programmers write programs from the program specification package created during analysis. Just as the SDLC follows an organized set of activities, so does program development. These program development activities are known as the **program development life cycle (PDLC)**.

The PDLC follows these six steps: (1) analyze the problem, (2) design the programs, (3) code the programs, (4) test the programs, (5) formalize the solution, and (6) maintain the programs. Chapter 15 explains the PDLC in depth. The important concept to understand now is that the PDLC is a part of the implementation phase, which is part of the SDLC.

Install and Test the New System

If the company acquires new hardware or software, someone must install and test it. It is extremely important the hardware and software be tested thoroughly. Obviously, you should test individual programs. You also should be sure all the programs work together in the system. It is better to find errors early in the process, so you can correct them before placing the system into production. You do not want errors in the system after you deliver it to the users.

System developers perform three types of tests:

- **Systems Test** – Verifies all programs in an application work together properly.
- **Integration Test** – Verifies an application works with other applications.
- **Acceptance Test** – Performed by end-users, checks that the new system works with actual data.

Train Users

For a system to be effective, users must be trained properly on its functionality. **Training** involves showing users exactly how they will use the new hardware and software in the system. This training could be one-on-one sessions or classroom-style lectures (Figure 14-26). Whichever technique you use, it should include hands-on sessions using realistic sample data. Users should practice on the actual system during training. Users also should receive user manuals for reference. It is the systems analyst's responsibility to create user manuals.

Figure 14-26 Organizations must ensure that users are trained properly on the new system. One training method is classroom-style lectures.

Convert to the New System

The final activity in implementation is to change from the old system to the new system. This change can take place using one or more of the following conversion strategies: direct, parallel, phased, or pilot (Figure 14-27).

With **direct conversion**, the user stops using the old system and begins using the new system on a certain date. The advantage of this strategy is it requires no transition costs and is a quick implementation technique. Some systems analysts call this technique an **abrupt cutover.** The disadvantage is it is extremely risky and can disrupt operations seriously if the new system does not work correctly the first time.

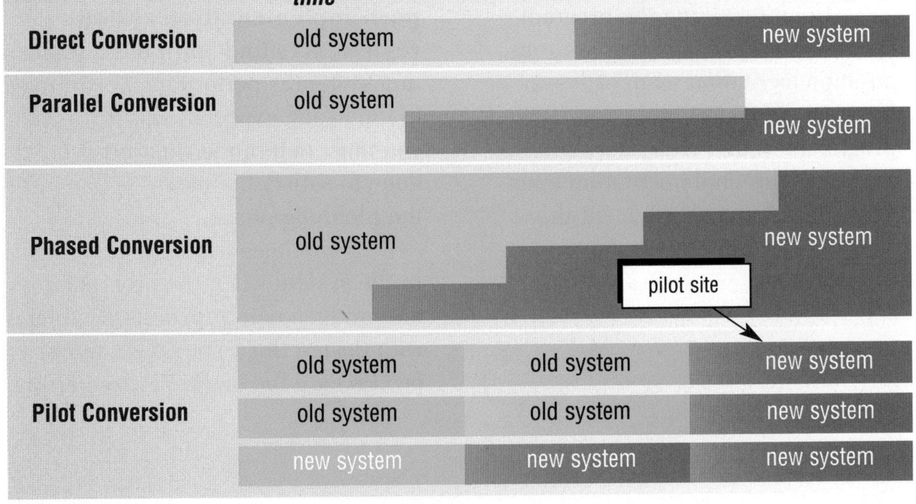

Figure 14-27 Converting from the old system to the new system usually follows one of these strategies.

ISSUE

Workers at Play

The Learning Curve and Employee Productivity

From 1950 to 1970, productivity — output per hour of work — increased almost three percent annually. Since that time, however, despite an expanding use of computer information systems, annual increases in productivity have been substantially less. Research indicates that during the last few years, growth was less than one percent. Economists are baffled. Some argue that information systems make the most positive impact where productivity is hard to measure, such as in finance and health care. Others suspect that advancing technology causes workers to spend more time learning new systems than the workers using systems to be more productive. Still others claim workers spend too much time on non-productive computer activities, such as surfing the Web or playing games. Which, if any, of these explanations do you think is correct? Why? What other reasons might there be? How can companies ensure that information systems will make their workers more productive?

For more information on worker productivity, visit the Discovering Computers 2002 Issues Web page (**scsite.com/dc2002/issues.htm**) and click Chapter 14 Issue #4.

Parallel conversion consists of running the old system alongside the new system for a specified time period. Results from both systems are compared. If the results are the same, the company either terminates the old system abruptly or phases it out. The advantage of this strategy is that you can fix any problems in the new system before you terminate the old system. The disadvantage is it is costly to operate two systems at the same time.

Larger systems that have multiple sites often use a phased conversion. With a **phased conversion**, or **location conversion**, each site converts at a separate time. For example, an accounting system might convert accounts receivable, accounts payable, general ledger, and payroll sites in separate phases. Each site can use a direct or parallel conversion.

With a **pilot conversion**, only one location in the company uses the new system — so it can be tested. Once the pilot site approves the new system, other sites convert using one of the other conversion strategies.

At the beginning of the conversion, existing data must be made ready for the new system. Converting existing manual and computer files so the new system can use them is known as **data conversion**.

Implementation at Web Lane Café

Upon receiving the program specification package, Sadie forms an implementation team of Jesse Martinez, Webmaster; Andrea Travnik, programmer; and Kelly Sarkis, data modeler. The implementation team works together to implement the Vendor Web System.

Sadie works closely with the team to answer questions about the design and to check the progress of their work. When the team completes its work, they ask Sadie to test it. She does and it works great!

Sadie arranges a training class for the employees of the marketing and customer service departments. During the training session, she shows them how to use the new Vendor Information page on the company's Web site. Sadie gives each attendee a user guide. She wants to prepare everyone thoroughly for the new Web pages once they are posted. Sadie also sends a letter to all existing vendors informing when this new service will be available and how to use it.

SUPPORT PHASE

The purpose of the **support phase** is to provide ongoing assistance for an information system and its users after the system is implemented. The support phase consists of four major activities: (1) conduct a post-implementation system review, (2) identify errors, (3) identify enhancements, and (4) monitor system performance.

One of the first activities the company performs in the support phase is to meet with users. The purpose of this meeting, called the **post-implementation system review**, is to find out if the information system is performing according to the users' expectations. If it is not, you must determine what must be done to satisfy the users — back to the planning phase.

Sometimes users identify errors in the system when the program does not produce correct results. Problems with design (logic) or programming (syntax) are the cause of these errors.

TECHNOLOGY TRAILBLAZER

TOM **DEMARCO**

Ever wonder why software is so expensive? Tom DeMarco knows why. As author of *Why Does Software Cost So Much? (And Other Puzzles of the Information Age)*, he has explored the successes and the absurdities of the software development process. In more than 100 books, articles, and papers, DeMarco focuses on productive business principles for project management.

He is a principal for The Atlantic Systems Guild, Inc., a software think tank exploring issues facing the computer industry. DeMarco's efforts center on software specification and design, software metrics, people-aware project management, and risk management. He believes that good managers focus on motivating employees and designing organizations to work efficiently; they do not pressure their employees to produce under extreme deadlines. In contrast, poor managers exert pressure because they know of no other solution. Project managers should apply the principles they learned in kindergarten — tell the truth and work together — as behavior guidelines.

For more information on Tom DeMarco, visit the Discovering Computers 2002 People Web page (**scsite.com/dc2002/people.htm**) and click Tom DeMarco.

Often these errors are minor. For example, the total of a column might be incorrect on a daily order summary. Other times, however, the error requires more serious investigation — back to the planning phase.

In some cases, users would like the system to do more. Maybe they have additional requirements. **System enhancement** involves modifying or expanding an existing application system — back to the planning phase.

During the support phase, the systems analyst monitors performance of the new or modified information system. The purpose of **performance monitoring** is to determine if the system is inefficient at any point. If so, is the inefficiency causing a problem? Is the time it takes to download vendor information reasonable? If not, the systems analyst must investigate solutions to make the download time more acceptable — back to the planning phase.

Support at Web Lane Café

During the post-implementation system review, Sadie learns many hits have been made to the new Web page. Vendors are using it and they like it! Customer service regularly receives e-mail messages from vendors that appreciate the new service. Carla says her staff has much more time to spend on other tasks.

Six months after the Vendor Web System has been in operation, Carla would like to add more information to the Vendor Information page. She sends an e-mail message to Sadie requesting the change. Sadie asks her to fill out a Request for System Services and puts her on the agenda of the next steering committee meeting. Back to the planning phase again!

CHAPTER SUMMARY

This chapter discussed the phases in the system development life cycle. The guidelines for system development also were presented. The chapter addressed activities that occur during the entire SDLC such as project management, feasibility assessment, data and information gathering, and documentation. Throughout the chapter, a case study about Web Lane Café illustrated and reinforced activities performed during each phase of the life cycle.

ISSUE

Everyone Is Complaining

Costly System Errors

Eighteen months after a $5 million information system was placed in full operation, workers for a New York county were grumbling that the system was plagued with errors. The head of the county's Civil Service Employees Association reported complaints from almost every department. The cost of remedying the flawed system was prohibitive, and county legislators were incensed. During system development, problems are easier and less expensive to fix at some phases in the system development life cycle than at others. When would it be simplest and least costly to identify and solve problems? Why? At what phase would it be more expensive? Why? If you were the project leader, how would your beliefs influence the way you manage each phase of the SDLC?

For more information on the SDLC, visit the Discovering Computers 2002 Issues Web page (**scsite.com/dc2002/issues.htm**) and click Chapter 14 Issue #5.

Systems Analyst

One of the most in-demand IT positions is that of systems analyst. The primary nature of this type of work is to design and develop new hardware and software systems and to incorporate new technologies.

To be successful as a systems analyst, you must be willing to embrace new technologies and be prepared for continual learning. Typically, systems analysts are more involved in design issues than in day-to-day coding. Systems analyst is a somewhat arbitrary title, however, as different companies define the role differently. Some emerging paradigms for the systems analyst include e-commerce, enterprise-wide networking, and intranet technologies. Given the technology available today, telecommuting is common for computer professionals, including the systems analyst. Many analysts work as consultants.

Minimum educational requirements are a bachelor's degree, but many people opt for a masters. Because this is one of the top three fastest growing occupations in the IT field, salaries are excellent. They range from $40,000 to $80,000 and up. Recent reports indicate graduates are receiving offers in excess of $50,000 per year.

To learn more about the field of systems analyst as a career, visit the Discovering Computers 2002 Careers Web page (**scsite.com/dc2002/careers.htm**) and click Systems Analyst.

E-RESEARCH

SEARCH AND YE SHALL FIND

Info on the Web

Have you ever wondered which Beatles albums turned platinum? What is the manufacturer's suggested retail price of a 2002-model Corvette? How low is the lowest price for a new CD-ROM for your computer? These facts and figures are at your fingertips — if you know where to locate them on the Internet.

Unlike the days when you used the Dewey Decimal Classification or the Library of Congress systems to locate reference materials easily, you will not find Internet documents organized in any systematic manner. And no helpful, patient reference librarian is working behind a desk to assist you in your quest for information. Instead, you are on your own when you navigate the tangled Web. But you have some tools: search engines and subject directories.

Yahoo!, AltaVista, Go.com, Northern Light, Excite, FAST Search, and Google are some of the more popular search engines. They crawl through a Web page, and with the help of programs such as spiders and robots, they record each word in their enormous databases. When you enter a key term, search text, or query, in their search boxes, the search engines scan the databases and list the Web sites that contain the specified search text. As shown in Figure 14-28, the Yahoo! search result for the phrase, CD-R drive, lists nearly 45,000 Web sites.

The key to effective searching on the Web is composing search queries that narrow the search results and place the most relevant Web sites at the top of the list. Think of major terms that describe the issue or item you are researching and use Boolean operators — and, or, and not — to help retrieve appropriate Web sites. The Go.com search locates Web sites describing the Beatles' platinum albums and eliminates Web sites describing platinum jewelry or Beatles' memorabilia, as shown in Figure 14-29.

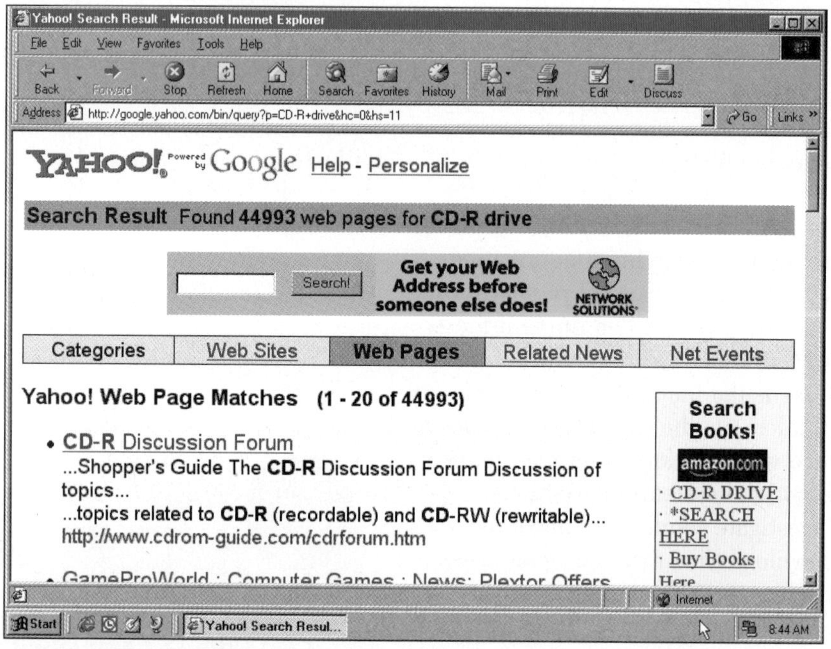

Figure 14-28 Yahoo! features organized information on tens of thousands of computers linked to the Internet.

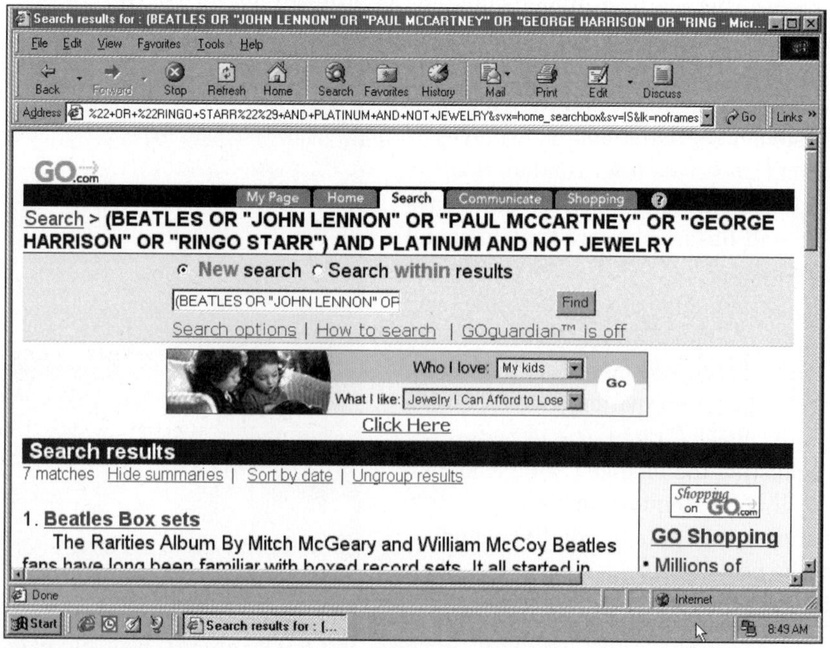

Figure 14-29 The Walt Disney Company's Go.com Web site features seearches, shopping, and news.

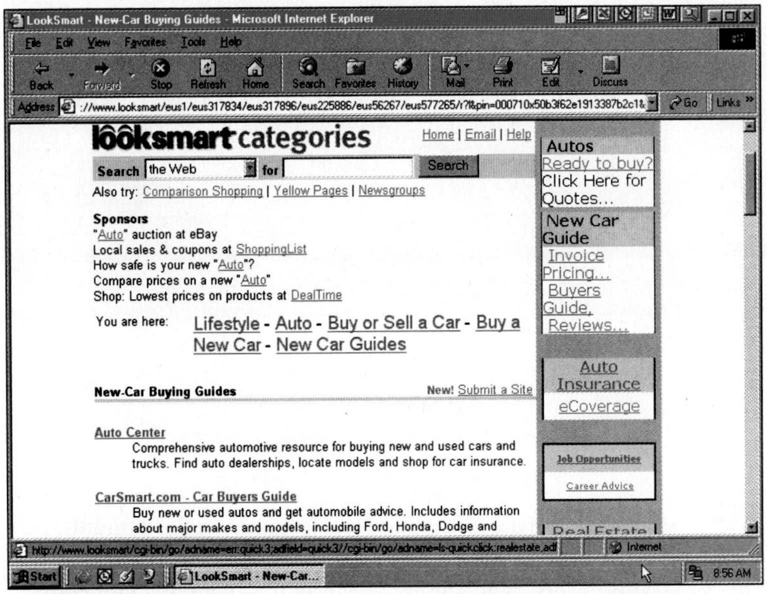

Figure 14-30 Webrarians index millions of Web pages into more than 200,000 categories.

RESEARCH WEB SITES	URL
Search Engines	
Yahoo!	yahoo.com
AltaVista	altavista.com
Go.com	go.com
Northern Light	northernlight.com
Excite	excite.com
FAST Search	fastsearch.com
Google	google.com
Subject Directories	
Yahoo!	yahoo.com
LookSmart	looksmart.com
About	about.com
Argus Clearinghouse	clearinghouse.net
The Internet Public Library	ipl.org
The WWW Virtual Library	vlib.org

For an updated list of research Web sites, visit scsite.com/dc2002/e-rev.htm.

Figure 14-31 Web users can find information by using search engines and subject directories.

For example, searching on Beatles, or John Lennon, or Paul McCartney, or George Harrison, or Ringo Starr, along with platinum and not jewelry can help you narrow the list of results.

Even when using these search techniques, one search engine only can explore 20 percent of the 200 million Internet pages. All the search engines combined can rummage through less than half of these Web sites.

Another search tool is a subject directory, which is a collection of related Web sites. Yahoo! and LookSmart have two of the most comprehensive subject directories on the Web. Their organized lists often are called trees because a few main categories, such as Entertainment, Computing, Lifestyle, and Work, branch out to more specific subtopics. Figure 14-30 shows LookSmart's tree for buying a new car. The list begins with the Lifestyle main category and branches to Auto, Buy or Sell a Car, Buy a New Car, and finally New Car Guides.

For more information on searching on the Web and for an updated list of research Web sites, visit the Discovering Computers 2002 e-Revolution Web page (scsite.com/dc2002/e-rev.htm) and click Research.

eREVOLUTION E-RESEARCH *applied:*

1. This chapter discusses acquiring hardware and software during the design phase of the Systems Development Life Cycle and displays Sony's and Approved Systems' Web sites. Use two of the search engines listed in Figure 14-31 to find three Web sites reviewing the latest digital cameras from Sony and Kodak. Make a table listing the search engines, Web site names, and the cameras' model numbers, suggested retail price, megapixels, memory, and features.

2. If money were no object, virtually everyone would have an exquisite car. On the other hand, drivers need a practical vehicle to drive around town daily. Use one of the subject directories listed in Figure 14-31 to research your dream car and another directory to research your practical car. Write a paragraph about each car describing the particular subject directory tree you used, the MSRP of the car, standard and optional equipment, engine size, miles per gallon, and safety features.

In Summary

Web Instructions: To display this page from the Web, start your browser and enter the URL scsite.com/dc2002/ch14/summary.htm. Click the links for current and additional information. To listen to an audio version of this In Summary, click the Audio button. To play the audio, RealPlayer must be installed on your computer (download by clicking here).

1 Describe the Phases in the System Development Life Cycle.

The system development life cycle (SDLC) is an organized set of activities that guides those involved through the development of an information system and to maintain and monitor ongoing activities. The activities of the SDLC are grouped into five **phases**, some of which are performed concurrently and others sequentially. The **planning phase** involves reviewing and prioritizing project requests, allocating resources, and identifying the project development team. The **analysis phase** consists of conducting a preliminary investigation and performing detailed analysis activities. The **design phase** calls for acquiring the necessary hardware and software and developing details of the system. The **implementation phase** includes developing programs, installing and testing the new system, training and educating users, and converting to the new system. The **support phase** entails conducting post-implementation system review, identifying errors and enhancements, and monitoring system performance.

2 What Are the Guidelines for System Development?

The development of an information system should follow three general guidelines. First, use a phased approach to group activities or tasks. Second, involve the **users**, including anyone for whom the system is being built. Third, develop standards, or sets of rules and procedures, that the organization expects employees to accept and follow.

3 What Are Some of the Responsibilities of IT Professionals?

IT professionals with whom the system analyst might work include other analysts; database analysts and administrating users, who submit requests for change; a **steering committee**, which is responsible for decision making; programmers; network administrators; vendors; Webmaster; and managers.

4 Why Are Project Management, Feasibility Assessment, Data and Information Gathering Techniques, and Documentation Important?

Project management is the process of planning, scheduling, and then controlling the activities during the SDLC. The goal is to deliver an acceptable system in an agreed-upon time frame, while maintaining costs. The project plan generally is recorded and monitored using a **Gantt chart** and **project management software**. **Feasibility** is a measure of how suitable the development of a system will be to an organization. Analysts use four criteria to test feasibility: **operational feasibility**, **schedule feasibility**, **technical feasibility**, and **economic feasibility**. Data and information gathering techniques supply system developers with accurate and timely data in order to keep the project on schedule, assess feasibility, and ensure that the system is meeting requirements. **Documentation** is the compilation and summarization of data and information.

In Summary

5 How Are Structured Tools such as Entity-Relationship Diagrams and Data Flow Diagrams Used in Analysis and Design?

A system analyst uses graphics to present a systems analysis in a way that can be understood by the project team. An **entity-relationship diagram** (**ERD**) is a tool that graphically represents the associations between entities (vendors, orders, customers, jobs, and so on) in the project. A **data flow diagram (DFD)** is a tool that graphically represents the flow of data (input or output of data or information) in a system.

6 What is the Difference between Packaged Software and Custom Software?

When a steering committee discusses the **system proposal** and determines which alternative to implement, it often faces a build-or-buy decision. The committee must decide whether to buy packaged software or build custom software. **Packaged software** is pre-written software available for purchase. **Custom software** is application software developed by the user or at the user's request. Custom software matches an organization's requirements but usually is more expensive than packaged software and takes longer to design and implement.

7 How Is Program Development Part of the System Development Life Cycle?

If the project development team decides to write custom software, then programmers develop programs from the program specification package created during analysis. The **program development life cycle** (**PDLC**) is part of the **implementation phase** of the SDLC and follows an organized set of six activities. These six steps are: (1) analyze the problem, (2) design the programs, (3) code the programs, (4) test the programs, (5) formalize the solution, and (6) maintain the programs.

8 What Techniques Are Used to Convert to a New System?

The final activity in implementation is to change from the old system to the new system. This is called conversion. Moving to a new system can take place using one or more strategies. With **direct conversion**, the user stops using the old system and begins using the new system on a certain date. **Parallel conversion** consists of running the old system alongside the new system for a specified period of time. **Phased conversion** is used with larger systems that are split into individual sites, each of which converts separately at different times using either a direct or parallel conversion. With a **pilot conversion**, only one location in the organization uses the new system — so it can be tested.

9 How Do IT Professionals Support an Information System?

In the **support phase**, systems analysts perform four major activities. They conduct a post-implementation system review, which is a meeting with users to determine if the information system is performing according to their specifications. Second, they identify errors. Third, they identify **system enhancements**. Finally, they do **performance monitoring** to determine if the system is inefficient at any point.

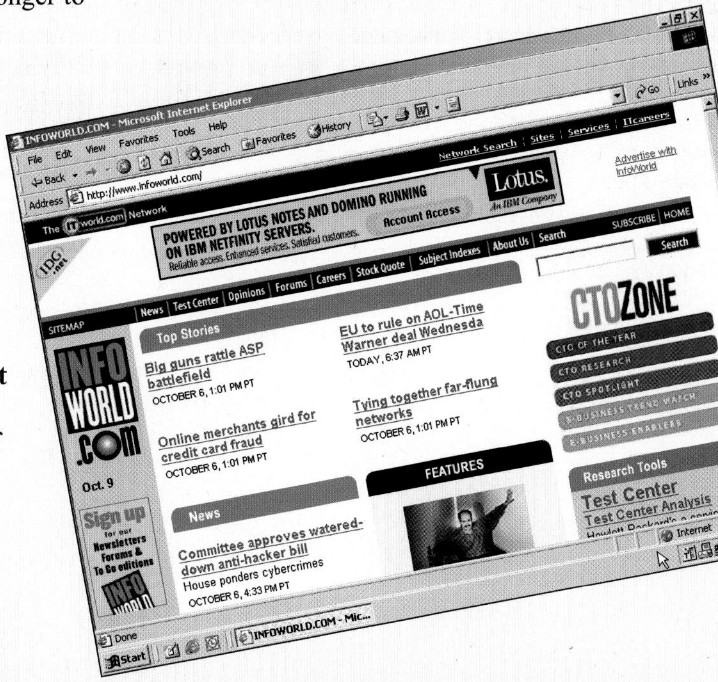

Key Terms

Web Instructions: To display this page from the Web, start your browser and enter the URL scsite.com/dc2002/ch14/terms.htm. Scroll through the list of terms. Click a term to display its definition and a picture. Click the To WEB button for current and additional information about the term from the Web. To see animations, Shockwave and Flash Player must be installed on your computer (download by clicking here).

abrupt cutover (14.31)
acceptance test (14.30)
agent (14.17)
analysis phase (14.13)
benchmark test (14.25)
commercial off-the-shelf software (14.19)
computer-aided software engineering (CASE) (14.29)
context diagram (14.17)
cost/benefit feasibility (14.7)
custom software (14.20)
cybercafe´ (14.11)
data conversion (14.32)
data dictionary (14.19)
data flow (14.17)
data flow diagram (DFD) (14.17)
data store (14.17)
decision table (14.18)
decision tree (14.18)
deliverable (14.6)
design phase (14.21)
detailed analysis (14.15)
direct conversion (14.31)
documentation (14.7)
economic feasibility (14.7)
electronic magazine (14.22)
end-user license agreement (EULA) (14.26)
entity (14.16)
entity-relationship diagram (E-R diagram or ERD) (14.16)
e-zine (14.22)
feasibility (14.6)
feasibility study (14.13)
Gantt chart (14.5)
horizontal market software (14.20)
implementation phase (14.30)
information system (IS) (14.2)
integration test (14.30)
joint-application design (JAD) session (14.8)
layout chart (14.27)
location conversion (14.32)
logic (14.28)
logical design (14.15)
mockup (14.27)
operational feasibility (14.6)
packaged software (14.19)
parallel conversion (14.32)
performance monitoring (14.33)
phased conversion (14.32)
phases (14.2)
physical design (14.26)
pilot conversion (14.32)
planning phase (14.12)
post-implementation system review (14.32)

SYSTEM DEVELOPMENT LIFE CYCLE (SDLC)
Organized set of activities that guides those involved through the development of an information system. The phases in the SDLC are planning, analysis, design, implentation, and support. (14.2)

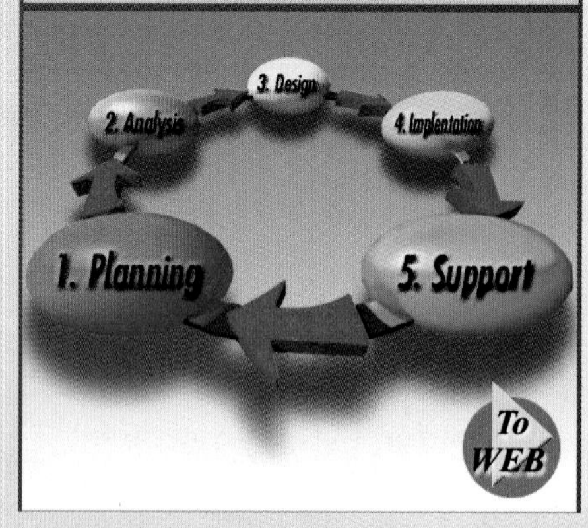

preliminary investigation (14.13)
process (14.17)
program development life cycle (PDLC) (14.30)
program specification package (14.28)
project dictionary (14.17)
project leader (14.5)
project management (14.5)
project management software (14.6)
project notebook (14.7)
project plan (14.5)
project request (14.10)
project team (14.5)
prototype (14.28)
rapid application development (RAD) (14.28)
repository (14.17)
request for information (RFI) (14.23)
request for proposal (RFP) (14.23)
request for quotation (RFQ) (14.22)
request for system services (14.10)
schedule feasibility (14.6)
scope (14.5)
software engineering (14.2)
source (14.17)
standards (14.4)
steering committee (14.5)
structured analysis and design (14.15)
structured English (14.18)
structured walkthrough (14.30)
support phase (14.32)
system (14.2)
system development life cycle (SDLC) (14.2)
system enhancement (14.33)
system proposal (14.19)
systems analyst (14.5)
systems flowchart (14.28)
systems test (14.30)
technical feasibility (14.7)
trade publication (14.20)
training (14.30)
turnkey solution (14.24)
users (14.3)
value-added reseller (VAR) (14.23)
vertical market software (14.20)
warranty (14.23)

Learn It Online

Web Instructions: To display this page from the Web, start your browser and enter the URL scsite.com/dc2002/ch14/learn.htm.

1. Web Guide

Click Web Guide to display the Guide to World Wide Web Sites and Searching Techniques page. Click Reference and then click Webopedia. Search for CASE. Click one of the CASE links. Use your word processing program to prepare a brief report on your findings and submit your assignment to your instructor.

2. Scavenger Hunt

Click Scavenger Hunt. Print a copy of the Scavenger Hunt page; use this page to write down your answers as you search the Web. Submit your completed page to your instructor.

3. Who Wants to Be a Computer Genius?

Click Computer Genius to find out if you are a computer genius. Directions on how to play the game will display. When you are ready to play, click the PLAY button. Submit your score to your instructor.

4. Wheel of Terms

Click Wheel of Terms to reinforce important terms you learned in this chapter by playing the Shelly Cashman Series version of this popular game. Directions on how to play the game will display. When you are ready to play, click the PLAY button. Submit your score to your instructor.

5. Career Corner

Click Career Corner to display the WomenCentral page. Click one of the search results links and then review the information. Write a brief report describing what you learned. Submit the report to your instructor.

6. Search Sleuth

Click Search Sleuth to learn search techniques that will help make you a research expert. Submit the completed assignment to your instructor.

7. Crossword Puzzle Challenge

Click Crossword Puzzle Challenge. Complete the puzzle to reinforce skills you learned in this chapter. Directions on how to play the game will display. When you are ready to play, click the PLAY button. Submit the completed puzzle to your instructor.

8. Practice Test

Click Practice Test. Answer each question. When completed, enter your name and click the Grade Test button to submit the quiz for grading. Make a note of any missed questions. If required, print a copy to submit to your instructor.

Checkpoint

Web Instructions: To display this page from the Web, start your browser and enter the URL scsite.com/dc2002/ch14/check.htm. Click the links for current and additional information. To experience the animation and interactivity, Shockwave and Flash Player must be installed on your computer (download by clicking here).

LABEL THE FIGURE

Instructions: Identify the phases in the system development life cycle.

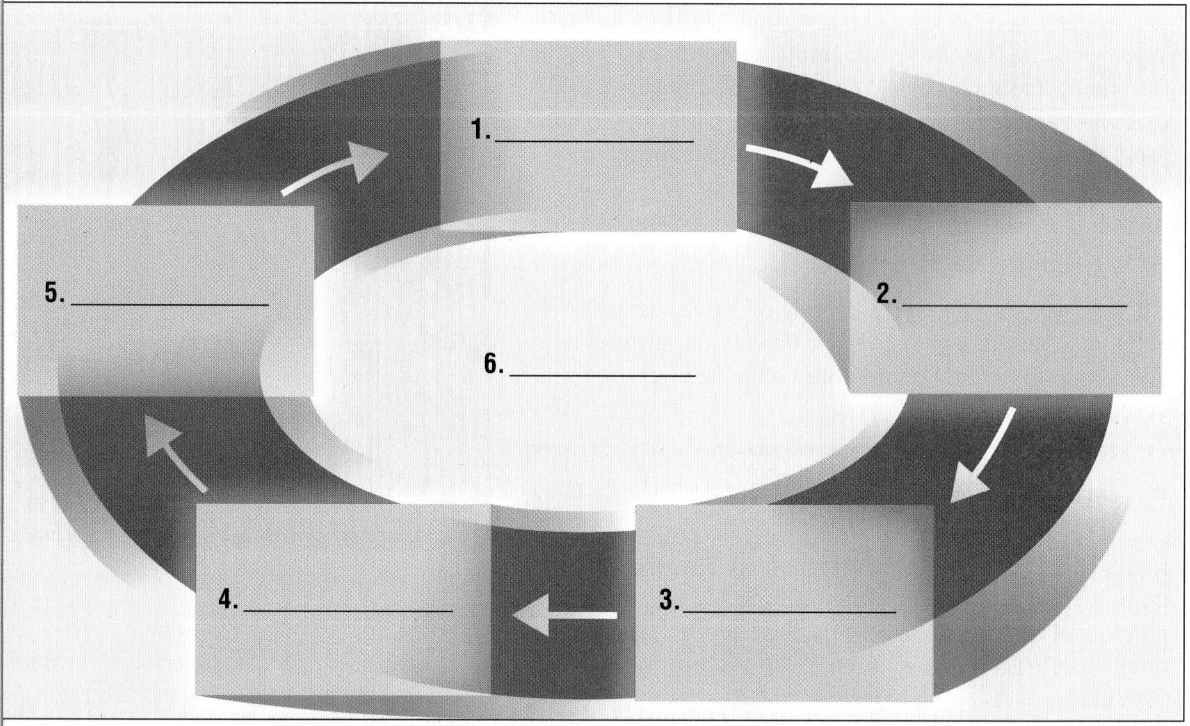

MATCHING

Instructions: Match each term from the column on the left with the best description from the column on the right.

_______ 1. benchmark test
_______ 2. data dictionary
_______ 3. direct conversion
_______ 4. pilot conversion
_______ 5. systems analyst

a. Only one location in the company uses the new system.
b. Measures the performance of hardware or software.
c. Contains data about each file in the database.
d. Manages and controls the budget and schedule of the project.
e. User stops using the old system and begins using the new system on a certain date.
f. Responsible for designing and developing an information system.
g. Running the old system alongside the new system for a specified period of time.

Checkpoint

MULTIPLE CHOICE

Instructions: Select the letter of the correct answer for each of the following questions.

1. A(n) __________ supports daily, short-term, and long-range activities of users.
   a. information system
   b. systems analyst
   c. project manager
   d. conversion specialist
2. __________ is the third phase of the SDLC.
   a. Implementation
   b. Support
   c. Design
   d. Planning
3. Sets of rules and procedures that a company expects employees to follow are called __________.
   a. proposal
   b. solutions
   c. standards
   d. guidelines
4. A __________ uses horizontal bars to show project phases or activities.
   a. timeline
   b. planning guide
   c. project guide
   d. Gantt Chart
5. In a(n) __________, a vendor quotes a price for the listed product(s).
   a. RFQ
   b. RFP
   c. BID
   d. RFI

SHORT ANSWER

Instructions: Write a brief answer to each of the following questions.

1. What is a project plan? __________ How is a Gantt chart used within a project plan? __________
2. What is feasibility? __________ List and briefly describe the four tests a system analyst uses to evaluate feasibility. __________
3. What is JAD? __________ How would a system analyst use JAD? __________
4. What are the two structured analysis graphical design tools? __________ How are they different? __________
5. What is a data dictionary? __________ How does a systems analyst use a data dictionary? __________

WORKING TOGETHER

Instructions: Working with a group of your classmates, complete the following team exercise.

Identify a problem on campus or a common problem within your community. One or two individuals assume the position of system analyst. The remaining students assume the role of one of the people identified in Chapter 14 in Figure 14.3 on page 14.4. Some students are users and others are members of the project team. Brainstorm and determine a feasible solution for the problem. Using a software program such as Microsoft Project, design a plan and a schedule for implementing your solution. To learn more about project management, use your browser to link to scsite.com/dc2002/ch14/check.htm.

In The Lab

Web Instructions: To display this page from the Web, start your browser and enter the URL scsite.com/dc2002/ch14/lab.htm. Click the links for current and additional information.

Traffic Sign Tutorial

1

Insert the Discover Data Disk into drive A. See the inside back cover of this book for instructions for downloading the Discover Data Disk or see your instructor for information on accessing the files required in this book. Click the Start button on the taskbar and then click Run on the Start menu. In the Open text box, type `a:traffic.exe` and then press the ENTER key to display the Traffic Sign Tutorial window. This program was written in Visual Basic. Drag the signs to their correct containers. Click Options on the menu bar and then click Clear to reset the tutorial. Click Options on the menu bar and then click Show. Click Options on the menu bar and then click Clear. Click Options on the menu bar and then click Quiz. Answer the quiz questions.

Dr. Watson

2

This exercise uses Windows 98 or Windows 2000 procedures. Dr. Watson is a Windows diagnostic tool used to identify faults in a system. To find out more about Dr. Watson, click the Start button on the taskbar and then click Help on the Start menu. Click the Index tab. Type `Dr. Watson` in the Type in the keyword to find text box and then click the Display button. Click an appropriate Help topic in the Topics Found dialog box, click the Display button, and answer the following questions:

- How is Dr. Watson used to diagnose system faults?
- How can you open Dr. Watson from the Start menu?
- How do you use Dr. Watson to create a system snapshot?

Click the Close button to close the Windows Help window.

Creating a Drawing

3

Click the Start button on the taskbar, point to Programs on the Start menu, point to Accessories on the Programs submenu, and then click Paint on the Accessories submenu. If necessary, maximize the Paint window and drag the lower-right corner of the white rectangle to the right to increase its size. Change the background color to orange by clicking the color orange in the color box at the bottom of the Paint window, clicking the Fill With Color tool (row 2, column 2) in the toolbox on the left edge of the window, and clicking the white rectangle. Change the foreground color to red by clicking the color red in the color box. Use the Rectangle tool (row 7, column 1) and the Line tool (row 6, column 1) in the toolbox to draw the box (Figure 14-32). Use the Fill With Color tool (row 2, column 2) in the toolbox and color box to color the box. If you make a mistake, click Edit on the menu bar and then click Undo to erase your last draw. Click File on the menu bar and then click Save. With a floppy disk in drive A, type `a:\h14-3` in the File name text box. Click the Save button. Click File on the menu bar and then click Print. Click the OK button. Close the Paint window.

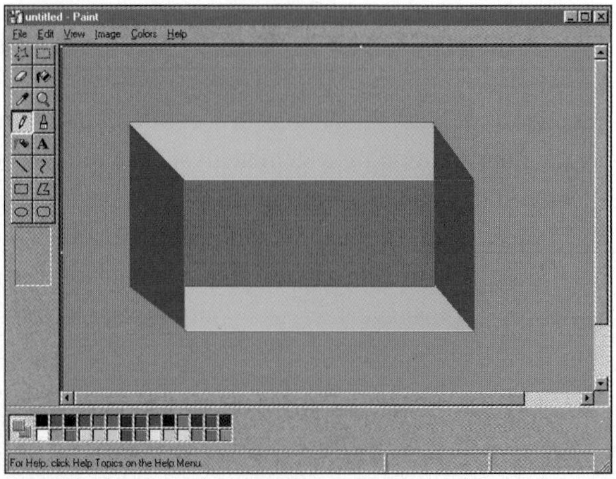

Figure 14-32

Capturing Screen Images

4

Click the Start button on the taskbar, point to Programs on the Start menu, and point to Accessories on the Programs submenu. Press the PRINT SCREEN key on your keyboard. Click WordPad on the Accessories submenu. In WordPad, type your name followed by `Below is a Windows Screen Shot:` and then press the ENTER key twice. Click Edit on the menu bar and then click Paste. Use the scroll bar to scroll through the document. Click the Print button on the toolbar to print the file. Close WordPad. Do not save the file unless your instructor tells you to do so.

Web Work

Web Instructions: To display this page from the Web, start your browser and enter the URL scsite.com/dc2002/ch14/web.htm. To view At The Movies in exercise 1, RealPlayer must be installed on your computer (download by clicking here).

1 BizTech & Productivity

To view the BizTech & Productivity movie, click the button to the left or click the Play button to the right. Watch the movie, and then complete the exercise by answering the question below. For decades, business productivity climbed at a comfortable, steady rate. Then, in the 1990s, expanding implementation of computer applications, the proliferation of personal computers, and the advent of the Internet caused the percentage of productivity gain to more than double by the year 2000. What new technologies or Internet-like medium do you foresee keeping these high-gain rates going?

2 Customizing Your E-Mail Program

Many e-mail programs can be customized. To customize your e-mail program, click the button to the left to display your e-mail service. Enter your Login Name and Password. When the In-Box screen displays, click Options. On the Options sheet, click the Filters link in the Mail Handling column. Follow the directions on the Options: Filters sheet to block senders of mail you do not want to receive and direct incoming messages to specific folders. Click the OK button. On the Options sheet, click the Signature link in the Additional Options column. Follow the directions on the Options: Signature sheet to create a signature that will be added to outgoing messages. Click the OK button. Read any new mail. When you have read all of your messages, click Log Out to quit your e-mail program.

3 System Development Life Cycle (SDLC)

People deal with problems in a variety of ways. An anthropologist studying workers in Silicon Valley tells the story of an engineer who kept a list of dilemmas with possible answers. When the list got too long, the engineer's solution simply was to combine the problems into a shorter list. The core of the SDLC is based on a standard, more effective approach to problem solving. To learn about different approaches, click the button to the left and complete this exercise.

4 Computer-Aided Software Engineering (CASE)

A difficult task in the design phase is to organize all of the information needed by an organization and to document the flow of data within the organization. One estimate indicates that the amount of material amassed in this phase is greater than the quantity of information an average person in the seventeenth century would acquire in a lifetime. To learn more about one of the many CASE products available for managing information and tracking data, click the button to the left and complete this exercise.

5 In the News

When teams from around the world gathered in France for the World Cup soccer championship, more than 60 groups of researchers met at a Paris café for another event — the annual Robot Football World Cup. Click the button to the left and read a news article about an innovative development or use of a computer information system. Who developed or used the system? In what way is the development or use of the system original?

CHAPTER 15

Program Development and Programming Languages

What a relief! After a day of midterms, your last exam finally is finished. Earlier today, all of your friends completed their tests, and they are waiting for you at Java Joint, a local coffee house. With all the homework and studies this semester, fun and relaxing times with friends are rare. Your excitement builds.

When you join the group, they are in the middle of a conversation about Java. You decide to order the house specialty, vanilla iced latte. It hits the spot! Now you can focus on the group's discussion. Yes, you agree this new Java is great. Your friends describe it as simple and robust, but you think of it more as savory and delectable.

Java applet, you hear one friend mention. Instantly you realize it has happened again. Your computer-major friends have not been talking about the house special at all. They are talking about a Web programming language. As you sit back in your chair with your latte, you hope no one will notice the dialogue is way over your head. You resolve to surf the Internet tomorrow to learn more about Java — the programming language.

OBJECTIVES

After completing this chapter, you will be able to:

- Explain the six steps in the program development life cycle
- Describe top-down program design
- Explain structured program design and the three basic control structures
- Explain the differences among the categories of programming languages
- Describe the object-oriented approach to progam development
- Identify programming languages commonly used today
- Identify the uses of application generators, macros, and RAD tools
- Describe various Web page development tools, including HTML, DHTML, XML, and WML
- Identify uses of multimedia authoring packages

WHAT IS A COMPUTER PROGRAM?

A **computer program** is a set of instructions that directs a computer to perform tasks. Computer programmers use program development tools that generate these instructions automatically or use a programming language to write these instructions themselves. A programming language is a set of words, symbols, and codes that enables a programmer to communicate instructions to a computer.

It is possible you will use a program development tool. Although you may never write a computer program, information you request may require that a programmer modify or write a program. Thus, you should understand how programmers develop programs to meet information requirements.

THE PROGRAM DEVELOPMENT LIFE CYCLE

The **program development life cycle (PDLC)** is a set of steps programmers use to build computer programs. As presented in Chapter 14, the SDLC guides information technology (IT) professionals through the development of an information system. Likewise, the PDLC guides computer programmers through the development of a program. The PDLC consists of six steps (Figure 15-1):

1. Analyze Problem
2. Design Programs
3. Code Programs
4. Test Programs
5. Formalize Solution
6. Maintain Programs

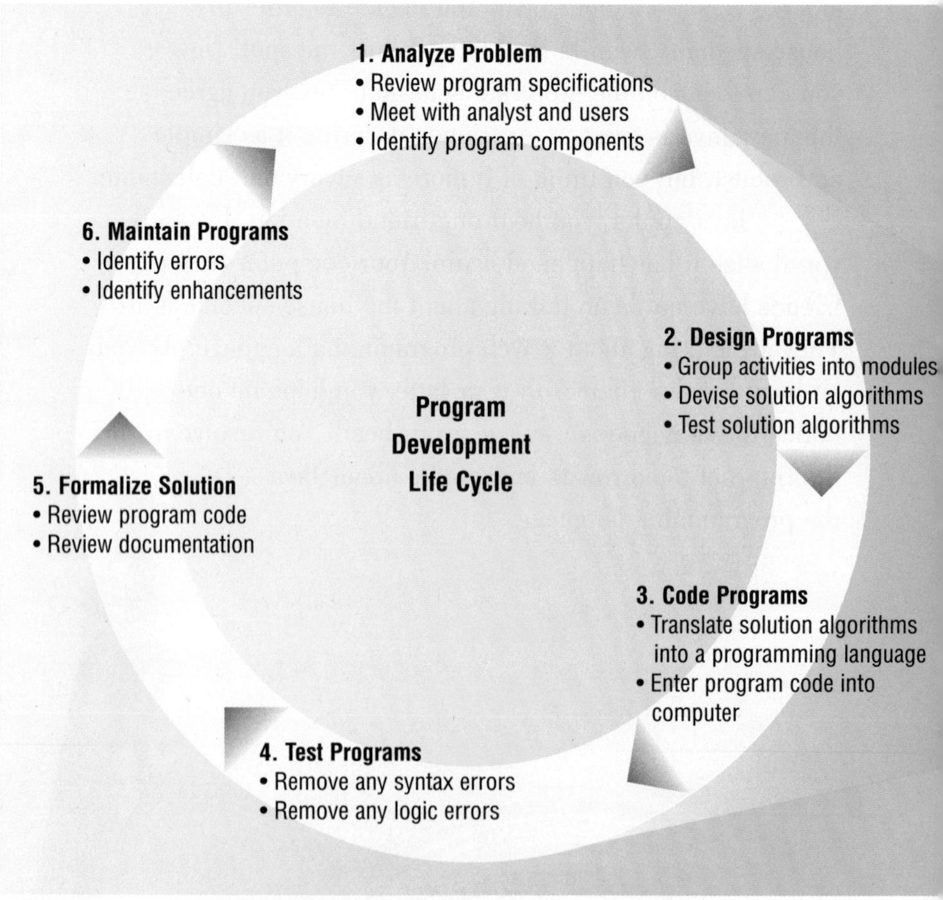
1. Analyze Problem
• Review program specifications
• Meet with analyst and users
• Identify program components
2. Design Programs
• Group activities into modules
• Devise solution algorithms
• Test solution algorithms
3. Code Programs
• Translate solution algorithms into a programming language
• Enter program code into computer
4. Test Programs
• Remove any syntax errors
• Remove any logic errors
5. Formalize Solution
• Review program code
• Review documentation
6. Maintain Programs
• Identify errors
• Identify enhancements
Program Development Life Cycle

Figure 15-1 The program development life cycle consists of six steps that form a loop.

As shown in Figure 15-1, the steps in the PDLC form a loop. Program development is an ongoing process within system development. The Maintain Programs step connects to the Analyze Problem step to form the loop. Each time someone identifies errors in or improvements to a program and requests program modifications, the Analyze Problem step begins again.

What Initiates the Program Development Life Cycle?

As discussed in Chapter 14, the system development life cycle (SDLC) consists of five phases: planning, analysis, design, implementation, and support. During the analysis phase, the development team recommends how to handle software needs. Choices include building custom software, purchasing packaged software, or outsourcing the entire IT operation.

If the company decides to build custom software, it then faces additional decisions. Should it develop the software in-house using its own IT staff? Should it contract the services of an outside source to develop the software? Or, should it consider some combination of these two alternatives?

If the company opts for in-house development, the design and implementation phases of the SDLC become quite extensive. In the design phase, the analyst creates a detailed set of requirements for the programmers. These design specifications, called the **program specification package**, identify the input, output, processing, and data requirements of each program and the relationships among programs. Once the programmers receive the program specification package, the implementation phase begins. At this time, the programmer analyzes the problem to be solved. The PDLC thus begins at the start of the implementation phase (Figure 15-2).

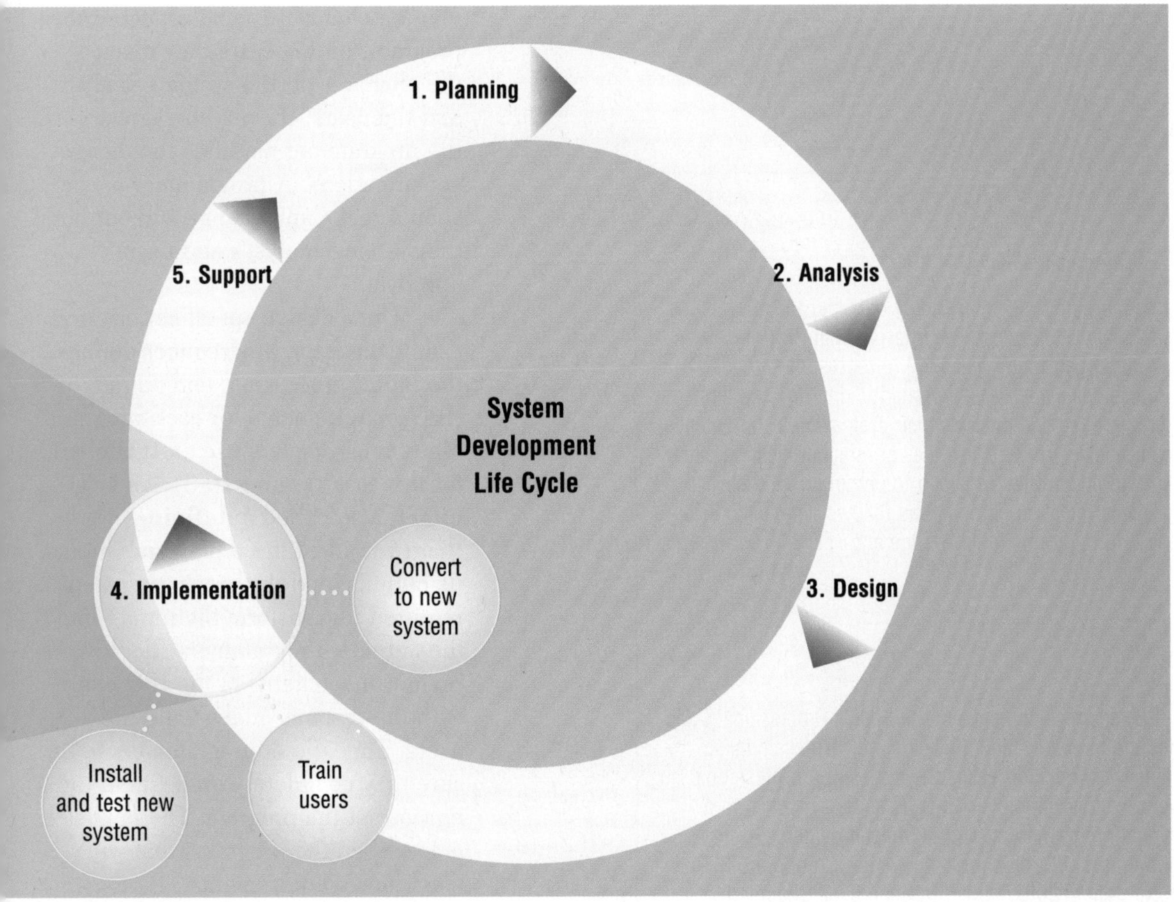

Figure 15-2 The program development life cycle is part of the implementation phase of the system development life cycle.

The scope of the program specification package largely determines how many programmers work on the program development. If scope is large, a **programming team** that consists of a group of programmers may develop the programs. If the specifications are fairly simple, a single programmer might complete all of the development tasks. Whether a single programmer or a programming team, all of the programmers involved must interact with users and members of the development team throughout the PDLC.

By following the steps in the PDLC, programmers can create programs that are correct (produce accurate information) and maintainable (easy to modify). Interacting with the development team further helps programmers build programs to meet user requirements.

The following sections address each of the steps in the PDLC.

STEP 1 – ANALYZE PROBLEM

The first step in the PDLC is to analyze the problem the program(s) should solve so you can begin to develop an appropriate solution. In most cases, the solution requires more than one program. This analysis step consists of three major tasks: (1) review the program specifications package, (2) meet with the systems analyst and users, and (3) identify each program's input, output, and processing components.

First, the programmer reviews the program specifications package. This package identifies the input, output, processing, and data requirements for each program. It also shows relationships among programs.

The program specifications package contains a variety of deliverables such as charts, diagrams, and reports. These deliverables document various aspects of the users' requirements. For example, screen and report layout charts show input and output requirements. System flowcharts, structured English, decision tables, and decision trees convey program design (processing) requirements. The data dictionary identifies the data requirements. By thoroughly reviewing these deliverables, the programmer understands the nature and requirements of each program.

During this step, the programmer also meets with the systems analyst and the users. This enables the programmer to understand the purpose of the program from the users' perspective. Recall from Chapter 14 that a guideline of system development is to involve users throughout the entire SDLC.

After reviewing the program specifications package and meeting with the systems analyst and users, the programmers may wish to recommend a change to some aspect of the program. In this case, they discuss the change with the systems analyst and the users. If everyone agrees, the programmer modifies the design specifications. A programmer never should make any change without both the systems analyst's and users' approval.

Once design specifications are established, the programmer defines the input, processing, and output (IPO) requirements for each program. Many programmers use an IPO chart for this task (Figure 15-3). An **IPO chart**, also called a **defining diagram**, identifies a program's inputs, its outputs, and the processing steps required to transform the inputs into the outputs. Programmers should review the contents of the IPO chart with the systems analyst and the users. This allows programmers to be sure they completely understand the purpose of the program. The next step is to design the programs that will meet these requirements.

APPLY IT!

Programmers' Code of Ethics

If your career goal is to be a programmer, you should consider the advantages of belonging to a professional organization. The International Programmer Guild (IPG) is a professional organization designed to represent and assist programmers. Many professionals such as accountants, doctors, lawyers, teachers, and so on are required to demonstrate their professional competence through certification and licensing. The IPG provides several certification paths and encourages members to be certified as a way to demonstrate their professional competence. The certification paths are as follows, with each level representing an increase in programming knowledge and skills:

- Junior Member
- Interim Member
- Fellow Programmer
- Senior Programmer
- Master Programmer

Membership in the IPG requires adherence to the Guild's Professional Code of Ethics, which outlines the principles and guidelines for professionalism in the programming field. This code addresses the duties of a professional programmer to the public, to their employer, in independent practice to a client, to other professional programmers, and to himself or herself.

For more information on the IPG, visit the Discovering Computers 2002 Apply It Web page (**scsite.com/dc2002/apply.htm**) and click Chapter 15 Apply It #1.

STEP 2 – DESIGN PROGRAMS

Designing the programs involves three tasks: (1) grouping each program's activities into modules, (2) devising a solution algorithm for each module, and (3) testing the solution algorithms. The first task is called top-down design. The last two tasks are part of a process called structured design.

Top-down design continues to focus on *what* the program should do (the requirements). Structured design determines *how* to build the programs based on the requirements. The following sections present details about top-down and structured design.

Top-Down Design

Top-down design breaks down the original set of program specifications into smaller, more manageable sections. It is easier to design smaller sections one at a time than to design the entire program at once. With top-sections. It is easier to design smaller sections one at a time than to design the entire program at once. With top-down design, the programmer uses a telescopic approach to view a program. The programmer begins with the big picture and then zooms in on the details.

The first step in top-down design is to identify the major function of a program, sometimes called the main routine. Next, you decompose (break down) the main routine into smaller sections. These smaller sections often are called subroutines because they are subordinate to the main routine. Then, analyze each subroutine to determine if it can be decomposed further. You continue decomposing subroutines until each one performs a single function. A section of a program that performs a single function is a **module**. Each subroutine also is a module. The main routine often is called the main module.

Web Link

For more information on top-down design, visit the Discovering Computers 2002 Chapter 15 WEB LINK page (**scsite.com/dc2002/ch15/weblink.htm**) and click Top-Down Design.

ISSUE

Calling All High School Students

Recruiting Programmers

The U.S. Department of Commerce predicts that there is a need for more than a million new technology workers. Computer scientists, computer engineers, systems analysts, programmers, and network technicians are just some of the high-demand skill sets needed. When it comes to applicants, supply is not keeping up with demand. To ease the shortage, companies are recruiting high-school students by offering them attractive training programs that lead to lucrative jobs. Will students who begin technological training right out of high school have a background general enough for other pursuits if their interest fades or the market withers? Do you think companies should be allowed to sign high-school students? Why or why not? What can be done to address long-term concerns?

For more information on IT workers in demand, visit the Discovering Computers 2002 Issues Web page (**scsite.com/dc2002/issues.htm**) and click Chapter 15 Issue #1.

INPUT	PROCESSING	OUTPUT
Regular Time Hours Worked	Read regular time hours worked, overtime hours worked, hourly pay rate.	Gross Pay
Overtime Hours Worked	Calculate regular time pay.	
Hourly Pay Rate	If employee worked overtime, calculate overtime pay.	
	Calculate gross pay.	
	Print gross pay.	

Figure 15-3 An IPO (Input Process Output) chart is a tool that assists the programmer in analyzing a program.

Web Link

For more information on structured design, visit the Discovering Computers 2002 Chapter 15 WEB LINK page (**scsite.com/dc2002/ch15/weblink.htm**) and click Structured Design.

Programmers use a **hierarchy chart**, also called a **structure chart** or **top-down chart**, to show program modules graphically (Figure 15-4). A hierarchy chart contains rectangles and lines. The rectangles are the modules. The main module is at the top of the chart. You place all other modules below the main module, connecting modules with lines to indicate their relationships. In Figure 15-4, for example, the initialization, process, and wrap-up modules are subordinate to the main module.

Programs developed using the top-down approach benefit from the simplicity of their design. They usually are reliable and easy to read and maintain. For these reasons, many IT professionals and programmers recommend the top-down approach to program design.

Structured Design

Using top-down design, the programmer identified the modules for a program (the *what*). The next step is to use structured design to identify the logical order of the tasks required to accomplish the function of each module (the *how*).

Structured design is a technique that builds all program logic from a combination of three control structures. A **control structure**, also known as a **construct**, is a design that determines the logical order of program instructions. Each module in a program typically contains more than one control structure. Structured design uses three basic control structures: sequence, selection, and repetition.

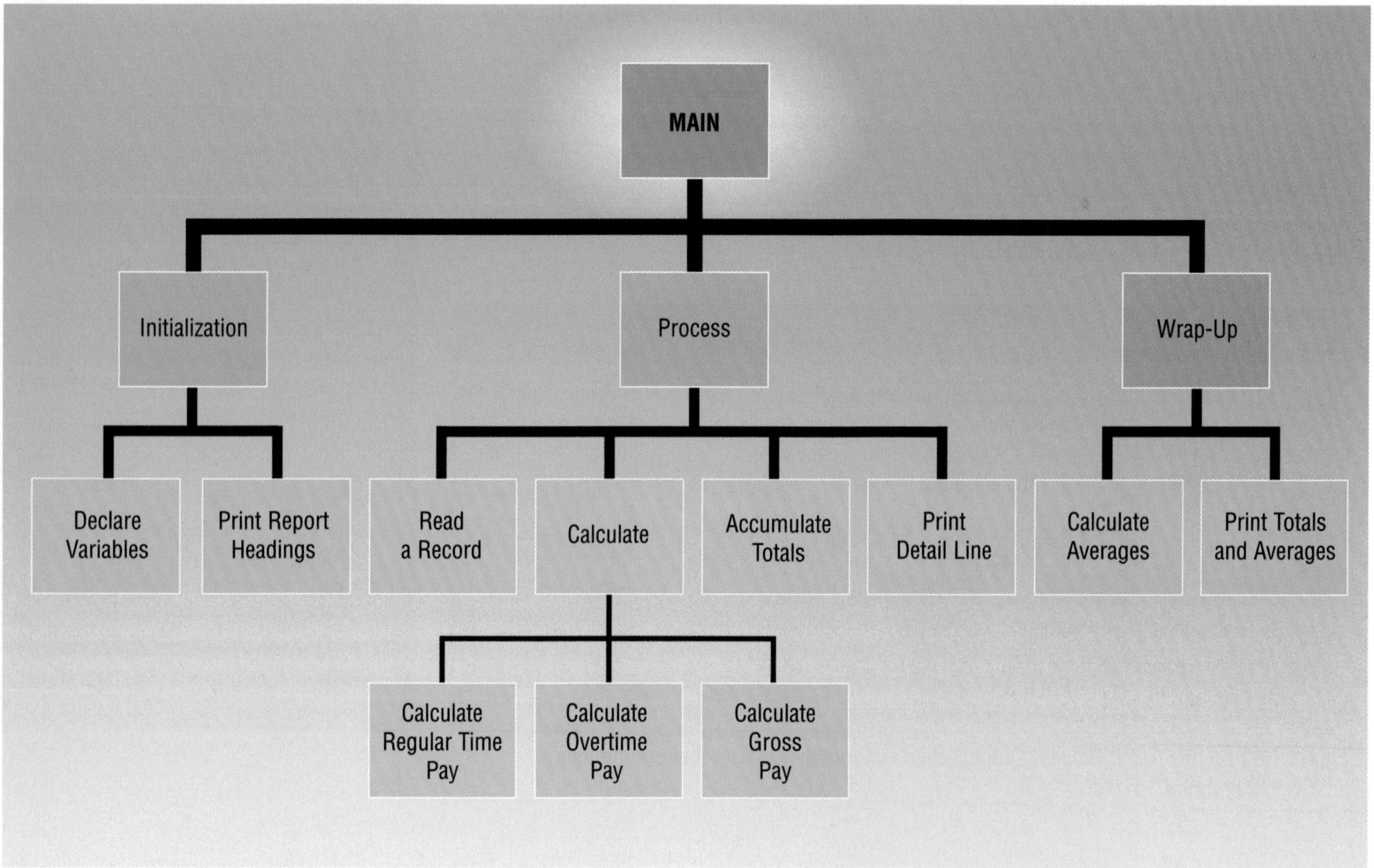

Figure 15-4 The hierarchy chart is a tool the programmer uses during top-down design. On the hierarchy chart, the program modules are drawn as rectangles. All modules are subordinate to the main module.

SEQUENCE CONTROL STRUCTURE

A **sequence control structure** shows one or more actions following each other in order (Figure 15-5). Actions include inputs, processes, and outputs. Examples of actions are reading a record, calculating averages or totals, and printing totals.

SELECTION CONTROL STRUCTURE

A **selection control structure** tells the program which action to take, based on a certain condition. Two common types of selection control structures are the if-then-else and the case.

When a program evaluates the condition in an **if-then-else control structure**, it yields one of two possibilities: true or false. Figure 15-6 shows the condition as a diamond symbol. If the result of the condition is true, then the program performs one action. If the result is false, the program performs a different (or possibly no) action. For example, the selection control structure can determine if an employee should receive overtime pay. A possible condition might be the following: Is Overtime Hours greater than 0? If the response is yes (true), then the action would calculate overtime pay. If the response is no (false), then the action would set overtime pay equal to zero.

With the **case control structure**, a condition can yield one of three or more possibilities (Figure 15-7). The size of a soft drink, for example, might be one of these options: small, medium, large, or extra large. A case control structure would determine the price of the soft drink based on the size purchased.

Selection Control Structure

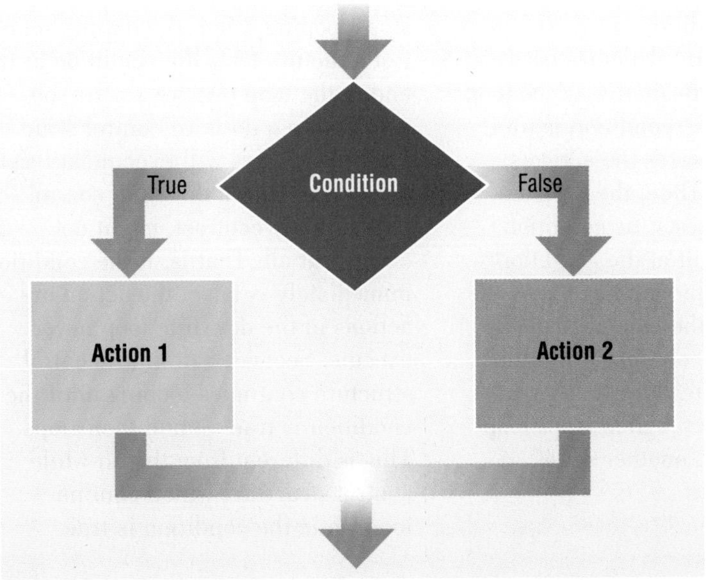

Figure 15-6 The if-then-else control structure directs the program toward one course of action or another based on the evaluation of a condition.

Sequence Control Structure

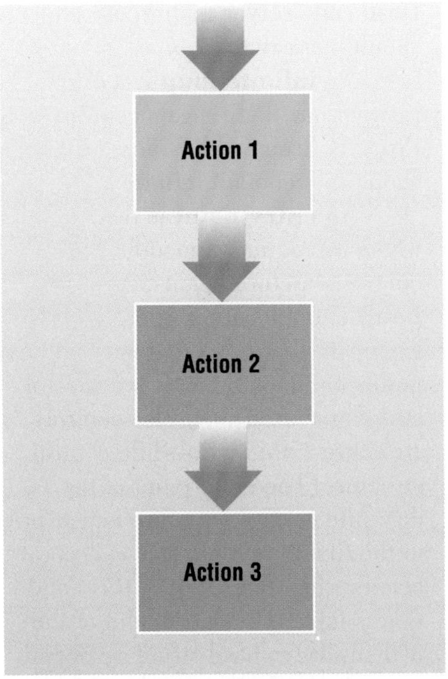

Figure 15-5 The sequence control structure shows one or more actions followed by another.

Case Control Structure

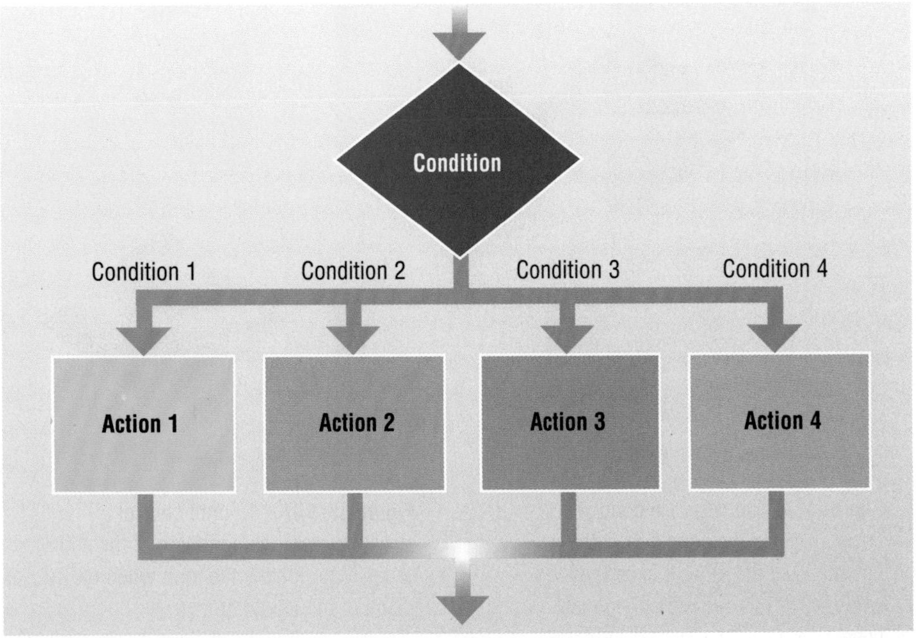

Figure 15-7 The case control structure allows for more than two alternatives when a condition is evaluated.

REPETITION CONTROL STRUCTURE Use the **repetition control structure**, also called the **iteration control structure**, when a program performs one or more actions repeatedly as long as a certain condition is met. Many programmers refer to this construct as a **loop**. Two forms of the repetition control structure are the do-while and do-until.

The **do-while control structure** repeats one or more times as long as a condition is true (Figure 15-8). This control structure tests a condition at the beginning of the loop. If the result of the condition is true, the program executes the action(s) inside the loop. Then, the program loops back and tests the condition again. If the result of the condition still is true, the program executes the action(s) inside the loop again. This looping process continues until the condition being tested becomes false. At that time, the program stops looping and moves to another set of actions.

Programmers frequently use the do-while control structure to process all records in a file. A payroll program using a do-while control structure, for example, loops once for each employee. This program stops looping when it processes the last employee's record.

The **do-until control structure** is similar to the do-while but has two major differences: where it tests the condition and when it stops looping. First, the do-until control structure tests the condition at the end of the loop (Figure 15-9). The action(s) in a do-until control structure thus always will execute at least once. The loop in do-while control structure, by contrast, might not execute at all. That is, if the condition immediately is false, the action or actions in the do-while loop never execute. Second, a do-until control structure continues looping until the condition is true — and then stops. This is different from the do-while control structure, which continues to loop while the condition is true.

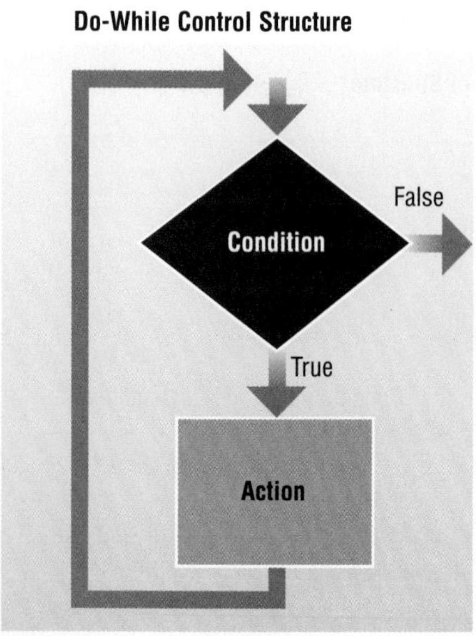

Figure 15-8 The do-while control structure tests the condition at the beginning of the loop. It exits the loop when the result of the condition is false.

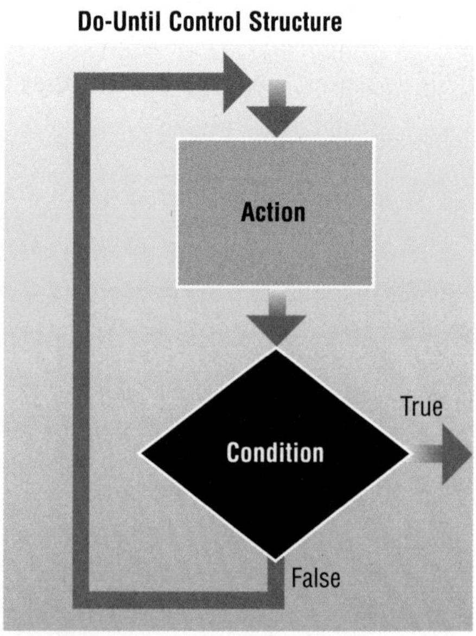

Figure 15-9 The do-until control structure tests the condition at the end of the loop. It exits the loop when the result of the condition is true.

Proper Program Design

Programs designed using top-down and structured techniques are simple, yet effective. These programs also are reliable and easy to use and maintain. When using top-down and structured techniques, a programmer must be sure to follow the guidelines of a proper program. To write a **proper program**, the programmer must make certain that the program, each of its modules, and each of its control structures has the following characteristics:

1. No dead code
2. No infinite loops
3. One entry point
4. One exit point

Dead code is any code, or program instruction, that a program never executes. When programmers write a program, they write a section of code in the program. Sometimes they decide not to use the code, but leave it in the program anyway. This unused code is known as dead code. Dead code serves no purpose and should not exist.

An **infinite loop** is a set of instructions that repeats continuously. Properly designed business programs should not contain infinite loops.

An **entry point** is the location where a program, a module, or a control structure begins. An **exit point** is the location where it ends. Figure 15-10 shows the entry and exit points of a module with two control structures: an if-then-else control structure within a do-while control structure. The entry point of the do-while control structure is just prior to the first condition. The exit point occurs when the result of this condition is false. The entry point of the if-then-else control structure occurs just prior to the second condition. The exit point occurs just after the program executes one of the two actions.

A properly designed program, module, or control structure has only one entry point and one exit point. Prior to the introduction of this concept, programmers often designed programs with multiple entry and exit points. This caused the program to jump frequently from one section of code to another. Some people use the term, spaghetti code, to refer to these poorly designed programs. This is because if you draw a line connecting all of the jumps together, the resulting line would look like cooked spaghetti! If you restrict program logic to the three basic control structures, your programs naturally will follow the single entry and single exit point rule.

Design Tools

A **solution algorithm,** also called **program logic**, is a graphical or written description of the step-by-step procedures in a module. Determining the logic for a program usually is a programmer's most challenging task. It requires that the programmer understand structured design concepts, as well as creativity. Defining the solution algorithm is both a skill and an art.

To help develop a solution algorithm, programmers use **design tools**. Three design tools are program flowcharts, Nassi-Schneiderman charts, and pseudocode.

PROGRAM FLOWCHART A **program flowchart**, or simply **flowchart**, graphically shows the logic in a solution algorithm. The American National Standards Institute (ANSI) published a set of standards for program flowcharts in the early 1960s. These standards, still used today, specify symbols for various operations in a program's logic (Figure 15-11).

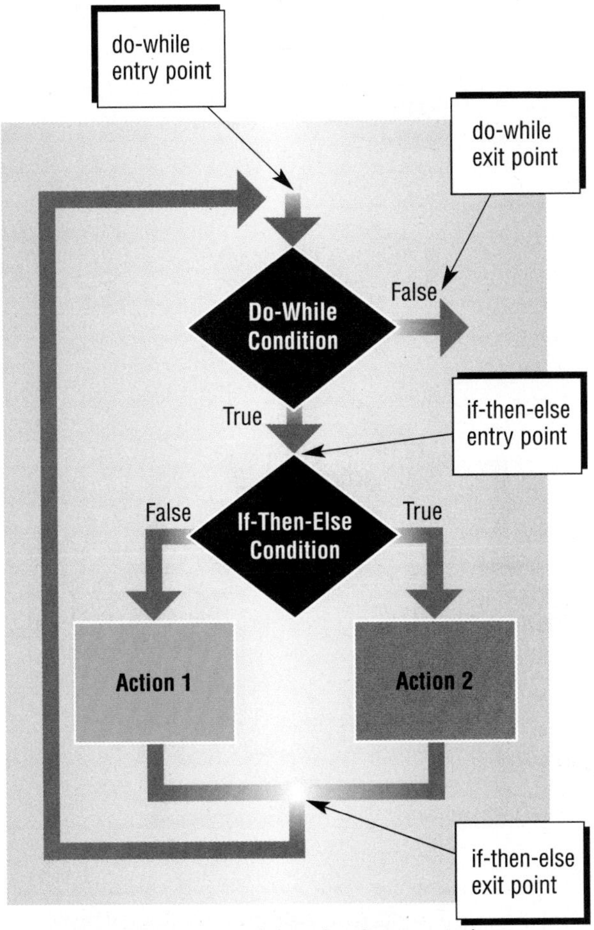

Figure 15-10 Program modules often have control structures nested inside one another, each of which should have one entry point and one exit point. In this example, an if-then-else is nested inside a do-while. The entry and exit points adhere to proper program design.

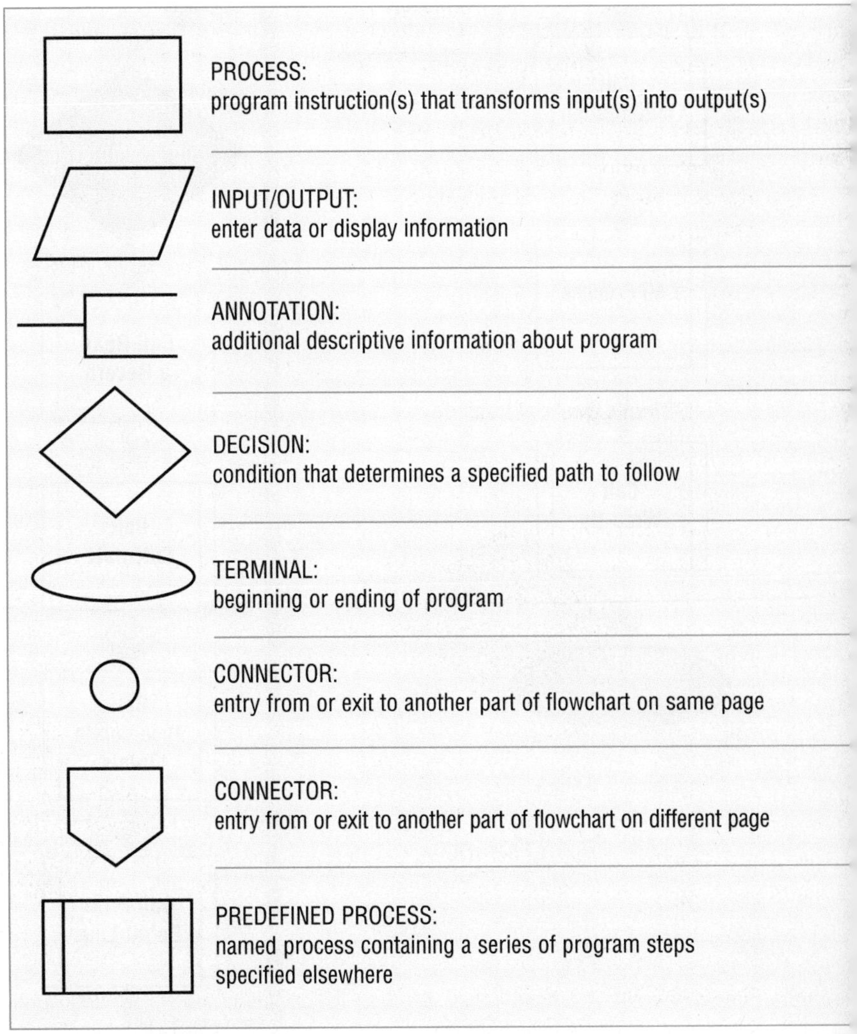

Figure 15-11 Standard symbols used to create program flowcharts.

Web Link

For more information on flowcharting software, visit the Discovering Computers 2002 Chapter 15 WEB LINK page (**scsite.com/dc2002/ch15/weblink.htm**) and click Flowcharting Software.

Programmers connect most symbols on a program flowchart with solid lines. These lines show the direction of the program. Dotted lines on a flowchart connect comment symbols. A **comment symbol**, also called an **annotation symbol**, explains or clarifies logic in the solution algorithm. Figure 15-12 shows the program flowchart for three modules of the program shown in the hierarchy chart in Figure 15-4 on page 15.6.

In the past, programmers used a template to trace the symbols for a flowchart on paper. Today, programmers use commercial **flowcharting software** to develop flowcharts. This software makes it easy to modify and update flowcharts (Figure 15-13).

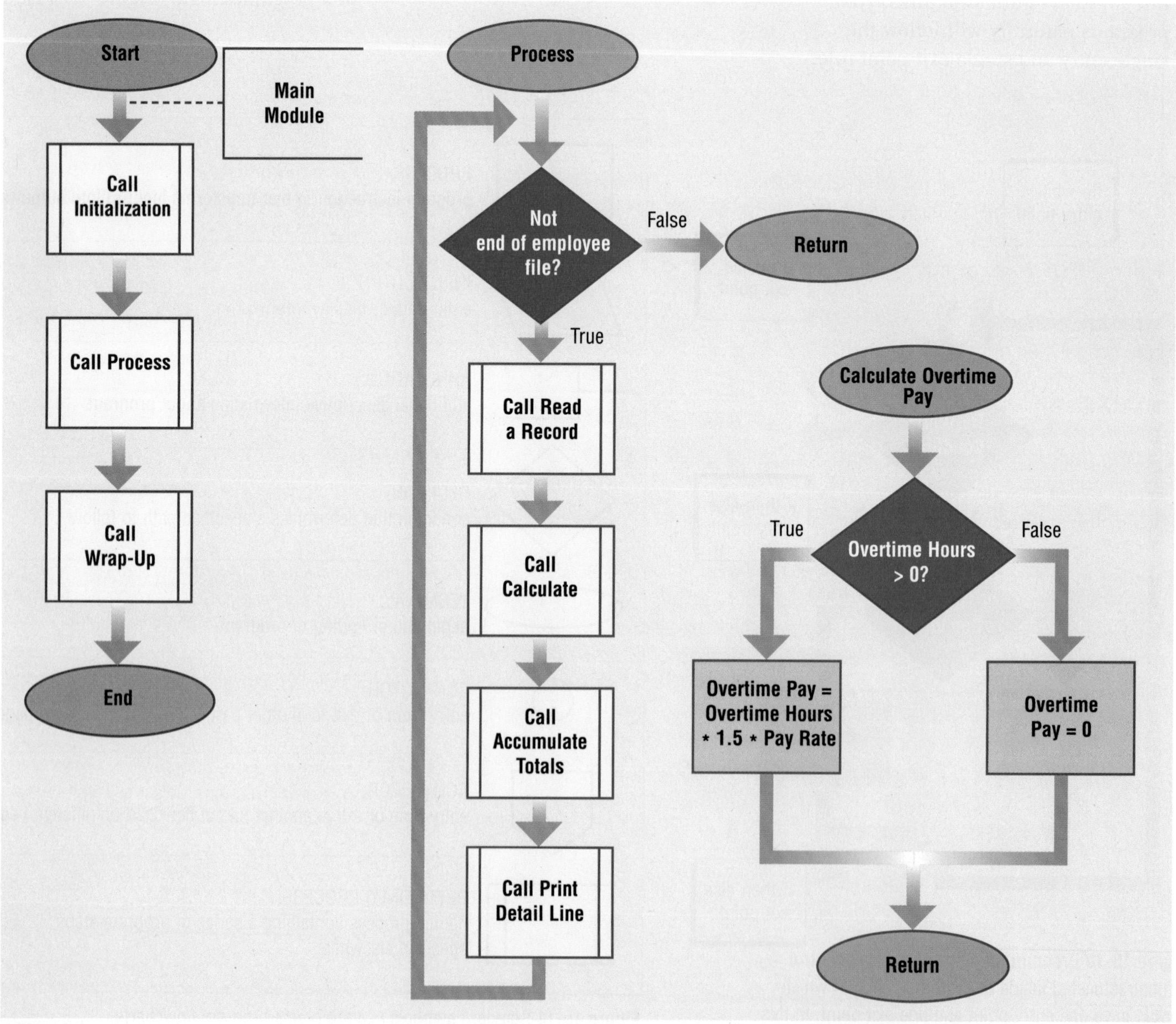

Figure 15-12 A program flowchart is drawn for each module on the hierarchy chart. Three modules from Figure 15-4 on page 15.6 are shown in this figure: main, process, and calculate overtime pay. Notice the main module is terminated with the word, End; whereas, the subordinate modules end with the word, Return, because they return to a higher-level module.

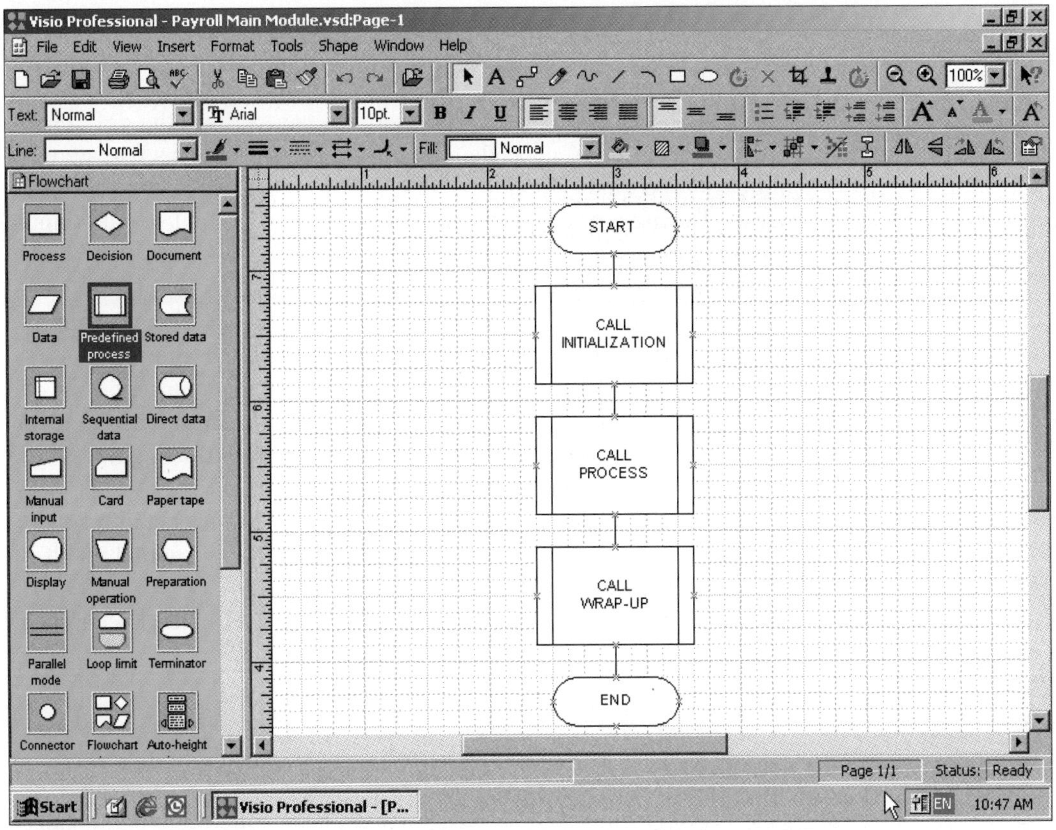

Figure 15-13 Visio is a popular flowcharting software package.

NASSI-SCHNEIDERMAN CHART A **Nassi-Schneiderman (N-S) chart** also graphically shows the logic in a solution algorithm. N-S charts sometimes are called **structured flowcharts** because they easily represent each of the three basic control structures. Unlike a program flowchart, an N-S chart does not use lines to show direction. Instead, N-S charts use a series of rectangular boxes, one below the next, with the flow always moving from top to bottom. Figure 15-14 shows N-S charts for the same three program modules shown as flowcharts in Figure 15-12.

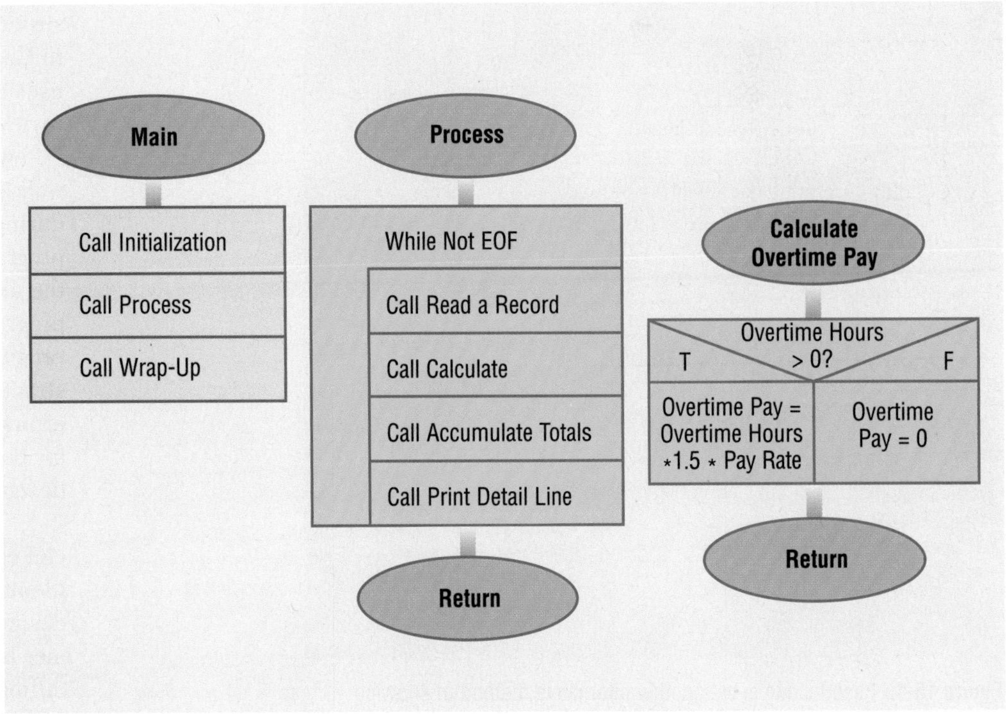

Figure 15-14 An N-S chart is an alternative method of showing program logic. This figure shows the same three modules (main, process, and calculate overtime pay) as illustrated in Figure 15-12 with program flowcharts.

PSEUDOCODE Some programmers prefer to explain the logic of a solution algorithm with words, instead of a graphical flowcharting technique. **Pseudocode** uses a condensed form of English to convey program logic. It also uses indentation to identify the three basic control structures. The beginning and ending of the module start at the left margin. You indent the actions within the module. The actions within a selection or repetition control structure are indented again. This allows you to identify clearly the beginning and ending of the control structure. Figure 15-15 shows the pseudocode for the same three program modules as in Figure 15-12 on page 15.10 and Figure 15-14 on the previous page.

```
MAIN MODULE:

        CALL Initialization
        CALL Process
        CALL Wrap-Up

END

PROCESS MODULE:

        DO WHILE Not EOF
            CALL Read a Record
            CALL Calculate
            CALL Accumulate Totals
            CALL Print Detail Line
        ENDDO

RETURN

CALCULATE OVERTIME PAY MODULE:

        IF Overtime Hours > 0 THEN
            Overtime Pay = Overtime Hours * 1.5 * Pay Rate
        ELSE
            Overtime Pay = 0
        ENDIF

RETURN
```

Figure 15-15 Pseudocode is yet another alternative method of showing program logic. This figure shows the same three modules (main, process, and calculate overtime pay) as illustrated in Figure 15-12 on page 15.10 with program flowcharts and Figure 15-14 on the previous page with N-S charts.

Quality Review Techniques

Once programmers develop the solution algorithm using a program flowchart, an N-S chart, or pseudocode, they should perform a quality review of the program. During a **quality review**, the programmer checks the logic for correctness and attempts to uncover logic errors. A **logic error** is a flaw in the design that causes inaccurate results. Two techniques for reviewing a solution algorithm are a desk check and a structured walkthrough.

When you **desk check** a program, you use test data to step through its logic. **Test data** is sample data that mimics data the program might process once it is in production. The programmer that developed the solution algorithm usually performs the desk check, but another programmer also can perform the desk check. Desk checking involves five steps.

1. Developing sets of test data (inputs)
2. Determining the expected result (output) for each set of data, without using the solution algorithm
3. Stepping through the solution algorithm using one set of test data and writing down the actual result obtained (output) using the solution algorithm
4. Comparing the expected result from Step 2 to the actual result from Step 3
5. Repeating Steps 3 and 4 for each set of test data

If the expected result and actual result do not match for any set of data, the program has a logic error. When this occurs, the programmer must review the logic of the solution algorithm to determine the reason for the error and then correct it.

A more formal technique for checking the solution algorithm is a structured walkthrough. As discussed in Chapter 14, a systems analyst often uses a structured walkthrough to review deliverables during the SDLC. Likewise, a programmer can request a walkthrough of a solution algorithm during the PDLC. In this case, the programmer explains the logic of the algorithm while members of the programming team step through the program logic. The purpose of this structured walkthrough is to identify errors in the program logic and check for possible improvements in program design.

Usually, a programmer easily can correct errors or improvements identified at this point. Once program design is complete and the programmer begins coding, errors are more difficult to fix. Thus, detecting errors and making improvements early in the PDLC reduces the overall time and cost of program development.

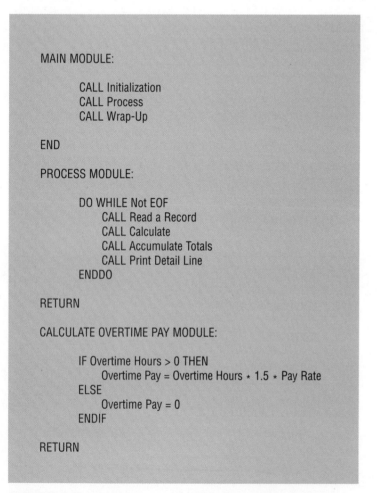

STEP 3 – CODE PROGRAMS

Coding a program involves two steps: (1) translating the solution algorithm into a programming language and (2) entering the programming language code into the computer. Of all tasks, programmers usually find coding the most tedious.

As previously mentioned, many different programming languages exist. Each of these has a particular syntax. A language's **syntax** is the set of grammar and rules that specifies how to write instructions for a solution algorithm. For example, a programmer writes an instruction to add three numbers differently in each language, according to its syntax.

As you enter a program into the computer, you should take time to document the program code thoroughly. Thus far, the programmer has created external program documentation in the form of flowcharts, N-S charts, or pseudocode. A program also has its own documentation, called **comments** or **remarks**.

Programs should include both global and internal comments (Figure 15-16). **Global comments** explain the program's purpose and identify the program name, its author, and the date written. Generally, global comments are at the top of the program. Internal comments, by contrast, appear throughout the body of the program. **Internal comments** explain the purpose of the code statements within the program. Programs that include global and internal comments are much easier to maintain.

STEP 4 – TEST PROGRAMS

Once a programmer codes and enters the program, the next step is to test it. Thorough testing is very important. Once the program is put into use, many users rely on the program and its output to support their daily activities and decisions. Users should assist in the development of test data.

The goal of program testing is to ensure the program runs correctly and is error free. Errors uncovered during this step usually are one of two types: (1) syntax errors or (2) logic errors.

A **syntax error** occurs when the code violates the syntax, or grammar, of the programming language. Misspelling a command, leaving out required punctuation, or typing command words out of order all will cause syntax errors. You usually discover syntax errors the first time you execute the program code on the computer. When a syntax error is located, a message either displays on the screen immediately or is written to a log file. Either way, the programmer must review and correct all syntax errors. The procedure for testing for logic errors at this step is much like the desk checking techniques used in the Design Programs step. First, you develop test data. In the Design Programs step, the programmer develops the test data. In this Test Programs step, by contrast, the systems analyst usually develops the test data. The test data should include both valid (correct) and invalid (incorrect) input data. When valid test data is input, the program should produce the correct result. If the expected result and actual result do not match, the program has a logic error. In this case, the programmer must review the logic of the program code to determine the cause of the logic error and then correct it.

Another purpose of using test data is to try to crash the system. For example, the programmer will deliberately try to cause **run time errors**, or make the program fail while it is running. If the pay rate for employees cannot exceed $55 per hour, then the test data should use some valid pay rates, such as $25 and $10.50, as well as some invalid ones, such as $-32.00 and $72.50. When you input an invalid pay rate, the program should display an error message and allow you to re-enter the pay rate. If, however, the program accepts an invalid pay rate, it contains a logic error.

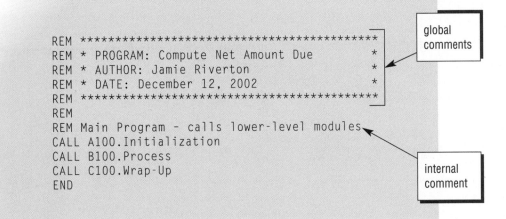

```
REM *****************************************
REM * PROGRAM: Compute Net Amount Due       *
REM * AUTHOR: Jamie Riverton                *
REM * DATE: December 12, 2002               *
REM *****************************************
REM
REM Main Program - calls lower-level modules
CALL A100.Initialization
CALL B100.Process
CALL C100.Wrap-Up
END
```

global comments

internal comment

Figure 15-16 Thorough documentation leads to maintainable programs. A program should contain global comments (at the top of the program) and internal comments (throughout the body of the program). In this QuickBASIC program, comments are identified by the letters, REM, which are an abbreviation for REMARK.

The process of locating and correcting syntax and logic errors in a program is known as **debugging** the program. The errors themselves are the bugs. Thus, removing the errors is de*bug*ging. It is said that the term bug originated when the failure of one of the first computers was traced to an actual bug. A moth lodged in the computer's electronic components was the cause of the failure (Figure 15-17).

Most programming languages include a debug utility. A **debug utility**, or **debugger**, allows you to identify syntax errors and to find logic errors. With these utilities, you can examine program values (such as the result of a calculation) while the program runs in slow motion.

A bug that had the potential to cause serious financial losses for computers around the world was the millennium bug. The **millennium bug**, or **Y2K bug**, took effect when the computer date rolled over to January 1, 2000. At this time, non-Y2K compliant computers read the date as 01/01/00. Computers that used just the last two digits of a year could not distinguish 01/01/1900 from 01/01/2000. Most companies prepared themselves thoroughly for the Y2K bug and made necessary corrections to dates in hardware and software well in advance of January 1, 2000. Even with proper preparation, some computer hardware and software had problems.

If a program is well designed during the Design Programs step, then testing should not require much time. When a programmer does not test the solution algorithm thoroughly during design, many logic errors may exist and testing can take longer. As a general rule, the more time and effort programmers spend analyzing and designing the solution algorithm, the less time they will spend debugging the program.

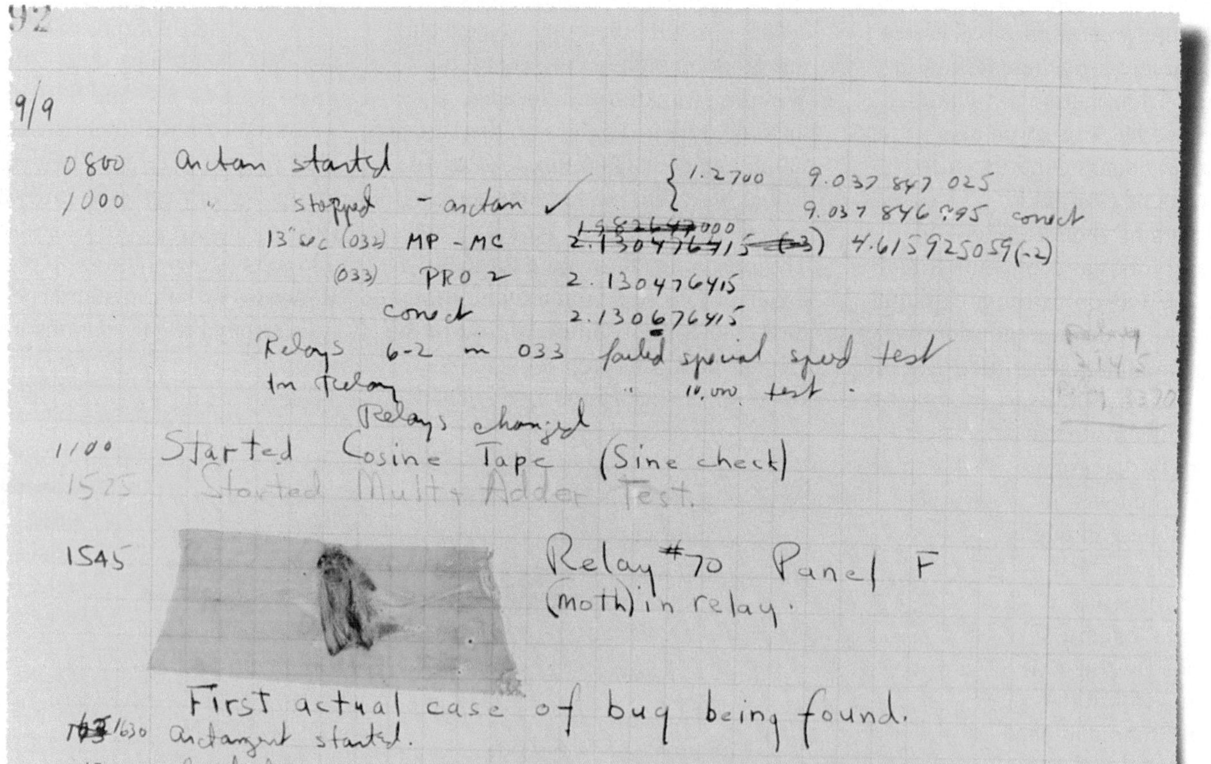

Figure 15-17 The temporary failure of one of the first computers was traced to a dead moth (shown taped to the log book) caught in the electrical components. Some say this event is the origin of the term bug, which means computer error.

STEP 5 – FORMALIZE SOLUTION

In formalizing the solution, the programmer performs two activities: (1) review the program code and (2) review all the documentation.

First, programmers review the program for any dead code and remove it. Then, they should run the program one final time to verify it still works.

After reviewing the program code, the programmer gives the program and all of its documentation to the systems analyst. The documentation includes the following: a hierarchy chart; a solution algorithm in the form of a program flowchart, an N-S chart, or pseudocode; test data; and program code listings that contain global and internal comments.

The programmer should be sure all documentation is complete and accurate. This becomes especially valuable if the program requires changes at a later date. One year later, a new programmer might have to update these programs. Proper documentation greatly reduces the amount of time a new programmer spends learning about existing programs.

STEP 6 – MAINTAIN PROGRAMS

Maintaining programs involves two activities: (1) correcting errors and (2) adding enhancements. Once programs are **implemented**, or placed into production, users interact with the programs. These programs process actual, also known as live, transactions.

During the course of their use, programs may require maintenance. One type of maintenance occurs when users encounter program errors. If the programmer and systems analyst thoroughly tested the solution algorithm and program code in the earlier steps, the number of errors found during production should be very small.

A more common type of maintenance occurs when a user would like the program to have new features or functionality. **Program enhancement** involves modifying existing programs to improve their functionality.

When users identify errors or enhancements, they typically notify the systems analyst. The systems analyst then contacts and meets with a programmer. Sometimes, the systems analyst meets with the programmer who wrote the original program. If the programmer is not available, the systems analyst meets with a different programmer. During the initial meeting, the systems analyst and the programmer begin analyzing the problem or enhancement, which is Step 1 of the PDLC. The PDLC thus completes its loop and begins again.

ISSUE

Coping with Bugs

Huge Costs of Computer Bugs

The consequences of bugs in computer programs can be staggering. One mistake in the code controlling a Canadian nuclear facility caused more than 3,000 gallons of radioactive water to be spilled. A bug in AT&T's long-distance switching software cost the company $60 million. Despite sophisticated debugging utilities, experts estimate that one in every 5,000 lines of code contains an error. Given that many programs contain hundreds of thousands, even millions, of code lines, is it possible to remove all the bugs from a program? Why or why not? What can be done to reduce the number of software bugs? If software bugs are inevitable, or at least to be expected depending on the complexity of the code, what steps can people relying on computer programs take to deal with the bugs? Should programmers be held responsible for these bugs?

For more information on debugging programs, visit the Discovering Computers 2002 Issues Web page (**scsite.com/dc2002/issues.htm**) and click Chapter 15 Issue #2.

PROGRAMMING LANGUAGES AND PROGRAM DEVELOPMENT TOOLS

A computer programmer can select from a variety of programming languages or program development tools to create solutions to information system requirements. A **programming language** is a set of words, symbols, and codes that enables a programmer to communicate a solution algorithm to the computer. Just as humans understand a variety of spoken languages (English, Spanish, French, and so on), you can use a variety of programming languages to code a program.

A **program development tool** consists of user-friendly software products designed to assist both programmers and nontechnical users with the creation of information system solutions. If you use a program development tool, you often do not need to learn a programming language. Program development tools automatically generate the programming language instructions necessary to communicate with the computer.

The following sections discuss programming languages and program development tools.

CATEGORIES OF PROGRAMMING LANGUAGES

Several hundred programming languages exist today. Each language has its own syntax, or rules. Some languages work with only certain computers. Other languages are for specific purposes, such as scientific or business applications. Many languages, however, run on several types of computers. These programming languages often follow standards set by the American National Standards Institute (ANSI). ANSI standard programs can run on many different types of computers, as well as many different operating systems.

Five major categories of programming languages exist: machine languages, assembly languages, third-generation languages, fourth-generation languages, and fifth-generation languages. These languages are classified as either low level or high level.

A **low-level language** is a programming language that is machine dependent. A **machine-dependent language** only runs on one particular computer. These programs are not portable to other computers. Machine and assembly languages are low-level languages.

A **high-level language**, by contrast, is a language that is machine independent. A **machine-independent language** can run on many different types of computers and operating systems. Third-generation, fourth-generation, and fifth-generation languages are high-level languages.

The following sections discuss each of the five major categories of programming languages.

Machine Languages (First-Generation Language)

Machine language is the first generation of programming languages. The only language the computer directly understands is **machine language** (Figure 15-18). Machine language instructions use a series of binary digits (1s and 0s) or a combination of numbers and letters that represent binary digits. The binary digits correspond to the on and off electrical states of a computer. As you might imagine, coding in machine language can be tedious and time-consuming.

Assembly Languages (Second-Generation Languages)

Assembly languages are the second generation of programming languages. With an **assembly language**, a programmer writes instructions using symbolic instruction codes (Figure 15-19). **Symbolic instruction codes**, or **mnemonics**, are meaningful abbreviations and codes. With an assembly language, a programmer writes codes such as A for addition, C for compare, L for load, and M for multiply.

Assembly languages also use symbolic addresses. A **symbolic address** is a meaningful name that identifies a storage location. For example, a programmer can use the name RATE to refer to the storage location that contains the pay rate.

Despite these advantages, assembly languages can be difficult to learn. In addition, you must convert an assembly language program into machine language before the computer can understand it. The computer cannot understand or execute the assembler source program. A **source program** is the program that contains the assembly language code. To convert the assembly language source program into machine language, you use an **assembler**.

One assembly language instruction usually translates into one machine language instruction. In some cases, however, the assembly language includes macros. This type of **macro** generates multiple machine language instructions for a single assembly language instruction. Macros save the programmer time during program development.

```
                                          00090
000090  50E0   30B2                       010B4
000094  1B44
000096  1B77
000098  1B55
00009A  F273   30D6   2C81   010D8        00C83
0000A0  4F50   30D6                       010D8
0000A4  F275   30D6   2C7B   010D8        00C7D
0000AA  4F70   30D6                       010D8
0000AE  5070   304A                       0104C
0000B2  1C47
0000B4  5050   304E                       01050
0000B8  58E0   30B2                       010B4
0000BC  07FE
                                          000BE
0000BE  50E0   30B6                       010B8
0000C2  95F1   2C85          00C87
0000C6  4770   20D2          000D4
0000CA  1B55
0000CC  5A50   35A6                       015A8
0000D0  47F0   2100          00102
0000D4  95F2   2C85          00C87
0000D8  4770   20E4          000E6
0000DC  1B55
0000DE  5A50   35AA                       015AC
0000E2  47F0   2100          00102
000102  1B77
000104  5870   304E                       01050
000108  1C47
00010A  4E50   30D6                       010D8
00010E  F075   30D6   003E   010D8        0003E
000114  4F50   30D6                       010D8
000118  5050   3052                       01054
00011C  58E0   30B6                       010B8
000120  07FE
                                          00122
000122  50E0   30BA                       010BC
000126  1B55
000128  5A50   304E                       01050
00012C  5B50   3052                       01054
000130  5050   305A                       0105C
000134  58E0   30BA                       010BC
000138  07FE
```

Figure 15-18 A sample machine language program.

```
*          THIS MODULE CALCULATES THE REGULAR TIME PAY
CALCSTPY   EQU    *
           ST     14,SAVERTPY
           SR     4,4
           SR     7,7
           SR     5,5
           PACK   DOUBLE,RTHRSIN
           CVB    4,DOUBLE
           PACK   DOUBLE,RATEIN
           CVB    7,DOUBLE
           ST     7,RATE
           MR     4,7
           ST     5,RTPAY
           L      14,SAVERTPY
           BR     14
*          THIS MODULE CALCULATES THE OVERTIME PAY
CALCOTPY   EQU    *
           ST     14,SAVEOTPY
TEST1      CLI    CODEIN,C'0'
           BH     TEST2
           SR     5,5
           A      5,=F'0'
           ST     5,OTPAY
           B      AROUND
TEST2      SR     4,4
           SR     7,7
           SR     5,5
           PACK   DOUBLE,OTHRSIN
           CVB    4,DOUBLE
           PACK   DOUBLE,RATEIN
           CVB    7,RATE
           MR     4,7
           MR     4,=F'1.5'
           ST     5,OTPAY
AROUND     L      14,SAVEOTPY
           BR     14
*          THIS MODULE CALCULATES THE GROSS PAY
CALCGPAY   EQU    *
           ST     14,SAVEGPAY
           SR     5,5
           A      5,RTPAY
           A      5,OTPAY
           ST     5,GRPAY
           L      14,SAVEGPAY
           BR     14
```

Figure 15-19 An excerpt from an assembly language program. The code shows the computations for regular time pay, overtime pay, and gross pay, and the decision to evaluate the overtime hours.

Third-Generation Languages

The disadvantages of low-level machine and assembly languages led to the development of third generation languages in the late 1950s and 1960s. A programmer uses a series of English-like words to write a **third-generation language (3GL)** instruction. For example, ADD stands for addition or PRINT means to print. Many 3GLs also use arithmetic operators such as * for multiplication and + for addition. These English-like words and arithmetic symbols simplify the program development process for the programmer.

Third-generation languages are procedural languages. A **procedural language** requires the program instructions tell the computer *what* to accomplish and *how* to do it. With most 3GLs a programmer can use both the top-down approach (modules) and structured constructs (sequence, selection, and repetition) within each module to develop these procedures.

Like an assembly language program, the 3GL code is called the source program. You must convert this source program into machine language before the computer can understand it. This translation process often is very complex, because one 3GL source program instruction translates into many machine language instructions. For 3GLs, you typically use either a compiler or an interpreter to perform this translation.

A **compiler** converts the entire source program into machine language before executing it. The machine language version that results from compiling the 3GL is called the **object code** or **object program**. The compiler stores the object code on disk for execution at a later time.

While it is compiling the source program into object code, the compiler checks the source program's syntax. It also makes sure the program properly defines the data it will use in calculations or comparisons. The compiler then produces a program listing, which contains the source code and a list of any syntax errors. This listing helps the programmer make necessary changes to the source code and debug the program. Figure 15-20 shows the process of compiling a source program.

A compiler translates an entire program before executing it. An interpreter, by contrast, translates and executes one program code statement at a time. An **interpreter** reads a code statement, converts it to one or more machine language instructions, and then executes those machine language instructions. It does this all before moving to the next code statement in the program. Each time you run the source program, the interpreter translates and executes it, statement by statement. An interpreter does not produce an object program. Figure 15-21 shows the process of interpreting a program.

One advantage of an interpreter is it immediately displays feedback when it finds a syntax error. The programmer can correct the error, or debug the code, before the interpreter translates the next line. The disadvantage is that interpreted programs do not run as fast as compiled programs. This is because an interpreter must translate the source program to machine language each time you execute it. Once you compile a program, however, you simply execute the object code to run the program.

Many programming languages include both an interpreter and a compiler. In this case, the programmer can use the interpreter to debug the program. Once debugged, the programmer can compile the program so it runs faster when it is placed into production.

```
*    COMPUTE REGULAR TIME PAY
     MULTIPLY REGULAR-TIME-HOURS BY HOURLY-PAY-RATE
         GIVING REGULAR-TIME-PAY.

*    COMPUTE OVERTIME PAY
     IF OVERTIME-HOURS > 0
          COMPUTE OVERTIME-PAY = OVERTIME-HOURS * 1.5 * HOURLY-PAY-RATE
     ELSE
         MOVE 0 TO OVERTIME-PAY.

*    COMPUTE GROSS PAY
     ADD REGULAR-TIME-PAY TO OVERTIME-PAY
         GIVING GROSS-PAY.

*    PRINT GROSS PAY
     MOVE GROSS-PAY TO GROSS-PAY-OUT.
     WRITE REPORT-LINE-OUT FROM DETAIL-LINE
         AFTER ADVANCING 2 LINES.
```

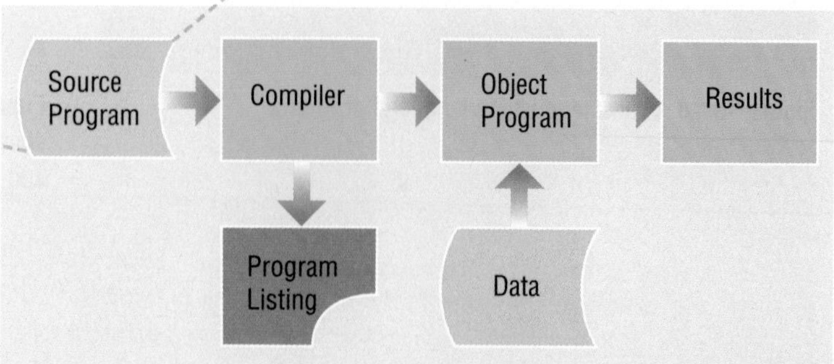

Figure 15-20 With a compiler, the entire source program is converted into a machine language object program. If the compiler encounters any errors, it records them in the program-listing file, which the programmer may print when the entire compilation is complete. When the user wants to run the program, the object program is loaded into the memory of the computer and the program instructions begin executing.

Fourth-Generation Languages

Like a 3GL, a **fourth-generation language** (**4GL**) uses English-like statements. The syntax of 4GL, however, is closer to human language than that of a 3GL. A 4GL is a nonprocedural language. With a **nonprocedural language**, the programmer only specifies *what* the program should accomplish without explaining how. Consequently, programmers spend much less time and effort coding programs with a 4GL. These languages tend to be quite easy to use. Thus, users with very little programming background also can develop programs using a 4GL.

Many 4GLs work with a database and its project dictionary. These powerful languages allow database administrators to define the database and its structure. They also help users maintain and query the data in the database. As discussed in Chapter 13, SQL is a popular ANSI-standard 4GL used with relational DBMSs (Figure 15-22). Recall that SQL is a **query language** enabling users and programmers to retrieve data from database tables. One query, for example, might request a list of all employees receiving overtime pay.

Some DBMSs provide a report writer. As discussed in Chapter 13, a **report writer** or **report generator** is software that allows you to design a report on the screen, retrieve data into the report design, and then display or print the report. Behind the scenes, these report writers build a 4GL query that enables you to access the data.

One advantage of a report writer is that you can retrieve data without having to learn a query language. Another advantage is you easily can include page numbers and dates; report titles and column headings; subtotals and totals; numeric formatting (such as dollars and cents); and other formatting features such as fonts, font sizes, color, and shading. Report writers usually are menu-driven and have a graphical user interface.

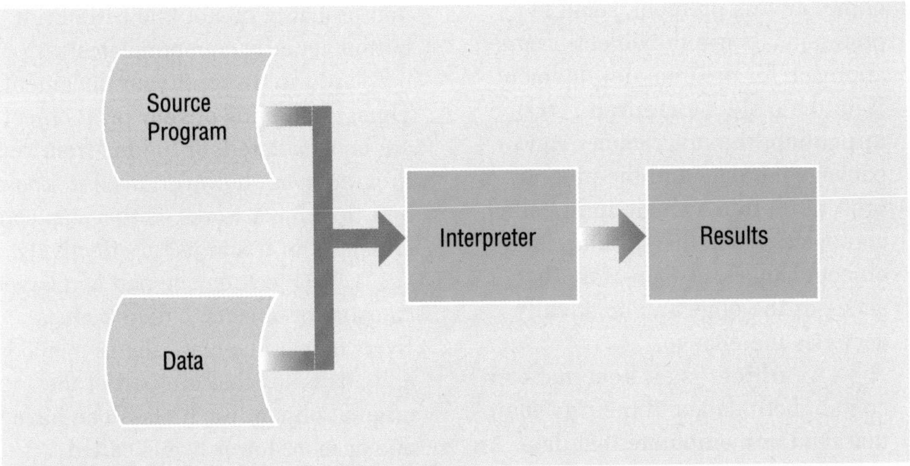

Figure 15-21 With an interpreter, one line of the source program at a time is converted into machine language and then immediately executed by the computer. If the interpreter encounters an error while converting a line of code, an error message immediately displays on the screen and the interpretation stops.

```
SELECT LAST_NAME, FIRST_NAME, GROSS_PAY

FROM EMPLOYEE

WHERE OVERTIME_HOURS > 0

ORDER BY LAST_NAME;

LAST_NAME     FIRST_NAME     GROSS_PAY

Antiqua       Martin            780.00
Charles       Leslie            715.00
Guillan       Anita             847.50
.
.
.
```

Figure 15-22 SQL is a fourth-generation language that can be used to query database tables. This query produces an alphabetical list of those employees who receive overtime pay; that is, their overtime hours are greater than zero.

Fifth-Generation Languages

A **fifth-generation language** (**5GL**) is one that provides a visual or graphical interface for creating the source code. The 5GL often converts the source code to machine language using a 3GL or a 4GL compiler. Object-oriented and Web development tools sometimes use a 5GL. Visual Basic, which is illustrated in Figure 15-25 on page 15.23, is a 5GL.

ISSUE

What's the Secret?

Sharing Program Code

Linux is a fast-growing, innovative new operating system. Linux differs from other operating systems because of its open source code, which means there are no proprietary restrictions to the operating system code. Anyone may alter the code to his or her own needs without asking for, or receiving, any permission. Something else that makes Linux different from other operating systems is that the program is downloadable right from the Web, and at no cost. Since its introduction in 1991, hundreds of programmers, each adding their expertise to make the code better, have altered, adapted, and improved Linux. While Linux is an open-source program, application code for other operating systems is a zealously guarded secret. At a large software developer firm, an employee claims that system programmers have little opportunity to contribute to application programs because they have no access to the application program source code. Why are many commercial software developers reluctant to share program code? What are the advantages of making program code public? What are the disadvantages?

For more information on open source code, visit the Discovering Computers 2002 Issues Web page (**scsite.com/dc2002/issues.htm**) and click Chapter 15 Issue #3.

OBJECT-ORIENTED PROGRAM DEVELOPMENT

As discussed earlier in this chapter, the introduction of structured program design and its three basic constructs largely solved the problem of spaghetti code. Structured program design, however, does not provide a way to keep the data and the program (or procedure) together. Each program has to define how it will use the data for a particular program. This can result in redundant programming code that must change every time the structure of the data changes. To eliminate this problem, some IT professionals use the object-oriented approach for program development. With the **object-oriented (OO) approach**, the programmer can package the data and the program (or procedure) into a single unit, called an object. When the structure of an object changes, any program that accesses the object automatically accesses the change.

An **object** is an item that can contain both data and the procedures that read or manipulate that data. An Employee object might contain data about an employee (Employee ID, First Name, Last Name, Address, and so on) and instructions on how to print the employee record or the formula required to calculate the employee's gross pay. The procedure in the object, called a **method** or **operation**, contains activities that read or manipulate the data. The data elements are called **attributes** or **variables**. For example, automobile manufacturers can program their assembly line cars (objects) to send messages to paint booths asking for an available slot and color (attributes).

Encapsulation, also called **information hiding**, is the concept of packaging methods and attributes into a single object. That is, an object encapsulates, or *hides*, the details of the object from the programmer. Think of an object as a box and you cannot see inside the box. The box sends and receives messages. It also contains code and data. Users do not need to look into the box because the object package is self-sufficient. When you want to print a document, you click the Print button (the object). You probably do not know the Print button actually communicates with the hardware to print your document. Thus, the details of your print object are encapsulated, or hidden from you. Programmers, however, need to know how the object works so they can send messages to it and use it effectively.

An object may be part of a larger category of objects, called a **class**. Every object in a class shares methods and attributes that are part of the original object. Each class can have one or more lower levels called **subclasses** (Figure 15-23). For example, ink-jet printer, laser printer, and thermal printer are all subclasses of a higher-level class, called printer. The higher-level class is called a **superclass**. Each subclass inherits the methods and attributes of the objects in its superclass. All printers have a weight (which would be an attribute in the printer object), but only ink-jet printers have ink-filled print cartridges. This concept of lower levels inheriting methods and attributes of higher levels is called **inheritance**.

A specific occurrence of an object or object class is called an **object instance**. For example, a Hewlett-Packard DeskJet printer in your home is an object instance of the ink-jet printer object.

To make an object do something, you send it a message. A **message** tells the object what to do. It indicates the name of the method to be used. For example, print a document might be a method of the printer object.

A major benefit of the OO approach is the ability to reuse and modify existing objects. If a program had to test the performance of 20 printers, a programmer could reuse the printer object over and over. The OO approach saves programming time when developing programs.

With the OO approach, the development team uses different analysis, design, and programming techniques and tools from those used in structured program development. Many developers today use Unified Modeling Language. **UML (Unified Modeling Language**) contains the standard notation for analysis, design, and documentation for the OO approach. Several CASE tools now include UML notations. Recall from Chapter 14 that a systems analyst uses CASE tools to automate activities in the system development process.

In the late 1990s, the Object Management Group adopted UML as a standard. The **Object Management Group** (**OMG**) is an international organization that establishes guidelines and specifications for OO application development. In addition to UML, the OMG also has adopted CORBA as a programming standard. **CORBA** (**Common Object Request Broker Architecture**) defines how objects in separate programs on a network can communicate with each other.

Object-Oriented Programming

With the OO approach, a programmer uses an **object-oriented programming** (**OOP**) **language** to implement the OO design. An OOP language is event-driven. **Event** is simply the OOP term for message. An event-driven program checks for and responds to a set of events. An event could be pressing a key on the keyboard, clicking the mouse, or typing a value into a text box. Some programming languages are not OOP languages, but they are event-driven. Others, such as C++, are complete object-oriented languages. The following section covers specific examples of these and other programming languages in more detail.

Web Link

For more information on object-oriented programming languages, visit the Discovering Computers 2002 Chapter 15 WEB LINK page (**scsite.com/dc2002/ch15/weblink.htm**) and click Object-Oriented Programming Languages.

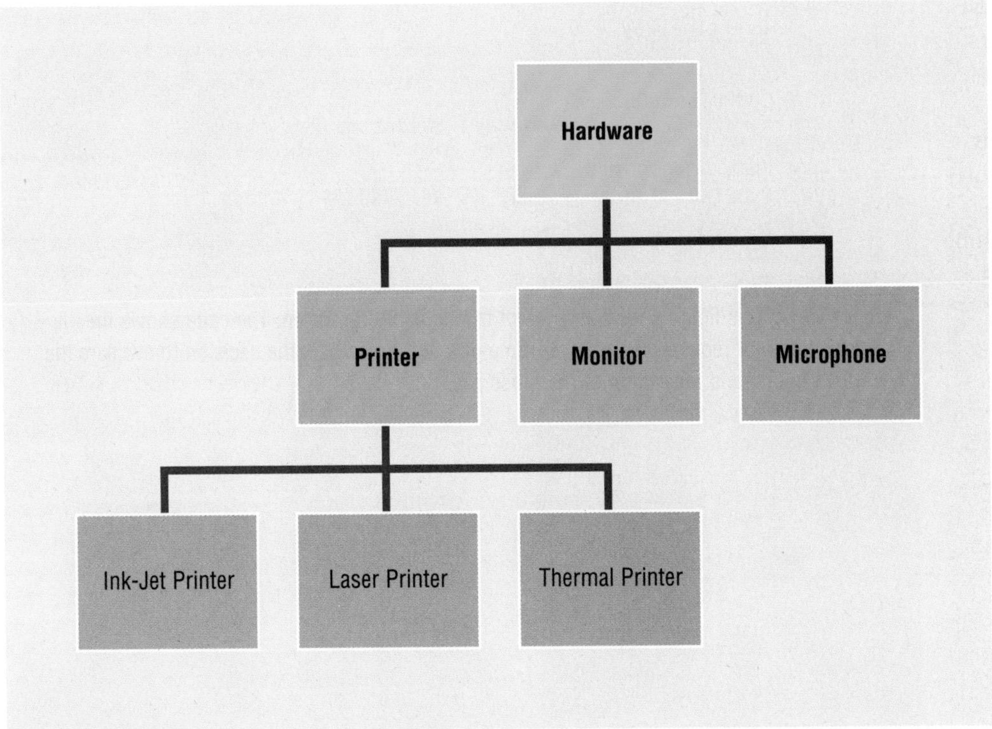

Figure 15-23 A generalization hierarchy is an object-oriented analysis tool that shows relationships between classes of an object. In this figure, printer has three subclasses. A subclass inherits (or acquires) the attributes and methods of its higher class.

PROGRAMMING LANGUAGES

Hundreds of programming languages exist. Only a few, however, are used widely enough today for the industry to recognize them as standards. Most of these are high-level languages that work on a variety of computers. This section discusses these programming languages, their origins, and their primary purpose. Languages used for Web page development and multimedia applications are discussed later in the chapter.

To illustrate the similarities and differences among programming languages, figures on the following pages show program code in several programming languages. The code solves a simple payroll problem — computing the gross pay for an employee. The steps to compute gross pay can vary from one system to another. The examples on the following pages use a simple algorithm to help you easily compare one programming language to another.

To compute the gross pay, first you multiply the regular time hours worked by the hourly rate of pay to obtain the regular time pay. If the employee has overtime hours, their overtime pay is 1.5 times their hourly rate of pay multiplied by overtime hours. Then, you add the regular time pay and overtime pay together.

BASIC

John Kemeny and Thomas Kurtz developed a programming language called **B**eginner's **A**ll-purpose **S**ymbolic **I**nstruction **C**ode, or **BASIC**, in the mid-1960s at Dartmouth College. Kemeny and Kurtz designed BASIC for use as a simple, interactive problem-solving language (Figure 15-24). BASIC originally was intended as, and sometimes is still, the language used in a student's first programming course because it is so easy to learn and use. Today, BASIC is used on both personal computers and minicomputers to develop some business applications. Many versions of BASIC exist, including QBasic, QuickBASIC, and MS-BASIC.

Visual Basic

Developed by Microsoft Corporation in the early 1990s, **Visual Basic** is a Windows-based application that assists programmers in developing other event-driven Windows-based applications. The first step in building a Visual Basic application is to design the graphical user interface using Visual Basic objects (Steps 1 and 2 in Figure 15-25). Visual Basic objects, or controls, include items such as command buttons, text boxes, and labels.

Next, you write any code needed to define program events (Step 3 in Figure 15-25). An event in Visual Basic might be the result of an action initiated by a user. When a user

```
REM COMPUTE REGULAR TIME PAY
Regular.Time.Pay = Regular.Time.Hours * Hourly.Pay.Rate

REM COMPUTE OVERTIME PAY
If Overtime.Hours > 0 THEN
    Overtime.Pay = Overtime.Hours * 1.5 * Hourly.Pay.Rate
ELSE
    Overtime.Pay = 0
END IF

REM COMPUTE GROSS PAY
Gross.Pay = Regular.Time.Pay + Overtime.Pay

REM PRINT GROSS PAY
PRINT USING "The gross pay is $##,###.##"; Gross.Pay
```

Figure 15-24 This figure shows an excerpt from a BASIC program. The code shows the computations for regular time pay, overtime pay, and gross pay; the decision to evaluate the overtime hours; and the output of the gross pay.

clicks an object in a Visual Basic application, the application executes the Click event. You define Visual Basic events using code statements written in Visual Basic's own programming language. This language is very similar to BASIC and easy to learn and use. Once you have completed these steps, you can generate and test the final application (Step 4 in Figure 15-25).

Beginning programmers can create professional Windows-based applications using Visual Basic because the program is easy to use.

Web Link

For more information on Visual Basic, visit the Discovering Computers 2002 Chapter 15 WEB LINK page (**scsite.com/dc2002/ch15/weblink.htm**) and click Visual Basic.

Figure 15-25 CREATING A VISUAL BASIC APPLICATION

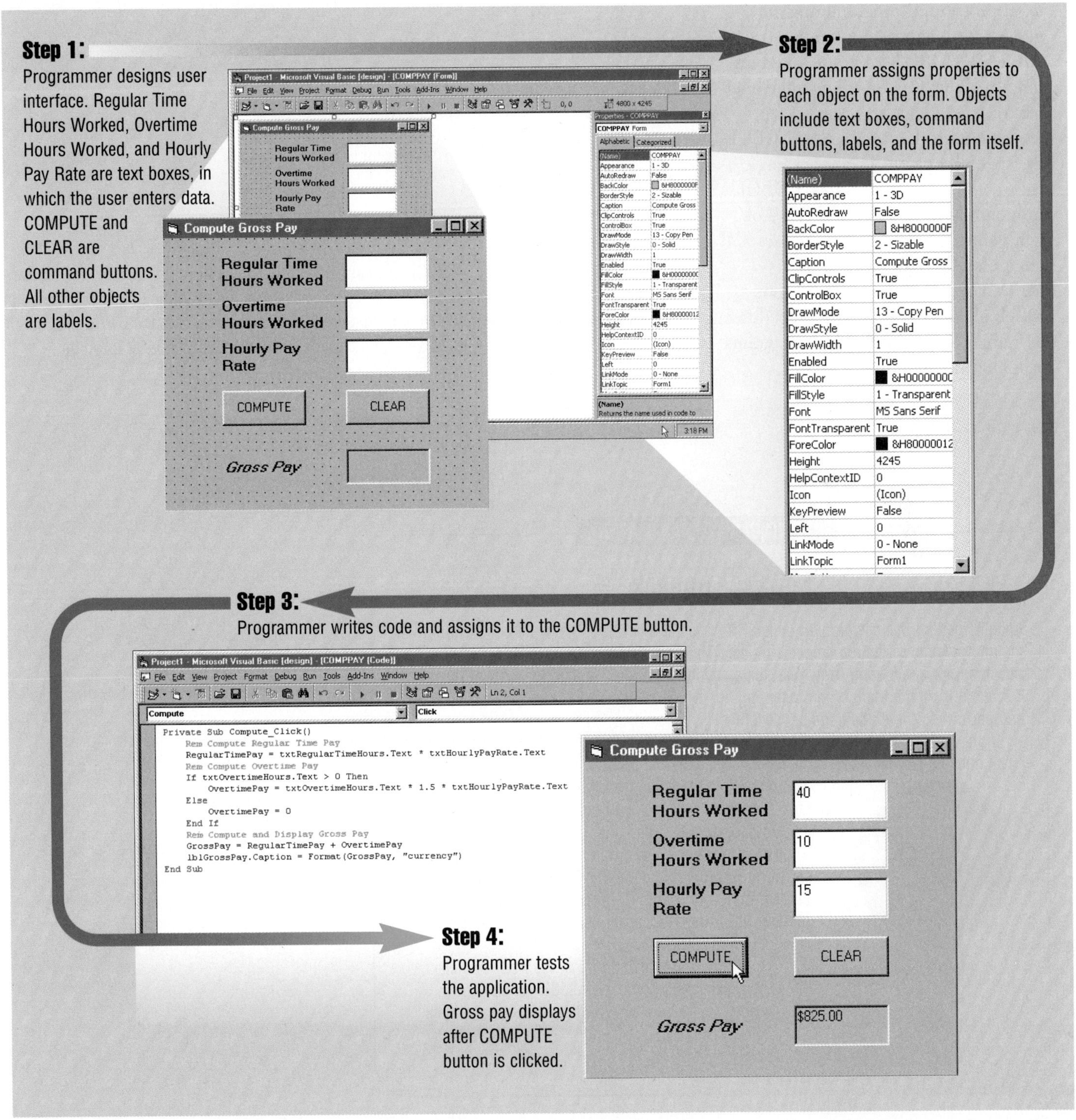

COBOL

COBOL (**CO**mmon **B**usiness-**O**riented **L**anguage) developed out of a joint effort between the United States government, businesses, and major universities in the early 1960s. Naval officer Grace Hopper, a pioneer in computer programming, was a prime developer of the COBOL language.

COBOL is one of the more widely used procedural programming languages for business applications. Although COBOL programs often are lengthy, their English-like statements make the code easy to read, write, and maintain (Figure 15-26). COBOL is especially useful for processing transactions on mainframes. COBOL programs also run on other types of computers. The most popular personal computer COBOL program is MERANT Micro Focus Net Express, which allows you to create procedural and object-oriented COBOL programs and migrate them to the Web.

```
*    COMPUTE REGULAR TIME PAY
     MULTIPLY REGULAR-TIME-HOURS BY HOURLY-PAY-RATE
         GIVING REGULAR-TIME-PAY.

*    COMPUTE OVERTIME PAY
     IF OVERTIME-HOURS > 0
         COMPUTE OVERTIME-PAY = OVERTIME-HOURS * 1.5 * HOURLY-PAY-RATE
     ELSE
         MOVE 0 TO OVERTIME-PAY.

*    COMPUTE GROSS PAY
     ADD REGULAR-TIME-PAY TO OVERTIME-PAY
         GIVING GROSS-PAY.

*    PRINT GROSS PAY
     MOVE GROSS-PAY TO GROSS-PAY-OUT.
     WRITE REPORT-LINE-OUT FROM DETAIL-LINE
         AFTER ADVANCING 2 LINES.
```

Figure 15-26 An excerpt from a COBOL program. The code shows the computations for regular time pay, overtime pay, and gross pay; the decision to evaluate the overtime hours; and the output of the gross pay. Notice how much wordier this program is compared with the BASIC program in Figure 15-24 on page 15.22. It is, however, much more readable than the BASIC program.

TECHNOLOGY TRAILBLAZER

GRACE **HOPPER**

Imagine getting this assignment on your first day at a new job: "have the coefficients for the interpolation of the arc tangents by next Thursday." That was Grace Hopper's first mission upon graduating from Yale University in 1934. And she had to perform these calculations on the Mark I "computer engine," which measured 51 feet by 8 feet by 8 feet and performed three additions per second.

In the next years she found herself programming the Mark I to find the angles to aim naval guns in varying weather conditions, building and programming the Navy's Mark II and III computers, and building the UNIVAC I computer. She is credited with finding the first computer "bug" shown in Figure 15-17 on page 15.14.

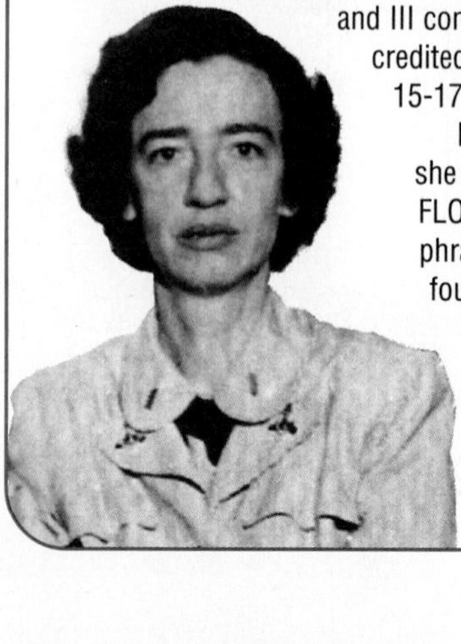

In an effort to make programming easier for laypeople, she developed the first compiler. She also created the FLOW-MATIC programming language, which used English phrases in business applications. This language laid the foundation for COBOL.

For more information on Grace Hopper, visit the Discovering Computers 2002 People Web page (**scsite.com/dc2002/people.htm**) and click Grace Hopper.

C

The **C** programming language, developed in the early 1970s by Dennis Ritchie at Bell Laboratories, originally was designed for writing system software. Today, a variety of software programs are written in C. This includes operating systems and application software such as word processing and spreadsheet programs.

C is a powerful language that requires professional programming skills. Many programmers use C for business and scientific problems (Figure 15-27). C runs on almost any type of computer with any operating system, but it most often is used with the UNIX operating system. In fact, most of the UNIX operating system is written in C.

C++

Developed in the 1980s by Bjarne Sroustrup at Bell Laboratories, **C++** (pronounced SEE-plus-plus) is an object-oriented programming language. C++ is an extension of the C programming language. It includes all the elements of the C language plus has additional features for working with objects, classes, events, and other object-oriented concepts. Programmers commonly use C++ to develop application software, such as word processing and spreadsheet programs, as well as database and Web applications. Although C++ is an outgrowth of the C programming language, you do not need C programming experience to be a successful C++ programmer.

Some programmers use a newer programming language called C# (pronounced SEE-sharp). **C#** combines features of C and C++ and is best suited for development of Web applications.

```
/* Compute Regular Time Pay                                */
rt_pay = rt_hrs * pay_rate;

/* Compute Overtime Pay                                    */
if (ot_hrs > 0)
    ot_pay = ot_hrs * 1.5 * pay_rate;
else
    ot_pay = 0;

/* Compute Gross Pay                                       */
gross = rt_pay + ot_pay

/* Print Gross Pay                                         */
printf("The gross pay is %d\n", gross);
```

Figure 15-27 An excerpt from a C or C++ program. The code shows the computations for regular time pay, overtime pay, and gross pay; the decision to evaluate the overtime hours; and the output of the gross pay.

TECHNOLOGY TRAILBLAZER

DENNIS **RITCHIE**

Children learn their ABCs; programmers learn their BCC++s. Many of today's Internet applications and commercial software packages are written using C++, a useful object-oriented language. C++ is an expansion of C, which Dennis Ritchie developed at Bell Labs in the early 1970s.

At that time, systems programmers were using the UNIX operating system on meager Digital Equipment Corporation PDP-11 computers with 24 KB of memory and a programming language called B, which was developed by Ken Thompson. Ritchie tweaked B to make it portable, so it could be installed easily on computers other than the PDP-11 without extensive software rewrites. C became extremely popular outside of Bell Labs after 1980.

President Bill Clinton awarded Ritchie and Thompson the National Medal of Technology, the country's highest prize for achievement in technology, in 1999.

Besides being a powerful force behind Bell Labs' Computer Sciences Research Center, Ritchie also drove a tractor-trailer for the Roush Racing Valvoline/Cummings NASCAR team and served as a mechanic on Mark Martin's racecar and a front tire carrier during pit stops.

For more information on Dennis Ritchie, visit the Discovering Computers 2002 People Web page (**scsite.com/dc2002/people.htm**) and click Dennis Ritchie.

Web Link

For more information on C++, visit the Discovering Computers 2002 Chapter 15 WEB LINK page (**scsite.com/dc2002/ch15/weblink.htm**) and click C++.

RPG

In the early 1960s, IBM introduced **RPG**, which stands for **R**eport **P**rogram **G**enerator, to assist businesses in generating reports (Figure 15-28). Today, businesses also use RPG for complex computations and file updating. Because RPG is a nonprocedural language, many users of RPG (and other report generators) claim it paved the way for 4GLs. RPG primarily is used for application development on IBM midrange computers, such as the AS/400. A version with limited functionality is available for the personal computer.

```
C* COMPUTE REGULAR TIME PAY
C          RTHRS      MULT RATE                RTPAY     72
C*
C* COMPUTE OVERTIME PAY
C          OTHRS      IFGT 0
C          RATE       MULT 1.5                 OTRATE    72
C          OTRATE     MULT OTHRS               OTPAY     72
                      ELSE
C                     INZ                      OTPAY     72
C
C* COMPUTE GROSS PAY
C          RTPAY      ADD  OTPAY               GRPAY     72
C
C* PRINT GROSS PAY
C                     EXCPTDETAIL
C
C*
O* OUTPUT SPECIFICATIONS
OQPRINT  E            DETAIL
O                                     23 'THE GROSS PAY IS $'
O                     GRPAY  J        34
```

Figure 15-28 This figure shows an excerpt from an RPG program. The code shows the computations for regular time pay, overtime pay, and gross pay; the decision to evaluate the overtime hours; and the output of the gross pay.

Other Programming Languages

In addition to the programming languages just discussed, programmers sometimes do use other languages. Figure 15-29 lists some of these languages and their primary applications.

ADA	Derived from Pascal, developed by the U.S. Department of Defense, named after Augusta Ada Lovelace Byron, who is thought to be the first female computer programmer
ALGOL	ALGOrithmic Language, the first structured procedural language
APL	A Programming Language, a scientific language designed to manipulate tables of numbers
FORTH	Similar to C, used for device control applications
FORTRAN	FORmula TRANSlator, one of the first high-level programming languages used for scientific applications
HYPERTALK	An object-oriented programming language developed by Apple to manipulate cards that can contain text, graphics, and sound
LISP	LISt Processing, a language used for artificial intelligence applications
LOGO	An educational tool used to teach programming and problem-solving to children
MODULA-2	A successor to Pascal used for developing systems software
PASCAL	Developed to teach students structured programming concepts, named in honor of Blaise Pascal, who developed one of the earliest calculating machines
PILOT	Programmed Inquiry Learning Or Teaching, used to write computer-aided instruction programs
PL/I	Programming Language One, a business and scientific language that combines many features of Fortran and COBOL
PROLOG	PROgramming LOGic, used for development of artificial intelligence applications
SMALLTALK	Object-oriented programming language

Figure 15-29 Other programming languages.

Is Generic Okay?

One Programming Language for all Applications

Different languages are used for different applications because each programming language has its strengths and weaknesses. Some authorities believe, however, it would be best to develop a single programming language that could be used for all applications. SQL is a language that is probably one of the most standardized, but even within SQL there are variations. What would be the advantages of writing all applications using the same programming language? What would be the disadvantages? Do you think such a generic programming language ever will be developed? Why or why not?

For more information on programming languages, visit the Discovering Computers 2002 Issues Web page (**scsite.com/dc2002/issues.htm**) and click Chapter 15 Issue #4.

PROGRAM DEVELOPMENT TOOLS

Program development tools are user-friendly software products designed to help both program developers and nontechnical users create solutions to information requirements. With these tools, IT professionals develop systems faster. Program development tools also **empower** nontechnical users by giving them the ability to write simple programs and satisfy information requests on their own. This allows programmers and other IT professionals to focus development efforts on larger projects.

Examples of program development tools include query languages and report writers, which were discussed earlier in this chapter and Chapter 13. In addition to query languages and report writers, other software development tools include application generators, macros, and RAD tools.

Application Generators

An **application generator**, sometimes called a **program generator**, is a program that allows you to build an application without writing the extensive code required by a 3GL. Programmers that use application generators can be more productive in a shorter time frame. In addition, many users that are unfamiliar with programming concepts can build applications with an application generator. Application generators empower users by providing them with the ability to create applications on their own.

When using an application generator, the developer (a programmer or user) works with menu-driven tools that have graphical user interfaces. Some application generators create source code. Others simply create object code. Some application generators are available as stand-alone programs. Most often they are bundled with or part of a DBMS. An application generator typically includes a report writer, form, and menu generator.

As discussed in Chapter 13, a report writer allows you to design a report on the screen, retrieve data into the report design, and then display or print the report. A form is a window on the screen that provides areas for entering or changing data in a database.

With both a report writer and a form, developers type titles and headings directly on the screen. Then, they describe the data elements to be used usually by clicking the location where the data elements should display or print. The data dictionary contains characteristics about the data elements. When the developer uses an existing data element, the report writer or form accesses the data dictionary for the format specifications of the data element. Figure 15-30 shows a sample form design and the resulting form it generates.

Figure 15-30a (form design)

Figure 15-30b (resulting form)

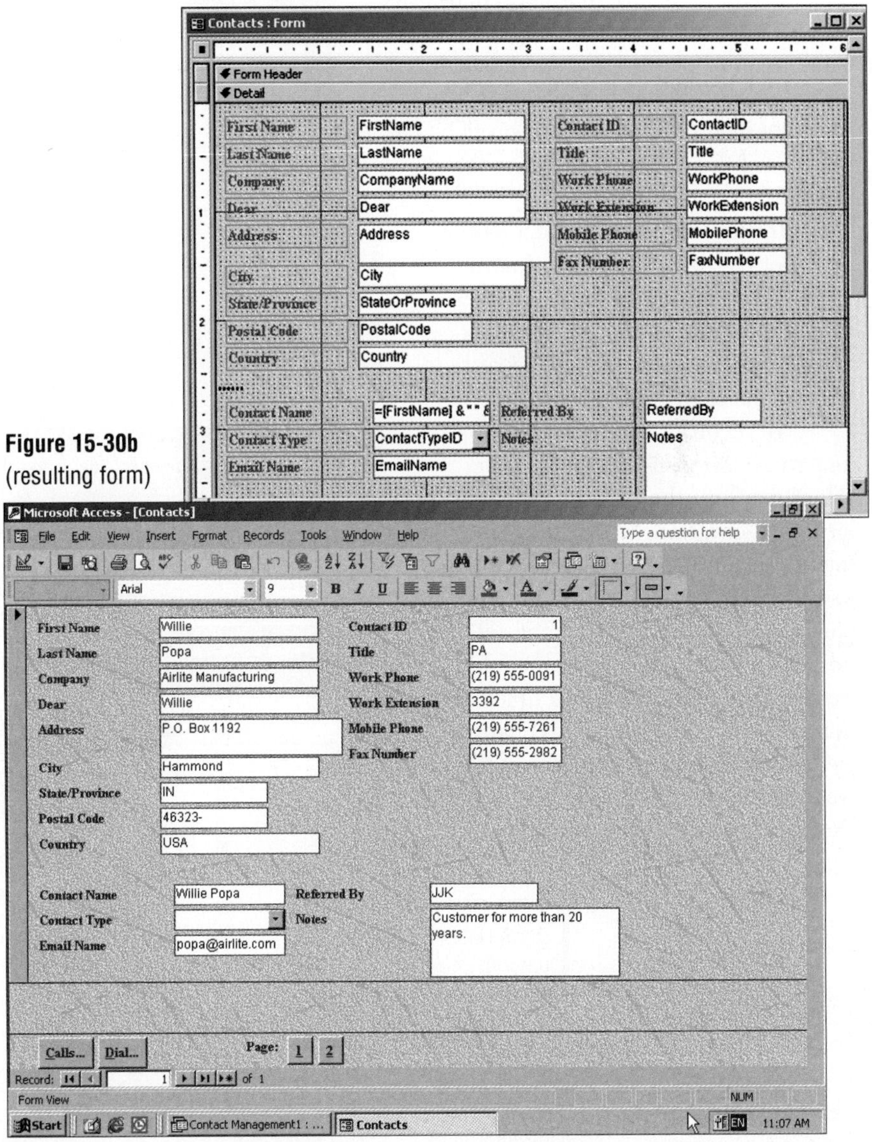

Figure 15-30 A form design and the resulting form created with Microsoft Access.

A **menu generator** allows the developer to create a menu, or list of choices, for the application options. If you create three reports and two forms for an application, for example, your menu would contain at least six options: one for each report, one for each form, and one to exit, or quit, the application.

Macros

Empowered users also can create simple programs within applications by writing macros. A **macro** is a series of statements that instructs an application how to complete a task. Macros can automate routine, repetitive, or difficult tasks in an application such as word processing, spreadsheet, or database programs. You usually create a macro in one of two ways: (1) record the macro or (2) write the macro.

If you want to automate a routine or repetitive task such as formatting or editing, you would record a macro. A **macro recorder** is similar to a movie camera because both record all actions until turned off.

To record a macro, start the macro recorder in the application. Then, perform the steps to be part of the macro, such as clicks of the mouse or keystrokes. Once the macro is recorded, you can run it any time you want to perform that same set of actions. For example, you could record the actions required to format a number as a subscript. To change a selected number in a document to a subscript, you would run the Format Number As Subscript macro.

Once familiar with programming techniques, you can write your own macros instead of recording them. Many applications use **Visual Basic for Applications (VBA)** or a similar language as their macro programming language. Macros written in VBA use the three basic structured programming constructs (sequence, selection, and iteration) within modules. They also use objects, classes, and other object-oriented concepts. The objects in a VBA macro apply only to the specific application for which the macro was developed. In a spreadsheet, an object might be a cell, a range of cells, a chart, or the workbook.

The macro in Figure 15-31a shows an Excel macro that automates the data entry process to determine the interest and principal for a car loan. Figure 15-31b shows the dialog box generated from the macro that prompts the user to enter the purchase price of the vehicle.

Figure 15-31a (VBA macro)

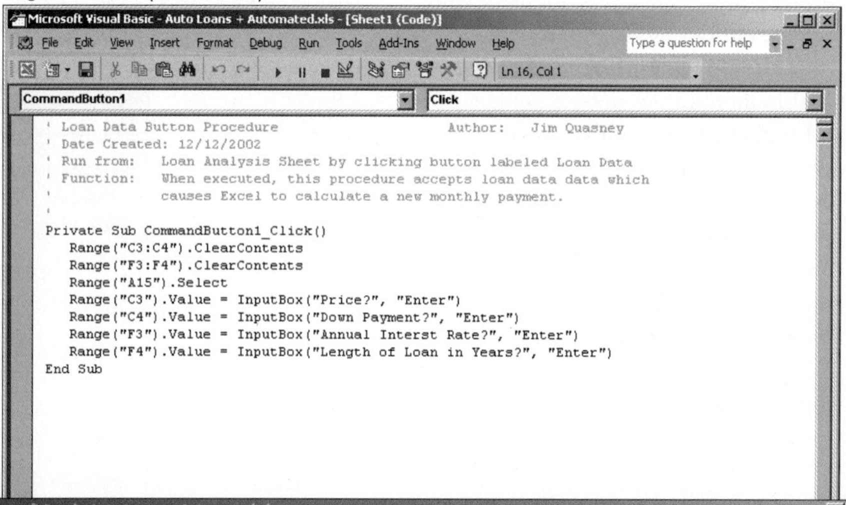

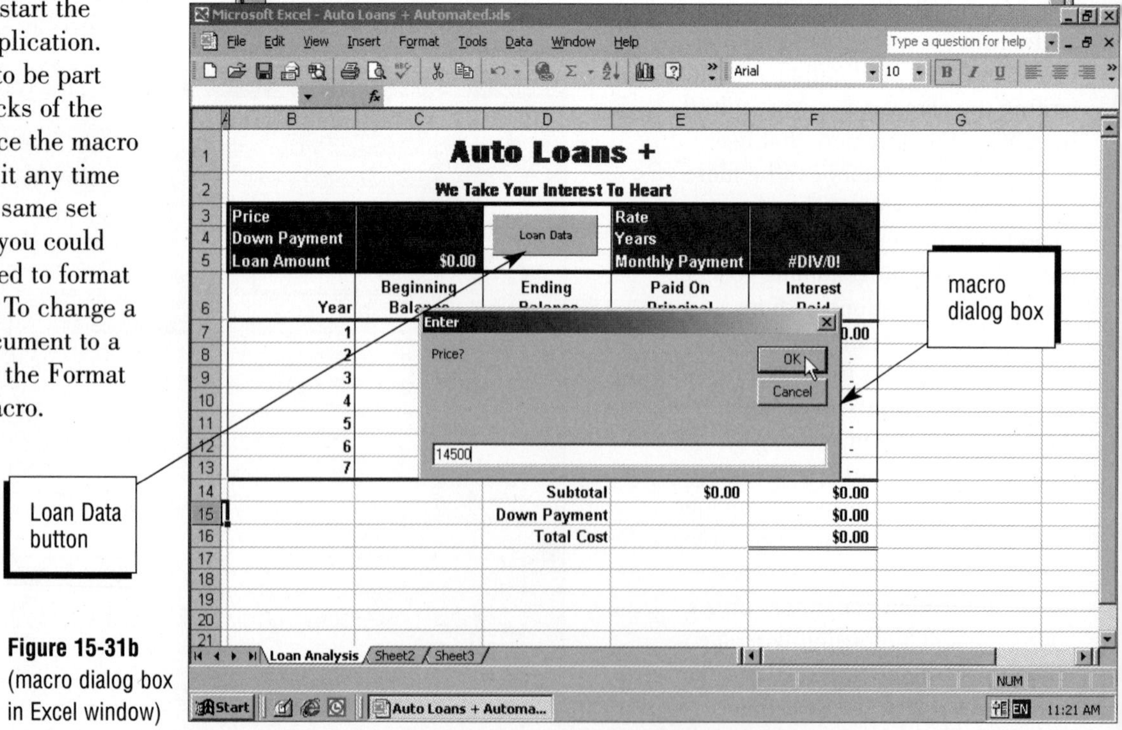

Figure 15-31b (macro dialog box in Excel window)

Figure 15-31 The top screen shows a VBA macro used to automate an auto loan computation. After a macro is written, the user clicks the Loan Data button to launch the macro. The bottom screen shows the macro guiding the user through the data entry process.

RAD Tools: Visual Basic, Delphi, and PowerBuilder

Rapid application development (**RAD**) is the concept of developing software throughout the system development process. Chapter 14 discussed that software development typically occurs in the implementation phase. RAD is an alternative to this technique.

A common technique of RAD is prototyping. As discussed in Chapter 14, a prototype is a working model of the proposed system. With a prototype, system developers can implement a solution more quickly than without a prototype. That is, they can develop the application rapidly.

Rapid application development uses RAD tools. These tools allow you to develop easy-to-maintain, component-based applications. **Component** is simply another term for object. A RAD tool typically includes an object-oriented programming language. Three popular RAD tools are Visual Basic, Delphi, and PowerBuilder.

VISUAL BASIC As discussed earlier in this chapter, Visual Basic is a Windows-based application that assists programmers in developing other event-driven Windows-based applications. Visual Basic was one of the first programming environments to provide a visual programming environment. A **visual programming environment** (**VPE**) allows developers to drag-and-drop objects to build programs. Visual Basic is a popular RAD tool because it is easy-to-use and event-driven.

DELPHI **Delphi** is another popular RAD tool. This powerful tool offers a drag-and-drop VPE. Delphi provides full object-oriented capabilities. This is different from Visual Basic, which is only an event-driven language. Delphi has more functionality and features than Visual Basic, making it slightly more difficult to learn and use.

Web Link

For more information on rapid application development, visit the Discovering Computers 2002 Chapter 15 WEB LINK page (**scsite.com/dc2002/ch15/weblink.htm**) and click Rapid Application Development.

APPLY IT!

Creating Macros in Microsoft Office

A macro consists of a series of commands that are grouped together as a single command. The single command is a convenient way to automate a difficult or lengthy task. Macros often are used for repetitive formatting or editing activities, to combine multiple commands into a single command, or to select an option within a dialog box with a single keystroke. To create macros in Microsoft Office 2000 requires the use of Visual Basic for Applications (VBA). This programming language is integrated into Access, Excel, FrontPage, Outlook, PowerPoint, and Word.

Within each of the above listed applications are two options for creating macros: record a macro or create a macro using the Visual Basic Editor. To record a macro, complete the following procedure:

1. On the Tools menu, point to Macro, and then click Record New Macro.
2. Change the default macro name if you would like and then click the OK button to start the recorder.
3. Record the series of actions you want to automate.
4. Click the Stop Recording button on the Stop Recording toolbar.

To create a macro using the Visual Basic Editor requires that you know VBA programming commands. To create a macro with the Visual Basic Editor, complete the following procedure:

1. On the Tools menu, point to Macro, and then click Visual Basic Editor to open the VB Editor window.
2. Type your programming commands to create the series of actions you want to automate.
3. On the File menu, click Save Normal or Close and Return to [application name].

For more information on macros, visit the Discovering Computers 2002 Apply It Web page (**scsite.com/dc2002/apply.htm**) and click Chapter 15 Apply It #2.

POWERBUILDER Another RAD tool, called **PowerBuilder**, uses a proprietary object-oriented language for its application development (Figure 15-32). This language, called PowerScript, is similar to BASIC and C. PowerBuilder can create powerful applications. Many developers use PowerBuilder for Web-based applications. PowerBuilder can be more difficult to learn than Visual Basic because of its extended functionality.

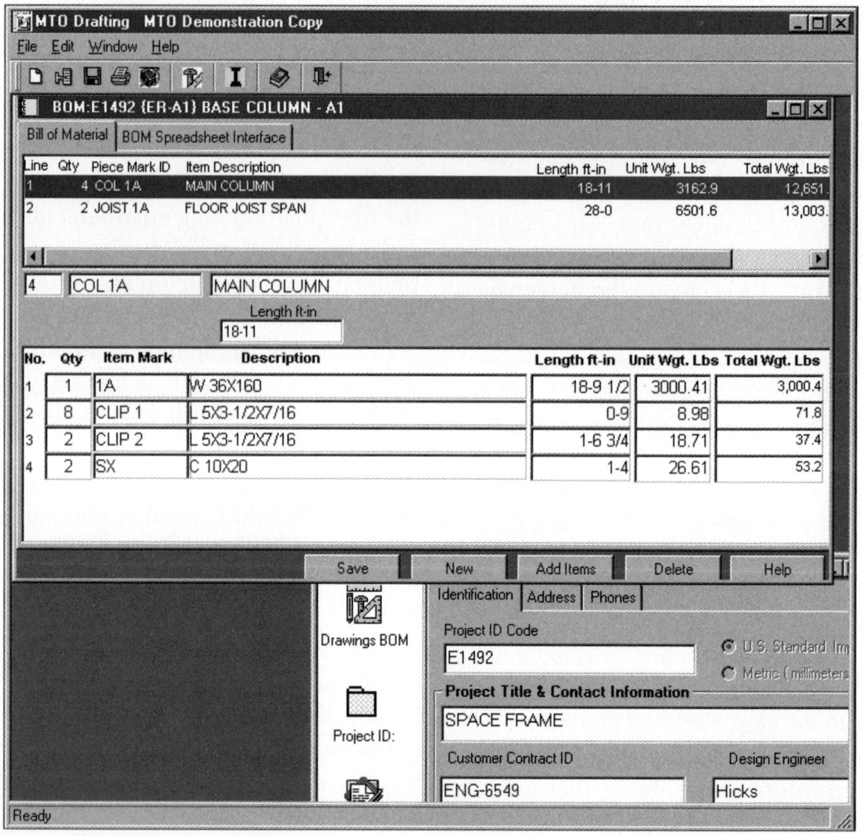

Figure 15-32 Shown above is a material take off utility and bill of material application that is used in the structural steel industry. The application was created using PowerBuilder.

COMPANY ON THE CUTTING EDGE

SYBASE®

PowerBuilder Users Get Top Technical Support

After waiting on hold for hours on the telephone listening to boring music, you are at your wits' end. You are having a problem with your software and just need to talk to a knowledgeable person for a few minutes.

Maybe if you would have chosen to work with the software programs PowerBuilder Enterprise, Powersoft, PowerStudio, or Adaptive Component Architecture, you might not be having this problem. What you need more than anything right now is a good customer support service. *InfoWorld* readers selected Sybase's online newsgroups as the *Best Customer Support* in the computer industry. These newsgroups are supported by Sybase support employees as well as dedicated customers.

No doubt some queries discuss the optimal method for using PowerBuilder, Sybase's RAD tool, because it helps developers efficiently create Internet applications and client/server programs. Developers at Blue Cross & Blue Shield in Rhode Island used this product to build a Y2K-compliant customer service system in record time. In addition, the National Marrow Donor Program in Minneapolis, MN, used Sybase products to create an application that searches a database and matches transplant donors with patients, and devoted tennis fans can watch the Sybase Open tournament via a Web site powered by Sybase technology.

For more information on Sybase, visit the Discovering Computers 2002 Companies Web page (**scsite.com/dc2002/companies.htm**) and click Sybase.

WEB PAGE PROGRAM DEVELOPMENT

As discussed in Chapter 2, the collection of linked documents accessible on the Internet is known as the World Wide Web, or simply, the Web. Each document posted on the Web, called a Web page, is a linked document that can contain text, graphics, video, and audio. The designers of Web pages, called **Web page authors**, use a variety of techniques to develop Web pages. The following sections discuss these techniques.

HTML

Hypertext markup language (HTML) is a special formatting language that programmers use to create Web pages. You view a Web page written with HTML in a Web browser such as Microsoft Internet Explorer or Netscape Navigator.

HTML is not actually a programming language. It is, however, a language that has specific syntax rules for defining the placement and format of text, graphics, video, and audio on a Web page. HTML uses **tags**, or **markups**, which are codes that specify links to other documents and indicate how the Web page displays when viewed on the Web. A Web page, thus, is a file that contains both text and HTML tags. Examples of tags are <B> to bold text, <P> to indicate a new paragraph, and <HR> to display a horizontal rule across the page. Figure 15-33 shows part of the HTML code used to create the Web page shown in Figure 15-34.

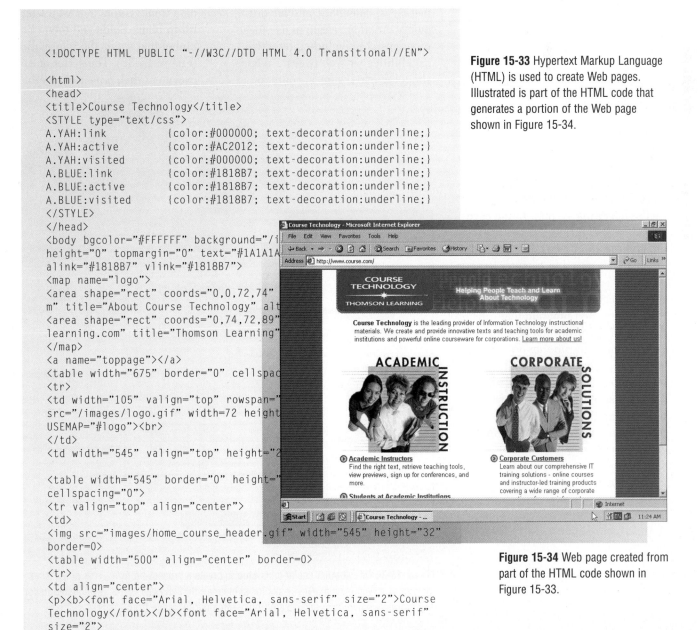

```
<!DOCTYPE HTML PUBLIC "-//W3C//DTD HTML 4.0 Transitional//EN">

<html>
<head>
<title>Course Technology</title>
<STYLE type="text/css">
A.YAH:link          {color:#000000; text-decoration:underline;}
A.YAH:active        {color:#AC2012; text-decoration:underline;}
A.YAH:visited       {color:#000000; text-decoration:underline;}
A.BLUE:link         {color:#1818B7; text-decoration:underline;}
A.BLUE:active       {color:#1818B7; text-decoration:underline;}
A.BLUE:visited      {color:#1818B7; text-decoration:underline;}
</STYLE>
</head>
<body bgcolor="#FFFFFF" background="/i
height="0" topmargin="0" text="#1A1A1A
alink="#1818B7" vlink="#1818B7">
<map name="logo">
<area shape="rect" coords="0,0,72,74"
m" title="About Course Technology" al
<area shape="rect" coords="0,74,72,89"
learning.com" title="Thomson Learning"
</map>
<a name="toppage"></a>
<table width="675" border="0" cellspac
<tr>
<td width="105" valign="top" rowspan="
src="/images/logo.gif" width=72 height
USEMAP="#logo"><br>
</td>
<td width="545" valign="top" height="2

<table width="545" border="0" height="
cellspacing="0">
<tr valign="top" align="center">
<td>
<img src="images/home_course_header.gif" width="545" height="32"
border=0>
<table width="500" align="center" border=0>
<tr>
<td align="center">
<p><b><font face="Arial, Helvetica, sans-serif" size="2">Course
Technology</font></b><font face="Arial, Helvetica, sans-serif"
size="2">
is the leading provider of Information Technology instructional
materials.
```

Figure 15-33 Hypertext Markup Language (HTML) is used to create Web pages. Illustrated is part of the HTML code that generates a portion of the Web page shown in Figure 15-34.

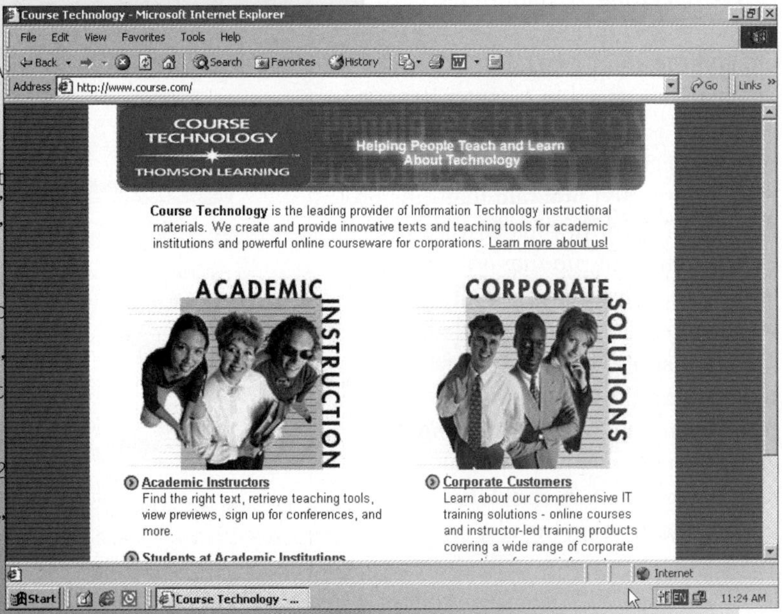

Figure 15-34 Web page created from part of the HTML code shown in Figure 15-33.

You can write HTML code using any text editor such as Notepad. The HTML code also can be entered into any standard word processing software package, such as Microsoft Word. You must save the code, however, as an ASCII file with an .htm or .html extension, instead of as a formatted word processing document.

Scripts, Applets, Servlets, and ActiveX Controls

HTML tells the browser how to display text and images, set up lists and option buttons, and establish hyperlinks on a Web page. These Web pages come to life when you add dynamic content and interactive elements such as scrolling messages, animated graphics, forms, pop-up windows, and interaction. To add these elements, you write small programs called scripts, applets, servlets, and ActiveX controls.

Scripts, applets, servlets, and ActiveX controls are short programs that run inside of another program. This is different from programs discussed thus far, which are executed by the operating system. In the case of Web pages, the Web browser executes these short programs.

As discussed in Chapter 9, your computer is the client computer when it is connected to the Web. A **script** is an interpreted program that runs on the client. A script runs on your computer, instead of running on a Web server. An **applet** also usually runs on the client, but it is compiled. Thus, an applet usually runs faster than a script. Scripts and applets shift the computational work from the Web server to your computer because they run on the client. A **servlet** is an applet that runs on the server.

Similar to an applet, an **ActiveX control** is a small program that runs on your computer, instead of the server. ActiveX controls use ActiveX technology. **ActiveX** is a set of object-oriented technologies by Microsoft that allow components on a network to communicate with one another. To run an ActiveX control, your browser must support ActiveX technology. If it does not, you will need a plug-in program to run ActiveX controls.

One reason for using scripts, applets, servlets, and ActiveX controls is to add special multimedia effects to Web pages. Examples include animated graphics, scrolling messages, calendars, and advertisements. Another reason to use these programs is to include interactive capabilities on Web pages. Cookies, shopping carts, games, counters, image maps, and processing forms, are types of scripts, applets, servlets, and ActiveX controls that allow you to transfer information to and from a Web server.

A **counter** tracks the number of visitors to a Web site. An image map is a graphical image that points to a URL. Web pages use **image maps** in place of, or in addition to, plain text hyperlinks. When you click a certain part of the graphical image, your Web browser sends the coordinates of the clicked location to the Web server, which in turn locates the corresponding URL and sends the Web page to your computer.

A **processing form** collects data from visitors to a Web site, who fill in blank fields and then click a button that sends the information (Figure 15-35). The script or applet executes when a user clicks this

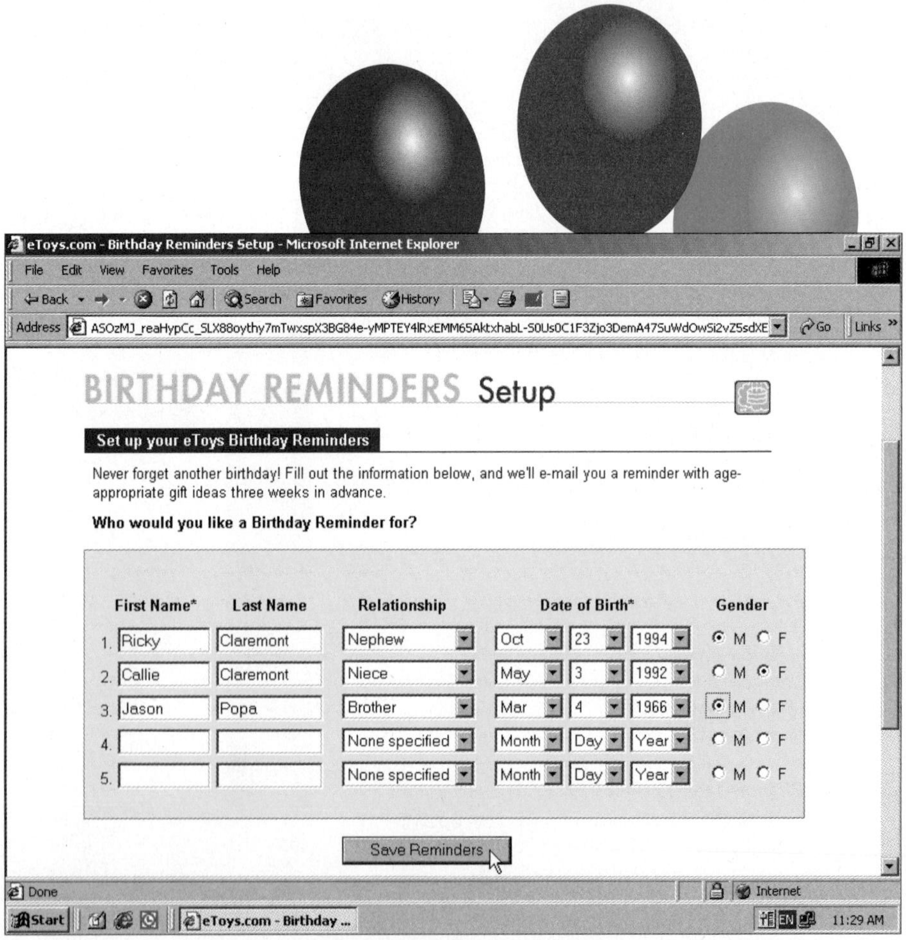

Figure 15-35 One popular use of a script is to create a processing form. This processing form from a Web page at eToys asks for someone's first and last name, relationship to you, and birthdate so you can receive a birthday reminder message from eToys.

button on the processing form. It transmits the data to the server, processes it, and then, if appropriate, sends information back to your Web browser via the server.

To send and receive information between your computer and a Web server, the script, applet, or servlet uses the common gateway interface. The **common gateway interface** (**CGI**) is the communications standard that defines how a Web server communicates with outside sources. Many times, the outside source is a database. The program that manages the sending and receiving across the CGI is a **CGI script**, also called a **CGI program**. The steps in Figure 15-36 show how a CGI program works.

A CGI program can be in the form of a script, applet, servlet, or ActiveX control. You can download CGI programs from the Web and purchase them. If one does not exist that meets your needs, you can write your own CGI program.

Web Link

For more information on CGI programs, visit the Discovering Computers 2002 Chapter 15 WEB LINK page (**scsite.com/dc2002/ch15/weblink.htm**) and click CGI Programs.

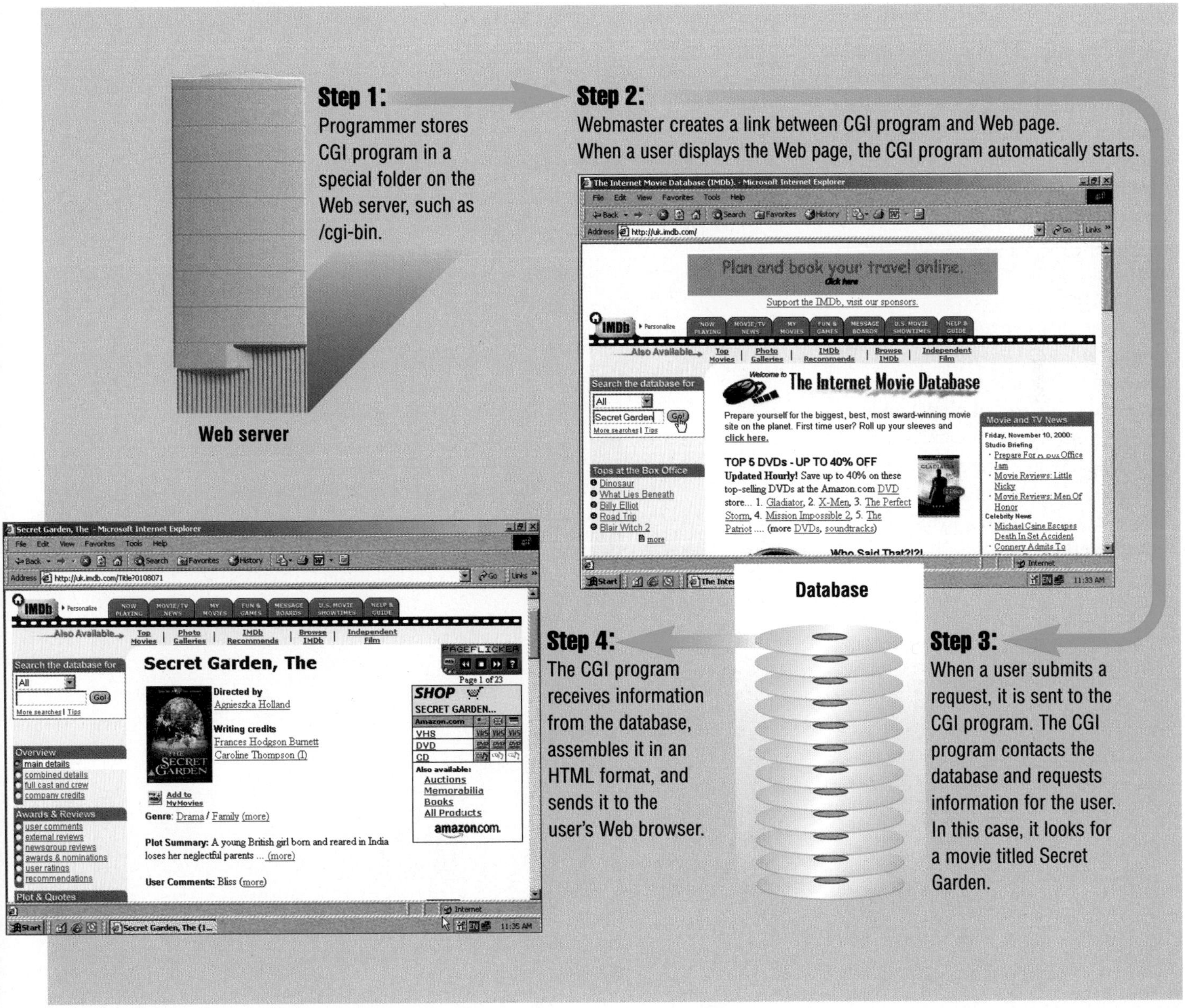

Step 1:
Programmer stores CGI program in a special folder on the Web server, such as /cgi-bin.
Web server
Step 2:
Webmaster creates a link between CGI program and Web page. When a user displays the Web page, the CGI program automatically starts.
The Internet Movie Database
Database
Step 3:
When a user submits a request, it is sent to the CGI program. The CGI program contacts the database and requests information for the user. In this case, it looks for a movie titled Secret Garden.
Step 4:
The CGI program receives information from the database, assembles it in an HTML format, and sends it to the user's Web browser.
Secret Garden, The

Figure 15-36 HOW A CGI PROGRAM WORKS

Java, JavaScript, VBScript, and Perl

You can write a CGI program using a variety of languages. These include some of the languages previously discussed, such as C, C++, and Visual Basic. Many programmers choose to use scripting languages to write CGI scripts. A **scripting language** is an interpreted language that typically is easy to learn and use. Popular scripting languages include JavaScript, VBScript, and Perl. Programmers often use Java for applets and servlets. The following paragraphs discuss each of these languages.

JAVA Developed by Sun Microsystems, **Java** is a compiled object-oriented programming language used to write stand-alone applications, as well as applets and servlets. Java applet examples might include input forms, rotating images, fireworks, interactive animations, or a game. Figure 15-37 shows a sample Java program and its resulting screen.

The Java language is very similar to C++. One difference is that Java source code is compiled into **bytecode**, instead of object code. The operating system cannot execute bytecode. A Java interpreter executes the bytecode. Java-enabled Web browsers contain Java bytecode interpreters.

Web Link

For more information on Java, visit the Discovering Computers 2002 Chapter 15 WEB LINK page (**scsite.com/dc2002/ch15/weblink.htm**) and click Java.

Figure 15-37a (Java applet code)

```
/*
    Project 3:      Making Decision
    Programmer:     Joy Starks
    Date:           November 2, 2002
    Program Name:   CandleApplet
*/

import java.awt.*;
import java.applet.*;
import java.awt.event.*;

public class CandleApplet extends Applet implements ItemListener
{
   //Create components for applet
   Label companyNameLabel = new Label ("CandleLine--Candles Online");

   Label priceLabel = new Label ("Please enter the total dollar amount of your order:");
      TextField priceField = new TextField(35);

   Label shippingLabel = new Label ("Please choose your method of shipping:");

   CheckboxGroup shippingGroup = new CheckboxGroup();
      Checkbox oneDayBox = new Checkbox("Priority (Overnight)",false,shippingGroup);
      Checkbox twoDayBox = new Checkbox("Express (2 business days)",false,shippingGroup);
      Checkbox moreDaysBox = new Checkbox("Standard (3 to 7 business
           days)",false,shippingGroup);
      Checkbox hiddenBox = new Checkbox("",true,shippingGroup);

   Label outputLabel = new Label("We guarantee on time delivery, or your money back.");

   public void init()
   {
      //Add components to window and set colors
      setBackground(Color.cyan);
      add(companyNameLabel);
      add(priceLabel);
      add(priceField);
         priceField.requestFocus();
      add(shippingLabel);
      add(oneDayBox);
         oneDayBox.addItemListener(this);
      add(twoDayBox);
         twoDayBox.addItemListener(this);
      add(moreDaysBox);
         moreDaysBox.addItemListener(this);
      add(outputLabel);
   }

   public void itemStateChanged(ItemEvent choice)
   {
      try
      {
         double shipping;
         double price = Double.parseDouble(priceField.getText());
```

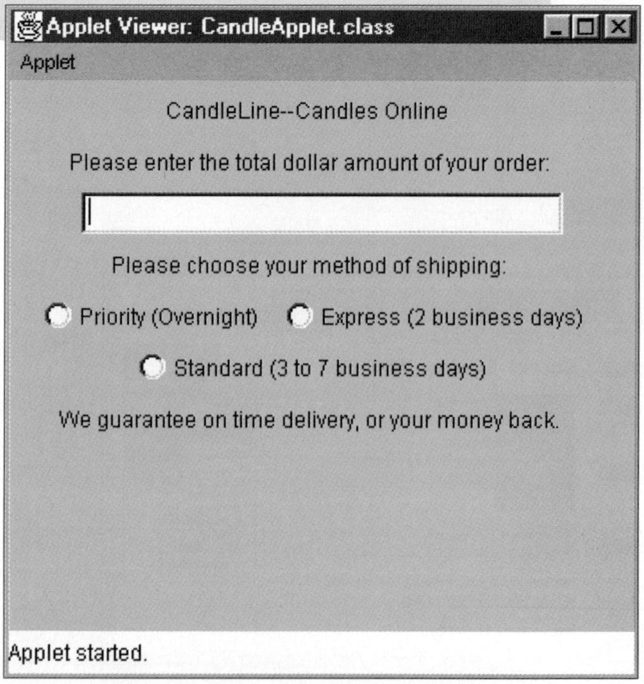

Figure 15-37b (resulting screen)

Figure 15-37 Sample Java applet code and the screen it displays.

Code segments used to create a Java application are called **JavaBeans**, or **Beans**. A JavaBean is platform independent. This enables the code to run on any computer or operating system. Many programmers believe that Java will be the programming language of the future because of its simplicity, robustness, and portability.

JAVASCRIPT **JavaScript** is an interpreted language that allows the programmer to add dynamic content and interactive elements to a Web page (Figure 15-38). These elements include alert messages, scrolling text, animations, drop-down menus, data input forms, pop-up windows, and interactive quizzes. You insert JavaScript code directly into an HTML document. Although it shares many of the features of the full Java language, JavaScript is a much simpler language.

Figure 15-38a (JavaScript code)

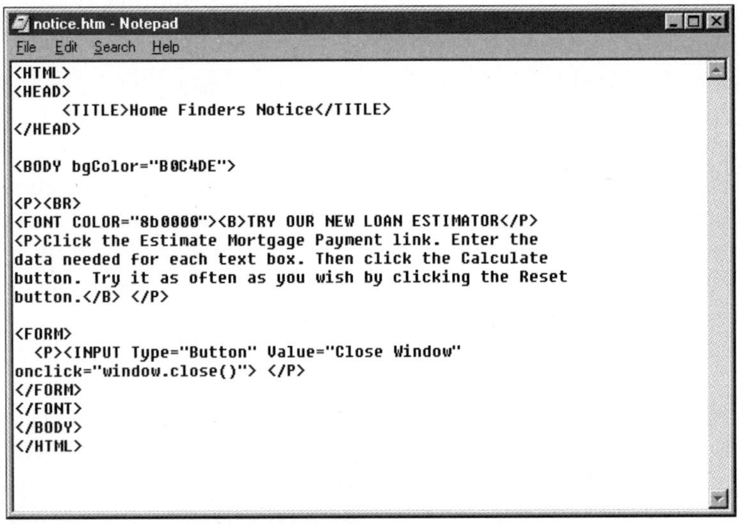


```
<HTML>
<HEAD>
     <TITLE>Home Finders Notice</TITLE>
</HEAD>

<BODY bgColor="B0C4DE">

<P><BR>
<FONT COLOR="8b0000"><B>TRY OUR NEW LOAN ESTIMATOR</P>
<P>Click the Estimate Mortgage Payment link. Enter the
data needed for each text box. Then click the Calculate
button. Try it as often as you wish by clicking the Reset
button.</B> </P>

<FORM>
  <P><INPUT Type="Button" Value="Close Window"
onclick="window.close()"> </P>
</FORM>
</FONT>
</BODY>
</HTML>
```

Figure 15-38b (pop-up window)

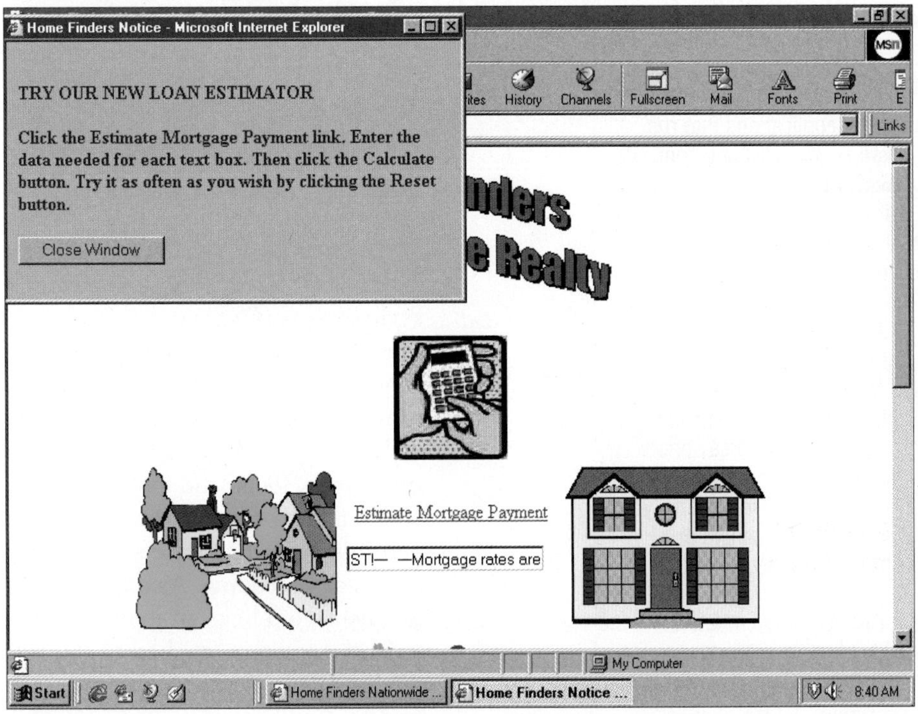

Figure 15-38 Shown here is a pop-up window that displays on a Web page and its associated JavaScript code.

ISSUE

100% Pure

Standardizing Java

"100% Pure Java" may soon be as familiar on software packages as it is on coffee shop menus. Java is called the programming language of the future. A simple language, Java utilizes an object-oriented approach, module orientation, and an easy-to-use GUI. In addition, Java offers a cross-platform capability that allows it to be used in any computing environment. Some software companies, however, are releasing nonstandard Java applications. This contaminated Java, which incorporates certain proprietary elements, runs only on specific computers. A number of vendors want standard Java applications to be awarded a "100% Pure Java" logo. Do you think this is a good idea? Why or why not? Who would test, and confirm, the purity of Java applications? Who might oppose this certification? Why?

For more information on Java, visit the Discovering Computers 2002 Issues Web page (**scsite.com/dc2002/issues.htm**) and click Chapter 15 Issue #5.

JavaScript is the result of a joint venture between Sun Microsystems and Netscape Communications Corporation. Netscape originally began developing a scripting language called LiveScript. Simultaneously, Sun tried to simplify its Java programming language. Today, many software companies endorse JavaScript. The program is an **open language**, which means anyone can use it without purchasing a license. JavaScript thus allows the programmer to improve the appearance of Web pages without spending a large amount of money.

To run a JavaScript program, your browser must support it. Netscape supports it. Internet Explorer supports a subset of JavaScript, called **JScript**.

Web Link

For more information on JavaScript, visit the Discovering Computers 2002 Chapter 15 WEB LINK page (**scsite.com/dc2002/ch15/weblink.htm**) and click JavaScript.

VBSCRIPT **Visual Basic Scripting Edition**, also called **VBScript**, is a subset of the Visual Basic language that allows you to add intelligence and interactivity to Web pages. As with JavaScript, you embed VBScript code directly into an HTML document. Programmers already familiar with Visual Basic choose VBScript as their scripting language, so they do not have to learn a new scripting language. The latest version of Internet Explorer includes VBScript.

PERL **Perl** (**P**ractical **E**xtraction and **R**eport **L**anguage) originally was developed by Larry Wall at NASA's Jet Propulsion Laboratory as a procedural language similar to C. The latest release of PERL, however, is an interpreted scripting language. PERL has powerful text processing capabilities, enabling it to become a popular language for writing scripts.

Dynamic HTML

Dynamic HTML (**DHTML**) is a newer type of HTML that allows you to include more graphical interest and interactivity in a Web page, without the Web page accessing the Web server. When a programmer uses DHTML to create Web pages, the client's computer automatically can update and change its own content. These Web pages display much faster than Web pages created with basic HTML.

Typically, Web pages created with DHTML are much more animated and responsive to user interaction. Once these pages have downloaded, the page seems to come to life. Colors change, font sizes grow, objects appear and disappear as you move the mouse, and animations dance around the screen. Figure 15-39 shows an example of a Web page containing DHTML.

Dynamic HTML works by using the document object model, style sheets, and scripting languages. The **document object model** (**DOM**) defines every item on a Web page as an object. Fonts, graphics, headlines, tables, and every other page element are objects. With DOM, you can change properties such as color or size, of any or all of these objects on the Web page.

A style sheet contains descriptions of a document's characteristics. Many word processing documents use style sheets to define formats of characters and paragraphs. **Cascading style sheets** (**CSS**) contain the formats for how a particular object should display in a Web browser. For example, the CSS specify items such as background colors and images and link colors, fonts, and font sizes. A single HTML document can contain multiple cascading style sheets, thus, the name cascading. As a user moves the mouse or clicks an item, a new style sheet can be applied to change the appearance of the screen.

APPLY IT!

JavaScript Magic

JavaScript is a scripting language that lets you create applications that run over the Internet. A scripting language is like a macro — it is a list of commands that can be executed without user interaction. JavaScript is an open language anyone can use without purchasing a license. Although Netscape developed JavaScript, Microsoft Internet Explorer and other browsers support it. If you are developing Web pages and wish to include dynamic content, then consider adding JavaScript.

Compared with programming languages like Java, Visual Basic, and C, JavaScript is fairly simple to learn and use. Other options are available if, however, you do not have the time or inclination to devote to learning this scripting language. The Internet contains a wealth of resources. You can find example code, free tutorials, references, and even thousands of free scripts. For instance, you easily can create Web pages that include games such as checkers, interactive jigsaw puzzles, crosswords, and others. Or perhaps, you want to let users choose their own background color or add banners or a guest book. You can accomplish all of this, and much more, by cutting and pasting these free scripts into your Web page.

For more information on JavaScript, visit the Discovering Computers 2002 Apply It Web page (**scsite.com/dc2002/apply.htm**) and click Chapter 15 Apply It #3.

Once you have defined and formatted objects on a Web page, a scripting language manipulates them. A script can move, display, hide, or change the appearance of an object as the mouse moves over the object.

XHTML, XML, and WML

XHTML (eXtensible HTML) includes features of HTML and XML. **XML (eXtensible Markup Language)** allows Web page developers to create customized tags, as well as use predefined tags. With XML, you can define a link that points to multiple Web sites instead of a single site. XML uses **XSL (eXtensible Stylesheet Language)** as its style sheet specification.

XML separates the Web page content from its format, allowing your browser to display Web page contents in a form appropriate for your display device. For example, a handheld computer, a laptop computer, and a desktop computer all could display the same XML page. A Web page written with only HTML probably would require multiple versions to run on each of these types of computers.

Web Link

For more information on dynamic HTML, visit the Discovering Computers 2002 Chapter 15 WEB LINK page (**scsite.com/dc2002/ch15/weblink.htm**) and click Dynamic HTML.

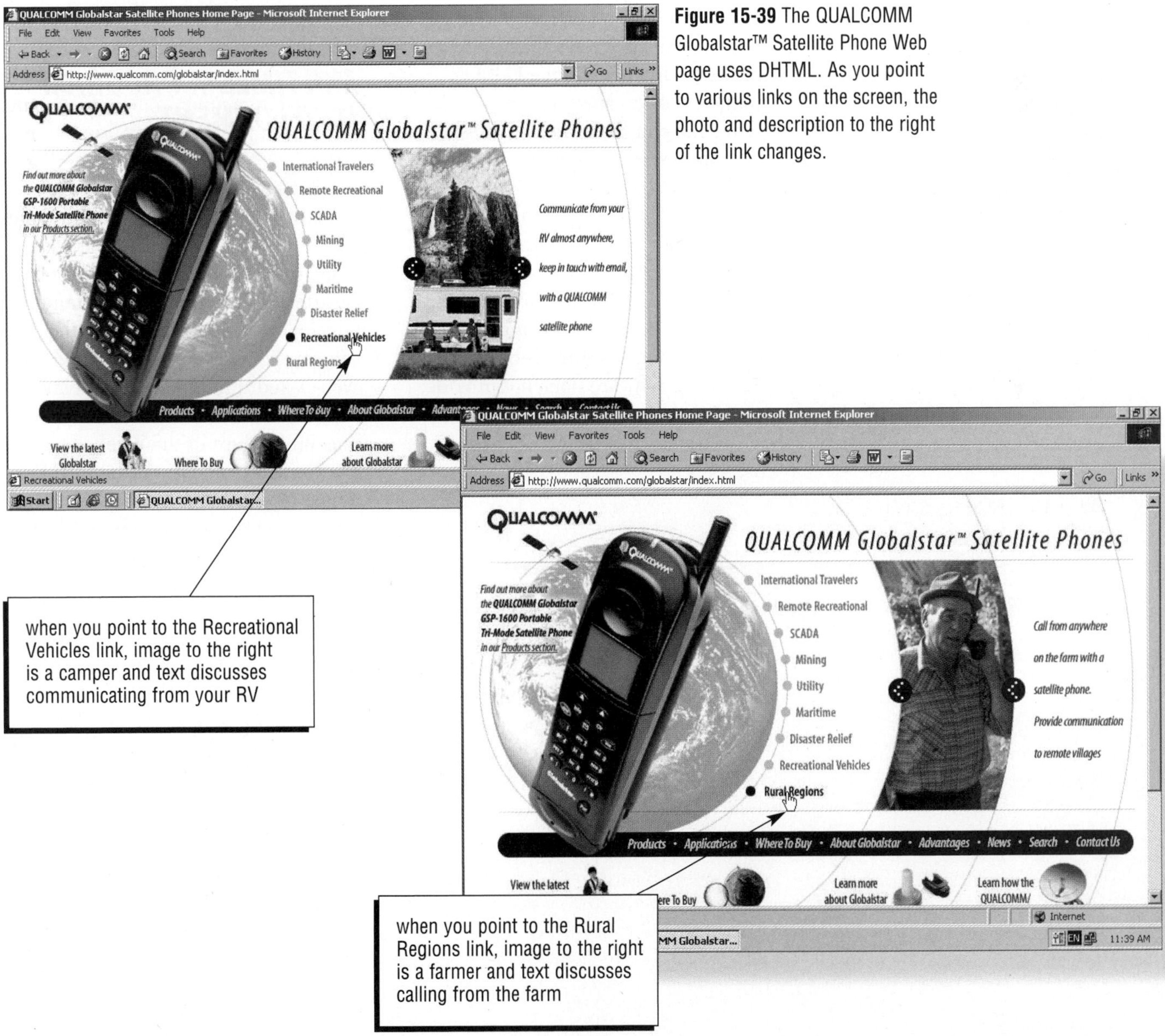
when you point to the Recreational Vehicles link, image to the right is a camper and text discusses communicating from your RV
when you point to the Rural Regions link, image to the right is a farmer and text discusses calling from the farm

Figure 15-39 The QUALCOMM Globalstar™ Satellite Phone Web page uses DHTML. As you point to various links on the screen, the photo and description to the right of the link changes.

Wireless devices use a subset of XML called WML. **WML (wireless markup language)** allows Web page developers to design pages specifically for microbrowsers. Many Web-enabled handheld computers, PDAs, cellular phones, and pagers use WML as their markup language. WML uses the **wireless application protocol (WAP)**, a standard that specifies how wireless devices communicate with the Web.

Web Link
For more information on WML, visit the Discovering Computers 2002 Chapter 15 WEB LINK page (**scsite.com/dc2002/ch15/weblink.htm**) and click WML.

Before using XHTML, DHTML, or WML, be sure your browser supports them. The World Wide Web Consortium (W3C) is developing standards for new HTML features.

Web Page Authoring Software

As discussed in Chapter 3, you do not need to learn HTML to develop a Web page. Both new and experienced users can create fascinating Web sites with Web page authoring software. **Web page authoring software**, sometimes called an **HTML editor**, allows you to create sophisticated Web pages that include graphical images, video, audio, animation, and other special effects. Popular Web page authoring packages include Adobe GoLive, Lotus FastSite, Macromedia Dreamweaver, Macromedia Flash, and Microsoft FrontPage.

Web page authoring software generates HTML tags from your Web page design. With the Web page authoring software, you can view or modify the HTML associated with a Web page. Sometimes you may add an HTML tag that the Web page authoring software does not provide. The benefits to learning HTML basics enable you to fine-tune Web page formats created with authoring software.

Many application software packages also include Web page authoring features. With packages such as Microsoft Word or Excel, you can create basic Web pages that contain text and graphical images. Instead of or along with Web page authoring software, many Web developers use multimedia authoring software. This software allows developers to add additional special multimedia effects to Web pages. The next section discusses multimedia authoring software.

MULTIMEDIA PROGRAM DEVELOPMENT

Multimedia authoring software, sometimes called **authorware**, allows you to combine text, graphics, animation, audio, and video into an interactive presentation. Many developers use multimedia authoring software for computer-based and Web-based training environments.

As discussed in the Multimedia Special Feature in this book, **computer-based training (CBT)** is a type of education in which students learn by using and completing exercises with instructional software

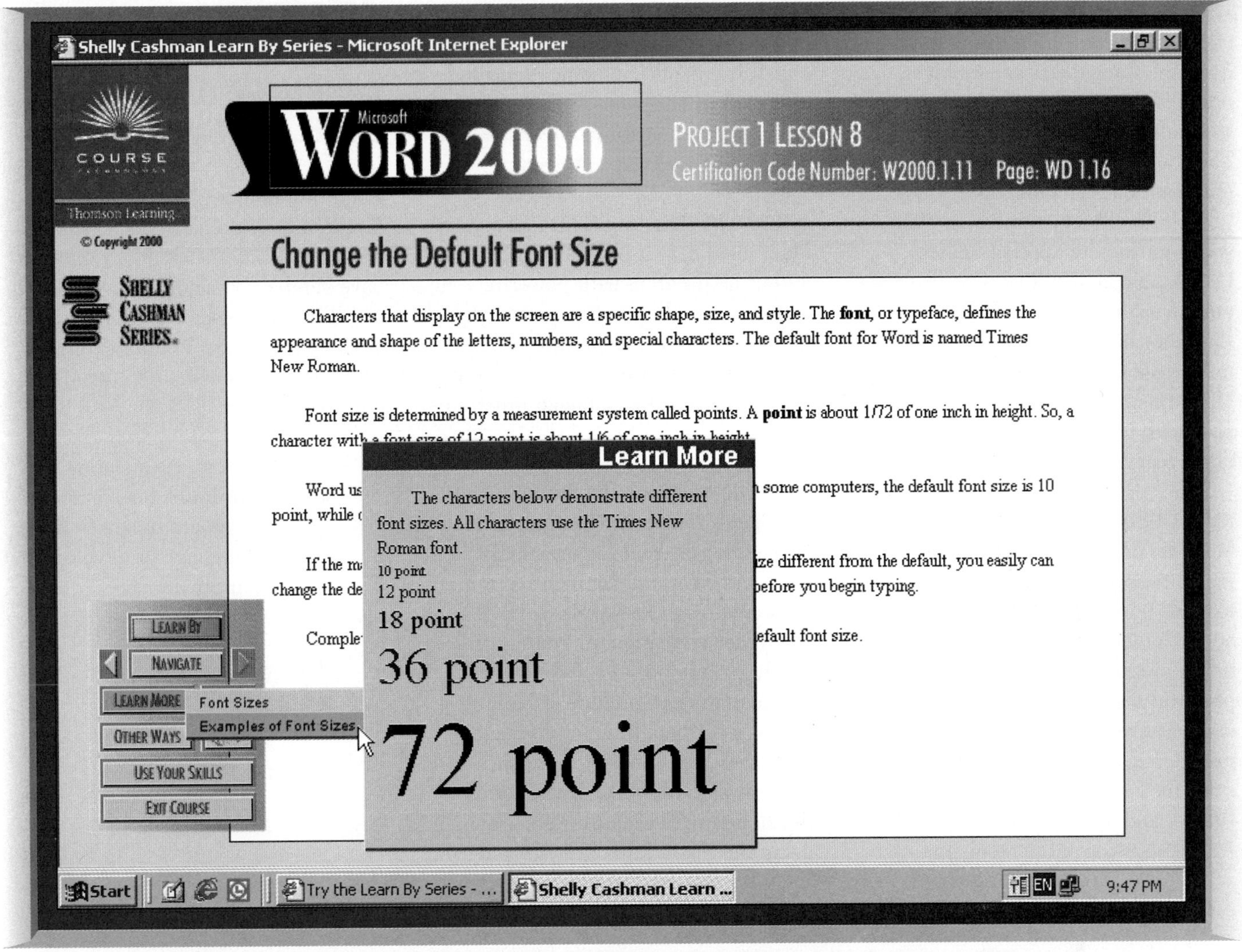

Figure 15-40 Computer-based training such as the Learn By Series is designed so students can choose learning activities that complement their learning styles. Five distinctive Learn By activities and a simulated environment where students use their skills guarantee an effective learning experience.

(Figure 15-40). Also called **computer-aided instruction (CAI)**, this type of training is popular in business, industry, and schools to teach new skills or enhance the existing skills of employees, teachers, or students. Interactive CBT software called **courseware** usually is available on CD-ROM or DVD-ROM or shared over a network.

Web-based training (WBT) is an approach to computer-based training (CBT) that uses the technologies of the Internet and the Web. Today, many major companies provide employees with some type of WBT to teach new skills or upgrade their current skills.

WBT, CBT, and other materials often are combined as materials for distance learning courses. **Distance learning**, also called **distance education** or **online learning**, is the delivery of education at one location while the learning takes place at other locations. Many national and international companies, as well as colleges and universities, offer distance-learning training and courses.

Toolbook, Authorware, Director, and Flash

You can buy many CBT and WBT programs from a local retailer or merchant on the Web. You also can write them yourself using multimedia authoring software. Most of today's popular authoring packages share similar features and are capable of creating similar applications. Popular packages include Toolbook, Authorware, and Director.

TOOLBOOK **ToolBook**, from click2learn.com, Inc., has a graphical user interface and uses an object-oriented approach so you can design your applications using basic objects. These objects include buttons, fields, graphics, backgrounds, and pages.

In ToolBook, you can convert your multimedia application into HTML and Java so it can be distributed over the Internet. Figure 15-41 shows a sample application developed in ToolBook that generated DHTML. Many businesses and colleges use ToolBook to create content for distance learning courses.

AUTHORWARE **Authorware**, from Macromedia, is a multimedia authoring software package that provides the tools developers need to build interactive multimedia training and educational programs. Authorware offers a powerful authoring environment for the development of interactive multimedia magazines, catalogs, reference titles for CD-ROMs and DVD-ROMs, and applications for kiosks. Authorware also offers tools for bundling the content, student tracking, and course management components of a WBT or other distance learning course. You can view Authorware applications distributed over the Web using the Shockwave plug-in.

DIRECTOR **Director**, also from Macromedia, is a popular multimedia authoring program with powerful features that allow you to create highly interactive multimedia applications. The CBT application shown in Figure 15-40 on the previous page illustrates a multimedia application created in Director.

Director includes Lingo, a built-in object-oriented scripting language. Director's powerful features make it well suited for developing electronic presentations, CD-ROMs or DVD-ROMs for education and entertainment, and simulations. Web-based applications can include streaming audio and video, interactivity, and multiuser functionality. As with Authorware, you view applications developed in Director on the Web using the Shockwave browser plug-in.

SELECTING A PROGRAMMING LANGUAGE OR PROGRAM DEVELOPMENT TOOL

Each programming language and program development tool has its own unique characteristics. Many, however, have similar characteristics — making it difficult to select one for a program development task. When deciding which to use, you should consider the following factors.

1. Standards of the organization. Many organizations have standards that require programmers to use a particular language or development tool for all applications.

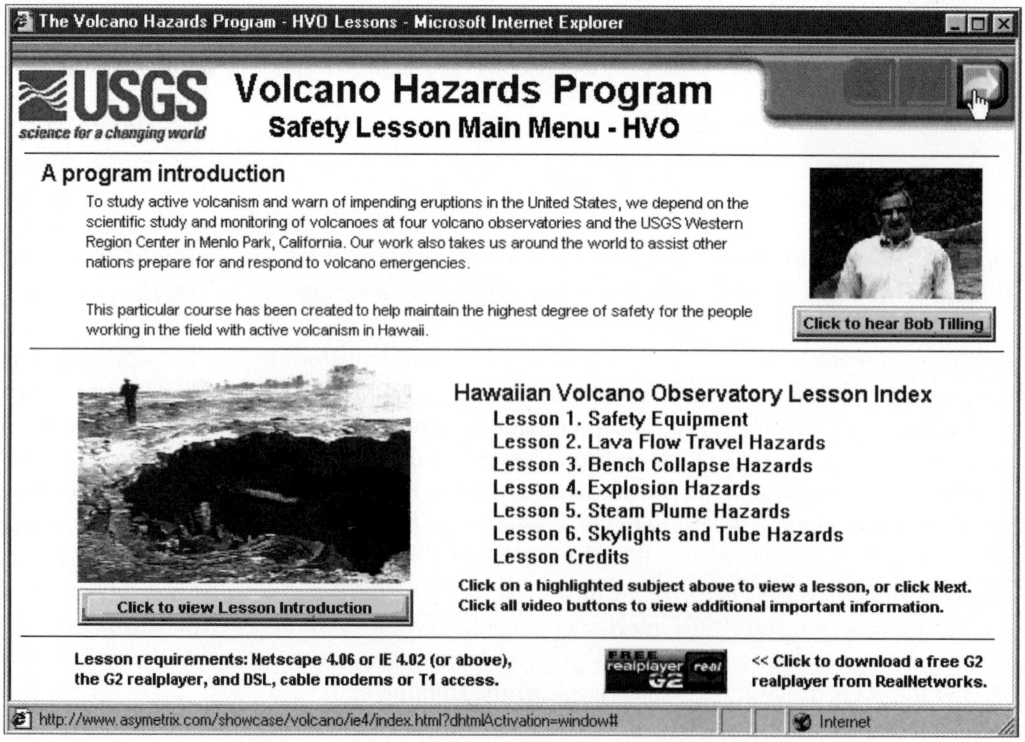

Figure 15-41 A sample Toolbook application that uses DHTML.

2. Interface with other programs. If a program is to work with other programs, you should write it in the same language or with the same development tool as the other programs or a language or development tool compatible with the other programs.
3. Suitability of the language to the application. Most languages and development tools are designed to work with particular applications such as business applications or scientific applications.
4. Portability to other systems. If an application runs on multiple types of computers (hardware platforms) and operating systems (software platforms), select a language or development tool common to these platforms.

CHAPTER SUMMARY

This chapter discussed each step in the program development life cycle and presented the tools used to make this process efficient. This chapter also explained various programming languages and program development tools used to write and develop computer programs. Finally, it presented a variety of Web development and multimedia development tools.

COMPANY ON THE CUTTING EDGE

macromedia

Multimedia Dominates Web Sites

Want to demo a Lexus sports sedan without leaving your house? Check the features on a Timex I-Control watch on your laptop computer? Create fun and educational science projects with your handheld computer? You can, with the help of Macromedia's lineup of splashy products, including Dreamweaver, Flash Player, and Shockwave.

More than 1 million professional Web developers use Macromedia software worldwide to author, produce, deliver, and analyze Web content that is rich in motion, sound, and graphics. They make the most of the high-quality, interactive user interfaces, which have been translated in eight languages. Dreamweaver is the leading platform in 70 percent of the market. More than 1.4 million copies of Flash Player are downloaded from Macromedia's Web site daily, making it the most widely Web-distributed software in history. Nearly 20 million users have registered their copies of Shockwave, with an average of 70,000 new users each day.

For more information on Macromedia, visit the Discovering Computers 2002 Companies Web page (**scsite.com/dc2002/companies.htm**) and click Macromedia.

Programmer

If you are curious, creative, and enjoy problem solving and detailed work, then consider a career in programming. Programmers write the code that tells computers what to do. Most programmers specialize in one of three fields: systems programming, application programming, and Web development programming.

Some jobs may require that the programmer develop the entire program, while others require program maintenance. Likewise, you may work for a small company where you are responsible for the entire System Development Life Cycle or you may work for a larger company where you are part of a team and the duties are very specialized.

Academic credentials are essential for success in this career. A good foundation in programming logic is the key to your success with any programming language. Some of the more popular languages to consider are Visual Basic, Java, C, and C++. Surveys indicate that average salaries for junior level programmers are about $40,000 and approximately $70,000 for senior programmers.

To learn more about a career in programming, visit the Discovering Computers 2002 Careers Web page (**scsite.com/dc2002/careers.htm**) and click Programmer.

E-CAREER

IN SEARCH OF THE PERFECT JOB

Web Helps Career Hunt

If you choose a job you love, you never will have to work a day in your life, according to Confucius. Does that sound good? All you need to do is find that perfect job, but that is no easy feat.

While your teachers give you valuable training to prepare you for a career, they rarely teach you how to begin that career. On-campus interviews are a start, but you can broaden your horizons by searching on the Internet for career information and job openings.

First, examine some of the job search Web sites. These resources list thousands of openings in hundreds of fields, companies, and locations. For example, the Monster Web site, shown in Figure 15-42, allows you to choose a broad job area, such as healthcare, then narrow your search to specific fields within that area, and then search for specific salary ranges, locations, and job functions. Other job search Web sites are listed in Figure 15-43.

Next, prepare your resume. Some Web sites have forms that allow you to type pertinent information into a blank form. Other Web sites want you to submit, or post a document. If so, write your resume using nouns to describe your skills and experience, such as team player, Spanish, and Microsoft Word. Be certain to spell check and scan the document for viruses. When you write your cover letter, use words the company incorporated in its job posting. Many companies use computer software applications, not humans, to find interviewees. The software searches for particular buzzwords, called keywords, in the files and then lists the documents that contain the most matches.

When a company contacts you for an interview, learn as much about it and the

Figure 15-42 Monster.com's global online network connects companies with career-minded individuals.

CAREER WEB SITES	URL
Job Search	
BestJobsUSA.com	bestjobsusa.com
Career Magazine	careermag.com
CareerBuilder	careerbuilder.com
CareerExchange.com	careerexchange.com
Careernet	careernet.com
College Grad Job Hunter	collegegrad.com
Headhunter.net	headhunter.net
HotJobs.com	hotjobs.com
JobBank USA	jobbankusa.com
JobOptions™	www.espan.com
JOBTRAK	jobtrak.com
JobWeb	www.jobweb.org
Monster Board	monster.com
The Employment Guide's CareerWeb	cweb.com
Company/Industry Information	
AmericanCompanies.com	www.americancompanies.com
Argus Clearinghouse	clearinghouse.net
Career ResourceCenter	www.resourcecenter.com
FORTUNE.com	fortune.com
Hoover's Online	hoovers.com
Occupational Outlook Handbook	stats.bls.gov/ocohome.htm

For an updated list of career Web sites, visit scsite.com/dc2002/e-rev.htm.

Figure 15-43 Career Web sites provide a variety of job openings and information on major companies worldwide.

industry as possible before the interview. Many of the Web sites listed in Figure 15-43 have detailed company profiles and links to their corporate Web sites. For instance, company information on Southwest Airlines is displayed in the Hoover's Online Web site, as shown in Figure 15-44. Also, look at Web sites for professional organizations and discussion groups for further insights.

For more information on using the Web for career information and for an updated list of career Web sites, visit the Discovering Computers 2002 E-Revolution Web page (scsite.com/dc2002/e-rev.htm) and click Careers.

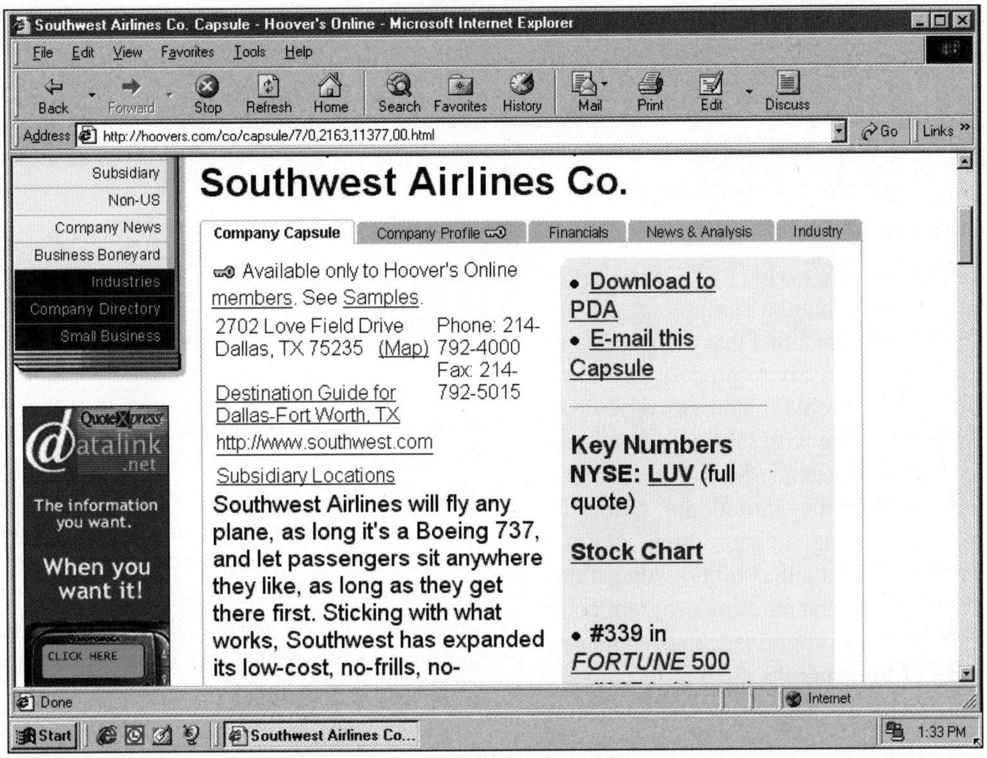

Figure 15-44 Company and industry information forms the core of Hoover's Online Web site.

eREVOLUTION E-CAREER *applied:*

1. Use two of the job search Web sites listed in Figure 15-43 to find three companies with job openings in your field. Make a table listing the Web site name, position available, description, salary, location, desired education, and desired experience.

2. It is a good idea to acquire information prior to graduation about the industry in which you would like to work. Are you interested in the automotive manufacturing industrtoy, the restaurant service industry, or the financial industry? Use two of the company/industry information Web sites listed in Figure 15-43 to research a particular career related to your major. Write a paragraph naming the Web sites and the specific information you found, such as the nature of the work, recommended training and qualifications, employment outlook, and earnings. Then, use two other Web sites to profile three companies with positions available in this field. Write a paragraph about each of these companies, describing the headquarters' location, sales and earnings for the previous year, total number of employees, working conditions, perks, and competitors.

In Summary

Web Instructions: To display this page from the Web, start your browser and enter the URL scsite.com/dc2002/ch15/summary.htm. Click the links for current and additional information. To listen to an audio version of this In Summary, click the Audio button. To play the audio, RealPlayer must be installed on your computer (download by clicking here).

1 What Are the Six Steps in the Program Development Life Cycle?

The **program development life cycle (PDLC)** is a set of steps that programmers use to build a computer program. That program is the set of instructions that directs the computer to perform the steps necessary to process data into information. Step 1, analyze problem, consists of reviewing program specifications; meeting with the analyst and users; and identifying program components. Step 2, design programs, involves grouping activities into modules, devising **solution algorithms**, and testing the algorithms. Step 3, code programs, entails translating the solution algorithm into a programming language and entering program code into the computer. Step 4, test programs, consists of correcting **syntax errors** or **logic errors**. Step 5, formalize solution, includes reviewing program code and documentation. Step 6, maintain programs, involves correcting errors and adding enhancements.

2 What Is Top-Down Program Design?

Top-down design breaks the original set of program specifications into smaller, more manageable sections. A **module** is a section of program dedicated to performing a single function. Programmers use a **hierarchy chart** to graphically represent program modules. Programs developed using the top-down approach usually are reliable and easy to read and maintain.

3 What Are Structured Program Design and Control Structures?

Structured design is an approach wherein all program logic is constructed from a combination of three **control structures**, or designs, that direct the order in which program instructions are executed. A **sequence control structure** shows one or more actions following each other in sequence. A **selection control structure** tells the program which action to take based on a certain condition. Programmers use a **repetition control structure** when one or more actions are to be performed repeatedly as long as a certain condition is met.

4 How Are the Categories of Programming Languages Different?

A **programming language** is a set of words, symbols, and codes that enable a programmer to communicate a solution algorithm to the computer. **Machine language** uses a series of binary digits that correspond to the on and off electrical states of a computer. **Assembly language** instructions are written using abbreviations, codes, and **symbolic addresses**. **Third-generation language** (**3GL**) instructions use a series of English-like words. They are called **procedural languages** because the computer must be told what to accomplish and how to do it. A **fourth-generation language** (**4GL**), which also uses English-like statements, is a **nonprocedural language** because a programmer specifies only what the program should accomplish without explaining how. A **fifth-generation language** (**5GL**) provides a visual graphical interface for creating the source code. Machine and assembly languages are **low-level languages** written to run on one particular computer. Third-, fourth-, and fifth-generation languages are **high-level languages** that can run on various computers.

5 What Is the Object-Oriented Approach to Program Development?

With the **object-oriented (OO) approach**, a programmer can package the data and the procedure into a single unit called an **object**. The data elements in the object are called **attributes**, and the procedures are called **methods**. An **object-oriented programming** (**OOP**) **language** is used to implement the object-oriented approach to program development.

6 What Programming Languages Are Commonly Used Today?

BASIC is a simple, interactive problem-solving language sometimes used in an introductory programming course. **Visual Basic** is a programming language used to develop Windows-based applications. **COBOL** is a procedural programming language widely used for business applications. The **C** programming language is used to develop a variety of software, including operating systems and application programs. **C++** is an object-oriented extension of the C programming language. **RPG** is a nonprocedural language used for application development on IBM midrange computers.

7 Why Are Application Generators, Macros, and RAD Tools Used?

Program development tools such as application generators, macros, and RAD are user-friendly software products designed to create solutions to information systems requirements. An **application generator** is a program used to build an application without writing extensive code. A **macro** is a series of statements that instructs an application how to complete a routine, repetitive, or sometimes difficult task. **Rapid application development** (**RAD**) tools — such as **Visual Basic**, **Delphi**, and **PowerBuilder** — are used to develop software throughout the system development process instead of waiting until the implementation phase.

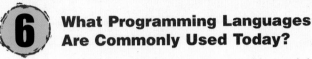

8 What Are the HTML, DHTML, XML, and WML Web Page Development Tools?

Hypertext markup language (HTML) is a special language used to create Web pages. It uses specific syntax rules for defining the placement and format of text, graphics, video, and sound on a Web page. **Dynamic HTML** (**DHTML**) is a newer type of HTML used to include more graphical interest and interactivity, without accessing the Web server. **eXtensible Markup Language** (**XML**) allows Web page developers to create customized **tags** (codes that specify links to other documents and indicate how the Web page displays), as well as use predefined tags. XML allows you to define a link that points to multiple Web sites. **WML** is a subset of XML and is used to design pages specifically for microbrowsers. **Scripts**, **applets**, and **servlets** are short programs that are executed inside of another program. The more common **scripting languages** are **VBScript**, **JavaScript**, and **Perl**. Applets and servlets commonly are written using **Java**.

9 Why are Multimedia Authoring Software Programs Used?

Multimedia authoring software allows you to combine text, graphics, animation, audio, and video into an interactive presentation. Applications created for **computer-based training** (**CBT**) and **Web-based training (WBT)** use this technology.

Key Terms

Web Instructions: To display this page from the Web, start your browser and enter the URL scsite.com/dc2002/ch15/terms.htm. Scroll through the list of terms. Click a term to display its definition and a picture. Click the To WEB button for current and additional information about the term from the Web. To see animations, Shockwave and Flash Player must be installed on your computer (download by clicking here).

ActiveX (15.32)
ActiveX control (15.32)
annotation symbol (15.10)
applet (15.32)
application generator (15.27)
assembler (15.17)
assembly language (15.16)
attributes (15.20)
authorware (15.38)
Authorware (15.40)
BASIC (15.22)
Beans (15.35)
bytecode (15.34)
C (15.25)
C# (15.25)
C++ (15.25)
cascading style sheets (CSS) (15.36)
case control structure (15.7)
CGI program (15.33)
CGI script (15.33)
class (15.20)
COBOL (15.24)
coding (15.13)
comment symbol (15.10)
comments (15.13)
common gateway interface (CGI) (15.33)
compiler (15.18)
component (15.29)
computer program (15.2)
computer-aided instruction (CAI) (15.39)
computer-based training (CBT) (15.38)
construct (15.6)
control structure (15.6)
CORBA (Common Object Request Broker Architecture) (15.21)

INFINITE LOOP
Set of instructions that repeats indefinitely, or forever. (15.8)

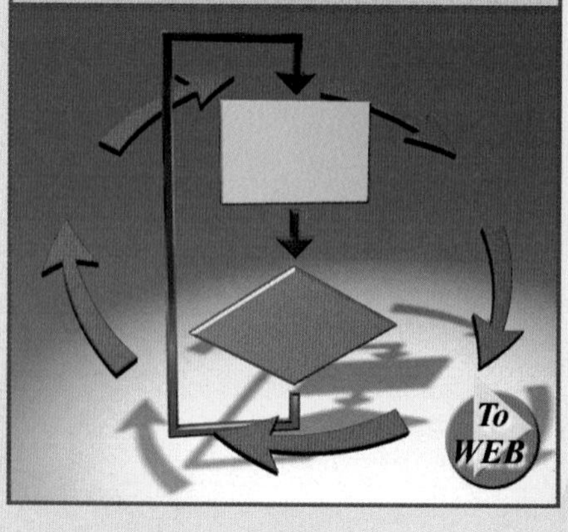

counter (15.32)
courseware (15.39)
dead code (15.8)
debug utility (15.14)
debugger (15.14)
debugging (15.14)
defining diagram (15.4)
Delphi (15.29)
design tools (15.9)
desk check (15.12)
Director (15.40)
distance education (15.39)
distance learning (15.39)
document object model (DOM) (15.36)
do-until control structure (15.8)
do-while control structure (15.8)
dynamic HTML (DHTML) (15.36)
empower (15.27)
encapsulation (15.20)
entry point (15.8)
event (15.21)
exit point (15.8)
fifth-generation language (5GL) (15.20)
flowchart (15.9)
flowcharting software (15.10)
fourth-generation language (4GL) (15.19)
global comments (15.13)
hierarchy chart (15.6)
high-level language (15.16)
HTML editor (15.38)
hypertext markup language (HTML) (15.31)
if-then-else control structure (15.7)
image maps (15.32)
implemented (15.15)
infinite loop (15.8)
information hiding (15.20)
inheritance (15.20)
internal comments (15.13)
interpreter (15.18)
IPO chart (15.4)
iteration control structure (15.8)
Java (15.34)
JavaBeans (15.35)
JavaScript (15.35)
JScript (15.36)
logic error (15.12)
loop (15.8)
low-level language (15.16)
machine language (15.16)
machine-dependent language (15.16)
machine-independent language (15.16)
macro (15.17, 15.28)
macro recorder (15.28)
maintaining (15.15)
markups (15.31)
menu generator (15.28)
message (15.21)
method (15.20)
millennium bug (15.14)
mnemonics (15.16)
module (15.5)
multimedia authoring software (15.38)
Nassi-Schneiderman (N-S) chart (15.11)
nonprocedural language (15.19)
object (15.20)
object code (15.18)
object instance (15.21)
Object Management Group (OMG) (15.21)
object program (15.18)
object-oriented (OO) approach (15.20)
object-oriented programming (OOP) language (15.21)
online learning (15.39)
open language (15.36)
operation (15.20)
Perl (15.36)
PowerBuilder (15.30)
procedural language (15.18)
processing form (15.32)
program development life cycle (PDLC) (15.2)
program development tool (15.16)
program enhancement (15.15)
program flowchart (15.9)
program generator (15.27)
program logic (15.8)
program specification package (15.2)
programming language (15.16)
programming team (15.4)
proper program (15.8)
pseudocode (15.12)
quality review (15.12)
query language (15.19)
rapid application development (RAD) (15.29)
remarks (15.13)
repetition control structure (15.8)
report generator (15.19)
report writer (15.19)
RPG (15.26)
run time errors (15.13)
script (15.32)
scripting language (15.34)
selection control structure (15.7)
sequence control structure (15.7)
servlet (15.32)
solution algorithm (15.8)
source program (15.17)
structure chart (15.6)
structured design (15.6)
structured flowcharts (15.12)
subclasses (15.20)
superclass (15.20)
symbolic address (15.16)
symbolic instruction codes (15.16)
syntax (15.13)
syntax error (15.13)
tags (15.31)
test data (15.12)
third-generation language (3GL) (15.18)
ToolBook (15.40)
top-down chart (15.6)
top-down design (15.5)
UML (Unified Modeling Language) (15.21)
variables (15.20)
VBScript (15.36)
Visual Basic Scripting Edition (15.36)
Visual Basic (15.22)
Visual Basic for Applications (VBA) (15.28)
visual programming environment (VPE) (15.29)
Web page authoring software (15.38)
Web page authors (15.31)
Web-based training (WBT) (15.39)
wireless application protocol (WAP) (15.38)
WML (wireless markup language) (15.38)
XHTML (eXtensible HTML) (15.37)
XML (eXtensible Markup Language) (15.37)
XSL (eXtensible Stylesheet Language) (15.37)
Y2K Bug (15.14)

Learn It Online

Web Instructions: To display this page from the Web, start your browser and enter the URL scsite.com/dc2002/ch15/learn.htm.

1. Web Guide

Click Web Guide to display the Guide to World Wide Web Sites and Searching Techniques page. Click Reference and then click Webopedia. Search for Visual Basic. Click one of the Visual Basic links. Use your word processing program to prepare a brief report on your findings and submit your assignment to your instructor.

2. Scavenger Hunt

Click Scavenger Hunt. Print a copy of the Scavenger Hunt page; use this page to write down your answers as you search the Web. Submit your completed page to your instructor.

3. Who Wants to Be a Computer Genius?

Click Computer Genius to find out if you are a computer genius. Directions on how to play the game will display. When you are ready to play, click the PLAY button. Submit your score to your instructor.

4. Wheel of Terms

Click Wheel of Terms to reinforce important terms you learned in this chapter by playing the Shelly Cashman Series version of this popular game. Directions on how to play the game will display. When you are ready to play, click the PLAY button. Submit your score to your instructor.

5. Career Corner

Click Career Corner to display the IBM page. Click one of the Facts and Information links and then review the information. Write a brief report describing what you learned. Submit the report to your instructor.

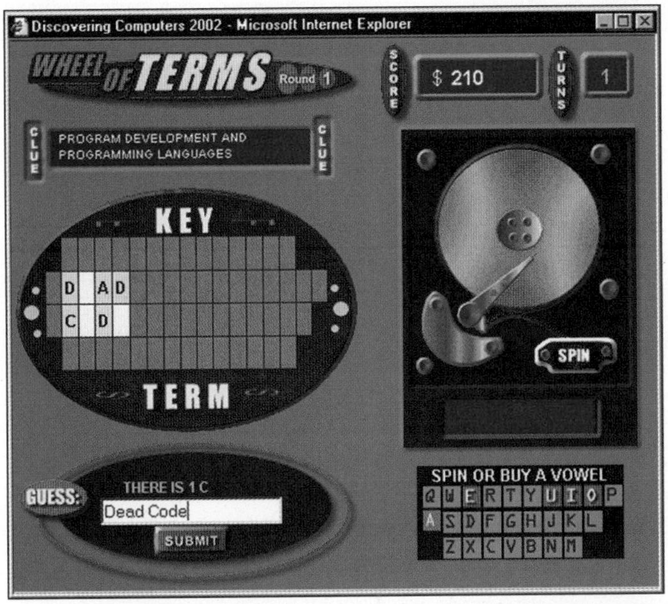

6. Search Sleuth

Click Search Sleuth to learn search techniques that will help make you a research expert. Submit the completed assignment to your instructor.

7. Crossword Puzzle Challenge

Click Crossword Puzzle Challenge. Complete the puzzle to reinforce skills you learned in this chapter. Directions on how to play the game will display. When you are ready to play, click the PLAY button. Submit the completed puzzle to your instructor.

8. Practice Test

Click Practice Test. Answer each question. When completed, enter your name and click the Grade Test button to submit the quiz for grading. Make a note of any missed questions. If required, print a copy to submit to your instructor.

Web Instructions: To display this page from the Web, start your browser and enter the URL scsite.com/dc2002/ch15/check.htm. Click the links for current and additional information. To experience the animation and interactivity, Shockwave and Flash Player must be installed on your computer (download by clicking here.)

LABEL THE FIGURE

Instructions: Identify the steps in the program development lifecycle (PDLC).

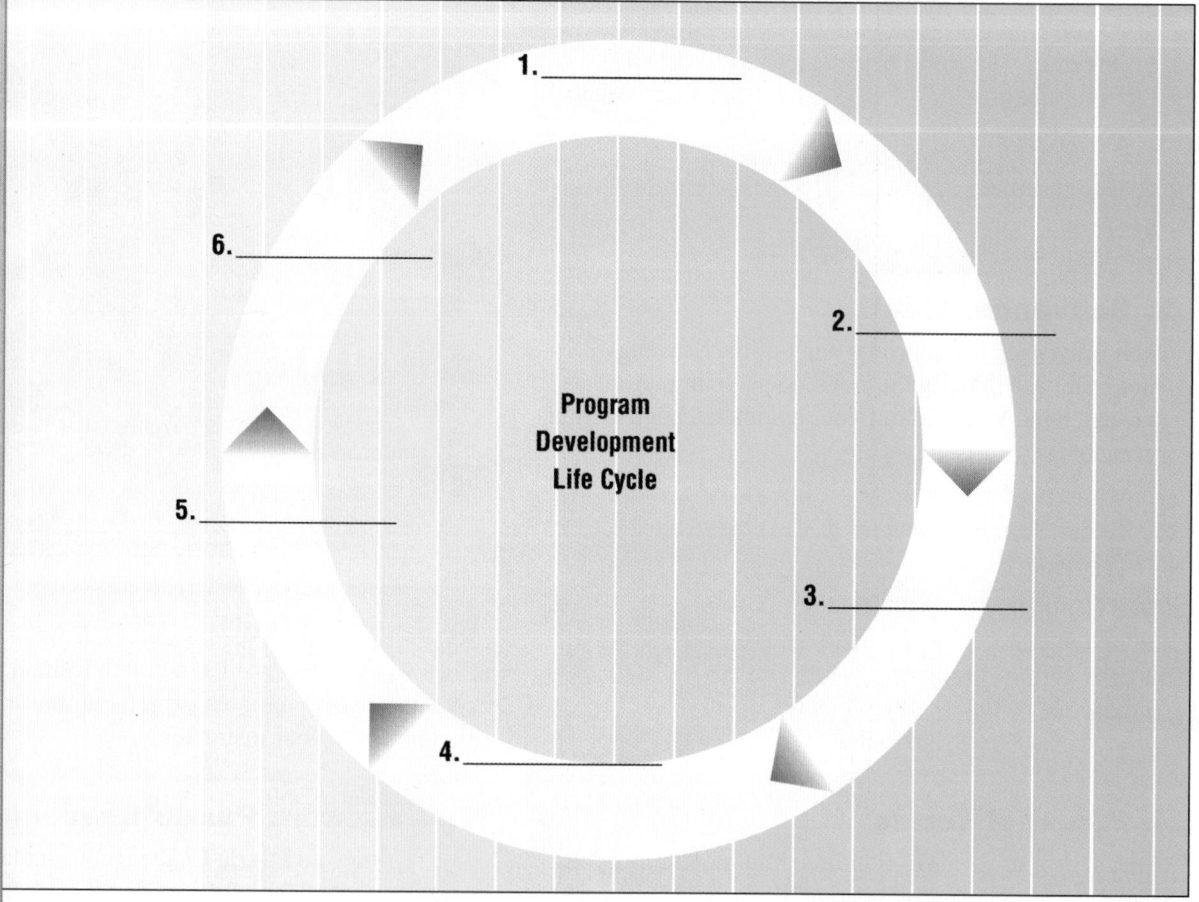

MATCHING

Instructions: Match each term from the column on the left with the best description from the column on the right.

_______ 1. annotation
_______ 2. terminal
_______ 3. process
_______ 4. decision
_______ 5. input/output

a. Program instructions that transform input into output.
b. Beginning or ending of program.
c. Entry from or exit to another part of flowchart on the same page.
d. Entry from or exit to another part of flowchart on a different page.
e. Condition that determines a specified path to follow.
f. Enter date or display information.
g. Additional descriptive information about the program.

Checkpoint

MULTIPLE CHOICE

Instructions: Select the letter of the correct answer for each of the following questions.

1. A tool the programmer uses during top-down design where the program modules are drawn as rectangles is a(n) __________ .
   a. IPO chart
   b. hierarchy chart
   c. Nassi-Schneiderman chart
   d. program flowchart
2. A(n) __________ structure shows one or more actions following each other in order.
   a. sequence control
   b. selection control
   c. case control
   d. if-then-else
3. A Windows-based application programming language is __________ .
   a. COBOL
   b. BASIC
   c. Visual Basic
   d. C
4. With a(n) __________, you can build an application without writing extensive programming code.
   a. Nassi-Schneiderman chart
   b. Delphi
   c. HTML
   d. application generator
5. __________ is a compiled object-oriented programming language used to write applets.
   a. C
   b. RPG
   c. JavaScript
   d. Java

SHORT ANSWER

Instructions: Write a brief answer to each of the following questions.

1. How is the if-then-else control structure different from the case control structure? __________ How is the do-while control structure different from the do-until control structure? __________
2. What is proper program design? __________ What are dead code, infinite loops, entry points, and exit points? __________
3. How is a compiler different from an interpreter? __________ What is an advantage of an interpreter? __________
4. What factors should be considered when selecting a programming language? __________
5. What is a CGI script? __________ What is the difference between Jscript and JavaScript? __________ What is an applet? __________

WORKING TOGETHER

Instructions: Working with a group of your classmates, complete the following team exercise.

If you work in an office and use a computer, you probably have experienced an out-of-date computer or last year's software. To address this problem, software industry predictions indicate we are moving into the next wave of the Web where software and services are delivered online. Microsoft's Office Online, for example, provides a choice for Office customers who prefer the benefits of centrally managed software. Investigate the possibilities of online software. Create a three- to five-page report, addressing the positives and negatives of offering software online. In particular, focus your report on software errors and how those errors could impact this offering. To learn more about software online, visit scsite.com/dc2002/ch15/check.htm.

In The Lab

Web Instructions: To display this page from the Web, start your browser and enter the URL scsite.com/dc2002/ch15/lab.htm. Click the links or current and additional information.

1 Searching for Executable Files

This exercise uses Windows 98 procedures. In Windows, application files have an .exe extension, meaning that they are executable. To find the executable program files on your computer, click the Start button on the taskbar, point to Find on the Start menu, and then click Files or Folders on the Find submenu. In the Find: All Files window, click the Name & Location tab, click View on the menu bar, and then click Details. Type `*.exe` in the Named text box. Type `c:\` in the Look in text box. Make certain the Include subfolders check box is selected. Click the Find Now button. Sort the files alphabetically by name by clicking the Name column heading. Scroll through the list of files and find the file name, Notepad. In what folder is Notepad located? How large is the file? Close the Find window.

2 Movie Box Office Simulation

Insert the Discover Data Disk into drive A. See the inside back cover of this book for instructions for downloading the Discover Data Disk or see your instructor for information on accessing the files required in this book. Click the Start button on the taskbar and then click Run on the Start menu. In the Open text box, type `a:movie.exe` and then press the ENTER key. This program was written in Visual Basic. The first customer wishes to purchase three tickets to a matinee performance of *The Abyss*. Notice the amount due and then click the Enter button. Enter the following transactions and write down the amount due for each transaction: (1) *The Client*, no matinee, 3 tickets; (2) *Forrest Gump*, matinee, 1 ticket; (3) *Beverly Hills Cop*, matinee, 2 tickets.

3 Adjusting Keyboard Speed

Windows allows users to adjust the keyboard to their own specifications. To customize the keyboard, click the Start button on the taskbar, point to Settings on the Start menu, and then click Control Panel on the Settings submenu. Double-click the Keyboard icon in the Control Panel window. When the Keyboard Properties dialog box displays, if necessary, click the Speed tab (Figure 15-45). Use the Question Mark button on the title bar to answer the following questions: What is Repeat delay? What is Repeat rate? Click the Cancel button. Close the Control Panel window.

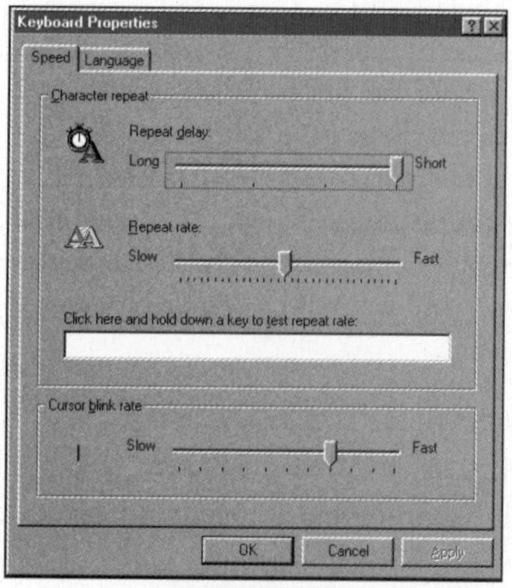

Figure 15-45

4 Loan Payment Calculator

Insert the Discover Data Disk into drive A. See the Preface at the front of this book for instructions for downloading the Discover Data Disk or see your instructor for information on accessing the files required in this book. Click the Start button on the taskbar, and then click Run on the Start menu to display the Run dialog box. In the Open text box, type `a:loancalc.exe` and then press the ENTER key to open the Loan Payment Calculator window. This program was written in Visual Basic. Type `12500` in the LOAN AMOUNT text box. Click the YEARS right scroll arrow or drag the scroll box until YEARS equals 15. Click the APR right scroll arrow or drag the scroll box until APR equals 8.5. Click the Calculate button. Write down the monthly payment and sum of payments. Click the Clear button. What are the monthly payment and sum of payments for each of these loan amounts, years, and APRs? (1) 28000, 5, 7.25; (2) 98750, 30, 9; (3) 6000, 3, 8.75; and (4) 62500, 15, 9.25. Close the Loan Payment Calculator.

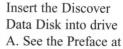

Web Work

Web Instructions: To display this page from the Web, start your browser and enter the URL scsite.com/dc2002/ch15/web.htm. To view At The Movies in exercise 1, RealPlayer must be installed on your computer (download by clicking here). To use the Shelly Cashman Series Choosing a Programming Language Lab from the Web, Shockwave and Flash Player must be installed on your computer (download by clicking here).

1

Java Victory

To view the Java Victory movie, click the button to the left or click the Play button to the right. Watch the movie, and then complete the exercise by answering the questions below. Developed by Sun Microsystems, Java is an important language used in Web site development, particularly in the creation of graphic elements such as moving banners, ads, and logos. Java was designed by Sun as an easy-to-use, cross-platform language that would run on any computer. Sun licensed Java to others with the hope that Java would become the standard language of the future. Microsoft, an early licensee, chose to modify its version of Java only to run on Microsoft operating systems. Sun sued, and subsequently won the case. What are the benefits of standardization? Do consumers or companies benefit more?

2

Shelly Cashman Series Choosing a Programming Language Lab

Follow the instructions in Web Work 2 on page 1.47 to start and use the Choosing a Programming Language Lab. If you are running from the Web, enter the URL, www.scsite.com/sclabs/menu.htm; or display the Web Work page (see instructions at the top of this page) and then click the button to the left.

3

Image Maps

One common use of a script is to create an image map — a Web page picture that points to a URL and is used in place of, or in addition to, plain text hyperlinks (Figure 15-46). When you click a part of the picture, the Web browser locates the corresponding URL and sends the Web page to you computer. To work with image maps on Web pages, click the button to the left and complete this exercise.

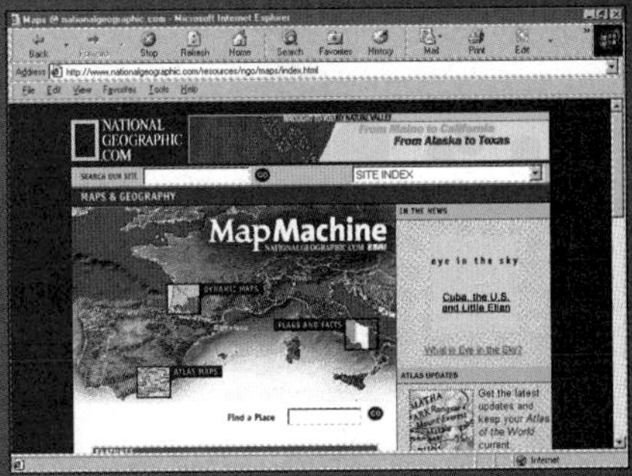

Figure 15-46

4

Application Generators

When using an application generator, a developer works with menu-driven tools that have easy-to-use graphical interfaces. To use an application generator to produce Web pages, click the button to the left and complete this exercise.

5

In the News

Programming is not just for programmers anymore. Yaroze is a Japanese expression meaning, let us work together. Net Yaroze is a new project that lets anyone with a computer and some programming experience work together with Sony to create their own games for Sony's Playstation. Increasingly, entertainment and productivity applications are offering tools, such as macros, that allow users to program their own innovations. Click the button to the left and read a news article about programming. Who is doing the programming? How is the programming different?

CHAPTER 16

Computer Careers and Certification

College life has been much more than you anticipated … more demanding, more challenging, more rewarding, and more fun! It took a few weeks to coordinate all your classes and activities, but now with your first semester well under way, you feel quite comfortable with the school atmosphere. Classes are intense, but all the hard work and efforts are paying off. Your grades so far have been good. Best of all, you have made many new friends. In fact, you just joined a few of them in the school cafeteria for lunch.

The group's conversation centers on registration, which starts tomorrow. You, and most of your friends, are in the General Studies program. The dilemma now is selecting a major. That decision will determine which classes you take next semester. You have not made an appointment with an advisor yet because you have no idea what career path you plan to take.

One friend mentions that some departments offer one-credit courses that explore careers in a field of study. He is interested in computers, so he plans to sign up for the Computing Careers course next semester. You like working with computers. Immediately, you add the Computing Careers course to your schedule.

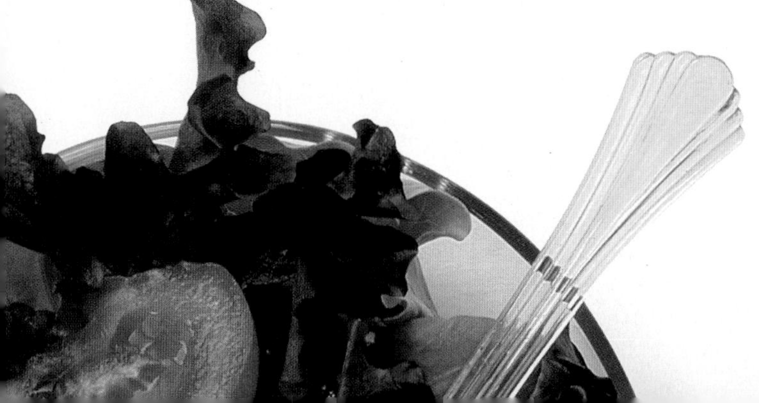

CAREERS IN THE COMPUTER INDUSTRY

In today's technology-rich world, a great demand for computer and information technology (IT) professionals exists and continues to grow. In fact, the U.S. Department of Labor's Bureau of Labor Statistics recently reported that by the year 2006, American businesses and schools will require more than 5.6 million new systems analysts, computer scientists, engineers, and programmers. Nearly 20 percent of the U.S. information technology careers — or 800,000 jobs — are open today. Currently, however, fewer than three percent of college freshmen are majoring in a computer-related field. When you consider these three facts together, it is clear that computer and IT professionals are in demand. For individuals worldwide, this means that incredible opportunities increase daily.

As presented in the Career Corner feature in each chapter of this book, the computer and IT industry offers many rewarding careers, which can require a unique combination of hands-on skills, creative problem solving, and an understanding of business needs. This chapter discusses the careers available, preparing for a job, and planning for career development in the computer and IT industry.

With annual sales of nearly $400 billion, the computer industry is one of the larger worldwide industries. Approximately one-half of this $400 billion total is related to equipment sales; the other half comes from software and service sales.

OBJECTIVES

After completing this chapter, you will be able to:

- Describe career opportunities in the computer industry
- Discuss how to prepare for a career in the computer industry
- Define the term certification
- Describe types of IT certification
- List the benefits of certification
- Explain considerations for choosing a certification
- Describe methods of preparation for certification
- Discuss features of certification examinations and recertification requirements
- Understand how to keep informed about changes in certification

Web Link

For more information on employment projections, visit the Discovering Computers 2002 Chapter 16 WEB LINK page (**scsite.com/dc2002/ch16/weblink.htm**) and click Employment Projections.

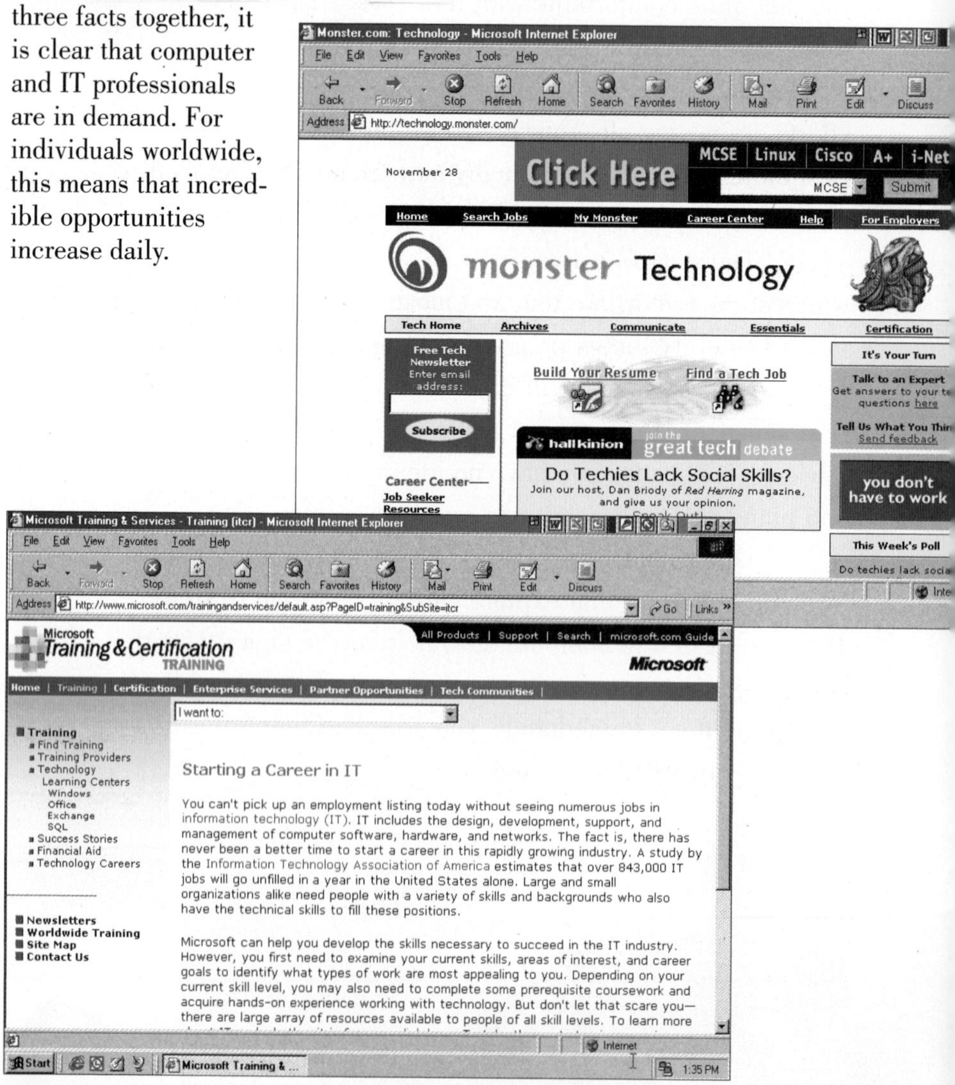

Figure 16-1 Information on computer-related jobs is available on many Web sites on the World Wide Web.

Job opportunities in the industry are found primarily in four areas:

- Companies that manufacture computer-related equipment (hardware)
- Companies that develop software
- Companies that hire IT professionals to work with these products
- Companies and organizations that provide computer-related training and education

As in any major industry, the computer industry includes many service companies that support each of these four areas. Examples of such companies include firms that sell computer supplies or provide consultation on analysis, design, programming, and networking projects. You can find information on specific careers in each of these industries via typical job-searching methods, as well as on career-oriented sites on the World Wide Web (Figure 16-1).

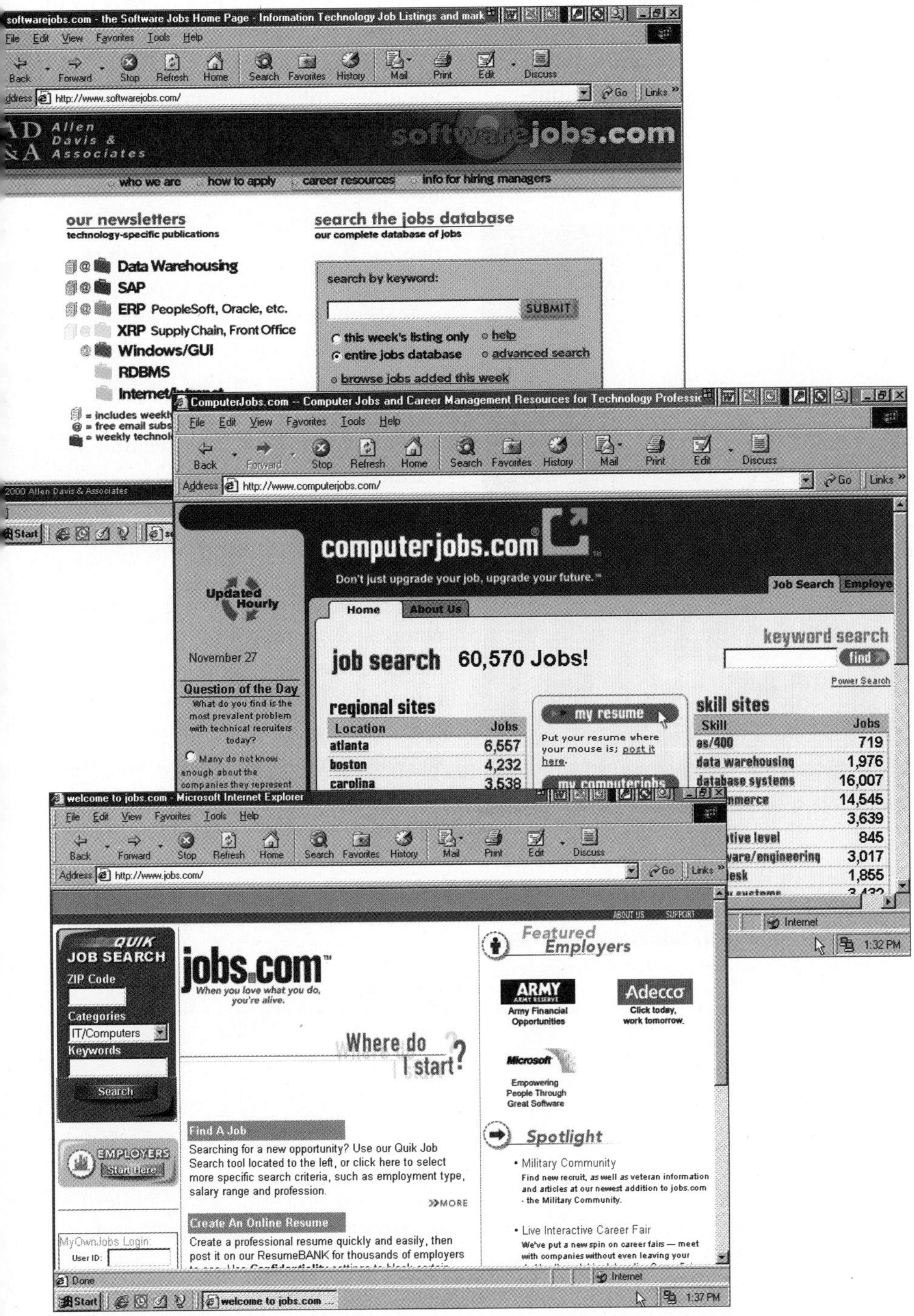

Foreign Workers

H1B Visa Expansion Program

Millions of Americans are employed today in computer and telecommunications industries. In order for companies to remain competitive as the economy continues to grow, a technologically literate workforce is needed. In the United States, however, a major shortage of IT workers exists. The U.S. Congress has responded to this worker shortage by lifting the cap on the number of foreign workers that can be imported to fill these jobs. Many argue that the expansion of the H1B Visa skilled-labor immigration program (see URL below) is crucial to the future development of the economy in the United States. They contend that some of the world's best high-tech employees come from places other than the United States, so there should be legislation expanding the H1B Visa program. Others argue that this is a method for American companies to bring in cheap labor and drive down salaries of American workers. Should Congress expand the immigration program for additional IT workers? Why or why not? Should a time limit be set on those migrating to the United States? Should a minimum wage be established for IT workers?

For more information on the IT worker shortage and the Web site mentioned above, visit the Discovering Computers 2002 Issues Web page (**scsite.com/dc2002/issues.htm**) and click Chapter 16 Issue #1.

Web Link

For more information on Web resources, visit the Discovering Computers 2002 Chapter 16 WEB LINK page (**scsite.com/dc2002/ch16/weblink.htm**) and click Web Resources.

The Computer Equipment Industry

The computer hardware industry consists of manufacturers and distributors of computers and computer-related equipment such as disk and tape drives, monitors, printers, and communications equipment (Figure 16-2).

Computer equipment manufacturers include such companies as Apple, Cisco, Compaq, Dell, Gateway, Hewlett-Packard, IBM, Intel, Lucent, QUALCOMM, Sun Microsystems, and 3Com. Many of these firms are huge organizations with thousands of employees worldwide. IBM, for example, is one of the largest computer companies with more than 307,000 employees and annual sales of more than $87 billion.

The computer equipment industry also is well known for the many start-up companies that appear each year. These new companies take advantage of rapid changes in equipment technology, such as wireless communications, networking, multimedia, and fiber optics, to create new products and new job opportunities. Often these companies offer stock options to induce college graduates to join their firm instead of the larger, more established companies. Many young graduates have become millionaires overnight by taking a chance with a start-up company.

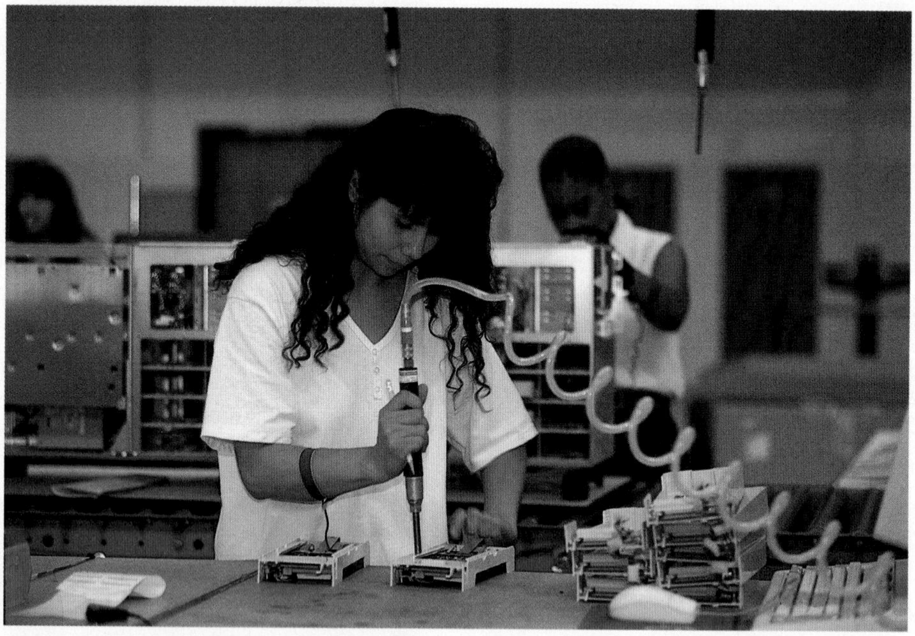

Figure 16-2 A computer is assembled carefully.

In addition to the companies that make end-user equipment, thousands of companies build components that most users never see. These companies manufacture chips, motherboards, power supplies, peripherals, and the hundreds of other parts that are inside a computer.

Some of the more popular job titles that involve the design and manufacture of computer equipment are described in Figure 16-3. In larger companies there are several levels to each job title, including management careers.

Many companies list their job openings, internship opportunities, and career opportunities on their Web sites. The right column in Figure 16-4 lists the Web site addresses of some of the major computer equipment companies. If you are serious about interviewing with a company, you often can obtain a wealth of information about the firm and its employment opportunities by visiting the company's Web site. Some companies even allow you to submit your resume online.

The Computer Software Industry

The computer software industry is composed of companies that develop, manufacture, and support a wide range of software products, such as operating systems and other systems software; productivity software; network software; software development tools; and Internet software and technologies.

Web Link

For more information on salaries, visit the Discovering Computers 2002 Chapter 16 WEB LINK page (**scsite.com/dc2002/ch16/weblink.htm**) and click Salaries.

COMPUTER EQUIPMENT INDUSTRY POSITIONS

Title	**Median Salary Range** *(in thousands of $)*		
	1999	2000	Change %
Digital signal processor (DSP) designer	80.0	87.5	9.3
Integrated circuit (IC) designer	90.7	101.1	11.5
Systems integrator	76.8	84.8	10.4
Wireless designer	77.4	84.1	8.7

Figure 16-3 Popular job titles involving the design and manufacture of computer equipment.
(Source: EE Times Salary & Opinion Survey, CMP Media Inc.)

WEB SITE ADDRESSES FOR MAJOR COMPANIES

Hardware Company	URL
Apple Computer, Inc.	apple.com/jobs
Cisco Systems, Inc.	cisco.com/jobs
Compaq Computer Corporation	vcmproapp04.compaq.com/jobs/index.html
Dell Computer Corporation	dellapp.us.dell.com/careers
Gateway, Inc.	jobs.gateway.com
Hewlett-Packard Company	jobs.hp.com
IBM Corporation	www.empl.ibm.com
Intel Corporation	intel.com/jobs/students
Lucent Technologies	lucent.com/work/work.html
QUALCOMM Incorporated	www.qualcomm.com/HR
Sun Microsystems, Inc.	sun.com/corp_emp/zone/index.html
3Com Corporation	3com.com/inside/college
Software Company	**URL**
Adobe Systems, Inc.	www.adobe.com/aboutadobe/careeropp
Computer Associates International, Inc.	cai.com/career/cajobs.htm
IBM Corporation	www.empl.ibm.com
Intuit Inc.	intuit.com/corporate/hr
Macromedia, Inc.	macromedia.com/macromedia/hr
Microsoft Corporation	microsoft.com/jobs
Network Associates, Inc.	job4.cbdr.com/networkassoc
Novell, Inc.	www.novell.com/company/careers
Oracle Corporation	oracle.com/corporate/employment
Sybase, Inc.	sybase.com/corporate/careers
Symantec Corporation	symantec.com/corporate/hr/index.html
Internet Company	**URL**
Amazon.com. Inc.	amazon.com
America Online, Inc.	corp.aol.com/careers
EarthLink, Inc.	www.earthlink.com/about/jobs
eBay Inc.	ebaycareers.com
E*Trade Securities, Inc.	e-trade.com
At Home Corporation (Excite)	corp.excite.com/jobs
Lycos, Inc.	lycos.com/careers
Microsoft Corporation	microsoft.com/jobs
RealNetworks, Inc.	real.com/company/index.html
theglobe.com	theglobe.com
Music.com, Inc.	music.com/company
Yahoo! Inc.	join.yahoo.com
Noncomputer-Related Company	**URL**
AT&T	att.com/hr/ur
The Boeing Company	boeing.com/employment/college.html
Caterpillar, Inc.	cat.com/about_cat/employment/employment.html
Chevron Corporation	www.chevron.com/about/hr
Disney	disney.go.com/DisneyCareers
General Motors Corporation	generalmotors.com/company/careers
McDonald's Corporation	mcdonalds.com/corporate/careers
Merck & Co., Inc.	merck.com
Merrill Lynch & Co., Inc.	ml.com/careers
Pfizer Inc.	pfizer.com/pfizerinc/career
The Procter & Gamble Company	pg.com/jobs/sectionmain.jhtml
Union Carbide	unioncarbide.com/recruit/uccrec.html
Wal-Mart Stores, Inc.	walmartstores.com/careers

Figure 16-4 This table lists the Web site addresses for the major hardware, software, Internet, and noncomputer-related companies. When you visit a Web site, you may have to click a link, such as About or Company Information, to obtain a list of employment opportunities and other career-related information.
For an updated list, visit scsite.com/dc2002/ch16/careers.htm.

APPLY IT!

Resume Online

The days of putting pencil to paper and wearing out the soles of your shoes during a job search are in the past. Today, you are more likely to wear out your keyboard. The Internet can provide a point of introduction between you and potential employers around the world. Just publish your resume on a Web site, sit back, and wait for the job offers. Before publishing your resume online, you may want to use resume building software such as Web Resume Writer.

To publish your resume, you can select from several options. You may want to use one of the free Web page sites such as GeoCities or Tripod. A second option is to have your own Web site. Several Web sites offer free Web site hosting services.

Third, many job seekers use the resume database feature supported by many of the online career recruitment Web sites. Most of these Web sites, such as Monster.com, provide e-forms into which you can publish your information. If you use one of the forms, the first step is to start with a plain, simple resume. Use a simple font like Courier or Times New Roman. Avoid columns and tabs and formatting with bold, italics, script, graphics, and borders.

For more information on online resumes and the Web sites mentioned above, visit the Discovering Computers 2002 Apply It Web page (**scsite.com/dc2002/apply.htm**) and click Chapter 16 Apply It #1.

Web Link

For more information on benefits, visit the Discovering Computers 2002 Chapter 16 WEB LINK page (**scsite.com/dc2002/ch16/weblink.htm**) and click Benefits.

Some software companies specialize in a particular type of software product such as business productivity software, utility programs, or multimedia and graphic design tools. Other software companies, especially larger firms, produce and sell multiple software products.

The software industry is a huge one, with annual sales exceeding $200 billion. Leading software companies include Adobe Systems, Computer Associates, IBM, Intuit, Macromedia, Microsoft, Novell, Oracle, Sybase, and Symantec. The largest software company, Microsoft, has more than 300 products and technologies, 39,900 employees, and annual sales of more than $33 billion.

Career opportunities in the software industry involve designing and programming all kinds of software products, including application software for business, productivity software, educational programs, entertainment software, and systems software. Figure 16-5 describes some of the popular job titles used for careers related to the development of software.

The right column in Figure 16-4 on the previous page lists the Web site addresses of some of the major software companies. As with the computer equipment companies, you may wish to visit a software company's Web site to obtain information on specific job openings and career opportunities.

IT Professionals

In many companies, the IT department includes professionals who set up and manage the computer equipment and software to ensure that it produces information for the end user. In addition to other jobs, IT professionals include programmers and systems analysts that companies hire to work in an IT department. The next section discusses these and other careers available within most IT departments. In the fast-paced world of technology, job titles are not standardized. Some companies are shrinking their number of titles, while others invent new ones each time someone is hired.

IT Career Opportunities

Without computers, very few companies could operate in today's economy. For some, computers help ensure smooth communications between corporate offices. Other firms use computers to order raw materials automatically, control manufacturing, and ship finished goods. In many cases, the only time a human is involved in the process is in designing and writing the programs that tell the computer what to do each step of the way. This dependency on computers has created thousands of new high-tech jobs, even in noncomputer-related companies. For many firms, the use of technology separates them from their

Web Link

For more information on the computer software industry, visit the Discovering Computers 2002 Chapter 16 WEB LINK page (**scsite.com/dc2002/ch16/weblink.htm**) and click Computer Software Industry.

COMPUTER SOFTWARE INDUSTRY POSITIONS

Title	Function	Minimum Education	Median Salary Range *(in thousands of $)*
Programmer/ Analyst	Design, write, and test computer programs	B.S. in Computer Science or Information Technology	62.5
Project engineer	Analyze software requirements, design software solutions, and oversee the software development process	B.S. in Computer Science or Electrical Engineering	74.7
Software engineer	Develop system software such as operating systems, utilities, and software drivers	B.S. in Computer Science or Electrical Engineering	71.3

Figure 16-5 Popular job titles for software development careers.

(Sources: EE Times Salary & Opinion Survey, CMP Media Inc.; Information Technology Salary Survey, kforce.com)

competitors and is a distinction they highlight on their Web sites (see Figure 16-4 on page 16.5).

Because of rapid changes in technology, many current jobs did not even exist just a few years ago. For example, the World Wide Web, which began in 1993, has spawned thousands of Internet Content/Commerce/Provider companies (see Figure 16-4) that demand Web designers and network specialists to create and maintain their Web sites. These jobs are described in Figure 16-6.

The following sections describe some current career opportunities in an IT department.

Web Link

For more information on career mobility, visit the Discovering Computers 2002 Chapter 16 WEB LINK page (**scsite.com/dc2002/ch16/weblink.htm**) and click Career Mobility.

INTERNET INDUSTRY POSITIONS

Title	Function	Minimum Education	Median Salary Range (in thousands of $)
Project manager	Supervises the development and execution of Internet or e-commerce systems; works with the company's marketing and customer service divisions	B.S. in Management Information Technology	81.5
Web administrator	Oversees Web site performance; maintains Web link between company's Web server and ISP	B.S. in Information Technology	57.5
Web developer	Analyzes, designs, implements, and supports Web applications. Works with HTML, JavaScript, and multimedia	B.S. in Information Technology	63.2
Web graphic designer	Develops graphical content using Photoshop, Flash, and multimedia	B.S. in Information Technology	64.9
Web programmer	Supports the company's Internet strategy by analyzing, designing, implementing, and supporting Web-related applications	A.A.S. or A.S. in Information Technology	66.9
Webcaster	Creates and delivers Webcasts featuring streaming rich media, including audio, video, and Web-based multimedia	A.A.S. or A.S. in Information Technology	62.5
Webmaster	Maintains an organization's Web site; creates or helps users create Web pages	B.S. in Information Technology	52.2

Figure 16-6 This table shows some of the jobs available in the Internet field.
(Sources: Information Technology Salary Survey, kforce.com; Occupational Outlook Handbook, Bureau of Labor Statistics, U.S. Department of Labor)

TECHNOLOGY TRAILBLAZER

MARC ANDREESSEN

Drinking a great cup of coffee and sleeping until 3:00 p.m. make Marc Andreessen happy. But he certainly is happy, too, about the success of his programs, Mosaic and Netscape Navigator.

As a computer science student at the University of Illinois, Andreessen worked as a part-time programmer at the university's National Center for Supercomputing Applications (NCSA) and became familiar with the Internet, which was primarily a text-based resource used almost exclusively by scientists and scholars.

Andreessen and a friend worked 18 hours a day to create NCSA Mosaic in 6 weeks. Although slow and unstable, the program gave users a user-friendly graphical tool to browse the Web by jumping from links to other Web pages with a click of the mouse.

After graduating in 1994, Andreessen accepted a job as a programmer in California's Silicon Valley. He and some colleagues from NCSA met with Jim Clark, who invested $4 million in a new company, called Netscape Communications. They decided to "create a Mosaic killer" and developed the Netscape browser.

Today, Andreessen works at Loudcloud, a company he co-founded to provide technology and software to Internet startups.

For more information on Marc Andreessen, visit the Discovering Computers 2002 People Web page (**scsite.com/dc2002/people.htm**) and click Marc Andreessen.

Working in an IT Department

The people in an IT department work together as a team to meet the information demands of their organization. Several jobs have been discussed previously, including database administrators (Chapter 13), systems analysts (Chapter 14), and programmers (Chapter 15). In addition to these jobs, many other careers exist. Generally, these jobs fall into five main groups:

1. Management
2. Operations
3. System development
4. Technical services
5. End-user computing

The table in Figure 16-7 shows some of the jobs in each group in a typical IT department. The management group directs the planning, research, development, evaluation, and integration of technology. The operations group is responsible for operating the centralized computer equipment and administering the network including both data and voice communications. The system development group is responsible for analyzing, designing, developing, and implementing new information technology and maintaining and improving existing systems. The technical services group is responsible for evaluating and integrating new technologies, administering the organization's data resources, and supporting the centralized computer operating system or servers. The end-user computing group is responsible for assisting end users in working with existing systems and in using productivity software and query languages to obtain the information necessary to perform their jobs.

An IT department provides career opportunities for people with a variety of skills and talents. Other information industry jobs are found in the areas of education and training, sales, service and repair, and consulting.

COMPANY ON THE CUTTING EDGE

divine interVentures™
The Internet Zaibatsu™

Creating Commerce for Chicago

When you think of Chicago, you most likely envision windy weather, Michael Jordan, and pizza. If Andrew "Flip" Filipowski is successful, you might add Internet technology to your list of Chicago's claims to fame.

Filipowski is the head of divine interVentures, an Internet holding company. He believes that Chicago is ripe for a thriving Internet economy due to its 8,000 technology-based corporations, top educational institutions, and hard-working residents. A multitude of other investors agrees, including Microsoft, Dell Computer, Compaq Computer, Hewlett-Packard, Aon Corporation, the Chicago Tribune, and Michael Jordan.

In 2000, Filipowski offered shares in divine to public investors. These backers share his passion to create an Internet *Zaibatsu*™ community, which is a Japanese term for a family of businesses working collaboratively to create mutual opportunity and gain. Using this model, entrepreneurs will be able to focus on their core businesses while divine supplies managerial expertise, networking resources, and industry knowledge. Filipowski believes these relationships and synergies will help Chicago build its high-tech industry.

For more information on divine interVentures, visit the Discovering Computers 2002 Companies Web page (**scsite.com/dc2002/companies.htm**) and click divine interVentures.

INFORMATION TECHNOLOGY POSITIONS

Group	Job Title	Function	Minimum Education	Median Salary Range (*in thousands of $*)
Management	MIS director/CIO	Directs the company's information service and communications functions	B.S. in Management Information Technology	129
	Project leader	Coordinates projects; performs systems analysis and programming tasks	B.S. in Management Information Technology	72.6
	Project manager	Oversees all assigned projects; allocates resources, selects teams, conducts performance appraisals	B.S. in Management Information Technology	81.5
Operations	Computer operator	Performs equipment-related activities such as monitoring performance, running jobs, backup, and restore	A.A.S. or A.S. in Information Technology	33.5
	Data communications analysts	Evaluates, installs, and monitors data and/or voice communications equipment and software and maintains connections to the Internet and other wide area networks	B.S. in Management Information Technology or Electrical Engineering Technology	47.6
	Network (LAN) administrator	Installs and maintains local area networks; identifies and resolves connectivity issues	B.S. in Management Information Technology or Electrical Engineering Technology	59.4
System development	Application programmer	Converts the system design into the appropriate computer language, such as Visual Basic, Java, C, and C++	A.A.S. or A.S. in Information Technology	46.7
	Computer science engineer/ Software engineer	Specifies, designs, implements, tests, and documents high-quality software in a variety of fields, including robotics, operating systems, animation, and applications	B.S. in Computer Science	62.9
	Technical writer	Works with the analysts, programmers, and users to create system documentation and user materials	A.A.S. or A.S. in Information Technology; B.A. in English	51.1
	Systems analyst	Works closely with users to analyze their requirements, design and develop new hardware and software systems, and incorporate new technologies	B.S. in Management Information Technology	54.3
Technical services	Database analyst/Data modeler	Uses data modeling techniques and tools to analyze, tune, and specify data usage within an application area	B.S. in Computer Science or Information Technology	71.1
	Desktop publishing specialist	Produces documents such as newsletters, brochures, and books by combining text and graphics	Certificate	39.1
	Graphic designer/ illustrator	Creates visual impressions of products and advertisements in the fields of graphics, theater, interior design, jewelry, and fashion	Certificate	31.7
	Network security specialist	Configures routers and firewalls; specifies Web protocols and enterprise technologies	B.S. in Computer Science or Information Technology	64.0
	Quality assurance specialist	Reviews programs and documentation to ensure they meet the organization's standards	B.S. in Information Technology	61.6
	System programmer	Installs and maintains operation system software and provides technical support to the programming staff	B.S. in Computer Science or Information Technology	78.3
End-user computing	Computer technician/ Computer service technician	Installs and supports personal computer equipment and software; troubleshoots client and/or server problems	A.A.S. or A.S. in Information Technology	33.9
	Help desk specialist	Solves procedural and software questions in person and over the telephone for hardware, software, or telecommunications systems	A.A.S. or A.S. in Information Technology	39.7

Figure 16-7 This table shows some of the careers available in each of the five main groups in a typical IT department.
(Sources: Information Technology Salary Survey, kforce.com; Occupational Outlook Handbook, Bureau of Labor Statistics, U.S. Department of Labor)

Education and Training

The increased sophistication and complexity of today's computer products has opened extensive opportunities in computer-related education and training (Figure 16-8). Schools, colleges, universities, and private companies all need qualified instructors. The high demand for instructors, in fact, has led to a shortage of qualified instructors at the university level as educators increasingly are lured into private industry by the promise of higher pay. This shortage probably will not end in the near future because the supply of educators with Ph.D. degrees is not keeping pace with the demand.

Sales

Sales representatives must have a general understanding of computers and a specific knowledge of the product they are selling. Strong interpersonal, or people, skills are important, including listening ability and strong oral and written communications skills. Companies usually pay sales representatives based on the amount of product they sell; top sales representatives often are among an organization's more highly compensated employees.

Some sales representatives work directly for hardware and software manufacturers (see Figure 16-4 on page 16.5). Others work for resellers, including retailers that sell personal computer products such as CompUSA, Best Buy, and OfficeMax (Figure 16-9).

Service and Repair

Being a service and repair technician is a challenging job for individuals who like to troubleshoot and solve problems and have a strong background in electronics (Figure 16-10). In the early days of computers,

Figure 16-8 A high demand exists in schools and industry for qualified instructors who can teach IT subjects.

Figure 16-9 Computer retailers need sales people who understand personal computers and have good people skills.

technicians often made repairs at the site of the computer equipment. Today, however, technicians first will replace a malfunctioning component, such as a hard disk, and then take the faulty part back for repair at their office or at a special repair facility. Many computer equipment manufacturers include special diagnostic software with their computer equipment that helps service technicians identify any problems. Some computers even use a modem to telephone a computer automatically at a service technician's office to leave a message that a malfunction has been detected.

Consulting

After building experience in one or more computer and IT-related areas, an individual might decide to become a **consultant**, someone who draws upon his or her experiences to give advice to others. Consultants not only must have strong technical skills in their area of expertise, but they also must have the people skills necessary to communicate their suggestions effectively to their clients. Qualified consultants are in high demand for tasks such as computer selection, system design, communications, network design and installation, and Web development.

PREPARING FOR A CAREER IN THE COMPUTER INDUSTRY

To prepare for a career in the computer industry, you first must decide on the area in which you are interested and then obtain education in that field. According to the U.S. Bureau of Labor Statistics, the fastest growing computer jobs through the year 2008 will be computer engineer, computer support specialist, systems analyst, database administrator, and desktop publishing specialist (Figure 16-11).

Figure 16-10 Computer service and repair require knowledge of electronics.

Web Link

For more information on the computer equipment industry, visit the Discovering Computers 2002 Chapter 16 WEB LINK page **(scsite.com/dc2002/ch16/weblink.htm)** and click Computer Equipment Industry.

Web Link

For more information on information systems consulting, visit the Discovering Computers 2002 Chapter 16 WEB LINK page **(scsite.com/dc2002/ch16/weblink.htm)** and click Information Systems Consulting.

FASTEST GROWING IT POSITIONS

Title	Employment		Change	
	1998	2008	Number	%
Computer engineer	299,000	622,000	323,000	108
Computer support specialist	429,000	869,000	439,000	102
Systems analyst	617,000	1,194,000	577,000	94
Database administrator	87,000	155,000	67,000	77
Desktop publishing specialist	26,000	44,000	19,000	73

Figure 16-11 Projected growth rates for the five fastest-growing IT jobs.

(Source: Occupational Outlook Handbook, Bureau of Labor Statistics, U.S. Department of Labor)

The Web sites listed in the Getting Started category in Figure 16-12 will guide you through the prerequisites and opportunities in each field. The Microsoft Skills Web site is especially helpful. You also can obtain career information by visiting the Web sites listed in the Professional Organizations and Job Opportunities categories in Figure 16-12.

Choosing the Right Course of Study

Three broad disciplines in higher education produce the majority of entry-level employees in the computer industry: computer information systems, computer science (also referred to as software engineering), and computer engineering. The characteristics of each program are summarized in Figure 16-13 and discussed in the following paragraphs.

Computer information systems (CIS) programs emphasize the practical aspects of computing. After two years of study, students often receive an Applied Associate in Science (A.A.S.) degree or an Associate in Science (A.S.) degree with an emphasis in application programming. In four-year programs, students work toward and receive a Bachelor of Science (B.S.) degree with an emphasis in systems programming, systems analysis and design, or networking. In many cases, local community colleges offer the A.A.S. or A.S. degree. Students then transfer to a four-year college or university to complete their B.S. degree.

Web Link

For more information on U.S. Commerce reports, visit the Discovering Computers 2002 Chapter 16 WEB LINK page (**scsite.com/dc2002/ch16/weblink.htm**) and click U.S. Commerce Reports.

CAREER PREPARATION WEB SITES

WEB SITE	URL
Getting Started	
Bureau of Labor Statistics	stats.bls.gov/blshome.htm
Careers in Computing	tcm.org/html/resources/cmp-careers cnc-topdrawer.html
Computer Programmers	stats.bls.gov/oco/ocos110.htm
Green Thumb/Microsoft Skills	www.greenthumb.org
Making College Count	makingitcount.com/yournextjob/start
Scholarships	fastweb.com
Professional Organizations	
Association for Computing Machinery	acm.org
Association for Information Systems	aisnet.org
Association of Information Technology Professionals (formerly DPMA)	aitp.org
IEEE Computer Society	computer.org
Institute of Electrical and Electronics Engineers	ieee.org
Job Opportunities	
CareerBuilder	careerbuilder.com
ComputerJobs.com	computerjobs.com
HotJobs.com	hotjobs.com/htdocs/channels/tech
JobOptions	joboptions.com
Monster.com	monster.com
Computer Industry Training	
Microsoft Training and Certification	microsoft.com/trainingandservices/training
Novell Education and Certification	www.novell.com/education
Certification	
Adobe Certified Training Provider Program	partners.adobe.com/asn/training
Cisco Connection Online	cisco.com
Computing Technology Industry Association (CompTIA)	comptia.org
Institute for Certification of Computer Professionals	www.iccp.org
Microsoft Training and Certification	microsoft.com/traingandservice/mcp
Novell Professional Certifications	www.novell.com/education/certinfo
Sun Educational Services	suned.sun.com/HQ/certification
Certified Internet Webmaster	ciwcertified.com
Publications and Web News	
Computerworld	computerworld.com
InfoWorld.com	infoworld.com
EarthWeb Datamation	datamation.earthweb.com
internet.com	internet.com
eWeek	zdnet.com/eweek

Figure 16-12 These Web sites help in career preparation in the computer industry. *For an updated list, visit scsite.com/dc2002/ch16/careers.htm.*

DISCIPLINE DIFFERENCES

Computer Information Systems	Computer Science/ Software Engineering	Computer Engineering
Practical and application-oriented	Theoretical oriented	Design oriented
Business and management oriented	Mathematics and science oriented	Mathematics and science oriented
Understanding how to design and implement information systems	Understanding the fundamental nature of software	Understanding the fundamental nature of hardware
Degrees include A.A.S., B.S., M.S., Ph.D.	Degrees include B.S., M.S., Ph.D.	Degrees include B.S., M.S., Ph.D.

Figure 16-13 The major differences among the computer information systems, computer science/software engineering, and computer engineering disciplines.

If you are attending a community college, ask your advisor if the school has an **articulation agreement** with a nearby college or university. An articulation agreement ensures that, if you transfer to a college or university, you will receive credit for most of the courses you took at the community college level. In general, a computer information systems program does not require its majors to have a strong mathematics and science background, but those courses do help.

Computer science (**CS**), also called **software engineering** (**SE**), programs stress the theoretical side of programming. A computer science curriculum typically emphasizes systems programming, rather than applications programming. In general, CS programming courses are more rigorous than CIS programming courses. Students thus are required to take several mathematics and science courses before enrolling in the majority of computer science courses.

Computer engineering (**CE**) programs teach students how to design and develop the electronic components found in computers and peripheral devices. Students usually are required to take mathematics, physics, and basic engineering courses before taking the more in-depth computer engineering design and development courses.

As in most other industries, individuals with advanced degrees in specific fields have a better chance of success. Thus, to round out their education, instead of continuing down a narrow path with a second degree in the computer area, many graduates with a computer degree change direction and obtain a Masters in Business Administration (M.B.A.) degree.

Attending a Trade School

An alternative to enrolling in a college or university is to attend a trade school. Trade schools offer programs primarily in the areas of programming and maintenance. One advantage of attending a trade school is time; students often can complete trade school programs in a shorter time than college and university programs because generally they are not required to take science or humanities courses. As with any post-secondary school, when deciding on a trade school, you should compare curricula, laboratory facilities, instructors, and the types of jobs the school's graduates have obtained. While not having a college degree may limit a person's opportunities for securing a top position, it neither will prevent entry into nor preclude success in the computer industry.

Web Link

For more information on IT training, visit the Discovering Computers 2002 Chapter 16 WEB LINK page (**scsite.com/dc2002/ch16/weblink.htm**) and click IT Training.

TECHNOLOGY TRAILBLAZER

JERRY **YANG**

As self-proclaimed "Chief Yahoo," Jerry Yang says he feels proud and satisfied to have lead Yahoo! to the top spot among Internet portals. But he adds that he does not consider himself successful yet. "So much that I want to do remains to be done," he explains. "It's important to continue to be modest and paranoid."

Born in Taiwan in 1967, Yang was 10 years old and knew very little English when he came to the United States with his mother and his younger brother. In college at Stanford University, he completed both his bachelor's and master's degrees in electrical engineering in just four years. At Stanford, David Filo was the teaching assistant for one of Yang's classes. In late 1993, Yang and Filo worked in a trailer on campus and began creating Jerry's Guide to the World Wide Web, the precursor to today's Yahoo!.

Yang and Filo left Stanford's Ph.D. program to work on their growing company. Yang says he might go back to college because "Being in school was very fun, and maybe someday I'll go back to do something else!"

For more information on Jerry Yang, visit the Discovering Computers 2002 People Web page (**scsite.com/dc2002/people.htm**) and click Jerry Yang.

Planning for Career Development

The computer- and IT-related industry is one of the more fluid parts of today's marketplace. Someone who is an expert today can be a has-been tomorrow. As a computer professional, you must find methods to keep up to date on industry trends and technologies, to develop new skills, and to increase recognition among peers within your company. Three primary ways to achieve these objectives are through professional organizations, certification, and professional growth and continuing education activities. Numerous computer publications also can help an individual keep up with changes in the computer industry.

Professional Organizations

Computer professionals with common interests and a desire to extend their proficiency have formed computer-related professional organizations to share their knowledge. Two professional organizations that have been influential in the industry are the Association for Computing Machinery (ACM) and the Association of Information Technology Professionals (AITP). The **Association for Computing Machinery (ACM)** is a scientific and educational organization dedicated to advancing information technology. The ACM is composed of professionals and students working and interested in computer science and computer science education. A large number of college and university computer educators are members of the ACM. The **Association of Information Technology Professionals**, formerly called the Data Processing Management Association (DPMA), is a professional association of programmers, systems analysts, and information processing managers. Both ACM and AITP offer the following features and benefits:

- Chapters throughout the United States, for both professionals and students
- Monthly meetings
- Workshops, seminars, and conventions
- Publications, including magazines, journals, and books that help computing professionals negotiate industry and career challenges
- Special Interest Groups (SIGs), that bring together members with shared interests, needs, knowledge, and experience
- Programs to help with continuing education needs

Attending professional meetings provides an excellent opportunity for students to learn about the information processing industry and to meet and talk with professionals in the field. Figure 16-12 on page 16.12 presents a list of professional organizations and their URLs.

In addition to these and other professional organizations, user groups exist for a wide range of computers, operating systems, application software, and more. A **user group** is a collection of people with common computer equipment or software interests that meets regularly to share information. Most metropolitan areas have one or more local computer user groups that convene monthly to discuss mutual interests about personal computers. Figure 16-14 shows a list of major user group organizations and their URLs. For anyone employed or simply interested in the computer industry, these groups can be an effective and rewarding way to learn and continue career development.

Web Link

For more information on IT careers, visit the Discovering Computers 2002 Chapter 16 WEB LINK page (**scsite.com/dc2002/ch16/weblink.htm**) and click IT Careers.

Professional Growth and Continuing Education

Staying aware of new products and services in the computer industry can be a challenging task because technology changes so rapidly. One way to stay informed about the industry is to participate in professional growth and continuing education activities. This broad category includes events such as workshops, seminars, conferences, conventions, and trade shows. These events provide both general and specific information on equipment, software, services, and issues affecting the industry. Workshops and seminars usually last one or two days, while conferences, conventions, and trade shows can run for a week. One of the larger technology trade shows in the world, **COMDEX**, brings together more than 2,100 vendors and 200,000 attendees (Figure 16-15).

USER GROUP ORGANIZATION

Organization	URL
Apple User Groups	apple.com/usergroups/program
Association of Personal Computer User Groups (APCUG)	www.apcug.org
Microsoft Mindshare User Group Program	microsoft.com/mindshare/default.asp
User Group Relations	ugr.com

Figure 16-14 The Web sites for the major user group organizations. *For an updated list, visit scsite.com/dc2002/careers.htm.*

Many companies also offer training on their products in the form of books, video-based training, computer-based training (CBT), Web-based training (WBT), and instructor-led training in a classroom.

Computer Publications

Another way to stay informed about happenings in the computer industry is to read one or more computer industry publications regularly (Figure 16-16) or visit the Web News sites listed in Figure 16-12 on page 16.12. Hundreds of publications are available from which to choose. Some magazines, such as *PC Week*, *Computerworld*, and *InfoWorld*, are similar to newspapers and cover a wide range of issues. Other periodicals are oriented toward a particular topic such as communications, personal computers, or a specific equipment manufacturer. You can find many of the more popular publications in public or school libraries; most of them also have Web sites you can visit for news on the latest developments in the computer industry. For exact Web site addresses, review the Publications and Web News category in Figure 16-12.

Figure 16-15 COMDEX, held each November in Las Vegas, Nevada, is one of the larger technology trade shows in the world. More than 2,100 vendors display their newest products and services to more than 200,000 attendees.

Web Link
For more information on IT professionals, visit the Discovering Computers 2002 Chapter 16 WEB LINK page **(scsite.com/dc2002/ch16/weblink.htm)** and click IT Professionals.

Web Link
For more information on professional organizations, visit the Discovering Computers 2002 Chapter 16 WEB LINK page **(scsite.com/dc2002/ch16/weblink.htm)** and click Professional Organizations.

Web Link
For more information on issues, visit the Discovering Computers 2002 Chapter 16 WEB LINK page **(scsite.com/dc2002/ch16/weblink.htm)** and click Issues.

Figure 16-16 Numerous computer industry publications are available.

WHAT IS COMPUTER CERTIFICATION?

Certification is a way for employers to ensure a level of competency, skills, or quality in a particular area. Companies are looking for certified professionals with the knowledge and skills to work with and maintain complex systems. Now more than ever, computer innovations are spawning major opportunities in new occupations within the IT industry. Certification continues to ensure quality and workmanship standards and is one way companies can help ensure their workforce remains up to date on computers and technology.

Computer certification demonstrates the mastery of a skill set and knowledge base in a specific IT area. Computing professionals typically obtain a certification by passing an examination. The certification process requires experience or special classes, many of which are offered by community colleges and adult education centers. After certification requirements are met, proficiency in an area is acknowledged.

Many vendors such as Microsoft and Novell offer technical certification programs for their software products. These vendors use examinations to determine if a person is qualified for certification. Some of the benefits of certification include:

- Proof of professional achievement, a level of competence commonly accepted and valued by the industry.
- Enhancement of job opportunities. Many employers give preference in hiring applicants with certification. They view this as proof that a new hire knows the procedures and technologies required.
- Opportunity for advancement. Certification can be a plus when an employer awards job advancements and promotions.

The hottest IT trends bring with them a vast array of certifications. As shown in Figure 16-17, a sponsoring organization develops and administers each certification. These **sponsors** include computer hardware and software vendors, independent training companies, and professional organizations. Both IT professionals and computer services end-users should be familiar with IT certifications, know certification benefits and limitations, and recognize the more popular certification designations. These topics are explained in this section. Also included is information about certification preparation, examinations, and resources. Finally, career development after certification is discussed. Each month, more

TYPES OF COMPUTER CERTIFICATION

The IT industry has grown by phenomenal proportions, and certification has grown as quickly. Today, more than 200 certifications are available. Each month, more

Figure 16-17 Many certifications are available in the information technology industry.

certifications are announced. Some certifications have a broad focus, while others require an in-depth knowledge of a single computing aspect. Often, a sponsor establishes a series of related certifications to show levels of expertise within a single area.

As shown in Figure 16-18, certifications usually are classified based on the computer industry area to which they most closely relate: software applications, operating systems, programming, hardware, networking, Internet, and database systems. Some certifications are closely related to more than one category. For example, a certification in networking also may indicate knowledge of hardware and operating systems.

A GUIDE TO COMPUTER CERTIFICATION

This section describes the major certifications and certification sponsors. The certifications are categorized by their role in the IT industry: software applications, operating systems, programming, hardware, networks, the Internet, and database systems.

Some certifications have components that fall into multiple categories. In this case, they are placed in the area for which they are known best. Each category includes an overview. In addition, APPLY IT boxes describe the requirements for several popular certifications. Tables within each area list the URLs for major certification sponsors.

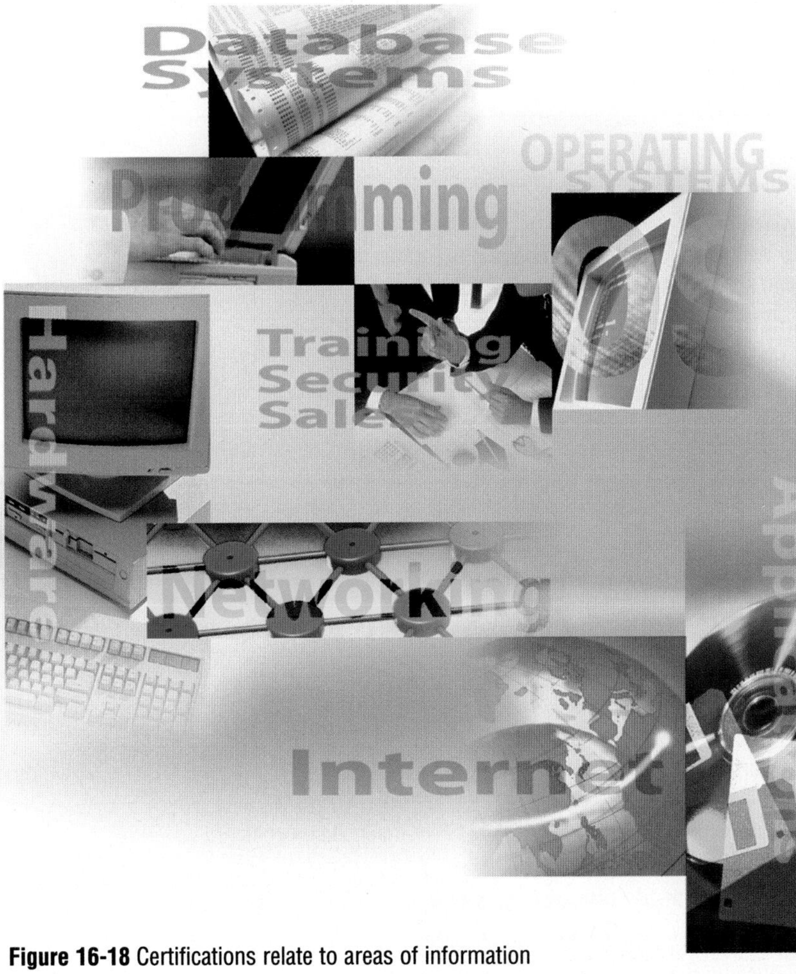

Figure 16-18 Certifications relate to areas of information technology.

Web Link

For more information on certification, visit the Discovering Computers 2002 Chapter 16 WEB LINK page (**scsite.com/dc2002/ch16/weblink.htm**) and click Certification.

ISSUE

Certification – Is It Worth the Price?

The Value of Certifications

Certification has developed as part of the computer industry itself, and for the most part, as a commercial enterprise. No one organization oversees or sets standards for certifications. Some certifications are more respected and have a higher demand than others. Certifying sponsors set their own certification requirements. Some certifications are extremely rigorous, requiring an individual to complete extensive training and pass a number of tests. Other certifications have been compared with a rubber stamp. Even certifications offered by the same sponsor have varying worth. When more certifications are conferred than the market can support, a certification loses its value. In this case, it is to the sponsor's advantage to adjust the test to increase the certification's value. Already organizations such as the American Association of Internet Professionals (AIP) are establishing systems of accreditation to provide quality control and rank certifications (see URL below). How important is it to investigate a certification to determine its worth? Should the certification sponsor adjust the degree of difficulty of a test? Are certifications more important than college degrees?

For more information on the value of certification, visit the Discovering Computers 2002 Issues Web page (**scsite.com/dc2002/issues.htm**) and click Chapter 16 Issue #2.

Software Applications Certifications

Although numerous software packages exist, several have achieved national recognition for use as productivity tools, including Microsoft Office Professional, Adobe Photoshop, Autodesk AutoCad, and Lotus Notes. As with most certifications, professionals can take an end-user certification test by registering with a vendor-authorized testing facility. The companies listed in the table in Figure 16-19 have a partner training program and encourage computer-training centers to become authorized training representatives.

Obtaining an end-user certification is very helpful to anyone who works in the computer industry, such as application trainers, help desk operators, and personal computer sales representatives. People who work in the following areas can benefit from software application certifications:

- Desktop publishers
- Draftspeople
- Graphical designers
- Layout editors
- Office managers/workers
- Photographers

Operating Systems Certifications

Several options representing different knowledge levels are available for those seeking operating system certifications. These certifications focus on particular skills — the user, the operator, the system administrator, and the system engineer. Since the inception of the Internet, networking has grown in importance, spawning new certifications that include operating system and networking components. For example, the Microsoft Certified Professional (MCP) and Microsoft Certified Systems Engineer (MCSE) are two certifications that validate a professional's knowledge of Microsoft's operating systems. The Red Hat Certified Engineer (RHCE) program validates mastery of the Linux operating system. IBM certifications are UNIX oriented, but they are specific to particular computers manufactured by its namesake.

If you are interested in an occupation as an operating system administrator or engineer, you also may benefit from certifications in networking, hardware, and the Internet. These additional certifications are closely linked to the operating system and would serve to broaden your expertise in that area.

The table in Figure 16-20 lists a few of the certifications available in the operating system area. People in the following jobs may be interested in a certification in operating systems:

- Computer consultants
- Hardware technicians
- Help desk operators
- System administrators

SOFTWARE APPLICATIONS

Certifications	URL
Adobe Systems Inc. Adobe Certified Expert (ACE)	partners.adobe.com/asn/training
Autodesk, Inc. AutoCAD Certified Professional (ACP)	autodesk.com/exams
Lotus Certified Lotus Specialist (CLS)	lotus.com/education
Microsoft Microsoft Office User Specialist (MOUS)	mous.net

Figure 16-19 Web sites for software applications certifications.
For an updated list of training centers, visit scsite.com/cert.htm.

OPERATING SYSTEMS

Certifications	URL
IBM IBM Certified Specialist	ibm.com/education/certify
Microsoft Microsoft Certified Professional (MCP) Microsoft Certified Systems Engineer (MCSE)	microsoft.com/train_cert
Redhat Red Hat Certified Engineer (RHCE)	redhat.com
Sun Microsystems Certified System Administrator	suned.sun.com

Figure 16-20 Web sites for operating systems certifications.
For an updated list of training centers, visit scsite.com/cert.htm.

Programming Certifications

Various certifications are available in the programming area. These certifications are valuable in two ways. First, a programming certification usually is supported with training programs that prepare applicants for the certification test. Secondly, programmers can add to their knowledge and skill base. The preparation classes for certifications provide excellent methods for approaching programming programs and an opportunity for professionals to share ideas.

APPLY IT!

Microsoft Office User Specialist

The Microsoft Office User Specialist (MOUS pronounced mouse) program is a Microsoft certification designed to measure and validate users' skills with these areas of Microsoft Office: Word, Excel, PowerPoint, Access, and Outlook (see URL below). Core and expert certification levels exist for most Office releases. You can take a Core examination for a single application within Office to obtain the User Specialist title. You are issued the Expert Specialist designation by passing an Expert level exam in one application area. The Microsoft Office Master designation is achieved by successfully completing the highest level exam for each of the five Office applications.

Requirements to become MOUS certified are as follows:

1. Register for an exam in your chosen area of expertise and certification level.
2. Take the exam and pass with a score of 80 percent or better.

The cost of the exam is \$65 to \$100 for each test, and testing format is computer-based performance.

Authorized training centers, including many colleges and adult education programs, are available to prepare for certification. Educational costs are \$60 to \$200 per class, which may vary in length from two to four hours. The tests can be taken without attending a training program. Alternate training methods may be used.

For more information on Microsoft and the MOUS certification, visit the Discovering Computers 2002 Apply It Web page (**scsite.com/dc2002/apply.htm**) and click Chapter 16 Apply It #2.

APPLY IT!

Microsoft Certified Systems Engineer and Microsoft Certified Professional

The Microsoft Certified Systems Engineer (MCSE) is one of seven certification tracks in the Microsoft Certified Professionals Program (see URL below). MCSEs operate in a range of environments using the Microsoft Windows 2000 platform and Microsoft server software. After passing one exam in the MCSE track, an individual is awarded the entry-level Microsoft Certified Professional (MCP) designation.

Requirements for the MCSE are as follows:

1. Take five core exams and meet passing criteria.
2. Take two elective exams in supporting areas.

The cost of the exam is \$400 for core and \$200 for elective exams. Testing format is three computer-based multiple choice formats — short form (30 items, 60 minutes), long form (50 to 70 items, 90 minutes), and adaptive testing form (15 to 25 items, 60 minutes).

Microsoft authorized training centers are available to prepare a registrant for certification. Many community colleges and adult education programs provide this instruction. Educational training costs are approximately \$300 to \$450 per day. To complete the training, costs could total from \$5,000 to \$12,000. The tests can be taken without attending a training program. Alternate training methods may be used.

Microsoft made significant changes to the MSCE exam to protect test security, retain its validity, and meet organizations' technical needs. Microsoft eliminated the MCP + Internet certification when it retired its Windows NT 4.0 exam on December 21, 2000.

For more information on Microsoft and the MCSE certification, visit the Discovering Computers 2002 Apply It Web page(**scsite.com/dc2002/apply.htm**) and click Chapter 16 Apply It #3.

APPLY IT!

Certified Computing Professional

The recipient of the Certified Computing Professional (CCP) from the Institute for Certification of Computing Professionals (ICCP) has demonstrated a broad understanding of the computer as a business tool (see URL below). The knowledge base includes data resource management, communications and business information systems, fundamental principles of system security, office information systems, microcomputing and networks, programming development and software design, programming skills in two languages, such as BASIC and COBOL, and software engineering. The certification is not vendor specific; test takers are allowed to select from approximately 20 specialty areas, the more popular being management and systems development.

Requirements for the CCP certification are as follows:

1. Apply with ICCP for test authorization and take the tests within 90 days.
2. Take the Core exam and two specialty exams and pass with scores of 70 percent or better.
3. Meet the 48-month full-time work in computer-based information systems experience requirement.
4. Sign a document agreeing to comply with the ICCP Code of Ethics.
5. Pay an ICCP membership fee of \$50.

CCPs can renew certification every 3 years and receive 120 hours of continuing education (CE) credit during the 3-year period. The cost of the exam is \$195 per test, and testing format is computer-based multiple choice. Each test contains 110 items. The tests can be taken without attending a training program. ICCP offers training guides. Training resources are available through the ICCP Education Foundation.

In addition to the CCP, the organization also sponsors a second entry-level certification, the Associate Computing Professional (ACP), requiring only the Core IT Skill exam and one specialty exam.

For more information on the CCP, visit the Discovering Computers 2002 Apply It Web page (**scsite.com/dc2002/apply.htm**) and click Chapter 16 Apply It #4.

If you are interested in writing application programs, you also may benefit from certifications in networking and Web design. These certifications are tied closely to programming and broaden employment opportunities.

The table shown in Figure 16-21 represents a few of the certifications available in the programming area. People in the following jobs may be interested in a certification in programming:

- ActiveX, Perl, or Java programmers
- Network administrators
- Oracle database managers
- Programming consultants
- SQL programmers
- Web page designers

Hardware Certifications

The IT industry recognizes that knowledge of the hardware and the controlling software is necessary to set up, maintain, and repair a computer. Hardware certifications may vary in scope from a narrow focus with an emphasis on the repair of a specific device to an integrated hardware solution that addresses a company's current and future computing needs. Obtaining an advanced certification in hardware implies that you have achieved a standard of competence in assessing a company's hardware needs, and you can implement solutions to help the company achieve its computing goals.

If hardware is your forte, you also may benefit from networking and operating system software certifications. These certifications are tied closely to advanced hardware knowledge.

The table in Figure 16-22 represents a few available hardware certifications. People in the following careers may be interested in hardware certification:

- Cable installation technicians
- Personal computer consultants
- Personal computer field technicians
- Personal computer help desk specialists
- Personal computer repair technicians
- Personal computer trainers
- System engineers and administrators
- Technology coordinators

Networking Certifications

Professionals with the know-how to design, administer, and maintain a network are rewarded for their skills. MCSE, CCIE, and CNE certification holders with successful networking experience typically earn between $60,000 and $80,000. With multiple certifications and more experience, the networking professional may command a six-digit salary.

PROGRAMMING

Sponsor and Certifications	URL
IBM IBM Certified Developer Associate IBM Certified Specialist	ibm.com/education/certify
Microsoft Microsoft Certified Solution Developer (MCSD) Windows 2000 MCSE	microsoft.com/train_cert
Sun Certified Java Programmer Certified Java Developer Sun Certified Architect for Java Technology	suned.sun.com

Figure 16-21 Web sites for programming certifications.
For an updated list of training centers, visit scsite.com/cert.htm.

HARDWARE

Sponsor and Certifications	URL
Computing Technology Industry A+	comptia.com
International Business Machines (IBM) IBM Certified Professional Server Specialists (PSS)	ibm.com/education/certify
National Association of Communication System Engineers (NACSE) Associate and Senior Network Specialist Technician (NNT)	nacse.com

Figure 16-22 Web sites for hardware certifications.
For an updated list of training centers, visit scsite.com/cert.htm.

APPLY IT!

Sun Certified Programmer for the Java 2 Platform

In 1995, Sun introduced Java Technology, which became the first universal software platform designed from the ground up for the Internet and corporate intranets. A multivendor collaboration with Sun, IBM, Novell, and Sun-Netscape resulted from the expansion of the Certification Initiative for Enterprise Development. These companies agreed to establish a common certification for Java training to help address personnel shortages and assure a common platform for applications. Sun offers several certifications in Java and networking.

Receiving Sun Certified Programmer (SCP) certification indicates a programmer can create sophisticated Java applets; call Java applets from HTML (hypertext markup language); create a minimal TCP/IP server and client that communicates through sockets; generate simple and complex stand-alone applications and multithreaded programs; utilize GUI components, as well as simple and complex graphics; and use streams to read and write data and text files (see URL below).

Requirements for the SCP certification are as follows:

1. Purchase test voucher (good for one year) from Sun Educational Services.
2. Take one exam and pass with a score of 71 percent or higher.

The cost is $150 per test, and testing format is computer-based multiple-choice and short answer; 59 questions; 2 hours.

Sun Educational Services provides three types of courseware for its SCP certification: instructor-led training, self-paced training, and Web seminars. The instructor-led Java Programming Language is a five-day course. Other independent training companies may become Sun authorized training sites, and they often charge for classes on a daily basis. Sun also provides a self-paced CD-ROM course, JavaTutor, and a 30-day Java Programming Language Bundle on the Internet.

For more information on Sun Educational Services and the SCP certification, visit the Discovering Computers 2002 Apply It Web page (**scsite.com/dc2002/apply.htm**) and click Chapter 16 Apply It #5.

APPLY IT!

A+ Certification

The A+ Certification, sponsored by Computing Technology Industry Association (CompTIA), is designed to affirm the competency level of computer repair technicians (see URL below). A+ certification indicates the IT professional has obtained a knowledge of PC setup, configuration, maintenance, troubleshooting, and system software that meets industrial standards. Certification indicates technicians have at least six months experience in the field. A+ certification integrates concepts with common setup and maintenance problems in the Windows and DOS environments.

Requirements for the A+ certification are as follows:

1. Take two tests, Core and DOS/Windows Operating Systems, and pass with scores of 65 to 66 percent or better.
2. Must take the tests within 90 days of each other.

The cost is $128 per test, and the testing format is computer-based multiple choice; 69 item core, 70 item operating system.

CompTIA provides curriculum objectives. Independent computer training centers use the objectives supplied by CompTia to develop A+ training programs. Prices for these programs may range from $700 to $1,400, depending on course length. The tests can be taken without attending a training program. CompTIA is a computer industry association established in 1982. Additional certification areas CompTIA offers include Certified Document Imaging Architect, Network+, and I–Net+. The I-Net+ is the newest certification sponsored by CompTIA and already has received the endorsement of major software companies.

For more information on the A+ certification, visit the Discovering Computers 2002 Apply It Web page (**scsite.com/dc2002/apply.htm**) and click Chapter 16 Apply It #6.

APPLY IT!

Cisco Certified Internetworking Expert

The CCIE, sponsored by Cisco Systems, is one of the more valued certifications today (see URL below). A CCIE certifies an individual is qualified to work with Internetworking technologies and protocols at very complex levels. The CCIE certificate is valuable to both network and Internet experts. CCIEs specialize in one of three areas: WAN Switching, ISP-Dial, or Routing and Switching. Cisco places a high emphasis on experience by requiring a comprehensive hands-on laboratory examination that requires considerable knowledge to pass. Although not required, candidates first may qualify for the lower-level certifications before receiving the CCIE certification.

Requirements for the CCIE certification are as follows:

1. Take the CCIE exam and pass with a score of 70 percent or better.
2. After passing the written exam, pass a two-day, hands-on laboratory examination.

Recertification is available by completing authorized classroom training and passing one recertification examination every two years. The cost of the test is $100 to $200 for the written exam, and $1,000 plus travel expenses for the hands-on exam. The testing format is computer-based multiple choice (2 hours) and hands-on laboratory. Authorized training centers are available to prepare for certification. Educational costs range from $150 to $1,400 per class. Total training costs are reported from $10,000 to $30,000. The tests can be taken without attending a training program. Alternate training methods may be used.

Cisco Systems is a leading manufacturer of networking hardware and Internet solutions. The company controls over 80 percent of the networking router market. Because the system is highly proprietary, Cisco certifications are in high demand. Additional certifications offered by Cisco include Cisco Certified Networking Associate (CCNA), Cisco Certified Networking Professional (CCNP), Cisco Certified Design Associate (CCDA), and Cisco Certified Design Professional (CCDP).

For more information on Cisco Systems and CCIE certification, visit the Discovering Computers 2002 Apply It Web page (**scsite.com/dc2002/apply.htm**) and click Chapter 16 Apply It #7.

APPLY IT!

Certified Novell Engineer

The Certified Novell Engineer (CNE), sponsored by Novell Corporation was the first vendor-sponsored certification and is a highly recognized credential (see URL below). A candidate earning the CNE demonstrates in-depth knowledge of the Novell network system. A CNE selects one of five specialization areas associated with a high level of networking knowledge. These skills include administration, design, configuration, and implementation of NetWare or GroupWare. The Certified Novell Administrator (CNA) is a stepping stone credential earned by taking one exam on the path to the CNE.

Requirements for the CNE certification are as follows:

1. Take one core exam and pass with a score of 75 percent or better.
2. Take five additional specialization exams.
3. All exams must be taken within a one-year time frame.

Recertification is renewed periodically by meeting Continuing Certification Requirements. The cost of the test is $95 per exam, and the testing format is computer-based multiple choice or adaptive testing; 63 to 73 items per test.

Authorized training centers are available to prepare for certification. Educational costs range from $300 to $400 per day. The tests can be taken without attending a training program. Alternate training methods may be used.

For more information on the Novell Corporation and CNE, visit the Discovering Computers 2002 Apply It Web page (**scsite.com/dc2002/apply.htm**) and click Chapter 16 Apply It #8.

NETWORK

Certifications	URL
Cisco Cisco Certified Network Professional (CCNP) Cisco Certified Internetwork Expert (CCIE)	cisco.com/certification
Computing Technology Industry Network +	comptia.com
Microsoft Microsoft Certified Systems Engineer (MCSE)	microsoft/train_cert
Novell Certified Novell Associate (CNA) Certified Novell Engineer (CNE)	education.novell.com

Figure 16-23 Web sites for network certifications.
For an updated list of training centers, visit scsite.com/cert.htm.

Network expertise is acquired through years of experience and training because so many variables exist for a total network solution. Obtaining an advanced certification in networking implies that you have achieved a standard of competence, enabling you to address the complex issues that arise when planning, installing, managing, and troubleshooting a network.

The table shown in Figure 16-23 represents a few of the certifications available in the network area. People in the following careers may be interested in network certification:

- Hardware service technicians
- Help desk personnel
- Network consultants
- Network managers
- Networking engineers
- System administrators

Internet Certifications

A variety of Internet certification tracks are available. Some of these certifications are hardware based. They cover technology often used by an Internet service provider or for a large company developing an intranet system. These certifications are demanding and require technical expertise in networking hardware and configuration before enrollment in the training program. Web management and Web programming certifications also are among the tracks. Certification in these tracks are for people interested in designing, implementing, and maintaining Web sites. Web development certifications also are demanding. Success in the field requires special resources, including an aptitude for programming, marketing and graphic design skills, a customer service-oriented attitude, and good communications skills.

If you are interested in working in an Internet-related occupation, you can benefit from certifications in hardware, networking, operating systems, and programming. These certifications are tied closely to the Internet and broaden your opportunities to acquire Internet and Internetworking knowledge quickly.

The table shown in Figure 16-24 represents a few of the certifications available in the Internet area. People in the following careers may be interested in Internet certification:

- Internet and intranet managers
- Internet service provider staff
- Java, Perl, or ActiveX programmers
- Network administrators
- Web page designers
- Webmasters

INTERNET

Certifications	URL
Cisco Cisco Certified Internetwork Expert (CCIE)	cisco.com/certification
International Webmasters Association Certified Web Professional (CWP)	irwa.org
Microsoft MCSE + Internet	microsoft.com/train_cert
Novell Certified Internet Professional	education.novell.com
ProsoftTraining.com Certified Internet Webmaster (CIW)	ciwcertified.com

Figure 16-24 Web sites for Internet certifications.
For an updated list of training centers, visit scsite.com/cert.htm.

COMPANY ON THE CUTTING EDGE

RealNetworks

Delivering Multimedia Content

Imagine having 200,000 new users visit your home page each day! That is the success RealNetworks has experienced with its RealPlayer®, amounting to a 300 percent growth since 1998. The RealNetworks family of Web sites is one of the 20th most popular Internet destinations. RealPlayer also is the fourth most popular application among United States' home users, according to Media Metrix. No wonder *PC Magazine* ranks the company 15th on its list of the 100 most influential companies in the world.

More than 400,000 companies rely on RealNetworks' software to deliver audio, video, and other multimedia services to personal computers and other electronic devices. Despite continued competition, RealNetworks' formats are used in 85 percent of Web pages using streaming media.

Founder Rob Glaser introduced the first version of RealAudio in 1995, and his company has set the standard for sending multimedia content across the Internet. Today, the two most popular products are RealPlayer and RealJukebox. RealPlayer, released in 1995, has more than 160 million unique registered users. RealJukebox is the favorite music jukebox system among U.S. listeners, with 50 million unique registered users. In addition, more that 2,500 live radio stations and broadcasters rely on RealAudio to deliver live sports, music, news, and entertainment.

For more information on RealNetworks, visit the Discovering Computers 2002 Companies Web page (**scsite.com/dc2002/companies.htm**) and click RealNetworks.

APPLY IT!

Certified Internet Webmaster

The Certified Internet Webmaster (CIW) Internet certification program, sponsored by ProsoftTraining.com, targets Internet professionals who plan, produce, manage, maintain, and provide Web presence security (see URL below). Foundations, a Level 1 certification, introduces the Web as a commerce opportunity. Level 2 contains seven specialty areas. Each area represents a role in the Internet industry. The certifications are Site Designer, Application Developer, Enterprise Developer, Server Administrator, Internet-working Professional, Security Profes-sional, and E-Commerce Professional.

Requirements for the CIW Certification are as follows:

1. Take the CIW Foundations test and pass it with a score of 75 percent or better.
2. After passing the Level 1 test, take any Level 2 specialty certification exam.

The cost of the test is $100, and the testing format is computer-based multiple-choice.

ProsoftTraining.com offers the Prosoft Certified Training Center (PCTC) partnership and educational materials to resellers and independent computer training centers. The complete CIW Level 1 and Level 2 certification is a 55-day curriculum and has a cost of approximately $500 per training day. The tests can be taken without attending a training program. Alternate training methods may be used.

ProsoftTraining.com is an Internet-solutions company committed to providing instructor-led curriculum for comprehensive Internet skills and vendor-neutral certification to obtain Internet skills. In addition to the CIW program, ProsoftTraining.com provides a certification for Linux and UNIX Administration and training courses and educational materials for CompTIA's Network+ and I-Net+ certification. ProsoftTraining.com offers more than 50 instructor-led Internet skills courses that range from one-day end-user workshops to 10-day certification programs.

For more information on ProsoftTraining.com certification and its Web site, visit the Discovering Computers 2002 Apply It Web page (**scsite.com/dc2002/apply.htm**) and click Chapter 16 Apply It #9.

Database Systems Certifications

Supporting a large database management system requires a professional staff. The job roles the staff assumes are a core around which the database management certifications are based. If you are interested in working with a database management system, you also may benefit from certifications in hardware, Internet, networking, and programming.

The table shown in Figure 16-25 represents a few of the certifications available in the database systems area. People in the following careers may be interested in database certification:

- Database administrators
- Database analysts
- Database application developers
- Database designers
- Database specialists

DATABASE

Sponsor and Certifications	URL
IBM IBM Certified Solutions Expert DB2 UDB V6.1 IBM Database Administration for UNIX, Windows, and OS/2	ibm.com/education/certify
Informix Informix Certified Database Specialist	informix.com/informix/training
Microsoft Microsoft Certified Database Administrator (MCDBA)	microsoft.com/training_cert
Oracle Application Developer, Oracle Developer Release 1 Track	education.oracle.com/certification
Sybase Certified Sybase Professional – Database Administrator (CSP-DBA)	slc.sybase.com/certification

Figure 16-25 Web sites for database systems certifications.
For an updated list of training centers, visit scsite.com/cert.htm.

CERTIFICATION BENEFITS

When it comes to certification, organizations send IT professionals a clear message: certifications offer many benefits to companies and employees. IT certification can enhance employees' careers and provide them with a better standing as industry professionals. As shown in Figure 16-26, a salary survey

APPLY IT!

Oracle Certified Database Administrator

The DBA certification, sponsored by the Oracle Corporation identifies the skills necessary for setting up, maintaining, diagnosing, and troubleshooting Oracle databases in a networked or non-networked environment (see URL below). It also indicates knowledge of security systems and data access, auditing, and backup. This certification assumes that candidates have at least six months of database administrative experience before taking the exam.

Requirements for the DBA are as follows:

1. Take 4 or 5 exams (depending on the track selected) and pass with scores of 75 percent or better.

The cost of the exams is $125 each, and the testing format is computer-based multiple-choice; 60 to 65 items, 90 minutes.

Authorized training centers are available to prepare for certification. Educational costs are $8,200 for a five-exam training package. The tests can be taken without attending a training program. Alternate training methods may be used.

The Oracle database product line has become one of the more respected database management products in the computer industry. It is designed for portability and can be used in network, intranet, and Internet environments.

For more information on the Oracle Corporation and the DBA certification, visit the Discovering Computers 2002 Apply It Web page (**scsite.com/dc2002/apply.htm**) and click Chapter 16 Apply It #10.

conducted by Microsoft reported that more than one-half of the respondents had a salary increase due to certification, with 13 percent of these workers reporting significant raises of more than 25 percent. Many job listings ask for specific skills represented by certifications, and the number of companies requiring these skills is expected to continue growing in the future. Figure 16-27 describes three benefits derived from certification.

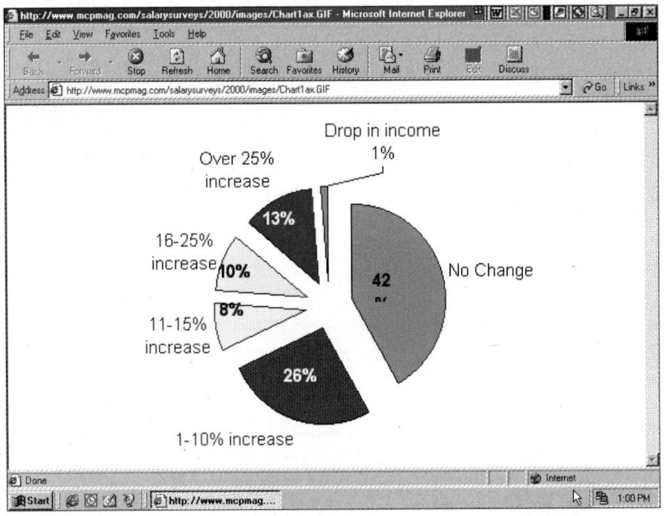

Figure 16-26 Microsoft's Fifth Annual Salary Survey of Microsoft Certified Professionals shows that certification can increase salary.

BENEFITS OF CERTIFICATION

Benefit	Description
Career	Certification accomplishments are one of the first listings an employer notices on a resume. Certification provides a benchmark, or a means to measure a person's skills. It can set an individual apart from other potential candidates who may be vying for a similar advancement or position. Often a professional studies and takes training to move into another area of the computer industry. Even for those not currently looking for a career change, certification can serve as insurance.
Professional	Certification is a personal achievement that adds credibility among peers and employers. To identify certified individuals, sponsors award certificates of accomplishment. Certification also authorizes the person to use the product's official logo or symbol on items, such as business cards and Web pages. These emblems represent a person's skills and knowledge in a concise form. As an additional bonus, some certification training can be used for college credit.
Salary	Numerous salary surveys have shown that certification is one of the top factors influencing raises. Companies often pay a bonus as an incentive for certification. Individuals with more than one area of expertise can command even higher salaries.

Figure 16-27 Employees benefit from computer certification in three major ways.

ISSUE

Marketing Strategy or Product Support?

Vendor-Specific Certification

Some feel a self-created demand exists for certain vendor-specific certifications based on brand-name association. Vendors may sponsor a number of certifications to gain industry recognition. Occasionally vendors even require resellers employ a certain number of certified individuals. In addition, certifications are used as major moneymakers in their own right. Training has grown into a major part of the computer industry, with tuition costing thousands of dollars.

On the other hand, each particular computer product has unique features that are not covered in a general examination. Vendor-specific certifications confirm a professional knows the distinctive details of a particular system. Computer products also undergo continual updates. To ensure certified individuals have up-to-date knowledge, vendors constantly modify the examinations to reflect the latest alterations in their product technology. Should certificate holders be required to renew their certification frequently? How often? Should they be required to review for each product update? Should the sponsoring company offer a price break for certification updates?

For more information on the vendor-specific certification, visit the Discovering Computers 2002 Issues Web page (**scsite.com/dc2002/issues.htm**) and click Chapter 16 Issue #3.

Vendor-sponsored certifications offer many special benefits as incentives. As shown in Figure 16-28, vendors often provide special privileges to certified professionals, such as access to technical and product information. This may include access to secure online electronic resources, special technical support, automatic notification of updates, and access to **beta products** — those still in the testing stage — and early releases. In addition, vendors may offer advanced training opportunities to certification holders. Free vendor magazine subscriptions and discounts on product-support publications and tools sometimes are available. Some vendors even have authorized clothing lines with T-shirts embellished with the certification logo. Although nothing guarantees job security, certification helps to give the IT professional peace of mind.

The certified professional is not the only beneficiary of certification. As mentioned earlier, vendors also benefit from the product recognition and support that certification brings. Employers and customers profit, too, for they know they hired a professional with the training and skills needed to work on their particular system.

Professional organizations, such as the Institute for Certification of Computer Professionals (ICCP), establish standards to raise the competence level for the computer industry. Certification beneficiaries are described in Figure 16-29.

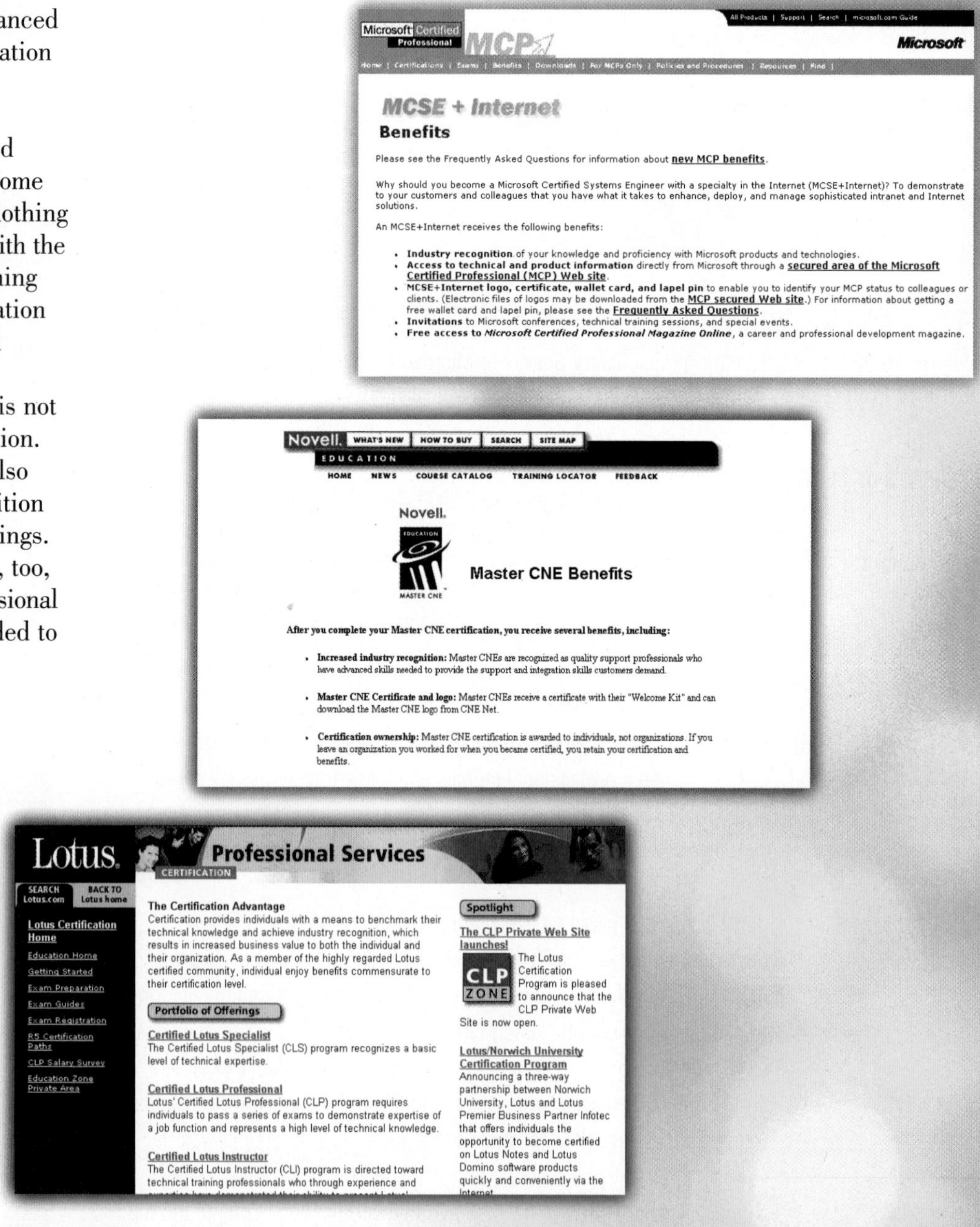

Figure 16-28 Sponsors offer a variety of benefits to certificate holders.

CHOOSING A COMPUTER CERTIFICATION

With certification, one size does not fit all. Just as all computers are not alike inside the box, all certifications are not the same when it comes to training and options. Selecting a certification is a personal process that requires careful thought and research. If you are considering obtaining a certification, reflect on your career goals and interests. Consider your career path during the long term. Then, assess your background knowledge and experience.

Finally, research certifications to find those that best match your needs. Figure 16-30 describes factors to consider. If you are new to the computer field, it is best to start with a general, entry-level certification.

BENEFICIARIES OF CERTIFICATION

Benefit	Description
Customers	Customers are becoming aware of the benefits of certification. They gain confidence when the IT professional has earned a certification. Multiple certifications show the professional can deal with many aspects of a problem, using several areas of expertise. As an added benefit, certification implies motivation to expend extra effort to go beyond basic job requirements.
Employers	An industry-sponsored study indicates certified workers are more productive and knowledgeable than non-certified employees. Certified help desk technicians are able to handle more support calls. Companies with certified personnel experience less network downtime. As an added bonus, end users are more satisfied with the company's work, and the professional employees within the company have higher morale and job contentment. Certification is an incentive for employees to upgrade their skills continuously.
Industry	Certification is a form of industry self-regulation. It sets computer professionals' competence standards and raises the level of expertise and knowledge in the IT industry as a whole. This, in turn, enhances the reputation of the professionals within the industry. As more people become certified, the industry professionals are perceived as reliable and capable support for the computers on which society has come to rely.

Figure 16-29 Certification benefits extend beyond the certified individual.

Web Link

For more information on loans, visit the Discovering Computers 2002 Chapter 16 WEB LINK page (**scsite.com/dc2002/ch16/weblink.htm**) and click Loans.

FACTORS TO CONSIDER IN SELECTING A CERTIFICATION

- Consider the expenses and the time involved to obtain the certification.
- Examine employment projections.
- Look at job listings to see what skills currently are needed.
- Read evaluations of certifications.
- Talk to people in the industry.
- Think about complementary combinations of certifications to meet your goals.

Figure 16-30 Factors in selecting a certification.

Otherwise, you may wish to choose a certification that has immediate benefits for your current job. Alternately, consider building on your existing experience with a certification that helps to reach your career goals. A certification represents a major commitment in time and money. Thoughtful research and planning can serve to guide your career to your chosen destination.

PREPARING FOR COMPUTER CERTIFICATION

Most certification programs do not require academic coursework. Test results determine certification entirely. Very few professionals, however, have the experience and skill set to take a certification exam without preparation. Most people prefer to follow a study program to prepare for the test. Even with experience, study serves as a review and may help to fill gaps in knowledge.

Training options are available to suit every learning style. You can study on your own using a variety of educational materials, including those available from online suppliers. Or you can take online training classes. A third option is to select an instructor-led class to guide you through the training process. In addition, the Internet contains many resources. Most people prefer to use a combination of these options, which are described in the table in Figure 16-31. Figure 16-32 shows Web sites for many of these training methods.

CERTIFICATION STUDY PROGRAMS

Method	Description
Self-Study	Flexible self-study programs help professionals prepare for certification at their own pace and supplement other training methods. Self-study requires high motivation and discipline, but many people like the convenience of setting their own pace while studying at home or in the office. Although self-study is the least expensive option, it can be the most time-consuming. Hundreds of books, workbooks, videotapes, and computer-based training packages on CD-ROM or disk are available.
Online Training Classes	Many online training classes are available on the Internet and by many companies that have set up intranets to provide online training within their organizations. Online training allows students to set their own pace in an interactive environment and combines the technological advantages of computer-based training with the connectivity of the Internet. Some programs allow students to take certification examinations online. Online programs can cost approximately one-third the price of the traditional instructor-led programs.
Instructor-Led Training	Estimates show that 80 percent of all certification preparation is classroom-based. Instructor-led training is available in a variety of forms, including seminars, which traditionally are held for several days within the span of one week; boot camps, which immerse students in intensive coursework for up to two weeks; and academic-style classes, which span a period of several weeks or months. Some sponsors operate their own training sessions and also authorize independent training centers.
Web Resources	The certification sponsor's Web site generally contains descriptions of the available certifications, with frequently asked questions (FAQ) and links to authorized training and testing centers. Many sites include detailed course objectives, training guides, and sample test questions. Some sponsors have online resources to help you plan and track your training program. Most sell books and other training resources. Many sites offer practice test sessions, chat rooms, and discussion groups. Individuals often set up sites to offer their own views and tips on the testing process.

Figure 16-31 Study programs help professionals prepare for certification examinations.

ISSUE

Certification Versus Experience

Substituting Certification for Experience

New contenders entering the IT industry often use certification to jump-start their careers. Although certification cannot replace job experience, most employers today look at a certification as a complement, not a replacement, to experience. Certification is an objective measurement of achievement. It represents a knowledge- and skill-base a person can draw on to perform a job. IT training is not mandatory. Neither is college. As with college, however, IT certification can take a career to new heights. Certification cannot replace the decision-making and troubleshooting skills gained through experience, but it can open doors to employment and help gain advancement for those already employed. Can certification help someone become a successful employee? How important are certifications without experience? Will IT certified specialists continue to be in high demand?

For more information on the value of certification, visit the Discovering Computers 2002 Issues Web page (**scsite.com/dc2002/issues.htm**) and click Chapter 16 Issue #4.

COMPUTER CERTIFICATION EXAMINATIONS

Authorized testing companies, such as Sylvan Prometrics (sylvanprometric.com), Virtual University Enterprises (vue.com), and e-certifications (tekmetrics.com) provide most certification exams. Certification sponsors often have a link to the testing company's site from their own Web page. At the training company's site, you can use the test center locator to find a list of centers near you. The list includes addresses and telephone numbers. Most companies enable you to pay for the test either online or by telephone with a credit card. On the day of the test, you must present two forms of identification, one of which is a photo identification.

At the testing centers, examinations are taken using computers. These systems process the results as you take a test; you will know immediately whether you pass the examination. Most tests are in a multiple-choice format. Figure 16-33 shows a sample of the types of questions that appear on a certification exam. A new technique known as

TRAINING WEB SITES

Online Suppliers	URL
Amazon.com	amazon.com
Barnes and Noble	b&n.com
computerprep.com	computerprep.com
Fatbrain	fatbrain.com
VCSS – Virtual Computer Super Store	vcss.com
Online Training	**URL**
CyberState University at Bad Dog's Training Planet	trainingplanet.com
DigitalThink	digitalthink.com
Learning Tree International	learningtree.com
Magellan University	magellan.edu
Instructor-Led Training	**URL**
Global Knowledge	globalknowledge.com
New Horizons	newhorizons.com
The Institute for Technology Training and Excellence (ITTE)	itte.org
Virtual University Enterprises (VUE)	vue.com/training
Study Resources	**URL**
Cramsession	cramsession.com
gocertifiy.com	gocertify.com
mcsetutor.com	mcsetutor.com
The Mining Company	certification.miningco.com

Figure 16-32 Study options include obtaining materials from online suppliers, viewing online training, attending instructor-led training, and using Web resources.

Web Link
For more information on self-study, visit the Discovering Computers 2002 Chapter 16 WEB LINK page (**scsite.com/dc2002/ch16/weblink.htm**) and click Self-Study.

Web Link
For more information on instructor-led training, visit the Discovering Computers 2002 Chapter 16 WEB LINK page (**scsite.com/dc2002/ch16/weblink.htm**) and click Instructor-Led Training.

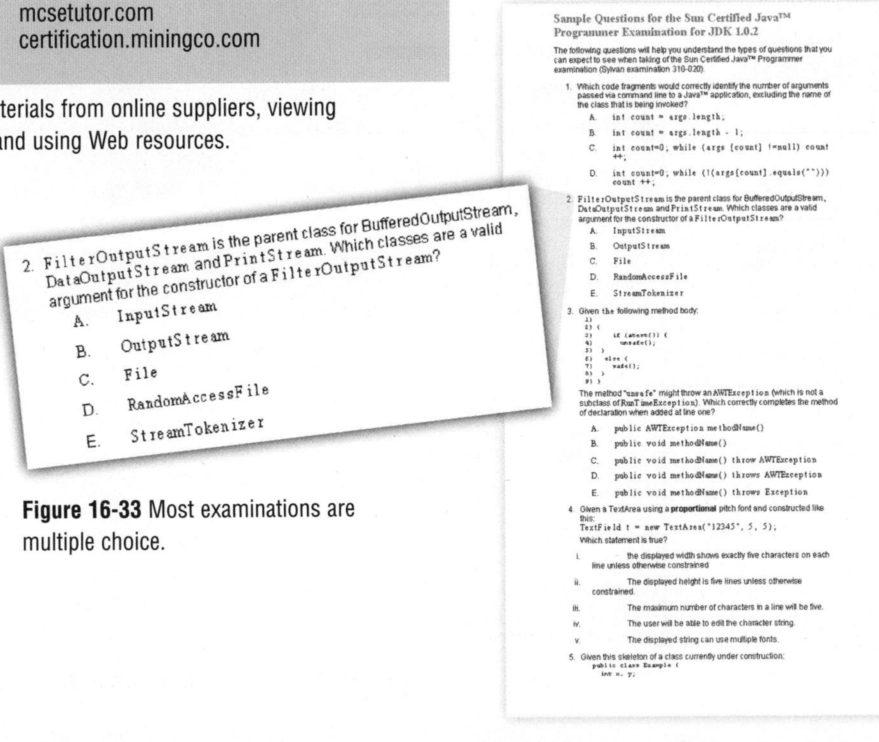

Figure 16-33 Most examinations are multiple choice.

computerized adaptive testing (CAT) may be used; these tests analyze a person's responses while taking the test. The number and order of the test questions are modified to correspond to each individual's progress and demonstrated ability. Occasionally, a certification requires a hands-on lab test. The certification sponsor typically administers these tests. These examinations are much more expensive than the traditional tests. In addition, the number of testing facilities is limited.

If you do not pass an exam, you must pay the fee again to retake the test. In some cases, you can retake the test immediately. Most people, however, opt to review before trying to take the test again. Some training centers offer a guarantee for their program. They provide discounts or even free sessions for individuals who have completed their program, yet do not pass a test. Most sponsors allow candidates a set time period, such as a year, in which to complete the test.

CAREER DEVELOPMENT AFTER COMPUTER CERTIFICATION

Knowledge is an endless quest for IT professionals. Professionals realize that to keep pace with this revolutionary industry, they must maintain and continually monitor technological developments. As shown in Figure 16-34, sponsors often provide restricted-access Web resources specifically for certificate holders.

Web Link

For more information on examinations, visit the Discovering Computers 2002 Chapter 16 WEB LINK page (**scsite.com/dc2002/ch16/weblink.htm**) and click Examinations.

Figure 16-34 Certified professionals have access to resources to help them maintain their skills.

Most certifications expire after a set time period because product-based skills remain current for only about 18 months. Sponsors specify training or examinations to maintain the certification. In addition, if a vendor issues a product update, certificate holders must retrain almost immediately.

CHAPTER SUMMARY

This chapter discussed the strong demand for computer and IT professionals and focused on the available careers, job preparation, and career development planning. Also included was information about certification preparation, examinations, and resources. Finally, career development after certification was discussed.

Computer and IT Teachers

Computer and IT teachers are more in demand than ever. From K-12, to higher education, to business and corporate training, skilled teachers are being encouraged and enticed with many benefits and rewards not offered previously to teachers.

To teach in K-12 requires at least a bachelor's degree with some computer-related courses. Most higher education institutions require at least a master's degree with 18 graduate hours in the subject area. To teach software and/or hardware design generally requires a master's and/or a Ph.D. in engineering. Those looking to teach at the community college level or in technical schools, can take several teaching paths — from office applications and help desk to Internet development to programming to networking and even multimedia.

Qualifications for the corporate world are not quite so stringent as those for educational institutions. Many companies hire instructors with trainer certifications. Examples are the Microsoft Certified Trainer (MCT) and Cisco Certified Trainer. Distance learning management programs, such as WebCT, also are offering certification programs.

Salaries range widely. For those who work in a traditional educational setting, the salaries vary from around $30,000 to $60,000, depending on area of expertise, years of experience, and the state in which one works. In the corporate world, salaries are considerably higher, ranging from $35,000 to $80,000 or more.

To learn more about the field of computer and IT teacher as a career, visit the Discovering Computers 2002 Careers Web page (**scsite.com/dc2002/careers. htm**) and click Computer and IT Teacher.

Certification Tests

Critics say that certification tests cannot truly measure a person's ability to work with actual computers. Certification tests are composed primarily of multiple-choice questions. The critics believe the tests do not reflect the multitude of real-world possibilities an individual might encounter.

Another concern is that individuals may study to pass the test, focusing on how to answer particular questions instead of gaining a broad knowledge of the field. Indeed, some Web sites post specific advice on passing the tests, based on information garnered from people who already have taken the tests. In addition, a few feel that some forms of training — where intense, short-term sessions culminate in an exam — rely on the accumulation of the collection of facts needed for short-term success instead of long-term skill development.

Certification sponsors are addressing these issues by continually improving the tests. Simulations and problem solving are used in the examinations to measure an individual's ability to work with a system. Can skills be measured by a multiple-choice question test? Should all certification tests include simulations and problem solving? Some sponsors now require individuals taking the tests to sign nondisclosure statements. Should someone have to sign these statements or should sponsors randomize and vary their tests? Adaptive testing techniques tailor a test to the individual being tested. This means that each person's testing experience is unique. Is this a more valid way of administering a test? Is it better than simulation? Or, should it be combined with simulation?

For more information on certification testing, visit the Discovering Computers 2002 Issues Web page (**scsite.com/dc2002/issues.htm**) and click Chapter 16 Issue #5.

E-ARTS E-LITERATURE

FIND SOME CULTURE

Get Ready to Read, Paint, and Dance

Brush up your Shakespeare. Start quoting him now. Brush up your Shakespeare. And the women you will wow. This refrain to one of the songs in Broadway's hit musical, Cole Porter's *Kiss Me Kate*, emphasizes the value of knowing the Bard of Avon's words. You can expand your knowledge of Shakespeare and other literary greats with a little help from the Internet.

For example, Shakespeare.com provides in-depth reviews and news of the world's most famous playwright and his works. The Gale's Literary Index Web site has a master index of the authors and titles of popular literature series, such as Shakespearean Criticism, Hispanic Writers, and Twentieth-Century Romance and Historical Writers. At the Fantastic Web Fiction site, you can peruse an online bibliography database of science fiction authors and book titles. The Electronic Literature Directory allows you to search for genres, titles, authors, and publishers.

The full text of hundreds of books is available online from the Bibliomania (Figure 16-35) and Project Gutenberg Web sites. If you are not keen on reading all of Dostoevsky's *Crime and Punishment* or Homer's *Iliad* on your desktop computer monitor, you can download these works to your e-book or handheld computer.

When you are ready to absorb more culture, you can turn to various art Web sites on the Internet. Many museums have images of their collections online. Among them are the J. Paul Getty Museum in Los Angeles, the Montreal Museum of Fine Arts (Figure 16-36), the Children's Museum of Indianapolis, and the Louvre Museum in Paris (Figure 16-37). Comprehensive glimpses of galleries, museums, and other

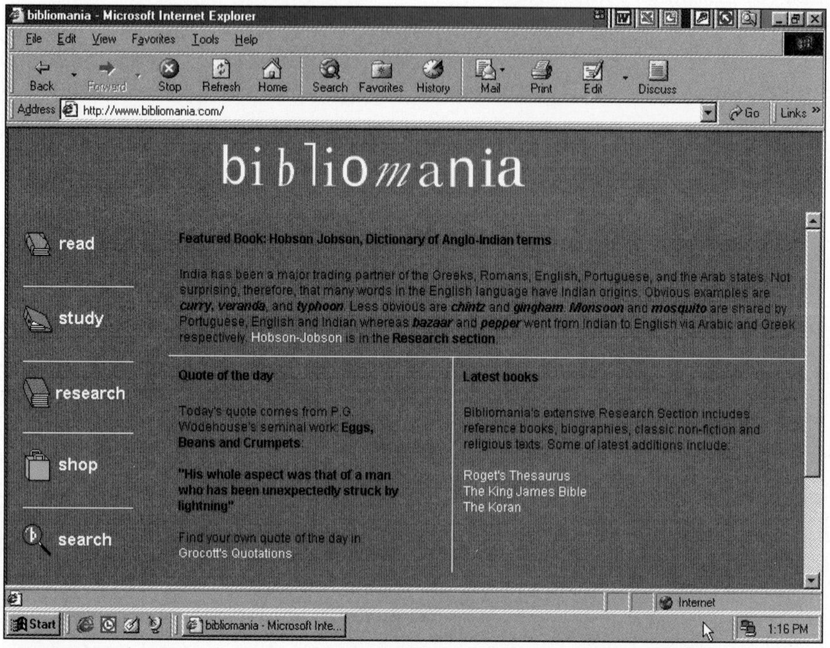

Figure 16-35 Classic fiction, short stories, drama, poetry, and dictionaries are available for viewing or dowloading from Bibliomania and other Web sites.

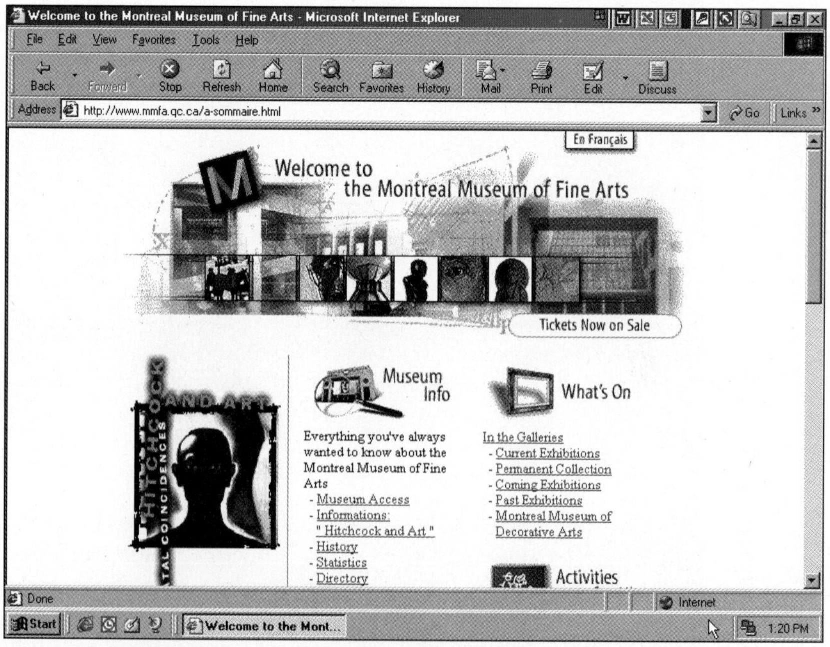

Figure 16-36 Permanent, temporary, and virtual exhibitions, educational activities, a boutique, and a bookstore are featured on the Montreal Museum of Fine Arts Web site.

cultural meccas throughout the world as well as paintings and sculptures are found on such Web sites as Absolutearts.com, and the Gallery Guide.

The Argus Clearinghouse, Access Place Arts, and CyberTimes arts@large focus on the arts and humanities and provide fascinating glimpses into the worlds of dance, music, performance, cinema, and other topics pertaining to human's creative expression.

So brush up your knowledge of Shakespeare, grab a canvas, and put on your dancing shoes. The visual arts and literature Web sites on the Internet are about to sweep you off your cyber feet.

For more information on arts and literature Web sites, visit the Discovering Computers 2002 E-Revolution Web page (scsite.com/dc2002/e-rev.htm) and click Arts and Literature.

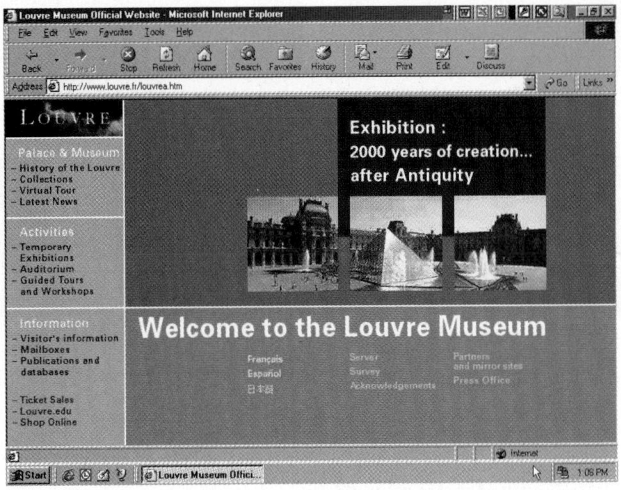

Figure 16-37 Established in 1793 by the French Republic, the Louvre Museum is one of the earliest European museums. You can view its collections online.

ARTS AND LITERATURE WEB SITES	URL
Arts	
Absolutearts.com	absolutearts.com
Access Place Arts	accessplace.com/arts.htm
Argus Clearinghouse	clearinghouse.net/arthum.html
Cyber Times art@large	nytimes.com/library/tech/reference/index/artatlarge.html
Gallery Guide	galleryguide.org
J. Paul Getty Museum	www.getty.edu
Louvre Museum	www.louvre.fr
Montreal Museum of Fine Arts	www.mmfa.qc.ca
The Children's Museum of Indianapolis	childrensmuseum.org
Literature	
Bibliomania	www.bibliomania.com
Electronic Literature Directory	directory.eliterature.org
Fantastic Fiction	fantasticfiction.co.uk
Gale's Literary Index	www.galenet.com/servlet/LitIndex
Modern Library eBooks	randomhouse.com/modernlibrary/ebookslist.html
Project Gutenberg	promo.net/pg
Shakespeare.com	shakespeare.com

For an updated list of art and literature Web sites, visit scsite.com/dc2002/e-rev.htm.

Figure 16-38 Discover culture throughout the world by visiting these art and literature Web sites.

eREVOLUTION E-ARTS E-LITERATURE *applied:*

1. Visit the Modern Library eBooks Web site listed in Figure 16-38, and view one book in the 20th Century Novels, 19th Century Novels, British Literature, and History sections. Create a table with columns for the book name, author, cost, online store, local store, and description. Then, read the excerpt from each of the four books and write a paragraph describing which of these four books is the most interesting to you. What are the advantages and disadvantages of reading classic literature electronically?

2. Using the arts Web sites listed in Figure 16-38, search for three temporary exhibitions in galleries throughout the world. Describe the venues, the artists, and the works. What permanent collections are found in these museums? Some people shop for gifts in the museums' stores. View and describe three items for sale.

In Summary

Web Instructions: To display this page from the Web, start your browser and enter the URL scsite.com/dc2002/ch16/summary.htm. Click the links for current and additional information. To listen to an audio version of this In Summary, click the Audio button. To play the audio, RealPlayer must be installed on your computer (download by clicking here).

1 What Are Some Careers Opportunities in the Computer Industry?

Job opportunities in the computer industry are found primarily in four areas – hardware, software, IT professionals, and training and education. In the computer hardware industry, jobs exist in manufacturing of computers, computer components, and peripherals. Career opportunities in the software industry involve designing and programming, including application software for business, productivity software, educational programs, entertainment software, and systems software. In many companies, IT professionals set up and manage the computer equipment and software. The IT professional may work in management, operations, system development, technical services, and end user computing. Companies and organizations that provide computer-related training and education also provide opportunities for teachers and trainers. Other IT careers include sales, service and repair, and consulting.

2 How Do You Prepare for a Career in the Computer Industry?

To prepare for a career in the computer industry, you first must decide on the area in which you are interested and then obtain education in that field. Begin your preparation by visiting professional organizations and job opportunity Web sites. After making your decision, you must choose a course of study. Three broad disciplines in higher education are **computer information technology**, **computer science**, and **computer engineering**. At the community college level, students can obtain an A.S. or an A.A.S degree. Trade schools are an alternative to enrolling in a college or university.

3 What Is Certification?

Certification demonstrates the mastery of a skill set and knowledge base in a specific IT area and ensures a level of competency, skills, or quality in a particular area. Certification can help companies ensure that their workforce remains current on computers and technology.

4 What Are the Different Types of IT Certification?

More than 200 certifications are available within the IT industry. Most of the certifications are developed by **sponsors**. Some certifications have a broad focus, while others require an in-depth knowledge. Some sponsors have a series of related certifications tied to different levels of expertise. Software application certifications include Microsoft Office Professional, Adobe Photoshop, Autodesk AutoCad, and Lotus Notes. Operating systems certifications focus on the user, the operator, the system administrator, and the system engineer. **Microsoft's MCP** and **MCSE** certifications demonstrate knowledge of Microsoft's operating systems. The **Red Hat Certified Engineer Program (RHCE)** validates mastery of the Linux operating system, while IBM certifications are UNIX oriented. Microsoft, Sun, and IBM offer certifications in the programming area. Several companies provide hardware certifications. One of the most popular is A+, provided by Computing Technology Industry (CompTIA), which also relates to network certification. A variety of network certifications are available, including Microsoft's MCSE, Cisco's CCIE and CCNP, and Novell's CNE. Several Internet certifications are available and include both hardware and software tracks. Within the database area, certifications are in hardware, Internet, networking, and programming.

In Summary

5 What Are the Benefits of Certification?

Some of the benefits include proof of professional achievement, enhancement of job opportunities, salary increases, and opportunities for advancement. Vendor-sponsored certifications may provide special privileges, such as access to technical and product information or access to **beta products**. Vendors also benefit from the product recognition and support the certification brings.

6 What Are the Considerations for Choosing a Certification?

Selecting a certification is a personal process that requires careful thought and research. Consider your career goals and interest and then assess your background knowledge and expertise.

7 What Are the Methods of Preparation for Certification?

Test results determine certification. Most people follow a study program to prepare for the test. Training options include studying on your own with educational materials, taking online classes, or attending an instructor-led class, or using a combination of these options.

8 What Are the Features of Certification Examinations and Recertification Requirements?

Authorized testing companies provide most certification and recertification exams. At the testing centers, examinations are delivered via computer, and most tests are in a multiple-choice format. Some tests use the **computerized adaptive testing (CAT)** technique. Some training centers provide a program guarantee and offer discounts or free sessions for those individuals who complete the program, but do not pass the test.

9 How Do You Keep Informed about Changes in Certification?

To keep pace with the changes in information technology, professionals must maintain and continually monitor technological developments. Most certifications expire after a set time limit. If a product update is released, certificate holders must retrain almost immediately.

Key Terms

Web Instructions: To display this page from the Web, start your browser and enter the URL scsite.com/dc2002/ch16/terms.htm. Scroll through the list of terms. Click a term to display its definition and a picture. Click the To WEB button for current and additional information about the term from the Web. To see animations, Shockwave and Flash Player must be installed on your computer (download by clicking here).

A+ certification (16.21)
Adobe Certified Expert (ACE) (16.18)
Application Developer, Oracle Developer Release 1 Track (16.24)
application programmer (16.9)
articulation agreement (16.13)
Associate and Senior Network Specialist Technician (NNT) (16.20)
Association for Computing Machinery (ACM) (16.14)
Association of Information Technology Professionals (16.14)
AutoCAD Certified Professional (ACP) (16.18)
beta products (16.26)
certification (16.16)
Certified Computing Professional (CCP) (16.19)
Certified Internet Professional (16.23)
Certified Internet WebMaster (CIW) (16.23)
Certified Java Developer (16.20)
Certified Java Programmer (16.20)
Certified Lotus Specialist (CLS) (16.18)
Certified Novell Associate (CNA) (16.22)
Certified Novell Engineer (CNE) (16.22)
Certified Sybase Professional – Database Administrator (CSP-DBA) (16.24)
Certified System Administrator (16.18)
Certified Web Professional (CWP) (16.23)
Cisco Certified Internetwork Expert (CCIE) (16.21, 16.22, 16.23)
Cisco Certified Network Professional (CCNP) (16.22)
COMDEX (16.14)
computer engineer (16.11)
computer engineering (CE) (16.13)
computer operator (16.9)
computer science (CS) (16.13)
computer science engineer/software engineer (16.9)
computer support specialist (16.11)
computer technician/computer service technician (16.9)
computerized adaptive testing (CAT) (16.30)
consultant (16.11)
data communications analyst (16.9)
database administrator (16.11)
database analyst/data modeler (16.9)
desktop publishing specialist (16.9, 16.11)
digital signal processor (DSP) designer (16.4)
graphic designer/illustrator (16.9)
help desk specialist (16.9)
IBM Certified Developer Associate (16.20)
IBM Certified Professional Server Specialists (PSS) (16.20)
IBM Certified Solutions Expert DB2 UDB V6.1 (16.24)
IBM Certified Specialist (16.18, 16.20)

CERTIFICATION
A way for employers to ensure a level of competency, skills, or quality in a specific area. (16.16)

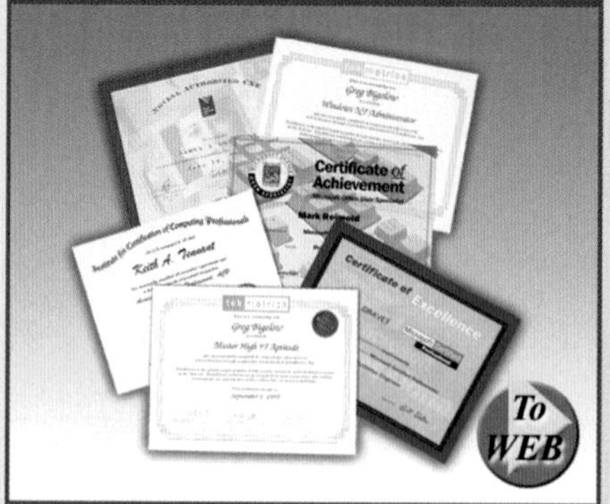

IBM Database Administration for UNIX, Windows, and OS/2 (16.24)
Informix Certified Database Specialist (16.24)
integrated circuit (IC) designer (16.4)
MCSE + Internet (16.23)
Microsoft Certified Database Administrator (MCDBA) (16.24)
Microsoft Certified Professional (MCP) (16.18)
Microsoft Certified Solution Developer (MCSD) (16.20)
Microsoft Certified Systems Engineer (MCSE) (16.18, 16.19, 16.22)
Microsoft Office User Specialist (MOUS) (16.18, 16.19)
MIS director/CIO (16.9)
network (LAN) administrator (16.9)
Network + (16.22)
network security specialist (16.9)
programmer/analyst (16.5)
project engineer (16.6)
project leader (16.9)
project manager (16.7, 16.9)
quality assurance specialist (16.9)
Red Hat Certified Engineer (RHCE) (16.18)
software engineer (16.6)
software engineering (SE) (16.13)
Sun Certified Architect for JavaTechnology (16.20)
system programmer (16.9)
systems analyst (16.9, 16.11)
systems integrator (16.4)
technical writer (16.9)
user group (16.14)
Web administrator (16.7)
Web developer (16.7)
Web graphic designer (16.7)
Web programmer (16.7)
Webcaster (16.7)
Webmaster (16.7)
Windows 2000 MCSE (16.20)
wireless designer (16.4)

Learn It Online

Web Instructions: To display this page from the Web, start your browser, and then enter the URL scsite.com/dc2002/ch16/learn.htm.

1. Web Guide

Click Web Guide to display the Guide to World Wide Web Sites and Searching Techniques Web page. Click Reference and then click About.com. Search for electronic commerce. Click one of the electronic commerce links. Use your word processing program to prepare a brief report on your findings and submit your assignment to your instructor.

2. Scavenger Hunt

Click Scavenger Hunt. Print a copy of the Scavenger Hunt page; use this page to write down your answers as you search the Web. Submit your completed page to your instructor.

3. Who Wants to Be a Computer Genius?

Click Computer Genius to find out if you are a computer genius. Directions on how to play the game will display. When you are ready to play, click the PLAY button. Submit your score to your instructor.

4. Wheel of Terms

Click Wheel of Terms to reinforce important terms you learned in this chapter by playing the Shelly Cashman Series version of this popular game. Directions on how to play the game will display. When you are ready to play, click the PLAY button. Submit your score to your instructor.

5. Career Corner

Click Career Corner to display the CareerBuilder Web site. Click the My Job link and search for an IT job. Scroll through the results until you find a job in which you are interested. Write a brief report on the job you selected and what you discovered. Submit the report to your instructor.

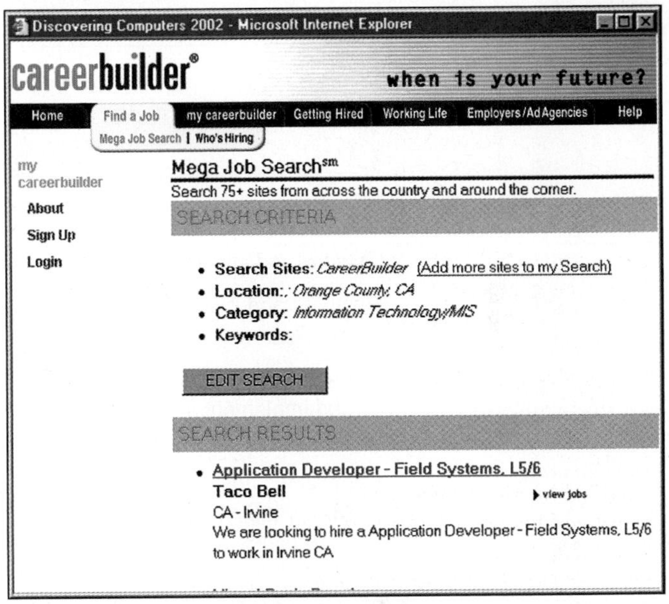

6. Search Sleuth

Click Search Sleuth to learn search techniques that will help make you a research expert. Submit the completed assignment to your instructor.

7. Crossword Puzzle Challenge

Click Crossword Puzzle Challenge. Complete the puzzle to reinforce skills you learned in this chapter. Directions on how to play the game will display. When you are ready to play, click the PLAY button. Submit the completed puzzle to your instructor.

8. Practice Test

Click Practice Test. Answer each question. When completed, enter your name and click the Grade Test button to submit the quiz for grading. Make a note of any missed questions. If required, print a copy to submit to your instructor.

Checkpoint

Web Instructions: To display this page from the Web, start your browser and enter the URL scsite.com/dc2002/ch16/check.htm. Click the links for current and additional information. To experience the animation and interactivity, Shockwave and Flash Player must be installed on your computer (download by clicking here.)

LABEL THE FIGURE

Instructions: Identify the different computer disciplines.

1.__________	2.__________	3.__________
Practical and application-oriented	Theoretical oriented	Design oriented
Business and management oriented	Mathematics and science oriented	Mathematics and science oriented
Understanding how to design and implement information systems	Understanding the fundamental nature of software	Understanding the fundamental nature of hardware
Degrees include A.A.S., B.S., M.S., Ph.D.	Degrees include B.S., M.S., Ph.D.	Degrees include B.S., M.S., Ph.D.

MATCHING

Instructions: Match each term from the column on the left with the best description from the column on the right.

_______ 1. sponsor
_______ 2. certification
_______ 3. beta products
_______ 4. computerized adaptive testing
_______ 5. Red Hat Certified Engineer program

a. Validates mastery of the Linux operating system.
b. A hardware certification.
c. Computer hardware and software vendors.
d. Validates mastery of Cisco networking.
e. Ensures a level of competency, skills, or quality in a particular area.
f. Products that are still in the testing stage.
g. Analyze a person's responses.

Checkpoint

MULTIPLE CHOICE

Instructions: Select the letter of the correct answer for each of the following questions.

1. An example of a hardware certification is ___________.
   a. A+
   b. UNIX
   c. Java
   d. Oracle DBA
2. The most frequently encountered format for a certification examinion is ___________.
   a. hands-on
   b. multiple-choice
   c. adaptive testing
   d. simulation
3. An office manager has excelled in word processing, spreadsheets, and desktop publishing. He would most likely be interested in a(n) ___________ certification.
   a. database
   b. operating system
   c. hardware
   d. software applications
4. Most people prefer to prepare for a certification exam by using ___________ as a training option.
   a. beta products
   b. computerized adaptive testing
   c. the H1B Visa program
   d. a combination of self-study, online, and instructor-led classes
5. ___________ companies manufacture and distribute computer systems and computer-related equipment.
   a. Hardware
   b. Software
   c. Networking
   d. Programming

SHORT ANSWER

Instructions: Write a brief answer to each of the following questions.

1. Job opportunities in the computer industry are found in what four areas? ___________ List some of the leading software companies offering certifications. ___________
2. Describe IT professionals. ___________ What are some IT career positions? ___________
3. What skills are necessary for a computer consultant? ___________ What are some tasks that a consultant may perform? ___________
4. What are the three computer disciplines within higher education? ___________ How are they different? ___________ What is the difference between and A.S. and an A.A.S. degree? ___________
5. What is a professional organization? ___________ How does involvement in a professional organization benefit computer professionals? ___________ List some of the more popular professional organizations. ___________

WORKING TOGETHER

Instructions: Working with a group of your classmates, complete the following team exercise.

Study options for obtaining certifications include self-study, online courses, and instructor-led courses. Use the Internet to find a Web site for self-study materials, a second for online training, a third for seminar-style instructor-led training, and a fourth Web site for academic-style instructor-led training. Select a common certification track available from each training center. Compare the training programs. Consider the number of classes required, the cost per class, and the duration of each class. Prepare a report and a PowerPoint presentation to share with your class.

In The Lab

Web Instructions: To display this page from the Web, start your browser and enter the URL scsite.com/dc2002/ch16/lab.htm. Click the links for current and additional information.

1 Using the Character Map Utility

This exercise uses Windows 98 procedures. The Character Map Utility lets you retrieve characters for use in other programs. Click the Start button on the taskbar, point to Programs on the Start menu, point to Accessories on the Programs submenu, point to System Tools on the Accessories submenu, and then click Character Map. When the Character Map window opens, click a character of your choice, and then click the Select button. Click a second character and click the Select button a second time. Click the Copy button. Close the Character Map window by clicking its Close button. Click the Start button on the taskbar, point to Programs on the Start menu, point to Accessories on the Programs submenu, and then click Notepad on the Accessories submenu. Click Edit on the menu bar and then click Set Font. Click Symbol in the Font list. Click the OK button in the Font dialog box. Click Edit on the menu bar and then click Paste to paste the characters into the Notepad window. Press the ENTER key and type your name. Click File on the menu bar and then click Save. When the Save As dialog box displays, make sure you have a floppy disk in drive A and then type `a:\h16-1` in the File name text box. Click the Save button in the Save As dialog box. After saving, close the Notepad window.

2 Adding a Scrap to the Desktop

To keep the contents of the Clipboard on your desktop for later reference, you can create a scrap. The are two ways to create a scrap are: drag-and-drop and copy and paste. You can recognize a scrap by its icon — it looks like a document file, except for a torn edge along the bottom. Click the Start button on the taskbar, point to Programs on the Start menu, point to Accessories on the Programs submenu, and then click WordPad on the Accessories submenu. Type your name and address. To use drag-and-drop, select the text and drag it to the desktop to create a scrap. To use copy and paste, select the text and click Copy on the Edit menu. Right-click the desktop and then click Paste on the shortcut menu to create a scrap containing the information copied to the Clipboard. To use the scrap in a document, drag it into the document. Or, right-click the scrap, click Copy on the shortcut menu, and then paste it into your document. Close Notepad. Do not save the file. Delete the scrap on the desktop by dragging it to the Recycle Bin.

3 Toggle Keys

The Microsoft's Accessible options allow you to sound a beep when the CAPS LOCK key is engaged. Click the Start button, point to Settings, and click Control Panel on the Settings submenu. Double-click the Accessibility Options icon. If necessary, click the Keyboard tab and click the Use Toggle Keys check mbox. Click the OK button. Close the Control Panel window. Press the CAPS LOCK key to hear the sound. Press it again to disengage it. This option functions the same for the NUM LOCK and SCROLL LOCK keys. To return the Toggle Keys to their original settings, in the Control Panel window, click the Accessibility Options icon and deselect the Use Toggle Keys check box. Click the OK button, and then close the Control Panel window.

4 Disk Maintenance

This exercise uses Windows 98 procedures. Hard disk maintance should be done on a regular basis. To check when these operations were last performed, right-click the Start button on the taskbar and then click Explore. Right-click the (C:) icon, and then click Properties on the shortcut menu. When the (C:) Properties dialog box displays, click the Tools tab. The status of each of these operations displays. Answer the following questions:

- When was the last day the drive was checked for errors?
- How many days has it been since the files were backed up?
- How many days has it been since the disk was defragmented?

Close the (C:) Properties dialog box and the Exploring - Start Menu window.

Web Work

Web Instructions: To display this page from the Web, start your browser and enter the URL scsite.com/dc2002/ch16/web.htm. To view At The Movies in exercise 1, RealPlayer must be installed on your computer (download by clicking here).

1 *Internet Economy*

To view the Internet Economy movie, click the button to the left or click the Play button to the right. Watch the movie, and then complete the exercise by answering the questions below. Skyrocketing growth of the Internet has created a massive shortfall of qualified employees. College graduates with degrees in engineering or computer science, however, can expect at least a dozen job offers upon graduation. Internet employment lures job seekers with the dream of latching onto a winner and becoming quick millionaires before hitting age 30. At the same time, chaos and uncertainty prevail in the industry as thousands of companies go under. If you are looking for an Internet-related job, what are the things to look for in a company? Where do you look for Internet-related jobs? What skills are required?

2 *Interviewing for an IT Career*

Making a good impression and preparing for an interview is one of the more important steps to getting a job. To begin your preparation, compose a list of common questions that you may be asked. Most employers will ask about experience, qualifications, and future plans. Next, prepare a list of questions that you can ask your potential employer. Some common questions are about benefits, types of training programs, and available career paths. Then practice, practice, practice. One way to practice in a safe environment is through a virtual interview. Click the button to the left and complete the virtual interview. Was the interview helpful? What questions were the most difficult?

3 *MOUS Certification*

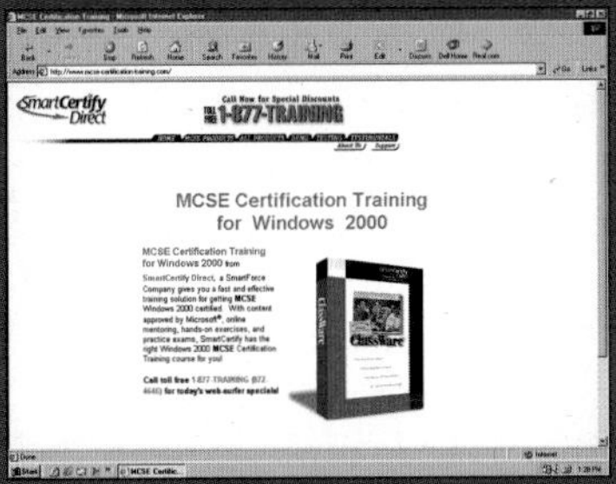

One of the more popular application certification programs is the Microsoft Office User Specialist (MOUS) certification. The certification program recognizes individuals who have achieved a certain level of mastery with Microsoft Office products and provides a framework for measuring end-user proficiency with the Microsoft Office applications. Attaining MOUS certification proves you have met an industry-recognized standard for measuring an individual's mastery of Office applications, demonstrates proficiency in a given Office application to employers, and provides a competitive edge in the job marketplace. Click the button to the left for a list of frequently asked questions (FAQs) about the MOUS program. Read the questions. What types of certifications are available? What kind of preparation is necessary for certification? Does your educational institution offer MOUS courses?

4 *In the News*

As the IT professionals shortage continues, several certification sponsors have started offering certification training and testing to high school students. The students choose computers as a major and take courses in certification programs such as A+ and MCSE. Many states have magnet schools where most of the curriculum is focused on technology. Click the button to the left and read a news article about a recent high school certification story. Could this trend cause a potential problem with students not attending college?

Figure 1
In the future, computers will have an even more important role in all aspects of your life by providing vast information resources, fast communications, and powerful support for activities in homes, schools, and businesses.

TRENDS 2002
A Look to the Future

WEB INSTRUCTIONS: *To gain World Wide Web access to additional and up-to-date information regarding this special feature, start your browser and enter the URL shown at the top of this page.*

Progress in computing no longer affects only computer scientists, engineers, and information technologists. Today, computer advances influence all individuals, families, organizations, and schools (Figure 1). As you have learned throughout this book, computers already are an essential part of people's daily lives; they quickly have become a mainstay, much as the automobile, television, and telephone have. In the future, computers will take on many new roles and become an even more pervasive and critical part of homes, schools, and businesses. This special feature looks at several computer technology trends that will influence the direction of the computer field and then looks at the impact those technologies will have on information technology in business.

TRENDS IN COMPUTER TECHNOLOGY

During the next several years, the greatest advances in computer technology will occur in areas such as hardware, software, communications and networks, mobile and wireless connectivity, and robotics.

Hardware

Manufacturers intensely are developing and producing new devices, including microdisplays and headsets, that will pervade all aspects of people's lives. This hardware will contain faster and smaller chips, which could be implanted in your body. Atomic Quantum computers and optical computers could process data at record-breaking speeds. Fluorescent multiplayer discs and digital books will revolutionize the ways information is stored and accessed. These hardware developments will affect learning and playing.

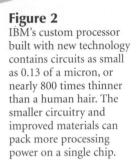

Figure 2
IBM's custom processor built with new technology contains circuits as small as 0.13 of a micron, or nearly 800 times thinner than a human hair. The smaller circuitry and improved materials can pack more processing power on a single chip.

UBIQUITOUS COMPUTING Computers are not yet everywhere, but as they get smaller, faster, and less expensive, they are being utilized in everything from toothbrushes and curling irons to cars and spaceships. Ralph Merkle, a research scientist at Xerox's Palo Alto Research Center, envisions a "not-so-distant future, maybe by 2020, definitely by 2050, [in which] we will have devices with the computational power of . . . roughly a billion Pentium computers." Having access to such enormous computational power will change the emphasis of computing from processing data to generating information to managing knowledge. Further, every device known to man, including the human body, will use some type of computer to help it function more efficiently and effectively.

NEXT-GENERATION CHIP Engineers are using extreme ultraviolet lithography (UVL) to turn their circuit designs into silicon chips. This technology uses ultrasmooth mirrors, rather than optical projection, to draw circuits that are 100 times more powerful than today's chips. Intel's Pentium® 4 processors run at speeds of 1.4 GHz and higher and contain 42 million transistors that are 0.13 of a micron wide. A micron is the width of a human hair (Figure 2). By 2005, chip manufacturers plan to introduce chips that will run at speeds up to 10 GHz with 400 million transistors that are just 0.03 of a micron wide. When the circuits are closer together, data travels shorter distances and consequently requires less time to process. Intel's 64-bit Itanium processor also will improve the speed of high-end workstations and servers.

Figure 3
Video and television images will appear right before your eyes with new visual appliances.

MICRODISPLAYS AND HEADSETS You will be seeing technology in a whole new way with the advent of visual devices that resemble sunglasses. One model replicates a 52-inch television screen or Sony PlayStation 2 on an LCD screen (Figure 3). Headsets plug into DVD players, notebook computers, desktop computers, and digital cameras and allow a display measuring one-tenth of an inch to look like a full-sized theater screen. Microdisplays the size of postage stamps fill your field of vision and appear as large as a regular monitor when magnified (Figure 4).

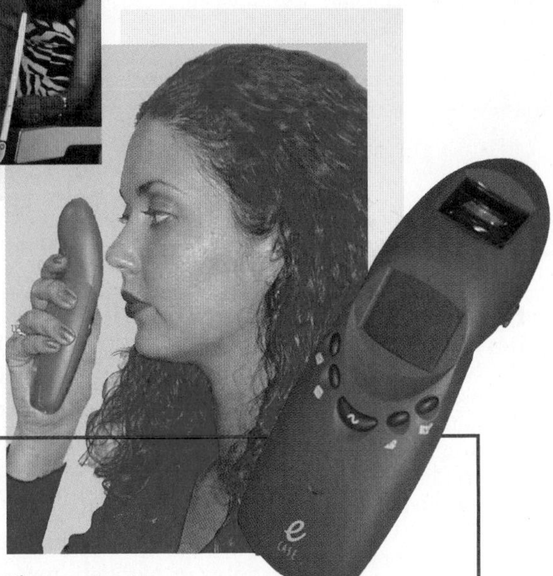

Figure 4
Microdisplays give you the visual equivalent of a 19-inch monitor and allow you to view Web pages, e-mail, maps, and calendars.

HUMAN COMPUTER INTEGRATION Some researchers believe the processor eventually will become an integral part of the most complex device known — the human body. Computers already are used inside the human body. Cochlear implants, for example, help some deaf people hear by stimulating the ear and the nerves that send information to the brain. The next step in human computer integration will involve implanting chips in the body to help it perform basic functions (Figure 5). A processor, for example, could help regulate the release of hormones in the same way that a processor regulates the fuel mixture in modern autos.

Canadian futurist Frank Ogden has conceived an even more futuristic use of embedded processors, called CyberSight. With CyberSight, a processor interfaces with a person's optic nerve to allow him or her to see information transmitted over a wireless link. The CyberSight system, for example, could transmit the floor plans of a building to a firefighter; the plans then would display in the vision of the firefighter, so that he or she can determine the best way to enter a burning building.

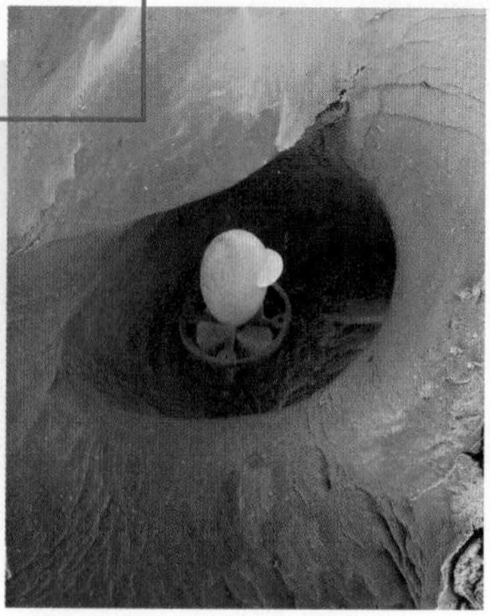

Figure 5
Doctors hope to use a microsubmarine to detect and repair defects in the human body. This device measures four millimeters in length and 0.65 millimeter in diameter.

ATOMIC QUANTUM COMPUTERS By the middle of this century, the computer on your desk could very well be filled with liquid instead of transistors and chips. It probably will be called a QC for Quantum computer, rather than a personal computer. In theory, the speed of Quantum computers could be up to a billion times faster than today's fastest Pentium® 4 computers. At that speed, a Quantum computer could search the entire Internet instantaneously or break any security code in a second. Quantum computers use quantum mechanics, rather than digital technology. In a Quantum computer, bits are replaced by atoms. Several computer companies, the federal government, and a number of independent research teams are working feverishly to put the theory of quantum computing into practice.

OPTICAL COMPUTERS Transmitting data using optical technology has become commonplace in CD-ROM drives, laser printers, photocopiers, and scanners and in fiber optic digital communications. Some engineers believe this technology will extend to computers using visible light or infrared beams to perform digital computations, increasing the speed of operations tenfold. Likewise, it should decrease the optical computers' physical size because the light beams can pass through each other without interacting.

FLUORESCENT MULTILAYER DISC (FMD) The next step in storage capacity is the Fluorescent Multilayer Disc. The first generation of this five-inch clear optical medium can hold 140 GB of data — almost 30 times more than a DVD-ROM disc can store. Data is recorded on fluorescent materials, which reflect light, on the disc's multiple layers. These discs could have as many as 100 layers of data, which will increase their storage capacity to one terabyte (one trillion bytes). Uses include high-definition television, digital cinema, and mobile applications, such as digital cameras. FMD-ROM drives currently are read-only, but engineers are perfecting recordable FMD technology.

Figure 6
Demand is expected to increase for electronic books (e-books). Some of these devices can hold up to 56,000 pages, or the equivalent of 150 books' worth of text.

DIGITAL BOOKS The Internet clearly will have a major impact on libraries. During this decade, many libraries will convert hard copy documents into digital form. Eventually, this could develop into online universal libraries to which all schools have access. While looking for a book in this online universal library, you could search a network of individual online libraries to find the book, view any checkout terms or fees, and then view or download it from the library Web site. Traditional libraries, however, still will exist, if only to house publicly accessible computers and a collection of books required to verify digitized versions.

Initial consumer reluctance for the electronic book, or e-book, is expected to subside in the next few years. Several companies have introduced these small book-sized computers (Figure 6) that can hold up to 56,000 pages, or about 150 books' worth of text. By pressing a button, you can move forward or backward through the text. You also can download Web pages and add notes or highlight text using a small pen input device. Although the tablet-sized displays will not have the clear resolution of ink on a page for years to come, Microsoft has developed ClearType, which significantly enhances the appearance of the font on a screen.

EDUCATION The use of personal computers in educational settings is another rapidly growing area. The Internet and the World Wide Web are affecting education, as distance education allows students to take classes or Webinars — online seminars — whenever they have time from home or workplace computers. Such courses are ideal for workers seeking advanced training but lacking the time to pursue on-campus studies or for undergraduates living far from campus. University professors will continue to develop entire courses using video lectures with coordinated demonstrations on virtual blackboards — all distributed to students over the Internet. Critics argue, however, that while the Internet can help with continuing education and professional retraining initiatives, a fully Internet-based education cannot capture the full value of the educational experience.

Imagine learning a new subject without ever going to class or opening a book. A further phase of human computer integration could involve making various disciplines such as mathematics, literature, and foreign languages available on processors. If you wanted to learn Dutch, you could purchase a chip from a local retail store, much as you purchase a CD. Once you upload the chip to your brain through an implanted port, immediately you will know Dutch — without ever taking a class. While this may seem farfetched, recent advances suggest it is possible.

ENTERTAINMENT For the younger members of the family, playing games using entertainment software always has had a large appeal. Many adults, however, find that entertainment software also provides them with hours of enjoyment. Popular types of entertainment software include arcade games, board games, and simulations.

Entertainment software also consists of a variety of interactive adventure games, which range from rescuing a princess from a castle's dungeon to solving a murder mystery. You can play many of these games in groups using a network or on the World Wide Web, or you can play with just the computer as your opponent. Entertainment software usually allows players to adjust the level of play to match their abilities — that is, beginner through advanced. With entertainment software, the computer becomes a fun, skillful, and challenging game partner.

Sega Corporation is developing an assortment of games to play on Motorola's new application-upgradable handsets. UIEvolution is working on interactive games, starting with chess, checkers, hangman, and Space Invaders, that allow users to play between multiple wireless handsets.

Virtual reality (VR) is the use of computers to simulate a real or imagined environment that appears as a three-dimensional (3-D) space. VR allows you to explore and manipulate controls to experience the 3-D space completely (Figure 7). One futurist suggests that VR someday will allow moviegoers to pretend they are one of the movie characters. In such an environment, the virtual reality technology would link the moviegoer's sensory system (sight, smell, hearing, taste, and touch) to the character's sensory system.

Figure 7
New Jersey bus driver trainees learn to maneuver their vehicles on virtual streets. New Jersey Transit says the virtual training saves the company thousands of dollars each year in training costs and also reduces accidents.

Software

A second major area of technology innovation involves the instructions that tell computers what tasks to perform. Software trends include improved user interfaces, enhanced Internet content, digital music, MP4 video compression, intelligent agents, speech recognition, and remote control of home appliances.

USER INTERFACE Most computers use a graphical user interface (GUI), which developers have dubbed the WIMP (windows, icons, menus, and pointer) interface. To use the WIMP interface, you must learn a new mode of communication that includes pointing, clicking, dragging, and so on. Next-generation operating systems will be more natural and human-centric, meaning they will allow you to interface with a computer using many of the methods you now use to communicate with humans. Such methods will include natural language, hand gestures, facial expressions, and of course, spoken words.

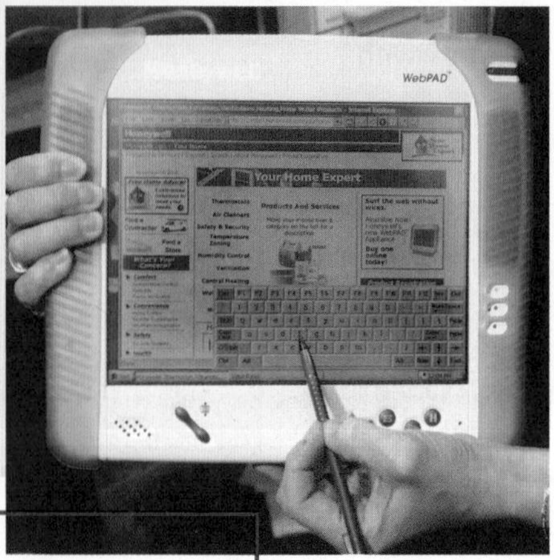

Figure 8
Web tablets offer consumers easy access to browsers and Web sites.

THE INTERNET AND THE WEB In this decade, the Internet and the Web promise many exciting developments. Already, the Internet is the fastest growing segment of the computer industry and is a major reason why consumers are buying personal computers and handheld devices at a record pace. Today, one half of U.S. homes have access to the Internet. At present, individuals primarily use the Internet to access information and communicate using e-mail. In the future, individuals increasingly will rely on two other Internet-based communication applications — telephony and videoconferencing.

Other developments will be Web tablets (Figure 8), which feature full-color touch screens allowing users easy access to the Internet, and the continued integration of television, networks, and computers. For now, the relatively inexpensive WebTV allows you to send e-mail and surf the Web using your television set. In the future, you will use WebTV in an interactive fashion to view your favorite movie, television show, concert, sporting event, or shopping guide.

MUSIC AND THE INTERNET As more digital music becomes available for download from the Internet, market analysts predict fewer consumers will buy CDs and will instead turn to MP3 and other digital audio players. MP3 technology compresses audio files, so music can be downloaded from Web pages and transmitted in e-mail messages much faster than with uncompressed files. Sales of players using this technology have soared from $126 million in 1999 to an expected $1.25 billion by the end of 2002. This growth is due, in part, to Shawn Fanning and his Napster software and company, which were created as a means of allowing music lovers to swap songs.

Legal proceedings for copyright infringement against Napster and its progeny helped spur consumer awareness that high-quality music is available on the Internet, and many musicians have released songs solely on the Web. Sony and many other entertainment companies are pursuing selling music via Internet-based pay-per-listen systems. Some analysts predict one-third of all consumers will have virtual music collections by 2005.

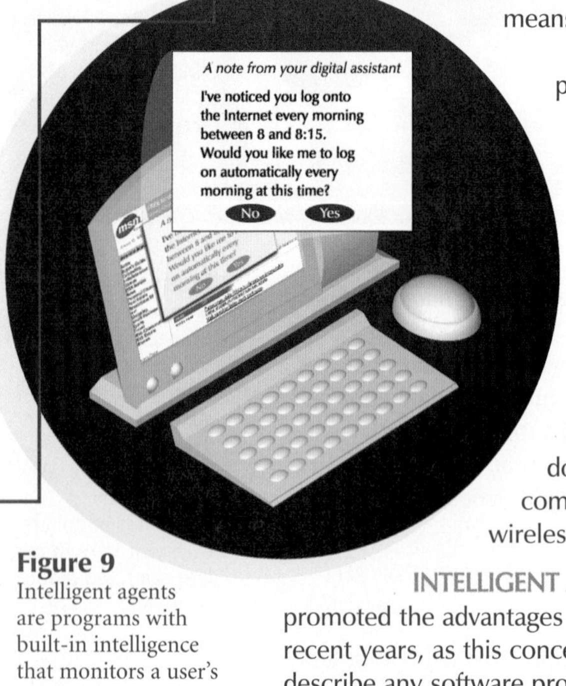

A note from your digital assistant
I've noticed you log onto the Internet every morning between 8 and 8:15. Would you like me to log on automatically every morning at this time?
No
Yes

Figure 9
Intelligent agents are programs with built-in intelligence that monitors a user's work patterns and carry out tasks independently.

MP4 VIDEO COMPRESSION Video files can be compressed to 10 percent of their original size with MP4 technology, which filters out images the eye cannot perceive. Using today's standards, a full-length compressed video would take two hours to download, but as broadband Internet access and data transfer rates increase, the download time should become more manageable. Entertainment companies are considering sending movie trailers and video messages on wireless handheld devices.

INTELLIGENT AGENTS For more than 40 years, artificial intelligence (AI) experts promoted the advantages of smart software — that is, software with built-in intelligence. In recent years, as this concept has become reality, the term, intelligent agent, has evolved to describe any software program that independently asks questions, pays attention to work patterns, and carries out tasks on behalf of a user (Figure 9).

Some intelligent agents are embedded and work within a single program. Other intelligent agents, sometimes called network agents, perform tasks on multiple remote computers with different platforms before bringing the results back to the user. Intelligent agents already are a part of several productivity software packages. Some e-mail software, for example, includes intelligent agents that allow individuals and businesses to filter incoming messages and request immediate notification of messages about specific subjects or from specific individuals. The Intellisense™ technology built into Microsoft Office also is based on an intelligent agent.

SPEECH RECOGNITION The ability to understand a natural language means that a computer will be capable of translating your spoken statements into computer instructions and responding in an appropriate fashion. The market for voice recognition software is expected to climb to $22.6 billion in 2003, up from $356 million in 1997. The newest version of Microsoft Office includes Office Speech Recognition software, which allows you to speak the names of menu commands, toolbar buttons, dialog box controls, text, and numbers. You also can instruct the computer to read a document or worksheet to you in a male or female voice. In the near future, computers will support continuous-speech voice recognition and use artificial intelligence to determine the meaning of your spoken words.

In an even more advanced use of speech recognition, computers will recognize your voice commands and respond in a computer-generated voice through an on-screen presence that resembles a person, animal, or other object. IBM and Apple, for example, have developed prototype interfaces that resemble the human head (Figure 10). When using this interface, you turn off the computer by telling the character to go to sleep. The character closes its eyes and droops its head as the computer begins to shut down.

Figure 10
Companies have prototype interfaces that resemble the human head to make voice recognition more realistic.

CONTROL OF HOME SYSTEMS The smart home of the future will include appliances that plug into the Internet (Figure 11). Electronics retailers will feature integrated systems to network your computer, television, security system, heating and air conditioning units, stove, refrigerator, DVD, VCR, video games, and monitoring devices. You then will be able to use a telephone or computer to change the operation of one of the control systems, such as turning lights on or off or viewing the contents of your storeroom by using a Web cam.

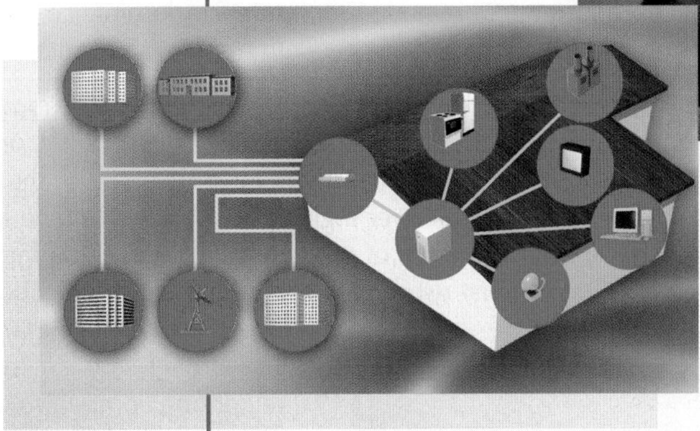

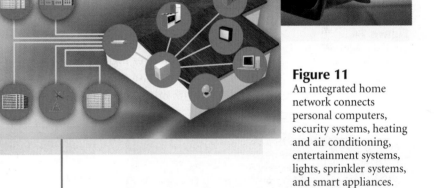

Figure 11
An integrated home network connects personal computers, security systems, heating and air conditioning, entertainment systems, lights, sprinkler systems, and smart appliances.

Smart appliances using the Sun Microsystems Java and Jini technologies can perform time-consuming chores. For example, your refrigerator or pantry will be linked through a home control system to the grocery store and order groceries without your intervention. Modern refrigerators will have Web panels that display recipes and then convert the recipes' ingredients to shopping lists, which can be forwarded to a handheld computer, mobile telephone, or online shopping service, such as Webvan (Figure 12). Dishwashers will communicate with their manufacturers to report malfunctions or maintenance problems and then be repaired remotely (Figure 13). Coffeemakers will download new functions as they become available. Entertainment media will download movies, games, music, and a week's worth of your favorite television programs from your cable company, satellite operator, or other video service.

Figure 12
Grocery shopping services deliver brand-name grocery and drugstore items to your doorstep.

Figure 13
Smart homes feature appliances that communicate with manufacturers and let you connect to the Internet for news, recipes, and cooking information.

Communications and Networks

The methods of transmitting and sharing data are about to change dramatically. Updates include Microsoft's .NET strategy, home wireless networks, wired broadband, wireless communication, the Bluetooth™ standard, mobile Internet access, global positioning systems, electronic paper and ink, and multiple-function telephones.

.NET AND SOFTWARE SUBSCRIPTIONS Microsoft's .NET strategy is a new environment for developing and running software applications. .NET will provide instant access to data and services in the context of your current task. Microsoft plans to shift the focus of software from the desktop to Web-based services. As part of its Office Online initiative, the company has granted permission to more than 20 application service providers to host Microsoft Office applications. A .NET version of Office is slated for a 2003 release.

HOME WIRELESS NETWORKS Most technology companies are taking sides and backing one of two competing wireless standards for the home, but others are backing both. Apple Computer, Dell Computer, Sony, 3Com, and 70 other companies are supporting the Wi-Fi, or 802.11B, standard, while Intel, Motorola, Hewlett-Packard, and 80 other corporations are backing the alternate HomeRF standard. IBM and other companies are backing both, reluctant to be caught with obsolete equipment. The battle for dominance likely is to continue as new Net appliances and wireless devices emerge, data transfer rates increase, and prices drop.

WIRED BROADBAND During the next few years, home and business users can expect much faster access to the Internet as cable and telephone companies provide broader bandwidth. As discussed in Chapter 9, bandwidth is a measure of the amount of data a communications channel can transmit over a given period of time. The key to speeding up Internet access is to increase the bandwidth of the communications channel between the user and the access provider. For most users, this part of the communications channel, which is called the last mile, often involves using a modem to dial up and connect to a server over slow analog telephone lines. Several cable and telephone companies are increasing the bandwidth of the last mile by using fiber optics, broadband cable (TV cable), and fast Digital Subscriber Lines (DSL). Higher-bandwidth communications channels will eliminate the use of dial-up modem connections and greatly increase Internet access speeds for streaming video, interactivity, and real-time applications.

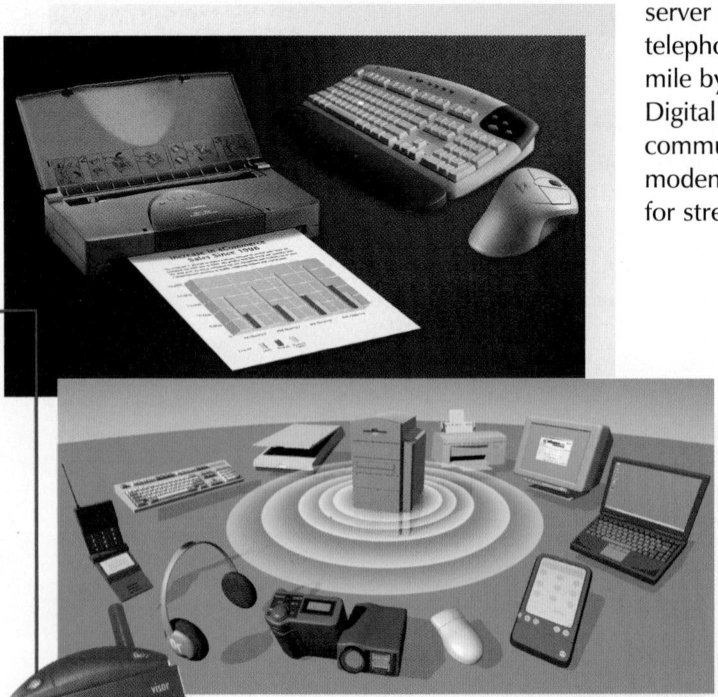

Figure 14
Wireless desktop connections will become commonplace in the next few years.

Mobile and Wireless Connectivity

As the personal-computing market matures, consumers are looking for new ways to access the Internet and to communicate. Cordless products are in high demand, and these devices with Bluetooth™ technology should flood the market in the next few years. Third-generation communications service will increase Internet services. Other advances will be made in global positioning systems, electronic paper and ink, and multiple-function telephones.

WIRELESS DEVICES Recent advances in digital wireless technology have focused on using mobile telephones and handheld computers and devices. During the next few years, as these wireless forms of communication become the norm, attention will turn towards developing cordless computers (Figure 14) and other household appliances. Palmtops are expected to be the top-selling wireless devices (Figure 15) with an average

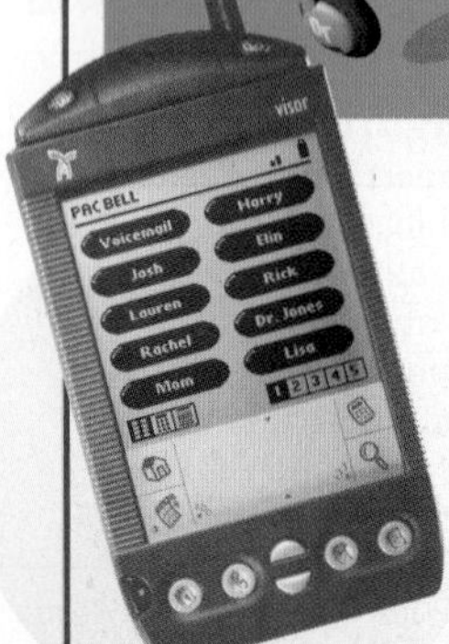

Figure 15
Wireless Internet connections will boost sales of handheld computers, particularly with expansion port add-ons such as keyboards, GPS modules, and bar code scanners.

annual growth of 28 percent through 2004. Palm, Inc., continues to dominate the wireless market, but products from Handspring and from companies using the Windows CE operating system will continue to erode Palm's market share.

BLUETOOTH™ Bluetooth™ technology allows cellular telephones, pagers, handheld computers and devices, and other wireless products to detect one another and communicate across short distances, usually a maximum of 30 feet. According to Cahners In-Stat Group, a leading industry analyst firm, manufactures should ship more than 1.4 billion Bluetooth™-enabled devices by 2005. The Bluetooth Special Interest Group (SIG) developers from the computing, networking, and telecommunications fields jointly are planning a wide range of applications, such as those that allow travelers to receive flight information automatically at airports or to be directed to the nearest coffee shop as they walk down a street. Shoppers with Bluetooth™-enabled cellular telephones could receive coupons as they walk past displays. Developers state this technology ultimately should add no more than $5 to the price of a chip.

Figure 16
NTT DoCoMo's i-mode mobile Internet service is immensely popular among Japanese consumers.

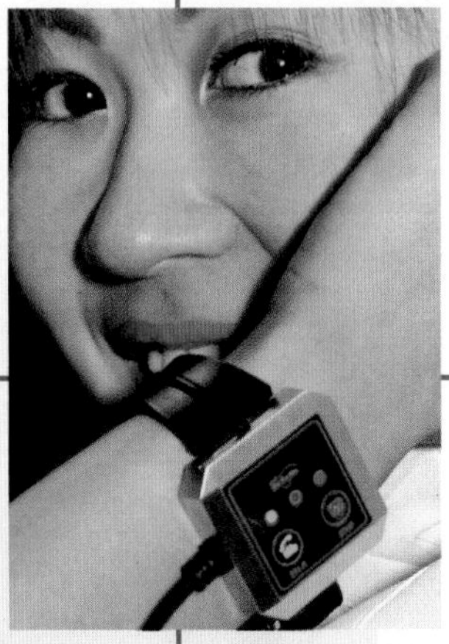

MOBILE INTERNET ACCESS Japan's pioneer mobile-Internet company, NTT DoCoMo, Inc., plans to lead the world's new phase of broadband services, Wideband Code Division Multiple Access (W-CDMA). This third-generation (3G) mobile communications service has the data-transmission capacity to download songs and short video clips. Each day, more than 50,000 new Japanese consumers subscribe to DoCoMo's mobile Internet service, i-mode (Figure 16), which provides access to thousands of official i-mode and independent news services, information, and entertainment, as well as such specialized services as airline reservations, online shopping and banking, and the ability to exchange digital images. In contrast, American consumers have been reluctant to subscribe to mobile services that offer shopping, weather updates, and e-mail. DoCoMo has invested $9.8 billion in AT&T's wireless unit, representing a venture to close the gap between wireless technologies in the two countries.

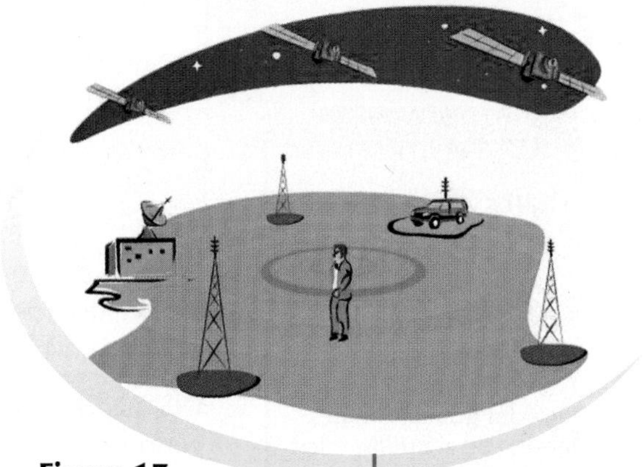

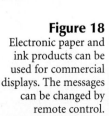

Figure 17
The Digital Angel provides location and monitoring information. Its microchip includes biosensors that measure body parameters and an antenna that communicates with GPS satellites.

GLOBAL POSITIONING SYSTEMS The U.S. Department of Defense developed the Global Positioning System (GPS) for national security, but today this technology is found 10 times more frequently in civilian, rather than military, applications. The already widespread use of GPS devices is about to increase dramatically in 2002 when cellular telephone companies will be able to locate the position of their callers to within 100 meters and when localized wireless advertising is available. Cellular telephones may contain GPS technology that can be used on a pay-per-use basis. Designed to be implanted in the human body, the Digital Angel's wearable patch (Figure 17) will send and receive GPS information along with medical diagnostic data. In another use, a wind-up generator may provide the power for recreational GPS users who travel without power, such as hikers, bikers, and kayakers.

ELECTRONIC PAPER/ELECTRONIC INK Engineers are developing electronic paper and ink products (Figure 18) that combine the strengths of digital technology with the qualities of paper, including its light weight and high contrast. Several companies are developing this rewriteable medium. Some use microscopic liquid particles or beads that are white on one side and black or red on the other and are suspended in a transparent plastic cavity. This display screen currently is as thick as a mouse pad, but eventually it will become as thin as four sheets of paper. The particles or beads respond to electronic impulses and move depending on the images requested. The next generation of e-paper will add organic light-emitting diodes (OLEDs) to the plastic sheets to display full color and full-motion video.

Figure 18
Electronic paper and ink products can be used for commercial displays. The messages can be changed by remote control.

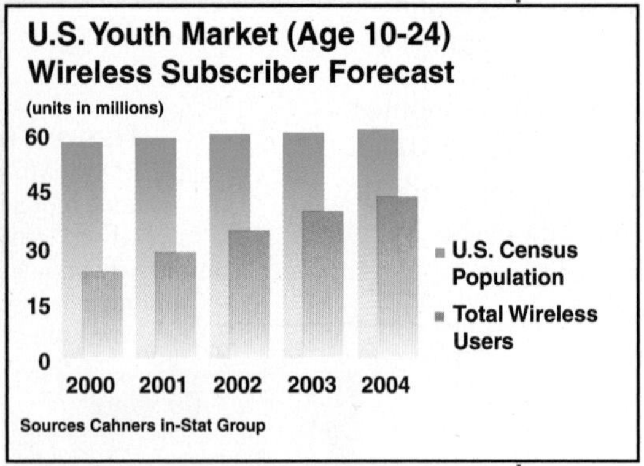

Figure 19
(Source: Cahners In-Stat Group) Cellular telephone manufacturers and carriers are aiming to lure young users to their products.

MULTIPLE-FUNCTION TELEPHONES Cellular telephones will be packed with new features. Some will be popular among young users — those between the ages of 10 and 24 — who are the target group for the newest products (Figure 19). The fastest growing cellular telephone application is e-mail messaging. Nearly every digital wireless telephone sold will feature this two-way text messaging, which allows users to type short messages into their telephones and then transmit the words to other wireless telephones. This service is very popular in Asia and Europe, especially in countries that do not have reliable or easily accessible wired telephone service. More than 10 billion text messages are sent each month. A joint venture between Ericsson and Microsoft should offer improved e-mail services on cellular telephones.

More people worldwide will be accessing the Internet via cellular telephones rather than by personal computers in 2003, according to industry executives. Fourth generation (4G) wireless standards are predicted to be in place by 2010, and they will offer even faster mobile Internet access.

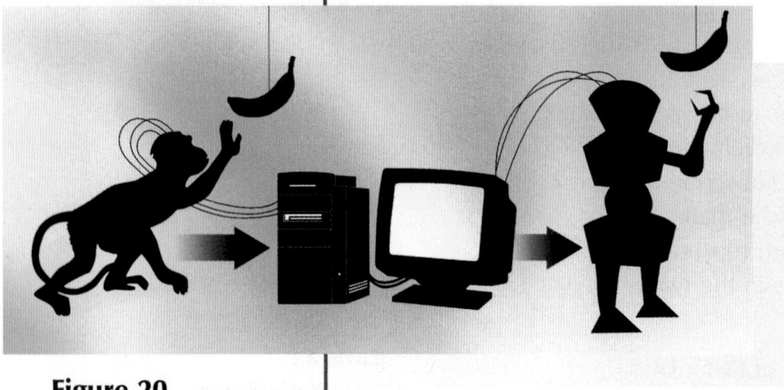

Figure 20
Research involing monkeys is helping researchers record brain cell activity. When the monkeys perform a learned task, their neurons generate brain waves that are transmitted to computers via wires implanted in the monkeys' brains. The computer decodes and sends the data to a robot that replicates the monkey's movements.

Robotics

Computers capable of performing human tasks will be seen everywhere from hospitals to your home. Medical breakthroughs achieved in hospitals include brain pacemaker implants and distance surgery. Homes are becoming lively and clean with the advent of robots for entertainment and vacuuming.

BRAIN PACEMAKER Scientists working with monkeys and studying how brain cells interact are perfecting a type of pacemaker to implant in the brain and send brain waves directly to a robot or device (Figure 20). One practical use is for reading the brain waves of people with seizure disorders, anticipating a seizure, and delivering drugs or electrical impulses that can stop or prevent a seizure.

DISTANCE SURGERY The next generation of health care will promote the use of robots to perform surgeries (Figure 21). The robots' precise skills and small sizes — less than one-fifth the size of traditional instruments — make surgeries less invasive and recovery times less prolonged. Surgeons view three-dimensional images of internal organs on large monitors and can control the robots' actions through voice commands.

Operating rooms will undergo another dramatic change when surgeons practice telemedicine. Through the use of videoconferencing and satellites, doctors can perform surgery when they are in locations other than the operating room.

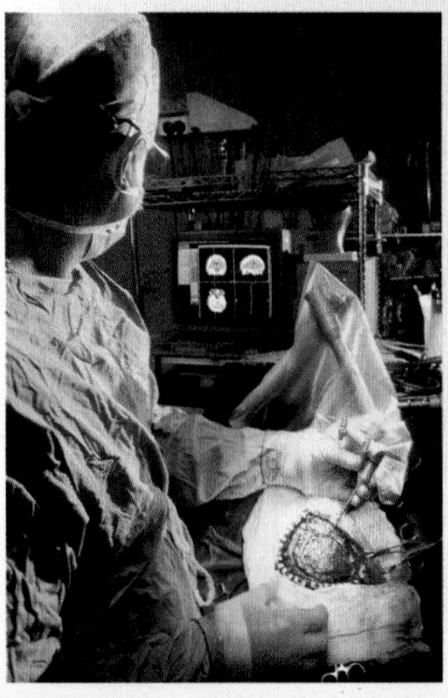

Figure 21
Robot-aided surgeries help surgeons remove brain tumors. Information regarding the precise location of the tumor displays on the monitor and is fed into the robot's computer. Robotic surgeries result in minimal damage to the surrounding brain tissue.

AIBO Now you can have mankind's best friend without the mess and expensive veterinarian bills. Sony Corporation's AIBO (Artificial Intelligence Robot), which coincidentally is the Japanese word for companion, is a breed of entertainment robot with voice recognition technology, emotions, instincts, the ability to learn 50 verbal commands, and four senses for touch, hearing, sight, and balance (Figure 22). AIBO is part of Sony's development efforts to create robots that coexist with people and create unlimited opportunities for humans to interact with computers.

CYE-SR You will not have to worry about AIBO shedding its fur around your house, but this problem is a given with a real dog. Why not let a robot clean your room? Just use your personal computer to program the Cye-SR robot that is attached to the Probotics cordless vacuum cleaner (Figure 23). Cye-SR will travel throughout your house in search of dust and dirt.

Figure 22
Each AIBO develops an individual personality based on its interaction with its environment.

THE FUTURE OF INFORMATION SYSTEMS IN BUSINESS

Although millions of homes now include one or more computers, businesses by far are the largest users of computers. Around the world, organizations install and use millions of computers of all types — mainframes, personal computers, and more — for applications such as inventory control, billing, and accounting. These computers often are part of a large information system that includes data, people, procedures, hardware, and software.

Existing business information systems will undergo profound changes as a result of the computer trends just described. As computers become increasingly ubiquitous and technologies converge, businesses will rely on computers for communications — and users at all levels will need to be computer literate. These new technologies will enhance security measures, provide computers for all employees, improve communications and health care in hospitals, and shape t-commerce and e-business.

Figure 23
The Probotics cordless vacuum cleaner comes with an added feature — the Cye-SR robot that scouts out dust.

AUTHENTICATION/SECURITY Public surveillance by businesses, government, and institutions is a growing industry, spurred by smaller and less expensive technology. According to the Security Industry Association, nearly $2 billion has been spent on computer controlled closed-circuit television networks, such as those being used in more than 60 U.S. cities to curb vandalism, prevent crime, and record incidents.

Surveillance is being taken to a higher level with software that converts images of faces to a series of 14 reference points, such as the eyebrows' bone structure and the distance between the eyes. This data is stored in databases and compared at rates of 45 million records per minute to people who pass by security cameras at countries' border crossings and who apply for new driver's licenses.

Upcoming software can be trained to recognize threatening behavior, such as when someone points a gun, and then alert the police. Applications also could help maintain security at automatic teller machines, where cardholders' facial images could be stored in a database and compared to a person using the machine (Figure 24). Computers also will use video cameras to record and identify individuals

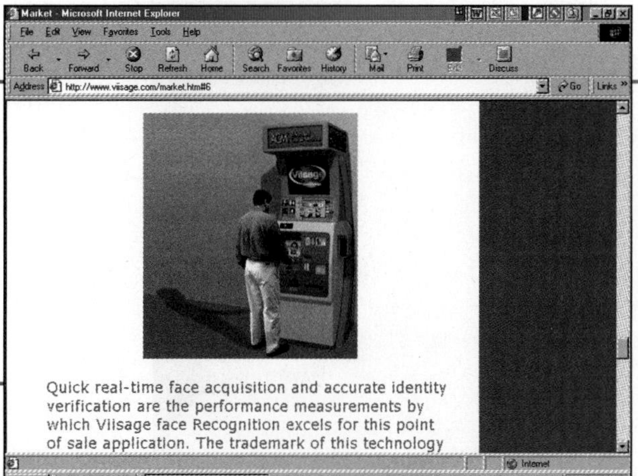

Market - Microsoft Internet Explorer
Quick real-time face acquisition and accurate identity verification are the performance measurements by which Viisage face Recognition excels for this point of sale application. The trademark of this technology

Figure 24
Instead of entering a PIN, automatic teller machine users can access their accounts securely using face recognition to verify their identities.

through facial expressions and fingerprint recognition (Figure 25). Industry experts project that surveillance cameras could become so prevalent that everyone could watch everyone at any time.

WIRING THE ENTIRE WORKFORCE For many years, computer use centered around white-collar professionals sitting at desks using wired computers. Indeed, of all employees, nearly 70 percent uses some type of computer during the workday. With the influx of wireless products, manufacturers are striving to wire the other 30 percent of workers holding mobile positions, such as mechanics, inspectors, messengers, and warehouse workers, so they can send and retrieve detailed information while keeping their hands free for other tasks. The Palm OS® and Windows® CE platforms are opening opportunities for the blue-collar world, as are hardware and software advances in speech recognition, wireless headsets, and wearable computers equipped with processing power equal to that of desktop computers.

Figure 25
A fingerprint reader captures the curves and indentations of a fingerprint.

HEALTH-CARE INDUSTRY The medical industry has been recognized, in general, as being one of the last fields to integrate the Internet and high-tech solutions. Recent cuts in insurance reimbursements and federal Medicare spending have decreased revenues, resulting in budget cutting measures. Many health facilities, however, are integrating online medical-records systems, electronic medical charts, and medical literature searches. Wireless products will help improve patient care and communications; for example, some emergency room personnel use Palm handheld computers to access patients' medical records.

T-COMMERCE Television advertising is taking a new turn with the advent of t-commerce. Instead of buying commercial time, advertisers embed their ads in actual television programs (Figure 26). Viewers use their remote controls to interact with the television programs and advertisements by replying to free offers, buying items, receiving sports scores, and participating in games. The Wink service is featured on CNN, The Weather Channel, ESPN, and "The Tonight Show with Jay Leno." This form of advertisement can be termed merchantainment – a combination of merchandising and entertainment.

Figure 26
Wink Communications uses t-commerce in a variety of television programs.

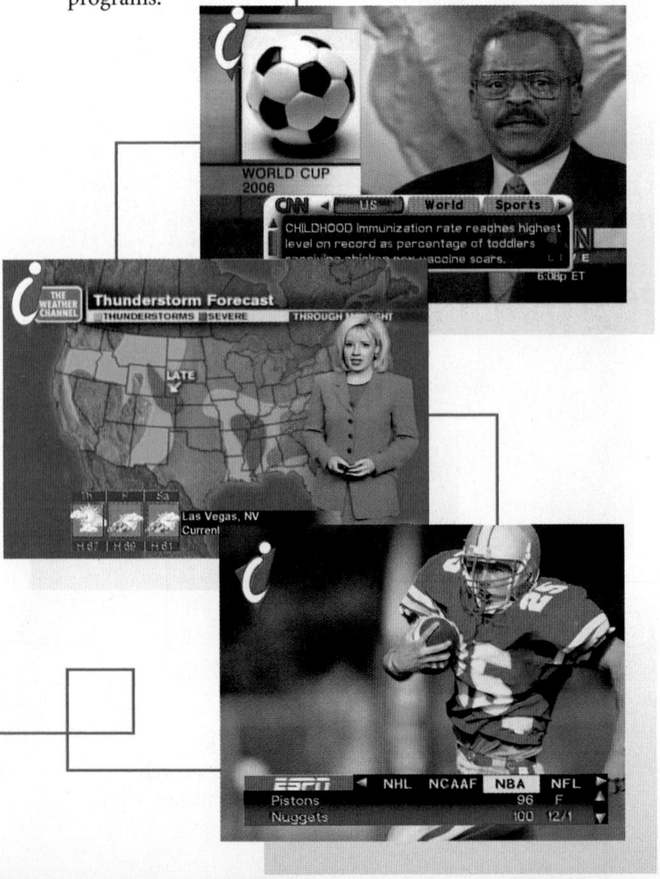

E-BUSINESS The volatile e-commerce marketplace has produced some winners and many losers. In 2000, more than one dot-com (Internet-only) company failed each day. Companies with greater successes were those with both Internet and physical presences, known as clicks-and-mortar businesses. Each year, individual and business consumers purchase more goods and services online; approximately 50 percent of Web users shop online, and the same percent of investors trade securities online. During the next few years, more e-commerce applications — and the technologies used to support them — will be developed. Many of these technologies will be focused on improving the security of and expediting credit card transactions.

FEATURE SUMMARY

Despite the surge in dot-com failures and employee layoffs in early 2001, the demand for high-tech workers continues to be extremely strong. According to the U.S. Department of Labor, more than 5.6 million new software engineers, Web programmers, optical networking specialists, programmers, and systems analysts will be needed by 2006. Indeed, amazing opportunities increase daily in the ubiquitous computer technology industry.

APPENDIX

Coding Schemes and Number Systems

CODING SCHEMES

As discussed in Chapter 4, a computer uses a coding scheme to represent characters. This section presents the ASCII, EBCDIC, and Unicode coding schemes and discusses parity.

ASCII and EBCDIC

Two widely used codes that represent characters in a computer are the ASCII and EBCDIC codes. **The American Standard Code for Information Interchange**, called ASCII (pronounced ASK-ee), is the most widely used coding system to represent data. Many personal computers and mid-range servers use ASCII. The **Extended Binary Coded Decimal Interchange Code**, or EBCDIC (pronounced EB-see-dic) is used primarily on mainframe computers. Figure A-1 summarizes these codes. Notice how the combination of bits (0s and 1s) is unique for each character.

When the ASCII or EBCDIC code is used, each character that is represented is stored in one byte of memory. Other binary formats exist, however, that the computer sometimes uses to represent numeric data. For example, a computer may store, or pack, two numeric characters in one byte of memory. The computer uses these binary formats to increase storage and processing efficiency.

Unicode

The 256 characters and symbols that are represented by ASCII and EBCDIC codes are sufficient for English and western European languages but are not large enough for Asian and other languages that use different alphabets. Further compounding the problem is that many of these languages use symbols, called **ideograms**, to represent multiple words and ideas. One solution to this situation is Unicode. **Unicode** is a 16-bit code that has the capacity of representing more than 65,000 characters and symbols.

ASCII	SYMBOL	EBCDIC
00110000	0	11110000
00110001	1	11110001
00110010	2	11110010
00110011	3	11110011
00110100	4	11110100
00110101	5	11110101
00110110	6	11110110
00110111	7	11110111
00111000	8	11111000
00111001	9	11111001
01000001	A	11000001
01000010	B	11000010
01000011	C	11000011
01000100	D	11000100
01000101	E	11000101
01000110	F	11000110
01000111	G	11000111
01001000	H	11001000
01001001	I	11001001
01001010	J	11010001
01001011	K	11010010
01001100	L	11010011
01001101	M	11010100
01001110	N	11010101
01001111	O	11010110
01010000	P	11010111
01010001	Q	11011000
01010010	R	11011001
01010011	S	11100010
01010100	T	11100011
01010101	U	11100100
01010110	V	11100101
01010111	W	11100110
01011000	X	11100111
01011001	Y	11101000
01011010	Z	11101001
00100001	!	01011010
00100010	“	01111111
00100011	#	01111011
00100100	$	01011011
00100101	%	01101100
00100110	&	01010000
00101000	(	01001101
00101001	)	01011101
00101010	*	01011100
00101011	+	01001110

Figure A-1

Unicode represents all the world's current languages using more than 34,000 characters and symbols (Figure A-2). In Unicode, 30,000 codes are reserved for future use, such as ancient languages, and 6,000 codes are reserved for private use. Existing ASCII coded data is fully compatible with Unicode because the first 256 codes are the same. Unicode currently is implemented in several operating systems, including Windows NT and OS/2, and major system developers have announced plans eventually to implement Unicode.

	041	042	043	044	045	046	047
0	А	Р	а	р		Ѡ	Ѱ
1	Б	С	б	с	ё	ѡ	ѱ
2	В	Т	в	т	ђ	Ѣ	Ѳ
3	Г	У	г	у	ѓ	ѣ	ѳ
4	Д	Ф	д	ф	є	Ѥ	Ѵ
5	Е	Х	е	х	ѕ	ѥ	ѵ
6	Ж	Ц	ж	ц	і	Ѧ	Ѷ
7	З	Ч	з	ч	ї	ѧ	ѷ
8	И	Ш	и	ш	ј	Ѩ	Ѹ
9	Й	Щ	й	щ	љ	ѩ	ѹ
A	К	Ъ	к	ъ	њ	Ѫ	Ѻ
B	Л	Ы	л	ы	ћ	ѫ	ѻ
C	М	Ь	м	ь	ќ	Ѭ	Ѽ
D	Н	Э	н	э		ѭ	ѽ
E	О	Ю	о	ю	ў	Ѯ	Ѿ
F	П	Я	п	я	џ	ѯ	ѿ

Figure A-2

Parity

Regardless of whether ASCII, EBCDIC, or other binary methods are used to represent characters in memory, it is important that the characters be stored accurately. For each byte of memory, most computers have at least one extra bit, called a **parity bit**, that is used by the computer for error checking. A parity bit can detect if one of the bits in a byte has been changed inadvertently. While such errors are extremely rare (most computers never have a parity error during their lifetime), they can occur because of voltage fluctuations, static electricity, or a memory failure.

Computers are either odd- or even-parity machines. In computers with odd parity, the total number of on bits in the byte (including the parity bit) must be an odd number. In computers with even parity, the total number of on bits must be an even number (Figure A-3). The computer checks parity each time it uses a memory location. When the computer moves data from one location to another in memory, it compares the parity bits of both the sending and receiving locations to see if they are the same. If the system detects a difference or if the wrong number of bits is on (e.g., an odd number in a system with even parity), an error message displays. Many computers use multiple parity bits that enable them to detect and correct a single-bit error and detect multiple-bit errors.

NUMBER SYSTEMS

This section describes the number systems that are used with computers. Whereas thorough knowledge of this subject is required for technical computer personnel, a general understanding of number systems and how they relate to computers is all most users need.

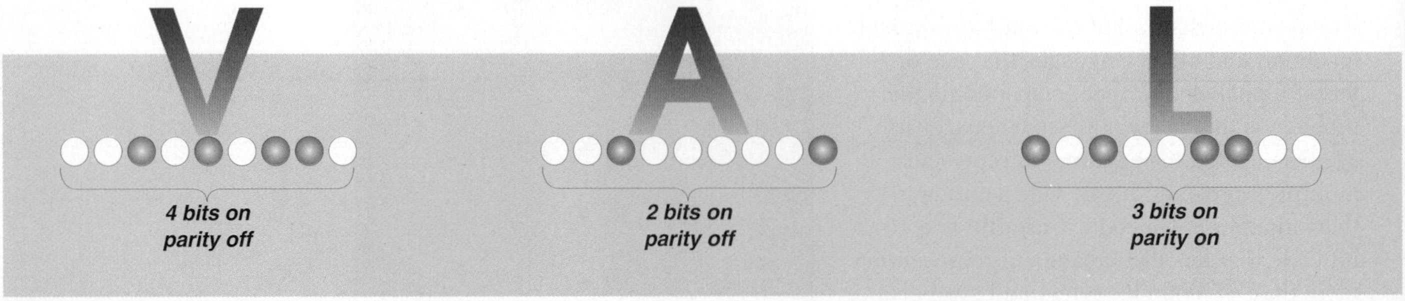

Figure A-3

The binary (base 2) number system is used to represent the electronic status of the bits in memory. It also is used for other purposes such as addressing the memory locations. Another number system that commonly is used with computers is **hexadecimal** (base 16). The computer uses the hexadecimal system to communicate with a programmer when a problem with a program exists, because it would be difficult for the programmer to understand the 0s and 1s of binary code. Figure A-4 shows how the decimal values 0 through 15 are represented in binary and hexadecimal.

The mathematical principles that apply to the binary and hexadecimal number systems are the same as those that apply to the decimal number system. To help you better understand these principles, this section starts with the familiar decimal system, then progresses to the binary and hexadecimal number systems.

DECIMAL	BINARY	HEXADECIMAL
0	0000	0
1	0001	1
2	0010	2
3	0011	3
4	0100	4
5	0101	5
6	0110	6
7	0111	7
8	1000	8
9	1001	9
10	1010	A
11	1011	B
12	1100	C
13	1101	D
14	1110	E
15	1111	F

Figure A-4

The Decimal Number System

The decimal number system is a base 10 number system (deci means ten). The base of a number system indicates how many symbols are used in it. The decimal number system uses 10 symbols: 0 through 9. Each of the symbols in the number system has a value associated with it. For example, 3 represents a quantity of three and 5 represents a quantity of five.

The decimal number system also is a positional number system. This means that in a number such as 143, each position in the number has a value associated with it. When you look at the decimal number 143, the 3 is in the ones, or units, position and represents three ones or (3 x 1); the 4 is in the tens position and represents four tens or (4 x 10); and the 1 is in the hundreds position and represents one hundred or (1 x 100). The number 143 is the sum of the values in each position of the number (100 + 40 + 3 = 143). The chart in Figure A-5 shows how you can calculate the positional values (hundreds, tens, and units) for a number system. Starting on the right and working to the left, the base of the number system, in this case 10, is raised to consecutive powers (10^0, 10^1, 10^2). These calculations are a mathematical way of determining the place values in a number system.

When you use number systems other than decimal, the same principles apply. The base of the number system indicates the number of symbols that are used, and each position in a number system has a value associated with it. By raising the base of the number system to consecutive powers beginning with zero, you can calculate the positional value.

power of 10	10^2	10^1	10^0
positional value	100	10	1
number	1	4	3

1 4 3 =

$(1 \times 10^2) + (4 \times 10^1) + (3 \times 10^0) =$

$(1 \times 100) + (4 \times 10) + (3 \times 1) =$

$100 + 40 + 3 = 143$

Figure A-5

The Binary Number System

As previously discussed, binary is a base 2 number system (bi means two), and the symbols it uses are 0 and 1. Just as each position in a decimal number has a place value associated with it, so does each position in a binary number. In binary, the place values, moving from right to left, are successive powers of two (2^0, 2^1, 2^2, 2^3) or (1, 2, 4, 8). To construct a binary number, you place ones in the positions where the corresponding values add up to the quantity you want to represent; you place zeros in the other positions. For example, in a four-digit binary number, the binary place values are (from right to left) 1, 2, 4, and 8. The binary number 1001 has ones in the positions for the values 1 and 8 and zeros in the positions for 2 and 4. Therefore, the quantity represented by binary 1001 is 9 (8 + 0 + 0 + 1) (Figure A-6).

The Hexadecimal Number System

The hexadecimal number system uses 16 symbols to represent values (hex means six, deci means ten). These include the symbols 0 through 9 and A through F (Figure A-4 on page A.3). The mathematical principles previously discussed also apply to hexadecimal (Figure A-7).

The primary reason why the hexadecimal number system is used with computers is because it can represent binary values in a more compact and readable form and because the conversion between the binary and the hexadecimal number systems is very efficient.

An eight-digit binary number (a byte) can be represented by a two-digit hexadecimal number. For example, in the ASCII code, the character M is represented as 01001101. This value can be represented in hexadecimal as 4D. One way to convert this binary number (4D) to a hexadecimal number is to divide the binary number (from right to left) into groups of four digits; calculate the value of each group; and then change any two-digit values (10 through 15) into the symbols A through F that are used in hexadecimal (Figure A-8).

Figure A-6

power of 2	2^3	2^2	2^1	2^0
positional value	8	4	2	1
binary	1	0	0	1

$$1 \quad 0 \quad 0 \quad 1 =$$
$$(1 \times 2^3) + (0 \times 2^2) + (0 \times 2^1) + (1 \times 2^0) =$$
$$(1 \times 8) + (0 \times 4) + (0 \times 2) + (1 \times 1) =$$
$$8 + 0 + 0 + 1 = 9$$

power of 16	16^1	16^0
positional value	16	1
hexadecimal	A	5

$$A \quad 5 =$$
$$(10 \times 16^1) + (5 \times 16^0) =$$
$$(10 \times 16) + (5 \times 1) =$$
$$160 + 5 = 165$$

Figure A-7

positional value	8421	8421
binary	0100	1101
decimal	4	13
hexadecimal	4	D

Figure A-8

INDEX

Exit point: Location where a program, module, or control structure ends. **15.8**
Expansion board: Circuit board that fits in an expansion slot. **4.23**
Expansion bus: Bus that allows the processor to communicate with peripheral devices. **4.30**-32
Expansion card: Circuit board that fits in an expansion slot; examples are a video card, sound card, network interface card, or modem card. 4.4, **4.23**-25
Expansion slot: Opening, or socket in the motherboard, into which a circuit board can be inserted, such as additional memory, higher-quality sound devices, a modem, or graphics capabilities. **4.23**
Expert system: Management information system that captures and stores the knowledge of human experts and then imitates human reasoning and decision making. **13.40**
Exposed drive bay, *see* External drive bay
Extended Binary Coded Decimal Interchange Code (EBCDIC): Coding system used primarily on mainframe computers. **4.14**
External cache, *see* Level 2 (L2) cache
External drive bay: Drive bay that allows access to the drive from outside the system unit; also called exposed drive bay. **4.32**
External modem: Modem that is a stand-alone (separate) device that attaches to a special serial port on a computer with a standard telephone cord connected to a telephone outlet. **9.28**
External sources: Sources of data from outside a company. **13.37**
Extranet: Network that allows customers or suppliers to access part of a company's extranet. **9.20**
Eyes
computer vision syndrome and, 11.31
iris recognition system, 12.12
E-zine: A publication available on the Web used as a research resource by systems analysts when identifying technical specifications for the new or modified system; the information can be located quickly and easily. Also called electronic magazine. **14.22**

Face recognition system: Biometric device that captures a live face image and compares it to a stored image to authenticate a user. **12.11**
Facsimile (fax) machine: Device that transmits and receives documents over telephone lines. Standalone fax machines scan an original document, convert the image into digitized data, and transmit the digitized image to a receiving fax, while fax modems send and receive electronic documents from a computer as faxes. **6.25**-26
Fair Credit Reporting Act: Federal law passed in 1970 that limits the rights of others viewing a credit report to those with a legitimate business need. The law has a loophole in that it does not define a legitimate need, resulting in just about anyone being able to say they have a legitimate need and gain access to a credit report. **12.33**
Fanning, Shawn, 1.30
FAQs (Frequently Asked Questions): Page that assists a user in finding answers to common questions. **3.36**
FAQs: Stands for frequently asked questions. **2.37**
Fast Ethernet: Ethernet standard that transmits data and information at speeds up to 10 times faster than the original standard. **9.19**
Fault-tolerant computer: Computer that continues to operate even if one of its components fails. **8.9**
Fax: Document that can contain handwritten or typed text, illustrations, photographs, or other graphics. **9.5**
Fax machine, *see* Facsimile (fax) machine
Fax modem: Modem used to send (and sometimes receive) electronic documents as faxes. **6.26**
Feasibility: Measure of how suitable the development of a system will be to the company. Feasibility is tested using these criteria: operational feasibility, schedule feasibility, technical feasibility, and economic feasibility. **14.6**
Feasibility assessment, 14.6-7
Feasibility report, 14.14
Feasibility study: Occurs during the analysis phase of the SDLC, an investigation by the systems analyst to decide whether the problem or improvement identified in a project request is worth pursuing. Also called preliminary investigation. **14.13**
Female connector: Connector that has matching holes to accept the pins on a male connector, similar to an electrical wall outlet. **4.26**
Fetching: Control unit operation that obtains a program instruction or data item from memory; part of the machine cycle. **4.5**
Fiber-optic cable: Transmission medium whose core consists of dozens or hundreds of thin strands of glass or plastic that use light to transmit signals. **9.34**
Field: Column in a table that contains a specific piece of information within a record. **3.16, 13.4**
Field camera: Portable digital camera that has many lenses and other attachments, often used by photojournalists. **5.19**
Field name: Unique identifier for a field. **13.4**
Field size: The maximum number of characters that a particular field can contain. **3.16, 13.5**
Fifth-generation language (5GL): Programming language that provides a visual or graphical interface for creating the source code; often converting the source code to machine language using a 3GL or 4GL compiler. **15.20**
File: Named collection of data, instructions, or information. **3.10**
backup, *see* Backup
graphics, 2.18
network management, 9.12
security and, 12.26
File (database), *see* Data file
File allocation table (FAT): Table of information that the operating system uses to locate files on a disk. **8.15**
File compression utility: Utility program that shrinks the size of a file. **8.28**
File maintenance: Procedures that keep data current. Also called data maintenance. **13.6**-10
File manager: Operating system program that performs functions related to storage and file management. **8.14**
File name: Unique combination of letters of the alphabet, numbers, and other characters that identifies a file. **3.10**
File processing environment, 13.13
File processing system: System used to store and manage data that involves each department or area within an organization having its own set of files, often creating data redundancy and data isolation. **13.11**
File server: Server that stores and manages files. **9.14**
File viewer: Utility program used to display and copy the contents of a file. **8.27**
File virus: Virus that attaches itself to program files. When the infected program is run, the virus loads into memory. Sometimes called a program virus. 12.2, **12.4**
Filo, David, 2.17
Finance, 11.14-16
Financial institutions, e-commerce and, 10.14
Financial management, for home users, 11.3
Find or search: Feature that locates all occurrences of a certain character, word, or phrase. **3.9**
network agent, 11.29
shopping online and, 10.15
Fingerprint scanner: Biometric device that captures curves and indentations of a fingerprint. **12.11**
FIR (fast infrared): High-speed IrDA port. **4.29**
Firewall: Security system consisting of hardware and/or software that prevents unauthorized access to data and information on a network. **9.20**, 9.29, **12.24**
network, 12.25
personal, 12.5, 12.23, 12.25
FireWire, *see* 1394 port
Firmware: ROM chips that contain permanently written data, instructions, or information, recorded on the chips when they are manufactured. **4.20**
Fixed disk: Hard disk inside the system unit of a desktop personal computer. **7.10**
Flame wars: Exchanges of flames. **2.37**
Flames: Abusive or insulting messages sent over the Internet. **2.37**
Flash BIOS: Type of BIOS that allows a computer easily to update the contents of the BIOS chip, if necessary. **4.21**
Flash memory cards: Removable device used in handheld computers and devices that stores flash memory, allowing the convenient transfer of data from those devices to a desktop computer. **4.21,** 4.25
Flash memory: Type of nonvolatile memory that can be erased electronically and reprogrammed; also known as flash ROM or flash RAM. 4.10, **4.21**
Flash RAM, *see* Flash memory
Flash ROM, *see* Flash memory
Flatbed scanner: Scanner that works similar to a copy machine except it creates a file of a document in memory instead of a paper copy. **5.25**
Flat-panel display: Display used by devices such as LCD monitors and LCD displays, using a lightweight, compact screen that consumes less than one-third of the power of a CRT monitor, making it ideal for mobile users or users with space limitations. **6.5**
Flip chip-PGA (FC-PGA) package: Higher-performance PGA chip package that places the chip on the opposite side (flip side) of the pins. **4.4**
Floating-point coprocessor: Coprocessor used to speed up engineering, scientific, or graphics applications; sometimes called a math or numeric coprocessor. **4.13**
Floppy disk: Portable, inexpensive storage medium that consists of a thin, circular, flexible plastic disk with a magnetic coating enclosed in a square-shaped plastic shell. Also called diskette. 1.7, 7.4, **7.6**-9
capacity of, 7.5, 7, 8
formatting, 8.15
viruses and, 3.4, 12.5
Floppy disk drive (FDD): Device that can read from and write on a floppy disk. 1.7, **7.6**
Flowchart: Design tool that graphically shows the logic in a solution algorithm, using symbols that represent various operations in a program's logic. Also called program flowchart. **15.9**
Flowcharting software: Software used to develop flowcharts that makes them easy to modify and update. **15.10**
Font: Name assigned to a specific design of characters. **3.10**
Font size: The size of the characters in a particular font, gauged by a measurement system called points. **3.10**
Font style: Emphasis added to a font, such as **bold**, *italic*, and underline. **3.10**
Footer: Text that appears at the bottom of each page. **3.9**
Foreground: When running multiple applications, describes the active application. **8.9**
Form: Window on a screen that provides areas for entering or changing data in a database. Sometimes called a data entry form. **13.17**
Formalizing solution, 15.15
Format: Process of changing a document's appearance. **3.10**
Formatting: Process of preparing a disk for reading and writing, usually performed in advance by floppy and hard disk manufacturers. **7.8, 8.15**
Formula: Group of symbols that performs calculations on data in a worksheet and displays the resulting value in a cell. **3.12**
Fortezza: Public key encryption technology that stores a user's private key and other information on a PC Card. **12.17**

Wide area network (WAN): Network that covers a large geographic area (such as a city, country, or the world) using a communications channel that combines many types of media such as telephone lines, cables, and air waves. A WAN can be one large network or can consist of two or more LANs connected together. The Internet is the world's largest WAN. 1.16, 1.33, **9.14**
Window: Rectangular area of the screen that displays a program, data, and/or information. **3.6**
Windows: Microsoft operating system with a graphical user interface. 1.9, 1.20, **8.18**
desktop, 3.4-5
features of, 8.19
graphical user interface, 1.12
starting computer and, 8.6
UNIX vs., 8.25
Windows 2000 Advanced Server: Microsoft operating system designed for e-commerce applications. **8.22**
Windows 2000 Datacenter Server: Microsoft operating system used for demanding, large-scale applications such as data warehousing. **8.22**
Windows 2000 (MCSE), 16.20
Windows 2000 Professional: Upgrade to Windows NT Workstation operating system that is a complete multitasking client operating system that has GUI. **8.18**
Windows 2000 Server: Microsoft operating system that is an upgrade to Windows NT Server, used for a typical business network. **8.22**
Windows 2000 Server family: Microsoft operating system products that meet various levels of server requirements; include Windows 2000 Server, Windows 2000 Advanced Server, and Windows 2000 Datacenter Server. **8.22**
Windows 3.x: Three early versions of Microsoft Windows: Windows 3.0, Windows 3.1, and Windows 3.11 that were operating environments, not operating systems. **8.18**
Windows 95: Microsoft multitasking operating system, written to be a true operating system and take advantage of the processing speed in 32-bit processors. **8.18**
Windows 98: Microsoft operating system that was an upgrade to Windows 95 and was more integrated with the Internet, provided faster system startup and shutdown, better file management, and support for multimedia technologies and the Universal Serial Bus (USB). **8.18**
Windows-based applications programming, 15.22
Windows CE: Scaled-down Windows operating system designed for use on wireless communications devices and smaller computers. **8.25**
Windows Explorer: Windows 98 file manager. **8.18**
WINDOWS key, 5.5
Windows Me, *see* Windows Millennium Edition
Windows Millennium Edition: Upgrade to Windows 98 operating system that has features specifically for the home user; also called Windows Me. **8.20**
Windows NT: Microsoft operating system designed for client/server networks; also called NT. **8.18**
Windows NT Server: Microsoft operating system for the server in client/server networks. **8.22**
Windows NT Workstation: Microsoft client operating system that could connect to a Windows NT Server. **8.18**
WinZip, 8.28
Wireless advertising, 9.38
Wireless Application Protocol (WAP): Communications protocol that allows wireless mobile devices to access the Internet and its services such as the Web and e-mail, using a client/server network. **15.38**
wireless designer, 16.4
Wireless LAN (WLAN): LAN that connects using wireless media such as radio waves. **9.12**, 9.36
Wireless modem: Modem that accesses the Web wirelessly from mobile devices, typically by using the same waves used by cellular telephones. **9.28**
Wireless mouse, *see* Cordless mouse
Wireless portal: Portal specifically designed for Web-enabled handheld computers and devices. **2.17**
Wireless service provider (WSP): Company that provides wireless Internet access to users with wireless modems or Web-enabled handheld computers or devices. **2.6**
Wireless transmission media: Media that sends communications signals through the air or space using radio, microwave, and infrared signals. **9.32**, 9.34-39
Wizard: Automated assistant used to complete a task by asking a user questions and then automatically performing actions based on the answers; included in many software applications. **3.37**
WML (wireless markup language): A subset of the XML Web development language that allows Web page developers to design pages specifically for microbrowsers, such as Web-enabled handheld computers, cellular telephones, and pagers. **15.38**
World Wide Web Consortium, 15.38
Woofer: Audio output device that produces low bass sounds. **6.23**
Word processing software, 3.8-9
Word processing software: One of the most widely used types of application software; allows users to create and manipulate documents that contain text and graphics. Sometimes called a word processor. **3.8**
Word processing technician, 3.37
Word processor, *see* Word processing software
Word size: The number of bits a processor can interpret and execute at a given time. **4.30**
Word wrap: Automatic positioning of text by a program at the beginning of the next line, if text is typed that extends beyond the right page margin. **3.9**
Workplace
computers in, 1.3
healthy environment at, 11.30-33
See also Ergonomics
Workgroup computing: Network hardware and software that enables group members to communicate, manage projects, schedule meetings, and make group decisions. **9.10**
Worksheet: The collection of rows and columns in a spreadsheet. **3.12**
Workstation: More expensive and powerful desktop computer designed for work that requires intense calculations and graphics capabilities. **1.21**
processors, 4.10
World Wide Web (WWW): Also called the Web, a worldwide collection of electronic documents. **2.9**-24
audio, 6.3
databases, 13.28-29
graphics, 6.3
home users, 1.29, 11.3, 11.4-5
multimedia on, 2.18-22
operating system and, 8.13
processors and, 4.11
searching for information on, 2.14-15
selling on, 1.37
See also Internet
World Wide Web Consortium (W3C): Group that oversees research and sets standards and guidelines for many areas of the Internet. **2.4**
Worm: Malicious-logic program that copies itself repeatedly in memory or on a disk drive until no memory or disk space remains, causing the computer to stop working. **12.4**
Wozniak, Stephen, 8.21, 11.5
Write-protect notch: Small opening on a floppy disk with a tab that slides to cover or expose the notch, used to protect the floppy disk from being accidentally erased. **7.9**
Writing: Process of transferring data, instructions, and information from memory to a storage medium. **7.4**
Xeon™: Intel processor used in workstations and low-end servers. **4.10**
XHTML (eXtensible HTML): Web development language that includes features of HTML and XML. **15.37**
XML (eXtensible Markup Language): Web development language that enables Web page developers to create customized tags and makes it possible to define a link that points to multiple Web sites instead of a single site. **15.37**
XSL (eXtensible Stylesheet Language): Used by XML as its style sheet specification. **15.37**

Y2K Bug: Bug that had the potential to cause serious financial losses for computers around the world. The bug took effect when the computer date rolled over to January 1, 2000. At that time, non-Y2K compliant computers read the date as 01/01/00. Computers that used just the last two digits of a year could not distinguish 01/01/1900 from 01/01/2000, which caused some computer hardware and software to operate according to the wrong date. Also called millennium bug. **15.14**
Yahoo, 2.17
Yahoo! Store, 10.21
Yang, Jerry, 2.17, 16.13
Yes/No data type, 13.5
Yourdon, Ed, 14.15

Zero-insertion force (ZIF) socket: Socket on a motherboard with a small lever or screw that facilitates the installation and removal of processor chips; used by many PGA (pin grid array) chips. **4.12**
Ziff Davis Media, 14.9
Zip® disk: 100 MB or 250 MB disk that is read from and written on using a Zip® drive. 1.7, **7.10**
viruses and, 3.4
Zip® drive: High-capacity disk drive developed by Iomega that reads from and writes on a 100 MB or 250 MB Zip® disk. 7.9, **7.10**
Zipped files: Compressed files that have a .zip extension. **8.28**

PHOTO CREDITS

Chapter 1: *Chapter opener Figures* Courtesy of Microsoft Corporation; IBM and the IBM Logo are Trademarks of International Business Machines Corporation. Courtesy of International Business Machines Corporation; AP/ Wide World Photos; Gateway and the Gateway stylized logo are trademarks of Gateway, Inc. Courtesy of Gateway, Inc.; *Figure 1-1a* Michael Newman/PhotoEdit; *Figure 1-1b* David Young-Wolff/ PhotoEdit; *Figure 1-1c (c)* Bob Daemmrich/The Image Works; *Figure 1-1d* Hunter Freeman/Stone; *Figure 1-1e (c)* Thomas Schweizer/The Stock Market; *Figure 1-2* Courtesy of ADP; *Figure 1-3a* Courtesy of International Business Machines Corporation; *Figure 1-3b* Courtesy of Intel Corporation; *Figure 1-3c* Courtesy of Labtec, Inc.; *Figure 1-3d* Courtesy of Gateway, Inc.; *Figure 1-3e* Courtesy of Eastman Kodak Company; *Figure 1-3f* Courtesy of Thomson Multimedia; *Figure 1-3g* Courtesy of Microsoft Corporation; *Figure 1-3h* Courtesy of Labtec, Inc.; *Figure 1-4a* Courtesy of Intel Corporation; *Figure 1-4b* Courtesy of Advanced Micro Devices, Inc.; *Figure 1-4c* Courtesy of Intel Corporation; *Figure 1-4d* Courtesy of Intel Corporation; *Figure 1-4e* Phil A. Harrington/Peter Arnold, Inc.; *Figure 1-4f* PhotoDisc; *Figure 1-5* Scott Goodwin Photography; *Figure 1-6* Courtesy of Seagate Technology; *Figure 1-7* Courtesy of Iomega Corporation; *Figure 1-8* Scott Goodwin Photography; *Figure 1-9* Courtesy of Eastman Kodak Company; *Figure 1-11* Scott Goodwin Photography; *Figure 1-14* Scott Goodwin Photography; *Figure 1-21* Courtesy of International Business Machines Corporation; *Figure 1-22* Courtesy of Apple Computer, Inc.; *Figure 1-23a* Courtesy of Toshiba America Information Systems, Inc.; *Figure 1-23b* Courtesy of Toshiba America Information Systems, Inc.; *Figure 1-24a* Courtesy of Gateway, Inc.; *Figure 1-24b* Courtesy of Apple Computer, Inc.; *Figure 1-26* Courtesy of Dell Computer; *Figure 1-27* Courtesy of Hewlett Packard Company; *Figure 1-28* Fisher/Thatcher/Stone; *Figure 1-29a* Courtesy of Compaq Computer Corporation; *Figure 1-29b* Courtesy of Nokia; *Figure 1-29c* Scott Goodwin Photography; *Figure 1-30* Courtesy of Intel Corporation; *Figure 1-31* Courtesy of Thomson Multimedia; *Figure 1-32* Courtesy of Hewlett Packard Company; *Figure 1-33* Courtesy of International Business Machines Corporation; *Figure 1-34* Courtesy of International Business Machines Corporation; *Figure 1-36a* PhotoDisc; *Figure 1-36b* PhotoDisc; *Figure 1-36c* Corbis; *Figure 1-36d* PhotoDisc; *Figure 1-36e* Bob Daemmrich/Stock Boston; *Figure 1-38* PhotoEdit; *Figure 1-40a* Corbis; *Figure 1-40b* Bob Daemmrich/Stock Boston; *Figure 1-40c* Courtesy of Nokia; *Figure 1-40d* David Young Wolff/PhotoEdit; *Figure 1-40e* Paul Barton/The Stock Market; *Figure 1-43* Courtesy of Kiosk Information Systems, Inc.; *Figure 1-44* Zigy Kaluzny/Stone; *Figure 1-45a* Bob Daemmrich/Stock Boston; *Figure 1-45b* Linda Phillips/Photo Researchers, Inc.; *Figure 1-45c* Frank Pedrick/The Image Works; *Figure 1-45d* James King-Holmes/Science Photo Library/Photo Researchers, Inc.; *Figure 1-46* Walter Hodges/Stone; **Timeline** 1937 Courtesy of Iowa State University; 1943 The Computer Museum History Center; 1945 Courtesy of the Institute for Advanced Studies; 1946 Courtesy of the University of Pennsylvania Archives; 1947 Courtesy of International Business Machines Corporation; 1951 Courtesy of Unisys Corporation; 1952 Hagley Museum and Library; 1953 Courtesy of M.I.T. Archives; 1957 Courtesy of International Business Machines Corporation; 1957 Courtesy of the Deparment of the Navy; 1958 Courtesy of M.I.T. Archives; 1959 Courtesy of International Business Machines Corporation; 1960 Hagley Museum and Library; 1964 Courtesy of International Business Machines Corporation; 1965 Courtesy of Dartmouth College News Service; 1965 Courtesy of Digital Equipment Corporation; 1970 Courtesy of International Business Machines Corporation; 1971 Courtesy of Intel Corporation; 1975 Courtesy of InfoWorld; 1975 The Computer Museum History Center; 1976 Courtesy of Apple Computer, Inc.; 1979 The Computer Museum History Center; 1980 Courtesy of International Business Machines Corporation; 1980 Courtesy of Microsoft Corporation; 1981 Courtesy of International Business Machines Corporation; 1983 Courtesy of Lotus Development Corporation; 1983 (c) 1982 Time Inc.; 1984 Courtesy of International Business Machines Corporation; 1984 Courtesy of Apple Computer, Inc.; 1984 Courtesy of Hewlett Packard Company; 1987 Courtesy of International Business Machines Corporation; 1989 Courtesy of Intel Corporation; 1989 Courtesy (c) 1997-1998 W3C (MIT,INRIA, Keio). All rights reserved; 1992 Courtesy of Microsoft Corporation; 1993 Courtesy of Intel Corporation; 1993 Jim Clark/ The Liaison Agency; 1993 Courtesy of Netscape Communications Corporation; 1994 Courtesy of Netscape Communications Corporation; 1995 Courtesy of Sun Microsystems, Inc.; 1995 Courtesy of Microsoft Corporation; 1996 Courtesy of Palm Computing, Inc.; 1996 Courtesy of Microsoft Corporation; 1996 Reuters/Rick T. Wilking/Archive Photos; 1996 Courtesy of WebTV Networks Inc.; 1997 I. Uimonen/CORBIS Sygma; 1997 Motion Picture & Television Archives; 1997 Courtesy of Denon Electronics; 1997 Courtesy of International Business Machines Corporation; 1998 Courtesy of Microsoft Corporation; 1998 Courtesy of Apple Computer, Inc.; 1999 Courtesy of Microsoft Corporation; 2000 Courtesy of Microsoft Corporation; 2000 Courtesy of Intel Corporation; 2001 Courtesy of RCA; **Chapter 2:** *Chapter opener Figures* Courtesy of Yahoo!, Inc.; Courtesy of America Online, Inc.; AP/Wide World Photos; Courtesy of Max Ramirez (c) 2000; AP/ Wide World Photos; *Figure 2-3b* Courtesy of Juniper Networks, Inc.; *Figure 2-8a* Scott Goodwin Photography; *Figure 2-8b* Courtesy of Motorola, Inc.; *Figure 2-18a* Courtesy of RCA; *Figure 2-18b* AP/Wide World Photos; *Figure 2-23* PhotoDisc; *Figure 2-26* PhotoDisc; *Figure 2-28* Courtesy of Juniper Networks, Inc.; *Figure 2-29* Jeff Zaruba/The Stock Market; **Chapter 3:** *Chapter opener Figures* (c) 1999 Kathleen King; Courtesy of Dan Bricklin; Courtesy of Microsoft Corporation; Courtesy of Adobe Systems, Inc.; *Figure 3-2* Courtesy of International Business Machines Corporation; *Figure 3-2* Figure Courtesy of Compaq Computer Corporation; *Figure 3-24* Courtesy of Microsoft Corporation; *Figure 3-27* Courtesy of Autodesk's Manufacturing Division; *Figure 3-29* Courtesy of Adobe Systems, Inc.; *Figure 3-30 (c)* Luke Wolbach; *Figure 3-31* Courtesy of click2learn; *Figure 3-33* Courtesy of Intuit; *Figure 3-34* Courtesy of Nolo Software; *Figure 3-35* Courtesy of Intuit; *Figure 3-39* Courtesy of Broderbund; *Figure 3-45* Courtesy of Metier Ltd.; *Figure 3-47* Scott Goodwin Photography; *Figure 3-48* Jose L. Pelaez/The Stock Market; **Chapter 4:** *Chapter opener Figures* Courtesy of Intel Corporation; Courtesy of Advanced Micro Devices, Inc.; Courtesy of Intel Corporation; Courtesy of Intel Corporation; *Figure 4-1a* Courtesy of Gateway, Inc.; *Figure 4-1b* Courtesy of Gateway, Inc.; *Figure 4-1c* Courtesy of International Business Machines Corporation; *Figure 4-1d* Courtesy of Palm, Inc.; *Figure 4-2a* Courtesy of Intel Corporation; *Figure 4-2b* Courtesy of Kingston Technology, Inc.; *Figure 4-2c* Courtesy of SMC Corporation; *Figure 4-2d* Courtesy of ATI Technologies, Inc.; *Figure 4-2g* Courtesy of the author; *Figure 4-3* Scott Goodwin Photography; *Figure 4-4a* Courtesy of Intel Corporation; *Figure 4-4b* PhotoDisc; *Figure 4-4c* Courtesy of Intel Corporation; *Figure 4-4d* Phil A. Harrington/ Peter Arnold, Inc.; *Figure 4-4e* Courtesy of Advanced Micro Devices, Inc.; *Figure 4-9a* Courtesy of Advanced Micro Devices, Inc.; *Figure 4-9b* Courtesy of Intel Corporation; *Figure 4-9b* Courtesy of Advanced Micro Devices, Inc.; *Figure 4-9d* Courtesy of Intel Corporation; *Figure 4-12* Scott Goodwin Photography; *Figure 4-18* George Schiavone/The Stock Market; *Figure 4-21* Scott Goodwin Photography; *Figure 4-25* Courtesy of Intel Corporation; *Figure 4-29* Scott Goodwin Photography; *Figure 4-30* Scott Goodwin Photography; *Figure 4-31* Courtesy of Sandisk, Inc.; *Figure 4-33* Courtesy of the author; *Figure 4-37* Courtesy of the author; *Figure 4-38* Courtesy of Hewlett Packard Company; *Figure 4-39* Courtesy of Intel Corporation; *Figure 4-42* Courtesy of the author; *Figure 4-43a* Scott Goodwin Photography; *Figure 4-43b* Courtesy of Handspring, Inc.; *Figure 4-44* Scott Goodwin Photography; *Figure 4-45* Scott Goodwin Photography; *Figure 4-46* Courtesy of Compaq Computer Corporation; *Figure 4-47a* PhotoDisc; *Figure 4-47b* PhotoDisc; *Figure 4-47c* Corbis; *Figure 4-47d* PhotoDisc; *Figure 4-47e* Bob Daemmrich/Stock Boston; *Figure 4-48* AP/Wide World Photos; **Chapter 5:** *Chapter opener Figures* Courtesy of Logitech, Inc.; Courtesy of Palm, Inc.; Courtesy of Handspring, Inc.; Courtesy of Doug Englebart; (c) Carol J. Kaelson and Robert Pearcy of Animals/Animals; *Figure 5-1a* PhotoDisc; *Figure 5-1b* Dick Blume/The Image Works; *Figure 5-1c* Dan Bosler/Stone; *Figure 5-1d* Michael Newman/PhotoEdit; *Figure 5-1e* David Young Wolff/PhotoEdit; *Figure 5-1f* PhotoDisc; *Figure 5-2* Courtesy of Compaq Computer Corporation; *Figure 5-3* Courtesy of Logitech, Inc.; *Figure 5-6a* Courtesy of Toshiba America Information Systems, Inc.; *Figure 5-6b* Courtesy of Hewlett Packard Company; *Figure 5-7* Courtesy of Think Outside, Inc.; *Figure 5-8* Courtesy of Microsoft Corporation; *Figure 5-10* Scott Goodwin Photography; *Figure 5-13* Scott Goodwin Photography; *Figure 5-14* Scott Goodwin Photography; *Figure 5-15* Scott Goodwin Photography; *Figure 5-16* Courtesy of Microsoft Corporation; *Figure 5-17* Courtesy of Fastpoint Technologies; *Figure 5-18* AP/ Wide World Photos; *Figure 5-19a* Michael Newman/PhotoEdit; *Figure 5-19b* PhotoDisc; *Figure 5-20* Courtesy of Wacom Technology Corporation; *Figure 5-21a* AP/ Wide World Photos; *Figure 5-21b* Raquel Ramirez/PhotoEdit; *Figure 5-23* David Hanover/Stone; *Figure 5-24* Courtesy of Handspring, Inc.; *Figure 5-25a* Courtesy of Palm, Inc; *Figure 5-25b* Courtesy of Palm. Inc.; *Figure 5-25c* Courtesy of Think Outside, Inc.; *Figure 5-25d* Courtesy of Eastman Kodak Company; *Figure 5-26a* Courtesy of Casio, Inc.; *Figure 5-26b* Courtesy of Eastman Kodak Company; *Figure 5-29* Courtesy of Intel Corporation; *Figure 5-30* Courtesy of Intel Corporation; *Figure 5-32* Steven Peters/Stone; *Figure 5-34a* Courtesy of Microtek Lab, Inc.; *Figure 5-34c* Courtesy of Visioneer, Inc.; *Figure 5-34d* Courtesy of Howtek, Inc.; *Figure 5-36* Scott Goodwin Photography; *Figure 5-37* Courtesy of Scantron; *Figure 5-38a* Scott Goodwin Photography; *Figure 5-38b* Chuck Savage/The Stock Market; *Figure 5-38c* Tony Freeman/PhotoEdit; *Figure 5-41* Scott Goodwin Photography; *Figure 5-42* Courtesy of Psion; *Figure 5-43* Courtesy of Orcca Technologies, Inc.; *Figure 5-45* Courtesy of Prentke Romich Company; *Figure 5-46a* PhotoDisc; *Figure 5-46b* PhotoDisc; *Figure 5-46c* Corbis; *Figure 5-46d* PhotoDisc; *Figure 5-46e* Bob Daemmrich/Stock Boston; *Figure 5-47* David Young-Wolff/PhotoEdit; **Chapter 6:** *Chapter opener Figures* Courtesy of Hewlett Packard Company; Courtesy of Hewlett Packard Company; Motorola and the Motorola logo are registered trademarks of Motorola, Inc. Courtesy of Motorola, Inc.; Courtesy of Heidi Van Arnem; Scott Goodwin Photography; *Figure 6-1b* Courtesy of Eastman Kodak Company; *Figure 6-1c* Courtesy of ViewSonics Corporation; *Figure 6-1d* Courtesy of Hewlett Packard Company; *Figure 6-1e* Courtesy of ViewSonics Corporation; *Figure 6-2* Courtesy of ViewSonics Corporation; *Figure 6-3* Courtesy of InFocus Corporation; *Figure 6-4* Courtesy of ViewSonics Corporation; *Figure 6-5a* Courtesy of International Business Machines Corporation; *Figure 6-5b* Courtesy of Compaq Computer Corporation; *Figure 6-6* Courtesy of Motorola, Inc.; *Figure 6-7* Courtesy of RCA; *Figure 6-8* Courtesy of Fujitsu General America, Fujitsu Plasmavision SlimScreen (r) ; *Figure 6-10* Courtesy of ATI Technologies,Inc.; *Figure 6-16a* Courtesy of Nokia; *Figure 6-16a* Courtesy of Nokia; *Figure 6-16b* Courtesy of Hewlett Packard Company; *Figure 6-17* Courtesy of Okidata Americas, Inc.; *Figure 6-18* Courtesy of Genicom Corporation; *Figure 6-19* Courtesy of Hewlett Packard Company; *Figure 6-21* Courtesy of the author; *Figure 6-22* Courtesy of Hewlett Packard Company; *Figure 6-24* Courtesy of Mitsubishi Digital Electronics America, Inc.; *Figure 6-26* Courtesy of Neopost Online; *Figure 6-27* Courtesy of Citizen America Corporation, www.citizen-america.com; *Figure 6-28* Corbis; *Figure 6-29* Courtesy of Dell Computer ; *Figure 6-30* AP/ Wide World Photos; *Figure 6-32* Courtesy of InFocus Corporation; *Figure 6-32* Courtesy of InFocus Corporation; *Figure 6-33* Stephen Welstead/The Stock Market; *Figure 6-35* Courtesy of Hewlett Packard Company; *Figure 6-36* Charlie Westerman/Stone; *Figure 6-37a* Steve Krongard/The Image Bank; *Figure 6-37b (c)* Bob Daemmrich Photo, Inc.; *Figure 6-39* Courtesy of Freedom Scientific, Inc.; *Figure 6-40a* PhotoDisc; *Figure 6-40b* PhotoDisc; *Figure 6-40c* Corbis; *Figure 6-40d* PhotoDisc; *Figure 6-40e* Bob Daemmrich/Stock Boston; **Multimedia** *Figure 8* AP/Wide World Photos; *Figure 18* Hank Morgan/Photo Researchers, Inc.; *Figure 19* Sam Ogen/Science Photo Library/Photo Researchers, Inc.; *Figure 22* Courtesy of Vance Design and Associates; **Chapter 7:** *Chapter opener Figures* Courtesy of EMC Corporation; Courtesy of Kingston Technology Company, Inc.; Courtesy of International Business Machines Research; Courtesy of Alan Shugart; *Figure 7-1a* eyewire.com; *Figure 7-1b* Courtesy of Maxtor Corporation; *Figure 7-1c* Courtesy of Advanced Computer and Netware Company; *Figure 7-1d* COGU2259; *Figure 7-1e* Courtesy of Excel/Meridian Data, Inc. (www.excelcdrom.com); *Figure 7-1f* Courtesy of Imation Corporation; *Figure 7-1g* Courtesy of Exabyte Corporation; *Figure 7-1g* Courtesy of Exabyte Corporation; *Figure 7-1h* Courtesy of Kingston Technology Company, Inc.; *Figure 7-1i* Courtesy of Sandisk, Inc.; *Figure 7-6* Corbis; *Figure 7-11* Courtesy of the author; *Figure 7-12* Courtesy of Seagate Technologies; *Figure 7-13* Courtesy of Maxtor Corporation; *Figure 7-17a* Courtesy of Iomega Corporation; *Figure 7-17b* Courtesy of Iomega Corporation; *Figure 7-18* Courtesy of Advanced Computer and Netware Company; *Figure 7-22* PhotoDisc; *Figure 7-25* PhotoDisc; *Figure 7-29* Sylvie Villegler/Explorer/Photo Researchers; *Figure 7-32a* Courtesy of Imation Corporation; *Figure 7-32b* Courtesy of Seagate Technologies; *Figure 7-34a* Courtesy of Advanced Computer and Netware Company; *Figure 7-34b* Courtesy of Exabyte Corporation; *Figure 7-34c* Courtesy of Excel/Meridian Data, Inc. (www.excelcdrom.com); *Figure 7-34e* Courtesy of Excel/Meridian Data, Inc. (www.excelcdrom.com); *Figure 7-35a* Courtesy of Nokia; *Figure 7-35b* Courtesy of Nokia; *Figure 7-37a* Scott Goodwin Photography; *Figure 7-37b* Courtesy of Sandisk, Inc.; *Figure 7-37c* Courtesy of International Business Machines Corporation; *Figure 7-37d* Courtesy of Sandisk, Inc.; *Figure 7-38* Courtesy of Brenner/ Lennon Photo Productions; *Figure 7-39* Courtesy of International Business Machines Corporation; *Figure 7-40* Courtesy of Eastman Kodak Company; *Figure 7-42a* PhotoDisc; *Figure 7-42b* PhotoDisc; *Figure 7-42c* Corbis; *Figure 7-42d* PhotoDisc; *Figure 7-42e* Bob Daemmrich/Stock Boston; *Figure 7-43* The Image Bank; **Chapter 8:** *Chapter opener Figures* Courtesy of (c) 1999, 2000 Linux.com; AP/Wide World Photos; Courtesy of Hildegard Katz; *Figure 8-1a* Scott Goodwin Photography; *Figure 8-1b* Courtesy of Kingston Technology Company, Inc.; *Figure 8-2* Scott Goodwin Photography; *Figure 8-21* Courtesy of Microsoft Corporation; *Figure 8-22* Courtesy of Apple Computer, Inc.; *Figure 8-23* Courtesy of International Business Machines Corporation; *Figure 8-25* Courtesy of (c) 1999 Red Hat, Inc.; *Figure 8-26* Courtesy of Clarion Corporation; *Figure 8-27* Courtesy of Compaq Computer Corporation; *Figure 8-27* Courtesy of Hewlett Packard Company; **Buyer's Guide** *Page 8.43* Courtesy of Adobe Systems, Inc.; *Page 8.45* Scott Goodwin Photography; *Page 8.56* Courtesy of Seagate Technologies, Inc.; *Figure 8* Courtesy of Compaq Computer Corporation; *Figure 9* Courtesy of Toshiba America Information Systems, Inc.; *Figure 10* Courtesy of Toshiba America Information Systems, Inc.; *Figure 11* Courtesy of InFocus Corporation; *Figure 13* Courtesy of Palm, Inc.; *Figure 14* Courtesy of Compaq Computer Corporation; **Chapter 9:** *Chapter opener Figures* Courtesy of 3Com Corporation; Courtesy of Compaq Computer Corporation; Courtesy of Sun Microsystems, Inc.; Courtesy of Cisco Technology, Inc.; *Figure 9-3a* Courtesy of Intel Corporation; *Figure 9-3b* Courtesy of RCA; *Figure 9-3c* Scott Goodwin Photography; *Figure 9-3d* Courtesy of Sprint; *Figure 9-6* Bruce Ayers/ Stone; *Figure 9-7* Courtesy of Microsoft Corporation; *Figure 9-20* Courtesy of Compaq Computer Corporation; *Figure 9-20d* Courtesy of Philips Consumer Electronics Company; *Figure 9-27a* Courtesy of U.S. Robotics Corporation; *Figure 9-27b* Courtesy of SONICBlue, Inc.; *Figure 9-29* Courtesy of SMC Corporation; *Figure 9-30* Courtesy of SMC Corporation; *Figure 9-38* Courtesy of SMC Corporation; *Figure 9-38* Courtesy of SMC Corporation; *Figure 9-40* PhotoDisc; *Figure 9-42* Courtesy of Clarinet Systems; *Figure 9-43 (c)* Mark Burnett/Stock Boston/PictureQuest; **A World without Wires** *Figure 1* Courtesy of Tower Group; *Figure 2* AP/Wide World Photos; *Figure 5* Courtesy of Compaq Computer Corporation; *Figure 6* Courtesy of Cybiko; *Figure 7* Courtesy of Gnnetcomm.com; *Figure 8* AP/Wide World Photos; *Figure 12* Courtesy of Magellan Corporation; *Figure 13* Courtesy of CPS Systems; **Chapter 10:** *Chapter opener Figures* Courtesy of Amazon.com, Inc.; Courtesy eBay, Inc.; (c) Sean Gallup; *Figure 10-1* Ed Bock/The Stock Market; *Figure 10-2* PhotoDisc; *Figure 10-4* Courtesy of Forrester Research, This chart is figure 2 of "Global eCommerce Approaches Hypergrowth," brief dated April 18, 2000.; *Figure 10-5* PhotoDisc; *Figure 10-15a* PhotoDisc; *Figure 10-15b* PhotoDisc; *Figure 10-15c* PhotoDisc; *Figure 10-15d* The Image Works; *Figure 10-15f* PhotoDisc; *Figure 10-15g* PhotoDisc; *Figure 10-15h* PhotoDisc; *Figure 10-24* Rachel Epstein/PhotoEdit; *Figure 10-25* (c) Ron Chapple/FPG International; **Chapter 11:** *Chapter opener Figures* AP/ Wide World Photos; Courtesy of Louis Fabian Bachrach; Courtesy of WebCT; Courtesy of Britannica.com Inc.; Courtesy of Al Luckow; *Figure 11-1a* Monica Graff/The Image Works; *Figure 11-1b (c)* Doug Martin/Photo Researchers, Inc.; *Figure 11-1c* Walter Hodges/Stone; *Figure 11-3* Courtesy of Intel Corporation; *Figure 11-4* Jose Luis Pelaez, Inc./The Stock Market ; *Figure 11-5a* Courtesy of Cybiko, Inc.; *Figure 11-5b* Courtesy of Compaq Computer Corporation; *Figure 11-5c* Courtesy of Compaq Computer Corporation; *Figure 11-6* Courtesy of Compaq Computer Corporation; *Figure 11-7* Peter Cade/Stone; *Figure 11-10c* Courtesy of InFocus Corporation; *Figure 11-10e* Telegraph Colour Library/FPG International; *Figure 11-10f* Telegraph Colour Library/FPG International; Figure *11-14* AP/Wide World Photos; *Figure 11-17a* PhotoDisc; *Figure 11-17b* J-Y Govin-Sorel/Stone; *Figure 11-17c* Rob Crandall/Stock Boston; Figure *11-17d* Bob Daemmrich The Image Works; *Figure 11-19* Walter Hodges Stone; *Figure 11-23a* Michael Newman PhotoEdit; *Figure 11-23b (c)* Syracuse Newspapers/Al Campanie/The Image Works; *Figure 11-25a* Walter Hodges Stone; *Figure 11-25c* Mug Shots/The Stock Market; Figure *11-26* Ziggy Kalzuny/Stone; *Figure 11-28* Courtesy of Precor, Inc.(c) 2000; *Figure 11-28* Courtesy of Precor, Inc.(c) 2000; *Figure 11-29* Walter Hodges Stone; *Figure 11-33a* Courtesy of OnStar; *Figure 11-33b* (c) General Motors; Figure 11-36 PhotoDisc; *Figure 11-38* Sam Ogden Science Photo Library/Photo Researchers; Figure 11-40a (c) Hank Morgan Photo Researchers, Inc.; Figure 11-40b Tony Freeman/PhotoEdit; *Figure 11-43* Gary A. Connor/PhotoEdit; *Figure 11-47* The Everett Collection; *Figure 11-48* Jon Riley/Stone; **Chapter 12:;** *Chapter opener Figures* Courtesy of Network Associates; Courtesy of Symantec Corporation; M. Ansin/Liaison Agency; Courtesy of Donn B. Parker; *Figure 12-10* Poulides/Thatcher/Stone; *Figure 12-11* Courtesy of Identix, Inc.; *Figure 12-12* Courtesy of Recognition Systems, Inc.; *Figure 12-13* Courtesy of eTrue, Inc.; *Figure 12-14* AP/ Wide World Photos; *Figure 12-15* Courtesy of Kensington Technology Group; *Figure 12-19* Screenshot of encrypted file provided by SAGRELTO Enterprises, Inc., distributor of Interbuz Software; *Figure 12-21* Courtesy of American Power Conversion; *Figure 12-22* Courtesy of American Power Conversion; *Figure 12-28* Courtesy of Network ICE Corporation; *Figure 12-29* AP/ Wide World Photos; **Chapter 13:** *Chapter opener Figures* Courtesy of Oracle Corporation "CBS" and the CBS Eye Device are registered trademarks of CBS Broadcasting, Inc. Switchboard is a registered service mark of Switchboard, Inc. Courtesy of CBS Switchboard.com; Courtesy of Sprint; *Figure 13-1a* Courtesy of Casio; *Figure 13-1b* PhotoDisc; *Figure 13-9a* David Roth/Stone; *Figure 13-9* PhotoDisc; *Figure 13-10a* David Roth/Stone; *Figure 13-16* David Young-Wolff/Stone; *Figure 13-33* PhotoDisc; **Chapter 14:** *Chapter opener Figures* Courtesy of Ed Yourdon; (c) Hein Van Steenis/Courtesy of Tom DeMarco; Courtesy of Visible Systems Corporation; Courtesy of Ziff Davis Media, Inc.; PhotoDisc; *Figure 14-5* Bruce Ayers/Stone; *Figure 14-*6a Courtesy of Ziff Davis Media, Inc.; *Figure 14-6b* Courtesy of Microsoft Corporation; *Figure 14-26* Peter Menzel/Stock Boston; **Chapter 15:** *Chapter opener Figures* The Computer Museum History Center; Courtesy of Lucent Technologies - Bell Laboratories; Powerbuilder is a registered rademark of Sybase, Inc.;Courtesy of Sybase, Inc.; Courtesy of Macromedia, Inc.; *Figure 15-32* Bill of Material System, by Greg Bloodworth/Corporate Technology Partners, Inc.; *Figure 15-33* PhotoDisc; **Chapter 16:** *Chapter opener Figures* Courtesy of Loudcloud; Courtesy of Divine Interventures; Courtesy of Yahoo! Inc.; *Figure 16-2* Bob Daemmrich/The Image Works; *Figure 16-8 (c)* K. Preuss/The Image Works; *Figure 16-9* Bill Aron/PhotoEdit; *Figure 16-10* Michael Newman/PhotoEdit; *Figure 16-16* Scott Goodwin Photography; *Figure 16-11* PhotoDisc; **Trends** *Figure 2* Courtesy of International Business Machines Corporation; *Figure 4* Courtesy of InViso.com; *Figure 5 (c)* Oilver Meskes/Eye of Science/Photo Researchers, Inc.; *Figure 6* Courtesy of RCA; *Figure 7 (c)* Michael Rosenthal/Photographer/NJ TRANSIT; *Figure 8* AP/WIDE World Photos. *Figure 12* AP/ Wide World Photos; *Figure 13* AP/ Wide World Photos; *Figure 14* Courtesy of Logitech, Courtesy of Canon; *Figure 15* Courtesy of Handspring, Inc.; *Figure 16* AP/ Wide World Photos; *Figure 17* Courtesy of Digital Angel.net, Inc.; *Figure 18* Courtesy of E Ink, Inc.; *Figure 21* Geoff Tompkinson/Science Photo Library/Photo Researchers, Inc.; *Figure 22* AP/ Wide World Photos; *Figure 23* Courtesy of Probotics, Inc.; *Figure 25* Courtesy of Identix, Inc.; *Figure 26* Courtesy of Wink Communications, Inc.